Essentials of Business Law & The Legal Environment

Richard A. Mann | Barry S. Roberts

CENGAGE
Learning·

Australia • Brazil • Japan • Korea • Mexico • Singapore • Spain • United Kingdom • United States

CENGAGE
Learning·

Essentials of Business Law & The Legal Environment

Essentials of Business Law & The Legal Environment, Eleventh Edition
Richard A. Mann | Barry S. Roberts

Executive Editors:
 Maureen Staudt
 Michael Stranz

Senior Project Development Manager:
 Linda deStefano

Marketing Specialist:
 Courtney Sheldon

Senior Production/Manufacturing Manager:
 Donna M. Brown

Production Editorial Manager:
 Kim Frv

Sr. Rights Acquisition Account Manager:
 Todd Osborne

This book contains select works from existing Cengage Learning resources and was produced by Cengage Learning Custom Solutions for collegiate use. As such, those adopting and/or contributing to this work are responsible for editorial content accuracy, continuity and completeness.

Compilation © 2012 Cengage Learning
ISBN-13: 978-1-285-00868-4

ISBN-10: 1-285-00868-5

Cengage Learning
5191 Natorp Boulevard
Mason, Ohio 45040
USA
Cengage Learning is a leading provider of customized learning solutions with office locations around the globe, including Singapore, the United Kingdom, Australia, Mexico, Brazil, and Japan. Locate your local office at:
international.cengage.com/region.

Cengage Learning products are represented in Canada by Nelson Education, Ltd.
For your lifelong learning solutions, visit **www.cengage.com/custom.**
Visit our corporate website at **www.cengage.com.**

Printed in the United States of America

Brief Contents

TABLE OF CASES

TABLE OF FIGURES

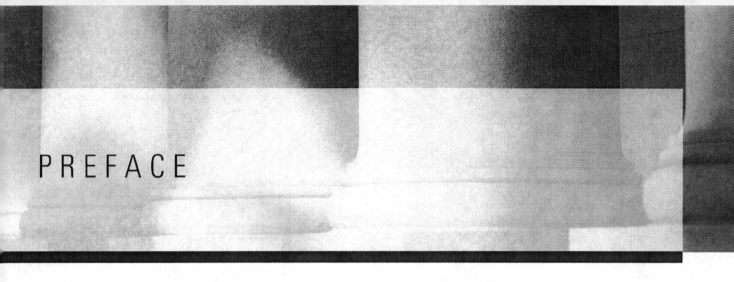

PREFACE

THE TRADITION CONTINUES

The eleventh edition of *Essentials of Business Law and the Legal Environment* continues the tradition of accuracy, comprehensiveness, and authoritativeness associated with its earlier editions. This text covers its subject material in a succinct, nontechnical but authoritative manner, and provides depth sufficient to ensure easy comprehension by today's students.

Certified Public Accountant Preparation

This text is designed for use in business law and legal environment courses generally offered in universities, colleges, and schools of business and management. Because of its broad coverage and variety of the material, this text may be readily adapted to specially designed courses in business law with emphasis on different combinations of the subject matter. All topics included in the business law section of the certified public accountant (CPA) exam are covered by the text. In addition, this text covers the legal responsibilities and liabilities of accountants section and the corporate governance portion of the business environment and concepts section of the CPA Exam. See the inside back cover of this text for a listing of the CPA exam topics covered in this text as well as the chapters covering each topic.

Uniform CPA Examination Content Specifications

The American Institute of CPAs (AICPA) Board of Examiners has approved and adopted content specification outlines (CSOs) for the four sections of the new computer-based Uniform CPA Examination: Auditing and Attestation, Financial Accounting and Reporting, Regulation, and Business Environment and Concepts. As revised and effective July 1, 2011, the CSOs include the following topics, which are covered in this textbook:

Regulation Section
I. Ethics, Professional, and Legal Responsibilities
   A. Legal Responsibilities and Liabilities [of accountants]
      1. Common law duties and liability to clients and third parties
      2. Federal statutory liability
   B. Privileged Communications and Confidentiality [of accountants]
II. Business Law
   A. Agency
      1. Formation and termination
      2. Authority of agents and principals
      3. Duties and liabilities of agents and principals
   B. Contracts
      1. Formation
      2. Performance
      3. Third-party assignments
      4. Discharge, breach, and remedies

    C. Uniform Commercial Code
      1. Sales contracts
      2. Negotiable instruments
      3. Secured transactions
      4. Documents of title and title transfer
    D. Debtor-Creditor Relationships
      1. Rights, duties, and liabilities of debtors, creditors, and guarantors
      2. Bankruptcy and insolvency
    E. Government Regulation of Business
      1. Federal securities regulation
      2. Other federal laws and regulations (antitrust, copyright, patents, labor, and employment)
    F. Business Structure (Selection of a Business Entity)
      1. Advantages, disadvantages, implications, and constraints
      2. Formation, operation, and termination
      3. Financial structure, capitalization, profit and loss allocation, and distributions
      4. Rights, duties, legal obligations, and authority of owners and management

Business Environment and Concepts Section

I. Corporate Governance
    A. Rights, Duties, Responsibilities, and Authority of the Board of Directors, Officers, and Other Employees

For more information, visit **www.cpa-exam.org**.

Business Ethics Emphasis

The Chapter 2 Business Ethics case studies require the student to make the value trade-offs that confront business people in their professional lives. (We gratefully acknowledge the assistance of James Leis in writing the Mykon's Dilemma case.) Two-thirds of the chapters also contain an "Ethical Dilemma," which presents a managerial situation involving ethical issues. A series of questions leads the student to explore the ethical dimensions of each situation. We wish to acknowledge and thank the following professors for their contributions in preparing the Ethical Dilemmas: Sandra K. Miller, professor of accounting and taxation, Widener University, and Gregory P. Cermignano, associate professor of accounting and business law, Widener University. In addition, to provide further application of ethics in different business contexts, an ethics question follows many cases. These questions are designed to encourage students to consider the ethical dimensions of the facts in the case or of the legal issue invoked by the facts.

NEW TO THIS EDITION

- **Taking Sides** In all chapters except for Chapters 1 and 2, we have added a feature that requires students to apply critical thinking skills to a case-based fact situation. The students are asked to identify the relevant legal rules and develop arguments for both parties to the dispute. In addition, the students are asked to explain how they think a court would resolve the dispute.
- **Up-to-Date Coverage** Chapters 7 and 8 have been revised to incorporate Volume 2 of the new Restatement of the Law Third, Torts: Liability for Physical and Emotional Harm, which was approved and published in 2011. The Dodd-Frank Wall Street Reform and Consumer Protection Act of 2010 has been extensively covered in Chapters 35, 36, 39, 44, 46, and 49. Recent amendments to the Revised Model Business Corporation Act have been included in the corporation chapters. The chapter on Securities Regulation has been updated to reflect recent U.S. Securities and Exchange Commission (SEC) regulations regarding proxy solicitations and disclosure of executive compensation and corporate governance. The Intellectual Property chapter covers the changes made by the Leahy-Smith America Invents Act of 2011. The antitrust chapter has been revised to reflect the Horizontal Merger Guidelines of 2010 that were issued jointly by the Justice Department and the Federal Trade Commission (FTC).

The Employment Law chapter has incorporated the Americans with Disabilities Act (ADA) Amendments of 2008. The Credit Card Accountability, Responsibility, and Disclosure Act is discussed in the Consumer Protection chapter.

- **Streamlined Coverage** Chapters 25 and 26 have been combined into one chapter, titled "Transfer and Holder in Due Course" to integrate the concepts covered.
- **New Cases** Twenty-one legal cases are new to this edition. (See Table of Cases.) The new cases include recent U.S. Supreme Court decisions such as *Rent-A-Center; West, Inc. v. Jackson; Williamson v. Mazda Motor of America, Inc.; Summers v. Earth Island Institute; FCC v. Fox Television Stations; Philip Morris USA v. Williams; Hamilton v. Lanning; Bilski v. Kappos; American Needle, Inc. v. National Football League; Ricci v. Destefano;* and *Morrison v. National Australia Bank Ltd.*

KEY FEATURES

Applying the Law

In a number of chapters we have included a feature that provides a systematic legal analysis of a single concept learned in that chapter. It begins with the facts of a hypothetical case, followed by an identification of the broad legal issue presented by those facts. We then state the rule—or applicable legal principles, including definitions, which aid in resolving the legal issue—and apply it to the facts. Finally we state a legal conclusion or decision in the case. We wish to acknowledge and thank Professor Ann Olazábal, University of Miami, for her contribution in preparing this feature.

Summarized Cases

From long classroom experience we are of the opinion that fundamental legal principles can be learned more effectively from text and case materials having at least a degree of human interest. Accordingly, we have included a large number of recent cases, as well as earlier landmark cases. The facts, decisions, and opinions for all of the cases are summarized for clarity. Each case is followed by an interpretation, which explains the significance of the case and how it relates to the textual material.

Case Critical Thinking Questions

Each case is also followed by a critical thinking question to encourage students to examine the legal policy or reasoning behind the legal principle of the case, or to apply it in a real-world context.

Business Law in Action

In a number of chapters we have included a scenario that illustrates the application of legal concepts in the chapter to business situations that commonly arise. We wish to acknowledge and thank Professor Ann Olazábal, University of Miami, for her contribution in preparing this feature.

Practical Advice

Each chapter contains a number of statements that illustrate how legal concepts can be applied to common business situations.

Chapter Outcomes

Each chapter begins with a list of learning objectives for the student.

Enhanced Readability

To improve readability throughout the text, all unnecessary "legalese" has been eliminated, while necessary legal terms have been printed in boldface and clearly defined, explained, and illustrated. Definitions of essential legal terms and legal concepts also appear in the margins. The text is enriched by numerous illustrative hypothetical and case examples that help students relate material to real-life experiences.

Classroom-Tested End-of-Chapter Materials

Classroom-tested problems appear at the end of the chapters to test the students' understanding of major concepts. We have used the problems and consider them excellent stimulants to classroom discussion. Students, in turn, have found the problems—many of which are taken from reported court decisions—helpful in enabling them to apply the basic rules of law to factual situations. Besides serving as a springboard for discussion, the problems readily suggest other and related problems to the inquiring, analytical mind.

Ample Illustrations

We have incorporated more than 220 classroom-tested figures, tables, diagrams, concept reviews, and chapter summaries. The figures, tables, and diagrams help the students conceptualize the many abstract concepts in the law; the concept reviews not only summarize prior discussions but also indicate relationships between different legal rules. Moreover, each chapter ends with a summary in the form of an annotated outline of the entire chapter, including key terms.

Pedagogical Benefits

Classroom use and study of this book should provide for the student the following benefits and skills:
1. Perception and appreciation of the scope, extent, and importance of the law.
2. Basic knowledge of the fundamental concepts, principles, and rules of law that apply to business transactions.
3. Knowledge of the function and operation of courts and government administrative agencies.
4. Ability to recognize the potential legal problems that may arise in a doubtful or complicated situation, and the necessity of consulting a lawyer and obtaining competent professional legal advice.
5. Development of analytical skills and reasoning power.

ONLINE RESOURCE ACCESS

The textbook companion site provides resources for both students and instructors.

Students: Access the following resources by going to **www.cengagebrain.com** and searching ISBN 9781133188636: Chapter Quizzes, Key Terms Flashcards, Chapter Summaries, and Court Case Updates.

Instructors: Access instructor resources by going to **login.cengage.com**, logging in with your faculty account username and password, and using ISBN 9781133188636 to search for and to add instructor resources to your account "Bookshelf."

COMPREHENSIVE LEARNING RESOURCES

Instructor's Resource CD (IRCD) (ISBN: 9781133626138) The IRCD contains the Instructor Manual, Test Bank in Microsoft® Word, PowerPoint® slides, and the ExamView® Test Bank. All IRCD resources except the ExamView® Test Bank are also available on the instructor companion site.
- The **Microsoft® Word Instructor's Manual** prepared by Richard A. Mann, Barry S. Roberts, and Beth D. Woods contains chapter outlines, teaching notes, answers to problems, key terms, recommendations for transparency masters and acetates, and part openers (which provide suggested research and outside activities for students).
- **PowerPoint® Slides** clarify course content and guide student note-taking during lectures.
- The **Microsoft® Word Test Bank** contains thousands of true-false, multiple-choice, case questions, and challenging test questions.

- The **ExamView**® **Test Bank** contains all of the questions from the Word® Test Bank and makes test preparation, scoring, and grading easy. This easy-to-use, computerized test creation software is compatible with Microsoft® Windows®. Add or edit questions, instructions, and answers, and select questions by previewing them on the screen, selecting them randomly, or selecting them by number. Instructors can also create and administer quizzes online, whether over the Internet, a local area network (LAN), or a wide area network (WAN). Contact your Cengage Learning representative for more information. The ExamView Test Bank Test Bank is only available on the IRCD.

ADDITIONAL COURSE TOOLS

Business Law Digital Video Library Featuring more than seventy-five video clips that spark class discussion and clarify core legal principles, the Business Law Digital Video Library is organized into six series: Legal Conflicts in Business (includes specific modern business and e-commerce scenarios); Ask the Instructor (presents straightforward explanations of concepts for student review); Drama of the Law (features classic business scenarios that spark classroom participation); LawFlix (contains clips from many popular films); Real World Legal (presents legal scenarios encountered in real businesses); and Business Ethics (presents ethical dilemmas in business scenarios). For more information about the Digital Video Library, visit www.cengage.com/blaw/dvl. Access for students is free when bundled with a new textbook or can be purchased separately. Students must register for and purchase access to the Digital Video Library at www.cengagebrain.com.

Student Guide to the Sarbanes-Oxley Act (ISBN 9780324827194) This brief overview for undergraduate business students explains the Sarbanes-Oxley Act, describes its requirements, and shows how it potentially affects students in their business life. The guide is available as an optional package with this text.

A Handbook of Basic Law Terms, *Black's Law Dictionary* **Series** This paperback dictionary, prepared by the editor of the popular *Black's Law Dictionary*, can be packaged with this text for a small additional cost.

TextChoice® **and WestLaw**® **Access** Instructors can select individual cases from TextChoice® to create a customized casebook for their course. Offered through Cengage Learning Custom Solutions, the TextChoice® database offers hundreds of case choices and is searchable by topic or state. Qualified adopters can also receive ten free hours of Westlaw®, an online legal portal with access to more than 15,000 databases of information including cases, public records, court dockets, legal forms, research materials, and the WestLaw® Directory. Please contact your Cengage Learning sales representative to request access to Westlaw® or to learn more about TextChoice® options.

Cengage Learning Custom Solutions Whether you need print, digital, or hybrid course materials, Cengage Learning Custom Solutions can help you create your perfect learning solution. Draw from Cengage Learning's extensive library of texts and collections, add or create your own original work, and create customized media and technology to match your learning and course objectives. Our editorial team will work with you through each step, allowing you to concentrate on the most important thing—your students. Learn more about all our services at **www.cengage.com/custom**.

The Cengage Global Economic Watch (GEW) Resource Center This is your source for turning today's challenges into tomorrow's solutions. This online portal houses the most current and up-to-date content concerning the economic crisis. Organized by discipline, the GEW Resource Center offers the solutions instructors and students need in an easy-to-use format. Included are an overview and timeline of the historical events leading up to the crisis, links to the latest news and resources, discussion and testing content, an instructor feedback forum, and a Global Issues Database. Visit **www.cengage.com/thewatch** for more information.

ACKNOWLEDGMENTS

We express our gratitude to the following professors for their helpful comments:

Stephanie Campbell, Mineral Area College; Dora J. L. Dye, City College of San Francisco; J. P. Giovacchini, Western Nevada College; Suzanne Gradisher, University of Akron; H. Daniel Holt, Southeastern Illinois College; Keith Kasper, Univeristy of Vermont; Blake LeCrone, Baylor University; Sarah H. Ludwig, Mary Baldwin College; John H. Neu, Whittier College; Caroline W. Smith, College of Central Florida; Mary Torma, Lorain County Community College;

We also are grateful to those who provided us with comments regarding earlier editions of the book:

Michael E. Adighibe, Cheyney University; Martha Agee, Baylor University; Jessica Allen, Suffolk Community College; Dawn Bennett-Alexander, University of Northern Florida; Terence Baird, Antelope Valley College; Keith A. Beebe, SUNY-Cobleskill; Janie Blankenship, DelMar College; George S. Bohler, Embry-Riddle University; Joyce Boland-DeVito, St. John's University; Steven W. Bostian, Caston College; Norman E. Bradshaw, Alvin Community College; Donald R. Brenner, American University; Carroll Burrell, San Jacinto College; Jane Campbell, Jackson Community College; Stephanie Campbell, Mineral Area College; Vic Daniels, Tallahassee Community College; Ed Dash, Pierce Junior College; Joseph P. Davey, Hartnell College; David L. Davis, Tallahassee Community College; Sandra Defebaugh, Eastern Michigan University; Theodore M. Dinges, Longview Community College; Vernon P. Dorweiler, Michigan Technological University; Steve Easter, Mineral Area College; Robert Ek, Seminole Community College; Tony Enerva, Lakeland Community College; Karla Harbin Fox, University of Connecticut; Edward J. Gac, University of Colorado; George P. Generas, Jr., University of Hartford; Allan M. Gerson, Palm Beach Community College; Thomson Glover, Murray State University; Douglas C. Gordon, Arapahoe Community College; A. James Granito, Youngstown State University; Deborah C. Hanks, Cardinal Stritch University; E. Sharon Hayenga, Minneapolis Community College; James E. Holloway, East Carolina University; Trevor Howell, Belmont College; Gregory M. Huckabee, University of South Dakota; Dan Huss, Miami University; Robert Inama, Ricks College; Michael A. Katz, Delaware State University; Julia S. Kennedy, University of St. Francis; George Kepner, Hartwick College; Edward M. Kissling, Ocean County College; Daniel A. Levin, University of Colorado/Boulder; David Ludwich, Belmont College; Bradley Lutz, Hillsborough Community College; Richard Lynn, Belmont College; Kyle McFatter, McNeese State University; John F. Mastriani, El Paso Community College; Marian Matthews, Central New Mexico Community College; James Miles, Anoka-Ramsey Community College; Scott E. Miller, CPA, J.D., Gannon University; David J. Moser, Belmont University; André Nelson, Montgomery College; Brennan Neville, Bellevue University; L.K. O'Drudy, Jr., University of Virginia; Michael J. O'Hara, University of Nebraska; Dinah Payne, University of New Orleans; Mary Ellen Perri, SUNY-Farmingdale; Todd B. Piller, SUNY-Cobleskill; Richard W. Post, College of the Desert; LeGene Quesenberry, Clarion University; Roger E. Reinsch, Emporia State University; Darlington C. Richards, Morgan State University; M. Rose, Macomb County Community College; Herbert Rossman, Drexel University; Sylvia Samuels, Skyline College; Donald E. Sanders, Southwest Texas State University; Susan Schoeffler, Central Piedmont Community College; John E. H. Sherry, Cornell University; Owen T. Smith, Long Island University; Michael E. Sommerville, St. Mary's College; Dan Spielmann, University of Wisconsin-Green Bay; Art Stelly, Baylor University; Larry Stephens, Gulf Coast College; Stanley H. Stone, Valencia Community College–East Campus; Patricia S. Tulin, Central Connecticut State University; Robert J. Votta, Pierce Junior College; Edward C. Wachter, Jr., Point Park College; Pamela Poole Weber, Seminole Community College; Hugh Wilkoff, Cerritos College; Kim Wong Central New Mexico Community College.

We express our thanks and appreciation to Debra Corvey for administrative assistance. For their support, we extend our thanks to Karlene Fogelin Knebel and Joanne Erwick Roberts. And we are grateful to Devanand Srinivasan and Andrea Clemente of Cenveo Publisher Services, and Vicky True-Baker, Kendra Brown, and Scott Dillon of South-Western Legal Studies in Business for their invaluable assistance and cooperation in connection with the preparation of this text.

This text is dedicated also to our children Lilli-Marie Knebel Mann, Justin Erwick Roberts, and Matthew Charles Roberts.

Richard A. Mann
Barry S. Roberts

PART I

Introduction to Law and Ethics

CHAPTER **1**

Introduction to Law

The life of law has not been logic; it has been experience.

Oliver Wendell Holmes (1881)

CHAPTER OUTCOMES

After reading and studying this chapter, you should be able to:

1. Identify and describe the basic functions of law.

2. Distinguish between (a) law and justice and (b) law and morals.

3. Distinguish between (a) substantive and procedural law, (b) public and private law, and (c) civil and criminal law.

4. Identify and describe the sources of law.

5. Explain the principle of *stare decisis*.

L aw concerns the relations between individuals as such relations affect the social and economic order. It is both the product of civilization and the means by which civilization is maintained. As such, law reflects the social, economic, political, religious, and moral philosophy of society.

Law is an instrument of social control. Its function is to regulate, within certain limitations, human conduct and human relations. Accordingly, the laws of the United States affect the life of every U.S. citizen. At the same time, the laws of each state influence the life of each of its citizens and the lives of many noncitizens as well. The rights and duties of all individuals, as well as the safety and security of all people and their property, depend on the law.

The law is pervasive. It permits, forbids, or regulates practically every human activity and affects all persons either directly or indirectly. Law is, in part, prohibitory: certain acts must not be committed. For example, one must not steal; one must not murder. Law is also partly mandatory: certain acts must be done or be done in a prescribed way. Thus, taxes must be paid; corporations must make and file certain reports with state or federal authorities; traffic must keep to the right. Finally, law is permissive: certain acts may be done. For instance, one may or may not enter into a contract; one may or may not dispose of one's estate by will.

Because the areas of law are so highly interrelated, you will find it helpful to begin the study of the different areas of business law by first considering the nature, classification, and sources of law. This will enable you not only to understand better each specific area of law but also to understand its relationship to other areas of law.

NATURE OF LAW

The law has evolved slowly, and it will continue to change. It is not a pure science based on unchanging and universal truths. Rather, it results from a continuous striving to develop a workable set of rules that balance the individual and group rights of a society.

Definition of Law

Scholars and citizens in general often ask a fundamental but difficult question regarding law: what is it? Numerous philosophers and jurists (legal scholars) have attempted to define it. American jurists and Supreme Court Justices Oliver Wendell Holmes and Benjamin Cardozo defined law as predictions of the way in which a court will decide specific legal questions. The English jurist William Blackstone, on the other hand, defined law as "a rule of civil conduct prescribed by the supreme power in a state, commanding what is right, and prohibiting what is wrong."

Because of its great complexity, many legal scholars have attempted to explain the law by outlining its essential characteristics. Roscoe Pound, a distinguished American jurist and former dean of the Harvard Law School, described law as having multiple meanings:

> First we may mean the legal order, that is, the régime of ordering human activities and relations through systematic application of the force of politically organized society, or through social pressure in such a society backed by such force. We use the term "law" in this sense when we speak of "respect for law" or for the "end of law."
>
> Second we may mean the aggregate of laws or legal precepts; the body of authoritative grounds of judicial and administrative action established in such a society. We may mean the body of received and established materials on which judicial and administrative determinations proceed. We use the term in this sense when we speak of "systems of law" or of "justice according to law."
>
> Third we may mean what Justice Cardozo has happily styled "the judicial process." We may mean the process of determining controversies, whether as it actually takes place, or as the public, the jurists, and the practitioners in the courts hold it ought to take place.

Functions of Law

At a general level the primary function of law is to maintain stability in the social, political, and economic system while simultaneously permitting change. The law accomplishes this basic function by performing a number of specific functions, among them dispute resolution, protection of property, and preservation of the state.

Disputes, which arise inevitably in any modern society, may involve criminal matters, such as theft, or noncriminal matters, such as an automobile accident. Because disputes threaten social stability, the law has established an elaborate and evolving set of rules to resolve them. In addition, the legal system has instituted societal remedies, usually administered by the courts, in place of private remedies such as revenge.

A second crucial function of law is to protect the private ownership of property and to assist in the making of voluntary agreements (called contracts) regarding exchanges of property and services. Accordingly, a significant portion of law, as well as this text, involves property and its disposition, including the law of property, contracts, sales, commercial paper, and business associations.

A third essential function of the law is preservation of the state. In our system, law ensures that changes in political structure and leadership are brought about by political action, such as elections, legislation, and referenda, rather than by revolution, sedition, and rebellion.

Law and Morals

Although moral concepts greatly influence the law, morals and law are not the same. You might think of them as two intersecting circles (see Figure 1-1). The more darkly shaded area common to both circles includes the vast body of ideas that are both moral and legal. For instance, "Thou shall not kill" and "Thou shall not steal" are both moral precepts and legal constraints.

On the other hand, that part of the legal circle that does not intersect the morality circle (the lightly shaded portion) includes many rules of law that are completely unrelated to morals, such as the rules stating that you must drive on the right side of the road and that you must register before you can vote. Likewise, the part of the morality circle that does not intersect the legal circle includes moral precepts not enforced by legal sanctions, such as the idea that you should not silently stand by and watch a blind man walk off a cliff or that you should provide food to a starving child.

Law and Justice

Law and justice represent separate and distinct concepts. Without law, however, there can be no justice. Although defining justice is at least as difficult as defining law, justice generally may be

Figure 1-1 Law and Morals

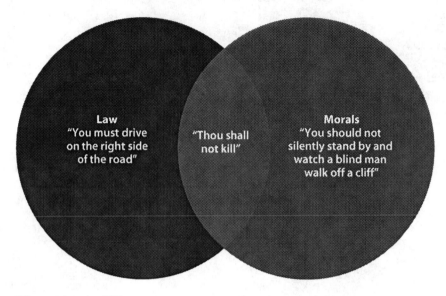

© Cengage Learning 2013

defined as the fair, equitable, and impartial treatment of the competing interests and desires of individuals and groups with due regard for the common good.

On the other hand, law is no guarantee of justice. Some of history's most monstrous acts have been committed pursuant to "law." Examples include the actions of Nazi Germany during the 1930s and 1940s and the actions of the South African government under apartheid from 1948 until 1994. Totalitarian societies often have shaped formal legal systems around the atrocities they have sanctioned.

CLASSIFICATION OF LAW

Right
legal capacity to require another person to perform or refrain from performing an act

Because the subject is vast, classifying the law into categories is helpful. Though a number of categories are possible, the most useful ones are (1) substantive and procedural, (2) public and private, and (3) civil and criminal. See Figure 1-2, which illustrates a classification of law.

Basic to understanding these classifications are the terms *right* and *duty*. A **right** is the capacity of a person, with the aid of the law, to require another person or persons to perform, or

Figure 1-2 Classification of Law

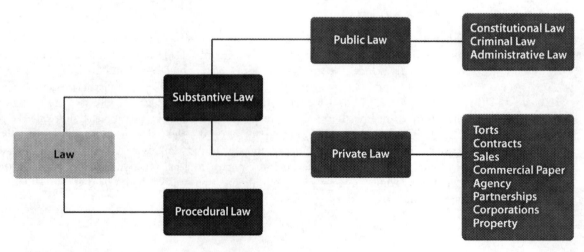

© Cengage Learning 2013

Duty
legal obligation requiring a person to perform or refrain from performing an act

Substantive law
the basic law creating rights and duties

Procedural Law
rules for enforcing substantive law

Public law
the law dealing with the relationship between government and individuals

Private law
the law involving relationships among individuals and legal entities ·

Civil law
the law dealing with the rights and duties of individuals among themselves

Criminal law
the law that involves offenses against the entire community

Sue
to begin a lawsuit in a court

Defendant
the person against whom a legal action is brought

Plaintiff
the person who initiates a civil suit

Prosecute
to bring a criminal proceeding

to refrain from performing, a certain act. Thus, if Alice sells and delivers goods to Bob for the agreed price of $500 payable at a certain date, Alice is capable, with the aid of the courts, of enforcing the payment by Bob of the $500. A **duty** is the obligation the law imposes upon a person to perform, or to refrain from performing, a certain act. Duty and right are correlatives: no right can rest upon one person without a corresponding duty resting upon some other person, or in some cases upon all other persons.

Substantive and Procedural Law

Substantive law creates, defines, and regulates legal rights and duties. Thus, the rules of contract law that determine a binding contract are rules of substantive law. On the other hand, **procedural law** sets forth the rules for enforcing those rights that exist by reason of the substantive law. Thus, procedural law defines the method by which to obtain a remedy in court.

Public and Private Law

Public law is the branch of substantive law that deals with the government's rights and powers and its relationship to individuals or groups. Public law consists of constitutional, administrative, and criminal law. **Private law** is that part of substantive law governing individuals and legal entities (such as corporations) in their relationships with one another. Business law is primarily private law.

Civil and Criminal Law

The **civil law** defines duties, the violation of which constitutes a wrong against the party injured by the violation. In contrast, the **criminal law** establishes duties, the violation of which is a wrong against the whole community. Civil law is a part of private law, whereas criminal law is a part of public law. (The term *civil law* should be distinguished from the concept of a civil law *system*, which is discussed later in this chapter.) In a civil action the injured party **sues** to recover *compensation* for the damage and injury sustained as a result of the **defendant's** wrongful conduct. The party bringing a civil action (the **plaintiff**) has the burden of proof, which the plaintiff must sustain by a *preponderance* (greater weight) *of the evidence*. The purpose of the civil law is to compensate the injured party, not, as in the case of criminal law, to punish the wrongdoer. The principal forms of relief the civil law affords are a judgment for money damages and a decree ordering the defendant to perform a specified act or to desist from specified conduct.

A crime is any act prohibited or omission required by public law in the interest of protecting the public and made punishable by the government in a judicial proceeding brought (**prosecuted**) by it. The government must prove criminal guilt *beyond a reasonable doubt,* which is a significantly higher burden of proof than that required in a civil action. Crimes are prohibited and punished on the grounds of public policy, which may include the safeguarding of government, human life, or private property. Additional purposes of criminal law include deterrence and rehabilitation. See Concept Review 1-1 for a comparison of civil and criminal law.

CONCEPT REVIEW 1-1

Comparison of Civil and Criminal Law

	Civil Law	Criminal Law
Commencement of Action	Aggrieved individual (plaintiff) sues	State or federal government prosecutes
Purpose	Compensation Deterrence	Punishment Deterrence Rehabilitation Preservation of peace
Burden of Proof	Preponderance of the evidence	Beyond a reasonable doubt
Principal Sanctions	Monetary damages Equitable remedies	Capital punishment Imprisonment Fines

SOURCES OF LAW

The sources of law in the U.S. legal system are the federal and state constitutions, federal treaties, interstate compacts, federal and state statutes and executive orders, the ordinances of countless local municipal governments, the rules and regulations of federal and state administrative agencies, and an ever-increasing volume of reported federal and state court decisions.

The *supreme law* of the land is the U.S. Constitution, which provides in turn that federal statutes and treaties shall be paramount to state constitutions and statutes. Federal legislation is of great significance as a source of law. Other federal actions having the force of law are executive orders by the President and rules and regulations set by federal administrative officials, agencies, and commissions. The federal courts also contribute considerably to the body of law in the United States.

The same pattern exists in every state. The paramount law of each state is contained in its written constitution. (Although a state constitution cannot deprive citizens of federal constitutional rights, it can guarantee rights beyond those provided in the U.S. Constitution.) State constitutions tend to be more specific than the U.S. Constitution and, generally, have been amended more frequently. Subordinate to the state constitution are the statutes enacted by the state's legislature and the case law developed by its judiciary. Likewise, rules and regulations of state administrative agencies have the force of law, as do executive orders issued by the governors of most states. In addition, cities, towns, and villages have limited legislative powers to pass ordinances and resolutions within their respective municipal areas. See Figure 1-3, which illustrates this hierarchy.

Constitutional Law

Constitution
fundamental law of a government establishing its powers and limitations

A **constitution**—the fundamental law of a particular level of government—establishes the governmental structure and allocates power among governmental levels, thereby defining political relationships. One of the fundamental principles on which our government is founded is that of separation of powers. As incorporated into the U.S. Constitution, this means that government consists of three distinct and independent branches—the federal judiciary, the Congress, and the executive branch.

A constitution also restricts the powers of government and specifies the rights and liberties of the people. For example, the Constitution of the United States not only specifically states what rights and authority are vested in the national government but also specifically enumerates certain rights and liberties of the people. Moreover, the Ninth Amendment to the U.S. Constitution makes it clear that this enumeration of rights does not in any way deny or limit other rights that the people retain.

Judicial review
authority of the courts to determine the constitutionality of legislative and executive acts

All other law in the United States is subordinate to the federal Constitution. No law, federal or state, is valid if it violates the federal Constitution. Under the principle of **judicial review**, the Supreme Court of the United States determines the constitutionality of *all* laws.

Judicial Law

Common law system
body of law originating in England and derived from judicial decisions

The U.S. legal system, a **common law system** like the system first developed in England, relies heavily on the judiciary as a source of law and on the adversary system for settling disputes. In an **adversary system** the parties, not the court, must initiate and conduct litigation. This approach is based on the belief that the truth is more likely to emerge from the investigation and presentation of evidence by two opposing parties, both motivated by self-interest, than from judicial investigation motivated only by official duty. In addition to the United States and England, the common law system is used in other English-speaking countries, including Canada and Australia.

Adversary system
system in which opposing parties initiate and present their cases

In distinct contrast to the common law system are civil law systems, which are based on Roman law. **Civil law systems** depend on comprehensive legislative enactments (called codes) and an inquisitorial system of determining disputes. In the **inquisitorial system**, the judiciary initiates litigation, investigates pertinent facts, and conducts the presentation of evidence. The civil law system prevails in most of Europe, Scotland, the state of Louisiana, the province of Quebec, Latin America, and parts of Africa and Asia.

Civil law system
body of law derived from Roman law and based upon comprehensive legislative enactments

Inquisitorial system
system in which the judiciary initiates, conducts, and decides cases

Common Law   The courts in common law systems have developed a body of law that serves as precedent for determining later controversies. In this sense, common law, also called case law or

Figure 1-3 Hierarchy of Law

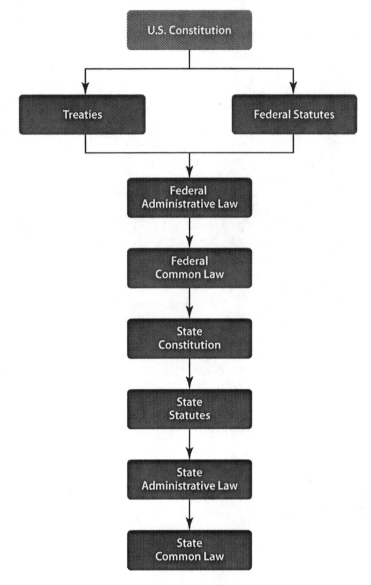

© Cengage Learning 2013

judge-made law, is distinguished from other sources of law, such as legislation and administrative rulings.

To evolve in a stable and predictable manner, the common law has developed by application of *stare decisis* ("to stand by the decisions"). Under the principle of **stare decisis**, courts adhere to and rely on rules of law that they or superior courts relied on and applied in prior similar decisions. Judicial decisions thus have two uses: (1) to determine with finality the case currently being decided and (2) to indicate how the court will decide similar cases in the future. *Stare decisis* does not, however, preclude courts from correcting erroneous decisions or from choosing among conflicting precedents. Thus, the doctrine allows sufficient flexibility for the common law to change. The strength of the common law is its ability to adapt to change without losing its sense of direction.

Stare decisis
principle that courts should apply rules decided in prior cases in deciding substantially similar cases

Equity As the common law developed in England, it became overly rigid and beset with technicalities. As a consequence, in many cases no remedies were provided because the judges insisted that a claim must fall within one of the recognized forms of action. Moreover, courts of common law could provide only limited remedies; the principal type of relief obtainable was a monetary judgment. Consequently, individuals who could not obtain adequate relief from monetary awards began to petition the king directly for justice. He, in turn, came to delegate these petitions to his chancellor.

Equity
body of law based upon
principles distinct from
common law and providing
remedies not available at law

Decree
decision of a court of equity

Specific performance
decree ordering a party to
perform a contractual duty

Injunction
decree ordering a party to
do or refrain from doing a
specified act

Reformation
equitable remedy rewriting a
contract to conform with the
original intent of the
contracting parties

Rescission
an equitable remedy
invalidating a contract

Maxim
a general legal principle

Gradually, there evolved what was in effect a new and supplementary system of needed judicial relief for those who could not receive adequate remedies through the common law. This new system, called **equity**, was administered by a court of chancery presided over by the chancellor. The chancellor, deciding cases on "equity and good conscience," regularly provided relief where common law judges had refused to act or where the remedy at law was inadequate. Thus, there grew up, side by side, two systems of law administered by different tribunals, the common law courts and the courts of equity.

An important difference between common law and equity is that the chancellor could issue a **decree**, or order, compelling a defendant to do, or refrain from doing, a specified act. A defendant who did not comply with this order could be held in contempt of court and punished by fine or imprisonment. This power of compulsion available in a court of equity opened the door to many needed remedies not available in a court of common law.

Courts of equity in some cases recognized rights that were enforceable at common law, but they provided more effective remedies. For example, in a court of equity, for breach of a land contract the buyer could obtain a decree of **specific performance** commanding the defendant seller to perform his part of the contract by transferring title to the land. Another powerful and effective remedy available only in the courts of equity was the **injunction**, a court order requiring a party to do or refrain from doing a specified act. Another remedy not available elsewhere was **reformation**, where, upon the ground of mutual mistake, an action could be brought to reform or change the language of a written agreement to conform to the actual intention of the contracting parties. An action for **rescission** of a contract, which allowed a party to invalidate a contract under certain circumstances, was another remedy.

Although courts of equity provided remedies not available in courts of law, they granted such remedies only at their discretion, not as a matter of right. This discretion was exercised according to the general legal principles, or **maxims**, formulated by equity courts over the years.

In nearly every jurisdiction in the United States, courts of common law and equity have merged into a single court that administers both systems of law. Vestiges of the old division remain, however. For example, the right to a trial by jury applies only to actions at law, but not, under federal law and in almost every state, to suits filed in equity.

Restatements of Law   The common law of the United States results from the independent decisions of the state and federal courts. The rapid increase in the number of decisions by these courts led to the establishment of the American Law Institute (ALI) in 1923. The ALI is composed of a distinguished group of lawyers, judges, and law teachers who set out to prepare

> an orderly restatement of the general common law of the United States, including in that term not only the law developed solely by judicial decision, but also the law that has grown from the application by the courts of statutes that were generally enacted and were in force for many years.

Regarded as the authoritative statement of the common law of the United States, the Restatements cover many important areas of the common law, including torts, contracts, agency, property, and trusts. Although not law in themselves, they are highly persuasive, and courts frequently have used them to support their opinions. Because they provide a concise and clear statement of much of the common law, relevant portions of the Restatements are relied on frequently in this book.

Legislative Law

Since the end of the nineteenth century, legislation has become the primary source of new law and ordered social change in the United States. The annual volume of legislative law is enormous. Justice Felix Frankfurter's remarks to the New York City Bar in 1947 are even more appropriate in the twenty-first century:

> Inevitably the work of the Supreme Court reflects the great shift in the center of gravity of lawmaking. Broadly speaking, the number of cases disposed of by opinions has not changed from term to term. But even as late as 1875 more than 40 percent of the controversies before the Court were common-law litigation, fifty years later only 5 percent, while today cases not resting on statutes are reduced almost to zero. It is therefore accurate to say that courts have ceased to be the primary makers of law in the sense in which they "legislated" the common law. It is certainly true of the Supreme Court that almost every case has a statute at its heart or close to it.

This emphasis on legislative or statutory law has occurred because common law, which develops evolutionarily and haphazardly, is not well suited for making drastic or comprehensive changes. Moreover, while courts tend to be hesitant about overruling prior decisions, legislatures commonly repeal prior enactments. In addition, legislatures may choose the issues they wish to address, whereas courts may deal only with those issues presented by actual cases. As a result, legislatures are better equipped to make the dramatic, sweeping, and relatively rapid changes in the law that technological, social, and economic innovations compel.

See Concept Review 1-2 for a comparison of law and equity.

While some business law topics, such as contracts, agency, property, and trusts, still are governed principally by the common law, most areas of commercial law, including partnerships, corporations, sales, commercial paper, secured transactions, insurance, securities regulation, antitrust, and bankruptcy have become largely statutory. Because most states enacted their own statutes dealing with these branches of commercial law, a great diversity developed among the states and hampered the conduct of commerce on a national scale. The increased need for greater uniformity led to the development of a number of proposed uniform laws that would reduce the conflicts among state laws.

The most successful example is the ***Uniform Commercial Code*** (UCC), which was prepared under the joint sponsorship and direction of the National Conference of Commissioners on Uniform State Laws (NCCUSL) and the ALI. All fifty states (although Louisiana has adopted only Articles 1, 3, 4, 5, 7, and 8), the District of Columbia, and the Virgin Islands have adopted the UCC.

The NCCUSL has drafted more than 250 uniform laws, including the Uniform Partnership Act, the Uniform Limited Partnership Act, and the Uniform Probate Code. The ALI has developed a number of model statutory formulations, including the Model Code of Evidence, the Model Penal Code, and a Model Land Development Code. In addition, the American Bar Association has promulgated the Model Business Corporation Act.

Treaty
an agreement between or among independent nations

Treaties A **treaty** is an agreement between or among independent nations. The U.S. Constitution authorizes the President to enter into treaties with the advice and consent of the Senate, "providing two thirds of the Senators present concur."

Treaties may be entered into only by the federal government, not by the states. A treaty signed by the President and approved by the Senate has the legal force of a federal statute. Accordingly, a federal treaty may supersede a prior federal statute, while a federal statute may supersede a prior treaty. Like statutes, treaties are subordinate to the federal Constitution and subject to judicial review.

Executive order
legislation issued by the President or a governor

Executive Orders In addition to the executive functions, the President of the United States also has authority to issue laws, which are called **executive orders**. This authority typically derives from specific delegation by federal legislation. An executive order may amend, revoke, or supersede a prior executive order. An example of an executive order is the one issued by President Johnson in 1965 prohibiting discrimination by federal contractors on the basis of race, color, sex, religion, or national origin in employment on any work the contractor performed during the period of the federal contract.

The governors of most states enjoy comparable authority to issue executive orders.

CONCEPT REVIEW 1-2

Comparison of Law and Equity

	Law	Equity
Availability	Generally	Discretionary: if remedy at law is inadequate
Precedents	*Stare decisis*	Equitable maxims
Jury	If either party demands	None in federal and almost all states
Remedies	Judgment for monetary damages	Decree of specific performance, injunction, reformation, rescission

Administrative Law

Administrative law
law dealing with the establishment, duties, and powers of agencies in the executive branch of government

Administrative law is the branch of public law that is created by administrative agencies in the form of rules, regulations, orders, and decisions to carry out the regulatory powers and duties of those agencies. It also deals with controversies arising among individuals and these public officials and agencies. Administrative functions and activities concern general matters of public health, safety, and welfare, including the establishment and maintenance of military forces, police, citizenship and naturalization, taxation, environmental protection, and the regulation of transportation, interstate highways, waterways, television, radio, and trade and commerce.

Because of the increasing complexity of the nation's social, economic, and industrial life, the scope of administrative law has expanded enormously. In 1952 Justice Jackson stated that "the rise of administrative bodies has been the most significant legal trend of the last century, and perhaps more values today are affected by their decisions than by those of all the courts, review of administrative decisions apart." This is evidenced by the great increase in the number and activities of federal government boards, commissions, and other agencies. Certainly, agencies create more legal rules and decide more controversies than all the legislatures and courts combined.

LEGAL ANALYSIS

Decisions in state trial courts generally are not reported or published. The precedent a trial court sets is not sufficiently weighty to warrant permanent reporting. Except in New York and a few other states where selected opinions of trial courts are published, decisions in trial courts are simply filed in the office of the clerk of the court, where they are available for public inspection. Decisions of state courts of appeals are published in consecutively numbered volumes called "reports." In most states, court decisions are found in the official state reports of that state. In addition, state reports are published by West Publishing Company in a regional reporter called the National Reporter System, composed of the following: Atlantic (A., A.2d, or A.3d); South Eastern (S.E. or S.E.2d); South Western (S.W., S.W.2d, or S.W.3d); New York Supplement (N.Y.S. or N.Y.S.2d); North Western (N.W. or N.W.2d); North Eastern (N.E. or N.E.2d); Southern (So., So.2d, or So.3d); and Pacific (P., P.2d, or P.3d). At least twenty states no longer publish official reports and have designated a commercial reporter as the authoritative source of state case law. After they are published, these opinions, or "cases," are referred to ("cited") by giving (1) the name of the case; (2) the volume, name, and page of the official state report, if any, in which it is published; (3) the volume, name, and page of the particular set and series of the National Reporter System; and (4) the volume, name, and page of any other selected case series. For instance, *Lefkowitz v. Great Minneapolis Surplus Store, Inc.*, 251 Minn. 188, 86 N.W.2d 689 (1957), indicates that the opinion in this case may be found in Volume 251 of the official Minnesota Reports at page 188 and in Volume 86 of the North Western Reporter, Second Series, at page 689, and that the opinion was delivered in 1957.

The decisions of courts in the federal system are found in a number of reports. U.S. District Court opinions appear in the Federal Supplement (F.Supp. or F.Supp.2d). Decisions of the U.S. Court of Appeals are found in the Federal Reporter (Fed., F.2d, or F.3d), while the U.S. Supreme Court's opinions are published in the U.S. Supreme Court Reports (U.S.), Supreme Court Reporter (S.Ct.), and Lawyers Edition (L.Ed.). While all U.S. Supreme Court decisions are reported, not every case decided by the U.S. District Courts and the U.S. Courts of Appeals is reported. Each circuit has established rules determining which decisions are published.

In reading the title of a case, such as "*Jones v. Brown*," the "*v.*" or "*vs.*" means versus or against. In the trial court, Jones is the **plaintiff**, the person who filed the suit, and Brown is the **defendant**, the person against whom the suit was brought. When the case is appealed, some, but not all, courts of appeals or appellate courts place the name of the party who appeals, or the **appellant**, first, so that "*Jones v. Brown*" in the trial court becomes, if Brown loses and hence becomes the appellant, "*Brown v. Jones*" in the appellate court. Therefore, it is not always possible to determine from the title itself who was the plaintiff and who was the defendant. You must carefully read the facts of each case and clearly identify each party in your mind to understand the discussion by the appellate court. In a criminal case the caption in the trial court will first designate the prosecuting governmental unit and then will indicate the defendant, as in "*State v. Jones*" or "*Commonwealth v. Brown*."

Appellant
party who appeals

The study of reported cases requires an understanding and application of legal analysis. Normally, the reported opinion in a case sets forth (1) the essential facts, the nature of the

APPLYING THE LAW

Introduction

Facts Jackson bought a new car and planned to sell his old one for about $2,500. But before he did so, he happened to receive a call from his cousin, Trina, who had just graduated from college. Among other things, Trina told Jackson she needed a car but did not have much money. Feeling generous, Jackson told Trina he would give her his old car. But the next day a coworker offered Jackson $3,500 for his old car, and Jackson sold it to the coworker.

Issue Did Jackson have the right to sell his car to the coworker, or legally had he already made a gift of it to Trina?

Rule of Law A gift is the transfer of ownership of property from one person to another without anything in return. The person making the gift is called the donor, and the person receiving it is known as the donee. A valid gift requires (1) the donor's present intent to transfer the property and (2) delivery of the property.

Application In this case, Jackson is the would-be donor and Trina the would-be donee. To find that Jackson had already made a gift of the car to Trina, both Jackson's intent to give it to her and delivery of the car to Trina would

need to be demonstrated. It is evident from their telephone conversation that Jackson did intend at that point to give the car to Trina. It is equally apparent from his conduct that he later changed his mind, because he sold it to someone else the next day. Consequently, he did not deliver the car to Trina.

Conclusion Because the donor did not deliver the property to the donee, legally no gift was made. Jackson was free to sell the car.

© Cengage Learning 2013

action, the parties, what happened to bring about the controversy, what happened in the lower court, and what pleadings are material to the issues; (2) the issues of law or fact; (3) the legal principles involved; (4) the application of these principles; and (5) the decision.

You can and should use this same legal analysis when learning the substantive concepts presented in this text and applying them to the end-of-chapter questions and case problems. By way of example, in a number of chapters throughout the text we have included a boxed feature called **Applying the Law**, which provides a systematic legal analysis of a single concept learned in the chapter. This feature begins with the **facts** of a hypothetical case, followed by an identification of the broad legal **issue** presented by those facts. We then state the **rule**—or applicable legal principles, including definitions, which aid in resolving the legal issue—and **apply** it to the facts. Finally we state a legal **conclusion**, or decision in the case. An example of this type of legal analysis appears above.

CHAPTER SUMMARY

Nature of Law

Definition of Law "a rule of civil conduct prescribed by the supreme power in a state, commanding what is right, and prohibiting what is wrong" (William Blackstone)

Functions of Law to maintain stability in the social, political, and economic system through dispute resolution, protection of property, and the preservation of the state, while simultaneously permitting ordered change

Laws and Morals are different but overlapping; law provides sanctions while morals do not

Law and Justice are separate and distinct concepts; justice is the fair, equitable, and impartial treatment of competing interests with due regard for the common good

Classification of Law

Substantive and Procedural
- *Substantive Law* law creating rights and duties
- *Procedural Law* rules for enforcing substantive law

Public and Private
- *Public Law* law dealing with the relationship between government and individuals
- *Private Law* law governing the relationships among individuals and legal entities

Civil and Criminal

- *Civil Law* law dealing with rights and duties, the violation of which constitutes a wrong against an individual or other legal entity
- *Criminal Law* law establishing duties that, if violated, constitute a wrong against the entire community

---

Sources of Law

Constitutional Law fundamental law of a government establishing its powers and limitations

Judicial Law

- *Common Law* body of law developed by the courts that serves as precedent for determination of later controversies
- *Equity* body of law based upon principles distinct from common law and providing remedies not available at law

Legislative Law statutes adopted by legislative bodies

- *Treaties* agreements between or among independent nations
- *Executive Orders* laws issued by the President or by the governor of a state

Administrative Law is created by administrative agencies in the form of rules, regulations, orders, and decisions to carry out the regulatory powers and duties of those agencies

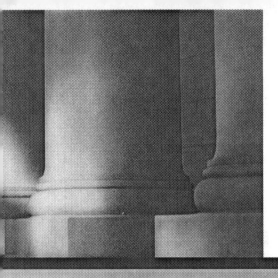

CHAPTER **2**

Business Ethics

Our characters are the result of our conduct.

Aristotle,
in Nicomachean Ethics (c. 335 BCE)

CHAPTER OUTCOMES

After reading and studying this chapter, you should be able to:

1. Describe the difference between law and ethics.

2. Compare the various ethical theories.

3. Describe cost-benefit analysis and explain when it should be used and when it should be avoided.

4. Explain Kohlberg's stages of moral development.

5. Explain the ethical responsibilities of business.

B
usiness ethics is a subset of ethics: no special set of ethical principles applies only to the world of business. Immoral acts are immoral, whether or not a businessperson has committed them. In the last few years, countless business wrongs, such as insider trading, fraudulent earnings statements and other accounting misconduct, price-fixing, concealment of dangerous defects in products, and bribery, have been reported almost daily. Companies such as Enron, WorldCom, Adelphia, Parmalat, Arthur Anderson, and Global Crossing have all violated the law, and some of these firms no longer exist as a result of these ethical lapses. In 2004, Martha Stewart was convicted of obstructing justice and lying to investigators about a stock sale. More recently, Bernie Madoff perpetrated the largest Ponzi scheme in history with an estimated loss of $20 billion in principal and approximately $65 billion in paper losses. In May 2011, Galleon Group (a hedge fund) billionaire, Raj Rajaratnam, was found guilty of fourteen counts of conspiracy and securities fraud.

Ethics can be defined broadly as the study of what is right or good for human beings. It attempts to determine what people ought to do, or what goals they should pursue. **Business ethics**, as a branch of applied ethics, is the study and determination of what is right and good in business settings. Business ethics seeks to understand the moral issues that arise from business practices, institutions, and decision making, and their relationship to generalized human values. Unlike legal analyses, analyses of ethics have no central authority, such as courts or legislatures, upon which to rely; nor do they follow clear-cut universal standards. Nonetheless, despite these inherent limitations, it still may be possible to make meaningful ethical judgments. To improve ethical decision making, it is important to understand how others have approached the task.

Some examples of the many business ethics questions may clarify the definition of business ethics. In the employment relationship, countless ethical issues arise regarding the safety and compensation of workers, their civil rights (such as equal treatment, privacy, and freedom from sexual harassment), and the legitimacy of whistle-blowing. In the relationship between business and its customers, ethical issues permeate marketing techniques, product safety, and consumer protection. The

Ethics
study of what is right or good for human beings

Business ethics
study of what is right and good in a business setting; includes the moral issues that arise from business practices, institutions, and decision making

© Kim Steele/Jupiter Images

13

relationship between business and its owners bristles with ethical questions involving corporate governance, shareholder voting, and management's duties to the shareholders. The relationship among competing businesses involves numerous ethical matters, including fair competition and the effects of collusion. The interaction between business and society at large presents additional ethical dimensions: pollution of the physical environment, commitment to the community's economic and social infrastructure, and depletion of natural resources. Not only do all of these issues recur at the international level, but also additional ones present themselves, such as bribery of foreign officials, exploitation of less-developed countries, and conflicts among differing cultures and value systems.

In resolving the ethical issues raised by business conduct, it is helpful to use a seeing–knowing–doing model. First, the decision maker should *see* (identify) the ethical issues involved in the proposed conduct, including the ethical implications of the various available options. Second, the decision maker should *know* (resolve) what to do by choosing the best option. Finally, the decision maker should *do* (implement) the chosen option by developing and implementing strategies.

This chapter first surveys the most prominent ethical theories (the knowing part of the decision, on which the great majority of philosophers and ethicists have focused). The chapter then examines ethical standards in business and the ethical responsibilities of business. It concludes with five ethical business cases, which give the student the opportunity to apply the seeing–knowing–doing model. The student (1) identifies the ethical issues presented in these cases; (2) resolves these issues by using one of the ethical theories described in the chapter, some other ethical theory, or a combination of the theories; and (3) develops strategies for implementing the ethical resolution.

Law versus Ethics

As discussed in Chapter 1, moral concepts strongly affect the law, but law and morality are not the same. Although it is tempting to say that "if it's legal, it's moral," such a proposition is generally too simplistic. For example, it would seem gravely immoral to stand by silently while a blind man walks off a cliff if one could prevent the fall by shouting a warning, even though one would not be legally obligated to do so. Similarly, moral questions arise concerning "legal" business practices, such as failing to fulfill a promise that is not legally binding; exporting products banned in the United States to developing countries where they are not prohibited; or slaughtering baby seals for fur coats. The mere fact that these practices are legal does not prevent them from being challenged on moral grounds.

Just as it is possible for legal acts to be immoral, it is equally possible for illegal acts to seem morally preferable to following the law. For example, it is the moral conviction of the great majority of people that those who sheltered Jews in violation of Nazi edicts during World War II and those who committed acts of civil disobedience in the 1950s and 1960s to challenge segregation laws in the United States were acting properly and that the laws themselves were immoral.

Ethical Theories

Philosophers have sought for centuries to develop dependable and universal methods for making ethical judgments. In earlier times, some thinkers analogized the discovery of ethical principles with the derivation of mathematical proofs. They asserted that people could discover fundamental ethical rules by applying careful reasoning *a priori*. (A priori reasoning is based on theory rather than experimentation and deductively draws conclusions from cause to effect and from generalizations to particular instances.) In more recent times, many philosophers have concluded that although careful reasoning and deep thought assist substantially in moral reasoning, experience reveals that the complexities of the world defeat most attempts to fashion precise, *a priori* guidelines. Nevertheless, a review of the most significant ethical theories can aid the analysis of business ethics issues.

Ethical Fundamentalism

Ethical fundamentalism
individuals look to a central authority or set of rules to guide them in ethical decision making

Under **ethical fundamentalism**, or absolutism, individuals look to a central authority or set of rules to guide them in ethical decision making. Some look to the Bible; others look to the Koran or to the writings of Karl Marx or to any number of living or deceased prophets. The essential characteristic of this approach is a reliance on a central repository of wisdom. In some cases, such reliance is total. In others, followers of a religion or a spiritual leader may believe that all members of the group are obligated to assess moral dilemmas independently, according to each person's understanding of the dictates of the fundamental principles.

Ethical Relativism

Ethical relativism
actions must be judged by what individuals subjectively feel is right or wrong for themselves

Ethical relativism is a doctrine asserting that actions must be judged by what individuals feel is right or wrong for themselves. It holds that when any two individuals or cultures differ regarding the morality of a particular issue or action, they are both correct because morality is relative. However, although ethical relativism promotes open-mindedness and tolerance, it has limitations. If each person's actions are always correct for that person, then his behavior is, by definition, moral and therefore exempt from criticism. Once a person concludes that criticizing or punishing behavior in some cases is appropriate, he abandons ethical relativism and faces the task of developing a broader ethical methodology.

Situational ethics
judging a person's actions by first putting oneself in the actor's situation

Although bearing a surface resemblance to ethical relativism, situational ethics actually differs substantially. **Situational ethics** holds that developing precise guidelines for effectively navigating ethical dilemmas is difficult because real-life decision making is so complex. To judge the morality of someone's behavior, the person judging must actually put herself in the other person's shoes to understand what motivated the other to choose a particular course of action. Situational ethics, however, does not cede the ultimate judgment of the propriety of an action to the actor; rather, it insists that, prior to evaluation, a person's decision or act be viewed from the actor's perspective.

Utilitarianism

Utilitarianism
moral actions are those that produce the greatest net pleasure compared with net pain

Utilitarianism is a doctrine that assesses good and evil in terms of the consequences of actions. Those actions that produce the greatest net pleasure compared with net pain are better in a moral sense than those that produce less net pleasure. As Jeremy Bentham, one of the most influential proponents of utilitarianism, proclaimed, a good or moral act is one that results in "the greatest happiness for the greatest number."

Act utilitarianism
each separate act must be assessed according to whether it maximizes pleasure over pain

Rule utilitarianism
supports rules that on balance produce the greatest good

The two major forms of utilitarianism are act utilitarianism and rule utilitarianism. **Act utilitarianism** assesses each separate act according to whether it maximizes pleasure over pain. For example, if telling a lie in a particular situation produces more overall pleasure than pain, then an act utilitarian would support lying as the moral thing to do. Rule utilitarians, disturbed by the unpredictability of act utilitarianism and its potential for abuse, follow a different approach. **Rule utilitarianism** holds that general rules must be established and followed even though, in some instances, following rules may produce less overall pleasure than not following them. It applies utilitarian principles in developing rules; thus, it supports rules that on balance produce the greatest satisfaction. Determining whether telling a lie in a given instance would produce greater pleasure than telling the truth is less important to the rule utilitarian than deciding whether a general practice of lying would maximize society's pleasure. If lying would not maximize pleasure generally, then one should follow a rule of not lying even though on occasion telling a lie would produce greater pleasure than would telling the truth.

Cost-benefit analysis
quantifies in monetary terms the benefits and costs of alternatives

Utilitarian notions underlie cost-benefit analysis, an analytical tool used by many business and government managers today. **Cost-benefit analysis** first quantifies in monetary terms and then compares the direct and indirect costs and benefits of program alternatives for meeting a specified objective. Cost-benefit analysis seeks the greatest economic efficiency according to the underlying notion that, given two potential acts, the act achieving the greatest output at the least cost promotes the greatest marginal happiness over the less-efficient act, other things being equal.

The chief criticism of utilitarianism is that in some important instances it ignores justice. A number of situations would maximize the pleasure of the majority at great social cost to a minority. Another major criticism of utilitarianism is that measuring pleasure and pain in the fashion its supporters advocate is extremely difficult, if not impossible.

Deontology

Deontology
holds that actions must be judged by their motives and means as well as their results

Deontological theories (from the Greek word *deon*, meaning duty or obligation) address the practical problems of utilitarianism by holding that certain underlying principles are right or wrong regardless of any pleasure or pain calculations. Believing that actions cannot be measured simply by their results but must be judged by means and motives as well, deontologists judge the morality of acts not so much by their consequences but by the motives that lead to them. A person not only must achieve just results but also must employ the proper means.

The best-known deontological theory was proffered by the eighteenth-century philosopher Immanuel Kant. Under Kant's *categorical imperative*, for an action to be moral it (1) must potentially be a universal law that could be applied consistently and (2) must respect the autonomy and rationality of all human beings and not treat them as an expedient. That is, one should not do anything that he or she would not have everyone do in a similar situation. For example, you should not lie to colleagues unless you support the right of all colleagues to lie to one another. Similarly, you should not cheat others unless you advocate everyone's right to cheat. We apply Kantian reasoning when we challenge someone's behavior by asking: what if everybody acted that way?

Under Kant's approach, it would be improper to assert a principle to which one claimed personal exception, such as insisting that it was acceptable for you to cheat but not for anyone else to do so. This principle could not be universalized because everyone would then insist on similar rules from which only they were exempt.

Kant's philosophy also rejects notions of the end justifying the means. To Kant, every person is an end in himself or herself. Each person deserves respect simply because of his or her humanity. Thus, any sacrifice of a person for the greater good of society would be unacceptable to Kant.

In many respects, Kant's categorical imperative is a variation of the Golden Rule; and, like the Golden Rule, the categorical imperative appeals to the individual's self-centeredness.

As does every theory, Kantian ethics has its critics. Just as deontologists criticize utilitarians for excessive pragmatism and flexible moral guidelines, utilitarians and others criticize deontologists for rigidity and excessive formalism. For example, if one inflexibly adopts as a rule to tell the truth, one ignores situations in which lying might well be justified. A person hiding a terrified wife from her angry, abusive husband would seem to be acting morally by falsely denying that the wife is at the person's house. Yet a deontologist, feeling bound to tell the truth, might ignore the consequences of truthfulness, tell the husband where his wife is, and create the possibility of a terrible tragedy. Another criticism of deontological theories is that the proper course may be difficult to determine when values or assumptions conflict.

Social Ethics Theories

Social ethical theories focus on a person's obligations to other members in society and on the individual's rights and obligations

Social egalitarians believe that society should provide all members with equal amounts of goods and services irrespective of their relative contributions

Distributive justice stresses equality of opportunity rather than of results

Libertarians stress market outcomes as the basis for distributing society's rewards

Social ethics theories assert that special obligations arise from the social nature of human beings. Such theories focus not only on each person's obligations to other members of society but also on the individual's rights and obligations within the society. For example, **social egalitarians** believe that society should provide each person with equal amounts of goods and services regardless of the contribution each makes to increase society's wealth.

Two other ethics theories have received widespread attention in recent years. One is the theory of **distributive justice** proposed by Harvard philosopher John Rawls, which seeks to analyze the type of society that people in a "natural state" would establish if they could not determine in advance whether they would be talented, rich, healthy, or ambitious, relative to other members of society. According to distributive justice, the society contemplated through this "veil of ignorance" is the one that should be developed because it considers the needs and rights of all its members. Rawls did not argue that such a society would be strictly egalitarian and that it would unfairly penalize those who turned out to be the most talented and ambitious. Instead, Rawls suggested that such a society would stress equality of opportunity, not of results. On the other hand, Rawls stressed that society would pay heed to the least advantaged to ensure that they did not suffer unduly and that they enjoyed society's benefits. To Rawls, society must be premised on justice. Everyone is entitled to his or her fair share in society, a fairness all must work to guarantee.

In contrast to Rawls, another Harvard philosopher, Robert Nozick, stressed liberty, not justice, as the most important obligation that society owes its members. **Libertarians** stress market outcomes as the basis for distributing society's rewards. Only to the extent that one meets market demands does one deserve society's benefits. Libertarians oppose social interference in the lives of those who do not violate the rules of the marketplace; that is, in the lives of those who do not cheat others and who disclose honestly the nature of their transactions with others. The fact that some end up with fortunes while others accumulate little simply proves that some can play in the market effectively while others cannot. To libertarians, this is not unjust. What is unjust to them is any attempt by society to take wealth earned by citizens and distribute it to those who did not earn it.

These theories and others (e.g., Marxism) judge society in moral terms by its organization and by the way in which it distributes goods and services. They demonstrate the difficulty of ethical decision making in the context of a social organization: behavior that is consistently ethical from individual to individual may not necessarily produce a just society.

Other Theories

The preceding theories do not exhaust the possible approaches to evaluating ethical behavior; several other theories also deserve mention. **Intuitionism** holds that a rational person possesses inherent powers to assess the correctness of actions. Though an individual may refine and strengthen these powers, they are just as basic to humanity as our instincts for survival and self-defense. Just as some people are better artists or musicians, some people have more insight into ethical behavior than others. Consistent with intuitionism is the **good person philosophy**, which declares that if individuals wish to act morally, they should seek out and emulate those who always seem to know the right choice in any given situation and who always seem to do the right thing. One variation of these ethical approaches is the *Television Test*, which directs us to imagine that every ethical decision we make is being broadcast on nationwide television. An appropriate decision is one we would be comfortable broadcasting on national television for all to witness.

ETHICAL STANDARDS IN BUSINESS

In this section, we explore the application of the theories of ethical behavior to the world of business.

Choosing an Ethical System

In their efforts to resolve the moral dilemmas facing humankind, philosophers and other thinkers have struggled for years to refine the various systems previously discussed. All of the systems are limited, however, in terms of applicability and tend to produce unacceptable prescriptions for action in some circumstances. But to say that each system has limits is not to say it is useless. On the contrary, a number of these systems provide insight into ethical decision making and help us formulate issues and resolve moral dilemmas. Furthermore, concluding that moral standards are difficult to articulate and that moral boundaries are imprecise is not the same as concluding that moral standards are unnecessary or nonexistent.

Research by the noted psychologist Lawrence Kohlberg provides some insight into ethical decision making and lends credibility to the notion that moral growth, like physical growth, is part of the human condition. **Kohlberg** observed that people progress through sequential **stages of moral development** according to two major variables: age and reasoning. During the first level—the *preconventional level*—a child's conduct is a reaction to the fear of punishment and, later, to the pleasure of reward. Although people who operate at this level may behave in a moral manner, they do so without understanding why their behavior is moral. The rules are imposed upon them. During adolescence—Kohlberg's *conventional level*—people conform their behavior to meet the expectations of groups, such as family, peers, and eventually society. The motivation for conformity is loyalty, affection, and trust. Most adults operate at this level. According to Kohlberg, some reach the third level—the *postconventional level*—at which they accept and conform to moral principles because they understand *why* the principles are right and binding. At this level, moral principles are voluntarily internalized, not externally imposed. Moreover, individuals at this stage develop their own universal ethical principles and may even question the laws and values that society and others have adopted (see Figure 2-1 for Kohlberg's stages of moral development).

Figure 2-1 Kohlberg's Stages of Moral Development

Levels	Perspective	Justification
Preconventional (Childhood)	Self	Punishment/Reward
Conventional (Adolescent)	Group	Group Norms
Postconventional (Adult)	Universal	Moral Principles

Intuitionism
a rational person possesses inherent powers to assess the correctness of actions

Good person philosophy
holds that individuals seek out and emulate good role models

Kohlberg's stages of moral development
see Figure 2-1

Kohlberg believed that not all people reach the third, or even the second, stage. He therefore argued that essential to the study of ethics was the exploration of ways to help people achieve the advanced stage of postconventional thought. Other psychologists assert that individuals do not pass sequentially from stage to stage but rather function in all three stages simultaneously.

Whatever the source of our ethical approach, we cannot avoid facing moral dilemmas that challenge us to recognize and do the right thing. Moreover, for those who plan business careers, such dilemmas necessarily will have implications for many others—employees, shareholders, suppliers, customers, and society at large.

Corporations as Moral Agents

Corporations as moral agents

because a corporation is a statutory entity, it is difficult to resolve whether it should be morally accountable

Because corporations are not persons but rather artificial entities created by the state, whether they can or should be held morally accountable is difficult to determine. Though, clearly, individuals within corporations can be held morally responsible, the corporate entity presents unique problems.

Commentators are divided on the issue. Some insist that only people can engage in behavior that can be judged in moral terms. Opponents of this view concede that corporations are not persons in any literal sense but insist that the attributes of responsibility inherent in corporations are sufficient to justify judging corporate behavior from a moral perspective.

ETHICAL RESPONSIBILITIES OF BUSINESS

Many people assert that the only responsibility of business is to maximize profit and that this obligation overrides any ethical or social responsibility. Although our economic system of modified capitalism is based on the pursuit of self-interest, it also contains components to check this motivation of greed. Our system has always recognized the need for some form of regulation, whether it be by the "invisible hand" of competition, the self-regulation of business, or government regulation.

Regulation of Business

As explained and justified by Adam Smith in *The Wealth of Nations* (1776), the capitalistic system is composed of six "institutions": economic motivation, private productive property, free enterprise, free markets, competition, and limited government. As long as all these constituent institutions continue to exist and operate in balance, the factors of production—land, capital, and labor—combine to produce an efficient allocation of resources for individual consumers and for the economy as a whole. To achieve this outcome, however, Smith's model requires that a number of conditions be satisfied: "standardized products, numerous firms in markets, each firm with a small share and unable by its actions alone to exert significant influence over price, no barriers to entry, and output carried to the point where each seller's marginal cost equals the going market price." E. Singer, *Antitrust Economics and Legal Analysis.*

History has demonstrated that the actual operation of the economy has satisfied almost none of these assumptions. More specifically, the actual competitive process falls considerably short of the assumptions of the classic economic model of perfect competition:

> Competitive industries are never perfectly competitive in this sense. Many of the resources they employ cannot be shifted to other employments without substantial cost and delay. The allocation of those resources, as between industries or as to relative proportions within a single industry, is unlikely to have been made in a way that affords the best possible expenditure of economic effort. Information is incomplete, motivation confused, and decision therefore ill informed and often unwise. Variations in efficiency are not directly reflected in variations of profit. Success is derived in large part from competitive selling efforts, which in the aggregate may be wasteful, and from differentiation of products, which may be undertaken partly by methods designed to impair the opportunity of the buyer to compare quality and price.
>
> *C. Edwards, Maintaining Competition*

In addition to capitalism's failure to allocate resources efficiently, it cannot be relied on to achieve all of the social and public policy objectives a pluralistic democracy requires. For example, the free enterprise model simply does not address equitable distribution of wealth, national defense, conservation of natural resources, full employment, stability in economic cycles, protection against economic dislocations, health and safety, social security, and other important social

Regulation of business
government regulation is necessary because all the conditions for perfect competition have not been satisfied and free competition cannot by itself achieve other social goals

and economic goals. Increased **regulation of business** has occurred not only to preserve the competitive process in our economic system but also to achieve social goals extrinsic to the efficient allocation of resources, the "invisible hand" and self-regulation by business having failed to bring about these desired results. Such intervention attempts (1) to regulate both "legal" monopolies, such as those conferred by law through copyrights, patents, and trade symbols, and "natural" monopolies, such as utilities, transportation, and communications; (2) to preserve competition by correcting imperfections in the market system; (3) to protect specific groups, especially labor and agriculture, from marketplace failures; and (4) to promote other social goals. Successful government regulation involves a delicate balance between regulations that attempt to preserve competition and those that attempt to advance other social objectives. The latter should not undermine the basic competitive processes that provide an efficient allocation of economic resources.

Corporate Governance

Corporate governance
vast amounts of wealth and power have become concentrated in a small number of corporations, which in turn are controlled by a small group of people, and it is argued that they therefore have a responsibility to undertake projects to benefit society

In addition to the broad demands of maintaining a competitive and fair marketplace, another factor demanding the ethical and social responsibility of business is the sheer size and power of individual corporations. The five thousand largest U.S. firms currently produce more than half of the nation's gross national product.

In a classic study published in 1932, Adolf Berle and Gardner Means concluded that great amounts of economic power had been concentrated in a relatively few large corporations, that the ownership of these corporations had become widely dispersed, and that the shareholders had become far removed from active participation in management. Since their original study, these trends have continued steadily. The five hundred to one thousand large publicly held corporations own the great bulk of the industrial wealth of the United States. Moreover, these corporations are controlled by a small group of corporate officers.

Historically, the boards of many publicly held corporations consisted mainly or entirely of inside directors (corporate officers who also serve on the board of directors). During the past two decades, however, as a result of regulations by the U.S. Securities and Exchange Commission and the stock exchanges, the number and influence of outside directors has increased substantially. Now the boards of the great majority of publicly held corporations consist primarily of outside directors, and these corporations have audit committees consisting entirely of outside directors. Nevertheless, a number of instances of corporate misconduct have been revealed in the first years of this century. In response to these business scandals—involving companies such as Enron, WorldCom, Global Crossing, Adelphia, and Arthur Andersen—in 2002 Congress passed the Sarbanes-Oxley Act. This legislation seeks to prevent these types of scandals by increasing corporate responsibility through the imposition of additional corporate governance requirements on publicly held corporations. (This statute is discussed further in Chapters 6, 35, 39, and 43.)

These developments raise a large number of social, policy, and ethical issues about the governance of large, publicly owned corporations. Many observers insist that companies playing such an important economic role should have a responsibility to undertake projects that benefit society in ways that go beyond mere financial efficiency in producing goods and services. In some instances, the idea of corporate obligations comes from industrialists themselves.

Arguments against Social Responsibility

A number of arguments oppose business involvement in socially responsible activities: profitability, unfairness, accountability, and expertise.

Profitability
the business of business should be to return as much money as possible to shareholders

Profitability   As Milton Friedman and others have argued, businesses are artificial entities established to permit people to engage in profit-making, not social, activities. Without profits, they assert, there is little reason for a corporation to exist and no real way to measure the effectiveness of corporate activities. Businesses are not organized to engage in social activities; they are structured to produce goods and services for which they receive money. Their social obligation is to return as much of this money as possible to their direct stakeholders. In a free market with significant competition, the selfish pursuits of corporations will lead to maximizing output, minimizing costs, and establishing fair prices. All other concerns distract companies and interfere with achieving these goals.

Unfairness
whenever corporations engage in social activities, they divert funds rightfully belonging to shareholders and/or employees

Unfairness Whenever companies stray from their designated role of profit-maker, they take unfair advantage of company employees and shareholders. For example, a company may support the arts or education or spend excess funds on health and safety; however, these funds rightfully belong to the shareholders or employees. The company's decision to disburse these funds to others who may well be less deserving than the shareholders and employees is unfair. Furthermore, consumers can express their desires through the marketplace, and shareholders and employees can decide privately whether they wish to make charitable contributions. In most cases, senior management consults the board of directors about supporting social concerns but does not seek the approval of the company's major stakeholders, thereby effectively disenfranchising these shareholders from actions that reduce their benefits from the corporation.

Accountability
a corporation is subject to less public accountability than public bodies

Accountability Corporations, as previously noted, are private institutions that are subject to a lower standard of accountability than are public bodies. Accordingly, a company may decide to support a wide range of social causes and yet submit to little public scrutiny. But a substantial potential for abuse exists in such cases. For one thing, a company could provide funding for a variety of causes its employees or shareholders did not support. It also could provide money "with strings attached," thereby controlling the recipients' agendas for less than socially beneficial purposes. For example, a drug company that contributes to a consumer group might implicitly or explicitly condition its assistance on the group's agreement never to criticize the company or the drug industry.

This lack of accountability warrants particular concern because of the enormous power corporations wield in modern society. Many large companies, like Walmart, Toyota, or ExxonMobil, generate and spend more money in a year than all but a handful of the world's countries. If these companies suddenly began to vigorously pursue their own social agendas, their influence might well rival, and perhaps undermine, that of their national government. In a country like the United States, founded on the principles of limited government and the balance of powers, too much corporate involvement in social affairs might well present substantial problems. Without clear guidelines and accountability, companies pursuing their private visions of socially responsible behavior might well distort the entire process of governance.

There is a clear alternative to corporations engaging in socially responsible action. If society wishes to increase the resources devoted to needy causes, it has the power to do so. Let the corporations seek profits without the burden of a social agenda, let the consumers vote in the marketplace for the products and services they desire, and let the government tax a portion of corporate profits for socially beneficial causes.

Expertise
although a corporation may have a high level of expertise in selling its goods and services, there is absolutely no guarantee that any promotion of social activities will be carried on with the same degree of competence

Expertise Even though a corporation has an expertise in producing and selling its product, it may not possess a talent for recognizing or managing socially useful activities. Corporations become successful in the market because they can identify and meet the needs of their customers. Nothing suggests that this talent spills over into nonbusiness arenas. In fact, critics of corporate participation in social activities worry that corporations will prove unable to distinguish the true needs of society from their own narrow self-interests.

Arguments in Favor of Social Responsibility

First, it should be recognized that even the critics of business acknowledge that the prime responsibility of business is to make a reasonable return on its investment by producing a quality product at a reasonable price. They do not suggest that business entities be charitable institutions. They do assert, however, that business has certain obligations beyond making a profit or not harming society. Such critics contend that business must help to resolve societal problems, and they offer a number of arguments in support of their position.

The social contract
because society allows for the creation of corporations and gives them special rights, including a grant of limited liability, corporations owe a responsibility to society

The Social Contract Society creates corporations and gives them a special social status, including the granting of limited liability, which insulates owners from liability for debts their organizations incur. Supporters of social roles for corporations assert that limited liability and other rights granted to companies carry a responsibility: corporations, just like other members of society, must contribute to its betterment. Therefore, companies owe a moral debt to society to contribute to its overall well-being. Society needs a host of improvements, such as pollution control, safe products, a free marketplace, quality education, cures for illness, and freedom from crime. Corporations can help in each of these areas. Granted, deciding which social needs deserve corporate attention is difficult; however, this challenge does not lessen a company's obligation to choose a cause. Corporate America cannot ignore the multitude of pressing needs that remain, despite the efforts of government and private charities.

Stakeholder model

corporations have fiduciary duty to all of their stakeholders, not just their stockholders

A derivative of the social contract theory is the **stakeholder model** for the societal role of the business corporation. Under the stakeholder model, a corporation has fiduciary responsibilities—duty of utmost loyalty and good faith—to all of its stakeholders, not just its stockholders. Historically, the stockholder model for the role of business has been the norm. Under this theory, a corporation is viewed as private property owned by and for the benefit of its owners—the stockholders of the corporation. (For a full discussion of this legal model, see Chapter 35.) The stakeholder model, on the other hand, holds that corporations are responsible to society at large and more directly to all those constituencies on which they depend for their survival. Thus, it is argued that a corporation should be managed for the benefit of all of its stakeholders—stockholders, employees, customers, suppliers, and managers, as well as the local communities in which it operates. (See Figure 2-2 for the stakeholder model of corporate responsibility; compare it with Figure 35-1.)

Less government regulation

by taking a more proactive role in addressing society's problems, corporations create a climate of trust and respect that has the effect of reducing government regulation

Less Government Regulation   According to another argument in favor of corporate social responsibility, the more responsibly companies act, the less the government must regulate them. This idea, if accurate, would likely appeal to those corporations that typically view regulation with distaste, perceiving it as a crude and expensive way of achieving social goals. To them, regulation often imposes inappropriate, overly broad rules that hamper productivity and require extensive recordkeeping procedures to document compliance. If companies can use more flexible, voluntary methods of meeting a social norm, such as pollution control, then government will be less tempted to legislate norms.

The argument can be taken further. Not only does anticipatory corporate action lessen the likelihood of government regulation, but also social involvement by companies creates a climate of trust and respect that reduces the overall inclination of government to interfere in company business. For example, a government agency is much more likely to show some leniency toward a socially responsible company than toward one that ignores social plights.

Long-run profits

corporate involvement in social causes creates goodwill, which simply makes good business sense

Long-Run Profits   Perhaps the most persuasive argument in favor of corporate involvement in social causes is that such involvement actually makes good business sense. Consumers often support good corporate images and avoid bad ones. For example, consumers generally prefer to patronize stores with "easy return" policies. Even though such policies are not required by law, companies institute them because they create goodwill—an intangible though indispensable asset for ensuring repeat customers. In the long run, enhanced goodwill often rebounds to stronger profits. Moreover, corporate actions to improve the well-being of their communities make these communities more attractive to citizens and more profitable for business.

Figure 2-2 The Stakeholder Model

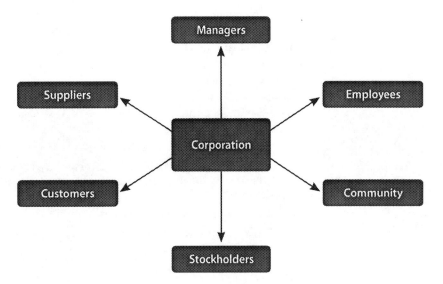

CHAPTER SUMMARY

Definitions

Ethics study of what is right or good for human beings

Business Ethics study of what is right and good in a business setting

Ethical Theories

Ethical Fundamentalism individuals look to a central authority or set of rules to guide them in ethical decision making

Ethical Relativism asserts that actions must be judged by what individuals subjectively feel is right or wrong for themselves

Situational Ethics one must judge a person's actions by first putting oneself in the actor's situation

Utilitarianism moral actions are those that produce the greatest net pleasure compared with net pain

- *Act Utilitarianism* assesses each separate act according to whether it maximizes pleasure over pain
- *Rule Utilitarianism* supports rules that on balance produce the greatest pleasure for society
- *Cost-Benefit Analysis* quantifies the benefits and costs of alternatives

Deontology holds that actions must be judged by their motives and means as well as their results

Social Ethics Theories focus on a person's obligations to other members in society and on the individual's rights and obligations within society

- *Social Egalitarians* believe that society should provide all its members with equal amounts of goods and services regardless of their relative contributions
- *Distributive Justice* stresses equality of opportunity rather than results
- *Libertarians* stress market outcomes as the basis for distributing society's rewards

Other Theories

- *Intuitionism* a rational person possesses inherent power to assess the correctness of actions
- *Good Person* individuals should seek out and emulate good role models

Ethical Standards in Business

Choosing an Ethical System Kohlberg's stages of moral development is a widely accepted model (see Figure 2-1.)

Corporations as Moral Agents because a corporation is a statutorily created entity, it is not clear whether it should be held morally responsible

Ethical Responsibilities of Business

Regulation of Business government regulation has been necessary because all the conditions for perfect competition have not been satisfied and free competition cannot by itself achieve other societal objectives

Corporate Governance vast amounts of wealth and power have become concentrated in a small number of corporations, which in turn are controlled by a small group of corporate officers

Arguments against Social Responsibility

- *Profitability* because corporations are artificial entities established for profit-making activities, their only social obligation should be to return as much money as possible to shareholders
- *Unfairness* whenever corporations engage in social activities, such as supporting the arts or education, they divert funds rightfully belonging to shareholders and/or employees to unrelated third parties
- *Accountability* a corporation is subject to less public accountability than public bodies are
- *Expertise* although a corporation may have a high level of expertise in selling its goods and services, there is absolutely no guarantee that any promotion of social activities will be carried on with the same degree of competence

Arguments in Favor of Social Responsibility

- *The Social Contract* because society allows for the creation of corporations and gives them special rights, including a grant of limited liability, corporations owe a responsibility to society

- *Less Government Regulation* by taking a more proactive role in addressing society's problems, corporations create a climate of trust and respect that has the effect of reducing government regulation
- *Long-Run Profits* corporate involvement in social causes creates goodwill, which simply makes good business sense

QUESTIONS

1. You have an employee who has a chemical imbalance in the brain that causes him to be severely unstable. The medication that is available to deal with this schizophrenic condition is extremely powerful and decreases the taker's life span by one to two years for every year that the user takes it. You know that his doctors and family believe that it is in his best interest to take the medication. What course of action should you follow?

2. You have a very shy employee who is from another country. After a time, you notice that the quality of her performance is deteriorating rapidly. You find an appropriate time to speak with her and determine that she is extremely distraught. She tells you that her family has arranged a marriage for her and that she refuses to obey their contract. She further states to you that she is thinking about committing suicide. Two weeks later, after her poor performance continues, you determine that she is on the verge of a nervous breakdown; and once again she informs you that she is going to commit suicide. What should you do? Consider further that you can petition a court to have her involuntarily committed to a mental hospital. You know, however, that her family would consider such a commitment an extreme insult and that they might seek retribution. Does this prospect alter your decision?

3. You receive a telephone call from a company you never do business with requesting a reference on one of your employees, Mary Sunshine. You believe Mary performs in a generally incompetent manner, and you would be delighted to see her take another job. You give her a glowing reference. Is this right? Explain.

4. You have just received a report suggesting that a chemical your company uses in its manufacturing process is very dangerous. You have not read the report, but you are generally aware of its contents. You believe that the chemical can be replaced fairly easily, but that if word gets out, panic may set in among employees and community members. A reporter asks if you have seen the report, and you say no. Is your behavior right or wrong? Explain.

5. You and Joe Jones, your neighbor and friend, bought lottery tickets at the corner drugstore. While watching the lottery drawing on television with you that night, Joe leaped from the couch, waved his lottery ticket, and shouted, "I've got the winning number!" Suddenly, he clutched his chest, keeled over, and died on the spot. You are the only living person who knows that Joe, not you, bought the winning ticket. If you substitute his ticket for yours, no one will know of the switch and you will be $10 million richer. Joe's only living relative is a rich aunt whom he despised. Will you switch his ticket for yours? Explain.

6. Omega, Inc., a publicly held corporation, has assets of $100 million and annual earnings in the range of $13 to $15 million. Omega owns three aluminum plants, which are profitable, and one plastics plant, which is losing $4 million a year.

Because of its very high operating costs, the plastics plant shows no sign of ever becoming profitable, and there is no evidence that the plant and the underlying real estate will increase in value. Omega decides to sell the plastics plant. The only bidder for the plant is Gold, who intends to use the plant for a new purpose: to introduce automation, and to replace all existing employees. Would it be ethical for Omega to turn down Gold's bid and keep the plastics plant operating indefinitely, for the purpose of preserving the employees' jobs? Explain.

7. You are the sales manager of a two-year-old electronics firm. At times, the firm has seemed on the brink of failure, but recently it has begun to be profitable. In large part, the profitability is due to the aggressive and talented sales force you have recruited. Two months ago, you hired Alice North, an honors graduate from the State University, who decided that she was tired of the Research Department and wanted to try sales.

   Almost immediately after you sent Alice out for training with Brad West, your best salesperson, he began reporting to you an unexpected turn of events. According to Brad, "Alice is terrific: she's confident, smooth, and persistent. Unfortunately, a lot of our buyers are good old boys who just aren't comfortable around young, bright women. Just last week, Hiram Jones, one of our biggest customers, told me that he simply won't continue to do business with 'young chicks' who think they invented the world. It's not that Alice is a know-it-all. She's not. It's just that these guys like to booze it up a bit, tell some off-color jokes, and then get down to business. Alice doesn't drink, and, although she never objects to the jokes, it's clear she thinks they're offensive." Brad felt that several potential deals had fallen through "because the mood just wasn't right with Alice there." Brad added, "I don't like a lot of these guys' styles myself, but I go along to make the sales. I just do not think Alice is going to make it."

   When you call Alice in to discuss the situation, she concedes the accuracy of Brad's report but indicates that she's not to blame and insists that she be kept on the job. You feel committed to equal opportunity but don't want to jeopardize your company's ability to survive. What should you do?

8. Major Company subcontracted the development of part of a large technology system to Start-up Company, a small corporation specializing in custom computer systems. The contract, which was a major breakthrough for Start-up Company and crucial to its future, provided for an initial development fee and subsequent progress payments, as well as a final date for completion.

   Start-up Company provided Major Company with periodic reports indicating that everything was on schedule. After several months, however, the status reports stopped coming, and the company missed delivery of the schematics, the second major milestone. As an in-house technical consultant for Major Company, you visited Start-up Company and found not only that it was far behind schedule but also that it had lied about its previous progress. Moreover, you determined that this slippage put the schedule for the entire project in severe jeopardy. The cause of Start-up's slippage was the removal of personnel from your project to work on short-term contracts to obtain money to meet the weekly payroll.

Your company decided that you should stay at Start-up Company to monitor its work and to assist in the design of the project. After six weeks and some progress, Start-up is still way behind its delivery dates. Nonetheless, you are now familiar enough with the project to complete it in-house with Major's personnel.

Start-up is still experiencing severe cash flow problems and repeatedly requests payment from Major. But your CEO, furious with Start-up's lies and deceptions, wishes to "bury" Start-up and finish the project using Major Company's internal resources. She knows that withholding payment to Start-up will put it out of business. What do you do? Explain.

9. A customer requested certain sophisticated tests on equipment he purchased from your factory. Such tests are very expensive and must be performed by a third party. The equipment was tested as requested and met all of the industry standards, but showed anomalies which could not be explained. Though the problem appeared to be very minor, you decided to inspect the unit to try to understand the test data—a very expensive and time-consuming process. You informed the customer of this decision. A problem was found, but it was minor and was highly unlikely ever to cause the unit to fail. Rebuilding the equipment would be very expensive and time-consuming; moreover, notifying the customer that you were planning to rebuild the unit would also put your overall manufacturing procedures in question. Should you fix the problem, ship the equipment as is, or inform the customer?

10. You are a project manager for a company making a major proposal to a Middle Eastern country. Your major competition is from Japan.

a. Your local agent, who is closely tied to a very influential sheikh, would receive a 5 percent commission if the proposal were accepted. Near the date for the decision, the agent asks you for $150,000 to grease the skids so that your proposal is accepted. What do you do?

b. What do you do if, after you say no, the agent goes to your vice president, who provides the money?

c. Your overseas operation learns that most other foreign companies in this Middle Eastern location bolster their business by exchanging currency on the gray market. You discover that your division is twice as profitable as budgeted due to the amount of domestic currency you have received on the gray market. What do you do?

BUSINESS ETHICS CASES

The business ethics cases that follow are based on the kinds of situations that companies regularly face when conducting business. You should first read each case carefully and in its entirety before attempting to analyze it. Second, you should identify the most important ethical issues arising from the situation. Often it is helpful to prioritize these issues. Third, you should identify the viable options for addressing these issues and the ethical implications of the identified options. This might include examining the options from the perspectives of the various ethical theories as well as the affected stakeholders. Fourth, you should reach a definite resolution of the ethical issues by choosing what you think is the best option. You should have a well-articulated rationale for your resolution. Finally, develop a strategy for implementing your resolution.

PHARMAKON DRUG COMPANY

Background

William Wilson, senior vice president of research, development, and medical (RD&M) at Pharmakon Drug Company, received both his Ph.D. in biochemistry and his M.D. from the University of Oklahoma. Upon completion of his residency, Dr. Wilson joined the faculty at Harvard Medical School. He left Harvard after five years to join the research group at Merck & Co. Three years later, he went to Burroughs-Wellcome as director of RD&M, and, after eight years, Dr. Wilson joined Pharmakon in his current position.

William Wilson has always been highly respected as a scientist, a manager, and an individual. He has also been an outstanding leader in the scientific community, particularly in the effort to attract more minorities into the field.

Pharmakon concentrates its research efforts in the areas of antivirals (with a focus on HIV), cardiovascular, respiratory, muscle relaxants, gastrointestinal, the central nervous system, and consumer health care (i.e., nonprescription or over-the-counter [OTC] medicines). Dr. Wilson is on the board of directors of Pharmakon and the company's executive committee. He reports directly to the chairman of the board and CEO, Mr. Jarred Swenstrum.

Declining Growth

During the previous eight years, Pharmakon experienced tremendous growth: 253 percent overall with yearly growth ranging from 12 percent to 25 percent. During this period, Pharmakon's RD&M budget grew from $79 million to $403 million, and the number of employees rose from 1,192 to 3,273 (see Figure 2-3). During the previous two years, however, growth in revenue and earnings had slowed considerably. Moreover, in the current year, Pharmakon's revenues of $3.55 billion and earnings before taxes of $1.12 billion were up only 2 percent from the previous year. Furthermore, both revenues and earnings are projected to be flat or declining for the next five years.

The cessation of this period's tremendous growth and the likelihood of future decline have been brought about principally by two causes. First, a number of Pharmakon's most important patents have expired and competition from generics has begun and could continue to erode its products' market shares. Second, as new types of health-care delivery organizations evolve, pharmaceutical companies' revenues and earnings will in all likelihood be adversely affected.

Problem and Proposed Solutions

In response, the board of directors has decided that the company must emphasize two conflicting goals: increase the number of new drugs brought to market and cut back on the workforce in anticipation of rising labor and marketing costs and declining revenues. Accordingly, Dr. Wilson has been instructed to cut costs significantly and to reduce his workforce by 15 percent over the next six months.

Dr. Wilson called a meeting with his management team to discuss the workforce reduction. One of his managers, Leashia Harmon, argued that the layoffs should be made "so that recent gains in minority hiring are not wiped out." The percentage of minority employees had increased from 2.7 percent eight years ago to 8.3 percent in the previous year (see Figure 2-3). The minority population in communities in which Pharmakon has major facilities has remained over the years at approximately 23 percent. About 20 percent of the RD&M workforce have a Ph.D. in a physical science or in pharmacology, and another 3 percent have an M.D.

Dr. Harmon, a Ph.D. in pharmacology and head of clinical studies, is the only minority on Dr. Wilson's seven-member management team. Dr. Harmon argued that RD&M has worked long and hard to increase minority employment and has been a leader in promoting Pharmakon's affirmative action plan (see Figure 2-4). Therefore, she asserted, all layoffs should reflect this commitment, even if it meant disproportionate layoffs of nonminorities.

Dr. Anson Peake, another member of Dr. Wilson's management team and director of new products, argued that Pharmakon's RD&M division has never discharged a worker except for cause and should adhere as closely as possible to that policy by terminating individuals solely based on merit. Dr. Rachel Waugh, director of product development, pointed out that the enormous growth in employment over the last eight years—almost a trebling of the workforce—had made the company's employee performance evaluation system less than reliable. Consequently, she contended that because laying off 15 percent of her group would be extremely difficult and subjective, she preferred to follow a system of seniority.

Dr. Wilson immediately recognized that any system of reducing the workforce would be difficult to implement. Moreover, he was concerned about fairness to employees and maintaining the best qualified group to carry out the area's mission. He was very troubled by a merit or seniority system if it could not maintain the minority gains. In fact, he had even thought about the possibility of using this difficult situation to increase the percentage of minorities to bring it more in line with the minority percentage of the communities in which Pharmakon had major facilities.

Figure 2-3 Pharmakon Employment

Attribute/Years Ago	1	2	3	4	5	6	7	8
Total Employment	3,273	3,079	2,765	2,372	1,927	1,619	1,306	1,192
Minority	272	238	196	143	109	75	53	32
Employment	(8.35%)	(7.7%)	(7.15%)	(6.0%)	(5.7%)	(4.6%)	(4.1%)	(2.7%)
Revenue ($ million)	3,481	3,087	2,702	2,184	1,750	1,479	1,214	986
Profit ($ million)	1,106	1,021	996	869	724	634	520	340
RD&M Budget ($ million)	403	381	357	274	195	126	96	79

© Cengage Learning 2013

Figure 2-4 Pharmakon Affirmative Action Program

> **Pharmakon Drug Company**
> **Equal Employment Opportunity Affirmative Action Program**
>
> **POLICY**
>
> It is the policy of Pharmakon Drug Co. to provide equal employment opportunities without regard to race, color, religion, sex, national origin, sexual orientation, disability, and veteran status. The Company will also take affirmative action to employ and advance individual applicants from all segments of our society. This policy relates to all phases of employment, including, but not limited to, recruiting, hiring, placement, promotion, demotion, layoff, recall, termination, compensation, and training. In communities where Pharmakon has facilities, it is our policy to be a leader in providing equal employment for all of its citizens.
>
> **RESPONSIBILITY FOR IMPLEMENTATION**
>
> The head of each division is ultimately responsible for initiating, administering, and controlling activities within all areas of responsibility necessary to ensure full implementation of this policy.
> The managers of each location or area are responsible for the implementation of this policy.
> All other members of management are responsible for conducting day-to-day activities in a manner to ensure compliance with this policy.

© Cengage Learning 2013

MYKON'S DILEMMA

Jack Spratt, the newly appointed CEO of Mykon Pharmaceuticals, Inc., sat at his desk and scratched his head for the thousandth time that night. His friends never tired of telling him that unless he stopped this habit he would remove what little hair he had left. Nevertheless, he had good reason to be perplexed—the decisions he made would determine the future of the company and, literally, the life or death of thousands of people.

As a young, ambitious scientist, Spratt had gained international fame and considerable fortune while rising quickly through the ranks of the scientists at Mykon. After receiving a degree from the Executive MBA program at the Kenan-Flagler Business School, University of North Carolina at Chapel Hill, he assumed, in rapid succession, a number of administrative positions at the company, culminating in his appointment as CEO. But no one had told him that finding cures for previously incurable diseases would be fraught with moral dilemmas. Although it was 3:00 A.M., Spratt remained at his desk, unable to stop thinking about his difficult choices. His preoccupation was made worse by the knowledge that pressure from governments and consumers would only increase each day he failed to reach a decision. This pressure had mounted relentlessly since the fateful day he announced that Mykon had discovered the cure for AIDS. But the cure brought with it a curse: there was not enough to go around.

Background

Mykon, a major international research-based pharmaceutical group, engages in the research, development, manufacture, and marketing of human health-care products for sale in both the prescription and over-the-counter (OTC) markets. The company's principal prescription medicines include a range of products in the following areas: antiviral, neuromuscular blocking, cardiovascular, anti-inflammatory, immunosuppressive, systemic antibacterial, and central nervous system. Mykon also manufactures other products such as muscle relaxants, antidepressants, anticonvulsants, and respiratory stimulants. In addition, the company markets drugs for the treatment of congestive heart failure and the prevention of organ rejection following transplant.

Mykon's OTC business primarily consists of cough and cold preparations and several topical antibiotics. The company seeks to expand its OTC business in various ways, including the reclassification of some of its prescription drugs to OTC status. Mykon's OTC sales represented 14 percent of the company's sales during last year.

Mykon has a long tradition of excellence in research and development (R&D). The company's expenditures on R&D for the last three financial years constituted 15 percent of its sales.

Mykon focuses its R&D on the following selected therapeutic areas, listed in descending order of expenditure amount: antivirals and other antibiotics, cardiovascular, central nervous system, anticancer, anti-inflammatory, respiratory, and neuromuscular.

Mykon sells its products internationally in more than 120 countries and has a significant presence in two of the largest pharmaceutical markets—the United States and Europe—and a growing presence in Japan. It generated approximately 43 percent and 35 percent of the company's sales from the previous year in the United States and Europe, respectively. The company sells essentially the same range of products throughout the world.

Production

Mykon carries out most of its production in Rotterdam in the Netherlands and in Research Triangle Park, North Carolina, in the United States. The latter is the company's world headquarters. The company's manufacturing processes typically consist of three stages: the manufacture of active chemicals, the incorporation of these chemicals into products designed for use by the consumer, and packaging. The firm has an ongoing program of capital expenditure to provide up-to-date production facilities and relies on advanced technology, automation, and computerization of its manufacturing capability to help maintain its competitive position.

Production facilities are also located in ten other countries to meet the needs of local markets and to overcome legal restrictions on the importation of finished products. These facilities principally engage in product formulation and packaging, although plants in certain countries manufacture active chemicals. Last year, Mykon had more than seventeen thousand employees, 27 percent of whom were in the United States. Approximately 21 percent of Mykon's employees were engaged in R&D, largely in the Netherlands and the United States. Although unions represent a number of the firm's employees, the firm has not experienced any significant labor disputes in recent years, and it considers its employee relations to be good.

Research and Development

In the pharmaceutical industry, R&D is both expensive and prolonged, entailing considerable uncertainty. The process of producing a commercial drug typically takes between eight and twelve years as it proceeds from discovery through development to regulatory approval and finally to the product launch. No assurance exists that new compounds will survive the development process or obtain the requisite regulatory approvals. In addition, research conducted by other pharmaceutical companies may lead at any time to the introduction of competing or improved treatments.

Figure 2-5 Mykon R&D Expenditures

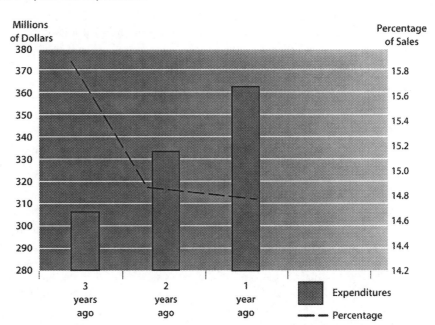

© Cengage Learning 2013

Last year Mykon incurred approximately 95 percent of its R&D expenditures in the Netherlands and the United States. Figure 2-5 sets out the firm's annual expenditure on R&D in dollars and as a percentage of sales for each of the last three financial years.

Jack Spratt

Every society, every institution, every company, and most important, every individual should follow those precepts that society holds most dear. The pursuit of profits must be consistent with and subordinate to these ideals, the most important of which is the Golden Rule. To work for the betterment of humanity is the reason I became a scientist in the first place. As a child, Banting and Best were my heroes. I could think of no vocation that held greater promise to help mankind. Now that I am CEO I intend to have these beliefs included in our company's mission statement.

These sentiments, expressed by Jack Spratt in a newsmagazine interview, capture the intensity and drive that animate the man. None who knew him was surprised when he set out years ago—fueled by his prodigious energy, guided by his brilliant mind, and financed by Mykon—for the inner reaches of the Amazon Basin to find naturally occurring medicines. Spratt considered it to be his manifest destiny to discover the cure for some dread disease.

His search was not totally blind. Some years earlier, Frans Berger, a well-known but eccentric scientist, had written extensively about the variety of plant life and fungi that flourished in the jungles of the Bobonaza River region deep in the Amazon watershed. Although he spent twenty years there and discovered nothing of medical significance, the vast number and intriguing uniqueness of his specimens convinced Spratt that it was just a matter of time before a major breakthrough would occur.

Spratt also had some scientific evidence. While working in Mykon's laboratory to finance his graduate education in biology and genetics, Spratt and his supervisors had noticed that several fungi could not only restore damaged skin but, when combined with synthetic polymers, had significant effects on internal cells. Several more years of scientific expeditions and investigations proved promising enough for Mykon to send Spratt and a twenty-person exploration team to the Amazon Basin for two years. Two years became five, and the enormous quantity of specimens sent back eventually took over an entire wing of the company's sizable laboratories in Research Triangle Park, North Carolina.

Upon Spratt's return, he headed up a group of Mykon scientists who examined the Amazonian fungi for pharmacological activity. After several years of promising beginnings and disappointing endings, they discovered that one fungus destroyed the recently identified virus HIV. Years later, the company managed to produce enough of the drug (code named Sprattalin) derived from the fungus to inform the Food and Drug Administration (FDA) that it was testing what appeared to be a cure for HIV. It was the happiest moment of Jack Spratt's life. The years of determined effort, not to mention the $800 million Mykon had invested, would now be more than fully rewarded.

Spratt's joy was short-lived, though. Public awareness of the drug quickly spread, and groups pressured the FDA to shorten or eliminate its normal approval process, which ordinarily takes more than seven years. People dying from the virus's effects demanded immediate access to the drug.

The Drug

Mirroring the insidiousness of HIV itself, the structure of Sprattalin is extraordinarily complex. Consequently, it takes four to seven months to produce a small quantity, only 25 percent of which is usable. It is expensive; each unit of Sprattalin costs Mykon $20,000 to produce. The projected dosage ranges from ten units for asymptomatic HIV-positive patients who have normal white blood cell counts to fifty units for patients with low white blood cell counts and full-blown AIDS. The drug appears to eliminate the virus from all patients regardless of their stage of the disease. However, it does not have any restorative effect on patients' compromised immune systems. Accordingly, it is expected that asymptomatic HIV-positive patients will revert to their normal life expectancies. It is not clear what the life expectancy will be of patients with full-blown AIDS, although it is almost certain that their life expectancy would be curtailed.

Supply of Sprattalin   The company has estimated that the first two years of production would yield enough Sprattalin to cure 6 percent of all asymptomatic HIV-positive patients. Alternatively, the supply would be sufficient to treat 4 percent of all patients with full-blown AIDS.

Figure 2-6 UNAIDS/WHO

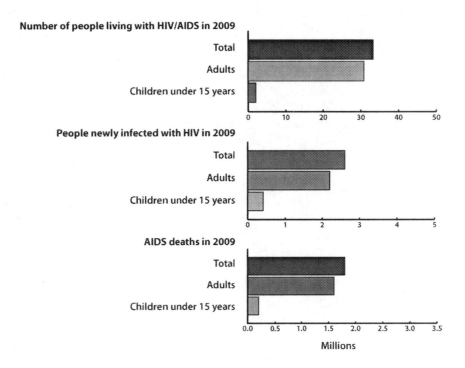

Global Summary of the HIV/AIDS Epidemic, December 2009

Children constitute 7.5 percent of all people living with HIV/AIDS. See Figures 2-6 and 2-7 for statistics on the HIV/AIDS epidemic.

Interested parties have argued that the solution to production problems is clear: build larger facilities. However, even with production levels as low as they are, the bottleneck in supply occurs elsewhere. The fungus on which the whole process depends is incredibly rare, growing only in two small regions near Jatun Molino, Ecuador, along the Bobonaza River. At current harvesting rates, scientists predict that all known deposits will be depleted in three years, and many of them insist that production should be scaled back to allow the fungus to regenerate itself.

Presently there are no known methods of cultivating the fungus in the laboratory. Apparently, the delicate ecology that allows it to exist in only one region of the earth is somehow distressed enough by either transport or lab conditions to render it unable to grow and produce the drug's precursor. Scientists are feverishly trying to discover those factors that will support successful culture. However, with limited quantities of the starting material and most of that pressured into production, the company has enjoyed no success in this endeavor. Because of Sprattalin's complexity, attempts to synthesize the drug have failed completely, mainly because, like aspirin, it is not known how the drug works; thus, Sprattalin's effectiveness remains shrouded in mystery.

Figure 2-7 Regional Statistics for HIV and AIDS End of 2009 (in millions)

Region	Persons with HIV/AIDS	Persons Newly Infected	Adult Infection Rate	Deaths
Sub-Saharan Africa	22.5	1.8	5.0%	1.3
East Asia	0.77	0.082	0.1%	0.036
South and South-East Asia	4.1	0.27	0.3%	0.26
Oceania	0.057	0.005	0.3%	0.001
Eastern Europe & Central Asia	1.4	0.13	0.8%	0.076
Western & Central Europe	0.82	0.031	0.2%	0.009
North Africa & Middle East	0.46	0.075	0.2%	0.024
North America	1.5	0.07	0.5%	0.026
Caribbean	0.24	0.017	1.0%	0.012
Latin America	1.4	0.092	0.5%	0.058
Global Total	33.3	2.6	0.8%	1.8

Allocation of Sprattalin   In response to the insufficient supply, a number of powerful consumer groups have made public their suggestions regarding the allocation of Sprattalin. One proposition advanced would use medical records to establish a waiting list of possible recipients based on the length of time they have been in treatment for the virus. The argument is that those people who have waited the longest and are most in danger of dying should be the first to find relief.

Other groups propose an opposite approach, arguing that because supply is so drastically short, Mykon should make Sprattalin available only to asymptomatic HIV patients. They require the least concentrations of the drug to become well, thus extending the drug's supply. They also have the greatest likelihood of returning to full life expectancies. Under this proposal, people who have full-blown AIDS would be ineligible for treatment. Such patients have previously come to terms with their impending mortality, have fewer psychological adjustments to make, and represent, on a dosage basis, two to five healthier patients. In meting the drug out in this manner, proponents argue, the drug can more readily meet the highest public health objectives to eradicate the virus and prevent further transmission.

Others propose that only patients who contracted the virus through no fault of their own should have priority. This approach would first make Sprattalin available to children who were born with the virus, hemophiliacs and others who got the virus from blood transfusions, rape victims, and health-care workers.

One member of Sprattalin's executive committee has suggested a free market approach: the drug should go to the highest bidder.

Pricing of Sprattalin   In addition to supply problems, Mykon has come under considerable criticism for its proposed pricing structure. Because of extraordinarily high development and production costs, the company has tentatively priced the drug at levels unattainable for most people afflicted with HIV. Perhaps never before in the history of medicine has the ability to pay been so starkly presented as those who can pay will live, while those who cannot will die.

Even at these prices, though, demand far exceeds supply. Jack Spratt and the rest of the Mykon executives predict that the company could easily sell available supplies at twice the proposed price.

A growing number of Mykon executives disagree with the passive stance the company has taken in pricing the product. In their view, a 20 percent markup represents a meager return for the prolonged risk and high levels of spending that the company incurred to develop the drug. Moreover, it leaves little surplus for future investment. Furthermore, eight years is too long to amortize the R&D expenses because Sprattalin, though the first, is unlikely to be the last anti-HIV drug, now that Mykon has blazed a path. Other, more heavily capitalized companies are racing to reverse engineer the drug, and the availability of competing drugs remains only a matter of time. Accordingly, the company cannot realistically count on an eight-year window of opportunity.

Foreign markets further exacerbate the pricing perplexity. Other countries, with less privatized health care, have already promised their citizens access to Sprattalin at any price. Some industrial countries, for instance, are willing to pay up to $2 million per patient. They do not, however, wish to subsidize the drug for the United States. At the same time, some voices in the United States insist that supplies should go first to U.S. citizens.

On the other hand, countries with the most severe concentration of the HIV infection cannot afford to pay even Mykon's actual costs. Some regions in Africa and Asia have experienced rapid growth of the disease, reporting 50 percent to 80 percent of their population at some stage in the HIV cycle. Jack Spratt feels a very real moral obligation to help at least some of these people, whether they can pay or not.

Making the Decision

In the past few months, Jack Spratt had seen many aspects of the most important project in his life become not only public knowledge but also public domain. Because of the enormous social and political consequences of the discovery, it is unlikely that the government will allow Mykon to control the destiny of either Sprattalin or ultimately the company.

Addressing the public's concern over access to the drug while ensuring future prosperity of his company had become like walking a tightrope with strangers holding each end of the rope. He knew of no way to satisfy everyone. As Jack Spratt sat at his desk, sleep remained an eon away.

OLIVER WINERY, INC.

Background

Paul Oliver, Sr., immigrated to the United States in 1930 from Greece. After working for several wineries, he started Oliver Winery, Inc., which eventually found a market niche in nonvarietal jug wines. Through mass-marketing techniques, the company established a substantial presence in this segment of the market. Ten years ago, Paul, Jr., joined the firm after receiving a degree in enology (the study of wine making). He convinced his father of the desirability of entering a different segment of the wine market: premium varietals. To do this, the company needed a large infusion of capital to purchase appropriate vineyards. Reluctantly, Paul, Sr., agreed to take the company public. The initial public offering succeeded, and 40 percent of the company's stock went into outsiders' hands. Also, for the first time, outsiders served on the board of directors. Although Paul, Jr., wanted to use a new name for the premium varietal to appeal to a more upscale market, his father insisted on using the name Oliver.

Board Meeting

The board of directors met, along with Janet Stabler, the director of marketing of Oliver Winery, Inc. The following directors were in attendance:

Paul Oliver, Sr.,
    chairman of the board, founder of the company
Paul Oliver, Jr., CEO,
    has an advanced degree in enology
Cyrus Abbott, CFO,
    has an MBA
Arlene Dale, comptroller,
    has a CPA with a master's degree in accounting
Raj Ray, COO,
    has a master's degree in industrial engineering
LaTasha Lane, VP Legal,
    has a J.D. degree
Elisabeth Constable, union representative to the board,
    has a GED degree
Rev. John W. Calvin, outside director,
    has a Doctor of Divinity degree
Carlos Menendez, outside director,
    has an MFA degree

Oliver, Sr.: The next item on the agenda is a proposal to develop a new line of wines. Janet Stabler will briefly present the proposal.

Stabler: Thank you. The proposal is to enter the fortified wine market. It's the only type of wine in which unit sales are increasing. We'll make the wines cheaply and package them in pint bottles with screw-on caps. Our chief competitors are Canandaigua with Richard's Wild Irish Rose, Gallo with Thunderbird and Night Train Express, and Mogen David with MD 20/20. We'll market the wine with little or no media advertising by strategically sampling the product to targeted consumers. That's it in a nutshell.

Oliver, Sr.: Any questions before we vote?

Menendez: Who'll buy this wine?

Calvin: From what I know about the consumers of your competitors, it appears to me that it's bought by homeless winos.

Stabler: Not entirely. For example, pensioners on a fixed income would find the price of the wine appealing. Thunderbird has been recently introduced into England and has become very popular with the yuppie crowd.

Calvin: Then why put it in pint bottles?

Stabler: For the convenience of consumers.

Menendez: Why would pensioners want a small bottle?

Calvin: Homeless people want it in pints so they can fit it in their hip pockets. They obviously don't have a wine cellar to lay away their favorite bottles of Mad Dog.

Stabler: The pint size also keeps the price as low as possible.

Calvin: Translation: The homeless don't have to panhandle as long before they can make a purchase. Also, why would you increase the alcoholic content to 18 percent and make it so sweet if it weren't for the wino market?

Stabler: Many people like sweet dessert wines and 18 percent is not that much more than other types of wines that have 12 percent alcohol.

Menendez: Is it legal?

Lane: Sure. We sell to the retailers. It may be against the law to sell to intoxicated persons, but that's the retailers' business. We cannot control what they do.

Calvin: Isn't this product intended for a perpetually intoxicated audience that many people consider to be ill? Wouldn't we be taking advantage of their illness by selling highly sugared alcohol that suppresses their appetite? I've spoken to drinkers who claim to live on a gallon of this type of product a day.

Oliver, Jr.: What will this do to our image? We're still trying to get our premium wines accepted.

Stabler: Of course we won't use the Oliver name on these wines. We will use another name.

Menendez: Is it OK to do that?

Stabler: Why not? Canandaigua, Gallo, and Mogen David all do the same thing. None of them put their corporate name on this low-end product.

Abbott: We're getting away from the crux of the matter. Profit margins would be at least 10 percent higher on this line than our others. Moreover, unit sales might increase over time. Our other lines are stagnant or decreasing. The public shareholders are grousing.

Dale: Not to mention that our stock options have become almost worthless. I'm only a few years from retirement. We need to increase the profitability of the company.

Ray: Operationally, this proposal is a great fit. We can use the grapes we reject from the premium line. It will also insulate us from bad grape years because any grape will do for this wine. We can fill a lot of our unused capacity.

Constable: And hire back some of the workers who were laid off!

Stabler: It's a marketing dream. Just give out some samples to "bell cows."

Menendez: What are bell cows?

Stabler: Opinion leaders who will induce other consumers to switch to our brand.

Calvin: You mean wino gurus?

Oliver, Sr.: Look, if we don't do it, others will. In fact, they already have.

Abbott: And they'll get richer and we'll get poorer.

Lane: Gallo pulled out of several of these skid-row markets as did Canandaigua. Little good it did. The alcoholics just switched to malt liquor, vodka, or anything they could get their hands on.

Dale: I think our concern is misplaced. These people are the dregs of society. They contribute nothing.

Calvin: They're human beings who need help. We're profiting off their misfortune and misery.

Oliver, Sr.: We can take that up when we decide on what charities to support. Anyone opposed to the proposal?

Calvin: Is this a done deal? I believe we should contribute half of our profits from this product to support homeless shelters and other programs that benefit indigent and homeless people. If not, I must resign from this board.

Sources

Carrie Dolan, "Gallo Conducts Test to Placate Critics of Its Cheap Wine," *The Wall Street Journal*, June 16, 1989, p. B3.

Alix M. Freedman, "Winos and Thunderbird Are a Subject Gallo Doesn't Like to Discuss," *The Wall Street Journal*, February 25, 1988, p. 1.

Frank J. Prial, "Experiments by a Wine Maker Fails to Thwart Street Drunks," *The New York Times*, February 11, 1990, p. A29.

JLM, Inc.

Background

Sitting in her office, Ellen Fulbright, director of human resources (HR) for JLM, Inc., thought over the decisions confronting her. To help her decide, she mentally reviewed how they had arisen.

After receiving her MBA and J.D. degrees from a highly regarded university, she joined a prestigious New York law firm where she specialized in employment law. After seven years at the law firm, she was hired by one of the firm's clients as general counsel. When that company was acquired by JLM, she joined its legal staff and within a few years had been promoted to her current position.

Fulbright's rapid advancement resulted from her having made a positive impression on Rasheed Raven, JLM's CEO. Raven is a hard-driving, bottom-line-oriented pragmatist in his early forties. Raven, a graduate of Howard University, had begun his business career on Wall Street, which he astounded with his aggressive but successful takeover strategies. After acquiring fifteen unrelated manufacturing companies, he decided to try his hand at the turnaround business. He organized JLM as an umbrella for his acquired companies. Soon he earned the reputation as the best in the business by transforming JLM into the leader in the industry.

JLM is a highly successful turnaround company. Typically, JLM purchases companies that are in serious financial trouble and manages them until they become successful companies. At that time, JLM either retains them in its own portfolio of companies or sells them off to other enterprises.

Reference Letter Policy

About a year after Fulbright had become HR director, Raven called her into his office and showed her a newspaper article. It reported, in somewhat sensational fashion, that several defamation suits had resulted in multimillion dollar judgments against companies that had written negative letters of references about former employees. Raven told her that he was concerned about this and that he wanted her to develop an HR policy covering letters of reference.

In researching the issue, she discovered several articles in which the authors decried the recent spate of companies that had decided to stop writing letters of reference. According to their data, they believed that these companies had overreacted to the actual risk posed by defamation suits. Based on these articles and her own inclination toward full disclosure, she proposed that the company continue to permit letters of reference but that all letters with negative comments must be reviewed by her.

Raven did not receive her proposal favorably and sought a second opinion from her old law firm. His analysis of the firm's advice was: "We get nothing but brownie points for writing reference letters, but we face the possibility of incurring the cost of a legal defense or, worse yet, a court judgment. This is a 'no-brainer.' We have no upside and all downside." Raven ordered that, henceforth, company employees would no longer write letters of reference but would simply verify dates of employment.

Although Fulbright was personally and professionally miffed by his decision, she drew up the policy statement as directed. Fulbright believed that because JLM frequently took over companies that needed immediate downsizing, this policy would be unfair and extremely detrimental to longtime employees of newly purchased companies.

Takeover of Diversified Manufacturing, Inc.

After a number of years of steady growth, Diversified Manufacturing began experiencing huge financial losses and its immediate survival was in serious doubt. After careful consideration, Raven decided that Diversified was an ideal takeover target in that its core businesses were extremely strong and presented great long-term economic viability.

Upon acquiring Diversified, JLM quickly decided that it had to rid Diversified of some of its poorly performing companies and that it had to reduce the size of Diversified's home office staff by 25 percent. Raven relentlessly orchestrated the reduction in force, but at Fulbright's urging he provided the discharged executives with above-average severance packages, including excellent outplacement services.

The Problem

The reduction in force was disruptive and demoralizing in all the usual ways. But for Fulbright there was a further complication: the "no reference letter" policy. She was extremely troubled by its application to three discharged Diversified employees and to one discharged JLM employee.

The Salacious Sales Manager Soon after taking over Diversified, Fulbright became all too aware of the story of Ken Byrd, Diversified's then national sales manager. Ken is an affable man of fifty who had been an unusually effective sales manager. Throughout his career, his sales figures had always doubled those of his peers. He achieved rapid advancement despite a fatal flaw: he is an inveterate and indiscreet womanizer. He could not control his hands, which slapped backs so well, nor his tongue, which persuaded so eloquently. He had two approaches to women. With a woman of equal or superior rank in the company, he would politely, but inexorably, attempt to sweep her off her feet. With these women, he would be extremely charming and attentive, taking great care to avoid being offensive or harassing. In contrast, with a woman of subordinate rank, he would physically harass her. Less openly, but much too often, he would come up behind a woman, reach around her, and grab her. He invariably found this amusing—his victims, however, did not.

Fulbright could not believe that such a manager had stayed employed at Diversified so long, let alone been continually promoted to positions of greater responsibility and power. As Fulbright investigated the situation, she discovered that numerous sexual harassment complaints had been filed with Diversified concerning Byrd's behavior. To protect Byrd, Diversified dealt with these complaints by providing money and undeserved promotions to the complainants to smooth over their anger. Thus, Diversified successfully kept the complaints in-house and away from the courts and the Equal Employment Opportunity Commission.

After JLM's takeover of Diversified, Fulbright quickly discharged Byrd. Her satisfaction in getting rid of him was short-lived, however. His golden tongue and stellar sales record had landed him several job offers. Her dilemma was that she was uncomfortable about unleashing this deviant on an unsuspecting new employer. But JLM's policy forbade her from writing any letters or answering questions from prospective employers.

The Fruitless Juice Melissa Cuthbertson had been a vice president in procurement for Diversified's Birch-Wood division with direct responsibility over the ordering of supplies and raw materials. Birch-Wood manufactured a full line of baby food products, including fruit juices that were labeled "100% fruit juice." To cut costs, Stanley Aker, the division's president, had arranged for an unscrupulous supplier to provide high-fructose corn syrup labeled as juice concentrate. Because standard testing in the industry was unable to detect the substitution, the company did not get caught. Emboldened, Aker gradually increased the proportion of corn syrup until there were only trace amounts of fruit juice left in the "juice." A company employee discovered the practice and after the takeover brought the matter to Fulbright's attention through JLM's internal whistle-blowing channel, which Fulbright had established. She referred the matter to Raven, who called in Aker and Cuthbertson and confronted them with the accusation. They admitted it all, explaining that nutritionally the corn syrup was equivalent to the fruit juice. But at 60 percent of the cost of fruit juice, the corn syrup made a big difference to the bottom line. Raven told them that such conduct was not permitted and that they must properly dispose of the adulterated juice.

That night Aker and Cuthbertson had the juice moved from Birch-Wood's New York warehouse and shipped to its Puerto Rico warehouse. Over the course of the next few days, the "juice" was sold in Latin America as "apple juice." Aker reported to Raven that the juice had been properly disposed of and that Birch-Wood had sustained only a small loss during that quarter. When Raven discovered the truth, he immediately discharged Aker and Cuthbertson, telling them "that if he had anything to do with it, neither of them would ever work again." Fulbright was to meet soon with Raven to discuss what should be done about Aker and Cuthbertson.

The Compassionate CFO Jackson Cobb, JLM's former chief financial officer, is a brilliant analyst. Through hard work, he had earned an excellent education that honed his innate mathematical gifts. His natural curiosity led him to read widely, and this enabled him to bring disparate facts and concepts to bear on his often novel analyses of financial matters. But he had no interest in implementing his insights, for his only enjoyment was the process of discovering connections. Fortune—or fate—had brought him together with Raven, who is twenty years younger than Cobb. Theirs was definitely a case of opposites attracting. Raven cared little about ideas; he cared primarily about money. Cobb cared little about money; he cared primarily about ideas. Raven took Cobb's insights and translated them into action with spectacular success. Their relationship brought new meaning to the concept of synergy. When Raven formed JLM, he brought Cobb on as CFO and installed him in an adjoining office.

Their relationship continued to flourish, as did JLM's bottom line, until Cobb's wife became terminally ill. During the eighteen months she languished, Cobb spent as much time as he could taking care of her. After forty years of marriage, he was unwilling to leave her welfare to the "kindness of strangers." At his own expense, he installed a state-of-the-art communication center in his home. By virtue of computers, modems, video cameras, faxes, copiers, mobile telephones, and the like, he had available to him the same data and information as he had at his office. He could be reached by telephone at all times. But he was not in the office next to Raven; he was not present at Raven's daily breakfast meetings; he was not on the corporate jet en route to business meetings. After their many years of working together, Raven was enraged at the loss of immediate access to Cobb. He felt that Cobb had betrayed him and demanded that Cobb resume his old working hours. Cobb refused, and Raven fired him. Because of his age, Cobb was experiencing difficulty in finding new employment, and Fulbright wanted to write a letter on his behalf.

SWORD TECHNOLOGY, INC.

Background

Sitting in his office, Stephen Hag, CEO of Sword Technology, Inc., contemplated the problems that had been perplexing him for some time. They had begun when he took his company international, and they kept coming. But today he was no more successful in devising a solution than he had been previously. Slowly, his thoughts drifted to those early days years ago when he and his sister Marian started the company.

The company's first product was an investment newsletter stressing technical analysis in securities investing. A few years later, he developed what became a "killer app": a computer program that defines an entirely new market and through customer loyalty substantially dominates that market. His software program enabled investors to track their investments in stocks, bonds, and futures. By combining powerful analytical tools with an accessible graphical interface, it appealed to both professional and amateur investors. Moreover, it required users to download information from the company's database. With one of the most extensive databases and the cheapest downloading rates in the industry, the company soon controlled the U.S. market. Sword then went public through a highly successful IPO (an initial public offering of the company's common stock), and its stock is traded on the NASDAQ Stock Market. The company is required to file periodic reports with the Securities and Exchange Commission.

The company used cash from sales of software, online charges, and the IPO to try to enter the hardware side of the computer industry. It began manufacturing modems and other computer peripherals. A nagging problem, however, plagued the company's manufacturing efforts. Although Sword's modem could convert data more quickly and efficiently than most of its competitors, because of high labor costs it was unable to market its modem successfully. To reduce manufacturing costs, especially labor costs, the company decided to move its manufacturing facilities overseas. And that's when the trouble began.

Stephen's thoughts returned to the present. He reopened the folder labeled "Confidential: International Issues" and began perusing its contents.

Transfer Pricing

The first item he saw was an opinion letter from the company's tax attorney. It dealt with Excalibur Technology, the first overseas company Sword established. Excalibur, a wholly owned subsidiary of Sword, is incorporated in Tolemac, an emerging country with a rapidly growing economy. To encourage foreign investment, Tolemac taxes corporate profits at a significantly lower rate than the United States and other industrial nations. Excalibur manufactures modems for Sword pursuant to a licensing agreement under which Excalibur pays Sword a royalty equal to a specified percentage of the modems' gross sales. Excalibur sells all of its output at a fair market price to Sword, which then markets the modems in the United States. Stephen had been closely involved in structuring this arrangement and had insisted on keeping the royalty rate low to minimize taxable income for Sword. Stephen reread the opinion letter:

> Section 482 of the Internal Revenue Code authorizes the Internal Revenue Service to allocate gross income, deductions, credits, and other common allowances among two or more organizations, trades, or businesses under common ownership or control whenever it determines that this action is necessary "in order to prevent evasion of taxes or clearly to reflect the income of any such organizations, trades, or businesses." IRS Regulation 1.482–2(e) governing the sale or trade of intangibles between related persons mandates an appropriate allocation to reflect the price that an unrelated party under the same circumstances would have paid, which normally includes profit to the seller. The Regulations provide four methods for determining an arm's-length price. In our opinion, under the only method applicable to the circumstances of Sword Technology, Inc., and Excalibur Technology, the royalty rate should be at least three times the current one. If the IRS were to reach the same conclusion, then the company would be liable for the taxes it underpaid because of the understatement of income. Moreover, the company would be liable for a penalty of either 20 percent or 40 percent of the tax deficiency, unless the company can show that it had reasonable cause and acted in good faith.

Stephen had spoken to the tax attorney at length and learned that the probability of an audit was about 10 percent and that many multinational companies play similar "games" with their transfer pricing. The attorney also told him that he believed that if the company were audited, there was at least a 90 percent probability that the IRS would agree with his conclusion and at least a 70 percent probability that it would impose a penalty. Because the dollar amount of the contingent tax liability was not an insignificant amount, Stephen had been concerned about it for the six weeks since he had received the letter.

Customs and Customs

Soon after Excalibur had manufactured the first shipment of modems, a new problem arose: getting them out of Tolemac. It took far too long to clear customs, thus undermining their carefully planned just-in-time manufacturing schedules. Stephen hired a local export broker, who distributed cash gifts to customs officials. Miraculously, the clearance time shortened and manufacturing schedules were maintained. The export broker billed the company for his services and the amount of the cash gifts. Although the broker assured Stephen that such gifts were entirely customary, Stephen was not entirely comfortable with the practice.

The Thorn in His Side

Tolemac was not Stephen's only problem. Six months after commencing operations in Tolemac, Sword began serious negotiations to enter the Liarg market. Liarg is a developing country with a large population and a larger national debt. Previously, Sword had encountered great difficulties in exporting products to Liarg. Stephen's sister, Marian, COO of Sword, took on the challenge of establishing a Liarg presence.

They decided that setting up a manufacturing facility in Liarg would achieve two objectives: greater access to the Liarg marketplace and lower-cost modems. At first, the Liarg government insisted that Sword enter into a joint venture, with the government having a 51 percent interest. Sword was unwilling to invest in such an arrangement, countering with a proposal for a wholly owned subsidiary. Marian conducted extensive negotiations with the government, assisted by a Liarg consulting firm that specialized in lobbying governmental officials. As part of these negotiations, Sword made contributions to the reelection campaigns of key Liarg legislators who were opposed to wholly owned subsidiaries of foreign corporations. After the legislators' reelection, the negotiations quickly reached a successful conclusion. On closing the contract, Sword flew several Liarg officials and their wives to Lake Tahoe for a lavish three-day celebration. All of these expenses were reported in the company's financial statements as payments for legal and consulting fees.

Marian then hired an international engineering firm to help design the manufacturing plant. Two weeks later, they submitted plans for the plant and its operations that fully complied with

Liarg regulations regarding worker health and safety as well as environmental protection. But, as Marian had explained to Stephen, the plant's design fell far short of complying with U.S. requirements. Marian noted that, under the proposed design, the workers would face exposure to moderately high levels of toxic chemicals and hazardous materials. The design also would degrade the water supply of nearby towns. However, the design would generate significant savings in capital and operational costs as compared with the design used in their U.S. facility. Marian assured Stephen that all quality control systems were in place so the modems produced in this plant would be indistinguishable from their U.S. counterparts. Stephen and Marian have had long discussions about what to do about the plant.

Stephen then took from the folder an article that had appeared in a number of U.S. newspapers.

Children and Chips

A twelve-year-old Liarg child recently spoke at an international conference in New York denouncing the exploitation of children in the Liarg computer chip industry. The child informed the outraged audience that he had worked in such a plant from age four to age ten. He asserted that he was just one of many children who were so employed. He described the deplorable working conditions: poor ventilation, long hours, inadequate food, and substandard housing. The pay was low. But, because their families could not afford to keep them at home, the children were hired out to the factory owners, who especially wanted young children because their small fingers made them adept at many assembly processes.

Stephen had read the article countless times, thinking about his own children. He knew that if they set up a plant in Liarg, they would have to buy chip components from Liarg suppliers. He also knew that there would be no way for Sword to ensure that the chips had not been made with child labor.

Another labor issue also troubled Stephen. Marian told him that she had met considerable resistance from the Liarg executives they had hired when she suggested that women should be hired at the supervisory level. They maintained that it was not done and would make it impossible to hire and control a satisfactory workforce at the plant. Moreover, they insisted on hiring their relatives as supervisors. When Marian protested this nepotism, they assured her that it was customary and asserted that they could not trust anyone not related to them.

To Outsource or Not to Outsource

Once again Stephen glanced over the cost data. Sword's labor costs for supporting its database services and hardware were eviscerating the company's profits. After racking his brain endlessly, he had concluded that wherever it made financial and strategic sense Sword should utilize business process outsourcing (BPO); that is, long-term contracting out of non-core business processes to an outside provider in order to lower costs and thereby increase shareholder value.

Stephen had examined a number of potential countries on the basis of many factors, including time zone, communications infrastructure, technical training, English language skills of the workforce, and—most critically—costs. Liarg had emerged as the optimal choice. He anticipated reducing labor and associated overhead costs by 45 to 50 percent.

He planned to start by offshoring half of the call center operations, soon to be followed by a third of the low-end software development such as maintenance and coding. Assuming all went as he envisioned, he expected to move offshore back-office operations and higher-level software development. As his imagination soared, he saw the potential to amplify the company's operations with round-the-clock development.

Stephen realized that embarking on this course would result in reducing the staffing at the company's U.S. call centers. He expected he could achieve some reductions through attrition and reassignment, but considerable layoffs would be necessary. He hoped that outsourcing the low-end software development would enable the company to redeploy its software developers to higher-level and more profitable assignments. Moreover, the recent rollback in the number of visas had resulted in difficulty in hiring sufficient numbers of software developers with the necessary skills. If Sword were to offshore back-office operations, Stephen expected an impact on current employees comparable to offshoring the call centers.

On top of all these concerns had come a letter from the company's outside legal counsel regarding payments made to foreign officials.

Memorandum of Law

The Foreign Corrupt Practices Act makes it unlawful for any domestic company or any of its officers, directors, employees, or agents or its stockholders acting on its behalf to offer or give anything of value directly or indirectly to any foreign official, political party, or political official for the purpose of

1. influencing any act or decision of that person or party in his or its official capacity,
2. inducing an act or omission in violation of his or its lawful duty, or
3. inducing such person or party to use its influence to affect a decision of a foreign government in order to assist the domestic concern in obtaining or retaining business.

An offer or promise to make a prohibited payment is a violation even if the offer is not accepted or the promise is not performed. The 1988 amendments explicitly excluded facilitating or expediting payments made to expedite or secure the performance of routine governmental actions by a foreign official, political party, or party official. Routine governmental action does not include any decision by a foreign official regarding the award of new business or the continuation of old business. The amendments also added an affirmative defense for payments that are lawful under the written laws or regulations of the foreign official's country. Violations are punishable by fines of up to $2 million for companies; individuals may be fined a maximum of $100,000 or imprisoned up to five years, or both. Fines imposed upon individuals may not be paid directly or indirectly by the domestic company on whose behalf they acted. In addition, the courts may impose civil penalties of up to $16,000.

The statute also imposes internal control requirements on all reporting companies. Such companies must

1. make and keep books, records, and accounts, that in reasonable detail, accurately and fairly reflect the transactions and dispositions of the assets of the company; and
2. devise and maintain a system of internal controls that ensure that transactions are executed as authorized and recorded in conformity with generally accepted accounting principles, thereby establishing accountability with regard to assets and ensuring that access to those assets is permitted only with management's authorization.

Any person who knowingly circumvents or knowingly fails to implement a system of internal accounting controls or knowingly falsifies any book, record, or account is subject to criminal liability.

VULCAN, INC.

The Company

Vulcan, Inc. is a multinational Fortune 200 company engaging principally in the exploration for and extraction of minerals. It is listed on the New York Stock Exchange and has more than 615 million shares outstanding.

The Meeting (March 7)

On March 5, Stewart Myer, the company's CEO, personally telephoned Martha Bordeaux, the vice president for finance; Lamont Johnson, the chief geologist; and Natasha Bylinski, the vice president for acquisitions, to arrange a March 7 meeting at the Atlanta airport. He emphasized to each of them the need for the utmost secrecy, directing them to arrange their travel to Atlanta as a connection to other and different destinations. When they all arrived at the meeting room, Myer reemphasized the need for complete secrecy. He then asked Johnson to present his report.

The Report

Johnson read his report:

Over the past few years we have conducted extensive aerial geophysical surveys of the areas west of the Great Plains. These revealed numerous anomalies or extreme variations in the conductivity of rocks. One appeared particularly encouraging, so late last year we began a ground geophysical survey of the southwest portion of the Z segment in Montana. This survey confirmed the presence of anomalies. Accordingly, on January 14 we drilled some core samples and sent them to our lab. The results were so extraordinarily promising that on February 10 we obtained more core samples and had them chemically assayed. On February 25, we received the assay, which revealed an average mineral content of 1.17 percent copper and 8.6 percent zinc over 600 feet of the sample's 650-foot length.

Johnson then commented, "In my forty years in the business I have never seen such remarkable test results. On a scale of one to ten, this is an eleven."

The Reaction

Bordeaux exclaimed, "Our stock price will go through the roof!" Bylinski retorted, "So will land prices!"

The Strategy

Myer interrupted, "Look, we're not here to celebrate. There are a lot of better places to do that. We can't keep a lid on this for very long so we have to strike soon. We need to line up the right agents to acquire the land. We must fragment the acquisitions to keep the sellers in the dark. Most critical is maintaining absolute secrecy. No one else in the company must know this. I will decide who needs to know and I will tell them. It is your duty to the company to keep totally quiet. Now, let's discuss the acquisition plan."

When asked how he had managed to obtain core samples without tipping off the owners of the land, Johnson explained, "We pretended to be a motion picture company looking for locations to remake the movie *High Noon*. We drilled the samples in isolated areas and quickly filled the holes. To further cover our tracks we drilled some barren core samples from land we owned and hid the cores on our land."

The Plan

Bylinski outlined the plan to acquire the land. "We only own about 20 percent of the land we want and we have options on another 15 percent. However, we currently own none of the principal portion. So we have a lot of work to do. We will employ several agents to negotiate the purchases. We will instruct them not to disclose that they are acting for us. In fact, we will order them not to disclose they are acting for anyone. We need to acquire approximately twenty square miles of additional land."

Bordeaux asked, "What if the locals start getting curious?"

Myer replied, "I'll deal with that later if it arises."

Stock Options

On March 15, Vulcan issued stock options at $23.50 per share to thirty of its executives, including Myer, Bordeaux, Johnson, and Bylinski. At this time neither the stock option committee nor the board of directors had been informed of the strike or the pending land acquisition program.

The Rumors

While the land acquisition plan was nearing completion, rumors about a major strike by Vulcan began circulating throughout the business community. On the morning of March 20, Bordeaux read an account in a national newspaper reporting that ore samples had been sent out of Montana and inferring from that fact that Vulcan had made a rich strike. Bordeaux called Myer and told him about the article.

The Press Release

Myer prepared the following press release, which appeared in morning newspapers of general circulation on March 21:

> During the past few days the press has reported drilling activities by Vulcan and rumors of a substantial copper discovery. These reports greatly exaggerate. Vulcan has engaged in normal geophysical explorations throughout the West. We routinely send core samples to verify our visual examinations. Most of the areas drilled have been barren or marginal. When we have additional information we will issue a statement to shareholders and the public.

Land Acquired

On April 6, Vulcan completed its land acquisition program. It had employed seven different agents. In total, it had acquired thirty-seven parcels from twenty-two different sellers at prices ranging from $300 to $600 per acre. The land cost a total of approximately $6 million.

Official Announcement

At 10:00 A.M. on April 11, Myer released on behalf of Vulcan an official announcement of a strike in Montana containing at least 30 million tons of high-grade copper and zinc ore. The

Figure 2-8 Stock Price of Vulcan, Inc. (note irregular intervals on time axis)

release appeared on the wire services at 10:30 A.M. The price of Vulcan stock shot up eleven points to $38 by the close of business that day and continued to rise, reaching a price of $56 on May 16. (Figures 2-8 and 2-9 show the price and volume of Vulcan stock.)

Loose Lips

Prior to the April 11 official announcement, a number of people purchased Vulcan stock with knowledge of the mineral discovery. Some people also purchased land adjacent to Vulcan's holdings in Montana. These purchasers included the following:

The Vulcan Executives   Myer, Bordeaux, Johnson, and Bylinski each purchased shares or calls on several occasions during this time period. See Figure 2-10 for a listing of their purchases.

Figure 2-9 Average Daily Volume of Vulcan, Inc., Stock for Week (in 1,000s)

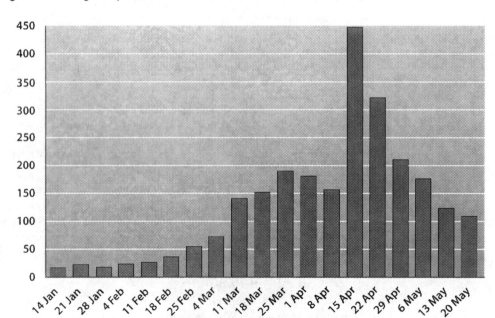

Figure 2-10 Purchases of Vulcan Stock by Selected Executives

Purchaser	Date	Shares	Price	Calls	Price
Myer	Jan. 20	10,000	18.00		
	Feb. 25	10,000	20.00		
	March 2	15,000	21.25		
	March 7			5,000	22.25
	March 15			5,000	23.75
Bordeaux	March 7	10,000	22.00		
	March 15			7,500	23.75
	March 18	5,000	24.00		
Johnson	Jan. 20	5,000	18.00		
	Feb. 25	8,000	20.00		
	March 1	12,000	21.00		
	March 7	6,000	22.00		
	March 15	4,000	23.50		
Bylinski	March 7	5,000	22.00		
	March 15	3,000	23.50		
	March 18			4,000	24.25

The Eager Eavesdropper   After leaving the March 7 meeting, Bordeaux and Bylinski went to the airport lounge to wait for their flights. They excitedly—and loudly—discussed what they had learned at the meeting. Several people overheard their remarks, and one of them, Rae Bodie, immediately called her broker and bought fifteen hundred shares of Vulcan stock. Ms. Bodie also purchased a large tract of land next to Vulcan's site in Montana for approximately $600 per acre.

The Crestfallen Security Guard   On March 9, Johnson went into the home office very early to finish up the exploratory work on the new find. At the elevator he encountered Celia Tidey, one of the company's security guards. Johnson knew her fairly well since they both had worked for Vulcan for more than fifteen years. Noting her despondent visage, Johnson asked her what was wrong. She related to him her tale of woe: her husband had become disabled and lost his job while her son needed an expensive medical procedure and their health insurance did not cover it. Johnson felt great empathy for her plight. He told her that big doings were afoot at Vulcan and that if she bought Vulcan stock soon she would make a lot of money in a month or so. She took her savings and bought two hundred shares of Vulcan stock, which were as many shares as she could buy.

The Avaricious Agent   William Baggio, one of the agents hired to acquire the land, inferred that whatever was up had to be good for Vulcan. Accordingly, on March 21, he purchased twenty-five hundred shares of Vulcan and five thousand acres of land adjacent to the Vulcan property.

The Trusted Tippee   On March 8, Myer called Theodore Griffey, his oldest and dearest friend. After getting Griffey to swear absolute confidentiality, Myer told him all the details of the strike. After hanging up the telephone, Griffey immediately purchased fifteen thousand shares of Vulcan stock. Griffey then told his father and sister about the land; both of them bought fifteen thousand shares.

The Scampering Stockbroker   Morris Lynch, Myer's stockbroker, was intrigued by Myer's purchases of an unusually large volume of Vulcan shares. During the last two weeks of March, he put a number of his other clients into Vulcan, telling them, "I've looked at this stock and it's good for you." About a dozen of his clients purchased a total of eight thousand shares.

The Land Grab

After the official announcement on April 11, several of Vulcan's competitors began exploring the area and purchased large tracks of land, bidding up the price of land to $2,250 per acre. Both Bodie and Baggio sold their newly acquired land to Vulcan competitors at this higher price.

PART II

The Legal Environment of Business

CHAPTER **3**

Civil Dispute Resolution

Laws are a dead letter without courts to expound and define their true meaning and operation.

Alexander Hamilton,
The Federalist (1788)

CHAPTER OUTCOMES

After reading and studying this chapter, you should be able to:

1. List and describe the courts in the federal court system and in a typical state court system.

2. Distinguish among exclusive federal jurisdiction, concurrent federal jurisdiction, and exclusive state jurisdiction.

3. Distinguish among (a) subject matter jurisdiction and jurisdiction over the parties and (b) the three types of jurisdiction over the parties.

4. List and explain the various stages of a civil proceeding.

5. Compare and contrast litigation, arbitration, conciliation, and mediation.

A
s we discussed in Chapter 1, substantive law sets forth the rights and duties of individuals and other legal entities, whereas procedural law determines how these rights are asserted. Procedural law attempts to accomplish two competing objectives: (1) to be fair and impartial and (2) to operate efficiently. The judicial process in the United States represents a balance between these two objectives as well as a commitment to the adversary system.

In the first part of this chapter, we will describe the structure and function of the federal and state court systems. The second part deals with jurisdiction; the third part discusses civil dispute resolution, including the procedure in civil lawsuits.

THE COURT SYSTEM

Courts are impartial tribunals (seats of judgment) established by governmental bodies to settle disputes. A court may render a binding decision only when it has jurisdiction over the dispute and the parties to that dispute; that is, when it has a right to hear and make a judgment in a case. The United States has a dual court system: the federal government has its own independent system, as does each of the fifty states and the District of Columbia.

THE FEDERAL COURTS

Article III of the U.S. Constitution states that the judicial power of the United States shall be vested in one Supreme Court and such lower courts as Congress may establish. Congress has established a lower federal court system consisting of a number of special courts, district courts, and courts of appeals. Judges in the federal court system are appointed for life by the President, subject to confirmation by the Senate. The structure of the federal court system is illustrated in Figure 3-1.

Figure 3-1 Federal Judicial System

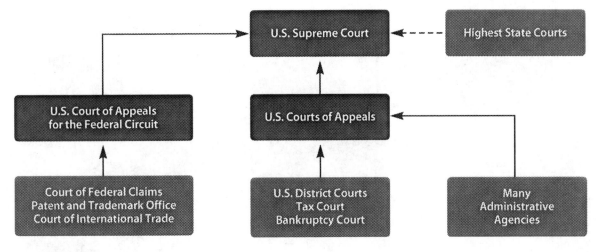

© Cengage Learning 2013

District Courts

District Courts

trial courts of general jurisdiction that can hear and decide most legal controversies in the federal system

The **district courts** are general trial courts in the federal system. Most federal cases begin in the district court, and it is here that issues of fact are decided. The district court is generally presided over by *one* judge, although in certain cases three judges preside. In a few cases, an appeal from a judgment or decree of a district court is taken directly to the Supreme Court. In most cases, however, appeals go to the Circuit Court of Appeals of the appropriate circuit, the decision of which is final in most cases.

Congress has established ninety-four federal judicial districts, each of which is located entirely in a particular state. All states have at least one district, while certain states contain more than one district. For instance, New York has four districts, Illinois has three, and Wisconsin has two, while a number of less populated states each make up a single district.

Courts of Appeals

Courts of Appeals

hear appeals from the district courts and review orders of certain administrative agencies

Reverse

set aside the lower court's judgment

Modify

change the lower court's judgment

Remand

send the case back to the lower court

Affirm

uphold the lower court's judgment

Congress has established twelve judicial circuits (eleven numbered circuits plus the D.C. circuit), each having a court known as the Court of Appeals, which primarily hears appeals from the district courts located within its circuit (see Figure 3-2). In addition, these courts review decisions of many administrative agencies, the Tax Court, and the Bankruptcy Courts. Congress has also established the U.S. Court of Appeals for the Federal Circuit, which is discussed later in the section on "Special Courts." The U.S. Courts of Appeals generally hear cases in panels of three judges, although in some instances all judges of the circuit will sit *en banc* to decide a case.

The function of appellate courts is to examine the record of a case on appeal and to determine whether the trial court committed prejudicial error (error substantially affecting the appellant's rights and duties). If so, the appellate court will **reverse** or **modify** the judgment of the lower court and, if necessary, **remand** or send it back to the lower court for further proceeding. If there is no prejudicial error, the appellate court will **affirm** the decision of the lower court.

The Supreme Court

The Supreme Court

the nation's highest court whose principal function is to review decisions of the Federal Courts of Appeals and the highest state courts

Appeal by right

mandatory review by a higher court

The nation's highest tribunal is the U.S. Supreme Court, which consists of nine justices (a Chief Justice and eight Associate Justices) who sit as a group in Washington, D.C. A quorum consists of any six justices. In certain types of cases, the U.S. Supreme Court has original jurisdiction (the right to hear a case first). The Court's principal function, nonetheless, is to review decisions of the Federal Courts of Appeals and, in some instances, decisions involving federal law resolved by the highest state courts. Cases reach the Supreme Court under its appellate jurisdiction by one of two routes. Very few come by way of **appeal by right**. The Court must hear these cases if one of the parties requests the review. In 1988 Congress enacted legislation that almost completely eliminated the right to appeal to the U.S. Supreme Court.

Figure 3-2 Circuit Courts of the United States

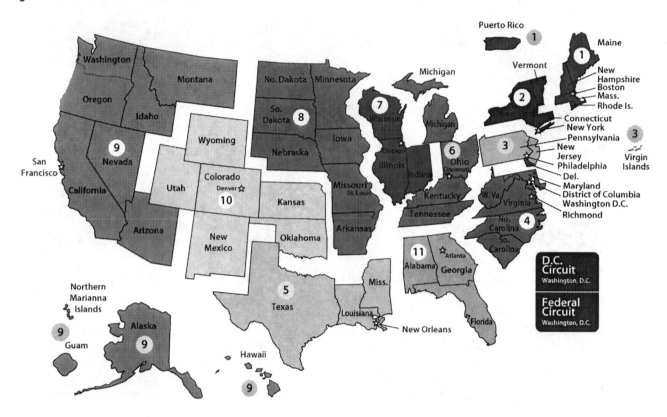

Source: Administrative Office of The United States Courts, January 1983

Writ of *certiorari*
discretionary review by
a higher court

The second way in which the Supreme Court may review a decision of a lower court is by the discretionary **writ of *certiorari***, which requires a lower court to produce the records of a case it has tried. Now almost all cases reaching the Supreme Court come to it by means of writs of *certiorari*. If four Justices vote to hear the case, the Court grants writs when there is a federal question of substantial importance or a conflict in the decisions of the U.S. Circuit Courts of Appeals. Only a small percentage of the petitions to the Supreme Court for review by *certiorari* are granted, however, because the Court uses the writ as a device to choose which cases it wishes to hear.

Special Courts

Special courts
have jurisdiction over
cases in a particular area of
federal law and include the
U.S. Court of Federal Claims,
the Tax Court, the U.S.
Bankruptcy Courts, and the
U.S. Court of Appeals for the
Federal Circuit

The **special courts** in the federal judicial system include the U.S. Court of Federal Claims, the U.S. Bankruptcy Courts, the U.S. Tax Court, and the U.S. Court of Appeals for the Federal Circuit. These courts have jurisdiction over particular subject matter. The U.S. Court of Federal Claims has national jurisdiction to hear claims against the United States. The U.S. Bankruptcy Courts have jurisdiction to hear and decide certain matters under the Federal Bankruptcy Code, subject to review by the U.S. District Court. The U.S. Tax Court has national jurisdiction over certain cases involving federal taxes. The U.S. Court of Appeals for the Federal Circuit has national jurisdiction and reviews decisions of the Court of Federal Claims, the Patent and Trademark Office, patent cases decided by U.S. District Courts, the U.S. Court of International Trade, the Merit Systems Protection Board, and the U.S. Court of Veterans Appeals.

STATE COURTS

Each of the fifty states and the District of Columbia has its own independent court system. In most states, the voters elect judges for a stated term. The structure of state court systems varies from state to state. Figure 3-3 shows a typical system.

Figure 3-3 State Court System

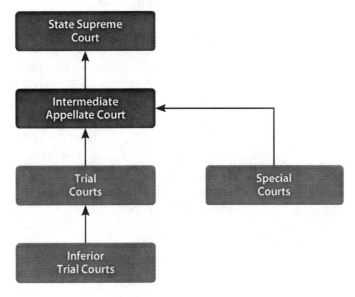

© Cengage Learning 2013

Inferior trial courts
hear minor criminal cases such as traffic offenses and civil cases involving small amounts of money and conduct preliminary hearings in more serious criminal cases

Small claims courts
inferior trial courts with jurisdiction over civil cases involving a limited dollar amount

Trial courts
have general jurisdiction over civil and criminal cases

Special trial courts
trial courts, such as probate courts and family courts, which have jurisdiction over a particular area of state law

Appellate courts
include one or two levels; the highest court's decisions are final except in those cases reviewed by the U.S. Supreme Court

Inferior Trial Courts

At the bottom of the state court system are the **inferior trial courts**, which decide the least serious criminal and civil matters. Usually, inferior trial courts do not keep a complete written record of trial proceedings. Minor criminal cases such as traffic offenses are heard in inferior trial courts, which are referred to as municipal courts, justice of the peace courts, or traffic courts. These courts also conduct preliminary hearings in more serious criminal cases.

Small claims courts are inferior trial courts that hear civil cases involving a limited amount of money. Usually there is no jury, the procedure is informal, and neither side employs an attorney. An appeal from a small claims court is taken to the trial court of general jurisdiction, where a new trial (called a trial *de novo*), in which the small claims court's decision is given no weight, is begun.

Trial Courts

Each state has **trial courts** of general jurisdiction, which may be called county, district, superior, circuit, or common pleas courts. (In New York the trial court is called the Supreme Court.) These courts do not have a dollar limitation on their jurisdiction in civil cases and hear all criminal cases other than minor offenses. Unlike the inferior trial courts, these trial courts of general jurisdiction maintain formal records of their proceedings as procedural safeguards.

Many states have **special trial courts** that have jurisdiction over particular areas. For example, many states have probate courts with jurisdiction over the administration of wills and estates as well as family courts with jurisdiction over divorce and child custody cases.

Appellate Courts

At the summit of the state court system is the state's court of last resort, a reviewing court generally called the supreme court of the state. Except for those cases in which review by the U.S. Supreme Court is available, the decision of the highest state tribunal is final. In addition, most states also have created intermediate appellate courts to handle the large volume of cases in which review is sought. Review by such a court is usually by right. Further review is in most cases at the highest court's discretion.

JURISDICTION

Jurisdiction means the power or authority of a court to hear and decide a given case. To resolve a lawsuit, a court must have two kinds of jurisdiction. The first is jurisdiction over the subject

Jurisdiction
authority of a court to hear and decide a case

matter of the lawsuit. If a court lacks jurisdiction over the subject matter of a case, no action it takes in the case will have legal effect.

The second kind of jurisdiction is over the parties to a lawsuit. This jurisdiction is required for the court to render an enforceable judgment that affects the parties' rights and duties. A court usually may obtain jurisdiction over the defendant in a lawsuit if the defendant lives and is present in the court's territory or the transaction giving rise to the case has a substantial connection to the court's territory. The court obtains jurisdiction over the plaintiff when the plaintiff voluntarily submits to the court's power by filing a complaint with the court.

SUBJECT MATTER JURISDICTION

Subject matter jurisdiction
authority of a court to decide a particular kind of case

Subject matter jurisdiction refers to the authority of a particular court to judge a controversy of a particular kind. Federal courts have *limited* subject matter jurisdiction. State courts have jurisdiction over *all* matters that the Constitution or the Congress neither denies them nor gives exclusively to the federal courts.

Federal Jurisdiction

Exclusive federal jurisdiction
jurisdiction that permits only the federal courts to hear a case

The federal courts have, to the exclusion of the state courts, subject matter jurisdiction over some areas. Such jurisdiction is called **exclusive federal jurisdiction**. Federal jurisdiction is exclusive only if Congress so provides, either explicitly or implicitly. If Congress does not so provide and the area is one over which federal courts have subject matter jurisdiction, they share this jurisdiction with the state courts. Such jurisdiction is known as **concurrent federal jurisdiction**.

Concurrent federal jurisdiction
authority of federal or state courts to hear the same case

Exclusive Federal Jurisdiction The federal courts have exclusive jurisdiction over federal criminal prosecutions; admiralty, bankruptcy, antitrust, patent, trademark, and copyright cases; suits against the United States; and cases arising under certain federal statutes that expressly provide for exclusive federal jurisdiction.

Federal question
any case arising under the Constitution, statutes, or treaties of the United States

Concurrent Federal Jurisdiction The two types of concurrent federal jurisdiction are federal question jurisdiction and diversity jurisdiction. The first arises whenever there is a federal question over which the federal courts do not have exclusive jurisdiction. A **federal question** is any case arising under the Constitution, statutes, or treaties of the United States. There is no minimum dollar requirement in federal question cases. When a state court hears a concurrent federal question case, it applies *federal* substantive law but its own procedural rules.

The second type of concurrent federal jurisdiction occurs in a civil suit where there is diversity of citizenship and the amount in controversy exceeds $75,000. As the following case explains, the jurisdictional requirement is satisfied if the claim for the amount is made in good faith, unless it is clear to a legal certainty that the claim does not meet or exceed the required amount. *Diversity of citizenship* exists (1) when the plaintiffs are citizens of a state or states different from the state or states of which the defendants are citizens; (2) when a foreign country brings an action against citizens of the United States; or (3) when the controversy is between citizens of a state and citizens of a foreign country. The citizenship of an individual litigant (party in a lawsuit) is the state in which the individual resides or is domiciled, whereas that of a corporate litigant is both the state of incorporation and the state in which its principal place of business is located. For example, if the amount in controversy exceeds $75,000, then diversity of citizenship jurisdiction would be satisfied if Ada, a citizen of California, sues Bob, a citizen of Idaho. If, however, Carol, a citizen of Virginia, and Dianne, a citizen of North Carolina, sue Evan, a citizen of Georgia, and Farley, a citizen of North Carolina, there is *not* diversity of citizenship, because both Dianne, a plaintiff, and Farley, a defendant, are citizens of North Carolina.

When a federal district court hears a case solely under diversity of citizenship jurisdiction, no federal question is involved; and, accordingly, the federal courts must apply *state* substantive law. The conflict of law rules of the state in which the district court is located determine which state's substantive law is to be used in the case. (Conflict of laws is discussed later.) Federal courts apply federal procedural rules in diversity cases.

PRACTICAL ADVICE

If you have the option, consider whether you want to bring your lawsuit in a federal or state court.

In any case involving concurrent jurisdiction, the plaintiff has the choice of bringing the action in either an appropriate federal court or state court. If the plaintiff brings the case in a state court, however, the defendant usually may have it removed (shifted) to a federal court for the district in which the state court is located.

White v. FCI USA, Inc.
United States Court of Appeals, Fifth Circuit, 2003
319 F.3d 672
http://caselaw.lp.findlaw.com/data2/circs/5th/0250890p.pdf

FACTS On March 29, 2001, the plaintiff, Regina White (White), brought suit in a Texas state court against the defendant FCI USA, Inc. (FCI), White's former employer, for wrongful termination based on her refusal to perform illegal acts. White sought punitive damages, attorneys' fees, prejudgment interest, court costs, and compensatory damages for lost pay, lost fringe benefits, loss of wage earning capacity, harm to White's credit and credit reputation, and mental anguish and emotional distress. White did not specify how much monetary relief she was seeking. On May 25, 2001, FCI sought to remove the case to a federal district court on the basis of diversity asserting that the amount in controversy exceeded $75,000. White filed a motion opposing removal.

The district court concluded it was "more probable than not" that the lengthy list of compensatory and punitive damages sought by White, when combined with attorneys' fees, would exceed $75,000. In fact, the district court concluded that the compensatory damages or punitive damages alone would "in all likelihood" exceed $75,000. The district court also noted White's admission that her damages "[did] not yet equal" $75,000 but "it [was] possible that [they] will exceed $75,000.00 at the time of trial."

DECISION District court's decision affirmed.

OPINION Diversity jurisdiction only exists where the parties are citizens of different states and the amount in controversy exceeds $75,000. The amount in controversy is determined at the time of filing. However, White never specified the total amount of monetary relief she was seeking. Where the plaintiff fails to allege a specific amount of damages, the party invoking federal jurisdiction must prove by a preponderance of the evidence that the amount

in controversy exceeds the jurisdictional amount. The district court must first examine the complaint to determine whether it is "facially apparent" that the claims exceed the jurisdictional amount. If it is not thus apparent, the court may rely on "summary judgment-type" evidence to ascertain the amount in controversy.

In its Requests for Admission, FCI asked White to admit or deny that she was seeking damages of $75,000 or more. White admitted that her damages "[did] not yet equal" $75,000 but "it [was] possible that [they] will exceed $75,000.00 at the time of trial." Through this language, White implied that the amount in controversy was not limited to the damages she suffered before her filing. Instead, White indicated that she was seeking continuing and future damages as well.

The jurisdictional facts that support removal must be judged at the time of the removal. At the time of removal, it was apparent from the face of the complaint and the evidence presented by FCI that the amount in controversy exceeded $75,000. Once a defendant is able to show that the amount in controversy exceeds the jurisdictional amount, removal is proper, provided the plaintiff has not shown that it is legally certain that her recovery will not exceed the amount stated. White has failed to show that it was legally certain that her recovery will not exceed $75,000.

INTERPRETATION Federal diversity jurisdiction exists if the preponderance of the evidence indicates that the amount in controversy is over $75,000.

CRITICAL THINKING QUESTION Why has Congress imposed a jurisdictional minimum for diversity of citizenship cases?

Exclusive State Jurisdiction

The state courts have exclusive jurisdiction over all other matters. All matters not granted to the federal courts in the Constitution or by Congress are solely within the jurisdiction of the states. Accordingly, exclusive state jurisdiction would include cases involving diversity of citizenship where the amount in controversy is $75,000 or less. In addition, the state courts have exclusive jurisdiction over all cases to which the federal judicial power does not reach, including, but by no means limited to, property, torts, contract, agency, commercial transactions, and most crimes.

A court in one state may be a proper forum for a case even though some or all of the relevant events occurred in another state. For example, a California plaintiff may sue a Washington defendant in Washington over a car accident that occurred in Oregon. Because of Oregon's connections to the accident, Washington may choose, under its **conflict of laws** rules, to apply the substantive law of Oregon. Conflict of laws rules vary from state to state.

The jurisdiction of the federal and state courts is illustrated in Figure 3-4. Also, see Concept Review 3-1.

PRACTICAL ADVICE

Consider including in your contracts a choice-of-law provision specifying which jurisdiction's law will apply.

Figure 3-4 Federal and State Jurisdiction

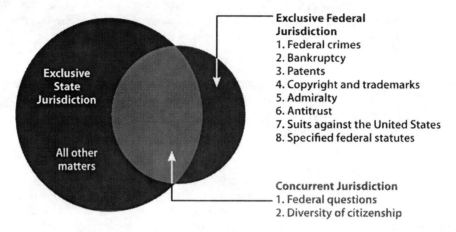

© Cengage Learning 2013

Stare Decisis in the Dual Court System

The doctrine of *stare decisis* presents certain problems when there are two parallel court systems. As a consequence, in the United States, *stare decisis* works approximately as follows (also illustrated in Figure 3-5):

1. The U.S. Supreme Court has never held itself to be bound rigidly by its own decisions, and lower federal courts and state courts have followed that course with respect to their own decisions.
2. A decision of the U.S. Supreme Court on a federal question is binding on all other courts, federal or state.
3. On a federal question, although a decision of a federal court other than the Supreme Court may be persuasive in a state court, it is not binding.
4. A decision of a state court may be persuasive in the federal courts, but it is not binding except in cases in which federal jurisdiction is based on diversity of citizenship. In such a case, the federal courts must apply state law as determined by the highest state tribunal.
5. Decisions of the federal courts (other than the U.S. Supreme Court) are not binding on other federal courts of equal or inferior rank unless the latter owe obedience to the deciding court. For example, a decision of the Fifth Circuit Court of Appeals binds district courts in the Fifth Circuit but binds no other federal court.
6. A decision of a state court is binding on all courts inferior to it in its jurisdiction. Thus, the decision of the supreme court in a state binds all other courts in that state.
7. A decision of a state court is not binding on courts in another state except in cases in which the latter courts are required, under their conflict of laws rules, to apply the law of the first state as determined by the highest court in that state. For example, if a North Carolina court is required to apply Virginia law, it must follow decisions of the Virginia Supreme Court.

CONCEPT REVIEW 3-1

Subject Matter Jurisdiction

Type of Jurisdiction	Court	Substantive Law Applied	Procedural Law Applied
Exclusive federal	Federal	Federal	Federal
Concurrent: federal question	Federal	Federal	Federal
	State	Federal	State
Concurrent: diversity	Federal	State	Federal
	State	State	State
Exclusive state	State	State	State

© Cengage Learning 2013

Figure 3-5 *Stare Decisis* in the Dual Court System

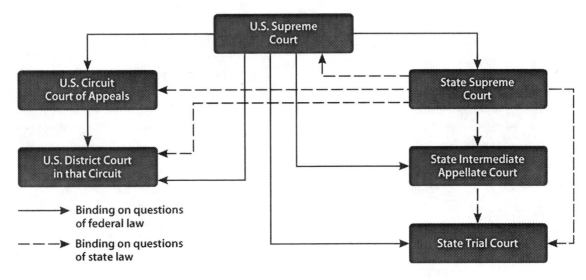

© Cengage Learning 2013

JURISDICTION OVER THE PARTIES

Jurisdiction over the parties

power of a court to bind the parties to a suit

PRACTICAL ADVICE

Consider including in your contracts a choice-of-forum provision specifying what court will have jurisdiction over any litigation arising from the contract.

The second essential type of jurisdiction a court must have is the power to bind the parties involved in the dispute. This type of jurisdiction is called **jurisdiction over the parties**. The court obtains jurisdiction over the *plaintiff* when she voluntarily submits to the court's power by filing a complaint with the court. With respect to the *defendant,* a court may meet the requirements of this type of jurisdiction in any of three ways: (1) *in personam* jurisdiction, (2) *in rem* jurisdiction, or (3) attachment jurisdiction. In addition, the exercise of jurisdiction must satisfy the constitutionally imposed requirements of reasonable notification and a reasonable opportunity to be heard. Moreover, the court's exercise of jurisdiction is valid under the Due Process Clause of the U.S. Constitution only if the defendant has minimum contacts with the state sufficient to prevent the court's assertion of jurisdiction from offending "traditional notions of fair play and substantial justice." For a court constitutionally to assert jurisdiction over a defendant, the defendant must have engaged in either purposeful acts in the state or acts outside the state that are of such a nature that the defendant could reasonably foresee being sued in that state, as discussed in the next case.

World-Wide Volkswagen Corp. v. Woodson
Supreme Court of the United States, 1980
444 U.S. 286, 100 S.Ct. 559, 62 L.Ed.2d 490
http://laws.findlaw.com/us/444/286.html

FACTS Harry and Kay Robinson purchased a new Audi automobile from Seaway Volkswagen, Inc. (Seaway) in Massena, New York. The Robinsons, who had resided in New York for years, left for a new home in Arizona. As they drove through Oklahoma, another car struck their Audi from behind, causing a fire that severely burned Kay and her two children.

The Robinsons brought a products-liability suit in the District Court in Oklahoma, claiming their injuries resulted from defective design of the Audi gas tank and fuel system. They joined as defendants the manufacturer (Audi), the regional distributor (World-Wide Volkswagen Corp.), and the retail distributor (Seaway).

World-Wide and Seaway entered special appearances, asserting that Oklahoma's exercise of jurisdiction over them offended limitations on state jurisdiction imposed by the Due Process Clause of the Fourteenth Amendment. The Oklahoma Supreme Court upheld the assertion of state jurisdiction, and World-Wide and Seaway appealed.

DECISION Judgment of Oklahoma Supreme Court reversed.

OPINION The Due Process Clause of the Fourteenth Amendment limits the power of a state court to render a valid personal judgment against a nonresident defendant. A judgment rendered in violation of due process is void in the rendering state and is not entitled to full faith and credit elsewhere. A state court may exercise personal jurisdiction over a nonresident defendant only so long as there exist "minimum contacts" between the defendant and the forum state. The defendant's contacts with the forum state must be such that maintenance of the suit does not offend traditional notions of fair play and justice.

World-Wide is incorporated and has its place of business in New York. It distributes vehicles, parts, and accessories to retail dealers in New York, New Jersey, and Connecticut. Seaway, one of those retail dealers, is incorporated and has its place of business in New York. There is no evidence that either World-Wide or Seaway does any business in Oklahoma, ships or sells any products to or in that state, has an agent to receive process there, or purchases advertisements in any media calculated to reach Oklahoma. In fact, there is no showing that any automobile sold by World-Wide or Seaway has ever entered Oklahoma with the single exception of the Robinsons' Audi. Thus, in this case, there is a total absence of those affiliating circumstances, or minimum contacts, that are a necessary predicate to any exercise of state court jurisdiction.

INTERPRETATION Sufficient minimal contacts between the defendant and the state must exist for a state to exercise jurisdiction.

CRITICAL THINKING QUESTION Explain the public policy reasons for subjecting nonresidents doing business in a state to the *in personam* jurisdiction of the courts within that state.

In Personam Jurisdiction

In personam jurisdiction
jurisdiction based upon claims against a person in contrast to jurisdiction over his property

In personam jurisdiction, or personal jurisdiction, is the jurisdiction of a court over the parties to a lawsuit, in contrast to its jurisdiction over their property. A court obtains *in personam* jurisdiction over a defendant either (1) by serving process on the party within the state in which the court is located or (2) by reasonable notification to a party outside the state in those instances where a "long-arm statute" applies. To *serve process* means to deliver a summons, which is an order to respond to a complaint lodged against a party. (The terms *summons* and *complaint* are explained more fully later in this chapter.)

Personal jurisdiction may be obtained by personally serving process upon a defendant within a state if that person is domiciled in that state. The U.S. Supreme Court has held that a state may exercise personal jurisdiction over a nonresident defendant who is temporarily present if the defendant is personally served in that state. Personal jurisdiction may also arise from a party's consent. For example, parties to a contract may agree that any dispute concerning that contract will be subject to the jurisdiction of a specific court.

Most states have adopted **long-arm statutes** to expand their jurisdictional reach beyond those persons who may be personally served within the state. These statutes allow courts to obtain jurisdiction over nonresident defendants under the following conditions, as long as the exercise of jurisdiction does not offend traditional notions of fair play and substantial justice: if the defendant (1) has committed a tort (civil wrong) within the state, (2) owns property within the state and if that property is the subject matter of the lawsuit, (3) has entered into a contract within the state, or (4) has transacted business within the state and if that business is the subject matter of the lawsuit.

In Rem Jurisdiction

In rem jurisdiction
jurisdiction based on claims against property

Courts in a state have the jurisdiction to adjudicate claims to property situated within the state if the plaintiff gives those persons who have an interest in the property reasonable notice and an opportunity to be heard. Such jurisdiction over property is called **in rem jurisdiction**. For example, if Carpenter and Miller are involved in a lawsuit over property located in Kansas, then an appropriate court in Kansas would have *in rem* jurisdiction to adjudicate claims over this property as long as both parties are given notice of the lawsuit and a reasonable opportunity to contest the claim.

Attachment Jurisdiction

Quasi in rem jurisdiction
jurisdiction over property not based on claims against it

Attachment jurisdiction, or **quasi in rem jurisdiction**, like *in rem* jurisdiction, is jurisdiction over property rather than over a person. But attachment jurisdiction is invoked by seizing the defendant's property located within the state to obtain payment of a claim against the defendant that is *unrelated* to the property seized. For example, Allen, a resident of Ohio, has obtained a valid judgment in the amount of $20,000 against Bradley, a citizen of Kentucky. Allen can attach Bradley's automobile, which is located in Ohio, to satisfy his court judgment against Bradley.

See Figure 3-6, which outlines the concepts of subject matter and party jurisdiction.

Venue

Venue
particular geographical place where a court with jurisdiction may hear a case

Venue, which often is confused with jurisdiction, concerns the geographic area in which a lawsuit *should* be brought. The purpose of venue is to regulate the distribution of cases within a specific court system and to identify a convenient forum. In the federal court system, venue determines the district or districts in a given state in which suit may be brought. State rules of venue typically

Figure 3-6 Jurisdiction

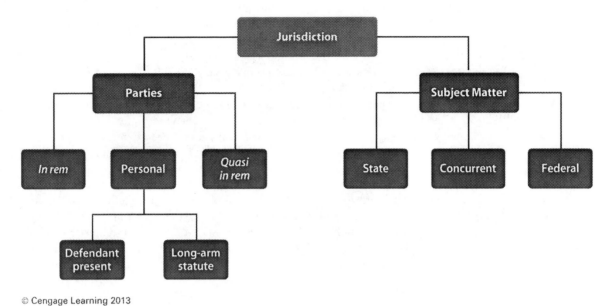

© Cengage Learning 2013

require that a suit be initiated in a county where one of the defendants lives. In matters involving real estate, most venue rules require that a suit be initiated in the county where the property is situated.

CIVIL DISPUTE RESOLUTION

As mentioned in Chapter 1, one of the primary functions of law is to provide for the peaceful resolution of disputes. Accordingly, our legal system has established an elaborate set of governmental mechanisms to settle disputes. The most prominent of these is judicial dispute resolution, called *litigation*. Judicial resolution of civil disputes is governed by the rules of civil procedure, which we will discuss in the first part of this section. Judicial resolution of criminal cases is governed by the rules of criminal procedure, which are covered in Chapter 6. Dispute resolution by administrative agencies, which is also common, is discussed in Chapter 5.

As an alternative to governmental dispute resolution, several nongovernmental methods of dispute resolution, such as arbitration, have developed. We will discuss these in the second part of this section.

CIVIL PROCEDURE

A civil dispute that enters the judicial system must follow the rules of civil procedure. These rules are designed to resolve the dispute justly, promptly, and inexpensively.

To acquaint you with civil procedure, we will carry a hypothetical action through the trial court to the highest court of review in the state. Although there are technical differences in trial and appellate procedure among the states and the federal courts, the following illustration will give you a general understanding of the trial and appeal of cases. Assume that Pam Pederson, a pedestrian, is struck while crossing a street in Chicago by an automobile driven by David Dryden. Pederson suffers serious personal injuries, incurs heavy medical and hospital expenses, and is unable to work for several months. She desires that Dryden pay her for the loss and damages she sustained. After attempts at settlement fail, Pederson brings an action at law against Dryden. Thus, Pederson is the plaintiff and Dryden the defendant. Each is represented by a lawyer. Let us follow the progress of the case.

The Pleadings

The **pleadings** are a series of responsive, formal, written statements in which each side to a lawsuit states its claims and defenses. The purpose of pleadings is to give notice and to establish the

PRACTICAL ADVICE

If you become involved in litigation, make full disclosure to your attorney and do not discuss the lawsuit without consulting your attorney.

Pleadings

series of responsive, formal, written statements by each side to a lawsuit issues of fact and law the parties dispute. An "issue of fact" is a dispute between the parties regarding the events that gave rise to the lawsuit. In contrast, an "issue of law" is a dispute between the parties as to what legal rules apply to these facts. Issues of fact are decided by the jury, or by the judge when there is no jury, whereas issues of law are decided by the judge.

Complaint
initial pleading by the plaintiff stating his case

Summons
notice given to inform a person of a lawsuit against her

Complaint and Summons A lawsuit begins when Pederson, the plaintiff, files with the clerk of the trial court a **complaint** against Dryden that contains (1) a statement of the claim and supporting facts showing that she is entitled to relief and (2) a demand for that relief. Pederson's complaint alleges that while exercising due and reasonable care for her own safety, she was struck by Dryden's automobile, which was being driven negligently by Dryden, causing her personal injuries and damages of $50,000, for which Pederson requests judgment.

Once the plaintiff has filed a complaint, the clerk issues a **summons** to be served upon the defendant to notify him that a suit has been brought against him. If the defendant has contacts with the state sufficient to show that the state's assertion of jurisdiction over the defendant is constitutional, proper service of the summons establishes the court's jurisdiction over the person of the defendant. The county sheriff or a deputy sheriff serves a summons and a copy of the complaint on Dryden, the defendant, commanding him to file his appearance and answer with the clerk of the court within a specific time, usually thirty days from the date the summons was served.

Default judgment
judgment against a defendant who fails to respond to a complaint

Demurrer
motion to dismiss for failure to state a claim

Responses to Complaint At this point, Dryden has several options. If he fails to respond at all, a **default judgment** will be entered against him. He may make *pretrial motions* contesting the court's jurisdiction over him or asserting that the action is barred by the statute of limitations, which requires suits to be brought within a specified time. Dryden also may move, or request, that the complaint be made more definite and certain, or he may instead move that the complaint be dismissed for failure to state a claim on which relief may be granted. Such a motion is sometimes called a **demurrer**; it essentially asserts that even if all of Pederson's allegations were true, she still would not be entitled to the relief she seeks and that therefore there is no need for a trial of the facts. The court rules on this motion as a matter of law. If it rules in favor of the defendant, the plaintiff may appeal the ruling.

Answer
defendant's pleading in response to the plaintiff's complaint

Reply
plaintiff's pleading in response to the defendant's answer

If he does not make any pretrial motions, or if they are denied, Dryden will respond to the complaint by filing an **answer**, which may contain denials, admissions, affirmative defenses, and counterclaims. Dryden might answer the complaint by denying its allegations of negligence and stating that he was driving his car at a low speed and with reasonable care (a *denial*) when his car struck Pederson (an *admission*), who had dashed across the street in front of his car without looking in any direction to see whether cars or other vehicles were approaching; that, accordingly, Pederson's injuries were caused by her own negligence (an *affirmative defense*); and that, therefore, she should not be permitted to recover any damages. Dryden might further state that Pederson caused damage to his car and request a judgment for $2,000 (a *counterclaim*). These pleadings create an issue of fact regarding whether Dryden or Pederson, or both, failed to exercise due and reasonable care under the circumstances and were thus negligent and liable for their carelessness.

Pretrial procedure
process requiring the parties to disclose what evidence is available to prove the disputed facts; designed to encourage settlement of cases or to make the trial more efficient

If the defendant counterclaims, the plaintiff must respond through a **reply**, which also may contain admissions, denials, and affirmative defenses.

Pretrial Procedure

Judgment on the Pleadings After the pleadings, either party may move for **judgment on the pleadings**, which requests the judge to rule as a matter of law whether the facts as alleged in the pleadings of the nonmoving party are sufficient to warrant granting the requested relief.

Judgment on the pleadings
final binding determination on the merits made by the judge after the pleadings

Discovery
pretrial exchange of information between opposing parties to a lawsuit

Discovery In preparation for trial and even before completion of the pleadings stage, each party has the right to obtain relevant evidence, or information that may lead to evidence, from the other party. This procedure, known as **discovery**, includes (1) pretrial *depositions* consisting of sworn testimony, taken out of court, of the opposing party or other witnesses; (2) sworn answers by the opposing party to *written interrogatories*, or questions; (3) *production* of documents and physical objects in the possession of the opposing party or, by a court-ordered subpoena, in the possession of nonparties; (4) *court-ordered examination* by a physician of the opposing party, as needed; and (5) admissions of facts obtained by a *request for admissions* submitted to the opposing party. By using discovery properly, each party may become fully informed of relevant evidence and avoid surprise at trial. Another purpose of this procedure is to facilitate settlements by giving both parties as much relevant information as possible.

Pretrial Conference   Also furthering these objectives is the pretrial conference between the judge and the attorneys representing the parties. The basic purposes of the **pretrial conference** are (1) to simplify the issues in dispute by amending the pleadings, admitting or stipulating facts, and identifying witnesses and documents to be presented at trial; and (2) to encourage settlement of the dispute without trial. (More than 90 percent of all cases are settled before going to trial.) If no settlement occurs, the judge will enter a pretrial order containing all of the amendments, stipulations, admissions, and other matters agreed to during the pretrial conference. The order supersedes the pleadings and controls the remainder of the trial.

Summary Judgment   The evidence disclosed by discovery may be so clear that a trial to determine the facts becomes unnecessary. If this is so, either party may move for a summary judgment, which requests the judge to rule that, because there are no issues of fact to be determined by trial, the party thus moving should prevail as a matter of law. A **summary judgment** is a final binding determination on the merits made by the judge before a trial. The following case involving actress Shirley MacLaine explains the rules courts use to determine whether to grant summary judgment.

Margin notes:

Pretrial conference
a conference between the judge and the attorneys to simplify the issues in dispute and to attempt to settle the dispute without trial

Summary judgment
binding determinations on the merits made by the judge before trial

---

Parker v. Twentieth Century-Fox Film Corp.
Supreme Court of California, 1970
3 Cal.3d 176, 89 Cal.Rptr. 737, 474 P.2d 689
http://scholar.google.com/scholar_case?case=8204943341098207403&q=474+P.2d+689&hl=en&as_sdt=2,34

FACTS Shirley MacLaine Parker, a well-known actress, contracted with Twentieth Century-Fox Film Corporation in August 1965 to play the female lead in Fox's upcoming production of *Bloomer Girl*, a motion picture musical that was to be filmed in California. Fox agreed to pay Parker $750,000 for fourteen weeks of her services. Fox decided to cancel its plans for *Bloomer Girl* before production had begun and, instead, offered Parker the female lead in another film, *Big Country, Big Man*, a dramatic western to be filmed in Australia. The compensation offered was identical, but Parker's right to approve the director and screenplay would have been eliminated or altered by the *Big Country* proposal. She refused to accept and brought suit to recover the $750,000 for Fox's breach of the *Bloomer Girl* contract. Fox's sole defense in its answer was that it owed no money to Parker because she had deliberately failed to mitigate or reduce her damages by unreasonably refusing to accept the *Big Country* lead. Parker filed a motion for summary judgment. Fox, in opposition to the motion, claimed, in effect, only that the *Big Country* offer was not employment different from or inferior to that under the *Bloomer Girl* contract. The trial court granted Parker a summary judgment and Fox appealed.

DECISION Summary judgment affirmed.

OPINION The matter to be determined by a trial court on a motion for summary judgment is whether facts have been

presented which give rise to a triable factual issue. The trial court may not pass upon the issue itself. Summary judgment is proper only if the affidavits or declarations in support of Parker, the moving party, would be sufficient to sustain a judgment in her favor and her opponent does not by affidavit show facts sufficient to present a triable issue of fact. The affidavits of the moving party are strictly construed, and doubts as to the propriety of summary judgment should be resolved against granting the motion. Such summary procedure is drastic and should be used with caution so that it does not become a substitute for the open trial method of determining facts.

Here, it is clear that the trial court correctly ruled that Parker's failure to accept Fox's tendered substitute employment could not be applied in mitigation of damages because the offer of the *Big Country* lead was of employment both different and inferior, and that no factual dispute was presented on that issue. Therefore, summary judgment in favor of Parker is granted for $750,000.

INTERPRETATION A court will grant summary judgment when there are no issues of fact to be determined by trial.

CRITICAL THINKING QUESTION When should a court grant summary judgment? Explain.

Trial

Trial
determines the facts and the outcome of the case

In all federal civil cases at common law involving more than $20, the U.S. Constitution guarantees the right to a jury trial. In addition, nearly every state constitution provides a similar right. In addition, federal and state statutes may authorize jury trials in cases not within the constitutional guarantees. Under federal law and in almost all states, jury trials are *not* available in equity cases. Even in cases in which a jury trial is available, the parties may waive (choose not to have) a trial by jury. When a trial is conducted without a jury, the judge serves as the fact finder and will make separate findings of fact and conclusions of law. When a trial is conducted *with* a jury, the judge determines issues of law and the jury determines questions of fact.

Voir dire
preliminary examination of potential jurors

Jury Selection   Assuming a timely demand for a jury has been made, the trial begins with the selection of a jury. The jury selection process involves a **voir dire**, an examination by the parties' attorneys (or in some courts by the judge) of the potential jurors. Each party has an unlimited number of *challenges for cause*, which allow the party to prevent a prospective juror from serving if the juror is biased or cannot be fair and impartial. In addition, each party has a limited number of *peremptory challenges* for which no cause is required to disqualify a prospective juror. The Supreme Court has held that the U.S. Constitution prohibits discrimination in jury selection on the basis of race or gender.

Edmonson v. Leesville Concrete Company, Inc.
Supreme Court of the United States, 1991
500 U.S. 614, 111 S.Ct. 2077, 114 L.Ed.2d 660
http://laws.findlaw.com/us/500/614.html

FACTS Thaddeus Donald Edmonson, a construction worker, was injured in a job-site accident at Fort Polk, Louisiana. Edmonson sued Leesville Concrete Company for negligence in the U.S. District Court for the Western District of Louisiana, claiming that a Leesville employee permitted one of the company's trucks to roll backward and pin him against some construction equipment. Edmonson invoked his Seventh Amendment right to a trial by jury. During *voir dire*, Leesville used two of its three peremptory challenges authorized by statute to remove black persons from the prospective jury. When Edmonson, who is himself black, requested that the District Court require Leesville to articulate a race-neutral explanation for striking the two jurors, the District Court ruled that the precedent on which Edmonson's request relied applied only to criminal cases and allowed the strikes to stand. A jury of eleven whites and one black brought in a verdict for Edmonson, assessing total damages at $90,000. It also attributed 80 percent of the fault to Edmonson's contributory negligence and awarded him only $18,000. On appeal, a divided *en banc* panel affirmed the judgment of the District Court, concluding that the use of peremptory challenges by private litigants did not constitute state action and, as a result, did not violate constitutional guarantees against racial discrimination. The U.S. Supreme Court granted *certiorari*.

DECISION Judgment for Edmonson.

OPINION Although the conduct of private parties lies beyond the Constitution's scope in most instances, governmental authority may dominate an activity to such an extent that its participants must be deemed to act with the authority of the government and, as a result, be subject to Constitutional constraints. In determining whether a particular course of action is governmental in character, it is relevant to examine (1) the extent to which the actor relies on governmental assistance and benefits, (2) whether the actor is performing a traditional governmental function, and (3) whether the

injury caused is aggravated in a unique way by the incidents of governmental authority. The Court held that, based on these three principles, the exercise of peremptory challenges by the defendant in the district court was pursuant to a course of state action and therefore subject to Constitutional protection against discrimination on the basis of race.

Without significant participation of the government, the whole jury trial system, of which the peremptory challenge is a part, could not exist. In fact, peremptory challenges have no utility outside the jury system. Further, government statutes prescribe the qualifications for jury service, the procedures for jury selection, and lawful excuse from jury service. Trials are held in governmental buildings and presided over by judges who are state actors charged to use the utmost care to see that justice is done. And in all jurisdictions, a verdict will be incorporated in a judgment, which is enforceable by the state. When private litigants participate in the judicial process—including the selection of jurors—they serve an important function within the government and act with its substantial assistance. Finally, the injury caused by discrimination in peremptory challenges is made more severe because it has occurred within the courthouse, where the law itself unfolds in an ongoing expression of Constitutional authority. To permit racial exclusion in this official forum offends the integrity of the court and compounds the racial insult inherent in judging a citizen by the color of his or her skin.

INTERPRETATION The U.S. Constitution imposes restrictions against racial discrimination in the jury selection process.

ETHICAL QUESTION What are ethical grounds for an attorney to exercise a peremptory challenge? Explain.

CRITICAL THINKING QUESTION What grounds should be disallowed in the exercise of peremptory challenges? Explain.

Conduct of Trial   After the jury has been selected, both attorneys make an **opening statement** about the facts that they expect to prove in the trial. The plaintiff and plaintiff's witnesses then testify on **direct examination** by the plaintiff's attorney. Each is subject to **cross-examination** by

Conduct of trial
consists of opening statements by attorneys, direct and cross-examination of witnesses, and closing arguments

Directed verdict
final binding determination on the merits made by the judge after a trial has begun but before the jury renders a verdict

the defendant's attorney. Pederson and her witnesses testify that the traffic light at the street intersection where she was struck was green for traffic in the direction in which she was crossing but changed to yellow when she was about one-third of the way across the street.

During the trial, the judge rules on the admission and exclusion of evidence on the basis of its relevance and reliability. If the judge does not allow certain evidence to be introduced or certain testimony to be given, the attorney must make an *offer of proof* to preserve for review on appeal the question of its admissibility. The offer of proof consists of oral statements of counsel or witnesses showing for the record the evidence that the judge has ruled inadmissible; it is not regarded as evidence and is not heard by the jury.

After cross-examination, followed by redirect examination of each of her witnesses, Pederson rests her case. At this time, Dryden may move for a directed verdict in his favor. A **directed verdict** is a final binding determination on the merits made by the judge after a trial has begun but before the jury renders a verdict. If the judge concludes that the evidence introduced by Pederson, which is assumed for the purposes of the motion to be true, would not be sufficient for the jury to find in favor of the plaintiff, then the judge will grant the directed verdict in favor of the defendant. In some states, the judge will deny the motion for a directed verdict if there is *any* evidence on which the jury might possibly render a verdict for the plaintiff.

If the judge denies the motion for a directed verdict, however, the defendant then has the opportunity to present evidence. Dryden and his witnesses testify that he was driving his car at a low speed when it struck Pederson and that Dryden at the time had the green light at the intersection. After the defendant has presented his evidence, the plaintiff and the defendant may be permitted to introduce rebuttal evidence. Once both parties have rested (concluded), then either party may move for a directed verdict. By this motion, the party contends that the evidence is so clear that reasonable persons could not differ about the outcome of the case. If the judge grants the motion for a directed verdict, he takes the case away from the jury and enters a judgment for the party making the motion.

If these motions are denied, then Pederson's attorney makes a *closing argument* to the jury, reviewing the evidence and urging a verdict in favor of Pederson. Then Dryden's attorney makes a closing argument, summarizing the evidence and urging a verdict in favor of Dryden. Pederson's attorney is permitted to make a short argument in rebuttal.

Jury instructions
judge gives the jury the particular rules of law that apply to the case

Jury Instructions   The attorneys have previously given possible written jury instructions on the applicable law to the trial judge, who gives to the jury those instructions that he approves and denies those that he considers incorrect. The judge also may give the jury instructions of his own. **Jury instructions** (called "charges" in some states) advise the jury of the particular rules of law that apply to the facts the jury determines from the evidence.

Verdict
formal decision by the jury on questions submitted to it

Verdict   The jury then retires to the jury room to deliberate and to reach its **verdict** in favor of one party or the other. If the jury finds the issues in favor of Dryden, its verdict is that he is not liable. If, however, it finds the issues for Pederson and against Dryden, its verdict will be that the defendant is liable and will specify the amount of the plaintiff's damages. In this case, the jury found that Pederson's damages were $35,000. On returning to the jury box, the foreperson either announces the verdict or hands it in written form to the clerk to give to the judge, who reads the verdict in open court. In some jurisdictions, a *special verdict*, by which the jury makes specific written findings on each factual issue, is used. The judge then applies the law to these findings and renders a judgment. In the United States the prevailing litigant is ordinarily *not* entitled to collect attorneys' fees from the losing party, unless otherwise provided by statute or an enforceable contract allocating attorneys' fees.

Motions challenging verdict
include motions for a new trial and a motion for judgment notwithstanding the verdict

Motions Challenging Verdict   The unsuccessful party may then file a written motion for a new trial or for judgment notwithstanding the verdict. A *motion for a new trial* may be granted if (1) the judge committed prejudicial error during the trial, (2) the verdict is against the weight of the evidence, (3) the damages are excessive, or (4) the trial was not fair. The judge has the discretion to grant a motion for a new trial (on grounds 1, 3, or 4) even if the verdict is supported by substantial evidence. On the other hand, the motion for judgment notwithstanding the verdict (also called a judgment n.o.v.) must be denied if any substantial evidence supports the verdict. This motion is similar to a motion for a directed verdict, only it is made *after* the jury's

Judgment notwithstanding the verdict

a final binding determination on the merits made by the judge after and contrary to the jury's verdict

Appeal

determines whether the trial court committed prejudicial error

verdict. To grant the motion for **judgment notwithstanding the verdict**, the judge must decide that the evidence is so clear that reasonable people could not differ as to the outcome of the case. If a judgment n.o.v. is reversed on appeal, a new trial is *not* necessary, and the jury's verdict is entered. If the judge denies the motions for a new trial and for a judgment notwithstanding the verdict, he enters *judgment on the verdict* for $35,000 in favor of the plaintiff.

Appeal

The purpose of an **appeal** is to determine whether the trial court committed prejudicial error. Most jurisdictions permit an appeal only from a final judgment. As a general rule, only errors of law are reviewed by an appellate court. Errors of law include the judge's decisions to admit or exclude evidence; the judge's instructions to the jury; and the judge's actions in denying or granting a motion for a demurrer, a summary judgment, a directed verdict, or a judgment n.o.v. Appellate courts review errors of law *de novo*. Errors of fact will be reversed only if they are so clearly erroneous that they are considered to be an error of law.

Let us assume that Dryden directs his attorney to appeal. The attorney files a notice of appeal with the clerk of the trial court within the prescribed time. Later, Dryden, as appellant, files in the reviewing court the record on appeal, which contains the pleadings, a transcript of the testimony, rulings by the judge on motions made by the parties, arguments of counsel, jury instructions, the verdict, posttrial motions, and the judgment from which the appeal is taken. In states having an intermediate court of appeals, such court usually will be the reviewing court. In states having no intermediate court of appeal, a party may appeal directly from the trial court to the state supreme court.

Dryden, as appellant, is required to prepare a condensation of the record, known as an abstract, or pertinent excerpts from the record, which he files with the reviewing court together with a brief and argument. His *brief* contains a statement of the facts, the issues, the rulings by the trial court that Dryden contends are erroneous and prejudicial, grounds for reversal of the judgment, a statement of the applicable law, and arguments on his behalf. Pederson, the appellee, files an answering brief and argument. Dryden may, but is not required to, file a reply brief. The case is now ready to be considered by the reviewing court.

The appellate court does not hear any evidence; rather, it decides the case on the record, abstracts, and briefs. After **oral argument** by the attorneys, if the court elects to hear one, the court takes the case under advisement, or begins deliberations. Then, having made a decision based on majority rule, the appellate court prepares a written opinion containing the reasons for its decision, the rules of law that apply, and its judgment. The judgment may affirm the judgment of the trial court, or, if the appellate court finds that reversible error was committed, the judgment may be reversed or modified or returned to the lower court (remanded) for a new trial. In some instances the appellate court will affirm the lower court's decision in part and will reverse it in part. The losing party may file a petition for rehearing, which is usually denied.

If the reviewing court is an intermediate appellate court, the party losing in that court may decide to seek a reversal of its judgment by filing within a prescribed time a notice of appeal, if the appeal is by right, or a petition for leave to appeal to the state supreme court, if the appeal is by discretion. This petition corresponds to a petition for a writ of *certiorari* in the U.S. Supreme Court. The party winning in the appellate court may file an answer to the petition for leave to appeal. If the petition is granted, or if the appeal is by right, the record is certified to the Supreme Court, where each party files a new brief and argument. The Supreme Court may hear oral argument or simply review the record; it then takes the case under advisement. If the Supreme Court concludes that the judgment of the appellate court is correct, it affirms. If it decides otherwise, it reverses the judgment of the appellate court and enters a reversal or an order of remand. The unsuccessful party may again file a petition for a rehearing, which is likely to be denied. Barring the remote possibility of an application for still further review by the U.S. Supreme Court, the case either has reached its termination or, on remand, is about to start its second journey through the courts, beginning, as it did originally, in the trial court.

Enforcement

plaintiff with an unpaid judgment may resort to a writ of execution to have the sheriff seize property of the defendant and to garnishment to collect money owed to the defendant by a third party

Enforcement

If Dryden does not appeal, or if the reviewing court affirms the judgment if he does appeal, and Dryden does not pay the judgment, the task of enforcement will remain. Pederson must request the clerk to issue a *writ of execution* demanding payment of the judgment, which is served by the sheriff on the defendant. If the writ is returned "unsatisfied," that is, if Dryden still does not

Figure 3-7 Stages in Civil Procedure

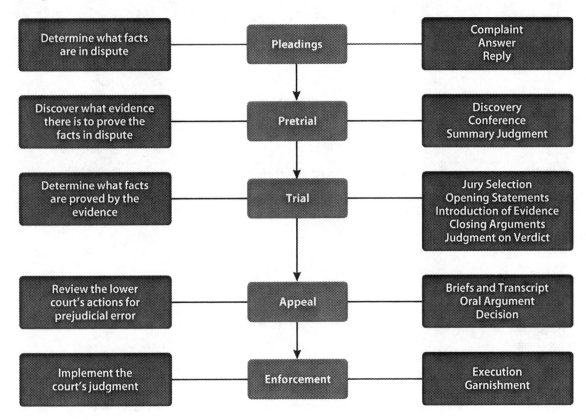

© Cengage Learning 2013

pay, Pederson may post bond or other security and order a levy on and sale of specific non-exempt property belonging to the defendant, which is then seized by the sheriff, advertised for sale, and sold at a public sale under the writ of execution. If the sale does not produce enough money to pay the judgment, Pederson's attorney may begin another proceeding in an attempt to locate money or other property belonging to Dryden. In an attempt to collect the judgment, Pederson's attorney may also proceed by *garnishment* against Dryden's employer to collect from his wages or against a bank in which he has an account.

If Pederson cannot satisfy the judgment with Dryden's property located within Illinois (the state where the judgment was obtained), Pederson will have to bring an action on the original judgment in other states where Dryden owns property. Because the U.S. Constitution requires each state to accord judgments of other states **full faith and credit**, Pederson will be able to obtain a local judgment that may be enforced by the methods described above.

The various stages in civil procedure are illustrated in Figure 3-7.

ALTERNATIVE DISPUTE RESOLUTION

Litigation is complex, time consuming, and expensive. Furthermore, court adjudications involve long delays, lack special expertise in substantive areas, and provide only a limited range of remedies. Additionally, litigation is structured so that one party takes all with little opportunity for compromise and often causes animosity between the disputants. Consequently, in an attempt to overcome some of the disadvantages of litigation, several nonjudicial methods of dealing with disputes have developed. The most important of these alternatives to litigation is arbitration. Others include conciliation, mediation, and "mini-trials."

The various techniques differ in a number of ways, including (1) whether the process is voluntary, (2) whether the process is binding, (3) whether the disputants represent themselves or are represented by attorneys, (4) whether the decision is made by the disputants or by a third party, (5) whether the procedure used is formal or informal, and (6) whether the basis for the decision is law or some other criterion.

CONCEPT REVIEW 3-2

Comparison of Court Adjudication, Arbitration, and Mediation/Conciliation

	Court Adjudication	Arbitration	Mediation/Conciliation
Advantages	Binding	Binding	Preserves relations
	Public norms	Parties control process	Parties control process
	Precedents	Privacy	Privacy
	Uniformity	Special expertise	Flexible
	Publicly funded	Speedy resolution	
	Compels participation		
Disadvantages	Expensive	No public norms	Not binding
	Time consuming	No precedent	Lacks finality
	Long delays	No uniformity	No compelled participation
	Limited remedies		No precedent
	Lacks special expertise		No uniformity
	No compromise		
	Disrupts relationships		
	Publicity		

Source: Adapted from Table 4 of *Report of the Ad Hoc Panel on Dispute Resolution and Public Policy*, prepared by the National Institute for Dispute Resolution.

Which method of civil dispute resolution—litigation or one of the nongovernmental methods—is better for a particular dispute depends on several factors, including the financial circumstances of the disputants, the nature of the relationship (commercial or personal, ongoing or limited) between them, and the urgency of a quick resolution. Alternative dispute resolution methods are especially suitable when privacy, speed, preservation of continuing relations, and control over the process—including the flexibility to compromise—are important to the parties. Nevertheless, the disadvantages of using alternative dispute mechanisms may make court adjudication more appropriate. For example, with the exception of arbitration, only courts can compel participation and provide a binding resolution. In addition, only courts can establish precedents and create public duties. Furthermore, the courts provide greater due process protections and uniformity of outcome. Finally, the courts are independent of the parties and are publicly funded.

See Concept Review 3-2 for a comparison of adjudication, arbitration, and mediation/conciliation.

PRACTICAL ADVICE
Consider including in your contracts a provision specifying what means of dispute resolution will apply to the contract.

Arbitration

Arbitration
nonjudicial proceeding where a neutral third party selected by disputants renders a binding decision

In **arbitration**, the parties select a *neutral* third person or persons—the arbitrator(s)—who render(s) a binding decision after hearing arguments and reviewing evidence. Because the presentation of the case is less formal and the rules of evidence are more relaxed, arbitration usually takes less time and costs less than litigation. Moreover, in many arbitration cases, the parties are able to select an arbitrator with special expertise concerning the subject of the dispute. Thus, the quality of the arbitrator's decision may be higher than that available through the court system. In addition, arbitration normally is conducted in private, thus avoiding unwanted publicity. Arbitration is commonly used in commercial and labor management disputes.

Consensual arbitration
arbitration voluntarily entered into by the parties

Types of Arbitration There are two basic types of arbitration—consensual, which is by far the most common, and compulsory. **Consensual arbitration** occurs whenever the parties to a dispute agree to submit the controversy to arbitration. They may do this in advance by agreeing in their contract that disputes arising out of their contract will be resolved by arbitration. Or they may do so after a dispute arises by then agreeing to submit the dispute to arbitration. In either instance, such agreements are enforceable under the Federal Arbitration Act (FAA) and statutes in more than forty states. The great majority of these states have adopted the Uniform Arbitration Act (UAA); the others have adopted substantially similar legislation. (In 2000, the National

Conference of Commissioners on Uniform State Laws promulgated the Revised UAA to provide state legislatures with a more up-to-date statute to resolve disputes through arbitration. To date, at least fourteen states have adopted the Revised UAA.) In **compulsory arbitration**, which is relatively infrequent, a federal or state statute requires arbitration for specific types of disputes, such as those involving public employees, including police officers, teachers, and firefighters.

Compulsory arbitration
arbitration required by statute for specific types of disputes

Procedure Usually the parties' agreement to arbitrate specifies how the arbitrator or arbitrators will be chosen. If it does not, the FAA and state statutes provide methods for selecting arbitrators. Although the requirements for arbitration hearings vary from state to state, they generally consist of opening statements, case presentation, and closing statements. Case presentations may include witnesses, documentation, and site inspections. The parties may cross-examine witnesses and may be represented by attorneys.

The decision of the arbitrator, called an **award**, is binding on the parties. Nevertheless, it is subject to *very* limited judicial review. Under the FAA and the Revised UAA these include (1) the award was procured by corruption, fraud, or other undue means; (2) the arbitrators were partial or corrupt; (3) the arbitrators were guilty of misconduct prejudicing the rights of a party to the arbitration proceeding; and (4) the arbitrators exceeded their powers. Historically, the courts were unfriendly to arbitration; however, they have dramatically changed their attitude and now favor arbitration.

Award
the decision of an arbitrator

International Arbitration Arbitration is a commonly used means for resolving international disputes. The United Nations Committee on International Trade Law (UNCITRAL) and the International Chamber of Commerce have promulgated arbitration rules that have won broad international adherence. The FAA has provisions implementing the United Nations Convention on the Recognition and Enforcement of Foreign Arbitral Awards. A number of states have enacted laws specifically governing international arbitration; some of the statutes have been based on the Model Law on International Arbitration drafted by UNCITRAL.

Court-Annexed Arbitration A growing number of federal and state courts have adopted court-annexed arbitration in civil cases in which the parties seek limited amounts of damages. The arbitrators are usually attorneys. Appeal from this type of *nonbinding* arbitration is by trial *de novo*. Many states have enacted statutes requiring the arbitration of medical malpractice disputes.

Rent-A-Center, West, Inc. v. Jackson
Supreme Court of the United States, 2010
561 U.S. ___, 130 S.Ct. 2772, 177 L.Ed.2d 403
http://scholar.google.com/scholar_case?case=10589677176860191748&q=Rent-A-Center&hl=en&as_sdt=2,34

FACTS On February 1, 2007, the plaintiff, Antonio Jackson, filed an employment-discrimination suit against his former employer in the United States District Court for the District of Nevada. The defendant, Rent-A-Center, West, Inc., filed a motion under the Federal Arbitration Act (FAA) to dismiss the proceedings, and to compel arbitration based on an arbitration agreement (Agreement), which Jackson signed on February 24, 2003 as a condition of his employment. The Agreement provided for arbitration of all "past, present or future" disputes arising out of Jackson's employment with Rent-A-Center. It also provided that "[t]he Arbitrator, and not any federal, state, or local court or agency, shall have exclusive authority to resolve any dispute relating to the interpretation, applicability, enforceability or formation of this Agreement including, but not limited to any claim that all or any part of this Agreement is void or voidable."

Jackson opposed the motion on the ground that "the arbitration agreement in question is clearly unenforceable in that it is unconscionable" under Nevada law. Rent-A-Center responded that Jackson's unconscionability claim was not properly before the court because Jackson had expressly agreed that the arbitrator would have exclusive authority to resolve any dispute about the enforceability of the Agreement. It also disputed the merits of Jackson's unconscionability claims.

The District Court granted Rent-A-Center's motion to dismiss the proceedings and to compel arbitration. The court found that the Agreement gives the arbitrator exclusive authority to decide whether the Agreement is enforceable, and, because Jackson challenged the validity of the Agreement as a whole, the issue was for the arbitrator. The Court of Appeals for the Ninth Circuit reversed in relevant part, holding that where "a party challenges an arbitration agreement as unconscionable, and thus asserts that he could not meaningfully assent to the agreement, the threshold question of unconscionability is for the court." The U.S. Supreme Court granted *certiorari*.

DECISION The judgment of the Court of Appeals for the Ninth Circuit is reversed.

OPINION The FAA reflects the fundamental principle that arbitration is a matter of contract. Section 2, provides:

A written provision in ... a contract evidencing a transaction involving commerce to settle by arbitration a controversy thereafter arising out of such contract ... shall be valid, irrevocable, and enforceable, save upon such grounds as exist at law or in equity for the revocation of any contract.

Thus the FAA places arbitration agreements on an equal footing with other contracts and requires courts to enforce them according to their terms. Like other contracts, however, they may be invalidated by generally applicable contract defenses, such as fraud, duress, or unconscionability.

The Agreement here contains two relevant arbitration provisions. The first provides for arbitration of all "past, present or future" disputes arising out of Jackson's employment with Rent-A-Center. The second (the "delegation provision") states that "[t]he Arbitrator ... shall have exclusive authority to resolve any dispute relating to the ... enforceability ... of this Agreement including, but not limited to any claim that all or any part of this Agreement is void or voidable." The dispute between the parties is whether the Agreement is unconscionable. It is the second provision, which delegates resolution of that dispute to the arbitrator, that Rent-A-Center seeks to enforce.

The delegation provision is an agreement to arbitrate threshold issues concerning the arbitration agreement. Reflecting the principle that arbitration is a matter of contract, the Supreme Court has recognized that parties can agree to arbitrate "gateway" questions of "arbitrability," such as whether the parties have agreed to arbitrate or whether their agreement covers a particular controversy. An agreement to arbitrate a gateway issue is simply an additional, antecedent agreement the party seeking arbitration asks the federal court to enforce, and the FAA operates on this additional arbitration agreement just as it does on any other. The question is whether the delegation provision is valid under Section 2.

There are two types of validity challenges under Section 2: "One type challenges specifically the validity of the agreement to arbitrate," and "[t]he other challenges the contract as a whole, either on a ground that directly affects the entire agreement (e.g., the agreement was fraudulently induced), or on the ground that the illegality of one of the contract's provisions renders the whole contract invalid." Only the first type of challenge is relevant to a court's determination whether the arbitration agreement at issue is enforceable. That is because Section 2 states that a "written provision" "to settle by arbitration a controversy" is "valid, irrevocable, and enforceable" without mention of the validity of the contract in which it is contained. Thus, a party's challenge to another provision of the contract, or to the contract as a whole, does not prevent a court from enforcing a specific agreement to arbitrate. "[A]s a matter of substantive federal arbitration law, an arbitration provision is severable from the remainder of the contract."

But that agreements to arbitrate are severable does not mean that they are unassailable. If a party challenges the validity under Section 2 of the precise agreement to arbitrate at issue, the federal court must consider the challenge before ordering compliance with that agreement. In some cases the claimed basis of invalidity for the contract as a whole will be much easier to establish than the same basis as applied only to the severable agreement to arbitrate. Thus, in an employment contract many elements of alleged unconscionability applicable to the entire contract (outrageously low wages, for example) would not affect the agreement to arbitrate alone. But even where that is not the case, for example, where the alleged fraud that induced the whole contract equally induced the agreement to arbitrate which was part of that contract, the basis of challenge nonetheless must be directed specifically to the agreement to arbitrate before a court will intervene.

Here, Rent-A-Center asks for enforcement of the delegation provision that gave the arbitrator "exclusive authority to resolve any dispute relating to the ... enforceability ... of this Agreement." The "remainder of the contract," is the rest of the agreement to arbitrate claims arising out of Jackson's employment with Rent-A-Center. In this case, the underlying contract is itself an arbitration agreement. But that makes no difference. Application of the severability rule does not depend on the substance of the remainder of the contract. Section 2 operates on the specific "written provision" to "settle by arbitration a controversy" that the party seeks to enforce. Accordingly, unless Jackson challenged the delegation provision specifically, it must be treated as valid under Section 2, leaving any challenge to the validity of the Agreement as a whole for the arbitrator.

The District Court correctly concluded that Jackson challenged only the validity of the contract as a whole. Nowhere in his opposition to Rent-A-Center's motion to compel arbitration did he even mention the delegation provision.

As required to make out a claim of unconscionability under Nevada law, Jackson contended that the Agreement was both procedurally and substantively unconscionable. It was procedurally unconscionable, he argued, because it "was imposed as a condition of employment and was non-negotiable." But because Jackson's substantive unconscionability challenges were *not* specific to the delegation provision, they are not to be considered. First, he argued that the Agreement's coverage was one sided in that it required arbitration of claims an employee was likely to bring—contract, tort, discrimination, and statutory claims—but did not require arbitration of claims Rent-A-Center was likely to bring—intellectual property, unfair competition, and trade secrets claims. This one-sided-coverage argument clearly did not go to the validity of the delegation provision.

Jackson's other two substantive unconscionability arguments assailed arbitration procedures that were to be used under *both* the agreement to arbitrate employment-related disputes *and* the delegation provision. It may be that had Jackson challenged the delegation provision by arguing that these common procedures as applied to the delegation provision rendered that provision unconscionable, the challenge should have been considered by the court. Jackson, however, did not make any arguments specific to the delegation provision; he argued that the procedures rendered the entire Agreement invalid.

Jackson's appeal to the Ninth Circuit confirms that he did not contest the validity of the delegation provision in particular. In his brief to the Supreme Court, Jackson made the contention for the first time that the delegation provision itself is substantively unconscionable. He brought this challenge to the delegation provision too late, and it will not be considered.

INTERPRETATION Under the FAA, where an arbitration agreement includes a delegation provision stating that the arbitrator will determine the enforceability of the arbitration agreement, (1) if a party challenges specifically the enforceability of the delegation provision, the district court considers the challenge, but (2) if a party challenges the enforceability of the arbitration agreement as a whole, the arbitrator considers the challenge.

CRITICAL THINKING QUESTION How likely is it that the parties in this case would have thought that they had agreed that an arbitrator would decide whether they had a valid arbitration agreement?

BUSINESS LAW *IN ACTION*

In any given year, a large company like Dobashi Motors has lots of litigation exposure. In its vehicle manufacturing division it employs thousands of workers, who bring numerous claims arising out of such matters as workplace injuries and alleged employment discrimination. Nationwide it has a network of hundreds of dealers, who may have contract disagreements with Dobashi, some of which inevitably escalate to the point they end up in court.

Naturally the company also regularly contends with payment disputes involving its many service providers and parts suppliers, sometimes initiating suit and other times finding itself on the other side as a defendant. And together with its financing division, Dobashi Motors deals with thousands of buyers and potential buyers, who sue not so infrequently, typically based on state deceptive practices statutes or federal laws governing access to credit. Every year, adverse judgments arise from at least some of each of these types of legal disputes. Judgments aside, even if Dobashi were to win every case, the company still would spend millions of dollars in attorneys' fees and other litigation expenses annually.

Legal disagreement is inherent in a business's contractual relationships. Recognizing this, Dobashi can choose to include predispute arbitration agreements in its employment contracts, written distribution and vendor arrangements, and financing deals. The regular use of such clauses would divert most of Dobashi's litigation out of the court system and into what has been acknowledged to be a much more inexpensive, faster, more private, and more flexible dispute resolution environment. Indeed, studies have shown that a company like Dobashi can save 50 percent or more in litigation expenses by choosing arbitration as its primary vehicle for resolving disputes.

Critics contend that arbitration results often are inconsistent with the law and that they can deprive the parties of certain remedies available only in court. Good drafting can eliminate the latter and, even if the former is true, it will operate rather evenhandedly: Dobashi may lose some cases it would have won in court, and vice versa. In the end, the cost savings are not inconsequential, both in the short term and over time.

Source: © Cengage Learning 2013

Conciliation

nonbinding process in which a third party acts as an intermediary between the disputing parties

Mediation

nonbinding process in which a third party acts as an intermediary between the disputing parties and proposes solutions for them to consider

Med-arb

binding process in which a third party serves first as a mediator and then as an arbitrator for those issues not resolved through mediation

Mini-trial

nonbinding process in which attorneys for the disputing parties present evidence to managers of the disputing parties and a neutral third party, and then the managers attempt to negotiate a settlement in consultation with the third party

Conciliation

Conciliation is a nonbinding, informal process in which a third party (the conciliator) selected by the disputing parties attempts to help them reach a mutually acceptable agreement. The duties of the conciliator include improving communications, explaining issues, scheduling meetings, discussing differences of opinion, and serving as an intermediary between the parties when they are unwilling to meet.

Mediation

Mediation is a process in which a third party (the mediator) selected by the disputants helps them to resolve their disagreement. In addition to employing conciliation techniques to improve communications, the mediator, unlike the conciliator, proposes possible solutions for the parties to consider. Like the conciliator, the mediator does not have the power to render a binding decision. Mediation has become commonly used by the judicial system in such tribunals as small claims courts, housing courts, family courts, and neighborhood justice centers. In 2001 the National Conference of Commissioners on Uniform State Laws promulgated the Uniform Mediation Act, which was amended in 2003. The Act establishes a privilege of confidentiality for mediators and participants. To date at least ten states have adopted it.

Sometimes the techniques of arbitration and mediation are combined in a procedure called "med-arb." In **med-arb**, the neutral third party serves first as a mediator and, if all issues are not resolved through such mediation, then serves as an arbitrator authorized to render a binding decision on the remaining issues.

Mini-Trial

A mini-trial is a structured settlement process that combines elements of negotiation, mediation, and trials. Mini-trials are most commonly used when both disputants are corporations. In a **mini-trial**, attorneys for the two corporations conduct limited discovery and then present evidence to a panel consisting of managers from each company, as well as to a neutral third party, who may be a retired judge or other attorney. After the lawyers complete their presentations, the managers try to negotiate a settlement without the attorneys. The managers may consult the third party on how a court might resolve the issues in dispute.

Summary jury trial
mock trial followed by
negotiations

Negotiation
consensual bargaining
process in which the parties
attempt to reach an
agreement resolving their
dispute without the
involvement of third parties

Summary Jury Trial

A **summary jury trial** is a mock trial in which the parties present their case to a jury. Though not binding, the jury's verdict does influence the negotiations in which the parties must participate following the mock trial. If the parties do not reach a settlement, they may have a full trial *de novo*.

Negotiation

Negotiation is a consensual bargaining process in which the parties attempt to reach an agreement resolving their dispute. Negotiation differs from other methods of alternate dispute resolution in that no third parties are involved.

CHAPTER SUMMARY

The Court System

Federal Courts

District Courts trial courts of general jurisdiction that can hear and decide most legal controversies in the federal system

Courts of Appeals hear appeals from the district courts and review orders of certain administrative agencies

The Supreme Court the nation's highest court, whose principal function is to review decisions of the federal Courts of Appeals and the highest state courts

Special Courts have jurisdiction over cases in a particular area of federal law and include the U.S. Court of Federal Claims, the U.S. Tax Court, the U.S. Bankruptcy Courts, and the U.S. Court of Appeals for the Federal Circuit

State Courts

Inferior Trial Courts hear minor criminal cases such as traffic offenses and civil cases involving small amounts of money and conduct preliminary hearings in more serious criminal cases

Trial Courts have general jurisdiction over civil and criminal cases

Special Trial Courts trial courts, such as probate courts and family courts, which have jurisdiction over a particular area of state law

Appellate Courts include one or two levels; the highest court's decisions are final except in those cases reviewed by the U.S. Supreme Court

Jurisdiction

Subject Matter Jurisdiction

Definition authority of a court to decide a particular kind of case
Federal Jurisdiction

- *Exclusive Federal Jurisdiction* federal courts have sole jurisdiction over federal crimes, bankruptcy, antitrust, patent, trademark, copyright, and other special cases
- *Concurrent Federal Jurisdiction* authority of more than one court to hear the same case; state and federal courts have concurrent jurisdiction over (1) federal question cases (cases arising under the Constitution, statutes, or treaties of the United States) which do not involve exclusive federal jurisdiction and (2) diversity of citizenship cases involving more than $75,000

Exclusive State Jurisdiction state courts have exclusive jurisdiction over all matters to which the federal judicial power does not reach

Jurisdiction over the Parties

Definition the power of a court to bind the parties to a suit
***In Personam* Jurisdiction** jurisdiction based on claims against a person, in contrast to jurisdiction over property
***In Rem* Jurisdiction** jurisdiction based on claims against property
Attachment Jurisdiction jurisdiction over a defendant's property to obtain payment of a claim not related to the property
Venue geographic area in which a lawsuit should be brought

Civil Dispute Resolution

Civil Procedure

The Pleadings series of statements that give notice and establish the issues of fact and law presented and disputed

- *Complaint* initial pleading by the plaintiff stating his case
- *Summons* notice given to inform a person of a lawsuit against her
- *Answer* defendant's pleading in response to the plaintiff's complaint
- *Reply* plaintiff's pleading in response to the defendant's answer

Pretrial Procedure process requiring the parties to disclose what evidence is available to prove the disputed facts; designed to encourage settlement of cases or to make the trial more efficient

- *Judgment on Pleadings* a final ruling in favor of one party by the judge based on the pleadings
- *Discovery* right of each party to obtain evidence from the other party
- *Pretrial Conference* a conference between the judge and the attorneys to simplify the issues in dispute and to attempt to settle the dispute without trial
- *Summary Judgment* final ruling by the judge in favor of one party based on the evidence disclosed by discovery

Trial determines the facts and the outcome of the case

- *Jury Selection* each party has an unlimited number of challenges for cause and a limited number of peremptory challenges
- *Conduct of Trial* consists of opening statements by attorneys, direct and cross-examination of witnesses, and closing arguments
- *Directed Verdict* final ruling by the judge in favor of one party based on the evidence introduced at trial
- *Jury Instructions* judge gives the jury the particular rules of law that apply to the case
- *Verdict* the jury's decision based on those facts the jury determines the evidence proves
- *Motions Challenging Verdict* include motions for a new trial and a motion for judgment notwithstanding the verdict

Appeal determines whether the trial court committed prejudicial error

Enforcement plaintiff with an unpaid judgment may resort to a writ of execution to have the sheriff seize property of the defendants and to garnishment to collect money owed to the defendant by a third party

Alternative Dispute Resolution

Arbitration nonjudicial proceeding in which a neutral third party selected by the disputants renders a binding decision (award)

Conciliation nonbinding process in which a third party acts as an intermediary between the disputing parties

Mediation nonbinding process in which a third party acts as an intermediary between the disputing parties and proposes solutions for them to consider

Mini-Trial nonbinding process in which attorneys for the disputing parties (typically corporations) present evidence to managers of the disputing parties and a neutral third party, after which the managers attempt to negotiate a settlement in consultation with the third party

Summary Jury Trial mock trial followed by negotiations

Negotiation consensual bargaining process in which the parties attempt to reach an agreement resolving their dispute without the involvement of third parties.

QUESTIONS

1. On June 15 a newspaper columnist predicted that the coast of State X would be flooded on the following September 1. Relying on this pronouncement, Gullible quit his job and sold his property at a loss so as not to be financially ruined. When the flooding did not occur, Gullible sued the columnist in a State X court for damages. The court dismissed the case for failure to state a cause of action under applicable state law. On appeal, the State X Supreme Court upheld the lower court. Three months after this ruling, the State Y Supreme Court heard an appeal in which a lower court had ruled that a reader could sue a columnist for falsely predicting flooding.

a. Must the State Y Supreme Court follow the ruling of the State X Supreme Court as a matter of *stare decisis*?

b. Should the State Y lower court have followed the ruling of the State X Supreme Court until the State Y Supreme Court issued a ruling on the issue?

c. Once the State X Supreme Court issued its ruling, could the U.S. Supreme Court overrule the State X Supreme Court?

d. If the State Y Supreme Court and the State X Supreme Court rule in exactly opposite ways, must the U.S. Supreme Court resolve the conflict between the two courts?

2. State Senator Bowdler convinced the legislature of State Z to pass a law requiring all professors to submit their class notes and transparencies to a board of censors to be sure that no "lewd" materials were presented to students at state universities. Professor Rabelais would like to challenge this law as being violative of his First Amendment rights under the U.S. Constitution.

a. May Professor Rabelais challenge this law in State Z courts?

b. May Professor Rabelais challenge this law in a federal district court?

3. While driving his car in Virginia, Carpe Diem, a resident of North Carolina, struck Butt, a resident of Alaska. As a result of the accident, Butt suffered more than $80,000 in medical expenses. Butt would like to know if he personally serves the proper papers to Diem whether he can obtain jurisdiction against Diem for damages in the following courts:

a. Alaska state trial court

b. Federal Circuit Court of Appeals for the Ninth Circuit (includes Alaska)

c. Virginia state trial court

d. Virginia federal district court

e. Federal Circuit Court of Appeals for the Fourth Circuit (includes Virginia and North Carolina)

f. Virginia equity court

g. North Carolina state trial court

4. Sam Simpleton, a resident of Kansas, and Nellie Naive, a resident of Missouri, each bought $85,000 in stock at local offices in their home states from Evil Stockbrokers, Inc. (Evil), a business incorporated in Delaware with its principal place of business in Kansas. Both Simpleton and Naive believe that they were cheated by Evil and would like to sue it for fraud. Assuming that no federal question is at issue, assess the accuracy of the following statements:

a. Simpleton can sue Evil in a Kansas state trial court.

b. Simpleton can sue Evil in a federal district court in Kansas.

c. Naive can sue Evil in a Missouri state trial court.

d. Naive can sue Evil in a federal district court in Missouri.

5. The Supreme Court of State A ruled that, under the law of State A, pit bull owners must either keep their dogs fenced or pay damages to anyone bitten by the dogs. Assess the accuracy of the following statements:

a. It is likely that the U.S. Supreme Court would issue a writ of *certiorari* in the "pit bull" case.

b. If a case similar to the "pit bull" case were to come before the Supreme Court of State B in the future, the doctrine of *stare decisis* would leave the court no choice but to rule the same way as the Supreme Court of State A ruled in the "pit bull" case.

6. The Supreme Court of State G decided that the U.S. Constitution requires professors to warn students of their right to remain silent before questioning the students about cheating. This ruling directly conflicts with a decision of the Federal Court of Appeals for the circuit that includes State G.

a. Must the Federal Circuit Court of Appeals withdraw its ruling?

b. Must the Supreme Court of State G withdraw its ruling?

CASE PROBLEMS

7. Thomas Clements brought an action in a court in Illinois to recover damages for breach of warranty against defendant, Signa Corporation. (A warranty is an obligation that the seller of goods assumes with respect to the quality of the goods sold.) Clements had purchased a motorboat from Barney's Sporting Goods, an Illinois corporation. The boat was manufactured by Signa Corporation, an Indiana corporation with its principal place of business in Decatur, Indiana. Signa has no office in Illinois and no agent authorized to do business on its behalf within Illinois. Clements saw Signa's boats on display at the Chicago Boat Show. In addition, literature on Signa's boats was distributed at the Chicago Boat Show. Several boating magazines, delivered to Clements in Illinois, contained advertisements for Signa's boats. Clements had also seen Signa's boats on display at Barney's Sporting Goods Store in Palatine, Illinois, where he eventually purchased the boat. A written warranty issued by Signa was delivered to Clements in Illinois. Although Signa was served with a summons, it failed to enter an appearance in this case. A default order was entered against Signa and subsequently a judgment of $6,220 was entered against Signa. Signa appealed. Decision?

8. Vette sued Aetna under a fire insurance policy. Aetna moved for summary judgment on the basis that the pleadings and discovered evidence showed a lack of an insurable interest in Vette. An "insurable interest" exists when the insured derives a monetary benefit or advantage from the preservation or continued existence of the property or would sustain an economic loss from its destruction. Aetna provided ample evidence to infer that Vette had no insurable interest in the contents of the burned building. Vette also provided sufficient evidence to put in dispute this factual issue. The trial court granted the motion for summary judgment. Vette appealed. Decision?

9. Mark Womer and Brian Perry were members of the U.S. Navy and were stationed in Newport, Rhode Island. On April 10, Womer allowed Perry to borrow his automobile so that Perry could visit his family in New Hampshire. Later that day, while operating Womer's vehicle, Perry was involved in an accident in Manchester, New Hampshire. As a result of the accident, Tzannetos Tavoularis was injured. Tavoularis brought this action against Womer in a New Hampshire superior court, contending that Womer was negligent in lending

the automobile to Perry when he knew or should have known that Perry did not have a valid driver's license. Womer sought to dismiss the action on the ground that the New Hampshire courts lacked jurisdiction over him, citing the following facts: (a) he did not live in New Hampshire; (b) he had no relatives in New Hampshire; (c) he neither owned property nor possessed investments in New Hampshire; and (d) he had never conducted business in New Hampshire. Did the New Hampshire courts have jurisdiction? Explain.

10. Mariana Deutsch worked as a knitwear mender and attended a school for beauticians. The sink in her apartment collapsed on her foot, fracturing her big toe and making it painful for her to stand. She claims that as a consequence of the injury she was compelled to abandon her plans to become a beautician because that job requires long periods of standing. She also asserts that she was unable to work at her current job for a month. She filed a tort claim against Hewes Street Realty for negligence in failing properly to maintain the sink. She brought the suit in federal district court, claiming damages of $85,000. Her medical expenses and actual loss of salary were less than $7,500; the rest of her alleged damages were for loss of future earnings as a beautician. Hewes Street moved to dismiss the suit on the basis that Deutsch's claim fell short of the jurisdictional requirement and therefore the federal court lacked subject matter jurisdiction over her claim. The district court dismissed the suit, and Deutsch appealed. Does the federal court have jurisdiction? Explain.

11. Kenneth Thomas brought suit against his former employer, Kidder, Peabody & Company, and two of its employees, Barclay Perry and James Johnston, in a dispute over commissions on sales of securities. When he applied to work at Kidder, Peabody & Company, Thomas had filled out a form, which contained an arbitration agreement clause. Thomas had also registered with the New York Stock Exchange (NYSE). Rule 347 of the NYSE provides that any controversy between a registered representative and a member company shall be settled by arbitration. Kidder, Peabody & Company is a member of the NYSE. Thomas refused to arbitrate, relying on Section 229 of the California Labor Code, which provides that actions for the collection of wages may be maintained "without regard to the existence of any private agreement to arbitrate." Perry and Johnston filed a petition in a California state court to compel arbitration under Section 2 of the Federal Arbitration Act, which was enacted pursuant to the Commerce Clause of the U.S. Constitution. Should the petition of Perry and Johnson be granted?

12. Steven Gwin bought a lifetime Termite Protection Plan for his home in Alabama from the local office of Allied-Bruce, a franchise of Terminix International Company. The plan provided that Allied-Bruce would "protect" Gwin's house against termite infestation, reinspect periodically, provide additional treatment if necessary, and repair damage caused by new termite infestations. Terminix International guaranteed the fulfillment of these contractual provisions. The plan also provided that all disputes arising out of the contract would be settled exclusively by arbitration. Four years later, Gwin had Allied-Bruce reinspect the house in anticipation of selling it. Allied-Bruce gave the house a "clean bill of health." Gwin then sold the house and transferred the Termite Protection Plan to Dobson. Shortly thereafter, Dobson found the house to be infested with termites. Allied-Bruce attempted to treat and repair the house, using materials from out of state, but these efforts failed to satisfy Dobson. Dobson then sued Gwin, Allied-Bruce, and Terminix International in an Alabama state court. Allied-Bruce and Terminix International asked for a stay of these proceedings until arbitration could be carried out as stipulated in the contract. The trial court refused to grant the stay. The Alabama Supreme Court upheld that ruling, citing a state statute that makes predispute arbitration agreements unenforceable. The court found that the Federal Arbitration Act, which preempts conflicting state law, did not apply to this contract because its connection to interstate commerce was too slight. Was the Alabama Supreme Court correct? Explain.

TAKING SIDES

John Connelly suffered personal injuries when a tire manufactured by Uniroyal failed while his 1969 Opel Kadett was being operated on a highway in Colorado. Connelly's father had purchased the automobile from a Buick dealer in Evanston, Illinois. The tire bore the name "Uniroyal" and the legend "made in Belgium" and was manufactured by Uniroyal, sold in Belgium to General Motors, and subsequently installed on the Opel when it was assembled at a General Motors plant in Belgium. The automobile was shipped to the United States for distribution by General Motors. It appears that between the years 1968 and 1971 more than 4,000 Opels imported into the United States from Antwerp, Belgium were delivered to dealers in Illinois each year; that in each of those years between 600 and 1,320 of the Opels delivered to Illinois dealers were equipped with tires manufactured by Uniroyal, and that the estimated number of Uniroyal tires mounted on Opels delivered in Illinois within each of those years ranged from 3,235 to 6,630. Connelly brought suit in Illinois against Uniroyal to recover damages for personal injuries. Uniroyal asserted that it was not subject to the jurisdiction of the Illinois courts because it is not registered to do business and has never had an agent, employee, representative or salesperson in Illinois; that it has never possessed or controlled any land or maintained any office or telephone listing in Illinois; that it has never sold or shipped any products into Illinois, either directly or indirectly; and that it has never advertised in Illinois.

a. What arguments could Connelly make in support of its claim that Illinois courts have jurisdiction over Uniroyal?

b. What arguments could Uniroyal make in support of its claim that Illinois courts do not have jurisdiction over it?

c. Who should prevail? Explain.

CHAPTER **4**

Constitutional Law

I have always regarded [the American] Constitution as the most remarkable work known to me in modern times to have been produced by the human intellect, at a single stroke (so to speak), in its application to political affairs.

William Gladstone
(British Prime Minister)

CHAPTER OUTCOMES

After reading and studying this chapter, you should be able to:

1. Explain the basic principles of constitutional law.

2. Describe the sources and extent of the power of the federal and state governments to regulate business and commerce.

3. Distinguish the three levels of scrutiny used by the courts to determine the constitutionality of government action.

4. Explain the effect of the First Amendment on (a) corporate political speech, (b) commercial speech, and (c) defamation.

5. Explain the difference between substantive and procedural due process.

You will recall from Chapter 1 that a constitution is the fundamental law of a particular level of government. It establishes the structure of government and defines the political relationships within it. It also places restrictions on the powers of government and guarantees the rights and liberties of the people.

The Constitution of the United States was adopted on September 17, 1787, by representatives of the thirteen newly created states. Its purpose is stated in the preamble:

> We the People of the United States, in Order to form a more perfect Union, establish Justice, insure domestic Tranquility, provide for the common defense, promote the general Welfare, and secure the Blessings of Liberty to ourselves and our Posterity, do ordain and establish this Constitution for the United States of America.

Although the framers of the U.S. Constitution stated precisely what rights and authority were vested in the new national government, they considered it unnecessary to list those liberties the people were to keep for themselves. Nonetheless, during the state conventions ratifying the document, people expressed fear that the federal government might abuse its powers. To calm these concerns, the first Congress approved ten amendments to the U.S. Constitution, now known as the Bill of Rights, which were adopted on December 15, 1791.

The Bill of Rights restricts the powers and authority of the federal government and establishes many of the civil and political rights enjoyed in the United States, including the right to due process of law and freedoms of speech, press, religion, assembly, and petition. Though the Bill of Rights does not apply directly to the states, the Supreme Court has held that the Fourteenth Amendment incorporates most of the principal guarantees of the Bill of Rights, thus making them applicable to the states.

This chapter concerns constitutional law as it applies to business and commerce. We will begin by surveying some of the basic principles of constitutional law and will then examine the allocation of power between the federal and state governments with respect to the regulation of business. Finally, we will discuss the constitutional restrictions on the power of government to regulate business.

BASIC PRINCIPLES

Constitutional law in the United States involves several basic concepts. These fundamental principles, which apply both to the powers of and to the limitations on government, are (1) federalism, (2) federal supremacy and preemption, (3) judicial review, (4) separation of powers, and (5) state action.

Federalism

Federalism
governing power is divided between the federal government and the states

Federalism is the division of governing power between the federal government and the states. The U.S. Constitution enumerates the powers of the federal government and specifically reserves to the states or the people the powers not expressly delegated to the federal government. Accordingly, the federal government is a government of enumerated, or limited, powers, and a specified power must authorize each of its acts. The doctrine of enumerated powers is not, however, a significant limitation on the federal government, because a number of these enumerated powers, in particular the power to regulate interstate and foreign commerce, have been broadly interpreted.

Furthermore, the Constitution grants Congress not only specified powers but also the power "[t]o make all Laws which shall be necessary and proper for carrying into Execution the foregoing Powers, and all other Powers vested by this Constitution in the Government of the United States, or in any Department or Officer thereof." U.S. Const. Art. I, Section 8, cl. 18. In the Supreme Court's view, the Necessary and Proper Clause enables Congress to legislate in areas not mentioned in the list of enumerated powers as long as such legislation reasonably relates to some enumerated power.

Federal Supremacy and Preemption

Supremacy Clause
federal law takes precedence over conflicting state laws

Although under our federalist system the states retain significant powers, the **Supremacy Clause** of the U.S. Constitution provides that, within its own sphere, federal law is supreme and that state law must, in case of conflict, yield. Accordingly, any state constitutional provision or law that conflicts with the U.S. Constitution or valid federal laws or treaties is unconstitutional and may not be given effect.

Federal preemption
first right of the federal government to regulate matters within its powers to the possible exclusion of state regulation

Under the Supremacy Clause, whenever Congress enacts legislation within its constitutional powers, the federal action **preempts** (overrides) any conflicting state legislation. Even if a state regulation is not in conflict, it must still give way if Congress clearly has intended its action to preempt state legislation. This intent may be specifically stated in the legislation or inferred from the scope of the legislation, the need for uniformity, or the danger of conflict between coexisting federal and state regulation.

When Congress has *not* intended to displace all state legislation, then nonconflicting state legislation is permitted. When Congress has not acted, the fact that it has the power to act does not prevent the states from acting. Until Congress exercises its power to preempt, state regulation is permitted.

Williamson v. Mazda Motor of America, Inc.
Supreme Court of the United States, 2011
562 U.S. ___, 131 S.Ct. 1131
http://www.law.cornell.edu/supct/html/08-1314.ZO.html

FACTS The 1989 version of Federal Motor Vehicle Safety Standard 208 (FMVSS 208) requires, among other things, that auto manufacturers install seatbelts on the rear seats of passenger vehicles. They must install lap-and-shoulder belts on seats next to a vehicle's doors or frames. But they have a choice about what to install on rear inner seats (middle seats or those next to a minivan's aisle). There they can install either (1) simple lap belts or (2) lap-and-shoulder belts.

In 2002, the Williamson family, riding in their 1993 Mazda minivan, was struck head on by another vehicle. Thanh Williamson was sitting in a rear aisle seat, wearing a lap belt; she died in the accident. Delbert and Alexa Williamson were wearing lap-and-shoulder belts; they survived. They, along with Thanh's estate, brought this California tort suit against Mazda. They claimed that Mazda should have installed lap-and-shoulder belts on rear aisle seats, and that Thanh died because Mazda equipped her seat with a lap belt instead.

The California trial court dismissed this tort claim on the basis of the pleadings. The California Court of Appeal affirmed, relying on a U.S. Supreme Court decision, *Geier v. American Honda Motor Co.* That case held that a different portion of an older version of FMVSS 208—which required installation of passive restraint devices—preempted a state tort suit that sought to hold an auto manufacturer liable for failure to install a particular kind of passive restraint, namely, airbags. The Williamsons sought *certiorari*, which was granted.

DECISION The judgment of the California Court of Appeal is reversed.

OPINION Did the state tort action here conflict with the federal regulation? Under ordinary conflict preemption principles, a state law that "stands as an obstacle to the accomplishment and execution of the full purposes and objectives" of a federal law is preempted. Like the regulation in *Geier*, the regulation in this case leaves the manufacturer with a choice, and the tort suit here would restrict that choice. But unlike *Geier*, the choice here is *not* a significant regulatory objective. The Department of Transportation (DOT) rejected a regulation requiring lap-and-shoulder belts in rear seats in 1984. But by 1989, changed circumstances led DOT to require manufacturers to install lap-and-shoulder belts for rear outer seats but to retain a manufacturer choice for rear inner seats. It was not concerned about consumer acceptance; it thought that lap-and-shoulder belts would increase safety and did not pose additional safety risks; and it was not seeking to use the regulation to spur development of alternative safety devices.

The more important reason why DOT did not require lap-and-shoulder belts for rear inner seats was that it thought that this requirement would not be cost-effective. The agency explained that it would be significantly more expensive for manufacturers to install lap-and-shoulder belts in rear middle and aisle seats than in seats next to the car doors. But the fact that DOT made a negative judgment about cost effectiveness cannot by itself show that DOT sought to forbid common-law tort suits in which a judge or jury might reach a different conclusion.

For one thing, DOT did not believe that costs would remain frozen. Rather it pointed out that costs were falling, as manufacturers were "voluntarily equipping more and more of their vehicles with rear seat lap/shoulder belts." For another thing, many, perhaps most, federal safety regulations embody some kind of cost-effectiveness judgment. While an agency could base a decision to preempt on its cost-effectiveness judgment, the rulemaking record at issue here discloses no such preemptive intent. And to infer from the mere existence of such a cost-effectiveness judgment that the federal agency intends to bar states from imposing stricter standards would treat all such federal standards as if they were maximum standards, eliminating the possibility that the federal agency seeks only to set forth a minimum standard potentially supplemented through state tort law. This consequence cannot be reconciled with a statutory saving clause that foresees the likelihood of a continued meaningful role for state tort law.

Finally, the Solicitor General represents that DOT's regulation does not preempt this tort suit, and the DOT has not expressed inconsistent views on this subject. As in *Geier*, "the agency's own views should make a difference."

> Congress has delegated to DOT authority to implement the statute; the subject matter is technical; and the relevant history and background are complex and extensive. The agency is likely to have a thorough understanding of its own regulation and its objectives and is "uniquely qualified" to comprehend the likely impact of state requirements.

Here the regulation's history, the agency's contemporaneous explanation, and its consistently held interpretive views indicated that the regulation did not seek to maintain manufacturer choice in order to further significant regulatory objectives. The Court therefore concluded that, even though the state tort suit may restrict the manufacturer's choice, it does not "stan[d] as an obstacle to the accomplishment ... of the full purposes and objectives" of federal law. Thus, the regulation does not preempt this tort action.

INTERPRETATION Providing manufacturers with a choice of belts for rear inner seats is not a significant objective of the federal regulation, and thus the regulation does not preempt the state tort suit.

CRITICAL THINKING QUESTION How does this decision affect the extent to which manufacturers can rely on federal safety regulations? Explain.

Judicial Review

Judicial review
power of the courts to determine the constitutionality of any legislative or executive act

Judicial review describes the process by which the courts examine government actions to determine whether they conform to the U.S. Constitution. If government action violates the U.S. Constitution, under judicial review the courts will invalidate that action. Judicial review extends to legislation, acts of the executive branch, and the decisions of inferior courts; such review scrutinizes actions of both the federal and state governments and applies to both the same standards of constitutionality. The U.S. Supreme Court is the final authority as to the constitutionality of any federal and state law.

Separation of Powers

Separation of powers
allocation of powers among the legislative, executive, and judicial branches of government

Another basic principle on which our government is founded is that of **separation of powers**. Our Constitution vests power in three distinct and independent branches of government—the executive, legislative, and judicial branches. The purpose of the doctrine of separation of powers is to prevent any branch of government from gaining too much power. The doctrine also permits each branch to function without interference from any other branch. Basically, the legislative branch is granted the power to make the law, the executive branch to enforce the law, and the judicial branch to interpret the law. This separation of powers is not complete, however. For example, the executive branch has veto power over legislation enacted by Congress; the legislative branch must approve a great number of executive appointments; and the judicial branch may declare both legislation and executive actions unconstitutional. Nevertheless, our government

Figure 4-1 Separation of Powers: Checks and Balances

© Cengage Learning 2013

generally operates under a three-branch scheme that provides for separation of powers and places checks and balances on the power of each branch, as illustrated by Figure 4-1.

State Action

State action

actions by governments as opposed to actions taken by private individuals

Most of the protections provided by the U.S. Constitution and its amendments apply only to government, or state, action. **State action** includes any actions of the federal and state governments and their subdivisions, such as city or county governments and agencies. Only the Thirteenth Amendment, which abolishes slavery or involuntary servitude, applies to the actions of private individuals. The protections that guard against state action, however, may be extended by *statute* to apply to private activity.

Additionally, action taken by private citizens may constitute state action if the state exercises coercive power over the challenged private action, has encouraged the action significantly, or was substantially involved with the action. For example, the Supreme Court found state action when the Supreme Court of Missouri ordered a lower court to enforce an agreement among white property owners that prohibited the transfer of their property to nonwhites. Moreover, if "private" individuals or entities engage in public functions, their actions may be considered state action subject to constitutional limitations. For example, the U.S. Supreme Court held that a company town was subject to the First Amendment because the state had allowed the company to exercise all of the public functions and activities usually conducted by a town government. Since that case, the Supreme Court has been less willing to find state action based upon the performance of public functions by private entities; the Court now limits such a finding to those functions "traditionally exclusively reserved to the state."

Brentwood Academy v. Tennessee Secondary School Athletic Association

Supreme Court of the United States, 2001

531 U.S. 288, 121 S.Ct. 924, 148 L.Ed.2d 807

http://laws.findlaw.com/us/000/99-901.html

FACTS The Tennessee Secondary School Athletic Association (Association) is a not-for-profit membership corporation organized to regulate interscholastic sport among the public and private high schools in Tennessee. No school is forced to join, but since there is no other authority regulating interscholastic athletics, it enjoys the memberships of almost all the state's public high schools (some 290 of them or 84 percent of the Association's voting membership), far outnumbering the fifty-five private schools that belong.

The Association's rulemaking arm is its legislative council, while its board of control tends to administration. The voting membership of each of these nine-person committees is limited

under the Association's bylaws to high school principals, assistant principals, and superintendents elected by the member schools, and the public school administrators who so serve typically attend meetings during regular school hours. Although the Association's staff members are not paid by the state, they are eligible to join the state's public retirement system for its employees. Member schools pay dues to the Association, though the bulk of its revenue is gate receipts at member teams' football and basketball tournaments. The constitution, bylaws, and rules of the Association set standards of school membership and the eligibility of students to play in interscholastic games. In 1997, a regulatory enforcement proceeding was brought against Brentwood Academy, a private parochial high school member of the Association. The Association's board of control found that Brentwood violated a rule prohibiting "undue influence" in recruiting athletes, when it wrote to incoming students and their parents about spring football practice. The Association placed Brentwood's athletic program on probation for four years, declared its football and boys' basketball teams ineligible to compete in playoffs for two years, and imposed a $3,000 fine.

Brentwood sued the Association and its executive director claiming that enforcement of the Rule was state action and a violation of the First and Fourteenth Amendments. The district court entered summary judgment for Brentwood and enjoined the Association from enforcing the Rule. The U.S. Court of Appeals for the Sixth Circuit reversed, saying that the district court was mistaken in seeing a symbiotic relationship between the state and the Association. It emphasized that the Association was neither engaging in a traditional and exclusive public function nor responding to state compulsion. The U.S. Supreme Court granted *certiorari* to resolve the conflict.

DECISION The judgment of the Court of Appeals for the Sixth Circuit is reversed, and the case is remanded for further proceedings consistent with this opinion.

OPINION State action may be found if, though only if, there is such a "close nexus between the State and the challenged action" that seemingly private behavior "may be fairly treated as that of the State itself." In this case, the Association is not an organization of natural persons acting on their own, but of schools, and of public schools to the extent of 84 percent of the total. Each member school is represented by its principal or a faculty member, who has a vote in selecting members of the governing legislative council and the board of control from eligible principals, assistant principals, and superintendents.

Although there is no express conclusion of law that public school officials act within the scope of their duties when they represent their institutions, no other view would be rational.

Interscholastic athletics obviously play an integral part in the public education of Tennessee, requiring some mechanism to produce rules and regulate competition. The mechanism is an organization overwhelmingly composed of public school officials who select representatives (all of them public officials at the time in question here), who in turn adopt and enforce the rules that make the system work. Many of the council or board meetings are held during official school hours, and the public schools have largely provided for the Association's financial support.

In sum, to the extent of 84 percent of its membership, the Association is an organization of public schools represented by their officials acting in their official capacity to provide an integral element of secondary public schooling. There would be no recognizable Association, legal or tangible, without the public school officials, who do not merely control but overwhelmingly perform all but the purely ministerial acts by which the Association exists and functions in practical terms. Only the 16 percent minority of private school memberships prevents this entwinement of the Association and the public school system from being total and their identities totally indistinguishable.

To complement the entwinement of public school officials with the Association from the bottom up, the State of Tennessee has provided for entwinement from top down. State Board members are assigned *ex officio* to serve as members of the board of control and legislative council, and the Association's ministerial employees are treated as state employees to the extent of being eligible for membership in the state retirement system. The entwinement down from the State Board is therefore unmistakable, just as the entwinement up from the member public schools is overwhelming.

INTERPRETATION If an association involves the pervasive entwinement of state school officials in its structure, the association's regulatory activity will be treated as state action.

CRITICAL THINKING QUESTION Should the actions of private parties be immune from federal constitutional limitations? Explain.

POWERS OF GOVERNMENT

The U.S. Constitution created a federal government of enumerated powers. Moreover, as the Tenth Amendment declares, "[t]he powers not delegated to the United States by the Constitution, nor prohibited by it to the States, are reserved to the States respectively, or to the people." Consequently, the legislation Congress enacts must be based on a specific power the Constitution grants to the federal government or be reasonably necessary to carry out an enumerated power.

Some government powers may be exercised only by the federal government. These exclusive federal powers include the power to establish laws regarding bankruptcy, to establish post offices, to grant patents and copyrights, to coin currency, to wage war, and to enter into treaties. Conversely, both the federal government and the states may exercise concurrent government powers, which include taxation, spending, and police power (regulation of public health, safety, and welfare).

In this part of the chapter, we will examine the sources and extent of the powers of the federal government—as well as the power of the states—to regulate business and commerce.

Federal Commerce Power

Commerce power
exclusive power granted by the U.S. Constitution to the federal government to regulate commerce with foreign countries and among the states

The U.S. Constitution provides that Congress has the power to regulate commerce with other nations and among the states. This Commerce Clause has two important effects: (1) it provides a broad source of **commerce power** for the federal government to regulate the economy and (2) it restricts state regulations that obstruct or unduly burden interstate commerce.

The U.S. Supreme Court interprets the Commerce Clause as granting virtually complete power to Congress to regulate the economy and business. More specifically, under the Commerce Clause, Congress has the power to regulate (1) the channels of interstate commerce, (2) the instrumentalities of interstate commerce, and (3) those activities having a substantial relation to interstate commerce. A court may invalidate legislation enacted under the Commerce Clause only if it is clear that (1) the activity the legislation regulates does not affect interstate commerce or (2) no reasonable connection exists between the selected regulatory means and the stated ends. For example, activities conducted solely within one state, such as the practice of law or real estate brokerage agreements, are subject to federal antitrust laws under the power granted by the Commerce Clause if those activities (1) substantially affect interstate commerce or (2) are in the flow of commerce.

Because of the broad and permissive interpretation of the commerce power, Congress currently regulates a vast range of activities. Many of the activities discussed in this text are regulated by the federal government through its exercise of the commerce power; such activities include federal crimes, consumer warranties and credit transactions, electronic funds transfers, trademarks, unfair trade practices, other consumer transactions, residential real estate transactions, consumer and employee safety, labor relations, civil rights in employment, transactions in securities, and environmental protection.

State Regulation of Commerce

State regulation of commerce
the Commerce Clause of the U.S. Constitution restricts the states' power to regulate activities if the result obstructs interstate commerce

The Commerce Clause, as we have previously discussed, specifically grants to Congress the power to regulate commerce among the states. In addition to acting as a broad source of federal power, the clause also implicitly restricts the states' power to regulate activities if the result obstructs or unduly burdens interstate commerce.

Regulations The Supreme Court ultimately decides the extent to which state regulation may affect interstate commerce. In doing so, the Court weighs and balances several factors: (1) the necessity and importance of the state regulation, (2) the burden it imposes on interstate commerce, and (3) the extent to which it discriminates against interstate commerce in favor of local concerns. The application of these factors involves case-by-case analysis. In general, in cases in which a state statute regulates evenhandedly to accomplish a legitimate state interest and its effects on interstate commerce are only incidental, the Court will uphold the statute unless the burden imposed on interstate commerce is clearly excessive compared with the local benefits. The Court will uphold a discriminatory regulation only if no other reasonable method of achieving a legitimate local interest exists.

Department of Revenue of Kentucky, et al., Davis
United States Supreme Court, 2008
553 U.S. 328, 128 S.Ct. 1801, 170 L.Ed.2d 685
http://www.law.cornell.edu/supct/html/06-666.ZS.html

FACTS Kentucky, like forty other states, exempts from state income taxes interest on bonds issued by it or its political subdivisions but not on bonds issued by other states and their subdivisions. The differential tax scheme in Kentucky benefits its residents who buy its bonds by effectively lowering interest rates. After paying state income tax on out-of-state municipal bonds, plaintiffs sued Kentucky for a refund, claiming that Kentucky's differential tax impermissibly discriminated against interstate commerce. The trial court ruled for Kentucky. The State Court of Appeals reversed, finding that Kentucky's scheme violated the Commerce Clause. The United States Supreme Court granted *certiorari*.

DECISION The judgment is reversed, and the case is remanded.

OPINION The significance of the differential tax scheme is immense. Between 1996 and 2002, Kentucky and its subdivisions

issued $7.7 billion in long-term bonds to pay for spending on transportation, public safety, education, utilities, and environmental protection, among other things. Across the United States during the same period, states issued over $750 billion in long-term bonds, with nearly a third of the money going to education, followed by transportation (13%) and utilities (11%). Municipal bonds currently finance roughly two-thirds of capital expenditures by state and local governments.

The "dormant" Commerce Clause implicitly restricts state regulatory measures designed to benefit in-state economic interests by burdening out-of-state competitors. Under the dormant Commerce Clause a challenged law that discriminates against interstate commerce is "virtually *per se* invalid" and will survive only if it "advances a legitimate local purpose that cannot be adequately served by reasonable nondiscriminatory alternatives." Absent discrimination for the forbidden purpose, however, the law "will be upheld unless the burden imposed on [interstate] commerce is clearly excessive in relation to the putative local benefits."

Kentucky treats income from municipal bonds of other states just like income from bonds privately issued in Kentucky or elsewhere; no preference is given to any local issuer, and none to any local holder, beyond what is entailed in the preference Kentucky grants itself when it engages in activities serving public objectives. These facts suggest that no state perceives any local advantage or disadvantage beyond the permissible ones open to a government and to those who deal with it when that government itself enters the market. The differential tax scheme is critical to the operation of an identifiable segment of the municipal financial market as it

currently functions, and this fact alone demonstrates that the unanimous desire of the states to preserve the tax feature is a far cry from the private protectionism that has driven the development of the dormant Commerce Clause.

INTERPRETATION State law exempting from state income taxes interest on bonds issued by that state or its political subdivisions but not on bonds issued by other states and their subdivisions does not impermissibly discriminate against interstate commerce.

CRITICAL THINKING QUESTION Had the Court invalidated Kentucky's taxing scheme, what would the impact have been on the states' ability to finance their operations?

Taxation The Commerce Clause, in conjunction with the Import-Export Clause, also limits the power of the state to tax. The Import-Export Clause provides: "No State shall, without the Consent of the Congress, lay any Imposts or Duties on Imports or Exports." U.S. Const. Art. I, Section 10, cl. 2. Together, the Commerce Clause and the Import-Export Clause exempt from state taxation goods that have entered the stream of commerce, whether they are interstate or foreign and whether they are imports or exports. The purpose of this immunity is to protect goods in commerce from both discriminatory and cumulative state taxes. Once the goods enter the stream of interstate or foreign commerce, the power of the state to tax ceases and does not resume until the goods are delivered to the purchaser or the owner terminates the movement of the goods through commerce.

The Due Process Clause of the Fourteenth Amendment also restricts the power of states to tax. Under the Due Process Clause, for a state tax to be constitutional, a sufficient nexus must exist between the state and the person, thing, or activity to be taxed.

Federal Fiscal Powers

The federal government exerts a dominating influence over the national economy through its control of financial matters. Much of this impact results from the exercise of its regulatory powers under the Commerce Clause, as previously discussed. In addition, the government derives a substantial portion of its influence from powers that are independent of the Commerce Clause. These include (1) the power to tax, (2) the power to spend, (3) the power to borrow and coin money, and (4) the power of eminent domain.

Taxation The federal government's power to tax, although extremely broad, has three major limitations: (1) direct taxes must be apportioned among the states, (2) all custom duties and excise taxes must be uniform throughout the United States, and (3) no duties may be levied on exports from any state.

Besides raising revenues, taxes also have regulatory and socioeconomic effects. For example, import taxes and custom duties can protect domestic industry from foreign competition. Graduated or progressive tax rates and exemptions may further social policies seeking the redistribution of wealth. Tax credits encourage investment in favored enterprises to the disadvantage of unfavored businesses. A tax that does more than just raise revenue will be upheld "so long as the motive of Congress and the effect of its legislative action are to secure revenue for the benefit of the general government."

Spending Power The Constitution authorizes the federal government to pay debts and to spend for the common defense and general welfare of the United States. Like the power to tax, the spending power of Congress is extremely broad; this power will be upheld so long as it does not violate a specific constitutional limitation on federal power.

Furthermore, through its spending power, Congress may accomplish indirectly what it may not do directly. For example, the Supreme Court has held that Congress may condition a state's receipt of federal highway funds on that state's mandating twenty-one as the minimum drinking age, even though the Twenty-first Amendment grants the states significant powers with respect to alcohol consumption within their respective borders. As the Court noted, "Constitutional limitations on Congress when exercising its spending power are less exacting than those on its authority to regulate directly." Whether directly or indirectly, the power of the federal government to spend money represents an important regulatory force in the economy and significantly affects the general welfare of the United States.

Borrowing and Coining Money   The U.S. Constitution also grants Congress the power to borrow money on the credit of the United States and to coin money. These two powers have enabled the federal government to establish a national banking system, the Federal Reserve System, and specialized federal lending programs such as the Federal Land Bank. Through these and other institutions and agencies, the federal government wields extensive control over national fiscal and monetary policies and exerts considerable influence over interest rates, the money supply, and foreign exchange rates.

Eminent domain

the power of a government to take private property for public use upon payment of fair compensation

Eminent Domain   The government's power to take private property for public use, known as the power of **eminent domain**, is recognized, in the federal Constitution and in the constitutions of the states, as one of the inherent powers of government. At the same time, however, the power is carefully limited. The Fifth Amendment to the federal Constitution contains a Takings Clause that provides that private property shall not be taken for public use without just compensation. Although this amendment applies only to the federal government, the Supreme Court has held that the Takings Clause is incorporated through the Fourteenth Amendment and is therefore applicable to the states. Moreover, similar or identical provisions are found in the constitutions of the states.

As the language of the Takings Clause indicates, the taking must be for a public use. Public use has been held to be synonymous with public purpose. Thus, private entities, such as railroads and housing authorities, may use the government's power of eminent domain so long as the entity's use of the property benefits the public. When the government or a private entity properly takes property under the power of eminent domain, the owners of the property must receive just compensation, which has been interpreted as the fair market value of the property.

The Supreme Court has held that the Takings Clause requires just compensation only if a government taking actually occurs, not if the government regulation only reduces the value of the property. If, however, a regulation deprives the owner of all economic use of the property, then a taking has occurred. Eminent domain is discussed further in Chapter 49.

Figure 4-2 summarizes the powers granted to the federal government, the states, and the people.

Figure 4-2 Powers of Government

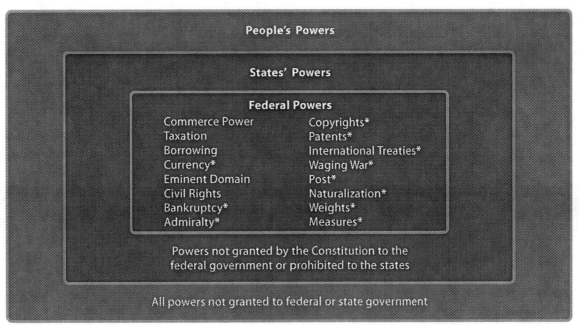

People's Powers

States' Powers

Federal Powers

Commerce Power	Copyrights*
Taxation	Patents*
Borrowing	International Treaties*
Currency*	Waging War*
Eminent Domain	Post*
Civil Rights	Naturalization*
Bankruptcy*	Weights*
Admiralty*	Measures*

Powers not granted by the Constitution to the federal government or prohibited to the states

All powers not granted to federal or state government

*Exclusive power

LIMITATIONS ON GOVERNMENT

As we have discussed, the U.S. Constitution grants certain specified powers to the federal government, while reserving other, unspecified powers to the states. The Constitution and its amendments, however, impose limits on the powers of both the federal government and the states. In this part of the chapter, we will discuss those limitations most applicable to business: (1) the Contract Clause, (2) the First Amendment, (3) due process, and (4) equal protection. The first of these—the Contract Clause—applies only to the actions of state governments, whereas the other three apply to both the federal government and the states.

None of these restrictions operates as an absolute limitation but instead triggers review or scrutiny by the courts to determine whether the government power exercised encroaches impermissibly upon the interest the Constitution protects. The U.S. Supreme Court has used different levels of scrutiny, depending on the interest affected and the nature of the government action. Although this differentiation among levels of scrutiny is most fully developed in the area of equal protection, it also occurs in other areas, including substantive due process and protection of free speech.

The least rigorous level of scrutiny is the **rational relationship test**, which requires that the regulation conceivably bear some rational relationship to a legitimate government interest that the regulation will attempt to further. The most exacting level of scrutiny is the **strict scrutiny test**, which requires that the regulation be necessary to promote a compelling government interest. Finally, under the **intermediate test**, the regulation must have a substantial relationship to an important government objective. These standards will be more fully explained below. See Concept Review 4-1 illustrating these limitations on government.

Contract Clause

Article I, Section 10, of the Constitution provides: "No State shall ... pass any ... Law impairing the Obligation of Contracts." The Supreme Court has used the **Contract Clause** to restrict states from retroactively modifying public charters and private contracts. However, the Court, holding that the Contract Clause does *not* preclude the states from exercising eminent domain or their police powers, has ruled: "No legislature can bargain away the public health or the public morals." Although the Contract Clause does not apply to the federal government, due process limits the federal government's power to impair contracts.

First Amendment

The First Amendment states:

> Congress shall make no law respecting an establishment of religion, or prohibiting the free exercise thereof; or abridging the freedom of speech, or of the press; or the right of the people peaceably to assemble, and to petition the Government for a redress of grievances.

The First Amendment's protection of **free speech** is not absolute. Some forms of speech, such as obscenity, receive no protection. Most forms of speech, however, are protected by the strict or exacting scrutiny standard, which requires the existence of a compelling and legitimate state interest to justify a restriction of speech. If such an interest exists, the legislature must use means that least restrict free speech. We will examine the application of the First Amendment's guarantee of free speech to (1) corporate political speech, (2) commercial speech, and (3) defamation.

Rational relationship test requirement that regulation bears a rational relationship to a legitimate government interest

Strict scrutiny test requirement that regulation be necessary to promote a compelling government interest

Intermediate test requirement that regulation have a substantial relationship to an important government objective

Contract Clause prohibition against the states' retroactively modifying public and private contracts

PRACTICAL ADVICE *The federal Constitution protects you from a state law that impairs a preexisting contract.*

Free speech First Amendment protects most speech by using a strict scrutiny standard

---

CONCEPT REVIEW 4-1

Limitations on Government

Test/Interest	Equal Protection	Substantive Due Process	Free Speech
Strict Scrutiny	Fundamental Rights Suspect Classifications	Fundamental Rights	Protected Noncommercial Speech
Intermediate	Gender Legitimacy		Commercial Speech
Rational Relationship	Economic Regulation	Economic Regulation	Nonprotected Speech

© Cengage Learning 2013

Corporate Political Speech   Freedom of speech is indispensable to the discovery and spread of political truth; indeed, "the best test of truth is the power of the thought to get itself accepted in the competition of the market." To promote this competition of ideas, the First Amendment's guarantee of free speech applies not only to individuals but also to corporations. Accordingly, corporations may not be prohibited from speaking out on political issues. For example, in *First National Bank v. Bellotti*, 435 U.S. 765 (1978), the Supreme Court has held unconstitutional a Massachusetts criminal statute that prohibited banks and business corporations from making contributions and expenditures with regard to most referenda issues. The Court held that if speech is otherwise protected, the fact that the speaker is a corporation does not alter the speech's protected status.

The Supreme Court retreated somewhat from its holding in *Bellotti* when it upheld a state statute prohibiting corporations, except media corporations, from using general treasury funds to make independent expenditures in elections for public office but permitting such expenditures from segregated funds used solely for political purposes. The Court held that the statute did not violate the First Amendment because the burden on corporations' exercise of political expression was justified by a compelling state interest in preventing corruption in the political arena: "the corrosive and distorting effects of immense aggregations of wealth that are accumulated with the help of the corporate form and that have little or no correlation to the public's support for the corporation's political ideas." The Court held that the statute was sufficiently narrowly tailored because it "is precisely targeted to eliminate the distortion caused by corporate spending while also allowing corporations to express their political views" by making expenditures through segregated funds. *Austin v. Michigan Chamber of Commerce*, 494 U.S. 652 (1990).

In a recent landmark five-to-four decision, *Citizens United v. Federal Election Commission*, 558 U.S. 50, 130 S.Ct. 876, 175 L. Ed. 2d 753 (2010), the Supreme Court explicitly overruled the *Austin* case. *Citizens United* involved a First Amendment challenge to a federal law that prohibited corporations and unions from using their general treasury funds to make independent expenditures for speech defined as an "electioneering communication" or for speech expressly advocating the election or defeat of a candidate. (An electioneering communication is "any broadcast, cable, or satellite communication" that "refers to a clearly identified candidate for Federal office" and is made within thirty days of a primary election.) The Supreme Court invalidated these provisions as conflicting with the First Amendment, holding: "We return to the principle established in ... *Bellotti* that the Government may not suppress political speech on the basis of the speaker's corporate identity. No sufficient governmental interest justifies limits on the political speech of nonprofit or for-profit corporations."

Commercial Speech   **Commercial speech** is expression related to the economic interests of the speaker and his audience, such as advertisements for a product or service. Since the mid-1970s, U.S. Supreme Court decisions have eliminated the doctrine that commercial speech is wholly outside the protection of the First Amendment. Rather, the Court has established the principle that speech proposing a commercial transaction is entitled to protection, which, although less than that accorded political speech, is still extensive. Protection is accorded commercial speech because of the interest such communication holds for the advertiser, consumer, and general public. Advertising and other similar messages convey important information for the proper and efficient distribution of resources in our free market system. At the same time, however, commercial speech is less valuable and less vulnerable than other varieties of speech and therefore does not merit complete First Amendment protection.

In cases determining the protection to be afforded commercial speech, a four-part analysis has developed. First, the court must determine whether the expression is protected by the First Amendment. For commercial speech to come within that provision, such speech, at the least, must concern lawful activity and not be misleading. Second, the court must determine whether the asserted government interest is substantial. If both inquiries yield positive answers, then, third, the court must determine whether the regulation directly advances the government interest asserted and, fourth, whether the regulation is not more extensive than is necessary to serve that interest. The Supreme Court recently held that government restrictions of commercial speech need not be absolutely the least severe so long as they are "narrowly tailored" to achieve the government objective.

Because the constitutional protection extended to commercial speech is based on the informational function of advertising, governments may regulate or suppress commercial messages that do not accurately inform the public about lawful activity. "The government may ban forms of communication more likely to deceive the public than to inform it, or commercial speech related to illegal activity." Therefore, government regulation of false and misleading advertising is permissible under the First Amendment.

Thompson v. Western States Medical Center
Supreme Court of the United States, 2002
535 U.S. 357, 122 S.Ct. 1497, 152 L.Ed.2d 563
http://laws.findlaw.com/us/000/01-344.html

FACTS Drug compounding is a process by which a pharmacist or doctor combines, mixes, or alters ingredients to create a medication tailored to the needs of an individual patient. Compounding is typically used to prepare medications that are not commercially available, such as medication for a patient who is allergic to an ingredient in a mass-produced product.

The Federal Food, Drug, and Cosmetic Act of 1938 (FDCA) regulates drug manufacturing, marketing, and distribution, providing that no person may sell any new drug unless approved by the Food and Drug Administration (FDA). The Food and Drug Administration Modernization Act of 1997 (FDAMA), which amends the FDCA, exempts compounded drugs from the FDCA's requirements provided the drugs satisfy a number of restrictions, including that the prescription must be "unsolicited," and the provider compounding the drug may "not advertise or promote the compounding of any particular drug, class of drug, or type of drug." The provider may, however, "advertise and promote the compounding service."

The plaintiffs are a group of licensed pharmacies that specialize in drug compounding. They filed a complaint in the U.S. District Court for the District of Nevada, arguing that the Act's requirement that they refrain from advertising and promoting their products if they wish to continue compounding violates the Free Speech Clause of the First Amendment. The district court agreed with the plaintiffs and granted their motion for summary judgment, holding that the provisions do not meet the test for acceptable government regulation of commercial speech set forth in *Central Hudson Gas & Elec. Corp. v. Public Serv. Comm'n of N.Y.* The Court of Appeals for the Ninth Circuit affirmed in relevant part agreeing that the provisions regarding advertisement and promotion are unconstitutional.

DECISION Judgment affirmed.

OPINION The parties agree that the advertising and soliciting prohibited by the FDAMA constitute commercial speech. Commercial speech receives First Amendment protection, because "It is a matter of public interest that [economic] decisions, in the aggregate, be intelligent and well-informed. To this end, the free flow of commercial information is indispensable." Although the First Amendment protects commercial speech, not all regulation of such speech is unconstitutional. *Central Hudson* articulated a test for determining whether a particular commercial speech regulation is constitutionally permissible. Under that test a threshold matter is whether the commercial speech concerns unlawful activity or is misleading. If so, then the speech is not protected by the First Amendment. If the speech concerns lawful activity and is not misleading, however, the next question is "whether the asserted governmental interest is substantial." If it is, then the courts "determine whether the regulation directly advances the governmental interest asserted," and, finally, "whether it is not more extensive than is necessary to serve that

interest." Each of these latter three inquiries must be answered in the affirmative for the regulation to be found constitutional.

The government asserted that three substantial interests underlie the FDAMA. The first is an interest in "preserving the effectiveness and integrity of the FDCA's new drug approval process and the protection of the public health that it provides." The second is an interest in "preserving the availability of compounded drugs for those individual patients who, for particularized medical reasons, cannot use commercially available products that have been approved by the FDA." Finally, the government argued that "achieving the proper balance between those two independently compelling but competing interests is itself a substantial governmental interest."

The government needs to be able to draw a line between small-scale compounding and large-scale drug manufacturing. That line must distinguish compounded drugs produced on such a small scale that they could not undergo safety and efficacy testing from drugs produced and sold on a large enough scale that they could undergo such testing and therefore must do so. The government argued that the FDAMA's speech-related provisions "directly advance the governmental interests asserted." Those provisions use advertising as the trigger for requiring FDA approval—essentially, as long as pharmacists do not advertise particular compounded drugs, they may sell compounded drugs without first undergoing safety and efficacy testing and obtaining FDA approval. If they advertise their compounded drugs, however, FDA approval is required.

Assuming it is true that drugs cannot be marketed on a large scale without advertising, the FDAMA's prohibition on advertising compounded drugs might indeed "directly advance" the government's interests. Even assuming that it does, however, the government has failed to demonstrate that the speech restrictions are "not more extensive than is necessary to serve [those] interests." In addressing this final prong of the *Central Hudson* test, previous cases have made clear that if the government could achieve its interests in a manner that does not restrict speech, or that restricts less speech, the government must do so. However, several non-speech-related means of drawing a line between compounding and large-scale manufacturing might be possible here.

Even if the government had argued that the FDAMA's speech-related restrictions were motivated by a fear that advertising compounded drugs would put people who do not need such drugs at risk by causing them to convince their doctors to prescribe the drugs anyway, that fear would fail to justify the restrictions. The Supreme Court has previously rejected the notion that the government has an interest in preventing the dissemination of truthful commercial information in order to prevent members of the public from making bad decisions with the information. In *Virginia Bd. of Pharmacy*, the state feared that if people received price advertising from pharmacists, they would "choose the low-cost, low-quality service and drive the 'professional' pharmacist out of business" and would "destroy the pharmacist-customer relationship" by going from one pharmacist to another. The Supreme Court found these fears insufficient to justify a ban on such advertising.

INTERPRETATION A government restriction on nonmisleading commercial speech concerning lawful activity is invalid under the First Amendment if the regulation is more extensive than necessary to directly advance a substantial government interest.

CRITICAL THINKING QUESTION Do you agree that the Court's suggested non-speech-related means of drawing a line between compounding and large-scale manufacturing would be effective? Explain.

Defamation
injury of a person's reputation by publication of false statements

Defamation **Defamation** is a civil wrong or tort that consists of disgracing or diminishing a person's reputation through the communication of a false statement. An example would be the publication of a statement that a person had committed a crime or had a loathsome disease. (Defamation is also discussed in Chapter 7.)

Because defamation involves a communication, it receives the protection extended to speech by the First Amendment. Moreover, the Supreme Court has ruled that a public official who is defamed in regard to his conduct, fitness, or role as public official may not recover in a defamation action unless the statement was made with *actual malice*, which requires clear and convincing proof that the defendant had knowledge of the falsity of the communication or acted in reckless disregard of its truth or falsity. This restriction on the right to recover for defamation is based on "a profound national commitment to the principle that debate on public issues should be uninhibited, robust and wide-open, and that it may well include vehement, caustic, and sometimes unpleasantly sharp attacks on government and public officials." The communication may deal with the official's qualifications for and performance in office, which would likely include most aspects of character and public conduct. In addition, the Supreme Court has extended the same rule to public figures and candidates for public office. (The Court, however, has not precisely defined the term *public figure*.)

In a defamation suit brought by a private person (one who is neither a public official nor a public figure), the plaintiff must prove that the defendant published the defamatory and false comment with malice *or* negligence.

Due Process

Due process
Fifth and Fourteenth Amendments prohibit the federal and state governments from depriving any person of life, liberty, or property without due process of law

The Fifth and Fourteenth Amendments prohibit the federal and state governments, respectively, from depriving any person of life, liberty, or property without **due process** of law. Due process has two different aspects: substantive and procedural. As we discussed in Chapter 1, substantive law creates, defines, or regulates legal rights, whereas procedural law establishes the rules for enforcing those rights. Accordingly, substantive due process concerns the compatibility of a law or government action with fundamental constitutional rights such as free speech. In contrast, procedural due process involves the review of the decision-making process that enforces substantive laws and results in depriving a person of life, liberty, or property.

Substantive due process
requirement that government action be compatible with individual liberties

Substantive Due Process Substantive due process, which involves a court's determination of whether a particular government action is compatible with individual liberties, addresses the constitutionality of a legal rule, not the fairness of the process by which the rule is applied. Legislation affecting economic and social interests satisfies substantive due process so long as the legislation is rationally related to legitimate government objectives. In cases in which a rule affects individuals' fundamental rights under the Constitution, however, the Court will carefully scrutinize the legislation to determine whether it is necessary to promote a compelling or overriding state interest.

Procedural due process
requirement that government action depriving a person of life, liberty, or property be done through a fair procedure

Procedural Due Process Procedural due process pertains to the government decision-making process that results in depriving a person of life, liberty, or property. As the Supreme Court has interpreted procedural due process, the government is required to provide an individual with a fair procedure if, but only if, the person faces deprivation of life, liberty, or property. When government action adversely affects an individual but does not deny life, liberty, or property, the government is not required to give the person any hearing at all.

Liberty
ability of individuals to engage in freedom of action and choice regarding their personal lives

Property
includes real property, personal property, and certain benefits conferred by government

For the purposes of procedural due process, **liberty** generally includes the ability of individuals to engage in freedom of action and choice regarding their personal lives. **Property** includes not only all forms of real and personal property but also certain benefits (entitlements) conferred by the government, such as social security payments and food stamps.

When applicable, procedural due process requires that a court use a fair and impartial procedure in resolving the factual and legal basis for a government action that results in a deprivation of life, liberty, or property.

Equal Protection

The Fourteenth Amendment provides that "nor shall any State ... deny to any person within its jurisdiction the equal protection of the laws." Although this amendment applies only to the actions of state governments, the Supreme Court has interpreted the Due Process clause of the Fifth Amendment to subject federal actions to the same standards of review. The most important constitutional concept protecting individual rights, the guarantee of **equal protection** basically requires that similarly situated persons be treated similarly by government actions.

Equal protection
requirement that similarly situated persons be treated similarly by government action

When government action involves classification of people, the equal protection guarantee comes into play. In determining whether government action satisfies the equal protection guarantee, the Supreme Court uses one of three standards of review, depending on the nature of the right involved. The three standards are (1) the rational relationship test, (2) the strict scrutiny test, and (3) the intermediate test.

Rational relationship test
a standard of review used to determine whether economic regulation satisfies the equal protection guarantee

Rational Relationship Test The **rational relationship test**, which applies to economic regulation, simply requires that the classification *conceivably* bear some rational relationship to a legitimate government interest the classification seeks to further. Under this standard of review, the government action is permitted to attack part of the evil to which the action is addressed. Moreover, there is a strong presumption that the action is constitutional. Therefore, the courts will overturn the government action *only* if clear and convincing evidence shows that there is *no* reasonable basis justifying the action.

Strict scrutiny test
exacting standard of review applicable to regulation affecting a fundamental right or involving a suspect classification

Strict Scrutiny Test The strict scrutiny test is far more exacting than the rational relationship test. Under this test, the courts do not defer to the government; rather, they independently determine whether a classification of persons is constitutionally permissible. This determination requires that the classification be necessary to promote a compelling or overriding government interest.

The strict scrutiny test is applied when government action affects fundamental rights or involves suspect classifications. Fundamental rights include most of the provisions of the Bill of Rights and certain other rights, such as interstate travel, voting, and access to criminal justice. Suspect classifications include those made on the basis of race or national origin. A classic and important example of strict scrutiny applied to classifications based upon race is found in the 1954 school desegregation case of *Brown v. Board of Education of Topeka*, in which the Supreme Court ruled that segregated public school systems violated the equal protection guarantee. Subsequently, the Court has invalidated segregation in public beaches, municipal golf courses, buses, parks, public golf courses, and courtroom seating.

A recent U.S. Supreme Court case again addressed the application of strict scrutiny to public schools. School districts in Seattle, Washington, and metropolitan Louisville, Kentucky, had voluntarily adopted student assignment plans that relied on race to determine which schools certain children may attend. In a five-to-four decision, the Court held that public school systems may not seek to achieve or maintain integration through measures that take explicit account of a student's race. The Court reaffirmed that when the government distributes burdens or benefits on the basis of individual racial classifications, that action is reviewed under strict scrutiny requiring the most exact connection between justification and classification. Therefore, the school districts must demonstrate that the use of individual racial classifications in their school assignment plans is narrowly tailored to achieve a compelling government interest. In reversing the lower courts' decisions upholding the schools' plans, the Court held: "The [school] districts have also failed to show that they considered methods other than explicit racial classifications to achieve their stated goals. Narrow tailoring requires 'serious, good faith consideration of workable race-neutral alternatives.'" *Parents Involved in Community Schools v. Seattle School District No.1*, 551 U.S. 701 (2007).

Brown v. Board of Education of Topeka
Supreme Court of the United States, 1954
347 U.S. 483, 74 S.Ct. 686, 98 L.Ed. 873
http://laws.findlaw.com/US/347/483.html

FACTS These were consolidated cases from Kansas, South Carolina, Virginia, and Delaware, each with a different set of facts and local conditions but also presenting a common legal question. Black minors, through their legal representatives, sought court orders to obtain admission to the public schools in their community on a nonsegregated basis. They had been denied admission to schools attended by white children under laws requiring or permitting segregation according to race. The Supreme Court had previously upheld such laws under the "separate but equal" doctrine, which provided that there was equality of treatment of the races through substantially equal, though separate, facilities; and the lower courts had found that the white schools and the black schools involved had been or were being equalized with respect to buildings, curricula, qualifications and salaries of teachers, and other "tangible" factors. The black minors contended, however, that segregated public schools were not and could not be made "equal," and that hence they had been deprived of the equal protection of the laws guaranteed by the Fourteenth Amendment.

DECISION Judgment for plaintiffs.

OPINION Segregation of children in public schools solely on the basis of race generates a feeling of inferiority that diminishes their motivation to learn and affects "their hearts and minds in a way unlikely ever to be undone." Though the physical facilities and other "tangible" factors may be equal, segregation of the races with the sanction of law retards the educational and mental development of black children and deprives them of equal educational opportunities. Since separate educational facilities are inherently unequal, the "separate but equal" doctrine has no place in the field of public education. Therefore, segregation denies the black children the equal protection of the laws guaranteed by the Fourteenth Amendment.

INTERPRETATION When a governmentally imposed classification involves fundamental rights or suspect classifications, equal protection requires the classification to be necessary to promote a compelling or overriding government interest.

CRITICAL THINKING QUESTION Is the equal protection clause of the U.S. Constitution violated when different public school districts spend significantly different amounts of money per student? Explain.

Intermediate test
standard of review applicable to regulation based on gender and legitimacy

Intermediate Test An **intermediate test** has been applied to government action based on gender and legitimacy. Under this test, the classification must have a substantial relationship to an important government objective. The intermediate standard eliminates the strong presumption of constitutionality to which the rational relationship test adheres. For example, the Supreme Court invalidated an Alabama law that allowed courts to grant alimony awards only

Ethical Dilemma

Who Is Responsible for Commercial Speech?

Facts Jane Stewart is an assistant manager of advertising for *Dazzling Magazine*, a fashion magazine aimed primarily at women between the ages of twenty-five and thirty-five. Offering regular columns on health, beauty, fashion, and current events, the magazine has a small circulation and handles its advertising internally.

Having experienced declining sales in recent years, the magazine has downsized its operations by eliminating jobs and implementing cost-cutting measures. To prevent further declines in revenue, *Dazzling*'s marketing and editorial staffs are attempting to expand the magazine's appeal to include younger audiences between the ages of sixteen and twenty-four. Jane is in charge of making recommendations to the advertising manager with regard to new advertisements. The

advertising manager, in turn, makes the final recommendation to the head of the advertising department. Because of the magazine's overall decline in sales, the advertising unit has come under increased pressure to generate revenue from advertisements. Compensation of advertising unit employees is based in part on the earning of "bonus points" related to first-year revenues from new clients.

Jane has received advertisement offers from two cigarette companies and from one swimsuit manufacturer. Although the cigarette advertisements would generate twice as much revenue as the swimsuit advertisement, Jane is concerned that the cigarette advertisements would lure young women to smoke. She has recommended to her supervisor, Agnes Scott, that the cigarette advertisements be rejected.

Scott adamantly disagrees. She strongly recommends to the head of the advertising department that the cigarette advertisements be accepted.

Social, Policy, and Ethical Considerations
1. What should Jane do? What is best for (a) her company and (b) society? Should Jane raise her concerns to the department head?
2. Identify the competing social values at stake with regard to cigarette advertising. What role should the government play in regulating speech that promotes products such as tobacco and alcohol?
3. Should the age of *Dazzling*'s prospective audience influence the choice of advertisements? Explain.

from husbands to wives and not from wives to husbands. Similarly, where an Idaho statute gave preference to males over females in qualifying for selection as administrators of estates, the Supreme Court invalidated the statute because the preference did not bear a fair and substantial relationship to any legitimate legislative objective. Moreover, the Supreme Court invalidated a state university's (Virginia Military Institute) admission policy excluding women. *U.S. v. Virginia*, 518 U.S. 515 (1996). On the other hand, not all legislation based on gender is invalid. For example, the Supreme Court has upheld a California statutory rape law that imposed penalties only on males, as well as the federal military Selective Service Act that exempted women from registering for the draft.

CHAPTER SUMMARY

Basic Principles

Federalism the division of governing power between the federal government and the states

Federal Supremacy federal law takes precedence over conflicting state law

Federal Preemption right of federal government to regulate matters within its power to the exclusion of regulation by the states

Judicial Review examination of government actions to determine whether they conform to the U.S. Constitution

Separation of Powers allocation of powers among executive, legislative, and judicial branches of government

State Action actions of governments to which constitutional provisions apply

Powers of Government

Federal Commerce Power exclusive power of federal government to regulate commerce with other nations and among the states

State Regulation of Commerce the Commerce Clause of the Constitution restricts the states' power to regulate activities if the result obstructs interstate commerce

Federal Fiscal Powers

- *Taxation and Spending* the Constitution grants Congress broad powers to tax and spend; such powers are important to federal government regulation of the economy
- *Borrowing and Coining Money* enables the federal government to establish a national banking system and to control national fiscal and monetary policy
- *Eminent Domain* the government's power to take private property for public use with the payment of just compensation

Limitations on Government

Contract Clause restricts states from retroactively modifying contracts

Freedom of Speech First Amendment protects most speech by using a strict scrutiny standard

- *Corporate Political Speech* First Amendment protects a corporation's right to speak out on political issues
- *Commercial Speech* expression related to the economic interests of the speaker and its audience; such expression receives a lesser degree of protection
- *Defamation* a tort consisting of a false communication that injures a person's reputation; such a communication receives limited constitutional protection

Due Process Fifth and Fourteenth Amendments prohibit the federal and state governments from depriving any person of life, liberty, or property without due process of law

- *Substantive Due Process* determination of whether a particular government action is compatible with individual liberties
- *Procedural Due Process* requires the government decision-making process to be fair and impartial if it deprives a person of life, liberty, or property

Equal Protection requires that similarly situated persons be treated similarly by government actions

- *Rational Relationship Test* standard of review used to determine whether economic regulation satisfies the equal protection guarantee
- *Strict Scrutiny Test* exacting standard of review applicable to regulation affecting a fundamental right or involving a suspect classification
- *Intermediate Test* standard of review applicable to regulation based on gender and legitimacy

QUESTIONS

1. In May, Patricia Allen left her automobile on the shoulder of a road in the city of Erehwon after the car stopped running. A member of the Erehwon city police department found the car later that day and placed on it a sticker stating that unless the car was moved, it would be towed. When after a week the car had not been removed, the police department authorized Baldwin Auto Wrecking Co. to tow it away and to store it on its property. Allen was told by a friend that her car was at Baldwin's. Allen asked Baldwin to allow her to take possession of her car, but Baldwin refused to relinquish the car until the $70 towing fee was paid. Allen could not afford to pay the fee, and the car remained at Baldwin's for six weeks. At that time, Baldwin requested the police department for a permit to dispose of the automobile. After the police department tried unsuccessfully to telephone Allen, the department issued the permit. In late July, Baldwin destroyed the automobile. Allen brings an action against the city and Baldwin for damages for loss of the vehicle, arguing that she was denied due process. Decision?

CASE PROBLEMS

2. In 1967, large oil reserves were discovered in the Prudhoe Bay area of Alaska. As a result, state revenues increased from $124 million in 1969 to $3.7 billion in 1981. In 1980, the state legislature enacted a dividend program that would distribute annually a portion of these earnings to the state's adult residents. Under the plan, each citizen eighteen years of age or older receives one unit for each year of residency subsequent to 1959, the year Alaska became a state. The state advanced three purposes justifying the distinctions made by the dividend program: (a) creation of a financial incentive for individuals to establish and maintain residence in Alaska; (b) encouragement of prudent management of the earnings; and (c) apportionment of benefits in recognition of undefined "contributions of various kinds, both tangible and intangible, which residents have made during their years of residency." Crawford, a resident since 1978, brings suit challenging the dividend distribution plan as violative of the equal protection guarantee. Did the dividend program violate the Equal Protection Clause of the Fourteenth Amendment? Explain.

3. Maryland enacted a statute prohibiting any producer or refiner of petroleum products from operating retail service stations within the state. The statute also required that any producer or refiner discontinue operating its company-owned retail service stations. Approximately 3,800 retail service stations in Maryland sell more than twenty different brands of gasoline. All of this gasoline is brought in from other states, as no petroleum products are produced or refined in Maryland. Only 5 percent of the total number of retailers are operated by a producer or refiner. Maryland enacted the statute because a survey conducted by the state comptroller indicated that gasoline stations operated by producers or refiners had received preferential treatment during periods of gasoline shortage. Seven major producers and refiners brought an action challenging the statute on the ground that it discriminated against interstate commerce in violation of the Commerce Clause of the U.S. Constitution. Are they correct? Explain.

4. The Federal Aviation Act provides that "The United States of America is declared to possess and exercise complete and exclusive national sovereignty in the airspace of the United States." The city of Orion adopted an ordinance that makes it unlawful for jet aircraft to take off from its airport between 11:00 P.M. of one day and 7:00 A.M. of the next day. Jordan Airlines, Inc., is adversely affected by this ordinance and brings suit challenging it under the Supremacy Clause of the U.S. Constitution as conflicting with the Federal Aviation Act or preempted by it. Is the ordinance valid? Explain.

5. The Public Service Commission of State X issued a regulation completely banning all advertising that "promotes the use of electricity" by any electric utility company in State X. The commission issued the regulation to conserve energy. Central Electric Corporation of State X challenges the order in the state courts, arguing that the commission had restrained commercial speech in violation of the First Amendment. Was its freedom of speech unconstitutionally infringed? Explain.

6. E-Z-Rest Motel is a motel with 216 rooms located in the center of a large city in State Y. It is readily accessible from two interstate highways and three major state highways. The motel solicits patronage from outside State Y through various national advertising media, including magazines of national circulation. It accepts convention trade from outside State Y, and approximately 75 percent of its registered guests are from out of State Y. An action under the Federal Civil Rights Act of 1964 has been brought against E-Z-Rest Motel alleging that the motel discriminates on the basis of race and color. The motel contends that the statute cannot be applied to it because it is not engaged in interstate commerce. Can the federal government regulate this activity under the Interstate Commerce Clause? Why?

7. State Z enacted a Private Pension Benefits Protection Act requiring private employers with one hundred or more employees to pay a pension funding charge for terminating a pension plan or closing an office in State Z. Acme Steel Company closed its offices in State Z, whereupon the state assessed the company $185,000 under the vesting provisions of the Act. Acme challenged the constitutionality of the Act under the Contract Clause of the U.S. Constitution. Was the Act constitutional? Explain.

8. A state statute empowered public school principals to suspend students for up to ten days without any notice or hearing. A student who was suspended for ten days challenges the constitutionality of his suspension on the ground that he was denied due process. Was due process denied? Explain.

9. Iowa enacted a statute prohibiting the use of sixty-five-foot double-trailer-truck combinations. All of the other midwestern and western states permit such trucks to be used on their roads. Despite these restrictions, Iowa's statute permits cities abutting the state line to enact local ordinances adopting the length limitations of the adjoining state. In cases in which a city has exercised this option, otherwise-oversized trucks are permitted within the city limits and in nearby commercial zones. Consolidated Freightways is adversely affected by this statute and brings suit against Iowa, alleging that the statute violates the Commerce Clause. The District Court found that the evidence established that sixty-five-foot doubles were as safe as the shorter truck units. Does the statute violate the Commerce Clause? Explain.

10. Metropolitan Edison Company is a privately owned and operated Pennsylvania corporation subject to extensive regulation by the Pennsylvania Public Utility Commission. Under a provision of its general tariff filed with the commission, Edison had the right to discontinue electric service to any customer on reasonable notice of nonpayment of bills. Catherine Jackson had been receiving electricity from Metropolitan Edison when her account was terminated because of her delinquency in payments. Edison later opened a new account for her residence in the name of James Dodson, another occupant of Jackson's residence. In August of the following year, Dodson moved away and no further payments were made to the account. Finally, in October, Edison disconnected Jackson's service without any prior notice. Jackson brought suit claiming that her electric service could not be terminated without notice and a hearing. She further argued that such action, allowed by a provision of Edison's tariff filed with the commission, constituted "state action" depriving her of property in violation of the Fourteenth Amendment's guarantee of due process of law. Should Edison's actions be considered state action? Explain.

11. The McClungs own Ollie's Barbecue, a restaurant located a few blocks from the interstate highway in Birmingham, Alabama, with dining accommodations for whites only and a take-out service for blacks. In the year preceding the passage of the Civil Rights Act of 1964, the restaurant had purchased a substantial portion of the food it served from outside the state. The restaurant has refused to serve blacks since its original opening in 1927 and asserts that if it were required to serve blacks it would lose much of its business. The McClungs sought a declaratory judgment to render unconstitutional the application of the Civil Rights Act to their restaurant because their admitted racial discrimination did not restrict or significantly impede interstate commerce. Decision?

12. Miss Horowitz was admitted as an advanced medical student at the University of Missouri–Kansas City. During the spring of her first year, several faculty members expressed dissatisfaction with Miss Horowitz's clinical performance, noting that it was below that of her peers, that she was erratic in attendance at her clinical sessions, and that she lacked a critical concern for personal hygiene. Upon the recommendation of the school's Council on Evaluation, she was advanced to her second and final year on a probationary basis. After subsequent unfavorable reviews during her second year and a negative evaluation of her performance by seven practicing physicians, the council recommended that Miss Horowitz be dismissed from the school for her failure to meet academic standards. The decision was approved by the dean and later affirmed by the provost after an appeal by Miss Horowitz. She brought suit against the school's Board of Curators, claiming that her dismissal violated her right to procedural due process under the Fourteenth Amendment and deprived her of "liberty" by substantially impairing her opportunities to continue her medical education or return to employment in a medically related field. Is her claim correct? Explain.

13. Alabama law imposes a fee of $97.60 per ton for hazardous waste generated outside the state and disposed of at a commercial facility in Alabama. The fee for hazardous wastes generated within Alabama is $25.60 per ton. Chemical Waste Management, Inc., which operates a commercial hazardous waste land disposal facility in Emelle, Alabama, filed suit requesting a declaratory judgment that the Alabama law violated the Commerce Clause of the U.S. Constitution. Alabama argued that the additional fee of $72.00 served a legitimate local purpose related to its citizens' health and safety, given recent large increases in the hazardous waste received into the state and the possible adverse effects of such waste. Judgment? Explain.

TAKING SIDES

Alabama was one of only sixteen states that permitted commercial hazardous waste landfills. From 1985 through 1989, the tonnage of hazardous waste received per year more than doubled. Of this, up to 90 percent of the hazardous waste was shipped in from other states. In response, Alabama imposed a hazardous waste disposal fee of $72 per ton on hazardous waste generated outside the state and disposed of at a commercial facility in Alabama. The fee does not apply to such waste having a source in Alabama. (This law imposes a fee of $97.60 per ton for hazardous waste generated outside Alabama compared with a fee of $25.60 per ton for hazardous wastes generated within Alabama.)

Chemical Waste Management, Inc., which operates a commercial hazardous waste land disposal facility in Emelle, Alabama, filed suit asserting that the Alabama law violated the Commerce Clause of the U.S. Constitution.

a. What arguments could Chemical Waste Management, Inc. make in support of its claim that the statute is unconstitutional?

b. What arguments could Alabama make to defend the constitutionality of the statute?

c. Who should prevail? Explain.

CHAPTER **5**

Administrative Law

In all tyrannical governments, . . . the right both of making and enforcing the law is vested in . . . one and the same body of men; and wherever these two powers are united together, there can be no public liberty.

William Blackstone
(British Jurist, 1775)

CHAPTER OUTCOMES

After reading and studying this chapter, you should be able to:

1. Explain the three basic functions of administrative agencies.

2. Distinguish among the three types of rules promulgated by administrative agencies.

3. Explain the difference between formal and informal methods of adjudication.

4. Identify (a) the questions of law determined by a court in conducting a review of a rule or order of an administrative agency and (b) the three standards of judicial review of factual determinations made by administrative agencies.

5. Describe the limitations imposed on administrative agencies by the legislative branch, the executive branch, and the legally required disclosure of information.

Administrative agency
government entity (other than a court or legislature) having authority to affect the rights of private parties

A dministrative law is the branch of public law that is created by administrative agencies in the form of rules, regulations, orders, and decisions to carry out the regulatory powers and duties of those agencies. **Administrative agencies** are government entities—other than courts and legislatures—having authority to affect the rights of private parties through their operations. Administrative agencies, referred to by names such as commission, board, department, agency, administration, government corporation, bureau, or office, regulate a vast array of important matters involving national safety, welfare, and convenience. For instance, federal administrative agencies are charged with responsibility for national security, citizenship and naturalization, law enforcement, taxation, currency, elections, environmental protection, consumer protection, regulation of transportation, telecommunications, labor relations, trade, commerce, and securities markets, as well as with providing health and social services.

Because of the increasing complexity of the social, economic, and industrial life of the nation, the scope of administrative law has expanded enormously. In 1952, Justice Jackson observed that "the rise of administrative bodies has been the most significant legal trend of the last century, and perhaps more values today are affected by their decisions than by those of all the courts, review of administrative decisions apart." This observation is even more true in the twenty-first century, as evidenced by the great increase in the number and activities of federal government boards, commissions, and other agencies. Certainly, agencies create more legal rules and adjudicate more controversies than all the nation's legislatures and courts combined.

State agencies also play a significant role in the functioning of our society. Among the more important state boards and commissions are those that supervise and regulate banking, insurance, communications, transportation, public utilities, pollution control, and workers' compensation.

Much of the federal, state, and local law in this country is established by countless administrative agencies. These agencies, which many label the "fourth branch of government," possess tremendous power and have long been criticized as being "in reality miniature independent governments . . . which are a haphazard deposit of irresponsible agencies." Presidential Task Force Report (1937).

Despite such criticism, these administrative entities clearly play a significant and necessary role in our society. Administrative agencies relieve legislatures from the impossible burden of fashioning legislation that deals with every detail of a specific problem. As a result, Congress can enact legislation, such as the Federal Trade Commission Act, which prohibits unfair and deceptive trade practices, without having to define such a phrase specifically or to anticipate all the particular problems that may arise. Instead, Congress may pass an enabling statute that creates an agency—in this example, the Federal Trade Commission (FTC)—to which it can delegate the power to issue rules, regulations, and guidelines to carry out the statutory mandate. In addition, the establishment of separate, specialized bodies enables administrative agencies to be staffed by individuals with expertise in the field being regulated. Administrative agencies can thus develop the knowledge and devote the time necessary to provide continuous and flexible solutions to evolving regulatory problems.

In this chapter, we will discuss federal administrative agencies. Such agencies can be classified as either independent or executive. Executive agencies are those housed within the executive branch of government, while independent agencies are not. Many federal agencies are discussed in other parts of the text. More specifically, the FTC and Department of Justice are discussed in Chapter 42; the FTC and the Consumer Product Safety Commission (CPSC) in Chapter 44; the Department of Labor, National Labor Relations Board (NLRB) and Equal Employment Opportunity Commission (EEOC) in Chapter 41; the Securities and Exchange Commission (SEC) in Chapters 39 and 43; and the Environmental Protection Agency (EPA) in Chapter 45.

OPERATION OF ADMINISTRATIVE AGENCIES

Administrative process
entire set of activities
engaged in by administrative
agencies while carrying out
their rulemaking,
enforcement, and
adjudicative functions

Most administrative agencies perform three basic functions: (1) rulemaking, (2) enforcement, and (3) adjudication of controversies. The term **administrative process** refers to the entire set of activities in which administrative agencies engage while carrying out these functions. Administrative agencies exercise powers that have been allocated by the Constitution to the three separate branches of government. More specifically, an agency exercises legislative power when it makes rules, executive power when it enforces its enabling statute and its rules, and judicial power when it adjudicates disputes. This concentration of power has raised questions regarding the propriety of having the same bodies that establish the rules also act as prosecutors and judges in determining whether those rules have been violated. To address this issue and to bring about certain additional procedural reforms, the Administrative Procedure Act (APA) was enacted in 1946.

Rulemaking
process by which an
administrative agency
promulgates rules of law

Rulemaking

Rule
agency statement of general
or particular applicability
designed to implement,
interpret, or process law or
policy

Rulemaking is the process by which an administrative agency enacts or promulgates rules of law. Under the APA, a **rule** is "the whole or a part of an agency statement of general or particular applicability and future effect designed to implement, interpret, or process law or policy." Once promulgated, rules are applicable to all parties. Moreover, the process of rulemaking notifies all parties that the impending rule is being considered and provides concerned individuals with an opportunity to be heard. Administrative agencies promulgate three types of rules: legislative rules, interpretative rules, and procedural rules.

PRACTICAL ADVICE
*Keep informed of the
regulations issued by
administrative agencies
that affect your business.*

Legislative rules
substantive rules issued by
an administrative agency
under the authority
delegated to it by the
legislature

Legislative Rules   Legislative rules, often called regulations, are in effect "administrative statutes." **Legislative rules** are those issued by an agency having the ability, under a legislative delegation of power, to make rules having the force and effect of law. For example, the FTC has rulemaking power with which to elaborate upon its enabling statute's prohibition of unfair or deceptive acts or practices.

Legislative rules have the force of law if they are constitutional, within the power granted to the agency by the legislature, and issued according to proper procedure. To be constitutional, regulations must not violate any provisions of the U.S. Constitution, such as due process or equal protection. In addition, they may not involve an unconstitutional delegation of legislative power from the legislature to the agency. To be constitutionally permissible, the enabling statute granting power to an agency must establish reasonable standards to guide the agency in implementing the statute. This requirement has been met by such statutory language as "to prohibit unfair methods of competition," "fair and equitable," "public interest, convenience, and necessity," and other equally broad expressions. In any event, agencies may not exceed the actual authority granted by the enabling statute.

Diersen v. Chicago Car Exchange
United States Court of Appeals, Seventh Circuit, 1997
110 F.3d 481, cert. denied, 522 U.S. 868, 118 S.Ct. 178, 139 L.Ed.2d 119 (1997)
http://laws.findlaw.com/7th/961588.html

FACTS David Diersen filed a complaint against the Chicago Car Exchange (CCE), an automobile dealership, alleging that the CCE fraudulently furnished him an inaccurate odometer reading when it sold him a 1968 Dodge Charger, in violation of the Vehicle Information and Cost Savings Act ("the Odometer Act" or "the Act"). The Odometer Act requires all persons transferring a motor vehicle to give an accurate, written odometer reading to the purchaser or recipient of the transferred vehicle. Under the Act, those who disclose an inaccurate odometer reading with the intent to defraud are subject to a private cause of action by the purchaser and may be held liable for treble damages or $1,500, whichever is greater. The CCE had purchased the vehicle from Joseph Slaski, who certified to the CCE that the mileage was approximately 22,600. The CCE did not suspect that the odometer reading was inaccurate. After purchasing the vehicle, Diersen conducted an extensive investigation and discovered that the vehicle's title documents previously listed its mileage as 75,000. Before Diersen filed this lawsuit, the CCE offered to have Diersen return the car for a complete refund. Diersen refused this offer and decided instead to sue the CCE under the Act. The district court granted the defendant's motion for summary judgment, relying upon a regulation promulgated by the National Highway Traffic Safety Administration (NHTSA), which purports to exempt vehicles that are at least ten years old (such as the one Diersen purchased from the CCE) from the Act's odometer disclosure requirements. Diersen then filed a motion for reconsideration of the court's summary judgment order, arguing that the older-car exemption created by the NHTSA lacked any basis in the Act and was therefore invalid. The court denied Diersen's motion to reconsider and Diersen appealed.

DECISION That portion of the district court opinion which relied upon the NHTSA regulation as a ground for ruling in favor of the CCE is reversed, but the grant of summary judgment is affirmed on other grounds.

OPINION The CCE argues that in considering the validity of the NHTSA regulation, we must defer to the NHTSA's interpretation of the Act, because the NHTSA is the agency charged with administering the Act and thus has familiarity and expertise that we do not possess. We do defer to an administrative agency's reasonable construction of a statute if (as is not the case here) the statute is silent or ambiguous. On the other hand, "[i]f the intent of Congress is clear, that is the end of the matter; for the court, as well as the agency must give effect to the unambiguously expressed intent of Congress." Because the text of the Odometer Act does not even suggest a legislative intent to exempt entire classes of vehicles from the disclosure requirements of the Act, we hold that the regulation is invalid.

Our holding that the older-car exemption is invalid supports the broad purposes of the Act, which are "to prohibit tampering with motor vehicle odometers; and to provide safeguards to protect purchasers in the sale of motor vehicles." The statutory statement of purpose, read concomitantly with the language of the Act, which does not specify any exemptions, establishes that Congress intended to protect all purchasers of motor vehicles from odometer tampering.

Finally, we observe that the Act provides for the levying of civil and criminal fines against violators at the discretion of the NHTSA. In the exercise of prosecutorial discretion, the NHTSA may opt to conserve its resources by declining to prosecute certain classes of vehicles (e.g., those cases involving older vehicles). However, the NHTSA does not, without statutory authority, have jurisdiction to tell victims of odometer fraud that they are without a remedy if the car they purchased was ten or more years old. This effectively removes a cause of action that Congress has unambiguously provided to all victims of odometer fraud, regardless of the age of the vehicle being purchased.

Although we agree with Diersen that the NHTSA regulation is invalid, this does not end our inquiry. In order to succeed on his claim of odometer fraud, Diersen must also demonstrate an intent to defraud, for which we found no evidence. Therefore, we affirm the entry of summary judgment in the defendant's favor.

INTERPRETATION To be valid, legislative rules must not exceed the actual authority granted to the agency by the enabling statute.

ETHICAL QUESTION Did Diersen act fairly in refusing the CCE's offer of a full refund? Explain.

CRITICAL THINKING QUESTION Do you agree with the court's distinction between the agency's power to exercise prosecutorial discretion and its lack of power to deprive purchasers of a statutory remedy? Explain.

Legislative rules must be promulgated in accordance with the procedural requirements of the APA, although the enabling statute may impose more stringent requirements. Most legislative rules are issued in accordance with the *informal rulemaking* procedures of the APA, which require that the agency provide the following:

1. prior notice of a proposed rule, usually by publication in the *Federal Register;*
2. an opportunity for interested parties to participate in the rulemaking; and
3. publication of a final draft containing a concise general statement of the rule's basis and purpose at least thirty days before its effective date.

In some instances the enabling statute requires that certain rules be made only after the opportunity for an agency hearing. This formal rulemaking procedure is far more complex than the informal procedures and is governed by the same APA provisions that govern an adjudication, discussed later in this chapter. In *formal rulemaking*, the agency must consider the record of the trial-like agency hearing and include a statement of "findings and conclusions, and the reasons or basis therefore, on all the material issues of fact, law, or discretion presented on the record" when making rules.

Some enabling statutes direct that the agency, in making rules, use certain procedures that are more formal than those in informal rulemaking but do not compel the full hearing that formal rulemaking requires. This intermediate procedure, known as *hybrid rulemaking*, results from combining the informal procedures of the APA with the additional procedures specified by the enabling statute. For example, an agency may be required to conduct a legislative-type hearing (formal) that permits no cross-examination (informal).

In 1990, Congress enacted the Negotiated Rulemaking Act to encourage the involvement of affected parties in the initial stages of the policy-making process prior to the publication of notice of a proposed rule. The Act authorizes agencies to use negotiated rulemaking but does not require it. If an agency decides to use negotiated rulemaking, the affected parties and the agency develop an agreement and offer it to the agency. If accepted, the agreement becomes a basis for the proposed regulation, which is then published for comment.

Interpretative Rules **Interpretative rules** are agency-issued statements that explain how the agency construes its governing statute. For instance, the SEC "renders administrative interpretations of the law and regulations thereunder to members of the public, prospective registrants and others, to help them decide legal questions about the application of the law and the regulations to particular situations and to aid them in complying with the law." *The Work of the SEC* (1980).

These interpretative rules, however, which are exempt from the APA's procedural requirements of notice and comment, are *not* automatically binding on the private parties the agency regulates or on the courts, although they are given substantial weight. As the Supreme Court has stated, "The weight of such [an interpretative rule] in a particular case will depend upon the thoroughness evident in its consideration, the validity of its reasoning, its consistency with earlier and later pronouncements, and all those factors which give it power to persuade."

Procedural Rules **Procedural rules** are also exempt from the notice and comment requirements of the APA and are not law. These rules establish rules of conduct for practice before the agency, identify an agency's organization, and describe its method of operation. For example, the SEC's Rules of Practice deal with matters such as who may appear before the commission; business hours and notice of proceedings and hearings; settlements, agreements, and conferences; presentation of evidence and the taking of depositions and interrogatories; and review of hearings.

See Concept Review 5-1.

PRACTICAL ADVICE
Participate as early as possible in the rulemaking process of administrative agencies that affect your business.

Interpretative rules
statements issued by an administrative agency indicating its construction of its governing statute

Procedural rules
rules issued by an administrative agency establishing its organization, method of operation, and rules of conduct for practice before it

CONCEPT REVIEW 5-1

Administrative Rulemaking

Rule	Procedure	Effect
Legislative	Subject to APA	Binding
Interpretative	Exempt from APA	Persuasive
Procedural	Exempt from APA	Persuasive

© Cengage Learning 2013

Enforcement

process by which agencies determine whether their rules have been violated

Enforcement

Agencies also investigate conduct to determine whether the enabling statute or the agency's legislative rules have been violated. In carrying out this executive function, the agencies traditionally have been accorded great discretion, subject to constitutional limitations, to compel the disclosure of information. These limitations require that (1) the investigation is authorized by law and undertaken for a legitimate purpose, (2) the information sought is relevant, (3) the demand for information is sufficiently specific and not unreasonably burdensome, and (4) the information sought is not privileged.

For example, the following explains some of the SEC's investigative and enforcement functions:

Most of the Commission's investigations are conducted privately. Facts are developed to the fullest extent possible through informal inquiry, interviewing witnesses, examining brokerage records and other documents, reviewing and trading data, and similar means. The Commission is empowered to issue subpoenas requiring sworn testimony and the production of books, records, and other documents pertinent to the subject matter under investigation. In the event of refusal to respond to a subpoena, the Commission may apply to a Federal court for an order compelling obedience. *The Work of the SEC* (1986).

Adjudication

After concluding an investigation, the agency may use informal or formal methods to resolve the matter. Because the caseload of administrative agencies is vast, far greater than that of the judicial system, most matters are informally adjudicated. Informal procedures include advising, negotiating, and settling. In 1990 Congress enacted the Administrative Dispute Resolution Act to authorize and encourage federal agencies to use mediation, conciliation, arbitration, and other techniques for the prompt and informal resolution of disputes. The Act does not, however, require agencies to use alternative dispute resolution, and the affected parties must consent to its use.

PRACTICAL ADVICE

When available, consider using alternative methods of dispute resolution with administrative agencies.

Adjudication

formal methods by which an agency resolves disputes

Order

a final disposition made by an agency

The formal procedure by which an agency resolves a matter (called **adjudication**) involves finding facts, applying legal rules to the facts, and formulating orders. An **order** "means the whole or a part of a final disposition, whether affirmative, negative, injunctive or declaratory in form, of an agency." In essence an administrative trial, adjudication is used when the enabling statute so requires.

The procedures employed by the various administrative agencies to adjudicate cases are nearly as varied as the agencies themselves. Nevertheless, the APA does establish certain mandatory standards for those federal agencies the Act covers. For example, an agency must give notice of a hearing. The APA also requires that the agency give all interested parties the opportunity to submit and consider "facts, arguments, offers of settlement, or proposals of adjustment." In many cases this involves testimony and cross-examination of witnesses. If no settlement is reached, then a hearing must be held.

The hearing is presided over by an administrative law judge (ALJ) and is prosecuted by the agency. ALJs are appointed by the agency through a professional merit selection system and may be removed only for good cause. There are more than twice as many ALJs as there are federal judges. Juries are never used. Thus, the agency serves as both the prosecutor and decision maker. To reduce the potential for a conflict of interest, the APA provides for a separation of functions between those agency members engaged in investigation and prosecution and those involved in decision making.

Oral and documentary evidence may be introduced by either party, and all sanctions, rules, and orders must be based upon "consideration of the whole record or those parts cited by a party and supported by and in accordance with the reliable, probative, and substantial evidence." All decisions must include a statement of findings of fact and conclusions of law and the reasons or basis for them, as well as a statement of the appropriate rule, order, sanction, or relief.

If such are authorized by law and within its delegated jurisdiction, an agency may impose in its orders sanctions such as penalties; fines; the seizing of property; the assessment of damages, restitution, compensation, or fees; and the act of requiring, revoking, or suspending a license. In most instances, orders are final unless appealed, and failure to comply with an order subjects the party to a statutory penalty. If the order is appealed, the governing body of the agency may decide the case *de novo*. Thus, the agency may hear additional evidence and arguments in deciding whether to revise the findings and conclusions it made in the initial decision.

Although administrative adjudications mirror to a large extent the procedures of judicial trials, there are many differences between the two.

> Agency hearings, especially those dealing with rulemaking, often tend to produce evidence of general conditions as distinguished from facts relating solely to the respondent. Administrative agencies in rulemaking and occasionally in formal adversarial adjudications more consciously formulate policy than do courts. Consequently, administrative adjudications may require that the administrative law judge consider more consciously the impact of his decision upon the public interest as well as upon the particular respondent. . . . An administrative hearing is tried to an **administrative law judge**, never to a **jury**. Since many of the rules governing the admission of proof in judicial trials are designed to protect the jury from unreliable and possibly confusing evidence, it has long been asserted that such rules need not be applied at all or with the same vigor in proceedings solely before an administrative law judge. . . . Consequently, the technical common law rules governing the admissibility of evidence have generally been abandoned by administrative agencies. *McCormick on Evidence*, 4th ed., Section 350, p. 605.

American Airlines, Incorporated v. Department of Transportation
United States Court of Appeals, Fifth Circuit, 2000
202 F.3d 788, cert. denied, 530 U.S. 1284, 120 S.Ct. 2762, 147 L.Ed.2d 1022 (2000)
http://laws.findlaw.com/5th/9960008cv0v3.html

FACTS Prior to 1968, Dallas and Fort Worth operated independent and competing airports, one of which was Dallas's Love Field. The Department of Transportation's (DOT's) predecessor agency, the Civil Aeronautics Board (CAB), found that the competition between Dallas's and Fort Worth's airports was harmful and in 1964 ordered the cities to build a jointly operated airport that would serve as the region's primary airport. The cities responded by creating the Dallas-Fort Worth (DFW) Board and by jointly adopting the 1968 Regional Airport Concurrent Bond Ordinance (the "Ordinance"). The Ordinance authorized the issuance of bonds to finance the DFW Airport and contained the cities' agreement to phase out operations at the old airports and to transfer these activities to the DFW Regional Airport. The eight CAB-certified air carriers who were using the Dallas and Fort Worth airports first signed "letter agreements" and then later signed "use agreements" with the DFW Board, agreeing to move their air services to DFW as specified in the Ordinance. Southwest Airlines, which was solely running intrastate flights from Love Field and thus was exempt from CAB certification and pressure, refused to move to DFW and did not sign a use agreement. Litigation ensued over efforts to force Southwest from Love Field, terminating with a decision by the Fifth Circuit Court of Appeals that Southwest Airlines Co. has a federally declared right to the continued use of and access to Love Field, so long as Love Field remains open.

Shortly after Congress deregulated the airline industry in 1978, Southwest applied for permission to provide interstate service between Love Field and New Orleans. The CAB granted the application, concluding that it lacked power to deny it. Congress responded by enacting the Wright Amendment, which generally bans interstate service from Love Field. However, it and the 1997 Shelby Amendments provide certain exemptions from this ban, including the following: (1) the commuter airline exemption, which allows interstate "air transportation provided by commuter airlines operating aircraft with a passenger capacity of 56 passengers or less"; and (2) the contiguous state exemption, which allows flights to and from Louisiana, Arkansas, Oklahoma, New Mexico, Kansas, Alabama, and Mississippi if the flights do not "provide any through service or ticketing with another air carrier" and do not "offer for sale transportation to or from . . . any point which is outside any such State."

The airlines began offering additional flights from and to Love Field. Lawsuits to block the proposed additional service from Love Field were brought in state and federal court. At the urging of several of the parties, and while both the federal and state actions were pending, DOT initiated an interpretative proceeding and ultimately issued a "Declaratory Order" ruling that included the following provisions: (1) services at Love Field authorized by federal law may not be restricted by the cities of Dallas and Fort Worth; (2) the Wright and Shelby Amendments preempt the ability of the City of Dallas to limit the type of airline service operated at Love Field; (3) the commuter airline exemption overrides any agreement between the Cities of Dallas and Fort Worth; and (4) the Dallas-Fort Worth International Airport Board may not enforce any contract provision that allegedly bars an airline from operating interstate airline service at another airport in the DFW metropolitan area. In an accompanying "Procedural Order," DOT rejected various procedural objections raised by the parties. DOT subsequently reaffirmed its rulings on reconsideration. Several of the parties appealed challenging DOT's declaratory order on procedural grounds that DOT violated the Administrative Procedure Act (APA).

DECISION DOT's orders affirmed.

OPINION DOT issued its declaratory order after conducting an informal adjudication, pursuant to its authority under § 554(e) to "issue a declaratory ruling to terminate a controversy or remove uncertainty." Several parties object to DOT's failure to adhere to the APA's notice requirements for formal adjudications. However, in the absence of a statute requiring an agency to conduct its adjudication "on the record after opportunity for agency hearing," an agency can define its own procedures for conducting an informal adjudication.

While the APA does not expressly require notice in informal adjudications, courts have inferred a requirement that there be "some sort of procedures for notice [and] comment . . . as a necessary means of carrying out our responsibility for a thorough and searching review [of agency action]." Here, DOT issued an order in which it specified the legal issues on which it would rule, allowed the parties to submit comments on these issues, and extended the comment period at the request of several parties. It then ruled on precisely the issues that it identified. The DOT's actions satisfied the minimum procedural notice requirements. Fort Worth contends that DOT failed to comply with § 554(b) by neglecting to notify parties that DOT would also be considering a factual issue: the effect of increased service at Love Field on DFW Airport. This argument fails for two reasons. First, as noted, the formal notice requirement of § 554(b) does not apply to an informal adjudication. Second, the parties were effectively on notice of this issue since it was one that they could reasonably expect to arise given the issues of which DOT gave notice. The DFW Board's argument that DOT's order amounts to a substantive rule subject to the notice and comment provision of the APA is rejected. Agencies have discretion to choose between adjudication and rulemaking as a means of setting policy. In determining whether an agency action constituted adjudication or rulemaking,

courts look to the product of the agency action and accord significant deference to an agency's characterization of its own action. Since the APA defines "adjudication" as the "agency process for formulating an order," and DOT classifies its ruling as a declaratory order, the agency engaged in adjudication rather than rulemaking. Furthermore, because DOT's order interpreted the rights of a small number of parties properly before it, DOT did not abuse its discretion by acting through an adjudicatory proceeding.

INTERPRETATION While the APA does not expressly require notice in informal adjudications, courts have inferred there must be some procedures for notice and comment.

CRITICAL THINKING QUESTION Why is it so important that administrative agencies provide prior notice of proposed rules and adjudications?

LIMITS ON ADMINISTRATIVE AGENCIES

An important and fundamental part of administrative law is the limits imposed by judicial review upon the activities of administrative agencies. On matters of policy, however, courts are not supposed to substitute their judgment for the agency's judgment. Additional limitations arise from the legislature and the executive branch, which, unlike the judiciary, may address the wisdom and correctness of an agency's decision or action. See Figure 5-1, which illustrates the limits on administrative agencies. Moreover, legally required disclosure of agency actions provides further protection for the public.

Judicial review

acts as a control or check by a court on a particular rule or order of an administrative agency

Judicial Review

As discussed in Chapter 4, judicial review describes the process by which the courts examine government action. Judicial review, which is available unless a statute precludes such review or

Figure 5-1 Limits on Administrative Agencies

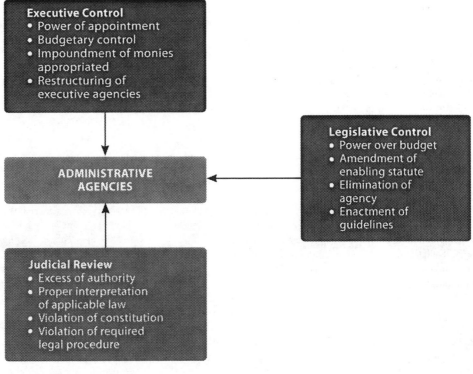

© Cengage Learning 2013

the agency action is committed to agency discretion by law, acts as a control or check on a particular rule or order of an administrative agency.

PRACTICAL ADVICE

Be sure to exhaust all of your administrative remedies before seeking judicial review of action taken by an administrative agency.

General Requirements Parties seeking to challenge agency action must have standing and must have exhausted their administrative remedies. Standing requires that the agency action injure the party in fact and that the party assert an interest that is in the "zone of interests to be protected or regulated by the statute in question." Judicial review is ordinarily available only for *final* agency action. Accordingly, if a party seeks review while an agency proceeding is in progress, a court will usually dismiss the action because the party has failed to exhaust his administrative remedies.

Summers v. Earth Island Institute
Supreme Court of the United States, 2009
555 U.S. 488, 129 S.Ct. 1142, 173 L.Ed.2d 1
http://scholar.google.com/scholar_case?case=5706931806999628341&q=555+U.S.+488&hl=en&as_sdt=2,34

FACTS In 1992, Congress enacted legislation requiring the Forest Service to establish a notice, comment, and appeal process for proposed actions of the Forest Service concerning projects and activities implementing land and resource management plans. The Forest Service's regulations implementing this legislation provided that certain of its procedures would not be applied to projects that the Service considered categorically excluded from the requirement to file an environmental impact statement (EIS) or environmental assessment (EA). Later amendments to the Forest Service's manual of implementing procedures, adopted by rule after notice and comment, provided that fire-rehabilitation activities on areas of less than 4,200 acres, and salvage-timber sales of 250 acres or less, did not cause a significant environmental impact and thus would be categorically exempt from the requirement to file an EIS or EA. This had the effect of excluding these projects from the notice, comment, and appeal process.

In the summer of 2002, fire burned a significant area of the Sequoia National Forest. In September 2003, the Service issued a decision memo approving the Burnt Ridge Project, a salvage sale of timber on 238 acres damaged by that fire. Pursuant to its categorical exclusion of salvage sales of less than 250 acres, the Forest Service did not provide notice in a form consistent with the Appeals Reform Act, did not provide a period of public comment, and did not make an appeal process available.

In December 2003, the plaintiffs—a group of organizations dedicated to protecting the environment ("Earth Island")—filed a complaint, challenging the failure of the Forest Service to apply to the Burnt Ridge Project its regulations implementing requiring prior notice and comment and setting forth an appeal procedure. The District Court granted a preliminary injunction against the sale, and the parties then settled their dispute as to Burnt Ridge. Although concluding that the sale was no longer at issue, and despite the government's argument that the plaintiffs therefore lacked standing to challenge the regulations, the court nevertheless proceeded to adjudicate the merits of their challenges, invalidating several regulations, including the notice and comment and the appeal provisions, and entered a nationwide injunction against their application.

The Ninth Circuit held that Earth Island's challenges to regulations not at issue in the Burnt Ridge Project were not ripe for adjudication because there was not a sufficient case or controversy before the court to sustain a challenge. It affirmed, however, the District Court's determination that the regulations applicable to the Burnt Ridge Project were contrary to law and upheld the nationwide injunction against their application. The government sought review of the question whether Earth Island could challenge the regulations at issue in the Burnt Ridge Project, and if so whether a nationwide injunction was appropriate relief. The U.S. Supreme Court granted *certiorari*.

DECISION The judgment of the Court of Appeals is reversed in part and affirmed in part.

OPINION In limiting the judicial power to "Cases" and "Controversies," Article III of the Constitution restricts courts to redressing or preventing actual or imminently threatened injury to persons caused by private or official violation of law. This limitation "is founded in concern about the proper—and properly limited—role of the courts in a democratic society."

The doctrine of standing reflects this fundamental limitation. It requires that "the plaintiff has 'alleged such a personal stake in the outcome of the controversy' as to warrant *his* invocation of federal-court jurisdiction." He bears the burden of showing that he has standing for each type of relief sought. To seek injunctive relief, a plaintiff must show that he is under threat of suffering "injury in fact" that is concrete and particularized; the threat must be actual and imminent, not conjectural or hypothetical; it must be fairly traceable to the challenged action of the defendant; and it must be likely that a favorable judicial decision will prevent or redress the injury.

The regulations under challenge here neither require nor forbid any action on the part of the plaintiffs. "[W]hen the plaintiff is not himself the object of the government action or inaction he challenges, standing is not precluded, but it is ordinarily 'substantially more difficult' to establish." Here, the plaintiffs can demonstrate standing only if application of the regulations by the government will affect *them* in the manner described above.

As organizations, the plaintiffs can assert the standing of their members. While generalized harm to the forest or the environment will not alone support standing, if that harm in fact affects the recreational or even the mere esthetic interests of the plaintiffs, that will suffice.

The plaintiffs' argument that they have standing based on Burnt Ridge fails because, after voluntarily settling the portion of their lawsuit relevant to Burnt Ridge, the plaintiffs and their members are no longer under threat of injury from that project. Moreover, the plaintiffs have identified no other application of the invalidated regulations that threatens imminent and concrete harm to the interests of their members

The plaintiffs argue that they have standing to bring their challenge because they have suffered procedural injury, namely that they have been denied the ability to file comments on some Forest Service actions and will continue to be so denied. But deprivation of a procedural right without some concrete interest that is affected by the deprivation is insufficient to create Article III standing.

INTERPRETATION The doctrine of standing requires a plaintiff seeking injunctive relief to show that he is under threat of suffer-

ing injury in fact that is concrete and particularized; the threat is actual and imminent; the threat is fairly traceable to the challenged action of the defendant; and it is likely that a favorable judicial decision will prevent or redress the injury.

CRITICAL THINKING QUESTION What policy reasons support and which oppose the standing requirement?

In exercising judicial review, the court may decide either to compel agency action unlawfully withheld or to set aside impermissible agency action. In making its determination, the court must review the whole record and may set aside agency action only if the error is prejudicial.

Questions of Law When conducting a review, a court decides all relevant questions of law, interprets constitutional and statutory provisions, and determines the meaning or applicability of the terms of an agency action. This review of questions of law includes determining whether the agency has (1) exceeded its authority, (2) properly interpreted the applicable law, (3) violated any constitutional provision, or (4) acted contrary to the procedural requirements of the law.

Questions of Fact When reviewing factual determinations, the courts use one of three different standards. Where informal rulemaking or informal adjudication has occurred, the standard generally is the *arbitrary and capricious* test, which requires only that the agency had a rational basis for reaching its decision. Where there has been a formal hearing, the substantial evidence test usually applies. It also applies to informal or hybrid rulemaking if the enabling statute so requires. The *substantial evidence* test requires the conclusions reached to be supported by "such relevant evidence as a reasonable mind might accept as adequate to support a conclusion." Finally, in rare instances, the reviewing court may apply the *unwarranted by the facts* standard, which permits the court to try the facts *de novo*. This strict review is available only when the enabling statute so provides, when the agency has conducted an adjudication with inadequate fact-finding procedures, or when issues that were not before the agency are raised in a proceeding to enforce nonadjudicative agency action.

FCC v. Fox Television Stations
Supreme Court of the United States, 2009
556 U.S. ___, 129 S.Ct. 1800, 173 L.Ed.2d 738
http://www.law.cornell.edu/supct/html/07-582.ZO.html

FACTS Federal law bans the broadcasting of "any . . . indecent . . . language," which includes references to sexual or excretory activity or organs. Congress has given the Federal Communications Commission (FCC) various means of enforcing this indecency ban, including civil fines, license revocations, and the denial of license renewals. The Commission first invoked the statutory ban on indecent broadcasts in 1975, declaring a daytime broadcast of George Carlin's "Filthy Words" monologue actionably indecent. In the ensuing years, the Commission took a cautious, but gradually expanding, approach to enforcing the statutory prohibition against indecent broadcasts. Although the Commission had expanded its enforcement beyond the "repetitive use of specific words or phrases," it preserved a distinction between literal and nonliteral (or "expletive") uses of evocative language. The Commission explained that each literal "description or depiction of sexual or excretory functions must be examined in context to determine whether it is patently offensive," but that "deliberate and repetitive use . . . is a requisite to a finding of indecency" when a complaint focuses solely on the use of nonliteral exple-

tives. In 2004, the FCC's *Golden Globes Order* declared for the first time that an expletive (nonliteral) use of the F-Word or the Sh-Word could be actionably indecent, even when the word is used only once. The first order to this effect dealt with an NBC broadcast of the Golden Globe Awards, in which the performer Bono commented, "This is really, really, f* * *ing brilliant."

This case concerns utterances in two live broadcasts aired by Fox Television Stations, Inc., and its affiliates prior to the Commission's *Golden Globes Order*. The first occurred during the 2002 Billboard Music Awards, when the singer Cher exclaimed, "I've also had critics for the last 40 years saying that I was on my way out every year. Right. So f* * * 'em." The second involved a segment of the 2003 Billboard Music Awards, during the presentation of an award by Nicole Richie and Paris Hilton, principals in a Fox television series called "The Simple Life." Ms. Hilton began their interchange by reminding Ms. Richie to "watch the bad language," but Ms. Richie proceeded to ask the audience, "Why do they even call it 'The Simple Life?' Have you ever tried to get cow s* * * out of a Prada purse? It's not so f* * *ing simple." Following each of these broadcasts, the Commission received numerous complaints from parents whose children were exposed to the language.

In 2006, the FCC found both broadcasts to have violated the prohibition against indecency. The FCC's order stated that the *Golden Globes Order* eliminated any doubt that fleeting expletives could be actionable; declared that under the new policy, a lack of repetition weighs against a finding of indecency, but is not a safe harbor; and held that both broadcasts met the new test because one involved a literal description of excrement and both invoked the F-Word. The order did not impose sanctions for either broadcast. The Second Circuit set aside the agency action, declining to address the constitutionality of the FCC's action but finding the FCC's reasoning inadequate under the Administrative Procedure Act (APA).

DECISION The judgment of the United States Court of Appeals for the Second Circuit is reversed, and the case is remanded.

OPINION The APA permits the setting aside of agency action that is "arbitrary" or "capricious." Under this narrow standard of review, an agency must "examine the relevant data and articulate a satisfactory explanation for its action." However, a court is not to substitute its judgment for that of the agency and should uphold a decision of less than ideal clarity if the agency's path may reasonably be discerned.

In overturning the Commission's judgment, the Court of Appeals relied in part on Circuit precedent requiring a more substantial explanation for agency action that changes prior policy. The Second Circuit has interpreted the APA and Supreme Court precedent as requiring agencies to make clear "why the original reasons for adopting the [displaced] rule or policy are no longer dispositive" as well as "why the new rule effectuates the statute as well as or better than the old rule."

There is no basis in the APA or in Supreme Court opinions for a requirement that all agency change be subjected to more searching review. The requirement that an agency provide reasoned explanation for its action would ordinarily demand that it display awareness that it *is* changing position. The agency must show that there are good reasons for the new policy. But it need not demonstrate to a court's satisfaction that the reasons for the new policy are *better* than the reasons for the old one; it suffices that the new

policy is permissible under the statute, that there are good reasons for it, and that the agency *believes* it to be better, which the conscious change of course adequately indicates. This means that the agency need not always provide a more detailed justification than what would suffice for a new policy created on a blank slate. Sometimes it must: for example, when its new policy rests upon factual findings that contradict those which underlay its prior policy or when its prior policy has engendered serious reliance interests that must be taken into account. It would be arbitrary or capricious to ignore such matters. In such cases it is not that further justification is demanded by the mere fact of policy change, but rather that a reasoned explanation is needed for disregarding facts and circumstances that underlay or were engendered by the prior policy.

Judged under these standards, the Commission's new enforcement policy and its order finding the broadcasts actionably indecent were neither arbitrary nor capricious. First, the Commission forthrightly acknowledged that its recent actions have broken new ground, taking account of inconsistent "prior Commission and staff action" and explicitly disavowing them as "no longer good law." There is no doubt that the Commission knew it was making a change. That is why it declined to assess penalties.

Moreover, the agency's reasons for expanding the scope of its enforcement activity were entirely rational. Even isolated utterances can be made in "pander[ing,] . . . vulgar and shocking" manners and can constitute harmful "first blow[s]" to children. It is rational to believe that a safe harbor for single words would "likely lead to more widespread use of the offensive language."

The Supreme Court is a court of final review, "not of first view." Because the Second Circuit did not definitively rule on the constitutionality of the Commission's orders, the Supreme Court declined to address the constitutional questions.

INTERPRETATION For agency action to be upheld on review under the Administrative Procedure Act's "arbitrary or capricious" standard, the agency must have examined relevant data and articulated a satisfactory explanation for its action.

CRITICAL THINKING QUESTION What policies support limitations on judicial review of agency action? Were these policies implicated in this case?

Legislative Control

The legislature may exercise control over administrative agencies in various ways. Through its budgetary power, it may greatly restrict or expand an agency's operations. Congress may amend an enabling statute to increase, modify, or decrease an agency's authority. Even more drastically, it may completely eliminate an agency. Or, Congress may establish general guidelines to govern agency action, as it did by enacting the APA. Moreover, it may reverse or change an agency rule or decision by specific legislation. In addition, each house of Congress has oversight committees that review the operations of administrative agencies. Finally, the Senate has the power of confirmation over some high-level appointments to administrative agencies.

In 1996 Congress enacted the Congressional Review Act, which subjects most rules to a new, extensive form of legislative control. With limited exceptions, the Act requires agencies to submit newly adopted rules to each house of Congress before they can take effect. If the rule is a major rule, it does not become final until Congress has had an opportunity to disapprove it. A **major rule** is any rule that the Office of Management and Budget (OMB) finds has resulted in or is likely to result in (1) an annual effect on the economy of at least $100 million; (2) a major increase in costs or prices; or (3) a significant adverse effect on competition, employment, investment, productivity, innovation, or international competitiveness of U.S. enterprises. If the rule is not a major rule, it takes effect as it otherwise would have after its submission to Congress; it is subject to possible disapproval by Congress. All rules covered by the Act shall not take effect if Congress adopts a joint resolution of disapproval. The President may veto the joint resolution, but Congress may then vote to override the veto. A rule that has been disapproved is treated as though it had never taken effect.

Control by Executive Branch

By virtue of their power to appoint and remove their chief administrators, U.S. Presidents have significant control over the administrative agencies housed within the executive branch. With respect to independent agencies, however, the President has less control because commissioners serve for a fixed term that is staggered with the President's term of office. Nevertheless, his power to appoint agency chairs and to fill vacancies confers considerable control, as does his power to remove commissioners for statutorily defined cause. The President's central role in the budgeting process of agencies also enables him to exert great control over agency policy and operations. Even more extreme is the President's power to impound monies appropriated to an agency by Congress. In addition, the President may radically alter, combine, or even abolish agencies of the executive branch unless either house of Congress disapproves such an act within a prescribed time.

Disclosure of Information

Requiring administrative agencies to disclose information about their actions makes them more accountable to the public. Accordingly, Congress has enacted disclosure statutes to enhance public and political oversight of agency activities. These statutes include the Freedom of Information Act (FOIA), the Privacy Act, and the Government in the Sunshine Act.

Freedom of Information Act First enacted in 1966, FOIA gives the public access to most records in the files of federal administrative agencies. Once a person has requested files, an agency must indicate within ten working days whether it intends to comply with the request and must within a reasonable time respond to the request. The agency may charge a fee for providing the records.

FOIA permits agencies to deny access to nine categories of records: (1) records specifically authorized in the interest of national defense or foreign policy to be kept secret; (2) records that relate solely to the internal personnel rules and practices of an agency; (3) records specifically exempted by statute from disclosure; (4) trade secrets and commercial or financial information that is privileged or confidential; (5) interagency or intraagency memorandums; (6) personnel and medical files, the disclosure of which would constitute a clearly unwarranted invasion of personal privacy; (7) investigatory records compiled for law enforcement purposes; (8) records that relate to the regulation or supervision of financial institutions; and (9) certain geological and geophysical information and data.

The Electronic FOIA Amendments require agencies to provide public access to information in an electronic format. Agencies must, within one year after their creation, make records available by computer telecommunications or other electronic means.

Privacy Act The Privacy Act protects certain government records pertaining to individuals that a federal agency maintains and retrieves by an individual's name or other personal identifier, including social security number. In general, the Privacy Act prohibits unauthorized disclosures of those records covered by the Act. It also gives individuals the right to review and copy records about themselves, to find out whether these records have been disclosed, and to request corrections or amendments of these records, unless the records are legally exempt. It also requires agencies to maintain in their records only that information about an individual that is relevant and necessary to accomplish an agency function and to collect information to the greatest extent practicable directly from the individual.

Government in the Sunshine Act The Government in the Sunshine Act requires meetings of many federal agencies to be open to the public. This Act applies to multimember bodies whose members the President appoints with the advice and consent of the Senate, such as the SEC, the FTC, the Federal Communications Commission, the CPSC, and the Commodity Futures Trading

PRACTICAL ADVICE

Be aware that the Freedom of Information Act may give the public access to information you provide to administrative agencies.

Ethical Dilemma

Should the Terminally Ill Be Asked to Await FDA Approval of Last-Chance Treatments?

Facts Mrs. Barnett is a seventy-three-year-old widow who has just been diagnosed with ovarian cancer. Because of the lack of adequate screening procedures for this type of cancer, Mrs. Barnett's cancer has long gone undetected and has progressed considerably.

Dr. Jason, Mrs. Barnett's doctor, will perform immediate surgery, but the surgery will not effectively cure the cancer. He has recommended that she undergo rigorous chemotherapy on a monthly basis for eighteen months following surgery. Thereafter, an exploratory operation can be conducted to assess the success of the treatment. The proposed chemotherapy will cause severe side effects, including nausea, oral lesions, and complete hair loss.

Dr. Jason has informed Mrs. Barnett and her two daughters, June and Sarina, that although chemotherapy will defer their mother's immediate death, her chances of a recovery are slim. Dr. Jason stated that while, on average, one in three patients undergoing such treatment could expect to recover, he believed Mrs. Barnett's recovery was highly unlikely. A second opinion from a reputable cancer treatment center confirmed Dr. Jason's diagnosis and recommendations for treatment.

Sarina has heard of an experimental cancer drug being tested in Europe. Thus far the results seem promising. Though the drug may be obtained in Europe, it is not yet legal in the United States. The Food and Drug Administration (FDA) has just begun to review the drug, but it will be years before the drug could receive FDA approval.

Sarina is strongly opposed to the painful regimen of chemotherapy that has been proposed, particularly because the treatment seems futile. She wants to fly to Europe, obtain the experimental drug, and return with it to the United States. Mrs. Barnett is much too ill to travel. June, on the other hand, is opposed to any course of treatment that does not have the approval of the FDA. Mrs. Barnett, who is weak and confused, is looking to her daughters for guidance.

Social, Policy, and Ethical Considerations

1. If Mrs. Barnett were your mother, what recommendation would you make? Under the circumstances, is it unethical to use a drug that has not been approved by the FDA?
2. As a policy matter, how should the FDA handle drugs for life-threatening diseases?
3. Should individuals be allowed absolute freedom to take risks with drug therapy?
4. Should the FDA apply different drug approval standards with regard to children who suffer from life-threatening diseases?
5. As policy matter, how should the government and nonprofit organizations allocate resources among research groups competing for funding? How should the government, through its administrative agencies, establish priorities for funding research on various illnesses?

Commission. The Act does not cover executive agencies such as the EPA, the Food and Drug Administration (FDA), and the National Highway Safety Administration (NHTSA).

Agencies generally may close meetings on the same grounds upon which they may refuse disclosure of records under FOIA. In addition, agencies such as the SEC and the Federal Reserve Board may close meetings to protect information the disclosure of which would lead to financial speculation or endanger the stability of financial institutions. The Sunshine Act also permits agencies to close meetings that concern agency participation in pending or anticipated litigation.

CHAPTER SUMMARY

Operation of Administrative Agencies

Rulemaking process by which an administrative agency promulgates rules of law

- *Legislative Rules* substantive rules issued by an administrative agency under the authority delegated to it by the legislature
- *Interpretative Rules* statements issued by an administrative agency indicating how it construes its governing statute
- *Procedural Rules* rules issued by an administrative agency establishing its organization, method of operation, and rules of conduct for practice before the agency

Enforcement process by which agencies determine whether their rules have been violated

Adjudication formal methods by which an agency resolves disputes

Limits on Administrative Agencies

Judicial Review acts as a control or check by a court on a particular rule or order of an administrative agency

Legislative Control includes control over the agency's budget and enabling statute

Control by Executive Branch includes the President's power to appoint members of the agency

Disclosure of Information congressionally required public disclosure enhances oversight of agency activities

CASE PROBLEMS

1. Congress passed the Emergency Price Control Act in the interest of national defense and security. The stated purpose of the Act was "to stabilize prices and to prevent speculative, unwarranted and abnormal increases in prices and rents." The Act established the Office of Price Administration, which was authorized to establish maximum prices and rents that were to be "generally fair and equitable and [were to] effectuate the purposes of this Act." Stark was convicted for selling beef at prices in excess of those set by the agency. Stark appeals on the ground that the Act unconstitutionally delegated to the agency the legislative power of Congress to control prices. Is Stark correct in this contention?

2. The Secretary of Commerce (Secretary) published a notice in the *Federal Register* inviting comments regarding flammability standards for mattresses. Statistical data were compiled, consultant studies were conducted, and seventy-five groups submitted comments. The Secretary then determined that all mattresses, including crib mattresses, must pass a cigarette test, consisting of bringing a mattress in contact with a burning cigarette. The department's staff supported this position by stating: "Exemption of youth and crib mattresses is not recommended. While members of these age groups do not smoke, their parents frequently do, and the accidental dropping of a lighted cigarette on these mattresses while attending to a child is a distinct possibility." Bunny Bear, Inc., now challenges the cigarette flammability test, asserting that the standard was not shown to be applicable to crib mattresses, as "infants and young children obviously do not smoke." Bunny Bear argues that the Secretary has not satisfied the burden of proof justifying the inclusion of crib mattresses within this general safety standard. Is Bunny Bear correct? Explain.

3. Reagan National Airport in Washington, D.C., is one of the busiest and most crowded airports in the nation. Accordingly, the Federal Aviation Administration (FAA) has restricted the number of commercial landing and takeoff slots at National to forty per hour. Allocation of the slots among the air carriers serving National had been by voluntary agreement through an airline scheduling committee (ASC). When a new carrier requested twenty slots during peak hours, National's ASC was unable to agree on a slot allocation schedule. The FAA engaged in informal rulemaking and invited public comment as a means to solve the slot allocation dilemma. The FAA then issued Special Federal Aviation Regulation 43 (SFAR 43) based on public comments and a proposal made at the last National ASC meeting, thereby decreasing the number of slots held by current carriers and shifting some slots to less desirable times. SFAR 43 also granted eighteen slots to New York Air. More specifically, SFAR 43 requires five carriers to give up one or more slots in specific hours during the day,

requires twelve carriers to shift one slot to the latest hour of operations, and then reserves and allocates the yielded slots among the new entrants and several other carriers. Northwest Airlines seeks judicial review of SFAR 43, claiming that it is arbitrary, capricious, and not a product of reasoned decision making, and that it capriciously favors the Washington–New York market as well as the new carrier. What standard would apply to the agency's actions? Should Northwest prevail? Explain.

4. Bachowski was defeated in a United Steelworkers of America union election. After exhausting his union remedies, Bachowski filed a complaint with Secretary of Labor Dunlop. Bachowski invoked the Labor-Management Reporting and Disclosure Act, which required Dunlop to investigate the complaint and determine whether to bring a court action to set aside the election. Dunlop decided such action was unwarranted. Bachowski then filed an action in a federal district court to order Dunlop to file suit to set aside the election. What standard of review would apply and what would Bachowski have to prove to prevail under that standard?

5. The Federal Crop Insurance Corporation (FCIC) was created as a wholly government-owned corporation to insure wheat producers against unavoidable crop failure. As required by law, the FCIC published in the *Federal Register* conditions for crop insurance. Specifically, the FCIC published that spring wheat reseeded on winter wheat acreage was ineligible for coverage. When farmer Merrill applied for insurance on his wheat crop, he informed the local FCIC agent that 400 of his 460 acres of spring wheat were reseeded on the winter acreage. The agent advised Merrill that his entire crop was insurable. When drought destroyed Merrill's wheat, Merrill tried to collect the insurance, but the FCIC refused to pay, asserting that Merrill is bound by the notice provided by publication of the regulation in the *Federal Register*. Is the FCIC correct? Explain.

6. The Department of Energy (DOE) issued a subpoena requesting information regarding purchases, sales, exchanges, and other transactions in crude oil from Phoenix Petroleum Company (Phoenix). The aim of the DOE audit was to uncover violations of the Emergency Petroleum Allocation Act of 1973 (EPAA). The EPAA contained provisions for summary, or expedited, enforcement of DOE decisions. However, after the subpoena was issued but before Phoenix had responded, the EPAA expired. The EPAA provided that

> The authority to promulgate and amend any regulation, or to issue any order under this Chapter shall expire at midnight September 30, 1981, but such expiration shall not affect any action or pending proceedings, administrative, civil or criminal action or proceeding, whether

or not pending, based upon any act committed or liability incurred prior to such expiration date.

Using the summary enforcement provisions of the now-defunct EPAA, the DOE sues to enforce the subpoena. Phoenix argues that because the EPAA has expired, the DOE lacks the authority either to issue the subpoena or to use the summary enforcement provisions. Is Phoenix correct? Why?

7. Under the Communications Act of 1934 the Federal Communications Commission may not impose common carrier obligations on cable operators. A common carrier is one that "makes a public offering to provide [communication facilities] whereby all members of the public who choose to employ such facilities may communicate or transmit." In May 1976, the Commission issued rules requiring cable television systems of a designated size (a) to develop a minimum ten-channel capacity by 1986; (b) to make available on a first-come, nondiscriminatory basis certain channels for access by third parties; and (c) to furnish equipment and facilities for such access. The purpose of these rules was to ensure public access to the cable systems. Midwest Video Corporation claimed that the access rules exceeded the Commission's jurisdiction granted it by the Communications Act of 1934, because the rules infringe upon the cable systems' journalistic freedom by in effect treating the cable operators as "common carriers." The Commission contended that its expansive mandate under the Communications Act to supervise and regulate broadcasting encompassed the access rules. Did the Commission exceed its authority under the Act?

8. Congress enacted the National Traffic and Motor Vehicle Safety Act of 1966 (the Act) for the purpose of reducing the number of traffic accidents that result in death or personal injury. The Act directs the Secretary of Transportation to issue motor vehicle safety standards in order to improve the design and safety features of cars. The Secretary has delegated authority to promulgate safety standards to the National Highway Traffic Safety Administration (NHTSA) under the informal rulemaking procedure of the APA. The Act also authorizes judicial review under the provisions of the Administrative Procedure Act (APA) of all orders establishing, amending, or revoking a federal motor vehicle safety standard issued by the NHTSA.

Pursuant to the Act, the NHTSA issued Motor Vehicle Safety Standard 208, which required all cars made after September 1982 to be equipped with passive restraints (either automatic seatbelts or airbags). The cost of implementing the standard was estimated to be around $1 billion. However, early in 1981, due to changes in economic circumstances and particularly due to complaints from the automotive industry, the NHTSA rescinded Standard 208. The NHTSA had originally assumed that car manufacturers would install airbags in 60 percent of new cars and passive seatbelts in 40 percent. However, by 1981 it appeared that manufacturers were planning to install seatbelts in 99 percent of all new cars. Moreover, the majority of passive seatbelts could be easily and permanently detached by consumers. Therefore, the NHTSA felt that Standard 208 would not result in any significant safety benefits. State Farm Mutual Automobile Insurance Company (State Farm) and the National Association of Independent Insurers (NAII) filed petitions in federal court for review of the NHTSA's rescission of Standard 208. What standard of review would apply to the recission? Should it be set aside? Explain.

TAKING SIDES

Section 7 (a)(2) of the Endangered Species Act of 1973 (ESA) provides (in relevant part) that

> [e]ach Federal agency shall, in consultation with and with the assistance of the Secretary (of the Interior), insure that any action authorized, funded, or carried out by such agency . . . is not likely to jeopardize the continued existence of any endangered species or threatened species or result in the destruction or adverse modification of habitat of such species which is determined by the Secretary, after consultation as appropriate with affected States, to be critical.

In 1978, the Fish and Wildlife Service and the National Marine Fisheries Service, on behalf of the Secretary of the Interior and the Secretary of Commerce respectively, promulgated a joint regulation stating that the obligations imposed by Section 7(a)(2) extend to actions taken in foreign nations. In 1983, the Interior Department proposed a revised joint regulation that would require consultation only for actions taken in the United States or on the high seas. Shortly thereafter, Defenders of Wildlife and other organizations filed an action against the Secretary of the Interior, seeking a declaratory judgment that the new regulation is in error as to the geographic scope of Section 7(a)(2) and an injunction requiring the Secretary to promulgate a new regulation restoring the initial interpretation. The Secretary asserted that the plaintiffs did not have standing to bring this action.

a. What arguments would support the plaintiff's standing to bring this action?
b. What arguments would support Secretary's claim that plaintiffs did not have standing to bring this action?
c. Which side's arguments are most convincing? Explain.

CHAPTER **6**

Criminal Law

These guys commit their crimes with a pencil instead of a gun.

Bronx District Attorney
(speaking about corporate crime to The New York Times, 1985)

CHAPTER OUTCOMES

After reading and studying this chapter, you should be able to:

1. Describe criminal intent and the various degrees of mental fault.

2. Identify the significant features of white-collar crimes, corporate crimes, and Racketeer Influenced and Corrupt Organizations Act (RICO).

3. List and define the crimes against business.

4. Describe the defenses of person or property, duress, mistake of fact, and entrapment.

5. List and explain the constitutional amendments affecting criminal procedure.

A s we discussed in Chapter 1, the civil law defines duties the violation of which constitutes a wrong against the injured party. The criminal law, on the other hand, establishes duties the violation of which is a societal wrong against the whole community. Civil law is a part of private law, whereas criminal law is a part of public law. In a civil action, the injured party sues to recover compensation for the damage and injury that he has sustained as a result of the defendant's wrongful conduct. The party bringing a civil action (the plaintiff) has the burden of proof, which he must sustain by a preponderance (greater weight) of the evidence. The purpose of the civil law is to compensate the aggrieved party.

Criminal law is designed to prevent harm to society by defining criminal conduct and establishing punishment for such conduct. In a criminal case, the defendant is prosecuted by the government, which must prove the defendant's guilt beyond a reasonable doubt, a significantly higher burden of proof than that required in a civil action. Moreover, under our legal system, guilt is never presumed. Indeed, the law presumes the innocence of the accused, and this presumption is unaffected by the defendant's failure to testify in her own defense. The government still has the burden of affirmatively proving the guilt of the accused beyond a reasonable doubt.

Of course, the same conduct may, and often does, constitute both a crime and a tort, which is a civil wrong. (We will discuss torts in Chapters 7 and 8.) But an act may be criminal without being tortious; by the same token, an act may be a tort but not a crime.

Because of the increasing use of criminal sanctions to enforce government regulation of business, criminal law is an essential part of business law. Moreover, businesses sustain considerable loss as victims of criminal actions. Accordingly, this chapter covers the general principles of criminal law and criminal procedure as well as specific crimes and defenses relevant to business.

NATURE OF CRIMES

A **crime** is any act or omission forbidden by public law in the interest of protecting society and made punishable by the government in a judicial proceeding brought by it.

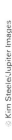

Crime

an act or omission in violation of a public law and punishable by the government

© Kim Steele/Jupiter Images

Punishment for criminal conduct includes fines, imprisonment, probation, and death. In addition, some states and the federal government have enacted victim indemnification statutes, which establish funds, financed by criminal fines, to provide indemnification in limited amounts to victims of criminal activity. Crimes are prohibited and punished on grounds of public policy, which may include the protection and safeguarding of government (as in treason), human life (as in murder), or private property (as in larceny). Additional purposes for criminal law include deterrence, rehabilitation, and retribution.

Historically, criminal law was primarily common law. In the twenty-first century, however, criminal law is almost exclusively statutory. All states have enacted comprehensive criminal law statutes (or codes) covering most, if not all, of the common law crimes. Moreover, these statutes have made the number of crimes defined in criminal law far greater than the number of crimes defined under common law. Some codes expressly limit crimes to those the code includes, thus abolishing common law crimes. Nonetheless, some states do not define all crimes statutorily; therefore, the courts must rely on common law definitions. Because there are no federal common law crimes, all federal crimes are statutory.

Within recent times the scope of the criminal law has increased greatly. The scope of traditional criminal behavior has been expanded by numerous regulations and laws, pertaining to nearly every phase of modern living, that contain criminal penalties. Typical examples in the field of business law are those laws concerning the licensing and conduct of a business, antitrust laws, and laws governing the sales of securities.

Essential Elements

Actus reus
wrongful or overt act

Mens rea
criminal intent or mental fault

In general, a crime consists of two elements: (1) the wrongful or overt act (*actus reus*) and (2) the criminal or mental intent (*mens rea*). For example, to support a larceny conviction it is not enough to show that the defendant stole another's goods; it must also be established that he intended to steal the goods. Conversely, criminal intent without an overt act is not a crime. For instance, Ann decides to rob the neighborhood grocery store and then really "live it up." Without more than the thought, Ann has committed no crime.

Actus reus refers to all the nonmental elements of a crime, including the physical act that must be performed, the circumstances under which it must be performed, and the consequences of that act. The *actus reus* required for specific crimes will be discussed later in this chapter.

Mens rea, or mental fault, refers to the mental element of a crime. Most common law and some statutory crimes require subjective fault, whereas other crimes require objective fault; some statutory crimes require no fault at all. The American Law Institute's proposed Model Penal Code and most modern criminal statutes recognize three possible types of **subjective fault**: purposeful, knowing, and reckless. A person acts *purposely* or *intentionally* if his conscious object is to engage in the prohibited conduct or to cause the prohibited result. Thus, if Arthur, with the desire to kill Donna, shoots his rifle at Donna, who is seemingly out of gunshot range, and in fact does kill her, Arthur had the purpose or intent to kill Donna. If Benjamin, desiring to poison Paula, places a toxic chemical in the water cooler in Paula's office and unwittingly poisons Gail and Ram, Benjamin will be found to have purposefully killed Gail and Ram, because Benjamin's intent to kill Paula is transferred to Gail and Ram, regardless of Benjamin's feelings toward Gail and Ram.

A person acts *knowingly* if he is aware that his conduct is of a prohibited type or is practically certain to cause a prohibited result. A person acts *recklessly* if he consciously disregards a substantial and unjustifiable risk that his conduct is prohibited or that it will cause a prohibited result.

Subjective fault
purposeful, knowing, or reckless

Objective fault
gross deviation from reasonable conduct

Objective fault involves a gross deviation from the standard of care that a reasonable person would observe under given circumstances. Criminal statutes refer to objective fault by terms such as carelessness or negligence. Such conduct occurs when a person *should* be aware of a substantial and unjustifiable risk that his conduct is prohibited or will cause a prohibited result. Examples of crimes requiring objective fault are involuntary manslaughter (negligently causing the death of another), carelessly driving an automobile, and, in some states, issuing a bad check.

Liability without fault
crime to do a specific act or cause a certain result without regard to the care exercised

Many regulatory statutes have totally dispensed with the mental element of a crime by imposing criminal **liability without fault**. Without regard to the care that a person exercises, criminal liability without fault makes it a crime for that person to do a specified act or to bring about a certain result. Statutory crimes imposing liability without fault include the sale of

---

CONCEPT REVIEW 6-1

Degrees of Mental Fault

Type	Fault Required	Examples
Subjective fault	Purposeful Knowing Reckless	Larceny Embezzlement
Objective fault	Negligent Careless	Careless driving Issuing bad checks (some states)
Liability without fault	None	Sale of alcohol to a minor Sale of adulterated food

© Cengage Learning 2013

---

adulterated food, the sale of narcotics without a prescription, and the sale of alcoholic beverages to a minor. Most of these crimes involve regulatory statutes dealing with health and safety and impose only fines for violations. See *State v. Morse* later in this chapter.

See the Concept Review 6-1 for an overview of degree of mental fault.

CLASSIFICATION

Mala in se (ma′ la in say)
wrongs in themselves or morally wrong

Mala prohibita
(ma′ la pro·hi′ bi·ta)
not morally wrong but declared wrongful by law

Felony
serious crime

Misdemeanor
less serious crime

Historically, crimes have been classified *mala in se* (wrongs in themselves or morally wrong, such as murder) or *mala prohibita* (not morally wrong but declared wrongful by law, such as the failure to drive on the right side of the road). From the standpoint of the seriousness of the offense, crimes are also classified as a **felony**, which is a serious crime (any crime punishable by death or imprisonment in the penitentiary), or as a **misdemeanor**, which is a less serious crime (any crime punishable by a fine or imprisonment in a local jail).

Vicarious Liability

Vicarious liability
liability imposed on one for acts of another

Vicarious liability is liability imposed upon one person for the acts of another. Employers are vicariously liable for the authorized criminal acts of their employees if the employer directed, participated in, or approved of the act. For example, if an employer directs its vice president of marketing to fix prices with its company's competitors, and the employee does so, both the employer and employee have criminally violated the Sherman Antitrust Act. On the other hand, employers ordinarily are not liable for the unauthorized criminal acts of their employees. As previously discussed, most crimes require mental fault; this element is not present, so far as criminal responsibility of the employer is concerned, where the employee's criminal act was not authorized.

PRACTICAL ADVICE
Because employers may be criminally liable for the acts of their employees, you should exercise due diligence in adequately checking the backgrounds of prospective employees.

Employers may, however, be subject to a criminal penalty for the unauthorized act of an adviser or manager acting in the scope of employment. Moreover, an employer may be criminally liable under a liability without fault statute for certain unauthorized acts of an employee, whether the employee is managerial or not. For example, many states have statutes that punish "every person who by himself or his employee or agent sells anything at short weight," or "whoever sells liquor to a minor and any sale by an employee shall be deemed the act of the employer as well."

Liability of a Corporation

Liability of a corporation
under certain circumstances a corporation may be convicted of crimes and punished by fines

Historically, corporations were not held criminally liable because, under the traditional view, a corporation could not possess the requisite criminal intent and, therefore, was incapable of committing a crime. The dramatic growth in size and importance of corporations changed this view. Under the modern approach, a corporation may be liable for violation of statutes imposing liability without fault. In addition, a corporation may be liable where the offense is perpetrated by a high corporate officer or the board of directors. The Model Penal Code provides that a corporation may be convicted of a criminal offense for the conduct of its employees if:

1. the legislative purpose of the statute defining the offense is to impose liability on corporations and the conduct is within the scope of the [employee's] office or employment;
2. the offense consists of an omission to discharge a specific, affirmative duty imposed upon corporations by law; or
3. the offense was authorized, requested, commanded, performed, or recklessly tolerated by the board of directors or by a high managerial agent of the corporation.

Punishment of a corporation for crimes is necessarily by fine, not imprisonment. Nonetheless, individuals bearing responsibility for the criminal act face fines, imprisonment, or both. The Model Penal Code provides that the corporate agent having primary responsibility for the discharge of the duty imposed by law on the corporation is as accountable for a reckless omission to perform the required act as though the law imposed the duty directly upon him.

On November 1, 1991 (updated in 2004 and 2010), the Federal Organizational Corporate Sentencing Guidelines took effect. The overall purpose of the guidelines is to impose sanctions that will provide just punishment and adequate deterrence. The guidelines provide a base fine for each criminal offense, but that fine can be increased or reduced. Factors that can increase a corporate fine include the corporation's involvement in or tolerance of criminal activity, its prior history, and whether it has obstructed justice. On the other hand, corporations can reduce their punishment by implementing an effective compliance and ethics program reasonably designed to prevent potential legal violations by the corporation and its employees.

PRACTICAL ADVICE

Companies should ensure that they have a satisfactory corporate compliance program.

An effective compliance and ethics program should include the following:
1. standards and procedures to prevent and detect criminal conduct;
2. responsibility at all levels and adequate resources, and authority for the program;
3. personnel screening related to program goals;
4. training at all levels;
5. auditing, monitoring, and evaluating program effectiveness;
6. nonretaliatory internal reporting systems;
7. incentives and discipline to promote compliance; and
8. reasonable steps to respond to and prevent further similar offenses upon detection of a violation.

The 2010 amendments to the guidelines expanded the availability of reduced sentencing for corporations meeting additional requirements. Under the previous guidelines, convicted corporations could receive a reduced fine for having an effective compliance and ethics program *only if* no high-level personnel were involved in, or willfully ignorant of, the crime. Under the 2010 amendments, a corporation can be eligible for a reduced fine based on an effective compliance and ethics program *despite* the involvement or willful ignorance of high-level personnel if the convicted corporation satisfies four additional criteria:
1. a direct and prompt communication channel exists between compliance personnel and the organization's governing authority (e.g., the board of directors or the audit committee of the board);
2. the compliance program discovered the criminal offense before discovery outside the company was reasonably likely;
3. the corporation promptly reported the offense to appropriate government authorities; and
4. no individual with operational responsibility for the compliance program participated in, condoned, or was willfully ignorant of the offense.

WHITE-COLLAR CRIME

White-collar crime

nonviolent crime involving deceit, corruption, or breach of trust

White-collar crime has been defined in various ways. The Justice Department defines it as nonviolent crime involving deceit, corruption, or breach of trust. It includes crimes committed by individuals—such as embezzlement and forgery—as well as crimes committed on behalf of a corporation—such as commercial bribery, product safety and health crimes, false advertising, and antitrust violations. Regardless of the definition, white-collar crime clearly costs society billions of dollars; according to the Federal Bureau of Investigation, white-collar crime is estimated to cost the United States between $300 and $660 billion per year. Historically, prosecution of white-collar crime was deemphasized because such crime was not considered violent. Now, however, many contend that white-collar crime often inflicts violence but does so impersonally. For example, unsafe products cause injury and death to consumers, while unsafe working conditions cause injury and death to employees. Indeed, many contend that white-collar criminals should receive stiff prison sentences due to the magnitude of their crimes.

In response to the business scandals involving companies such as Enron, WorldCom, Global Crossing, Adelphia, and Arthur Andersen, in 2002, Congress passed the Sarbanes-Oxley Act. The Act, according to former President George W. Bush, constitutes "the most far-reaching reforms of American business practices since the time of Franklin Delano Roosevelt [President from 1932 until 1945]." The legislation seeks to prevent such scandals by increasing corporate responsibility; adding new financial disclosure requirements; creating new criminal offenses and increasing the penalties of existing federal crimes; and creating a powerful new five-person Accounting Oversight Board with authority to review and discipline auditors.

The Sarbanes-Oxley Act establishes new criminal penalties, including the following: (1) making it a crime to defraud any person or to obtain any money or property fraudulently in connection with any security of a public company with penalties of a fine and/or up to twenty-five years imprisonment, and (2) imposing fines and/or imprisonment of up to twenty years for knowingly altering, destroying, mutilating, or falsifying any document with the intent of impeding a federal investigation. In addition, the Act substantially increases the penalties for existing crimes, including the following: (1) mail and wire fraud (five-year maximum increased to twenty-five-year maximum) and (2) violation of the Securities and Exchange Act (ten-year maximum increased to twenty-year maximum). The Act is discussed further in Chapters 35, 39, and 43.

In December 2008, Bernard L. Madoff admitted to perpetrating a massive Ponzi scheme with estimated losses of $20 billion in principal and approximately $65 billion dollars in paper losses. As a result, in 2010 the Securities and Exchange Commission began reforming and improving the way it operates to reduce the chances that such frauds will occur or be undetected in the future.

People v. Farell
Supreme Court of California, 2002
28 Cal. 4th 381, 121 Cal.Rptr.2d 603, 121 Cal.Rptr.2d 603
http://caselaw.lp.findlaw.com/data2/californiastatecases/s092183.doc

---

FACTS On April 18, 1997, the defendant, Farell, was charged with the theft of a trade secret based upon evidence that he had printed out confidential design specifications for certain computer chips on the last day of his employment as an electrical engineer at Digital Equipment Corporation. As a sentence enhancement, it was further alleged that the loss exceeded $2.5 million and, as a restriction on probation, that the theft was of an amount exceeding $100,000. Defendant pleaded no contest to the theft charge but objected to the potential application of Section 1203.044 to his sentence, which requires a ninety-day county jail sentence as condition of probation for theft of an amount exceeding $50,000. The trial court placed him on probation conditioned on the service of a term in county jail under Section 1203.044

A hearing was held in the superior court on the limited question of whether the amount of the theft applies to the theft of property other than money, including trade secrets. The court concluded that the provision applies to the theft of all property of a certain value, including trade secrets. The court suspended imposition of sentence and placed the defendant on probation for a period of three years on the condition that he serve three months in county jail. The court granted a stay of the jail term pending appeal.

The Court of Appeal reversed, holding that the statute applies only to the theft of what it termed "monetary property." The California Supreme Court granted the government's petition for review.

DECISION The judgment of the Court of Appeal is reversed.

OPINION Defendant stands convicted of theft, specifically a violation of a California statute that provides:

(b) Every person is guilty of theft who, with intent to deprive or withhold the control of a trade secret from its owner, or with an intent to appropriate a trade secret to his or her own use or to the use of another, does any of the following: (1) Steals, takes, carries away, or uses without authorization, a trade secret.

The statute defines the term "trade secret" as follows:

information, including a formula, pattern, compilation, program, device, method, technique, or process, that: (A) Derives independent economic value, actual or potential, from not being generally known to the public or to other persons who can obtain economic value from its disclosure or use; and (B) Is the subject of efforts that are reasonable under the circumstances to maintain its secrecy.

The trial court determined that Section 1203.044 applies to such a theft. This statute, entitled The Economic Crime Law of 1992, requires that a defendant who is convicted of certain theft offenses and is granted probation shall be sentenced to at least ninety days in the county jail as a condition of probation. Section 1203.044 applies only to a defendant convicted of a felony for theft of an amount exceeding fifty thousand dollars ($50,000) in a single transaction or occurrence.

The Court of Appeal determined that Section 1203.044 may not be applied to persons convicted of the theft of trade secrets. Based on the words of the statute and the legislative history of the enactment it concluded that the statute is at best ambiguous and accordingly applied the so-called rule of lenity to give the defendant the benefit of the doubt.

In interpreting a statute a court must first turn to the words of the statute themselves, recognizing that they generally provide the most reliable indicator of legislative intent. The California Supreme Court determined that the meaning of the phrase "convicted of a felony for theft of an amount exceeding fifty thousand dollars," does not specify that the theft must involve cash—or that it must involve what is referred to by the Court of Appeal as "monetary property." In the absence of evidence to the contrary, it must be inferred that when the legislature referred in Section 1203.044 to persons "convicted of a felony for theft," it had in mind the general definition of theft, including the broad categories of property that may be the subject of theft, including trade secrets.

As further evidence, the Court looked at the legislature's intent in regard to punishment of white-collar crime. The legislature declared in enacting Section 1203.044:

[M]ajor economic or "white collar" crime is an increasing threat to California's economy and the well-being of its citizens. The Legislature intends to deter that crime by ensuring that every offender, without exception, serves at least some time in jail and by requiring the offenders to divert a portion of their future resources to the payment of restitution to their victims.

Moreover, the term "white-collar crime" is a relatively broad one generally defined as "[a] nonviolent crime usu[ally] involving cheating or dishonesty in commercial matters. Examples include fraud, embezzlement, bribery, and insider trading."

INTERPRETATION The requirement imposing a minimum term in county jail applies to the theft of property other than money, including trade secrets.

CRITICAL THINKING QUESTION Should the penalty for theft vary depending on the dollar value of the property taken? Explain.

Computer Crime

Computer crime

crime by, with, or at a computer

One special type of white-collar crime is computer crime. **Computer crime**, or **cybercrime**, is best categorized based on whether the computer was the instrument or the target of the crime. Examples of cybercrimes using computers as the *instrument* of the crime include the distribution of child pornography, money laundering, illegal gambling, copyright infringement, illegal communication of trade secret, and fraud involving credit cards, e-commerce, and securities. Cybercrime with a computer as a *target* of the crime attacks a computer's confidentiality, integrity, or availability; examples include theft or destruction of proprietary information, vandalism, denial of service, website defacing and interference, and implanting malicious code. Detection of crimes involving computers is extremely difficult. In addition, computer crimes often are not reported because businesses do not want to give the impression that their security is lax. Nonetheless, losses due to computer crimes are estimated to be in the tens of billions of dollars. Moreover, given society's ever-increasing dependence upon computers, this type of crime will in all likelihood continue to increase.

As a consequence, enterprises are spending large sums of money to increase computer security. In addition, every state has enacted computer crime laws. Originally passed in 1984, the federal Computer Fraud and Abuse Act protects a broad range of computers that facilitate interstate and international commerce and communications. The Act was amended in 1986, 1994, 1996, 2001 2002, and 2008. The Act makes it a crime with respect to any computer that is used in interstate commerce or communications (1) to access or damage it without authorization, (2) to access it with the intent to commit fraud, (3) to traffic in passwords for it, and (4) to threaten to cause damage to it with the intent to extort money or anything of value. Furthermore, depending on the details of the crime, cybercriminals may also be prosecuted under other federal laws, such as copyright, mail fraud, or wire fraud laws. *Spam*—unsolicited commercial electronic mail—is currently estimated to account for well over half of all electronic mail. Congress has concluded that spam has become the most prevalent method used for distributing pornography, perpetrating fraudulent schemes, and introducing viruses, worms, and Trojan horses into personal and business computer systems. In response, Congress enacted the Controlling the Assault of Non-Solicited Pornography and Marketing Act of 2003, or the CAN-SPAM Act of 2003, which went into effect on January 1, 2004. In enacting the statute Congress determined that senders of spam should not mislead recipients as to the source or content of such mail and that recipients of spam have a right to decline to receive additional spam from the same source.

PRACTICAL ADVICE

Adequately protect the safety and security of all company electronic data and records.

Racketeer Influenced and Corrupt Organizations Act

RICO

federal law intended to stop organized crime from infiltrating legitimate businesses

The **Racketeer Influenced and Corrupt Organizations Act (RICO)** was enacted in 1970 with the stated purpose of terminating the infiltration by organized crime into legitimate business. The Act subjects to severe civil and criminal penalties enterprises that engage in a pattern of racketeering, defined as the commission of two or more predicate acts within a period of ten years. A "predicate act" is any of several criminal offenses listed in RICO. Included are nine major categories of state crimes and more than thirty federal crimes, such as murder, kidnapping, arson, extortion, drug dealing, mail fraud, and bribery. The most controversial issue concerning RICO is its application to businesses that are not engaged in organized crime but that do meet the "pattern of racketeering" test under the Act. Criminal conviction under the law may result in a prison term of up to twenty years plus a fine of up to $25,000 per violation. In addition, businesses forfeit any property obtained due to a RICO violation, and individuals harmed by RICO violations may invoke the statute's civil remedies, which include treble damage and attorneys' fees.

Other areas of federal law that impose both civil and criminal penalties include bankruptcy (Chapter 38), antitrust (Chapter 42), securities regulation (Chapter 43), and environmental regulation (Chapter 45).

CRIMES AGAINST BUSINESS

Criminal offenses against property greatly affect businesses, amounting to losses worth hundreds of billions of dollars each year. In this section we will discuss the following crimes against property: (1) larceny, (2) embezzlement, (3) false pretenses, (4) robbery, (5) burglary, (6) extortion and bribery, (7) forgery, and (8) bad checks.

Larceny

Larceny
trespassory taking and carrying away of the goods of another with the intent to permanently deprive

The crime of **larceny** is the (1) trespassory (2) taking and (3) carrying away of (or exercising dominion or control over) (4) personal property (5) of another (6) with the intent to deprive the victim permanently of the goods. All six elements must be present for the crime to exist. Thus, if Carol takes Dan's 1968 automobile without Dan's permission, intending to use it for a joyride and to then return it to Dan, Carol has not committed larceny because she did not intend to deprive Dan permanently of the automobile. (Carol nevertheless has committed the offense of unauthorized use of an automobile, which is a crime in most states.) On the other hand, if Carol left Dan's 1968 car in a junkyard after the joyride, Carol most likely would be held to have committed a larceny because of the high risk that Dan would be permanently deprived of the car.

Embezzlement

Embezzlement
taking the property of one's employer in violation of a trust

Embezzlement is the fraudulent conversion of another's property by one who was in lawful possession of it. A conversion is any act that seriously interferes with the owner's rights in the property; such acts may include exhausting the resources of the property, selling it, giving it away, or refusing to return it to its rightful owner. The key distinction between larceny and embezzlement, therefore, is whether the thief is in lawful possession of the property. Although both situations concern misuse of the property of another, in embezzlement, the thief lawfully possesses the property; in larceny, she does not.

False Pretenses

False pretenses
obtaining title to property of another by means of materially false representations of fact made with knowledge of their falsity and with the intent to defraud

False pretenses is the crime of obtaining title to property of another by making materially false representations of an existing fact with knowledge of their falsity and with the intent to defraud. Larceny does not cover this situation because here the victim voluntarily transfers the property to the thief. For example, a con artist who goes door to door and collects money by saying he is selling stereo equipment, when he is not, is committing the crime of false pretenses.

Other specialized crimes that are similar to false pretenses include mail, wire, and bank fraud as well as securities fraud. *Mail fraud*, unlike the crime of false pretenses, does not require the victim to be actually defrauded; it simply requires the defendant to use the mails (or private carrier) to carry out a scheme that attempts to defraud others. Due to its breadth and ease of use, mail fraud has been employed extensively by federal prosecutors. The *wire fraud* statute prohibits the transmittal by wire, radio, or television in interstate or foreign commerce of any information with the intent to defraud. The federal statute prohibiting *bank fraud* makes it a crime knowingly to execute or attempt to execute a scheme to defraud a financial institution or to obtain by false pretenses funds under the control or custody of a financial institution. *Securities fraud* is discussed in Chapter 39.

APPLYING THE LAW

Criminal Law

Facts Bivens worked as an accounts payable clerk for C&N Construction. Every Wednesday morning, the site foreman would call Bivens and give her the names of the employees working on the job and the number of hours they had worked. Bivens would then convey this information to a paycheck processing company, which would return unsigned payroll checks to C&N. After a designated officer of the company signed them, Bivens would forward the checks to the job site for distribution by the foreman. After working for the company for nearly eight years, Bivens began sending false information to the payroll service about employees and hours worked. The resulting checks were typically payable to employees who had worked for C&N in the recent past but who were not active on the current job. Bivens would intercept these "fake" checks after they were signed, forge the payees' names, and either cash them or deposit them into her bank account. Over a period of seventeen months, Bivens diverted tens of thousands of dollars to herself by forging more than one hundred fake paychecks. She spent all but a few hundred dollars of the money on meals and entertainment, jewelry, clothing, and shoes. C&N's vice president ultimately discovered Bivens's practice, fired her, and notified the authorities of her conduct.

Issue Has Bivens committed the crime of embezzlement?

Rule of Law A crime consists of two elements: (1) *actus reus*, or a wrongful act, and (2) *mens rea*, or criminal intent. The crime of embezzlement occurs when a person who is in lawful possession of another's property intentionally misuses the property or seriously interferes with the owner's rights in it. Possible defenses to a crime include defense of person or property, duress, and mistake of fact.

Application The *actus reus* in this case is exercising wrongful dominion and control over the property of another while in legal possession of it. Bivens was lawfully in possession of C&N's property in the form of the payroll checks. While her job description certainly did not authorize her to keep any of the checks or payroll funds for herself, Bivens's position at C&N did require her to record and transmit payroll information as well as to handle the checks themselves. While in legal possession of C&N paychecks, Bivens misused or seriously interfered with C&N payroll funds. Without permission or right, she cashed some of the checks and diverted to herself money that belonged to C&N. She has committed the necessary wrongful act.

The next question is whether she had the requisite state of mind. Bivens's paycheck scheme also reflects *mens rea*, or subjective fault. Her conduct with regard to the checks was clearly purposeful or intentional. While it might be possible to make an error in transmitting employee names or hours worked occasionally, Bivens could not have negligently transmitted incorrect information about former employees in more than one hundred instances. Moreover, the fact she separated out the fake checks from the genuine paychecks, surreptitiously took them from work, falsely endorsed them with the names of the former employee payees, and then cashed them and spent the money indicates she intended to steal the funds. This series of events benefiting Bivens could not possibly have happened unintentionally or through carelessness alone. Therefore the necessary *mens rea* is present.

Moreover, none of the defenses to a crime is applicable here. Bivens was not acting to protect herself, another person, or her property. Nor was she under duress; she was not threatened with immediate, serious bodily harm when she engaged in the paycheck scam. Finally, there is nothing to indicate that Bivens was mistaken about C&N's ownership of the payroll funds, about the names or hours worked by employees any given week, or that she could have mistakenly thought she was expected to or permitted to falsify payroll records so as to cause paychecks to be issued to former employees, paychecks which she would then take and cash for herself. Thus, Bivens has no valid legal defense.

Conclusion Bivens's conduct with regard to these checks constitutes embezzlement.

© Cengage Learning 2013

State of South Dakota v. Morse
Supreme Court of South Dakota, 2008
753 N.W.2d 915, 2008 SD 66
http://scholar.google.com/scholar_case?case=4959207354232635251&q=753+N.W.2d+915,&hl=en&as_sdt=2,22

FACTS Janice Heffron orally contracted with her neighbor, Wyatt Morse, to convert her second-floor bedroom into a bathroom in five weeks for $5,000. According to Janice, Morse repeatedly stated that he could do it "easy, quick, cheap." Janice told her mother, Maxine Heffron, who would finance the project, about Morse's offer. Maxine and Janice then went to Morse's home, where he showed them the bathroom he had restored. Janice and Maxine were impressed. Morse also told them that he had plumbing experience, that his work would be above and beyond code, and that the local inspector did not inspect his work because he was so good. Maxine wanted to pay using personal checks to assure a paper trail, but Morse convinced her to pay him with cash. According to Janice, he wanted to be paid in cash to avoid the Internal Revenue Service. They agreed that Morse would convert the room into a bathroom, install an antique claw-foot tub (one that he would provide personally), put wainscoting on the walls, install an old tin ceiling like the one in his bathroom, and install crown molding.

Morse began work in January 2006. His efforts continued until the second week of March. He installed plumbing fixtures and he removed the old water heater and installed a new one. He ran a freeze-proof spigot outside the house. He put in a bathroom vent with an antique vent cover. He custom built a bathroom cabinet at no extra cost to the Heffrons. He mounted wainscoting and crafted a surrounding shelf with rope lighting. He put in a faux tin ceiling, with crown molding and trim. He installed water pipes and a new drain stack. The project took longer and cost more than originally agreed. Morse ran into difficulties when he attempted to install a tankless water heater. He was never able to install the tankless heater and ended up installing a traditional tanked water heater. Morse also experienced problems with some of the pipes he installed. Janice told him that they were leaking. He repaired them and blamed the leaks on bad batches of solder.

Maxine paid Morse somewhere between $6,000 and $6,500 cash. In March 2006, Morse fell and aggravated his already bad back. Before Janice and Maxine hired him, Morse had told them that he had a back condition. After his fall in March, he came to the job site less and less. Then, after the second week in March he stopped coming entirely. The Heffrons tried contacting him through phone calls, personal visits, and certified mail. He never responded. After Morse abandoned the project, Janice contacted a licensed plumber, who examined Morse's work and gave Janice an estimate on the cost of completing the project. The plumber pointed out several deficiencies in Morse's work. In particular, Morse incorrectly installed the water heater, the pipes for the sink, lavatory, and bathtub. He used S-traps, illegal in South Dakota, and improperly vented the floor drains. Because he installed the water heater incorrectly, carbon monoxide was leaking into Janice's home. In sum, Morse's work on the bathroom, in the opinion of the licensed plumber, had no value to the home.

On October 12, 2006, Morse was indicted for grand theft by deception in violation of South Dakota law. A jury returned a guilty verdict. Morse was sentenced to five years in prison. He appeals asserting that the evidence was insufficient to sustain the verdict.

DECISION Judgment reversed.

OPINION Morse argues that the South Dakota failed to prove he had the requisite intent to defraud the Heffrons. He does not dispute that the work he did on Janice's home was faulty and resulted in the Heffrons having to pay considerably more in repairs. Nonetheless, he claims that his faulty work created a classic breach of contract claim, because when he entered into the agreement to remodel the bathroom, he believed he was capable of doing quality work and fully intended on completing the project. The state,

on the other hand, argues that Morse "created and reinforced the false impression in the minds of Jan and Maxine Heffron that he was licensed to, and capable of, installing a second floor bathroom" and in his ability to do the work. Theft by deception is a specific intent crime. Intent to defraud "means to act willfully and with the specific intent to deceive or cheat, ordinarily for the purpose of either causing some financial loss to another or bringing about some financial gain to one's self." Therefore, Morse must have had the "purpose to deceive."

The record indicates that Morse (1) failed to complete the project in five weeks for $5,000 as promised; (2) performed work that was not "above and beyond code" as promised; (3) lied about obtaining a building permit; (4) lied about the reasons he could not get the tankless water heater installed and why the pipes were leaking; (5) returned the water heater and did not give the $186 refund to Maxine; (6) never provided Janice or Maxine receipts for materials purchased; (7) quit working on the project prematurely and without explanation; and (8) never responded to the Heffrons' attempts to contact him.

These facts do not prove the elements of theft by deception. There is no evidence that Morse had a purpose to deceive or intended to defraud the Heffrons when he agreed to remodel Janice's bathroom. Although his work was not above and beyond code, the state never argued that Morse *knew* he would do faulty work. Janice and Maxine both testified that Morse took them up to his house and showed him the remodeling that he did to his own bathroom. They both said they were impressed. It cannot be inferred that Morse intended to defraud the Heffrons because his work product was not up to code.

Moreover, the state never argued or presented evidence that Morse took Maxine's money with the intention of never performing under their agreement. The parties made their agreement in December 2005, and no one disputes that Morse worked regularly on the project from January 2006 until the second week of March. While Morse failed to complete the project in five weeks for $5,000 as promised, the state never claimed that he *knew* it would take longer and charge more, and tricked the Heffrons into believing him. Neither Janice nor Maxine claimed that Morse deceived them into paying him more money when the project took longer than anticipated.

INTERPRETATION An essential element of a crime is the mental intent (*mens rea*) to commit the crime.

CRITICAL THINKING QUESTION When should circumstantial evidence be permitted to prove a crime has been committed? Explain.

Robbery

Robbery
larceny from a person by force or threat of force

Robbery is a larceny with two additional elements: (1) the property is taken directly from the victim or in the immediate presence of the victim and (2) the act is accomplished through either force or the threat of force. The defendant's force or threat of force need not be against the person from whom the property is taken. For example, a robber threatens Sam that unless Sam opens up his employer's safe, the robber will shoot Maria.

Many statutes distinguish between simple robbery and aggravated robbery. Robbery can be aggravated by any of several factors, including (1) robbery with a deadly weapon, (2) robbery where the robber has the intent to kill or would kill if faced with resistance, (3) robbery that involves serious bodily injury, or (4) robbery by two or more persons.

Burglary

Burglary

breaking and entering the home of another at night with intent to commit a felony

At common law, **burglary** was defined as breaking and entering the dwelling of another at night with the intent to commit a felony. Modern statutes differ from the common law definition. Many of them simply require that there be (1) an entry (2) into a building (3) with the intent to commit a felony in the building. Nevertheless, the modern statutes vary so greatly it is nearly impossible to generalize.

Extortion and Bribery

Extortion

making threats to obtain property

Although extortion and bribery are frequently confused, they are two distinct crimes. **Extortion**, or blackmail as it is sometimes called, is generally held to be the making of threats for the purpose of obtaining money or property. For example, Lindsey tells Jason that unless Jason pays her $10,000, she will tell Jason's customers that Jason was once arrested for disturbing the peace. Lindsey has committed the crime of extortion. In a few jurisdictions, however, the crime of extortion occurs only if the defendant actually causes the victim to relinquish money or property.

Bribery

offering property to a public official to influence the official's decision

Bribery, on the other hand, is the offer of money or property to a public official to influence the official's decision. The crime of bribery is committed when the illegal offer is made, whether accepted or not. Thus, if Andrea offered Edward, the mayor of Allentown, a 20 percent interest in Andrea's planned real estate development if Edward would use his influence to have the development proposal approved, Andrea would be guilty of criminal bribery. In contrast, if Edward had threatened Andrea that unless he received a 20 percent interest in Andrea's development, he would use his influence to prevent the approval of the development, Edward would be guilty of criminal extortion. Bribery of foreign officials is covered by the Foreign Corrupt Practices Act, discussed in Chapter 39.

Some jurisdictions have gone beyond the traditional bribery law to adopt statutes that make *commercial bribery* illegal. Commercial bribery is the use of bribery to acquire new business, obtain secret information or processes, or obtain kickbacks.

Forgery

Forgery

intentional falsification of a document in order to defraud

Forgery is the intentional falsification or false making of a document with the intent to defraud. Accordingly, if William prepares a false certificate of title to a stolen automobile, he is guilty of forgery. Likewise, if an individual alters some receipts to increase her income tax deductions, she has committed the crime of forgery. The most common type of forgery is the signing of another's name to a financial document.

Bad Checks

Bad checks

checks issued with funds insufficient to cover them

All jurisdictions have enacted laws making it a crime to issue **bad checks**; that is, writing a check when there is not enough money in the account to cover the check. Most jurisdictions simply require that the check be issued; they do not require that the issuer receive anything in return for the check. Also, though most jurisdictions require that defendants issue a check with knowledge that they do not have enough money to cover the check, a few jurisdictions require only that there be insufficient funds.

State v. Kelm
Superior Court of New Jersey, 1996
289 N.J. Super. 55, 672 A.2d 1261, cert. denied 146 N.J. 68, 679 A.2d 655 (1996)
http://lawlibrary.rutgers.edu/decisions/appellate/a1118-94.opn.html

---

FACTS On February 10, 1991, defendant Kelm secured a loan for $6,000 from Ms. Joan Williams. Kelm told Williams that the loan was to finance a real estate transaction. Five days later, Ms. Williams received a check drawn by Kelm in the amount of $6,000 from Kelm's attorney. Although the check was dated February 15, 1991, Kelm claims that she delivered the check to her attorney on February 10, 1991. The following week, Ms. Williams learned the check was uncollectible. Subsequently, Williams received assurances from Kelm but was unsuccessful in her efforts to obtain money from the drawee's bank. When Williams deposited the check, it was returned with a notation that it should not be presented again and that no account was on file. Bank records show that the account was closed on March 8, 1991, and that it had negative balances since February 10, 1991. Following a jury trial, Kelm was found guilty of issuing a bad check. Kelm appeals, asserting that an intent to defraud is an element of the statutory offense of issuing a bad check and that the statutory provision exempts postdated checks.

DECISION The jury verdict is affirmed.

OPINION The principal issue on appeal is whether an intent to defraud is an element of Section 2C:21-5 [issuing a bad check] of the New Jersey statutes. The statute provides:

> A person who issues or passes a check or similar sight order for the payment of money, knowing that it will not be honored by the drawee, commits an offense.... For the purposes of this section as well as in any prosecution for theft committed by means of a bad check, an issuer is presumed to know that the check or money order (other than a post-dated check or order) would not be paid, if:
>
> ***.
>
> (b) Payment was refused by the drawee for lack of funds, upon presentation within 30 days after issue, and the issuer failed to make good within 10 days after receiving notice of that refusal....

This statute, unlike its predecessor, does not contain the language "with intent to defraud." Kelm's reliance on cases interpreting the prior bad check statute is misplaced. An intent to defraud is not an element of the offense of issuing a bad check. Rather, the current statute requires mere knowledge at the time the check is issued or passed that it will not be honored by the drawee.

Addressing Kelm's second assertion, the statute's reference to postdated checks does not completely exempt such checks from its operation. That reference only exempts the drawer of a postdated check from the presumption of knowledge that the check will not be paid. In such cases, the state must prove such knowledge beyond a reasonable doubt.

The trial judge's charge to the jury correctly reflected the statutory requirement of knowledge. It also states that if the jury should find that the check was postdated, then the element of knowledge requires proof beyond a reasonable doubt. The jury was correctly instructed by this charge. Therefore, the jury's verdict is affirmed.

INTERPRETATION Under the New Jersey statute the offense of issuing a bad check requires mere knowledge at the time the check is issued or passed that the check will not be honored by the drawee.

CRITICAL THINKING QUESTION What elements do you believe are essential to a bad check law? Explain.

DEFENSES TO CRIMES

Even though a defendant is found to have committed a criminal act, he will not be convicted if he has a valid defense. The defenses most relevant to white-collar crimes and crimes against business include defense of property, duress, mistake of fact, and entrapment. In some instances, a defense proves the absence of a required element of the crime; other defenses provide a justification or excuse that bars criminal liability.

Defense of Person or Property

Defense of person or property
individuals may use reasonable force to protect themselves, other individuals, and their property

Individuals may use reasonable force to protect themselves, other individuals, and their property. This defense enables a person to commit, without any criminal liability, what otherwise would be considered the crime of assault, battery, manslaughter, or murder. Under the majority rule, deadly force is never reasonable to protect property because life is deemed more important than the protection of property. For this reason, individuals cannot use a deadly mechanical device, such as a spring gun, to protect their property. If, however, the defender's use of reasonable force in protecting his property is met with an attack upon his person, he then may use deadly force if the attack threatens him with death or serious bodily harm.

Duress

Duress
coercion by threat of serious bodily injury

A person who is threatened with immediate, serious bodily harm to himself or another unless he engages in criminal activity has the valid defense of **duress** (sometimes referred to as compulsion or coercion) to criminal conduct other than murder. For example, Ann threatens to kill Ben if Ben does not assist her in committing larceny. Ben complies. Because of duress, he would not be guilty of the larceny.

Mistake of Fact

Mistake of fact
honest and reasonable belief that conduct is not criminal is a defense

If a person reasonably believes the facts surrounding an act to be such that his conduct would not constitute a crime, then the law will treat the facts as he reasonably believes them to be. Accordingly, an honest and reasonable **mistake of fact** will justify the defendant's conduct. For example, if Ann gets into a car that she reasonably believes to be hers—the car is the same color, model, and year as hers, is parked in the same parking lot, and is started by her key—she will be relieved of criminal responsibility for taking Ben's automobile.

Entrapment

The defense of **entrapment** arises when a law enforcement official induces a person to commit a crime when that person would not have done so without the persuasion of the police official. The rationale behind the rule, which applies only to government officials and agents, not to private individuals, is to prevent law enforcement officials from provoking crime and from engaging in improper conduct.

CRIMINAL PROCEDURE

Each of the states and the federal government have procedures for initiating and coordinating criminal prosecutions. In addition, the first ten amendments to the U.S. Constitution (called the Bill of Rights) guarantee many defenses and rights of an accused. The Fourth Amendment prohibits unreasonable searches and seizures to obtain incriminating evidence. The Fifth Amendment requires indictment by a grand jury for capital crimes, prevents double jeopardy, protects against self-incrimination, and prohibits deprivation of life or liberty without due process of law. The Sixth Amendment requires that an accused receive a speedy and public trial by an impartial jury and that he be informed of the nature of the accusation, be confronted with the witnesses who testify against him, be given the power to obtain witnesses in his favor, and have the right to competent counsel for his defense. The Eighth Amendment prohibits excessive bail, excessive fines, and cruel or unusual punishment.

Most state constitutions have similar provisions to protect the rights of accused persons. In addition, the Fourteenth Amendment prohibits state governments from depriving any person of life, liberty, or property without due process of law. Moreover, the U.S. Supreme Court has held that most of the constitutional protections just discussed apply to the states through the operation of the Fourteenth Amendment.

Although various jurisdictions may differ in actual operational details, their criminal processes have a number of common objectives. The primary purpose of the process in any jurisdiction is the effective enforcement of the criminal law, but this purpose must be accomplished within the limitations imposed by other goals. These goals include advancing an adversary system of adjudication, requiring the government to bear the burden of proof, minimizing both erroneous convictions and the burdens of defense, respecting individual dignity, maintaining the appearance of fairness, and achieving equality in the administration of the process.

We will first discuss the steps in a criminal prosecution; we will then focus on the major constitutional protections for the accused in our system of criminal justice.

Steps in Criminal Prosecution

Although the particulars of criminal procedure vary from state to state, the following provides a basic overview of the **steps in criminal prosecution**. After arrest, the accused is booked and appears before the magistrate, commissioner, or justice of the peace, where he is given formal notice of the charges and is advised of his rights and where bail is set. Next, a **preliminary hearing** is held to determine whether there is probable cause to believe the defendant is the one who committed the crime. The defendant is usually entitled to be represented by counsel.

If the magistrate concludes that there is probable cause, she will bind the case over to the next stage, which is either an indictment or information, depending upon the jurisdiction. The federal system and about one-third of the states require indictments for all felony prosecutions (unless waived by the defendant), while the other states permit, but do not mandate, indictments. A grand jury issues an **indictment** or true bill if it finds sufficient evidence to justify a trial on the charge brought. The grand jury, which traditionally consists of no fewer than sixteen and no more than twenty-three people, is not bound by the magistrate's decision at the preliminary hearing. Unlike the preliminary hearing, the grand jury does not hear evidence from the defendant, nor does the defendant appear before the grand jury. In contrast, an **information** is a formal accusation of a crime brought by a prosecuting officer, not a grand jury. Such a procedure is used in misdemeanor cases and in some felony cases in those states that do not require indictments. The indictment or information at times precedes the actual arrest.

At the **arraignment**, the defendant is brought before the trial court, where he is informed of the charge against him and where he enters his plea. The arraignment must be held promptly after the indictment or information has been filed. If his plea is "not guilty," the defendant must stand trial. He is entitled to a jury trial for all felonies and for misdemeanors punishable by more than six months' imprisonment. Most states also permit a defendant to request a jury trial for lesser misdemeanors. If the defendant chooses, however, he may have his guilt or innocence determined by the court sitting without a jury, which is called a "bench trial."

Beyond a reasonable doubt
proof that is entirely convincing; satisfied to a moral certainty

A criminal trial is similar to a civil trial, but there are some significant differences: (1) the defendant is presumed innocent, (2) the burden of proof on the prosecution is to prove criminal guilt **beyond a reasonable doubt** (proof that is entirely convincing, satisfied to a moral certainty), and (3) the defendant is not required to testify. The trial begins with the selection of the jury and the opening statements by the prosecutor and the attorney for the defense. The prosecution presents evidence first; then the defendant presents his evidence. At the conclusion of the testimony, closing statements are made and the jury is instructed as to the applicable law and retires to arrive at a verdict. If the verdict is "not guilty," the matter ends there. The state has no right to appeal from an acquittal; and the accused, having been placed in "jeopardy," cannot be tried a second time for the same offense. If the verdict is "guilty," the judge will enter a judgment of conviction and set the case for sentencing. The defendant may make a motion for a new trial, asserting that prejudicial error occurred at his original trial, thus requiring a retrial of the case. He may appeal to a reviewing court, alleging error by the trial court and asking for either his discharge or a remand of the case for a new trial.

Fourth Amendment

Fourth Amendment
protects individuals against unreasonable searches and seizures

The **Fourth Amendment**, which protects all individuals against unreasonable searches and seizures, is designed to guard the privacy and security of individuals against arbitrary invasions by government officials. Although the Fourth Amendment by its terms applies only to acts of the federal government, the Fourteenth Amendment makes it applicable to state government actions as well.

Exclusionary rule
prohibition against the introduction of illegally seized evidence

When a violation of the Fourth Amendment has occurred, the general rule prohibits the introduction of the illegally seized evidence at trial. The purpose of this **exclusionary rule** is to discourage illegal police conduct and to protect individual liberty, not to hinder the search for the truth. Nonetheless, in recent years the Supreme Court has limited the exclusionary rule.

Probable cause
reasonable belief of the offense charged

To obtain a warrant to search a particular person, place, or thing, a law enforcement official must demonstrate to a magistrate that he has probable cause to believe that the search will reveal evidence of criminal activity. **Probable cause** means "[t]he task of the issuing magistrate is simply to make a practical, common-sense decision whether, given all the circumstances set forth … before him, … there is a fair probability that contraband or evidence of a crime will be found in a particular place." *Illinois v. Gates*, 462 U.S. 213 (1983). Even though the Fourth Amendment requires that a search and seizure generally be made after a valid search warrant has been obtained, in some instances a search warrant is not necessary. For example, it has been held that a warrant is not necessary when (1) there is hot pursuit of a fugitive, (2) the subject of the search voluntarily consents, (3) an emergency requires such action, (4) there has been a lawful arrest, (5) evidence of a crime is in plain view of the law enforcement officer, or (6) delay would present a significant obstacle to the investigation.

Fifth Amendment

Fifth Amendment
protects persons against self-incrimination, double jeopardy, and being charged with a capital crime except by grand jury indictment

The **Fifth Amendment** protects persons against self-incrimination, double jeopardy, and being charged with a capital or infamous crime except by grand jury indictment. The prohibitions against self-incrimination and double jeopardy also apply to the states through the due process clause of the Fourteenth Amendment; however, the grand jury clause does not.

The privilege against self-incrimination extends only to testimonial evidence, not to physical evidence. The Fifth Amendment privilege "protects an accused only from being compelled to testify against himself, or otherwise provide the state with evidence of a testimonial or communicative nature." Therefore, a person can be forced to stand in an identification lineup, provide a handwriting sample, or take a blood test. Significantly, the Fifth Amendment does not protect the records of a business entity, such as a corporation or partnership; it applies only to papers of individuals. Moreover, the Fifth Amendment does not prohibit examination of an individual's business records as long as the individual is not compelled to testify against himself.

CONCEPT REVIEW 6-2

Constitutional Protection for the Criminal Defendant

Amendment	Protection Conferred
Fourth	Freedom from unreasonable search and seizure
Fifth	Right to due process
	Right to indictment by grand jury for capital crimes*
	Freedom from double jeopardy
	Freedom from self-incrimination
Sixth	Right to speedy, public trial by jury
	Right to be informed of accusations
	Right to present witnesses
	Right to competent counsel
Eighth	Freedom from excessive bail
	Freedom from cruel and unusual punishment

*This right has *not* been applied to the states through the Fourteenth Amendment.

© Cengage Learning 2013

PRACTICAL ADVICE

A defendant has the right not to testify against himself and a jury cannot consider this against him.

The Fifth Amendment and the Fourteenth Amendment also guarantee due process of law, which is basically the requirement of a fair trial. All persons are entitled to have the charges or complaints against them made publicly and in writing, whether in civil or criminal proceedings, and are to be given the opportunity to defend themselves against such charges. In criminal prosecutions, due process includes the right to counsel, to confront and cross-examine adverse witnesses, to testify in one's own behalf if desired, to produce witnesses and offer other evidence, and to be free from any and all prejudicial conduct and statements.

Sixth Amendment

Sixth Amendment provides the accused with the right to a speedy and public trial, the opportunity to confront witnesses, have compulsory process for obtaining witnesses, and the right to counsel

The **Sixth Amendment** provides that the federal government shall provide the accused with a speedy and public trial by an impartial jury, inform him of the nature and cause of the accusation, confront him with the witnesses against him, have compulsory process for obtaining witnesses in his favor, and allow him to obtain the assistance of counsel for his defense. The Fourteenth Amendment extends these guarantees to the states.

See Concept Review 6-2 for a presentation of the constitutional protections provided the defendant in a criminal action.

CHAPTER SUMMARY

Nature of Crimes

Definition any act or omission forbidden by public law

Essential Elements

- *Actus reus* wrongful or overt act
- *Mens rea* criminal intent or mental fault
- *Felony* a serious crime
- *Misdemeanor* a less serious crime

Classification

Vicarious Liability liability imposed for acts of his or her employees if the employer directed, participated in, or approved of the acts

Liability of a Corporation under certain circumstances a corporation may be convicted of crimes and punished by fines

White-Collar Crime	**Definition** nonviolent crime involving deceit, corruption, or breach of trust
	Computer Crime use of a computer to commit a crime
	Racketeer Influenced and Corrupt Organizations Act federal law intended to stop organized crime from infiltrating legitimate businesses
Crimes against Business	**Larceny** trespassory taking and carrying away of personal property of another with the intent to deprive the victim permanently of the property
	Embezzlement taking of another's property by a person who was in lawful possession of the property
	False Pretenses obtaining title to property of another by means of representations one knows to be materially false, made with intent to defraud
	Robbery committing larceny with the use or threat of force
	Burglary under most modern statutes, an entry into a building with the intent to commit a felony
	Extortion the making of threats to obtain money or property
	Bribery offering money or property to a public official to influence the official's decision
	Forgery intentional falsification of a document in order to defraud
	Bad Checks knowingly issuing a check without funds sufficient to cover the check
Defenses to Crimes	**Defense of Person or Property** individuals may use reasonable force to protect themselves, other individuals, and their property
	Duress coercion by threat of serious bodily harm is a defense to criminal conduct other than murder
	Mistake of Fact honest and reasonable belief that conduct is not criminal is a defense
	Entrapment inducement by a law enforcement official to commit a crime is a defense
Criminal Procedure	**Steps in Criminal Prosecution** generally include arrest, booking, formal notice of charges, preliminary hearing to determine probable cause, indictment or information, arraignment, and trial
	Fourth Amendment protects individuals against unreasonable searches and seizures
	Fifth Amendment protects persons against self-incrimination, double jeopardy, and being charged with a capital crime except by grand jury indictment
	Sixth Amendment provides the accused with the right to a speedy and public trial, the opportunity to confront witnesses, have compulsory process for obtaining witnesses, and the right to counsel

QUESTIONS

1. Sam said to Carol, "Kim is going to sell me a good used car next Monday and then I'll deliver it to you in exchange for your computer but I'd like to have the computer now." Relying on this statement, Carol delivered the computer to Sam. Sam knew Kim had no car and would have none in the future, and he had no such arrangement with her. The appointed time of exchange passed, and Sam failed to deliver the car to Carol. Has a crime been committed? Discuss.

2. Sara, a lawyer, drew a deed for Robert by which Robert was to convey land to Rick. The deed was correct in every detail. Robert examined and verbally approved it but did not sign it. Then Sara erased Rick's name and substituted her own. Robert subsequently signed the deed with all required legal formalities without noticing the change. Was Sara guilty of forgery? Discuss.

3. Ann took Bonnie's watch without Bonnie knowing of the theft. Bonnie subsequently discovered her loss and was informed that Ann had taken the watch. Bonnie immediately pursued Ann. Ann pointed a loaded pistol at Bonnie, who, in fear of being shot, allowed Ann to escape. Was Ann guilty of robbery? Of any other crime?

4. Jones and Wilson were on trial, separately, for larceny of a $1,000 bearer bond (payable to the holder of the bond, not a named individual) issued by Brown, Inc. The commonwealth's evidence showed that the owner of the bond put it in an envelope bearing his name and address and dropped it accidentally in the street; that Jones found the envelope with the bond in it; that Jones could neither read nor write; that Jones presented the envelope and bond to Wilson, an educated man, and asked Wilson what he should do with it; that Wilson told Jones that the finder of lost property becomes the owner of it; that Wilson told Jones that the bond was worth $100 but that the money could be collected only at the issuer's home office; that Jones then handed the bond to Wilson, who redeemed it at the corporation's home office and received $1,000; that Wilson gave Jones $100 of the proceeds. What rulings?

5. Truck drivers for a hauling company, while loading a desk, found a $100 bill that had fallen out of the desk. They agreed to get it exchanged for small bills and divide the proceeds. En route to the bank, one of them changed his mind and refused to proceed with the scheme, whereupon the other pulled a

knife and demanded the bill. A police officer intervened. What crimes have been committed?

6. Peter, an undercover police agent, was trying to locate a laboratory where it was believed that methamphetamine, or "speed"—a controlled substance—was being manufactured illegally. Peter went to Mary's home and said that he represented a large organization that was interested in obtaining methamphetamine. Peter offered to supply a necessary ingredient for the manufacture of the drug, which was very difficult to obtain, in return for one-half of the drug produced. Mary agreed and processed the chemical given to her by Peter in Peter's presence. Later Peter returned with a search warrant and arrested Mary. Mary was charged with various narcotics law violations. Mary asserted the defense of entrapment. Should Mary prevail? Why?

7. The police obtained a search warrant based on an affidavit that contained the following allegations: (a) Donald was seen crossing a state line on four occasions during a five-day period and going to a particular apartment; (b) telephone records disclosed that the apartment had two telephones; (c) Donald had a reputation as a bookmaker and as an associate of gamblers; and (d) the Federal Bureau of Investigation was informed by a "confidential reliable informant" that Donald was conducting gambling operations from the apartment. The affidavit did not indicate how the informant knew of this in-

formation nor did it contain any information about the reliability of the informant. When a search was made based on the warrant, evidence was obtained that resulted in Donald's conviction of violating certain gambling laws. Donald challenged the constitutionality of the search warrant. Were Donald's constitutional rights violated? Explain your answer.

8. A national bank was robbed by a man with a small strip of tape on each side of his face. An indictment was returned against David. David was then arrested, and counsel was appointed to represent him. Two weeks later, without notice to David's lawyer, an agent with the Federal Bureau of Investigation arranged to have the two bank employees observe a lineup, including David and five or six other prisoners. Each person in the lineup wore strips of tape, as had the robber, and each was directed to repeat the words "Put the money in the bag," as had the robber. Both of the bank employees identified David as the robber. At David's trial he was again identified by the two, in the courtroom, and the prior lineup identification was elicited on cross-examination by David's counsel. David's counsel moved the court either to grant a judgment of acquittal or alternatively to strike the courtroom identifications on the ground that the lineup had violated David's Fifth Amendment privilege against self-incrimination and his Sixth Amendment right to counsel. Decision?

CASE PROBLEMS

9. Waronek owned and operated a trucking rig, transporting goods for L.T.L. Perishables, Inc., of St. Paul, Minnesota. He accepted an offer to haul a trailer load of beef from Illini Beef Packers, Inc., in Joslin, Illinois, to Midtown Packing Company in New York City. After his truck was loaded with ninety-five forequarters and ninety-five hindquarters of beef in Joslin, Waronek drove north to his home in Watertown, Wisconsin, rather than east to New York. While in Watertown, he asked employees of the Royal Meat Company to butcher and prepare four hindquarters of beef—two for himself and two for his friends. He also offered to sell ten hindquarters to one employee of the company at an alarmingly reduced rate. The suspicious employee contacted the authorities, who told him to proceed with the deal. When Waronek arrived in New York with his load short nineteen hindquarters, Waronek telephoned L.T.L. Perishables in St. Paul. He notified them "that he was short nineteen hindquarters, that he knew where the beef went, and that he would make good on it out of future settlements." L.T.L. told him to contact the New York police but he failed to do so. Shortly thereafter, he was arrested by the Federal Bureau of Investigation and indicted for the embezzlement of goods moving in interstate commerce. Explain whether Waronek was guilty of the crime of embezzlement.

10. Four separate cases involving similar fact situations were consolidated because they presented the same constitutional question. In each case, police officers, detectives, or prosecuting attorneys took a defendant into custody and interrogated him in a police station to obtain a confession. In none of these cases did the officials fully and effectively advise the defendant

of his rights at the outset of the interrogation. The interrogations produced oral admissions of guilt from each defendant, as well as signed statements from three of them, which were used to convict them at their trials. The defendants appealed, arguing that the officials should have warned them of their constitutional rights and the consequences of waiving them before the questioning began. It was contended that to permit any statements obtained without such a warning violated their Fifth Amendment privilege against self-incrimination. Were the defendants' constitutional rights violated? Discuss.

11. Officer Cyril Rombach of the Burbank Police Department, an experienced and well-trained narcotics officer, applied for a warrant to search several residences and automobiles for cocaine, methaqualone, and other narcotics. Rombach supported his application with information given to another police officer by a confidential informant of unproven reliability. He also based the warrant application on his own observations made during an extensive investigation: known drug offenders visiting the residences and leaving with small packages as well as a suspicious trip to Miami by two of the suspects. A state superior court judge in good faith issued a search warrant to Rombach based on this information. Rombach's searches netted large quantities of drugs and other evidence, which produced indictments of several suspects on charges of conspiracy to possess and distribute cocaine. The defendants moved to suppress the evidence on the grounds that the search warrant was defective in that Rombach had failed to establish the informant's credibility. Should the evidence be excluded or can it be placed into evidence since the police and courts acted in good faith? Why?

TAKING SIDES

Olivo was in the hardware area of a department store. A security guard saw him look around, take a set of wrenches, and conceal it in his clothing. Olivo looked around once more and proceeded toward an exit, passing several cash registers. The guard stopped him short of the exit.

a. What argument would support the prosecutor in finding Olivo guilty of larceny?

b. What argument would you make as Olivio's defense counsel for finding him not guilty of larceny?

c. Which side's argument do you find most convincing? Explain.

CHAPTER **7**

Intentional Torts

CHAPTER OUTCOMES

After reading and studying this chapter, you should be able to:

1. Identify and describe the torts that protect against **intentional harm to personal rights.**

2. Explain the application of the various privileges to defamation suits and how they are affected by whether the plaintiff is (a) a public figure, (b) a public official, or (c) a private person.

3. Describe and distinguish the four torts comprising invasion of privacy.

4. Identify and describe the torts that protect against harm to property.

5. Distinguish among interference with contractual relations, disparagement, and fraudulent misrepresentation.

Torts are infinitely various, not limited or confined, for there is nothing in nature but may be an instrument for mischief.

Charles Pratt
(quoted in *The Guide to American Law,* vol. 10)

Tort

a civil wrong causing injury to persons, their property, or their economic interests

All forms of civil liability are either (1) voluntarily assumed, as by contract, or (2) involuntarily assumed, as imposed by law. **Tort** liability is of the second type. Tort law gives persons relief from civil wrongs or injuries to their persons, property, and economic interests. Examples include assault and battery, automobile accidents, professional malpractice, and products liability. This law has three principal objectives: (1) to compensate persons who sustain harm or loss resulting from another's conduct, (2) to place the cost of that compensation only on those parties who should bear it, and (3) to prevent future harms and losses. Thus, the law of torts reallocates losses caused by human misconduct. In general, a tort is committed when (1) a duty owed by one person to another (2) is breached, (3) proximately causing (4) injury or damage to the owner of a legally protected interest.

Each person is legally responsible for the damages proximately caused by his tortious conduct. Moreover, as we will discuss in Chapter 29, businesses that conduct their business activities through employees are also liable for the torts their employees commit in the course of employment. The tort liability of employers makes the study of tort law essential to business managers.

Injuries may be inflicted intentionally, negligently, or without fault (strict liability). We will discuss intentional torts in this chapter and cover negligence and strict liability in Chapter 8.

The same conduct may, and often does, constitute both a crime and a tort. For example, let us assume that Johnson has committed an assault and battery against West. For the commission of this crime, the state may take appropriate action against Johnson. In addition, Johnson has violated West's right to be secure in his person, and so has committed a tort against West. Regardless of the criminal action brought by the state against Johnson, West may bring a civil tort action against Johnson for damages. But an act may be criminal without being tortious; by the same token, an act may be a tort but not a crime.

In a tort action, the injured party sues to recover compensation for the injury sustained as a result of the defendant's wrongful conduct. The purpose of tort law,

Punitive damages

damages awarded in excess of normal compensation to punish a defendant for a serious civil wrong

unlike criminal law, is to compensate the injured party, not to punish the wrongdoer. In certain cases, however, courts may award exemplary or **punitive damages**, which are damages over and above the amount necessary to compensate the plaintiff. Where the defendant's tortious conduct has been intentional—or in some states, reckless—and outrageous, showing malice or a fraudulent or evil motive, most courts permit a jury to award punitive damages. The allowance of punitive damages is designed to punish and make an example of the defendant and thus deter others from similar conduct.

Philip Morris USA v. Williams
Supreme Court of the United States, 2007
549 U.S. 346, 127 S.Ct. 1057, 166 L.Ed. 2d 940
http://www.law.cornell.edu/supct/pdf/05-1256P.ZS

FACTS This lawsuit arises out of the death of Jesse Williams, a heavy cigarette smoker. Williams' widow represents his estate in this state lawsuit for negligence and deceit against Philip Morris, the manufacturer of Marlboro, the brand that Williams smoked. A jury found that Williams' death was caused by smoking; that Williams smoked in significant part because he thought it was safe to do so; and that Philip Morris knowingly and falsely led him to believe that this was so. The jury found that both Philip Morris and Williams were negligent and that Philip Morris had engaged in deceit. In respect to deceit, it awarded compensatory damages of about $821,000 along with $79.5 million in punitive damages.

The trial judge subsequently found the $79.5 million punitive damages award "excessive" and reduced it to $32 million. Both sides appealed. The Oregon Court of Appeals rejected Philip Morris' arguments and restored the $79.5 million jury award. Subsequently, the Oregon Supreme Court rejected Philip Morris' arguments that the trial court should have instructed the jury that it could not punish Philip Morris for injury to persons not before the court and that the roughly 100:1 ratio of the $79.5 million punitive damages award to the compensatory damages amount was "grossly excessive."

The U.S. Supreme Court granted Philip Morris *certiorari* on its claims that (1) Oregon had unconstitutionally permitted it to be punished for harming nonparty victims; and (2) Oregon had in effect disregarded "the constitutional requirement that punitive damages be reasonably related to the plaintiff's harm."

DECISION The Oregon Supreme Court's judgment is vacated, and the case is remanded.

OPINION The Supreme Court has long made clear that "punitive damages may properly be imposed to further a State's legitimate interests in punishing unlawful conduct and deterring its repetition." At the same time, the Supreme Court has emphasized the need to avoid an arbitrary determination of an award's amount. Unless a state insists upon proper standards that will confine the jury's discretionary authority, its punitive damages system may deprive a defendant of "fair notice ... of the severity of the penalty that a State may impose"; it may threaten "arbitrary punishments;" and, where the amounts are sufficiently large, it may impose one state's "policy choice," as to the conditions under which (or even whether) certain products can be sold, upon other states" with different public policies.

For these and similar reasons, the Supreme Court has found that the Constitution imposes certain limits, in respect both to procedures for awarding punitive damages and to amounts forbidden as "grossly excessive." These opinions have required *de novo*

judicial review of the size of punitive awards; have held that excessiveness depends upon (1) the reprehensibility of the defendant's conduct, (2) whether the award bears a reasonable relationship to the actual and potential harm caused by the defendant to the plaintiff, and (3) the difference between the award and sanctions "authorized or imposed in comparable cases;" and have indicated that excessiveness is more likely where the ratio between punitive and compensatory damages exceeds single digits.

In the Court's view, the Constitution's Due Process Clause forbids a state to use a punitive damages award to punish a defendant for injury that it inflicts upon nonparties or those whom they directly represent, that is, injury that it inflicts upon those who are, essentially, strangers to the litigation. For one thing, the Due Process Clause prohibits a state from punishing an individual without first providing that individual with "an opportunity to present every available defense." Yet a defendant threatened with punishment for injuring a nonparty victim has no opportunity to defend against the charge, by showing, for example in a case such as this, that the other victim was not entitled to damages because he or she knew that smoking was dangerous or did not rely upon the defendant's statements to the contrary.

Finally, the Court has said that it may be appropriate to consider the reasonableness of a punitive damages award in light of the *potential* harm the defendant's conduct could have caused. But the Court has made clear that the potential harm at issue was harm potentially caused *the plaintiff*.

Evidence of actual harm to nonparties can help to show that the conduct that harmed the plaintiff also posed a substantial risk of harm to the general public, and so was particularly reprehensible—although counsel may argue in a particular case that conduct resulting in no harm to others nonetheless posed a grave risk to the public, or the converse. Yet for the reasons given above, a jury may not go further than this and use a punitive damages verdict to punish a defendant directly on account of harms it is alleged to have caused nonparties. The Court concluded that the Due Process Clause requires states to provide assurance that juries are not asking the wrong question, that is, seeking, not simply to determine reprehensibility, but also to punish for harm caused strangers.

The instruction that Philip Morris said the trial court should have given distinguishes between using harm to others as part of the "reasonable relationship" equation (which it would allow) and using it directly as a basis for punishment. This case was remanded so that the Oregon Supreme Court could apply the standard the Court set forth in this opinion. Because the application of this standard may lead to the need for a new trial, or a change in the level of the punitive damages award, the Court did not consider whether the award is constitutionally "grossly excessive."

INTERPRETATION In most states, a jury may award punitive damages if a defendant's tortious conduct is intentional and outrageous, but the amount of damages must not be grossly excessive and may not punish the defendant for harm caused to parties other than the plaintiff.

ETHICAL QUESTION Is it ethical to impose punishment in a civil case without the protections provided to defendants in a criminal proceeding? Explain.

CRITICAL THINKING QUESTION Can juries be adequately instructed to make the distinction required by the U.S. Supreme Court? Explain.

PRACTICAL ADVICE
When bringing a lawsuit for an intentional tort, consider whether it is appropriate to ask for punitive damages.

Tort law is primarily common law, and, as we mentioned in Chapter 1, the Restatements, prepared by the American Law Institute (ALI), present many important areas of the common law, including torts. You will recall that although they are not law in themselves, the Restatements are highly persuasive in the courts. Since then, the Restatement has served as a vital force in shaping the law of torts. Between 1965 and 1978, the institute adopted and promulgated a second edition of the Restatement of Torts, which revised and superseded the First Restatement. This text will refer to the second Restatement simply as the Restatement.

In 1996, the ALI approved the development of a new Restatement, called Restatement Third, Torts: Liability for Physical and Emotional Harm, which addresses the general or basic elements of the tort action for liability for accidental personal injury, property damage, and emotional harm but does not cover liability for economic loss. This work replaces comparable provisions in the Restatement Second, Torts. The final work is published in two volumes. Volume 1 was published in 2009 and covers liability for negligence causing physical harm, duty, strict liability, factual cause, and scope of liability (traditionally called proximate cause). Volume 2 covers affirmative duties, emotional harm, landowner liability, and liability of actors who retain independent contractors. Volume 2 was approved and published in 2011.

Because this new Restatement applies to nonintentional torts, it will be covered extensively in the next chapter and it will be cited as the "Third Restatement." A few of its provisions, however, do apply to intentional torts and will be included in this chapter. Comment c to Section 5 of the Third Restatement provides that the Second Restatement remains largely authoritative in explaining the details of specific intentional torts and their related defenses.

The Institute's Restatement Third, Torts: Economic Torts and Related Wrongs will update coverage on torts that involve economic loss or pecuniary harm *not* resulting from physical harm or physical contact to a person or property. The project will update coverage of economic torts in Restatement Second, Torts and address some topics not covered in prior Restatements. The Institute began this project in 2004 and after several years of inactivity the project was resumed in 2010. Thus far, no part of the work has been approved.

Intent
desire to cause the consequences of an act or knowledge that the consequences are substantially certain to result from the act

Intent, as used in tort law, does not require a hostile or evil motive. Rather, it means that the actor desires to cause the consequences of his act or that he believes the consequences are substantially (almost) certain to result from it. (See Figure 7-1, which illustrates intent.) The Third Restatement provides that "[a] person acts with the intent to produce a consequence if: (a) the person acts with the purpose of producing that consequence; or (b) the person acts knowing that the consequence is substantially certain to result."

The following examples illustrate the definition of intent: (1) If Mark fires a gun in the middle of the Mojave Desert, he intends to fire the gun; but when the bullet hits Steven, who is in the desert without Mark's knowledge, Mark does not intend that result. (2) Mark throws a bomb into Steven's office in order to kill Steven. Mark knows that Carol is in Steven's office and that the bomb is substantially certain to injure Carol, although Mark has no desire to harm her. Mark is, nonetheless, liable to Carol for any injury caused Carol. Mark's intent to injure Steven is *transferred* to Carol.

Infants (persons who have not reached the age of majority, which is eighteen years in almost all states) are held liable for their intentional torts. The infant's age and knowledge, however, are critical in determining whether the infant had sufficient intelligence to form the required intent. Incompetents, like infants, are generally held liable for their intentional torts.

Even though the defendant has intentionally invaded the interests of the plaintiff, the defendant will not be liable if such conduct was privileged. A defendant's conduct is *privileged* if it furthers an interest of such social importance that the law grants immunity from tort liability

Figure 7-1 Intent

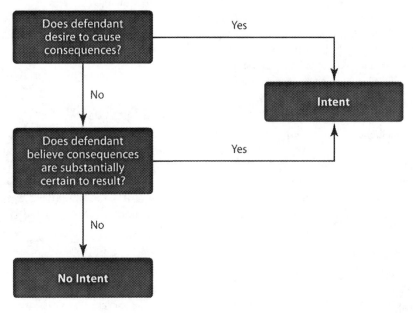

© Cengage Learning 2013

for damage to others. Examples of privilege include self-defense, defense of property, and defense of others. In addition, the plaintiff's consent to the defendant's conduct is a defense to intentional torts.

HARM TO THE PERSON

The law provides protection against harm to the person. Generally, intentional torts to the person entitle the injured party to recover damages for bodily harm, emotional distress, loss or impairment of earning capacity, reasonable medical expenses, and harm the tortious conduct caused to property or business.

Battery

Battery is an intentional infliction of harmful or offensive bodily contact. It may consist of contact causing serious injury, such as a gunshot wound or a blow on the head with a club. Or it may involve contact causing little or no physical injury, such as knocking a hat off of a person's head or flicking a glove in another's face. Bodily contact is offensive if it would offend a reasonable person's sense of dignity. Such contact may be accomplished through the use of objects, such as Gustav's throwing a rock at Hester with the intention of hitting her. If the rock hits Hester or any other person, Gustav has committed a battery.

> **Battery**
> intentional infliction of harmful or offensive bodily contact

Assault

Assault is intentional conduct by one person directed at another that places the other in apprehension of imminent (immediate) bodily harm or offensive contact. It is usually committed immediately before a battery, but if the intended battery fails, the assault remains. Assault is essentially a mental rather than a physical intrusion. Accordingly, damages for it may include compensation for fright and humiliation. The person in danger of immediate bodily harm must have *knowledge* of the danger and be apprehensive of its imminent threat to his safety.

> **Assault**
> intentional infliction of apprehension of immediate bodily harm or offensive contact

False Imprisonment

The tort of **false imprisonment** or *false arrest* is the act of intentionally confining a person against her will within fixed boundaries if the person is conscious of the confinement or harmed by it. Such restraint may be brought about by physical force, the threat of physical force, or by force directed against a person's property. Damages for false imprisonment may include compensation for loss of time, physical discomfort, inconvenience, physical illness, and mental

> **False imprisonment**
> intentional interference with a person's freedom of movement by unlawful confinement

suffering. Merely obstructing a person's freedom of movement is not false imprisonment so long as a reasonable alternative exit is available.

Merchants occasionally encounter potential liability for false imprisonment when they seek to question a suspected shoplifter. A merchant who detains an innocent person may face a lawsuit for false imprisonment. However, most states have statutes protecting the merchant, provided she detains the suspect with probable cause, in a reasonable manner, and for not more than a reasonable time.

Infliction of Emotional Distress

Infliction of emotional distress

extreme and outrageous conduct intentionally or recklessly causing severe emotional distress

Recklessness

conduct that evidences a conscious disregard of or an indifference to the consequences of the act committed

Under the Second and Third Restatements, a person is liable for **infliction of emotional distress** when that person by extreme and outrageous conduct intentionally or recklessly causes severe emotional distress to another. The person is liable for that emotional distress and, if the emotional distress causes bodily harm, also for the resulting bodily harm. **Recklessness** is conduct that evidences a conscious disregard of or an indifference to the consequences of the act committed. With respect to infliction of emotional distress, the Third Restatement explains that an

actor acts recklessly when the actor knows of the risk of severe emotional disturbance (or knows facts that make the risk obvious) and fails to take a precaution that would eliminate or reduce the risk even though the burden is slight relative to the magnitude of the risk, thereby demonstrating the actor's indifference.

Damages may be recovered for severe emotional distress even in the absence of any physical injury. Liability for infliction of emotional distress, however, arises only when the person seeking recovery has suffered *severe* emotional disturbance and when a reasonable person in the same circumstances would suffer severe disturbance. Thus, the Third Restatement is imposing an objective—not a subjective—test. Accordingly, there is no liability for mental harm suffered by an unusually vulnerable plaintiff, unless the defendant knew of the plaintiff's special vulnerability. Under the "extreme and outrageous" requirement, a person is liable only if the conduct goes beyond the bounds of human decency and would be regarded as intolerable in a civilized community. Ordinary insults and indignities are not enough for liability to be imposed, even if the person desires to cause emotional disturbance. Examples of this tort include sexual harassment on the job and outrageous and prolonged bullying tactics employed by creditors or collection agencies attempting to collect a debt, or by insurance adjusters trying to force a settlement of an insurance claim.

Ferrell v. Mikula
Court of Appeals of Georgia, 2008, reconsideration denied, 2008
627 S.E.2d 7
http://scholar.google.com/scholar_case?case=12901711244406213270&q=FERRELL+v.+MIKULA&hl=en&as_sdt=2,34

FACTS On Friday night, August 6, 2006, eighteen-year old Racquel Ferrell and thirteen-year-old Kristie Ferrell went to Ruby Tuesday. After they ate and paid their bill, the girls left the restaurant, got into their car, and drove out of the parking lot. As they entered the highway, Racquel noticed a black truck following her very closely with its headlights on high. A marked police car by the side of the road pulled onto the highway between the girls' car and the following truck and pulled the car over. The officer pulled Racquel out of the car, placed her in handcuffs, and put her in the back seat of his patrol car. Another officer removed Kristie from the car, placed her in handcuffs, and put her in the back of another patrol car.

All of the police officers gathered to talk to the driver of the truck that had been following the Ferrells, who turned out to be a uniformed off-duty police officer working as a security guard for Ruby Tuesday. The officer who arrested Racquel returned to the patrol car where she was being held and told her if she had not paid her Ruby Tuesday bill, she was going to jail. She protested,

and the officer conferred again with the other officers, then returned to the car and said, "It was a mistake." He explained that the manager at the restaurant had sent the off-duty officer after them because he said the girls had not paid their bill, but they did not fit the description of the two people who had walked out without paying. The officers removed the handcuffs from Racquel and Kristie and returned them to their car. After asking for Racquel's driver's license and obtaining information about both girls, the officer told them they were free to go.

Christian Mikula had been an assistant manager for about a month, and was the only manager at Ruby Tuesday that night. One of the servers, Robert, reported that his customers at Table 24 had a complaint, so Mikula talked to the couple and told them he would "take care of" the food item in question. The customers were a man and a woman in their late twenties to early thirties. Mikula left the table to discuss the matter with Robert, after which server Aaron told Mikula that the patrons at Table 24 had left without paying. Mikula looked at the table, confirmed they had not left any money for the bill, and went out the main entrance. He saw a car pulling out of the parking lot, and said to the off-duty officer, "Hey, I think they just left without paying." The officer said, "Who, them?" Mikula said, "I think so," and the officer got up and went to his vehicle.

Mikula knew the officer was going to follow the people in the car and would stop them, but did not ask the officer if he had seen who got into the car. He did not give the officer a description of the people at Table 24, and did not know the race, age, gender, or number of people in the car being followed. He did not know if there were people in any of the other cars in the parking lot. He did not ask any other people in the restaurant if they had seen the people at Table 24 leave the building, which had two exits. He did not know how long the people had been gone before Aaron told him they left, or whether another customer had picked up money from Table 24. He could have tried to obtain more information to determine whether the people in the car he pointed out were the people who had been sitting at Table 24, but did not do so.

Racquel Ferrell and the parents of Kristie Ferrell sued Ruby Tuesday, Inc. and its manager, Christian Mikula, for false imprisonment and intentional infliction of emotional distress. The trial court granted the defendants' motion for summary judgment on all counts. The Ferrells appealed.

DECISION Summary judgment on the claim for intentional infliction of emotional distress is affirmed; summary judgment on the claim for false imprisonment is reversed.

OPINION In this case, the Ferrells were detained without a warrant and thus have a claim for false imprisonment. False imprisonment is the unlawful detention of the person of another, for any length of time, whereby such person is deprived of his personal liberty. The only essential elements of the action being the detention and its unlawfulness; malice and the want of probable cause need not be shown.

The evidence in this case clearly establishes that the Ferrells were detained. Although "'imprisonment' was originally intended to have meant stone walls and iron bars, ... under modern tort law an individual may be imprisoned when his movements are restrained in the open street, or in a traveling automobile." Ruby Tuesday does not argue otherwise, but instead argues that the evidence established sufficient probable cause and the plaintiffs failed to establish that Mikula acted with malice. But malice is not an element of false imprisonment. Further, the mere existence of probable cause standing alone has no real defensive bearing on the issue of liability for false imprisonment.

Arresting or causing the arrest of a person without a warrant constitutes a tort, unless he can justify under some of the exceptions in which arrest and imprisonment without a warrant are permitted by law. Generally, one who causes or directs the arrest of another by an officer without a warrant may be held liable for false imprisonment, in the absence of justification, and the burden of proving that such imprisonment lies within an exception rests upon the person causing the imprisonment.

Accordingly, as the Ferrells have established an unlawful detention, the next issue to consider is whether Mikula "caused" the arrest. It is a factual question for the jury to determine whether a party (1) is potentially liable for false imprisonment by directly or indirectly urging a law enforcement official to begin criminal proceedings or (2) is not liable because he merely relates facts to an official who then makes an independent decision to arrest. The party need not expressly request an arrest and may be liable if his conduct and acts "procured and directed the arrest."

Here, Mikula told the officer that the car leaving the parking lot contained people who left without paying for their food, although he did not know or try to ascertain who was in the car. He also knew the officer was going to detain the people in the car and could have tried to stop him, but made no attempt to do so. Accordingly, the trial court erred in granting summary judgment to the defendants on the plaintiffs' false imprisonment claim.

The Ferrells also contend that the trial court erred in granting summary judgment to the defendants on their claim for intentional infliction of emotional distress. The elements of a cause of action for intentional infliction of emotional distress are: (1) intentional or reckless conduct; (2) that is extreme and outrageous; (3) a causal connection between the wrongful conduct and the emotional distress; and (4) severe emotional distress. Further,

> [l]iability for this tort has been found only where the conduct has been so outrageous in character, and so extreme in degree, as to go beyond all possible bounds of decency, and to be regarded as atrocious, and utterly intolerable in a civilized community. Generally, the case is one in which the recitation of the facts to an average member of the community would arouse his resentment against the actor, and lead him to exclaim, "Outrageous!"

In this case, the action upon which the Ferrells base their emotional distress claim is being stopped by the police, placed in handcuffs, and held in a patrol car for a short period of time before being released. While this incident was unfortunate, the question raised by the evidence was whether the restaurant manager's actions were negligent, not whether he acted maliciously or his conduct was extreme, atrocious, or utterly intolerable. Accordingly, the trial court did not err in granting the defendants' motion for summary judgment on the Ferrells' claim for intentional infliction of emotional distress.

INTERPRETATION False imprisonment is the unlawful detention of the person of another, for any length of time, whereby such person is deprived of his personal liberty unless there is a legally recognized justification. Liability is imposed under the tort of infliction of emotional distress for intentional or reckless conduct that is extreme and outrageous and that causes severe emotional distress.

CRITICAL THINKING QUESTION Do you agree that the manager's conduct was negligent at most and thus not reckless?

HARM TO THE RIGHT OF DIGNITY

The law also protects a person against intentional interference with, or harm to, his right of dignity. This protection covers a person's reputation, privacy, and right to freedom from unjustifiable litigation.

Defamation

Defamation
injury to a person's reputation by publication of false statements

As we discussed in Chapter 4, the tort of **defamation** is a false communication that injures a person's reputation by disgracing him and diminishing the respect in which he is held. An example would be the publication of a false statement that a person had committed a crime or had a loathsome disease.

Elements of Defamation   The elements of a defamation action are (1) a false and defamatory statement concerning another; (2) an unprivileged publication (communication) to a third party; (3) depending on the status of the defendant, negligence or recklessness on her part in knowing or failing to ascertain the falsity of the statement; and (4) in some cases, proof of special harm caused by the publication. The burden of proof is on the plaintiff to prove the falsity of the defamatory statement.

Libel
defamation communicated by writing, television, radio, or the like

If the defamatory communication is handwritten, typewritten, printed, pictorial, or in any other medium with similar communicative power, such as a television or radio broadcast, it is designated as **libel**. If it is spoken or oral, it is designated as **slander**. In either case, it must be communicated to a person or persons other than the one who is defamed, a process referred to as its *publication*. Thus, if Maurice writes a defamatory letter about Pierre's character that he hands or mails to Pierre, this is not a publication because it is intended only for Pierre. The publication must have been intentional or the result of the defendant's negligence.

Slander
oral defamation

Any living person, as well as corporations, partnerships, and unincorporated associations, may be defamed. Unless a statute provides otherwise, no action may be brought for defamation of a deceased person.

PRACTICAL ADVICE

Consider whether you should provide employment references for current and former employees, and if you decide to do so, take care in what you say. See the "Business Law in Action" feature on the next page.

A significant trend affecting business has been the bringing of defamation suits against former employers by discharged employees. It has been reported that such suits account for approximately one-third of all defamation lawsuits. The following case demonstrates the consequences of failing to be careful in discharging an employee.

Frank B. Hall & Co., Inc. v. Buck
Court of Appeals of Texas, Fourteenth District, 1984
678 S.W.2d 612, *cert. denied*, 472 U.S. 1009, 105 S.Ct. 2704, 86 L.Ed.2d 720 (1985)
http://scholar.google.com/scholar_case?case=17495651340574040653&q=678+S.W.2d+612&hl=en&as_sdt=2,34

FACTS On June 1, 1976, Larry W. Buck, an established salesman in the insurance business, began working for Frank B. Hall & Co. In the course of the ensuing months, Buck brought several major accounts to Hall and produced substantial commission income for the firm. In October 1976, Mendel Kaliff, then president of Frank B. Hall & Co. of Texas, informed Buck that his salary and benefits were being reduced because of his failure to generate sufficient income for the firm. On March 31, 1977, Kaliff and Lester Eckert, Hall's office manager, fired Buck. Buck was unable to procure subsequent employment with another insurance firm. He hired an investigator, Lloyd Barber, to discover the true reasons for his dismissal and for his inability to find other employment.

Barber contacted Kaliff, Eckert, and Virginia Hilley, a Hall employee, and told them he was an investigator and was seeking information about Buck's employment with the firm. Barber conducted tape-recorded interviews with the three in September and October of 1977. Kaliff accused Buck of being disruptive, untrustworthy, paranoid, hostile, untruthful, and of padding his expense account. Eckert referred to Buck as "a zero" and a "classical sociopath" who was ruthless, irrational, and disliked by other employees. Hilley stated that Buck could have been charged with theft for certain materials he brought with him from his former employer to Hall. Buck sued Hall for damages for defamation and was awarded over $1.9 million by a jury—$605,000 for actual damages and $1,300,000 for punitive damages. Hall then brought this appeal.

DECISION Judgment for Buck affirmed.

OPINION Any intentional or negligent communication of defamatory matter to a third person is a publication, unless the defamed individual authorized, invited, or procured the statement or statements and knew of their contents in advance. The Hall employees intentionally communicated disparaging remarks about Buck to Barber. While it may be true that Buck could assume the employees would express their opinion of him, he did not know they would defame him. Their accusations were not mere opinions but were untrue and derogatory statements of fact. Although the comments were directed at an individual acting at Buck's request, communication to an agent of the defamed individual qualifies as a publication unless the defamed individual or his agent invited the publication. In this case, neither Buck nor Barber induced the defamatory remarks.

INTERPRETATION The key elements of defamation are that the statements made are false, injure the plaintiff's reputation, and are published.

ETHICAL QUESTION Did Hall's employees act ethically? Did Buck act ethically in hiring an investigator to obtain the information? Explain.

CRITICAL THINKING QUESTION How should a company respond to inquiries for information about former or current employees? Explain.

BUSINESS LAW *IN ACTION*

If you own or manage a business, you can expect employees to leave for a variety of reasons. When your present or former employees apply for work elsewhere, their potential new employers may well call you to verify their employment history and ask your opinion of them as employees. Should you give that information?

Many employers have stopped giving meaningful references for former employees. Some employers verify only employment dates and job titles of former employees. Others give no information at all. The reason? Fear of liability for defamation and of incurring large legal expenses to defend a lawsuit.

Are those fears justified? Does the benefit of minimizing risk outweigh the cost of shutting down a legitimate and valuable information system? Consider the following points:

- A number of the states have enacted statutes that provide varying degrees of protection against liability for defamation to companies that give job references for current or former employees.
- An employer is liable for a false statement only if she was negligent in attempting to establish its truth.
- Employment references enjoy qualified privilege, unless the employer communicates the statements to people with no need to know their contents or publishes them out of spite.
- Employment references are valuable. Employers who expect to get useful information about job applicants should also be willing to give it.

You can reduce the risk of liability when giving employment references if you . . .

- Endeavor to ensure that all statements you publish about an employee are true. Your effort can be used as a defense against negligence.
- Make sure you publish statements only to people with a legitimate need to know (i.e., potential employers).
- Regulate the giving of references in your company. Make sure people who work for you understand who may give references and who may not. And make sure they know that no one is ever to publish statements maliciously.
- Ask your existing employees to give you written consent to provide references for them.

Source: Ramona L. Paetzold and Steven L. Wilborn, "Employer (Ir)rationality and the Demise of Employment References," *American Business Law Journal*, May 1992, 123–42.

Privilege

immunity from tort liability

Defenses to Defamation Privilege is immunity from tort liability granted when the defendant's conduct furthers a societal interest of greater importance than the injury inflicted upon the plaintiff. Three kinds of privileges apply to defamation: absolute, conditional, and constitutional.

Absolute privilege, which protects the defendant regardless of his motive or intent, has been confined to those few situations in which public policy clearly favors complete freedom of speech. Such privilege includes (1) statements made by participants in a judicial proceeding regarding that proceeding; (2) statements made by members of Congress on the floor of Congress and by members of state and local legislative bodies; (3) statements made by certain executive branch officers while performing their governmental duties; and (4) statements regarding a third party made between spouses when they are alone.

Qualified or *conditional privilege* depends on proper use of the privilege. A person has a conditional privilege to publish defamatory matter to protect her own legitimate interests or, in some cases, the interests of another. Conditional privilege also extends to many communications in which the publisher and the recipient have a common interest, such as letters of reference. Conditional privilege, however, is forfeited by a publisher who acts in an excessive manner, without probable cause, or for an improper purpose.

The First Amendment to the U.S. Constitution guarantees freedom of speech and freedom of the press. The U.S. Supreme Court has applied these rights to the law of defamation by extending a form of *constitutional privilege* to defamatory and false statements about public officials or public figures so long as it is done without malice. For these purposes, *malice* is not ill will but clear and convincing proof of the publisher's knowledge of falsity or reckless disregard of the truth. Thus, under constitutional privilege, the public official or public figure must prove that the defendant published the defamatory and false comment with knowledge or in reckless disregard of the comment's falsity and its defamatory character. However, in a defamation suit brought by a private person (one who is neither a public official nor a public figure), the plaintiff must prove that the defendant published the defamatory and false comment with malice *or* negligence.

Congress enacted Section 230 of the *Communications Decency Act of 1996 (CDA)* granting immunity to Internet service providers (ISPs) from liability for defamation when publishing information originating from a third party. A court has interpreted this provision of the CDA as immunizing an ISP that refused to remove or retract an allegedly defamatory posting made on its bulletin board. The immunity granted by the CDA to ISPs has spawned a number of lawsuits urging ISPs to reveal the identities of subscribers who have posted allegedly defamatory statements. To date, ISPs have complied, generating additional litigation by angry ISP patrons attempting to keep their identities protected by asserting that their right to free speech is being compromised.

Because Section 230 of the CDA grants immunity only to ISPs, there is the possibility that employers will be held liable for some online defamatory statements made by an employee. Section 577(2) of the Restatement of Torts provides that a person who intentionally and unreasonably fails to remove defamatory matter that she knows is exhibited on property in her possession or under her control is liable for its continued publication. Therefore, employers in control of e-forums, such as electronic bulletin boards and chat rooms, should act quickly to remove any defamatory statement brought to their attention.

Invasion of Privacy

The invasion of a person's right to privacy actually consists of four distinct torts: (1) appropriation of a person's name or likeness; (2) unreasonable intrusion on the seclusion of another; (3) unreasonable public disclosure of private facts; or (4) unreasonable publicity that places another in a false light in the public eye.

It is entirely possible and not uncommon for a person's right of privacy to be invaded in a manner entailing two or more of these related torts. For example, Bart forces his way into Cindy's hospital room, takes a photograph of Cindy, and publishes it to promote his cure for Cindy's illness along with false statements about Cindy that would be highly objectionable to a reasonable person. Cindy would be entitled to recover on any or all of the four torts comprising invasion of privacy.

PRACTICAL ADVICE

When using another person's identity for your own purposes, be sure to obtain that person's written consent.

Appropriation

unauthorized use of another person's name or likeness for one's own benefit

Appropriation **Appropriation** is the unauthorized use of another person's name or likeness for one's own benefit, as, for example, in promoting or advertising a product or service. The tort of appropriation, which seeks to protect the individual's right to the exclusive use of his identity, is also known as the "right of publicity." In the example above, Bart's use of Cindy's photograph to promote Bart's business constitutes the tort of appropriation. The following case involving Vanna White is also an example of appropriation.

White v. Samsung Electronics
United States Court of Appeals, Ninth Circuit, 1992
971 F.2d 1395, *cert. denied*, 508 U.S. 951, 113 S.Ct. 2443, 124 L.Ed.2d 660 (1993)
http://scholar.google.com/scholar_case?case=15763501998860364615&q=971+F.2d+1395&hl=en&as_sdt=2,34

FACTS Plaintiff, Vanna White, is the hostess of *Wheel of Fortune*, one of the most popular game shows in television history. Samsung Electronics and David Deutsch Associates ran an advertisement for videocassette recorders that depicted a robot dressed in a wig, gown, and jewelry chosen to resemble White's hair and dress. The robot was posed in a stance, for which White is famous, next to a game board, which is instantly recognizable as the *Wheel of Fortune* game show set. The caption of the ad read: "Longest-running game show. 2012 AD." Defendants referred to the ad as the "Vanna White" ad. White neither consented to the ads, nor was she paid for them. White sued Samsung and Deutsch under the California common law right of publicity. The district court granted summary judgment against White on this claim.

DECISION Judgment reversed.

OPINION The law protects a person's exclusive right to exploit the value of her identity. To state a cause of action under the California common law right of publicity, a plaintiff must allege (1) the defendant's use of the plaintiff's identity; (2) the appropriation of the plaintiff's name or likeness to the defendant's advantage, commercially or otherwise; (3) lack of consent; and

(4) resulting injury. In this case, the district court dismissed White's claim for failure to meet the second element. Although the robot ad did not make use of White's name or likeness, the common law right of publicity is not so confined. The "name or likeness" formulation originated not as an element of the right of publicity cause of action, but as a description of the types of cases in which the cause of action had been recognized. The case law has borne out that the right of publicity is not limited to the appropriation of name or likeness. The specific means of appropriation are relevant only for determining whether the defendant has in fact appropriated the plaintiff's identity. It is not important how the defendant has appropriated the plaintiff's identity, but whether the defendant has done so.

To consider the means of appropriation as dispositive would not only weaken the right of publicity but would effectively eviscerate it. The identities of the most popular celebrities are not only the most attractive for advertisers but also the easiest to evoke without resorting to obvious means such as name, likeness, or voice. Consider a hypothetical advertisement that depicts a mechanical robot with male features, an African-American complexion, and a bald head. The robot is wearing black high-top Air Jordan basketball sneakers and a red basketball uniform with black trim, baggy shorts, and the number 23 (though not revealing "Bulls" or "Jordan" lettering). The ad depicts the robot dunking a basketball one-handed, stiff-armed, legs extended like open scissors, and tongue hanging out. Now envision that this ad is run on television during professional basketball games. Considered individually, the robot's physical attributes, its dress, and its stance tell us little. Taken together, they lead to the only conclusion that any sports viewer who has registered a discernible pulse in the past five years would reach: the ad depicts Michael Jordan.

Viewed together, the individual aspects of the ad in the present case leave little doubt about the celebrity the ad is meant to depict.

Indeed, the defendants themselves referred to their ad as the "Vanna White" ad. Because White has alleged facts showing that Samsung and Deutsch had appropriated her identity, the district court erred by rejecting, on summary judgment, White's common law right of publicity claim.

INTERPRETATION The tort of appropriation protects a person's exclusive right to exploit the value of her identity.

CRITICAL THINKING QUESTION What are the interests protected by this tort?

Intrusion
unreasonable and highly offensive interference with the seclusion of another

Intrusion   **Intrusion** is the unreasonable and highly offensive interference with the solitude or seclusion of another. Such unreasonable interference includes improper entry into another's dwelling, unauthorized eavesdropping on another's private conversations, and unauthorized examination of another's private papers and records. The intrusion must be highly offensive or objectionable to a reasonable person and must involve private matters. Thus, there is no liability if the defendant examines public records or observes the plaintiff in a public place. This form of invasion of privacy is committed once the intrusion occurs—publicity is not required.

Public disclosure of private facts
highly offensive publicity given to private information about another person

Public Disclosure of Private Facts   Under the tort of **public disclosure of private facts**, liability is imposed for publicity given to private information about another, if the matter made public would be highly offensive and objectionable to a reasonable person. Like intrusion, this tort applies only to private, not public, information about an individual; unlike intrusion, it requires publicity. Under the Restatement, the publicity required differs in degree from "publication" as used in the law of defamation. This tort requires that private facts be communicated to the public at large or that they become public knowledge, whereas publication of a defamatory statement need be made only to a single third party. Thus Kathy, a creditor of Gary, will not invade Gary's privacy by writing a letter to Gary's employer informing the employer of Gary's failure to pay the debt, but Kathy would be liable if she posted in the window of her store a statement that Gary will not pay a debt owed to her. Some courts, however, have allowed recovery where the disclosure was made to only one person. Also, unlike defamation, this tort applies to truthful private information if the matter published would be offensive and objectionable to a reasonable person of ordinary sensibilities.

False light
highly offensive publicity placing another in a false light

False Light   The tort of **false light** imposes liability for highly offensive publicity placing another in a false light if the defendant knew that the matter publicized was false or acted in reckless disregard of the truth. For example, Edgar includes Jason's name and photograph in a public "rogues' gallery" of convicted criminals. Because Jason has never been convicted of any crime, Edgar is liable to Jason for placing him in a false light.

As with defamation, the matter must be untrue; unlike defamation, it must be "publicized," not merely "published." Although the matter must be objectionable to a reasonable person, it need not be defamatory. In many instances, the same facts will give rise to actions both for defamation and for false light.

Defenses   The defenses of absolute, conditional, and constitutional privilege apply to publication of any matter that is an invasion of privacy to the same extent that such defenses apply to defamation.

Misuse of Legal Procedure

Misuse of legal procedure
torts protecting an individual from unjustifiable litigation

Three torts comprise the **misuse of legal procedure**: malicious prosecution, wrongful civil proceedings, and abuse of process. Each protects an individual from being subjected to unjustifiable litigation. *Malicious prosecution* and *wrongful civil proceedings* impose liability for damages caused by improperly brought proceedings, including harm to reputation, credit, or standing; emotional distress; and the expenses incurred in defending against the wrongfully brought lawsuit. *Abuse of process* consists of using a legal proceeding (criminal or civil) to

CONCEPT REVIEW 7-1

CONCEPT REVIEW 7-1

Privacy

	Appropriation	Intrusion	Public Disclosure	False Light
Publicity	Yes	No	Yes	Yes
Private Facts	No	Yes	Yes	No
Offensiveness	No	Yes	Yes	Yes
Falsity	No	No	No	Yes

© Cengage Learning 2013

accomplish a purpose for which the proceeding is not designed. This misuse of procedure applies even when there is probable cause or when the plaintiff or prosecution succeeds in the litigation.

HARM TO PROPERTY

The law also provides protection against invasions of a person's interests in property. Intentional harm to property includes the torts of (1) trespass to real property, (2) nuisance, (3) trespass to personal property, and (4) conversion.

Real Property

Real property
land and anything attached
to it

Real property is land and anything attached to it, such as buildings, trees, and minerals. The law protects the possessor's rights to the exclusive use and quiet enjoyment of the land. Accordingly, damages for harm to land include compensation for the resulting diminution in the value of the land, the loss of use of the land, and the discomfort caused to the possessor of the land.

Trespass to real property
wrongful entry onto
another's land

Trespass   A person is liable for **trespass to real property** if he intentionally (1) enters or remains on land in the possession of another, (2) causes a thing or a third person to so enter or remain, or (3) fails to remove from the land a thing that he is under a duty to remove. Liability exists even though no actual damage is done to the land.

It is no defense that the intruder acted under the mistaken belief of law or fact that he was not trespassing. If the intruder intended to be on the particular property, his reasonable belief that he owned the land or had permission to enter on it is irrelevant. However, an intruder is not liable if his presence on the land of another is not caused by his own actions. For example, if Shirley is thrown onto Roy's land by Jimmy, Shirley is not liable to Roy for trespass, although Jimmy is.

PRACTICAL ADVICE

In using, manufacturing, and disposing of dangerous, noxious, or toxic materials take care not to create a nuisance.

A trespass may be committed on, beneath, or above the surface of the land, although the law regards the upper air, above a prescribed minimum altitude for flight, as a public highway. No aerial trespass occurs unless the aircraft enters into the lower reaches of the airspace and substantially interferes with the landowner's use and enjoyment.

Nuisance
nontrespassory invasion of
another's interest in the
private use and enjoyment of
his land

Nuisance   A **nuisance** is a nontrespassory invasion of another's interest in the private use and enjoyment of land. In contrast to trespass, nuisance does not require interference with another's right to exclusive possession of land but imposes liability for significant and unreasonable harm to another's use or enjoyment of land. Examples of nuisances include the emission of unpleasant odors, smoke, dust, or gas, as well as the pollution of a stream, pond, or underground water supply.

Personal Property

Personal property
any property other than an
interest in land

Personal property is any type of property other than an interest in land. The law protects a number of interests in the possession of personal property, including an interest in the property's physical condition and usability, an interest in the retention of possession, and an interest in the property's availability for future use.

Trespass to personal property
intentional dispossession or
unauthorized use of the
personal property of another

Trespass   **Trespass to personal property** consists of the intentional dispossession or unauthorized use of the personal property of another. Although the interference with the right to exclusive use and possession may be direct or indirect, liability is limited to instances in which the trespasser (1) dispossesses the other of the property; (2) substantially impairs the condition, quality, or value of the property; or (3) deprives the possessor of use of the property for a substantial time. For example, Albert parks his car in front of his house. Later, Ronald pushes Albert's car around the corner. Albert subsequently looks for his car but cannot find it for several hours. Ronald is liable to Albert for trespass.

Conversion
intentional exercise of dominion or control over another's personal property

Conversion   **Conversion** is an intentional exercise of dominion or control over another's personal property that so seriously interferes with the other's right of control as justly to require the payment of full value for the property. Thus, all conversions are trespasses, but not all trespasses are conversions. Conversion may consist of the intentional destruction of the personal property or the use of the property in an unauthorized manner. For example, Barbara entrusts an automobile to Ken, a dealer, for sale. After he drives the car eight thousand miles on his own business, Ken is liable to Barbara for conversion. On the other hand, in the example in which Ronald pushed Albert's car around the corner, Ronald would not be liable to Albert for conversion.

HARM TO ECONOMIC INTERESTS

Economic interests comprise a fourth set of interests the law protects against intentional interference. Economic or pecuniary interests include a person's existing and prospective contractual relations, a person's business reputation, a person's name and likeness (previously discussed under appropriation), and a person's freedom from deception. In this section, we will discuss business torts—those torts that protect a person's economic interests.

Interference with Contractual Relations

Interference with contractual relations
intentionally causing one of the parties to a contract not to perform the contract

Interference with contractual relations involves interfering intentionally and improperly with the performance of a contract by inducing one of the parties not to perform it. (Contracts are discussed extensively in Part III of this text.) The injured party may recover the economic loss resulting from the breach of the contract. The law imposes similar liability for intentional and improper interference with another's prospective contractual relation, such as a lease renewal or financing for construction.

PRACTICAL ADVICE

Recognize that inducing another person's employees to breach a valid agreement not to compete or not to disclose confidential information may be improper interference with contractual relations.

In either case, the rule requires that a person act with the purpose or motive of interfering with another's contract or with the knowledge that such interference is substantially certain to occur as a natural consequence of her actions. The interference may occur by prevention through the use of physical force or by threats. Frequently, the interference is accomplished by inducement, such as the offer of a better contract. For instance, Calvin may offer Becky, an employee of Fran under a contract that has two years left, a yearly salary of $5,000 per year more than the contractual arrangement between Becky and Fran. If Calvin is aware of the contract between Becky and Fran and of the fact that his offer to Becky will interfere with that contract, then Calvin is liable to Fran for intentional interference with contractual relations.

Texaco, Inc. v. Pennzoil, Co.
Court of Appeals of Texas, First District, 1987
729 S.W.2d 768, *cert. denied*, 485 U.S. 994, 108 S.Ct. 1305, 99 L.Ed.2d 686 (1988)
http://scholar.google.com/scholar_case?case=11763000609638124594&q=729+S.W.2d+768&hl=en&as_sdt=2,34

FACTS Pennzoil negotiated with Gordon Getty and the J. Paul Getty Museum over the purchase by Pennzoil of all the Getty Oil stock held by each. Gordon Getty, who was also a director of Getty Oil, held about 40.2 percent of the outstanding shares of Getty Oil. The Museum held 11.8 percent. On January 2, a Memorandum of Agreement was drafted, setting forth the terms reached by Pennzoil, Gordon Getty, and the Museum. After increasing the offering price to $110 per share plus a $5 "stub" or bonus, the board of directors of Getty Oil voted on January 3 to accept the Pennzoil deal. Accordingly, on January 4 both Getty Oil and Pennzoil issued press releases, announcing an agreement in principle on the terms of the Memorandum of Agreement but at the higher price.

Having learned of the impending sale of Getty Oil stock to Pennzoil, Texaco hurriedly called several in-house meetings, and hired an investment banker as well, to determine a feasible price range for acquiring Getty Oil. On January 5, Texaco decided on $125 per share and authorized its officers to take any steps necessary to conclude a deal. Texaco met first with a lawyer for the Museum, then with Gordon Getty. Texaco stressed to Getty that if he hesitated in selling his shares, he might be "locked out" in a minority position. On January 6, the Getty Oil board of directors voted to withdraw from the Pennzoil deal and unanimously voted to accept the $125-per-share Texaco offer. Pennzoil sued and won an award of $7.53 billion in compensatory damages and $3 billion in punitive damages based on tortious interference with a contract. Texaco appealed.

DECISION Judgment of trial court affirmed.

OPINION New York law requires knowledge by a defendant of the existence of contractual rights as an element of the tort of inducing breach of that contract. Since there was no direct evidence of Texaco's knowledge of a contract, the question is whether there was legally and factually sufficient circumstantial evidence from which the knowledge could be inferred. Among the evidence were (1) Texaco's carefully mapped strategy to defeat Pennzoil's deal; (2) the notice of a contract in a January 5 *Wall Street Journal* article, although Texaco claimed that no one at Texaco had seen it; (3) the knowledge of an agreement that would arise from comparing the Memorandum of Agreement with the Getty press release; and (4) demands made by the Museum and Trust for full indemnity by Texaco against any claims by Pennzoil based on the Memorandum of Agreement. Clearly, the inference by the jury that Texaco had knowledge of contractual relations between Pennzoil and Gordon Getty and the Museum is supported by the evidence.

Another necessary element is a showing that the defendant took an active part in persuading a party to a contract to breach it.

Merely entering into a contract with a party with the knowledge of that party's contractual obligations to someone else is not the same as inducing a breach. For tort liability to arise, it is necessary that there be some act of interference or of persuading a party to breach, such as by offering better terms or other incentives. The evidence shows that Texaco knew it had only twenty-four hours to "stop the Pennzoil train." Furthermore, the evidence also shows that Texaco's strategy included pressure on Gordon Getty, as well as on key people at the Museum. This evidence contradicts the contention that Texaco passively accepted a deal proposed by the other parties.

INTERPRETATION The tort of interference with contractual relations protects a party to a contract from a third party who intentionally and improperly induces the other contracting party not to perform the contract.

ETHICAL QUESTION Did Getty or Texaco act unethically? Explain.

CRITICAL THINKING QUESTION Does the protection afforded by this tort conflict with society's interest in free competition? Explain.

CONCEPT REVIEW 7-2

Intentional Torts

Interest Protected	Tort
Person	
Freedom from contact	Battery
Freedom from apprehension	Assault
Freedom of movement	False imprisonment
Freedom from distress	Infliction of emotional distress
Dignity	
Reputation	Defamation
Privacy	Appropriation
	Intrusion
	Public disclosure of private facts
	False light
Freedom from wrongful legal actions	Misuse of legal procedure
Property	
Real	Trespass
	Nuisance
Personal	Trespass
	Conversion
Economic	
Contracts	Interference with contractual rights
Goodwill	Disparagement
Freedom from deception	Fraudulent misrepresentation

Ethical Dilemma

What May One Do to Attract Clients from a Previous Employer?

Facts Carl Adle and Louise Bart formed a law firm as partners, and Anne Lily, Marvin Thomas, and Tim Jones joined the newly formed firm of Adle & Bart as associates (nonpartner employees). After about five years, Lily, Thomas, and Jones became disenchanted with the law firm and decided to form their own, to be called Lily, Thomas & Jones.

Lily and Thomas suggested to Jones that they contact approximately five hundred of Adle & Bart's current clients. Lily and Thomas had prepared a model letter to inform clients about the new law firm (Lily, Thomas & Jones) and to encourage them to leave Adle & Bart and to become clients of the new firm. The letter also indicated that Lily, Thomas & Jones would offer legal services far better than those of Adle & Bart: billing rates would be more reasonable, service more prompt, and legal representation more effective and successful. The reference to success was aimed, in part,

at three large clients who recently lost lawsuits under Adle & Bart representation. Although the losses had not resulted from malpractice or mishandling by Adle & Bart, Lily and Thomas knew that significant amounts of money had been at issue and that the clients were sensitive about the results of the lengthy litigation.

The letter included two postage-paid form letters for the prospective client to sign and mail. One form letter was addressed to Adle & Bart, informing them of the client's desire to discontinue the client-attorney relationship and requesting the firm to forward all files to Lily, Thomas & Jones. The other form letter, addressed to Lily, Thomas & Jones, requested representation.

Jones is reluctant about the proposed mailing. Lily and Thomas, in turn, argue that their new firm is not doing as well as they expected. They essentially give Jones an ultimatum: join in the letter or leave the firm. Jones, who has thoroughly alienated

Adle & Bart, does not believe he has any immediate alternative job opportunities.

Social, Policy, and Ethical Considerations
1. Should Jones agree to the proposed mailing? Is it ethical for those forming the new firm to use a client list of their former employer when seeking clients?
2. What practical steps could Jones take to assist him in his decision?
3. What are the competing social interests at stake in this controversy?
4. How would your answers differ, if at all, if the firms were accounting firms rather than law firms?
5. In what manner, if at all, should the law protect existing businesses from competition? Under what circumstances might competition become unfair, and how should laws be tailored to deter unfair practices?
6. Should Jones be concerned about the comparisons the letter makes between the new firm and Adle & Bart?

Disparagement

Disparagement
publication of false statements resulting in harm to another's monetary interests

PRACTICAL ADVICE
When commenting on the products or services offered by a competitor, take care not to make any false statements.

Fraudulent misrepresentation
false statement made with knowledge of its falsity and with intent to induce another to act

PRACTICAL ADVICE
When describing your products or services, take care not to make any false statements.

The tort of **disparagement** or injurious falsehood imposes liability upon one who publishes a false statement that results in harm to another's monetary interests if the publisher knows that the statement is false or acts in reckless disregard of its truth or falsity. This tort most commonly involves intentionally false statements that cast doubt on another's right of ownership in or on the quality of another's property or products. Thus Simon, while contemplating the purchase of a stock of merchandise that belongs to Marie, reads an advertisement in a newspaper in which Ernst falsely asserts he owns the merchandise. Ernst has disparaged Marie's property in the goods.

Absolute, conditional, and constitutional privileges apply to the same extent to the tort of disparagement as they do to defamation. In addition, a competitor has conditional privilege to compare her products favorably with those of a rival, even though she does not believe that her products are superior. No privilege applies, however, if the comparison contains false assertions of specific unfavorable facts about the competitor's property.

The pecuniary loss an injured person may recover is that which directly and immediately results from impairment of the marketability of the property disparaged. Damages also may be recovered for expenses necessary to counteract the false publication, including litigation expenses, the cost of notifying customers, and the cost of publishing denials.

Fraudulent Misrepresentation

Fraudulent misrepresentation imposes liability for the monetary loss caused by a justifiable reliance on a misrepresentation of fact intentionally made for the purpose of inducing the relying party to act. For example, Smith misrepresents to Jones that a tract of land in Texas is located in an area where oil drilling has recently commenced. Smith makes this statement knowing it is not true. In reliance upon the statement, Jones purchases the land from Smith. Smith is liable to Jones for intentional or fraudulent misrepresentation. Although fraudulent misrepresentation is a tort action, it is closely connected with contractual negotiations; we will discuss its relationship to contracts in Chapter 11.

CHAPTER SUMMARY

Harm to the Person

Battery intentional infliction of harmful or offensive bodily contact

Assault intentional infliction of apprehension of immediate bodily harm or offensive contact

False Imprisonment intentional confining of a person against her will

Infliction of Emotional Distress extreme and outrageous conduct intentionally or recklessly causing severe emotional distress

Harm to the Right of Dignity

Defamation false communication that injures a person's reputation
- *Libel* written or electronically transmitted defamation
- *Slander* spoken defamation

Invasion of Privacy
- *Appropriation* unauthorized use of a person's identity
- *Intrusion* unreasonable and highly offensive interference with the seclusion of another
- *Public Disclosure of Private Facts* highly offensive publicity of private information
- *False Light* highly offensive and false publicity about another

Misuse of Legal Procedure torts of malicious prosecution, wrongful civil proceeding, and abuse of process that protect an individual from unjustifiable litigation

Harm to Property

Real Property land and anything attached to it
- *Trespass to Real Property* wrongfully entering on land of another
- *Nuisance* a nontrespassory interference with another's use and enjoyment of land

Personal Property any property other than land
- *Trespass to Personal Property* an intentional taking or use of another's personal property
- *Conversion* intentional exercise of control over another's personal property

Harm to Economic Interests

Interference with Contractual Relations intentionally causing one of the parties to a contract not to perform

Disparagement publication of false statements about another's property or products

Fraudulent Misrepresentation a false statement, made with knowledge of its falsity, intended to induce another to act

QUESTIONS

1. The Penguin intentionally hits Batman with his umbrella. Batman, stunned by the blow, falls backward, knocking Robin down. Robin's leg is broken in the fall, and he cries out, "Holy broken bat bones! My leg is broken." Who, if anyone, has liability to Robin? Why?

2. CEO was convinced by his employee, M. Ploy, that a co-worker, A. Cused, had been stealing money from the company. At lunch that day in the company cafeteria, CEO discharged Cused from her employment, accused her of stealing from the company, searched through her purse over her objections, and finally forcibly escorted her to his office to await the arrival of the police, whom he had his secretary summon. Cused is indicted for embezzlement but subsequently is acquitted upon establishing her innocence. What rights, if any, does Cused have against CEO?

3. Ralph kisses Edith while she is asleep but does not waken or harm her. Edith sues Ralph for battery. Has a battery been committed?

4. Claude, a creditor seeking to collect a debt, calls on Dianne and demands payment in a rude and insolent manner. When Dianne says that she cannot pay, Claude calls Dianne a deadbeat and says that he will never trust Dianne again. Is Claude liable to Dianne? If so, for what tort?

5. Lana, a ten-year-old child, is run over by a car negligently driven by Mitchell. Lana, at the time of the accident, was acting reasonably and without negligence. Clark, a newspaper reporter, photographs Lana while she is lying in the street in great pain. Two years later, Perry, the publisher of a newspaper, prints Clark's picture of Lana in his newspaper as a lead to an article concerning the negligence of children. The caption under the picture reads: "They ask to be killed." Lana, who has recovered from the accident, brings suit against Clark and Perry. What is the result?

6. The *Saturday Evening Post* featured an article entitled "The Story of a College Football Fix," characterized in the subtitle as "A Shocking Report of How Wally Butts and Bear Bryant

Rigged a Game Last Fall." Butts was athletic director of the University of Georgia, and Bryant was head coach of the University of Alabama. The article was based on a claim by one George Burnett that he had accidentally overheard a long-distance telephone conversation between Butts and Bryant in the course of which Butts divulged information on plays Georgia would use in the upcoming game against Alabama. The writer assigned to the story by the *Post* was not a football expert, did not interview either Butts or Bryant, and did not personally see the notes Burnett had made of the telephone conversation. Butts admitted that he had a long-distance telephone conversation with Bryant but denied that any advance information on prospective football plays was given. Has Butts been defamed by the *Post*?

7. A patient confined in a hospital, Joan, has a rare disease that is of great interest to the public. Carol, a television reporter, requests Joan to consent to an interview. Joan refuses, but Carol, nonetheless, enters Joan's room over her objection and photographs her. Joan brings a suit against Carol. Is Carol liable? If so, for what tort?

8. Owner has a place on his land where he piles trash. The pile has been there for three months. John, a neighbor of Owner, without Owner's consent or knowledge, throws trash onto the trash pile. Owner learns that John has done this and sues him. What tort, if any, has John committed?

9. Chris leaves her car parked in front of a store. There are no signs that say Chris cannot park there. The store owner, however, needs the car moved to enable a delivery truck to unload. He releases the brake and pushes Chris's car three or four feet, doing no harm to the car. Chris returns and sees that her car has been moved and is very angry. She threatens to sue the store owner for trespass to her personal property. Can she recover?

10. Carr borrowed John's brand-new Ford for the purpose of going to the store. He told John he would be right back. Carr then decided, however, to go to the beach while he had the car. Can John recover from Carr the value of the automobile? If so, for what tort?

CASE PROBLEMS

11. Marcia Samms claimed that David Eccles had repeatedly and persistently called her at various hours, including late at night, from May to December, soliciting her to have illicit sexual relations with him. She also claimed that on one occasion Eccles came over to her residence to again solicit sex and indecently exposed himself to her. Mrs. Samms had never encouraged Eccles but had continuously repulsed his "insulting, indecent, and obscene" proposals. She brought suit against Eccles, claiming she suffered great anxiety and fear for her personal safety and severe emotional distress, demanding actual and punitive damages. Can she recover? If so, for what tort?

12. National Bond and Investment Company sent two of its employees to repossess Whithorn's car after he failed to complete the payments. The two repossessors located Whithorn while he was driving his car. They followed him and hailed him down in order to make the repossession. Whithorn refused to abandon his car and demanded evidence of their authority. The two repossessors became impatient and called a wrecker. They ordered the driver of the wrecker to hook Whithorn's car and move it down the street while Whithorn was still inside the vehicle. Whithorn started the car and tried to escape, but the wrecker lifted the car off the road and progressed seventy-five to one hundred feet until Whithorn managed to stall the wrecker. Has National Bond committed the tort of false imprisonment?

13. William Proxmire, a U.S. senator from Wisconsin, initiated the "Golden Fleece of the Month Award" to publicize what he believed to be wasteful government spending. The second of these awards was given to the federal agencies that had for seven years funded Dr. Hutchinson's research on stress levels in animals. The award was made in a speech Proxmire gave in the Senate; the text was also incorporated into an advance press release that was sent to 275 members of the national news media. Proxmire also referred to the research again in two subsequent newsletters sent to one hundred thousand constituents and during a television interview. Hutchinson then brought this action alleging defamation resulting in personal and economic injury. Assuming that Hutchinson proved that the statements were false and defamatory, would he prevail?

14. Capune was attempting a trip from New York to Florida on an eighteen-foot-long paddleboard. The trip was being covered by various media to gain publicity for Capune and certain products he endorsed. Capune approached a pier by water. The pier was owned by Robbins, who had posted signs prohibiting surfing and swimming around the pier. Capune was unaware of these notices and attempted to continue his journey by passing under the pier. Robbins ran up yelling and threw two bottles at Capune. Capune was frightened and tried to maneuver his paddleboard to go around the pier. Robbins then threw a third bottle that hit Capune on the head. Capune had to be helped out of the water and taken to the hospital. He suffered a physical wound that required twenty-four sutures and, as a result, had to discontinue his trip. Capune brought suit in tort against Robbins. Is Robbins liable? If so, for which tort or torts?

15. Ralph Nader, who has been a critic of General Motors Corp. for many years, claims that when General Motors learned that Nader was about to publish a book entitled *Unsafe at Any Speed*, criticizing one of its automobiles, the company decided to conduct a campaign of intimidation against him. Specifically, Nader claims that GMC (a) conducted a series of interviews with Nader's acquaintances, questioning them about his political, social, racial, and religious views; (b) kept him under surveillance in public places for an unreasonable length of time including close observation of him in a bank; (c) caused him to be accosted by women for the purpose of entrapping him into illicit relationships; (d) made threatening, harassing, and obnoxious telephone calls to him; (e) tapped his telephone and eavesdropped by means of mechanical and electronic equipment on his private conversations with others; and (f) conducted a "continuing" and harassing investigation of him. Nader brought suit against GMC for invasion of privacy. Which, if any, of the alleged actions would constitute invasion of privacy?

16. Bill Kinsey was charged with murdering his wife while working for the Peace Corps in Tanzania. After waiting six months in jail, he was acquitted at a trial that attracted wide publicity. Five years later, while a graduate student at Stanford University, Kinsey had a brief affair with Mary Macur. He abruptly ended the affair by telling Macur he would no longer be seeing her because another woman, Sally Allen, was coming from England to live with him. A few months later, Kinsey and Allen moved to Africa and were subsequently married. Soon after Bill ended their affair, Macur began a letter-writing campaign designed to expose Bill and his mistreatment of her. Macur sent several letters to both Bill and Sally Kinsey, their parents, their neighbors, their parents' neighbors, members of Bill's dissertation committee, other faculty, and the president of Stanford University. The letters contained statements accusing Bill of murdering his first wife, spending six months in jail for the crime, being a rapist, and other questionable behavior. The Kinseys brought an action for invasion of privacy, seeking damages and a permanent injunction. Will the Kinseys prevail? If so, for what tort?

17. Plaintiff, John W. Carson, was the host and star of *The Tonight Show*, a well-known television program broadcast by the National Broadcasting Company. Carson also appeared as an entertainer in nightclubs and theaters around the country. From the time he began hosting *The Tonight Show*, he had been introduced on the show each night with the phrase "Here's Johnny." The phrase "Here's Johnny" is still generally associated with Carson by a substantial segment of the television viewing public. To earn additional income, Carson began authorizing use of this phrase by outside business ventures.

    Defendant, Here's Johnny Portable Toilets, Inc., is a Michigan corporation engaged in the business of renting and selling "Here's Johnny" portable toilets. Defendant's founder was aware at the time he formed the corporation that "Here's Johnny" was the introductory slogan for Carson on *The Tonight Show*. He indicated that he coupled the phrase with a second one, "The World's Foremost Commodian," to make "a good play on a phrase." Carson brought suit for invasion of privacy. Should Carson recover? If so, for which tort?

18. Lemmie L. Ruffin, Jr., was an Alabama licensed agent for Pacific Mutual Life Insurance and for Union Fidelity Life Insurance Company. Union wrote group health insurance policies for municipalities, while Pacific did not. Plaintiffs Cleopatra Haslip, Cynthia Craig, Alma M. Calhoun, and Eddie Hargrove were employees of Roosevelt City, Alabama. Ruffin gave the city a single proposal for health and life insurance for its employees, which the city approved. Both companies provided the coverage; however, Union provided the health insurance and Pacific provided the life insurance. This packaging of coverage by two different and unrelated insurers was not unusual. Union would send its billings for health premiums to Ruffin at Pacific Mutual's office. The city clerk each month issued a check for those premiums and sent it to Ruffin. Ruffin, however, did not remit to Union the premium payments he received from the city; instead, he misappropriated most of them. When Union did not receive payment from the city, it sent notices of lapsed health coverage to the plaintiffs, who did not know that their health policies had been canceled.

    Plaintiff Haslip was subsequently hospitalized and because the hospital could not confirm her health coverage, it required her to make a partial payment on her bill. Her physician, when he was not paid, placed her account with a collec-

tion agency, which obtained against Haslip a judgment that damaged her credit. Plaintiffs sued Pacific Mutual and Ruffin for fraud. The case was submitted to a jury, which was instructed that if it found liability for fraud, it could award punitive damages. The jury returned verdicts for the plaintiffs and awarded Haslip $1,040,000, of which at least $840,000 was punitive damages. The Supreme Court of Alabama affirmed the trial court's judgment. Pacific Mutual appealed. Decision?

19. Susan Jungclaus Peterson was a twenty-one-year-old student at Moorhead State University who had lived most of her life on her family farm in Minnesota. Though Susan was a dean's list student her first year, her academic performance declined after she became deeply involved in an international religious cult organization known locally as The Way of Minnesota, Inc. The cult demanded an enormous psychological and monetary commitment from Susan. Near the end of her junior year, her parents became alarmed by the changes in Susan's physical and mental well-being and concluded that she had been "reduced to a condition of psychological bondage by The Way." They sought help from Kathy Mills, a self-styled "deprogrammer" of minds brainwashed by cults.

    On May 24, Norman Jungclaus, Susan's father, picked up Susan at Moorhead State. Instead of returning home, they went to the residence of Veronica Morgel, where Kathy Mills attempted to deprogram Susan. For the first few days of her stay, Susan was unwilling to discuss her involvement. She lay curled in a fetal position in her bedroom, plugging her ears and hysterically screaming and crying while her father pleaded with her to listen. By the third day, however, Susan's demeanor changed completely. She became friendly and vivacious and communicated with her father. Susan also went roller skating and played softball at a nearby park over the following weekend. She spent the next week in Columbus, Ohio, with a former cult member who had shared her experiences of the previous week. While in Columbus, she spoke daily by telephone with her fiancé, a member of The Way, who begged her to return to the cult. Susan expressed the desire to get her fiancé out of the organization, but a meeting between them could not be arranged outside the presence of other members of The Way. Her parents attempted to persuade Susan to sign an agreement releasing them from liability for their actions, but Susan refused. After nearly sixteen days of "deprogramming" Susan left the Morgel residence and returned to her fiancé and The Way. Upon the direction of The Way ministry, she brought an action against her parents for false imprisonment. Will Susan prevail? Explain.

20. Debra Agis was a waitress in a restaurant owned by the Howard Johnson Company. On May 23, Roger Dionne, manager of the restaurant, called a meeting of all waitresses at which he informed them "there was some stealing going on." Dionne also stated that the identity of the party or parties responsible was not known and that he would begin firing all waitresses in alphabetical order until the guilty party or parties were detected. He then fired Debra Agis, who allegedly "became greatly upset, began to cry, sustained emotional distress, mental anguish, and loss of wages and earnings." Mrs. Agis brought this complaint against the Howard Johnson Company and Roger Dionne, alleging that the defendants acted recklessly and outrageously, intending to cause emotional distress and anguish. The defendants argued that damages for emotional distress are not recoverable unless physical injury occurs as a result of the distress. Will Agis be successful on her complaint?

TAKING SIDES

Edith Mitchell, accompanied by her thirteen-year-old daughter, went through the checkout at Walmart and purchased several items. As they exited, the Mitchells passed through an electronic antitheft device, which sounded an alarm. Robert Canady, employed by Walmart as a "people greeter" and security guard, forcibly stopped Edith Mitchell at the exit, grabbed her bag, and told her to step back inside. The security guard never touched Edith or her daughter and never threatened to touch either of them. Nevertheless, Edith Mitchell described the security guard's actions in her affidavit as "gruff, loud, rude behavior." The security guard removed every item Mitchell had just purchased and ran it through the security gate. One of the items still had a security code unit on it, which an employee admitted could have been overlooked by the cashier. When the security guard finished examining the contents of Mitchell's bag, he put it on the checkout counter. This examination of her bag took ten or fifteen minutes. Once her bag had been checked, no employee of Walmart ever told Mitchell she could not leave. Mitchell was never threatened with arrest. Mitchell brought a tort action against Walmart.

a. Explain on which torts should Mitchell base her claim against Walmart?

b. What arguments would support Walmart denial of liability for these torts?

c. Which party should prevail? Explain.

CHAPTER **8**

Negligence and Strict Liability

Nothing is so easy as to be wise after the event.

B. Branwell (1859)

CHAPTER OUTCOMES

After reading and studying this chapter, you should be able to:

1. List and describe the three required elements of an action for negligence.

2. Explain the duty of care that is imposed on (a) adults, (b) children, (c) persons with a physical disability, (d) persons with a mental deficiency, (e) persons with superior knowledge, and (f) persons acting in an emergency.

3. Differentiate among the duties that possessors of land owe to trespassers, licensees, and invitees.

4. Identify the defenses that are available to a tort action in negligence and those that are available to a tort action in strict liability.

5. Identify and describe those activities giving rise to a tort action in strict liability.

Whereas intentional torts deal with conduct that has a substantial certainty of causing harm, negligence involves conduct that creates an unreasonable risk of harm. The basis of liability for negligence is the failure to exercise reasonable care under the circumstances for the safety of another person or his property, which failure proximately causes injury to such person or damage to his property, or both. Thus, if the driver of an automobile intentionally runs down a person, she has committed the intentional tort of battery. If, on the other hand, the driver hits and injures a person while driving with no reasonable regard for the safety of others, she is negligent.

Strict liability is not based on the negligence or intent of the defendant but rather on the nature of the activity in which he is engaging. Under this doctrine, defendants who engage in certain activities, such as keeping animals or carrying on abnormally dangerous conditions, are held liable for injuries they cause, even if they have exercised the utmost care. The law imposes this liability to bring about a just reallocation of loss, given that the defendant engaged in the activity for his own benefit and probably is better prepared than the plaintiff is to manage the risk inherent in the activity through insurance or otherwise.

As mentioned in Chapter 7, the American Law Institute (ALI) has published the Restatement Third, Torts: Liability for Physical and Emotional Harm (the "Third Restatement"). This new Restatement addresses the general or basic elements of the tort action for liability for accidental personal injury, property damage, and emotional harm, but does not cover liability for economic loss. "Physical harm" is defined as bodily harm (physical injury, illness, disease, and death) or property damage (physical impairment of real property or tangible personal property). The Third Restatement replaces comparable provisions in the Restatement Second, Torts. However, the Third Restatement does not cover the following matters, which remain governed by the Second Restatement: protection of reputation or privacy, economic loss, or domestic relations; determination of the recoverable damages and their amount; and the standards for liability of professionals for malpractice. Otherwise, this chapter reflects the Third Restatement's provisions.

The ALI's Restatement Third, Torts: Economic Torts and Related Wrongs will update coverage on torts that involve economic loss or pecuniary harm *not* resulting from physical harm or physical contact to a person or property. This project will update coverage of economic torts in Restatement Second, Torts and address some topics not covered in prior Restatements. The ALI began this project in 2004, and after several years of inactivity, the project was resumed in 2010. Thus far, no part of the work has been approved by the ALI.

NEGLIGENCE

Negligence
conduct that falls below the standard established by law for the protection of others against unreasonable risk of harm

A person acts negligently if the person does not exercise reasonable care under all the circumstances. Moreover, the general rule is that a person is under a duty to all others at all times to exercise reasonable care for the safety of other persons and their property.

As the comments to the Third Restatement explain, an action for **negligence** consists of five elements, each of which the plaintiff must prove:

1. **Duty of care:** that a legal duty required the defendant to conform to the standard of conduct established for the protection of others;
2. **Breach of duty:** that the defendant failed to exercise reasonable care;
3. **Factual cause:** that the defendant's failure to exercise reasonable care in fact caused the harm the plaintiff sustained;
4. **Harm:** that the harm sustained is of a type protected against negligent conduct; and
5. **Scope of liability:** that the harm sustained is within the "scope of liability," which historically has been referred to as "proximate cause."

We will discuss the first two elements in the next section, "Breach of Duty of Care"; we will cover the last three elements in subsequent sections.

BREACH OF DUTY OF CARE

Negligence consists of conduct that creates an unreasonable risk of harm. In determining whether a given risk of harm was unreasonable, the following factors are considered: (1) the foreseeable probability that the person's conduct will result in harm, (2) the foreseeable gravity or severity of any harm that may follow, and (3) the burden of taking precautions to eliminate or reduce the risk of harm. Thus, the standard of conduct, which is the basis for the law of negligence, is usually determined by a cost-benefit or risk-benefit analysis.

Reasonable Person Standard

Reasonable person standard
degree of care that a reasonable person would exercise under all the circumstances

The duty of care imposed by law is measured by the degree of carefulness that a reasonable person would exercise in a given situation. The **reasonable person** is a fictitious individual who is always careful and prudent and never negligent. What the judge or jury determines a reasonable person would have done in light of the facts revealed by the evidence in a particular case sets the standard of conduct for that case. The reasonable person standard is thus *external* and *objective*.

Children
must conform to conduct of a reasonable person of the same age, intelligence, and experience

Children   A child is a person below the age of majority, which in almost all states has been lowered from twenty-one to eighteen. The standard of conduct to which a child must conform to avoid being negligent is that of a reasonably careful person of the same age, intelligence, and experience under all the circumstances. The law applies a test that acknowledges these three factors, because children do not have the judgment, intelligence, knowledge, and experience of adults. Moreover, children as a general rule do not engage in activities entailing high risk to others, and their conduct normally does not involve a potential for harm as great as that of adult conduct. A child who engages in a dangerous activity that is characteristically undertaken by adults, however, such as flying an airplane or driving a boat or car, is held in almost all states to the standard of care applicable to adults.

Physical Disability

If a person is ill or otherwise physically disabled, the standard of conduct to which he or she must conform to avoid being negligent is that of a reasonably careful person with the same disability. Thus, a blind person must act as a reasonable person who is blind. However, the conduct of a person during a period of sudden incapacitation or loss of consciousness resulting from physical illness is negligent only if the sudden incapacitation or loss of consciousness was reasonably foreseeable to the actor. Examples of sudden incapacitation include heart attack, stroke, epileptic seizure, and diabetes.

Mental Disability

A person's mental or emotional disability is not considered in determining whether conduct is negligent unless the person is a child. The defendant is held to the standard of conduct of a reasonable person who is not mentally or emotionally disabled, even though the defendant is, in fact, incapable of conforming to the standard. When a person's intoxication is voluntary, it is not considered as an excuse for conduct that is otherwise lacking in reasonable care.

Superior Skill or Knowledge

If a person has skills or knowledge beyond those possessed by most others, these skills or knowledge are circumstances to be taken into account in determining whether the person has acted with reasonable care. Thus, persons who are qualified and who practice a profession or trade that requires special skill and expertise are required to use the same care and skill that members of their profession or trade normally possess. This standard applies to such professionals as physicians, dentists, attorneys, pharmacists, architects, accountants, and engineers and to those who perform a skilled trade such as an airline pilot, electrician, carpenter, and plumber. If a member of a profession or skilled trade possesses greater skill than that common to the profession or trade, she is required to exercise that greater degree of skill.

Emergencies

An **emergency** is a sudden and unexpected event that calls for immediate action and permits no time for deliberation. In determining whether a defendant's conduct was reasonable, the fact that he was at the time confronted with a sudden and unexpected emergency is taken into consideration. The standard is still that of a reasonable person under the circumstances—the emergency is simply part of the circumstances. If, however, the defendant's own negligent or tortious conduct created the emergency, he is liable for the consequences of this conduct even if he acted reasonably in the resulting emergency situation. Moreover, failure to anticipate an emergency may itself constitute negligence.

Violation of Statute

The reasonable person standard of conduct may be established by legislation or administrative regulation. Some statutes do so by expressly imposing civil liability on violators. Where a statute does not expressly provide for civil liability, courts may adopt the requirements of the statute as the standard of conduct if the statute is designed to protect against the type of accident the defendant's conduct causes and the accident victim is within the class of persons the statute is designed to protect.

If the statute is found to apply, the great majority of the courts hold that an unexcused violation is **negligence *per se***; that is, the violation conclusively shows negligent conduct (breach of duty of care). In a minority of states, the violation is considered merely to be evidence of negligence. In either event, the plaintiff must also prove legal causation and injury.

For example, a statute enacted to protect employees from injuries requires that all factory elevators be equipped with specified safety devices. Arthur, an employee in Leonard's factory, and Marian, a business visitor to the factory, are injured when the elevator fails because the safety devices have not been installed. The court may adopt the statute as a standard of conduct as to Arthur, and hold Leonard negligent *per se* as to Arthur, but not as to Marian, because Arthur, not Marian, is within the class of persons the statute is intended to protect. Marian would have to establish that a reasonable person in the position of Leonard under the circumstances would have installed the safety device. (See Figure 8-1 illustrating negligence and negligence *per se*.)

On the other hand, compliance with a legislative enactment or administrative regulation does not prevent a finding of negligence if a reasonable person would have taken additional precautions. For instance, driving at the speed limit may not constitute due care when traffic or road conditions require a lower speed. Legislative or administrative rules normally establish *minimum* standards.

Figure 8-1 Negligence and Negligence *per se*

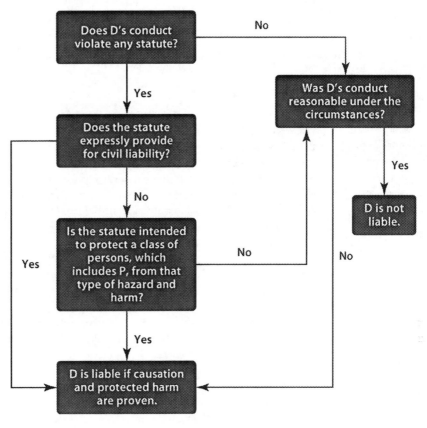

© Cengage Learning 2013

Ryan v. Friesenhahn
Court of Appeals of Texas, 1995
911 S.W.2d 113, aff'd, 41 Tex. Sup. J. 261, 960 S.W.2d 656 (1998)
http://scholar.google.com/scholar_case?case=5075518384525866053&q=911+S.W.2d+113&hl=en&as_sdt=2,34

FACTS Todd Friesenhahn, son of Nancy and Frederick Friesenhahn, held an "open invitation" party at his parents' home that encouraged guests to "bring your own bottle." Sabrina Ryan attended the party, became intoxicated, and was involved in a fatal accident after she left the party. Sandra and Stephen Ryan, Sabrina's parents, sued the Friesenhahns for negligence, alleging that the Friesenhahns were aware of the underage drinking at the party and of Sabrina's condition when she left the party. The trial court granted summary judgment for the Friesenhahns.

DECISION Judgment reversed.

OPINION Accepting the Ryans' allegations as true, the Friesenhahns were aware that minors possessed and consumed alcohol on their property and specifically allowed Sabrina to become intoxicated. The Texas Alcoholic Beverage Code provides that a person commits an offense if, with criminal negligence, that person "makes available an alcoholic beverage to a minor." A violation of a statute constitutes negligence *per se* if the injured party is a member of the class protected by the statute. The Alcoholic Beverage Code was designed to protect the general public and minors in particular. Therefore, Sabrina was a member of the protected class, and we find that the Ryans have stated a cause of action against the Friesenhahns for violation of the Alcoholic Beverage Code.

In considering common-law negligence as a basis for social host liability, courts have relied on *Graff v. Board*, a prior Texas Supreme Court decision in which it was held that no third party liability should be imposed on social hosts who provide alcohol to adult guests. The Texas Supreme Court gave two reasons for its holding in *Graff*: first, the host cannot reasonably know the extent of his guests' alcohol consumption level; second, the host cannot reasonably be expected to control his guests' conduct. However, this rationale does not apply where the guest is a minor. The adult social host need not estimate the extent of a minor's alcohol consumption, because serving minors any amount of alcohol is a criminal offense. Furthermore, the social host may control the minor, with whom there is a special relationship, in a manner analogous to that of parent-child.

While one adult has no general duty to control the behavior of another adult, one would hope that adults would exercise special diligence in supervising minors. When a party is for the purpose of engaging in the consumption of alcohol by minors, adults certainly have a greater duty of care. Moreover, in view of the legislature's determination that minors are not competent to understand the effects of alcohol, the court found sufficient legislative intent to support its holding that a duty exists between the adult social host and the minor guest. Accordingly, the court found that the Ryans' petition stated a common-law cause of action.

INTERPRETATION A violation of a statute constitutes negligence *per se* if the injured party is a member of the class protected by the statute.

ETHICAL QUESTION When should a parent be held liable for her child's negligence? Explain.

CRITICAL THINKING QUESTION Should a court extend social host liability for providing alcohol to an adult guest? Explain?

Duty to act

a person is under a duty to all others at all times to exercise reasonable care for the safety of the others' person and property; however, except in special circumstances, no one is required to aid another in peril

Duty to Act

As stated above, the general rule is that a person is under a duty to all others at all times to exercise reasonable care for the safety of the others' person and property. On the other hand, subject to several exceptions, a duty of care does not exist when the other's person or property is at risk for reasons other than the conduct of the person. This rule applies even though the person may be in a position to help another in peril. For example, Adolf, an adult standing at the edge of a steep cliff, observes a baby carriage with a crying infant in it slowly heading toward the edge and certain doom. Adolf could easily prevent the baby's fall at no risk to his own safety. Nonetheless, Adolf does nothing, and the baby falls to its death. Adolf is under no legal duty to act and therefore incurs no liability for failing to do so.

Nonetheless, special relations between the parties may impose an affirmative duty of reasonable care on the defendant to aid or protect the other with respect to risks that arise within the scope of the relationship. Thus, in the example above, if Adolf were the baby's parent or babysitter, Adolf would be under a duty to act and therefore would be liable for not taking action. The special relations giving rise to an affirmative duty to aid or protect another include (1) a common carrier with its passengers, (2) an innkeeper with its guest, (3) an employer with its employees, (4) a school with its students, (5) a landlord with its tenants with respect to common areas under the landlord's control, (6) a business open to the public with its customers, and (7) custodian with those in its custody including parents with their children. The Third Restatement leaves it to the courts whether to recognize additional relationships as sufficient to impose an affirmative duty. Furthermore, state and federal statutes and administrative regulations as well as local ordinances may impose an affirmative duty to act for the protection of another.

In addition, when a person's prior conduct, even though not tortious, creates a continuing risk of physical harm, the person has a duty to exercise reasonable care to prevent or minimize the harm. For example, Alice innocently drives her car into Frank, rendering him unconscious. Alice leaves Frank lying in the middle of the road, where he is run over by a second car driven by Rebecca. Alice is liable to Frank for the additional injuries inflicted by Rebecca. Moreover, a person who begins a rescue by taking charge of another who is imperiled and unable to protect himself incurs a duty to exercise reasonable care under the circumstances. Furthermore, a person who discontinues aid or protection is under a duty of reasonable care not to leave the other in a worse position. For example, Ann finds Ben drunk and stumbling along a dark sidewalk. Ann leads Ben halfway up a steep and unguarded stairway, where she then abandons him. Ben attempts to climb the stairs but trips and falls, suffering serious injury. Ann is liable to Ben for having left him in a worse position. Most states have enacted Good Samaritan statutes to encourage voluntary emergency care. These statutes vary considerably, but they typically limit or disallow liability for some rescuers under specified circumstances.

There are special relationships in which one person has some degree of control over another person, including (1) a parent with dependent children, and (2) an employer with employees when the employment facilitates the employee's causing harm to third parties. The parent and the employer each owe a duty of reasonable care under the circumstances to third persons with regard to foreseeable risks that arise within the scope of the relationship. Depending on the circumstances, reasonable care may require controlling the activities of the other person or merely providing a warning. Generally, the duty of parents is limited to dependent children; thus when children reach majority or are no longer dependent, parents no longer have control and the duty of reasonable care ceases. The duty of employers includes the duty to exercise reasonable care in the hiring, training, supervision, and retention of employees. This duty of employers is independent of the vicarious liability of an employer for an employee's tortious conduct during the course of employment, and extends to conduct by the employee that occurs both inside and outside the scope of employment so long as the employment facilitates the employee causing harm to third parties. The Third Restatement provides the following example of an employer's duty:

Don is employed by Welch Repair Service, which knows that Don had several episodes of assault in his previous employment. Don goes to Traci's residence, where he had previously been dispatched by Welch, and misrepresents to Traci that he is there on Welch business to check repairs that had previously been made in Traci's home. After Traci admits Don, he assaults Traci. Welch is subject to a duty under this subsection with regard to Don's assault on Traci.

Soldano v. O'Daniels
California Court of Appeals, Fifth District, 1983
141 Cal.App.3d 443, 190 Cal.Rptr. 310
http://scholar.google.com/scholar_case?case=6364984666656533477&q=190+Cal.Rptr.+310&hl=en&as_sdt=2,34

FACTS On August 9, the plaintiff's father, Darrell Soldano, was shot and killed at the Happy Jack Saloon. The defendant owns and operates the Circle Inn, an eating establishment across the street from the Happy Jack Saloon. On the night of the shooting, a patron of the Happy Jack Saloon came into the Circle Inn and informed the Circle Inn bartender that a man had been threatened at Happy Jack's. The patron requested that the Circle Inn bartender either call the police or allow the patron to use the Circle Inn phone to call the police. The bartender refused either to make the call or to allow the Happy Jack patron to use the phone. The plaintiff alleges that the actions of the Circle Inn employee were a breach of the legal duty that the Circle Inn owed to the decedent. The defendant maintains that there was no legal obligation to take any action, and therefore there was no duty owed to the decedent. The trial court dismissed the case on the defendant's motion for summary judgment.

DECISION The appellate court reversed and remanded the case for trial.

OPINION Defendant points to the established rule that one who has not created a peril ordinarily does not have a duty to take affirmative action to assist an imperiled person. The courts have increased the instances in which affirmative duties are imposed, not by direct rejection of the common law rule but by expanding the list of special relationships that will justify departure from that rule. In this case, however, there was no special relationship between the defendant and the deceased. Nonetheless, the court determined to reexamine the common law rule of nonliability for nonfeasance in the special circumstances of this case. Imposing such a duty to third parties requires an examination and balancing of foreseeability of harm, certainty that the plaintiff would suffer injury, the connection between defendant's conduct and the injury, moral blame attached to defendant's conduct, the prevention of future harm, extent of the burden to the defendant, consequences to the community of imposing a duty to exercise care, and the availability, cost, and prevalence of insurance for the particular risk involved. The court concluded, on these facts, that the Circle Inn's employee's conduct displayed a disregard for human life in that the burden on the defendant to respond was minimal. Balancing these factors, the court concluded that there was an affirmative duty on the defendant's part to respond and that his failure to respond resulted in a legal breach of duty of care. It bears emphasizing that the duty in this case does not require that one go to the aid of another. Rather, the use of a telephone, in the public portion of a business open to the public, during business hours, should not be refused for a legitimate emergency call.

INTERPRETATION Although a person may not have a duty to help another, in a case such as this, a person has a duty not to hinder others who are trying to help.

CRITICAL THINKING QUESTION Should the courts go beyond the rule of this case and impose an affirmative duty to go to the aid of another person who is in peril if it can be done without endangerment? Explain.

Duties of Possessors of Land

The right of possessors of land to use that land for their own benefit and enjoyment is limited by their duty to do so in a reasonable manner. By the use of their land, possessors of land cannot cause unreasonable risks of harm to others. Liability for breach of this obligation may arise from conduct in any of the three areas of torts discussed in this and the preceding chapter: intentional harm, negligence, or strict liability. Most of these cases fall within the classification of negligence.

In conducting activities on her land, the possessor of land is required to exercise reasonable care to protect others who are not on her property. For example, a property owner who constructs a factory on her premises must take reasonable care that it is not unreasonably dangerous to people off the site. Moreover, a business or other possessor of land that holds its premises open to the public owes those who are lawfully on the premises a duty of reasonable care with regard to risks that arise within the scope of the relationship.

In most states and under the Second Restatement, the duty of a possessor of land to persons who come on the land usually depends on whether those persons are trespassers, licensees, or invitees. In about fifteen states, however, licensees and invitees are owed the same duty. In addition, at least nine states have abandoned these distinctions and simply apply ordinary negligence principles of foreseeable risk and reasonable care to all entrants on the land including trespassers. The Third Restatement has adopted this last—the unitary—approach.

Second Restatement

a land possessor owes the following duties: (1) not to injure intentionally *trespassers*; (2) to warn *licensees* of known dangerous conditions licensees are unlikely to discover for themselves; and (3) to exercise reasonable care to protect *invitees* against dangerous conditions land possessor should know of but invitees are unlikely to discover

Trespasser

person who enters or remains on the land of another without permission or privilege to do so

Licensee

person privileged to enter or remain on land by virtue of the consent of the lawful possessor

Invitee

person invited upon land as a member of the public or for a business purpose

Third Restatement

adopts a unitary duty of reasonable care to all entrants on the land except for flagrant trespassers: a land possessor must use reasonable care to investigate and discover dangerous conditions and must use reasonable care to eliminate or improve those dangerous conditions that are known or should have been discovered by the exercise of reasonable care

Second Restatement In accordance with the historical—and still majority—approach to the duties of possessors of land, the Second Restatement provides for varying duties depending on the status of the entrant on the land.

A **trespasser** is a person who enters or remains on the land of another without the possessor's consent or a legal privilege to do so. The possessor of the land is *not* liable to adult trespassers for his failure to maintain the land in a reasonably safe condition. Nonetheless, the possessor is not free to inflict intentional injury on a trespasser. Moreover, most courts hold that upon discovery of the presence of trespassers on the land, the lawful possessor is required to exercise reasonable care for their safety in carrying on her activities and to warn the trespassers of potentially dangerous conditions that the trespassers are not likely to discover.

A **licensee** is a person who is privileged to enter or remain on land only by virtue of the lawful possessor's consent. Licensees include members of the possessor's household, social guests, and salespersons calling at private homes. A licensee will become a trespasser, however, if he enters a portion of the land to which he is not invited or remains on the land after his invitation has expired. The possessor owes a higher duty of care to licensees than to trespassers. The possessor must warn the licensee of dangerous activities and conditions (1) of which the possessor has knowledge or reason to know and (2) the licensee does not and is not likely to discover. If he is not warned, the licensee may recover if the activity or dangerous condition resulted from the possessor's failure to exercise reasonable care to protect him from the danger. To illustrate: Henry invites a friend, Anne, to his place in the country at 8:00 P.M. on a winter evening. Henry knows that a bridge in his driveway is in a dangerous condition that is not noticeable in the dark. Henry does not inform Anne of this fact. The bridge gives way under Anne's car, causing serious harm to Anne. Henry is liable to Anne.

An **invitee** is a person invited upon land as a member of the public or for a business purpose. A *public invitee* is a person who is invited to enter or remain on land as a member of the public for a purpose for which the land is held open to the public. Such invitees include those who use public parks, beaches, or swimming pools, as well as those who use government facilities, such as a post office or an office of the recorder of deeds, where business with the public is transacted openly. A *business visitor* is a person invited to enter or remain on premises for a purpose directly or indirectly concerning business dealings with the possessor of the land, such as one who enters a store or a worker who enters a residence to make repairs. With respect to the condition of the premises, the possessor of land is under a duty to exercise reasonable care to protect invitees against dangerous conditions they are unlikely to discover. This liability extends not only to those conditions of which the possessor actually knows but also to those of which she would discover by the exercise of reasonable care. For example, David's store has a large glass front door that is well lighted and plainly visible. Maxine, a customer, mistakes the glass for an open doorway and walks into the glass, injuring herself. David is not liable to Maxine. If, on the other hand, the glass was difficult to see and a person foreseeably might have mistaken the glass for an open doorway, then David would be liable to Maxine if Maxine crashed into the glass while exercising reasonable care.

Third Restatement The status-based duty rules just discussed have been rejected by the Third Restatement, which adopts a unitary duty of reasonable care to entrants on the land.

[Except for "flagrant trespassers,"] a land possessor owes a duty of reasonable care to entrants on the land with regard to:
1. conduct by the land possessor that creates risks to entrants on the land;
2. artificial conditions on the land that pose risks to entrants on the land;
3. natural conditions on the land that pose risks to entrants on the land; * * *

This rule is similar to the duty land possessors owed to invitees under the Second Restatement except that it extends the duty to all who enter the land, including trespassers, with the exception of "flagrant trespassers." This rule requires a land possessor to use reasonable care to investigate and discover dangerous conditions and to use reasonable care to eliminate or improve those dangerous conditions that are known or should have been discovered by the exercise of reasonable care. However, some risks cannot reasonably be discovered, and the land possessor is not subject to liability for those risks. In addition, a land possessor is not liable to an ordinary trespasser whose unforeseeable presence results in an unforeseeable risk.

A different rule applies to "flagrant trespassers." The Third Restatement requires that a land possessor only (1) refrain from intentional, willful, or wanton conduct that harms a flagrant trespasser and (2) exercise reasonable care on behalf of flagrant trespassers who are imperiled and helpless. The Third Restatement does not define "flagrant trespassers" but instead leaves it to each jurisdiction to determine at what point an ordinary trespasser becomes a "flagrant trespasser." The comments to the Third Restatement explain:

> The idea behind distinguishing particularly egregious trespassers for different treatment is that their presence on another's land is so antithetical to the rights of the land possessor to exclusive use and possession of the land that the land possessor should not be subject to liability for failing to exercise the ordinary duty of reasonable care otherwise owed to them as entrants on the land. It stems from the idea that when a trespass is sufficiently offensive to the property rights of the land possessor it is unfair to subject the possessor to liability for mere negligence.

PRACTICAL ADVICE

Take care to inspect your premises regularly to detect any dangerous conditions and either remedy the danger or post prominent warnings of any dangerous conditions you discover.

The Third Restatement provides an illustration of a flagrant trespasser: "Herman engaged in a late-night burglary of the Jacob liquor store after it had closed. While leaving the store after taking cash from the store's register, Herman slipped on a slick spot on the floor, fell, and broke his arm. Herman is a flagrant trespasser * * *."

Love v. Hardee's Food Systems, Inc.
Court of Appeals of Missouri, Eastern District, Division Two, 2000
16 S.W.3d 739
http://scholar.google.com/scholar_case?case=12304910341505965816&hl=en&as_sdt=2&as_vis=1&oi=scholarr

---

FACTS At about 3:15 P.M. on November 15, 1995, plaintiff, Jason Love, and his mother, Billye Ann Love, went to the Hardee's Restaurant in Arnold, Missouri, owned by defendant, Hardee's Food Systems, Inc. There were no other customers in the restaurant between 3:00 P.M. and 4:00 P.M., but two or three workmen were in the back doing construction. The workmen reported that they did not use the restroom and did not see anyone use the restroom. When Jason went to use the restroom, he slipped on water on the restroom floor. He fell backwards, hit his head, and felt a shooting pain down his right leg. He found himself lying in an area of dirty water, which soaked his clothes. There were no barricades, warning cones, or anything else that would either restrict access to the bathroom or warn of the danger.

Jason stated after the fall that his back and leg were "hurting pretty bad." His mother reported the fall. The supervisor filled out an accident report form, which reported that the accident occurred at 3:50 P.M.. The supervisor testified that the water appeared to have come from someone shaking his hands after washing them. The supervisor could not recall the last time the restroom had been checked. Jason was taken to a hospital emergency room. As a result of his injuries, he underwent two back surgeries, missed substantial time from work, and suffered from continuing pain and limitations on his physical activities.

Hardee's had a policy requiring that the restroom be checked and cleaned every hour by a maintenance person, who was scheduled to work until 3:00 P.M., but normally left at 1:00 P.M.. The supervisor could not recall whether the maintenance person left at 1:00 P.M. or 3:00 P.M. on November 15, and the defendant was unable to produce the time clock report for that day.

It was also a store policy that whenever employees cleaned the tables, they would check the restroom. If an employee had to use the restroom, then that employee was also supposed to check the restroom. The restaurant supervisor did not ask if any employees had been in the restroom, or if they had checked it in the hour prior to the accident, and did not know if the restroom

was actually inspected or cleaned at 3:00 P.M.. The restaurant had shift inspection checklists on which the manager would report on the cleanliness of the restrooms and whether the floors were clean and dry. However, the checklists for November 15 were thrown away.

Jason Love filed a lawsuit against Hardee's Food Systems, Inc. to recover damages for negligence. The jury returned a verdict in the plaintiff's favor in the amount of $125,000.

DECISION The judgment of the trial court is affirmed.

OPINION In order to have made a submissible case, the plaintiff had to show that defendant knew or, by using ordinary care, could have known of the dangerous condition and failed to use ordinary care to remove it, barricade it, or warn of it, and plaintiff sustained damage as a direct result of such failure. In order to establish constructive notice, the condition must have existed for a sufficient length of time or the facts must be such that the defendant should have reasonably known of its presence.

In this case the accident took place in the restaurant's restroom, which is provided for the use of employees and customers. The cause of the accident was water, which is provided in the restroom. The restaurant owner could reasonably foresee that anyone using the restroom, customers or employees, would use the tap water provided in the restroom and could spill, drop, or splash water on the floor. Accordingly, the restaurant owner was under a duty to use due care to guard against danger from water on the floor.

There was substantial evidence to support submissibility. First, there was evidence that the water came from the use of the restroom. It was on the floor of the restroom and the supervisor testified it appeared that someone had shaken water from his hands on the floor. If the water was caused by a nonemployee, the water was on the floor for at least fifty minutes, or longer, because no other customers were in the store to use the restroom after 3:00 P.M. and the workmen on the site had not used the restroom. In addition, the defendant's employees had the opportunity to observe the hazard. The restroom was to be used by the employees and was supposed to be checked by them when they used it; employees cleaning tables were supposed to check the restroom when they cleaned the tables; and a maintenance man was supposed to check and clean the restroom every hour.

There was evidence that the maintenance man charged with cleaning the restroom every hour did not clean the restroom at 3:00 P.M. as scheduled on the day of the accident. There was testimony that the maintenance man usually left at 1:00 P.M.. The supervisor could not recall what time the maintenance man left that day and defendant was unable to produce the time clock reports for that day, which would have shown when the maintenance man clocked out. This could have created a span of two hours and fifty minutes during which there was no employee working at the restaurant whose primary responsibility was to clean the restroom.

INTERPRETATION The owner or possessor of property is liable to an invitee if the owner knew or, by using ordinary care, could have known of the dangerous condition and failed to use ordinary care to remove it, barricade it, or warn of it, and the invitee sustained damage as a direct result of such failure.

CRITICAL THINKING QUESTION Should customers be required to look for dangers?

Res Ipsa Loquitur

Res ipsa loquitur
"the thing speaks for itself"; permits the jury to infer both negligent conduct and causation

A rule of circumstantial evidence has developed that permits the jury to infer both negligent conduct and causation from the mere occurrence of certain types of events. This rule, called *res ipsa loquitur*, meaning "the thing speaks for itself," applies when the accident causing the plaintiff's physical harm is a type of accident that ordinarily happens as a result of the negligence of a class of actors of which the defendant is the relevant member. For example, Camille rents a room in Leo's motel. During the night, a large piece of plaster falls from the ceiling and injures Camille. In the absence of other evidence, the jury may infer that the harm resulted from Leo's negligence in permitting the plaster to become defective. Leo is permitted, however, to introduce evidence to contradict the inference of negligence.

FACTUAL CAUSE

Factual cause
liability for the negligent conduct of a defendant requires that his conduct in fact caused harm to the plaintiff

But-for test
the defendant's conduct is a factual cause of the harm when the harm would not have occurred absent the conduct

Liability for the negligent conduct of a defendant requires that the conduct in fact caused harm to the plaintiff. The Third Restatement states: "Tortious conduct must be a factual cause of physical harm for liability to be imposed." A widely applied test for causation in fact is the **but-for test**: A person's conduct is a cause of an event if the event would not have occurred but for the person's negligent conduct. That is, conduct is a factual cause of harm when the harm would not have occurred absent the conduct. For instance, Arnold fails to erect a barrier around an excavation. Doyle is driving a truck when its accelerator becomes stuck. Arnold's negligence is not a cause in fact of Doyle's death if the runaway truck would have crashed through the barrier even if it had been erected. Similarly, failure to install a proper fire escape to a hotel is not the cause in fact of the death of a person who is suffocated by the smoke while sleeping in bed during a hotel fire.

If the tortious conduct of Adam is *insufficient* by itself to cause Paula's harm, but when Adam's conduct is combined with the tortious conduct of Barry, the combined conduct is sufficient to cause Paula's harm, then Adam and Barry are each considered a factual cause of Paula's harm.

The but-for test, however, is not satisfied when there are two or more causes, each of which is *sufficient* to bring about the harm in question and each of which is active at the time harm occurs. For example, Wilson and Hart negligently set fires that combine to destroy Kennedy's property. Either fire would have destroyed the property. Under the but-for test, either Wilson or Hart, or both, could argue that the fire caused by the other would have destroyed the property and that he, therefore, is not liable. The Third Restatement addresses this problem of multiple *sufficient* causes by providing, "If multiple acts exist, each of which alone would have been a factual cause under [the but-for test] of the physical harm at the same time, each act is regarded as a factual cause of the harm." Under this rule the conduct of both Wilson and Hart would be found to be a factual cause of the destruction of Kennedy's property.

SCOPE OF LIABILITY (PROXIMATE CAUSE)

Scope of liability
liability is limited to those harms that result from the risks that made the defendant's conduct tortious

As a matter of social policy, legal responsibility has not followed all the consequences of a negligent act. Tort law does not impose liability on a defendant for all harm factually caused by the defendant's negligent conduct. Liability has been limited—to a greater extent than with intentional torts—to those harms that result from the risks that made the defendant's conduct tortious. This "risk standard" limitation on liability also applies to strict liability cases. The Third Restatement provides the following example:

Richard, a hunter, finishes his day in the field and stops at a friend's house while walking home. His friend's nine-year-old daughter, Kim, greets Richard, who hands his loaded shotgun to her as he enters the house. Kim drops the shotgun, which lands on her toe, breaking it. Although Richard was negligent for giving Kim his shotgun, the risk that made Richard negligent was that Kim might shoot someone with the gun, not that she would drop it and hurt herself (the gun was neither especially heavy nor unwieldy). Kim's broken toe is outside the scope of Richard's liability, even though Richard's tortious conduct was a factual cause of Kim's harm.

Foreseeability

Determining the liability of a negligent defendant for unforeseeable consequences has proved to be troublesome and controversial. The Restatement and many courts have adopted the following position:

1. If the actor's conduct is a substantial factor in bringing about harm to another, the fact that the actor neither foresaw nor should have foreseen the extent of the harm or the manner in which it occurred does *not* prevent him from being liable.
2. The actor's conduct may be held not to be a legal cause of harm to another where, after the event and looking back from the harm to the actor's negligent conduct, it appears to the court highly extraordinary that it should have brought about the harm.

A comment to the Third Restatement explains that

the foreseeability test for proximate cause is essentially consistent with the standard set forth in this [Restatement]. Properly understood, both the risk standard and a foreseeability test exclude liability for harms that were sufficiently unforeseeable at the time of the actor's tortious conduct that they were not among the risks—potential harms—that made the actor negligent. Negligence limits the requirement of reasonable care to those risks that are foreseeable.

For example, Steven, while negligently driving an automobile, collides with a car carrying dynamite. Steven is unaware of the contents of the other car and has no reason to know about them. The collision causes the dynamite to explode, shattering glass in a building a block away. The shattered glass injures Doria, who is inside the building. The explosion also injures Walter, who is walking on the sidewalk near the collision. Steven would be liable to Walter because Steven should have realized that his negligent driving might result in a collision that would endanger pedestrians nearby. Doria's harm, however, was beyond the risks posed by Steven's negligent driving and he, accordingly, is not liable to Doria.

Palsgraf v. Long Island Railroad Co.
Court of Appeals of New York, 1928
248 N.Y. 339, 162 N.E. 99

FACTS Palsgraf was on the railroad station platform buying a ticket when a train stopped at the station. As it began to depart, two men ran to catch it. After the first was safely aboard, the second jumped onto the moving car. When he started to fall, a guard on the train reached to grab him and another guard on the platform pushed the man from behind. They helped the man to regain his balance, but in the process they knocked a small package out of his arm. The package, which contained fireworks, fell onto the rails and exploded. The shock from the explosion knocked over a scale resting on the other end of the platform, and it landed on Mrs. Palsgraf. She then brought an action against the Long Island Railroad Company to recover for the injuries she sustained. The railroad appealed from the trial and appellate courts' decisions in favor of Palsgraf.

DECISION Judgment for Palsgraf reversed.

OPINION Negligence is not actionable unless it involves the invasion of a legally protected interest or the violation of a right. In other words, in order for a given act to be held negligent, it must be shown that the charged party owed a duty to the complaining individual, the observance of which would have averted or avoided the injury.

Here, then, Palsgraf cannot recover because the railroad, although perhaps negligent as to the man carrying the package, was not negligent as to her. This was because the harm to her was not foreseeable. She cannot recover for injuries sustained merely because the railroad's agents were negligent as to the man they assisted.

INTERPRETATION Even if the defendant's negligent conduct in fact caused harm to the plaintiff, the defendant is not liable if the defendant could not have foreseen injuring the plaintiff or a class of persons to which the plaintiff belonged.

CRITICAL THINKING QUESTION Should a person be held liable for all injuries that her negligence in fact causes? Explain.

Superseding Cause

An intervening cause is an event or act that occurs after the defendant's negligent conduct and with that negligence causes the plaintiff's harm. If the intervening cause is deemed a **superseding cause**, it relieves the defendant of liability for that harm.

For example, Carol negligently leaves in a public sidewalk a substantial excavation without a fence or warning lights, into which Gary falls at night. Darkness is an intervening, but not a superseding, cause of harm to Gary because it is a normal consequence of the situation caused by Carol's negligence. Therefore, Carol is liable to Gary. In contrast, if Carol negligently leaves an excavation in a public sidewalk into which Barbara intentionally shoves Gary, under the Second Restatement as a matter of law Carol is not liable to Gary because Barbara's conduct is a superseding cause that relieves Carol of liability. The Third Restatement rejects this exception to liability, stating,

> Whether Gary's harm is within the scope of Carol's liability for her negligence is an issue for the factfinder. The factfinder will have to determine whether the appropriate characterization of the harm to Gary is falling into an unguarded excavation site or being deliberately pushed into an unguarded excavation site and, if the latter, whether it is among the risks that made Carol negligent.

An intervening cause that is a foreseeable or normal consequence of the defendant's negligence is not a superseding cause. Thus, a person who negligently places another person or his property in imminent danger is liable for the injury sustained by a third-party rescuer who attempts to aid the imperiled person or his property. The same is true of attempts by the endangered person to escape the peril, as, for example, when a person swerves off the road to avoid a head-on collision with an automobile driven negligently on the wrong side of the road. It is commonly held that a negligent defendant is liable for the results of necessary medical treatment of the injured party, even if the treatment itself is negligent.

Petition of Kinsman Transit Co.
United States Court of Appeals, Second Circuit, 1964
338 F.2d 708
http://scholar.google.com/scholar_case?case=7870539560920231106&q=338+F.2d+708&hl=en&as_sdt=2,34

FACTS The *MacGilvray Shiras* was a ship owned by the Kinsman Transit Company. During the winter months when Lake Erie was frozen, the ship and others moored at docks on the Buffalo River. As oftentimes happened, one night an ice jam disintegrated upstream, sending large chunks of ice downstream. Chunks of ice began to pile up against the *Shiras*, which at that time was without power and manned only by a shipman. The ship broke loose when a negligently constructed "deadman" to which one mooring cable was attached pulled out of the ground. The "deadman" was operated by Continental Grain Company. The ship began moving down the S-shaped river stern first and struck another ship, the *Tewksbury*. The *Tewksbury* also broke loose from its mooring, and the two ships floated down the river together. Although the crew manning the Michigan Avenue Bridge downstream had been notified of the runaway ships, they failed to raise the bridge in time to avoid a collision because of a mix-up in the shift changeover. As a result, both ships crashed into the bridge and were wedged against the bank of the river. The two vessels substantially dammed the flow of the river, causing ice and water to back up and flood installations as far as three miles upstream. The injured parties brought this action for damages against Kinsman, Continental, and the city of Buffalo. The trial court found the three defendants liable, and they appealed from that decree.

DECISION Decree of trial court affirmed as to liability.

OPINION A ship insecurely moored in a fast-flowing river is a known danger to the owners of all ships and structures down the river and to persons upon them. Kinsman and Continental, then, owed a duty of care to all within the foreseeable reach of the ships' destructive path. Similarly, the city is liable to those who foreseeably could have been injured by its negligent failure to raise the bridge in time to prevent the collision. Finally, although the exact type of harm that occurred was not foreseeable, this does not prevent liability. The damage resulted from the same physical forces whose existence required the exercise of greater care than was displayed and was of the same general type that was foreseeable. In short, the unforeseeability of the exact developments and of the extent of the loss will not limit liability where the persons injured and the general nature of the damage done were foreseeable.

INTERPRETATION The unforeseeability of the exact manner and extent of a loss will not limit liability where the persons injured and the general nature of the damage were foreseeable.

CRITICAL THINKING QUESTION Compare this decision with that in the *Palsgraf* case and attempt to reconcile the two decisions.

Harm

Harm to legally protected interest
courts determine which interests are protected from negligent interference

The plaintiff must *prove* that the defendant's negligent conduct proximately caused **harm to a legally protected interest**. Certain interests receive little or no protection against such conduct, while others receive full protection. The courts determine the extent of protection for a particular interest as a matter of law on the basis of social policy and expediency. For example, negligent conduct that is the proximate cause of harmful contact with the person of another is actionable. Thus, if Bob while driving his car negligently runs into Julie, a pedestrian, who is carefully crossing the street, Bob is liable for physical injuries Julie sustains as a result of the collision. On the other hand, if Bob's careless driving causes the car's side view mirror to brush Julie's coat but results in no physical injuries to her or damage to the coat, thus causing only offensive contact with Julie's person, Bob is not liable because Julie did not sustain harm to a legally protected interest.

The courts traditionally have been reluctant to allow recovery for negligently inflicted emotional distress. This view has gradually changed, and the majority of courts now hold a person liable for negligently causing emotional distress if bodily harm—such as a heart attack—results from the distress. And though, in the majority of states, a defendant is not liable for conduct resulting solely in emotional disturbance, some courts have recently allowed recovery of damages for negligently inflicted emotional distress even in the absence of physical harm when a person's negligent conduct places another in immediate danger of bodily harm. The Third Restatement follows the minority approach: a person whose negligent conduct places another in immediate danger of bodily harm is subject to liability to the other for serious emotional disturbance caused by reaction to the danger even though the negligent conduct did not cause any impact or bodily harm to the other. Furthermore, in a majority of states and under the Third Restatement liability for negligently inflicted emotional distress arises in the following situation: A negligently causes serious bodily injury to B. If C is a close family member of B and witnesses the injury to B, then A is liable to C for serious emotional disturbance C suffers from witnessing the event.

Defenses to Negligence

Although a plaintiff has established by a preponderance of the evidence all the required elements of a negligence action, he may nevertheless fail to recover damages if the defendant proves a valid defense. As a general rule, any defense to an intentional tort is also available in an action in negligence. In addition, certain defenses are available in negligence cases that are not defenses to intentional torts. These are contributory negligence, comparative negligence, and assumption of risk. (See Figure 8-2 illustrating the defenses to a negligence action.)

Contributory Negligence

Contributory negligence
failure of a plaintiff to exercise reasonable care such that her failure is a legal cause of the plaintiff's harm

Contributory negligence is defined as conduct on the part of the plaintiff that falls below the standard to which he should conform for his own protection and that is a legal cause of the plaintiff's harm. The Third Restatement's definition of negligence as the failure of a person to exercise reasonable care under all the circumstances applies to the contributory negligence of the plaintiff. In those few jurisdictions that have not adopted comparative negligence (Alabama, Maryland, North Carolina, Virginia, and Washington, D.C.), the contributory negligence of the plaintiff, whether slight or extensive, prevents him from recovering *any* damages from the defendant.

Last clear chance
final opportunity to avoid an injury

Notwithstanding the contributory negligence of the plaintiff, if the defendant had a **last clear chance** to avoid injury to the plaintiff but did not avail himself of such a chance, the contributory negligence of the plaintiff does not bar his recovery of damages.

Comparative Negligence

Comparative negligence
doctrine dividing damages between the plaintiff and defendant where the negligence of each has caused the harm

The harshness of the contributory negligence doctrine has caused all but a few states to reject its all-or-nothing rule and to substitute the doctrine of **comparative negligence**, which is also called comparative fault or comparative responsibility. (In states adopting comparative negligence, the doctrine of last clear chance has been abandoned.)

Approximately a dozen states have judicially or legislatively adopted "pure" comparative negligence systems. (The ALI's recently promulgated Third Restatement of Torts: Apportionment of Liability advocates this form of comparative negligence.) Under *pure comparative negligence* damages are divided between the parties in proportion to the degree of fault or negligence

Figure 8-2 Defenses to a Negligence Action

© Cengage Learning 2013

found against them. For instance, Matthew negligently drives his automobile into Nancy, who is crossing against the light. Nancy sustains damages in the amount of $10,000 and sues Matthew. If the trier of fact (the jury or judge, depending on the case) determines that Matthew's negligence contributed 70 percent to Nancy's injury and that Nancy's contributory negligence contributed 30 percent to her injury, then Nancy would recover $7,000.

Most states have adopted the doctrine of "modified" comparative negligence. Under *modified comparative negligence* the plaintiff recovers as in pure comparative negligence unless her contributory negligence was equal to or greater than that of the defendant, in which case the plaintiff recovers nothing. Thus, in the example above, if the trier of fact determined that Matthew's negligence and Nancy's contributory negligence contributed 40 percent and 60 percent, respectively, to her injury, then Nancy would not recover anything from Matthew.

Moore v. Kitsmiller
Court of Appeals of Texas, Twelfth District, Tyler, 2006
201 S.W.3d 147, *review denied*
http://www.12thcoa.courts.state.tx.us/opinions/HTMLopinion.asp?OpinionID=7549

FACTS In the spring of 2001, Kitsmiller purchased a house in Van Zandt County to use as rental property. In mid-June, he hired B & H Shaw Company, Inc. (B & H) to install a replacement septic tank in the back yard. The septic tank was located about two or three feet from a concrete stoop at the back door of the garage. B & H mounded dirt over the septic tank and the lateral lines going out from it upon completion. Sometime after B & H installed the septic tank, Kitsmiller smoothed out the mounds of dirt over the septic tank and lateral lines. Kitsmiller then leased the property to Moore and his wife on July 27. Kitsmiller testified that he viewed the back yard about a week or ten days prior to leasing the property to the Moores and stated that the dirt around the septic system looked firm.

On August 7, the Moores moved in. On August 11, Moore and his wife went into the back yard for the first time, and as he stepped off the stoop, he was unable to see the ground and could only see his wife and the bag of trash in his left arm. His wife testified that the ground looked flat. Moore testified that he had only taken a few steps off the stoop when his left leg sank into a hole, causing him to fall forward into his wife. As he tried to steady himself with his right foot, it hung and then sank, causing him to fall backward on his head and back. Moore testified that the injury to his back required surgery and affected his ability to earn a living.

Moore filed suit against Kitsmiller and B & H. He sought damages for past and future pain and suffering, past and future mental anguish, past and future physical impairment, and past and future loss of earning capacity. In their answers to Moore's suit, both Kitsmiller and B & H pleaded the affirmative defense of contributory negligence.

During the jury trial, Moore testified Kitsmiller should have notified him where the septic tank and lateral lines were located and that the dirt should have remained mounded over the tank and lines. Martin, an on-site septic tank complaint investigator for both the Texas Commission on Environmental Quality and Van Zandt County, testified that dirt should have been mounded over the septic tank and lateral lines, so that when the dirt settled, there would be no holes in the ground around the septic tank or lateral lines.

The jury determined that (1) both Kitsmiller and Moore were negligent, but B & H was not; (2) Kitsmiller was 51 percent negligent and Moore was 49 percent negligent; and (3) Moore was entitled to $210,000 in damages. On September 29, 2004, the trial court entered a judgment in favor of Moore and against Kitsmiller in the amount of $210,000 plus interest and costs. Applying comparative negligence, the trial court entered a modified final judgment on November 1, 2004, awarding Moore $107,100 plus interest and costs based upon Moore's contributory negligence. Moore appealed all issues involving his contributory negligence.

DECISION The judgment of the trial court is affirmed.

OPINION Contributory negligence contemplates an injured person's failure to use ordinary care regarding his or her own safety. This affirmative defense requires proof that the plaintiff was negligent and that the plaintiff's negligence proximately caused his or

her injuries. Negligence requires proof of proximate cause. Proximate cause requires proof of both cause in fact and foreseeability. The test for cause in fact is whether the negligent act or omission was a substantial factor in bringing about an injury without which the harm would not have occurred. Foreseeability requires that a person of ordinary intelligence should have anticipated the danger created by a negligent act or omission.

Because comparative responsibility involves measuring the party's comparative fault in causing the plaintiff's injuries, it requires a preliminary finding that the plaintiff was in fact contributorily negligent. The standards and tests for determining contributory negligence ordinarily are the same as those for determining negligence. The burden of proof on the whole case is on the plaintiff. However, the burden of proof is on the defendant to prove the defense contributory negligence by a preponderance of the evidence.

The trier of fact may draw reasonable and logical inferences from the evidence. It is within the province of the jury to draw one reasonable inference from the evidence although another inference could have been made.

Moore testified that when he stepped off the stoop into the back yard for the first time on August 11, 2001, he could only see his wife and the plastic bag of trash he was carrying in his left hand. The jury was allowed to draw an inference from this evidence that Moore was not watching where he was walking. An individual must keep a proper lookout where he is walking, and a jury is allowed to make a reasonable inference that failure to do so was the proximate cause of his injuries. It was reasonable for the jury to make an inference from Moore's testimony that his failure to keep a proper lookout where he was walking contributed to the occurrence.

Moore contends that the only reasonable inference the jury could have made was that, even if he had been watching where he was walking, he would not have been able to avoid stepping in the holes because they were not visible to the naked eye. The jury could have made that inference, but chose not to do so. Thus the jury made a reasonable inference from the evidence in finding Moore contributorily negligent.

INTERPRETATION Where both the plaintiff and defendant are negligent, under comparative negligence the law apportions damages between the parties in proportion to the degree of fault or negligence found against them.

CRITICAL THINKING QUESTION Is it fair that the plaintiff recovers damages despite being contributorily negligent? Explain.

Assumption of Risk

Express assumption of the risk
plaintiff's express consent to encounter a known danger

A plaintiff who has voluntarily and knowingly assumed the risk of harm arising from the negligent or reckless conduct of the defendant cannot recover for such harm. In **express assumption of the risk**, the plaintiff expressly agrees to assume the risk of harm from the defendant's conduct. Usually, but not always, such an agreement is by contract. Courts usually construe these exculpatory contracts strictly and will hold that the plaintiff has assumed the risk only if the terms of the agreement are clear and unequivocal. Moreover, some contracts for assumption of risk are considered unenforceable as a matter of public policy. See Chapter 13.

In *implied assumption of the risk*, the plaintiff voluntarily proceeds to encounter a known danger. Thus, a spectator entering a baseball park may be regarded as consenting that the players may proceed with the game without taking precautions to protect him from being hit by the ball. Most states have abolished or modified the defense of implied assumption of risk. Some have abandoned it entirely while others have merged implied assumption of risk into their comparative negligence systems.

Reflecting this general trend the Third Restatement of Torts: Apportionment of Liability has abandoned the doctrine of implied voluntary assumption of risk: it is no longer a defense that the plaintiff was aware of a risk and voluntarily confronted it. But if a plaintiff's conduct in the face of a known risk is unreasonable, it might constitute contributory negligence, thereby reducing the plaintiff's recovery under comparative negligence. This new Restatement limits the defense of assumption of risk to express assumption of risk, which consists of a contract between the plaintiff and another person to absolve the other person from liability for future harm. Contractual assumption of risk may occur by written agreement, express oral agreement, or conduct that creates an implied-in-fact contract, as determined by the applicable rules of contract law. Some contractual assumptions of risk, however, are not enforceable under other areas of substantive law or as against public policy.

PRACTICAL ADVICE

Consider having customers and clients sign waivers of liability and assumption of risk forms, but realize that many courts limit their effectiveness.

STRICT LIABILITY

Strict liability
liability for nonintentional and nonnegligent conduct

In some instances a person may be held liable for injuries he has caused even though he has not acted intentionally or negligently. Such liability is called **strict liability**, absolute liability, or liability without fault. The courts have determined that certain types of otherwise socially desirable activities pose sufficiently high risks of harm regardless of how carefully they are conducted, and that therefore those who carry on these activities should bear the cost of any harm that such activities cause. The doctrine of strict liability is not based on any particular fault of the defendant but on the nature of the activity in which he is engaging.

ACTIVITIES GIVING RISE TO STRICT LIABILITY

We will discuss in this section the following activities that give rise to strict liability: (1) performing abnormally dangerous activities and (2) keeping animals. In addition, strict liability is imposed upon other activities. For example, nearly all states have imposed a limited form of strict product liability upon manufacturers and merchants who sell goods in a *defective condition* unreasonably dangerous to the user or consumer. This topic is covered in Chapter 22.

Abnormally dangerous activity

strict liability is imposed for any activity that (1) creates a foreseeable and highly significant risk of harm and (2) is not one of common usage

Abnormally Dangerous Activities

A person who carries on an abnormally dangerous activity is subject to strict liability for physical harm resulting from the activity. The Third Restatement provides that "An **activity** is **abnormally dangerous** if: (1) the activity creates a foreseeable and highly significant risk of physical harm even when reasonable care is exercised by all actors; and (2) the activity is not one of common usage." The court determines whether an activity is abnormally dangerous by applying these factors. Activities to which the rule has been applied include collecting water or sewage in such quantity and location as to make it dangerous; storing explosives or flammable liquids in large quantities; blasting or pile driving; crop dusting; drilling for or refining oil in populated areas; and emitting noxious gases or fumes into a settled community. On the other hand, courts have refused to apply the rule where the activity is a "natural" use of the land, such as drilling for oil in the oil fields of Texas or transmitting gas through a gas pipe or electricity through electric wiring.

PRACTICAL ADVICE

Determine if any of your activities involve abnormally dangerous activities for which strict liability is imposed and be sure to obtain adequate insurance.

Klein v. Pyrodyne Corporation
Supreme Court of Washington, 1991
117 Wash.2d 1, 810 P.2d 917
http://scholar.google.com/scholar_case?case=7983277736024137446&q=810--P.2d--917&hl=en&as_sdt=2,34

FACTS Pyrodyne Corporation contracted to display the fireworks at the Western Washington State Fairgrounds in Puyallup, Washington, on July 4, 1987. During the fireworks display, one of the five-inch mortars was knocked into a horizontal position. A shell inside ignited and discharged, flying five hundred feet parallel to

the earth and exploding near the crowd of onlookers. Danny and Marion Klein were injured by the explosion. Mr. Klein suffered facial burns and serious injuries to his eyes. The parties provided conflicting explanations for the improper discharge, and because all the evidence had exploded, there was no means of proving the cause of the misfire. The Kleins brought suit against Pyrodyne under the theory of strict liability for participating in an abnormally dangerous activity.

DECISION Judgment for the Kleins.

OPINION Under the modern doctrine of strict liability for abnormally dangerous activities, a defendant will be liable when he damages another by a thing or activity unduly dangerous and inappropriate to the place where it is maintained, in light of the character of that place and its surroundings. The Restatement of Torts provides that any party carrying on an "abnormally dangerous activity" is strictly liable and lists six factors that courts are to consider in determining whether an activity is "abnormally dangerous." These factors are (1) the existence of a high degree of risk of some harm to the person, land, or chattels of others; (2) the likelihood that the harm resulting from the activity will be great; (3) the inability to eliminate the risk by the exercise of reasonable care; (4) the extent to which the activity is not a matter of common usage; (5) the inappropriateness of the activity to the place where it is carried on; and (6) the extent to which the activity's dangerous attributes outweigh its value to the community. Any one of these is not necessarily sufficient, and ordinarily a finding of strict liability will require several of them. The essential question is whether the risk the activity creates is so unusual as to justify the imposition of strict liability even though the activity is conducted with all reasonable care.

Factors (1), (2), and (3) are present in this case. Any time a person ignites aerial shells or rockets with the intention of sending them aloft in the presence of large crowds of people, a high risk of serious personal injury or property damage is created. That risk arises because of the possibility that a shell or rocket will malfunction or be misdirected. Furthermore, no matter how much care pyrotechnicians exercise, they cannot entirely eliminate the high risk inherent in setting off powerful explosives, such as fireworks, near crowds. Moreover, since relatively few persons conduct public fireworks displays, factor (4) is also present. Since the fairgrounds were an appropriate place for the fireworks and we as a society value fireworks on the Fourth of July more than we fear the risks, factors (5) and (6) are not present. Finding that four of the six conditions were present, the court holds that conducting public fireworks displays is an abnormally dangerous activity justifying strict liability.

INTERPRETATION The courts impose strict liability for harm resulting from an abnormally dangerous activity, as determined in light of the place, time, and manner in which the activity was conducted.

CRITICAL THINKING QUESTION If an activity is abnormally dangerous, should the law abolish it? Explain.

Keeping of Animals

Strict liability for harm caused by animals existed at common law and continues today with some modification. As a general rule, those who possess animals for their own purposes do so at their peril and must protect against harm those animals may cause to people and property.

Trespassing Animals Owners and possessors of animals, except for dogs and cats, are subject to strict liability for any physical harm their animals cause by trespassing on the property of another. There are two exceptions to this rule: (1) keepers of animals are not strictly liable for animals incidentally straying upon land immediately adjacent to a highway on which they are being lawfully driven, although the owner may be liable for negligence if he fails to control them properly and (2) in some western states, keepers of farm animals, typically cattle, are not strictly liable for harm caused by their trespassing animals that are allowed to graze freely.

Nontrespassing Animals Owners and possessors of wild animals are subject to strict liability for physical harm caused by such animals, whether or not they are trespassing. Accordingly the owner or possessor is liable even if she has exercised reasonable care in attempting to restrain the wild animal. *Wild animals* are defined as those that, in the particular region in which they are kept, are known to be likely to inflict serious damage and that cannot be considered safe, no matter how domesticated they are. The Third Restatement has a similar definition: "A wild animal is an animal that belongs to a category of animals that have not been generally domesticated and that are likely, unless restrained, to cause personal injury." The court determines whether a category of animals is wild. Animals included in this category are bears, lions, elephants, monkeys, tigers, deer, and raccoons. On the other hand, iguanas, pigeons, and manatees are not considered wild animals because they do not pose a risk of causing substantial personal injury.

Domestic animals are those animals that are traditionally devoted to the service of humankind and that as a class are considered safe. Examples of domestic animals are dogs, cats, horses, cattle, and sheep. Owners and possessors of domestic animals are subject to strict liability if they knew, or had reason to know, of an animal's dangerous tendencies abnormal for the animal's category. The animal's dangerous propensity must be the cause of the harm. For example, a keeper is not liable for a dog that bites a human merely because he knows that the dog has a propensity to fight with

Ethical Dilemma

What Are the Obligations of a Bartender to His Patrons?

Facts John Campbell, age twenty-two, was recently hired as a management trainee for the Stanton Hotel. The Stanton features a health club, swimming pool, ski slopes, and boating facilities. The management trainee program is an eighteen-month program during which the trainees rotate jobs to gain exposure to all phases of hotel operations. There is no formal orientation, and each trainee is randomly assigned to jobs.

John's first assignment was at the restaurant/bar working with Mr. Arnold, a bartender who was fifty years old and quite experienced. Mr. Arnold commented to John that John was lucky to be working the bar during the skiing season. Mr. Arnold explained that skiers frequently come in from the slopes to warm up. He told John

that all tips are shared equally and that the more it snows and the colder it gets, the better the bar business.

One day, John observed that Mr. Arnold was serving drinks to two young men who appeared to be about twenty-two or twenty-three. John overheard the men planning to ski an hour or so more and then drive over to meet friends at a neighboring hotel. One of the men appeared self-contained and unaffected by the drinks. His friend, however, was gradually getting louder, although he was not making a disturbance.

John noticed that Mr. Arnold had already served three rounds of bourbon to the men. When Mr. Arnold was preparing the fourth round, John said to him, "Don't you think they've had enough? They're

going back on the slopes." Mr. Arnold replied, "Kid, you've got a lot to learn."

Social, Policy, and Ethical Considerations
1. What action, if any, should John take?
2. What are the potential risks to the two men who are drinking? Are public safety issues involved?
3. What management policies should the hotel institute with regard to its liquor policies and athletic operations?
4. Do the drinking companions bear an ethical responsibility for each other's drinking?
5. How should society balance the interests of freedom of business and individual conduct (i.e., drinking) with the competing interests of protecting public safety?

© Cengage Learning 2013

other dogs. On the other hand, a person whose 150-pound Old English sheepdog has a propensity to jump enthusiastically on visitors would be liable for any damage caused by the dog's playfulness. About half of the states statutorily impose strict liability in dog cases even where the owner or possessor does not know, and did not have reason to know, of the dog's dangerous tendencies.

DEFENSES TO STRICT LIABILITY

Contributory negligence is *not* a defense to strict liability

Comparative negligence some states apply this doctrine to some strict liability cases

Assumption of risk express assumption of risk is a defense to an action based upon strict liability; some states apply implied assumption of risk to strict liability cases

Because the strict liability of one who carries on an abnormally dangerous activity or keeps animals is not based on his negligence, the ordinary **contributory negligence** of the plaintiff is *not* a defense to such liability. The law in imposing strict liability places the full responsibility for preventing harm on the defendant. Nevertheless, some states apply the doctrine of **comparative negligence** to some types of strict liability. The Third Restatement provides that if the plaintiff has been contributorily negligent in failing to take reasonable precautions, the plaintiff's recovery in a strict-liability claim for physical harm caused by abnormally dangerous activities or keeping of animals is reduced in accordance with the share of comparative responsibility assigned to the plaintiff.

Under the Second Restatement of Torts voluntary **assumption of risk** is a defense to an action based on strict liability. If the owner of an automobile knowingly and voluntarily parks the vehicle in a blasting zone, he may not recover for harm to his automobile. The assumption of risk, however, must be voluntary. Where blasting operations are established, for example, the possessor of nearby land is not required to move away and may recover for harm suffered.

The Third Restatement of Torts: Apportionment of Liability has abandoned the doctrine of implied voluntary assumption of risk in tort actions generally: it is no longer a defense that the plaintiff was aware of a risk and voluntarily confronted it. This new Restatement limits the defense of assumption of risk to express assumption of risk, which consists of a contract between the plaintiff and another person to absolve the other person from liability for future harm.

The Third Restatement: Liability for Physical and Emotional Harm recognizes a limitation on strict liability for abnormally dangerous activities and keeping of animals when the victim suffers harm as a result of exposure to the animal or activity resulting from the victim's securing some benefit from that exposure. The Third Restatement gives the following example: "if the plaintiff is a veterinarian or a groomer who accepts an animal such as a dog from the defendant, the plaintiff is deriving financial benefits from the acceptance of the animal, and is beyond the scope of strict liability, even if the dog can be deemed abnormally dangerous."

CHAPTER SUMMARY

Negligence

Breach of Duty of Care

Definition of Negligence conduct that falls below the standard established by law for the protection of others against unreasonable risk of harm

Reasonable Person Standard degree of care that a reasonable person would exercise under all the circumstances

- *Children* must conform to conduct of a reasonable person of the same age, intelligence, and experience under all the circumstances
- *Physical Disability* a disabled person's conduct must conform to that of a reasonable person under the same disability
- *Mental Disability* a mentally disabled person is held to the reasonable person standard of a reasonable person who is not mentally deficient
- *Superior Skill or Knowledge* if a person has skills or knowledge beyond those possessed by most others, these skills or knowledge are circumstances to be taken into account in determining whether the person has acted with reasonable care
- *Emergencies* the reasonable person standard applies, but an unexpected emergency is considered part of the circumstances
- *Violation of Statute* if the statute applies, the violation is negligence *per se* in most states

Duty to Act a person is under a duty to all others at all times to exercise reasonable care for the safety of the others' person and property; however, except in special circumstances, no one is required to aid another in peril

Duties of Possessors of Land

- *Second Restatement* a land possessor owes the following duties: (1) not to injure intentionally *trespassers*; (2) to warn *licensees* of known dangerous conditions licensees are unlikely to discover for themselves; and (3) to exercise reasonable care to protect *invitees* against dangerous conditions land possessor should know of but invitees are unlikely to discover
- *Third Restatement* adopts a unitary duty of reasonable care to all entrants on the land except for flagrant trespassers: a land possessor must use reasonable care to investigate and discover dangerous conditions and must use reasonable care to eliminate or improve those dangerous conditions that are known or should have been discovered by the exercise of reasonable care

Res Ipsa Loquitur permits the jury to infer both negligent conduct and causation

Factual Cause and Scope of Liability

Factual Cause the defendant's conduct is a factual cause of the harm when the harm would not have occurred absent the conduct

Scope of Liability (Proximate Cause) Liability is limited to those harms that result from the risks that made the defendant's conduct tortious

- *Foreseeability* excludes liability for harms that were sufficiently unforeseeable at the time of the defendant's tortious conduct that they were not among the risks that made the defendant negligent
- *Superseding Cause* an intervening act that relieves the defendant of liability

Harm

Burden of Proof plaintiff must prove that defendant's negligent conduct caused harm to a legally protected interest

Harm to Legally Protected Interest courts determine which interests are protected from negligent interference

Defenses to Negligence

Contributory Negligence failure of a plaintiff to exercise reasonable care for his own protection, which in a few states prevents the plaintiff from recovering anything

Comparative Negligence damages are divided between the parties in proportion to their degree of negligence; applies in almost all states

Assumption of Risk plaintiff's express consent to encounter a known danger; some states still apply implied assumption of the risk

Strict Liability

Activities Giving Rise to Strict Liability	**Definition of Strict Liability** liability for nonintentional and nonnegligent conduct
	Abnormally Dangerous Activity strict liability is imposed for any activity that (1) creates a foreseeable and highly significant risk of harm and (2) is not one of common usage
	Keeping of Animals strict liability is imposed for wild animals and usually for trespassing domestic animals
Defenses to Strict Liability	**Contributory Negligence** is not a defense to strict liability
	Comparative Negligence some states apply this doctrine to some strict liability cases
	Assumption of Risk express assumption of risk is a defense to an action based upon strict liability; some states apply implied assumption of risk to strict liability cases

QUESTIONS

1. A statute that requires railroads to fence their tracks is construed as intended solely to prevent injuries to animals straying onto the right-of-way. B & A Railroad Company fails to fence its tracks. Two of Calvin's cows wander onto the track. Nellie is hit by a train. Elsie is poisoned by weeds growing beside the track. For which cow(s), if any, is B & A Railroad Company liable to Calvin? Why?

2. Martha invites John to come to lunch. Martha knows that her private road is dangerous to travel, having been heavily eroded by recent rains. She doesn't warn John of the condition, reasonably believing that he will notice the deep ruts and exercise sufficient care. John's attention, while driving over, is diverted from the road by the screaming of his child, who has been stung by a bee. He fails to notice the condition of the road, hits a rut, and skids into a tree. If John is not contributorily negligent, is Martha liable to John?

3. Nathan is run over by a car and left lying in the street. Sam, seeing Nathan's helpless state, places him in his car for the purpose of taking him to the hospital. Sam drives negligently into a ditch, causing additional injury to Nathan. Is Sam liable to Nathan?

4. Vance was served liquor while he was an intoxicated patron of the Clear Air Force Station Noncommissioned Officers' Club. He later injured himself as a result of his intoxication. An Alaska state statute makes it a crime to give or to sell liquor to intoxicated persons. Vance has brought an action seeking damages for the injuries he suffered. Could Vance successfully argue that the United States was negligent *per se* by its employee's violation of the statute?

5. A statute requires all vessels traveling on the Great Lakes to provide lifeboats. One of Winston Steamship Company's boats is sent out of port without a lifeboat. Perry, a sailor, falls overboard in a storm so heavy that had there been a lifeboat it could not have been launched. Perry drowns. Is Winston liable to Perry's estate?

6. Lionel is negligently driving an automobile at excessive speed. Reginald's negligently driven car crosses the center line of the highway and scrapes the side of Lionel's car, damaging its fenders. As a result, Lionel loses control of his car, which goes into the ditch, wrecking the car and causing personal injuries to Lionel. What can Lionel recover?

7. Ellen, the owner of a baseball park, is under a duty to the entering public to provide a reasonably sufficient number of screened seats to protect those who desire such protection against the risk of being hit by batted balls. Ellen fails to do so.
   a. Frank, a customer entering the park, is unable to find a screened seat and, although fully aware of the risk, sits in an unscreened seat. Frank is struck and injured by a batted ball. Is Ellen liable?
   b. Gretchen, Frank's wife, has just arrived from Germany and is viewing baseball for the first time. Without asking any questions, she follows Frank to a seat. After the batted ball hits Frank, it caroms into Gretchen, injuring her. Is Ellen liable to Gretchen?

8. CC Railroad is negligent in failing to give warning of the approach of its train to a crossing and thereby endangers Larry, a blind man who is about to cross. Mildred, a bystander, in a reasonable effort to save Larry, rushes onto the track to push Larry out of danger. Although Mildred acts as carefully as possible, she is struck and injured by the train.
   a. Can Mildred recover from Larry?
   b. Can Mildred recover from CC Railroad?

9. Two thugs in an alley in Manhattan held up an unidentified man. When the thieves departed with his possessions, the man quickly gave chase. He had almost caught one when the thief managed to force his way into an empty taxicab stopped at a traffic light. The Peerless Transport Company owned the cab. The thief pointed his gun at the driver's head and ordered him to drive on. The driver started to follow the directions while closely pursued by a posse of good citizens, but then suddenly jammed on the brakes and jumped out of the car to safety. The thief also jumped out, but the car traveled on, injuring Mrs. Cordas and her two children. The Cordases then brought an action for damages, claiming that the cab driver was negligent in jumping to safety and leaving the moving vehicle uncontrolled. Was the cab driver negligent? Explain.

10. Timothy keeps a pet chimpanzee that is thoroughly tamed and accustomed to playing with its owner's children. The chimpanzee escapes, despite every precaution to keep it on

the owner's premises. It approaches a group of children. Wanda, the mother of one of the children, erroneously thinking the chimpanzee is about to attack the children, rushes to her child's assistance. In her hurry and excitement, she stumbles and falls, breaking her leg. Can Wanda recover from Timothy for her personal injuries?

CASE PROBLEMS

11. Hawkins slipped and fell on a puddle of water just inside the automatic door to the H. E. Butt Grocery Company's store. The water had been tracked into the store by customers and blown through the door by a strong wind. The store manager was aware of the puddle and had mopped it up several times earlier in the day. Still, no signs had been placed to warn store patrons of the danger. Hawkins brought an action to recover damages for injuries sustained in the fall. Was the store negligent in its conduct?

12. Escola, a waitress, was injured when a bottle of soda exploded in her hand while she was putting it into the restaurant's cooler. The bottle came from a shipment that had remained under the counter for thirty-six hours after being delivered by the bottling company. The bottler had subjected the bottle to the method of testing for defects commonly used in the industry, and there is no evidence that Escola or anyone else did anything to damage the bottle between its delivery and the explosion. Escola brought an action against the bottler for damages. Because she is unable to show any specific acts of negligence on its part, she seeks to rely on the doctrine of *res ipsa loquitur*. Should she be able to recover on this theory? Explain.

13. Hunn injured herself when she slipped and fell on a loose plank while walking down some steps. The night before, while entering the hotel, she had noticed that the steps were dangerous, and although she knew from her earlier stays at the hotel that another exit was available, she chose that morning to leave via the dangerous steps. The hotel was aware of the hazard, as one of three other guests who had fallen that night had reported his accident to the desk clerk then on duty. Still, the hotel did not place cautionary signs on the steps to warn of the danger, and the steps were not roped off or otherwise excluded from use. Hunn brought an action against the hotel for injuries she sustained as a result of her fall. Should she recover? Explain.

14. Fredericks, a hotel owner, had a dog named Sport that he had trained as a watchdog. When Vincent Zarek, a guest at the hotel, leaned over to pet the dog, it bit him. Although Sport had never bitten anyone before, Fredericks was aware of the dog's violent tendencies and, therefore, did not allow it to roam around the hotel alone. Vincent brought an action for injuries sustained when the dog bit him. Is Fredericks liable for the actions of his dog? Explain.

15. Led Foot drives his car carelessly into another car. The second car contains dynamite, a fact which Led had no way of knowing. The collision causes an explosion that shatters a window of a building half a block away on another street. The flying glass inflicts serious cuts on Sally, who is working at a desk near the window. The explosion also harms Vic, who is walking on the sidewalk near the point of the collision. Toward whom is Led Foot negligent?

16. A foul ball struck Marie Uzdavines on the head while she was watching the Metropolitan Baseball Club (The Mets) play the Philadelphia Phillies at the Mets' home stadium in New York.

The ball came through a hole in a screen designed to protect spectators sitting behind home plate. The screen contained several holes that had been repaired with baling wire, a lighter weight wire than that used in the original screen. Although the manager of the stadium makes no formal inspections of the screen, his employees do try to repair the holes as they find them. Weather conditions, rust deterioration, and baseballs hitting the screen are the chief causes of these holes. The owner of the stadium, the city of New York, leases the stadium to the Mets and replaces the entire screen every two years. Uzdavines sued the Mets for negligence under the doctrine of *res ipsa loquitur*. Is this an appropriate case for *res ipsa loquitur*? Explain.

17. Two-year-old David Allen was bitten by Joseph Whitehead's dog while he was playing on the porch at the Allen residence. Allen suffered facial cuts, a severed muscle in his left eye, a hole in his left ear, and scarring over his forehead. Through his father, David sued Whitehead, claiming that, as owner, Whitehead is responsible for his dog's actions. Whitehead admitted that (a) the dog was large, mean-looking, and frequently barked at neighbors; (b) the dog was allowed to roam wild; and (c) the dog frequently chased and barked at cars. He stated, however, that (a) the dog was friendly and often played with his and neighbors' children; (b) he had not received previous complaints about the dog; (c) the dog was neither aggressive nor threatening; and (d) the dog had never bitten anyone before this incident. Is Whitehead liable?

18. Larry VanEgdom, in an intoxicated state, bought alcoholic beverages from the Hudson Municipal Liquor Store in Hudson, South Dakota. An hour later, VanEgdom, while driving a car, struck and killed Guy William Ludwig, who was stopped on his motorcycle at a stop sign. Lela Walz, as special administrator of Ludwig's estate, brought an action against the city of Hudson, which operated the liquor store, for the wrongful death of Ludwig. Walz alleged that the store employee was negligent in selling intoxicating beverages to VanEgdom when he knew or could have observed that VanEgdom was drunk. Decision?

19. Carolyn Falgout accompanied William Wardlaw as a social guest to Wardlaw's brother's camp. After both parties had consumed intoxicating beverages, Falgout walked onto a pier that was then only partially completed. Wardlaw had requested that she not go on the pier. Falgout said, "Don't tell me what to do," and proceeded to walk on the pier. Wardlaw then asked her not to walk past the completed portion of the pier. She ignored his warnings and walked to the pier's end. When returning to the shore, Falgout got her shoe caught between the boards. She fell, hanging by her foot, with her head and arms in the water. Wardlaw rescued Falgout, who had seriously injured her knee and leg. She sued Wardlaw for negligence. Decision?

20. Joseph Yania, a coal strip-mine operator, and Boyd Ross visited a coal strip-mining operation owned by John Bigan to discuss a business matter with Bigan. On Bigan's property

there were several cuts and trenches he had dug to remove the coal underneath. While there, Bigan asked the two men to help him pump water from one of these cuts in the earth. This particular cut contained water eight to ten feet in depth with sidewalls or embankments sixteen to eighteen feet in height. The two men agreed, and the process began with Ross and Bigan entering the cut and standing at the point where the pump was located. Yania stood at the top of one of the cut's sidewalls. Apparently, Bigan taunted Yania into jumping into the water from the top of the sidewall—a height of sixteen to eighteen feet. As a result, Yania drowned. His widow brought a negligence action against Bigan. She claims that Bigan was negligent "(1) by urging, enticing, taunting, and inveigling Yania to jump into the water; (2) by failing to warn Yania of a dangerous condition on the land; and (3) by failing to go to Yania's rescue after he jumped into the water." Was Bigan negligent?

TAKING SIDES

Rebecca S. Dukat arrived at Mockingbird Lanes, a bowling alley in Omaha, Nebraska, at approximately 6:00 P.M. to bowl in her league game. The bowling alley's parking lot and adjacent sidewalk were covered with snow and ice. Dukat proceeded to walk into the bowling alley on the only sidewalk provided in and out of the building. She testified that she noticed the sidewalk was icy. After bowling three games and drinking three beers, Dukat left the bowling alley at approximately 9:00 P.M. She retraced her steps on the same sidewalk, which was still covered with ice and in a condition that, according to Frank Jameson, general manager of Mockingbird Lanes, was "unacceptable" if the bowling alley were open to customers. As Dukat proceeded along the sidewalk to her car, she slipped, attempted to catch herself by reaching toward a car, and fell. She suffered a fracture of both bones in her left ankle as well as a ruptured ligament. Dukat sued Mockingbird Lanes, seeking damages for her for personal injuries. Mockingbird denied liability for Dukat's personal injuries.

a. What arguments would support Dukat's claim for her personal injuries?

b. What arguments would support Mockingbird's denial of liability for Dukat's personal injuries?

c. Which side should prevail? Explain.

PART III

Contracts

CHAPTER **9**

Introduction to Contracts

A promise is a debt, and I certainly wish to keep all my promises to the letter; I can give no better advice.

The Man of Law in the *Canterbury Tales*, Geoffrey Chaucer (fourteenth century)

CHAPTER OUTCOMES

After reading and studying this chapter, you should be able to:

1. Distinguish between contracts that are covered by the Uniform Commercial Code and those covered by the common law.

2. List the essential elements of a contract.

3. Distinguish among (a) express and implied contracts; (b) unilateral and bilateral contracts; (c) valid, void, voidable, and unenforceable agreements; and (d) executed and executory contracts.

4. Explain the doctrine of promissory estoppel.

5. Identify the three elements of enforceable quasi contract and explain how it differs from a contract.

Every business enterprise, whether large or small, must enter into contracts with its employees, its suppliers of goods and services, and its customers in order to conduct its business operations. Thus, contract law is an important subject for the business manager. Contract law is also basic to fields of law treated in other parts of this book, such as agency, partnerships, corporations, sales of personal property, negotiable instruments, and secured transactions.

Even the most common transaction may involve many contracts. For example, in a typical contract for the sale of land, the seller promises to transfer title, or right of ownership, to the land; and the buyer promises to pay an agreed-upon purchase price. In addition, the seller may promise to pay certain taxes, and the buyer may promise to assume a mortgage on the property or to pay the purchase price to a creditor of the seller. If the parties have lawyers, they very likely have contracts with these lawyers. If the seller deposits the proceeds of the sale in a bank, he enters into a contract with the bank. If the buyer rents the property, he enters into a contract with the tenant. When one of the parties leaves his car in a parking lot to attend to any of these matters, he assumes a contractual relationship with the owner of the lot. In short, nearly every business transaction is based on contract and the expectations the agreed-upon promises create. It is, therefore, essential that you know the legal requirements for making binding contracts.

DEVELOPMENT OF THE LAW OF CONTRACTS

Contract law, like the law as a whole, is not static. It has undergone—and is still undergoing—enormous changes. In the nineteenth century, almost total freedom in forming contracts was the rule. However, contract formation also involved many technicalities, and the courts imposed contract liability only when the parties complied strictly with the required formalities.

During the twentieth century, many of the formalities of contract formation were relaxed, and as a result, contractual obligations usually are recognized whenever the parties clearly intend to be bound. In addition, an increasing number of promises are now enforced in certain circumstances, even though such promises do not comply strictly with the basic requirements of a contract. In brief, the twentieth century left its mark on contract law by limiting the absolute freedom of contract and, at the same time, by relaxing the requirements of contract formation. Accordingly, we can say that it is considerably easier now both to get into a contract and to get out of one.

Common Law

Contracts are primarily governed by state common law. An orderly presentation of this law is found in the Restatements of the Law of Contracts, a valuable authoritative reference work extensively relied on and quoted in reported judicial opinions.

The Uniform Commercial Code

Uniform Commercial Code (UCC)
Article 2 of the UCC governs the sales of goods

Sale
the transfer of title from seller to buyer

Goods
tangible personal property

Personal property
property other than an interest in land

The sale of personal property is a large part of commercial activity. Article 2 of the **Uniform Commercial Code** (the Code, or UCC) governs such sales in all states except Louisiana. A **sale** consists of the passing of title to goods from seller to buyer for a price. A contract for sale includes both a present sale of goods and a contract to sell goods at a future time. The Code essentially defines **goods** as tangible personal property. **Personal property** is any property other than an interest in real property (land). For example, the purchase of a television set, an automobile, or a textbook is a sale of goods. All such transactions are governed by Article 2 of the Code, but where the Code has not specifically modified general contract law, the common law of contracts continues to apply. In other words, the law of sales is a specialized part of the general law of contracts, and the law of contracts governs unless specifically displaced by the Code. See *Pittsley v. Houser* in Chapter 19.

Amendments to Article 2 were promulgated in 2003 to accommodate electronic commerce and to reflect development of business practices, changes in other law, and other practical issues. To date no states have adopted them. However, at least forty-one of the states have adopted the 2001 Revisions to Article 1, which applies to all of the articles of the Code.

Types of Contracts Outside the Code

Common law
most contracts are primarily governed by state common law, including contracts involving employment, services, insurance, real property, patents, and copyrights

Real property
land and anything attached to it

General contract law (**common law**) governs all contracts outside the scope of the Code. Such contracts play a significant role in commercial activities. For example, the Code does *not* apply to employment contracts, service contracts, insurance contracts, contracts involving **real property** (land and anything attached to it, including buildings, as well as any right, privilege, or power in the real property, including leases, mortgages, options, and easements), and contracts for the sale of intangibles such as patents and copyrights. These transactions continue to be governed by general contract law. Figure 9-1 summarizes the types of law governing contracts.

See *Fox v. Mountain West Electric, Inc.*, later in this chapter.

Figure 9-1 Law Governing Contracts

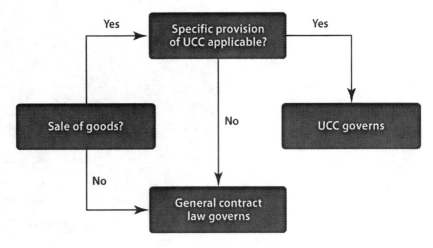

© Cengage Learning 2013

DEFINITION OF CONTRACT

Contract
binding agreement that the courts will enforce

Put simply, a **contract** is a binding agreement that the courts will enforce. The Restatement Second, Contracts more precisely defines a contract as "a promise or a set of promises for the breach of which the law gives a remedy, or the performance of which the law in some way recognizes a duty." A *promise* manifests or demonstrates the intention to act or to refrain from acting in a specified manner.

Breach
failure to properly perform a contractual obligation

Those promises that meet *all* of the essential requirements of a binding contract are contractual and will be enforced. All other promises are *not* contractual, and usually no legal remedy is available for a **breach** of, or a failure to properly perform, these promises. (The remedies provided for breach of contract, which include compensatory damages, equitable remedies, reliance damages, and restitution, are discussed in Chapter 18.) Thus, a promise may be contractual (and therefore binding) or noncontractual. In other words, all contracts are promises, but not all promises are contracts, as illustrated by Figure 9-2.

REQUIREMENTS OF A CONTRACT

The four basic requirements of a contract are as follows:

1. **Mutual assent.** The parties to a contract must manifest by words or conduct that they have agreed to enter into a contract. The usual method of showing mutual assent is by offer and acceptance.
2. **Consideration.** Each party to a contract must intentionally exchange a legal benefit or incur a legal detriment as an inducement to the other party to make a return exchange.
3. **Legality of object.** The purpose of a contract must not be criminal, tortious, or otherwise against public policy.
4. **Capacity.** The parties to a contract must have contractual capacity. Certain persons, such as adjudicated incompetents, have no legal capacity to contract, while others, such as minors, incompetent persons, and intoxicated persons, have limited capacity to contract. All others have full contractual capacity.

In addition, though in a limited number of instances a contract must be evidenced by a writing to be enforceable, in most cases an oral contract is binding and enforceable. Moreover, there must be an *absence* of invalidating conduct, such as duress, undue influence, misrepresentation,

Figure 9-2 Contractual and Noncontractual Promises

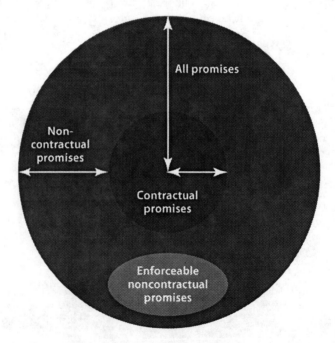

© Cengage Learning 2013

Figure 9-3 Validity of Agreements

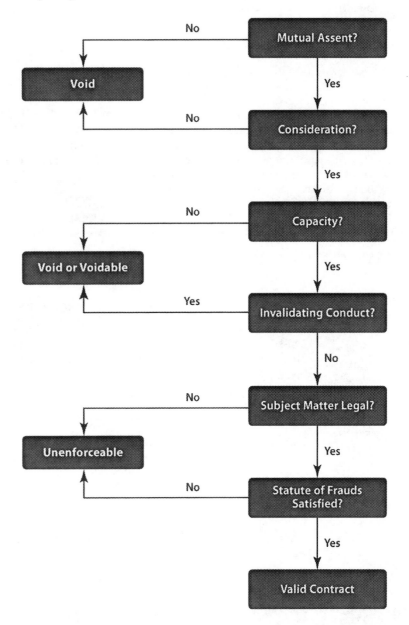

© Cengage Learning 2013

or mistake. (See Figure 9-3.) As the *Steinberg v. Chicago Medical School* case shows, a promise meeting all of these requirements is contractual and legally binding. However, if any requirement is unmet, the promise is noncontractual. We will consider these requirements separately in succeeding chapters.

Steinberg v. Chicago Medical School
Illinois Court of Appeals, 1976
41 Ill.App.3d 804, 354 N.E.2d 586
http://scholar.google.com/scholar_case?case=13765816040578352414&q=354+N.E.2d+586&hl=en&as_sdt=2,34

FACTS Robert Steinberg applied for admission to the Chicago Medical School as a first-year student and paid an application fee of $15. The school, a private educational institution, rejected his application. Steinberg brought an action against the school, claiming that it did not evaluate his and other applications according to the academic entrance criteria printed in the school's bulletin.

Instead, he argues, the school based its decisions primarily on nonacademic considerations, such as family connections between the applicant and the school's faculty and members of its board of trustees and the ability of the applicant or his family to donate large sums of money to the school. Steinberg asserts that by evaluating his application according to these unpublished criteria, the school breached the contract it had created when it accepted his application fee. The trial court granted the defendant's motion to dismiss, and Steinberg appealed.

DECISION Trial court's dismissal reversed and case remanded.

OPINION A contract is a promise or set of promises for the breach of which the law gives a remedy. "A contract's essential requirements are: competent parties, valid subject matter, legal consideration, mutuality of obligation and mutuality of agreement." Generally, parties may contract in any situation where there is no legal prohibition. To be binding, however, the terms must be "reasonably certain and definite." The contract must also be supported by consideration. Defined in its most general terms, consideration is some benefit accruing to one party or some detriment undertaken by the other, such as the payment of or promise to pay money. In addition, the parties must mutually agree to the contract's essential terms and conditions to make the contract

binding. Mutual consent is gathered from the language employed by the parties or manifested by their words or acts.

In this situation, the school's promise to evaluate the applications according to academic standards is stated in a "definitive manner" in its bulletin. Steinberg accepted this in good faith, and his $15 application fee served as valid consideration. When the school accepted this money, it bound itself to honor the obligations stated in its bulletin. Therefore, its failure to use the stated academic criteria in evaluating applications constituted a breach of its contractual obligation to Steinberg.

INTERPRETATION An agreement meeting all of the requirements of a contract is binding and legally enforceable.

ETHICAL QUESTION Is it ethical for a school to consider any factors other than an applicant's merit? Explain.

CRITICAL THINKING QUESTION Should the courts resolve this type of dispute on the basis of contract law? Explain.

PRACTICAL ADVICE
Whenever possible, try to use written express contracts that specify all of the important terms rather than using implied in fact contracts.

Implied in fact contract
contract in which agreement of the parties is inferred from their conduct

Express contract
agreement of parties that is stated in words either in writing or orally

CLASSIFICATION OF CONTRACTS

Contracts can be classified according to various characteristics, such as method of formation, content, and legal effect. The standard classifications are (1) express or implied contracts; (2) bilateral or unilateral contracts; (3) valid, void, voidable, or unenforceable contracts; and (4) executed or executory contracts. These classifications are not mutually exclusive. For example, a contract may be express, bilateral, valid, and executory.

Express and Implied Contracts

Parties to a contract may indicate their assent either in words or by conduct implying such willingness. For instance, a regular customer known to have an account at a drugstore might pick up an item at the drugstore, show it to the clerk, and walk out. This is a perfectly valid contract. The clerk knows from the customer's conduct that she is buying the item at the specified price and wants it charged to her account. Her actions speak as effectively as words. Such a contract, formed by conduct, is an implied or, more precisely, an **implied in fact contract**; in contrast, a contract in which the parties manifest assent in words is an **express contract**. Both are contracts, equally enforceable. The difference between them is merely the manner in which the parties manifest their assent.

Fox v. Mountain West Electric, Inc.
Supreme Court of Idaho, 2002
137 Idaho 703, 52 P.3d 848; rehearing denied, 2002
http://caselaw.lp.findlaw.com/data2/idahostatecases/sc/1026/fox8.pdf

FACTS Lockheed Martin Idaho Technical Company (LMITCO) requested bids for a comprehensive fire alarm system in its twelve buildings located in Idaho Falls. Mountain West Electric (MWE) was in the business of installing electrical wiring, conduit and related hookups, and attachments. Fox provided services in designing, drafting, testing, and assisting in the installation of fire alarm systems. The parties decided that it would be better for them to work together with MWE taking the lead on the project. The parties prepared a document defining each of their roles and jointly prepared a bid. MWE was awarded the LMITCO fixed-price contract. In May 1996, Fox began performing various services at the direction of MWE's manager.

During the course of the project, many changes and modifications to the LMITCO contract were made. MWE and Fox dis-

agreed on the procedure for the compensation of the change orders. MWE proposed a flow-down procedure, whereby Fox would receive whatever compensation LMITCO decided to pay MWE. Fox found this unacceptable and suggested a bidding procedure to which MWE objected. Fox and MWE could not reach an agreement upon a compensation arrangement with respect to change orders. Fox left the project on December 9, 1996, after delivering the remaining equipment and materials to MWE. MWE contracted with Life Safety Systems to complete the LMITCO project.

Fox filed a complaint in July 1998 seeking money owed for materials and services provided to MWE by Fox. MWE answered and counterclaimed seeking monetary damages resulting from the alleged breach of the parties' agreement by Fox. The district court found in favor of MWE holding that an implied in fact contract existed. Fox appealed.

DECISION The decision of the district court is affirmed.

OPINION The Court recognizes three types of contractual relationships: (1) an express contract in which the parties expressly agree regarding a transaction; (2) an implied in fact contract in which there is no express agreement, but the conduct of the parties implies an agreement from which an obligation in contract exists; and (3) an implied in law contract, or quasi contract, which is not a contract at all, but an obligation imposed by law for the purpose of bringing about justice and equity without reference to the intent or the agreement of the parties.

An implied in fact contract is one in which the terms and existence of the contract are manifested by the conduct of the parties with the request of one party and the performance by the other often being inferred from the circumstances attending the performance. An implied in fact contract is grounded in the parties' agreement and tacit understanding.

Using the district court's finding that pricings submitted by Fox were used by MWE as estimates for the change orders, the Court held that the district court did not err in finding that there was an implied in fact contract using the industry standard's flow-down method of compensation for the change orders rather than a series of fixed price contracts between MWE and Fox.

A second question that was raised is whether this contract should be governed by the Uniform Commercial Code (UCC). For that to be the case, the contract would have to be predominantly for the sale of goods. Fox argued the predominant factor of this transaction was the fire alarm system, not the methodology of how the system was installed, and, therefore, the UCC should govern.

MWE contended that the UCC should not be used, despite the fact that goods accounted for one-half of the contract price, because the predominant factor at issue is services and not the sale of goods. MWE points out that the primary issue is the value of Fox's services under the change orders and the cost of obtaining replacement services after Fox left the job.

The Court held that the predominant factor test should be used to determine whether the UCC applies to transactions involving the sale of both goods and services as explained in *Pittsley v. Houser* (see Chapter 19).

The test for inclusion or exclusion is not whether they are mixed, but, granting that they are mixed, whether their predominant factor, their thrust, and their purpose, reasonably stated, is the rendition of service, with goods incidentally involved (e.g., contract with artist for painting) or is a transaction of sale, with labor incidentally involved (e.g., installation of a water heater in a bathroom). This test essentially involves consideration of the contract in its entirety, applying the UCC to the entire contract or not at all.

The district court found that the contract at issue in this case contained both goods and services; however, the predominant factor was Fox's services while the goods provided by Fox were merely incidental to the services he provided. The Court held that the district court did not err in finding that the predominant factor of the underlying transaction was services and that the UCC did not apply.

INTERPRETATION An implied in fact contract is formed by the conduct of the parties; where a contract provides for both goods and services, the common law applies if the predominant factor of the contract is the provision of services.

CRITICAL THINKING QUESTION Why should the legal rights of contracting parties depend on whether a contract is or is not for the sale of goods?

Bilateral and Unilateral Contracts

Bilateral contract
contract in which both parties exchange promises

Promisor
person making a promise

Promisee
person to whom a promise is made

In the typical contractual transaction, each party makes at least one promise. For example, if Adelle says to Byron, "If you promise to mow my lawn, I will pay you $10," and Byron agrees to mow Adelle's lawn, Adelle and Byron have made mutual promises, each agreeing to do something in exchange for the promise of the other. When a contract is formed by the exchange of promises, each party is under a duty to the other. This kind of contract is called a **bilateral contract**, because each party is both a **promisor** (a person making a promise) and a **promisee** (the person to whom a promise is made).

Unilateral contract
contract in which only one party makes a promise

But suppose that only one of the parties makes a promise. Adelle says to Byron, "If you will mow my lawn, I will pay you $10." A contract will be formed when Byron has finished mowing the lawn and not before. At that time, Adelle becomes contractually obligated to pay $10 to Byron. Adelle's offer was in exchange for Byron's act of mowing the lawn, not for his promise to mow it. Because Byron never made a promise to mow the lawn, he was under no duty to mow it. This is a **unilateral contract** because only one of the parties has made a promise.

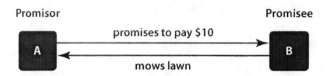

Thus, whereas a bilateral contract results from the exchange of a promise for a return promise, a unilateral contract results from the exchange of a promise either for performing an act or for refraining from doing an act. In cases in which it is not clear whether a unilateral or bilateral contract has been formed, the courts presume that the parties intended a bilateral contract. Thus, if Adelle says to Byron, "If you will mow my lawn, I will pay you $10," and Byron replies, "OK, I will mow your lawn," a bilateral contract is formed.

Valid, Void, Voidable, and Unenforceable Contracts

By definition a **valid contract** is one that meets all of the requirements of a binding contract. It is an enforceable promise or agreement.

A **void contract** is an agreement that does not meet all of the requirements of a binding contract. Thus, it is no contract at all; it is merely a promise or an agreement that has no legal effect. An example of a void agreement is an agreement entered into by a person whom the courts have declared incompetent.

A **voidable contract**, on the other hand, though defective, is not wholly lacking in legal effect. A voidable contract is a contract; however, because of the manner in which the contract was formed or a lack of capacity of a party to it, the law permits one or more of the parties to avoid the legal duties the contract creates. If the contract is voided, both of the parties are relieved of their legal duties under the agreement. For instance, through intentional misrepresentation of a material fact (fraud), Thomas induces Regina to enter into a contract. Regina may, upon discovery of the fraud, notify Thomas that by reason of the misrepresentation, she will not perform her promise, and the law will support Regina. Although the contract induced by fraud is not void, it is voidable at the election of Regina, the defrauded party. Thomas, the fraudulent party, may make no such election. If Regina elects to avoid the contract, Thomas will be released from his promise under the agreement, although he may be liable for damages under tort law for fraud.

A contract that is neither void nor voidable may nonetheless be unenforceable. An **unenforceable contract** is one for the breach of which the law provides no remedy. For example, a contract may be unenforceable because of a failure to satisfy the requirements of the statute of frauds, which requires certain kinds of contracts to be evidenced by a writing to be enforceable. Also, the statute of limitations imposes restrictions on the time during which a party has the right to bring a lawsuit for breach of contract. After the statutory time period has passed, a contract is referred to as unenforceable, rather than void or voidable. Figure 9-3 lists the requirements of a binding contract and the consequences of failing to satisfy each requirement.

Executed and Executory Contracts

A contract that has been fully carried out by all of the parties to it is an **executed contract**. Strictly speaking, an executed contract is no longer a contract, because all of the duties under it have been performed; but having a term for such a completed contract is useful. By comparison, the term **executory contract** applies to contracts that are still partially or entirely unperformed by one or more of the parties.

PROMISSORY ESTOPPEL

As a general rule, promises are not enforceable if they do not meet all the requirements of a contract. Nevertheless, in certain circumstances, the courts enforce noncontractual promises under the doctrine of **promissory estoppel** to avoid injustice. A noncontractual promise is enforceable when it is made under circumstances that should lead the promisor reasonably to expect that the promisee, in reliance on the promise, would be induced by it to take definite and substantial action or to forbear, and the promisee does take such action or does forbear (see Figure 9-2). For example, Gordon promises Constance not to foreclose for a period of six months on a mortgage Gordon owns on Constance's land. Constance then expends $100,000 to construct a building on the land. His promise not to foreclose is binding on Gordon under the doctrine of promissory estoppel.

PRACTICAL ADVICE

Because it is uncertain whether the offeree in a unilateral contract will choose to perform, use bilateral contracts wherever possible.

Valid contract

contract that meets all of the requirements of a binding contract

Void contract

an agreement without legal effect

Voidable contract

contract capable of being made void

Unenforceable contract

contract for the breach of which the law does not provide a remedy

PRACTICAL ADVICE

Be careful to avoid entering into void, voidable, and unenforceable contracts.

Executed contract

contract fully performed by all of the parties

Executory contract

contract not fully performed

Promissory estoppel

doctrine enforcing noncontractual promises for which there has been justifiable reliance on the promise and justice requires enforcement

PRACTICAL ADVICE

Take care not to make promises on which others may detrimentally rely.

Skebba v. Kasch
Court of Appeals of Wisconsin, 2006
2006 WI App 232, 724 N.W.2d 408; review denied, 2007 WI 59
http://www.wicourts.gov/ca/opinion/DisplayDocument.html?content=html&seqNo=26899

FACTS Kasch and his brother owned M.W. Kasch Co. Kasch hired Skebba as a sales representative, and over the years promoted him first to account manager, then to customer service manager, field sales manager, vice president of sales, senior vice president of sales and purchasing, and finally to vice president of sales. When M.W. Kasch Co. experienced serious financial problems in 1993, Skebba was approached by another company to leave Kasch and work for them. When Skebba told Kasch he was accepting the new opportunity, Kasch asked what it would take to get him to stay. Skebba told Kasch that he needed security for his retirement and family and would stay if Kasch agreed to pay Skebba $250,000 if one of these three conditions occurred: (1) the company was sold; (2) Skebba was lawfully terminated; or (3) Skebba retired. Kasch agreed to this proposal and promised to have the agreement drawn up. Skebba turned down the job opportunity and stayed with Kasch from December 1993 through 1999 when the company assets were sold.

Over the years, Skebba repeatedly but unsuccessfully asked Kasch for a written summary of this agreement. Eventually, Kasch sold the business receiving $5.1 million dollars for his fifty-one percent share of the business. Upon the sale of the business, Skebba asked Kasch for the $250,000 Kasch had previously promised to him. Kasch refused and denied ever having made such an agreement. Instead, Kasch gave Skebba a severance agreement, which had been drafted by Kasch's lawyers in 1993. This agreement promised two years of salary continuation on the sale of the company, but only if Skebba was not hired by the successor company. The severance agreement also required a set-off against the salary continuation of any sums Skebba earned from any activity during the two years of the severance agreement. Skebba sued, alleging breach of contract and promissory estoppel.

The jury found there was no contract, but that Kasch had made a promise upon which Skebba relied to his detriment, that the reliance was foreseeable, and that Skebba was damaged in the amount of $250,000. The trial court concluded that, based on its reading of applicable case law, it could not specifically enforce the promise the jury found Kasch made to Skebba because there were other ways to measure damages. The trial court held that since Skebba could not establish what he had lost by relying on Kasch's promise he had not proved his damages.

DECISION Order of trial court reversed and case remanded.

OPINION Kasch did not promise to pay Skebba more than Skebba would have earned at the job Skebba turned down. Kasch did not promise that total income to Skebba would be greater than in the turned-down job, no matter how long he remained with Kasch. Kasch only promised that if Skebba stayed, Kasch would pay Skebba $250,000 (the sum Skebba wanted for his retirement), at the time the earliest of three conditions occurred. Kasch sold the business while Skebba was still employed by Kasch. Kasch refused to pay as promised.

The purpose of promissory estoppel is to enforce promises where the failure to do so is unjust. The requirements of promissory estoppel follow: (1) Was the promise one which the promisor should reasonably expect to induce action or forbearance of a definite and substantial character on the part of the promisee? (2) Did the promise induce such action or forbearance? (3) Can injustice be avoided only by enforcement of the promise? The first two of these requirements are facts to be found by a jury or other factfinder, while the third is a policy decision to be made by the court.

A court, in fashioning a remedy, can consider any equitable or legal remedy, which will "prevent injustice." Moreover, the

> amount allowed as damages may be determined by the plaintiff's expenditures or change of position in reliance as well as by the value to him of the promised performance.... In determining what justice requires, the court must remember all of its powers, derived from equity, law merchant, and other sources, as well as the common law. Its decree should be molded accordingly.

Wisconsin is one of a small group of states which recognizes that to fulfill the purpose of promissory estoppel (i.e., prevent injustice) a court must be able to fashion a remedy that restores the promisee to where he or she would be if the promisor had fulfilled the promise. In this case, Skebba performed in reliance on Kasch's promise to pay $250,000 to him if one of three conditions occurred. Kasch enjoyed the fruits of Skebba's reliance—he kept on a top salesperson to help the company through tough financial times and he avoided the damage that he believed Skebba's leaving could have had on M.W. Kasch's reputation in the industry. Accordingly, to prevent injustice, the equitable remedy for Skebba to receive is Kasch's specific performance: the promised payment of the $250,000.

Skebba's loss has nothing to do with what he might have earned on another job. Income from the rejected job was never a part of the calculus of the promise made and relied upon.

INTERPRETATION The courts will enforce a promise that the promisor should reasonably expect to induce detrimental reliance by the promisee if the promisee takes such action and justice requires enforcement.

ETHICAL QUESTION Did Kasch act ethically? Explain.

CRITICAL THINKING QUESTION What could Skebba have done to better protect his interests? Explain.

QUASI CONTRACTS

In addition to express and implied in fact contracts, there are implied in law or quasi contracts, which were not included in the previous classification of contracts for the reason that a quasi (meaning "as if") contract is not a contract at all but based in restitution. The term *quasi contract* is used because the remedy granted for quasi contract is similar to one of the remedies available for breach of contract.

Quasi contract
obligation *not* based upon contract that is imposed to avoid injustice

A quasi contract is not a contract because it is based neither on an express nor on an implied promise. Rather, a *contract implied in law* or **quasi contract** is an obligation imposed by law to avoid injustice. For example, Willard by mistake delivers to Roy a plain, unaddressed envelope containing $100 intended for Lucia. Roy is under no contractual obligation to return it, but Willard is permitted to recover the $100 from Roy. The law imposes a quasi-contractual obligation on Roy to prevent his unjust enrichment at the expense of Willard. Such a recovery requires three essential elements: (1) a benefit conferred upon the defendant (Roy) by the plaintiff (Willard); (2) the defendant's (Roy's) appreciation or knowledge of the benefit; and (3) acceptance or retention of the benefit by the defendant (Roy) under circumstances making it inequitable for him to retain the benefit without compensating the plaintiff for its value.

Not infrequently, quasi contracts are used to provide a remedy when the parties enter into a void contract, an unenforceable contract, or a voidable contract that is avoided. In such a case, the law of quasi contracts will determine what recovery is permitted for any performance rendered by the parties under the invalid, unenforceable, or invalidated agreement.

Weichert Co. Realtors v. Ryan
Supreme Court of New Jersey, 1992
128 N.J. 427, 608 A.2d 280

FACTS In March 1987, William Tackaberry, a real estate agent for Weichert Co. Realtors, informed Thomas Ryan, a local developer, that he knew of property Ryan might be interested in purchasing. Ryan indicated he was interested in knowing more about the property. Tackaberry disclosed the property's identity and the seller's proposed price. Tackaberry also stated that the purchaser would have to pay Weichert a 10 percent commission. Tackaberry met with the property owner and gathered information concerning the property's current leases, income, expenses, and development plans. Tackaberry also collected tax and zoning documents relevant to the property. In a face-to-face meeting on April 4, Tackaberry gave Ryan the data he had gathered and presented Ryan with a letter calling for a 10 percent finder's fee to be paid to Weichert by Ryan upon "successfully completing and closing of title." Tackaberry arranged a meeting, held three days later, where Ryan contracted with the owner to buy the land. Ryan refused, however, to pay the 10 percent finder's fee to Weichert. The trial and appellate courts found that Ryan and Weichert had entered into a binding contract. Ryan appealed.

DECISION Judgment for Weichert modified and remanded to the trial court to determine the amount of plaintiff's recovery.

OPINION This case presents two issues: whether Ryan and Tackaberry entered into an enforceable agreement and, if not, whether Weichert is entitled to recover the reasonable value of Tackaberry's services on a theory of *quantum meruit*. The record is insufficient to support a finding that Tackaberry and Ryan mutually manifested assent to the essential terms of the contract. First, Ryan never expressly assented to the terms of Tackaberry's offer. Although Ryan expressed interest in learning more about the property, neither his expression of interest nor his agreement to meet with Tackaberry to learn more about the transaction was

sufficient to establish the "unqualified acceptance" necessary to manifest express assent. Moreover, Ryan refused to agree to the 10 percent figure during the April meeting and thereafter consistently rejected that term. Thus, the parties never formed an express contract.

In some circumstances, courts will allow recovery even though the parties' words and actions are insufficient to manifest an intention to agree to the proffered terms. Recovery based on a quasi contract, sometimes referred to as a contract implied in law, is wholly unlike recovery based on an express or implied in fact contract in that the law imposes it for the purpose of bringing about justice without reference to the parties' intentions. Applying that principle, courts have allowed quasi-contractual recovery for services rendered when a party confers a benefit with a reasonable expectation of payment. That type of quasi-contractual recovery, known as *quantum meruit*, entitles the performing party to recoup the reasonable value of the services he has rendered. In this case, Tackaberry furnished Ryan with information about the property with an expectation that Ryan would pay a brokerage fee, and Ryan himself admitted at trial that he had always intended to compensate Tackaberry for his services. To deny Tackaberry compensation for services rendered would unjustly enrich Ryan. The commission amount should be determined on the basis of proofs showing the reasonable value of Tackaberry's services, including evidence of customary brokers' fees for similar transactions.

INTERPRETATION The courts impose a quasi-contractual obligation to pay the reasonable value of a benefit conferred in order to avoid unjust enrichment.

CRITICAL THINKING QUESTION Why does the law allow a recovery in quasi contract?

CONCEPT REVIEW 9-1

Contracts, Promissory Estoppel, and Quasi Contracts

	Contract	Promissory Estoppel	Quasi Contract
Type of Promise	Contractual	Noncontractual	None Void Unenforceable Invalidated
Requirements	All of the essential elements of a contract	Detrimental and justifiable reliance	Benefit conferred and knowingly accepted
Remedies	Equitable Compensatory Reliance Restitution	Promise enforced to the extent necessary to avoid injustice	Reasonable value of benefit conferred

© Cengage Learning 2013

BUSINESS LAW *IN ACTION*

Armed with a hastily scribbled work order, Jonas, an employee of Triton Painting Service, heads to 109 Millard Road. He works for two full days power cleaning, priming, and painting the exterior of the house. Satisfied with his work, Jonas moves on to his next job. When the homeowners, the Prestons, return from their vacation several days later, they are shocked to see their formerly "Palatial Peach" home painted "Santa Fe Sand." They are even more surprised when they receive a call from Triton demanding payment for the paint job.

Errors such as this sometimes occur in business. It was the homeowners at 104

Millard Road who had contracted to pay Triton $1,200 for an exterior paint job using Santa Fe Sand. But Jonas felt sure enough he had the correct house number, and no one stopped him from doing the work. And even though the Prestons had not chosen the color, they now have a freshly painted house because of Triton's error. Should the Prestons have to pay? If so, how much? What does the law say about this?

To begin with, there was no contract between Triton and the Prestons. Therefore Triton cannot sue the Prestons for breach of contract. A suit in quasi contract is Triton's best bet, but to prevail Triton must

prove unjust enrichment. One factor affecting Triton's success is whether the Prestons, in good faith, dislike the new color. However, even if they do not dislike Santa Fe Sand, another factor is whether the house needed repainting. It would be unfair to require the Prestons to pay for an unnecessary service. Moreover, because the Prestons were out of town they could not have stopped Jonas from doing the work. Finally, because they received services rather than goods, they cannot now give back the service. Under these circumstances, it is hardly equitable to make the Prestons pay for what was clearly Triton's mistake.

CHAPTER SUMMARY

Development of the Law of Contracts

Common Law most contracts are primarily governed by state common law, including contracts involving employment, services, insurance, real property (land and anything attached to it), patents, and copyrights

The Uniform Commercial Code (UCC) Article 2 of the UCC governs the sales of goods

- *Sale* the transfer of title from seller to buyer
- *Goods* tangible personal property (personal property is all property other than an interest in land)

Definition of a Contract

Contract binding agreement that the courts will enforce

Breach failure to properly perform a contractual obligation

Requirements of a Contract

Mutual Assent the parties to a contract must manifest by words or conduct that they have agreed to enter into a contract

Consideration each party to a contract must intentionally exchange a legal benefit or incur a legal detriment as an inducement to the other party to make a return exchange

Legality of Object the purpose of a contract must not be criminal, tortious, or otherwise against public policy

Capacity the parties to a contract must have contractual capacity

Classification of Contracts

Express and Implied Contracts
- *Implied in Fact Contract* contract in which the agreement of the parties is inferred from their conduct
- *Express Contract* an agreement that is stated in words either orally or in writing

Bilateral and Unilateral Contracts
- *Bilateral Contract* contract in which both parties exchange promises
- *Unilateral Contract* contract in which only one party makes a promise

Valid, Void, Voidable, and Unenforceable Contracts
- *Valid Contract* one that meets all of the requirements of a binding contract
- *Void Contract* no contract at all; without legal effect
- *Voidable Contract* contract capable of being made void
- *Unenforceable Contract* contract for the breach of which the law provides no remedy

Executed and Executory Contracts
- *Executed Contract* contract that has been fully performed by all of the parties
- *Executory Contract* contract that has yet to be fully performed

Promissory Estoppel

Definition a doctrine enforcing some noncontractual promises

Requirements a promise made under circumstances that should lead the promisor reasonably to expect that the promise would induce the promisee to take definite and substantial action, and the promisee does take such action

Remedy a court will enforce the promise to the extent necessary to avoid injustice

Quasi Contract

Definition an obligation not based upon contract that is imposed by law to avoid injustice; also called an implied in law contract

Requirements a court will impose a quasi contract when (1) the plaintiff confers a benefit upon the defendant, (2) the defendant knows or appreciates the benefit, and (3) the defendant's retention of the benefit is inequitable

Remedy the plaintiff recovers the reasonable value of the benefit she conferred upon the defendant

QUESTIONS

1. Owen telephones an order to Hillary's store for certain goods, which Hillary delivers to Owen. Nothing is said by either party about price or payment terms. What are the legal obligations of Owen and Hillary?

2. Minth is the owner of the Hiawatha Supper Club, which he leased for two years to Piekarski. During the period of the lease, Piekarski contracted with Puttkammer for the resurfacing of the access and service areas of the supper club. Puttkammer performed the work satisfactorily. Minth knew about the contract and the performance of the work. The work, including labor and materials, had a reasonable value of $2,540, but Puttkammer was never paid because Piekarski went bankrupt. Puttkammer brought an action against Minth to recover the amount owed to him by Piekarski. Will Puttkammer prevail? Explain.

3. Jonathan writes to Willa, stating, "I'll pay you $150 if you reseed my lawn." Willa reseeds Jonathan's lawn as requested. Has a contract been formed? If so, what kind?

4. Calvin uses fraud to induce Maria to promise to pay money in return for goods he has delivered to her. Has a contract been formed? If so, what kind? What are the rights of Calvin and Maria?

5. Anna is about to buy a house on a hill. Prior to the purchase, she obtains a promise from Betty, the owner of the adjacent property, that Betty will not build any structure that would block Anna's view. In reliance on this promise, Anna buys the house. Is Betty's promise binding? Why or why not?

CASE PROBLEMS

6. Mary Dobos was admitted to Boca Raton Community Hospital in serious condition with an abdominal aneurysm. The hospital called upon Nursing Care Services, Inc., to provide around-the-clock nursing services for Mrs. Dobos. She received two weeks of in-hospital care, forty-eight hours of postrelease care, and two weeks of at-home care. The total bill was $3,723.90. Mrs. Dobos refused to pay, and Nursing Care Services, Inc., brought an action to recover. Mrs. Dobos maintained that she was not obligated to render payment in that she never signed a written contract, nor did she orally agree to be liable for the services. The necessity for the services, reasonableness of the fee, and competency of the nurses were undisputed. After Mrs. Dobos admitted that she or her daughter authorized the forty-eight hours of postrelease care, the trial court ordered compensation of $248 for that period. It did not allow payment of the balance, and Nursing Care Services, Inc., appealed. Decision?

7. St. Charles Drilling Co. contracted with Osterholt to install a well and water system that would produce a specified quantity of water. The water system failed to meet its warranted capacity, and Osterholt sued for breach of contract. Does the Uniform Commercial Code apply to this contract?

8. Helvey brought suit against the Wabash County REMC (REMC) for breach of implied and express warranties. He alleged that REMC furnished electricity in excess of 135 volts to Helvey's home, damaging his 110-volt household appliances. This incident occurred more than four years before Helvey brought this suit. In defense, REMC pleads that the Uniform Commercial Code's (UCC's) Article 2 statute of limitations of four years has passed, thereby barring Helvey's suit. Helvey argues that providing electrical energy is not a transaction in goods under the UCC but rather a furnishing of services that would make applicable the general contract six-year statute of limitations. Is the contract governed by the UCC? Why?

9. Jack Duran, president of Colorado Carpet Installation, Inc., began negotiations with Fred and Zuma Palermo for the sale and installation of carpeting, carpet padding, tile, and vinyl floor covering in their home. Duran drew up a written proposal that referred to Colorado Carpet as "the seller" and to the Palermos as the "customer." The proposal listed the quantity, unit cost, and total price of each item to be installed. The total price of the job was $4,777.75. Although labor was expressly included in this figure, Duran estimated the total labor cost at $926. Mrs. Palermo in writing accepted Duran's written proposal soon after he submitted it to her. After Colorado Carpet delivered the tile to the Palermo home, however, Mrs. Palermo had a disagreement with Colorado Carpet's tile man and arranged for another contractor to perform the job. Colorado Carpet brought an action against the Palermos for breach of contract. Does the Uniform Commercial Code apply to this contract?

10. On November 1, the Kansas City Post Office Employees Credit Union merged into the Kansas City Telephone Credit Union to form the Communications Credit Union (Credit Union). Systems Design and Management Information (SDMI) develops computer software programs for credit unions, using Burroughs (now Unisys) hardware. SDMI and Burroughs together offered to sell to Credit Union both a software package, called the Generic System, and Burroughs hardware. Later in November, a demonstration of the software was held at SDMI's offices, and the Credit Union agreed to purchase the Generic System software. This agreement was oral. After Credit Union was converted to the SDMI Generic System, major problems with the system immediately became apparent, so SDMI filed suit against Credit Union to recover the outstanding contract price for the software. Credit Union counterclaimed for damages based upon breach of contract and negligent and fraudulent misrepresentation. Does the Uniform Commercial Code apply to this contract?

11. Insul-Mark is the marketing arm of Kor-It Sales, Inc. Kor-It manufactures roofing fasteners and Insul-Mark distributes them nationwide. In late 1985, Kor-It contracted with Modern Materials, Inc., to have large volumes of screws coated with a rust-proofing agent. The contract specified that the coated screws must pass a standard industry test and that Kor-It would pay according to the pound and length of the screws coated. Kor-It had received numerous complaints from customers that the coated screws were rusting, and Modern Materials unsuccessfully attempted to remedy the problem. Kor-It terminated its relationship with Modern Materials and brought suit for the deficient coating. Modern Materials counterclaimed for the labor and materials it had furnished to Kor-It. The trial court held that the contract (a) was for performance of a service, (b) not governed by the Uniform Commercial Code, (c) governed by the common law of contracts, and (d) therefore, barred by a two-year statute of limitations. Insul-Mark appealed. Decision?

12. Max E. Pass, Jr., and his wife, Martha N. Pass, departed in an aircraft owned and operated by Mr. Pass from Plant City, Florida, bound for Clarksville, Tennessee. Somewhere over Alabama the couple encountered turbulence, and Mr. Pass lost control of the aircraft. The plane crashed, killing both Mr. and Mrs. Pass. Approximately four and a half months prior to the flight in which he was killed, Mr. Pass had taken his airplane to Shelby Aviation, an aircraft service company, for inspection and service. In servicing the aircraft, Shelby Aviation replaced both rear wing attach point brackets on the plane. Three and one half years after the crash, Max E. Pass, Sr., father of Mr. Pass and administrator of his estate, and Shirley Williams, mother of Mrs. Pass and administratrix of her estate, filed suit against Shelby Aviation. The lawsuit alleged that the rear wing attach point brackets sold and installed by Shelby Aviation were defective because they lacked the bolts necessary to secure them properly to the airplane. The plaintiffs asserted claims against the defendant for breach of express and implied warranties under Article 2 of the Uniform Commercial Code (UCC), which governs the sale of goods. Shelby Aviation contended that the transaction with Mr. Pass had been primarily for the sale of services, rather than of goods, and that consequently Article 2 of the UCC did not cover the transaction. Does the UCC apply to this transaction? Explain.

TAKING SIDES

Richardson hired J. C. Flood Company, a plumbing contractor, to correct a stoppage in the sewer line of her house. The plumbing company's "snake" device, used to clear the line leading to the main sewer, became caught in the underground line. To release it, the company excavated a portion of the sewer line in Richardson's backyard. In the process, the company discovered numerous leaks in a rusty, defective water pipe that ran parallel with the sewer line. To meet public regulations, the water pipe, of a type no longer approved for such service, had to be replaced either then or later, when the yard would have to be excavated again. The plumbing company proceeded to repair the water pipe. Though Richardson inspected the company's work daily and did not express any objection to the extra work involved in replacing the water pipe, she refused to pay any part of the total bill after the company completed the entire operation. J. C. Flood Company then sued Richardson for the costs of labor and material it had furnished.

a. What arguments would support J. C. Flood's claim for the costs of labor and material it had furnished?

b. What arguments would support Richardson's refusal to pay the bill?

c. For what, if anything, should Richardson be liable? Explain.

CHAPTER **10**

Mutual Assent

It is elementary that for a contract to exist there must be an offer and acceptance.

Zeller v. First National Bank & Trust, Tales, 79 Ill. App. 3d 170, 34 Ill. Dec. 473, 398 N.E.2d 148 (1979)

CHAPTER OUTCOMES

After reading and studying this chapter, you should be able to:

1. Identify the three essentials of an offer and explain briefly the requirements associated with each.

2. State the seven ways by which an offer may be terminated other than by acceptance.

3. Compare the traditional and modern theories of definiteness of acceptance of an offer, as shown by the common law "mirror image" rule and by the rule of the Uniform Commercial Code.

4. Describe the five situations limiting an offeror's right to revoke her offer.

5. Explain the various rules that determine when an acceptance takes effect.

Though each of the requirements for forming a contract is essential to its existence, mutual assent is so basic that frequently a contract is referred to as an agreement between the parties. Enforcing the contract means enforcing the agreement; indeed, the agreement between the parties is the very core of the contract. As we discussed in Chapter 9, a contractual agreement always involves either a promise exchanged for a promise (*bilateral contract*) or a promise exchanged for a completed act or forbearance to act (*unilateral contract*).

The way in which parties usually show mutual assent is by offer and acceptance. One party makes a proposal (offer) by words or conduct to the other party, who agrees by words or conduct to the proposal (acceptance).

A contract may be formed by conduct. Thus, though there may be no definite offer and acceptance, or definite acceptance of an offer, a contract exists if both parties' actions manifest (indicate) a recognition by each of them of the existence of a contract. To form a contract, the agreement must be objectively manifested. The important thing is what the parties indicate to one another by spoken or written words or by conduct. The law, therefore, applies an *objective* standard and is concerned only with the assent, agreement, or intention of a party as it reasonably appears from his words or actions. The law of contracts is not concerned with what a party may have actually thought or the meaning that he intended to convey even if his subjective understanding or intention differed from the meaning he objectively indicated by word or conduct. For example, if Joanne seemingly offers to sell to Bruce her Chevrolet automobile but intended to offer and believes that she is offering her Ford automobile, and Bruce accepts the offer, reasonably believing it was for the Chevrolet, a contract has been formed for the sale of the Chevrolet. Subjectively, Joanne and Bruce are not in agreement as to the subject matter. Objectively, however, there is agreement, and the objective manifestation is binding.

The Uniform Commercial Code's (UCC's or Code's) treatment of mutual assent is covered in greater detail in Chapter 19.

OFFER

Offer
a proposal indicating a willingness to enter into a contract

Offeror
person making the offer

Offeree
person to whom the offer is made

Communication
offeree must have knowledge of the offer and the offer must be made by the offeror or her authorized agent to the offeree

Intent
determined by an objective standard of what a reasonable offeree would have believed

An **offer** is a definite undertaking or proposal made by one person to another indicating a willingness to enter into a contract. The person making the proposal is the **offeror**. The person to whom it is made is the **offeree**. When it is received, the offer confers on the offeree the power to create a contract by acceptance, which is an expression of the offeree's willingness to comply with the terms of the offer. Until the offeree exercises this power, the outstanding offer creates neither rights nor liabilities.

ESSENTIALS OF AN OFFER

An offer need not take any particular form to have legal effect. To be effective, however, it must (1) be communicated to the offeree; (2) manifest an intent to enter into a contract; and (3) be sufficiently definite and certain. If these essentials are present and the offer has not terminated, the offer gives the offeree the power to form a contract by accepting the offer.

Communication

To provide his part of the mutual assent required to form a contract, the offeree must know about the offer; he cannot agree to something about which he has no knowledge. Accordingly, the offeror must communicate the offer in an intended manner. For example, Oscar signs a letter containing an offer to Ellen and leaves it on top of the desk in his office. Later that day, Ellen, without prearrangement, goes to Oscar's office, discovers that he is away, notices the letter on his desk, reads it, and then writes on it an acceptance that she dates and signs. No contract is formed because the offer never became effective: Ellen became aware of the offer by chance, not by Oscar's intentional communication of it.

Not only must the offer be communicated to the offeree, but the communication must also be made or authorized by the offeror. If Jones tells Black that she plans to offer White $600 for a piano, and Black promptly informs White of Jones's intention, no offer has been made. There was no authorized communication of any offer by Jones to White. By the same token, if David should offer to sell to Lou his diamond ring, an acceptance of this offer by Tia would not be effective, as David made no offer to Tia.

An offer need not be stated or communicated by words. Conduct from which a reasonable person may infer a proposal in return for either an act or a promise amounts to an offer.

An offer may be made to the general public. No person can accept such an offer, however, until and unless he knows that the offer exists. For example, if a person, without knowing of an advertised reward for information leading to the return of a lost watch, gives information leading to the return of the watch, he is not entitled to the reward. His act was not an acceptance of the offer because he could not accept something of which he had no knowledge.

Intent

To have legal effect, an offer must manifest an intent to enter into a contract. The **intent** of an offer is determined objectively from the words or conduct of the parties. The meaning of either party's manifestation is based on what a reasonable person in the other party's position would have believed.

Occasionally, a person exercises her sense of humor by speaking or writing words that—taken literally and without regard to context or surrounding circumstances—could be construed as an offer. The promise is intended as a joke, however, and the promisee as a reasonable person should understand it to be such. Therefore, it is not an offer. Because the person to whom it is made realizes or should realize that it is not made in earnest, it should not create a reasonable expectation in his mind. No contractual intent exists on the part of the promisor, and the promisee is or reasonably ought to be aware of that fact. If, however, the intended joke is so real that the promisee as a reasonable person under all the circumstances believes that the joke is in fact an offer, and so believing accepts, the objective standard applies and the parties have entered into a contract.

A promise made under obvious excitement or emotional strain is likewise not an offer. For example, Charlotte, after having her month-old Cadillac break down for the third time in two days, screams in disgust, "I will sell this car to anyone for $10!" Lisa hears Charlotte and hands her a $10 bill. Under the circumstances, Charlotte's statement was not an offer if a reasonable person in Lisa's position would have recognized it merely as an excited, nonbinding utterance.

It is important to distinguish language that constitutes an offer from that which merely solicits or invites offers. Such proposals, although made in earnest, lack the intent to enter into a contract and are therefore not deemed offers. As a result, a purported acceptance does not bring about a contract but operates only as an offer. Proposals that invite offers include preliminary negotiations, advertisements, and auctions.

PRACTICAL ADVICE
Make sure that you indicate by words or conduct what agreement you wish to enter.

Catamount Slate Products, Inc. v. Sheldon
Supreme Court of Vermont, 2004
2003 VT 112, 845 A.2d 324
http://scholar.google.com/scholar_case?case=12161607133389120155&q=2003+VT+112&hl=en&as_sdt=2,22

FACTS The Reed Family owns and operates Catamount Slate Products, Inc. (Catamount), a slate quarry and mill, on 122 acres in Fair Haven, Vermont. The Sheldons own neighboring property. Since 1997, the parties have been litigating the Reeds' right to operate their slate business and to use the access road leading to the quarry. In 2000, the parties agreed to try to resolve their disputes in a state-funded mediation with retired Judge Arthur O'Dea serving as mediator. Prior to the mediation, Judge O'Dea sent each party a Mediation Agreement outlining the rules governing the mediation. Paragraph nine of the Mediation Agreement stated that—

i. all statements, admissions, confessions, acts, or exchanges ... are acknowledged by the parties to be offers in negotiation of settlement and compromise, and as such inadmissible in evidence, and not binding upon either party unless reduced to a final agreement of settlement. Any final agreement of settlement must be in writing and signed by every party sought to be charged.

The mediation was held on September 5, 2000. Judge O'Dea began the session by reaffirming the statements made in the Mediation Agreement. After ten hours, the parties purportedly reached an agreement on all major issues. Judge O'Dea then orally summarized the terms of the resolution with the parties and counsel present. The attorneys took notes on the terms of the agreement with the understanding that they would prepare the necessary documents for signature in the coming days.

The resolution required the Reeds to pay the Sheldons $250 a month for the right to use the access road, with payments to commence on October 1, 2000. The parties also agreed to a series of terms governing the operation of the slate quarry. These terms were to be memorialized in two distinct documents, a Lease Agreement and a Settlement Agreement.

On September 7, 2000, two days after the mediation, the Sheldons' attorney, Emily Joselson, drafted a letter outlining the terms of the settlement and sent copies to James Leary, the Reeds' attorney, and Judge O'Dea. Within a week, Leary responded by letter concurring in some respects and outlining the issues on which the Reeds disagreed with Joselson's characterization of the settlement.

On October 1, 2000, the Reeds began paying the $250 monthly lease payments, but, since the settlement agreement was not final, the parties agreed that the money would go into an escrow account maintained by the Sheldons' counsel. The check was delivered to the Sheldons' attorney with a cover memo stating, "This check is forwarded to you with the understanding that the funds will be disbursed to your clients only after settlement agreement becomes final. Of course, if the settlement agreement does not come to fruition, then the funds must be returned to my

clients." The parties continued to exchange letters actively negotiating the remaining details of the Lease and Settlement Agreements for the better part of the next five months.

In February 2001, while drafts were still being exchanged, Christine Stannard, the Reeds' daughter, saw a deed and map in the Fair Haven Town Clerk's Office which led her to believe that the disputed road was not owned by the Sheldons, but was a town highway. The Reeds then refused to proceed any further with negotiating the settlement agreement. A written settlement agreement was never signed by either party.

The Sheldons then filed a motion to enforce the settlement agreement. The trial court granted the option, finding that the attorneys' notes taken at the end of the mediation and the unsigned drafts of the Lease and Settlement Agreements sufficiently memorialized the agreement between the parties and thus constituted an enforceable settlement agreement.

DECISION Judgment of the trial is reversed and remanded.

OPINION The question is whether the oral agreement reached at mediation, when combined with the unexecuted documents drafted subsequently, constituted a binding, enforceable settlement agreement. Parties are free to enter into a binding contract without memorializing their agreement in a fully executed document. In such an instance, the mere intention or discussion to commit their agreement to writing will not prevent the formation of a contract prior to the document's execution.

"On the other hand, if either party communicates an intent not to be bound until he achieves a fully executed document, no amount of negotiation or oral agreement to specific terms will result in the formation of a binding contract." The freedom to determine the exact moment in which an agreement becomes binding encourages the parties to negotiate as candidly as possible, secure in the knowledge that they will not be bound until the execution of what both parties consider to be a final, binding agreement.

We look to the intent of the parties to determine the moment of contract formation. Intent to be bound is a question of fact. "To discern that intent a court must look to the words and deeds [of the parties] which constitute objective signs in a given set of circumstances." In determining whether the parties intended to be bound in the absence of a fully executed document the court will "consider (1) whether there has been an express reservation of the right not to be bound in the absence of a writing; (2) whether there has been partial performance of the contract; (3) whether all of the terms of the alleged contract have been agreed upon; and (4) whether the agreement at issue is the type of contract that is usually committed to writing." The language of the parties' correspondence and other documentary evidence presented reveals an intent by the mediation participants not to be bound prior to the execution of a final document. The Mediation Agreement Judge O'Dea sent to the parties prior to the mediation clearly contemplates that any settlement agreement emanating from the mediation would be binding only after being put in writing and signed. Further, Judge O'Dea reminded the parties of these ground rules at the outset of the mediation. The Reeds testified that they relied on these statements and assumed that, as indicated, they would not be bound until they signed a written agreement. Even more compelling evidence of the Reeds' lack of intent to be bound in the absence of a writing is the statement in the cover letter accompanying the Reeds' $250 payments to the Sheldons' attorney saying, "This check is forwarded to you with the understanding that the funds will be disbursed to your clients only after settlement agreement becomes final. Of course, if the settlement agreement does not come to fruition, then the funds must be returned to my clients."

No evidence was presented of partial performance of the settlement agreement. The third factor is whether there is anything left to negotiate. The lengthy correspondence in this case makes clear that several points of disagreement and ambiguity arose during the drafting process. Resolution of these issues was clearly impor-

tant enough to forestall final execution until the language of the documents could be agreed upon. In such a case, where the parties intend to be bound only upon execution of a final document, for the court to determine that, despite continuing disagreement on substantive terms, the parties reached a binding, enforceable settlement agreement undermines their right to enter into the specific settlement agreement for which they contracted.

The fourth and final factor, whether the agreement at issue is the type of contract usually put into writing, also weighs in the Reeds' favor. Being a contract for an interest in land, the Lease Agreement is subject to the Statute of Frauds and thus generally must be in writing.

In conclusion, three of the four factors indicate that the parties here did not intend to be bound until the execution of a final written document, and therefore the parties never entered into a binding settlement agreement.

INTERPRETATION The intent of the parties to be bound to a contract is determined by an objective standard of what a reasonable person would have believed based on the words and conduct of the parties.

CRITICAL THINKING QUESTION Does the decision rendered by the court establish a policy that is best for society? Explain.

Preliminary Negotiations If a communication creates in the mind of a reasonable person in the position of the offeree an expectation that his acceptance will conclude a contract, then the communication is an offer. If it does not, then the communication is a preliminary negotiation. Initial communications between potential parties to a contract often take the form of preliminary negotiations, through which the parties either request or supply the terms of an offer that may or may not be made. A statement that may indicate a willingness to make an offer is not in itself an offer. For instance, if Brown writes to Young, "Will you buy my automobile for $3,000?" and Young replies, "Yes," there is no contract. Brown has not made an offer to sell her automobile to Young for $3,000. The offeror must demonstrate an intent to enter into a contract, not merely a willingness to enter into a negotiation.

Advertisements Merchants desire to sell their merchandise and thus are interested in informing potential customers about the goods, terms of sale, and price. But if they make widespread promises to sell to each person on their mailing list, the number of acceptances and resulting contracts might conceivably exceed their ability to perform. Consequently, a merchant might refrain from making offers by merely announcing that he has goods for sale, describing the goods, and quoting prices. He is simply inviting his customers and, in the case of published advertisements, the public, to make offers to him to buy his goods. His advertisements, circulars, quotation sheets, and displays of merchandise are *not* offers because (1) they do not contain a promise and (2) they leave unexpressed many terms that would be necessary to the making of a contract. Accordingly, his customers' responses are not acceptances because no offer to sell has been made.

Nonetheless, a seller is not free to advertise goods at one price and then raise the price once demand has been stimulated. Although as far as contract law is concerned, the seller has made no offer, such conduct is prohibited by the Federal Trade Commission as well as by legislation in most states. Moreover, in some circumstances a public announcement or advertisement may constitute an offer if the advertisement or announcement contains a definite promise of something in exchange for something else and confers a power of acceptance on a specified person or class of persons. The typical offer of a reward is an example of a definite offer, as is the situation presented in the landmark *Lefkowitz v. Great Minneapolis Surplus Store, Inc.* case, which follows.

Lefkowitz v. Great Minneapolis Surplus Store, Inc.
Supreme Court of Minnesota, 1957
251 Minn. 188, 86 N.W.2d 689
http://scholar.google.com/scholar_case?case=1365398257799813577&q=251+Minn.+188&hl=en&as_sdt=2,22

FACTS On April 6, 1956, Great Minneapolis Surplus Store published an advertisement in a Minneapolis newspaper reporting that "Saturday, 9:00 A.M. sharp; 3 brand new fur coats worth up to $100; first come, first served, $1 each." Lefkowitz was the first to arrive at the store, but the store refused to sell him the fur coats because the "house rule" was that the offers were intended for women only and sales would not be made to men. The following week, Great Minneapolis published a similar advertisement for the sale of two mink scarves and a black lapin stole. Again Lefkowitz was the first to arrive at the store on Saturday morning, and once again the store refused to sell to him, this time because Lefkowitz knew of the house rule. This appeal was from a judgment awarding the plaintiff the sum of $138.50 as damages for breach of contract.

DECISION Judgment for Lefkowitz affirmed.

OPINION Whether a newspaper advertisement constitutes an offer, rather than a mere invitation to make an offer, depends upon the intention of the parties and the surrounding circumstances. If the facts show that some performance was promised in positive terms in return for something requested, then a newspaper advertisement addressed to the general public may lead to a binding obligation. Here the newspaper advertisements were clear, definite, and explicit, and left nothing open for negotiation. Lefkowitz was the first to arrive at the store and to offer to purchase the furs and, therefore, was entitled to performance on the part of the store.

INTERPRETATION Although advertisements generally do not constitute offers, under some circumstances they do.

ETHICAL QUESTION Should Lefkowitz be entitled to damages? Why?

CRITICAL THINKING QUESTION Should an advertisement generally be construed as *not* constituting an offer? Explain.

Auction Sales The auctioneer at an auction sale does not make offers to sell the property being auctioned but invites offers to buy. The classic statement by the auctioneer is, "How much am I offered?" The persons attending the auction may make progressively higher bids for the property, and each bid or statement of a price or a figure is an offer to buy at that figure. If the bid is accepted, customarily indicated by the fall of the hammer in the auctioneer's hand, a contract results. A bidder is free to withdraw his bid at any time prior to its acceptance. The auctioneer is likewise free to withdraw the goods from sale *unless* the sale is advertised or announced to be without reserve.

Without reserve
auctioneer may not withdraw the goods from the auction

If the auction sale is advertised or announced in explicit terms to be **without reserve**, the auctioneer may not withdraw an article or lot put up for sale unless no bid is made within a reasonable time. Unless so advertised or announced, the sale is with reserve. A bidder at either type of sale may retract his bid at any time prior to its acceptance by the auctioneer; such retraction, however, does not revive any previous bid.

Definiteness

Definiteness
offer's terms must be clear enough to provide a court with a basis for giving an appropriate remedy

PRACTICAL ADVICE
To make an offer that will result in an enforceable contract, make sure you include all the necessary terms.

The terms of a contract, all of which are usually contained in the offer, must be clear enough to provide a court with a reasonable basis for determining the existence of a breach and for giving an appropriate remedy. It is a fundamental policy that contracts should be made by the parties, not by the courts; accordingly, remedies for a breach must in turn have their basis in the parties' contract. Where the parties have intended to form a contract, the courts will attempt to find a basis for granting a remedy. Missing terms may be supplied by course of dealing, usage of trade, or inference. Thus, uncertainty as to incidental matters seldom will be fatal so long as the parties intended to form a contract. Nevertheless, the more terms the parties leave open, the less likely it is that they have intended to form a contract. Moreover, given the great variety of contracts, stating the terms that are essential to all contracts is impossible. In most cases, however, material terms would include the parties, subject matter, price, quantity, quality, and time of performance.

See *DiLorenzo v. Valve and Primer Corporation* in Chapter 12.

Open Terms With respect to agreements for the sale of goods, the UCC provides standards by which the courts may determine omitted terms, provided the parties intended to enter into a binding contract. The Code provides missing terms in a number of instances, where, for example, the contract fails to specify the price, the time or place of delivery, or payment terms. The

Restatement has adopted an approach similar to the Code's in supplying terms omitted from the parties' contract.

Under the Code, an offer for the purchase or sale of goods may leave open particulars of performance to be specified by one of the parties. Any such specification must be made in good faith and within limits set by commercial reasonableness. **Good faith** is defined as honesty in fact in the conduct or transaction concerned. Under the 2001 Revised UCC Article 1, good faith means honesty in fact and the observance of reasonable commercial standards of fair dealing. **Commercial reasonableness** is a standard determined in terms of the business judgment of reasonable persons familiar with the practices customary in the type of transaction involved and in terms of the facts and circumstances of the case.

See *DiLorenzo v. Valve and Primer Corporation* in Chapter 12.

Output and Requirements Contracts   An **output contract** is an agreement of a buyer to purchase a seller's entire output for a stated period. In comparison, a **requirements contract** is an agreement of a seller to supply a buyer with all his requirements for certain goods. Even though the exact quantity of goods is not specified and the seller may have some degree of control over his output and the buyer over his requirements, under the Code and the Restatement, such agreements are enforceable by the application of an objective standard based on the good faith of both parties. Thus, a seller who operated a factory only eight hours a day before the agreement was made cannot operate the factory twenty-four hours a day and insist that the buyer take all of the output. Nor can the buyer expand his business abnormally and insist that the seller still supply all of his requirements.

DURATION OF OFFERS

An offer confers upon the offeree a power of acceptance, which continues until the offer terminates. The ways in which an offer may be terminated, other than by acceptance, are through (1) lapse of time; (2) revocation; (3) rejection; (4) counteroffer; (5) death or incompetency of the offeror or offeree; (6) destruction of the subject matter to which the offer relates; and (7) subsequent illegality of the type of contract the offer proposes.

Lapse of Time

The offeror may specify the time within which the offer is to be accepted, just as he may specify any other term or condition in the offer. Unless otherwise terminated, the offer remains open for the *specified* time. Upon the expiration of that time, the offer no longer exists and cannot be accepted. Any purported acceptance of an expired offer will serve only as a new offer.

If the offer does not state the time within which the offeree may accept, the offer will terminate after a *reasonable* time. Determining a "reasonable" time is a question of fact, depending on the nature of the contract proposed, the usages of business, and other circumstances of the case (including whether the offer was communicated by electronic means). For instance, an offer to sell a perishable good would be open for a far shorter period of time than an offer to sell undeveloped real estate.

Good faith

honesty in fact

Commercial reasonableness

judgment of reasonable persons familiar with the business transaction

Output contract

an agreement of a buyer to purchase the entire output of a seller's factory

Requirements contract

an agreement of a seller to supply a buyer with all his requirements for certain goods

Lapse of time

offer remains open for the time period specified or, if no time is stated, for a reasonable period of time

PRACTICAL ADVICE

Because of the uncertainty as to what is a "reasonable time," it is advisable to specify clearly the duration of offers you make.

Sherrod v. Kidd
Court of Appeals of Washington, Division 3, 2007
155 P.3d 976
http://scholar.google.com/scholar_case?case=7607426217314840344&q=155+P.3d+976&hl=en&as_sdt=2,22

FACTS David and Elizabeth Kidd's dog bit Mikaila Sherrod. Mikaila through her guardian ad litem (GAL) made a claim for damages against the Kidds (defendants). On June 14, 2005, the Kidds offered to settle the claim for $31,837. On July 12, Mikaila through her GAL sued the Kidds. On July 20, the Kidds raised their settlement offer to $32,843. The suit was subject to mandatory arbitration. The parties proceeded to arbitration on April 28, 2006. On May 5, the arbitrator awarded Mikaila $25,069.47. On May 9, the GAL wrote to the Kidds and purported to accept their

last offer of $32,843, made the year before. The GAL on Mikaila's behalf moved to enforce the settlement agreement. The court concluded the offer was properly accepted because it had not been withdrawn and it entered judgment in the amount of the first written offer.

DECISION The decision of the trial judge is reversed.

OPINION An offer to form a contract is open only for a reasonable time, unless the offer specifically states how long it is open for acceptance. How much time is reasonable is usually a question of fact. A reasonable time "is the time that a reasonable person in the exact position of the offeree would believe to be satisfactory to the offeror." A reasonable time for an offeree to accept an offer depends on the "nature of the contract and the character of the business in which the parties were engaged."

Implicit in an offer (and an acceptance) to settle a personal injury suit is the party's intent to avoid a less favorable result at the hands of a jury, a judge or, in this case, an arbitrator. The defendant runs the risk that the award might be more than the offer.

The plaintiff, of course, runs the risk that the award might be less than the offer. Both want to avoid that risk. And it is those risks that settlements avoid. In this case the offer expired when the arbitrator announced the award and thus was not subject to being accepted.

INTERPRETATION An offer is open for a reasonable period of time.

CRITICAL THINKING QUESTION Should the courts consider the social and public policy in a case such as this? Explain.

Revocation

Revocation

cancellation of an offer by an offeror; generally, an offer may be terminated at any time before it is accepted

The offeror generally may cancel or *revoke* an offer (**revocation**) at any time *prior* to its acceptance. If the offeror originally promises that the offer will be open for thirty days but wishes to terminate it after five days, he may do so merely by giving the offeree notice that he is withdrawing the offer. This notice may be given by any means of communication and effectively terminates the offer when *received* by the offeree. A very few states, however, have adopted a rule that treats revocations the same as acceptances, thus making them effective upon dispatch. An offer made to the general public is revoked only by giving to the revocation publicity equivalent to that given the offer.

Notice of revocation may be communicated indirectly to the offeree through reliable information from a third person that the offeror has disposed of the property he has offered for sale or has otherwise placed himself in a position indicating an unwillingness or inability to perform the promise contained in the offer. For example, Aaron offers to sell his portable television set to Ted and tells Ted that he has ten days in which to accept. One week later, Ted observes the television set in Celia's house and is informed that Celia purchased it from Aaron. The next day, Ted sends to Aaron an acceptance of the offer. There is no contract because Aaron's offer was effectively revoked when Ted learned of Aaron's inability to sell the television set to Ted because he had sold it to Celia.

Certain limitations, however, restrict the offeror's power to revoke the offer at any time prior to its acceptance. These limitations apply to the following five situations.

Option

contract providing that an offer will stay open for a specified period of time

Consideration

the inducement to enter into a contract, consisting of an act or promise that has legal value

Option Contracts   An **option** is a contract by which the offeror is bound to hold open an offer for a specified period of time. It must comply with all of the requirements of a contract, including the offeree's giving of consideration to the offeror. (**Consideration**, or the inducement to enter into a contract consisting of an act or promise that has legal value, is discussed in Chapter 12.) For example, if Ellen, in return for the payment of $500 to her by Barry, grants Barry an option, exercisable at any time within thirty days, to buy Blackacre at a price of $80,000, Ellen's offer is irrevocable. Ellen is legally bound to keep the offer open for thirty days, and any communication by Ellen to Barry giving notice of withdrawal of the offer is ineffective. Though Barry is not bound to accept the offer, the option contract entitles him to thirty days in which to accept.

Firm offer

irrevocable offer by a merchant to sell or buy goods, made in a signed writing that gives assurance that it will not be revoked for up to three months

Firm Offers under the Code   The Code provides that a *merchant* is bound to keep an offer to buy or sell *goods* open for a stated period (or, if no time is stated, for a reasonable time) not exceeding three months if the merchant gives assurance in a *signed writing* that the offer will be held open. The Code, therefore, makes a merchant's **firm offer** (written promise not to revoke an offer for a stated period of time) enforceable even though no consideration is given to the offeror for that promise (i.e., an option contract does not exist). A *merchant* is defined as a person (1) who is a dealer in a given type of goods, or (2) who by his occupation holds himself out as having knowledge or skill peculiar to the goods or practices involved, or (3) who employs an agent or broker whom he holds out as having such knowledge or skill.

Statutory irrevocability

offer made irrevocable by statute

Statutory Irrevocability   Certain offers, such as bids made to the state, municipality, or other government body for the construction of a building or some public work, are made irrevocable by statute. Another example is preincorporation stock subscription agreements, which are irrevocable for a period of six months under many state corporation statutes.

Irrevocable offer of unilateral contracts
a unilateral offer may not be revoked for a reasonable time after performance is begun

Irrevocable Offers of Unilateral Contracts Where the offer contemplates a *unilateral* contract—that is, a promise for an act—injustice to the offeree may result if revocation is permitted after the offeree has started to perform the act requested in the offer and has substantially but not completely accomplished it. Such an offer is not accepted and no contract is formed until the offeree has completed the requested act. By simply starting performance, the offeree does not bind himself to complete performance; historically, he did not bind the offeror to keep the offer open, either. Thus, the offeror could revoke the offer at any time before the offeree's completion of performance. For example, Jordan offers Karlene $300 if Karlene will climb to the top of the flagpole in the center of campus. Karlene starts to climb, but when she is five feet from the top, Jordan yells to her, "I revoke."

The Restatement deals with this problem by providing that where the performance of the requested act necessarily requires the offeree to expend time and effort, the offeror is obligated not to revoke the offer for a reasonable time. This obligation arises when the offeree begins performance. If, however, the offeror does not know of the offeree's performance and has no adequate means of learning of it within a reasonable time, the offeree must exercise reasonable diligence to notify the offeror of the performance.

PRACTICAL ADVICE
When making an offer, be careful to make it irrevocable only if you so desire.

APPLYING THE LAW

Mutual Assent

Facts Taylor and Arbuckle formed a partnership for the purpose of practicing pediatric medicine together. They found new medical office space to lease and thereafter, among other things, they set about furnishing the waiting room in a way that children would find inviting. In addition to contracting with a mural painter, they decided to purchase a high-definition flat-panel television on which they could show children's programming. On a Monday, Taylor and Arbuckle visited a local retailer with a reputation for competitive pricing, called Today's Electronics. In addition to comparing the pictures on the various models on display, the doctors discussed the pros and cons of LCD (liquid crystal display) versus plasma with the store's owner, Patel.

While they were able to narrow their options down significantly, Taylor and Arbuckle nonetheless could not decide on the exact size set to purchase because they had not yet determined the configuration of the seating to be installed in the waiting room. Sensing that the doctors were considering shopping around, Patel offered them a sizeable discount: only $999 for the forty-inch LCD screen they had chosen, or the fifty-inch plasma model they favored for only $1,299. As they were leaving the store, Patel gave the doctors his business card, on which he had jotted the model numbers and

discount prices, his signature, and the notation "we assure you this offer is open through Sun., April 27."

Anxious to have the waiting room completed, Taylor and Arbuckle quickly agreed on a feasible seating arrangement for the waiting room, ordered the necessary furniture, and decided that the fifty-inch television would be too big. On Friday, April 25, Taylor returned to Today's Electronics. But before she could tell Patel that they had decided on the forty-inch LCD, Patel informed her that he could not honor the discounted prices because he no longer had in stock either model the doctors were considering.

Issue Is Patel free to revoke his offer notwithstanding having agreed to hold it open through the weekend?

Rule of Law The general rule is that an offeror may revoke, or withdraw, an offer any time before it has been accepted. However there are several limitations on an offeror's power to revoke an offer before acceptance. One of these is the Uniform Commercial Code's (UCC's) "merchant's firm offer" rule. Under the UCC, a merchant's offer to buy or sell goods is irrevocable for the stated period (or, if no period is stated, for a reasonable time) not exceeding three months, when he has signed a writing assuring the offeree that

the offer will be kept open for that period. The Code defines a merchant as one who trades in the types of goods in question or who holds himself out, either personally or by way of an agent, to be knowledgeable regarding the goods or practices involved in the transaction.

Application The proposed contract between the doctors and Today's Electronics is governed by Article 2 of the Code because it involves a sale of goods, in this case a television set. Both Patel and Today's Electronics are considered merchants of televisions under the Code's definition, because Patel and his store regularly sell electronics, including television sets. Patel offered to sell to Taylor and Arbuckle either the forty-inch LCD television for $999 or the fifty-inch plasma for $1,299. By reducing his offer to a signed writing, and by promising in that writing that the stated prices were assured to be open through Sun., April 27, Patel has made a firm offer that he cannot revoke during that six-day period. Whether he still has either model in stock does not affect the irrevocability of the offer.

Conclusion Patel's offer is irrevocable through Sunday, April 27. Therefore Patel's attempt to revoke it is ineffective, and Taylor may still accept it.

Promissory Estoppel As discussed in the previous chapter, a noncontractual promise may be enforced when it is made under circumstances that should lead the promisor reasonably to expect that the promise will induce the promisee to take action in reliance on it. This doctrine has been used in some cases to prevent an offeror from revoking an offer prior to its acceptance.

Thus, Ramanan Plumbing Co. submits a written offer for plumbing work to be used by Resolute Building Co. as part of Resolute's bid as a general contractor. Ramanan knows that Resolute is relying on Ramanan's bid, and in fact Resolute submits Ramanan's name as the plumbing subcontractor in the bid. Ramanan's offer is irrevocable until Resolute has a reasonable opportunity to notify Ramanan that Resolute's bid has been accepted.

Rejection

An offeree is at liberty to accept or reject the offer as he sees fit. If he decides not to accept it, he is not required to reject it formally but may simply wait until the offer terminates by lapse of time. A **rejection** of an offer is a manifestation by the offeree of his unwillingness to accept. A communicated rejection terminates the power of acceptance. From the effective moment of rejection, which is the receipt of the rejection by the offeror, the offeree may no longer accept the offer. Rejection by the offeree may consist of express language or may be implied from language or conduct.

Counteroffer

A **counteroffer** is a counterproposal from the offeree to the offeror that indicates a willingness to contract but on terms or conditions different from those contained in the original offer. It is not an unequivocal acceptance of the original offer, and by indicating an unwillingness to agree to the terms of the offer, it generally operates as a rejection. It also operates as a new offer. To illustrate further, assume that Worthy writes Joanne a letter stating that he will sell to Joanne a secondhand color television set for $300. Joanne replies that she will pay Worthy $250 for the set. This is a counteroffer that, on *receipt* by Worthy, terminates the original offer. Worthy may, if he wishes, accept the counteroffer and thereby create a contract for $250. If, on the other hand, Joanne in her reply states that she wishes to consider the $300 offer but is willing to pay $250 at once for the set, she is making a counteroffer that does *not* terminate Worthy's original offer. In the first instance, after making the $250 counteroffer, Joanne may not accept the $300 offer. In the second instance, she may do so, because the counteroffer was stated in such a manner as not to indicate an unwillingness to accept the original offer; Joanne therefore did not terminate it. In addition, a mere inquiry about the possibility of obtaining different or new terms is not a counteroffer and does not terminate the original offer.

Another common type of counteroffer is the **conditional acceptance**, which claims to accept the offer but expressly makes the acceptance contingent on the offeror's assent to additional or different terms. Nonetheless, it is a counteroffer and generally terminates the original offer. The Code's treatment of acceptances containing terms that vary from the offer is discussed later in this chapter.

Giannetti v. Cornillie
Court of Appeals of Michigan, 1994
204 Mich. app. 234, 514 N.W.2d 221

FACTS Defendants listed with a real estate agent a home for sale. Plaintiffs, Patrick and Anne Giannetti, offered $155,000 for the home and submitted a deposit in the amount of $2,500. The defendants countered the offer with an offer to sell the house for $160,000. The plaintiffs then inquired whether certain equipment and items of furniture could be included with the sale of the house. The defendants refused to include the questioned items in the sale. The plaintiffs then accepted the $160,000 offer, but changed the mortgage amount from $124,000 to $128,000. The agent failed to show this change to the defendants but instead told the defendants that the plaintiffs had accepted their counteroffer. Defendants then signed all papers, but before the closing sought to invalidate the agreement. The plaintiffs brought this action for specific performance to enforce the sale. The trial court granted plaintiffs' motion and the defendants appealed.

DECISION Judgment for the defendants.

OPINION Defendants' argue that, "[a]n offer is a unilateral declaration of intention, and is not a contract. A contract is made when both parties have executed or accepted it, and not before. A counterproposition is not an acceptance." An acceptance must be "unambiguous and in strict conformance with an offer." Moreover, "[A] proposal to accept, or an acceptance, upon terms varying from those offered, is a rejection of the offer, and puts an end to the negotiation, unless the party who made the original offer renews it, or assents to the modification suggested." Thus, "[a]ny material departure from the terms of an offer invalidates the offer as made and results in a counter proposition, which, unless accepted, cannot be enforced." Before the change, plaintiffs were obligated to buy the property if they obtained a mortgage for $124,000; after the change, no obligation to buy arose unless they obtained a $128,000 mortgage. Thus, the modification changed the contract and it was therefore material.

INTERPRETATION A counteroffer generally operates as a rejection and thus terminates the power of acceptance.

ETHICAL QUESTION Was the defendant morally obligated to sell the property? Explain.

CRITICAL THINKING QUESTION What could the plaintiffs have done to protect themselves while at the same time seeking different terms?

Death or Incompetency

Death or incompetency of either the offeror or the offeree terminates the offer

The **death or incompetency** of either the offeror or the offeree ordinarily terminates an offer. On his death or incompetency, the offeror no longer has the legal capacity to enter into a contract; thus, all outstanding offers are terminated. Death or incompetency of the offeree also terminates the offer, because an ordinary offer is not assignable (transferable) and may be accepted only by the person to whom it was made. When the offeree dies or ceases to have legal capability to enter into a contract, no one else has the power to accept the offer. Therefore, the offer necessarily terminates.

The death or incompetency of the offeror or offeree, however, does *not* terminate an offer contained in an option.

Destruction of Subject Matter

Destruction of subject matter of an offer terminates the offer

Destruction of the specific subject matter of an offer terminates the offer. Suppose that Sarah, owning a Buick, offers to sell the car to Barbara and allows Barbara five days in which to accept. Three days later the car is destroyed by fire. On the following day, Barbara, without knowledge of the destruction of the car, notifies Sarah that she accepts Sarah's offer. There is no contract. The destruction of the car terminated Sarah's offer.

Subsequent Illegality

Subsequent illegality of the purpose or subject matter of the offer terminates the offer

One of the essential requirements of a contract, as we previously mentioned, is legality of purpose or subject matter. If performance of a valid contract is subsequently made illegal, the obligations of both parties under the contract are discharged. Illegality taking effect after the making of an offer but prior to acceptance has the same effect: the offer is legally terminated.

For an illustration of the duration of revocable offers, see Figure 10-1.

ACCEPTANCE OF OFFER

Acceptance manifestation of a willingness to enter into a contract on the terms of the offer

The acceptance of an offer is essential to the formation of a contract. Once an effective acceptance has been given, the contract is formed. **Acceptance** of an offer for a bilateral contract is some overt act by the offeree that manifests his assent to the terms of the offer, such as speaking or sending a letter, a telegram, or other explicit or implicit communication to the offeror. If the offer is for a unilateral contract, acceptance is the performance of the requested act with the intention of accepting. For example, if Joy publishes an offer of a reward to anyone who returns the diamond ring that she has lost (an offer to enter into a unilateral contract) and Bob, with knowledge of the offer, finds and returns the ring to Joy, Bob has accepted the offer.

COMMUNICATION OF ACCEPTANCE

General Rule

Because acceptance is the manifestation of the offeree's assent to the offer, it must necessarily be communicated to the offeror. This is the rule as to all offers to enter into bilateral contracts. In the case of unilateral offers, however, notice of acceptance to the offeror usually is not required. If, however, the offeree in a unilateral contract has reason to know that the offeror has no adequate means of learning of the offeree's performance with reasonable promptness and

Figure 10-1 Duration of Revocable Offers

© Cengage Learning 2013

certainty, then the offeree must make reasonable efforts to notify the offeror of acceptance or lose the right to enforce the contract.

Silence as Acceptance

An offeree is generally under no legal duty to reply to an offer. Silence or inaction therefore does *not* indicate acceptance of the offer. By custom, usage, or course of dealing, however, the offeree's silence or inaction may operate as an acceptance. Thus, the silence or inaction of an offeree who fails to reply to an offer operates as an acceptance and causes a contract to be formed. Through previous dealings, for example, the offeree has given the offeror reason to understand that the offeree will accept all offers unless the offeree sends notice to the contrary. Another example of silence operating as an acceptance occurs when the prospective member of a mail-order club agrees that his failure to return a notification card rejecting offered goods will constitute his acceptance of the club's offer to sell the goods.

Furthermore, if an offeror sends unordered or unsolicited merchandise to a person, stating that the goods may be purchased at a specified price and that the offer will be deemed to have been accepted unless the goods are returned within a stated period of time, the offer is one for an inverted unilateral contract (i.e., an act for a promise). This practice has led to abuse, however, prompting the federal government as well as most states to enact statutes that provide that in such cases the offeree-recipient of the goods may keep them as a gift and is under no obligation either to return them or to pay for them.

Effective Moment

As we discussed previously, an offer, a revocation, a rejection, and a counteroffer are effective when they are *received*. An acceptance is generally effective upon *dispatch*. This is true unless the offer specifically provides otherwise, the offeree uses an unauthorized means of communication, or the acceptance follows a prior rejection.

Stipulated Provisions in the Offer   If the offer specifically stipulates the means of communication to be used by the offeree, the acceptance must conform to that specification. Thus, if an offer states that acceptance must be made by registered mail, any purported acceptance not made by registered mail would be ineffective. Moreover, the rule that an acceptance is effective when

Effective moment
acceptance effective upon dispatch unless the offer specifically provides otherwise or the offeree uses an unauthorized means of communication

Stipulated provisions in the offer
the communication of acceptance must conform to the specifications in the offer

PRACTICAL ADVICE
Consider whether you should specify in your offers that acceptances are valid only upon receipt.

dispatched or sent does not apply in cases in which the offer provides that the acceptance must be received by the offeror. If the offeror states that a reply must be received by a certain date or that he must hear from the offeree or uses other language indicating that the acceptance must be received by him, the effective moment of the acceptance is when the offeror receives it, not when the offeree sends or dispatches it.

Authorized Means Historically, an authorized means of communication was either the means the offeror expressly authorized in the offer or, if none was authorized, the means the offeror used in presenting the offer. If in reply to an offer by mail, the offeree places in the mail a letter of acceptance properly stamped and addressed to the offeror, a contract is formed at the time and place that the offeree mails the letter. This assumes, of course, that the offer was open at that time and had not been terminated by any of the methods previously discussed. The reason for this rule is that the offeror, by using the mail, impliedly authorized the offeree to use the same means of communication. It is immaterial if the letter of acceptance goes astray in the mail and is never received.

Authorized means
usually any reasonable means of communication

The Restatement and the Code both now provide that where the language in the offer or the circumstances do not otherwise indicate, an offer to make a contract shall be construed as authorizing acceptance in any reasonable manner. Thus, an **authorized means** is usually any *reasonable* means of communication. These provisions are intended to allow flexibility of response and the ability to keep pace with new modes of communication.

See Figure 10-2 for an overview of offer and acceptance.

Osprey L.L.C. v. Kelly-Moore Paint Co., Inc.
Supreme Court of Oklahoma 1999
1999 OK 50, 984 P.2d 194
http://scholar.google.com/scholar_case?case=15066374301719252497&q=1999+OK+50&hl=en&as_sdt=2,22

FACTS In 1977, the defendant, Kelly-Moore Paint Company, entered into a fifteen-year commercial lease with the plaintiff, Osprey, for a property in Edmond, Oklahoma. The lease contained two five-year renewal options. The lease required that the lessee give notice of its intent to renew at least six months prior to its expiration. It also provided that the renewal "may be delivered either personally or by depositing the same in United States mail, first class postage prepaid, registered or certified mail, return receipt requested." Upon expiration of the original fifteen-year lease, Kelly-Moore timely informed the lessor by certified letter of its intent to extend the lease an additional five years. The first five-year extension was due to expire on August 31, 1997. On the last day of the six-month notification deadline, Kelly-Moore faxed a letter of renewal notice to Osprey's office at 5:28 P.M. In addition, Kelly-Moore sent a copy of the faxed renewal notice letter by Federal Express that same day. Osprey denies ever receiving the fax, but it admits receiving the Federal Express copy of the notice on the following business day. Osprey rejected the notice, asserting that it was late, and it filed an action to remove the defendant from the premises. After a trial on the merits, the trial court granted judgment in favor of Kelly-Moore, finding that the faxed notice was effective. Osprey appealed. The Court of Civil Appeals reversed, determining that the plain language of the lease required that it be renewed by delivering notice either personally or by mail, and that Kelly-Moore had done neither. Kelly-Moore appealed.

DECISION The decision of the Court of Appeals is vacated and the decision of the trial court is affirmed.

OPINION A lease is a contract and, in construing a lease, the usual rules for the interpretation of contractual writings apply. Language in a contract is given its plain and ordinary meaning, unless some technical term is used in a manner meant to convey a specific technical concept. A contract term is ambiguous only if it can be interpreted as having two different meanings. The lease does not appear to be ambiguous. "Shall" is ordinarily construed as mandatory and "may" is ordinarily construed as permissive. The contract clearly requires that notice "shall" be in writing. The provision for delivery, either personally or by certified or registered mail, uses the permissive "may" and it does not bar other modes of transmission which are just as effective.

The purpose of providing notice by personal delivery or registered mail is to ensure the delivery of the notice and to settle any dispute which might arise between the parties concerning whether the notice was received. A substituted method of notice that performs the same function and serves the same purpose as an authorized method of notice is not defective. Here, the contract provided that time was of the essence. Although Osprey denies that it ever received the fax, the fax activity report and telephone company records confirm that the fax was transmitted successfully and that it was sent to Osprey's correct facsimile number on the last day of the deadline to extend the lease. The fax provided immediate written communication similar to personal delivery and would be timely if it were properly transmitted before the deadline. Kelly-Moore's use of the fax served the same function and the same purpose as the two methods suggested by the lease, and it was transmitted before the expiration of the deadline to renew. Under these facts, the faxed or facsimile delivery of the written notice to renew the commercial lease was sufficient to exercise timely the renewal option of the lease.

INTERPRETATION Where the language in the offer or the circumstances does not otherwise indicate, an offer to make a contract shall be construed as authorizing acceptance in any reasonable manner.

CRITICAL THINKING QUESTION Are there instances in which an offeror should require a certain mode for acceptance? When?

Figure 10-2 Mutual Assent

© Cengage Learning 2013

Unauthorized Means   When the method of communication used by the offeree is unauthorized, the traditional rule is that acceptance is effective when and if received by the offeror, provided that it is received within the time during which the authorized means would have arrived. The Restatement goes further by providing that if these conditions are met, then the effective time for the acceptance is the moment of dispatch.

Acceptance Following a Prior Rejection   An acceptance sent after a prior rejection is not effective when sent by the offeree, but only when and if *received* by the offeror before he receives the rejection. Thus, when an acceptance follows a prior rejection, the *first communication* the offeror receives is the effective one. For example, Carlos in New York sends by airmail to Paula in San Francisco an offer that is expressly stated to be open for one week. On the fourth day, Paula sends to Carlos by airmail a letter of rejection, which is delivered on the morning of the sixth day. At noon on the fifth day, Paula dispatches a telegram of acceptance that Carlos receives before the close of business on that day. A contract was formed when Carlos received Paula's telegram of acceptance—it was the first communication he received.

Unauthorized means
acceptance effective when received, provided that it is received within the time within which the authorized means would have arrived

Acceptance following a prior rejection
first communication received by the offeror is effective

Defective Acceptances

A late or defective acceptance does not create a contract. After the offer has expired, it cannot be accepted. However, a late or defective acceptance does manifest a willingness on the part of the offeree to enter into a contract and therefore constitutes a new offer. To create a contract based on this offer, the original offeror must accept the new offer by manifesting his assent to it.

VARIANT ACCEPTANCES

A variant acceptance—one that contains terms different from or additional to those in the offer—receives distinctly different treatment under the common law and under the Code.

Common Law

An acceptance must be *positive* and *unequivocal*. It may not change, add to, subtract from, or qualify in any way the provisions of the offer. In other words, it must be the **mirror image** of the offer. Any communication by the offeree that attempts to modify the offer is not an acceptance but a counteroffer, which does not create a contract.

Code

The common law mirror image rule, by which the acceptance cannot vary or deviate from the terms of the offer, is modified by the Code. This modification is necessitated by the realities of modern business practices. A vast number of business transactions use standardized business forms. For example, a merchant buyer sends to a merchant seller on the buyer's order form a purchase order for one thousand cotton shirts at $60 per dozen with delivery by October 1 at the buyer's place of business. On the reverse side of this standard form are twenty-five numbered paragraphs containing provisions generally favorable to the buyer. When the seller receives the buyer's order, he agrees to the buyer's quantity, price, and delivery terms and sends to the buyer on his acceptance form an unequivocal acceptance of the offer. However, on the back of his acceptance form, the seller has thirty-two numbered paragraphs generally favorable to himself and in significant conflict with the provisions on the buyer's form. Under the common law's *mirror image* rule, no contract would exist; for the seller has not accepted unequivocally all of the material terms of the buyer's offer.

The Code attempts to alleviate this **battle of the forms** by focusing on the intent of the parties. If the offeree does not expressly make her acceptance conditional upon the offeror's assent to the additional or different terms, a contract is formed. The issue then becomes whether the offeree's different or additional terms become part of the contract. If both offeror and offeree are merchants, such *additional* terms may become part of the contract provided that they do not materially alter the agreement and are not objected to either in the offer itself or within a reasonable period of time. If either of the parties is not a merchant or if the additional terms materially alter the offer, then the additional terms are merely construed as proposals to the contract. *Different* terms proposed by the offeree will not become part of the contract unless accepted by the offeror. The courts are divided over what terms to include when the terms differ or conflict. Most courts hold that the offeror's terms govern; other courts hold that the terms cancel each other out and look to the Code to provide the missing terms. Some states follow a third alternative and apply the additional terms test to different terms. (See Figure 19-1 in Chapter 19.)

Let us apply the Code to the previous example involving the seller and the buyer: because both parties are merchants and the seller's acceptance was not conditional upon assent to the seller's additional or different terms, then either (1) the contract will be formed without the seller's different terms unless the buyer specifically accepts them; (2) the contract will be formed without the seller's additional terms (unless they are specifically accepted by the buyer) because the additional terms materially alter the offer; or (3) depending upon the jurisdiction, either (a) the buyer's conflicting terms will be included in the contract, (b) the Code will provide the missing terms, because the conflicting terms cancel each other out, or (c) the additional terms test is applied.

See Concept Review 10-1 explicating the effective time and effect of communications involved in offers and acceptances.

CONCEPT REVIEW 10-1

Offer and Acceptance

	Time Effective	Effect
Communications by Offeror		
• Offer	Received by offeree	Creates power to form a contract
• Revocation	Received by offeree	Terminates power
Communications by Offeree		
• Rejection	Received by offeror	Terminates offer
• Counteroffer	Received by offeror	Terminates offer
• Acceptance	Sent by offeree	Forms a contract
• Acceptance after prior rejection	Received by offeror	If received before rejection forms a contract

© Cengage Learning 2013

BUSINESS LAW *IN ACTION*

Business-to-consumer, or "B2C," transactions on the Internet allow buyers to purchase goods for delivery as quickly as overnight—everything from sports equipment and welding tools to bath towels and fresh cut flowers. And increasingly consumers can buy services in cyberspace, too, like vacation packages and movie theater tickets.

The contracting process is easy. In addition to requiring the purchaser to input data like payment details and shipping and billing addresses, Web-based providers use radio buttons or check boxes for the customer to make various selections. In some cases the customer must uncheck or deselect items, and in others, the consumer must affirmatively click on a button or series of buttons labeled "I agree," or "I

accept." These cybercontracts are sometimes called "clickwrap" or "click on" agreements.

By filling in the required blanks, selecting or deselecting various options, and otherwise completing the transaction, the purchaser is indicating his or her assent to be bound by the seller's offer. Sales of goods can be relatively simple and straightforward. But services available on the Internet, particularly those that involve an ongoing relationship between the user and the provider, usually require more complex contract provisions.

Offers for video rental club memberships and software licenses, for example, frequently contain restrictions on use and such other terms as warranty disclaimers and arbitration clauses as well as privacy

policy disclosures, all written primarily in legalese and taking up multiple screens of text. The reality is that many buyers simply do not read them. Nonetheless, depending on how the agreement process is set up, these terms are likely binding.

Whether a buyer's nonverbal assent to these lengthy contract provisions will pass legal muster is dependent on the online contracting process. Even if the buyer does not read the proposed terms, they will be enforced if the buyer has had the opportunity to review them, either by way of an automatic screen or a link. And, equally as important, the cyberoffer's terms will be binding when the site requires the buyer to actively select them or to click on a button or type words affirmatively indicating his or her assent.

CHAPTER SUMMARY

Offer

Essentials of an Offer

Definition indication of willingness to enter into a contract

Communication offeree must have knowledge of the offer and the offer must be made by the offeror or her authorized agent to the offeree

Intent determined by an objective standard of what a reasonable offeree would have believed

Definiteness offer's terms must be clear enough to provide a court with a basis for giving an appropriate remedy

Duration of Offers

Lapse of Time offer remains open for the time period specified or, if no time is stated, for a reasonable period of time

Revocation generally, an offer may be terminated at any time before it is accepted, subject to the following exceptions

- *Option Contracts* contract that binds offeror to keep an offer open for a specified time
- *Firm Offer* a merchant's irrevocable offer to sell or buy goods in a signed writing that ensures that the offer will not be terminated for up to three months
- *Statutory Irrevocability* offer made irrevocable by statute
- *Irrevocable Offer of Unilateral Contracts* a unilateral offer may not be *revoked* for a reasonable time after performance is begun
- *Promissory Estoppel* noncontractual promise that binds the promisor because she should reasonably expect that the promise will induce the promisee (offeree) to take action in reliance on it

Rejection refusal to accept an offer terminates the power of acceptance

Counteroffer counterproposal to an offer that generally terminates the original offer

Death or Incompetency of either the offeror or the offeree terminates the offer

Destruction of Subject Matter of an offer terminates the offer

Subsequent Illegality of the purpose or subject matter of the offer terminates the offer

---

Acceptance of Offer

Requirements

Definition positive and unequivocal expression of a willingness to enter into a contract on the terms of the offer

Mirror Image Rule except as modified by the Code, an acceptance cannot deviate from the terms of the offer

Communication of Acceptance

General Rule acceptance effective upon dispatch unless the offer specifically provides otherwise or the offeree uses an unauthorized means of communication

Silence as Acceptance generally does not indicate acceptance of the offer

Effective Moment generally upon dispatch

- *Stipulated Provisions in the Offer* the communication of acceptance must conform to the specifications in the offer
- *Authorized Means* the Restatement and the Code provide that, unless the offer provides otherwise, acceptance is authorized to be in any reasonable manner
- *Unauthorized Means* acceptance effective when received, provided that it is received within the time within which the authorized means would have arrived
- *Acceptance Following a Prior Rejection* first communication received by the offeror is effective

Defective Acceptance does not create a contract but serves as a new offer

QUESTIONS

1. Ames, seeking business for his lawn maintenance firm, posted the following notice in the meeting room of the Antlers, a local lodge: "To the members of the Antlers—Special this month. I will resod your lawn for $4.00 per square foot using Fairway brand sod. This offer expires July 15."

   The notice also included Ames's name, address, and signature and specified that the acceptance was to be in writing.

   Bates, a member of the Antlers, and Cramer, the janitor, read the notice and were interested. Bates wrote a letter to Ames saying he would accept the offer if Ames would use Putting Green brand sod. Ames received this letter July 14 and wrote to Bates saying he would not use Putting Green sod. Bates received Ames's letter on July 16 and promptly wrote Ames that he would accept Fairway sod. Cramer wrote to Ames on July 10 saying he accepted Ames's offer.

   By July 15, Ames had found more profitable ventures and refused to resod either lawn at the specified price. Bates and Cramer brought an appropriate action against Ames for breach of contract. Decisions as to the respective claims of Bates and Cramer?

2. Justin owned four speedboats named *Porpoise, Priscilla, Providence,* and *Prudence.* On April 2, Justin made written offers to sell the four boats in the order named for $4,200 each to Charles, Diane, Edward, and Fran, respectively, allowing ten days for acceptance. In which, if any, of the following four situations was a contract formed?

   a. Five days later, Charles received notice from Justin that he had contracted to sell *Porpoise* to Mark. The next day, April 8, Charles notified Justin that he accepted Justin's offer.

b. On the third day, April 5, Diane mailed a rejection to Justin that reached Justin on the morning of the fifth day. At 10:00 A.M. on the fourth day, Diane sent an acceptance by telegram to Justin, who received it at noon the same day.

c. Edward, on April 3, replied that he was interested in buying *Providence* but declared the price appeared slightly excessive and wondered if, perhaps, Justin would be willing to sell the boat for $3,900. Five days later, having received no reply from Justin, Edward accepted Justin's offer by letter, and enclosed a certified check for $4,200.

d. Fran was accidentally killed in an automobile accident on April 9. The following day, the executor of her estate mailed an acceptance of Justin's offer to Justin.

3. Alpha Rolling Mill Corporation (Alpha Corporation), by letter dated June 8, offered to sell Brooklyn Railroad Company (Brooklyn Company) two thousand to five thousand tons of fifty-pound iron rails on certain specified terms and added that, if the offer was accepted, Alpha Corporation would expect to be notified prior to June 20. Brooklyn Company, on June 16, by telegram, referring to Alpha Corporation's offer of June 8, directed Alpha Corporation to enter an order for one thousand two hundred tons of fifty-pound iron rails on the terms specified. The same day, June 16, Brooklyn Company, by letter to Alpha Corporation, confirmed the telegram. On June 18, Alpha Corporation, by telegram, declined to fulfill the order. Brooklyn Company, on June 19, telegraphed Alpha Corporation: "Please enter an order for two thousand tons of rails as per your letter of the eighth. Please forward written contract. Reply." In reply to Brooklyn Company's repeated inquiries concerning whether the order for two thousand tons of rails had been entered, Alpha denied the existence of any contract between Brooklyn Company and itself. Thereafter, Brooklyn Company sued Alpha Corporation for breach of contract. Decision?

4. On April 8, Crystal received a telephone call from Akers, a truck dealer, who told Crystal that a new model truck in which Crystal was interested would arrive in one week. Although Akers initially wanted $10,500, the conversation ended after Akers agreed to sell and Crystal agreed to purchase the truck for $10,000, with a $1,000 down payment and the balance on delivery. The next day, Crystal sent Akers a check for $1,000, which Akers promptly cashed.

One week later, when Crystal called Akers and inquired about the truck, Akers informed Crystal he had several prospects looking at the truck and would not sell for less than $10,500. The following day Akers sent Crystal a properly executed check for $1,000 with the following notation thereon: "Return of down payment on sale of truck."

After notifying Akers that she will not cash the check, Crystal sues Akers for damages. Should Crystal prevail? Explain.

5. On November 15, Gloria, Inc., a manufacturer of crystalware, mailed to Benny Buyer a letter stating that Gloria would sell to Buyer one hundred crystal "A" goblets at $100 per goblet and that "the offer would remain open for fifteen (15) days." On November 18, Gloria, noticing the sudden rise in the price of crystal "A" goblets, decided to withdraw her offer to Buyer and so notified Buyer. Buyer chose to ignore Gloria's letter of revocation and gleefully watched as the price of crystal "A" goblets continued to skyrocket. On November 30, Buyer mailed to Gloria a letter accepting Gloria's offer to sell the goblets. The letter was received by Gloria on December 4. Buyer demands delivery of the goblets. What is the result?

6. On May 1, Melforth Realty Company offered to sell Greenacre to Dallas, Inc., for $1 million. The offer was made by telegraph and stated that the offer would expire on May 15. Dallas decided to purchase the property and sent a registered letter to Melforth on May 10 accepting the offer. As a result of unexplained delays in the postal service, the letter was not received by Melforth until May 22. Melforth wishes to sell Greenacre to another buyer who is offering $1.2 million for the tract of land. Has a contract resulted between Melforth and Dallas?

7. Rowe advertised in newspapers of wide circulation and otherwise made known that she would pay $5,000 for a complete set, consisting of ten volumes, of certain rare books. Ford, not knowing of the offer, gave Rowe all but one volume of the set of rare books as a Christmas present. Ford later learned of the offer, obtained the one remaining book, tendered it to Rowe, and demanded the $5,000. Rowe refused to pay. Is Ford entitled to the $5,000?

8. Scott, manufacturer of a carbonated beverage, entered into a contract with Otis, owner of a baseball park, whereby Otis rented to Scott a large signboard on top of the center field wall. The contract provided that Otis should letter the sign as Scott desired and would change the lettering from time to time within forty-eight hours after receipt of written request from Scott. As directed by Scott, the signboard originally stated in large letters that Scott would pay $100 to any ballplayer hitting a home run over the sign.

In the first game of the season, Hume, the best hitter in the league, hit one home run over the sign. Scott immediately served written notice on Otis instructing Otis to replace the offer on the signboard with an offer to pay $50 to every pitcher who pitched a no-hit game in the park. A week after receipt of Scott's letter, Otis had not changed the wording on the sign; and on that day, Perry, a pitcher for a scheduled game, pitched a no-hit game and Todd, one of his teammates, hit a home run over Scott's sign.

Scott refuses to pay any of the three players. What are the rights of Scott, Hume, Perry, and Todd?

9. Barney accepted Clark's offer to sell to him a portion of Clark's coin collection. Clark forgot at the time of the offer and acceptance that her prized $20 gold piece was included in the portion that she offered to sell to Barney. Clark did not intend to include the gold piece in the sale. Barney, at the time of inspecting the offered portion of the collection, and prior to accepting the offer, saw the gold piece. Is Barney entitled to the $20 gold piece?

10. Small, admiring Jasper's watch, asked Jasper where and at what price he had purchased it. Jasper replied, "I bought it at West Watch Shop about two years ago for around $85, but I am not certain as to that." Small then said, "Those fellows at West are good people and always sell good watches. I'll buy that watch from you." Jasper replied, "It's a deal." The next morning, Small telephoned Jasper and said he had changed his mind and did not wish to buy the watch.

Jasper sued Small for breach of contract. In defense, Small has pleaded that he made no enforceable contract with Jasper because (a) the parties did not agree on the price to be paid for the watch and (b) the parties did not agree on the place and time of delivery of the watch to Small. Are either, or both, of these defenses good?

11. Jeff says to Brenda, "I offer to sell you my PC for $900." Brenda replies, "If you do not hear otherwise from me by Thursday, I have accepted your offer." Jeff agrees and does not hear from Brenda by Thursday. Does a contract exist between Jeff and Brenda? Explain.

12. On November 19, Hoover Motor Express Company sent to Clements Paper Company a written offer to purchase certain real estate. Sometime in December, Clements authorized Williams to accept the offer. Williams, however, attempted to bargain with Hoover to obtain a better deal, specifically that Clements would retain easements on the property. In a telephone conversation on January 13 of the following year, Williams first told Hoover of his plan to obtain the easements. Hoover replied, "Well, I don't know if we are ready. We have not decided, we might not want to go through with it." On January 20, Clements sent a written acceptance of Hoover's offer. Hoover refused to buy, claiming it had revoked its offer through the January 13 phone conversation. Clements then brought suit to compel the sale or obtain damages. Did Hoover successfully revoke its offer?

13. Walker leased a small lot to Keith for ten years at $100 a month, with a right for Keith to extend the lease for another ten-year term under the same terms except as to rent. The renewal option provided:

> Rental will be fixed in such amount as shall actually be agreed upon by the lessors and the lessee with the monthly rental fixed on the comparative basis of rental values as of the date of the renewal with rental values at this time reflected by the comparative business conditions of the two periods.

> Keith sought to exercise the renewal right and, when the parties were unable to agree on the rent, brought suit against Walker. Who prevails? Why?

CASE PROBLEMS

14. The Brewers contracted to purchase Dower House from McAfee. Then, several weeks before the May 7 settlement date for the purchase of the house, the two parties began to negotiate for the sale of certain items of furniture in the house. On April 30, McAfee sent the Brewers a letter containing a list of the furnishings to be purchased at specific prices; a payment schedule including a $3,000 payment due on acceptance; and a clause reading: "If the above is satisfactory, please sign and return one copy with the first payment."

    On June 3, the Brewers sent a letter to McAfee stating that enclosed was a $3,000 check; that the original contract had been misplaced and could another be furnished; that they planned to move into Dower House on June 12; and that they wished that the red desk also be included in the contract. McAfee then sent a letter dated June 8 to the Brewers listing the items of furniture they had purchased.

    The Brewers moved into Dower House in the middle of June. Soon after they moved in, they tried to contact McAfee at his office to tell him that there had been a misunderstanding relating to their purchase of the listed items. They then refused to pay him any more money, and he brought this action to recover the outstanding balance unless the red desk was also included in the sale. Will McAfee be able to collect the additional money from the Brewers?

15. The Thoelkes were owners of real property located in Florida, which the Morrisons agreed to purchase. The Morrisons signed a contract for the sale of that property and mailed it to the Thoelkes in Texas on November 26. Subsequently, the Thoelkes executed the contract and placed it in the mail addressed to the Morrisons' attorney in Florida. After the executed contract was mailed but before it was received in Florida, the Thoelkes called the Morrisons' attorney in Florida and attempted to repudiate the contract. Does a contract exist between the Thoelkes and the Morrisons? Discuss.

16. Lucy and Zehmer met while having drinks in a restaurant. During the course of their conversation, Lucy apparently offered to buy Zehmer's 471.6-acre farm for $50,000 cash. Although Zehmer claims that he thought the offer was made in jest, he wrote the following on the back of a pad: "We hereby agree to sell to W. O. Lucy the Ferguson Farm complete for $50,000, title satisfactory to buyer." Zehmer then signed the writing and induced his wife Ida to do the same. She claims, however, that she signed only after Zehmer assured her that it was only a joke. Finally, Zehmer claims that he was "high as a Georgia pine" at the time but admits that he was not too drunk to make a valid contract. Explain whether the contract is enforceable.

17. On July 31, Lee Calan Imports advertised a used Volvo station wagon for sale in the *Chicago Sun-Times*. As part of the information for the advertisement, Lee Calan Imports instructed the newspaper to print the price of the car as $1,795. However, due to a mistake made by the newspaper, without any fault on the part of Lee Calan Imports, the printed ad listed the price of the car as $1,095. After reading the ad and then examining the car, O'Brien told a Lee Calan Imports salesman that he wanted to purchase the car for the advertised price of $1,095. Calan Imports refuses to sell the car to O'Brien for $1,095. Is there a contract? If so, for what price?

18. On May 20, cattle rancher Oliver visited his neighbor Southworth, telling him, "I know you're interested in buying the land I'm selling." Southworth replied, "Yes, I do want to buy that land, especially because it adjoins my property." Although the two men did not discuss the price, Oliver told Southworth he would determine the value of the property and send that information to Southworth so that he would have "notice" of what Oliver "wanted for the land." On June 13, Southworth called Oliver to ask if he still planned to sell the land. Oliver answered, "Yes, and I should have the value of the land determined soon." On June 17, Oliver sent a letter to Southworth listing a price quotation of $324,000. Southworth then responded to Oliver by letter on June 21, stating that he accepted Oliver's offer. However, on June 24 Oliver wrote back to Southworth saying, "There has never been a firm offer to sell, and there is no enforceable contract between us." Oliver maintains that a price quotation alone is not an offer. Southworth claims a valid contract has been made. Who wins? Discuss.

19. On August 12, Mr. and Mrs. Mitchell, the owners of a small secondhand store, attended Alexander's Auction, where they bought a used safe for $50. The safe, part of the Sumstad

estate, contained a locked inside compartment. Both the auctioneer and the Mitchells knew this fact. Soon after the auction, the Mitchells had the compartment opened by a locksmith, who discovered $32,207 inside. The Everett Police Department impounded the money. The city of Everett brought an action against the Sumstad estate and the Mitchells to determine the owner of the money. Who should receive the money? Why?

20. Irwin Schiff is a self-styled "tax rebel" who has made a career, and substantial profit, out of his tax protest activities. On February 7, Schiff appeared live on CBS News *Nightwatch*, a late-night program with a viewer participation format. During the broadcast Schiff repeated his assertion that nothing in the Internal Revenue Code stated that an individual was legally required to pay federal income tax. Schiff then challenged, "If anybody calls this show—I have the Code—and cites any section of this Code that says an individual is required to file a tax return, I will pay them $100,000." Call-in telephone numbers were periodically flashed on the screen. John Newman, an attorney, did not see Schiff's live appearance on *Nightwatch*. Newman did, however, see a two-minute videotaped segment, including Schiff's challenge, which was rebroadcast several hours later on the *CBS Morning News*. Newman researched the matter that same day, and on the following day, February 9, placed a call using directory assistance to *CBS Morning News* stating that the call was performance of the consideration requested by Mr. Schiff in exchange for his promise to pay $100,000. When Schiff refused to pay, Newman sued. Should Newman prevail? Explain.

TAKING SIDES

Cushing filed an application with the office of the Adjutant General of the State of New Hampshire for the use of the Portsmouth Armory to hold a dance on the evening of April 29. The application, made on behalf of the Portsmouth Area Clamshell Alliance, was received by the Adjutant General's office on or about March 30. On March 31 the Adjutant General mailed a signed contract after agreeing to rent the armory for the evening requested. The agreement required acceptance by the renter affixing his signature to the agreement and then returning the copy to the Adjutant General within five days after receipt. Cushing received the contract offer, signed it on behalf of the Alliance, and placed it in the outbox for mailing on April 3. At 6:30 on the evening of April 4, Cushing received a telephone call from the Adjutant General revoking the rental offer. Cushing stated during the conversation that he had already signed and mailed the contract. The Adjutant General sent a written confirmation of the withdrawal on April 5. On April 6 the Adjutant General's office received by mail from Cushing the signed contract dated April 3 and postmarked April 5.

a. What are the arguments that a binding contract exists?
b. What are the arguments that a contract does not exist or should not exist?
c. What is the proper outcome? Explain.

CHAPTER **11**

Conduct Invalidating Assent

CHAPTER OUTCOMES

After reading and studying this chapter, you should be able to:

1. Identify the types of duress and describe the legal effect of each.

2. Define undue influence and identify some of the situations giving rise to a confidential relationship.

3. Identify the types of fraud and the elements that must be shown to establish the existence of each.

4. Define the two types of nonfraudulent misrepresentation.

5. Identify and explain the situations involving voidable mistakes.

Fraud—A generic term embracing all multifarious means which human ingenuity can devise, and which are resorted to by one individual to get advantage over another by false suggestion or by suppression of the truth.

Johnson v. McDonald, 170 Okl. 117, 39 P.2d 150

I n addition to requiring offer and acceptance, the law requires that the agreement be voluntary and knowing. If these requirements are not met, then the agreement is either voidable or void. This chapter deals with situations in which the consent manifested by one of the parties to the contract is not effective because it was not knowingly and voluntarily given. We consider five such situations in this chapter: duress, undue influence, fraud, nonfraudulent misrepresentation, and mistake.

DURESS

A person should not be held to an agreement he has not entered voluntarily. Accordingly, the law will not enforce any contract induced by **duress**, which in general is any wrongful or unlawful act or threat that overcomes the free will of a party.

Physical Compulsion

Duress is of two basic types. The first type, **physical duress**, occurs when one party compels another to manifest assent to a contract through actual physical force, such as pointing a gun at a person or taking a person's hand and compelling him to sign a written contract. This type of duress, while extremely rare, renders the agreement *void*.

Improper Threats

The second and more common type of duress involves the use of **improper threats** or acts, including economic and social coercion, to compel a person to enter into a contract. Though the threat may be explicit or may be inferred from words or conduct, in either case it must leave the victim with no reasonable alternative. This type of duress makes the contract *voidable* at the option of the coerced party. For example, if Ellen, a landlord, induces Vijay, an infirm, bedridden tenant, to enter into a new lease on the same apartment at a greatly increased rent by wrongfully threatening to terminate Vijay's lease and evict him, Vijay can escape or *avoid* the new lease by reason of the duress exerted on him.

Duress
wrongful or unlawful act or threat that overcomes the free will of a party

Physical duress
coercion involving physical force renders the agreement void

Improper threats
improper threats or acts, including economic and social coercion, render the contract voidable

© Kim Steele/Jupiter Images

The fact that the act or threat would not affect a person of average strength and intelligence is not important if it places fear in the person actually affected and induces her to act against her will. The test is *subjective*, and the question is this: did the threat actually induce assent on the part of the person claiming to be the victim of duress?

Ordinarily, the acts or threats constituting duress are themselves crimes or torts. But this is not true in all cases. The acts need not be criminal or tortious to be *wrongful*; they merely need to be contrary to public policy or morally reprehensible. For example, if the threat involves a breach of a contractual duty of good faith and fair dealing, it is improper.

Moreover, it generally has been held that contracts induced by threats of criminal prosecution are voidable, regardless of whether the coerced party had committed an unlawful act. Similarly, threatening the criminal prosecution of a close relative is also duress. To be distinguished from such threats of prosecution are threats that resort to ordinary civil remedies to recover a debt due from another. It is not wrongful to threaten a civil suit against an individual to recover a debt. What is prohibited is threatening to bring a civil suit when bringing such a suit would be abuse of process.

PRACTICAL ADVICE
If you entered into a contract due to improper threats, consider whether you wish to void the contract. If you decide to do so, act promptly.

Berardi v. Meadowbrook Mall Company
Supreme Court of Appeals of West Virginia, 2002
212 W.Va. 377, 572 S.E.2d 900
http://www.state.wv.us/wvsca/docs/fall02/30517.htm

FACTS Between 1985 and 1987, Jerry A. Berardi, Betty J. Berardi, and Bentley Corporation (the Berardis) leased space for three restaurants from Meadowbrook Mall Company. In 1990, the Berardis were delinquent in their rent. Meadowbrook informed Mr. Berardi that a lawsuit would be filed in Ohio requesting judgment for the total amount owed. Mr. Berardi then entered into a consent judgment with Meadowbrook granting judgment for the full amount owed. Meadowbrook in return promised that no steps to enforce the judgment would be undertaken provided the Berardis continued to operate their three restaurants.

In April 1996, Meadowbrook filed in the Circuit Court of Harrison County, West Virginia, the judgment of the Ohio lawsuits and obtained a lien on a building that was owned by the Berardis, the Goff Building. By so doing, Meadowbrook impeded the then-pending refinancing of the building by the Berardis.

In June 1997, the Berardis and Meadowbrook signed a "Settlement Agreement and Release" settling the 1990 Ohio judgments. In this document, the Berardis acknowledged the validity of the 1990 Ohio judgments and that the aggregate due under them was $814,375.97. The Berardis agreed to pay Meadowbrook $150,000 on the date the Goff Building refinancing occurred, and also to pay Meadowbrook $100,000 plus 8.5 percent interest per year on the third anniversary of the initial $150,000 payment. These payments would discharge the Berardis from all other amounts owed. The payment of the initial $150,000 would also result in Meadowbrook releasing the lien against the Goff Building.

The agreement additionally recited:

Berardis hereby release and forever discharge Meadowbrook, its employees, agents, successors, and assigns from any and all claims, demands, damages, actions, and causes of action of any kind or nature that have arisen or may arise as a result of the leases.

Nevertheless, on October 2, 2000, the Berardis filed a complaint against Meadowbrook alleging that Meadowbrook breached the October 1990 agreement by attempting to enforce the 1990 Ohio judgments and that Meadowbrook extorted by duress and coercion the 1997 agreement. Meadowbrook filed a motion to dismiss under the 1997 settlement. Meadowbrook sought summary judgment, which the circuit court granted. Berardi now appeals.

DECISION Summary judgment affirmed.

OPINION Courts are generally reluctant to overturn settlement agreements as long as they are legally sound. The law favors and encourages the resolution of controversies by contracts of compromise and settlement rather than by litigation; and it is the policy of the law to uphold and enforce such contracts if they are fairly made and are not in contravention of some law or public policy.

The concept of "economic duress" may be generally stated as follows: Where the plaintiff is forced into a transaction as a result of unlawful threats or wrongful, oppressive, or unconscionable conduct on the part of the defendant which leaves the plaintiff no reasonable alternative but to acquiesce, the plaintiff may void the transaction and recover any economic loss.

Duress is not readily accepted as an excuse to avoid a contract. Thus, to establish economic duress, in addition to their own statements, the plaintiffs must produce objective evidence of their duress. Evidence of duress is not shown just because one party to the contract has driven a hard bargain or that market or other conditions now make the contract more difficult to perform by one of the parties or that financial circumstances may have caused one party to make concessions.

Mr. Berardi is a sophisticated businessman who has operated a number of commercial enterprises. Typically, "where an experienced businessman takes sufficient time, seeks the advice of counsel and understands the content of what he is signing he cannot claim the execution of the release was a product of duress."

Given the facts, the law's disfavor of economic duress, its support of settlements, the sophisticated nature of the parties, and the extremely high evidentiary burden the Berardis must overcome, the circuit court did not render an incorrect decision.

INTERPRETATION Economic duress consists of unlawful threats or wrongful, oppressive, or unconscionable conduct by one party which leaves the other party no reasonable alternative but to acquiesce to the terms of a contract.

ETHICAL QUESTION Did Meadowbrook act in a proper manner? Explain.

CRITICAL THINKING QUESTION Did Berardi really have a reasonable alternative to signing the release? Explain.

Undue Influence

Undue influence is the unfair persuasion of a person by a party in a dominant position based on a *confidential relationship*. The law very carefully scrutinizes contracts between those in a relationship of trust and confidence that is likely to permit one party to take unfair advantage of the other. Examples are the relationships of guardian–ward, trustee–beneficiary, agent–principal, spouses, parent–child, attorney–client, physician–patient, and clergy–parishioner.

A transaction induced by undue influence on the part of the dominant party is *voidable*. The ultimate question in undue influence cases is whether the transaction was induced by dominating either or both the mind or emotions of a submissive party. The weakness or dependence of the person persuaded is a strong indicator of whether the persuasion may have been unfair. For example, Abigail, a person without business experience, has for years relied on Boris, who is experienced in business, for advice on business matters. Boris, without making any false representations of fact, induces Abigail to enter into a contract with Boris's confederate, Cassius. The contract, however, is disadvantageous to Abigail, as both Boris and Cassius know. The transaction is voidable on the grounds of undue influence.

Rea v. Paulson
Court of Appeals of Oregon, 1994
131 Or.App. 743, 887 P.2d 355

FACTS Plaintiff (Ken Rea), as personal representative of his mother's estate, brought this action to set aside a deed from his mother to defendant Larry Paulson, a son of decedent by a second marriage. Decedent died on January 31, 1988, leaving four children: Ken, Donald, Barbara, and Larry. She had purchased a home in Rainier, the property that is the subject of this lawsuit, in 1983, for $21,300. At that time, she had a will that she had executed in 1967, leaving all of her property to her four children in equal shares. That will was never changed. After she moved into the house in Rainier, Ken and his wife, and Barbara and Don, helped decedent, who suffered from arthritis in both hands, renal failure, congestive heart failure, and diabetes, as a result of which she had trouble getting around and, during the last part of her life, used an electric cart. She was taking several medications, including Prozac, Prednisone, Zantac, and Procardia, and was receiving insulin daily and dialysis an average of three times a week. Although there is no evidence that she was mentally incompetent, the medications and treatments made her drowsy, tired, and depressed, and caused mood swings. It is undisputed that she was dependent on the help of others in her daily living.

Larry was not in the Rainier area when his mother moved there and did not visit her. The other children and her neighbor helped her. The other children reroofed the house for her, picked fruit and stored it, and mowed the lawn; her daughter helped her with her finances and had a joint account with her, which the daughter never used. All of those children visited her frequently, and at least one of them saw her every day. Decedent expressed concern about losing the house because of her medical bills and suggested that she put the house in Ken's name; he and Barbara looked into the situation and concluded that it was not necessary, and so advised their mother. At some point—it is not clear when—Larry was told by state welfare authorities, as Ken and Barbara had learned, that so long as his mother maintained her house as her primary residence and was not receiving Medicaid, she was not in danger of losing her house to the state.

Some time in early 1987, Larry and his then girlfriend (later his wife) moved in with decedent and took over her care. Larry expressed his concern to his mother that the state might take her house. Not long thereafter, Larry rented a house in Longview in his name and persuaded his mother to move in with him, his girlfriend, and her child. After decedent moved to Longview, she rented her house in Rainier; the rent was used to maintain the house in Longview. At that time decedent had a savings account with approximately $2,000 in it; Larry held his mother's power of attorney. At the time of her death in January 1988, that account was exhausted, although her medical expenses were being paid by Medicare. Larry admitted that he used some of that money to buy a bicycle and a guitar. He had also used her credit card, on which there was a substantial balance after her death, which he did not pay. He said that that debt "died with his mother." On numerous occasions, Larry expressed to his mother his concern that the state would take her house if she kept it in her name. She was fearful of that, in spite of what she had been told by Ken and Barbara. Larry told her that they were wrong, and frequently urged her to make up her mind "about the deed."

Decedent was hospitalized three times during 1987. Finally, on September 30, 1987, Larry suggested to his mother that they go to a title company in Rainier to get a deed. Decedent signed the deed and gave up all of her rights in the property. Larry then had it recorded. He did not mention it to any of his half-brothers or -sister until two months later when he boasted of it to his half-sister.

The trial court, sitting in equity, found in favor of plaintiff on his complaint.

DECISION Judgment affirmed in favor of plaintiff.

OPINION Clearly, decedent had trust and confidence in Larry and was completely dependent on him during the time she lived with him. He helped her with her finances and held her power of attorney. After she moved in with Larry, she depended on him to take her places. Because Larry made it clear to decedent's other children that they were not welcome in his home, he drove a wedge between them and their mother, with whom they had previously had a very close relationship. He did not even advise them of her death. There was a confidential relationship between decedent and Larry and he held a position of dominance over her.

Although one who claims that another has asserted undue influence has the burden to prove it, an inference of undue influence arises when, in addition to a confidential relationship, there are suspicious circumstances. Circumstances that give rise to suspicions of undue influence are present here. Larry took his mother to the title company, where he procured the deed, filled it out in his own handwriting, and then took his mother to a notary public. Although he contends that it was his mother's idea, if it was, it was the result of his having persuaded her that she would lose the house if she did not deed the property to him. Larry knew that the state would not take her home away from her as long as it was her primary residence. When he suggested that she rent her house and move in with him, it seems that he was trying to increase the chance that she would lose the house unless she deeded it to someone.

Another important factor is the absence of independent advice. Although Ken and Barbara had advised decedent that she would not lose her house to the state, Larry persuaded her that Ken was wrong. Larry breached his fiduciary duty to her by not seeing that she get independent advice.

Also to be considered is the change in attitude of decedent toward her other children after Larry took charge of his mother. Larry conceded that he had little good to say about his half-brothers and-sister, and they were not welcome at his home. When Barbara tried to call her mother, Larry would get on another phone to interfere.

There is no reason to doubt that decedent was grateful to Larry for his help, or that she loved him. However, the circumstances leading up to the conveyance, and the preparation and signing of the deed, lead to the conclusion that it was the product of undue influence exerted by Larry on his mother.

INTERPRETATION Undue influence is the unfair persuasion of a person by a party in a dominant position based upon a confidential relationship.

ETHICAL QUESTION Did the court correctly decide this case? Explain.

CRITICAL THINKING QUESTION Should the courts get involved in this type of controversy? Explain.

Fraud

Another factor affecting the validity of consent given by a contracting party is fraud, which prevents assent from being knowingly given. There are two distinct types of fraud: fraud in the execution and fraud in the inducement.

Fraud in the Execution

Fraud in the execution
a misrepresentation that deceives the other party as to the very nature of the contract; renders the agreement void

Fraud in the execution, which is extremely rare, consists of a misrepresentation that deceives the defrauded person as to the very nature of the contract. Such fraud occurs when a person does not know, or does not have reasonable opportunity to know, the character or essence of a proposed contract because the other party misrepresents its character or essential terms. Fraud in the execution renders the transaction **void**.

For example, Melody delivers a package to Ray, requests that Ray sign a receipt for it, holds out a simple printed form headed "Receipt," and indicates the line on which Ray is to sign. This line, which appears to Ray to be the bottom line of the receipt, is actually the signature line of a promissory note cleverly concealed underneath the receipt. Ray signs where directed without knowing that he is signing a note. This is fraud in the execution. The note is void and of no legal effect, for, although the signature is genuine and appears to manifest Ray's assent to the terms of the note, there is no actual assent. The nature of Melody's fraud precluded consent to the signing of the note because it prevented Ray from reasonably knowing what he was signing.

Fraud in the Inducement

Fraud in the inducement
misrepresentation regarding the subject matter of a contract that induces the other party to enter into the contract; renders the contract voidable

Fraud in the inducement, generally referred to as fraud or deceit, is an intentional misrepresentation of material fact by one party to the other, who consents to enter into a contract in justifiable reliance on the misrepresentation. Fraud in the inducement renders the contract **voidable** by the defrauded party. For example, Alice, in offering to sell her dog to Bob, tells Bob that the dog won first prize in its class in the recent national dog show. In truth, the dog had not even been entered in the show. However, Alice's statement induces Bob to accept the offer and pay a high price for the dog. There is a contract, but it is voidable by Bob because Alice's fraud induced his assent.

The requisites for fraud in the inducement are as follows:

1. a false representation
2. of a fact
3. that is material and
4. made with knowledge of its falsity and the intention to deceive (scienter) and
5. which representation is justifiably relied on.

Misrepresentation
some positive statement or conduct that is not in accord with the facts

Concealment
action taken to keep another from learning of a fact

PRACTICAL ADVICE
Consider bargaining with the other party to promise to give you full disclosure.

PRACTICAL ADVICE
When entering into contract negotiations, first determine what duty of disclosure you owe to the other party.

Fiduciary
person who owes a duty of trust, loyalty, and confidence to another

Fact
an event that took place or a thing that exists

Opinion
belief in the existence of a fact or a judgment as to value

False Representation A basic element of fraud is a false representation or a **misrepresentation** (i.e., misleading conduct or an assertion not in accord with the facts, made through a positive statement). In contrast, **concealment** is an action intended or known to be likely to keep another from learning a fact he otherwise would have learned. Active concealment can form the basis for fraud, as, for example, when a seller puts heavy oil or grease in a car engine to conceal a knock. Truth may be suppressed by concealment as much as by misrepresentation. Expressly denying knowledge of a fact that a party knows to exist is a misrepresentation if it leads the other party to believe that the fact does not exist or cannot be discovered. Moreover, a statement of misleading half-truth is considered the equivalent of a false representation.

Generally, *silence* or nondisclosure alone does not amount to fraud when the parties deal at arm's length. An *arm's-length transaction* is one in which the parties owe each other no special duties and each is acting in his or her self-interest. In most business or market transactions, the parties deal at arm's length and generally have no obligation to tell the other party everything they know about the subject of the contract. Thus, it is not fraud when a buyer possesses advantageous information about the seller's property, information of which he knows the seller to be ignorant, and does not disclose such information to the seller. A buyer is under no duty to inform the seller of the greater value or other advantages of the property for sale. Assume, for example, that Sid owns a farm that, as a farm, is worth $100,000. Brenda, who knows that there is oil under Sid's farm, also knows that Sid is ignorant of this fact. Without disclosing this information to Sid, Brenda makes an offer to Sid to buy the farm for $100,000. Sid accepts the offer, and a contract is duly made. Sid, on later learning the facts, can do nothing about the matter, either at law or in equity. As one case puts it, "a purchaser is not bound by our laws to make the man he buys from as wise as himself."

Although nondisclosure usually does not constitute a misrepresentation, in certain situations it does. One such situation arises when (1) a person fails to disclose a fact known to him; (2) he knows that the disclosure of that fact would correct a mistake of the other party as to a basic assumption on which that party is making the contract; and (3) nondisclosure of the fact amounts to a failure to act in good faith and in accordance with reasonable standards of fair dealing. Accordingly, if the property at issue in the contract contains a substantial latent (hidden) defect, one that would not be discovered through an ordinary examination, the seller may be obliged to reveal it. Suppose, for example, that Judith owns a valuable horse, which she knows is suffering from a disease discoverable only by a competent veterinary surgeon. Judith offers to sell this horse to Curt but does not inform him about the condition of her horse. Curt makes a reasonable examination of the horse and, finding it in apparently normal condition, purchases it from Judith. Curt, on later discovering the disease in question, can have the sale set aside. Judith's silence, under the circumstances, was a misrepresentation.

In other situations, the law imposes a duty of disclosure. For example, one may have a duty of disclosure because of prior representations innocently made before entering into the contract, which are later discovered to be untrue. Another instance in which silence may constitute fraud is a transaction involving a fiduciary. A **fiduciary** is a person in a confidential relationship who owes a duty of trust, loyalty, and confidence to another. For example, an agent owes a fiduciary duty to his principal, as does a trustee to the beneficiary of the trust and a partner to her copartners. A fiduciary may not deal at arm's length, as a party in most everyday business or market transactions may, but owes a duty to disclose fully all relevant facts when entering into a transaction with the other party to the relationship.

Fact The basic element of fraud is the misrepresentation of a material fact. A **fact** is an event that actually took place or a thing that actually exists. Suppose that Dale induces Mike to purchase shares in a company unknown to Mike at a price of $100 per share by representing that she had paid $150 per share for them during the preceding year, when in fact she had paid only $50. This representation of a past event is a misrepresentation of fact.

Actionable fraud rarely can be based on what is merely a statement of **opinion**. A representation is one of opinion if it expresses only the uncertain belief of the representer as to the existence of a fact or his judgment as to quality, value, authenticity, or other matters of judgment.

The line between fact and opinion is not an easy one to draw and in close cases presents an issue for the jury. The solution often will turn on the superior knowledge of the person making the statement and the information available to the other party. Thus, if Dale said to Mike that the shares were "a good investment," she was merely stating her opinion; and normally Mike ought to regard it as no more than that. Other common examples of opinion are statements of value, such as "This is the best car for the money in town" or "This deluxe model will give you twice the wear of a cheaper model." Such exaggerations and commendations of articles offered for sale are to be expected from dealers, who are merely **puffing** their wares with "sales talk." If the representer is a professional advising a client, the courts are more likely to regard an untrue statement of opinion as actionable. Such a statement expresses the opinion of one holding himself out as having expert knowledge, and the tendency is to grant relief to those who have sustained loss by reasonable reliance on expert evaluation, as the next case shows.

Puffing

sales talk that is considered general bragging or overstatement

Also to be distinguished from a representation of fact is a *prediction*. Predictions are similar to opinions, as no one can know with certainty what will happen in the future, and normally they are not regarded as factual statements. Likewise, promissory statements ordinarily do not constitute a basis of fraud, because a breach of promise does not necessarily indicate that the promise was fraudulently made. However, a promise that the promisor, at the time of making, had no intention of keeping is a misrepresentation of fact.

Historically, courts held that representations of *law* were not statements of fact but of opinion. The present trend is to recognize that a statement of law may have the effect of either a statement of fact or a statement of opinion. For example, a statement asserting that a particular statute has been enacted or repealed has the effect of a statement of fact. On the other hand, a statement as to the legal consequences of a particular set of facts is a statement of opinion.

Maroun v. Wyreless Systems, Inc.

Supreme Court of Idaho, 2005

141 Idaho 604, 114 P.3d 974

http://scholar.google.com/scholar_case?case=18286843461461582750&hl=en&as_sdt=2&as_vis=1&oi=scholarr

FACTS Tony Y. Maroun (Maroun) was employed by Amkor when he accepted an offer to work for Wyreless, a start-up company. Wyreless promised Maroun, among other items, the following: (1) annual salary of $300,000; (2) $300,000 bonus for successful organization of Wyreless Systems, Inc.; (3) 15 percent of the issued equity in Wyreless Systems, Inc.; (4) the equity and "organization bonus" will need to be tied to agreeable milestones; (5) full medical benefits; and (6) the position of Chief Executive Officer, President, and board member. Maroun began working for Wyreless but was terminated a few months later. Maroun then filed suit alleging he had not received 15 percent of issued equity and had not received $429,145, which represented the remainder of the $600,000. Wyreless filed a motion for summary judgment. The district court granted the motion, and Maroun appealed.

DECISION Judgment of the district court affirmed.

OPINION Maroun argues the district court erred in granting summary judgment in favor of Robinson on the fraud claim. In opposition to the defendants' motion for summary judgment, Maroun filed an affidavit that stated Robinson made the following representations to Maroun:

1. That Wyreless was to be a corporation of considerable size, with initial net revenues in excess of several hundred million dollars.
2. That Robinson would soon acquire one and one-half million dollars in personal assets, which Robinson would make available to personally guaranty payment of my compensation from Wyreless.
3. That he would have no difficulty in obtaining the initial investments required to capitalize Wyreless as a large, world

leading corporation with initial net revenues in excess of several hundred million dollars.
4. That he had obtained firm commitments from several investors and that investment funds would be received in Wyreless' bank account in the near future.

An action for fraud or misrepresentation will not lie for statements of future events. A promise or a statement as to a future event will not serve as a basis for fraud. Statements numbered one and two both address future events. The representation forming the basis of a claim for fraud must concern past or existing material facts. Neither of these statements constitutes a statement or a representation of past or existing fact. A promise or statement that an act will be undertaken, however, is actionable, if it is proven that the speaker made the promise without intending to keep it. There is no indication that Robinson did not intend to fulfill those representations to Maroun at the time he made the statements.

Opinions or predictions about the anticipated profitability of a business are generally not actionable as fraud. Statement number three is merely Robinson's opinion. As to statement number four, no evidence was submitted that Robinson had not received commitments at the time he made the statement to Maroun. Accordingly, the district court's grant of summary judgment against Maroun on the fraud claim is affirmed.

INTERPRETATION Fraud generally must be based on a material fact and not on predictions or a person's opinion.

ETHICAL QUESTION Did Wyreless act in an ethical manner?

CRITICAL THINKING QUESTION When should an employer be held to its "promises"?

Material

of substantial importance; likely to induce a reasonable person to enter into the contract

Materiality In addition to the requirement that a misrepresentation be one of fact, it must also be material. A misrepresentation is **material** if (1) it would be likely to induce a reasonable person to manifest assent or (2) the maker knows that it would be likely to induce the recipient to do so. Thus, in the sale of a racehorse, it may not be material whether the horse was ridden in its most recent race by a certain jockey, but its running time for the race probably would be. The Restatement of Contracts provides that a contract justifiably induced by a misrepresentation is voidable if the misrepresentation is either fraudulent or material. Therefore, a fraudulent misrepresentation does not have to be material to obtain rescission, but it must be material to recover damages.

The *Reed v. King* case presents an unusual factual situation involving the duty to disclose a "material" fact.

Reed v. King
California Court of Appeals, 1983
145 Cal.App.3d 261, 193 Cal.Rptr. 130
http://scholar.google.com/scholar_case?case=575864357603110085&q=193+Cal.Rptr.+130&hl=en&as_sdt=2,34

FACTS Dorris Reed bought a house from Robert King for $76,000. King and his real estate agent knew that a woman and her four children had been murdered in the house ten years earlier and allegedly knew that the event had materially affected the market value of the house. They said nothing about the murders to Reed, and King asked a neighbor not to inform her of them. After the sale, neighbors told Reed about the murders and informed her that the house was consequently worth only $65,000. Reed brought an action against King and the real estate agent, alleging fraud and seeking rescission and damages. The complaint was dismissed, and Reed appealed.

DECISION Judgment reversed.

OPINION The requisite elements of fraud are "(1) a *false representation* or concealment of a material fact (or, in some cases, an opinion) susceptible of knowledge, (2) made with *knowledge* of its falsity or without sufficient knowledge on the subject to warrant a representation, (3) with the *intent* to induce the person to whom it is made to act upon it; and such person must (4) act in *reliance* upon the representation (5) to his *damage*." The trial court determined that Reed failed to allege concealment of a material fact. Concealment, however, may include mere silence when a party has a duty to disclose. This duty falls upon the seller of real property where he (1) knows of facts that have a material effect upon the value or desirability of the property and (2) knows that these facts are unknown to the buyer and inaccessible to the buyer through the exercise of ordinary diligence. The second of these conditions clearly applies. King knew that Reed was unaware of the murders, and Reed cannot reasonably be expected to anticipate and discover such an unlikely possibility. The issue therefore turns upon the question of materiality. Material nondisclosures in real property cases generally pertain to physical defects of the property or to legal impediments to its use. Murder, however, is a particularly disturbing event that may cause a buyer to be unable to live in a house where it has occurred and may thus deprive the buyer of the intended use of the property. Moreover, the content of the information not disclosed by the seller need not be the crucial factor. If Reed can prove that the murders significantly and measurably affected the market value of the premises, she should receive a favorable judgment on the issue of materiality and duty to disclose.

INTERPRETATION A representation is material if it is likely to influence or affect a reasonable person.

ETHICAL QUESTION Should King have revealed the information to Reed? Explain.

CRITICAL THINKING QUESTION What is material information, and how should it be determined?

Scienter (sci·en′·ter)

guilty knowledge

Knowledge of Falsity and Intention to Deceive To establish fraud, the misrepresentation must have been known by the one making it to be false and must be made with an intent to deceive. This element of fraud is known as **scienter**. Knowledge of falsity can consist of (1) actual knowledge, (2) lack of belief in the statement's truthfulness, or (3) reckless indifference as to its truthfulness.

Justifiable reliance

reasonably influenced by the misrepresentation

Justifiable Reliance A person is not entitled to relief unless she has **justifiably relied** on the misrepresentation. If the complaining party's decision was in no way influenced by the misrepresentation, she must abide by the terms of the contract. She is not deceived if she does not rely on the misrepresentation. Justifiable reliance requires that the misrepresentation contribute substantially to the misled party's decision to enter into the contract. If the complaining party knew or it was obvious that the representation of the defendant was untrue, but she still entered into the contract, she has not justifiably relied on that representation. Moreover, where the misrepresentation is fraudulent, the party who relies on it is entitled to relief even though she does not investigate the statement or is contributorily negligent in relying on it. Not knowing or discovering the facts before making a contract does not make a person's reliance unjustified unless her reliance amounts to a failure to act in good faith and in accordance with reasonable standards of fair dealing. Thus, most courts will not allow a person who concocts a deliberate and elaborate scheme to defraud—one that the defrauded party should readily detect—to argue that the defrauded party did not justifiably rely upon the misrepresentation.

NONFRAUDULENT MISREPRESENTATION

Negligent misrepresentation
made without due care

Innocent misrepresentation
misrepresentation made without knowledge of its falsity but with due care

Nonfraudulent misrepresentation is a material, false statement that induces another to rely justifiably but is made *without* scienter. Such representation may occur in one of two ways. **Negligent misrepresentation** is a false representation that is made without due care in ascertaining its truthfulness; such representation renders an agreement voidable. **Innocent misrepresentation**, which also renders a contract voidable, is a false representation made without knowledge of its falsity but with due care. To obtain relief for nonfraudulent misrepresentation, all of the other elements of fraud must be present *and* the misrepresentation must be material. The remedies that may be available for nonfraudulent misrepresentation are rescission and damages (see Chapter 18).

MISTAKE

Mistake
an understanding that is not in accord with existing fact

A **mistake** is a belief that is not in accord with the facts. Where the mistaken facts relate to the basis of the parties' agreement, the law permits the adversely affected party to avoid or reform the contract under certain circumstances. But because permitting avoidance for mistake undermines the objective approach to mutual assent, the law has experienced considerable difficulty in specifying those circumstances that justify permitting the subjective matter of mistake to invalidate an otherwise objectively satisfactory agreement. As a result, establishing clear rules to govern the effect of mistake has proven elusive.

The Restatement and modern cases treat mistakes of law in existence at the time of making the contract *no* differently than mistakes of fact. For example, Susan contracts to sell a parcel of land to James with the mutual understanding that James will build an apartment house on the land. Both Susan and James believe that such a building is lawful. Unknown to them, however, three days before they entered into their contract, the town in which the land was located had enacted an ordinance precluding such use of the land. In states that regard mistakes of law and fact in the same light, this mistake of law would be treated as a mistake of fact that would lead to the consequences discussed below.

Mutual Mistake

Mutual mistake
both parties have a common but erroneous belief forming the basis of a contract

Mutual mistake occurs when *both* parties are mistaken as to the same set of facts. If the mistake relates to a basic assumption on which the contract is made and has a material effect on the agreed exchange, then it is *voidable* by the adversely affected party unless he bears the risk of the mistake.

CONCEPT REVIEW 11-1			
Misrepresentation			
	Fraudulent	Negligent	Innocent
False Statement of Fact	Yes	Yes	Yes
Materiality	Yes for damages No for rescission	Yes	Yes
Fault	Scienter	Without due care (knowledge and intent)	Without due care and knowledge
Reliance	Yes	Yes	Yes
Injury	Yes for damages No for rescission	Yes for damages No for rescission	Yes for damages No for rescission
Remedies	Damages Rescission	Damages Rescission	Damages Rescission

© Cengage Learning 2013

APPLYING THE LAW

Conduct Invalidating Assent

Facts In the summer of 2008, Gillian bought a 2006 model year car from a luxury automobile dealer for $36,000. At the time of her purchase, the odometer and title documentation both indicated that the car had 21,445 miles on it. But after just a little more than a year, the engine failed, and Gillian had to take the car to a mechanic. The problem was the water pump, which needed to be replaced. Surprised that a water pump should fail in a car with so few miles on it, the mechanic more closely examined the odometer and determined that someone had cleverly tampered with it. According to the mechanic, the car probably had about sixty thousand miles on it when Gillian bought it. At the time Gillian bought the car, the retail value for the same vehicle with sixty thousand miles on it was approximately $30,000.

Gillian decided that under these conditions she no longer wanted the car. She contacted the dealership, which strenuously denied having tampered with the odometer. In fact, the dealership's records reflect that it purchased Gillian's car at auction for $34,000, after a thorough inspection that revealed no mechanical deficiencies or alteration of the car's odometer.

Issue Is Gillian's contract voidable by her?

Rule of Law Innocent misrepresentation renders a contract voidable. Innocent misrepresentation is proven when the following elements are established: (1) a false representation, (2) of fact, (3) that is material, (4) made without knowledge of its falsity but with due care, and (5) the representation is justifiably relied upon.

Application Gillian can prove all five elements of innocent misrepresentation. First, the dealership's false representation was that the mileage on the car was 21,445, when the car actually had about sixty thousand miles on it. Second, the mileage of the car at the time of sale is an actual event not an opinion or prediction. Third, as the mileage of a used car is probably the most critical determinant of its value, this misrepresentation was material to the parties' agreed sale price, inducing the formation of the contract. Indeed, while Gillian might still have purchased this car with sixty thousand miles on it, she most certainly would have done so only at a lower price. Fourth, it is highly unlikely that the dealership was aware of the incorrect odometer reading. We know

this because it paid $34,000 for the car, which should have sold for something less than $30,000 in the wholesale market if the true mileage had been known. Moreover, the dealership appears to have conducted appropriate due diligence to support both its own purchase price and the price at which it offered the car to Gillian. The odometer tampering was cleverly concealed, so much so that neither the dealerships' inspection before purchase nor Gillian's mechanic's initial inspection revealed it. Fifth, Gillian's reliance on the ostensible odometer reading is justified. The car was only two years old when she bought it, and 21,445 miles is within an average range of mileage for a used car of that age. Unless the car's physical condition or something in the title paperwork should have alerted her to an inconsistency between the stated mileage and the car's actual mileage, Gillian was entitled to rely on what appeared to be a correct odometer reading.

Conclusion Because all the elements of innocent misrepresentation can be shown, Gillian's contract is voidable by Gillian.

© Cengage Learning 2013

Usually, market conditions and the financial situation of the parties are not considered basic assumptions. Thus, if Gail contracts to purchase Pete's automobile under the belief that she can sell it at a profit to Jesse, she is not excused from liability if she is mistaken in this belief. Nor can she rescind the agreement simply because she was mistaken as to her estimate of what the automobile was worth. These are the ordinary risks of business, and courts do not undertake to relieve against them. But suppose that the parties contract upon the assumption that the automobile is a 2010 Cadillac with fifteen thousand miles of use, when in fact the engine is that of a cheaper model and has been run in excess of fifty thousand miles. Here, a court likely would allow a rescission because of mutual mistake of a material fact. In a New Zealand case, the plaintiff purchased a "stud bull" at an auction. There were no express warranties as to "sex, condition, or otherwise." Actually, the bull was sterile. Rescission was allowed, the court observing that it was a "bull in name only."

Lesher v. Strid
Court of Appeals of Oregon, 2000
165 Or.App. 34, 996 P.2d 988
http://caselaw.findlaw.com/scripts/getcase.pl?court=OR&vol=A99602&invol=1

FACTS In May 1995, the plaintiffs, Vernon and Janene Lesher, agreed to purchase an eighteen-acre parcel of real property from defendant with the intention of using it to raise horses. In purchasing the property, the plaintiffs relied on their impression that at least

four acres of the subject property had a right to irrigation from Slate Creek. The earnest money agreement to the contract provided:

> D. **Water Rights** are being conveyed to Buyer at the close of escrow.... Seller will provide Buyer with a written explanation of

the operation of the irrigation system, water right certificates, and inventory of irrigation equipment included in sale.

The earnest money agreement also provided:

> **THE SUBJECT PROPERTY IS BEING SOLD "AS IS"** subject to the Buyer's approval of the tests and conditions as stated herein. Buyer declares that Buyer is not depending on any other statement of the Seller or licensees that is not incorporated by reference in this earnest money contract [Bold in original].

Before signing the earnest money agreement, the defendants presented to the plaintiffs a 1977 Water Resources Department water rights certificate and a map purporting to show an area of the subject property to be irrigated ("area to be irrigated" map), which indicated that the property carried a four-acre water right. Both parties believed that the property carried the irrigation rights and that the plaintiffs needed such rights for their horse farm. The plaintiffs did not obtain the services of an attorney or a water rights examiner before purchasing the property.

After purchasing the property and before establishing a pasture, the plaintiffs learned that the property did not carry a four-acre water right. The plaintiffs sought rescission of the contract for sale, alleging mutual mistake of fact or innocent misrepresentation regarding the existence of water rights. The trial court ruled in favor of the plaintiffs and the defendant appeals.

DECISION Judgment of the trial court affirmed.

OPINION Grounds for rescission on the basis of a mutual mistake of fact or innocent misrepresentation must be proved by clear and convincing evidence. An innocent misrepresentation of fact renders a contract voidable by a party if the party is relying on the material misrepresentation by the other party. A mutual mistake of fact renders a contract voidable by the adversely affected party, if the mistake is so fundamental that it frustrates the purpose of the contract.

Even though it appears that the trial court did not apply the clear and convincing standard, the plaintiffs' evidence meets that standard. Both defendant and plaintiffs testified that they believed that the four acres of water rights were appurtenant to the subject property. Defendant does not dispute that the 1977 water rights certificate and the "area to be irrigated" map are her representation about the water right. Plaintiffs also established by clear and convincing evidence that the existence of the four-acre water right was material and essential to the contract. Vernon testified that the motivation for the purchase was to expand his ability to raise horses from property they already owned where they had a two-acre irrigation right and that the subject property's water right was essential to the contract. Certainly, a smaller water right would limit, not expand, the plaintiffs' ability to raise horses. The mistake, therefore, goes to the very essence of the contract.

The defendant argues that the plaintiffs bore the risk of that mistake. The Restatement (Second) of Contracts § 154 explains that a party bears the risk of a mistake, in part, if the risk is allocated to the party by agreement of the parties, or if the risk is allocated to the party "by the court on the ground that it is reasonable in the circumstances to do so." There is nothing in the contract that would allocate to plaintiffs the risk of a mistake as to the existence of a four-acre water right. Defendant argues in the alternative that the plaintiffs' mistake of fact is the result of the defendant's misrepresentation, on which plaintiffs could not reasonably rely. An "innocent misrepresentation may support a claim for rescission of a real estate agreement if the party who relied on the misrepresentations of another establishes a right to have done so." Defendant argues that her representations about the four-acre water right were extrinsic to the contract and that the contract's "as is" clause expressly excluded reliance on such extrinsic representations. The "as is" clause specifically contemplated reliance on any statements by the seller that were "incorporated by reference" in the earnest money agreement. The earnest money agreement specifically referred to the conveyance of water rights.

INTERPRETATION If both parties to a contract have a common but erroneous belief as to a basic assumption on which the contract is made, the contract is voidable.

CRITICAL THINKING QUESTION Should all contracts provide for this type of situation? If so, how? Explain.

Unilateral Mistake

Unilateral mistake
erroneous belief on the part of only one of the parties to a contract

Unilateral mistake occurs when only one of the parties is mistaken. Courts have been hesitant to grant relief for unilateral mistake, even though it relates to a basic assumption on which a party entered into the contract and has a material effect on the agreed exchange. Nevertheless, relief will be granted where the nonmistaken party knows, or reasonably should know, that such a mistake has been made (palpable unilateral mistake) or where the mistake was caused by the fault of the nonmistaken party. For example, suppose a building contractor makes a serious error in his computations and consequently submits a job bid that is one-half the amount it should be. If the other party knows that the contractor made such an error, or reasonably should have known it, she cannot, as a general rule, take advantage of the other's mistake by accepting the offer. In addition, many courts and the Restatement allow rescission where the effect of unilateral mistake makes enforcement of the contract unconscionable.

Assumption of Risk of Mistake

Assumption of risk of mistake
a party may assume the risk of a mistake

A party who has undertaken to bear the risk of a mistake will not be able to avoid the contract, even though the mistake (which may be either mutual or unilateral) would have otherwise permitted the party to do so. This allocation of risk may occur by agreement of the parties. For instance, a ship at sea may be sold "lost or not lost." In such case the buyer is liable whether the ship was lost or not lost at the time the contract was made. There is no mistake; instead, there is a conscious allocation of risk.

CONCEPT REVIEW 11-2

Conduct Invalidating Assent

Conduct	Effect
Duress by physical force	Void
Duress by improper threat	Voidable
Undue influence	Voidable
Fraud in the execution	Void
Fraud in the inducement	Voidable

© Cengage Learning 2013

Effect of fault upon mistake

not a bar to avoidance unless the fault amounts to a failure to act in good faith

The risk of mistake also may be allocated by conscious ignorance when the parties recognize that they have limited knowledge of the facts. For example, the Supreme Court of Wisconsin refused to set aside the sale of a stone for which the purchaser paid $1 but that was subsequently discovered to be an uncut diamond valued at $700. The parties did not know at the time of sale what the stone was and knew they did not know. Each consciously assumed the risk that the value might be more or less than the selling price.

Effect of Fault upon Mistake

The Restatement provides that a mistaken party's fault in not knowing or discovering a fact before making a contract does not prevent him from avoiding the contract "unless his fault amounts to a failure to act in good faith and in accordance with reasonable standards of fair dealing." This rule does not, however, apply to a failure to read a contract. As a general proposition, a party is held to what she signs. Her signature authenticates the writing, and she cannot repudiate that which she has voluntarily approved. Generally, one who assents to a writing is presumed to know its contents and cannot escape being bound by its terms merely by contending that she did not read them; her assent is deemed to cover unknown as well as known terms.

Mistake in Meaning of Terms

Somewhat related to mistakes of fact is the situation in which the parties misunderstand their manifestations of mutual assent. A famous case involving this problem is *Raffles v. Wichelhaus*, 2 Hurlstone & Coltman 906 (1864), popularly known as the *Peerless* case. A contract of purchase was made for 125 bales of cotton to arrive on the *Peerless* from Bombay. It happened, however, that there were two ships by the name of *Peerless* each sailing from Bombay, one in October and the other in December. The buyer had in mind the ship that sailed in October, while the seller reasonably believed the agreement referred to the *Peerless* sailing in December. Neither party was at fault, but both believed in good faith that a different ship was intended. The English court held that no contract existed.

The Restatement is in accord: There is no manifestation of mutual assent in cases in which the parties attach materially different meanings to their manifestations and neither party knows or has reason to know the meaning attached by the other. If blame can be ascribed to either party, however, that party will be held responsible. Thus, if the seller knew of the sailing from Bombay of two ships by the name of *Peerless*, then he would be at fault, and the contract would be for the ship sailing in October as the buyer expected. If neither party is to blame or both are to blame, there is no contract at all; that is, the agreement is void.

CHAPTER SUMMARY

Duress

Definition wrongful act or threat that overcomes the free will of a party

Physical Compulsion coercion involving physical force renders the agreement void

Improper Threats improper threats or acts, including economic and social coercion, render the contract voidable

Undue Influence	**Definition** taking unfair advantage of a person by reason of a dominant position based on a confidential relationship
	Effect renders contract voidable
Fraud	**Fraud in the Execution** a misrepresentation that deceives the other party as to the nature of a document evidencing the contract; renders agreement void
	Fraud in the Inducement renders the agreement voidable if the following elements are present:

  - *False Representation* positive statement or conduct that misleads
  - *Fact* an event that occurred or thing that exists
  - *Materiality* of substantial importance
  - *Knowledge of Falsity and Intention to Deceive* (called scienter) and includes (1) actual knowledge, (2) lack of belief in statement's truthfulness, or (3) reckless indifference to its truthfulness
  - *Justifiable Reliance* a defrauded party is reasonably influenced by the misrepresentation

Nonfraudulent Misrepresentation	**Negligent Misrepresentation** misrepresentation made without due care in ascertaining its truthfulness; renders agreement voidable
	Innocent Misrepresentation misrepresentation made without knowledge of its falsity but with due care; renders contract voidable
Mistake	**Definition** an understanding that is not in accord with existing fact
	Mutual Mistake both parties have a common but erroneous belief forming the basis of the contract; renders the contract voidable by either party
	Unilateral Mistake courts are unlikely to grant relief unless the error is known or should be known by the nonmistaken party
	Assumption of Risk of Mistake a party may assume the risk of a mistake
	Effect of Fault upon Mistake not a bar to avoidance unless the fault amounts to a failure to act in good faith

QUESTIONS

1. Anita and Barry were negotiating, and Anita's attorney prepared a long and carefully drawn contract that was given to Barry for examination. Five days later and prior to its execution, Barry's eyes became so infected that it was impossible for him to read. Ten days thereafter and during the continuance of the illness, Anita called Barry and urged him to sign the contract, telling him that time was running out. Barry signed the contract despite the fact he was unable to read it. In a subsequent action by Anita, Barry claimed that the contract was not binding on him because it was impossible for him to read and he did not know what it contained prior to his signing it. Should Barry be held to the contract?

2. a. William tells Carol that he paid $150,000 for his farm in 2005, and that he believes it is worth twice that at the present time. Relying upon these statements, Carol buys the farm from William for $225,000. William did pay $150,000 for the farm in 2005, but its value has increased only slightly, and it is presently not worth $300,000. On discovering this, Carol offers to reconvey the farm to William and sues for the return of her $225,000. Result?

   b. Modify the facts in (a) by assuming that William had paid $100,000 for the property in 2005. What is the result?

3. On September 1, Adams in Portland, Oregon, wrote a letter to Brown in New York City offering to sell to Brown one thousand tons of chromite at $48 per ton, to be shipped by *S.S. Malabar* sailing from Portland, Oregon, to New York City via the Panama Canal. Upon receiving the letter on September 5, Brown immediately mailed to Adams a letter stating that she accepted the offer. There were two ships by the name of *S.S. Malabar* sailing from Portland to New York City via the Panama Canal, one sailing in October and the other sailing in December. At the time of mailing her letter of acceptance, Brown knew of both sailings and further knew that Adams knew only of the December sailing. Is there a contract? If so, to which *S.S. Malabar* does it relate?

4. Adler owes Perreault, a police captain, $500. Adler threatens Perreault that unless Perreault gives him a discharge from the debt, Adler will disclose the fact that Perreault has on several occasions become highly intoxicated and has been seen in the company of certain disreputable persons. Perreault, induced by fear that such a disclosure would cost him his position or in any event lead to social disgrace, gives Adler a release but subsequently sues to set it aside and recover on his claim. Will Adler be able to enforce the release?

5. Harris owned a farm that was worth about $600 an acre. By false representations of fact, Harris induced Pringle to buy the

farm at $1,500 an acre. Shortly after taking possession of the farm, Pringle discovered oil under the land. Harris, on learning this, sues to have the sale set aside on the ground that it was voidable because of fraud. Result?

6. On February 2, Phillips induced Mallor to purchase from her fifty shares of stock in the XYZ Corporation for $10,000, representing that the actual book value of each share was $200. A certificate for fifty shares was delivered to Mallor. On February 16, Mallor discovered that the February 2 book value was only $50 per share. Thereafter, Mallor sues Phillips. Will Mallor be successful in a lawsuit against Phillips? Why?

7. Dorothy mistakenly accused Fred's son, Steven, of negligently burning down Dorothy's barn. Fred believed that his son was guilty of the wrong and that he, Fred, was personally liable for the damage, because Steven was only fifteen years old. Upon demand made by Dorothy, Fred paid Dorothy $25,000 for the damage to Dorothy's barn. After making this payment, Fred learned that his son had not caused the burning of Dorothy's barn and was in no way responsible for its burning. Fred then sued Dorothy to recover the $25,000 that he had paid her. Will he be successful?

8. Jones, a farmer, found an odd-looking stone in his fields. He went to Smith, the town jeweler, and asked him what he thought it was. Smith said he did not know but thought it might be a ruby. Jones asked Smith what he would pay for it, and Smith said $200, whereupon Jones sold it to Smith for $200. The stone turned out to be an uncut diamond worth $3,000. Jones brought an action against Smith to recover the stone. On trial, it was proved that Smith actually did not know the stone was a diamond when he bought it, but he thought it might be a ruby. Can Jones void the sale? Explain.

9. Decedent, Joan Jones, a bedridden, lonely woman, eighty-six years old, owned outright Greenacre, her ancestral estate. Biggers, her physician and friend, visited her weekly and was held in the highest regard by Joan. Joan was extremely fearful of pain and suffering and depended on Biggers to ease her anxiety and pain. Several months before her death, Joan deeded Greenacre to Biggers for $5,000. The fair market value of Greenacre at this time was $125,000. Joan was survived by two children and six grandchildren. Joan's children challenged the validity of the deed. Should the deed be declared invalid due to Biggers' undue influence? Explain.

CASE PROBLEMS

10. In February, Gardner, a schoolteacher with no experience in running a tavern, entered into a contract to purchase for $40,000 the Punjab Tavern from Meiling. The contract was contingent upon Gardner's obtaining a five-year lease for the tavern's premises and a liquor license from the state. Prior to the formation of the contract, Meiling had made no representations to Gardner concerning the gross income of the tavern. Approximately three months after the contract was signed, Gardner and Meiling met with an inspector from the Oregon Liquor Control Commission (OLCC) to discuss transfer of the liquor license. Meiling reported to the agent, in Gardner's presence, that the tavern's gross income figures for February, March, and April were $5,710, $4,918, and $5,009 respectively. The OLCC granted the required license, the transaction was closed, and Gardner took possession on June 10. After discovering that the tavern's income was very low and that the tavern had very few female patrons, Gardner contacted Meiling's bookkeeping service and learned that the actual gross income for those three months had been approximately $1,400 to $2,000. Will a court grant Gardner rescission of the contract? Explain.

11. Dorothy and John Huffschneider listed their house and lot for sale with C. B. Property. The asking price was $165,000, and the owners told C. B. that the property contained 6.8 acres. Dean Olson, a salesman for C. B., advertised the property in local newspapers as consisting of six acres. James and Jean Holcomb signed a contract to purchase the property through Olson after first inspecting the property with Olson and being assured by Olson that the property was at least 6.6 acres. The Holcombs never asked for nor received a copy of the survey. In actuality, the lot was only 4.6 acres. Can the Holcombs rescind the contract? Explain.

12. Christine Boyd was designated as the beneficiary of a life insurance policy issued by Aetna Life Insurance Company on the life of Christine's husband, Jimmie Boyd. The policy insured against Jimmie's permanent total disability and

provided for a death benefit to be paid on Jimmie's death. Several years after the policy was issued, Jimmie and Christine separated. Jimmie began to travel extensively, and, therefore, Christine was unable to keep track of his whereabouts or his state of health. Jimmie nevertheless continued to pay the premiums on the policy until Christine tried to cash in the policy to alleviate her financial distress. A loan previously had been made on the policy, however, leaving its cash surrender value, and thus the amount Christine received, at only $4.19. Shortly thereafter, Christine learned that Jimmie had been permanently and totally disabled before the surrender of the policy. Aetna also was unaware of Jimmie's condition, and Christine requested the surrendered policy be reinstated and that the disability payments be made. Jimmie died soon thereafter, and Christine then requested that Aetna pay the death benefit. Decision?

13. Treasure Salvors and the state of Florida entered into a series of four annual contracts governing the salvage of the *Nuestra Senora de Atocha*. The *Atocha* is a Spanish galleon that sank in 1622, carrying a treasure now worth well over $250 million. Both parties had contracted under the impression that the seabed on which the *Atocha* lay was land owned by Florida. Treasure Salvors agreed to relinquish 25 percent of the items recovered in return for the right to salvage on state lands. In accordance with these contracts, Treasure Salvors delivered to Florida its share of the salvaged artifacts. Subsequently the U.S. Supreme Court held that the part of the continental shelf on which the *Atocha* was resting had *never* been owned by Florida. Treasure Salvors then brought suit to rescind the contracts and to recover the artifacts it had delivered to the state of Florida. Should Treasure Salvors prevail?

14. Jane Francois married Victor H. Francois. At the time of the marriage, Victor was a fifty-year-old bachelor living with his elderly mother, and Jane was a thirty-year-old, twice-divorced mother of two. Victor had a relatively secure financial portfolio; Jane, on the other hand, brought no money or property to the marriage.

The marriage deteriorated quickly over the next couple of years, with disputes centered on financial matters. During this period, Jane systematically gained a joint interest and took control of most of Victor's assets. Three years after they married Jane contracted Harold Monoson, an attorney, to draw up divorce papers. Victor was unaware of Jane's decision until he was taken to Monoson's office, where Monoson presented for Victor's signature a "Property Settlement and Separation Agreement." Monoson told Victor that he would need an attorney, but Jane vetoed Victor's choice. Monoson then asked another lawyer, Gregory Ball, to come into the office. Ball read the agreement and strenuously advised Victor not to sign it because it would commit him to financial suicide. The agreement transferred most of Victor's remaining assets to Jane. Victor, however, signed it because Jane and Monoson persuaded him that it was the only way that his marriage could be saved. In October of the following year, Jane informed Victor that she had sold most of his former property and that she was leaving him permanently. Can Victor have the agreement set aside as a result of undue influence?

15. Iverson owned Iverson Motor Company, an enterprise engaged in the repair and sale of Oldsmobile, Rambler, and International Harvester Scout automobiles. Forty percent of the business's sales volume and net earnings came from the Oldsmobile franchise. Whipp contracted to buy Iverson Motors, which Iverson said included the Oldsmobile franchise. After the sale, however, General Motors refused to transfer the franchise to Whipp. Whipp then returned the property to Iverson and brought this action seeking rescission of the contract. Should the contract be rescinded? Explain.

16. On February 10, Mrs. Sunderhaus purchased a diamond ring from Perel & Lowenstein for $6,990. She was told by the company's salesman that the ring was worth its purchase price, and she also received at that time a written guarantee from the company attesting to the diamond's value, style, and trade-in value. When Mrs. Sunderhaus went to trade the ring for another, however, she was told by two jewelers that the ring was valued at $3,000 and $3,500, respectively. Mrs. Sunderhaus knew little about the value of diamonds and claims to have relied on the oral representation of the Perel & Lowenstein's salesman and the written representation as to the ring's value. Mrs. Sunderhaus seeks rescission of the contract or damages in the amount of the sales price over the ring's value. Will she prevail? Explain.

17. Division West Chinchilla Ranch advertised on television that a five-figure income could be earned by raising chinchillas with an investment of only $3.75 per animal per year and only thirty minutes of maintenance per day. The minimum investment was $2,150 for one male and six female chinchillas. Division West represented to the plaintiffs that chinchilla ranching would be easy and that no experience was required to make ranching profitable. The plaintiffs, who had no experience raising chinchillas, each invested $2,150 or more to purchase Division's chinchillas and supplies. After three years without earning a profit, the plaintiffs sued Division West for fraud. Do these facts sustain an action for fraud in the inducement?

18. William Schmalz entered into an employment contract with Hardy Salt Company. The contract granted Schmalz six months' severance pay for involuntary termination but none for voluntary separation or termination for cause. Schmalz was asked to resign from his employment. He was informed that if he did not resign he would be fired for alleged misconduct. When Schmalz turned in his letter of resignation, he signed a release prohibiting him from suing his former employer as a consequence of his employment. Schmalz consulted an attorney before signing the release and, upon signing it, received $4,583.00 (one month's salary) in consideration. Schmalz now sues his former employer for the severance pay, claiming that he signed the release under duress. Is Schmalz correct in his assertion?

19. Glen Haumont, who owned an equipment retail business in Broken Bow, Nebraska, owed the Security State Bank more than $628,000 due to improper selling practices as well as business and inventory loans. Several times Glen tried to persuade his parents, Lee and Letha Haumont, to financially back his business debts, but each time they refused. Glen then told his parents that, according to his attorney and the bank, Glen could be prosecuted and sent to jail. Soon afterwards, David Schweitz, the president of the bank, drove out to the elder Haumonts' farm to convince them to sign as guarantors of Glen's debt. Both Schweitz and Glen stressed to the Haumonts that unless they agreed to guarantee his debt, Glen would go to jail. Letha asked that her attorney be allowed to read over the guarantee agreement, but Schweitz told her that he did not have time to wait and that she must decide right then whether Glen was to go to jail. As a result, the Haumonts signed the agreement, encumbering their previously debt-free family farm for more than $628,000. Should the guarantee agreement be set aside due to duress?

20. Conrad Schaneman was a Russian immigrant who could neither read nor write the English language. In 2008, Conrad deeded (conveyed) a farm he owned to his eldest son, Laurence, for $23,500, which was the original purchase price of the property in 1978. The value of the farm in 2008 was between $145,000 and $160,000. At the time he executed the deed, Conrad was an eighty-two-year-old invalid, severely ill, and completely dependent on others for his personal needs. He weighed between 325 and 350 pounds, had difficulty breathing, could not walk more than fifteen feet, and needed a special jackhoist to get in and out of the bathtub. Conrad enjoyed a long-standing, confidential relationship with Laurence, who was his principal adviser and handled Conrad's business affairs. Laurence also obtained a power of attorney from Conrad and made himself a joint owner of Conrad's bank account and $20,000 certificate of deposit. Conrad brought this suit to cancel the deed, claiming it was the result of Laurence's undue influence. Explain whether the deed was executed as a result of undue influence.

21. At the time of her death Olga Mestrovic was the owner of a large number of works of art created by her late husband, Ivan Mestrovic, an internationally known sculptor and artist whose works were displayed throughout Europe and the United States. By the terms of Olga's will, all the works of art created by her husband were to be sold and the proceeds distributed to members of the Mestrovic family. Also included in the estate of Olga Mestrovic was certain real property which 1st Source Bank (the Bank), as personal representative of the estate of Olga Mestrovic, agreed to sell to Terrence and Antoinette Wilkin. The agreement of purchase and sale made no mention of any works of art, although it did provide for the sale of such personal property as a dishwasher, drapes, and French doors stored in the attic. Immediately after closing on the real estate, the Wilkins complained to the Bank of the

clutter left on the premises; the Bank gave the Wilkins an option of cleaning the house themselves and keeping any personal property they desired, to which the Wilkins agreed. At the time these arrangements were made, neither the Bank nor the Wilkins suspected that any works of art remained on the premises. During cleanup, however, the Wilkins found eight drawings and a sculpture created by Ivan Mestrovic to which the Wilkins claimed ownership based upon their agreement with the Bank that, if they cleaned the real property, they could keep such personal property as they desired. Who is entitled to ownership of the works of art?

22. Frank Berryessa stole funds from his employer, the Eccles Hotel Company. His father, W. S. Berryessa (Berryessa), learned of his son's trouble and, thinking the amount involved was about $2,000, gave the hotel a promissory note for $2,186 to cover the shortage. In return, the hotel agreed not to publicize the incident or notify the bonding company. (A bonding company is an insurer that is paid a premium for agreeing to reimburse an employer for thefts by an employee.) Before this note became due, however, the hotel discovered that Frank had actually misappropriated $6,865. The hotel then notified its bonding company, Great American Indemnity Company, to collect the entire loss. W. S. Berryessa claims that the agent for Great American told him that unless he paid them $2,000 in cash and signed a note for the remaining $4,865, Frank would be prosecuted (which note would replace the initial note). Berryessa agreed, signed the note, and gave the agent a cashier's check for $1,500 and a personal check for $500. He requested that the agent not cash the personal check for about a month. Subsequently, Great American sued Berryessa on the note. He defends against the note on the grounds of duress and counterclaims for the return of the $1,500 and the cancellation of the uncashed $500 check. Who should prevail?

23. Ronald D. Johnson is a former employee of International Business Machines Corporation (IBM). As part of a downsizing effort, IBM discharged Johnson. In exchange for an enhanced severance package, Johnson signed a written release and covenant not to sue IBM. IBM's downsizing plan provided that surplus personnel were eligible to receive benefits, including outplacement assistance, career counseling, job retraining, and an enhanced separation allowance. These employees were eligible, at IBM's discretion, to receive a separation allowance of two weeks' pay. However, employees who signed a release could be eligible for an enhanced severance allowance equal to one week's pay for each six months of accumulated service with a maximum of twenty-six weeks' pay. Surplus employees could also apply for alternate, generally lower-paying, manufacturing positions. Johnson opted for the release and received the maximum twenty-six weeks' pay. He then alleged, among other claims, that IBM subjected him to economic duress when he signed the release and covenant-not-to-sue, and he sought to rescind both. What will Johnson need to show in order to prove his cause of action?

TAKING SIDES

Mrs. Audrey E. Vokes, a widow of fifty-one years and without family, purchased fourteen separate dance courses from J. P. Davenport's Arthur Murray, Inc., School of Dance. The fourteen courses totaled in the aggregate 2,302 hours of dancing lessons at a cost to Mrs. Vokes of $31,090.45. Mrs. Vokes was induced continually to reapply for new courses by representations made by Mr. Davenport that her dancing ability was improving, that she was responding to instruction, that she had excellent potential, and that they were developing her into an accomplished dancer. In fact, she had no dancing ability or aptitude and had trouble "hearing the musical beat." Mrs. Vokes brought action to have the contracts set aside.

a. What are the arguments that the contract should be set aside?
b. What are the arguments that the contract should be enforced?
c. What is the proper outcome? Explain.

CHAPTER **12**

Consideration

Nuda pactio obligationem non parit. (A naked agreement, that is, one without consideration, does not beget an obligation.)

Legal Maxim

CHAPTER OUTCOMES

After reading and studying this chapter, you should be able to:

1. Define *consideration* and explain what is meant by legal sufficiency.

2. Describe illusory promises, output contracts, requirements contracts, exclusive dealing contracts, and conditional contracts.

3. Explain whether preexisting public and contractual obligations satisfy the legal requirement of consideration.

4. Explain the concept of bargained-for exchange and whether this element is present with past consideration and third-party beneficiaries.

5. Identify and discuss those contracts that are enforceable even though they are not supported by consideration.

Consideration
inducement to make a promise enforceable

Gratuitous promise
promise made without consideration

Legal sufficiency
benefit to the promisor or detriment to the promisee

Legal detriment
(1) doing an act that one is not legally obligated to do or (2) refraining from doing an act that one has a legal right to do

Legal benefit
obtaining something to which one had no legal right

C onsideration is the primary—but not the only—basis for the enforcement of promises in our legal system. **Consideration** is the inducement to make a promise enforceable. The doctrine of consideration ensures that promises are enforced only in cases in which the parties have exchanged something of value in the eye of the law. **Gratuitous** (gift) **promises**—those made without consideration—are not legally enforceable, except under certain circumstances, which are discussed later in the chapter.

Consideration, or that which is exchanged for a promise, is present only when the parties intend an exchange. The consideration exchanged for the promise may be an act, a forbearance to act, or a promise to do either of these. Thus, there are two basic elements to consideration: (1) legal sufficiency (something of value in the eye of the law) and (2) bargained-for exchange. Both must be present to satisfy the requirement of consideration.

LEGAL SUFFICIENCY

To be **legally sufficient**, the consideration for the promise must be either a legal detriment to the promisee or a legal benefit to the promisor. In other words, in return for the promise, the promisee must give up something of legal value or the promisor must receive something of legal value.

Legal detriment means (1) the doing of (or the undertaking to do) that which the promisee was under no prior legal obligation to do or (2) the refraining from the doing of (or the undertaking to refrain from doing) that which he was previously under no legal obligation to refrain from doing. On the other hand, **legal benefit** means the obtaining by the promisor of that which he had no prior legal right to obtain. In most, if not all, cases where there is legal detriment to the promisee, there is also a legal benefit to the promisor. However, the presence of either is sufficient.

203

FACTS Harold Pearsall and Joe Alexander were friends for over twenty-five years. About twice a week they would get together after work and proceed to a liquor store, where they would purchase what the two liked to refer as a "package"—a half-pint of vodka, orange juice, two cups, and two lottery tickets. Occasionally these lottery tickets would yield modest rewards of two or three dollars, which the pair would then "plow back" into the purchase of additional tickets. On December 16, 1982, Pearsall and Alexander visited the liquor store twice, buying their normal "package" on both occasions. For the first package, Pearsall went into the store alone, and when he returned to the car, he said to Alexander, in reference to the tickets, "Are you in on it?" Alexander said, "Yes." When Pearsall asked him for his half of the purchase price, though, Alexander replied that he had no money. When they went to Alexander's home, Alexander snatched the tickets from Pearsall's hand and "scratched" them, only to find that they were both worthless. Later that same evening Alexander returned to the liquor store and bought a second "package." This time, Pearsall snatched the tickets from Alexander and said that he would "scratch" them. Instead, he gave one to Alexander, and each man scratched one of the tickets. Alexander's was a $20,000 winner. Alexander cashed the ticket and refused to give Pearsall anything. Pearsall brought suit against Alexander, claiming breach of an agreement to share the proceeds. The trial court dismissed Pearsall's complaint, and Pearsall appealed.

DECISION Judgment reversed and remanded with instructions to enter judgment in favor of Pearsall.

OPINION The record supports Pearsall's contention that an agreement to share the proceeds existed. The conduct of the two men on December 16, when the ticket was purchased, clearly demonstrates a meeting of the minds. After purchasing the first pair of tickets, Pearsall asked Alexander if he was "in on it." Not only did Alexander give his verbal assent, but also he snatched both tickets from Pearsall and "scratched" them. It is clear that Alexander considered himself "in on" an agreement to share in the fortunes of the tickets. It is also clear that in giving over the tickets he purchased, Pearsall gave his assent to the agreement he had proposed earlier. This conduct took place within the context of a long-standing pattern of similar conduct, which included the parties' practice of "plowing back" small returns from tickets to purchase additional tickets. It is clear that by exchanging mutual promises to share in the proceeds, the parties entered into a valid, enforceable contract.

INTERPRETATION Consideration can either be a legal benefit to the promisor or a legal detriment to the promisee.

CRITICAL THINKING QUESTION Would it have been preferable to have this continuing agreement put in writing? Explain.

Adequacy

Legal sufficiency has nothing to do with **adequacy of consideration**. The items or actions that the parties agree to exchange do not need to have the same value. Rather, the law will regard the consideration as adequate if the parties have freely agreed to the exchange. The requirement of legally sufficient consideration is, therefore, not at all concerned with whether the bargain was good or bad or whether one party received disproportionately more or less than what he gave or promised in exchange. (Such facts, however, may be relevant to the availability of certain defenses—such as fraud, duress, or undue influence—or certain remedies—such as specific performance.) The requirement of legally sufficient consideration is simply (1) that the parties have agreed to an exchange and (2) that, with respect to each party, the subject matter exchanged, or promised in exchange, either imposed a legal detriment on the promisee or conferred a legal benefit on the promisor. If the purported consideration is clearly without value, however, such that the transaction is a sham, many courts would hold that consideration is lacking.

Unilateral Contracts

In a unilateral contract, a promise is exchanged for a completed act or a forbearance to act. Because only one promise exists, only one party, the *offeror*, makes a promise, and is therefore the **promisor** while the other party, the *offeree*, is the person receiving the promise and, thus, is the **promisee**. For example, A promises to pay B $2,000 if B paints A's house. B paints A's house.

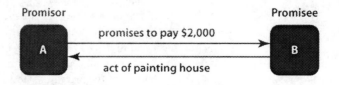

A's promise is binding only if it is supported by consideration consisting of either a legal detriment to B, the promisee (offeree), or a legal benefit to A, the promisor (offeror). B's painting the house is a legal detriment to B, the promisee, because she was under no prior legal duty to paint A's house. Also, B's painting of A's house is a legal benefit to A, the promisor, because A had no prior legal right to have his house painted by B.

A unilateral contract may also consist of a promise exchanged for a forbearance. To illustrate, A negligently injures B, for which B may recover damages in a tort action. A promises B $5,000 if B forbears from bringing suit. B accepts by not suing.

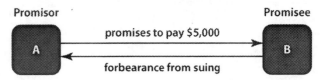

A's promise to pay B $5,000 is binding because it is supported by consideration; B, the promisee (offeree), has incurred a legal detriment by refraining from bringing suit, which he was under no prior legal obligation to refrain from doing. A, the promisor (offeror), has received a legal benefit because she had no prior legal right to B's forbearance from bringing suit.

Bilateral Contracts

In a bilateral contract there is an exchange of promises. Thus, each party is *both* a promisor and a promisee. For example, if A (the offeror) promises (offers) to purchase an automobile from B for $20,000, and B (the offeree) promises to sell the automobile to A for $20,000 (accepts the offer), the following relationship exists:

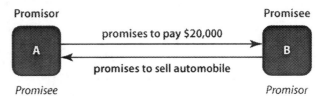

A (offeror) as promisor: A's promise (the offer) to pay B $20,000 is binding if that promise is supported by legal consideration from B (offeror), which may consist of either a legal detriment to B, the *promisee*, or a legal benefit to A, the *promisor*. B's promise to sell A the automobile is a legal detriment to B because he was under no prior legal duty to sell the automobile to A. Moreover, B's promise is also a legal benefit to A because A had no prior legal right to that automobile. Consequently, A's promise to pay $20,000 to B is supported by consideration and is enforceable.

B (offeree) as promisor: For B's promise (the acceptance) to sell the automobile to A to be binding, it likewise must be supported by consideration from A (offeror), which may be either a legal detriment to A, the *promisee*, or a legal benefit to B, the *promisor*. A's promise to pay B $20,000 is a legal detriment to A because he was under no prior legal duty to pay $20,000 to B. At the same time, A's promise is also a legal benefit to B because B had no prior legal right to the $20,000. Thus, B's promise to sell the automobile is supported by consideration and is enforceable.

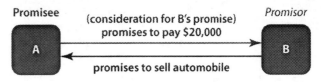

Consideration in Unilateral and Bilateral Contracts

Type of Contract	Offer	Acceptance	Consideration
Unilateral	Promise by A	Performance of requested act or forbearance by B	*Promise* by A *Performance* of requested act or forbearance by B
Bilateral	Promise by A	Return promise by B to perform requested act or forbearance	*Promise* by A *Return promise* by B to perform requested act or forbearance

To summarize, for A's *promise* to B to be binding, it must be supported by legally sufficient consideration, which requires that the promise A receives from B in exchange either provides a legal benefit to A or constitutes a legal detriment to B. B's return promise to A must also be supported by consideration. Thus, in a bilateral contract, each promise is the consideration for the other, a relationship that has been referred to as **mutuality of obligation**. A general consequence of mutuality of obligation is that each promisor in a bilateral contract must be bound or neither is bound. See Concept Review 12.1 for an overview of consideration in both unilateral and bilateral contracts. Also see the Ethical Dilemma for a situation dealing with the disputed enforceability of a promise.

Illusory Promises

Words of promise that make the performance of the purported promisor entirely optional do not constitute a promise at all. Consequently, they cannot serve as consideration. In this section, we will distinguish such illusory promises from promises that do impose obligations of performance upon the promisor and thus can be legally sufficient consideration.

An **illusory promise** is a statement that is in the form of a promise but imposes no obligation upon the maker of the statement. An illusory promise is not consideration for a return promise. Thus, a statement committing the promisor to purchase such quantity of goods as he may "desire" or "want" or "wish to buy" is an illusory promise because its performance is entirely optional. For example, if ExxonMobil offers to sell to Gasco as many barrels of oil as Gasco shall choose at $40 per barrel, there is no consideration. An offer containing such a promise, although accepted by the offeree, does not create a contract because the promise is illusory—Gasco's performance is entirely optional and no constraint is placed on its freedom. It is not bound to do anything, nor can ExxonMobil reasonably expect it to do anything. Thus, Gasco, by its promise, suffers no legal detriment and confers no legal benefit.

Output and Requirements Contracts   The agreement of a seller to sell her entire production to a particular purchaser is called an **output contract**. It gives the seller an ensured market for her product. Conversely, a purchaser's agreement to purchase from a particular seller all the materials of a particular kind that the purchaser needs is called a **requirements contract**. It ensures the buyer of a ready source of inventory or supplies. These contracts are *not* illusory. The buyer under a requirements contract does not promise to buy as much as she desires to buy, but to buy as much as she *needs*. Similarly, under an output contract, the seller promises to sell to the buyer the seller's entire production, not merely as much as the seller desires.

Furthermore, the Code imposes a good faith limitation upon the quantity to be sold or purchased under an output or requirements contract. Thus, this type of contract involves such actual output or requirements as may occur in good faith, except that no quantity unreasonably disproportionate to any stated estimate or, in the absence of a stated estimate, to any normal prior output or requirements may be tendered or demanded. Therefore, after contracting to sell to Adler, Inc., its entire output, Benevito Company cannot increase its production from one eight-hour shift per day to three eight-hour shifts per day.

Illusory promise
promise imposing no obligation on the promisor

PRACTICAL ADVICE
Because an agreement under which one party may perform at his discretion is not a binding contract, be sure that you make a promise and receive a promise that is not optional.

Output contract
agreement to sell all of one's production

Requirements contract
agreement to buy all of one's needs

PRACTICAL ADVICE
If you use an output or requirements contract, be sure to act in good faith and do not take unfair advantage of the situation.

Exclusive dealing
sole right to sell goods in a
defined market

Exclusive Dealing Contracts An **exclusive dealing** agreement is a contract in which a manufacturer of goods grants to a distributor an exclusive right to sell its products in a designated market. Unless otherwise agreed, an implied obligation is imposed on the manufacturer to use its best efforts to supply the goods and on the distributor to use her best efforts to promote their sale. These implied obligations are sufficient consideration to bind both parties to the exclusive dealing contract.

Conditional promise
obligations contingent upon
a stated event

Conditional Promises A **conditional promise** is a promise the performance of which depends upon the happening or nonhappening of an event not certain to occur (the condition). A conditional promise is sufficient consideration *unless* the promisor knows at the time of making the promise that the condition cannot occur.

Thus, if Joanne offers to pay Barry $8,000 for Barry's automobile, provided that Joanne receives such amount as an inheritance from the estate of her deceased uncle, and Barry accepts the offer, the duty of Joanne to pay $8,000 to Barry is *conditioned* on her receiving $8,000 from her deceased uncle's estate. The consideration moving from Barry to Joanne is the transfer of title to the automobile. The consideration moving from Joanne to Barry is the promise of $8,000 subject to the condition.

Preexisting Public Obligations

**Preexisting public
obligations**
performance of public duties
such as those imposed by
tort or criminal law is neither
a legal detriment nor a legal
benefit

The law does not regard the performance of, or the promise to perform, a preexisting legal duty, public or private, as either a legal detriment or a legal benefit. A **public duty** does not arise out of a contract; rather, it is imposed on members of society by force of the common law or by statute. Illustrations, as found in the law of torts, include the duty not to commit assault, battery, false imprisonment, or defamation. The criminal law also imposes many public duties. Thus, if Norton promises to pay Holmes, the village ruffian, $100 not to injure him, Norton's promise is unenforceable because both tort and criminal law impose a preexisting public obligation on Holmes to refrain from such abuse.

Public officials, such as the mayor of a city, members of a city council, police, and firefighters, are under a preexisting obligation to perform their duties by virtue of their public office. See *Denney v. Reppert* below.

**Preexisting contractual
duty**
performance of a preexisting
contractual duty is not
consideration

The performance of, or the promise to perform, a **preexisting contractual duty**, a duty the terms of which are neither doubtful nor the subject of honest dispute, is also legally insufficient consideration because the doing of what one is legally bound to do is neither a detriment to a promisee nor a benefit to the promisor. For example, if Anita employs Ben for one year at a salary of $1,000 per month, and at the end of six months promises Ben that in addition to the salary she will pay Ben $3,000 if Ben remains on the job for the remainder of the period originally agreed on, Anita's promise is not binding for lack of legally sufficient consideration. However, if Ben's duties were by agreement changed in nature or amount, Anita's promise would be binding because Ben's new duties are a legal detriment to Ben and a legal benefit to Anita.

The following case deals with both preexisting public and contractual obligations.

Denney v. Reppert
Court of Appeals of Kentucky, 1968
432 S.W.2d 647
http://scholar.google.com/scholar_case?case=14895092933351248292&q=432+S.W.2d+647&hl=en&as_sdt=2,34

FACTS In June, three armed men entered and robbed the First State Bank of Eubank, Kentucky, of $30,000. Acting on information supplied by four employees of the bank, Denney, Buis, McCollum, and Snyder, three law enforcement officials apprehended the robbers. Two of the arresting officers, Godby and Simms, were state policemen, and the third, Reppert, was a deputy sheriff in a neighboring county. All seven claimed the reward for the apprehension and conviction of the bank robbers. The trial court held that only Reppert was entitled to the reward, and Denney appealed.

DECISION Judgment affirmed.

OPINION In general, when a reward is offered to the general public for the performance of some specified act, the reward may be claimed by the person who performs that act unless that person is an agent, employee, or public official acting within the scope of his employment or official duties. For this reason, the bank employees cannot recover. At the time of the robbery, they were under a duty to protect the bank's resources and to safeguard the institution furnishing them employment. Thus, in assisting the police officers in apprehending the bank robbers, the bank employees were merely doing their duty and, therefore, are not entitled to share in the reward.

Similarly, the state policemen, Godby and Simms, were exercising their duty as police officers in arresting the bank robbers and, thus, are not entitled to share in the reward. Reppert, on the other hand, was out of his jurisdiction at the time and, thus, was under no legal duty to arrest the bank robbers.

INTERPRETATION The law does not regard the performance of a preexisting duty as either a legal detriment or a legal benefit.

ETHICAL QUESTION Did the court treat all the parties fairly? Explain.

CRITICAL THINKING QUESTION Do you agree with the preexisting duty rule? Explain.

Modification of a preexisting contract

under the common law, a modification of a preexisting contract must be supported by mutual consideration; under the Uniform Commercial Code a contract can be modified without new consideration

PRACTICAL ADVICE

If you modify a contract governed by the common law, be sure to provide additional consideration to make the other party's new promise enforceable.

Modification of a Preexisting Contract A **modification of a preexisting contract** occurs when the parties to the contract mutually agree to change one or more of its terms. Under the common law, as shown in the following case, a modification of an existing contract must be supported by mutual consideration to be enforceable. In other words, the modification must be supported by some new consideration beyond that which is already owed under the original contract. Thus, there must be a separate and distinct modification contract. For example, Diane and Fred agree that Diane shall put in a gravel driveway for Fred at a cost of $2,000. Subsequently, Fred agrees to pay an additional $3,000 if Diane will blacktop the driveway. Because Diane was not bound by the original contract to provide blacktop, she would incur a legal detriment in doing so and is therefore entitled to the additional $3,000. Similarly, consideration may consist of the promisee's refraining from exercising a legal right.

The Code has modified the common law rule for contract modification by providing that the parties can effectively modify a contract for the sale of goods without new consideration, provided they both intend to modify the contract and act in good faith. Moreover, the Restatement has moved toward this position by providing that a modification of an executory contract is binding if it is fair and equitable in the light of surrounding facts that the parties had not anticipated when the contract was made. Figure 12-1 demonstrates when consideration is required to modify an existing contract.

Figure 12-1 Modification of a Preexisting Contract

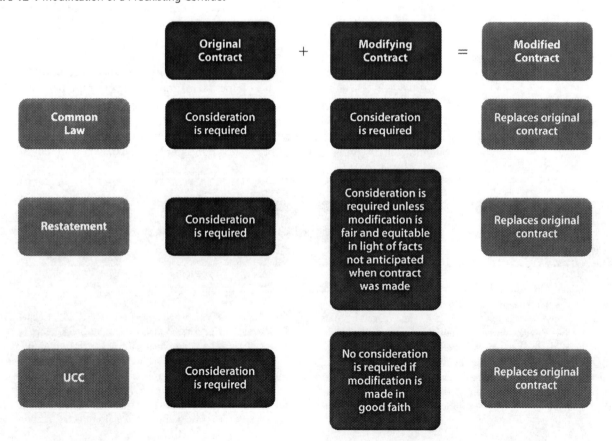

New England Rock Services, Inc. v. Empire Paving, Inc.
Appellate Court of Connecticut, 1999
53 Conn.App. 771, 731 A.2d 784, cert. denied, 250 Conn. 921, 738 A.2d 658
http://scholar.google.com/scholar_case?case=2815205762460431873&q=731+A.2d+784&hl=en&as_sdt=2,34

FACTS On October 26, 1995, the defendant, Empire Paving, Inc., entered into a contract with Rock Services under which Rock Services would provide drilling and blasting services as a subcontractor on the Niles Hill Road sewer project on which Empire was the general contractor and the city of New London was the owner. Rock Services was to be paid an agreed-upon price of $29 per cubic yard with an estimated amount of five thousand cubic yards, or on a time and materials basis, whichever was less. From the outset, Rock Services experienced problems on the job, the primary problem being the presence of a heavy concentration of water on the site. The water problem hindered Rock Services' ability to complete its work as anticipated. It is the responsibility of the general contractor to control the water on the work site and, on this particular job, Empire failed to control the water on the site properly. Rock Services attempted alternative methods of dealing with the problem, but was prevented from using them by the city. Thereafter, in order to complete its work, Rock Services was compelled to use a more costly and time-consuming method.

In late November 1995, Rock Services advised Empire that it would be unable to complete the work as anticipated because of the conditions at the site and requested that Empire agree to amend the contract to allow Rock Services to complete the project on a time and materials basis. On December 8, Empire signed a purchase order that so modified the original agreement. Upon completion of the work, Empire refused to pay Rock Services for the remaining balance due on the time and materials agreement in the amount of $58,686.63, and Rock Services instituted this action. The trial court concluded that the modified agreement was valid and ruled in favor of Rock Services. Empire brings this appeal.

DECISION Judgment in favor of Rock Services affirmed.

OPINION The general rule of contracts is that in the absence of consideration an executory promise is unenforceable. A modification of an agreement must be supported by valid consideration and requires a party to do, or promise to do, something further than, or different from, that which he is already bound to do. So, when a party negotiates a modification resulting in greater pay for the same, already-owed work, that modification is not valid without additional consideration. However, an exception to the preexisting duty rule occurs:

> [W]here a contract must be performed under burdensome conditions not anticipated, and not within the contemplation of the parties at the time when the contract was made, and the promisee measures up to the right standard of honesty and fair dealing, and agrees, in view of the changed conditions, to pay what is then reasonable, just, and fair, such new contract is not without consideration within the meaning of that term, either in law or in equity.

Empire argues that the water conditions on the site cannot qualify as a new circumstance that was not anticipated at the time the original contract was signed. The court, however, ruled that Empire's duty to control or remove the water on the job site arose in accordance with the custom and practice in the industry and, therefore, Empire's failure to control or remove the water on the site constituted a new circumstance that Rock Services did not anticipate at the time the original contract was signed.

INTERPRETATION The Restatement provides that a modification of an executory contract is binding if it is fair and equitable in the light of surrounding facts that the parties had not anticipated when the contract was made.

CRITICAL THINKING QUESTION Which rule for contract modification do you believe is best: the common law, the Restatement's, or the Uniform Commercial Code's? Why?

Substituted contract
parties rescind their original contract and enter into a new one

Settlement of an undisputed debt
payment of a lesser sum of money to discharge an undisputed debt does not constitute legally sufficient consideration

Undisputed debt
obligation whose existence and amount are not contested

Substituted Contracts A **substituted contract** results when the parties to a contract mutually agree to rescind their original contract and enter into a new one. This situation actually involves three separate contracts: the original contract, the contract of rescission, and the substitute contract. Substituted contracts are perfectly valid, allowing the parties to effectively discharge the original contract and to impose obligations under the new one. The rescission is binding in that, as long as each party still had rights under the original contract, each has, by giving up those rights, provided consideration to the other.

Settlement of an Undisputed Debt An **undisputed debt** is an obligation that is not contested as to its existence or its amount. Under the common law, the payment of a lesser sum of money than is owed in consideration of a promise to discharge a fully matured, undisputed debt is legally insufficient to support the promise of discharge. To illustrate, assume that Barbara owes Arnold $100, and in consideration of Barbara's paying him $50, Arnold agrees to discharge the debt. In a subsequent suit by Arnold against Barbara to recover the remaining $50, at common law Arnold is entitled to a judgment for $50 on the ground that Arnold's promise of discharge is not binding, because Barbara's payment of $50 was no legal detriment to the promisee, Barbara, because she was under a *preexisting legal obligation* to pay that much and more. Consequently, the consideration for Arnold's promise of discharge was legally insufficient, and Arnold is not bound by his promise. If, however, Arnold had accepted from Barbara any new or different consideration, such as the sum of $40 and a fountain pen worth $10 or less, or even the fountain pen with no payment of money, in full satisfaction of the $100 debt, the consideration moving from Barbara would be legally sufficient because Barbara was under no legal obligation to give a fountain pen to Arnold. In this example, consideration would also exist if Arnold had agreed to accept $50 *before* the debt became due, in full satisfaction of the debt. Barbara was under no legal obligation to pay any of the debt before its due date. Consequently, Barbara's early payment would constitute a legal detriment to Barbara as well as a legal benefit to Arnold. The common law is not concerned with the amount of the discount, because that is simply a question of adequacy. Likewise, Barbara's payment of a lesser amount on the due date at an agreed-upon different place of payment would be legally sufficient consideration. The Restatement, however, requires that the new consideration "differ[s] from what was required by the duty in a way which reflects more than a pretense of bargain."

Settlement of a disputed debt

payment of a lesser sum of money to discharge a disputed debt is legally sufficient consideration

Disputed debt

obligation whose existence or amount is contested

Settlement of a Disputed Debt   A **disputed debt** is an obligation whose existence or amount is contested. A promise to settle a validly disputed claim in exchange for an agreed payment or other performance is supported by consideration. Where the dispute is based on contentions without merit or not made in good faith, the debtor's surrender of such contentions is not a legal detriment to the claimant. The Restatement adopts a different position by providing that the settlement of a claim that proves invalid is consideration if at the time of the settlement (1) the claimant honestly believed that the claim was valid or (2) the claim was in fact doubtful because of uncertainty as to the facts or the law.

For example, where a person has requested professional services from an accountant or a lawyer and no agreement has been made about the amount of the fee to be charged, the client has a legal obligation to pay the reasonable value of the services performed. Because no definite amount was agreed on, the client's obligation is uncertain. When the accountant or lawyer sends the client a bill for services rendered, even though the amount stated in the bill is an estimate of the reasonable value of the services, the debt does not become undisputed until and unless the client agrees to pay the amount of the bill. If the client honestly disputes the amount that is owed and offers in full settlement an amount less than the bill, acceptance of the lesser amount by the accountant or lawyer discharges the debt. Thus, if Andy sends to Bess, an accountant, a check for $120 in full payment of his debt to Bess for services rendered, which services Andy considered worthless but for which Bess billed Andy $600, Bess's acceptance (cashing) of the check releases Andy from any further liability. Andy has given up his right to dispute the billing further, and Bess has forfeited her right to further collection. Thus, there is mutuality of consideration.

PRACTICAL ADVICE

If your contract is validly disputed, carefully consider whether to accept any payment marked "payment in full."

BARGAINED-FOR EXCHANGE

Bargained-for exchange

mutually agreed-upon exchange

The central idea behind consideration is that the parties have intentionally entered into a **bargained-for exchange** with each other and have each given to the other something in a mutually agreed-upon exchange for his promise or performance. Thus, a promise to give someone a birthday present is without consideration, because the promisor received nothing in exchange for her promise of a present.

PRACTICAL ADVICE

Because a promise to make a gift is generally not legally enforceable, obtain delivery of something that shows your control or ownership of the item to make it an executed gift.

Past Consideration

Past consideration

unbargained-for past events

Consideration, as previously defined, is the inducement for a promise or performance. The element of exchange is absent where a promise is given for an act already done. Therefore, unbargained-for past events are not consideration, despite their designation as **past consideration**. A promise made on account of something that the promisee has already done is not enforceable. For example, Diana installs Tom's complex new car stereo and speakers. Tom subsequently promises to reimburse Diana for her expenses, but his promise is not binding because there is no bargained-for exchange. See *DiLorenzo v. Valve and Primer Corporation* later in this chapter.

Third Parties

Consideration to support a promise may be given to a person other than the promisor if the promisor bargains for that exchange. For example, A promises to pay B $15 if B delivers a specified book to C.

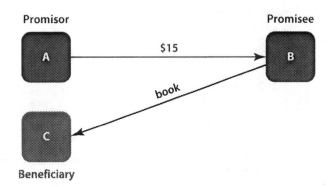

A's promise is binding because B incurred a legal detriment by delivering the book to C, because B was under no prior legal obligation to do so, and A had no prior legal right to have the book given to C. A and B have bargained for A to pay B $15 in return for B's delivering the book to C. A's promise to pay $15 is also consideration for B's promise to give C the book.

Conversely, consideration may be given by some person other than the promisee. For example, A promises to pay B $25 in return for D's promise to give a radio to A. A's promise to pay $25 to B is consideration for D's promise to give a radio to A and *vice versa*.

CONTRACTS WITHOUT CONSIDERATION

Certain transactions are enforceable even though they are not supported by consideration.

Promises to Perform Prior Unenforceable Obligations

In certain circumstances the courts will enforce new promises to perform an obligation that originally was not enforceable or that has become unenforceable by operation of law. These situations include promises to pay debts barred by the statute of limitations, debts discharged in bankruptcy, and voidable obligations. In addition, some courts will enforce promises to pay moral obligations.

Promise to Pay Debt Barred by the Statute of Limitations Every state has a **statute of limitations** stating that legal actions to enforce a debt must be brought within a prescribed period of time after the rights to bring the action arose. Actions not begun within the specified period—such periods vary among the states and also with the nature of the legal action—will be dismissed.

An exception to the past consideration rule extends to promises to pay all or part of a contractual or quasi-contractual debt barred by the statute of limitations. The new promise is binding according to its terms, without consideration, for a second statutory period. Any recovery under the new promise is limited to the terms contained in the new promise. Most states require that new promises falling under this rule, except those partially paid, must be in writing to be enforceable.

Promise to Pay Debt Discharged in Bankruptcy A promise to pay a debt that has been discharged in bankruptcy is also enforceable without consideration. The Bankruptcy Code, however, imposes a number of requirements that must be met before such a promise may be enforced. These requirements are discussed in Chapter 38.

Voidable Promises Another promise that is enforceable without new consideration is a new promise to perform a voidable obligation that has not previously been avoided. The power of avoidance may be based on lack of capacity, fraud, misrepresentation, duress, undue influence, or mistake. For instance, a promise to perform an antecedent obligation made by a minor upon

Promise to pay debt barred by the statute of limitations
a new promise by the debtor to pay the debt renews the running of the statute of limitations for a second statutory period

Statute of limitation
time period within which a lawsuit must be initiated

Promise to pay debt discharged in bankruptcy
may be enforceable without consideration

Voidable promises
a new promise to perform a voidable obligation that has not been previously avoided is enforceable

reaching the age of majority is enforceable without new consideration. To be enforceable, the promise itself must not be voidable. For example, if the new promise is made without knowledge of the original fraud or by a minor before reaching the age of majority, then the new promise is not enforceable.

Moral obligation

a promise made to satisfy a preexisting moral obligation is generally unenforceable for lack of consideration

Moral Obligation Under the common law and in most states, a promise made to satisfy a preexisting moral obligation is made for past consideration and therefore is unenforceable for lack of consideration. Instances involving such moral obligations include promises to pay another for board and lodging previously furnished to one's needy relative and promises to pay debts owed by a relative.

The Restatement and a minority of states recognize moral obligations as consideration. The Restatement provides that a promise made for "a benefit previously received by the promisor from the promisee is binding to the extent necessary to prevent injustice." For instance, under the Restatement, Tim's subsequent promise to Donna to reimburse her for expenses she incurred in rendering emergency services to Tim's son is binding even though it is not supported by new consideration.

Promissory estoppel

doctrine that prohibits a party from denying his promise when the promisee takes action or forbearance to his detriment reasonably based upon the promise

Promissory Estoppel

As discussed in Chapter 9, in certain circumstances in which there has been detrimental reliance, the courts enforce noncontractual promises under the doctrine of promissory estoppel. When applicable, the doctrine makes gratuitous promises enforceable to the extent necessary to avoid injustice. The doctrine applies when a promise that the promisor should reasonably expect to induce detrimental reliance does induce such action or forbearance.

Promissory estoppel does not mean that a promise given without consideration is binding simply because it is followed by a change of position on the part of the promisee. Such a change of position in justifiable reliance on the promise creates liability if injustice can be avoided only by the enforcement of the promise. For example, Ann promises Larry not to foreclose for a period of six months on a mortgage Ann owns on Larry's land. Larry then changes his position by spending $100,000 to construct a building on the land. Ann's promise not to foreclose is binding on her under the doctrine of promissory estoppel.

The most common application of the doctrine of promissory estoppel is to charitable subscriptions. Numerous churches, memorials, college buildings, stadiums, hospitals, and other structures used for religious, educational, or charitable purposes have been built with the assistance of contributions made through fulfillment of pledges or promises to contribute to particular worthwhile causes. Although the pledgor regards herself as making a gift for a charitable purpose and gift promises tend not to be enforceable, the courts have generally enforced charitable subscription promises. Although various reasons and theories have been advanced in support of liability, the one most commonly accepted is that the subscription has induced a change of position by the promisee (the church, school, or charitable organization) in reliance on the promise. The Restatement, moreover, has relaxed the reliance requirement for charitable subscriptions so that actual reliance need not be shown; the probability of reliance is sufficient.

DiLorenzo v. Valve & Primer Corporation
Appellate Court of Illinois, First District, Fifth Division, 2004
807 N.E.2d 673, 283 Ill.Dec. 68
http://www.state.il.us/court/Opinions/AppellateCourt/2003/1stDistrict/June/Html/1012803.htm

---

FACTS DiLorenzo, a forty-year employee of Valve & Primer, was also an officer, director, and shareholder of one hundred shares of stock. DiLorenzo claims that in 1987 Valve & Primer offered him a ten-year stock option that would allow DiLorenzo to purchase an additional three hundred shares at the fixed price of $250 per share. DiLorenzo claims that in reliance on that employment agreement, he stayed in his job for over nine additional years and did not follow up on any of several recruitment offers from other companies. Valve & Primer claims the 1987 employment agreement between it and DiLorenzo did not contain a stock purchase

agreement. The only purported proof of the agreement is an unsigned copy of board meeting minutes of which DiLorenzo had the only copy.

In January 1996, DiLorenzo entered into a semi-retirement agreement with Valve & Primer, and he attempted to tender his remaining one hundred shares pursuant to a stock redemption agreement. Shortly thereafter, Valve & Primer fired DiLorenzo. DiLorenzo argued before the trial court that, even if the purported agreement was not found to be valid, it should be enforced on promissory estoppel grounds. Valve & Primer's moved for summary judgment, which the trial court granted for lack of consideration. The trial court denied the promissory estoppel claim because of insufficient reliance. DiLorenzo appealed.

DECISION The trial court's grant of Valve & Primer's motion for summary judgment is affirmed.

OPINION Whether the 1987 corporate minutes are authentic is not an issue on appeal. The purported minutes of the June 8, 1987, special meeting contain the following relevant language:

> That in order to retain and reward such dedication ... that Ralph DiLorenzo be given an option to purchase additional shares not to exceed 300. Said option to be exercised within 10 years from below date at the price of $250.00 per share.

The first question is whether there was consideration for the stock options. DiLorenzo could have exercised the option the moment it was purportedly made, then immediately quit, thereby giving nothing to the employer. Though the exercise of the option would require the transfer of money for the stock, the option itself carries with it no detriment to DiLorenzo. Therefore, there was no consideration for the option.

The second issue is whether DiLorenzo is entitled to the value of the shares of stock based upon the theory of promissory estoppel.

DiLorenzo argues that he detrimentally relied upon Valve & Primer's promise in that he worked at Valve & Primer for an additional period in excess of nine years in reliance on the stock option agreement.

There is nothing in the language of the corporate minutes or any other source to be found in this record to suggest that Valve & Primer conditioned the alleged stock option on DiLorenzo's promise to remain in his employment. Since the corporate minutes lack a mandatory obligation on which DiLorenzo could have reasonably detrimentally relied, and he could have elected to buy the shares of stock immediately, DiLorenzo's decision to remain on the job for the additional period of over nine years must be viewed as a voluntary act. Under those circumstances, promissory estoppel would not apply.

INTERPRETATION Past consideration is not legal consideration to support a promise; promissory estoppel requires detrimental reliance.

ETHICAL QUESTION Did the parties act ethically? Explain.

CRITICAL THINKING QUESTION What would have satisfied the consideration requirement in this case?

Contracts under seal
where still recognized, the seal acts as a substitute for consideration

Contracts under Seal

Under the common law, when a person desired to bind himself by bond, deed, or solemn promise, he executed his promise under seal. He did not have to sign the document; rather, his delivery of a document to which he had affixed his seal was sufficient. No consideration for his promise was necessary. In some states a promise under seal is still binding without consideration.

Nevertheless, most states have abolished by statute the distinction between contracts under seal and written unsealed contracts. In these states, the seal is no longer recognized as a substitute for consideration. The Code also has adopted this position, specifically eliminating the use of seals in contracts for the sale of goods.

Promises Made Enforceable by Statute

Some gratuitous promises that otherwise would be unenforceable have been made binding by statute. Most significant among these are (1) contract modifications, (2) renunciations, and (3) irrevocable offers.

Contract Modifications As mentioned previously, the Uniform Commercial Code (UCC) has abandoned the common law rule requiring that a modification of an existing contract be supported by consideration to be valid. Instead, the Code provides that a contract for the sale of goods can be effectively modified without new consideration, provided the modification is made in good faith.

Renunciations Under the Code, any claim or right arising out of an alleged breach of contract can be discharged in whole or in part without consideration by a written waiver or renunciation signed and delivered by the aggrieved party. Under the Revised UCC Article 1, a claim or right arising out of an alleged breach may be discharged in whole or in part without consideration by agreement of the aggrieved party in an authenticated record. This section is subject to the obligation of good faith and, as with all sections of Article 1, applies to a transaction to the extent that it is governed by one of the other article of the UCC.

Firm Offers Under the Code, a firm offer, a written offer signed by a merchant offeror to buy or sell goods, is not revocable for lack of consideration during the time within which it is stated to be open, not to exceed three months or, if no time is stated, for a reasonable time. For a summary of consideration, see Figure 12-2.

Figure 12-2 Consideration

Ethical Dilemma

Should a Spouse's Promise Be Legally Binding?

Facts Joan Kantor is a social worker for the employees of Surf & Co., a towel manufacturer. Stan Koronetsky, a Surf employee, has confided the following problems to Kantor.

Koronetsky and his wife, Paula, have been married for ten years. Koronetsky states that three years ago his wife was unfaithful and Koronetsky began a divorce proceeding. When Paula Koronetsky promised to refrain from further infidelity and to attend marital counseling sessions, Koronetsky agreed to stop the divorce proceeding. However, although Stan dropped the divorce proceeding, his wife never attended counseling.

Koronetsky is also upset because he and his wife had agreed that she would attend medical school while he worked to support her. In exchange for his promise to put her through medical school, Paula promised that she would support him while he obtained his MBA degree. But after Paula became a doctor, she refused to support him; consequently, Stan never got his master's degree.

Social, Policy, and Ethical Considerations

1. What should Joan Kantor do in this situation? What is the scope of her counseling responsibilities?

2. Should agreements between married parties be enforced in a court of law? If so, what types of agreements should be enforceable?

3. What are the individual interests at stake in this situation? Is it reasonable to assume that spouses make many private agreements, and that generally these agreements are made without the intention of their being legally binding?

BUSINESS LAW *IN ACTION*

Computer Castle agreed to custom configure seventy-five personal computers and deliver them to Delber Data Corp. within ninety days. The price of each computer was $899, and Delber Data also agreed to a "Service-Pak" extended warranty plan for each unit purchased.

Computer Castle's employees worked diligently to get the order ready and had only five computers left to configure when a next-generation operating system hit the market. Prices for computers carrying the old operating system plummeted. Delber Data quickly sought to change its order, but Computer Castle had already built nearly all the computers. Delber admitted it could still use the computers with the old

operating system but felt that at a minimum Computer Castle should grant a price concession.

The computers Delber Data had agreed to buy could now be sold for only $699 each at most. Not wanting to lose a possible long-term business relationship, Computer Castle agreed to lower the price of the Delber Data computers to $799 each. Computer Castle faxed a short note to Delber confirming the new price. Thus, Delber Data has given no consideration to support the new contract price—indeed Delber is getting the very same computers for *less* than it originally agreed to pay.

Whether Computer Castle's price reduction will be enforceable depends on what

law governs the parties' contract. Though Delber did purchase the warranty plan, a service, the contract is clearly one for the sale of goods—the predominant purpose of the contract is the purchase of configured personal computers. The price reduction, then, is a modification of a sales contract and is governed by the Uniform Commercial Code. Despite the lack of consideration, the Code permits enforcement of this contract modification, as the change was agreed to by both parties and sought by Delber in good faith, here based on the unanticipated emergence of newer technology.

© Cengage Learning 2013

CHAPTER SUMMARY

Consideration	**Definition** the inducement to enter into a contract
	Elements legal sufficiency and bargained-for exchange
Legal Sufficiency of Consideration	**Definition** consists of either a benefit to the promisor or a detriment to the promisee
	• *Legal Benefit* obtaining something to which one had no prior legal right
	• *Legal Detriment* doing an act one is not legally obligated to do or not doing an act that one has a legal right to do

Adequacy of Consideration not required where the parties have freely agreed to the exchange

Illusory Promise promise that imposes no obligation on the promisor; the following promises are not illusory

- *Output Contract* agreement to sell all of one's production to a single buyer
- *Requirements Contract* agreement to buy all of one's needs from a single producer
- *Exclusive Dealing Contract* grant to a franchisee or licensee by a manufacturer of the sole right to sell goods in a defined market
- *Conditional Contract* a contract in which the obligations are contingent upon the occurrence of a stated event

Preexisting Public Obligations public duties such as those imposed by tort or criminal law are neither a legal detriment nor a legal benefit

Preexisting Contractual Obligation performance of a preexisting contractual duty is not consideration

- *Modification of a Preexisting Contract* under the common law a modification of a preexisting contract must be supported by mutual consideration; under the Code a contract can be modified without new consideration
- *Substituted Contracts* the parties agree to rescind their original contract and to enter into a new one; rescission and new contract are supported by consideration
- *Settlement of an Undisputed Debt* payment of a lesser sum of money to discharge an undisputed debt (one whose existence and amount are not contested) does not constitute legally sufficient consideration
- *Settlement of a Disputed Debt* payment of a lesser sum of money to discharge a disputed debt (one whose existence or amount is contested) is legally sufficient consideration

Bargained-for Exchange

Definition a mutually agreed-upon exchange

Past Consideration an act done before the contract is made is not consideration

Contracts without Consideration

Promises to Perform Prior Unenforceable Obligations

- *Promise to Pay Debt Barred by the Statute of Limitations* a new promise by the debtor to pay the debt renews the running of the statute of limitations for a second statutory period
- *Promise to Pay Debt Discharged in Bankruptcy* may be enforceable without consideration
- *Voidable Promises* a new promise to perform a voidable obligation that has not been previously avoided is enforceable
- *Moral Obligation* a promise made to satisfy a preexisting moral obligation is generally unenforceable for lack of consideration

Promissory Estoppel doctrine that prohibits a party from denying his promise when the promisee takes action or forbearance to his detriment reasonably based upon the promise

Contracts under Seal where still recognized, the seal acts as a substitute for consideration

Promises Made Enforceable by Statute some gratuitous promises have been made enforceable by statute; the Code makes enforceable (1) contract modifications, (2) renunciations, and (3) firm offers

QUESTIONS

1. In consideration of $1,800 paid to him by Joyce, Hill gave Joyce a written option to purchase his house for $180,000 on or before April 1. Prior to April 1, Hill verbally agreed to extend the option until July 1. On May 18, Hill, known to Joyce, sold the house to Gray, who was ignorant of the unrecorded option. On May 20 Joyce sent an acceptance to Hill who received it on May 25. Is there a contract between Joyce and Hill? Explain.

2. a. Ann owed $2,500 to Barry for services Barry rendered to Ann. The debt was due June 30, 2011. In March 2012, the debt was still unpaid. Barry was in urgent need of ready cash and told Ann that if she would pay $1,500 on the debt at once, Barry would release her from the balance. Ann paid $1,500 and stated to Barry that all claims had been paid in full. In August 2012, Barry demanded the unpaid balance and subsequently sued Ann for $1,000. Result?

   b. Modify the facts in (a) by assuming that Barry gave Ann a written receipt stating that all claims had been paid in full. Result?

c. Modify the facts in (a) by assuming that Ann owed Barry the $2,500 on Ann's purchase of a motorcycle from Barry. Result?

3. a. Judy orally promises her daughter, Liza, that she will give her a tract of land for her home. Liza, as intended by Judy, gives up her homestead and takes possession of the land. Liza lives there for six months and starts construction of a home. Is Judy bound to convey the real estate?

b. Ralph, knowing that his son, Ed, desires to purchase a tract of land, promises to give him the $25,000 he needs for the purchase. Ed, relying on this promise, buys an option on the tract of land. Can Ralph rescind his promise?

4. George owed Keith $800 on a personal loan. Neither the amount of the debt nor George's liability to pay the $800 was disputed. Keith had also rendered services as a carpenter to George without any agreement as to the price to be paid. When the work was completed, an honest and reasonable difference of opinion developed between George and Keith with respect to the value of Keith's services. Upon receiving Keith's bill for the carpentry services for $600, George mailed in a properly stamped and addressed envelope his check for $800 to Keith. In an accompanying letter, George stated that the enclosed check was in full settlement of both claims. Keith endorsed and cashed the check. Thereafter, Keith unsuccessfully sought to collect from George an alleged unpaid balance of $600. May Keith recover the $600 from George?

5. The Snyder Mfg. Co., being a large user of coal, entered into separate contracts with several coal companies. In each contract, it was agreed that the coal company would supply coal during the year in such amounts as the manufacturing company might desire to order, at a price of $55 per ton. In February of that year, the Snyder Company ordered one thousand tons of coal from Union Coal Company, one of the contracting parties. Union Coal Company delivered five hundred tons of the order and then notified Snyder Company that no more deliveries would be made and that it denied any obligation under the contract. In an action by Union Coal to collect $55 per ton for the five hundred tons of coal delivered, Snyder files a counterclaim, claiming damages of $1,500 for failure to deliver the additional five hundred tons of the order and damages of $4,000 for breach of agreement to deliver coal during the balance of the year. What contract, if any, exists between Snyder and Union?

6. On February 5, Devon entered into a written agreement with Gordon whereby Gordon agreed to drill a well on Devon's property for the sum of $5,000 and to complete the well on or before April 15. Before entering into the contract, Gordon had made test borings and had satisfied himself as to the character of the subsurface. After two days of drilling, Gordon struck hard rock. On February 17, Gordon removed his equipment and advised Devon that the project had proved unprofitable and that he would not continue. On March 17, Devon went to Gordon and told Gordon that he would assume the risk of the enterprise and would pay Gordon $100 for each day required to drill the well, as compen-

sation for labor, the use of Gordon's equipment, and Gordon's services in supervising the work, provided Gordon would furnish certain special equipment designed to cut through hard rock. Gordon said that the proposal was satisfactory. The work was continued by Gordon and completed in an additional fifty-eight days. Upon completion of the work, Devon failed to pay, and Gordon brought an action to recover $5,800. Devon answered that he had never become obligated to pay $100 a day and filed a counterclaim for damages in the amount of $500 for the month's delay based on an alleged breach of contract by Gordon. Explain who will prevail and why.

7. Discuss and explain whether there is valid consideration for each of the following promises:

a. A and B entered into a contract for the purchase and sale of goods. A subsequently promised to pay a higher price for the goods when B refused to deliver at the contract price.

b. A promised in writing to pay a debt, which was due from B to C, on C's agreement to extend the time of payment for one year.

c. A orally promised to pay $150 to her son, B, solely in consideration of past services rendered to A by B, for which there had been no agreement or request to pay.

8. Alan purchased shoes from Barbara on open account. Barbara sent Alan a bill for $10,000. Alan wrote back that two hundred pairs of the shoes were defective and offered to pay $6,000 and give Barbara his promissory note for $1,000. Barbara accepted the offer, and Alan sent his check for $6,000 and his note in accordance with the agreement. Barbara cashed the check, collected on the note, and one month later sued Alan for $3,000. Is Barbara bound by her acceptance of the offer?

9. Nancy owed Sharon $1,500, but Sharon did not initiate a lawsuit to collect the debt within the time period prescribed by the statute of limitations. Nevertheless, Nancy promises Sharon that she will pay the barred debt. Thereafter, Nancy refuses to pay. Sharon brings suit to collect on this new promise. Is Nancy's new promise binding? Explain.

10. Anthony lends money to Frank, who dies without having repaid the loan. Frank's widow, Carol, promises Anthony to repay the loan. Upon Carol's refusal to pay the loan, Anthony brings suit against Carol for payment. Is Carol bound by her promise to pay the loan?

11. The parties entered into an oral contract in June under which the plaintiff agreed to construct a building for the defendant on a time and materials basis, at a maximum cost of $56,146, plus sales tax and extras ordered by the defendant. When the building was 90 percent completed, the defendant told the plaintiff he was unhappy with the whole job as "the thing just wasn't being run right." The parties then, on October 17, signed a written agreement lowering the maximum cost to $52,000 plus sales tax. The plaintiff thereafter completed the building at a cost of $64,155. The maximum under the June oral agreement, plus extras and sales tax, totaled $61,040. Explain whether the defendant is obligated to pay only the lower maximum fixed by the October 17 agreement.

CASE PROBLEMS

12. Taylor assaulted his wife, who then took refuge in Ms. Harrington's house. The next day, Mr. Taylor entered the house and began another assault on his wife. Taylor's wife knocked him down and, while he was lying on the floor, attempted to cut his head open or decapitate him with an ax. Harrington intervened to stop the bloodshed and was hit by the ax as it was descending. The ax fell upon her hand, mutilating it badly, but sparing Taylor his life. Afterwards, Taylor orally promised to compensate Harrington for her injury. Is Taylor's promise enforceable? Explain.

13. Jonnel Enterprises, Inc., contracted to construct a student dormitory at Clarion State College. On May 6, Jonnel entered into a written agreement with Graham and Long as electrical contractors to perform the electrical work and to supply materials for the dormitory. The contract price was $70,544.66. Graham and Long claim that they believed the May 6 agreement obligated them to perform the electrical work on only one wing of the building, but that three or four days after work was started, a second wing of the building was found to be in need of wiring. At that time, Graham and Long informed Jonnel that they would not wire both wings of the building under the present contract, so the parties orally agreed upon a new contract. Under the new contract, Graham and Long were obligated to wire both wings and were to be paid only $65,000, but they were relieved of the obligations to supply entrances and a heating system. Graham and Long resumed their work, and Jonnel made seven of the eight progress payments called for. When Jonnel did not pay the final payment, Graham and Long brought this action. Jonnel claims that the May 6 contract is controlling. Is Jonnel correct in its assertion? Why?

14. Baker entered into an oral agreement with Healey, the state distributor of Ballantine & Sons' liquor products, that Ballantine would supply Baker with its products on demand and that Baker would have the exclusive agency for Ballantine within a certain area of Connecticut. Shortly thereafter, the agreement was modified to give Baker the right to terminate at will. Eight months later, Ballantine & Sons revoked its agency. May Baker enforce the oral agreement? Explain.

15. PLM, Inc., entered into an oral agreement with Quaintance Associates, an executive "headhunter" service, for the recruitment of qualified candidates to be employed by PLM. As agreed, PLM's obligation to pay Quaintance did not depend on PLM actually hiring a qualified candidate presented by Quaintance. After several months Quaintance sent a letter to PLM, admitting that it had so far failed to produce a suitable candidate, but included a bill for $9,806.61, covering fees and expenses. PLM responded that Quaintance's services were only worth $6,060.48, and that payment of the lesser amount was the only fair way to handle the dispute. Accordingly, PLM enclosed a check for $6,060.48, writing on the back of the check "IN FULL PAYMENT OF ANY CLAIMS QUAINTANCE HAS AGAINST PLM, INC." Quaintance cashed the check and then sued PLM for the remaining $3,746.13. Decision?

16. Red Owl Stores told the Hoffman family that upon the payment of approximately $518,000 a grocery store franchise would be built for them in a new location. On the advice of Red Owl, the Hoffmans bought a small grocery store in their hometown in order to get management experience. After the Hoffmans operated at a profit for three months, Red Owl advised them to sell the small grocery, assuring them that Red Owl would find them a larger store elsewhere. Although selling at that point would cost them much profit, the Hoffmans followed Red Owl's directions. Additionally, to raise the required money for the deal, the Hoffmans sold their bakery business in their hometown. The Hoffmans also sold their house and moved to a new home in the city where their new store was to be located. Red Owl then informed the Hoffmans that it would take $524,100, not $518,000, to complete the deal. The family scrambled to find the additional funds. However, when told by Red Owl that it would now cost them $534,000 to get their new franchise, the Hoffmans decided to sue instead. Should Red Owl be held to its promises? Explain.

17. The plaintiff, Brenner, entered into a contract with the defendant, Little Red School House, Ltd., which stated that in return for a nonrefundable tuition of $1,080, Brenner's son could attend the defendant's school for a year. When Brenner's ex-wife refused to enroll their son, the plaintiff sought and received a verbal promise of a refund. The defendant now refuses to refund the plaintiff's money for lack of consideration. Did mutual consideration exist between the parties? Explain.

18. Tender Loving Care, Inc. (TLC), a corporation owned and operated by Virginia Bryant, eventually went out of business. The Secretary of State canceled its corporate charter, and a check drawn on TLC's account made out to the Department of Human Resources (DHR) to pay state unemployment taxes was returned for insufficient funds. Subsequently, Bryant filed individually for bankruptcy, listing the DHR as a creditor. This claim was not allowed, because Bryant was held not to be personally liable on the debts of TLC to the DHR. The DHR later called Bryant to its offices, where she was told that she needed to pay the debt owed to the DHR by TLC. Unable to contact her lawyer, Bryant was persuaded to sign a personal guarantee to cover the debt. Later, when Bryant refused to pay, the DHR filed suit. Decision?

19. Ben Collins was a full professor with tenure at Wisconsin State University in 2007. In March 2007, Parsons College, in an attempt to lure Dr. Collins from Wisconsin State, offered him a written contract promising him the rank of full professor with tenure and a salary of $65,000 for the 2007–08 academic year. The contract further provided that the College would increase his salary by $2,000 each year for the next five years. In return, Collins was to teach two trimesters of the academic year beginning in October 2007. In addition, the contract stipulated, by reference to the College's faculty bylaws, that tenured professors could be dismissed only for just cause and after written charges were filed with the Professional Problems Committee. The two parties signed the contract, and Collins resigned his position at Wisconsin State.

In February 2009, the College tendered a different contract to Collins to cover the following year. This contract reduced his salary to $55,000 with no provision for annual increments, but left his rank of full professor intact. It also required that Collins waive any and all rights or claims existing under any previous employment contracts with the College. Collins refused to sign this new contract and Parsons College soon notified him that he would not be employed the following year. The College did not give any grounds for his dismissal; nor did it file charges with the Professional Problems Committee. As a result, Collins was forced to take a teaching position at the University of North Dakota at a substantially reduced salary. He sued to recover the difference between the salary Parsons College promised him until 2013 and the amount he earned. Will he prevail? Explain.

20. Rodney and Donna Mathis (Mathis) filed a wrongful death action against St. Alexis Hospital and several physicians, arising out of the death of their mother, Mary Mathis. Several weeks before trial, an expert consulted by Mathis notified the trial court and Mathis's counsel that, in his opinion, Mary

Mathis's death was not proximately caused by the negligence of the physicians. Shortly thereafter, Mathis voluntarily dismissed the wrongful death action. Mathis and St. Alexis entered into a covenant-not-to-sue in which Mathis agreed not to pursue any claims against St. Alexis or its employees in terms of the medical care of Mary Mathis. St. Alexis, in return, agreed not to seek sanctions, including attorney fees and costs incurred in defense of the previously dismissed wrongful death action. Subsequently, Mathis filed a second wrongful death action against St. Alexis Hospital, among others. Mathis asked the court to rescind the covenant-not-to-sue, arguing that because St. Alexis was not entitled to sanctions in connection with the first wrongful death action, there was no consideration for the covenant-not-to-sue. Is this contention correct? Explain.

TAKING SIDES

Anna Feinberg began working for the Pfeiffer Company in 1965 at age seventeen. By 2002, she had attained the position of bookkeeper, office manager, and assistant treasurer. In appreciation for her skill, dedication, and long years of service, the Pfeiffer board of directors resolved to increase Feinberg's monthly salary to $4,000 and to create for her a retirement plan. The plan allowed that Feinberg would be given the privilege of retiring from active duty at any time she chose and that she would receive retirement pay of $2,000 per month for life, although the Board expressed the hope that Feinberg would continue to serve the company for many years. Feinberg, however, chose to retire two years later. The Pfeiffer Company paid Feinberg her retirement pay until 2011. The company thereafter discontinued payments.

a. What are the arguments that the company's promise to pay Feinberg $2,000 per month for life is enforceable?

b. What are the arguments that the company's promise is not enforceable?

c. What is the proper outcome? Explain.

CHAPTER **13**

Illegal Bargains

Pactis privatorum juri publico non derogatur. (Private contracts do not derogate from public law.)

Legal Maxim

CHAPTER OUTCOMES

After reading and studying this chapter, you should be able to:

1. Identify and explain the types of contracts that may violate a statute and distinguish between the two types of licensing statutes.

2. Describe when a covenant not to compete will be enforced and identify the two situations in which these types of covenants most frequently arise.

3. Explain when exculpatory agreements, agreements involving the commitment of a tort, and agreements involving public officials will be held to be illegal.

4. Distinguish between procedural and substantive unconscionability.

5. Explain the usual effects of illegality and the major exceptions to this rule.

Violations of statutes
the courts will not enforce agreements declared illegal by statute

License
formal authorization to engage in certain practices

A legal objective is essential for a promise or agreement to be binding. When the formation or performance of an agreement is criminal, tortious, or otherwise contrary to public policy, the agreement is illegal and *unenforceable* (as opposed to being void). The law does *not* provide a remedy for the breach of an unenforceable agreement and thus "leaves the parties where it finds them." (It is preferable to use the term *illegal bargain* or *illegal agreement* rather than *illegal contract*, because the word *contract*, by definition, denotes a legal and enforceable agreement.) The illegal bargain is made unenforceable (1) to discourage such undesirable conduct in the future and (2) to avoid the inappropriate use of the judicial process in carrying out the socially undesirable bargain.

In this chapter, we will discuss (1) agreements in violation of a statute, (2) agreements contrary to public policy, and (3) the effect of illegality on agreements.

VIOLATIONS OF STATUTES

The courts will not enforce an agreement declared illegal by statute. For example, "wagering or gambling contracts" are specifically **declared** unenforceable in most states. Likewise, an agreement induced by criminal conduct will not be enforced. For example, if Alice enters into an agreement with Brent Co. through the bribing of Brent Co.'s purchasing agent, the agreement would be unenforceable.

Licensing Statutes

Every jurisdiction has laws requiring a **license** for those who engage in certain trades, professions, or businesses. Common examples are licensing statutes that apply to lawyers, doctors, dentists, accountants, brokers, plumbers, and contractors. Some licensing statutes mandate schooling and/or examination, while others require only financial responsibility and/or good moral character. Whether a person who has failed to comply with a licensing requirement may recover for services rendered depends on the terms or type of licensing statute.

The statute itself may expressly provide that an unlicensed person engaged in a business or profession for which a license is required shall not recover for services rendered. Where there is no express statutory provision, the courts commonly distinguish between regulatory statutes and those enacted merely to raise revenue through the issuance of licenses. If the statute is regulatory, a person cannot recover for professional services unless he has the required license as long as the public policy behind the regulatory purpose clearly outweighs the person's interest in being paid for his services. Some courts balance the penalty suffered by the unlicensed party against the benefit received by the other party. In contrast, if the law is for revenue purposes only, agreements for unlicensed services are enforceable.

A **regulatory license** is a measure designed to protect the public from unqualified practitioners. Examples are licenses issued under statutes prescribing standards for those who seek to practice law or medicine or, as demonstrated by the case below, to engage in the construction business. A **revenue license**, on the other hand, does not seek to protect against incompetent or unqualified practitioners but serves simply to raise money. An example is a statute requiring a license of plumbers but not establishing standards of competence for those who practice the trade. The courts regard this as a taxing measure lacking any expression of legislative intent to prevent unlicensed plumbers from enforcing their business contracts.

Gambling Statutes

In a **wager**, the parties stipulate that one shall win and the other lose depending on the outcome of an event in which their only "interest" is the possibility of such gain or loss. All states have legislation on gambling or wagering, and U.S. courts generally refuse to recognize the enforceability of a gambling agreement. Thus, if Smith makes a bet with Brown on the outcome of a ball game, the agreement is unenforceable by either party. Some states, however, now permit certain

Regulatory license
measure to protect the public interest

Revenue license
measure to raise money

PRACTICAL ADVICE
Obtain all necessary licenses before beginning to operate your business.

Wager (gambling)
agreement that one party will win and the other lose depending upon the outcome of an event in which their only interest is the possible gain or loss

---

Pacific Custom Pools, Inc. v. Turner Construction Company
Court of Appeal, Second District, Division 4, California, 2000
79 Cal.App.4th 1254, 94 Cal.Rptr.2d 756
http://scholar.google.com/scholar_case?case=8999574054725846170&q=79+Cal.App.4th+1254&hl=en&as_sdt=2,22

FACTS Universal City Studios, Inc. (Universal) entered into a general contract with Turner Construction Company (Turner) for the construction of the Jurassic Park ride. Turner entered into a subcontract with Pacific Custom Pools, Inc. (PCP), for PCP to furnish and install all water treatment work for the project for the contract price of $959,131. PCP performed work on the project from April 1995 until June 1996 for which it was paid $897,719. PCP's contractor's license, however, was under suspension from October 12, 1995, to March 14, 1996. In addition, PCP's license had expired as of January 31, 1996, and it was not renewed until May 5, 1996. PCP brought suit against Universal and Turner, the defendants, for the remainder of the contract price. The trial court granted the defendants' motion for summary judgment on the basis that PCP had not been licensed in California and thus could not bring suit. PCP appealed.

DECISION Summary judgment in favor of defendants affirmed.

OPINION California law (Section 7031) provides that a contractor may not maintain an action for the recovery of compensation for the performance of work requiring a license unless it was "a duly licensed contractor at all times during the performance of that" work. The purpose of the licensing law is to protect the public from incompetence and dishonesty in those who provide building and construction services. Section 7031 advances this purpose by withholding judicial aid from those who seek compensation for unlicensed contract work. The statutory intent is to discourage persons who have failed to comply with the licensing law from

offering or providing their unlicensed services for pay. It is well settled that Section 7031 applies despite injustice to the unlicensed contractor.

An exception may be made if the contractor proves that it had been licensed before performing work, acted reasonably in trying to maintain a license, and did not know or reasonably should not have known that it was not licensed. Such a case might occur where noncompliance with licensure requirements was the result of inadvertent clerical error or other error or delay not caused by the negligence of the licensee. In this case, however, (1) PCP was aware in November 1995 that its license was suspended for failure to file a judgment bond and that the deadline date for license renewal was January 31, 1996; (2) PCP knew shortly after February 23, 1996, that a renewal application sent in February 1996 was untimely; and (3) PCP was advised on April 22, 1996, that its license had not been renewed because PCP's filing fee check had been dishonored. The court found under these facts that PCP did not act reasonably or in good faith to maintain its license.

INTERPRETATION A regulatory license is a measure to protect the public from unqualified practitioners; the failure to comply with such a regulation prevents the noncomplying party from recovering for services rendered.

CRITICAL THINKING QUESTION When should the failure to obtain a license to operate a business prevent the owner or operator from receiving compensation for services?

Usury statute

law establishing a maximum rate of interest

kinds of regulated gambling. Wagering conducted by government agencies, principally state-operated lotteries, has come to constitute an increasingly important source of public revenues.

Usury Statutes

A **usury statute** is a law establishing a maximum rate of permissible interest for which a lender and borrower of money may contract. Although historically every state had a usury statute, the recent trend is to limit or relax such statutes. Maximum permitted rates vary greatly from state to state and among types of transactions. These statutes typically are general in their application, and certain types of transactions are exempted altogether. For example, many states impose no limit on the rate of interest that may be charged on loans to corporations. Furthermore, some states permit the parties to contract for any rate of interest on loans made to individual proprietorships or partnerships for the purpose of carrying on a business. Moreover, there are not many protections remaining for typical consumer transactions, including those involving credit cards. (More than half of the states have no interest rate limits on credit card transactions.)

In addition to the exceptions affecting certain designated types of borrowers, a number of states have exempted specific lenders. For example, the majority of states have enacted installment loan laws, which permit eligible lenders a higher return on installment loans than otherwise would be permitted under the applicable general interest statute. These specific lender usury statutes, which have all but eliminated general usury statutes, vary greatly but generally encompass small consumer loans, retail installment sales acts, corporate loans, loans by small lenders, real estate mortgages, and numerous other transactions.

For a transaction to be usurious, courts usually require evidence of the following factors: (1) a loan (2) of money (3) that is repayable absolutely and in all events (4) for which an interest charge is exacted in excess of the interest rate allowed by law. Nevertheless, the law does permit certain expenses or charges in addition to the maximum legal interest, such as payments made by a borrower to the lender for expenses incurred or for services rendered in good faith in making a loan or in obtaining security for its repayment. Permissible expenses commonly incurred by a lender include the costs of examining title, investigating the borrower's credit rating, drawing necessary documents, and inspecting the property. If not excessive, such expenses are not considered in determining the rate of interest under the usury statutes. As shown in the following case, however, payments made to the lender from which he derives an advantage are considered if they exceed the reasonable value of services he actually rendered.

Dunnam v. Burns
Court of Appeals of Texas, El Paso, 1995
901 S.W.2d 628
http://scholar.google.com/scholar_case?case=11789131696441466691&q=901+S.W.2d+628&hl=en&as_sdt=2,34

FACTS Defendant (Louis Dunnam) and Steve Oualline jointly borrowed $35,000 from plaintiff (Ken Burns) and agreed to repay the principal plus $5,000 six months later. After defendant defaulted on the loan, plaintiff sued to recover. Dunnam defended by claiming the loan was usurious. The trial court ruled in favor of the plaintiff, and defendant appealed.

DECISION Judgment for defendant.

OPINION Defendant claims the trial court erred by refusing to submit his usury defense to the jury. Usury is interest in excess of the amount permitted by law. For most transactions between private persons, the maximum allowable rate of interest is 18 percent if the parties agree on a rate of interest and 6 percent if they do not. Persons who contract for or collect usurious interest are subject to penalties that may exceed the total value of the contract.

When money is advanced in exchange for an obligation to repay the advance plus an additional amount, the added amount

is interest that may not exceed the statutory maximum. Thus, defendant's absolute obligation to pay $5,000 in addition to the principal renders the additional amount interest. Plaintiff argues that he did not "charge" such interest because the instrument was drafted by defendant and because plaintiff was actually interested in collecting only the principal amount. However, a document that contains an absolute obligation to repay a loan together with interest in excess of the amount permitted by statute is usurious on its face. The specific intent of the lender is immaterial because it is presumed to be reflected in the document he signs. The drafter of the usurious promissory note is simply irrelevant. The instrument embodies a usurious transaction, and plaintiff, as the lender, contracted for usurious interest.

INTERPRETATION Usury statutes establish a maximum rate of interest for which a lender may charge a borrower.

CRITICAL THINKING QUESTION Should the law establish maximum rates of interest? If so, in what situations?

The legal effect of a usurious loan varies from state to state. In a few states, the lender forfeits both principal and interest. In some jurisdictions, the lender can recover the principal but forfeits all interest. In other states, only that portion of interest exceeding the permitted maximum is forfeited, whereas in still other states, the amount forfeited is a multiple (double or treble) of the interest charged. How the states deal with usurious interest already paid also varies. Some states do not allow the borrower to recover any of the usurious interest she has paid; others allow recovery of such interest or a multiple of it.

VIOLATIONS OF PUBLIC POLICY

The reach of a statute may extend beyond its language. Sometimes the courts, by analogy, use a statute and the policy it embodies as a guide in determining a person's rights under a private contract. Conversely, the courts frequently must express the "public policy" of the state without significant help from statutory sources. This judicially declared public policy is very broad in scope, it often being said that agreements having "a tendency to be injurious to the public or the public good" are contrary to public policy. Contracts raising questions of public policy include agreements that (1) restrain trade, (2) excuse or exculpate a party from liability for his own negligence, (3) are unconscionable, (4) involve tortious conduct, (5) tend to corrupt public officials or impair the legislative process, (6) tend to obstruct the administration of justice, or (7) impair family relationships. This section will focus on the first five of these types of agreements.

Common Law Restraint of Trade

Restraint of trade
agreement that eliminates or tends to eliminate competition

A **restraint of trade** is any contract or agreement that eliminates or tends to eliminate competition or otherwise obstructs trade or commerce. One type of restraint of trade is a **covenant not to compete**, which is an agreement to refrain from entering into a competing trade, profession, or business.

Covenant not to compete
agreement to refrain from entering into a competing trade, profession, or business

Today, an agreement to refrain from a particular trade, profession, or business is enforceable if (1) the purpose of the restraint is to protect a property interest of the promisee and (2) the restraint is no more extensive than is reasonably necessary to protect that interest. Restraints typically arise in two situations: (1) the sale of a business and (2) employment contracts.

Covenant in sale of a business
the promise by the seller of a business not to compete in that particular business in a reasonable geographic area for a reasonable period of time is enforceable

Sale of a Business As part of an agreement to sell a business, the seller frequently promises not to compete in that particular type of business in a defined area for a stated period of time to protect the business's goodwill (an asset that the buyer has purchased). The courts will enforce such a covenant (promise) if the restraint is within reasonable limitations. The reasonableness of the restraint depends on the geographic area the restraint covers, the period for which it is to be effective, and the hardship it imposes on the promisor and the public.

For example, the promise of a person selling a service station business in Detroit not to enter the service station business in Michigan for the next twenty-five years is unreasonable as to both area and time. The business interest would not include the entire state, so the protection of the purchaser does not require that the seller be prevented from engaging in the service station business in all of Michigan or perhaps, for that matter, in the entire city of Detroit. Limiting the area to the neighborhood in which the station is located or to a radius of a few miles probably would be adequate protection. However, in the case of a citywide business, such as a laundry or cleaning establishment with neighborhood outlets, a covenant restraining competition anywhere in the city might well be reasonable.

The same type of inquiry must be made about time limitations. In the sale of a service station, a twenty-five-year ban on competition from the seller would be unreasonable, but a one-year ban probably would not. The courts consider each case on its own facts to determine what is reasonable under the particular circumstances.

Covenant in employment contracts
an employment contract prohibiting an employee from competing with his employer for a reasonable period following termination is enforceable provided the restriction is necessary to protect legitimate interests of the employer

Employment Contracts Salespeople, management personnel, and other employees are frequently required to sign employment contracts prohibiting them from competing with their employers during their employment and for some additional stated period after their termination. The same is also frequently true among corporations or partnerships involving professionals such as accountants, lawyers, investment brokers, stockbrokers, or doctors. Though the courts readily enforce a covenant not to compete during the period of employment, they subject the promise not to compete after termination of employment to a test of reasonableness stricter even than that applied to noncompetition promises included in a contract for the sale of a business.

A court order enjoining (prohibiting) a former employee from competing in a described territory for a stated period of time is the usual way in which an employer seeks to enforce an employee's promise not to compete. However, before the courts will grant such injunctions, the employer must demonstrate that the restriction is necessary to protect his legitimate interests, such as trade secrets or customer lists. Because the injunction may have the practical effect of placing the employee out of work, the courts must carefully balance the public policy favoring the employer's right to protect his business interests against the public policy favoring full opportunity for individuals to gain employment. Some courts, rather than refusing to enforce an unreasonable restraint, will modify the restrictive covenant to make it reasonable under the circumstances.

Thus, one court has held unreasonable a contract covenant requiring a travel agency employee after termination of her employment to not engage in a like business in any capacity in either of two named towns or within a sixty-mile radius of those towns for two years. There was no indication that the employee had enough influence over customers to cause them to move their business to her new agency, nor was it shown that any trade secrets were involved.

PRACTICAL ADVICE

If you include a covenant not to compete to protect your property interests, be careful to select a reasonable duration and geographic scope.

Due to the rapid evolution of business practices in the Internet industry, it has been argued that noncompetition agreements for Internet company employees need their own rules. *National Business Services, Inc. v. Wright* addressed the geographic scope of an Internet noncompetition agreement, upholding a one-year time restriction and a territorial clause that prevented the employee from taking another Internet-related job anywhere in the United States. The court stated, "Transactions involving the Internet, unlike traditional 'sales territory' cases, are not limited by state boundaries."

Payroll Advance, Inc. v. Yates
Missouri Court of Appeals, 2008
270 S.W.3d 428
http://scholar.google.com/scholar_case?case=12029870438647495616&q=270+S.W.3d+428&hl=en&as_sdt=2,22

FACTS In June of 1998, Payroll Advance, Inc. entered into an employment contract with Barbara Yates, which contained a covenant not to compete. It is customary for each of Payroll's branch offices to employ a sole employee at each branch and that sole employee is the manager of that particular branch. On November 19, 1999, as a condition of her continued employment, Payroll presented Yates with the Employment Agreement which included a provision entitled "NON-COMPETE" ("the covenant not to compete"). This provision provided:

> [Yates] agrees not to compete with [Payroll] as owner, manager, partner, stockholder, or employee in any business that is in competition with [Payroll] and within a fifty-mile radius of [Payroll's] business for a period of two (2) years after termination of employment or [Yates] quits or [Yates] leaves employment of [Payroll].

On November 8, 2007, Yates was fired for cause. Approximately thirty-two days after being terminated Yates obtained employment with Check Please, one of the Payroll's competitors. At Check Please, Yates performed basically the same duties as she had when employed with Payroll.

On February 7, 2008, Payroll filed a complaint against Yates for: (1) injunctive relief to prevent Yates from soliciting its clients for her new employer, and to stop her from using client information she purportedly obtained from her time with Payroll and (2) damages for breach of contract for violation of the covenant not to compete together with attorney fees and costs. The trial court found

> [n]o evidence exists that, following [Payroll's] termination of [Yates'] ten year period of employment, [Yates] removed any cus-

tomer list or other documents from [Payroll's] place of business [or] … made any personal or other contact with any previous or present customer of [Payroll's] business or intends to do so.

The trial court further determined that that if the covenant not to compete were enforced as requested, Yates would be prohibited from engaging in employment with any payday loan business in at least 126 cities situated in Missouri, Arkansas, and Tennessee. Further, Yates could also be prohibited from employment at a bank, savings and loan company, credit union, pawnshop, or title-loan company within Missouri, Arkansas, and Tennessee. Accordingly, the trial court found in favor of Yates holding that the Employment Agreement's noncompete covenant signed by the parties was not valid in that it was "unreasonable under the facts and circumstances of the particular industry, agreement, and geographic location here involved." Payroll appealed.

DECISION Judgment affirmed.

OPINION Because covenants not to compete are generally considered to be restraints on trade, they are presumptively void and are enforceable only to the extent that they are demonstratively reasonable. Thus, covenants not to compete are not favored in the law, and the party attempting to enforce a noncompetition agreement has the burden of demonstrating both the necessity to protect the claimant's legitimate interests and that the agreement is reasonable as to time and space. Non-compete agreements are typically enforceable so long as they are reasonable. In practical terms, a non-compete agreement is reasonable if it is no more restrictive than is necessary to protect the legitimate interests of the employer. In order to obtain an injunction it is not necessary for the employer to show that actual damage has occurred.

In this case, it is clear the trial court took umbrage with the covenant's restrictive provisions and geographical limitations on Yates' ability to find employment. The question of reasonableness of a restraint is to be determined according to the facts of the particular case and hence requires a thorough consideration of all surrounding circumstances, including the subject matter of the contract, the purpose to be served, the situation of the parties, the extent of the restraint, and the specialization of the business. Here, the covenant not to compete grandly declares that Yates cannot "compete with Appellant [Payroll] as owner, manager, partner, stockholder, or employee *in any business* that is in competition with [Payroll] and within a fifty-mile radius of [Payroll's] business...." There was evidence from Payroll's representative at trial that Payroll has seventeen branch offices in Missouri and still other locations in Arkansas. Thus under the plain meaning of the covenant not to compete as written, the covenant not to compete would prevent Yates not only from working at a competing business within fifty miles of the branch office in Kennett, Missouri, but Yates would also be barred from working in a competing business within fifty miles of *any* of Payroll's branch offices. Under this interpretation, Yates would be greatly limited in the geographic area she could work.

Additionally, the covenant not to compete bars Yates from working at "any business that is in competition with [Payroll]." Yet, it fails to set out with precision what is to be considered a competing business and certainly does not specify that it only applies to other payday loan businesses.

INTERPRETATION Noncompete clauses in employment agreements can be enforced only to the extent necessary to protect the employer's legitimate interests and only if reasonably limited in duration and geographic scope.

CRITICAL THINKING QUESTION How should courts balance the protection of employers with the freedom of employees to change jobs? Explain.

Exculpatory Clauses

Exculpatory clause
a provision excusing one party from fault or liability

Some contracts contain an **exculpatory clause** that excuses one party from liability for her own tortious conduct. Although there is general agreement that exculpatory clauses relieving a person from tort liability for harm caused intentionally or recklessly are unenforceable as violating public policy, exculpatory clauses that excuse a party from liability for harm caused by negligent conduct undergo careful scrutiny by the courts, which often require that the clause be conspicuously placed in the contract and clearly written. Accordingly, an exculpatory clause on the reverse side of a parking lot claim check, which attempts to relieve the parking lot operator of liability for negligently damaging the customer's automobile, generally will be held unenforceable as against public policy.

PRACTICAL ADVICE

Because many courts do not favor exculpatory clauses, carefully limit its applicability, make sure that it is clear and understandable, put it in writing, and have it signed.

Where one party's superior bargaining position has enabled him to impose an exculpatory clause upon the other party, the courts are inclined to nullify the provision. Such a situation may arise in residential leases exempting a landlord from liability for his negligence. Moreover, an exculpatory clause may be unenforceable for unconscionability.

Anderson v. McOskar Enterprises, Inc.
Court of Appeals of Minnesota, 2006
712 N.W. 2d 796
http://caselaw.lp.findlaw.com/scripts/getcase.pl?court=mn&vol=apppub\0605\opa051546-0502&invol=1

FACTS Plaintiff, Tammey J. Anderson, on April 2, 2003, joined the fitness club Curves for Women, which was owned and operated by McOskar Enterprises. As part of the registration requirements, Anderson read an "AGREEMENT AND RELEASE OF LIABILITY," initialed each of the three paragraphs in the document, and dated and signed it. The first paragraph purported to release Curves from liability for injuries Anderson might sustain in participating in club activities or using club equipment:

In consideration of being allowed to participate in the activities and programs of Curves for Women and to use its facilities, equipment and machinery in addition to the payment of any fee or charge, I do hereby waive, release and forever discharge Curves International Inc., Curves for Women, and their officers, agents, employees, representatives, executors, and all others (Curves representatives) from any and all responsibilities or liabilities from injuries or damages arriving [sic] out of or connected with my attendance at Curves for Women, my participation in all activities, my use of equipment or machinery, or any act or omission, including negligence by Curves representatives.

The second paragraph provided for Anderson's acknowledgment that fitness activities "involve a risk of injury" and her agreement "to expressly assume and accept any and all risks of injury or death."

After completing the registration, Anderson began a workout under the supervision of a trainer. About fifteen or twenty minutes later, having used four or five machines, Anderson developed a headache in the back of her head. She contends that she told the trainer, who suggested that the problem was likely just a previous lack of use of certain muscles and that Anderson would be fine. Anderson continued her workout and developed pain in her neck, shoulder, and arm. She informed the trainer but continued to exercise until she completed the program for that session. The pain persisted when Anderson returned home. She then sought medical attention and, in June 2003, underwent a cervical diskectomy. She then filed this lawsuit for damages, alleging that Curves had been negligent in its acts or omissions during her workout at the club. Curves moved for summary judgment on the ground that Anderson had released the club from liability for negligence. The district court agreed and granted the motion. Anderson appealed.

DECISION Judgment of the district court is affirmed.

OPINION It is settled law that, under certain circumstances, "parties to a contract may, without violation of public policy, protect themselves against liability resulting from their own negligence." The public interest in freedom of contract is preserved by recognizing release and exculpatory clauses as valid.

Releases of liability, however, are not favored by the law and are strictly construed against the benefited party. "If the clause is either ambiguous in scope or purports to release the benefited party from liability for intentional, willful or wanton acts, it will not be enforced." Furthermore, even if a release clause is unambiguous in scope and is limited only to negligence, courts must still ascertain whether its enforcement will contravene public policy. On this issue, a two-prong test is applied:

Before enforcing an exculpatory clause, both prongs of the test are examined, to-wit: (1) whether there was a disparity of bargaining power between the parties (in terms of a compulsion to sign a contract containing an unacceptable provision and the lack of ability to negotiate elimination of the unacceptable provision) ... and (2)

the types of services being offered or provided (taking into consideration whether it is a public or essential service).

The two-prong test describes what is generally known as a "contract of adhesion." There is nothing in the Curves release that expressly exonerates the club from liability for any intentional, willful, or wanton act. Thus, the question is whether the release is ambiguous in scope. In the context of a release in connection with an athletic, health, or fitness activity, the consumer surely is entitled to know precisely what liability is being exonerated. A release that is so vague, general, or broad as to fail to specifically designate the particular nature of the liability exonerated is not enforceable. It is clear from this release that the unmistakable intent of the parties is that Curves would not be held liable for acts of negligence.

Even if a release is unambiguously confined to liability for negligence, it still will be unenforceable if it contravenes public policy. Anderson contends that the Curves contract is one of adhesion characterized by such a disparity in bargaining power that she was compelled to sign it without any ability to negotiate. In this case there was neither proof of disparity in bargaining ability nor was there a showing that the services provided by Curves are necessary and unobtainable elsewhere.

INTERPRETATION An exculpatory clause is valid if it is limited in scope, not ambiguous, and not contrary to public policy.

ETHICAL QUESTION Did Curves act unethically? Explain.

CRITICAL THINKING QUESTION When should an exculpatory clause be held invalid? Explain.

Unconscionable Contracts

Unconscionable
unfair or unduly harsh

The Uniform Commercial Code provides that a court may scrutinize every contract for the sale of goods to determine whether in its commercial setting, purpose, and effect the contract is unconscionable, or unfair. The court may refuse to enforce an **unconscionable** contract or any part of the contract it finds to be unconscionable. The Restatement has a similar provision.

Though neither the Code nor the Restatement defines the word *unconscionable*, the term is defined in the *New Webster's Dictionary* (Deluxe Encyclopedic Edition) as "contrary to the dictates of conscience; unscrupulous or unprincipled; exceeding that which is reasonable or customary; inordinate, unjustifiable."

The doctrine of unconscionability has been justified on the basis that it permits the courts to resolve issues of unfairness explicitly in terms of that unfairness without recourse to formalistic rules or legal fictions. In policing contracts for fairness, the courts have again demonstrated their willingness to limit freedom of contract to protect the less advantaged from overreaching by dominant contracting parties. The doctrine of unconscionability has evolved through its application by the courts to include both procedural and substantive unconscionability. **Procedural unconscionability** involves scrutiny for the presence of "bargaining naughtiness." In other words, was the negotiation process fair? Or were there procedural irregularities, such as burying important terms of the agreement in fine print or obscuring the true meaning of the contract with impenetrable legal jargon?

Procedural unconscionability
unfair or irregular bargaining

Substantive unconscionability
oppressive or grossly unfair contractual terms

By comparison, in searching for **substantive unconscionability**, the courts examine the actual terms of a contract for oppressive or grossly unfair provisions such as exorbitant prices or unfair exclusions or limitations of contractual remedies. An all-too-common example of such a provision involves a buyer in pressing need who is in an unequal bargaining position with a seller who consequently obtains an exorbitant price for his product or service. In one case, a price of $749 ($920 if the purchaser wished to pay on credit over time) for a vacuum cleaner that

PRACTICAL ADVICE

When negotiating a contract, keep in mind that if your bargaining techniques or the contract terms are oppressive, a court may refuse to enforce the contract in part or in full.

cost the seller $140 was held unconscionable. In another case, the buyers, welfare recipients, purchased by a time payment contract a home freezer unit for $900 that, when time credit charges, credit life insurance, credit property insurance, and sales tax were added, cost $1,235. The purchase resulted from a visit to the buyers' home by a salesperson representing Your Shop At Home Service, Inc.; the maximum retail value of the freezer unit at the time of purchase was $300. The court held the contract unconscionable and reformed it by reducing the price to the total payment ($620) the buyers had managed to make. Another landmark case follows.

Williams v. Walker-Thomas Furniture Co.
United States Court of Appeals, District of Columbia Circuit, 1965
350 F.2d 445
http://scholar.google.com/scholar_case?case=9052480984854382590&q=350+F.2d+445&hl=en&as_sdt=2,34

FACTS Between 1957 and 1962, Williams purchased a number of household items on credit from Walker-Thomas Furniture Co., a retail furniture store. Walker-Thomas retained the right in its contracts to repossess an item if Williams defaulted on an installment payment. Each contract also provided that each installment payment by Williams would be credited *pro rata* to all outstanding accounts or bills owed to Walker-Thomas. As a result of this provision, an unpaid balance would remain on every item purchased until the entire balance due on all items, whenever purchased, was paid in full. Williams defaulted on a monthly installment payment in 1962, and Walker-Thomas sought to repossess all the items that Williams had purchased since 1957. Williams claimed that the contracts were unconscionable and therefore unenforceable. The trial court granted judgment for Walker-Thomas, and the District of Columbia Court of Appeals affirmed.

DECISION Judgment reversed and remanded to determine the possible unconscionability of the contracts.

OPINION In general, one who signs an agreement without knowledge of its terms is bound and is held to have assumed the risk that the bargain was one sided. But if a party with little bargaining

power and, therefore, no meaningful choice enters into a commercially unreasonable contract with little or no knowledge or understanding of its terms, one cannot say that the supposed acceptance was an objective manifestation of assent to all of the terms of the contract. In cases involving allegedly unconscionable terms, the court will examine the reasonableness or fairness of the term at the time that the contract was entered into to determine whether it should be enforced. Generally, the suspect term is evaluated in light of general commercial background and the particular reason for the term's inclusion. If the term is found to be so extreme as to be unconscionable, enforcement of that term should be denied. The contract provision as to prorating each payment on all purchases whenever made is unconscionable and therefore unenforceable.

INTERPRETATION The doctrine of unconscionability includes both procedural and substantive unconscionability.

ETHICAL QUESTION Did Walker-Thomas Furniture Co. act unethically? Explain.

CRITICAL THINKING QUESTION What is the appropriate penalty to apply in this type of situation? Explain.

Some courts hold that for a contract to be unenforceable both substantive and procedural unconscionability must be present. Nevertheless, they need not exist to the same degree; the more oppressive one is, the less evidence of the other is required.

Closely akin to the concept of unconscionability is the doctrine of contracts of adhesion. An *adhesion contract*, a standard-form contract prepared by one party, generally involves the preparer offering the other party the contract on a "take-it-or-leave-it" basis. Such contracts are not automatically unenforceable but are subject to greater scrutiny for procedural or substantive unconscionability. See the Ethical Dilemma at the end of this chapter.

Tortious conduct
an agreement that requires a person to commit a tort is unenforceable

Tortious Conduct

An agreement that requires a person to commit a tort is an illegal agreement and thus is unenforceable. The courts will not permit contract law to violate the law of torts. Any agreement attempting to do so is considered contrary to public policy. For example, Ada and Bernard enter into an agreement under which Ada promises Bernard that in return for $5,000, she will disparage the product of Bernard's competitor, Cone, in order to provide Bernard with a competitive advantage. Ada's promise is to commit the tort of disparagement and is unenforceable as contrary to public policy.

Corrupting Public Officials

Agreements that may adversely affect the public interest through the corruption of public officials or the impairment of the legislative process are unenforceable. Examples include using

Southwestern Casualty Insurance (SCI) has issued automobile insurance policies in the southwestern United States for a number of years. Its standard-form policies historically have covered its policyholders for accidents occurring in Mexico. After reassessing the company's liabilities, SCI determined that inserting an exclusion for accidents occurring within Mexico's borders would both assist in keeping premiums in check and contribute positively to the company's bottom line. It therefore issued a new standard-form policy that was the same in all respects as its old policy, but which now contained the Mexico exclusion in a long paragraph of other policy exclusions.

Rather than simply send the new form to its customers along with a premium notice when their policies are up for renewal, SCI must take pains to make its customers aware of the change in coverage. If it does not, there is a good chance in many jurisdictions that SCI will be stopped from enforcing the exclusion, and therefore will be required to provide coverage according to its customers' reasonable expectations.

Standard-form insurance policies generally are contracts of adhesion. This is because, while some provisions regarding limits and types of coverage may be bargained for, these agreements consist largely of boilerplate provisions that are not negotiated and that often are not, nor are they expected to be, read or fully understood by the insured. Standard-form insur-

ance contracts are useful in commerce; by narrowing the consumer's choice from a limited number of meaningful features rather than an endless combination of possible coverages, they focus the time and effort of the insurer and insured, thereby reducing costs to the benefit of all. The adhesive nature of the agreement, however, imposes an obligation of good faith on the insurer, which has been translated into a rule that insureds do not assent to standard-form terms the insurer has reason to believe that the consumer would not have accepted.

© Cengage Learning 2013

improper means to influence legislation, to secure some official action, or to procure a government contract. Contracts to pay lobbyists for services to obtain or defeat official action by means of persuasive argument are to be distinguished from illegal influence-peddling agreements.

For example, a bargain by a candidate for public office to make a certain appointment following his election is illegal. In addition, an agreement to pay a public officer something extra for performing his official duty, such as promising a bonus to a police officer for strictly enforcing the traffic laws on her beat, is illegal. The same is true of an agreement in which a citizen promises to perform, or to refrain from performing, duties imposed on her by citizenship. Thus, a promise by Carl to pay $50 to Rachel if she will register and vote is opposed to public policy and illegal.

EFFECT OF ILLEGALITY

With few exceptions, illegal contracts are *unenforceable*. In most cases, neither party to an illegal agreement can sue the other for breach or recover for any performance rendered. It is often said that where parties are *in pari delicto* (in pa˙re de·lik'tow)—in equal fault—a court will leave them where it finds them. The law will provide neither with any remedy. This strict rule of unenforceability is subject to certain exceptions, however, which are discussed as follows.

Party Withdrawing before Performance

A party to an illegal agreement may, before performance, withdraw from the transaction and recover whatever she has contributed, if the party has not engaged in serious misconduct. A common example is recovery of money left with a stakeholder for a wager before it is paid over to the winner.

Party Protected by Statute

Sometimes an agreement is illegal because it violates a statute designed to protect persons from the effects of the prohibited agreement. For example, state and federal statutes prohibiting the sale of unregistered securities are designed primarily to protect investors. In such case, even though there is an unlawful agreement, the statutes usually expressly give the purchaser a right to withdraw from the sale and recover the money paid.

Ethical Dilemma

Is It Fair to Mandate an Arbitration Clause?

Facts Delivery drivers at Figaro's Factory drive their own car in making deliveries. Their hourly wages range from the legal minimum wage to approximately $0.50 above minimum wage. Figaro's Pizza Factory reimburses them at a fixed rate of $0.80 per delivery regardless of the number of miles driven or actual expenses incurred. All drivers are required to sign an arbitration agreement that states (1) any dispute that the parties are unable to resolve informally will be submitted to binding arbitration before an arbitrator selected from a panel of a designated arbitration service and approved by both parties; (2) the parties give up the right to a jury trial; (3) the arbitration fees will be borne by Figaro's Pizza Factory and, except as otherwise required by law, each party will bear its own attorneys' fees and costs; (4) small claims may be resolved by a summary small claims procedure; and (5) the parties give up the right to bring class arbitration. In actuality, the arbitration provider designated by Figaro's Pizza Factory includes only one arbitrator.

Social, Policy, and Ethical Considerations

1. Is the bargaining power of the employer too great to assume that the terms of the arbitration agreement resulted from a fair negotiation process?
2. Do the terms of this agreement appear fair and reasonable to both parties?
3. What concerns are raised by the lack of real choice by the employees in selecting the arbitrator?
4. Is the compensation paid by Figaro's Pizza Factory fair?

© Cengage Learning 2013

Party Not Equally at Fault

Where one of the parties is less at fault than the other, he may be allowed to recover payments made or property transferred. For example, this exception would apply where one party induces the other to enter into an illegal bargain through the exercise of fraud, duress, or undue influence.

Excusable Ignorance

An agreement that appears to be entirely permissible on its face may, nevertheless, be illegal by reason of facts and circumstances of which one of the parties is completely unaware. For example, a man and woman make mutual promises to marry, but unknown to the woman, the man is already married. This is an agreement to commit the crime of bigamy, and the marriage, if entered into, is void. In such case, the courts permit the party who is ignorant of the illegality to maintain a lawsuit against the other party for damages.

A party may also be excused for ignorance of legislation of a minor character. For instance, Jones and Old South Building Co. enter into a contract to build a factory that contains specifications in violation of the town's building ordinance. Jones did not know of the violation and had no reason to know. Old South's promise to build would not be rendered unenforceable on grounds of public policy, and Jones consequently would have a claim against Old South for damages for breach of contract.

Partial Illegality

A contract may be partly unlawful and partly lawful. The courts view such a contract in one of two ways. First, the partial illegality may be held to taint the entire contract with illegality, so that it is wholly unenforceable. Second, the court may determine it possible to separate the illegal from the legal part, in which case the illegal part only will be held unenforceable, while the legal part will be enforced. For example, if a contract contains an illegal covenant not to compete, the covenant will not be enforced, though the rest of the contract may be.

CHAPTER SUMMARY

Violations of Statutes

General Rule the courts will not enforce agreements declared illegal by statute

Licensing Statutes require formal authorization to engage in certain trades, professions, or businesses

- *Regulatory License* licensing statute that is intended to protect the public against unqualified persons; an unlicensed person may not recover for services he has performed

- *Revenue License* licensing statute that seeks to raise money; an unlicensed person may recover for services he has performed

Gambling Statutes prohibit wagers, which are agreements that one party will win and the other lose depending on the outcome of an event in which their only interest is the gain or loss

Usury Statutes establish a maximum rate of interest

Violations of Public Policy

Common Law Restraint of Trade unreasonable restraints of trade are not enforceable

- *Sale of a Business* the promise by the seller of a business not to compete in that particular business in a reasonable geographic area for a reasonable period of time is enforceable

- *Employment Contracts* an employment contract prohibiting an employee from competing with his employer for a reasonable period following termination is enforceable provided the restriction is necessary to protect legitimate interests of the employer

Exculpatory Clauses the courts generally disapprove of contractual provisions excusing a party from liability for his own tortious conduct

Unconscionable Contracts unfair or unduly harsh agreements are not enforceable

- *Procedural Unconscionability* unfair or irregular bargaining

- *Substantive Unconscionability* oppressive or grossly unfair contractual terms

Tortious Conduct an agreement that requires a person to commit a tort is unenforceable

Corrupting Public Officials agreements that corrupt public officials are not enforceable

Effect of Illegality

Unenforceability neither party may recover (unenforceable) under an illegal agreement where both parties are *in pari delicto* (in equal fault)

Exceptions permit one party to recover payments

- *Party Withdrawing before Performance*
- *Party Protected by Statute*
- *Party Not Equally at Fault*
- *Excusable Ignorance*
- *Partial Illegality*

QUESTIONS

1. Johnson and Wilson were the principal shareholders in Matthew Corporation, located in the city of Jonesville, Wisconsin. This corporation was engaged in the business of manufacturing paper novelties, which were sold over a wide area in the Midwest. The corporation was also in the business of binding books. Johnson purchased Wilson's shares in Matthew Corporation and, in consideration thereof, Wilson agreed that for a period of two years he would not (a) manufacture or sell in Wisconsin any paper novelties of any kind that would compete with those sold by Matthew Corporation or (b) engage in the bookbinding business in the city of Jonesville. Discuss the validity and effect, if any, of this agreement.

2. Wilkins, a Texas resident licensed by that state as a certified public accountant (CPA), rendered service in his professional capacity in Louisiana to Coverton Cosmetics Company. He was not registered as a CPA in Louisiana. His service under his contract with the cosmetics company was not the only occasion on which he had practiced his profession in that state. The company denied liability and refused to pay him, relying on a Louisiana statute declaring it unlawful for any person to perform or offer to perform services as a CPA for compensation until he has been registered by the designated agency of the state and holds an unrevoked registration card.

The statute provides that a CPA certificate may be issued without examination to any applicant who holds a valid unrevoked certificate as a CPA under the laws of any other state. The statute provides further that rendering services of the kind performed by Wilkins, without registration, is a misdemeanor punishable by a fine or imprisonment in the county jail or by both fine and imprisonment. Discuss whether Wilkins would be successful in an action against Coverton seeking to recover a fee in the amount of $1,500 as the reasonable value of his services.

3. Michael is interested in promoting the passage of a bill in the state legislature. He agrees with Christy, an attorney, to pay Christy for her services in writing the required bill, obtaining its introduction in the legislature, and making an argument for its passage before the legislative committee to which it will be referred. Christy renders these services. Subsequently, on Michael's refusal to pay Christy, Christy sues Michael for damages for breach of contract. Will Christy prevail? Explain.

4. Anthony promises to pay McCarthy $100,000 if McCarthy reveals to the public that Washington is a communist. Washington is not a communist and never has been. McCarthy successfully persuades the media to report that Washington is a communist and now seeks to recover the $100,000 from

Anthony, who refuses to pay. McCarthy initiates a lawsuit against Anthony. What will be the result?

5. The Dear Corporation was engaged in the business of making and selling harvesting machines. It sold everything pertaining to its business to the HI Company, agreeing "not again to go into the manufacture of harvesting machines anywhere in the United States." The Dear Corporation, which had a national and international goodwill in its business, now begins the manufacture of such machines contrary to its agreement. Should the court stop it from doing so? Explain.

6. Charles Leigh, engaged in the industrial laundry business in Central City, employed Tim Close, previously employed in the home laundry business, as a route salesperson. Leigh rents linens and industrial uniforms to commercial customers; the soiled linens and uniforms are picked up at regular intervals by the route drivers and replaced with clean ones. Every employee is assigned a list of customers whom she services. The contract of employment stated that in consideration of being employed, on termination of his employment, Close would not "directly or indirectly engage in the linen supply business or any competitive business within Central City, Illinois, for a period of one year from the date when his employment under this contract ceases." On May 10 of the following year, Close's employment was terminated by Leigh for valid reasons. Close then accepted employment with Ajax Linen Service, a direct competitor of Leigh in Central City. He began soliciting former customers he had called on for Leigh and obtained some of them as customers for Ajax. Will Leigh be able to enforce the provisions of the contract?

7. On July 5, 2012, Bill and George entered into a bet on the outcome of the 2012 presidential election. On January 28, 2013, Bill, who bet on the winner, approached George, seeking to collect the $3,000 George had wagered. George paid Bill the wager but now seeks to recover the funds from Bill. Result?

8. Carl, a salesperson for Smith, comes to Benson's home and sells him a complete set of "gourmet cooking utensils" that are worth approximately $300. Benson, an eighty-year-old man who lives alone in a one-room efficiency apartment, signs a contract to buy the utensils for $1,450 plus a credit charge of $145 and to make payments in ten equal monthly installments. Three weeks after Carl leaves with the signed contract, Benson decides he cannot afford the cooking utensils and has no use for them. What can Benson do? Explain.

9. Consider the facts in question 8 but assume that the price was $350. Assume further that Benson wishes to avoid the contract based on the allegation that Carl befriended and tricked him into the purchase. Discuss.

10. Adrian rents a bicycle from Barbara. The bicycle rental contract Adrian signed provides that Barbara is not liable for any injury to the renter caused by any defect in the bicycle or the negligence of Barbara. Adrian is injured when she is involved in an accident due to Barbara's improper maintenance of the bicycle. Adrian sues Barbara for damages. Will Barbara be protected from liability by the provision in their contract?

11. Emily was a Java programmer employed with Sun Microsystems in Palo Alto, California. Upon beginning employment, Emily signed a contract which included a noncompetition clause that prevented her from taking another Java programming position with any of five companies Sun listed as "direct competitors" within three months of terminating her employment. Later that year Emily resigned and two months later accepted a position with Hewlett-Packard (HP) in Houston, Texas. HP was listed in Emily's contract as a "direct competitor," but she argues that due to the significant geographic distance between both jobs, the contract is not enforceable. Explain whether the contract is enforceable.

CASE PROBLEMS

12. Merrill Lynch employed Post and Maney as account executives. Both men elected to be paid a salary and to participate in the firm's pension and profit-sharing plans rather than take a straight commission. Thirteen years later, Merrill Lynch terminated the employment of both Post and Maney without cause. Both men began working for a competitor of Merrill Lynch. Merrill Lynch then informed them that all of their rights in the company-funded pension plan had been forfeited pursuant to a provision of the plan that permitted forfeiture in the event an employee directly or indirectly competed with the firm. Is Merrill Lynch correct in its assertion?

13. Tovar applied for the position of resident physician in Paxton Community Memorial Hospital. The hospital examined his background and licensing and assured him that he was qualified for the position. Relying upon the hospital's promise of permanent employment, Tovar resigned from his job and began work at the hospital. He was discharged two weeks later, however, because he did not hold a license to practice medicine in Illinois as required by state law. He had taken the examination but had never passed it. Tovar claims that the hospital promised him a position of permanent employment and that by discharging him, it breached their employment contract. Who is correct? Discuss.

14. Carolyn Murphy, a welfare recipient with very limited education and with four minor children, responded to an advertisement that offered the opportunity to purchase televisions without a deposit or credit history. She entered into a rent-to-own contract for a twenty-five-inch television set that required seventy-eight weekly payments of $16 (a total of $1,248, which was two and one-half times the retail value of the set). Under the contract, the renter could terminate the agreement by returning the television and forfeiting any payments already made. After Murphy had paid $436 on the television, she read a newspaper article criticizing the lease plan. She stopped payment and sued the television company. In response, the television company has attempted to take possession of the set. What will be the outcome?

15. Albert Bennett, an amateur cyclist, participated in a bicycle race conducted by the United States Cycling Federation. During the race, Bennett was hit by an automobile. He claims that employees of the Federation improperly allowed the car onto the course. The Federation claims that it cannot be held liable to Bennett because Bennett signed a release exculpating the Federation from responsibility for any personal injury resulting from his participation in the race. Is the exculpatory clause effective?

16. In February, Brady, a general contractor, signed a written contract with the Fulghums to build for them a house in North Carolina. The contract price of the house was $206,850, and construction was to begin in March of that year. Neither during the contract negotiations nor during the commencement of construction was Brady licensed as a general contractor as required by North Carolina law. In fact, Brady did not obtain his license until late October of that year, at which time he had completed more than two-thirds of the construction on the Fulghums' house. The Fulghums submitted to Brady total payments of $204,000 on the house. Brady sues for $2,850 on the original contract and $29,000 for additions and changes requested by the Fulghums during construction. Is Fulghum liable to Brady? Explain.

17. Robert McCart owned and operated an H&R Block tax preparation franchise. When Robert became a district manager for H&R Block, he was not allowed to continue operating a franchise. So, in accordance with company policy, he signed over his franchise to his wife June. June signed the new franchise agreement, which included a covenant not to compete for a two-year period within a fifty-mile radius of the franchise territory should the H&R Block franchise be terminated, transferred, or otherwise disposed of. June and Robert were both aware of the terms of this agreement, but June chose to terminate her franchise agreement anyway. Shortly thereafter, June sent out letters to H&R Block customers, criticizing H&R Block's fees and informing them that she and Robert would establish their own tax preparation services at the same address as the former franchise location. Each letter included a separate letter from Robert detailing the tax services to be offered by the McCart's new business. Should H&R Block be able to obtain an injunction against June? Against Robert?

18. Michelle Marvin and actor Lee Marvin began living together, holding themselves out to the general public as man and wife without actually being married. The two orally agreed that while they lived together they would share equally any and all property and earnings accumulated as a result of their individual and combined efforts. In addition, Michelle promised to render her services as "companion, homemaker, housekeeper, and cook" to Lee. Shortly thereafter, she gave up her lucrative career as an entertainer to devote her full time to being Lee's companion, homemaker, housekeeper, and cook. In return he agreed to provide for all of her financial support and needs for the rest of her life. After living together for six years, Lee compelled Michelle to leave his household but continued to provide for her support. One year later, however, he refused to provide further support. Michelle sued to recover support payments and half of their accumulated property. Lee contends that their agreement is so closely related to the sup-

posed "immoral" character of their relationship that its enforcement would violate public policy. The trial court granted Lee's motion for judgment on the pleadings. Decision?

19. Richard Brobston was hired by Insulation Corporation of America (ICA) in 2002. Initially, he was hired as a territory sales manager but was promoted to national account manager in 2006 and to general manager in 2010. In 2012, ICA was planning to acquire computer-assisted design (CAD) technology to upgrade its product line. Prior to acquiring this technology, ICA required that Brobston and certain other employees sign employment contracts that contained restrictive covenants or be terminated and changed their employment status to "at will" employees. These restrictive covenants provided that in the event of Brobston's termination for any reason, Brobston would not reveal any of ICA's trade secrets or sales information and would not enter into direct competition with ICA within three hundred miles of Allentown, Pennsylvania, for a period of two years from the date of termination. The purported consideration for Brobston's agreement was a $2,000 increase in his base salary and proprietary information concerning the CAD system, customers, and pricing. Brobston signed the proffered employment contract. In October 2012, Brobston became vice president of special products, which included responsibility for sales of the CAD system products as well as other products. Over the course of the next year, Brobston failed in several respects to properly perform his employment duties and on August 13, 2013, ICA terminated Brobston's employment. In December 2013, Brobston was hired by a competitor of ICA who was aware of ICA's restrictive covenants. Can ICA enforce the employment agreement by enjoining Brobston from disclosing proprietary information about ICA and by restraining him from competing with ICA? If so, for what duration and over what geographic area?

20. Henrioulle, an unemployed widower with two children, received public assistance in the form of a rent subsidy. He entered into an apartment lease agreement with Marin Ventures that provided "INDEMNIFICATION: Owner shall not be liable for any damage or injury to the tenant, or any other person, or to any property, occurring on the premises, or any part thereof, and Tenant agrees to hold Owner harmless for any claims for damages no matter how caused." Henrioulle fractured his wrist when he tripped over a rock on a common stairway in the apartment building. At the time of the accident, the landlord had been having difficulty keeping the common areas of the apartment building clean. Will the exculpatory clause effectively bar Henrioulle from recovery? Explain.

TAKING SIDES

EarthWeb provided online products and services to business professionals in the information technology (IT) industry. EarthWeb operated through a family of websites offering information, products, and services for IT professionals to use for facilitating tasks and solving technology problems in a business setting. EarthWeb obtained this content primarily through licensing agreements with third parties. Schlack began his employment with EarthWeb in its New York City office. His title at EarthWeb was Vice President, Worldwide Content, and he was responsible for the content of all of EarthWeb's websites. Schlack's employment contract stated that he was an employee at will and included a section titled "Limited Agreement Not To Compete." That section provided:

> (c) For a period of twelve (12) months after the termination of Schlack's employment with EarthWeb, Schlack shall not, directly or indirectly:
>
> (1) work as an employee … or in any other … capacity for any person or entity that directly competes with EarthWeb. For

the purpose of this section, the term "directly competing" is defined as a person or entity or division on an entity that is

> (i) an online service for Information Professionals whose primary business is to provide Information Technology Professionals with a directory of third party technology, software, and/or developer resources; and/or an online reference library, and or
>
> (ii) an online store, the primary purpose of which is to sell or distribute third party software or products used for Internet site or software development.

About one year later, Schlack tendered his letter of resignation to EarthWeb. Schlack revealed at this time that he had accepted a position with ITworld.com.

a. What arguments would support EarthWeb's enforcement of the covenant not to compete?

b. What arguments would support Schlack's argument that the covenant is not enforceable?

c. Which side should prevail? Explain.

CHAPTER 14

Contractual Capacity

> *Youth is a blunder, manhood a struggle, old age a regret.*
>
> Benjamin Disraeli (1805–1881), *Coningsby* (book iii, ch. i)

CHAPTER OUTCOMES

After reading and studying this chapter, you should be able to:

1. Explain how and when a minor may ratify a contract.

2. Describe the liability of a minor who (a) disaffirms a contract or (b) misrepresents his age.

3. Define as necessary and explain how it affects the contracts of a minor.

4. Distinguish between the legal capacity of a person under guardianship and a mentally incompetent person who is not under guardianship.

5. Explain the rule governing an intoxicated person's capacity to enter into a contract and contrast this rule with the law governing minors and incompetent persons.

A binding promise or agreement requires that the parties to the agreement have contractual capacity. Everyone is regarded as having such capacity unless the law, for public policy reasons, holds that the individual lacks such capacity. We will consider this essential ingredient of a contract by discussing those classes and conditions of persons who are legally limited in their capacity to contract: minors, incompetent persons, and intoxicated persons.

MINORS

Minor
person under age of legal majority

A **minor**, also called an infant, is a person who has not attained the age of legal majority. At common law, a minor was an individual who had not reached the age of twenty-one years. Today the age of majority has been changed by statute in nearly all jurisdictions, usually to age eighteen. Almost without exception a minor's contract, whether executory or executed, is *voidable* at his guardian's option. Thus, the minor is in a favored position by having the option to disaffirm the contract or to enforce it. The adult party to the contract cannot avoid her contract with a minor. Even an "emancipated" minor, one who, because of marriage or other reasons, is no longer subject to strict parental control, may nevertheless avoid contractual liability in most jurisdictions. Consequently, business-people deal at their peril with minors and in situations of consequence generally require an adult to cosign or guarantee the performance of the contract. Nevertheless, most states recognize special categories of contracts that cannot be avoided (such as student loans or contracts for medical care) or that have a lower age for capacity (such as bank accounts, marriage, and insurance contracts).

Liability on contracts
minor's contracts are voidable at the minor's option

Liability on Contracts

Disaffirmance
avoidance of a contract

Ratification
affirmation of a contract

A minor's contract is not entirely void and of no legal effect; rather, as we have said, it is voidable at the minor's option. The exercise of this power of avoidance, called a **disaffirmance**, releases the minor from any liability on the contract. On the other hand, after the minor comes of age, he may choose to adopt or ratify the contract, in which case he surrenders his power of avoidance and becomes bound by his **ratification**.

Disaffirmance As we stated earlier, a minor has the power to avoid liability. The minor or, in some jurisdictions, her guardian, may exercise the power to disaffirm a contract through words or conduct showing an intention not to abide by it.

A minor may disaffirm a contract at any time before reaching the age of majority. Moreover, a minor generally may disaffirm a contract within a reasonable time after coming of age as long as she has not already ratified the contract. A notable exception is that a minor cannot disaffirm a sale of land until after reaching her majority.

In most states, determining a reasonable time depends on circumstances such as the nature of the transaction, whether either party has caused the delay, and the extent to which either party has been injured by the delay. Some states, however, statutorily prescribe a time period, generally one year, in which the minor may disaffirm the contract.

Disaffirmance may be either *express* or *implied.* No particular form of language is essential, so long as it shows an intention not to be bound. This intention also may be manifested by acts or by conduct. For example, a minor agrees to sell property to Andy and then sells the property to Betty. The sale to Betty constitutes a disaffirmance of the contract with Andy.

A troublesome yet important problem in this area pertains to the minor's duty upon disaffirmance. The courts do not agree on this question. The majority hold that the minor must return any property received from the other party to the contract, provided she is in possession of it at the time of disaffirmance. Nothing more is required. If the minor disaffirms the purchase of an automobile and the vehicle has been wrecked, she need only return the wrecked vehicle. Other states require at least the payment of a reasonable amount for the use of the property or of the amount by which the property depreciated while in the hands of the minor. (See *Berg v. Traylor* below.) A few states, however, either by statute or court ruling, recognize a duty on the part of the minor to make *restitution*—that is, to return an equivalent of what has been received so that the seller will be in approximately the same position he would have occupied had the sale not occurred.

Finally, can a minor disaffirm and recover property that he has sold to a buyer who in turn has sold it to a good-faith purchaser for value? Traditionally, the minor could avoid the contract and recover the property, even though the third person gave value for it and had no notice of the minority. Thus, in the case of the sale of real estate, a minor could take back a deed of conveyance even against a third-party good-faith purchaser of the land who did not know of the minority. The Uniform Commercial Code (UCC), however, has changed this principle in connection with sales of goods by providing that a person with voidable title (e.g., the person buying goods from a minor) has power to transfer valid title to a good-faith purchaser for value. For example, a minor sells his car to an individual who resells it to a used-car dealer, a good-faith purchaser for value. The used-car dealer would acquire legal title even though he bought the car from a seller who had only voidable title.

PRACTICAL ADVICE
In all significant contracts entered into with a minor, have an adult cosign or guarantee the written agreement.

Berg v. Traylor
Court of Appeal, Second District, Division 2, California, 2007
148 Cal.App.4th 809, 56 Cal.Rptr.3d 140
http://scholar.google.com/scholar_case?case=15409397777753786246&q=56+Cal.Rptr.3d+140&hl=en&as_sdt=2,22

FACTS Sharyn Berg (Berg), plaintiff, brought this action against Meshiel Cooper Traylor (Meshiel) and her minor son Craig Lamar Traylor (Craig) for unpaid commissions under a contract between Berg, Meshiel, and Craig for Berg to serve as the personal manager of Craig. On January 18, 1999, Berg entered into a two-page "Artist's Manager's Agreement" (agreement) with Meshiel and Craig, who was then ten years old. Meshiel signed the agreement and wrote Craig's name on the signature page where he was designated "Artist." Craig did not sign the agreement. The agreement provided that Berg was to act as Craig's exclusive personal manager in exchange for a commission of 15 percent of all monies paid to him as an artist during the three-year term of the agreement. The agreement expressly provided that any action Craig "may take in the future pertaining to disaffirmance of this agreement, whether successful or not," would not affect Meshiel's liability

for any commissions due Berg. The agreement also provided that any disputes concerning payment or interpretation of the agreement would be determined by arbitration in accordance with the rules of Judicial Arbitration and Mediation Services, Inc. (JAMS).

In June 2001, Craig obtained a role on the Fox Television Network show "Malcolm in the Middle" (show). On September 11, 2001, four months prior to the expiration of the agreement, Meshiel sent a certified letter to Berg stating that while she and Craig appreciated her advice and guidance, they no longer needed her management services and could no longer afford to pay Berg her 15 percent commission because they owed a "huge amount" of taxes. On September 28, 2001, Berg responded, informing appellants that they were in breach of the agreement.

The arbitration hearing was held in February 2005. The arbitrator awarded Berg commissions and interest of $154,714.15, repayment of personal loans and interest of $5,094, and attorney fees and costs of $13,762. He also awarded Berg $405,000 "for future earnings projected on a minimum of six years for national syndication earnings." The defendants then filed a petition with the state trial court to vacate the arbitration award. Following a hearing, the trial court trial court entered a judgment in favor of Berg against Meshiel and Craig consistent with the arbitrator's award.

DECISION The decision against Craig is reversed but the judgment against Meshiel is affirmed.

OPINION One who provides a minor with goods and services does so at her own risk. The agreement here in question expressly contemplated this risk, requiring that Meshiel remain obligated for commissions due under the agreement regardless of whether Craig disaffirmed the agreement. Thus, Craig is permitted to and did disaffirm the agreement and any of its obligations, while Meshiel is liable under the agreement and resulting judgment. Craig's minority status entitled him to disaffirm the agreement and the arbitration award and judgment.

"As a general proposition, parental consent is required for the provision of services to minors for the simple reason that minors may disaffirm their own contracts to acquire such services." A contract of a minor may be disaffirmed by the minor before majority or within a reasonable time afterwards. The law shields minors from their lack of judgment and experience. This is so even though in many instances such disaffirmance may be a hardship upon those who deal with an infant, the right to avoid his contracts is conferred by law upon a minor for his protection against his own improvidence and the designs of others. It is the policy of the law to protect a minor against himself and his indiscretions and immaturity as well as against the machinations of other people and to discourage adults from contracting with an infant. No specific language is required to communicate an intent to disaffirm. "A contract (or conveyance) of a minor may be avoided by any act or declaration disclosing an unequivocal intent to repudiate its binding force and effect." Express notice to the other party is unnecessary. Craig disaffirmed both the agreement and the arbitration award.

Berg offers two reasons this rule is inapplicable. First, she without justification or legal support argues that a minor may not disaffirm an agreement signed by a parent. Second, Berg argues that Craig cannot disaffirm the agreement because it was for his and his family's necessities. This agreement, however, is not a contract to pay for the necessities of life for Craig or his family. A contract to secure personal management services for the purpose of advancing Craig's acting career does not constitute a necessity. Moreover, there is no evidence that Meshiel was unable to provide for the family in 1999 at the time of the agreement.

A disaffirmance of an agreement by a minor does not operate to terminate the contractual obligations of the parent who signed the agreement. There is no legal reason for Meshiel to avoid her independent obligations under the agreement.

INTERPRETATION A minor may disaffirm his contracts during minority and for a reasonable time thereafter; nevertheless, the minor's right to disaffirm does not extend to an adult party to the agreement.

CRITICAL THINKING QUESTION Under what circumstances should minors be able to disaffirm their contracts and receive their full consideration? Explain.

Ratification   A minor has the option of ratifying a contract after reaching the age of majority. Ratification makes the contract binding *ab initio* (from the beginning). That is, the result is the same as if the contract had been valid and binding from its inception. Ratification, once effected, is final and cannot be withdrawn; furthermore, it must be in total, validating the entire contract. The minor can ratify the contract only as a whole, both as to burdens and benefits. He cannot,

BUSINESS LAW *IN ACTION*

Using his own money, fifteen-year-old Zach bought $160 worth of video games and DVDs at a local electronics warehouse. His parents were furious about the purchase, but initially they did nothing. Several months later Zach's father learned about the so-called infancy doctrine and insisted that Zach return the games and movies. Zach took the items back to the store and asked for a refund. But the clerk refused, pointing to the store's "Return Policy," which permitted returns on opened items like those Zach had bought only within thirty days of purchase and only for the same title when necessary to replace defects. After speaking to the manager and getting a similar result, Zach's father considered filing suit against the store in small claims court. Does a minor's right of disaffirmation void override the store's return policy in a case like this?

Generally speaking, minors may disaffirm contracts entered into during their minority. In a majority of jurisdictions this is true even if the child or teenager cannot return the consideration he or she received and even if the minor misrepresented his or her age when entering into the transaction with the adult. However, this rule of incapacity does not excuse minors from paying the reasonable value of any necessaries for which they may have contracted. There is little question here that the purchases Zach made do not qualify as necessaries, things that supply his basic needs. Therefore, Zach is entitled to disaffirm his contract and receive a refund, although some states perhaps would subject the refund to a deduction of some amount representing depreciation of the items or the use or benefit he received.

Nonetheless, retailers need not fear or refuse transactions with minors, especially relatively insignificant ones. Most people will not go to the trouble and expense of bringing litigation to recover a small amount of money. It is also foreseeable that many courts, if given the opportunity, would not allow a minor to take unfair advantage of her minority. Moreover, teens make up a growing and lucrative segment of the retail market, with their purchases tallying in the billions of dollars each year.

for example, ratify so as to retain the consideration received and escape payment or other performance on his part; nor can the minor retain part of the contract and disaffirm another part.

Note that a minor has *no* power to ratify a contract while still a minor. A ratification based on words or conduct occurring while the minor is still underage is no more effective than his original contractual promise. The ratification must take place after the individual has acquired contractual capacity by attaining his majority.

Ratification can occur in three ways: (1) through express language, (2) as implied from conduct, and (3) through failure to make a timely disaffirmance. Suppose that a minor makes a contract to buy property from an adult. The contract is voidable by the minor, and she can escape liability. But suppose that after reaching her majority she promises to go through with the purchase. The minor has *expressly* ratified the contract she entered when she was a minor. Her promise is binding, and the adult can recover for breach if the minor fails to carry out the terms of the contract.

Ratification also may be *implied* from a person's conduct. Suppose that the minor, after attaining majority, uses the property involved in the contract, undertakes to sell it to someone else, or performs some other act showing an intention to affirm the contract. She may not thereafter disaffirm the contract but is bound by it. Perhaps the most common form of implied ratification occurs when a minor, after attaining majority, continues to use the property purchased as a minor. This use is obviously inconsistent with the nonexistence of a contract. Whether the contract is performed or still partly executory, the continued use of the property amounts to a ratification and prevents a disaffirmance by the minor. Simply keeping the goods for an unreasonable time after attaining majority has also been construed as a ratification.

In re The Score Board, Inc.
United States District Court, District of New Jersey, 1999
238 B.R. 585
http://lawlibrary.rutgers.edu/fed/html/ca99-259-1.html

FACTS During the spring of 1996, Kobe Bryant (Bryant), then a seventeen-year old star high school basketball player, declared his intention to forgo college and enter the 1996 National Basketball Association (NBA) lottery draft. The Score Board Inc., a company in the business of licensing, manufacturing, and distributing sports and entertainment-related memorabilia, entered into negotiations with Bryant's agent, Arn Tellem (Agent) and Bryant's father, former NBA star Joe "Jelly Bean" Bryant, to sign Bryant to a contract. In early July 1996, Score Board sent Bryant a signed written licensing agreement (agreement). The agreement granted Score Board the right to produce licensed products, such as trading cards, with Bryant's image. Bryant was obligated to make two personal appearances on behalf of Score Board and provide between a minimum of 15,000 and a maximum of 32,500 autographs. Bryant was to receive a $2 stipend for each autograph, after the first 7,500. Under the agreement, Bryant could receive a maximum of $75,000 for the autographs. In addition to being compensated for the autographs, Bryant was entitled to receive a base compensation of $10,000.

Bryant rejected this proposed agreement, and on July 11, 1996, while still a minor, made a counteroffer (counteroffer), signed it, and returned it to Score Board. The counteroffer made several changes to Score Board's agreement, including the number of autographs. Score Board claimed that they signed the counteroffer and placed it into its files. The copy signed by Score Board was subsequently misplaced and has never been produced by Score Board during these proceedings. Rather, Score Board has produced a copy signed only by Bryant.

On August 23, 1996, Bryant turned eighteen. Three days later, Bryant deposited the check for $10,000 into his account. Bryant subsequently performed his contractual duties for about a year and a half. By late 1997, Bryant grew reluctant to sign any more

autographs under the agreement and his Agent came to the conclusion that a fully executed contract did not exist. By this time, Agent became concerned with Score Board's financial condition because it failed to make certain payments to several other players. Score Board claims that the true motivation for Bryant's reluctance stems from his perception that he was becoming a "star" player, and that his autograph was "worth" more than $2.

On March 17, 1998, Score Board mistakenly sent Bryant a check for $1,130 as compensation for unpaid autographs. Bryant was actually entitled to $10,130 and the check for $1,130 was based on a miscalculation.

On March 18, 1998, Score Board filed a voluntary Chapter 11 bankruptcy petition. On March 23, 1998, Agent returned the $1,130 check. Included with the check was a letter that directed Score Board to "immediately cease and desist from any use of" Kobe Bryant's name, likeness, or other publicity rights. Subsequently, Score Board began to sell its assets, including numerous executory contracts with major athletes, including Bryant. Bryant argued that Score Board could not do this, because he believed that a contract never existed. In the alternative, if a contract had been created, Bryant contended that it was voidable because it had been entered into while he was a minor. The Bankruptcy Court ruled in favor of Score Board. Bryant appealed.

DECISION Judgment affirmed.

OPINION Bryant challenges the Bankruptcy Court's finding that he ratified the agreement upon attaining majority. Contracts made during minority are voidable at the minor's election within a reasonable time after the minor attains the age of majority. The infant's conduct upon reaching the age of majority may amount to ratification.

After Bryant deposited the $10,000 check sent to him from Score Board, he performed his contractual duties by signing autographs. It is clear that Bryant ratified the contract from the facts. Bryant asserts, however, that he acted at the insistence of his Agent, who believed that he was contractually obligated to perform. Yet, neither Bryant nor his Agent disputed the existence of a contract until the March 23, 1998, letter by the Agent. That Bryant may have relied on his Agent is irrelevant to this Court's inquiry and is proper evidence only in a suit against the Agent. To the contrary, by admitting that he acted because he was under the belief that a contract existed, Bryant confirms the existence of the contract. Moreover, it was Bryant who deposited the check, signed the autographs, and made personal appearances.

INTERPRETATION Ratification of a contract may be implied from a person's conduct after the person attains his majority.

CRITICAL THINKING QUESTION What criteria should a court employ in determining what is a reasonable period of time for disaffirmance by a person who has attained majority?

Liability for necessaries
a minor is liable for the reasonable value of necessary items

Necessaries
items that reasonably supply a person's needs

Liability for Necessaries

Contractual incapacity does not excuse a minor from an obligation to pay for **necessaries**, those things, such as food, shelter, medicine, and clothing, that suitably and reasonably supply his personal needs. Even here, however, the minor is not contractually liable for the agreed price but for the *reasonable* value of the items furnished. Recovery is based on quasi-contract. Thus, if a clothier sells a minor a suit that the minor needs, the clothier can successfully sue the minor. The clothier's recovery, however, is limited to the reasonable value of the suit only, even if this amount is much less than the agreed-upon selling price. In addition, a minor is not liable for anything on the ground that the item is a necessary, unless it has been actually furnished to him and used or consumed by him. In other words, a minor may disaffirm his executory contracts for necessaries and refuse to accept such clothing, lodging, or other items.

Defining "necessaries" is a difficult task. In general, the states regard as necessary those things that the minor needs to maintain himself in his particular station in life. Items necessary for subsistence and health, such as food, lodging, clothing, medicine, and medical services, are included. But other less essential items, such as textbooks, school instruction, and legal advice, may be included as well. Furthermore, some states enlarge the concept of necessaries to include articles of property and services that a minor needs to earn the money required to provide the necessities of life for himself and his dependents. Nevertheless, many states limit necessaries to items that are not provided to the minor. Thus, if a minor's guardian provides her with an adequate wardrobe, a blouse the minor purchased would *not* be considered a necessary.

Ordinarily, luxury items, such as cameras, tape recorders, stereo equipment, television sets, and motorboats, do not qualify as necessaries. The question concerning whether automobiles and trucks are necessaries has caused considerable controversy, but some courts have recognized that under certain circumstances, an automobile may be a necessary where it is used by the minor for his business activities.

Zelnick v. Adams
Supreme Court of Virginia, 2002
263 Va. 601, 561 S.E.2d 711
http://caselaw.lp.findlaw.com/scripts/getcase.pl?court=va&vol=1011390&invol=1

FACTS Jonathan Ray Adams (Jonathan) was born on April 5, 1980, the son of Mildred A. Adams (Adams or mother) and Cecil D. Hylton, Jr. (Hylton or father). Jonathan's parents were never married. Nevertheless, the Florida courts did determine Hylton's paternity of Jonathan. Jonathan's grandfather, Cecil D. Hylton, Sr. (Hylton Sr.), died in 1989 and had established certain trusts under his will, which provided that the trustees had sole discretion to determine who qualified as "issue" under the will.

In 1996, Adams met with an attorney, Robert J. Zelnick (Zelnick), about protecting Jonathan's interest as a beneficiary of the trusts after she had unsuccessfully attempted to get Jonathan recognized as an heir. Adams explained that she could not afford to pay Zelnick's hourly fee and requested legal services on her son's behalf on a contingency fee basis. Zelnick subsequently informed Adams that he had examined a copy of the will and that he was willing to accept the case. Adams went to Zelnick's office the next day, where Zelnick explained that the gross amount of the estate was very large. Nevertheless, Adams signed a retainer agreement (the contract) for Zelnick's firm to represent Jonathan on a one-third contingency fee.

In May 1997, Zelnick initiated a legal action on Jonathan's behalf. A consent decree was entered on January 23, 1998, which ordered that Jonathan was "declared to be the grandchild and issue of Cecil D. Hylton" and was entitled to all benefits under the Will and Trusts of Cecil D. Hylton.

In March 1998, Jonathan's father brought suit against Adams and Zelnick, on Jonathan's behalf, to have the contract with Zelnick declared void. Upon reaching the age of majority, Jonathan filed a petition to intervene, in which he disaffirmed the contract. Jonathan filed a motion for summary judgment asserting that the contract was "void as a matter of law" because it was not a contract for necessaries. Jonathan argued that the 1997 suit was unnecessary due to the Florida paternity decree which conclusively established Hylton's paternity.

The trial court granted Jonathan's motion for summary judgment and ruled that the contingency fee agreement was not binding on Jonathan because he was "in his minority" when the contract was executed. This appeal followed.

DECISION Judgment reversed and remanded.

OPINION Under well- and long-established Virginia law, a contract with an infant is not void, only voidable by the infant upon attaining the age of majority. When a court is faced with a defense of infancy, the court has the initial duty to determine, as a matter of law, whether the "things supplied" to the infant under a contract may fall within the general class of necessaries, and were in fact necessary in the instant case. If not, the provider of the goods cannot recover under the disaffirmed contract.

If a necessary, the party who provided the goods or services to the infant is entitled to the "reasonable value" of the things furnished. "Things supplied," which fall into the class of necessaries, include "board, clothing, and education." Things that are "necessary to [an infant's] subsistence and comfort, and to enable [an infant] to live according to his real position in society" are also considered part of the class of necessaries.

Certainly, the provision of legal services may fall within the class of necessaries for which an infant may not be avoided or disaffirmed on the grounds of infancy. Generally, contracts for legal services related to prosecuting personal injury actions and protecting an infant's personal liberty, security, or reputation are considered contracts for necessaries. Other states have also broadened the definition of "necessaries" to include contracts for legal services for the protection of an infant's property rights.

The trier of fact must also conclude that "under all the circumstances, the things furnished were actually necessary to the position and condition of the infant ... and whether the infant was already sufficiently supplied." If the contract does fall within the "general classes of necessaries," but upon consideration of all of the circumstances, the trier of fact determines that the provision of the particular services or things was not actually necessary, the plea of infancy must be sustained.

Because the trial court erred in its determination, on this record, on summary judgment, that the doctrine of necessaries did not apply, the decision must be reversed and remanded for further proceedings, including the taking of evidence on the issue of the factual determination of necessity "under all of the circumstances." Should the trial court upon remand hold that the evidence is sufficient to defeat Jonathan's plea of infancy, the trial court shall receive evidence of the reasonable value of the services rendered.

INTERPRETATION Contractual incapacity does not excuse a minor from an obligation to pay the reasonable value of a necessary.

ETHICAL QUESTION Did Jonathan act ethically? Explain.

CRITICAL THINKING QUESTION What factors should a court use in determining whether goods or services are necessary? Explain.

Liability for misrepresentation of age prevailing view is that a minor may disaffirm the contract

PRACTICAL ADVICE
In all significant contracts, if you have doubts about the age of your customers, have them prove that they are of legal age.

Liability for Misrepresentation of Age

The states do not agree whether a minor who fraudulently misrepresents her age when entering into a contract has the power to disaffirm. Suppose a contracting minor says that she is eighteen years of age (or twenty-one, if that is the year of attaining majority) and actually looks that old or even older. By the prevailing view in this country, despite her misrepresentation, the minor may nevertheless disaffirm the contract. Some states, however, prohibit disaffirmance if a minor misrepresented her age to an adult who, in good faith, reasonably relied on the misrepresentation. As shown in the case of *Keser v. Chagnon*, other states not following the majority rule either (1) require the minor to restore the other party to the position he occupied before making the contract or (2) allow the defrauded party to recover damages against the minor in tort.

Keser v. Chagnon
Supreme Court of Colorado, 1966
159 Colo. 209, 410 P.2d 637
http://scholar.google.com/scholar_case?case=4555401252219612466&q=410+P.2d+637&hl=en&as_sdt=2,34

FACTS On June 11, 1964, Chagnon bought a 1959 Edsel from Keser for $995. Chagnon, who was then a twenty-year-old minor, obtained the contract by falsely advising to Keser that he was over twenty-one years old, the age of majority. On September 25, 1964, two months and four days after his twenty-first birthday, Chagnon disaffirmed the contract and, ten days later, returned the Edsel to Keser. He then brought suit to recover the money he had paid for the automobile. Keser counterclaimed that he suffered damages as the direct result of Chagnon's false representation of his age. A trial was had to the court, sitting without a jury, all of which culminated in a judgment in favor of Chagnon against Keser in the sum of $655.78. This particular sum was arrived at by the trial court in the following manner: the trial court found that Chagnon initially purchased the Edsel for the sum of $995 and that he was entitled to the return of his $995; and then, by way of setoff, the trial court subtracted from the $995 the sum of $339.22, apparently representing the difference between the purchase price paid for the vehicle and the reasonable value of the Edsel on October 5, 1964, the date when the Edsel was returned to Keser.

DECISION Judgment affirmed except as to the calculation of damages for misrepresentation.

OPINION If a minor does not exercise his right to disaffirm a contract within a "reasonable time" after he reaches the age of majority, he loses that right. Here, however, Chagnon's disaffirmance just two months after reaching majority was within a reasonable time. Under the general rule, once he returned the car—the only consideration in his possession—he was entitled to recover the full $995. While a false representation of his age does not destroy a minor's right to disaffirm, it does permit the seller to deduct from the buyer's compensation any damages that the seller suffered due

to the false representation. The measure of damages for the seller is the difference between the reasonable value of the property on the date of delivery and its reasonable value on the date of return. Since Chagnon obtained the contract by false representation of his age, he will not recover his full $995. Instead, his recovery is decreased by the amount of Keser's damages—the loss of the Edsel's reasonable value.

INTERPRETATION States vary on the rights of a minor and a defrauded party when a minor fraudulently misrepresents her age when entering into a contract.

ETHICAL QUESTION If a minor misrepresents his age, should he forfeit the right to avoid the contract? Explain.

CRITICAL THINKING QUESTION What rule would you apply in this case? Explain.

Liability for Tort Connected with Contract

Liability for tort connected with contract
if a tort and a contract are so intertwined that to enforce the tort the court must enforce the contract, the minor is not liable in tort

It is well settled that minors are generally liable for their torts. There is, however, a legal doctrine that if a tort and a contract are so "interwoven" that the court must enforce the contract to enforce the tort action, the minor is not liable in tort. Thus, a minor who rents an automobile from an adult enters into a contractual relationship obliging him to exercise reasonable care to protect the property from injury. By negligently damaging the automobile, he breaches that contractual undertaking. But his contractual immunity protects him from an action by the adult based on the contract. By the majority view, the adult cannot successfully sue the minor for damages on a tort theory. For, it is reasoned, a tort recovery would, in effect, be an enforcement of the contract and would defeat the protection that contract law gives the minor. Should the minor depart, however, from the terms of the agreement (e.g., by using a rental automobile for an unauthorized purpose) and in so doing negligently cause damage to the automobile, most courts would hold that the tort is independent and that the adult can collect from the minor.

INCOMPETENT PERSONS

In this section, we will discuss the contract status of incompetent persons who are under court-appointed guardianship and those who are not adjudicated incompetents.

Person under Guardianship

Person under guardianship
contracts made by a person placed under guardianship by court order are void

Guardianship
the relationship under which a person (the guardian) is appointed by a court to preserve and control the property of another (the ward)

If a person is under **guardianship** by *court order*, her contracts are *void* and of no legal effect. A court appoints a *guardian*, generally under the terms of a statute, to control and preserve the property of a person (the *ward* or *adjudicated incompetent*) whose impaired capacity prevents her from managing her own property. Nonetheless, a party dealing with an individual under guardianship may be able to recover the fair value of any necessaries provided to the incompetent. Moreover, the contracts of the ward may be ratified by her guardian during the period of guardianship or by the ward on termination of the guardianship.

Mental Illness or Defect

Mental illness or defect
a contract entered into by a mentally incompetent person (one who is unable to understand the nature and consequences of his acts) is voidable

Mentally incompetent
unable to understand the nature and effect of one's acts

Because a contract is a consensual transaction, the parties to a valid contract must have a certain level of mental capacity. If a person lacks such capacity, or is **mentally incompetent**, the agreement is *voidable*.

Under the traditional cognitive ability test, a person is mentally incompetent if he is unable to comprehend the subject of the contract, its nature, and its probable consequences. Though he need not be proved permanently incompetent to avoid the contract, his mental defect must be something more than a weakness of intellect or a lack of average intelligence. In short, a person is competent unless he is unable to understand the nature and effect of his actions, in which case he may disaffirm the contract even if the other party did not know or had no reason to know of the incompetent's mental condition.

A second type of mental incompetence recognized by the Restatement and some states is a mental condition that impairs a person's ability to act in a reasonable manner. In other words, the person understands what he is doing but cannot control his behavior in order to act in a reasonable and rational way. If the contract he enters is entirely executory or grossly unfair, it is voidable. If, however, the contract is executed and fair and the competent party had no reason to suspect the incompetency of the other, the incompetent must restore the competent party to the *status quo* by returning the consideration he has received or its equivalent in money. If restoration to the *status quo* is impossible, avoidance will depend upon the equities of the situation.

Like minors and persons under guardianship, an incompetent person is liable on the principle of quasi-contract for *necessaries* furnished him, the amount of recovery being the reasonable value of the goods or services. Moreover, an incompetent person may *ratify* or *disaffirm* voidable contracts during a lucid period or when he becomes competent.

PRACTICAL ADVICE

If you have doubts about the capacity of the other party to a contract, have an individual with full legal capacity cosign the contract.

Intoxicated persons

a contract entered into by an intoxicated person (one who cannot understand the nature and consequence of her actions) is voidable

INTOXICATED PERSONS

A person may *avoid* any contract that he enters into if the other party has reason to know that the person, because of his intoxication, is unable to understand the nature and consequences of his actions or unable to act in a reasonable manner. Such contracts, as in the case that follows, are **voidable**, although they may be ratified when the intoxicated person regains his capacity. Slight intoxication will not destroy one's contractual capacity; on the other hand, to make a contract voidable, a person need not be so drunk that he is totally without reason or understanding.

The effect that the courts allow intoxication to have on contractual capacity is similar to the effect they allow contracts that are voidable because of incompetency, although the courts are even more strict with intoxication due to its voluntary nature. Most courts, therefore, require that, to avoid a contract, the intoxicated person on regaining his capacity must act promptly to disaffirm and generally must offer to restore the consideration he has received. Individuals who are taking prescribed medication or who are involuntarily intoxicated are treated the same as those who are incompetent under the cognitive ability test. As with incompetent persons, intoxicated persons are liable in quasi-contract for necessaries furnished during their incapacity.

First State Bank of Sinai v. Hyland
Supreme Court of South Dakota, 1987
399 N.W.2d 894
http://scholar.google.com/scholar_case?case=9646538788520684587&q=399+N.W.2d+894&hl=en&as_sdt=2,34

FACTS Randy Hyland, unable to pay two promissory notes due September 19, 1981, negotiated with The First State Bank of Sinai (Bank) for an extension. The Bank agreed on the condition that Randy's father, Mervin, act as cosigner. Mervin, a good customer of the Bank, had executed and paid on time over sixty promissory notes within a seven-year period. Accordingly, the Bank drafted a new promissory note with an April 20, 1982, due date, which Randy took home for Mervin to sign. On April 20, 1982, the new note was unpaid. Randy, on May 5, 1982, brought the Bank a check signed by Mervin to cover the interest owed on the unpaid note and asked for another extension. The Bank agreed to a second extension, again on the condition that Mervin act as cosigner. Mervin, however, refused to sign the last note; and Randy subsequently declared bankruptcy. The Bank sued Mervin on December 19, 1982. Mervin responded that he was not liable since he had been incapacitated by liquor at the time he signed the note. He had been drinking heavily throughout this period, and in fact had been involuntarily committed to an alcoholism treatment hospital twice during the time of these events. In between commitments, however, Mervin had executed and paid his own promissory note with the Bank and had transacted business in connection with his farm. The trial court held that Mervin's contract as cosigner was void due to alcohol-related incapacity, and the Bank appealed.

DECISION Judgment for the Bank.

OPINION Mervin's obligation on the note was voidable, not void, due to his alcohol-related incapacity. Voidable contracts may be disaffirmed by the temporarily disabled party. Disaffirmance, however, must be prompt upon the recovery of the intoxicated person, or upon notice of the agreement if the once-disabled person has forgotten it. A voidable contract may also be ratified by the party who contracted while disabled, resulting in a fully valid legal obligation. Ratification may be either express or implied by conduct. Furthermore, failure to disaffirm over a period of time may itself ripen into ratification, especially when voiding the contract will significantly prejudice the other party. Mervin had notice, both from Randy and the Bank, that the note he cosigned was overdue. Nevertheless, Mervin wrote a check paying the interest due. Such action amounts to ratification by conduct. Mervin also ratified the contract by waiting several months before attempting to disaffirm. The Bank has been significantly prejudiced by Mervin's delay since Randy has now been discharged through bankruptcy. Through his failure to disaffirm and subsequent ratification, the once-voidable contract is now fully binding on Mervin.

INTERPRETATION An intoxicated party ratifies a contract by not disaffirming it when she is not intoxicated and learns of its existence and by making interest payments on it when she is not intoxicated.

CRITICAL THINKING QUESTION When should a person be allowed to invalidate an agreement because of intoxication? Explain.

Figure 14-1 summarizes the voidability of contracts made by persons with contractual incapacity.

Figure 14-1 Incapacity: Minors, Nonadjudicated Incompetents, and Intoxicated

Ethical Dilemma

Should a Merchant Sell to One Who Lacks Capacity?

Facts Alice Richards is a salesclerk for an exclusive department store in Connecticut. She was working in the children's clothing department when an elderly woman, Carrie Johnson, entered the area and began to browse. Because part of her compensation is based on commissions and it had been a slow season, Richards was eager to help her. However, when Richards asked Johnson if she needed any help, Johnson replied, "No, I'm just looking for a new pocketbook." When Richards attempted to direct Johnson to the pocketbooks, Johnson did not appear to respond. Puzzled, Richards began to wonder whether the woman was mentally alert.

Johnson picked out infant's clothing and accessories worth approximately $250. At the cashier's counter she exclaimed how lovely everything was and explained that the jumpers and bath toys would go well with the other new clothes she had purchased for her son, who would soon be back from a cruise in the Bahamas.

Worried that the woman did not know what she was purchasing, Richards asked her manager for assistance. The manager said that the sale should be completed, as long as the store's credit policies were satisfied.

Social, Policy, and Ethical Considerations
1. What would you do?
2. What responsibility does a retail store have in stopping a sale where a reasonable person would assume that the customer lacks capacity? What business policies are appropriate?
3. What are the dangers in assuming a protective position? How can a retailer avoid discrimination and extend appropriate protection?
4. What alternatives does a family have when an elderly member begins to lose capacity?

CHAPTER SUMMARY

Minors

Definition person who is under the age of majority (usually eighteen years)

Liability on Contracts minor's contracts are voidable at the minor's option

- *Disaffirmance* avoidance of the contract; may be done during minority and for a reasonable time after reaching majority

- *Ratification* affirmation of the entire contract; may be done upon reaching majority

Liability for Necessaries a minor is liable for the reasonable value of necessary items (those that reasonably supply a person's needs)

Liability for Misrepresentation of Age prevailing view is that a minor may disaffirm the contract

Liability for Tort Connected with Contract if a tort and a contract are so intertwined that to enforce the tort the court must enforce the contract, the minor is not liable in tort

Incompetent and
Intoxicated Persons

Person under Guardianship contracts made by a person placed under guardianship by court order are void

Mental Illness or Defect a contract entered into by a mentally incompetent person (one who is unable to understand the nature and consequences of his acts) is voidable

Intoxicated Persons a contract entered into by an intoxicated person (one who cannot understand the nature and consequence of her actions) is voidable

QUESTIONS

1. Mark, a minor, operates a one-man automobile repair shop. Rose, having heard of Mark's good work on other cars, takes her car to Mark's shop for a thorough engine overhaul. Mark, while overhauling Rose's engine, carelessly fits an unsuitable piston ring on one of the pistons, with the result that Rose's engine is seriously damaged. Mark offers to return the sum that Rose paid him for his work, but refuses to pay for the damage. Rose sues Mark in tort for the damage to her engine. Can Rose recover from Mark in tort for the damage to her engine? Why?

2. a. On March 20, Andy Small became seventeen years old, but he appeared to be at least eighteen (the age of majority). On April 1, he moved into a rooming house in Chicago and orally agreed to pay the landlady $800 a month for room and board, payable at the end of each month. On April 30, he refused to pay his landlady for his room and board for the month of April.

   b. On April 4, he went to Honest Hal's Carfeteria and signed a contract to buy a used car on credit with a small down payment. He made no representation as to his age, but Honest Hal represented the car to be in top condition, which it subsequently turned out not to be. On April 25, he returned the car to Honest Hal and demanded a refund of his down payment.

   c. On April 7, Andy sold and conveyed to Adam Smith a parcel of real estate that he owned. On April 28, he demanded that Adam Smith reconvey the land although the purchase price, which Andy received in cash, had been spent in riotous living.

   Explain the outcome of each transaction.

3. Jones, a minor, owned a 2010 automobile. She traded it to Stone for a 2011 car. Jones went on a three-week trip and found that the 2011 car was not as good as the 2010 car. She asked Stone to return the 2010 car but was told that it had been sold to Tate, who did not know that the car had been obtained by Stone from a minor. Jones thereupon sued Tate for the return of the 2010 car. Is Jones entitled to regain ownership of the 2010 car? Explain.

4. On May 7, Roy, a minor, a resident of Smithton, purchased an automobile from Royal Motors, Inc., for $12,750 in cash. On the same day, he bought a motor scooter from Marks, also a minor, for $1,750 and paid him in full. On June 5, two days before attaining his majority, Roy disaffirmed the contracts and offered to return the car and the motor scooter to the respective sellers. Royal Motors and Marks each refused the offers. On June 16, Roy brought separate appropriate actions against Royal Motors and Marks to recover the purchase price of the car and the motor scooter. By agreement on July 30, Royal Motors accepted the automobile. Royal then filed a counterclaim against Roy for the reasonable rental value of the car between June 5 and July 30. The car was not damaged during this period. Royal knew that Roy lived twenty-five miles from his place of employment in Smithton and that he probably used the car, as he did, for transportation. What is the decision as to (a) Roy's action against Royal Motors, Inc., and its counterclaim against Roy; and (b) Roy's action against Marks?

5. On October 1, George Jones entered into a contract with Johnson Motor Company, a dealer in automobiles, to buy a car for $10,600. He paid $1,100 down and agreed to make monthly payments thereafter of $325 each. Although he made the first payment on November 1, he failed to make any more payments. Jones was seventeen years old at the time he made the contract, but he represented to the company that he was twenty-one years old because he was afraid the company would not sell the car to him if it knew his real age. His appearance was that of a man of twenty-one years of age. On December 15, the company repossessed the car under the terms provided in the contract. At that time, the car had been damaged and was in need of repairs. On December 20, George Jones became of age and at once disaffirmed the contract and demanded the return of the $1,425 paid on the contract. When the company refused to do so, Jones brought an action to recover the $1,425, and the company set up a counterclaim of $1,500 for expenses it incurred in repairing the car. Who will prevail? Why?

6. Rebecca entered into a written contract to sell certain real estate to Mary, a minor, for $80,000, payable $4,000 on the execution of the contract and $800 on the first day of each month thereafter until paid. Mary paid the $4,000 down payment and eight monthly installments before attaining her majority. Thereafter, Mary made two additional monthly payments and caused the contract to be recorded in the county where the real estate was located. Mary was then advised by her lawyer that the contract was voidable. After being so advised, Mary immediately tendered the contract to Rebecca, together with a deed reconveying all of Mary's interest in the property to Rebecca. Also, Mary demanded that Rebecca return the money paid under the contract. Rebecca refused the tender and declined to repay any portion of the money paid to her by Mary. Can Mary cancel the contract and recover the amount paid to Rebecca? Explain.

7. Anita sold and delivered an automobile to Marvin, a minor. Marvin, during his minority, returned the automobile to Anita, saying that he disaffirmed the sale. Anita accepted the automobile and said she would return the purchase price to Marvin the next day. Later in the day, Marvin changed his mind, took the automobile without Anita's knowledge, and sold it to Chris. Anita had not returned the purchase price

when Marvin took the car. On what theory, if any, can Anita recover from Marvin? Explain.

8. Ira, who in 2009 had been found not guilty of a criminal offense because of insanity, was released from a hospital for the criminally insane during the summer of 2010 and since that time has been a reputable and well-respected citizen and businessperson. On February 1, 2011, Ira and Shirley entered into a contract in which Ira would sell his farm to Shirley for $300,000. Ira now seeks to void the contract. Shirley insists that Ira is fully competent and has no right to avoid the contract. Who will prevail? Why?

9. Daniel, while under the influence of alcohol to the extent that he did not know the nature and consequences of his acts, agreed to sell his 2010 automobile to Belinda for $13,000. The next morning when Belinda went to Daniel's house with the $13,000 in cash, Daniel stated that he did not remember the transaction but that "a deal is a deal." One week after completing the sale, Daniel decides that he wishes to avoid the contract. What is the result?

CASE PROBLEMS

10. Langstraat, age seventeen, owned a motorcycle that he insured against liability with Midwest Mutual Insurance Company. He signed a notice of rejection attached to the policy indicating that he did not desire to purchase uninsured motorists' coverage from the insurance company. Later he was involved in an accident with another motorcycle owned and operated by a party who was uninsured. Langstraat now seeks to recover from the insurance company, asserting that his rejection was not valid because he is a minor. Can Langstraat recover from Midwest? Explain.

11. G.A.S. married his wife, S.I.S., on January 19, 1994. He began to have mental health problems in 2007; that year, he was hospitalized at the Delaware State Hospital for eight weeks. Similar illnesses occurred in 2005 and in the early part of 2011, with G.A.S. suffering from symptoms such as paranoia and loss of a sense of reality. In early 2012, G.A.S. was still committed to the Delaware State Hospital, attending a regular job during the day and returning to the hospital at night. G.A.S., however, was never adjudicated to be incompetent by any court. During this time, he entered into a separation agreement prepared by his wife's attorney which was grossly unfair to G.A.S. However, G.A.S. never spoke with the attorney about the contents of the agreement; nor did he read it prior to signing. Moreover, G.A.S. was not independently represented by counsel when he executed this agreement. Can G.A.S. disaffirm the separation agreement? Explain.

12. L. D. Robertson bought a pickup truck from King and Julian, who did business as the Julian Pontiac Company. At the time of purchase, Robertson was seventeen years old, living at home with his parents, and driving his father's truck around the county to different construction jobs. According to the sales contract, he traded in a passenger car for the truck and was given $723 credit toward the truck's $1,743 purchase price, agreeing to pay the remainder in monthly installments. After he paid the first month's installment, the truck caught fire and was rendered useless. The insurance agent, upon finding that Robertson was a minor, refused to deal with him. Consequently, Robertson sued to exercise his right as a minor to rescind the contract and to recover the purchase price he had already paid ($723 credit for the car traded in plus the one month's installment). The defendants argue that Robertson, even as a minor, cannot rescind the contract because it was for a necessary item. Are they correct?

13. A fifteen-year-old minor was employed by Midway Toyota, Inc. On August 18, 2010, the minor, while engaged in lifting heavy objects, injured his lower back. In October 2010 he underwent surgery to remove a herniated disk. Midway Toyota paid him the appropriate amount of temporary total disability payments ($153.36 per week) from August 18, 2010, through November 15, 2011. In February 2012 a final settlement was reached for 150 weeks of permanent partial disability benefits totaling $18,403.40. Tom Mazurek represented Midway Toyota in the negotiations leading up to the agreement and negotiated directly with the minor and his mother, Hermoine Parrent. The final settlement agreement was signed by the minor only. Mrs. Parrent was present at the time and did not object to the signing, but neither she nor anyone else of "legal guardian status" cosigned the agreement. The minor later sought to disaffirm the agreement and reopen his workers' compensation case. The workers' compensation court denied his petition, holding that Mrs. Parrent "participated fully in consideration of the offered final settlement and ... ratified and approved it on behalf of her ward ... to the same legal effect as if she had actually signed [it]...." The minor appealed. Decision?

14. Rose, a minor, bought a new Buick Riviera from Sheehan Buick. Seven months later, while still a minor, he attempted to disaffirm the purchase. Sheehan Buick refused to accept the return of the car or to refund the purchase price. Rose, at the time of the purchase, gave all the appearance of being of legal age. The car had been used by him to carry on his school, business, and social activities. Can Rose successfully disaffirm the contract?

15. Haydocy Pontiac sold Jennifer Lee an automobile for $7,500, of which $6,750 was financed with a note and security agreement. At the time of the sale, Lee, age twenty, represented to Haydocy that she was twenty-one years old, the age of majority then, and capable of contracting. After receiving the car, Lee allowed John Roberts to take possession of it. Roberts took the car and has not returned. Lee has failed to make any further payments on the car. Haydocy has sued to recover on the note, but Lee disaffirms the contract, claiming that she was too young to enter into a valid contract. Can Haydocy recover the money from Lee? Explain.

16. Carol White ordered a $225 pair of contact lenses through an optometrist. White, an emancipated minor, paid $100 by check and agreed to pay the remaining $125 at a later time. The doctor ordered the lenses, incurring a debt of $110. After the lenses were ordered, White called to cancel her order and stopped payment on the $100 check. The lenses could be used by no one but White. The doctor sued White for the value of the lenses. Will the doctor be able to recover the money from White? Explain.

17. Halbman, a minor, purchased a 2007 Mercury from Lemke for $11,250. Under the terms of the contract, Halbman would pay $1,000 down and the balance in $250 weekly installments.

Halbman purchased the car as a way to get around and have some fun. Upon making the down payment, Halbman received possession of the car, but Lemke retained the title until the balance was paid. After Halbman had made his first four payments, a connecting rod in the car's engine broke. Lemke denied responsibility but offered to help Halbman repair the engine if Halbman would provide the parts. Halbman, however, placed the car in a garage where the repairs cost $1,637.40. Halbman never paid the repair bill.

Hoping to avoid any liability for the vehicle, Lemke transferred title to Halbman even though Halbman never paid the balance owed. Halbman returned the title with a letter disaffirming the contract and demanded return of the money paid. Lemke refused. As the repair bill remained unpaid, the garage removed the car's engine and transmission and towed the body to Halbman's father's house. Vandalism during the period of storage rendered the car unsalvageable. Several times Halbman requested Lemke to remove the car. Lemke refused. Halbman sued Lemke for the return of his consideration, and Lemke countersued for the amount still owed on the contract. Decision?

18. On April 29, 2010, Kirsten Fletcher and John E. Marshall III jointly signed a lease to rent an apartment for the term beginning on July 1, 2010, and ending on June 30, 2011, for a monthly rent of $525 per month. At the time the lease was signed, Marshall was not yet eighteen years of age. Marshall turned eighteen on May 30, 2010. The couple moved into the apartment. About two months later, Marshall moved out to attend college, but Fletcher remained. She paid the rent herself for the remaining ten months of the lease and then sought contribution for Marshall's share of the rent plus court costs in the amount of $2,500. Can Fletcher collect from Marshall?

19. Rogers was a nineteen-year-old (the age of majority then being twenty-one) high school graduate pursuing a civil engineering degree when he learned that his wife was expecting a child. As a result, he quit school and sought assistance from Gastonia Personnel Corporation in finding a job. Rogers signed a contract with the employment agency providing that he would pay the agency a service charge if it obtained suitable employment for him. The employment agency found him such a job, but Rogers refused to pay the service charge, asserting that he was a minor when he signed the contract. Gastonia sued to recover the agreed-upon service charge from Rogers. Should Rogers be liable under his contract? If so, for how much?

TAKING SIDES

Joseph Eugene Dodson, age sixteen, purchased a used pickup truck from Burns and Mary Shrader. The Shraders owned and operated Shrader's Auto Sales. Dodson paid $14,900 in cash for the truck. At the time of sale, the Shraders did not question Dodson's age, but thought he was eighteen or nineteen. Dodson made no misrepresentation concerning his age. Nine months after the date of purchase, the truck began to develop mechanical problems. A mechanic diagnosed the problem as a burnt valve but could not be certain. Dodson, who could not afford the repairs, continued to drive the truck until one month later, when the engine "blew up." Dodson parked the vehicle in the front yard of his parents' home and contacted the Shraders to rescind the purchase of the truck and to request a full refund.

a. What arguments would support Dodson's termination of the contract?

b. What arguments would support Shrader's position that the contract is not voidable?

c. Which side should prevail? Explain.

CHAPTER **15**

Contracts in Writing

To break an oral agreement which is not legally binding is morally wrong.

Talmud

CHAPTER OUTCOMES

After reading and studying this chapter, you should be able to:

1. Identify and explain the five types of contracts covered by the general contract statute of frauds and the contracts covered by the Uniform Commercial Code (UCC) statute of frauds provision.

2. Describe the writings that are required to satisfy the general contract and the UCC statute of frauds provisions.

3. Identify and describe the other methods of complying with the general contract and the UCC statute of frauds provisions.

4. Explain the parol evidence rule and identify the situations to which the rule does not apply.

5. Discuss the rules that aid in the interpretation of a contract.

An *oral* contract, that is, one not in writing, is in every way as enforceable as a written contract *unless* otherwise provided by statute. Although most contracts do not need to be in writing to be enforceable, it is highly desirable that significant contracts be written. Written contracts avoid many problems that proving the terms of oral contracts inevitably involve. The process of setting down the contractual terms in a written document also tends to clarify the terms and bring to light problems the parties might not otherwise foresee. Moreover, the terms of a written contract do not change over time, whereas the parties' recollections of the terms might.

When the parties do reduce their agreement to a complete and final written expression, the law (under the parol evidence rule) honors this document by not allowing the parties to introduce any evidence in a lawsuit that would alter, modify, or vary the terms of the written contract. Nevertheless, the parties may differ as to the proper or intended meaning of language contained in the written agreement where such language is ambiguous or susceptible to different interpretations. To determine the proper meaning requires an interpretation, or construction, of the contract. The rules of construction permit the parties to introduce evidence to resolve ambiguity and to show the meaning of the language employed and the sense in which both parties used it.

In this chapter, we will examine (1) the types of contracts that must be in writing to be enforceable, (2) the parol evidence rule, and (3) the rules of contractual interpretation.

STATUTE OF FRAUDS

The **statute of frauds** requires that certain designated types of contracts be evidenced by a writing to be enforceable. Many more types of contracts are not subject to the statute of frauds than are subject to it. Most oral contracts, as previously indicated, are

Statute of frauds
specifies those contracts that
must be in writing to be
enforceable

PRACTICAL ADVICE
Significant contracts should
be memorialized in a
writing signed by both
parties.

as enforceable and valid as written contracts. If, however, a given contract subject to the statute of frauds is said to be within the statute, to be enforceable it must comply with the requirements of the statute. All other types of contracts are said to be "not within" or "outside" the statute and need not comply with its requirements to be enforceable.

The statute of frauds has no relation whatever to any kind of fraud practiced in the making of contracts. The rules relating to such fraud are rules of common law and are discussed in Chapter 11. The purpose of the statute is to prevent fraud in the proof of certain oral contracts by perjured testimony in court. This purpose is accomplished by requiring certain contracts to be proved by a signed writing. On the other hand, the statute does not prevent the performance of oral contracts if the parties are willing to perform. In brief, the statute relates only to the proof or evidence of a contract. It has nothing to do with the circumstances surrounding the making of a contract or with the validity of a contract.

CONTRACTS WITHIN THE STATUTE OF FRAUDS

The following five kinds of contracts are within the statute of frauds as most states have adopted it. Compliance requires a writing signed by the party to be charged (the party against whom the contract is to be enforced).

1. Promises to answer for the duty of another
2. Promises of an executor or administrator to answer personally for a duty of the decedent whose funds he is administering
3. Agreements upon consideration of marriage
4. Agreements for the transfer of an interest in land
5. Agreements not to be performed within one year

A sixth type of contract within the original English statute of frauds applied to contracts for the sale of goods. The Uniform Commercial Code (UCC) now governs the enforceability of contracts of this kind.

The various provisions of the statute of frauds apply independently. Accordingly, a contract for the sale of an interest in land may also be a contract in consideration of marriage, a contract not to be performed in one year, *and* a contract for the sale of goods.

In addition to those contracts specified in the original statute, most states require that other contracts be evidenced by a writing as well—for example, a contract to make a will, to authorize an agent to sell real estate, or to pay a commission to a real estate broker. In addition, UCC Article 9 requires that contracts creating certain types of security interests be in writing. On the other hand, UCC Revised Article 8, which all states have adopted, provides that the statute of frauds does *not* apply to contracts for the sale of securities. Finally, Article 1 of the UCC requires that contracts for the sale of other personal property for more than $5,000 be in writing. The 2001 Revisions to Article 1, however, has deleted this requirement.

Electronic Records

One significant impediment to e-commerce has been the questionable enforceability of contracts entered into through electronic means such as the Internet or e-mail because of the writing requirements under contract and sales law (statute of frauds). In response, the ***Uniform Electronic Transactions Act (UETA)*** was promulgated by the National Conference of Commissioners on Uniform State Laws (NCCUSL) in July 1999, and has been adopted by forty-seven states. The other three states, Illinois, New York, and Washington, have statutes pertaining to electronic transactions under consideration. UETA applies only to transactions between parties each of which has agreed to conduct transactions by electronic means. It gives full effect to electronic contracts, encouraging their widespread use, and develops a uniform legal framework for their implementation. UETA protects electronic signatures and contracts from being denied enforcement because of the statute of frauds. Section 7 of UETA accomplishes this by providing:

1. A record or signature may not be denied legal effect or enforceability solely because it is in electronic form.
2. A contract may not be denied legal effect or enforceability solely because an electronic record was used in its formation.

3. If a law requires a record to be in writing, an electronic record satisfies the law.
4. If a law requires a signature, an electronic signature satisfies the law.

Section 14 of UETA further validates contracts formed by machines functioning as electronic agents for parties to a transaction: "A contract may be formed by the interaction of electronic agents of the parties, even if no individual was aware of or reviewed the electronic agents' actions or the resulting terms and agreements." The Act excludes from its coverage wills, codicils, and testamentary trusts as well as all Articles of the UCC except Articles 2 and 2A.

In addition, Congress in 2000 enacted the *Electronic Signatures in Global and National Commerce (E-Sign)*. The Act, which uses language very similar to that of UETA, makes electronic records and signatures valid and enforceable across the United States for many types of transactions in or affecting interstate or foreign commerce. E-Sign does not generally preempt UETA. E-Sign does not require any person to agree to use or accept electronic records or electronic signatures. The Act defines transactions quite broadly to include the sale, lease, exchange, and licensing of personal property and services, as well as the sale, lease, exchange, or other disposition of any interest in real property. E-Sign defines an electronic record as "a contract or other record created, generated, sent, communicated, received, or stored by electronic means." It defines an electronic signature as "an electronic sound, symbol, or process, attached to or logically associated with a contract or other record and executed or adopted by a person with the intent to sign the record." Like UETA, E-Sign ensures that Internet and e-mail agreements will not be unenforceable because of the statute of frauds by providing that:

1. a signature, contract, or other record relating to such transaction may not be denied legal effect, validity, or enforceability solely because it is in electronic form; and
2. a contract relating to such transaction may not be denied legal effect, validity, or enforceability solely because an electronic signature or electronic record was used in its formation.

To protect consumers, E-Sign provides that they must consent *electronically* to conducting transactions with electronic records after being informed of the types of hardware and software required. Prior to consent, consumers must also receive a "clear and conspicuous" statement informing consumers of their right to (1) have the record provided on paper or in nonelectronic form; (2) after consenting to electronic records, receive paper copies of the electronic record; and (3) withdraw consent to receiving electronic records.

As defined by E-Sign, an electronic agent is a computer program or other automated means used independently to initiate an action or respond to electronic records or performances in whole or in part without review or action by an individual at the time of the action or response. The Act validates contracts or other records relating to a transaction in or affecting interstate or foreign commerce formed by electronic agents so long as the action of each electronic agent is legally attributable to the person to be bound.

E-Sign specifically excludes certain transactions, including (1) wills, codicils, and testamentary trusts; (2) adoptions, divorces, and other matters of family law; and (3) the UCC other than sales and leases of goods.

Suretyship Provision

Suretyship provision
promise to pay the debts of another

Surety
person who promises to pay the debt of another

Principal debtor
person whose debt is being supported

Collateral promise
undertaking to be secondarily liable; that is, liable if the principal debtor does not perform

The **suretyship provision** applies to a contractual promise by a **surety** (*promisor*) to a **creditor** (*promisee*) to perform the duties or obligations of a third person (**principal debtor**) if the principal debtor does not perform. Thus, if a mother tells a merchant to extend $1,000 worth of credit to her son and says, "If he doesn't pay, I will," the promise is a suretyship and must be evidenced by a writing (or have a sufficient electronic record) to be enforceable. The factual situation can be reduced to the simple idea that, "If X doesn't pay, I will." The promise is said to be a **collateral promise**, in that the promisor is not primarily liable. The mother does not promise to pay in any event; her promise is to pay only if the one primarily obligated, the son, defaults.

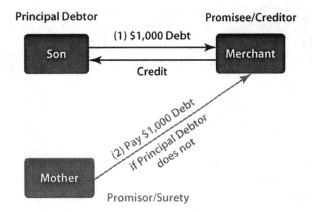

Thus, a suretyship involves three parties and two contracts. The primary contract, between the principal debtor and the creditor, creates the indebtedness. The collateral contract is made by the third person (surety) directly with the creditor, whereby the surety promises to pay the debt to the creditor in case the principal debtor fails to do so. For a complete discussion of suretyship, see Chapter 37. See *Rosewood Care Center, Inc. v. Caterpillar, Inc.* later in this chapter.

Original promise

promise to become primarily liable

Original Promise   If the promisor makes an **original promise** by undertaking to become primarily liable, then the statute of frauds does not apply. For example, a father tells a merchant to deliver certain items to his daughter and says, "I will pay $400 for them." The father is not promising to answer for the debt of another; rather, he is making the debt his own. It is to the father, and to the father alone, that the merchant extends credit; to the father alone the creditor may look for payment. The statute of frauds does not apply, and the promise may be oral.

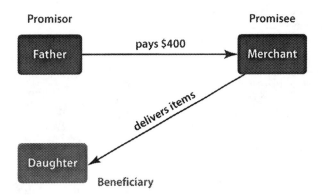

Main purpose

object of promisor/surety is to provide an economic benefit for herself

Main Purpose Doctrine   The courts have developed an exception to the suretyship provision called the "main purpose doctrine" or "leading object rule." In cases in which the **main purpose** of the promisor is to obtain an economic benefit for herself that she did not previously have, then the promise comes within the exception and is *outside* the statute. The expected benefit to the surety "must be such as to justify the conclusion that his main purpose in making the promise is to advance his own interest." The fact that the surety received consideration for his promise or that he might receive a slight and indirect advantage is insufficient to bring the promise within the main purpose doctrine.

Suppose that a supply company has refused to furnish materials on the credit of a building contractor. Faced with a possible slowdown in the construction of his building, the owner of the land promises the supplier that if the supplier will extend credit to the contractor, the owner will pay if the contractor does not. Here, the purpose of the promisor was to serve an economic interest of his own, even though the performance of the promise would discharge the duty of another. The intent to benefit the contractor was at most incidental, and courts will enforce oral promises of this type.

Rosewood Care Center, Inc., v. Caterpillar, Inc.
Supreme Court of Illinois, 2007
226 Ill.2d 559, 877 N.E.2d 1091, 315 Ill.Dec. 762
http://scholar.google.com/scholar_case?case=14227814297099210037&q=877+N.E.2d+1091&hl=en&as_sdt=2,22

FACTS On January 3, 2002, Caterpillar contacted HSM Management Services (HSM), the management agent for Plaintiff, Rosewood Care Center, Inc. (Rosewood), a skilled nursing facility. Caterpillar requested that Rosewood admit Betty Jo Cook, an employee of Caterpillar, on a "managed care basis (fixed rate)." HSM advised Caterpillar that Rosewood would not admit Cook on those terms. Shortly thereafter, on January 10, Dr. Norma Just, Caterpillar's employee in charge of medical care relating to workers' compensation claims, contacted HSM. Just told HSM that Cook had sustained a work-related injury and was receiving medical care at Caterpillar's expense under the workers' compensation laws. Just requested that Cook be admitted to Rosewood for skilled nursing care and therapy, and stated that the cost of Cook's care would be 100 percent covered and paid directly by Caterpillar to Rosewood with a zero deductible and no maximum limit. Just further advised HSM that Cook had been precertified for four weeks of care. Just asked that Rosewood send the bills for Cook's care to Caterpillar's workers' compensation division. On January 20, "Sue" from Dr. Just's office telephoned HSM and confirmed approval for Cook's transfer from the hospital to Rosewood. On January 30, Sue reconfirmed, via telephone, Caterpillar's authorization for Cook's care and treatment in accordance with the January 10 agreement, except that Sue now advised HSM that Cook was precertified for two weeks of care instead of the original four weeks. On January 30, Cook was admitted to Rosewood. Upon her admission, Cook signed a document entitled "Assignment of Insurance Benefits" as required by law. In this document, Cook assigned any insurance benefits she might receive to Rosewood and acknowledged her liability for any unpaid services. Caterpillar, through its health care management company, continued to orally "authorize" care for Cook and did so on February 8, February 25, March 11, March 21, April 8, April 18, May 16, and June 4. Cook remained at Rosewood until June 13, 2002. The total of Rosewood's charges for Cook's care amounted to $181,857. Caterpillar never objected to the bills being sent to it for Cook's care, nor did it ever advise Rosewood that treatment was not authorized. However, Caterpillar ultimately refused to pay for services rendered to Cook.

The plaintiff filed an action against Caterpillar seeking reimbursement for the services provided to Cook while she was a patient at Rosewood. In response, Caterpillar moved to dismiss the complaint, arguing that the alleged promise to pay for Cook's care was not enforceable because it was not in writing as required by the statute of frauds. The trial court granted Caterpillar's motion for summary judgment and Rosewood appealed. The appellate court reversed and remanded.

DECISION Judgment of the appellate court affirmed and remanded.

OPINION In general, the statute of frauds provides that a promise to pay the debt of another, that is, a suretyship agreement, is unenforceable unless it is in writing. According to Rosewood, Caterpillar's promise falls outside the statute of frauds pursuant to the "main purpose" or "leading object" rule. Under this rule, when the "main purpose" or "leading object" of the promisor/surety is to advance its own pecuniary or business interests, the promise does not fall within the statute. Caterpillar contended that the "main purpose" rule did not apply to its promises to Rosewood because the promises were not to promote its own interest. The question of whether Caterpillar's promise was within Caterpillar's "main purpose" or "leading object," is a factual one to be made based on evidence to be presented by the parties. Accordingly, this issue must be resolved by the trial court on remand.

INTERPRETATION When the "main purpose" or "leading object" of the surety is to advance its own pecuniary or business interests, the promise does not fall within the statute.

CRITICAL THINKING QUESTION Should the contracts of a surety have to be in writing? Explain.

Promise Made to Debtor The suretyship provision has been interpreted *not* to include promises made to a *debtor*. For example, D owes a debt to C. S promises D to pay D's debt. Because the promise of S was made to the debtor (D), not the creditor (C), the promise is enforceable even if it is oral.

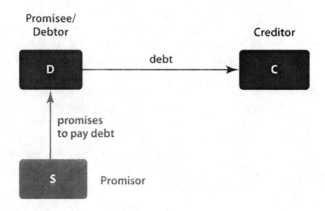

Executor-Administrator Provision

Executor-administrator provision
applies to promises to answer personally for a duty of the decedent

The **executor-administrator provision** applies to the promises of an executor of a decedent's will, or to those of the administrator of the estate if there is no will, to answer personally for a duty of the decedent. An **executor** or **administrator** is a person appointed by a court to carry out, subject to order of court, the administration of the estate of a deceased person. If the will of a decedent nominates a certain person as executor, the court usually appoints that person. (For a more detailed discussion of executors, administrators, and the differences between the two, see Chapter 50.) If an executor or administrator promises to answer personally for a duty of the decedent, the promise is unenforceable unless it is in writing or in proper electronic form. For example, Edgar, who is Donna's son and executor of Donna's will, recognizes that Donna's estate will not have enough funds to pay all of the decedent's debts. He orally promises Clark, one of Donna's creditors, that he will personally pay all of his mother's debts in full. Edgar's oral promise is not enforceable. This provision does not apply, however, to promises to pay debts of the deceased out of assets of the estate.

Executor/administrator
person appointed to settle a decedent's estate

The executor-administrator provision is thus a specific application of the suretyship provision. Accordingly, the exceptions to the suretyship provision also apply to this provision.

Marriage Provision

Marriage provision
applies to promises in consideration of marriage but not to mutual promises to marry

The notable feature of the marriage provision is that it does not apply to mutual promises to marry. Rather, the provision applies only if a promise to marry is made in consideration for some promise other than a mutual promise to marry. Therefore, this provision covers Adams's promise to convey title to a certain farm to Barnes if Barnes accepts Adams's proposal of marriage.

Land Contract Provision

Land contract provision
applies to promises to transfer any right, privilege, power, or immunity in real property

The land contract provision covers promises to transfer any **interest in land**, which includes any right, privilege, power, or immunity in real property. Thus, all promises to transfer, buy, or pay for an interest in land, including ownership interests, leases, mortgages, options, and easements, are within the provision.

Interest in land
any right, privilege, power, or immunity in real property

The land contract provision does not include contracts to transfer an interest in personal property. It also does not cover short-term leases, which by statute in most states are those for one year or less; contracts to build a building on a piece of land; contracts to do work on the land; or contracts to insure a building.

An oral contract for the transfer of an interest in land may be enforced if the party seeking enforcement has so changed his position in reasonable reliance on the contract that a court can prevent injustice only by enforcing the contract. In applying this *part performance* exception, many states require that the transferee has paid a portion or all of the purchase price *and* either has taken possession of the real estate or has started to make valuable improvements on the land. Payment of part or all of the price is not sufficient in itself to make the contract enforceable under this exception. For example, Jane orally agrees to sell land to Jack for $30,000. With Jane's consent, Jack takes possession of the land, pays Jane $10,000, builds a house on the land, and occupies it. Several years later, Jane repudiates the contract. The courts will enforce the contract against Jane.

An oral promise by a purchaser is also enforceable if the seller fully performs by conveying the property to the purchaser.

One-Year Provision

One-year provision
applies to contracts that cannot be performed within one year

The statute of frauds requires that all contracts that *cannot* be fully performed within one year of the making of the contract be in writing or in proper electronic form.

Possibility test
if it is possible for the agreement to be performed within one year it is not within the statute of frauds

The Possibility Test   To determine whether a contract falls within the one-year provision, the courts ask whether it is *possible* for the performance of the contract to be completed within a year. Under the majority rule, the **possibility test** does not ask whether the agreement is likely to be performed within one year from the date it was formed; nor does it ask whether the parties think that performance will occur within the year. The enforceability of the contract depends *not* on probabilities or on actual subsequent events but on whether the terms of the contract make it possible for performance to occur within one year. For example, an oral contract between Alice and Bill for Alice to build a bridge, which should reasonably take three years, is generally enforceable if it is possible, although extremely unlikely and difficult, for Alice to perform the contract in one year. Similarly, if Alice agrees to employ Bill for life, this contract is also not within

Iacono v. Lyons
Court of Appeals of Texas, 2000
16 S.W.3d 92, rehearing denied
http://scholar.google.com/scholar_case?case=11114784991765023339&hl=en&as_sdt=2&as_vis=1&oi=scholarr

FACTS The plaintiff, Mary Iacono, and the defendant, Carolyn Lyons, had been friends for almost thirty-five years. In late 1996, the defendant invited the plaintiff to join her on a trip to Las Vegas, Nevada, for which the defendant paid. The plaintiff contended she was invited to Las Vegas by the defendant because the defendant thought the plaintiff was lucky. Sometime before the trip, the plaintiff had a dream about winning on a Las Vegas slot machine. The plaintiff's dream convinced her to go to Las Vegas, and she accepted the defendant's offer to split "50–50" any gambling winnings. The defendant provided the plaintiff with money for the gambling.

The plaintiff and defendant started to gamble but after losing $47, the defendant wanted to leave to see a show. The plaintiff begged the defendant to stay, and the defendant agreed on the condition that the defendant put the coins into the machines because doing so took the plaintiff, who suffers from advanced rheumatoid arthritis and was in a wheelchair, too long. The plaintiff agreed and took the defendant to a dollar slot machine that looked like the machine in her dream. The machine did not pay on the first try. The plaintiff then said, "Just one more time," and the defendant looked at the plaintiff and said, "This one's for you, Puddin." They hit the jackpot, and the slot machine paid $1,908,064. The defendant refused to share the winnings with the plaintiff and denied they had an agreement to split any winnings. The defendant told Caesar's Palace that she was the sole winner and to pay her all the winnings.

The plaintiff sued the defendant for breach of contract. The defendant moved for summary judgment on the grounds that any oral agreement was unenforceable under the statute of frauds. The trial court entered summary judgment in favor of the defendant. The plaintiff appeals.

DECISION Summary judgment reversed and remanded.

OPINION The defendant asserted the agreement, if any, was unenforceable under the statute of frauds because it could not be performed within one year. There is no dispute that the winnings were to be paid over a period of twenty years. The one-year provision of the statute of frauds does not apply if the contract, from its terms, could possibly be performed within a year—however improbable performance within one year may be.

Assuming without deciding that the parties agreed to share their gambling winnings, such an agreement possibly could have been performed within one year. For example, if the plaintiff and defendant had won $200, they probably would have received all the money in one payout and could have split the winnings immediately.... Therefore, the defendant was not entitled to summary judgment based on her affirmative defense of the statute of frauds.

INTERPRETATION If a contract is possible to perform fully within one year, it does not fall within the statute of frauds.

ETHICAL QUESTION Is this result fair? Explain.

CRITICAL THINKING QUESTION Do you agree with the one-year provision? Explain.

---

the statute of frauds. It is possible that Bill may die within the year, in which case the contract would be completely performed. The contract is therefore one that is *fully performable* within a year. Contracts of indefinite duration are likewise excluded from the provision. On the other hand, an oral contract to employ another person for thirteen months could not possibly be performed within a year and is therefore unenforceable.

Computation of time
the year runs from the time the agreement is made

Computation of Time The year runs from the time the *agreement is made*, not from the time when the performance is to begin. For example, on January 1, 2011, A hires B to work for eleven months starting on May 1, 2011, under the terms of an oral contract. That contract will be fully performed on March 31, 2012, which is more than one year after January 1, 2011, the date the contract was made. Consequently, the contract is *within* the statute of frauds and unenforceable because it is oral.

Jan. 1, 2011 — A and B enter into oral contract

May 1, 2011 — B commences performance

Jan. 1, 2011 — Oral contract must be completed to be enforceable

March 31, 2012 — B finishes performance

Similarly, a contract for a year's performance that is to begin three days after the date of the making of the contract is within the statute and, if oral, is unenforceable. If, however, the performance is to begin the day following the making or, under the terms of the agreement, *could* have begun the following day, it is not within the statute and need not be in writing.

Full performance by one party

makes the promise of the other party enforceable under majority view

Full Performance by One Party   Where a contract has been fully performed by one party, most courts hold that the promise of the other party is enforceable even though by its terms its performance was not possible within one year. For example, Jane borrows $4,800 from Tom. Jane orally promises to pay Tom $4,800 in three annual installments of $1,600. Jane's promise is enforceable, despite the one-year provision, because Tom has fully performed by making the loan.

Sale of Goods

Sale of goods

a contract for the sale of goods for the price of $500 or more must be evidenced by a writing to be enforceable

The English statute of frauds, which applied to contracts for the sale of goods, has been used as a prototype for the UCC, Article 2, statute of frauds provision. The UCC provides that a contract for the sale of goods for the price of *$500 or more* is not enforceable unless there is some writing or record sufficient to indicate that a contract for sale has been made between the parties. The Code defines *goods* as movable personal property.

Admission

an admission in pleadings, testimony, or otherwise in court makes the contract enforceable for the quantity of goods admitted

Admission   The Code permits an oral contract for the sale of goods to be enforced against a party who, in his pleading, testimony, or otherwise, admits in court that a contract was made; but the Code limits enforcement to the quantity of goods he admits. Moreover, some courts hold that, by performing over a period of time, for example, a party may implicitly admit the existence of a contract. Some courts now apply this exception to other statute of frauds provisions.

Specially manufactured goods

an oral contract for specially manufactured goods is enforceable

Specially Manufactured Goods   The Code permits enforcement of an oral contract for goods specially manufactured for a buyer, but only if evidence indicates that the goods were made for the buyer and the seller can show that he has made a *substantial beginning* of their manufacture before receiving any notice of repudiation. If the goods, although manufactured on special order, may be readily resold in the ordinary course of the seller's business, this exception does not apply.

Kalas v. Cook
Appellate Court of Connecticut, 2002
70 Conn. App. 477, 800 A.2d 553, 47 U.C.C. Rep. Serv. 2d 1307
http://www.jud.state.ct.us/external/supapp/Cases/AROap/70ap412.pdf

---

FACTS   The plaintiff, Barbara H. Kalas, doing business as Clinton Press of Tolland, operated a printing press and, for several decades, provided written materials, including books and pamphlets, for Adelma G. Simmons. Simmons ordered these materials for use and sale at her farm, known as Caprilands Herb Farm (Caprilands). The defendant has not suggested that these materials could have been sold on the open market. Due to limited space at Caprilands, the plaintiff and Simmons agreed that the written materials would remain stored at the plaintiff's print shop until Simmons decided that delivery was necessary. The materials were delivered either routinely or upon request by Simmons and were paid for according to the invoice from plaintiff.

In early 1997, the plaintiff decided to close her business. The plaintiff and Simmons agreed that the materials printed for Caprilands and stored at the plaintiff's print shop would be delivered and paid for upon delivery. On December 3, 1997, Simmons died. The plaintiff submitted a claim against the estate for $24,599.38 for unpaid deliveries to Caprilands. (The defendant, Edward W. Cook, is the executor of the estate of Simmons). The defendant denied these allegations and raised a defense under the statute of frauds.

The trial ruled that as a contract for the sale of goods, its enforcement was not precluded by the Uniform Commercial Code (UCC) statute of frauds provision. Accordingly, the court rendered a judgment in favor of the plaintiff in the amount of $24,599.38. The defendant appealed.

DECISION   Judgment affirmed.

OPINION   On appeal, the defendant argued that the oral contract was invalid because a writing was required by the UCC. Contracts for the sale of goods at a price of $500 or more are presumptively unenforceable. However, under the Code, an oral contract for the sale of goods is enforceable if the goods in question are "specially manufactured." In determining whether goods are specially manufactured, courts generally apply a four-part standard:

> (1) the goods must be specially made for the buyer; (2) the goods must be unsuitable for sale to others in the ordinary course of the seller's business; (3) the seller must have substantially begun to have manufactured the goods or to have a commitment for their procurement; and (4) the manufacture or commitment must have been commenced under circumstances reasonably indicating that

the goods are for the buyer and prior to the seller's receipt of notification of contractual repudiation.

The term "specially manufactured," therefore, refers to the nature of the particular goods in question and not to whether the goods were made in an unusual, as opposed to the regular, business operation or manufacturing process of the seller. Printed material, particularly that, as in this case, names the buyer, has been deemed by both state and federal courts to fall within the exception set out for specially manufactured goods.

The printed materials in this case were specially manufactured goods. The materials were printed specifically for Caprilands. The materials included brochures and labels with the Caprilands' name, as well as books that were written and designed by Simmons. The plaintiff testified that the books were printed, as Simmons had requested, in a rustic style with typed inserts and hand-drawn pictures. Therefore, none of these materials was suitable for sale to others. Thus, the agreement for their production was not required to be in writing.

INTERPRETATION An oral contract for the sale of goods is enforceable if the goods in question are specially manufactured.

ETHICAL QUESTION Did the executor of Simmons' estate act ethically? Explain.

CRITICAL THINKING QUESTION Do you agree with the court's decision? Explain.

Delivery or payment and acceptance

validates the contract only for the goods that have been accepted or for which payment has been accepted

Delivery or Payment and Acceptance Under the Code, delivery and acceptance of part of the goods, or payment and acceptance of part of the price, validates the contract but only for the goods that have been accepted or for which payment has been accepted. To illustrate, Liz orally agrees to buy one thousand watches from David for $15,000. David delivers three hundred watches to Liz, who receives and accepts the watches. The oral contract is enforceable to the extent of three hundred watches ($4,500)—those received and accepted—but is unenforceable to the extent of seven hundred watches ($10,500).

A summary of the contracts within, and the exceptions to, the statute of frauds is provided in Concept Review 15-1.

Modification or rescission of contracts within the statute of frauds

oral contracts modifying existing contracts are unenforceable if the resulting contract is within the statute of frauds

Modification or Rescission of Contracts within the Statute of Frauds

Oral contracts modifying previously existing contracts are unenforceable if the resulting contract is within the statute of frauds. The reverse is also true: an oral modification of a prior contract is enforceable if the new contract is not within the statute of frauds.

Thus, examples of unenforceable oral contracts include an oral promise to guarantee the additional duties of another, an oral agreement to substitute different land for that described

---

CONCEPT REVIEW 15-1

The Statute of Frauds

Contracts within the Statute of Frauds	Exceptions
Suretyship—a promise to answer for the duty of another	• Main purpose rule • Original promise • Promise made to debtor
Executor–Administrator—a promise to answer personally for debt of decedent	• Main purpose rule • Original promise • Promise made to debtor
Agreements made upon consideration of marriage	• Mutual promises to marry
Agreements for the transfer of an interest in land	• Part performance plus detrimental reliance • Seller conveys property
Agreements not to be performed within one year	• Full performance by one party • Possibility of performance within one year
Sale of goods for $500 or more	• Admission • Specially manufactured goods • Delivery or payment and acceptance

in the original contract, and an oral agreement to extend an employee's contract for six months to a total of two years. On the other hand, an oral agreement to modify an employee's contract from two years to six months at a higher salary is not within the statute of frauds and is enforceable.

Under the UCC, the decisive point is the contract price after modification. If the parties enter into an oral contract to sell for $450 a motorcycle to be delivered to the buyer and later, prior to delivery, orally agree that the seller shall paint the motorcycle and install new tires and that the buyer shall pay a price of $550, the modified contract is unenforceable. Conversely, if the parties have a written contract for the sale of two hundred bushels of wheat at a price of $4 per bushel and later orally agree to decrease the quantity to one hundred bushels at the same price per bushel, the agreement as modified is for a total price of $400 and thus is enforceable.

An oral rescission is effective and discharges all unperformed duties under the original contract. For example, Jones and Brown enter into a written contract of employment for a two-year term. Later they orally agree to rescind the contract. The oral agreement is effective, and the written contract is rescinded. Where land has been transferred, however, an agreement to rescind the transaction is a contract to retransfer the land and is within the statute of frauds.

COMPLIANCE WITH THE STATUTE OF FRAUDS

Even a contract within the statute of frauds will be enforced if it is contained in a *writing, memorandum,* or *record* sufficient to satisfy the statute's requirements. As long as the writing or record meets those requirements, it need not be in any specific form, nor be an attempt by the parties to enter into a binding contract, nor represent their entire agreement.

General Contract Provisions

The English statute of frauds and most modern statutes of frauds require that the agreement be evidenced by a writing or record to be enforceable. The statute's purpose in requiring a writing or record is to ensure that the parties have actually entered into a contract. It is, therefore, not necessary that the writing or record be in existence when the parties initiate litigation; it is sufficient to show that the memorandum existed at one time. The note, memorandum, or record, which may be formal or informal, must

1. specify the parties to the contract;
2. specify with reasonable certainty the subject matter and the essential terms of the unperformed promises; and
3. be signed by the party to be charged or by her agent.

The memorandum may be such that the parties themselves view it as having no legal significance whatever. For example, a personal letter between the parties, an interdepartmental communication, an advertisement, or the record books of a business may serve as a memorandum. The writing need not have been delivered to the party who seeks to take advantage of it, and it may even contain a repudiation of the oral agreement. For example, Sid and Gail enter into an oral agreement that Sid will sell Blackacre to Gail for $5,000. Sid subsequently receives a better offer and sends Gail a signed letter, which begins by reciting all the material terms of the oral agreement. The letter concludes: "Because my agreement to sell Blackacre to you for $5,000 was oral, I am not bound by my promise. I have since received a better offer and will accept that one." Sid's letter constitutes a sufficient memorandum for Gail to enforce Sid's promise to sell Blackacre. Because Gail did not sign the memorandum, however, the writing does not bind her. Thus, a contract may be enforceable against only one of the parties.

The "signature" may be initials or may even be typewritten or printed, as long as the party intended it to authenticate the writing or record. Furthermore, the signature need not be at the bottom of the page or at the customary place for a signature.

The memorandum may consist of several papers or documents, none of which would be sufficient by itself. The several memoranda, however, must together satisfy all of the requirements of a writing to comply with the statute of frauds and must clearly indicate that they relate to the same transaction. The latter requirement can be satisfied if (1) the writings are physically connected, (2) the writings refer to each other, or (3) an examination of the writings shows them to be in reference to each other.

PRACTICAL ADVICE

When significantly modifying an existing common law contract, make sure that consideration is given and that the modification is in writing and signed by both parties.

Compliance: general contract law

the writing or writings must (1) specify the parties to the contract; (2) specify the subject matter and essential terms; and (3) be signed by the party to be charged or by her agent

PRACTICAL ADVICE

To avoid becoming solely liable by signing a contract before the other party signs, include a provision to the effect that no party is bound to the contract until all parties sign the contract.

Estate of Jackson v. Devenyns
Supreme Court of Wyoming, 1995
892 P.2d.786
http://wyomcases.courts.state.wy.us/applications/oscn/DeliverDocument.asp?CiteID=123305

FACTS On February 9, 1993, George Jackson and his neighbors, Karen and Steve Devenyn, drafted and signed a document that purports to convey a seventy-nine-acre parcel of land owned by Jackson. By the terms of the agreement, Jackson wished to reserve a 1.3 acre portion of the parcel. Although the agreement contained a drawing and dimensions of the conveyance, it did not contain a specific description of the parcel. Jackson died on May 8, 1993, and his estate refused to honor the agreement. The Devenyns then filed a petition with the probate court to order a conveyance. Based on the parol evidence rule, the estate of Jackson objected to the admission of the witnesses' testimony that they could point out the specific area based on conversations with Jackson. However, the probate court heard the testimony and determined that, with the witnesses' testimony, a sufficient description of the parcel could be determined. Accordingly, it granted the petition. The estate appeals.

DECISION Judgment reversed.

OPINION A written memorandum purporting to convey real estate must sufficiently describe the property to comply with the requirements of the statute of frauds and permit specific performance. A valid contract to convey land must expressly contain a description of the land, certain in itself or capable of being rendered certain by reference to an extrinsic source that the writing itself designates. It is expressly prohibited to supply the writing's essential provisions by inferences or presumptions deduced from oral testimony. This writing insufficiently describes the property it purports to convey, to reserve, and for which it grants an option to purchase. The writing's description of the property to be conveyed states: "George Jackson agrees to sell 79 acres...." Such a description is insufficiently definite to identify the land without recourse to extrinsic evidence. When a writing states only the total acreage without any description of the location of the land involved, the statute of frauds' requirement that the subject matter be reasonably certain is not satisfied and the contract is void. The present description provides only the total acreage and does not provide any certainty that this particular tract was intended to be conveyed. Therefore, this agreement is too uncertain to be enforced.

INTERPRETATION A writing to comply with the general contract statute of frauds must (1) specify the parties to the contract, (2) specify with reasonable certainty the subject matter and the essential terms of the promises, and (3) be signed by the party to be charged or by her agent.

CRITICAL THINKING QUESTION Should the statute of frauds provision mandate that the writing contain a reasonably certain description of the land? Explain.

Compliance: sale of goods
the writing or writings must (1) be sufficient to indicate that a contract has been made between the parties, (2) be signed by the party against whom enforcement is sought or by her authorized agent, and (3) specify the quantity of goods to be sold

Sale of Goods

The statute of frauds provision under Article 2 (Sales) of the UCC is more liberal. For a sale of goods, the Code requires merely a writing or record (1) sufficient to indicate that a contract has been made between the parties, (2) signed by the party against whom enforcement is sought or by her authorized agent or broker, and (3) specifying the *quantity* of goods or securities to be sold. The writing or record is sufficient even if it omits or incorrectly states an agreed-upon term; however, if the quantity term is misstated, the contract can be enforced only to the extent of the quantity stated in the writing or record.

As with general contracts, several related documents may satisfy the writing requirement. Moreover, the "signature" may be by initials or even typewritten or printed, so long as the party intended to authenticate the writing or record.

In addition, between merchants, if one party, within a reasonable time after entering into the oral contract, sends a written confirmation of the contract for a sale of goods to the other party and the written confirmation is sufficient against the sender, it is also sufficient against the recipient of the confirmation unless the recipient gives written notice of his objection within ten days after receiving the confirmation. This means that if these requirements have been met, the recipient of the writing or record is in the same position he would have assumed by signing it, and the confirmation, therefore, is enforceable against him.

PRACTICAL ADVICE

Merchants should examine written confirmations carefully and promptly to make certain that they are accurate.

For example, Brown Co. and ANM Industries enter into an oral contract that provides that ANM will deliver twelve thousand shirts to Brown at $6 per shirt. Brown sends a letter to ANM acknowledging the agreement. The letter is signed by Brown's president, contains the quantity term but not the price, and is mailed to ANM's vice president for sales. Brown is bound by the contract once its authorized agent signs the letter, while ANM cannot raise the defense of the statute of frauds ten days after receiving the letter if it does not object within that time.

EFFECT OF NONCOMPLIANCE

Under both the statute of frauds and the Code, the basic legal effect is the same: a contracting party has a defense to an action by the other party for enforcement of an *unenforceable* oral

BUSINESS LAW *IN ACTION*

When *should* a writing or record be used to memorialize a contract? The statute of frauds identifies those categories of contracts that must be evidenced by a writing or record to be enforced, but it does not prevent us from using written contracts where they are not legally called for nor does it preclude us from entering into an agreement without one.

Any time there is a doubt about the other party's ability to perform or a likelihood of future dispute over terms, the parties should have a writing—however brief or informal. For example, one should consider putting in writing service contracts

that will be completed in less than a year, such as construction contracts, professional contracts, or other contracts for personal service, even though they typically do not fall within the statute of frauds.

On the other hand, there are times when insisting on a writing might actually undermine an agreement. The most common reason for disregarding the statute of frauds is business expediency. Even though goods valued at greater than $500 may be involved, the seller may not want to "bother" with the formality of a writing, and there may be a buyer who is equally motivated to consummate the

transaction. Waiting for a written agreement might mean losing out on the deal. In such a case, however, both parties must understand that if the other party fails to perform, the agreement will be unenforceable.

Commerce is dynamic: depending on the type of agreement involved, it can be fast paced and fluid or it can be deliberate and painstaking. Understanding the statute of frauds is important, but one may also wish to consider other factors in deciding whether to put a contract in writing.

© Cengage Learning 2013

contract—that is, an oral contract that falls within the statute and does not comply with its requirements. For example, if Kirkland, a painter, and Riggsbee, a homeowner, make an oral contract under which Riggsbee is to give Kirkland a certain tract of land in return for the painting of Riggsbee's house, the contract is unenforceable under the statute of frauds. It is a contract for the sale of an interest in land. Either party can repudiate and has a defense to an action by the other to enforce the contract.

Full Performance

Full performance
statute does not apply to executed contracts

After *all* the promises of an oral contract have been *performed* by all the parties, the statute of frauds no longer applies. Accordingly, neither party may ask the court to rescind the executed oral contract on the basis that it did not meet the statute's requirements. Thus, the statute applies to executory contracts only.

Restitution

Restitution
is available in quasi-contract for benefits conferred in reliance on the oral contract

A party to a contract that is unenforceable because of the statute of frauds may have, nonetheless, acted in reliance upon the contract. In such a case, the party may recover in restitution the benefits he conferred upon the other in relying upon the unenforceable contract. Thus, if Wilton makes an oral contract to furnish services to Rochelle that are not to be performed within a year and Rochelle discharges Wilton after three months, Wilton may recover as restitution the value of the services he rendered during the three months. Most courts require, however, that the party seeking restitution not be in default.

Promissory Estoppel

Promissory estoppel
oral contracts will be enforced where the party seeking enforcement has reasonably and justifiably relied on the promise and the court can avoid injustice only by enforcement

A growing number of courts have used the doctrine of promissory estoppel to displace the requirement of a writing by enforcing oral contracts within the statute of frauds where the party seeking enforcement has reasonably and foreseeably relied upon a promise in such a way that the court can avoid injustice only by enforcing the promise. The remedy granted is limited, as justice requires, and depends on such factors as the availability of other remedies; the foreseeability, reasonableness, and substantiality of the reliance; and the extent to which reliance corroborates evidence of the promise. The use of promissory estoppel, however, to avoid the writing requirement of the statute of frauds has gained little acceptance in cases involving the sale of goods.

PAROL EVIDENCE RULE

A contract reduced to writing and signed by the parties is frequently the result of many conversations, conferences, proposals, counterproposals, letters, and memoranda; sometimes it is also the product of negotiations conducted, or partly conducted, by agents of the parties. At some stage in the negotiations, the parties or their agents may have reached tentative agreements that were superseded (or regarded as such by one of the parties) by subsequent negotiations. Offers may have been made and withdrawn, either expressly or by implication, or forgotten in the give-and-take of negotiations. Ultimately, though, the parties prepare and sign a final draft of the written contract, which may or may not include all of the points that they discussed and agreed on in the course of the negotiations. By signing the agreement, despite its potential omissions, the parties have declared it to be their contract, and the terms as contained in it represent the contract they have made. As a rule of substantive law, neither party is later permitted to show that the contract they made is different from the terms and provisions that appear in the written agreement. This rule, which also applies to wills and deeds, is called the "parol evidence" rule.

THE RULE

When the parties express their contract in a writing that is intended to be the complete and final expression of their rights and duties, the **parol evidence rule** excludes *prior* oral or written negotiations or agreements of the parties or their *contemporaneous* oral agreements that *vary* or *change* an integrated written contract. The word *parol* literally means "speech" or "words." The term *parol evidence* refers to any evidence, whether oral or in writing, that is outside the written contract and not incorporated into it either directly or by reference.

The parol evidence rule applies only to an **integrated contract**, that is, one contained in a certain writing or writings to which the parties have assented as being the statement of the complete and exclusive agreement or contract between them. When there is such an integration of a contract, the courts will not permit parol evidence of any prior or contemporaneous agreement to vary, change, alter, or modify any of the terms or provisions of the written contract.

The reason for the rule is that the parties, by reducing their entire agreement to writing, are regarded as having intended the writing that they signed to include the whole of their agreement. The terms and provisions contained in the writing are there because the parties intended them to be in their contract. Conversely, the courts regard the parties as having omitted intentionally any provision not in the writing. The rule, by excluding evidence that would tend to change, alter, vary, or modify the terms of the written agreement, safeguards the contract as made by the parties. The rule, which applies to all integrated written contracts, deals with what terms are part of the contract. The rule differs from the statute of frauds, which governs what contracts must be evidenced by a writing to be enforceable. Does the parol evidence rule or the statute of frauds apply to the situation presented in the Ethical Dilemma at the end of this chapter?

Parol evidence rule
excludes inconsistent prior and contemporaneous oral and written agreements not incorporated into an integrated contract

integrated contract
complete and exclusive agreement of the parties

PRACTICAL ADVICE

If your contract is intended to be the complete and final agreement, make sure that all terms are included and state your intention that the writing is complete and final. If you do not intend the writing to be complete or final, make sure that you so indicate in the writing itself.

Jenkins v. Eckerd Corporation
District Court of Appeal of Florida, First District, 2005
913 So.2d 43
http://scholar.google.com/scholar_case?case=12402686802007965629&hl=en&as_sdt=2&as_vis=1&oi=scholarr

---

FACTS In January 1991, Sandhill and K & B Florida Corporation (K & B), a pharmaceutical retailer, entered into lease agreement (K & B Lease) providing for the rental of a parcel of real property located in the Gulf Breeze Shopping Center in Gulf Breeze, Florida. Shortly before the execution of the K & B Lease, Sandhill had leased space in the shopping center to Delchamps, Inc., a regional supermarket chain, as the "anchor" tenant in the shopping center. Article 2B of the K & B Lease referred to the Delchamps lease and provided:

ARTICLE 2

B. Lessor represents to Lessee that Lessor has entered into leases with the following named concerns: with Delchamps, Inc. (Delchamps) for a minimum of 45,000 square feet for supermarket grocery store and that Lessor will construct and offer for lease individual retail shops for a minimum of 21,000 square feet for various retail uses, all located and dimensioned shown on the attached Plot Plan, ... The continued leasing and payment of rent for their store in the Shopping Center by Delchamps is part of the consideration to induce Lessee to lease and

pay rent for its store, ... Accordingly, should Delchamps fail or cease to lease and pay rent for its store in the Shopping Center during the Lease Term as hereinafter set out, Lessee shall have the right and privilege of: (a) canceling this Lease and of terminating all of its obligations hereunder at any time thereafter upon written notice by Lessee to Lessor, and such cancellation and termination shall be effective ninety (90) days after the mailing of such written notice; ...

The K & B Lease contained an integration clause which provided that "[t]his lease contains all of the agreements made between the parties hereto and may not be modified orally or in any manner other than by an agreement in writing." The Delchamps' lease included an assignment provision which granted Delchamps "the right, at any time after the commencement of the term hereof, to assign this lease."

In September 1997, Jitney Jungle Stores of America, Inc. (Jitney Jungle), another grocery store operator, acquired Delchamps and continued the operation of the Delchamps' grocery store in the shopping center. In 1998, Eckerd acquired the K & B drugstore. The K & B Lease was assigned to Eckerd, which began operating an Eckerd drugstore in the leased premises. In October 1999, Jitney Jungle filed for bankruptcy protection under Chapter 11 of the United States Bankruptcy Code. Thereafter, an order was entered in the bankruptcy proceeding approving Delchamps' assignment of its lease in the shopping center to Bruno's Supermarkets, Inc. (Bruno's). Since the assignment, Bruno's has occupied the leased premises under the assigned Delchamps' lease and has operated a Bruno's grocery store there. Sandhill did not provide notice to, or obtain consent from, Eckerd of this assignment. On June 22, 2001, Eckerd notified Sandhill that, because Delchamps had ceased to lease and pay rent for its store in the shopping center, pursuant to the K & B Lease, Eckerd was canceling its lease effective September 20, 2001. Sandhill filed suit against Eckerd for an alleged breach of the shopping center lease. At trial, Sandhill sought to introduce testimony relating to its negotiations of the K & B Lease to explain the parties' intent in drafting the allegedly ambiguous language in article 2B. The trial court prohibited the introduction of this evidence under the parol evidence rule. The district court entered a judgment in favor of Eckerd. This appeal was filed.

DECISION Judgment affirmed.

OPINION It is a fundamental rule of contract interpretation that a contract which is clear, complete, and unambiguous does not require judicial construction. The K & B Lease (article 2B) clearly and unambiguously gave the lessee the option to cancel the lease if Delchamps ceased to lease its store.

Sandhill argues that the trial court erred in applying the parol evidence rule and refusing to allow the introduction of extrinsic evidence in interpreting article 2B of the Lease. However, if a contract provision is "clear and unambiguous," a court may not consider extrinsic or "parol" evidence to change the plain meaning set forth in the contract. Sandhill contends that parol evidence was admissible below since the lease is incomplete and contains a latent ambiguity. A latent ambiguity arises when a contract on its face appears clear and unambiguous, but fails to specify the rights or duties of the parties in certain situations. Sandhill incorrectly argues that, while the reference in article 2B of the K & B Lease to the Delchamps' lease may be "unambiguous" when read literally, this reference was not "clear" or "complete" with regard to the operation of the lease should the Delchamps' lease be assigned. The operation of the parol evidence rule encourages parties to embody their complete agreement in a written contract and fosters reliance upon the written contract. "The parol evidence rule serves as a shield to protect a valid, complete and unambiguous written instrument from any verbal assault that would contradict, add to, or subtract from it, or affect its construction." The terms of an integrated (complete and exclusive) written contract can be varied by extrinsic evidence only to the extent that the terms are ambiguous and are given meaning by the extrinsic evidence. The K & B Lease is an integrated agreement complete in all essential terms.

Furthermore, article 2B is not in the least unclear or incomplete. It contains no latent or patent ambiguity. Although article 2B does not mention assignment by Delchamps, it unambiguously grants the lessee the right to terminate the K & B Lease if Delchamps ceases to lease and pay rent for its store in the shopping center *for any reason.*

INTERPRETATION The parol evidence rule encourages parties to embody their complete agreement in an integrated written contract and fosters reliance upon the written contract.

CRITICAL THINKING QUESTION Do you agree with the parol evidence rule? Explain.

SITUATIONS TO WHICH THE RULE DOES NOT APPLY

The parol evidence rule, in spite of its name, is not an exclusionary rule of evidence; nor is it a rule of construction or interpretation. Rather, it is a rule of substantive law that defines the limits of a contract. Bearing this in mind, as well as the reason underlying the rule, you will readily understand that the rule does **not** apply to any of the following situations (see Figure 15-1 for an overview of the parol evidence rule):

1. A contract that is *partly* written and partly oral; that is, a contract in which the parties do not intend the writing to be their entire agreement.
2. A clerical or *typographical error* that obviously does not represent the agreement of the parties. Where, for example, a written contract for the services of a skilled mining engineer provides that his rate of compensation is to be $8 per day, a court of equity would permit reformation (correction) of the contract to correct the mistake if both parties intended the rate to be $800 per day.
3. The lack of *contractual capacity* of one of the parties through, for instance, minority, intoxication, or mental incompetency. Such evidence would not tend to vary, change, or alter any of the terms of the written agreement but rather would show that the written agreement was voidable or void.
4. A *defense* of fraud, misrepresentation, duress, undue influence, mistake, illegality, lack of consideration, or other invalidating cause. Evidence establishing any of these defenses would not purport to vary, change, or alter any of the terms of the written agreement but rather would show such agreement to be voidable, void, or unenforceable.
5. A *condition precedent* to which the parties agreed orally at the time of the execution of the written agreement and to which the entire agreement was made subject. Such evidence does

Figure 15-1 Parol Evidence Rule

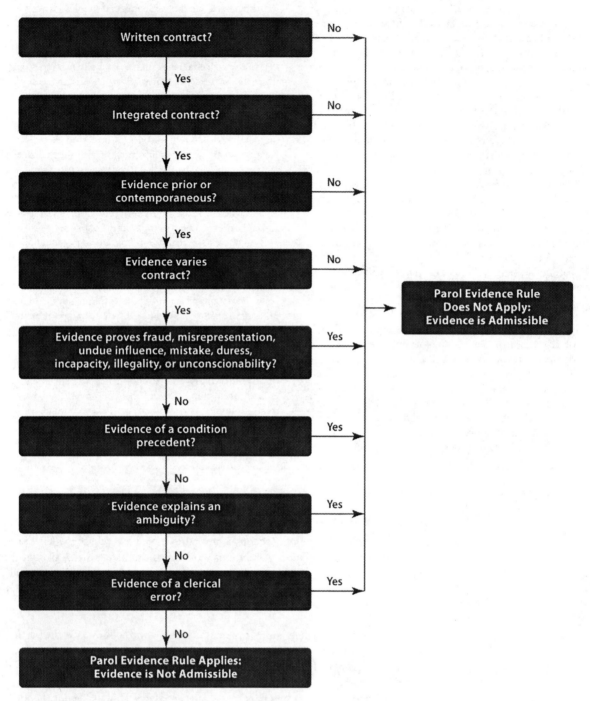

© Cengage Learning 2013

not tend to vary, alter, or change any of the terms of the agreement; rather, it shows whether the entire unchanged written agreement ever became effective.

6. A *subsequent mutual rescission* or *modification* of the written contract. Parol evidence of a later agreement does not tend to show that the integrated writing did not represent the contract between the parties at the time the writing was made.

7. Parol evidence is admissible to explain *ambiguous* terms in the contract. To enforce a contract, it is necessary to understand its intended meaning. Nevertheless, such interpretation is not to alter, change, or vary the terms of the contract.

8. A *separate contract*; the rule does not prevent a party from proving the existence of a separate, distinct contract between the same parties.

SUPPLEMENTAL EVIDENCE

Although a written agreement cannot be contradicted by evidence of a prior agreement or of a contemporaneous agreement, under the Restatement and the Code, a written contract may be explained or supplemented by (1) course of dealing between the parties; (2) usage of trade; (3) course of performance; or (4) evidence of consistent additional terms, unless the writing was intended by the parties to be a complete and exclusive statement of their agreement.

Course of dealing
previous conduct between the parties

A **course of dealing** is a sequence of previous conduct between the parties that a court may fairly regard as having established a common basis of understanding for interpreting their expressions and other conduct.

Usage of trade
practice engaged in by the trade or industry

A **usage of trade** is a practice or method of dealing regularly observed and followed in a place, vocation, or trade.

Course of performance
conduct between the parties concerning performance of the particular contract

Course of performance refers to the manner in which and the extent to which the respective parties to a contract have accepted without objection successive tenders of performance by the other party.

The Restatement and the Code permit *supplemental consistent evidence* to be introduced into a court proceeding. Such evidence, however, is admissible only if it does not contradict a term or terms of the original agreement and would probably not have been included in the original contract.

INTERPRETATION OF CONTRACTS

Although parol evidence may not change the written words or language in which the parties embodied their agreement or contract, the ascertainment (determination) of the meaning to be given to the written language is outside the scope of the parol evidence rule. Though the written words embody the terms of the contract, these words are but symbols; and, if their meaning is ambiguous, the courts may clarify this meaning by applying rules of interpretation or construction and by using extrinsic (external) evidence where necessary.

Interpretation
construction or meaning given the contract

The Restatement defines **interpretation** as the ascertainment of the meaning of a promise or agreement or of a term of the promise or agreement. Where the language in a contract is unambiguous, a court will not accept extrinsic evidence tending to show a meaning different from that which the words clearly convey. To perform its function of interpreting and construing written contracts and documents, the court adopts rules of interpretation to apply a legal standard to the words contained in the agreement. These are among the rules that aid interpretation:

1. Words and other conduct are interpreted in the light of all the circumstances, and if the principal purpose of the parties is ascertainable, it is given great weight.
2. A writing is interpreted as a whole, and all writings that are part of the same transaction are interpreted together.
3. Unless the parties manifest a different intention, language that has a commonly accepted meaning is interpreted in accordance with that meaning.
4. Unless a different intention is manifested, technical terms and words of art are given their technical meanings.
5. Wherever reasonable, the parties' manifestations of intention regarding a promise or agreement are interpreted as consistent with each other and with any relevant course of performance, course of dealing, or usage of trade.
6. An interpretation that gives a reasonable, lawful, and effective meaning to all the terms is preferred over an interpretation that leaves a part unreasonable, unlawful, or of no effect.
7. Specific and exact terms are given greater weight than general language.
8. Separately negotiated or added terms are given greater weight than standardized terms or other terms not separately negotiated.
9. Express terms, course of performance, course of dealing, and usage of trade are weighted in that order.
10. Where a term or promise has several possible meanings, it will be interpreted against the party who supplied the contract or the term.

Ethical Dilemma

What's (Wrong) in a Contract?

Facts Rick Davidson was an All-American point guard on Donaldson University's varsity basketball team. He was a four-year starter and, through the cooperation of several accommodating professors, was able to graduate on time—with one small catch: he really couldn't read or write. But his classroom experiences helped convince him that he could handle any situation, and when he was drafted in the first round by a National Basketball Association (NBA) team, he decided to act as his own agent.

During the negotiations, John Stock, general manager for the team, made Rick an offer of $2.4 million to play for the team for three years. After seeing that other first-round draft choices were receiving closer to $3 million for the same three years, Rick made it known to Stock that the team's offer was unacceptable. Stock told Rick that

because of the salary cap (each NBA team has a limit on the total amount of salaries it can pay its players), he would be willing to raise the offer to $2.8 million but that the extra $400,000 could not be written into the contract. This would be an oral agreement that would avoid disclosing the salary cap violation to the league. After considering the offer, Rick signed the contract for $2.4 million for three years' service, and he and Stock shook hands on the deal for the additional $400,000 for the same three years. The contract stated that it was the complete and final agreement between the parties.

After Rick's first year, it was obvious to the team that Rick was not worth the money, and Stock decided not to pay him the first year's portion of the extra $400,000. Stock claimed that because this

agreement was not in writing, it was not enforceable.

Social, Policy, and Ethical Considerations

1. What would you do?
2. Is the team legally obligated to pay the additional $400,000? Is it ethically obligated to do so?
3. What policy interests are served by the team's decision not to pay Rick the extra money? Would the fact that NBA policy makes it impossible for a player to leave a team and play for another NBA team change your answer?
4. What responsibility does the university bear in this situation?
5. What is the nature of Rick's responsibility with respect to the above facts? What should he do?

PRACTICAL ADVICE

Take care to ensure that your contracts are complete and understandable, especially if you drafted the contract.

11. Where written provisions are inconsistent with typed or printed provisions, the written provision is given preference. Likewise, typed provisions are given preference to printed provisions.

12. If the amount payable is set forth in both figures and words and the amounts differ, the words control the figures.

We may observe that, through the application of the parol evidence rule (where properly applicable) and the above rules of interpretation and construction, the law not only enforces a contract but also, in so doing, exercises great care both that the contract being enforced is the one the parties made and that the sense and meaning of the parties' intentions are carefully ascertained and given effect.

CHAPTER SUMMARY

Statute of Frauds

Contracts within the Statute of Frauds

Rule contracts within the statute of frauds must be evidenced by a writing to be enforceable

Electronic Records full effect is given to electronic contracts and signatures

Suretyship Provision applies to promises to pay the debt of another

- *Promise Must Be Collateral* promisor must be secondarily, not primarily, liable
- *Main Purpose Doctrine* if primary object is to provide an economic benefit to the surety, then the promise is not within the statute

Executor-Administrator Provision applies to promises to answer personally for a duty of the decedent

Marriage Provision applies to promises in consideration of marriage but not to mutual promises to marry

Land Contract Provision applies to promises to transfer any right, privilege, power, or immunity in real property

One-Year Provision applies to contracts that cannot be performed within one year

- *The Possibility Test* the criterion is whether it is possible, not likely, for the agreement to be performed within one year
- *Computation of Time* the year runs from the time the agreement is made
- *Full Performance by One Party* makes the promise of the other party enforceable under majority view

Sale of Goods a contract for the sale of goods for the price of $500 or more must be evidenced by a writing or record to be enforceable

- *Admission* an admission in pleadings, testimony, or otherwise in court makes the contract enforceable for the quantity of goods admitted
- *Specially Manufactured Goods* an oral contract for specially manufactured goods is enforceable
- *Delivery or Payment and Acceptance* validates the contract only for the goods that have been accepted or for which payment has been accepted

Modification or Rescission of Contracts within the Statute of Frauds oral contracts modifying existing contracts are unenforceable if the resulting contract is within the statute of frauds

Methods of Compliance

General Contract Provisions the writing(s) or record must
- specify the parties to the contract
- specify the subject matter and essential terms
- be signed by the party to be charged or by her agent

Sale of Goods provides a general method of compliance for all parties and an additional one for merchants

- *Writing(s) or Record* must (1) be sufficient to indicate that a contract has been made between the parties, (2) be signed by the party against whom enforcement is sought or by her authorized agent, and (3) specify the quantity of goods to be sold
- *Written Confirmation* between merchants, a written confirmation that is sufficient against the sender is also sufficient against the recipient unless the recipient gives written notice of his objection within ten days

Effect of Noncompliance

Oral Contract within Statute of Frauds is unenforceable

Full Performance statute does not apply to executed contracts

Restitution is available in quasi-contract for benefits conferred in reliance on the oral contract

Promissory Estoppel oral contracts will be enforced where the party seeking enforcement has reasonably and justifiably relied on the promise and the court can avoid injustice only by enforcement

Parol Evidence Rule and Interpretation of Contracts

The Parol Evidence Rule

Statement of Rule when parties express a contract in a writing that they intend to be the final expression of their rights and duties, evidence of their prior oral or written negotiations or agreements of their contemporaneous oral agreements that vary or change the written contract are not admissible

Situations to Which the Rule Does Not Apply
- a contract that is not an integrated document
- correction of a typographical error
- showing that a contract was void or voidable
- showing whether a condition has in fact occurred
- showing a subsequent mutual rescission or modification of the contract

Supplemental Evidence may be admitted

- *Course of Dealing* previous conduct between the parties
- *Usage of Trade* practice engaged in by the trade or industry
- *Course of Performance* conduct between the parties concerning performance of the particular contract
- *Supplemental Consistent Evidence*

Interpretation of Contracts

Definition the ascertainment of the meaning of a promise or agreement or a term of the promise or agreement

Rules of Interpretation include

- all the circumstances are considered and the principal purpose of the parties is given great weight
- a writing is interpreted as a whole
- commonly accepted meanings are used unless the parties manifest a different intention
- wherever possible, the intentions of the parties are interpreted as consistent with each other and with course of performance, course of dealing, or usage of trade
- technical terms are given their technical meaning
- specific terms are given greater weight than general language
- separately negotiated terms are given greater weight than standardized terms or those not separately negotiated
- the order for interpretation is express terms, course of performance, course of dealing, and usage of trade
- where a term has several possible meanings, the term will be interpreted against the party who supplied the contract or term
- written provisions are given preference over typed or printed provisions and typed provisions are given preference over printed provisions
- if an amount is set forth in both words and figures and they differ, words control the figures

QUESTIONS

1. Rafferty was the principal shareholder in Continental Corporation, and, as a result, he received the lion's share of Continental Corporation's dividends. Continental Corporation was anxious to close an important deal for iron ore products to use in its business. A written contract was on the desk of Stage Corporation for the sale of the iron ore to Continental Corporation. Stage Corporation, however, was cautious about signing the contract, and it did not sign until Rafferty called Stage Corporation on the telephone and stated that if Continental Corporation did not pay for the ore, he would pay. Business reversals struck Continental Corporation, and it failed. Stage Corporation sued Rafferty. What defense, if any, has Rafferty?

2. Green was the owner of a large department store. On Wednesday, January 26, he talked to Smith and said, "I will hire you to act as sales manager in my store for one year at a salary of $48,000. You are to begin work next Monday." Smith accepted and started work on Monday, January 31. At the end of three months, Green discharged Smith. On May 15, Smith brought an action against Green to recover the unpaid portion of the $48,000 salary. Is Smith's employment contract enforceable?

3. Rowe was admitted to the hospital suffering from a critical illness. He was given emergency treatment and later underwent surgery. On at least four occasions, Rowe's two sons discussed with the hospital the payment for services to be rendered by the hospital. The first of these four conversations took place the day after Rowe was admitted. The sons informed the treating physician that their father had no financial means but that they themselves would pay for such services. During the other conversations, the sons authorized whatever treatment their father needed, assuring the hospital that they would pay for the services. After Rowe's discharge, the hospital brought this action against the sons to recover the unpaid bill for the services rendered to their father. Are the sons' promises to the hospital enforceable? Explain.

4. Ames, Bell, Cain, and Dole each orally ordered LCD (liquid crystal display) televisions from Marvel Electronics Company, which accepted the orders. Ames's television was to be encased in a specially designed ebony cabinet. Bell, Cain, and Dole ordered standard televisions described as "Alpha Omega Theatre." The price of Ames's television was $1,800, and the televisions ordered by Bell, Cain, and Dole were $700 each. Bell paid the company $75 to apply on his purchase; Ames, Cain, and Dole paid nothing. The next day, Marvel sent Ames, Bell, Cain, and Dole written confirmations captioned "Purchase Memorandum," numbered 12345, 12346, 12347, and 12348, respectively, containing the essential terms of the oral agreements. Each memorandum was sent in duplicate with the request that one copy be signed and returned to the company. None of the four purchasers returned a signed copy. Ames promptly called the company and repudiated the oral contract, which it received before beginning manufacture of the set for Ames or making commitments to carry out the contract. Cain sent the company a letter reading in part, "Referring to your Contract No. 12347, please be advised I have canceled this contract. Yours truly, (Signed) Cain." The four televisions were duly tendered by Marvel to Ames, Bell, Cain, and Dole, all of whom refused to accept delivery. Marvel brings four separate actions against Ames, Bell, Cain, and Dole for breach of contract. Decide each claim.

5. Moriarity and Holmes enter into an oral contract by which Moriarity promises to sell and Holmes promises to buy Blackacre for $10,000. Moriarity repudiates the contract by writing a letter to Holmes in which she states accurately the terms of the bargain, but adds "our agreement was oral. It, therefore, is not binding upon me, and I shall not carry it out." Thereafter, Holmes sues Moriarity for specific performance of the contract. Moriarity interposes the defense of the statute of frauds, arguing that the contract is within the statute and hence unenforceable. What will be the result? Discuss.

6. On March 1, Lucas called Craig on the telephone and offered to pay him $90,000 for a house and lot that Craig owned. Craig accepted the offer immediately on the telephone. Later in the same day, Lucas told Annabelle that if she would marry

him, he would convey to her the property then owned by Craig that was the subject of the earlier agreement. On March 2 Lucas called Penelope and offered her $16,000 if she would work for him for the year commencing March 15, and she agreed. Lucas and Annabelle were married on June 25. By this time, Craig had refused to convey the house to Lucas. Thereafter, Lucas renounced his promise to convey the property to Annabelle. Penelope, who had been working for Lucas, was discharged without cause on July 5; Annabelle left Lucas and instituted divorce proceedings in July.

What rights, if any, have (a) Lucas against Craig for his failure to convey the property; (b) Annabelle against Lucas for failure to convey the house to her; and (c) Penelope against Lucas for discharging her before the end of the agreed term of employment?

7. Blair orally promises Clay to sell him five crops of potatoes to be grown on Blackacre, a farm in Idaho, and Clay promises to pay a stated price for them on delivery. Is the contract enforceable?

8. Rachel leased an apartment to Bertha for a one-year term beginning May 1, at $800 a month, "payable in advance on the first day of each and every month of said term." At the time the lease was signed, Bertha told Rachel that she received her salary on the tenth of the month, and that she would be unable to pay the rent before that date each month. Rachel replied that would be satisfactory. On June 2, Bertha not having paid the June rent, Rachel sued Bertha for the rent. At the trial, Bertha offered to prove the oral agreement as to the date of payment each month. Is the oral evidence admissible?

9. Ann bought a car from the Used Car Agency (Used) under a written contract. She purchased the car in reliance on Used's agent's oral representations that it had never been in a wreck and could be driven at least two thousand miles without adding oil. Thereafter, Ann discovered that the car had, in fact, been previously wrecked and rebuilt, that it used excessive quantities of oil, and that Used's agent was aware of these facts when the car was sold. Ann brought an action to rescind the contract and recover the purchase price. Used objected to the introduction of oral testimony concerning representations of its agent, contending that the written contract alone governed the rights of the parties. Should Ann succeed?

10. In a contract drawn up by Goldberg Company, it agreed to sell and Edwards Contracting Company agreed to buy wood shingles at $650. After the shingles were delivered and used, Goldberg Company billed Edwards Company at $650 per bunch of nine hundred shingles. Edwards Company refused to pay because it thought the contract meant $650 per thousand shingles. Goldberg Company brought action to recover on the basis of $650 per bunch. The evidence showed that there was no applicable custom or usage in the trade and that each party held its belief in good faith. Decision?

11. Amos orally agrees to hire Elizabeth for an eight-month trial period. Elizabeth performs the job magnificently, and after several weeks Amos orally offers Elizabeth a six-month extension at a salary increase of 20 percent. Elizabeth accepts the offer. At the end of the eight-month trial period, Amos discharges Elizabeth, who brings suit against Amos for breach of contract. Is Amos liable? Why?

CASE PROBLEMS

12. Halsey, a widower, was living without family or housekeeper in his house in Howell, New York. Burns and his wife claim that Halsey invited them to give up their house and business in Andover, New York, to live in his house and care for him. In return, they allege, he promised them the house and its furniture upon his death. Acting upon this proposal, the Burnses left Andover, moved into Halsey's house, and cared for him until he died five months later. No deed, will, or memorandum exists to authenticate Halsey's promise. McCormick, the administrator of the estate, claims the oral promise is unenforceable under the statute of frauds. Explain whether McCormick is correct.

13. Ethel Greenberg acquired the ownership of the Carlyle Hotel on Miami Beach but had little experience in the hotel business. She asked Miller to participate in and counsel her operation of the hotel, which he did. He claims that, because his efforts produced a substantial profit, Ethel made an oral agreement for the continuation of his services. Miller alleges that in return for his services, Ethel promised to marry him and to share the net income resulting from the operation of the hotel. Miller maintains that he rendered his services to Ethel in reliance upon her promises and that the couple planned to wed in the fall. Ethel, due to physical illness, decided not to marry. Miller sued for damages for Ethel's breach of agreement. Is the oral contract enforceable? Discuss.

14. Dean was hired on February 12 as a sales manager of the Co-op Dairy for a minimum period of one year with the dairy agreeing to pay his moving expenses. By February 26, Dean had signed a lease, moved his family from Oklahoma to Arizona, and reported for work. After he worked for a few days, he was fired. Dean then brought this action against the dairy for his salary for the year, less what he was paid. The dairy argues that the statute of frauds bars enforcement of the oral contract because the contract was not to be performed within one year. Is the dairy correct in its assertion?

15. Yokel, a grower of soybeans, had sold soybeans to Campbell Grain and Seed Company and other grain companies in the past. Campbell entered into an oral contract with Yokel to purchase soybeans from him. Promptly after entering into the oral contract, Campbell signed and mailed to Yokel a written confirmation of the oral agreement. Yokel received the written confirmation but did not sign it or object to its content. Campbell now brings this action against Yokel for breach of contract upon Yokel's failure to deliver the soybeans. Is the agreement binding?

16. Presti claims that he reached an oral agreement with Wilson by telephone in October to buy a horse for $60,000. Presti asserts that he sent Wilson a bill of sale and a postdated check, which Wilson retained. Presti also claims that Wilson told him that for tax reasons he wished not to consummate the transaction until January 1 of the following year. The check was neither deposited nor negotiated. Wilson denies that he ever agreed to sell the horse or that he received the check and bill of sale from Presti. Presti's claim is supported by a copy of his check stub and by the affidavit of his

executive assistant, who says that he monitored the telephone call and prepared and mailed both the bill of sale and the check. Wilson argues that the statute of frauds governs this transaction and that because there was no writing, the contract claim is barred. Is Wilson correct? Explain.

17. Louie E. Brown worked for the Phelps Dodge Corporation under an oral contract for approximately twenty-three years. In 2011, he was suspended from work for unauthorized possession of company property. In 2012, Phelps Dodge fired Brown after discovering that he was using company property without permission and building a trailer on company time. Brown sued Phelps Dodge for benefits under an unemployment benefit plan. According to the plan, "in order to be eligible for unemployment benefits, a laid-off employee must: (1) Have completed 2 or more years of continuous service with the company, and (2) Have been laid off from work because the company had determined that work was not available for him." The trial court held that the wording of the second condition was ambiguous and should be construed against Phelps Dodge, the party who chose the wording. A reading of the entire contract, however, indicates that the plan was not intended to apply to someone who was fired for cause. What is the correct interpretation of this contract?

18. Katz offered to purchase land from Joiner, and, after negotiating the terms, Joiner accepted. On October 13, over the telephone, both parties agreed to extend the time period for completing and mailing the written contract until October 20. Although the original paperwork deadline in the offer was October 14, Katz stated he had inserted that provision "for my purpose only." All other provisions of the contract remained unchanged. Accordingly, Joiner completed the contract and mailed it on October 20. Immediately after, however, Joiner sent Katz an overnight letter stating that "I have signed and returned contract, but have changed my mind. Do not wish to sell property." Joiner now claims an oral modification of a contract within the statute of frauds is unenforceable. Katz counters that the modification is not material and therefore does not affect the underlying contract. Explain who is correct.

19. When Mr. McClam died, he left the family farm, heavily mortgaged, to his wife and children. To save the farm from foreclosure, Mrs. McClam planned to use insurance proceeds and her savings to pay off the debts. She was unwilling to do so, however, unless she had full ownership of the property. Mrs. McClam wrote her daughter, stating that the daughter should deed over her interest in the family farm to her mother. Mrs. McClam promised that upon her death all the children would inherit the farm from their mother equally. The letter further explained that if foreclosure occurred, each child would receive very little, but if they complied with their mother's plan, each would eventually receive a valuable property interest upon her death. Finally, the letter stated that all the other children had agreed to this plan. The daughter also agreed. Years later, Mrs. McClam tried to convey the farm to her son Donald. The daughter challenged, arguing that the mother was contractually bound to convey the land equally to all children. Donald says this was an oral agreement to sell land and is unenforceable. The daughter says the letter satisfies the statute of frauds, making the contract enforceable. Who gets the farm? Explain.

20. Butler Brothers Building Company sublet all of the work in a highway construction contract to Ganley Brothers, Inc. Soon thereafter, Ganley brought this action against Butler for fraud in the inducement of the contract. The contract, however, provided: "The contractor [Ganley] has examined the said contracts ..., knows all the requirements, and is not relying upon any statement made by the company in respect thereto." Can Ganley introduce into evidence the oral representations made by Butler?

21. Alice solicited an offer from Robett Manufacturing Company to manufacture certain clothing that Alice intended to supply to the government. Alice contends that in a telephone conversation Robett made an oral offer that she immediately accepted. She then received the following letter from Robett, which, she claims, confirmed their agreement:

> Confirming our telephone conversation, we are pleased to offer the 3,500 shirts at $14.00 each and the trousers at $13.80 each with delivery approximately ninety days after receipt of order. We will try to cut this to sixty days if at all possible.
>
> This, of course, is quoted f.o.b. Atlanta and the order will not be subject to cancellation, domestic pack only.
>
> Thanking you for the opportunity to offer these garments, we are
>
> Very truly yours,
> ROBETT MANUFACTURING CO., INC.

Is the agreement enforceable against Robett?

22. Enrique Gittes was a financial consultant for NCC, an English holding company that invested capital in other businesses in return for a stake in those businesses. One of NCC's investments was a substantial holding in Simplicity Pattern Company. Gittes's consulting contract was subsequently transferred to Simplicity, and Gittes was elected to the Simplicity board of directors.

When NCC fell into serious financial straits, it became imperative that it sell its interest in Simplicity. Accordingly, a buyer was found. The buyer insisted that before closing the deal all current Simplicity directors, including Gittes, must resign. Gittes, however, refused to resign. Edward Cook, the largest shareholder of NCC and the one with the most to lose if the Simplicity sale was not completed, orally offered Gittes a five-year, $50,000-per-year consulting contract with Cook International if Gittes would resign from the Simplicity board.

Gittes and Cook never executed a formal contract. However, Cook International did issue two writings, a prospectus and a memo, that mentioned the employment of Gittes for five years at $50,000 per year. Neither writing described the nature of Gittes's job or any of his duties. In fact, Gittes was given no responsibilities, and was never paid. Gittes sued to enforce the employment contract. Cook International contended that the statute of frauds made the oral contract unenforceable. Decision?

23. Shane Quadri contacted Don Hoffman, an employee of Al J. Hoffman & Co. (Hoffman Agency), to procure car insurance. Later, Quadri's car was stolen. Quadri contacted Hoffman, who arranged with Budget Rent-a-Car for a rental car for Quadri until his car was recovered. Hoffman authorized Budget Rent-a-Car to bill the Hoffman Agency. Later, when the stolen car was recovered, Hoffman telephoned Goodyear and arranged to have four new tires put on Quadri's car to replace those damaged during the theft. Budget and Goodyear sued Hoffman for payment of the car rental and tires. Is Hoffman liable on his oral promise to pay for the car rental and the four new tires?

24. On July 5, 2000, Richard Price signed a written employment contract as a new salesman with the Mercury Supply Company. The contract was of indefinite duration and could be terminated by either party for any reason upon fifteen days' notice. Between 2000 and 2008, Price was promoted several times. In 2002, Price was made vice president of sales. In September of 2008, however, Price was told that his performance was not satisfactory and that if he did not improve he would be fired. In February of 2011, Price received notice of termination. Price claims that in 2005 he entered into a valid oral employment contract with Mercury Supply Company in which he was made vice president of sales for life or until he should retire. Is the alleged oral contract barred by the one-year provision of the statute of frauds?

25. Thomson Printing Company is a buyer and seller of used machinery. On April 10, the president of the company, James Thomson, went to the surplus machinery department of B.F. Goodrich Company in Akron, Ohio, to examine some used equipment that was for sale. Thomson discussed the sale, including a price of $9,000, with Ingram Meyers, a Goodrich employee and agent. Four days later, on April 14, Thomson sent a purchase order to confirm the oral contract for purchase of the machinery and a partial payment of $1,000 to Goodrich in Akron. The purchase order contained Thomson Printing's name, address, and telephone number, as well as certain information about the purchase, but did not specifically mention Meyers or the surplus equipment department. Goodrich sent copies of the documents to a number of its divisions, but Meyers never learned of the confirmation until weeks later, by which time the equipment had been sold to another party. Thomson Printing brought suit against Goodrich for breach of contract. Goodrich claimed that no contract had existed and that at any rate the alleged oral contract could not be enforced because of the statute of frauds. Is the contract enforceable? Why?

26. Plaintiffs leased commercial space from the defendant to open a florist shop. After the lease was executed, the plaintiffs learned that they could not place a freestanding sign along the highway to advertise their business because the Deschutes County Code allowed only one freestanding sign on the property, and the defendant already had one in place. The plaintiffs filed this action, alleging that defendant had breached the lease by failing to provide them with space in which they could erect a freestanding sign. Paragraph 16 of the lease provides as follows: "Tenant shall not erect or install any signs ... visible from outside the leased premises with out [sic] the previous written consent of the Landlord." Explain whether this evidence is admissible.

27. Jesse Carter and Jesse Thomas had an auto accident with a driver insured by Allstate. Carter and Thomas hired an attorney, Joseph Onwuteaka, to represent them. Mr. Onwuteaka sent a demand letter for settlement of the plaintiffs' claims to Allstate's adjustor, Ms. Gracie Weatherly. Mr. Onwuteaka claims Ms. Weatherly made, and he orally accepted, settlement terms on behalf of the plaintiffs. When Allstate did not honor the agreements, Carter and Thomas filed a suit for breach of contract. Discuss the enforceability of the oral agreement.

TAKING SIDES

Stuart Studio, an art studio, prepared a new catalog for the National School of Heavy Equipment, a school run by Gilbert and Donald Shaw. When the artwork was virtually finished, Gilbert Shaw requested Stuart Studio to purchase and supervise the printing of twenty-five thousand catalogs. Shaw told the art studio that payment of the printing costs would be made within ten days after billing and that if the "National School would not pay the full total that he would stand good for the entire bill." Shaw was chairman of the board of directors of the school, and he owned 100 percent of its voting stock and 49 percent of its nonvoting stock. The school became bankrupt, and Stuart Studio was unable to recover the sum from the school. Stuart Studio then brought an action against Shaw on the basis of his promise to pay the bill.

a. What are the arguments that Shaw is not liable on his promise?
b. What are the arguments that Shaw is liable on his promise?
c. Is Shaw obligated to pay the debt in question? Explain.

CHAPTER **16**

Third Parties to Contracts

The establishment of [the third-party beneficiary] doctrine ... is a victory of practical utility over theory, of equity over technical subtlety.

Brantly on Contracts, 2nd edition

CHAPTER OUTCOMES

After reading and studying this chapter, you should be able to:

1. Distinguish between an assignment of rights and a delegation of duties.

2. Identify (a) the requirements of an assignment of contract rights and (b) those rights that are not assignable.

3. Identify those situations in which a delegation of duties is not permitted.

4. Distinguish between an intended beneficiary and an incidental beneficiary.

5. Explain when the rights of an intended beneficiary vest.

I n prior chapters, we considered situations that essentially involved only two parties. In this chapter, we deal with the rights and duties of third parties, namely, persons who are not parties to the contract but who have a right to or an obligation for its performance. These rights and duties arise either by (1) an assignment of the rights of a party to the contract, (2) a delegation of the duties of a party to the contract, or (3) the express terms of a contract entered into for the benefit of a third person. In an assignment or delegation, the third party's rights or duties arise after the original contract is made, whereas in the third situation, the third-party beneficiary's rights arise at the time the contract is formed. We will consider these three situations in that order.

ASSIGNMENT OF RIGHTS

Every contract creates both rights and duties. A person who owes a duty under a contract is an **obligor**, while a person to whom a contractual duty is owed is an **obligee**. For instance, Ann promises to sell to Bart an automobile for which Bart promises to pay $10,000 by monthly installments over the next three years. Ann's right under the contract is to receive payment from Bart, whereas Ann's duty is to deliver the automobile. Bart's right is to receive the automobile; his duty is to pay for it.

Obligor / *Obligee* A — automobile → B Obligee / *Obligor*
$10,000

An **assignment of rights** is the voluntary transfer to a third party of the rights arising from the contract. In the above example, if Ann were to transfer her right under the contract (the installment payments due from Bart) to Clark for $8,500 in cash, this would constitute a valid assignment of rights. In this case, Ann would be the **assignor**, Clark would be the **assignee**, and Bart would be the *obligor*.

Obligor
party owing a duty under original contract

Obligee
party to whom a contractual duty of performance is owed

Assignment of rights
voluntary transfer to a third party of the rights arising from a contract

Assignor
party making an assignment

Assignee
party to whom contractual rights are assigned

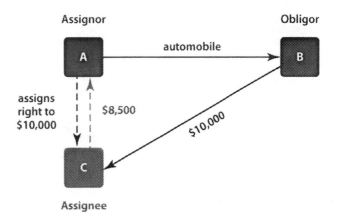

An effective assignment terminates the assignor's right to receive performance by the obligor. After an assignment, only the assignee has a right to the obligor's performance.

On the other hand, if Ann and Doris agree that Doris should deliver the automobile to Bart, this would constitute a delegation, not an assignment, of duties between Ann and Doris. A **delegation of duties** is a transfer to a third party of a contractual obligation. In this instance, Ann would be the **delegator**, Doris would be the **delegatee**, and Bart would be the *obligee*.

Delegation of duties
transfer to a third party of a contractual obligation

Delegator
party delegating his duty to a third party

Delegatee
third party to whom the delegator's duty is delegated

Requirements of an Assignment

The Restatement defines an assignment of a right as a manifestation of the assignor's intention to transfer the right so that the assignor's right to the performance of the obligor is extinguished either in whole or in part and the assignee acquires a right to such performance. No special form or particular words are necessary to create an assignment. Any words that fairly indicate an intention to make the assignee the owner of the right are sufficient.

Unless otherwise provided by statute, an assignment may be oral. The Uniform Commercial Code (UCC) imposes a writing requirement on all assignments beyond $5,000. The 2001 Revision to Article 1, however, has deleted this requirement. In addition, Article 9 requires certain assignments to be in writing.

Consideration is not required for an effective assignment. Consequently, gratuitous assignments are valid and enforceable. By giving value, or consideration, for the assignment, the assignee indicates his assent to the assignment as part of the bargained-for exchange. On the other hand, when the assignment is gratuitous, the assignee's assent is not always required. Any assignee who has not assented to an assignment may, however, disclaim the assignment within a reasonable time after learning of its existence and terms.

Revocability of assignment
when the assignee gives consideration, the assignor may not revoke the assignment without the assignee's consent

Revocability of Assignments   When the assignee gives consideration in exchange for an assignment, a contract exists between the assignor and the assignee. Consequently, the assignor may not revoke the assignment without the assignee's assent. In contrast, a gratuitous assignment is revocable by the assignor and is terminated by the assignor's death, incapacity, or subsequent assignment of the right, unless the assignor has made an effective delivery of the assignment to the assignee, as in the case of *Speelman v. Pascal*. Such delivery can be accomplished by transferring a deed or other document evidencing the right, such as a stock certificate or savings passbook. Delivery may also consist of physically delivering a signed, written assignment of the contract right. A gratuitous assignment is also made irrevocable if, before the attempted revocation, the donee-assignee receives payment of the claim from the obligor, obtains a judgment against the obligor, or obtains a new contract with the obligor.

PRACTICAL ADVICE
Be sure to make irrevocable assignments of only those rights you wish to transfer.

Speelman v. Pascal
Court of Appeals of New York, 1961
10 N.Y.2d 313, 222 N.Y.S.2d 324, 178 N.E.2d 723

FACTS In 1952, the estate of George Bernard Shaw granted to Gabriel Pascal Enterprises, Limited, the exclusive rights to produce a musical play and a motion picture based on Shaw's play *Pygmalion*.

The agreement contained a provision terminating the license if Gabriel Pascal Enterprises did not arrange for well-known composers, such as Lerner and Loewe, to write the musical and produce it within a specified period of time. George Pascal, owner of 98 percent of Gabriel Pascal Enterprises' stock, attempted to meet these requirements but died in July 1954 before negotiations had been completed. In February 1954, however, while the license had two years yet to run, Pascal had sent a letter to Kingman, his executive secretary, granting to her certain percentages of his share of the profits from the expected stage and screen productions of *Pygmalion*. Subsequently, Pascal's estate arranged for the writing and production of the highly successful *My Fair Lady*, based on Shaw's *Pygmalion*. Kingman then sued to enforce Pascal's gift assignment of the future royalties. The trial court entered judgment for Kingman.

DECISION Judgment for Kingman affirmed.

OPINION Assignments of rights to sums that are expected to become due to the assignor are enforceable. To make a gift of such

an assignment, the donor need only demonstrate a present intent to transfer irrevocably his right to the donee. Although at the time of the delivery of the letter there was no musical play or motion picture in existence, Pascal's letter was intended to transfer irrevocably by assignment a percentage of the royalties from the future productions to Kingman. Therefore, the assignment is enforceable as a valid gift.

INTERPRETATION A gratuitous assignment becomes irrevocable upon the assignor's making an effective delivery of the assignment to the assignee.

CRITICAL THINKING QUESTION Should the law enforce assignments of contractual rights not in existence at the time of the assignment? Explain.

Partial assignment transfer of a portion of contractual rights to one or more assignees

Partial Assignments   A **partial assignment** is a transfer of a portion of the contractual rights to one or more assignees, as in the case above. The obligor, however, may require all the parties entitled to the promised performance to litigate the matter in one action, thus ensuring that all parties are present and avoiding the undue hardship of multiple lawsuits. For example, Jack owes Richard $2,500. Richard assigns $1,000 to Mildred. Neither Richard nor Mildred can maintain an action against Jack if Jack objects, unless the other is joined in the proceeding against Jack.

Rights That Are Assignable

As a general rule, most contract rights, including rights under an option contract, are assignable. The most common contractual right that may be assigned is the right to the payment of money. A contract right to other property, such as land or goods, is likewise assignable.

Rights That Are Not Assignable

To protect the obligor or the public interest, some contract rights are not assignable. These non-assignable contract rights include those that (1) materially increase the duty, risk, or burden upon the obligor; (2) transfer highly personal contract rights; (3) are expressly prohibited by the contract; or (4) are prohibited by law.

Assignments That Materially Increase the Duty, Risk, or Burden   An assignment is ineffective if performance by the obligor to the assignee would differ materially from the obligor's performance to the assignor, that is, if the assignment would significantly change the nature or extent of the obligor's duty. Thus, an automobile liability insurance policy issued to Alex is not assignable by Alex to Betty. The risk assumed by the insurance company was liability for Alex's negligent operation of the automobile. Liability for Betty's operation of the same automobile would be a risk entirely different from the one the insurance company had assumed. Similarly, Candice would not be allowed to assign to Eunice, the owner of a twenty-five-room mansion, Candice's contractual right to have David paint her small, two-bedroom house. Clearly, such an assignment would materially increase David's duty of performance. By comparison, the right to receive monthly payments under a contract may be assigned, for mailing the check to the assignee costs no more than mailing it to the assignor. Moreover, if a contract explicitly provides that it may be assigned, then rights under it are assignable even if the assignment would change the duty, risk, or burden of performance on the obligor.

Reiser v. Dayton Country Club Company
United States Court of Appeals, 1992
972 F.2d 689

FACTS The Dayton Country Club Company (the Club) offers many social activities to its members. However, the privilege to play golf at the Club is reserved to a special membership category

for which additional fees are charged. The Club chooses golfing memberships from a waiting list of members according to detailed rules, regulations, and procedures. Magness and Redman were golfing members of the Club. Upon their filing for bankruptcy, their trustee sought to assign by sale their rights under these memberships to (1) other members on the waiting list, (2) other members not on the waiting list, or (3) the general public, provided the purchaser first acquired membership in the Club. The bankruptcy court found that the Club's rules governing golf membership were essentially anti-assignment provisions and therefore the estate could not assign rights contained in the membership agreement. On appeal to the district court, the bankruptcy court's ruling was affirmed. The district court added that this case was not a lease but rather a "non-commercial dispute over the possession of a valuable membership in a recreational and social club."

DECISION Judgment affirmed.

OPINION The court of appeals found that the memberships of Magness and Redman were personal contracts that are not assignable. A personal contract is one in which "the personality of one

of the parties is material." The determination of whether a contract is personal is a question of intent as shown by the language used in the contract and the nature of the contract. In this case, "[t]he contracts creating the complex relationships among the parties and others are not in any way commercial. They create personal relationships among individuals who play golf, who are waiting to play golf, who eat together, swim and play together." Therefore, the parties intended these contracts to be personal and thus they are nonassignable.

INTERPRETATION When rights under a contract are personal, they may not be assigned.

ETHICAL QUESTION Is the court's decision fair to the creditors of Magness and Redman? Explain.

CRITICAL THINKING QUESTION Which type of contracts should not be assignable because of their personal nature? Explain.

Assignments of Personal Rights When the rights under a contract are highly personal, in that they are limited to the person of the obligee, such rights are not assignable. An extreme example of such a contract is an agreement of two persons to marry one another. The prospective groom obviously may not transfer the prospective bride's promise to marry to some third party. A more typical example of contract involving personal rights would be a contract between a teacher and a school. The teacher could not assign her right to a faculty position to another teacher. Similarly, a student who is awarded a scholarship cannot assign his right to some other person. The *Aldana* case involves another example.

Express Prohibition against Assignment Though contract terms prohibiting assignment of rights under the contract are strictly construed, most courts interpret a general prohibition against assignments as a mere promise not to assign. As a consequence, the general prohibition, if violated, gives the obligor a right to damages for breach of the terms forbidding assignment but does not render the assignment ineffective.

The Restatement provides that, unless circumstances indicate the contrary, a contract term prohibiting assignment of the *contract* bars only the delegation to the assignee (delegatee) of the assignor's (delegator's) duty of performance, not the assignment of *rights*. Thus, Norman and Lucy contract for the sale of land by Lucy to Norman for $30,000 and provide in their contract that Norman may not assign the contract. Norman pays Lucy $30,000, thereby fulfilling his duty of performance under the contract. Norman then assigns his rights to George, who consequently is entitled to receive the land from Lucy (the obligor) despite the contractual prohibition of assignment.

Article 2 of the Code provides that a right to damages for breach of the whole contract or a right arising out of the assignor's due performance of his entire obligation can be assigned despite a contractual provision to the contrary. Article 2 also provides that, unless circumstances indicate the contrary, a contract term prohibiting assignment of the *contract* bars only the delegation to the assignee (delegatee) of the assignor's (delegator's) *duty* of performance, not the assignment of *rights*. Article 9 of the Code makes ineffective any term in a contract prohibiting the assignment of a security interest arising out of a sale of any right to payment for goods sold or leased or for services rendered.

PRACTICAL ADVICE

Consider including in your contract a provision prohibiting the assignment of any contractual rights without your written consent and making ineffective any such assignment.

Aldana v. Colonial Palms Plaza, Inc.
District Court of Appeal of Florida, Third District, 1991
591 So.2d 953

FACTS Colonial Palms Plaza, Inc. (Landlord) entered into a lease agreement with Abby's Cakes On Dixie, Inc. (Tenant). The lease included a provision in which Landlord agreed to pay Tenant a construction allowance of up to $11,250 after Tenant completed certain improvements. Prior to completion of the improvements,

Tenant assigned its right to receive the first $8,000 of the construction allowance to Robert Aldana in return for a loan of $8,000 to finance the construction. Aldana sent notice of the assignment to Landlord. When Tenant completed the improvements, Landlord ignored the assignment and paid Tenant the construction allowance. Aldana sued Landlord for the money due pursuant to the assignment. Landlord relied on an anti-assignment clause in the lease to argue that the assignment was void. That clause states in part:

> TENANT agrees not to assign, mortgage, pledge, or encumber this Lease, in whole or in part, to sublet in whole or any part of the DEMISED PREMISES ... without first obtaining the prior, specific written consent of the LANDLORD at LANDLORD'S sole discretion.... Any such assignment ... without such consent shall be void.

The trial court granted Landlord summary judgment.

DECISION Summary judgment reversed and case remanded.

OPINION Aldana argued that under ordinary contract principles the lease provision does not prevent the assignment of the right to receive contractual payments. The appellate court agreed. Tenant did not assign the lease but instead assigned a right to receive the construction allowance. The law in this area is summarized in the Restatement of Contracts as follows: "Unless the circumstances indicate the contrary, a contract term prohibiting assignment of 'the contract' bars only the delegation to an assignee of the performance by the assignor of a duty or condition." As a rule of construction, a prohibition against assignment of a contract (in this case, the lease) will prevent assignment of contractual duties but does not prevent assignment of the right to receive payments due—unless circumstances indicate otherwise. Having received notice of the assignment, Landlord was bound by the assignment.

INTERPRETATION Unless circumstances indicate the contrary, a contract term prohibiting assignment of the contract bars only delegation of the assignor's contractual duties.

ETHICAL QUESTION If the landlord had inadvertently ignored the notice of assignment, would the outcome of the case have been fair? Explain.

CRITICAL THINKING QUESTION Should the courts honor contractual prohibitions of assignments by rendering such assignments ineffective? Explain.

Assignments Prohibited by Law Various federal and state statutes, as well as public policy, prohibit or regulate the assignment of certain types of contract rights. For instance, assignments of future wages are subject to such statutes, some of which prohibit these assignments altogether, whereas others require the assignments to be in writing and subject them to certain restrictions. Moreover, an assignment that violates public policy will be unenforceable even in the absence of a prohibiting statute.

Rights of the Assignee

Rights of the assignee
assignee stands in the shoes of the assignor

Obtains Rights of Assignor The general rule is that an assignee *stands in the shoes* of the assignor. She acquires the rights of the assignor but no new or additional rights, and she takes with the assigned rights all of the defenses, defects, and infirmities to which they would be subject in an action against the obligor by the assignor. Thus, in an action brought by the assignee against the obligor, the obligor may plead fraud, duress, undue influence, failure of consideration, breach of contract, or any other defense arising out of the original contract against the assignor. The obligor may also assert rights of **setoff** or counterclaim arising out of entirely separate matters that he may have against the assignor, as long as they arose before he had notice of the assignment.

Setoff
claim by obligor against assignor arising out of an entirely separate transaction

The Code permits the buyer under a contract of sale to agree as part of the contract that he will not assert against an assignee any claim or defense that the buyer may have against the seller if the assignee takes the assignment for value, in good faith, and without notice of conflicting claims or of certain defenses. Such a provision in an agreement renders the seller's rights more marketable. The Federal Trade Commission, however, has invalidated such waiver of defense provisions in consumer credit transactions. This rule is discussed more fully in Chapter 25. Article 9 reflects this rule by essentially rendering waiver-of-defense clauses ineffective in consumer transactions. Most states also have statutes protecting buyers in consumer transactions by prohibiting waiver of defenses.

Notice The obligor need not receive notice for an assignment to be valid. Giving notice of assignment is advisable, however, because an assignee will lose his rights against the obligor if the obligor, without notice of the assignment, pays the assignor. Compelling an obligor to pay a claim a second time, when she was unaware that a new party was entitled to payment, would be unfair. For example, Donald owes Gary $1,000 due on September 1. Gary assigns the debt to Paula on August 1, but neither Gary nor Paula informs Donald. On September 1, Donald pays Gary. Donald is fully discharged from his obligation, whereas Gary is liable for $1,000 to Paula. On the other hand, if Paula had given notice of the assignment to Donald before September 1 and Donald had paid Gary nevertheless, Paula would then have the right to recover the $1,000 from either Donald or Gary. Furthermore, notice cuts off any defenses based on subsequent agreements between the obligor and assignor and, as already indicated, subsequent setoffs and counterclaims of the obligor that may arise out of entirely separate matters.

Implied Warranties of Assignor

An **implied warranty** is an obligation imposed by law upon the transferor of property or contract rights. In the absence of an express intention to the contrary, an assignor who receives value makes the following implied warranties to the assignee with respect to the assigned right:

1. that he will do nothing to defeat or impair the assignment;
2. that the assigned right actually exists and is subject to no limitations or defenses other than those stated or apparent at the time of the assignment;
3. that any writing that evidences the right and that is delivered to the assignee or exhibited to him as an inducement to accept the assignment is genuine and what it purports to be; and
4. that the assignor has no knowledge of any fact that would impair the value of the assignment.

Thus, Eric has a right against Julia and assigns it for value to Gwen. Later, Eric gives Julia a release. Gwen may recover damages from Eric for breach of the first implied warranty.

Express Warranties of Assignor

An **express warranty** is an explicitly made contractual promise regarding the property or contract rights transferred. The assignor is further bound by any specific express warranties he makes to the assignee about the right assigned. Unless he explicitly states as much, however, the assignor does not guarantee that the obligor will pay the assigned debt or otherwise perform.

Successive Assignments of the Same Right

The owner of a right could conceivably make successive assignments of the same claim to different persons. Although this action is morally and legally inappropriate, it raises the question of what rights successive assignees have. Assume, for example, that B owes A $1,000. On June 1, A for value assigns the debt to C. Thereafter, on June 15, A assigns it to D, who in good faith gives value and has no knowledge of the prior assignment by A to C. If the assignment is subject to Article 9, then the article's priority rules will control, as discussed in Chapter 37. Otherwise, the priority is determined by the common law. The majority rule in the United States is that the first assignee in point of time (C) prevails over later assignees. By way of contrast, in England and in a minority of the states, the first assignee to notify the obligor prevails.

The Restatement adopts a third view. A prior assignee is entitled to the assigned right and its proceeds to the exclusion of a subsequent assignee, *except* where the prior assignment is revocable or voidable by the assignor or the subsequent assignee in good faith and without knowledge of the prior assignment gives value and obtains one of the following: (1) payment or satisfaction of the obligor's duty, (2) a judgment against the obligor, (3) a new contract with the obligor, or (4) possession of a writing of a type customarily accepted as a symbol or evidence of the right assigned.

DELEGATION OF DUTIES

As we indicated, contractual *duties* are not assignable, but their performance generally may be delegated to a third person. A delegation of duties is a transfer of a contractual obligation to a third party. For example, A promises to sell B a new automobile, for which B promises to pay $10,000 by monthly installments over the next three years. If A and D agree that D should deliver the automobile to B, this would not constitute an assignment but would be a delegation of duties between A and D. In this instance, A would be the *delegator*, D would be the *delegatee*, and B would be the *obligee*. A delegation of duty does not extinguish the delegator's obligation to perform because A remains liable to B. When the delegatee accepts, or **assumes**, the delegated duty, *both* the delegator and delegatee are liable for performance of the contractual duty to the obligee.

Delegable Duties

Though contractual duties generally are delegable, a delegation will not be permitted if

1. the nature of the duties is personal in that the obligee has a substantial interest in having the delegator perform the contract;
2. the performance is expressly made nondelegable; or
3. the delegation is prohibited by statute or public policy.

PRACTICAL ADVICE

When it is important that the other party to a contract personally perform his contractual obligations, consider including a term in the contract prohibiting any delegation of duties without written consent.

The courts will examine a delegation more closely than an assignment because a delegation compels the nondelegating party to the contract (the obligee) to receive performance from a party with whom she has not dealt.

For example, a schoolteacher may not delegate her performance to another teacher, even if the substitute is equally competent, for this contract is personal in nature. On the other hand, under a contract in which performance by a party involves no special skill and in which no personal trust or confidence is involved, the party may delegate performance of his duty. For example, the duty to pay money, to deliver fungible goods such as corn, or to mow a lawn is usually delegable. The next case deals with this type of delegation.

Public Service Commission of Maryland. v. Panda-Brandywine, L.P.

Court of Appeals of Maryland, 2003

375 Md. 185, 825 A.2d 462

http://scholar.google.com/scholar_case?case=14283409950595264869&q=825+a.2d+462&hl=en&as_sdt=2,34

FACTS Potomac Electric Power Company (PEPCO) is an electric utility serving the metropolitan Washington, D.C., area. Panda-Brandywine, L.P. (Panda) is a "qualified facility" under the Public Utility Regulatory Policies Act of 1978. In August, 1991, PEPCO and Panda entered into a power purchase agreement (PPA) calling for (1) the construction by Panda of a new 230-megawatt cogenerating power plant in Prince George's County, Maryland; (2) connection of the facility to PEPCO's high-voltage transmission system by transmission facilities to be built by Panda but later transferred without cost to PEPCO; and (3) upon commencement of the commercial operation of the plant, for PEPCO to purchase the power generated by that plant for a period of twenty-five years. The plant was built at a cost of $215 million.

The PPA is 113 pages in length, single-spaced, and is both detailed and complex. It gave PEPCO substantial authority to review, influence, and, in some instances, determine important aspects of both the construction and operation of the Panda facility. Section 19.1 of the PPA provided that the agreement was not assignable and not delegable without the written consent of the other party, which consent could not be unreasonably withheld.

In 1999, Maryland enacted legislation calling for the restructuring of the electric industry in an effort to promote competition in the generation and delivery of electricity. PEPCO's proposed restructuring involved a complete divestiture of its electric generating assets and its various PPAs, to be accomplished by an auction. The sale to the winning bidder was to be accomplished by an Asset Purchase and Sale Agreement (APSA) that included the PPA to which PEPCO and Panda were parties. Under the APSA the buyer was authorized to take all actions that PEPCO could lawfully take under the PPA with Panda.

On June 7, 2000, Southern Energy, Inc. (SEI) was declared the winning bidder. On September 27, 2000, the Public Service Commission (PSC) entered an order declaring, among other things, that the provisions in the APSA did not constitute an assignment or transfer within the meaning of Section 19.1 of the Panda PPA, that PEPCO was not assigning "significant obligations and rights under the PPA," that Panda would not be harmed by the transaction, and that the APSA did not "fundamentally alter" the contract between Panda and PEPCO. The PSC thus concluded that Panda's consent to the proposed APSA was not required.

Panda disagreed and brought this lawsuit. The trial court ruled that the APSA effected an assignment of Panda's PPA and reversed the PSC order. PEPCO appealed and the appellate court concluded that, through the APSA, PEPCO effectively and improperly delegated its duties under the PPA to SEI.

DECISION Judgment affirmed.

OPINION In a bilateral contract, each party ordinarily has both rights and duties—the right to expect performance from the other party to the contract and the duty to perform what the party has agreed to perform. Although both are often the subjects of transfer, the law does distinguish between them, using the term "assignment" to refer to the transfer of contractual rights and the term "delegation" to refer to the transfer of contractual duties.

The Restatement (Second) of Contracts permits a contractual right to be assigned unless

> (1) the substitution of a right of the assignee for the right of the assignor would materially change the duty of the obligor, or materially increase the burden or risk imposed on him by his contract, or materially impair his chance of obtaining return performance, or materially reduce its value to him,
> (2) the assignment is forbidden by statute or is inoperative on grounds of public policy, or
> (3) "assignment is validly precluded by contract."

Section 19.1 of the PPA very clearly prohibits both the assignment of rights and the delegation of duties of performance, absent express written consent. The issue, then, is not whether PEPCO can make such an assignment or delegation but only whether it has, in fact, done so. The answer to that lies in the effect that the provisions of the APSA have on the contractual relationship between PEPCO and Panda.

The APSA involves a great deal more than merely a resale of electricity purchased from Panda and even more than the effective substitution of one customer for another. Much of Panda's control over its own facility and business was subject to the approval and cooperation of PEPCO; indeed, to a large extent, the operation of the facility was, in many important respects, almost a joint venture. In agreeing to that kind of arrangement, Panda necessarily was relying on its perceptions of PEPCO's competence and managerial style. One does not ordinarily choose a business partner by auction or lottery, and there is no evidence that Panda did so in this case. Panda has "a substantial interest in having [PEPCO] perform or control the acts promised." Under the APSA that control has been delegated irrevocably to SEI—a stranger to Panda—with the ability of SEI to delegate it to others. Virtually none of the rights and responsibilities transferred to SEI under the APSA are permitted under Section 19.1 of the PPA. Thus the APSA constitutes an assignment of rights and obligations under the PPA in contravention of Section 19.1 of that agreement and it is therefore invalid and unenforceable.

INTERPRETATION The extent to which contractual rights may be assigned and duties of performance delegated are subject to any valid contractual provision prohibiting assignment or delegation.

CRITICAL THINKING QUESTION If the APSA had involved only the resale of electricity purchased from Panda would the court have permitted the delegation?

Duties of the Parties

Delegation
delegator is still bound to perform original obligation

Novation
contract, to which the promisee is a party, substituting a new promisor for an existing promisor, who is consequently no longer liable on the original contract and is not liable as a delegator

Even when permitted, a **delegation** of a duty to a third person leaves the delegator bound to perform. If the delegator desires to be discharged of the duty, she may enter into an agreement by which she obtains the consent of the obligee to substitute a third person (the delegatee) in her place. This is a **novation**, whereby the delegator is discharged and the third party becomes directly bound on his promise to the obligee.

Though a delegation authorizes a third party to perform a duty for the delegator, the delegatee becomes liable for performance only if he assents to perform the delegated duties. Thus, if Frank owes a duty to Grace, and Frank delegates that duty to Henry, Henry is not obligated to either Frank or Grace to perform the duty unless Henry agrees to do so. If, however, Henry promises either Frank (the delegator) or Grace (the obligee) that he will perform Frank's duty, Henry is said to have *assumed the delegated duty* and becomes liable for nonperformance to both Frank and Grace. Accordingly, when there is both a delegation of duties *and* an assumption of the delegated duties, *both* the delegator and the delegatee are liable to the obligee for proper performance of the original contractual duty. The delegatee's promise to perform creates contract rights in the obligee, who may bring an action against the delegatee as a third-party beneficiary of the contract between the delegator and the delegatee. (Third-party contracts are discussed in the next section in this chapter.)

The question of whether a party has assumed contractual duties frequently arises in the following ambiguous situation: Marty and Carol agree to an assignment of Marty's contract with Bob. The Restatement and the Code clearly resolve this ambiguity by providing that unless the language or circumstances indicate the contrary, an assignment of "the contract" or of "all my rights under the contract" or an assignment in similar general terms is an assignment of rights *and* a delegation of performance of the duties of the assignor, and its acceptance by the assignee constitutes a promise to perform those duties. For example, Cooper Oil Company has a contract to deliver oil to Halsey. Cooper makes a written assignment to Lowell Oil Company "of all Cooper's rights under the contract." Lowell is under a duty to Halsey to deliver the oil called for by the contract, and Cooper is liable to Halsey if Lowell does not perform. You should also recall that the Restatement and the Code provide that a clause prohibiting an assignment of "the contract" is to be construed as barring only the delegation to the assignee (delegatee) of the assignor's (delegator's) performance, unless the circumstances indicate the contrary.

APPLYING THE LAW

Third Parties to Contracts

Facts Monica signed a twelve-month lease with Grandridge Apartments in Grand City. But after only two months she received a promotion that required her to move to Lakeville, three hundred miles away. Mindful of her lease obligation, she found an acquaintance, Troy, to rent the apartment for the remaining ten months. Troy promised Monica he would pay the rent directly to the landlord each month and would clean the place up before moving out at the end of the lease term.

After moving in, Troy personally delivered a check for the rent to the landlord each month until four months later when he lost his job, at which point he stopped paying rent altogether. The landlord evicted Troy and, as he was unable to find another suitable tenant, he sued Monica for the rent owed on the remainder of the lease. Monica claimed the landlord should have sued Troy.

Issue Is Monica liable for the remaining lease payments?

Rule of Law Performance of a contract obligation generally may be delegated to a third person who is willing to assume the liability. However, such a delegation by the obligor does not extinguish the obligor/delegator's duty to perform the contract. If the delegator wishes to be discharged from the contract prospectively, she should enter into a new agreement with the obligee, in which the obligee consents to the substitution of a third party (the delegatee) in the delegator's place. This is called a novation.

Application The lease is a contract obligation. Monica is the obligor, and the landlord is the obligee. Here, Monica delegated her performance under the lease to Troy. Troy assumed liability for the lease payments by agreeing to pay the rent. However, even though a valid delegation has been made, Monica is not relieved of her duty to pay the rent. Instead, both Troy and Monica are now obligated to the landlord for the remaining lease term.

Had Monica entered into a novation with the landlord, only Troy would be liable for the remaining rent. But the facts do not support finding a novation. Troy made the rent payments directly to the landlord, who ultimately evicted Troy from the apartment. Therefore, the landlord was aware that Troy had taken possession of the apartment and that Troy may have taken on some responsibility for rent payments. At most, the landlord tacitly consented to the informal assignment and delegation of the lease to Troy. However, the landlord never agreed to substitute Troy for Monica and thereby to release Monica from her legal obligations under the lease.

Conclusion In a suit by the landlord, Monica is responsible for the remaining rent payments.

© Cengage Learning 2013

THIRD-PARTY BENEFICIARY CONTRACTS

Third-party beneficiary contract

contract in which one party promises to render a performance to a third person

Intended beneficiary

third party intended by the two contracting parties to receive a benefit from their contract

A contract in which a party (the *promisor*) promises to render a certain performance not to the other party (the promisee) but to a third person (the beneficiary) is called a **third-party beneficiary contract**. The third person is merely a beneficiary of the contract, not a party to it. The law divides such contracts into two types: (1) intended beneficiary contracts and (2) incidental beneficiary contracts. An **intended beneficiary** is intended by the two parties to the contract (the promisor and promisee) to receive a benefit from the performance of their agreement. Accordingly, the courts generally permit intended beneficiaries to enforce third-party contracts. For example, Abbot promises Baldwin to deliver an automobile to Carson if Baldwin promises to pay $10,000. Carson is the intended beneficiary.

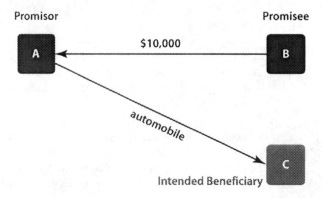

Incidental beneficiary

third party whom the two parties to the contract have no intention of benefiting by their contract and who acquires no rights under the contract

In an **incidental beneficiary** contract the third party is not intended to receive a benefit under the contract. Accordingly, courts do not enforce the third party's right to the benefits of the contract. For example, Abbot promises to purchase and deliver to Baldwin an automobile for $10,000. In all probability Abbot would acquire the automobile from Davis. Davis would be an incidental beneficiary and would have no enforceable rights against either Abbot or Baldwin.

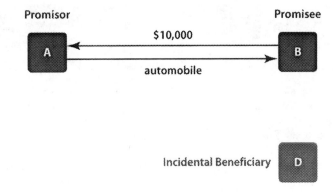

Intended Beneficiary

Unless otherwise agreed between the promisor and promisee, a beneficiary of a promise is an intended beneficiary if the parties intended this to be the result of their agreement. Thus, there are two types of intended beneficiaries: (1) donee beneficiaries and (2) creditor beneficiaries.

Donee beneficiary
a third party intended to receive a benefit from the contract as a gift

Donee Beneficiary   A third party is an intended donee beneficiary if the promisee's purpose in bargaining for and obtaining the contract with the promisor was to make a gift of the promised performance to the beneficiary. The ordinary life insurance policy illustrates this type of intended beneficiary third-party contract. The insured (the promisee) makes a contract with an insurance company (the promisor), which promises, in consideration of premiums paid to it by the insured, to pay upon the death of the insured a stated sum of money to the named beneficiary (generally a relative or close friend), who is an intended donee beneficiary.

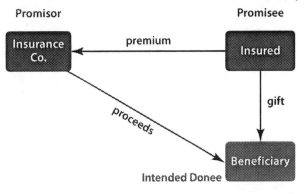

Creditor beneficiary
a third person intended to receive a benefit from the agreement to satisfy a legal duty owed to him

Creditor Beneficiary   A third person is an intended creditor beneficiary if the promisee intends the performance of the promise to satisfy a legal duty owed to the beneficiary, who is a creditor of the promisee. The contract involves consideration moving from the promisee to the promisor in exchange for the promisor's engaging to pay a debt or to discharge an obligation the promisee owes to the third person.

To illustrate: in the contract for the sale by Wesley of his business to Susan, she promises Wesley that she will pay all of his outstanding business debts, as listed in the contract. Wesley's creditors are intended creditor beneficiaries.

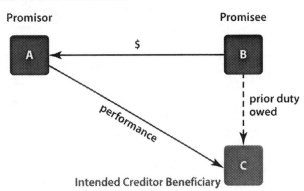

Stine v. Stewart
Supreme Court of Texas, 2002
80 S.W.3d 586
http://caselaw.lp.findlaw.com/scripts/getcase.pl?court=tx&vol=/sc/010896&invol=1

FACTS On April 26, 1984, Mary Stine (Stine) loaned her daughter (Mary Ellen) and son-in-law William Stewart $100,000 to purchase a home. In return, the Stewarts jointly executed a promissory note for $100,000, payable on demand to Stine. The Stewarts did not give a security interest or mortgage to secure the note. The Stewarts eventually paid $50,000 on the note, leaving $50,000, plus unpaid interest, due.

The Stewarts divorced on October 2, 1992. The couple executed an Agreement Incident to Divorce, which disposed of marital property, including the home (the agreement identifies the home as the Lago Vista property). The agreement provided that if Stewart sold the home, he agreed that "any monies owing to [Stine] are to be paid in the current principal sum of $50,000.00." The agreement further states:

> The parties agree that with regard to the note to Mary Nelle Stine, after application of the proceeds of the [Lago Vista property], if there are any amounts owing to [Stine] the remaining balance owing to her will be appropriated 50% to NANCY KAREN STEWART and 50% to WILLIAM DEAN STEWART, JR. and said 50% from each party will be due and payable upon the determination that the proceeds from the sale of said residence are not sufficient to repay said $50,000.00 in full.

Stine did not sign the agreement.

On November 17, 1995, Stewart sold the Lago Vista property for $125,000, leaving $6,820.21 in net proceeds. Stewart did not pay these proceeds to Stine and did not make any further payments on the $50,000 principal. Consequently, on July 27, 1998, Stine sued Stewart for breaching the agreement.

The trial court concluded that Stine was an intended third-party beneficiary of the agreement and that Stewart breached the agreement when he refused to pay Stine. The trial court awarded Stine $28,410 in damages from Stewart. The court of appeals reversed the judgment, concluding that Stine was neither an intended third-party donee beneficiary of the agreement nor an intended third-party creditor beneficiary of the agreement.

DECISION The court of appeals' judgment is reversed and case remanded.

OPINION A third party may recover on a contract made between other parties only if the parties intended to secure a benefit to that third party, and only if the contracting parties entered into the contract directly for the third party's benefit. A third party does not have a right to enforce the contract if she received only an incidental benefit. An agreement must clearly and fully express an intent to confer a direct benefit to the third party. To determine the parties' intent, courts must examine the entire agreement and give effect to all the contract's provisions so that none are rendered meaningless.

To qualify as an intended third-party beneficiary, a party must show that she is either a "donee" or "creditor" beneficiary of the contract. An agreement benefits a "donee" beneficiary if "the performance promised will, when rendered, come to him as a pure donation." In contrast, an agreement benefits a "creditor" beneficiary if "that performance will come to him in satisfaction of a legal duty owed to him by the promisee." This duty may be an indebtedness, contractual obligation, or other legally enforceable commitment owed to the third party.

The Court agreed with the court of appeals' determination that Stine was not an intended third-party donee beneficiary of the agreement. But, it concluded that Stine is a third-party creditor beneficiary. The agreement expressly provides that the Stewarts intended to satisfy an obligation to repay Stine the $50,000 that the Stewarts owed her. Specifically, the agreement refers to the monies owed to Stine as "the current principal sum of $50,000." Then, the agreement states that Stewart agreed to pay the property sale net proceeds "with regard to the note" to Stine. The agreement further provides that, if the property sale net proceeds did not cover the amount owed to Stine, the remainder would be immediately due and payable from the Stewarts, with each owing one half. Thus, the agreement expressly requires the Stewarts to satisfy their obligation to pay Stine.

The agreement's language clearly shows that Stewart intended to secure a benefit to Stine as a third-party creditor beneficiary. Consequently, Stewart breached the agreement when he refused to pay Stine the money owed to her as the agreement requires.

INTERPRETATION An intended third-party beneficiary of a contract may enforce that contract.

CRITICAL THINKING QUESTION Why did the court conclude that Stine was not an intended third-party donee beneficiary?

Rights of intended beneficiary

an intended donee beneficiary may enforce the contract against the promisor; an intended creditor beneficiary may enforce the contract against either or both the promisor and the promisee

Rights of Intended Beneficiary
Though an intended creditor beneficiary may sue either or both parties, an intended donee beneficiary may enforce the contract against the promisor only. He cannot maintain an action against the promisee, as the promisee was under no legal obligation to him.

Vesting of Rights
A contract for the benefit of an intended beneficiary confers upon that beneficiary rights that the beneficiary may enforce. Until these rights vest (take effect), however, the promisor and promisee may, by later agreement, vary or completely discharge them. There is considerable variation among the states as to when vesting occurs. Some states hold that vesting takes place immediately upon the making of the contract. In other states, vesting occurs when the third party learns of the contract and assents to it. In another group of states, vesting requires the third party to change his position in reliance upon the promise made for his benefit. The

Vesting of rights
if the beneficiary's rights vest, the promisor and promisee may not thereafter vary or discharge these vested rights

P R A C T I C A L   A D V I C E
To avoid uncertainty, consider specifying in the contract whether there are any third-party beneficiaries and, if so, who they are, what their rights are, and when their rights vest.

Defenses against beneficiary
in an action by the intended beneficiary to enforce the promise, the promisor may assert any defense that would be available to her if the action had been brought by the promisee

Incidental beneficiary
third party whom the two parties to a contract have no intention of benefiting by their contract

Restatement has adopted the following position: If the contract between the promisor and promisee provides that its terms may not be varied without the consent of the beneficiary, such a provision will be upheld. If there is no such provision, the parties to the contract may rescind or vary the contract unless the intended beneficiary (1) has brought an action on the promise, (2) has changed her position in reliance on it, or (3) has assented to the promise at the request of the promisor or promisee.

On the other hand, the promisor and promisee may provide that the benefits will never vest. For example, Mildred purchases an insurance policy on her own life, naming her husband as beneficiary. The policy, as such policies commonly do, reserves to Mildred the right to change her beneficiary or even to cancel the policy entirely.

Defenses against Beneficiary   In an action by the intended beneficiary to enforce the promise, the promisor may assert any defense that would be available to her if the action had been brought by the promisee. The rights of the third party are based upon the promisor's contract with the promisee. Thus, the promisor may assert the absence of mutual assent or consideration, lack of capacity, fraud, mistake, and the like against the intended beneficiary. Once an intended beneficiary's rights have vested, however, the promisor may not assert the defense of contractual modification or rescission entered into with the promisee.

Incidental Beneficiary

An incidental third-party beneficiary is a person to whom the parties to a contract did not intend a benefit but who nevertheless would derive some benefit by its performance. For instance, a contract to raze an old, unsightly building and to replace it with a costly modern house would benefit the owner of the adjoining property by increasing his property's value. He would have no rights under the contract, however, as the benefit to him would be unintended and incidental.

A third person who may benefit incidentally by the performance of a contract to which he is not a party has no rights under the contract, as neither the promisee nor the promisor intended that the third person benefit. Assume that for a stated consideration Charles promises Madeline that he will purchase and deliver to Madeline a new Sony television of the latest model. Madeline pays in advance for the television. Charles does not deliver the television to Madeline. Reiner, the local exclusive Sony dealer, has no rights under the contract, although performance by Charles would produce a sale from which Reiner would derive a benefit, for Reiner is only an incidental beneficiary.

C H A P T E R   S U M M A R Y

Assignment of Rights   **Definition of Assignment** voluntary transfer to a third party of the rights arising from a contract so that the assignor's right to performance is extinguished
- *Assignor* party making an assignment
- *Assignee* party to whom contract rights are assigned
- *Obligor* party owing a duty to the assignor under the original contract
- *Obligee* party to whom a duty of performance is owed under a contract

Requirements of an Assignment include intent but not consideration
- *Revocability of Assignment* when the assignee gives consideration, the assignor may not revoke the assignment without the assignee's consent
- *Partial Assignment* transfer of a portion of contractual rights to one or more assignees

Assignability most contract rights are assignable except:
- Assignments that materially increase the duty, risk, or burden upon the obligor
- Assignments of personal rights
- Assignments expressly forbidden by the contract
- Assignments prohibited by law

Rights of Assignee the assignee stands in the shoes of the assignor

* *Defenses of Obligor* may be asserted against the assignee
* *Notice* is not required but is advisable

Implied Warranties obligation imposed by law upon the assignor of a contract right

Express Warranty explicitly made contractual promise regarding contract rights transferred

Successive Assignments of the Same Right the majority rule is that the first assignee in point of time prevails over later assignees; minority rule is that the first assignee to notify the obligor prevails

Delegation of Duties

Definition of Delegation transfer to a third party of a contractual obligation

* *Delegator* party delegating his duty to a third party
* *Delegatee* third party to whom the delegator's duty is delegated
* *Obligee* party to whom a duty of performance is owed by the delegator and delegatee

Delegability most contract duties may be delegated except

* Duties that are personal
* Duties that are expressly nondelegable
* Duties whose delegation is prohibited by statute or public policy

Duties of the Parties

* *Delegation* delegator is still bound to perform original obligation
* *Novation Contract* a substituted contract to which the promisee is a party, which substitutes a new promisor for an existing promisor, who is consequently no longer liable on the original contract and is not liable as a delegator

Third-Party Beneficiary Contracts

Definition a third-party beneficiary contract is one in which one party promises to render a performance to a third person (the beneficiary)

Intended Beneficiaries third parties intended by the two contracting parties to receive a benefit from their contract

* *Donee Beneficiary* a third party intended to receive a benefit from the contract as a gift
* *Creditor Beneficiary* a third person intended to receive a benefit from the contract to satisfy a legal duty owed to him
* *Rights of Intended Beneficiary* an intended donee beneficiary may enforce the contract against the promisor; an intended creditor beneficiary may enforce the contract against either or both the promisor and the promisee
* *Vesting of Rights* if the beneficiary's rights vest, the promisor and promisee may not thereafter vary or discharge these vested rights

Defenses against Beneficiary in an action by the intended beneficiary to enforce the promise, the promisor may assert any defense that would be available to her if the action had been brought by the promisee

Incidental Beneficiary third party whom the two parties to the contract have no intention of benefiting by their contract and who acquires no rights under the contract

QUESTIONS

1. On December 1, Euphonia, a famous singer, contracted with Boito to sing at Boito's theater on December 31 for a fee of $45,000 to be paid immediately after the performance.
   a. Euphonia, for value received, assigns this fee to Carter.
   b. Euphonia, for value received, assigns this contract to sing to Dumont, an equally famous singer.
   c. Boito sells his theater to Edmund and assigns his contract with Euphonia to Edmund.
   State the effect of each of these assignments.

2. The Smooth Paving Company entered into a paving contract with the city of Chicago. The contract contained the clause "contractor shall be liable for all damages to buildings result-

ing from the work performed." In the process of construction, one of the bulldozers of the Smooth Paving Company struck and broke a gas main, causing an explosion and a fire that destroyed the house of John Puff. Puff brought an action for breach of the paving contract against the Smooth Paving Company to recover damages for the loss of his house. Can Puff recover under this contract? Explain.

3. Anne, who was unemployed, registered with the Speedy Employment Agency. A contract was then made under which Anne, in consideration of such position as the agency would obtain for her, agreed to pay the agency one half of her first month's salary. The contract also contained an assignment by

Anne to the agency of one half of her first month's salary. Two weeks later, the agency obtained a permanent position for Anne with the Bostwick Co. at a monthly salary of $1,900. The agency also notified Bostwick Co. of the assignment by Anne. At the end of the first month, Bostwick Co. paid Anne her salary in full. Anne then quit and disappeared. The agency now sues Bostwick Co. for $950 under the assignment. Who will prevail? Explain.

4. Georgia purchased an option on Greenacre from Pamela for $10,000. The option contract contained a provision by which Georgia promised not to assign the option contract without Pamela's permission. Georgia, without Pamela's permission, assigned the contract to Michael. Michael now seeks to exercise the option, and Pamela refuses to sell Greenacre to him. Must Pamela sell the land to Michael?

5. Julia contracts to sell to Hayden, an ice cream manufacturer, the amount of ice Hayden may need in his business for the ensuing three years to the extent of not more than 250 tons a week at a stated price per ton. Hayden makes a corresponding promise to Julia to buy such an amount of ice. Hayden sells his ice cream plant to Reed and assigns to Reed all Hayden's rights under the contract with Julia. On learning of the sale, Julia refuses to furnish ice to Reed. Can Reed successfully collect damages from Julia? Explain.

6. Brown enters into a written contract with Ideal Insurance Company under which, in consideration of Brown's payment of her premiums, the insurance company promises to pay Williams College the face amount of the policy, $100,000, on Brown's death. Brown pays the premiums until her death. Thereafter, Williams College makes demand for the $100,000, which the insurance company refuses to pay on the ground that Williams College was not a party to the contract. Can Williams successfully enforce the contract?

7. Grant and Debbie enter into a contract binding Grant personally to do some delicate cabinetwork. Grant assigns his rights and delegates performance of his duties to Clarence.

   a. On being informed of this, Debbie agrees with Clarence, in consideration of Clarence's promise to do the work, that Debbie will accept Clarence's work, if properly done, instead of the performance promised by Grant. Later, without cause, Debbie refuses to allow Clarence to proceed with the work, though Clarence is ready to do so, and makes demand on Grant that Grant perform. Grant refuses. Can Clarence recover damages from Debbie? Can Debbie recover from Grant?

   b. Instead, assume that Debbie refuses to permit Clarence to do the work, employs another carpenter, and brings an action against Grant, claiming as damages the difference between the contract price and the cost to employ the other carpenter. Explain whether Debbie will prevail.

8. Rebecca owes Lewis $2,500 due on November 1. On August 15, Lewis assigns this right for value received to Julia, who gives notice on September 10 of the assignment to Rebecca. On August 25, Lewis assigns the same right to Wayne, who in good faith gives value and has no prior knowledge of the assignment by Lewis to Julia. Wayne gives Rebecca notice of the assignment on August 30. What are the rights and obligations of Rebecca, Lewis, Julia, and Wayne?

9. Lisa hired Jay in the spring, as she had for many years, to set out in beds the flowers Lisa had grown in her greenhouses during the winter. The work was to be done in Lisa's absence for $300. Jay became ill the day after Lisa departed and requested his friend, Curtis, to set out the flowers, promising to pay Curtis $250 when Jay received his payment. Curtis agreed. On completion of the planting, an agent of Lisa's, who had authority to dispense the money, paid Jay, and Jay paid Curtis. Within two days, it became obvious that the planting was a disaster. Because he did not operate Lisa's automatic watering system properly, everything set out by Curtis had died of water rot.

   May Lisa recover damages from Curtis? May Lisa recover damages from Jay, and, if so, does Jay have an action against Curtis?

10. Caleb, operator of a window-washing business, dictated a letter to his secretary addressed to Apartments, Inc., stating, "I will wash the windows of your apartment buildings at $4.10 per window to be paid on completion of the work." The secretary typed the letter, signed Caleb's name, and mailed it to Apartments, Inc. Apartments, Inc., replied, "Accept your offer."

   Caleb wrote back, "I will wash them during the week starting July 10 and direct you to pay the money you will owe me to my son, Bernie. I am giving it to him as a wedding present." Caleb sent a signed copy of the letter to Bernie.

   Caleb washed the windows during the time stated and demanded payment to him of $8,200 (2,000 windows at $4.10 each), informing Apartments, Inc., that he had changed his mind about having the money paid to Bernie.

   What are the rights of the parties?

CASE PROBLEMS

11. On April 1, members of Local 100, Transport Workers Union of America (TWU), began an eleven-day mass transit strike that paralyzed the life and commerce of the city of New York. Jackson, Lewis, Schnitzler & Krupman, a Manhattan law firm, brought a class action suit against the TWU for the direct and foreseeable damages it suffered as a result of the union's illegal strike. The law firm sought to recover as a third-party beneficiary of the collective bargaining agreement between the union and New York City. The agreement contains a no-strike clause and states that the TWU agreed to cooperate with the city to provide a safe, efficient, and dependable mass transit system. The law firm argues that its members are a part of the general public that depends on the mass transit system to go to and from work. Therefore, they are in the class of persons for whose benefit the union has promised to provide dependable transportation service. Are the members of the class action suit entitled to recover? Explain.

12. Northwest Airlines leased space in the terminal building at the Portland Airport from the Port of Portland. Crosetti entered into a contract with the Port to furnish janitorial services for the building, which required Crosetti to keep the floor clean, to indemnify the Port against loss due to claims or lawsuits based upon Crosetti's failure to perform, and to provide public liability insurance for the Port and Crosetti. A patron of the

building who was injured by a fall caused by a foreign substance on the floor at Northwest's ticket counter brought suit for damages against Northwest, the Port, and Crosetti. Upon settlement of this suit, Northwest sued Crosetti to recover the amount of its contribution to the settlement and other expenses on the grounds that Northwest was a third-party beneficiary of Crosetti's contract with the Port to keep the floors clean and, therefore, within the protection of Crosetti's indemnification agreement. Will Northwest prevail? Why?

13. Tompkins-Beckwith, as the contractor on a construction project, entered into a subcontract with a division of Air Metal Industries. Air Metal procured American Fire and Casualty Company to be surety on certain bonds in connection with contracts it was performing for Tompkins-Beckwith and others. As security for these bonds, on January 3, Air Metal executed an assignment to American Fire of all accounts receivable under the Tompkins-Beckwith subcontract. On November 26 of that year, Boulevard National Bank lent money to Air Metal. To secure the loans, Air Metal purported to assign to the bank certain accounts receivable it had under its subcontract with Tompkins-Beckwith.

   In June of the following year, Air Metal defaulted on various contracts bonded by American Fire. On July 1, American Fire served formal notice on Tompkins-Beckwith of Air Metal's assignment. Tompkins-Beckwith acknowledged the assignment and agreed to pay. In August, Boulevard National Bank notified Tompkins-Beckwith of its assignment. Tompkins-Beckwith refused to recognize the bank's claim and, instead, paid all remaining funds that had accrued to Air Metal to American Fire. The bank then sued to enforce its claim under Air Metal's assignment. Is the assignment effective? Why?

14. The International Association of Machinists (the union) was the bargaining agent for the employees of Powder Power Tool Corporation. On August 24, the union and the corporation executed a collective bargaining agreement providing for retroactively increased wage rates for the corporation's employees effective as of the previous April 1. Three employees who were working for Powder before and for several months after April 1, but who were not employed by the corporation when the agreement was executed on August 24, were paid to the time their employment terminated at the old wage scale. The three employees assigned their claims to Springer, who brought this action against the corporation for the extra wages. Decision?

15. In March, Adrian Saylor sold government bonds owned exclusively by him and with $6,450 of the proceeds opened a savings account in a bank in the name of "Mr. or Mrs. Adrian M. Saylor." In June of the following year, Saylor deposited the additional sum of $2,132 of his own money in the account. There were no other deposits and no withdrawals prior to the death of Saylor in May a year later. Is the balance of the account on Saylor's death payable wholly to Adrian Saylor's estate, wholly to his widow, or half to each?

16. Linda King was found liable to Charlotte Clement as the result of an automobile accident. King, who was insolvent at the time, declared bankruptcy and directed her attorney, Prestwich, to list Clement as an unsecured creditor. The attorney failed to carry out this duty, and consequently King sued him for legal malpractice. When Clement pursued her judgment against King, she received a written assignment of King's legal malpractice claim against Prestwich. Clement has attempted to bring the claim, but Prestwich alleges that a claim for legal malpractice is not assignable. Decision?

17. Rensselaer Water Company contracted with the city of Rensselaer to provide water to the city for use in homes, public buildings, industry, and fire hydrants. During the term of the contract, a building caught fire. The fire spread to a nearby warehouse and destroyed it and its contents. The water company knew of the fire but failed to supply adequate water pressure at the fire hydrant to extinguish the fire. The warehouse owner sued the water company for failure to fulfill its contract with the city. Can the owner of the warehouse enforce the contract? Explain.

18. McDonald's has an undeviating policy of retaining absolute control over who receives new franchises. McDonald's granted to Copeland a franchise in Omaha, Nebraska. In a separate letter, it also granted him a right of first refusal for future franchises to be developed in the Omaha-Council Bluffs area. Copeland then sold all rights in his six McDonald's franchises to Schupack. When McDonald's offered a new franchise in the Omaha area to someone other than Schupack, he attempted to exercise the right of first refusal. McDonald's would not recognize the right in Schupack, claiming that it was personal to Copeland and, therefore, nonassignable without its consent. Schupack brought an action for specific performance, requiring McDonald's to accord him the right of first refusal. Is Schupack correct in his contention?

19. While under contract to play professional basketball for the Philadelphia 76ers, Billy Cunningham, an outstanding player, negotiated a three-year contract with the Carolina Cougars, another professional basketball team. The contract with the Cougars was to begin at the expiration of the contract with the 76ers. In addition to a signing bonus of $125,000, Cunningham was to receive under the new contract a salary of $100,000 for the first year, $110,000 for the second, and $120,000 for the third. The contract also stated that Cunningham "had special, exceptional and unique knowledge, skill and ability as a basketball player" and that Cunningham therefore agreed the Cougars could enjoin him from playing basketball for any other team for the term of the contract. In addition, the contract contained a clause prohibiting its assignment to another club without Cunningham's consent. In 1971, the ownership of the Cougars changed, and Cunningham's contract was assigned to Munchak Corporation, the new owners, without his consent. When Cunningham refused to play for the Cougars, Munchak Corporation sought to enjoin his playing for any other team. Cunningham asserts that his contract was not assignable. Was the contract assignable? Explain.

20. Pauline Brown was shot and seriously injured by an unknown assailant in the parking lot of National Supermarkets. Pauline and George Brown brought a negligence action against National, Sentry Security Agency, and T. G. Watkins, a security guard and Sentry employee. The Browns maintained that the defendants have a legal duty to protect National's customers, both in the store and in the parking lot, and that this duty was breached. The defendants denied this allegation. What will the Browns have to prove to prevail? Explain.

TAKING SIDES

Pizza of Gaithersburg and The Pizza Shops (Pizza Shops) contracted with Virginia Coffee Service (Virginia) to install vending machines in each of their restaurants. One year later, the Macke Company (a provider of vending machines) purchased Virginia's assets, and the vending machine contracts were assigned to Macke. Pizza Shops had dealt with Macke before but had chosen Virginia because they preferred the way it conducted its business. When Pizza Shops attempted to terminate their contracts for vending services, Macke brought suit for damages for breach of contract.

a. What arguments would support Pizza Shop's termination of the contracts?
b. What arguments would support Macke's suit for breach of contract?
c. Which side should prevail? Explain.

© Kim Steele/Jupiter Images

CHAPTER **17**

Performance, Breach, and Discharge

CHAPTER OUTCOMES

After reading and studying this chapter, you should be able to:

1. Identify and distinguish among the various types of conditions.

2. Distinguish between full performance and tender of performance.

3. Explain the difference between material breach and substantial performance.

4. Distinguish among a mutual rescission, substituted contract, accord and satisfaction, and novation.

5. Identify and explain the ways discharge may be brought about by operation of law.

Because contracting parties ordinarily expect that they will perform their obligations, they are usually more explicit in defining those obligations than in stating the consequences of their nonperformance.

Restatement of Contracts, Introductory Note

The subject of discharge of contracts concerns the termination of contractual duties. In earlier chapters we saw how parties may become contractually bound by their promises. It is also important to know how a person may become unbound from a contract. Although contractual promises are made for a purpose and the parties reasonably expect this purpose to be fulfilled by performance, performance of a contractual duty is only one method of discharge.

Whatever causes a binding promise to cease to be binding is a discharge of the contract. In general, there are four kinds of discharge: (1) performance by the parties, (2) material breach by one or both of the parties, (3) agreement of the parties, and (4) operation of law. Moreover, many contractual promises are not absolute promises to perform but are conditional—that is, they depend on the happening or nonhappening of a specific event. After we discuss the subject of conditions, we will cover the four kinds of discharge.

CONDITIONS

Condition
an uncertain event that affects the duty of performance

A **condition** is an event whose happening or nonhappening affects a duty of performance under a contract. Some conditions must be satisfied before any duty to perform arises; others terminate the duty to perform; still others either limit or modify the duty to perform. A condition is inserted in a contract to protect and benefit the promisor. The more conditions to which a promise is subject, the less content the promise has. For example, a promise to pay $8,000 provided that such sum is realized from the sale of an automobile, provided the automobile is sold within sixty days, and provided that the automobile, which has been stolen, can be found, is clearly different from, and worth considerably less than, an unconditional promise by the same promisor to pay $8,000.

A fundamental difference exists between the breach or nonperformance of a contractual promise and the failure or nonhappening of a condition. A breach of contract subjects the promisor to liability. It may or may not, depending on its materiality, excuse the nonbreaching party's nonperformance of his duty under the contract. The happening or nonhappening of a condition, on the other hand, either prevents a party from acquiring a right or deprives him of a right but subjects neither party to any liability.

Conditions may be classified by *how* they are imposed: express conditions, implied-in-fact conditions, or implied-in-law conditions (also called constructive conditions). They also may be classified by *when* they affect a duty of performance: conditions concurrent, conditions precedent, or conditions subsequent. These two ways of classifying conditions are not mutually exclusive; for example, a condition may be constructive and concurrent or express and precedent.

Express Conditions

An **express condition** is explicitly set forth in language. No particular form of words is necessary to create an express condition, as long as the event to which the performance of the promise is made subject is clearly expressed. An express condition is usually preceded by words such as "provided that," "on condition that," "if," "subject to," "while," "after," "upon," or "as soon as."

The basic rule applied to express conditions is that they must be fully and literally performed before the conditional duty to perform arises. However, when application of the full and literal performance test would result in a forfeiture, the courts usually apply to the completed portion of the condition a substantial satisfaction test, as discussed in this chapter under "Substantial Performance."

Satisfaction of a Contracting Party   The parties to a contract may agree that performance by one of them shall be to the **satisfaction** of the other, who will not be obligated to perform unless he is satisfied. This is an express condition to the duty to perform. Assume that tailor Ken contracts to make a suit of clothes to Dick's satisfaction, and that Dick promises to pay Ken $850 for the suit if he is satisfied with it when completed. Ken completes the suit using materials ordered by Dick. The suit fits Dick beautifully, but Dick tells Ken that he is not satisfied with it and refuses to accept or pay for it. Ken is not entitled to recover $850 or any amount from Dick because the express condition did not happen. This is so if Dick's dissatisfaction is honest and in good faith, even if it is unreasonable. Where satisfaction relates to a matter of personal taste, opinion, or judgment, the law applies the **subjective satisfaction** standard, and the condition has not occurred if the promisor is in good faith dissatisfied.

If the contract does not clearly indicate that satisfaction is subjective, or if the performance contracted for relates to mechanical fitness or utility, the law assumes an **objective satisfaction** standard. For example, the objective standard of satisfaction would apply to the sale of a building or standard goods. In such cases, the question would not be whether the promisor was actually satisfied with the performance by the other party but whether, as a reasonable person, he ought to be satisfied.

Michael Silvestri v. Optus Software, Inc.
Supreme Court of New Jersey, 2003
175 N.J. 113, 814 A.2d 602
http://lawlibrary.rutgers.edu/courts/supreme/a-95-01.opn.html

FACTS Optus Software, Inc. (Optus), a small computer software company, hired Michael Silvestri as its Director of Support Services at an annual salary of $70,000. Silvestri was responsible for supervising technical support services provided to the company's customers. More specifically, Silvestri was charged with supervision of the support services staff, responsibility for communication with resellers of the Optus computer software to end-users, and coordination of ongoing training for support staff and resellers of the company's products to maintain their proficiency in assisting end-users. Silvestri's two-year employment contract began on January 4, 1999, and contained a satisfaction clause that reserved to the company the right to terminate his employment for "failure or

refusal to perform faithfully, diligently or completely his duties ... to the satisfaction" of the company. Termination under that clause relieved the company of any further payment obligation to Silvestri.

During the first six months of his employment Silvestri enjoyed the full support of Joseph Avellino, the CEO of Optus. Avellino's attitude started to change during the summer months of 1999, when several clients and resellers communicated to Avellino their disappointment with the performance and attitude of the support services staff generally, and several complaints targeted Silvestri specifically. Avellino informed Silvestri of those criticisms. On September 17, 1999, Avellino terminated Silvestri

---

PRACTICAL ADVICE
Consider using conditions to place the risk of the nonoccurrence of critical, uncertain events on the other party to the contract.

Express condition
performance is explicitly made contingent on the happening or nonhappening of a stated event

Satisfaction
express condition making performance contingent upon one party's approval of the other's performance

Subjective satisfaction
approval based upon a party's honestly held opinion

Objective satisfaction
approval based upon whether a reasonable person would be satisfied

PRACTICAL ADVICE
In your contracts based on satisfaction, specify which standard—subjective satisfaction or objective satisfaction—should apply to each contractual duty of performance.

under the satisfaction clause. Silvestri filed an action for breach of contract.

Both parties moved for summary judgment relying on copies of the numerous e-mail communications between them. Optus also submitted copies of e-mail messages received from customers expressing difficulties with the delivery of support services, and with Silvestri's attitude toward them. In a written submission Avellino explained that he terminated Silvestri because Silvestri had failed to "exhibit the leadership and management skills necessary to perform his duties to the Company's satisfaction." He also maintained that Optus is a small company in the business of customer services, and difficulty with support to resellers and end-users of Optus's products carries the potential for significant consequences in such a business.

Silvestri did not assert that there was any reason for his termination other than Avellino's genuine dissatisfaction with his performance. Rather, Silvestri challenged the reasonableness of that dissatisfaction. He portrayed Avellino as a meddling microman-ager who overreacted to any customer criticism and thus could not reasonably be satisfied.

The trial court granted summary judgment in favor of Optus, refusing to substitute its judgment for that of the president and CEO of Optus. The Appellate Division reversed, holding that an employer must meet an objective, reasonable-person test when invoking a satisfaction clause permitting termination of employment. The Supreme Court of New Jersey granted review.

DECISION The judgment of the Appellate Division is reversed, and the case remanded for entry of summary judgment in favor of Optus.

Agreements containing a promise to perform in a manner satisfactory to another, or to be bound to pay for satisfactory performance, are a common form of enforceable contract. Such "satisfaction" contracts are generally divided into two categories: (1) contracts that involve matters of personal taste, sensibility, judgment, or convenience and (2) contracts that contain a requirement of satisfaction as to mechanical fitness, utility, or marketability. The standard for evaluating satisfaction depends on the type of contract. Satisfaction contracts of the first type are interpreted on a subjective basis, with satisfaction dependent on the personal, honest evaluation of the party to be satisfied. Absent language to the contrary, however, contracts of the second type—involving operative fitness or mechanical utility—are subject to an objective test of reasonableness, because in those cases the extent and quality of performance can be measured by objective tests.

A subjective standard typically is applied to satisfaction clauses in employment contracts because "there is greater reason and a greater tendency to interpret the contract as involving personal satisfaction," rather than the satisfaction of a hypothetical "reasonable" person. In the case of a high-level business manager, a subjective test is particularly appropriate to the flexibility needed by the owners and higher-level officers operating a competitive enterprise. When a manager has been hired to share responsibility for the success of a business entity, an employer is entitled to be highly personal and idiosyncratic in judging the employee's satisfactory performance in advancing the enterprise.

The Court held that a subjective test of performance governs the employer's resort to a satisfaction clause in an employment contract unless there is some language in the contract to suggest that the parties intended an objective standard. There is no such language here. Idiosyncratic judgments as to what constitutes satisfactory performance are expected and should be permitted. The employer, not some hypothetical reasonable person, is best suited to determine whether the employee's performance is satisfactory. Although the subjective standard obliges the employer to act "honestly in accordance with his duty of good faith and fair dealing," genuine dissatisfaction of the employer, honestly held, is sufficient for discharge.

INTERPRETATION A subjective test of performance governs an employer's use of a satisfaction clause in an employment contract unless language in the contract suggests that the parties intended an objective standard.

CRITICAL THINKING QUESTION Could an employee discharged under a satisfaction clause demonstrate that the employer was not honestly dissatisfied? Explain.

Satisfaction of a Third Party A contract may condition the duty of one contracting party to accept and pay for the performance of the other contracting party upon the approval of a third party who is not a party to the contract. For example, building contracts commonly provide that before the owner is required to pay, the builder shall furnish the architect's certificate stating that the building has been constructed according to the plans and specifications on which the builder and the owner agreed. For even though the price is being paid for the building, not for the certificate, the owner must have both the building and the certificate before she will be obliged to pay. The duty of payment was made expressly conditional on the presentation of the certificate.

Implied-in-fact condition
contingency understood but not expressed by the parties

Implied-in-Fact Conditions

Implied-in-fact conditions are similar to express conditions in that they must fully and literally occur and in that they are understood by the parties to be part of the agreement. They differ in that they are not stated in express language; rather, they are necessarily inferred from the terms of the contract, the nature of the transaction, or the conduct of the parties. Thus, if Edna, for $1,750, contracts to paint Sy's house any color Sy desires, it is necessarily implied in fact that Sy will inform Edna of the desired color before Edna begins to paint. The notification of choice of color is an implied-in-fact condition, an operative event that must occur before Edna is subject to the duty of painting the house.

Implied-in-Law Conditions

Implied-in-law condition
contingency that arises from
operation of law

An **implied-in-law condition**, or a constructive condition, is imposed by law to accomplish a just and fair result. It differs from an express condition and an implied-in-fact condition in two ways: (1) it is not contained in the language of the contract or necessarily inferred from the contract and (2) it need only be substantially performed. For example, Fernando contracts to sell a certain tract of land to Marie for $18,000, but the contract is silent as to the time of delivery of the deed and payment of the price. According to the law, the contract implies that payment and delivery of the deed are not independent of each other. The courts will treat the promises as mutually dependent and will therefore hold that a delivery or tender of the deed by Fernando to Marie is a condition to the duty of Marie to pay the price. Conversely, payment or tender of $18,000 by Marie to Fernando is a condition to the duty of Fernando to deliver the deed to Marie.

Concurrent Conditions

Concurrent condition
performance by the parties is
to occur simultaneously

Concurrent conditions occur when the mutual duties of performance are to take place simultaneously. As we indicated in the discussion of implied-in-law conditions, in the absence of agreement to the contrary, the law assumes that the respective performances under a contract are concurrent conditions.

Condition Precedent

Condition precedent
an event that must or must
not occur before
performance is due

A **condition precedent** is an event that must occur before performance is due under a contract. In other words, the immediate duty of one party to perform is subject to the condition that some event must first occur. For instance, Steve is to deliver shoes to Nancy on June 1, and Nancy is to pay for the shoes on July 15. Steve's delivery of the shoes is a condition precedent to Nancy's performance. Similarly, if Rachel promises to buy Justin's land for $50,000, provided Rachel can obtain financing in the amount of $40,000 at 10 percent or less for thirty years within sixty days of signing the contract, Rachel's obtaining the specified financing is a condition precedent to her duty. If the condition is satisfied, Rachel is bound to perform; if it is not met, she is not bound to perform. Rachel, however, is under an implied-in-law duty to use her best efforts to obtain financing under these terms.

Condition Subsequent

Condition subsequent
an event that terminates a
duty of performance

A **condition subsequent** is an event that terminates an existing duty. For example, when goods are sold under terms of "sale or return," the buyer has the right to return the goods to the seller within a stated period but is under an immediate duty to pay the price unless the parties have agreed on credit. The duty to pay the price is terminated by a return of the goods, which operates as a condition subsequent. Conditions subsequent occur very infrequently in contract law; conditions precedent are quite common.

DISCHARGE BY PERFORMANCE

Discharge
termination of a contractual
duty

Performance
fulfillment of a contractual
obligation

Tender
offer of performance

Discharge is the termination of a contractual duty. **Performance** is the fulfillment of a contractual obligation. Discharge by performance is undoubtedly the most frequent method of discharging a contractual duty. If a promisor exactly performs his duty under the contract, the promisor is no longer subject to that duty.

Every contract imposes upon each party a duty of good faith and fair dealing in its performance and its enforcement. As discussed in Chapter 19, the Uniform Commercial Code imposes a comparable duty.

Tender is an offer by one party—who is ready, willing, and able to perform—to the other party to perform his obligation according to the terms of the contract. Under a bilateral contract, the refusal or rejection of a tender, or offer of performance, by one party may be treated as a repudiation, excusing or discharging the tendering party from further duty of performance under the contract.

DISCHARGE BY BREACH

Breach
wrongful failure to perform
the terms of a contract

A **breach** of a contract is a wrongful failure to perform its terms. Breach of contract always gives rise to a cause of action for damages by the aggrieved (injured) party. It may, however, have a more important effect: an uncured (uncorrected) *material* breach by one party operates as an excuse for nonperformance by the other party and discharges the aggrieved party from any further duty under

Facts Davis manages commercial real estate. In April, Davis contracted with Bidley to acquire and plant impatiens in the flowerbeds outside fourteen office properties that Davis manages. Bidley verbally agreed to buy and plant the impatiens by May 31, for a total of $10,000. Bidley purchased the necessary plants from Ackerman, who delivered them to Bidley on May 26. Bidley completed the planting at thirteen of the office buildings by May 29, but because another job took much longer than anticipated, Bidley was unable to finish planting the flowers outside the fourteenth office building until June 1. When he received Bidley's invoice, Davis refused to pay any of the $10,000.

Issue Has Bidley's committed a material breach of the contract so as to discharge Davis's performance under the contract?

Rule of Law Breach of contract is defined as a wrongful failure to perform. An uncured material breach discharges the

aggrieved party's performance, serving as an excuse for the aggrieved party's nonperformance of his obligations under the contract. A breach is material if it significantly impairs the aggrieved party's contract rights. When a breach relates to timing of performance, failure to promptly perform a contract as promised is considered a material breach only if the parties have agreed that "time is of the essence," in other words that the failure to perform on time is material. If, on the other hand, the aggrieved party does get substantially that for which he bargained, the breach is not material. In such a case the aggrieved party is not discharged from the contract but has a right to collect damages for the injury sustained as a result of the breach.

Application Bidley failed to plant all of the flowers by May 31 as he promised. Therefore, he has breached the contract. However, Bidley's breach is not material. There is no indication that the parties agreed that time was

of the essence nor that there was any compelling reason the plants had to be in the ground by May 31. They simply agreed on May 31 as the date for performance.

Furthermore, Davis has gotten substantially that for which he bargained. In fact, as of May 31 Bidley had completed the planting at thirteen of the office buildings and had commenced the work at the fourteenth. One day later, the entire job was done. Given that Bidley's late performance did not significantly impair Davis's rights under the contract, the breach is not material. Therefore, Davis is entitled only to recover any damages he can prove were suffered as a result of Bidley's late performance.

Conclusion Bidley's breach is not material. Davis is not discharged from performance and must pay the $10,000 owed under the contract, less the value of any damages caused by the one-day delay in planting flowers at one office building.

© Cengage Learning 2013

the contract. If, on the other hand, the breach is not material, the aggrieved party is not discharged from the contract, although she may recover money damages. Under the Code's perfect tender rule, which applies only to sales transactions, *any* deviation discharges the aggrieved party.

Material Breach

Material breach
nonperformance that significantly impairs the aggrieved party's rights under the contract; discharges the injured party from any further duty under the contract

An unjustified failure to perform *substantially* the obligations promised in a contract is a **material breach**. The key is whether the aggrieved party obtained substantially what he had bargained for, despite the breach, or whether the breach significantly impaired his rights under the contract. A material breach discharges the aggrieved party from his duty of performance. For instance, Joe orders a custom-made, tailored suit from Peggy to be made of wool, but Peggy makes the suit of cotton instead. Assuming that the labor component of this contract predominates and thus the contract is not considered a sale of goods, Peggy has materially breached the contract. Consequently, Joe is discharged from his duty to pay for the suit, and he may also recover money damages from Peggy for her breach.

PRACTICAL ADVICE

If the timely performance of a contractual duty is important, use a "time-is-of-the-essence" clause to make failure to perform promptly a material breach.

Although there are no clear-cut rules as to what constitutes a material breach, several basic principles apply. First, partial performance is a material breach of a contract if it omits some essential part of the contract. Second, the courts will consider a breach material if it is quantitatively or qualitatively serious. Third, an intentional breach of contract is generally held to be material. Fourth, a failure to perform a promise promptly is a material breach if time is of the essence; that is, if the parties have clearly indicated that a failure to perform by a stated time is material; otherwise, the aggrieved party may recover damages only for loss caused by the delay. Fifth, the parties to a contract may, within limits, specify what breaches are to be considered material.

Prevention of performance
one party's substantial interference with or prevention of performance by the other constitutes a material breach and discharges the other party to the contract

Prevention of Performance One party's substantial interference with, or prevention of, performance by the other generally constitutes a material breach that discharges the other party to the contract. For instance, Dale prevents an architect from giving Lucy a certificate that is a condition to Dale's liability to pay Lucy a certain sum of money. Dale may not then use Lucy's failure to produce a certificate as an excuse for nonpayment. Likewise, if Matthew has contracted to grow a certain crop for Richard and Richard plows the field and destroys the seedlings Matthew has planted, his interference with Matthew's performance discharges Matthew from his duty under the contract. It does not, however, discharge Richard from his duty under the contract.

Perfect Tender Rule The Code greatly alters the common law doctrine of material breach by adopting what is known as the **perfect tender rule**. The perfect tender rule, which we will discuss more fully in Chapter 20, essentially provides that *any* deviation from the promised performance in a sales contract under the Code constitutes a material breach of the contract and discharges the aggrieved party from his duty of performance.

Substantial Performance

Substantial performance is performance that, though incomplete, does not defeat the purpose of the contract. If a party substantially, but not completely, performs her obligations under a contract, the common law generally will allow her to obtain the other party's performance, less any damages the partial performance caused. If no harm has been caused, the breaching party will obtain the other party's full contractual performance. Thus, in the specially ordered suit illustration, if Peggy, the tailor, used the correct fabric but improperly used black buttons instead of blue, she would be permitted to collect from Joe the contract price of the suit less the damage, if any, caused to Joe by the substitution of the wrongly colored buttons. The doctrine of substantial performance assumes particular importance in the construction industry in cases in which a structure is built on the aggrieved party's land. Consider the following: Adam builds a $300,000 house for Betty but deviates from the specifications, causing Betty $10,000 in damages. If the courts considered this a material breach, Betty would not have to pay for the house that is now on her land, a result that would clearly constitute an unjust forfeiture on Adam's part. Therefore, because Adam's performance has been substantial, the courts would probably not deem the breach material, and he would be able to collect $290,000 from Betty.

Anticipatory Repudiation

A breach of contract, as discussed, is a failure to perform the terms of a contract. Although it is logically and physically impossible to fail to perform a duty before the date on which that performance is due, a party may announce before the due date that she will not perform, or she may commit an act that makes her unable to perform. Either act is a repudiation of the contract, which notifies the other party that a breach is imminent. Such repudiation before the date fixed by the contract for performance is called an **anticipatory repudiation**. The courts, as shown in the leading case that follows, view it as a breach that discharges the nonrepudiating party's duty to perform and permits her to bring suit immediately. Nonetheless, the nonbreaching party may wait until the time the performance is due, to see whether the repudiator will retract his repudiation and perform his contractual duties. To be effective, the retraction must come to the attention of the injured party before she materially changes her position in reliance on the repudiation or before she indicates to the other party that she considers the repudiation to be final. If the retraction is effective and the repudiator does perform, then there is a discharge by performance; if the repudiator does not perform, there is a material breach.

Hochster v. De La Tour
Queen's Bench of England, 1853
2 Ellis and Blackburn Reports 678

FACTS On April 12, 1852, Hochster contracted with De La Tour to serve as a guide for De La Tour on his three-month trip to Europe, beginning on June 1 at an agreed-upon salary. On May 11, De La Tour notified Hochster that he would not need Hochster's services. He also refused to pay Hochster any compensation. Hochster brought this action to recover damages for breach of contract.

DECISION Judgment for Hochster.

OPINION Hochster may treat the repudiation by De La Tour as a breach of contract and immediately bring suit. Otherwise, Hochster would have to remain ready to perform and to refrain from accepting other employment in order to tender his services on June 1. It is far more rational, upon repudiation of the contract by one of the parties, to allow the other party to consider his performance under the contract as excused and seek other employment while retaining his right to sue for damages.

INTERPRETATION An anticipatory breach discharges the injured party and entitles her to bring suit immediately.

CRITICAL THINKING QUESTION What policy reasons support an injured party's right to bring suit immediately upon an anticipatory repudiation? Explain.

Material alteration of written contract
a material and fraudulent alteration of a written contract by a party to the contract discharges the entire contract

Material Alteration of Written Contract

An unauthorized alteration or change of any of the material terms or provisions of a written contract or document is a discharge of the entire contract. An alteration is material if it would vary any party's legal relations with the maker of the alteration or would adversely affect that party's legal relations with a third person. To constitute a discharge, the alteration must be material and fraudulent and must be the act of either a party to the contract or someone acting on his behalf. An unauthorized change in the terms of a written contract by a person who is not a party to the contract does not discharge the contract.

DISCHARGE BY AGREEMENT OF THE PARTIES

By agreement, the parties to a contract may discharge each other from performance under the contract. They may do this by rescission, substituted contract, accord and satisfaction, or novation.

Mutual Rescission

Mutual rescission
agreement of the parties to terminate their contractual duties

A **mutual rescission** is an agreement between the parties to terminate their respective duties under the contract. It is, literally, a contract to end a contract; and it must contain all of the essentials of a contract. In rescinding an executory, bilateral contract, each party furnishes consideration in giving up his rights under the contract in exchange for the other party's doing the same. If one party has already fully performed, however, a mutual rescission is not binding at common law because of lack of consideration.

Substituted Contracts

Substituted contract
a new contract accepted in satisfaction of the parties' duties under the original contract

A **substituted contract** is a new contract accepted by both parties in satisfaction of the parties' duties under the original contract. A substituted contract immediately discharges the original contract and imposes new obligations under its own terms.

Accord and Satisfaction

Accord and satisfaction
substituted performance (accord) and the discharge of the prior contractual obligation by performance of the new duty (satisfaction)

An **accord** is a contract by which an obligee promises to accept a stated performance in satisfaction of the obligor's existing contractual duty. The performance of the accord, called a **satisfaction**, discharges the original duty. Thus, if Dan owes Sara $500, and the parties agree that Dan will paint Sara's house in satisfaction of the debt, the agreement is an executory accord. When Dan performs the accord by painting Sara's house, he will by satisfaction discharge the $500 debt.

McDowell Welding & Pipefitting, Inc. v. United States Gypsum Co.
Supreme Court of Oregon, 2008
345 Or. 272, 193 P.3d 9
http://www.publications.ojd.state.or.us/S054626.htm

FACTS Defendant United States Gypsum (U.S. Gypsum) hired BE & K as general contractor on a new plant U.S. Gypsum was building in Columbia County. BE & K subcontracted with the plaintiff (McDowell Welding & Pipefitting, Inc.) to perform work on the project. During construction, the defendants asked the plaintiff to perform additional tasks, over and above the plaintiff's contractual obligations, and the defendants promised to pay the plaintiff for the additional work. After the plaintiff completed its work on the project, the parties disagreed over the amount that the defendants owed the plaintiff for the additional work.

The plaintiff filed an action against the defendants, alleging breach of contract. All of the plaintiff's claims arose out of the modification to the construction contract. BE & K's asserted an affirmative defense alleging that the plaintiff had agreed to settle its claims for a total payment of $896,000.

The trial court granted BE & K's motion to try its counterclaim before trying the plaintiff's claims against it. The plaintiff then filed a demand for a jury trial, which BE & K moved to strike, arguing that because its counterclaim was equitable, the plaintiff had no right to a jury trial on the counterclaim. The trial court granted BE & K's motion to strike the plaintiff's jury trial demand and, sitting as the trier of fact, found that the plaintiff had accepted the defendants' offer to settle its claims in return for the defendants' promise to pay the plaintiff $800,000. Although the defendants alleged that they promised to pay the plaintiff $896,000 in return for the plaintiff's promise to release its claims against them, the trial court found that the defendants had promised to pay only $800,000.

Based on its resolution of the defendants' counterclaim, the trial court entered a limited judgment directing the defendants to tender $800,000 to the court clerk and directing the plaintiff, after the defendants tendered that sum, to execute releases of its claims against the defendants. The plaintiff appealed, claiming a state constitutional right to a jury trial on the factual issues that the defendant's counterclaim had raised. A divided Court of Appeals affirmed the trial court's judgment. The Oregon Supreme Court allowed the plaintiff's petition for review.

DECISION Judgment of the Court of Appeals is affirmed in part, reversed in part, and remanded.

OPINION A settlement agreement may take one of three forms: an executory accord, an accord and satisfaction, or a substituted contract. When the Oregon Constitution was adopted, only a court of equity would enforce an executory accord. The law courts would not enforce executory accords because they suspended the underlying obligation; they did not discharge it. By contrast, an accord and satisfaction and a substituted contract discharged the underlying obligation, and both were enforceable in the law courts.

An executory accord is "an agreement for the future discharge of an existing claim by a substituted performance." Usually, an executory accord is a bilateral agreement; the debtor promises to pay an amount in return for the creditor's promise to release the underlying claim. When the parties enter into an executory accord, the underlying claim "is not [discharged] until the new agreement is performed. The right to enforce the original claim is merely suspended, and is revived by the debtor's breach of the new agreement."

Because an executory accord does not discharge the underlying claim but merely suspends it, the law courts refused to allow it to be pleaded as a bar to the underlying claim. Once the promised performance occurs, the accord has been executed or satisfied and the underlying claim is discharged, resulting in an accord and satisfaction. An accord and satisfaction may occur in one of two ways:

> The two parties may first make an executory accord, that is, a contract for the future discharge of the existing claim by a substituted performance still to be rendered. When this executory contract is fully performed as agreed, there is said to be an accord

and satisfaction, and the previously existing claim is discharged. It is quite possible, however, for the parties to make an accord and satisfaction without any preliminary executory accord or any other executory contract of any kind. [For example, a] debtor may offer the substituted performance in satisfaction of his debt and the creditor may receive it, without any binding promise being made by either party.

Because an accord and satisfaction discharges the underlying claim, that defense is legal, not equitable.

Finally, the parties may enter into a substituted contract; that is, the parties may agree to substitute the new agreement for the underlying obligation. A substituted contract differs from an executory accord in that the parties intend that entering into the new agreement will immediately discharge the underlying obligation. A substituted contract discharges the underlying obligation and could be asserted as a bar to an action at law.

In this case the defendants alleged that they agreed to pay the plaintiff $896,000 in exchange for a release of the plaintiff's claims against them. The defendants did not allege that they had paid the plaintiff the promised sum—an allegation necessary for an accord and satisfaction. Nor did they allege that, by entering into the settlement agreement, they extinguished the underlying obligation—an allegation necessary to allege a substituted contract. Rather, the defendants alleged that the plaintiff agreed to release its claims only after the defendants made the promised payment. Thus, the defendants alleged an executory accord.

The Oregon constitutional right to a jury trial in civil cases does not extend to the defendants' counterclaim of an executory accord.

INTERPRETATION When a debtor and a creditor enter into an executory accord, the underlying claim is not discharged until the new agreement is performed; the right to enforce the original claim is merely suspended, and is revived by the debtor's breach of the new agreement.

CRITICAL THINKING QUESTION In settling a contract dispute, what are the advantages and disadvantages of using an executory accord compared with using a substituted contract?

Novation

Novation
substituted contract
involving a new third-party
promisor or promisee

A **novation** is a substituted contract that involves an agreement among *three* parties to substitute a new promisee for the existing promisee or to replace the existing promisor with a new one. A novation discharges the old obligation by creating a new contract in which there is either a new promisee or a new promisor. Thus, if B owes A $500, and A, B, and C agree that C will pay the debt and B will be discharged, the novation is the substitution of the new promisor C for B. Alternatively, if the three parties agree that B will pay $500 to C instead of to A, the novation is the substitution of a new promisee (C for A). In each instance, the debt B owes A is discharged.

DISCHARGE BY OPERATION OF LAW

In this chapter, we have considered various ways by which contractual duties may be discharged. In all of these cases, the discharge resulted from the action of one or both of the parties to the contract. In this section, we will examine discharge brought about by the operation of law.

Impossibility

Subjective impossibility
the promisor—but not all promisors—cannot perform; does not discharge the promisor

Objective impossibility
performance cannot be done by anyone; generally discharges the promisor

PRACTICAL ADVICE
Use a clause in your contract specifying which events will excuse the nonperformance of the contract.

If a particular contracting party is unable to perform because of financial inability or lack of competence, for instance, this **subjective impossibility** does not excuse the promisor from liability for breach of contract, as the next case shows. Historically, the common law excused a party from contractual duties only for **objective impossibility**, that is, for situations in which no one could render performance. Thus, the death or illness of a person who has contracted to render personal services is a discharge of his contractual duty. Furthermore, the contract is discharged if, for example, a jockey contracts to ride a certain horse in the Kentucky Derby and the horse dies prior to the derby, for it is objectively impossible for this or any other jockey to perform the contract. Also, if Ken contracts to lease to Karlene a certain ballroom for a party on a scheduled future date, destruction of the ballroom by fire without Ken's fault before the scheduled event discharges the contract. Destruction of the subject matter or of the agreed-upon means of performance of a contract, without the fault of the promisor, is excusable impossibility.

Christy v. Pilkinton
Supreme Court of Arkansas, 1954
224 Ark. 407, 273 S.W.2d 533

FACTS The Christys entered into a written contract to purchase an apartment house from Pilkinton for $30,000. Pilkinton tendered a deed to the property and demanded payment of the unpaid balance of $29,000 due on the purchase price. As a result of a decline in the Christy's used car business, the Christys did not possess and could not borrow the unpaid balance and, thus, asserted that it was impossible for them to perform their contract. This suit was brought by Pilkinton to enforce the sale of the apartment house.

DECISION Judgment for Pilkinton.

OPINION There is an important distinction between objective impossibility, which amounts to saying, "the thing cannot be done," and subjective impossibility—"I cannot do it." The latter, which is well illustrated by a promisor's financial inability to pay, does not discharge the contractual duty.

INTERPRETATION Subjective impossibility (the promisor, but not all promisors, cannot perform) does not discharge the promisor's contractual duty.

ETHICAL QUESTION Is it fair to make contracting parties strictly liable for breach of contract? Explain.

CRITICAL THINKING QUESTION What type of fact situation would have excused the Christys' duty to perform? Explain.

Subsequent illegality
if performance becomes illegal or impractical as a result of a change in the law, the duty of performance is discharged

Subsequent Illegality   If the performance of a contract that was legal when formed becomes illegal or impractical because of a subsequently enacted law, the duty of performance is discharged. For example, Linda contracts to sell and deliver to Carlos ten cases of a certain whiskey each month for one year. A subsequent prohibition law makes the manufacture, transportation, or sale of intoxicating liquor unlawful. The contractual duties that Linda has yet to perform are discharged.

Frustration of purpose
principal purpose of a contract cannot be fulfilled because of a subsequent event

Frustration of Purpose   Where, after a contract is made, a party's principal purpose is substantially frustrated without his fault by the occurrence of an event whose nonoccurrence was a basic assumption on which the contract was made, his remaining duties to render performance are discharged, unless the party has assumed the risk. This rule developed from the so-called coronation cases. When, on the death of his mother, Queen Victoria, Edward VII became King of England, impressive coronation ceremonies were planned, including a procession along a designated route through London. Owners and lessees of buildings along the route made contracts to permit the use of rooms on the day scheduled for the procession. The king became ill, however, and the procession did not take place. Consequently, the rooms were not used. Numerous suits were filed, some by landowners seeking to hold the would-be viewers liable on their promises, and some by the would-be viewers seeking to recover money they had paid in advance for the rooms. Though the principle involved was novel, from these cases evolved the frustration of purpose doctrine, under which a contract is discharged if supervening circumstances make impossible the fulfillment of the purpose that both parties had in mind, unless one of the parties has contractually assumed that risk.

PRACTICAL ADVICE
Clearly state the basic assumptions of your contract and which risks are assumed by each of the parties.

Commercial impracticability

where performance can be accomplished only under unforeseen and unjust hardship, the contract is discharged under the Code and the Restatement

Commercial Impracticability   The Restatement and Code have relaxed the traditional test of objective impossibility by providing that performance need not be actually or literally impossible; rather, **commercial impracticability**, or unforeseen and unjust hardship, will excuse nonperformance. This does not mean mere hardship or an unexpectedly increased cost of performance. A party will be discharged from performing her duty only when her performance is made impracticable by a supervening event not caused by her own fault. Moreover, the nonoccurrence of the subsequent event must have been a "basic assumption" made by both parties when entering into the contract, neither party having assumed the risk that the event would occur.

Northern Corporation v. Chugach Electrical Association
Supreme Court of Alaska, 1974
518 P.2d 76

FACTS Northern Corporation (Northern) entered into a contract with Chugach Electrical Association (Chugach) in August 1966 to repair and upgrade the upstream face of Cooper Lake Dam in Alaska. The contract required Northern to obtain rock from a quarry site at the opposite end of the lake and to transport the rock to the dam during the winter across the ice on the lake. In December 1966, Northern cleared a road on the ice to permit deeper freezing, but thereafter water overflowed on the ice, preventing use of the road. Northern complained of the unsafe conditions of the lake ice, but Chugach insisted on performance. In March 1967, one of Northern's loaded trucks broke through the ice and sank. Northern continued to encounter difficulties and ceased operations with the approval of Chugach. However, on January 8, 1968, Chugach notified Northern that it would be in default unless all rock was hauled by April 1. After two more trucks broke through the ice, causing the deaths of the drivers, Northern ceased operations and notified Chugach that it would make no more attempts to haul across the lake. Northern advised Chugach that it considered the contract terminated for impossibility of performance and commenced suit to recover the cost incurred in attempting to complete the contract. The trial court found for Northern.

DECISION Judgment for Northern affirmed.

OPINION Northern's contract to perform was discharged by impossibility of performance. The particular method of performance specified in the contract presupposed the existence of ice frozen to sufficient depth to permit hauling of rock across the lake. This expectation by both parties was never fulfilled. A party is discharged from its contractual obligation, even if it is technically possible to perform, if the cost of performance would be so greatly disproportionate to that reasonably contemplated by the parties that performance would be commercially impracticable. In addition, a serious risk to life or health will excuse nonperformance.

INTERPRETATION Commercial impracticability (unforeseen and unjust hardship) will excuse performance.

ETHICAL QUESTION Did Chugach act ethically in insisting on performance by Northern in face of dangerous conditions? Explain.

CRITICAL THINKING QUESTION Do you think that the court used the proper standard in this case? Explain.

Bankruptcy

discharge available to a debtor who obtains an order of discharge by the bankruptcy court

Bankruptcy

Bankruptcy is a discharge of a contractual duty by operation of law available to a debtor who, by compliance with the requirements of the Bankruptcy Code, obtains an order of discharge by the bankruptcy court. It applies only to obligations that the Bankruptcy Code provides are dischargeable in bankruptcy. (We will treat the subject of bankruptcy in Chapter 38.)

Statute of limitations

after the statute of limitations has run, the debt is not discharged, but the creditor cannot maintain an action against the debtor

Statute of Limitations

At common law a plaintiff was not subject to any time limitation within which to bring an action. Now, however, all states have statutes providing such a limitation. The majority of courts hold that the running of the period of the statute of limitations does not operate to discharge the obligation but only to bar the creditor's right to bring an action.

For a summary of discharge of contracts, see Figure 17-1.

Figure 17-1 Discharge of Contracts

© Cengage Learning 2013

CHAPTER SUMMARY

Conditions

Definition of a Condition an event whose happening or nonhappening affects a duty of performance

Express Condition contingency explicitly set forth in language

- *Satisfaction* express condition making performance contingent on one party's approval of the other's performance
- *Subjective Satisfaction* approval based on a party's honestly held opinion
- *Objective Satisfaction* approval based on whether a reasonable person would be satisfied

Implied-in-Fact Condition contingency understood by the parties to be part of the agreement, though not expressed

Implied-in-Law Condition contingency not contained in the language of the contract but imposed by law; also called a constructive condition

Concurrent Conditions conditions that are to take place at the same time

Condition Precedent an event that must or must not occur before performance is due

Condition Subsequent an event that terminates a duty of performance

Discharge by Performance

Discharge termination of a contractual duty

Performance fulfillment of a contractual obligation resulting in a discharge

Discharge by Breach

Definition of Breach a wrongful failure to perform the terms of a contract that gives rise to a right to damages by the injured party

Material Breach nonperformance that significantly impairs the injured party's rights under the contract and discharges the injured party from any further duty under the contract

- *Prevention of Performance* one party's substantial interference with or prevention of performance by the other constitutes a material breach and discharges the other party to the contract
- *Perfect Tender Rule* standard under the Uniform Commercial Code that a seller's performance under a sales contract must strictly comply with contractual duties and that any deviation discharges the injured party

Substantial Performance performance that is incomplete but that does not defeat the purpose of the contract; does not discharge the injured party but entitles him to damages

Anticipatory Repudiation an inability or refusal to perform, before performance is due, that is treated as a breach, allowing the nonrepudiating party to bring suit immediately

Material Alteration of Written Contract a material and fraudulent alteration of a written contract by a party to the contract discharges the entire contract

Discharge by Agreement of the Parties

Mutual Rescission an agreement between the parties to terminate their respective duties under the contract

Substituted Contract a new contract accepted by both parties in satisfaction of the parties' duties under the original contract

Accord and Satisfaction substituted duty under a contract (accord) and the discharge of the prior contractual obligation by performance of the new duty (satisfaction)

Novation a substituted contract involving a new third-party promisor or promisee

Discharge by Operation of Law

Impossibility performance of contract cannot be done
- *Subjective Impossibility* the promisor—but not all promisors—cannot perform; does not discharge the promisor
- *Objective Impossibility* no promisor is able to perform; generally discharges the promisor
- *Subsequent Illegality* if performance becomes illegal or impractical as a result of a change in the law, the duty of performance is discharged
- *Frustration of Purpose* principal purpose of a contract cannot be fulfilled because of a subsequent event
- *Commercial Impracticability* where performance can be accomplished only under unforeseen and unjust hardship, the contract is discharged under the Code and the Restatement

Bankruptcy discharge available to a debtor who obtains an order of discharge by the bankruptcy court

Statute of Limitations after the statute of limitations has run, the debt is not discharged, but the creditor cannot maintain an action against the debtor

QUESTIONS

1. A-1 Roofing Co. entered into a written contract with Jaffe to put a new roof on the latter's residence for $1,800, using a specified type of roofing, and to complete the job without unreasonable delay. A-1 undertook the work within a week thereafter, and when all the roofing material was at the site and the labor 50 percent completed, the premises were totally destroyed by fire caused by lightning. A-1 submitted a bill to Jaffe for $1,200 for materials furnished and labor performed up to the time of the destruction of the premises. Jaffe refused to pay the bill, and A-1 now seeks payment from Jaffe. Should A-1 prevail? Explain.

2. By contract dated January 5, Rebecca agreed to sell to Nancy, and Nancy agreed to buy from Rebecca, a certain parcel of land then zoned commercial. The specific intent of Nancy, which was known to Rebecca, was to erect a manufacturing plant on the land; and the contract stated that the agreement was conditioned on Nancy's ability to construct such a plant on the land. The closing date for the transaction was set for April 1. On February 15, the city council rezoned the land from commercial to residential, which precluded the erection of the plant. As the closing date drew near, Nancy made it known to Rebecca that she did not intend to go through with the purchase because the land could no longer be used as intended. On April 1, Rebecca tendered the deed to Nancy, who refused to pay Rebecca the agreed purchase price. Rebecca brought an action against Nancy for breach of contract. Can Rebecca enforce the contract?

3. The Perfection Produce Company entered into a written contract with Hiram Hodges for the purchase of three hundred tons of potatoes to be grown on Hodges's farm in Maine at a stipulated price per ton. Though the land would ordinarily produce one thousand tons and although the planting and cultivation were properly done, Hodges was able to deliver only one hundred tons because an unprecedented drought caused a partial crop failure. Perfection accepted the one hundred tons but paid only 80 percent of the stipulated price per ton. Hodges sued the produce company to recover the unpaid balance of the agreed price for the one hundred tons of

potatoes accepted by Perfection. Perfection counterclaimed against Hodges for his failure to deliver the additional two hundred tons. Who will prevail? Why?

4. On November 23, Sally agreed to sell to Bart her Buick automobile for $7,000, delivery and payment to be made on December 1. On November 26, Bart informed Sally that he wished to rescind the contract and would pay Sally $350 if Sally agreed. Sally agreed and took the $350 in cash. On December 1, Bart tendered to Sally $6,650 and demanded that Sally deliver the automobile. Sally refused, and Bart initiated a lawsuit. May Bart enforce the original contract?

5. Webster, Inc., dealt in automobile accessories at wholesale. Although it manufactured a few items in its own factory, among them windshield wipers, Webster purchased most of its inventory from a large number of other manufacturers. In January, Webster entered into a written contract to sell Hunter two thousand windshield wipers for $1,900, delivery to be made June 1. In April, Webster's factory burned to the ground and Webster failed to make delivery on June 1. Hunter, forced to buy windshield wipers elsewhere at a higher price, is now trying to recover damages from Webster. Will Hunter be successful in its claim?

6. Erwick Construction Company contracted to build a house for Charles. The specifications called for the use of Karlene Pipe for all plumbing. Erwick, nevertheless, got a better price on Boynton Pipe and substituted the equally good Boynton Pipe for Karlene Pipe. Charles's inspection revealed the change, and Charles now refuses to make the final payment. The contract price was for $200,000, and the final payment is $20,000. Erwick now brings suit seeking the $20,000. Will Erwick succeed in its claim?

7. Green owed White $3,500, which was due and payable on June 1. White owed Brown $3,500, which was due and payable on August 1. On May 25, White received a letter signed by Green stating, "If you will cancel my debt to you, in the amount of $3,500, I will pay, on the due date, the debt you owe Brown, in the amount of $3,500." On May 28, Green received a letter signed by White stating, "I received your letter and agree to the proposals recited therein. You may consider your debt to me canceled as of the date of this letter." On June 1, White, needing money to pay his income taxes, made a demand upon Green to pay him the $3,500 due on that date. Is Green obligated to pay the money demanded by White?

8. By written contract, Ames agreed to build a house on Bowen's lot for $145,000, commencing within ninety days of the date of the contract. Prior to the date for beginning construction, Ames informed Bowen that he was repudiating the contract and would not perform. Bowen refused to accept the repudiation and demanded fulfillment of the contract. Eighty days after the date of the contract, Bowen entered into a new

contract with Curd for $142,000. The next day, without knowledge or notice of Bowen's contract with Curd, Ames began construction. Bowen ordered Ames from the premises and refused to allow him to continue. Will Ames be able to collect damages from Bowen? Explain.

9. Judy agreed in writing to work for Northern Enterprises, Inc., for three years as superintendent of Northern's manufacturing establishment and to devote herself entirely to the business, giving it her full time, attention, and skill, for which she was to receive $72,000 per annum in monthly installments of $6,000. Judy worked and was paid for the first twelve months, when, through no fault of her own or Northern's, she was arrested and imprisoned for one month. It became imperative for Northern to employ another, and it treated the contract with Judy as breached and abandoned, refusing to permit Judy to resume work on her release from jail. What rights, if any, does Judy have under the contract?

10. The Park Plaza Hotel awarded its valet and laundry concession to Larson for a three-year term. The contract contained the following provision: "It is distinctly understood and agreed that the services to be rendered by Larson shall meet with the approval of the Park Plaza Hotel, which shall be the sole judge of the sufficiency and propriety of the services." After seven months, the hotel gave a month's notice to discontinue services based on the failure of the services to meet its approval. Larson brought an action against the hotel, alleging that its dissatisfaction was unreasonable. The hotel defended on the ground that subjective or personal satisfaction may be the sole justification for termination of the contract. Who is correct? Explain.

11. Schlosser entered into an agreement to purchase a cooperative apartment from Flynn Company. The written agreement contained the following provision: "This entire agreement is conditioned on Purchaser's being approved for occupancy by the board of directors of the Cooperative. In the event approval of the Purchaser shall be denied, this agreement shall thereafter be of no further force or effect." When Schlosser unilaterally revoked her "offer," Flynn sued for breach of contract. Schlosser claims the approval provision was a condition precedent to the existence of a binding contract and, thus, she was free to revoke. Decision?

12. Jacobs, owner of a farm, entered into a contract with Earl Walker in which Walker agreed to paint the buildings on the farm. As authorized by Jacobs, Walker acquired the paint from Jones with the bill to be sent to Jacobs. Before the work was completed, however, Jacobs without good cause ordered Walker to stop. Walker made offers to complete the job, but Jacobs declined to permit Walker to fulfill his contract. Jacobs refused to pay Jones for the paint Walker had acquired for the job. Explain whether Jones and Walker would be successful in an action against Jacobs for breach of contract.

CASE PROBLEMS

13. Barta entered into a written contract to buy the K&K Pharmacy, located in a local shopping center. Included in the contract was a provision stating that "this Agreement shall be contingent upon Buyer's ability to obtain a new lease from Landlord for the premises presently occupied by Seller. In the event Buyer is unable to obtain a lease satisfactory to Buyer,

this Agreement shall be null and void." Barta planned to sell "high-traffic" grocery items, such as bread, milk, and coffee, to attract customers to his drugstore. A grocery store in the shopping center, however, already held the exclusive right to sell grocery items. Barta, therefore, could not obtain a leasing agreement meeting his approval. Barta refused to close the sale. In a suit by K&K Pharmacy against Barta for breach of contract, who will prevail? Explain.

14. Victor Packing Co. (Victor) contracted to supply Sun Maid Raisin Growers 1,800 tons of raisins from the current year's crop. After delivering 1,190 tons of raisins by August, Victor refused to supply any more. Although Victor had until the end of the crop season to ship the remaining 610 tons of raisins, Sun Maid treated Victor's repeated refusals to ship any more raisins as a repudiation of the contract. To prevent breaching its own contracts, Sun Maid went into the marketplace to "cover" and bought the raisins needed. Unfortunately, between the time Victor refused delivery and Sun Maid entered the market, disastrous rains had caused the price of raisins to skyrocket. May Sun Maid recover from Victor the difference between the contract price and the market price before the end of the current crop year?

15. On August 20, Hildebrand entered into a written contract with the city of Douglasville whereby he was to serve as community development project engineer for three years at a monthly fee of $1,583.33. This salary figure could be changed without affecting the other terms of the contract. One of the provisions for termination of the contract was written notice by either party to the other at any time at least ninety days prior to the intended date of termination. The contract listed a substantial number of services and duties Hildebrand was to perform for the city; among the lesser duties were (1) keeping the community development director (Hildebrand's supervisor) informed at all times of his whereabouts and how he could be contacted and (2) attending meetings at which his presence was requested. Two years later, by which time Hildebrand's fee had risen to $1,915.83 per month, the city fired Hildebrand effective immediately, citing "certain material breaches … of the … agreement." The city specifically charged that he did not attend the necessary meetings although requested to do so and seldom if ever kept his supervisor informed of his whereabouts and how he could be contacted. Will Hildebrand prevail in a suit against the mayor and city for the amount of $5,747.49 for breach of his employment contract because of the city's failure to give him ninety days' notice prior to termination?

16. Walker & Co. contracted to provide a sign for Harrison to place above his dry cleaning business. According to the contract, Harrison would lease the sign from Walker, making monthly payments for thirty-six months. In return, Walker agreed to maintain and service the sign at its own expense. Walker installed the sign in July, and Harrison made the first rental payment. Shortly thereafter, someone hit the sign with a tomato. Harrison also claims he discovered rust on its chrome and little spider webs in its corners. Harrison repeatedly called Walker for the maintenance work promised under the contract, but Walker did not respond immediately. Harrison then telegraphed Walker that, due to Walker's failure to perform the maintenance services, he held Walker in material breach of the contract. A week later, Walker sent out a crew, which did all of the requested maintenance services. Has Walker committed a material breach of contract? Explain.

17. In May, Watts was awarded a construction contract, based on its low bid, by the Cullman County Commission. The contract provided that it would not become effective until approved by the state director of the Farmers Home Administration (now part of the U.S. Department of Agriculture Rural Development Office). In September, construction still had not been

authorized and Watts wrote to the County Commission requesting a 5 percent price increase to reflect seasonal and inflationary price increases. The County Commission countered with an offer of 3.5 percent. Watts then wrote the commission, insisting on a 5 percent increase and stating that if this was not agreeable, it was withdrawing its original bid. The commission obtained another company to perform the project, and on October 14, informed Watts that it had accepted the withdrawal of the bid. Watts sued for breach of contract. Explain whether Watts will prevail and why or why not.

18. K & G Construction Co. was the owner of and the general contractor for a housing subdivision project. Harris contracted with the company to do excavating and earth-moving work on the project. Certain provisions of the contract stated that (1) K & G was to make monthly progress payments to Harris; (2) no such payments were to be made until Harris obtained liability insurance; and (3) all of Harris's work on the project must be performed in a workmanlike manner. On August 9, a bulldozer operator, working for Harris, drove too close to one of K & G's houses, causing the collapse of a wall and other damage. When Harris and his insurance carrier denied liability and refused to pay for the damage, K & G refused to make the August monthly progress payment. Harris, nonetheless, continued to work on the project until midSeptember, when the excavator ceased its operations due to K & G's refusal to make the progress payment. K & G had another excavator finish the job at an added cost of $450. It then sued Harris for the bulldozer damage, alleging negligence, and for the $450 damages for breach of contract. Harris claims that K & G defaulted first, having no legal right to refuse the August progress payment. Did K & G default first? Explain.

19. Mountain Restaurant Corporation (Mountain) leased commercial space in the ParkCenter Mall to operate a restaurant called Zac's Grill. The lease specified that the lessee shall "at all times have a non exclusive and non revocable right, together with the other tenants and occupants of … the shopping center, to use the parking area … for itself, its customers and employees." Zac's Grill was to be a fast-food restaurant where tables were anticipated to "turn over" twice during lunch. Zac's operated successfully until parking close to the restaurant became restricted. Two other restaurants opened and began competing for parking spaces, and the parking lot would become full between 12:00 and 12:30 P.M. Parking, however, was always available at other areas of the mall. Business declined for Zac's, which fell behind on the rent due to ParkCenter until finally the restaurant closed. Mountain claims that it was discharged from its obligations under the lease because of material breach. Is Mountain correct? Explain.

20. In late 2008 or early 2009, the plaintiff, Lan England, agreed to sell 258,363 shares of stock to the defendant, Eugene Horbach, for $2.75 per share, resulting in a total price of $710,498.25. Although the purchase money was to be paid in the first quarter of 2009, the defendant made periodic payments on the stock at least through September 2009. The parties met in May of 2010 to finalize the transaction. At this time, the plaintiff believed that the defendant owed at least $25,000 of the original purchase price. The defendant did not dispute that amount. The parties then reached a second agreement whereby the defendant agreed to pay to the plaintiff an

additional $25,000 and to hold in trust 2 percent of the stock for the plaintiff. In return, the plaintiff agreed to transfer the stock and to forgo his right to sue the defendant for breach of the original agreement.

In December 2011, the plaintiff made a demand for the 2 percent stock, but the defendant refused, contending that the 2 percent agreement was meant only to secure his payment of the additional $25,000. The plaintiff sued for breach of the 2 percent agreement. Prior to trial, the defendant discovered additional business records documenting that he had, before entering into the second agreement, actually overpaid the plaintiff for the purchase of the stock. The defendant asserts the plaintiff could not enforce the second agreement as an accord and satisfaction because (1) it was not supported by consideration and (2) it was based upon a mutual mistake that the defendant owed additional money on the original agreement. Is the defendant correct in his assertions? Explain.

21. An artist once produced a painting now called *The Plains of Meudon*. For a while, the parties in this case thought that the artist was Theodore Rousseau, a prominent member of the Barbizon school, and that the painting was quite valuable. With this idea in mind, the Kohlers consigned the painting to Leslie Hindman, Inc. (Hindman), an auction house. Among other things, the consignment agreement between the Kohlers and Hindman defined the scope of Hindman, Inc.'s authority as agent. First, Hindman was obliged to sell the painting according to the conditions of sale spelled out in the auction catalog. Those conditions provided that neither the consignors nor Hindman made any warranties of authenticity. Second, the consignment agreement gave Hindman extensive and exclusive discretionary authority to rescind sales if in its "sole discretion" it determined that the sale subjected the company or the Kohlers to any liability under a warranty of authenticity.

Despite having some doubts about its authenticity, Thune was still interested in the painting but wanted to have it authenticated before committing to its purchase. Unable to obtain an authoritative opinion about its authenticity before the auction, Leslie Hindman and Thune made a verbal agreement that Thune could return the painting within approximately thirty days of the auction if he was the successful bidder and if an expert then determined that Rousseau had not painted it. Neither Leslie Hindman nor anyone else at Hindman told the Kohlers about the questions concerning the painting or about the side agreement between Thune and Hindman. At the auction, Thune prevailed in the bidding with a high bid of $90,000, and he took possession of the painting without paying. He then sent it to an expert in Paris who decided that it was not a Rousseau. Thune returned the painting to Hindman within the agreed-upon period. Explain whether the Kohlers would be successful in a lawsuit against either Hindman or Thune.

TAKING SIDES

Associated Builders, Inc., provided labor and materials to William M. Coggins and Benjamin W. Coggins, doing business as Ben & Bill's Chocolate Emporium, to complete a structure on Main Street in Bar Harbor, Maine. After a dispute arose regarding compensation, Associated and the Cogginses executed an agreement stating that there existed an outstanding balance of $70,000 and setting forth the following terms of repayment:

It is agreed that, two payments will be made by the Cogginses to Associated Builders as follows: Twenty Five Thousand Dollars ($25,000.00) on or before June 1, 2010, and Twenty Five Thousand Dollars ($25,000.00) on or before June 1, 2011. No interest will be charged or paid providing payments are made as agreed. If the payments are not made as agreed then interest shall accrue at 10%

per annum figured from the date of default. It is further agreed that Associated Builders will forfeit the balance of Twenty Thousand Dollars and No Cents ($20,000.00) providing the above payments are made as agreed.

The Cogginses made their first payment in accordance with the agreement. The second payment, however, was delivered three days late on June 4, 2011. Claiming a breach of the contract, Associated contended that the remainder of the original balance of $20,000, plus interest and cost, were now due.

a. What arguments would support Associated's claim for $20,000?
b. What arguments would support the claim by the Cogginses that they were not liable for $20,000?
c. For what damages, if any, are the Cogginses liable? Explain.

CHAPTER **18**

Contract Remedies

The traditional goal of the law of contract remedies has not been the compulsion of the promisor to perform his promise but compensation of the promisee for the loss resulting from breach.

Restatement of Contracts

CHAPTER OUTCOMES

After reading and studying this chapter, you should be able to:

1. Explain how compensatory damages and reliance damages are computed.

2. Define (a) nominal damages, (b) incidental damages, (c) consequential damages, (d) foreseeability of damages, (e) punitive damages, (f) liquidated damages, and (g) mitigation of damages.

3. Define the various types of equitable relief and explain when the courts will grant such relief.

4. Explain how restitutionary damages are computed and identify the situations in which restitution is available as a contractual remedy.

5. Identify and explain the limitations on contractual remedies.

Kim Steele/Jupiter Images

W hen one party to a contract breaches the contract by failing to perform his contractual duties, the law provides a remedy for the injured party. Although the primary objective of contract remedies is to compensate the injured party for the loss resulting from the breach, it is impossible for any remedy to equal the promised performance. The relief a court can give an injured party is what it regards as an *equivalent* of the promised performance.

In this chapter, we will examine the most common remedies available for breach of contract: (1) monetary damages, (2) the equitable remedies of specific performance and injunction, and (3) restitution. Article 2 of the Uniform Commercial Code (UCC), which provides specialized remedies that we will discuss in Chapter 23, governs the sale of goods. Contract remedies are available to protect one or more of the following interests of the injured parties:

1. their *expectation interest*, which is their interest in having the benefit of their bargain by being put in a position as good as the one they would have been in had the contract been performed;

2. their *reliance interest*, which is their interest in being reimbursed for loss caused by reliance on the contract by being put in a position as good as the one they would have been in had the contract not been made; or

3. their *restitution interest*, which is their interest in having restored to them any benefit that they had conferred on the other party.

The contract remedies of compensatory damages, specific performance, and injunction protect the expectation interest. The contractual remedy of reliance damages protects the reliance interest, while the contractual remedy of restitution protects the restitution interest.

Monetary Damages

A judgment awarding monetary damages is the most frequently granted judicial remedy for breach of contract. Monetary damages, however, will be awarded only for losses that are foreseeable, established with reasonable certainty, and not avoidable. The equitable remedies discussed in this chapter are discretionary and are available only if monetary damages are inadequate.

Compensatory Damages

Compensatory damages
contract damages placing the injured party in a position as good as the one he would have held had the other party performed; equals loss of value minus loss avoided by injured party plus incidental damages plus consequential damages

The right to recover compensatory damages for breach of contract is always available to the injured party. The purpose in allowing **compensatory damages** is to place the injured party in a position as good as the one he would have been in had the other party performed under the contract. This involves compensating the injured party for the dollar value of the benefits he would have received had the contract been performed less any savings he experienced by not having to perform his own obligations under the contract. These damages are intended to protect the injured party's *expectation interest*, which is the value he expected to derive from the contract. Thus, the amount of compensatory damages is the loss of value to the injured party caused by the other party's failure to perform or by the other's deficient performance *minus* the loss or cost avoided by the injured party *plus* incidental damages *plus* consequential damages.

Loss of value
value of promised performance minus value of actual performance

Loss of Value   In general, **loss of value** is the *difference between the value of the promised performance* of the breaching party *and the value of the actual performance* rendered by the breaching party. If no performance is rendered at all, the loss of value is the value of the promised performance. If defective or partial performance is rendered, the loss of value is the difference between the value that the full performance would have had and the value of the performance actually rendered. Thus, when there has been a breach of warranty, the injured party may recover the difference between the value the goods would have had, had they been as warranted, and the value of the goods in the condition in which the buyer actually received them. To illustrate, Jacob sells an automobile to Juliet, expressly warranting that it will get forty-five miles per gallon; but the automobile gets only twenty miles per gallon. The automobile would have been worth $24,000 if as warranted, but it is worth only $20,000 as delivered. Juliet would recover $4,000 in damages for loss of value.

Cost avoided
loss or costs the injured party avoids by not having to perform

Cost Avoided   The recovery by the injured party is reduced, however, by any cost or loss she has avoided by not having to perform. For example, Clinton agrees to build a hotel for Debra for $11 million by September 1. Clinton breaches by not completing construction until October 1. As a consequence, Debra loses revenues for one month in the amount of $400,000 but saves operating expenses of $60,000. Therefore, she may recover damages for $340,000. Similarly, in a contract in which the injured party has not fully performed, the injured party's recovery is reduced by the value to the injured party of the performance the injured party promised but did not render. For example, Victor agrees to convey land to Joan in return for Joan's promise to work for Victor for two years. Joan repudiates the contract before Victor has conveyed the land to Joan. Victor's recovery for loss from Joan is reduced by the value to Victor of the land.

Incidental damages
damages arising directly out of a breach of contract

Incidental Damages   **Incidental damages** are damages that arise directly out of the breach, such as costs incurred to acquire the nondelivered performance from some other source. For example, Agnes employs Benton for nine months for $40,000 to supervise construction of a factory. She then fires Benton without cause after three weeks. Benton, who spends $850 in reasonable fees attempting to find comparable employment, may recover $850 in incidental damages in addition to any other actual loss he has suffered.

Consequential damages
damages not arising directly out of a breach but as a foreseeable result of the breach

Consequential Damages   **Consequential damages** are damages not arising directly out of a breach but arising as a foreseeable result of the breach. Consequential damages include lost profits and injury to person or property. Thus, if Tracy leases to Sean a defective machine that causes $40,000 in property damage and $120,000 in personal injuries, Sean may recover, in addition to damages for loss of value and incidental damages, $160,000 as consequential damages.

PRACTICAL ADVICE
If you are the provider of goods or services, consider including a contractual provision for the limitation or exclusion of consequential damages. If you are the purchaser of goods or services, avoid such limitations.

When contracting parties litigate over a breach, does the losing party have to pay the winner's attorneys' fees? These fees may appear to qualify as consequential damages, direct consequences of the breach of contract. However, courts in this country follow what is known as the "American Rule," which provides that each party pays its own attorneys' fees, regardless of who wins. This rule holds true unless there is an applicable statute or express contract clause to the contrary. (Some states have statutes that specifically provide for an award of reasonable attorneys' fees and costs to the pre-

vailing party in certain suits arising out of contract.)

Even though the general rule is that attorneys' fees are not awarded in breach of contract suits, proactive contracting parties can expressly provide in their contract that the losing party will pay the reasonable attorneys' fees of the prevailing party. Many written contracts, particularly those that are drafted by lawyers, contain so-called attorneys' fees provisions. An example of the language used follows: "In the event of any dispute arising out of the performance or breach of this agreement, the prevailing party will be entitled to an award of reason-

able attorneys' fees." Then if the parties end up litigating over the contract, the judge will be able to make the nonbreaching party whole by requiring the losing party to pay the winner's reasonable attorneys' fees, in addition to any other damages or relief granted.

However, absent an attorneys' fees clause in the parties' written agreement and without an attorneys' fees statute in place, the general rule applies and attorneys' fees will not be considered part of a litigating party's damages.

© Cengage Learning 2013

Reliance damages

contract damages placing the injured party in as good a position as he would have been in had the contract not been made

Reliance Damages

Instead of seeking compensatory damages, the injured party may seek reimbursement for foreseeable loss caused by her reliance on the contract. The purpose of **reliance damages** is to place the injured party in a position as good as the one she would have been in had the contract *not been made*. Reliance damages include expenses incurred in preparing to perform, in actually performing, or in forgoing opportunities to enter into other contracts. An injured party may prefer damages for reliance to compensatory damages when she is unable to establish her lost profits with reasonable certainty. For example, Donald agrees to sell his retail store to Gary, who spends $750,000 in acquiring inventory and fixtures. Donald then repudiates the contract, and Gary sells the inventory and fixtures for $735,000. Because neither party can establish with reasonable certainty what profit Gary would have made, Gary may recover from Donald as damages the loss of $15,000 he sustained on the sale of the inventory and fixtures plus any other costs he incurred in entering into the contract. An injured party may choose reliance damages instead of compensatory damages when the agreed-upon contract would be unprofitable. In such a case, however, if the breaching party can prove with reasonable certainty the amount of the loss, it will be subtracted from the injured party's reliance damages.

Nominal damages

a small sum awarded when a contract has been breached but the loss is negligible or unproved

Nominal Damages

An action to recover damages for breach of contract may be maintained even though the plaintiff has not sustained or cannot prove any injury or loss resulting from the breach. In such case he will be permitted to recover **nominal damages**—a small sum fixed without regard to the amount of loss. Such a judgment may also include an award of court costs.

Damages for Misrepresentation

The basic remedy for misrepresentation is rescission (avoidance) of the contract. When appropriate, restitution will also be required. At common law, an alternative remedy to rescission is a suit for damages. The Code liberalizes the common law by not restricting a defrauded party to an election of remedies. That is, the injured party may both rescind the contract by restoring the other party to the status quo and recover damages or obtain any other remedy available under the Code. In most states, the measure of damages for misrepresentation depends on whether the misrepresentation was fraudulent or nonfraudulent.

Out-of-pocket damages

difference between the value received and the value given

Benefit-of-the-bargain damages

difference between the value received and the value of the fraudulent party's performance as represented

Fraud   A party who has been induced by fraud to enter into a contract may recover general damages in a tort action. A minority of states allow the injured party to recover, under the "**out-of-pocket**" rule, general damages equal to the difference between the value of what she has received and the value of what she has given for it. The great majority of states, however, permit the intentionally defrauded party to recover, under the "**benefit-of-the-bargain**" rule, general damages that are equal to the difference between the value of what she has received and the value of the fraudulent party's performance as represented. The Restatement of Torts provides the fraudulently injured party with the option of either out-of-pocket or benefit-of-the-bargain damages. To illustrate, Emily intentionally misrepresents the capabilities of a printing press and thereby induces Melissa to purchase the machine for $20,000. Though the value of the press as delivered is $14,000, the machine would be worth $24,000 if it performed as represented. Under the out-of-pocket rule, Melissa would recover $6,000, whereas under the benefit-of-the-bargain rule, she would recover $10,000. In addition to a recovery of general damages under one of the measures just discussed, consequential damages may be recovered to the extent they are proved with reasonable certainty and to the extent they do not duplicate general damages. Moreover, where the fraud is gross, oppressive, or aggravated, punitive damages are permitted. See *Merritt v. Craig* later in this chapter.

Nonfraudulent Misrepresentation When the misrepresentation is negligent, the deceived party may recover general damages (under the out-of-pocket measure) and consequential damages. Furthermore, some states permit the recovery of general damages under the benefit-of-the-bargain measure. When the misrepresentation is neither fraudulent nor negligent, however, the Restatement of Torts limits damages to the out-of-pocket measure.

Punitive Damages

Punitive damages are generally not recoverable for breach of contract

Punitive damages are monetary damages in addition to compensatory damages awarded to a plaintiff in certain situations involving willful, wanton, or malicious conduct. Their purpose is to punish the defendant and thus discourage him, and others, from similar wrongful conduct. The purpose of allowing contract damages, on the other hand, is to compensate the plaintiff for the loss sustained because of the defendant's breach of contract. Accordingly, the Restatement provides that punitive damages are not recoverable for a breach of contract unless the conduct constituting the breach is also a tort for which the plaintiff may recover punitive damages. See *Merritt v. Craig* later in this chapter.

Liquidated Damages

Liquidated damages reasonable damages agreed to in advance by the parties to a contract

PRACTICAL ADVICE

Consider including a contractual provision for reasonable liquidated damages, especially where damages will be difficult to prove.

A contract may contain a **liquidated damages** provision by which the parties agree in advance to the damages to be paid in event of a breach. Such a provision will be enforced if it amounts to a reasonable forecast of the loss that may or does result from the breach. If, however, the sum agreed on as liquidated damages bears no reasonable relationship to the amount of probable loss, it is unenforceable as a penalty. (A penalty is a contractual provision designed to deter a party from breaching her contract and to punish her for doing so.) Such equivalence is required because the objective of contract remedies is compensatory, not punitive. By examining the substance of the provision, the nature of the contract, and the extent of probable harm that a breach may reasonably be expected to cause the promisee, the courts will determine whether the agreed amount is proper as liquidated damages or unenforceable as a penalty. If a liquidated damages provision is not enforceable, the injured party nevertheless is entitled to the ordinary remedies for breach of contract.

Arrowhead School District No. 75, Park County, Montana, v. James A. Klyap, Jr.
Supreme Court of Montana, 2003
318 Mont. 103, 79 P.3d 250
http://scholar.google.com/scholar_case?case=643756738100095281&q=79+p.3d+250&hl=en&as_sdt=2,34

FACTS Arrowhead School District No. 75 is located in Park County, Montana, and consists of one school, Arrowhead School (School). For the 1997–98 school year, the School employed eleven full-time teachers and several part-time teachers. During that school year, the School employed Klyap as a new teacher instructing math, language arts, and physical education for the sixth, seventh, and eighth grades. In addition, Klyap helped start a sports program and coached flag football, basketball, and volleyball. The School offered Klyap a contract for the 1998–99 school year in June 1998, which he accepted. This contract provided for a $20,500 salary and included a liquidated damages clause. The clause calculated liquidated damages as a percentage of annual salary determined by the date of breach; a breach of contract after July 20, 1998, required payment of 20 percent of salary as damages. Klyap also signed a notice indicating he accepted responsibility for familiarizing himself with the information in the teacher's handbook which also included the liquidated damages clause. On August 12, Klyap informed the School that he would not be returning for the 1998–99 school year even though classes were scheduled to start on August 26. The School then sought to enforce the liquidated damages clause in Klyap's teaching contract for the stipulated amount of $4,100.

After Klyap resigned, the School attempted to find another teacher to take Klyap's place. Although at the time that Klyap was offered his contract the School had eighty potential applicants, only two viable applicants remained available. Right before classes started, the School was able to hire one of those applicants, a less-experienced teacher, at a salary of $19,500.

After a bench trial, the District Court determined the clause was enforceable because the damages suffered by the School were impractical and extremely difficult to fix. Specifically, the court found the School suffered damages because it had to spend additional time setting up an interview committee, conducting interviews, training the new, less-experienced teacher, and reorganizing the sports program. After concluding that the School took appropriate steps to mitigate its damages, the court awarded judgment in favor of the School in the amount of $4,100. Klyap appealed.

DECISION Judgment affirmed.

OPINION The fundamental tenet of modern contract law is freedom of contract: parties are free to mutually agree to terms governing their private conduct as long as those terms do not conflict with public laws or policies. This tenet presumes that parties are in the best position to make decisions in their own interest. When one party breaches the contract, judicial enforcement of the contract ensures the nonbreaching party receives expectancy damages, compensation equal to what that party would receive if the contract were performed. By only awarding expectancy damages rather than additional damages intended to punish the breaching party for failure to perform the contract, court enforcement of private contracts supports the theory of efficient breach. In other words, if it is more efficient for a party to breach a contract and pay expectancy damages in order to enter a superior contract, courts will not interfere by requiring the breaching party to pay more than was due under their contract.

Liquidated damages are, in theory, an extension of these principles. Rather than wait until the occurrence of breach, the parties to a contract are free to agree in advance on a specific damage amount to be paid upon breach. This amount is intended to predetermine expectancy damages. Ideally, this predetermination is intended to make the agreement between the parties more efficient. Rather than requiring a postbreach inquiry into damages

between the parties, the breaching party simply pays the non-breaching party the stipulated amount. Furthermore, in this way, liquidated damages clauses allow parties to estimate damages that are impractical or difficult to prove, as courts cannot enforce expectancy damages without sufficient proof.

To determine whether a clause should be declared a penalty, courts attempt to measure the reasonableness of a liquidated damages clause. The threshold indicator of reasonableness is whether the situation involves damages of a type that are impractical or extremely difficult to prove. According to Restatement, damages must be reasonable in relation to the damages the parties anticipated when the contract was executed or in relation to actual damages resulting from the breach. Liquidated damages in a personal service contract induce performance by an employee by predetermining compensation to an employer if the employee leaves. However, the employer clearly prefers performance by the specific employee because that employee was chosen for hire. Furthermore, because personal service contracts are not enforceable by specific performance, liquidated damages are an appropriate way for employers to protect their interests.

After reviewing the facts of this case, the court held that while the 20 percent liquidated damages clause is definitely harsher than most, it is still within Klyap's reasonable expectations and is not unduly oppressive. First, as the School pointed out during testimony, at such a small school teachers are chosen in part depending on how their skills complement those of the other teachers. Therefore, finding someone who would provide services equivalent to Klyap at such a late date would be virtually impossible. Second, besides the loss of equivalent services, the School lost time for preparation for other activities in order to attempt to find equivalent services. Because Klyap was essential to the sports program, the School had to spend additional time reorganizing the sports program as one sport had to be eliminated with Klyap's loss. Therefore, because as a teacher Klyap would know teachers are typically employed for an entire school year and would know how difficult it is to replace equivalent services at such a small rural school, it was within Klyap's reasonable expectations to agree to a contract with a 20 percent of salary liquidated damages provision for a departure so close to the start of the school year.

INTERPRETATION A liquidated damages provision is enforceable if it is a reasonable forecast of the harm caused by the breach.

CRITICAL THINKING QUESTION What limitations, if any, should the law impose upon liquidated damages? Explain.

Limitations on Damages

To accomplish the basic purposes of contract remedies, the limitations of foreseeability, certainty, and mitigation have been imposed upon monetary damages. These limitations are intended to ensure that damages can be taken into account at the time of contracting, that they are compensatory and not speculative, and that they do not include loss that could have been avoided by reasonable efforts.

Foreseeability of Damages Contracting parties are generally expected to consider foreseeable risks at the time they enter into the contract. Therefore, compensatory or reliance damages are recoverable only for loss that the party in breach had reason to foresee as a *probable* result of a breach when the contract was made. The breaching party is not liable for loss that was not foreseeable at the time of entering into the contract. The test of **foreseeable damages** is *objective*, based on what the breaching party had reason to foresee. Loss may be deemed foreseeable

Foreseeable damages loss that the party in breach had reason to anticipate when the contract was made as a probable result of a breach because it followed from the breach (1) in the ordinary course of events or (2) as a result of special circumstances, beyond the ordinary course of events, about which the party in breach had reason to know.

A leading case on the subject of foreseeability of damages is *Hadley v. Baxendale*, decided in England in 1854.

Hadley v. Baxendale
Court of Exchequer, 1854
9 Ex. 341, 156 Eng.Rep. 145

FACTS The plaintiffs operated a flour mill at Gloucester. They had to stop operating the mill because of a broken crankshaft attached to the steam engine that furnished power to the mill. It was necessary to send the broken shaft to a foundry in Greenwich so that a new shaft could be made. The plaintiffs delivered the broken shaft to the defendants, who were common carriers, for immediate transportation from Gloucester to Greenwich but did not inform the defendants that the mill had ceased operating because of the broken crankshaft. The defendants received the shaft, collected the freight charges in advance, and promised the plaintiffs to deliver the shaft for repairs the following day. The defendants did not make prompt delivery as promised. As a result, the plaintiffs could not operate the mill for several days, thus losing profits that they otherwise would have received. The defendants contended that the loss of profits was too remote, and therefore unforeseeable, to be recoverable. In awarding damages to the plaintiffs, the jury was permitted to consider the loss of these profits.

DECISION Judgment for defendants.

OPINION The appellate court reversed the decision and ordered a new trial on the ground that the special circumstances that caused the loss of profits, namely, the continued stoppage of the mill while awaiting the return of the new crankshaft, had never been communicated by the plaintiffs to the defendants. A common carrier would not reasonably foresee that the plaintiff's mill would be shut down as a result of delay in transporting the broken crankshaft. Damages for

> breach of contract should be such as may fairly and reasonably be considered either arising naturally, i.e., according to the usual course of things, from such breach ... or such as may reasonably be supposed to have been in the contemplation of both parties at the time they made the contract, as the probable result of the breach of it.

INTERPRETATION Damages are recoverable only for those damages that were foreseeable at the time of entering into the contract.

ETHICAL QUESTION Is the court's decision fair? Explain.

CRITICAL THINKING QUESTION Should damages be limited to those that are foreseeable? Explain.

On the other hand, if the defendants in *Hadley v. Baxendale* had been informed that the shaft was necessary for the operation of the mill, or otherwise had reason to know this fact, they would be liable for the plaintiffs' loss of profit during that period of the shutdown caused by their delay. Under these circumstances, the loss would be the "foreseeable" and "natural" result of the breach.

Should a plaintiff's expected profit be extraordinarily large, the general rule is that the breaching party will be liable for such special loss only if he had reason to know of it. In any event, the plaintiff may recover for any ordinary loss resulting from the breach. Thus, if Madeline breaches a contract with Jane, causing Jane, due to special circumstances, $10,000 in damages when ordinarily such a breach would result in only $6,000 in damages, Madeline would be liable to Jane for $6,000, not $10,000, provided that Madeline was unaware of the special circumstances causing Jane the unusually large loss.

PRACTICAL ADVICE
Be sure to inform the other party to the contract of any "special circumstances" beyond the ordinary course of events that could result from a breach of contract.

Certainty of damages
damages are not recoverable beyond an amount that can be established with reasonable certainty

Mitigation of damages
the injured party may not recover damages for loss he could have avoided by reasonable effort

Certainty of Damages Damages are not recoverable for loss beyond an amount that the injured party can establish with reasonable certainty. If the injured party cannot prove a particular element of her loss with reasonable certainty, she nevertheless will be entitled to recover the portion of her loss that she can prove with reasonable certainty. The certainty requirement creates the greatest challenge for plaintiffs seeking the recovery of consequential damages for lost profits on related transactions. Similar difficulty arises in proving lost profits caused by breach of a contract to produce a sporting event or to publish a new book, for example.

Mitigation of Damages Under the doctrine of **mitigation of damages**, the injured party may not recover damages for loss that he could have avoided with reasonable effort and without undue risk, burden, or humiliation. Thus, if Earl is under a contract to manufacture goods for

Karl and Karl repudiates the contract after Earl has begun performance, Earl will not be allowed to recover for losses he sustains by continuing to manufacture the goods, if to do so would increase the amount of damages. The amount of loss that reasonably could have been avoided is deducted from the amount that otherwise would be recoverable as damages. On the other hand, if the goods were almost completed when Karl repudiated the contract, completing the goods might reduce the damages, because the finished goods may be resalable whereas the unfinished goods may not.

Similarly, if Harvey contracts to work for Olivia for one year for a weekly salary and after two months is wrongfully discharged by Olivia, Harvey must use reasonable efforts to mitigate his damages by seeking other employment. If, after such effort, he cannot obtain other employment of the same general character, he is entitled to recover full pay for the contract period during which he is unemployed. He is not obliged to accept a radically different type of employment or to accept work at a distant place. For example, a person employed as a schoolteacher or accountant who is wrongfully discharged is not obliged to accept employment as a chauffeur or truck driver. If Harvey does *not* seek other employment, then if Olivia proves with reasonable certainty that employment of the same general character was available, Harvey's damages are reduced by the amount he could have earned. The next case involving Shirley MacLaine turns on whether acting in a western is employment equivalent to singing and dancing in a musical.

PRACTICAL ADVICE

If the other party to the contract breaches, be sure to make reasonable efforts to avoid or mitigate damages.

Parker v. Twentieth Century-Fox Film Corp.
Supreme Court of California, 1970
3 Ca.3d 176, 89 Cal.Rptr. 737, 474 P.2d 689

FACTS Shirley MacLaine Parker, a well-known actress, contracted with Twentieth Century-Fox Film Corporation (Fox) in August 1965 to play the female lead in Fox's upcoming production of *Bloomer Girl*, a motion picture musical that was to be filmed in California. The contract provided that Fox would pay Parker a minimum "guaranteed compensation" of $750,000 for fourteen weeks of Parker's services, beginning May 23, 1966. By letter dated April 4, 1966, Fox notified Parker of its intention not to produce the film and, instead, offered to employ Parker in the female lead of another film entitled *Big Country, Big Man*, a dramatic western to be filmed in Australia. The compensation offered and most of the other provisions in the substitute contract were identical to the *Bloomer Girl* provisions, except that Parker's right to approve the director and screenplay would have been eliminated or reduced under the *Big Country* contract. Parker refused to accept and brought suit against Fox to recover $750,000 for breach of the *Bloomer Girl* contract. Fox contended that it owed no money to Parker because she had deliberately failed to mitigate or reduce her damages by unreasonably refusing to accept the *Big Country* lead. The trial court granted Parker a summary judgment. (The court's opinion with respect to the rules for determining whether to grant summary judgment appears in Chapter 3.)

DECISION Judgment for Parker affirmed.

OPINION A wrongfully discharged employee generally has a duty to mitigate her damages either by attempting to find or by actually finding substitute employment. The measure of recovery is typically the amount of salary promised under the original contract minus the amount the employer proves the employee has earned, or with reasonable effort might have earned, from other, "substantially similar" employment. The employee's rejection of or failure to seek other employment of a different or inferior kind cannot be used to mitigate damages.

Bloomer Girl was to be a musical revue calling upon Parker's talents as a dancer as well as an actress and was to be filmed in Los Angeles. On the other hand, *Big Country, Big Man* was a straight acting, western-type motion picture taking place in an opal mine in Australia. In addition, Parker would have had her right to approve the director and screenplay eliminated or impaired by the *Big Country* contract. Such disparities between the two projects render the substitute *Big Country* lead of a kind different and inferior to the *Bloomer Girl* role. Therefore, Parker need not accept or seek such inferior employment and could reject Fox's substitute offer with no reduction in her award for failure to mitigate.

INTERPRETATION An injured party's damages may not be reduced by mitigation for her failure to accept or seek other employment of a different or inferior kind.

ETHICAL QUESTION Was it fair for Twentieth Century-Fox Film Corporation to expect Parker to act in the substitute film? Explain.

CRITICAL THINKING QUESTION Why should an injured party be required to mitigate damages? Explain.

REMEDIES IN EQUITY

At times, damages will not adequately compensate an injured party. In these cases, equitable relief in the form of specific performance or an injunction may be available to protect the injured party's interest. Such remedies are not a matter of right but rest in the discretion of the court.

Consequently, they will not be granted when there is an adequate remedy at law; when it is impossible to enforce them, as when the seller has already transferred the subject matter of the contract to an innocent third person; when the terms of the contract are unfair; when the consideration is grossly inadequate; when the contract is tainted with fraud, duress, undue influence, mistake, or unfair practices; or when the relief would cause the defendant unreasonable hardship. See *Real Estate Analytics, LLC. v. Vallas* in this chapter.

On the other hand, a court may grant specific performance or an injunction despite a provision for liquidated damages. Moreover, a court will grant specific performance or an injunction even though a term of the contract prohibits equitable relief, if denying such relief would cause the injured party unreasonable hardship.

Reformation
equitable remedy correcting a written contract to conform with the original intent of the contracting parties

Another equitable remedy is **reformation**, a process whereby the court "rewrites" or "corrects" a written contract to make it conform to the true agreement of the parties. The purpose of reformation is not to make a new contract for the parties but to express adequately the contract they have made for themselves. The remedy of reformation is granted when the parties agree on a contract but write it in a way that inaccurately reflects their actual agreement. For example, Acme Insurance Co. and Bell agree that for good consideration, Acme will issue an annuity paying $500 per month. Because of a clerical error, the annuity policy is issued for $50 per month. A court of equity, upon satisfactory proof of the mistake, will reform the policy to provide for the correct amount—$500 per month. In addition, as discussed in Chapter 13, when a covenant not to compete is unreasonable, some courts will reform the agreement to make it reasonable and enforceable.

Specific Performance

Specific performance
court decree ordering a breaching party to render promised performance

Specific performance is the equitable remedy that compels the defaulting party to perform her contractual obligations. As with all equitable remedies, it is available only when there is no adequate remedy at law. Ordinarily, for instance, in a case in which a seller breaches a contract for the sale of personal property, the buyer has a sufficient remedy at law. When, however, the personal property contracted for is rare or unique, this remedy is inadequate. Examples of such property would include a famous painting or statue, an original manuscript or a rare edition of a book, a patent, a copyright, shares of stock in a closely held corporation, or an heirloom. Articles of this kind cannot be purchased elsewhere. Accordingly, on breach by the seller of the contract for the sale of any such article, money damages will not adequately compensate the buyer. Consequently, the buyer may avail herself of the equitable remedy of specific performance.

Although courts of equity will grant specific performance in connection with contracts for the sale of personal property only in exceptional circumstances, they will always grant it in case of breach of contract for the sale of real property. The reason for this is that every parcel of land is regarded as unique. Consequently, if the seller refuses to convey title to the real estate contracted for, the buyer may seek the aid of a court of equity to compel the seller to convey the title. Most courts of equity will likewise compel the buyer in a real estate contract to perform at the suit of the seller.

Courts of equity will not grant specific performance of contracts for personal services. In the first place, there is the practical difficulty, if not impossibility, of enforcing such a decree. In the second place, it is against the policy of the courts to force one person to work for or to serve another against his will, even though the person has contracted to do so. Such enforcement would closely resemble involuntary servitude. For example, if Carmen, an accomplished concert pianist, agrees to appear at a certain time and place to play a specified program for Rudolf, a court would not issue a decree of specific performance upon her refusal to appear.

Real Estate Analytics, LLC v. Vallas
Court of Appeal, Fourth District, Division 1, California, 2008
160 Cal.App.4th 463, 72 Cal.Rptr.3d 835, review denied 2008
http://scholar.google.com/scholar_case?case=16761955053572987435&q=72+cal.rptr.3d+835&hl=en&as_sdt=2,34

FACTS Real Estate Analytics, LLC (REA) is a limited liability company formed by Troy Shadian. In January 2004, Shadian and his business partner, Roshan Bhakta, became interested in Theodore Tee Vallas's 14.13-acre Lanikai Lane property located in Carlsbad, California, near the Pacific Coast Highway. The property contained a mobile home park with 147 individual mobile homes and numerous amenities, including a pool, playground, laundry facilities, and a long winding street. Vallas leased the property to a mobile home park operator, which managed the park and subleased the spaces to residents who owned their mobile homes. The lease began in 1951 and terminates in 2013.

REA's primary goal in purchasing the property was to make a profit for its investors and themselves. One proposed business model was to subdivide the property and sell the subdivided lots to the property's mobile home park residents. In March 2004, REA and Vallas entered into a written agreement for Vallas to sell the property to REA. Under the agreement, the sales price was $8.5 million, with REA to pay an immediate $100,000 deposit, and then pay $2.9 million at closing. In return, Vallas agreed to finance the remaining $5.5 million, with the unpaid balance to be paid over a five-year period, with the balance due on April 1, 2009. On June 14, Vallas cancelled the contract. The next day REA brought a breach of contract action seeking specific performance. The court, sitting without a jury, found Vallas breached the contract but refused to grant specific performance and instead awarded REA damages of $500,000, reflecting the difference between the contract price and the fair market value at the time of the breach. The court declined to award specific performance on the basis of its finding that damages would provide REA adequate relief.

DECISION Judgment is reversed, and the trial court is ordered to enter a new judgment granting specific performance.

OPINION To obtain specific performance after a breach of contract, a plaintiff must generally show the following: (1) the inadequacy of his legal remedy, (2) an underlying contract that is both reasonable and supported by adequate consideration, (3) the existence of a mutuality of remedies, (4) contractual terms which are sufficiently definite to enable the court to know what it is to enforce, and (5) a substantial similarity of the requested performance to that promised in the contract.

In this case, the trial court refused to specifically enforce the contract based on its finding that the first element (inadequacy of legal remedy) was not satisfied because REA sought to purchase the property as an investment, and not for some particular use of the land. REA contends this finding was incorrect as a matter of law and, alternatively, unsupported by the evidence.

A damage award is generally an inadequate remedy for a breach of real estate contract, and therefore courts generally grant a plaintiff's request for specific performance. Most jurisdictions have rules requiring special treatment of land sale contracts, reflecting the enduring view that (1) each parcel of land is unique and therefore there can be no adequate replacement after a breach and (2) monetary damages are difficult to calculate after a party refuses to complete a land sales contract, particularly expectation damages. In California, these principles are statutorily embodied in section 3387, which states the following:

> It is to be presumed that the breach of an agreement to transfer real property cannot be adequately relieved by pecuniary compensation. In the case of a single-family dwelling which the party seeking performance intends to occupy, this presumption is conclusive. In all other cases, this presumption is a presumption affecting the burden of proof.

By imposing a conclusive presumption for certain residential transactions, the California legislature decided that monetary damages can never be satisfactory compensation for a buyer who intends to live at a single-family home, regardless of the circumstances. But by establishing a rebuttable presumption with respect to other property, the legislature left open the possibility that damages can be an adequate remedy for a breach of a real estate contract. But the specific issue presented here is not whether a defendant can ever rebut the inadequacy of remedy presumption. The issue is whether Vallas did so in this case. And on this issue, the appellate court agreed with REA that Vallas did not make a sufficient evidentiary showing to establish damages were adequate to compensate REA for the breach. Given the statutory presumption that damages were inadequate and the largely undisputed evidence strongly supporting this presumption, Vallas had a high threshold to satisfy his burden to show damages would be an adequate remedy. Thus, although REA did not necessarily intend to benefit from its personal or commercial *use* of the land, the land did have a particular unique value because of the manner in which it could be used to earn profits upon a resale. Missing from the trial court's analysis was the recognition that to rebut the presumption that damages are an inadequate remedy, the defendant must come forward with evidence showing that damages will fully compensate the plaintiff for the breach. The record in this case was bereft of any such evidence.

INTERPRETATION Specific performance is an appropriate remedy when there is no adequate remedy at law.

CRITICAL THINKING QUESTION Should specific performance be available for all breaches of contract? Explain.

Injunctions

Injunction
court order prohibiting a party from doing a specific act

The **injunction**, as used as a contract remedy, is a formal court order enjoining (commanding) a person to refrain from doing a specific act or to cease engaging in specific conduct. A court of equity, at its discretion, may grant an injunction against breach of a contractual duty when damages for a breach would be inadequate. For example, Clint enters into a written contract to give Janice the right of first refusal on a tract of land owned by Clint. Clint, however, subsequently offers the land to Blake without first offering it to Janice. A court of equity may properly enjoin Clint from selling the land to Blake. Similarly, valid covenants not to compete may be enforced by an injunction.

An employee's promise of exclusive personal services may be enforced by an injunction against serving another employer as long as the probable result will not deprive the employee of other reasonable means of making a living. Suppose, for example, that Allan makes a contract with Marlene, a famous singer, under which Marlene agrees to sing at Allan's theater on certain dates for an agreed-upon fee. Before the date of the first performance, Marlene makes a contract with Craig to sing for Craig at his theater on the same dates. Although, as we have discussed, Allan cannot obtain specific performance of his contract by Marlene, a court of equity will, on suit by Allan against Marlene, issue an injunction against her ordering her not to sing for Craig. This is the situation in the case of *Madison Square Garden Corp., Ill. v. Carnera.*

When the services contracted for are *not* unusual or extraordinary in character, the injured party cannot obtain injunctive relief. His only remedy is an action at law for damages.

Madison Square Garden Corp., Ill. v. Carnera
Circuit Court of Appeals, Second Circuit, 1931
52 F.2d 47

FACTS Carnera (defendant) agreed with Madison Square Garden (plaintiff) to render services as a boxer in his next contest with the winner of the Schmeling-Stribling contest for the heavyweight championship title. The contract also provided that prior to the match Carnera would not engage in any major boxing contest without the permission of Madison Square Garden. Without obtaining such permission, Carnera contracted to engage in a major boxing contest with Sharkey. Madison Square Garden brought suit requesting an injunction against Carnera's performing his contract to box Sharkey. The trial court granted a preliminary injunction.

DECISION Order for Madison Square Garden affirmed.

OPINION The affidavits in support of the request for a preliminary injunction adequately show that Carnera's services are unique and extraordinary. While specific performance will not be ordered to compel Carnera to render personal services, the court will specifically enforce a negative covenant by injunctive order when damages are not readily ascertainable.

INTERPRETATION When damages are not adequate, an injunction may be used to enforce an agreement to perform exclusive services that are unusual and extraordinary.

CRITICAL THINKING QUESTION Should money damages have been an adequate remedy in this case? Explain.

RESTITUTION

Restitution
restoration of the injured party to the position he was in before the contract was made

One of the remedies that may be available to a party to a contract is restitution. **Restitution** is the act of returning to the aggrieved party the consideration, or its value, that he gave to the other party. The purpose of restitution is to restore the injured party to the position he was in before the contract was made. Therefore, the party seeking restitution must return what has been received from the other party.

Restitution is available in several contractual situations: (1) for a party injured by breach, as an alternative remedy; (2) for a party in default; (3) for a party who may not enforce a contract because of the statute of frauds; and (4) for a party wishing to rescind (avoid) a voidable contract.

Party Injured by Breach

Party injured by breach
may recover restitution if the other party totally breaches the contract by nonperformance or repudiation

A party is entitled to restitution if the other party totally breaches the contract by nonperformance or repudiation. For example, Benedict agrees to sell land to Beatrice for $60,000. After Beatrice makes a partial payment of $15,000, Benedict wrongfully refuses to transfer title. As an alternative to damages or specific performance, Beatrice may recover the $15,000 in restitution.

Party in Default

Party in default
for any benefit conferred in excess of the loss caused by the breach

Where a party, after having partly performed, commits a breach by nonperformance or repudiation that discharges the other party's duty to perform, the party in default is entitled to restitution for any benefit she has conferred in excess of the loss she has caused by the breach. For example, Nathan agrees to sell land to Milly for $60,000, and Milly makes a partial payment of $15,000. Milly then repudiates the contract. Nathan sells the land to Murray in good faith for $55,000. Milly may recover from Nathan in restitution the part payment of the $15,000 less the $5,000 damages Nathan sustained because of Milly's breach, which equals $10,000.

Statute of Frauds

Statute of frauds
when a contract is unenforceable because of the statute of frauds, a party may recover the benefits conferred on the other party in reliance on the contract

A party to a contract that is unenforceable because of the statute of frauds may, nonetheless, have acted in reliance on the contract. In such a case, that party may recover in restitution the

Figure 18-1 Contract Remedies

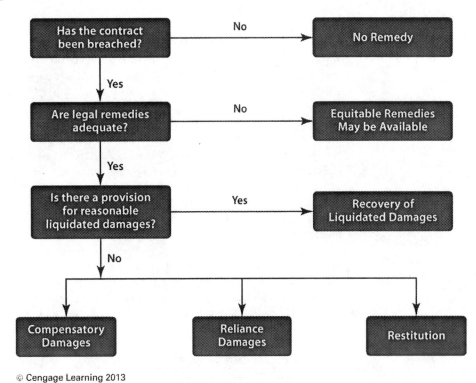

© Cengage Learning 2013

benefits he conferred on the other in relying on the unenforceable contract. In most states the party seeking restitution must not be in default. Thus, if Wilton makes an oral contract to furnish services to Rochelle that are not to be performed within a year, and Rochelle discharges Wilton after three months, Wilton may recover as restitution the value of the services rendered during the three months.

Voidable Contracts

Voidable contracts

a party who has avoided a contract is entitled to restitution for any benefit conferred on the other party

A party who has rescinded or avoided a contract for lack of capacity, duress, undue influence, fraud in the inducement, nonfraudulent misrepresentation, or mistake is entitled to restitution for any benefit he has conferred on the other. For example, Samuel fraudulently induces Edith to sell land for $60,000. Samuel pays the purchase price, and Edith conveys the land. She then discovers the fraud. Edith may disaffirm the contract and recover the land as restitution. Generally, the party seeking restitution must return any benefit that he has received under the agreement; however, as we found in our discussion of contractual capacity (Chapter 14), this is not always the case.

Figure 18-1 summarizes the remedies for breach of contract.

LIMITATIONS ON REMEDIES

Election of Remedies

Election of remedies

if remedies are not inconsistent, a party injured by a breach of contract may seek more than one remedy

If a party injured by a breach of contract has more than one remedy available, her manifestation of a choice of one remedy, such as bringing suit, does not prevent seeking another unless the remedies are inconsistent and the other party materially changes his position in reliance on the manifestation. For example, a party who seeks specific performance, an injunction, or restitution may be entitled to incidental damages, such as those brought about by delay in performance. Damages for total breach, however, are inconsistent with the remedies of specific performance, injunction, and restitution. Likewise, the remedy of specific performance or an injunction is inconsistent with that of restitution.

With respect to contracts for the sale of goods, the Code rejects any doctrine of election of remedies. Thus, the remedies it provides, which are essentially cumulative, include all of the remedies available for breach. Under the Code, whether one remedy prevents the use of another depends on the facts of the individual case.

Loss of Power of Avoidance

A party with a power of avoidance for lack of capacity, duress, undue influence, fraud, misrepresentation, or mistake may lose that power if (1) she affirms the contract, (2) she delays unreasonably in exercising the power of disaffirmance, or (3) the rights of third parties intervene.

Affirmance   A party who has the power to avoid a contract for lack of capacity, duress, undue influence, fraud in the inducement, nonfraudulent misrepresentation, or mistake will lose that power by affirming the contract. Affirmance occurs when the party, with full knowledge of the facts, either declares the intention to proceed with the contract or takes some other action from which such intention may reasonably be inferred. Thus, suppose that Pam was induced to purchase a ring from Sally through Sally's fraudulent misrepresentation. If, after learning the truth, Pam undertakes to sell the ring to Janet or does something else that is consistent only with her ownership of the ring, she may no longer rescind the transaction with Sally. In the case of incapacity, duress, or undue influence, affirmance is effective only after the circumstances that made the contract voidable cease to exist. When there has been fraudulent misrepresentation, the defrauded party may affirm only after he knows of the misrepresentation; if the misrepresentation is nonfraudulent or a mistake is involved, affirmance may occur only after the defrauded party knows or should know of the misrepresentation or mistake.

Merritt v. Craig
Court of Special Appeals of Maryland, 2000
130 Md.App. 350, 746 A.2d 923, cert. denied, 359 Md. 29, 753 A.2d 2 (2000)
http://scholar.google.com/scholar_case?case=10339288125936808164&q=746+a.2d+923&hl=en&as_sdt=2,34

FACTS In the fall of 1995, during their search for a new residence, the plaintiffs, Benjamin K. and Julie S. Merritt, advised the defendant, Virginia Craig, that they were interested in purchasing Craig's property contingent upon a satisfactory home inspection. On November 5, 1995, the plaintiffs, their inspector, and the defendant's husband Mark Craig conducted an inspection of the cistern and water supply pipes in the basement. The examination revealed that the cistern had been used to store a water supply reserve, but was not currently utilized. There were also two water lines that entered into the basement. One of the lines came from an eight-hundred-foot well that was located on the property, and the other line came from a well located on the adjacent property. The well located on the adjacent property supplied water to both the residence for sale and a guesthouse owned by Craig. The existence of the adjacent well was not disclosed to the plaintiffs.

On December 2, 1995, plaintiffs and Craig executed a contract of sale for the property, along with a "Disclosure Statement" signed by Craig and acknowledged by the plaintiffs affirming that there were no problems with the water supply to the house. Between November 5, 1995, and June 1996, Craig caused the water line from the guesthouse to the house purchased by the plaintiffs to be cut, and the cistern reactivated to store water from the existing well. On May 18, 1996, Craig's husband advised Dennis Hannibal, one of the real estate agents involved in the deal, that he had spent $4,196.79 to upgrade the water system on the property. On June 14, 1996, the plaintiffs and Craig closed the sale of the property. Later that afternoon, Craig's husband, without the plaintiffs' knowledge, excavated the inside wall of the house and installed a cap to stop a leaking condition on the water line that he had previously cut.

Upon taking possession of the house the plaintiffs noticed that the water supply in their well had depleted. The plaintiffs met with Craig to discuss a solution to the water failure problem, agreeing with Craig to conduct a flow test to the existing well and to contribute money for the construction of a new well. On October 29, 1996, the well was drilled and produced only one-half gallon of water per minute. Subsequently plaintiffs paid for the drilling of a second well on their property, but it failed to produce water. In January 1997, appellants contacted a plumber, who confirmed that the line from the guesthouse well had been cut flush with the inside surface of the basement wall and cemented closed. Plaintiffs continued to do further work on the house in an effort to cure the water problem. The plaintiffs brought suit against Craig, seeking rescission of the deed to the property and contract of sale, along with compensatory and punitive damages. The trial judge dismissed plaintiffs' claim for rescission on the ground that they had effectively waived their right to rescission. The jury returned a verdict in favor of the plaintiffs, awarding compensatory damages in the amount of $42,264.76 and punitive damages in the amount of $150,000. The plaintiffs appealed the trial court's judgment denying their right to rescind the contract. The defendant cross-appealed on the award of punitive damages.

DECISION Judgment of the trial court reversed, and the case is remanded.

OPINION Under Maryland law, when a party to a contract discovers that he or she has been defrauded, the party defrauded has either a right to retain the contract and collect damages for its breach, or a right to rescind the contract and recover his or her own expenditures, not both. These rights are inconsistent and mutually exclusive, and the discovery puts the purchaser to a prompt election. The plaintiffs may not successfully rescind the contract while simultaneously recovering compensatory and punitive damages. Restitution is "a party's unilateral unmaking of a contract for a legally sufficient reason, such as the other party's material breach" and it in effect "restores the parties to their pre-contractual position." The restoration of the parties to their original position is incompatible with the windfall of compensatory and punitive damages beyond incidental expenses.

Maryland law asserts, "A plaintiff seeking rescission must demonstrate that he [or she] acted promptly after discovery of the ground for rescission," otherwise the right to rescind is waived. Under the facts of this case, the plaintiffs must elect between damages or rescission. Because the plaintiffs were led to believe by the court that no election was required, the case is remanded to the lower court for the plaintiffs to make the proper election and for the case to be retried, pursuant to that election.

On the question whether the trial court erred by allowing the jury verdict awarding the plaintiffs punitive damages in the amount of $150,000 to stand, the plaintiffs are entitled to be awarded punitive damages resulting from Craig's actions. The jury believed that the representations made by Craig were undertaken with actual knowledge that the representations were false and with the intention to deceive the plaintiffs, which constitutes the actual malice required to support an award for punitive damages. The

jury could reasonably infer Craig's intention to defraud the plaintiffs by her representation that there were no problems with the water supply, and by subsequently making substantial changes in the water system by cutting off a water line which supplied water to the plaintiffs' residence immediately after the plaintiffs' inspector examined the system.

Craig also challenges the punitive damages award on the basis that the amount of the award was excessive, but Craig's conduct toward the plaintiffs was reprehensible and fully warranted punitive damages. Her conduct in willfully misrepresenting the condition of the water system, coupled with the actions of interfering and diverting the water flow subsequent to the inspection and sale of the property, constitute egregious conduct. As a result of Craig's conduct, the plaintiffs were forced to employ extreme water conservation practices due to an insufficient water supply and they attempted to ameliorate the problem by having two new wells drilled on the property, which proved to be unproductive.

INTERPRETATION A defrauded party may rescind a contract induced by fraud but may lose that power if he affirms the contract or delays unreasonably in exercising the power of rescission.

CRITICAL THINKING QUESTION What is the policy reason for requiring a defrauded party to elect between rescission and damages? Explain.

PRACTICAL ADVICE
If you have the power to avoid a contract, be sure to rescind within a reasonable time or you will forfeit your right to do so.

Delay The power of avoidance may be lost if the party who has the power to do so does not rescind within a reasonable time after the circumstances that made the contract voidable have ceased to exist. Determining a reasonable time depends on all the circumstances, including the extent to which the delay enables the party with the power of avoidance to speculate at the other party's risk. To illustrate, a defrauded purchaser of stock cannot wait unduly to see whether the market price or value of the stock appreciates sufficiently to justify retaining the stock.

Rights of Third Parties The intervening rights of third parties further limit the power of avoidance and the accompanying right to restitution. If A transfers property to B in a transaction that is voidable by A, and B sells the property to C (a good faith purchaser for value) before A exercises the power of avoidance, A will lose the right to recover the property.

Thus, if a third party (C), who is a good faith purchaser for value, acquires an interest in the subject matter of the contract before A has elected to rescind, no rescission is permitted. Because the transaction is voidable, B acquires a voidable title to the property. Upon a sale of the property by B to C, who is a purchaser in good faith and for value, C obtains good title and is allowed to retain the property. Because both A and C are innocent, the law will not disturb the title held by C, the good faith purchaser. In this case, as in all cases in which rescission is not available, A's only recourse is against B.

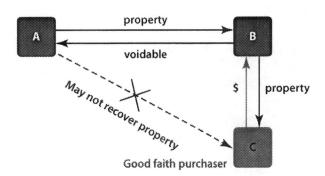

The one notable exception to this rule is the situation involving a sale, *other than a sale of goods*, by a minor who subsequently wishes to avoid the transaction, in which the property has been retransferred to a good faith purchaser. Under this special rule, a good faith purchaser is deprived of the protection generally provided such third parties. Therefore, the third party in a transaction not involving goods, real property being the primary example, is no more protected from the minor's disaffirmance than is the person dealing directly with the minor.

CHAPTER SUMMARY

Monetary Damages

Compensatory Damages contract damages placing the injured party in a position as good as the one he would have held had the other party performed; equals loss of value minus loss avoided by injured party plus incidental damages plus consequential damages

- *Loss of Value* value of promised performance minus value of actual performance
- *Cost Avoided* loss or costs the injured party avoids by not having to perform
- *Incidental Damages* damages arising directly out of a breach of contract
- *Consequential Damages* damages not arising directly out of a breach but arising as a foreseeable result of the breach

Reliance Damages contract damages placing the injured party in as good a position as she would have been in had the contract not been made

Nominal Damages a small sum awarded when a contract has been breached but the loss is negligible or unproved

Damages for Misrepresentation

- *Out-of-Pocket Damages* difference between the value given and the value received
- *Benefit-of-the-Bargain Damages* difference between the value of the fraudulent party's performance as represented and the value the defrauded party received

Punitive Damages are generally not recoverable for breach of contract

Liquidated Damages reasonable damages agreed to in advance by the parties to a contract

Limitations on Damages

- *Foreseeability of Damages* potential loss that the party now in default had reason to know of when the contract was made
- *Certainty of Damages* damages are not recoverable beyond an amount that can be established with reasonable certainty
- *Mitigation of Damages* injured party may not recover damages for loss he could have avoided by reasonable effort

Remedies in Equity

Availability only in cases in which there is no adequate remedy at law

Types

- *Specific Performance* court decree ordering the breaching party to render promised performance
- *Injunction* court order prohibiting a party from doing a specific act
- *Reformation* court order correcting a written contract to conform with the intent of the contracting parties

Restitution

Definition of Restitution restoration of the injured party to the position she was in before the contract was made

Availability

- *Party Injured by Breach* if the other party totally breaches the contract by nonperformance or repudiation
- *Party in Default* for any benefit conferred in excess of the loss caused by the breach
- *Statute of Frauds* where a contract is unenforceable because of the statute of frauds, a party may recover the benefits conferred on the other party in reliance on the contract
- *Voidable Contracts* a party who has avoided a contract is entitled to restitution for any benefit conferred on the other party

Limitations on Remedies

Election of Remedies if remedies are not inconsistent, a party injured by a breach of contract may seek more than one remedy

Loss of Power of Avoidance a party with the power to avoid a contract may lose that power by

- Affirming the contract
- Delaying unreasonably in exercising the power of avoidance
- Being subordinated to the intervening rights of third parties

QUESTIONS

1. Edward, a candy manufacturer, contracted to buy one thousand barrels of sugar from Marcia. Marcia failed to deliver, and Edward was unable to buy any sugar in the market. As a direct consequence he was unable to make candies to fulfill unusually lucrative contracts for the Christmas trade. (a) What damages is Edward entitled to recover? (b) Would it make any difference if Marcia had been told by Edward that he wanted the sugar to make candies for the Christmas trade and that he had accepted lucrative contracts for delivery for the Christmas trade?

2. Daniel agreed to erect an apartment building for Steven for $12 million, and that Daniel would suffer a deduction of $12,000 per day for every day of delay. Daniel was twenty days late in finishing the job, losing ten days because of a strike and ten days because the material suppliers were late in furnishing him with materials. Daniel claims that he is entitled to payment in full (a) because the agreement as to $12,000 a day is a penalty and (b) because Steven has not shown that he has sustained any damage. Discuss each contention and decide.

3. Sharon contracted with Jane, a shirtmaker, for one thousand shirts for men. Jane manufactured and delivered five hundred shirts, for which Sharon paid. At the same time, Sharon notified Jane that she could not use or dispose of the other five hundred shirts and directed Jane not to manufacture any more under the contract. Nevertheless, Jane made up the other five hundred shirts and tendered them to Sharon. Sharon refused to accept the shirts. Jane then sued for the purchase price. Is she entitled to the purchase price? If not, is she entitled to any damages? Explain.

4. Stuart contracts to act in a comedy for Charlotte and to comply with all theater regulations for four seasons. Charlotte promises to pay Stuart $1,800 for each performance and to allow Stuart one benefit performance each season. It is expressly agreed "Stuart shall not be employed in any other production for the period of the contract." Stuart and Charlotte, during the first year of the contract, have a terrible quarrel. Thereafter, Stuart signs a contract to perform in Elaine's production and ceases performing for Charlotte. Charlotte seeks (a) to prevent Stuart from performing for Elaine and (b) to require Stuart to perform his contract with Charlotte. What result?

5. Louis leased a building to Pam for five years at a rental of $1,000 per month. Pam was to deposit $10,000 as security for performance of all her promises in the lease, which was to be retained by Louis in case of any breach on Pam's part. Pam defaulted in the payment of rent for the last two months of the lease. Louis refused to return any of the deposit, claiming it as liquidated damages. Pam sued Louis to recover $8,000 (the $10,000 deposit less the amount of rent due Louis for the last two months). What amount of damages should Pam be allowed to collect from Louis? Explain.

6. In which of the following situations is specific performance available as a remedy?
   a. Mary and Anne enter into a written agreement under which Mary agrees to sell and Anne agrees to buy for $100 per share one hundred shares of the three hundred shares outstanding of the capital stock of the Infinitesimal Steel Corporation, whose shares are not listed on any exchange and are closely held. Mary refuses to deliver when tendered the $10,000.
   b. Modifying (a) above, assume that the subject matter of the agreement is stock of the U.S. Steel Corporation, which is traded on the New York Stock Exchange.
   c. Modifying (a) above, assume that the subject matter of the agreement is undeveloped farmland of little commercial value.

7. On March 1, Joseph sold to Sandra fifty acres of land in Oregon that Joseph at the time represented to be fine black loam, high, dry, and free of stumps. Sandra paid Joseph the agreed price of $140,000 and took from Joseph a deed to the land. Sandra subsequently discovered that the land was low, swampy, and not entirely free of stumps. Sandra, nevertheless, undertook to convert the greater part of the land into cranberry bogs. After one year of cranberry culture, Sandra became entirely dissatisfied, tendered the land back to Joseph, and demanded from Joseph the return of the $140,000. On Joseph's refusal to repay the money, Sandra brought an action at law against him to recover the $140,000. What judgment?

8. James contracts to make repairs to Betty's building in return for Betty's promise to pay $12,000 on completion of the repairs. After partially completing the repairs, James is unable to continue. Betty refuses to pay James and hires another builder, who completes the repairs for $5,000. The building's value to Betty has increased by $10,000 as a result of the repairs by James, but Betty has lost $500 in rents because of the delay caused by James's breach. James sues Betty. How much, if any, may James recover in restitution from Betty?

9. Linda induced Sally to enter into a purchase of a home theater receiver by intentionally misrepresenting the power output to be seventy-five watts at rated distortion, when in fact it delivered only forty watts. Sally paid $450 for the receiver. Receivers producing forty watts generally sell for $200, whereas receivers producing seventy-five watts generally sell for $550. Sally decides to keep the receiver and sue for damages. How much may Sally recover in damages from Linda?

10. Virginia induced Charles to sell Charles's boat to Virginia by misrepresentation of material fact on which Charles reasonably relied. Virginia promptly sold the boat to Donald, who paid fair value for it and knew nothing concerning the transaction between Virginia and Charles. Upon discovering the misrepresentation, Charles seeks to recover the boat. What are Charles's rights against Virginia and Donald?

CASE PROBLEMS

11. Felch was employed as a member of the faculty of Findlay College under a contract that permitted dismissal only for cause. He was dismissed by action of the President and Board of Trustees, which did not comply with a contractual provision for dismissal that requires a hearing. Felch requested the court to grant specific performance of the contract and require Findlay College to continue Felch as a member of the faculty and to pay him the salary agreed upon. Is Felch entitled to specific performance? Explain.

12. Copenhaver, the owner of a laundry business, contracted with Berryman, the owner of a large apartment complex, to allow Copenhaver to own and operate the laundry facilities within the apartment complex. Berryman terminated the five-year contract with Copenhaver with forty-seven months remaining. Within six months, Copenhaver placed the equipment into use in other locations and generated at least as much income as he would have earned at Berryman's apartment complex. He then filed suit, claiming that he was entitled to conduct the laundry operations for an additional forty-seven months and that, through such operations, he would have earned a profit of $13,886.58, after deducting Berryman's share of the gross receipts and other operating expenses. Decision?

13. Billy Williams Builders and Developers (Williams) entered into a contract with Hillerich under which Williams agreed to sell to Hillerich a certain lot and to construct on it a house according to submitted plans and specifications. The house built by Williams was defectively constructed. Hillerich brought suit for specific performance of the contract and for damages resulting from the defective construction and delay in performance. Williams argued that Hillerich was not entitled to have both specific performance and damages for breach of the contract because the remedies were inconsistent and Hillerich had to elect one or the other. Explain whether Williams is correct in this assertion.

14. Developers under a plan approved by the city of Rye had constructed six luxury cooperative apartment buildings and were to construct six more. To obtain certificates of occupancy for the six completed buildings, the developers were required to post a bond with the city to insure completion of the remaining buildings. The developers posted a $100,000 bond upon which Public Service Mutual Insurance Company, as guarantor or surety, agreed to pay $200 for each day after the contractual deadline that the remaining buildings were not completed. After the contractual deadline, more than five hundred days passed without completion of the buildings. The city claims that its inspectors and employees will be required to devote more time to the project than anticipated because it has taken extra years to complete. It also claims that it will lose tax revenues for the years the buildings are not completed. Should the city prevail in its suit against the developers and the insurance company to recover $100,000 on the bond? Explain.

15. Kerr Steamship Company sent a telegram at a cost of $26.78 to the Philippines through the Radio Corporation of America. The telegram, which contained instructions in unintelligible code for loading cargo on one of Kerr's ships, was mislaid and never delivered. Consequently, the ship was improperly loaded and the cargo was lost. Kerr sued the Radio Corporation for the $6,675.29 in profits the company lost on the cargo because of the Radio Corporation's failure to deliver the telegram. Should Kerr be allowed to recover damages from Radio? Explain.

16. El Dorado Tire Company fired Bill Ballard, a sales executive. Ballard had a five-year contract with El Dorado but was fired after only two years of employment. Ballard sued El Dorado for breach of contract. El Dorado claimed that any damages due to breach of the contract should be mitigated because of Ballard's failure to seek other employment after he was fired. El Dorado did not provide any proof showing the availability of comparable employment. Explain whether El Dorado is correct in its contention.

17. California and Hawaiian Sugar Company (C and H) is an agricultural cooperative in the business of growing sugarcane in Hawaii and transporting the raw sugar to its refinery in California for processing. Because of the seasonal nature of the sugarcane crop, availability of ships to transport the raw sugar immediately after harvest is imperative. After losing the services of the shipping company it had previously used, C and H decided to build its own ship, a Macababoo, which had two components, a tug and a barge. C and H contracted with Halter Marine to build the tug and with Sun Ship to build the barge. In finalizing the contract for construction of the barge, both C and H and Sun Ship were represented by senior management and by legal counsel. The resulting contract called for a liquidated damages payment of $17,000 per day that delivery of the completed barge was delayed. Delivery of both the barge and the tug was significantly delayed. Sun Ship paid the $17,000 per day liquidated damages amount and then sued to recover it, claiming that without the liquidated damages provision, C and H's legal remedy for money damages would have been significantly less than that paid by Sun Ship pursuant to the liquidated damages provision. Decision?

18. Bettye Gregg offered to purchase a house from Head & Seeman, Inc. (seller). Though she represented in writing that she had between $15,000 and $20,000 in equity in another home that she would pay to the seller after she sold the other home, she knew that she did not have such equity. In reliance upon these intentionally fraudulent representations, the seller accepted Gregg's offer and the parties entered into a land contract. After taking occupancy, Gregg failed to make any of the contract payments. The seller's investigations then revealed the fraud. Head & Seeman then brought suit seeking rescission of the contract, return of the real estate, and restitution. Restitution was sought for the rental value for the five months of lost use of the property and the seller's out-of-pocket expenses made in reliance upon the bargain. Gregg contends that under the election of remedies doctrine, the seller cannot both rescind the contract and recover damages for its breach. Is Gregg correct? Explain.

19. Watson agreed to buy Ingram's house for $355,000. The contract provided that Watson deposit $15,000 as earnest money and that "in the event of default by the Buyer, earnest money shall be forfeited to Seller as liquidated damages, unless Seller elects to seek actual damages or specific performance." Because Watson did not timely comply with all of the terms of the contract, nine months after the Watson sale was to occur, Ingram sold the house to a third party for $355,000. Is Ingram entitled to Watson's $15,000 earnest money as liquidated damages? Explain.

TAKING SIDES

Sanders agreed in writing to write, direct, and produce a motion picture on the subject of lithography (a method for printing using stone or metal) for the Tamarind Lithography Workshop. After the completion of this film, *Four Stones for Kanemitsu*, litigation arose concerning the parties' rights and obligations under their agreement. Tamarind and Sanders resolved this dispute by a written settlement agreement that provided for Tamarind to give Sanders a screen credit stating: "A Film by Terry Sanders." Tamarind did not comply with this agreement and failed to include the agreed-upon screen credit for Sanders. Sanders sued Tamarind seeking damages for breach of the settlement agreement and specific performance to compel Tamarind's compliance with its obligation to provide the screen credit.

a. What arguments would support Sander's claim for specific performance in addition to damages?

b. What arguments would support Tamarind's claim that Sanders was not entitled to specific performance in addition to damages?

c. Which side's arguments are most convincing? Explain.

Appendices

APPENDIX A

The Constitution of the United States of America

We the People of the United States, in Order to form a more perfect Union, establish Justice, insure domestic Tranquility, provide for the common defense, promote the general Welfare, and secure the Blessings of Liberty to ourselves and our Posterity, do ordain and establish this Constitution for the United States of America.

ARTICLE I

Section 1

All legislative Powers herein granted shall be vested in a Congress of the United States, which shall consist of a Senate and House of Representatives.

Section 2

The House of Representatives shall be composed of Members chosen every second Year by the People of the several States, and the Electors in each State shall have the Qualifications requisite for Electors of the most numerous Branch of the State Legislature.

No Person shall be a Representative who shall not have attained to the Age of twenty five Years, and been seven Years a Citizen of the United States, and who shall not, when elected, be an Inhabitant of that State in which he shall be chosen.

Representatives and direct Taxes shall be apportioned among the several States which may be included within this Union, according to their respective Numbers, which shall be determined by adding to the whole Number of free Persons, including those bound to Service for a Term of Years, and excluding Indians not taxed, three fifths of all other Persons. The actual Enumeration shall be made within three Years after the first Meeting of the Congress of the United States, and within every subsequent Term of ten Years, in such Manner as they shall by Law direct. The number of Representatives shall not exceed one for every thirty Thousand, but each State shall have at Least one Representative; and until such enumeration shall be made, the State of New Hampshire shall be entitled to chuse three, Massachusetts eight, Rhode Island and Providence Plantations one, Connecticut five, New-York six, New Jersey four, Pennsylvania eight, Delaware one, Maryland six, Virginia ten, North Carolina five, South Carolina five, and Georgia three. When vacancies happen in the Representation from any State, the Executive Authority thereof shall issue Writs of Election to fill such vacancies.

The House of Representatives shall chuse their Speaker and other Officers; and shall have the sole Power of Impeachment.

Section 3

The Senate of the United States shall be composed of two Senators from each State, chosen by the Legislature thereof, for six Years; and each Senator shall have one Vote.

Immediately after they shall be assembled in Consequence of the first Election, they shall be divided as equally as may be into three Classes. The Seats of the Senators of the first Class shall be vacated at the Expiration of the second Year, of the second Class at the Expiration of the fourth Year, and of the third Class at the Expiration of the sixth Year, so that one third may be chosen every second Year; and if Vacancies happen by Resignation or otherwise, during the Recess of the Legislature of any State, the Executive thereof may make temporary Appointments until the next Meeting of the Legislature, which shall then fill such Vacancies.

No Person shall be a Senator who shall not have attained to the Age of thirty Years, and been nine Years a Citizen of the United States, and who shall not, when elected, be an Inhabitant of that State for which he shall be chosen.

The Vice President of the United States shall be President of the Senate, but shall have no Vote, unless they be equally divided.

The Senate shall chuse their other Officers, and also a President pro tempore, in the Absence of the Vice President, or when he shall exercise the Office of President of the United States.

The Senate shall have the sole power to try all Impeachments. When sitting for that Purpose, they shall be an Oath or Affirmation. When the President of the United States is tried, the Chief Justice shall preside: And no Person shall be convicted without the Concurrence of two thirds of the Members present.

Judgment in Cases of Impeachment shall not extend further than to removal from Office, and disqualification to hold and enjoy any Office of honor, Trust or Profit under the United States: but the Party convicted shall nevertheless be liable and subject to Indictment, Trial, Judgment and Punishment, according to Law.

Section 4

The Times, Places and Manner of holding Elections for Senators and Representatives, shall be prescribed in each State by the Legislature thereof: but the Congress may at any time by Law make or alter such Regulations, except as to the Places of chusing Senators.

The Congress shall assemble at least once in every Year, and such Meeting shall be on the first Monday in December, unless they shall by Law appoint a different Day.

Section 5

Each House shall be the Judge of the Elections, Returns and Qualifications of its own Members, and a Majority of each shall constitute a Quorum to do Business; but a smaller Number may adjourn from day to day, and may be authorized to compel the Attendance of absent Members, in such Manner, and under such Penalties as each House may provide.

Each House may determine the Rules of its Proceedings, punish its Members for disorderly Behaviour, and, with the Concurrence of two thirds, expel a Member.

Each House shall keep a Journal of its Proceedings, and from time to time publish the same, excepting such Parts as may in their Judgment require Secrecy; and the Yeas and Nays of the Members of either House on any question shall, at the Desire of one fifth of those Present, be entered on the Journal.

Neither House, during the Session of Congress, shall, without the Consent of the other, adjourn for more than three days, nor to any other Place than that in which the two Houses shall be sitting.

Section 6

The Senators and Representatives shall receive a Compensation for their Services, to be ascertained by Law, and paid out of the Treasury of the United States. They shall in all Cases, except Treason, Felony and Breach of the Peace, be privileged from Arrest and Breach of the Peace, be privileged from Arrest during their Attendance at the Session of their respective Houses, and in going to and returning from the same; and for any Speech or Debate in either House, they shall not be questioned in any other Place.

No Senator or Representative shall, during the Time for which he was elected, be appointed to any civil Office under the Authority of the United States, which shall have been created, or the Emoluments whereof shall have been encreased during such time; and no Person holding any Office under the United States, shall be a Member of either House during his Continuance in Office.

Section 7

All Bills for raising Revenue shall originate in the House of Representatives; but the Senate may propose or concur with Amendments as on other Bills.

Every Bill which shall have passed the House of Representatives and the Senate, shall, before it become a Law, be presented to the President of the United States; If he approve he shall sign it, but if not he shall return it, with his Objections to that House in which it shall have originated, who shall enter the Objections at large on their Journal, and proceed to reconsider it. If after such Reconsideration two thirds of that House shall agree to pass the Bill, it shall be sent, together with the Objections, to the other House, by which it shall likewise be reconsidered, and if approved by two thirds of that House, it shall become a Law. But in all such Cases the Votes of both Houses shall be determined by Yeas and Nays, and the Names of the Persons voting for and against the Bill shall be entered on the Journal of each House respectively. If any Bill shall not be returned by the President within ten Days (Sundays excepted) after it shall have been presented to him, the Same shall be a Law, in like Manner as if he had signed it, unless the Congress by their Adjournment prevent its Return, in which Case it shall not be a Law.

Every Order, Resolution, or Vote to which the Concurrence of the Senate and House of Representatives may be necessary (except on a question of Adjournment) shall be presented to the President of the United States; and before the Same shall take Effect, shall be approved by him, or being disapproved by him, shall be repassed by two thirds of the Senate and House of Representatives, according to the Rules and Limitations prescribed in the Case of a Bill.

Section 8

The Congress shall have Power to lay and collect Taxes, Duties, Imposts and Excises, to pay the Debts and provide for the common Defense and general Welfare of the United States; but all Duties, Imposts and Excises shall be uniform throughout the United States;

To borrow Money on the credit of the United States;

To regulate Commerce with foreign Nations, and among the several States, and with the Indian Tribes;

To establish an uniform Rule of Naturalization, and uniform Laws on the subject of Bankruptcies throughout the United States;

To coin Money, regulate the Value thereof, and of foreign Coin, and fix the Standard of Weights and Measures;

To provide for the Punishment of counterfeiting the Securities and current Coin of the United States;

To establish Post Offices and post Roads;

To promote the Progress of Science and useful Arts, by securing for limited Times to Authors and Inventors the exclusive Right to their respective Writings and Discoveries;

To constitute Tribunals inferior to the supreme Court;

To define and punish Piracies and Felonies committed on the high Seas, and Offenses against the Law of Nations;

To declare War, grant Letters of Marque and Reprisal, and make Rules concerning Captures on Land and Water;

To raise and support Armies, but no Appropriation of Money to that Use shall be for a longer Term than two Years;

To provide and maintain a Navy;

To make Rules for the Government and Regulation of the land and naval Forces;

To provide for calling forth the Militia to execute the Laws of the Union, suppress Insurrections and repel Invasions;

To provide for organizing, arming, and disciplining, the Militia, and for governing such Part of them as may be employed in the Service of the United States, reserving to the States respectively, the Appointment of the Officers, and the Authority of training the Militia according to the discipline described by Congress;

To exercise exclusive Legislation in all Cases whatsoever, over such District (not exceeding ten Miles square) as may, by Cession of particular States, and the Acceptance of Congress, become the Seat of the Government of the United States, and to exercise like Authority over all Places purchased by the Consent of the Legislature of the State in which the Same shall be, for the Erection of Forts, Magazines, Arsenals, dock-Yards, and other needful Buildings;—And

To make all Laws which shall be necessary and proper for carrying into Execution the foregoing Powers, and all other Powers vested by this Constitution in the Government of the United States, or in any Department or Officer thereof.

Section 9

The Migration or Importation of such Persons as any of the States now existing shall think proper to admit, shall not be prohibited by the Congress prior to the Year one thousand eight hundred and eight, but a Tax of Duty may be imposed on such Importation, not exceeding ten dollars for each Person.

The Privilege of the Writ of Habeas Corpus shall not be suspended, unless when in Cases of Rebellion or Invasion the public Safety may require it.

No Bill of Attainder or ex post facto Law shall be passed.

No Capitation, or other direct, Tax shall be laid, unless in Proportion to the Census or Enumeration herein before directed to be taken.

No Tax or Duty shall be laid on Articles exported from any State.

No Preference shall be given by any Regulation of Commerce or Revenue to the Ports of one State over those of another; nor shall Vessels bound to, or from, one State, be obliged to enter, clear, or pay Duties in another.

No Money shall be drawn from the Treasury, but in Consequence of Appropriations made by Laws; and a regular Statement and Account of the Receipts and Expenditures of all public Money shall be published from time to time.

No Title of Nobility shall be granted by the United States: And no Person holding any Office of Profit or Trust under them, shall, without the Consent of the Congress, accept of any present, Emolument, Office, or Title, of any kind whatever, from any King, Prince, or foreign State.

Section 10

No State shall enter into any Treaty, Alliance, or Confederation; grant Letters of Marque and Reprisal; coin Money; emit Bills of Credit; make any Thing but gold and silver Coin a Tender in Payment of Debts; pass any Bill of Attainder, ex post facto Law, or Law impairing the Obligation of Contracts, or grant any Title of Nobility.

No State shall, without the Consent of the Congress, lay any Imposts or Duties on Imports or Exports, except what may be absolutely necessary for executing its inspection Laws: and the net Produce of all Duties and Imposts, laid by any State on Imports or Exports, shall be for the Use of the Treasury of the United States; and all such Laws shall be subject to the Revision and Controul of the Congress.

No State shall, without the Consent of Congress, lay any Duty of Tonnage, keep Troops, or Ships of War in time of Peace, enter into any Agreement or Compact with another State, or with a foreign Power, or engage in War, unless actually invaded, or in such imminent Danger as will not admit of delay.

ARTICLE II
Section 1

The executive Power shall be vested in a President of the United States of America. He shall hold his Office during the Term of four Years, and, together with the Vice President, chosen for the same Term, be elected, as follows:

Each State shall appoint, in such Manner as the Legislature thereof may direct, a Number of Electors, equal to the whole Number of Senators and Representatives to which the State may be entitled in the Congress: but no Senator or Representative, or Person holding an Office of Trust or Profit under the United States, shall be appointed an Elector.

The Electors shall meet in their respective States, and vote by Ballot for two Persons, of whom one at least shall not be an Inhabitant of the same State with themselves. And they shall make a list of all the Persons voted for, and of the Number of Votes for each; which List they shall sign and certify, and transmit sealed to the Seat of the Government of the United States, directed to the President of the Senate. The President of the Senate shall, in the presence of the Senate and House of Representatives, open all the Certificates, and the Votes shall be counted. The Person having the greatest Number of Votes shall be the President, if such Number be a Majority of the whole Number of Electors appointed; and if there be more than one who have such Majority, and have an equal Number of Votes, then the House of Representatives shall immediately chuse by Ballot one of them for President; and if no Person have a Majority, then from the five highest on the List the said House shall in like Manner chuse the President. But in chusing the President, the Votes shall be taken by States, the Representation from each State having one Vote; A quorum for this Purpose shall consist of a Member or Members from two thirds of the States, and a Majority of all the States shall be necessary to a Choice. In every Case, after the Choice of the President, the Person having the Greatest Number of Votes of the Electors shall be the Vice President. But if there should remain two or more who have equal Votes, the Senate shall chuse from them by Ballot the Vice President.

The Congress may determine the Time of Chusing the Electors, and the Day on which they shall give their Votes; which Day shall be the same throughout the United States.

No Person except a natural born Citizen, or a Citizen of the United States, at the time of the Adoption of this Constitution, shall be eligible to the Office of President; neither shall any Person be eligible to that Office who shall not have attained to the Age of thirty five Years, and been fourteen Years a Resident within the United States.

In Case of the Removal of the President from Office, or of his Death, Resignation, or Inability to discharge the Powers and Duties of the said Office, the Same shall devolve on the Vice President, and the Congress may by Law provide for the Case of Removal, Death, Resignation or Inability, both of the President and Vice President, declaring what Officer shall then act as President, and such Officer shall act accordingly, until the Disability be removed, or a President shall be elected.

The President shall, at stated Times, receive for his Services, a Compensation, which shall neither be encreased nor diminished during the Period for which he shall have been elected, and he shall not receive within that Period any other Emolument from the United States, or any of them.

Before he enter on the Execution of his Office, he shall take the following Oath or Affirmation:—"I do solemnly swear (or affirm) that I will faithfully execute the Office of President of the United States, and will to the best of my Ability, preserve, protect and defend the Constitution of the United States."

Section 2

The President shall be Commander in Chief of the Army and Navy of the United States, and of the Militia of the several States, when called into the actual Service of the United States; he may require the Opinion, in writing, of the principal Officer in each of the executive Departments, upon any Subject relating to the Duties of their respective Offices, and he shall have Power to grant Reprieves and Pardons for Offences against the United States, except in Cases of Impeachment.

He shall have Power, by and with the Advice and Consent of the Senate, to make Treaties, providing two thirds of the Senators present concur; and he shall nominate, and by and with the Advice and Consent of the Senate, shall appoint Ambassadors, other public Ministers and Consuls, Judges of the supreme Court, and all other Officers of the United States, whose Appointments are not herein otherwise provided for, and which shall be established by Law: but the Congress may by Law vest the Appointment of such inferior Officers, as they think proper, in the President alone, in the Courts of Law, or in the Heads of Departments.

The President shall have Power to fill up all Vacancies that may happen during the Recess of the Senate, by granting Commissions which shall expire at the End of their next Session.

Section 3

He shall from time to time give to the Congress Information of the State of the Union, and recommend to their Consideration such Measures as he shall judge necessary and expedient; he may, on extraordinary Occasions, convene both Houses, or either of them, and in Case of Disagreement between them, with Respect to the Time of Adjournment, he may adjourn them to such Time as he shall think proper, he shall receive Ambassadors and other public Ministers; he shall take Care that the Laws be faithfully executed, and shall Commission all the Offices of the United States.

Section 4

The President, Vice President and all civil Officers of the United States, shall be removed from Office on Impeachment for, and Conviction of, Treason, Bribery, or other high Crimes and Misdemeanors.

ARTICLE III
Section 1

The judicial Power of the United States, shall be vested in one supreme Court, and in such inferior Courts as the Congress may from time to time ordain and establish. The Judges, both of the supreme and inferior Courts, shall hold their Offices during good Behaviour, and shall, at Times, receive for their Services, a Compensation, which shall not be diminished during their Continuance in Office.

Section 2

The judicial Power shall extend to all Cases, in Law and Equity, arising under this Constitution, the Laws of the United States, and Treaties made, or which shall be made, under their Authority;—to all Cases affecting Ambassadors, other public Ministers and Consuls;—to all Cases of admiralty and maritime Jurisdiction;—to Controversies to which the United States shall be a Party;—to controversies between two or more States;—between a State and Citizens of another State;— between Citizens of different States;—between Citizens of the same State claiming Lands under Grants of different States; and between a State, or the Citizens thereof, and foreign States, Citizens or Subjects.

In all Cases affecting Ambassadors, other public Ministers and Consuls, and those in which a State shall be Party, the supreme Court shall have original Jurisdiction. In all the other Cases before mentioned, the supreme Court shall have appellate Jurisdiction, both as to Law and Fact, with such Exceptions, and under such Regulations as the Congress shall make.

The Trial of all Crimes, except in Cases of Impeachment, shall be by Jury; and such Trial shall be held in the State where the said Crimes shall have been committed; but when not committed within any State, the Trial shall be at such Place or Places as the Congress may by Law have directed.

Section 3

Treason against the United States, shall consist only in levying War against them, or in adhering to their Enemies, giving them Aid and Comfort. No Person shall be convicted of Treason unless on the Testimony of two Witnesses to the same overt Act, or on Confession in open Court.

The Congress shall have Power to declare the Punishment of Treason, but no Attainder of Treason shall work Corruption of Blood, or Forfeiture except during the Life of the Person attainted.

ARTICLE IV
Section 1

Full Faith and Credit shall be given in each State to the public Acts, Records, and judicial Proceedings of every other State. And the Congress may by general Laws prescribe the Manner in which such Arts, Records and Proceedings shall be proved, and the Effect thereof.

Section 2

The Citizens of each State shall be entitled to all Privileges and Immunities of Citizens in the several States.

A Person charged in any State with Treason, Felony, or other Crime, who shall flee from Justice, and be found in another State, shall on Demand of the executive Authority of the State from which he fled, be delivered up, to be removed to the State having Jurisdiction of the Crime.

No Person held to Service or Labour in one State, under the Laws thereof, escaping into another, shall, in Consequence of any Law or Regulation therein, be discharged from such Service or Labour, but shall be delivered up on Claim of the Party to whom such Service or Labour may be due.

Section 3
New States may be admitted by the Congress into this Union; but no new State shall be formed or erected within the Jurisdiction of any other State; nor any State be formed by the Junction of two or more States, or Parts of States, without the Consent of the Legislatures of the States concerned as well as the Congress.

The Congress shall have Power to dispose of and make all needful Rules and Regulations respecting the Territory or other Property belonging to the United States; and nothing in this Constitution shall be so construed as to Prejudice any Claims of the United States, or of any particular State.

Section 4
The United States shall guarantee to every State in this Union a Republican Form of Government, and shall protect each of them against Invasion; and on Application of the Legislature, or of the Executive (when the Legislature cannot be convened) against domestic Violence.

ARTICLE V
The Congress, whenever two thirds of both Houses shall deem it necessary, shall propose Amendments to this Constitution, or, on the Application of the Legislatures of two thirds of the several States, shall call a Convention for proposing Amendments, which, in either Case, shall be valid to all Intents and Purposes, as Part of this Constitution, when ratified by the Legislatures of three fourths of the several States, or by Conventions in three fourths thereof, as the one or the other Mode of Ratification may be proposed by the Congress; Provided that no Amendment which may be made prior to the Year One thousand eight hundred and eight shall in any Manner affect the first and fourth Clauses in the Ninth Section of the first Article; and that no State, without its Consent, shall be deprived of its equal Suffrage in the Senate.

ARTICLE VI
All Debts contracted and Engagements entered into, before the Adoption of this Constitution, shall be as valid against the United States under this Constitution, as under the Confederation.

This Constitution, and the Laws of the United States which shall be made in Pursuance thereof; and all Treaties made, or which shall be made, under the Authority of the United States, shall be the supreme Law of the Land; and the Judges in every State shall be bound thereby, any Thing in the Constitution or Laws of any State to the Contrary notwithstanding.

The Senators and Representatives before mentioned, and the Members of the several State Legislatures, and all executive and judicial Officers, both of the United States and of the Several States, shall be bound by Oath or Affirmation, to support this Constitution; but no religious Test shall ever be required as a Qualification to any Office or public Trust under the United States.

ARTICLE VII
The Ratification of the Conventions of nine States, shall be sufficient for the Establishment of this Constitution between the States so ratifying the Same.

Amendment I [1791]
Congress shall make no law respecting an establishment of religion, or prohibiting the free exercise thereof; or abridging the freedom of speech, or the press; or the right of the people peaceably to assemble, and to petition the Government for a redress of grievances.

Amendment II [1791]
A well regulated Militia, being necessary to the security for a free State, the right of the people to keep and bear Arms, shall not be infringed.

Amendment III [1791]
No Soldier shall, in time of peace be quartered in any house, without the consent of the Owner, nor in time of war, but in a manner to be prescribed by law.

Amendment IV [1791]
The right of the people to be secure in their persons, houses, papers, and effects, against unreasonable searches and seizures, shall not be violated, and no Warrants shall issue, but upon probable cause, supported by Oath or Affirmation, and particularly describing the place to be searched, and the persons or things to be seized.

Amendment V [1791]
No person shall be held to answer for a capital, or otherwise infamous crime, unless on a presentment or indictment of a Grand Jury, except in cases arising in the land or naval forces, or in the Militia, when in actual service in time of War or public danger; nor shall any person be subject for the same offense to be twice put in jeopardy of life or limb; nor shall be compelled in any criminal case to be a witness against himself, nor be deprived of life, liberty, or property, without due process of law; nor shall private property be taken for public use, without just compensation.

Amendment VI [1791]
In all criminal prosecutions, the accused shall enjoy the right to a speedy and public trial, by an impartial jury of the State and district wherein the crime shall have been committed, which district shall have been previously ascertained by law, and to be informed of the nature and cause of the accusation; to be confronted with the Witnesses against him; to have compulsory process for obtaining witnesses in his favor, and to have the Assistance of counsel for his defense.

Amendment VII [1791]
In suits at common law, where the value in controversy shall exceed twenty dollars, the right of trial by jury shall be preserved, and no fact tried by a jury, shall be otherwise re-examined in any Court of the United States, than according to the rules of the common law.

Amendment VIII [1791]
Excessive bail shall not be required, no excessive fines imposed, nor cruel and unusual punishments inflicted.

Amendment IX [1791]
The enumeration in the Constitution, of certain rights, shall not be construed to deny or disparage others retained by the people.

Amendment X [1791]
The powers not delegated to the United States by the Constitution, nor prohibited by it to the States, are reserved to the States respectively, or to the people.

Amendment XI [1798]
The judicial power of the United States shall not be construed to extend to any suit in law or equity, commenced or prosecuted against one of the United States by Citizens of another State, or by Citizens or Subjects of any Foreign State.

Amendment XII [1804]
The Electors shall meet in their respective states and vote by ballot for President and Vice-President, one of whom, at least, shall not be an inhabitant of the same state with themselves; they shall name in their ballots the person voted for as President, and in distinct ballots the person voted for as Vice-President, and they shall make distinct lists of all persons voted for as President, and of all persons voted for as Vice-President, and of the number of votes for each, which lists they shall sign and certify, and transmit sealed to the seat of the government of the United States, directed to the President of the Senate;—The President of the Senate shall, in the presence of the Senate and House of Representatives, open all the certificates and the votes shall then be counted;—The person having the greatest number of votes for President, shall be the President, if such a number be a majority of the whole number of Electors appointed; and if no person have such majority, then from the persons having the highest numbers not exceeding three on the list of those voted for as President, the House of Representatives shall

choose immediately, by ballot, the President. But in choosing the President, the votes shall be taken by states, the representation from each state having one vote; a quorum for this purpose shall consist of a member or members from two-thirds of the states, and a majority of all the states shall be necessary to a choice. And if the House of Representatives shall not choose a President whenever the right of choice shall devolve upon them, before the fourth day of March next following, then the Vice-President shall act as President, as in the case of the death or other constitutional disability of the President. The person having the greatest number of votes as Vice-President, shall be the Vice-President, if such number be a majority of the whole number of Electors appointed, and if no person have a majority, then from the two highest numbers on the list, the Senate shall choose the Vice-President; a quorum for the purpose shall consist of two-thirds of the whole number of Senators, and a majority of the whole number shall be necessary to a choice. But no person constitutionally ineligible to the office of President shall be eligible to that of the Vice-President of the United States.

Amendment XIII [1865]
Section 1
Neither slavery nor involuntary servitude, except as a punishment for crime whereof the party shall have been duly convicted, shall exist within the United States, or any place subject to their jurisdiction.

Section 2
Congress shall have power to enforce this article by appropriate legislation.

Amendment XIV [1868]
Section 1
All persons born or naturalized in the United States, and subject to the jurisdiction thereof, are citizens of the United States and of the State wherein they reside. No State shall make or enforce any law which shall abridge the privileges or immunities of citizens of the United States; nor shall any State deprive any person of life, liberty, or property, without due process of law; nor deny to any person within its jurisdiction the equal protection of the laws.

Section 2
Representatives shall be appointed among the several States according to their respective numbers, counting the whole number of persons in each State, excluding Indians not taxed. But when the right to vote at any election for the choice of electors for President and Vice President of the United States, Representatives in Congress, the Executive and Judicial officers of a State, or the members of the Legislature thereof, is denied to any of the male inhabitants of such State, being twenty-one years of age, and citizens of the United States, or in any way abridged, except for participation in rebellion, or other crime, the basis of representation therein shall be reduced in the proportion which the number of such male citizens shall bear the whole number of male citizens twenty-one years of age in such State.

Section 3
No person shall be a Senator or Representative in Congress, or elector of President and Vice President, or hold any office, civil or military, under the United States, or under any State, who, having previously taken an oath, as a member of Congress, or as an officer of the United States, or as a member of any State legislature, or as an executive or judicial officer of any State, to support the Constitution of the United States, shall have engaged in insurrection or rebellion against the same, or given aid or comfort to the enemies thereof. But Congress may by a vote of two-thirds of each House, remove such disability.

Section 4
The validity of the public debt of the United States, authorized by law, including debts incurred for payment of pensions and bounties for services in suppressing insurrection or rebellion, shall not be questioned. But neither the United States nor any State shall assume or pay any debt or obligation incurred in aid of insurrection of rebellion against the United States, or any claim for the loss or emancipation of any slave; but all such debts, obligations and claims shall be held illegal and void.

Section 5
The Congress shall have power to enforce, by appropriate legislation, the provisions of this article.

Amendment XV [1870]
Section 1
The right of citizens of the United States to vote shall not be denied or abridged by the United States or by any State on account of race, color, or previous condition of servitude.

Section 2
The Congress shall have power to enforce this article by appropriate legislation.

Amendment XVI [1913]
The Congress shall have power to lay and collect taxes on incomes, from whatever source derived, without apportionment among the several States, and without regard to any census or enumeration.

Amendment XVII [1913]
The Senate of the United States shall be composed of two Senators from each State, elected by the people thereof, for six years; and each Senator shall have one vote. The electors in each State shall have the qualifications requisite for electors of the most numerous branch of the State legislatures.

When vacancies happen in the representation of any State in the Senate, the executive authority of each State shall issue writs of election to fill such vacancies; Provided, That the legislature of any State may empower the executive thereof to make temporary appointments until the people fill the vacancies by election as the legislature may direct.

This amendment shall not be construed as to affect the election or term of any Senator chosen before it becomes valid as part of the Constitution.

Amendment XVIII [1919]
Section 1
After one year from the ratification of this article the manufacture, sale, or transportation of intoxicating liquors within, the importation thereof into, or the exportation thereof from the United States and all territory subject to the jurisdiction thereof for beverage purposes is hereby prohibited.

Section 2
The Congress and the several States shall have concurrent power to enforce this article by appropriate legislation.

Section 3
This article shall be inoperative unless it shall have been ratified as an amendment to the Constitution by the legislatures of the several States, as provided in the Constitution, within seven years from the date of the submission hereof to the States by the Congress.

Amendment XIX [1920]
The right of citizens of the United States to vote shall not be denied or abridged by the United States or by any State on account of sex.

Congress shall have power to enforce this article by appropriate legislation.

Amendment XX [1933]
Section 1
The terms of the President and Vice President shall end at noon on the 20th day of January, and the terms of Senators and Representatives at noon on the 3d day of January, of the years in which such terms would have ended if this article had not been ratified; and the terms of their successors shall then begin.

Section 2
The Congress shall assemble at least once in every year, and such meeting shall begin at noon on the 3d day of January, unless they shall by law appoint a different day.

Section 3

If, at the time fixed for the beginning of the term of the President, the President elect shall have died, the Vice President elect shall become President. If a President shall not have been chosen before the time fixed for the beginning of his term, or if the President elect shall have failed to qualify, then the Vice President elect shall act as President until a President shall have qualified; and the Congress may by law provide for the case wherein neither a President elect nor a Vice President elect shall have qualified, declaring who shall then act as President, or the manner in which one who is to act shall be selected, and such person shall act accordingly until a President or Vice President shall have qualified.

Section 4

The Congress may by law provide for the case of the death of any of the persons from whom the House of Representatives may choose a President whenever the right of choice shall have devolved upon them, and for the case of the death of any of the persons from whom the Senate may choose a Vice President whenever the right of choice shall have devolved upon them.

Section 5

Sections 1 and 2 shall take effect on the 15th day of October following the ratification of this article.

Section 6

This article shall be inoperative unless it shall have been ratified as an amendment to the Constitution by the legislatures of three-fourths of the several States within seven years from the date of its submission.

Amendment XXI [1933]
Section 1

The eighteenth article of amendment to the Constitution of the United States is hereby repealed.

Section 2

The transportation or importation into any State, Territory, or possession of the United States for delivery or use therein of intoxicating liquors, in violation of the laws thereof, is hereby prohibited.

Section 3

This article shall be inoperative unless it shall have been ratified as an amendment to the Constitution by conventions in the several States, as provided in the Constitution, within seven years from the date of the submission hereof to the States by the Congress.

Amendment XXII [1951]
Section 1

No person shall be elected to the office of the President more than twice, and no person who has held the office of President, or acted as President, for more than two years of a term to which some other person was elected President shall be elected to the office of the President more than once. But this Article shall not apply to any person holding the office of President when this Article was proposed by the Congress, and shall not prevent any person who may be holding the office of President, or acting as President, during the term within which this Article becomes operative from holding the office of President, or acting as President during the remainder of such term.

Section 2

This article shall be inoperative unless it shall have been ratified as an amendment to the Constitution by the legislatures of three-fourths of the several States within seven years from the date of its submission to the States by the Congress.

Amendment XXIII [1961]
Section 1

The District constituting the seat of Government of the United States shall appoint in such manner as the Congress may direct:

A number of electors of President and Vice President equal to the whole number of Senators and Representatives in Congress to which the District would be entitled if it were a State, but in no event more than the least populous State; they shall be in addition to those appointed by the States, but they shall be considered, for the purposes of the election of President and Vice President, to be electors appointed by a State; and they shall meet in the District and perform such duties as provided by the twelfth article of amendment.

Section 2

The Congress shall have power to enforce this article by appropriate legislation.

Amendment XXIV [1964]
Section 1

The right of citizens of the United States to vote in any primary or other election for President or Vice President, for electors for President or Vice President or for Senator or Representative in Congress, shall not be denied or abridged by the United States or any State by reason of failure to pay any poll tax or other tax.

Section 2

The Congress shall have power to enforce this article by appropriate legislation.

Amendment XXV [1967]
Section 1

In case of the removal of the President from office or of his death or resignation, the Vice President shall become President.

Section 2

Whenever there is a vacancy in the office of the Vice President, the President shall nominate a Vice President who shall take office upon confirmation by a majority vote of both Houses of Congress.

Section 3

Whenever the President transmits to the President pro tempore of the Senate and the Speaker of the House of Representatives his written declaration that he is unable to discharge the powers and duties of his office, and until he transmits to them a written declaration to the contrary, such powers and duties shall be discharged by the Vice President as Acting President.

Section 4

Whenever the Vice President and a majority of either the principal officers of the executive departments or of such other body as Congress may by law provide, transmit to the President pro tempore of the Senate and the Speaker of the House of Representatives their written declaration that the President is unable to discharge the powers and duties of his office, the Vice President shall immediately assume the powers and duties of the office as Acting President.

Thereafter, when the President transmits to the President pro tempore of the Senate and the Speaker of the House of Representatives his written declaration that no inability exists, he shall resume the powers and duties of his office unless the Vice President and a majority of either the principal officers of the executive department or of such other body as Congress may by law provide, transmit within four days to the President pro tempore of the Senate and the Speaker of the House of Representatives their written declaration that the President is unable to discharge the powers and duties of his office. Thereupon Congress shall decide the issue, assembling within forty-eight hours for that purpose if not in session. If the Congress, within twenty-one days after receipt of the latter written declaration, or, if Congress is not in session, within twenty-one days after Congress is required to assemble, determines by two-thirds vote of both Houses that the President is unable to discharge the powers and duties of his office, the Vice President shall continue to discharge the same as Acting President; otherwise, the President shall resume the powers and duties of his office.

Amendment XXVI [1971]
Section 1
The right of citizens of the United States, who are eighteen years of age or older, to vote shall not be denied or abridged by the United States or by any State on account of age.

Section 2
The Congress shall have power to enforce this article by appropriate legislation.

Amendment XXVII [1992]
No law, varying the compensation for the services of the Senators and Representatives, shall take effect, until an election of Representatives shall have intervened.

APPENDIX B
Uniform Commercial Code (Selected Provisions)

The Code consists of the following Articles:

1. General Provisions
2. Sales
2A. Leases
3. Commercial Paper
4. Bank Deposits and Collections
4A. Funds Transfers
5. Letters of Credit
6. Bulk Transfers
7. Warehouse Receipts, Bills of Lading and Other Documents of Title
8. Investment Securities
9. Secured Transactions: Sales of Accounts, Contract Rights and Chattel Paper
10. Effective Date and Repealer
11. Effective Date and Transition Provisions

REVISED ARTICLE 1: GENERAL PROVISIONS
Part 1—General Provisions
§1-101. Short Titles.
(a) This [Act] may be cited as the Uniform Commercial Code.

(b) This article may be cited as Uniform Commercial Code—General Provisions.

§1-102. Scope of Article.
This article applies to a transaction to the extent that it is governed by another article of [the Uniform Commercial Code].

§1-103. Construction of [Uniform Commercial Code] to Promote Its Purposes and Policies; Applicability of Supplemental Principles of Law.
(a) [The Uniform Commercial Code] must be liberally construed and applied to promote its underlying purposes and policies, which are:

(1) to simplify, clarify, and modernize the law governing commercial transactions;

(2) to permit the continued expansion of commercial practices through custom, usage, and agreement of the parties; and

(3) to make uniform the law among the various jurisdictions.

(b) Unless displaced by the particular provisions of [the Uniform Commercial Code], the principles of law and equity, including the law merchant and the law relative to capacity to contract, principal and agent, estoppel, fraud, misrepresentation, duress, coercion, mistake, bankruptcy, and other validating or invalidating cause supplement its provisions.

§1-104. Construction Against Implied Repeal.
[The Uniform Commercial Code] being a general act intended as a unified coverage of its subject matter, no part of it shall be deemed to be impliedly repealed by subsequent legislation if such construction can reasonably be avoided.

§1-105. Severability.
If any provision or clause of [the Uniform Commercial Code] or its application to any person or circumstance is held invalid, the invalidity does not affect other provisions or applications of [the Uniform Commercial Code] which can be given effect without the invalid provision or application, and to this end the provisions of [the Uniform Commercial Code] are severable.

§1-106. Use of Singular and Plural; Gender.
In [the Uniform Commercial Code], unless the statutory context otherwise requires:

(1) words in the singular number include the plural, and those in the plural include the singular; and

(2) words of any gender also refer to any other gender.

§1-107. Section Captions.
Section captions are part of [the Uniform Commercial Code].

§1-108. Relation to Electronic Signatures in Global and National Commerce Act.
This article modifies, limits, and supersedes the federal Electronic Signatures in Global and National Commerce Act, 15 U.S.C. Section 7001 et seq., except that nothing in this article modifies, limits, or supersedes Section 7001(c) of that Act or authorizes electronic delivery of any of the notices described in Section 7003(b) of that Act.

Part 2—General Definitions and Principles of Interpretation
§1-201. General Definitions.
(a) Unless the context otherwise requires, words or phrases defined in this section, or in the additional definitions contained in other articles of [the Uniform Commercial Code] that apply to particular articles or parts thereof, have the meanings stated.

(b) Subject to definitions contained in other articles of [the Uniform Commercial Code] that apply to particular articles or parts thereof:

(1) "Action", in the sense of a judicial proceeding, includes recoupment, counterclaim, set-off, suit in equity, and any other proceeding in which rights are determined.

(2) "Aggrieved party" means a party entitled to pursue a remedy.

(3) "Agreement", as distinguished from "contract", means the bargain of the parties in fact, as found in their language or inferred from other circumstances, including course of performance, course of dealing, or usage of trade as provided in Section 1-303.

(4) "Bank" means a person engaged in the business of banking and includes a savings bank, savings and loan association, credit union, and trust company.

(5) "Bearer" means a person in possession of a negotiable instrument, document of title, or certificated security that is payable to bearer or indorsed in blank.

(6) "Bill of lading" means a document evidencing the receipt of goods for shipment issued by a person engaged in the business of transporting or forwarding goods.

(7) "Branch" includes a separately incorporated foreign branch of a bank.

(8) "Burden of establishing" a fact means the burden of persuading the trier of fact that the existence of the fact is more probable than its nonexistence.

(9) "Buyer in ordinary course of business" means a person that buys goods in good faith, without knowledge that the sale violates the rights of another person in the goods, and in the ordinary course from a person, other than a pawnbroker, in the business of selling goods of that kind. A person buys goods in the ordinary course if the sale to the person comports with the usual or customary practices in the kind of business in which the seller is engaged or with the seller's own usual or customary practices. A person that sells oil, gas, or other minerals at the wellhead or minehead is a person in the business of selling goods of that kind. A buyer in ordinary course of business may buy for cash, by exchange of other property, or on secured or unsecured credit, and may acquire goods or documents of title under a preexisting contract for sale. Only a buyer that takes possession of the goods or has a right to recover the goods from the seller under Article 2 may be a buyer in ordinary course of business. "Buyer in ordinary course of business" does not include a person that acquires goods in a transfer in bulk or as security for or in total or partial satisfaction of a money debt.

(10) "Conspicuous", with reference to a term, means so written, displayed, or presented that a reasonable person against which it is to operate ought to have noticed it. Whether a term is "conspicuous" or not is a decision for the court. Conspicuous terms include the following:

    (A) a heading in capitals equal to or greater in size than the surrounding text, or in contrasting type, font, or color to the surrounding text of the same or lesser size; and

    (B) language in the body of a record or display in larger type than the surrounding text, or in contrasting type, font, or color to the surrounding text of the same size, or set off from surrounding text of the same size by symbols or other marks that call attention to the language.

(11) "Consumer" means an individual who enters into a transaction primarily for personal, family, or household purposes.

(12) "Contract", as distinguished from "agreement", means the total legal obligation that results from the parties' agreement as determined by [the Uniform Commercial Code] as supplemented by any other applicable laws.

(13) "Creditor" includes a general creditor, a secured creditor, a lien creditor, and any representative of creditors, including an assignee for the benefit of creditors, a trustee in bankruptcy, a receiver in equity, and an executor or administrator of an insolvent debtor's or assignor's estate.

(14) "Defendant" includes a person in the position of defendant in a counterclaim, cross-claim, or third-party claim.

(15) "Delivery", with respect to an instrument, document of title, or chattel paper, means voluntary transfer of possession.

(16) "Document of title" includes bill of lading, dock warrant, dock receipt, warehouse receipt or order for the delivery of goods, and also any other document which in the regular course of business or financing is treated as adequately evidencing that the person in possession of it is entitled to receive, hold, and dispose of the document and the goods it covers. To be a document of title, a document must purport to be issued by or addressed to a bailee and purport to cover goods in the bailee's possession which are either identified or are fungible portions of an identified mass.

(17) "Fault" means a default, breach, or wrongful act or omission.

(18) "Fungible goods" means:

    (A) goods of which any unit, by nature or usage of trade, is the equivalent of any other like unit; or

    (B) goods that by agreement are treated as equivalent.

(19) "Genuine" means free of forgery or counterfeiting.

(20) "Good faith," except as otherwise provided in Article 5, means honesty in fact and the observance of reasonable commercial standards of fair dealing.

(21) "Holder" means:

    (A) the person in possession of a negotiable instrument that is payable either to bearer or to an identified person that is the person in possession; or

    (B) the person in possession of a document of title if the goods are deliverable either to bearer or to the order of the person in possession.

(22) "Insolvency proceeding" includes an assignment for the benefit of creditors or other proceeding intended to liquidate or rehabilitate the estate of the person involved.

(23) "Insolvent" means:

    (A) having generally ceased to pay debts in the ordinary course of business other than as a result of bona fide dispute;

    (B) being unable to pay debts as they become due; or

    (C) being insolvent within the meaning of federal bankruptcy law.

(24) "Money" means a medium of exchange currently authorized or adopted by a domestic or foreign government. The term includes a monetary unit of account established by an intergovernmental organization or by agreement between two or more countries.

(25) "Organization" means a person other than an individual.

(26) "Party", as distinguished from "third party", means a person that has engaged in a transaction or made an agreement subject to [the Uniform Commercial Code].

(27) "Person" means an individual, corporation, business trust, estate, trust, partnership, limited liability company, association, joint venture, government, governmental subdivision, agency, or instrumentality, public corporation, or any other legal or commercial entity.

(28) "Present value" means the amount as of a date certain of one or more sums payable in the future, discounted to the date certain by use of either an interest rate specified by the parties if that rate is not manifestly unreasonable at the time the transaction is entered into or, if an interest rate is not so specified, a commercially reasonable rate that takes into account the facts and circumstances at the time the transaction is entered into.

(29) "Purchase" means taking by sale, lease, discount, negotiation, mortgage, pledge, lien, security interest, issue or reissue, gift, or any other voluntary transaction creating an interest in property.

(30) "Purchaser" means a person that takes by purchase.

(31) "Record" means information that is inscribed on a tangible medium or that is stored in an electronic or other medium and is retrievable in perceivable form.

(32) "Remedy" means any remedial right to which an aggrieved party is entitled with or without resort to a tribunal.

(33) "Representative" means a person empowered to act for another, including an agent, an officer of a corporation or association, and a trustee, executor, or administrator of an estate.

(34) "Right" includes remedy.

(35) "Security interest" means an interest in personal property or fixtures which secures payment or performance of an obligation. "Security interest" includes any interest of a consignor and a buyer of accounts, chattel paper, a payment intangible, or a promissory note in a transaction that is subject to Article 9. "Security interest" does not include the special property interest of a buyer of goods on identification of those goods to a contract for sale under Section 2-401, but a buyer may also acquire a "security interest" by complying with Article 9. Except as otherwise provided in Section 2-505, the right of a seller or lessor of goods under Article 2 or 2A to retain or acquire possession of the goods is not a "security interest", but a seller or lessor may also acquire a "security interest" by complying with Article 9. The retention or reservation of title by a seller of goods notwithstanding shipment or delivery to the buyer under Section 2-401 is limited in effect to a reservation of a "security interest." Whether a transaction in the form of a lease creates a "security interest" is determined pursuant to Section 1-203.

(36) "Send" in connection with a writing, record, or notice means:

    (A) to deposit in the mail or deliver for transmission by any other usual means of communication with postage or cost of transmission provided for and properly addressed and, in the case of an instrument, to an address specified thereon or otherwise agreed, or if there be none to any address reasonable under the circumstances; or

(B) in any other way to cause to be received any record or notice within the time it would have arrived if properly sent.

(37) "Signed" includes using any symbol executed or adopted with present intention to adopt or accept a writing.

(38) "State" means a State of the United States, the District of Columbia, Puerto Rico, the United States Virgin Islands, or any territory or insular possession subject to the jurisdiction of the United States.

(39) "Surety" includes a guarantor or other secondary obligor.

(40) "Term" means a portion of an agreement that relates to a particular matter.

(41) "Unauthorized signature" means a signature made without actual, implied, or apparent authority. The term includes a forgery.

(42) "Warehouse receipt" means a receipt issued by a person engaged in the business of storing goods for hire.

(43) "Writing" includes printing, typewriting, or any other intentional reduction to tangible form. "Written" has a corresponding meaning.

§1-202. Notice; Knowledge.

(a) Subject to subsection (f), a person has "notice" of a fact if the person:

(1) has actual knowledge of it;

(2) has received a notice or notification of it; or

(3) from all the facts and circumstances known to the person at the time in question, has reason to know that it exists.

(b) "Knowledge" means actual knowledge. "Knows" has a corresponding meaning.

(c) "Discover", "learn", or words of similar import refer to knowledge rather than to reason to know.

(d) A person "notifies" or "gives" a notice or notification to another person by taking such steps as may be reasonably required to inform the other person in ordinary course, whether or not the other person actually comes to know of it.

(e) Subject to subsection (f), a person "receives" a notice or notification when:

(1) it comes to that person's attention; or

(2) it is duly delivered in a form reasonable under the circumstances at the place of business through which the contract was made or at another location held out by that person as the place for receipt of such communications.

(f) Notice, knowledge, or a notice or notification received by an organization is effective for a particular transaction from the time it is brought to the attention of the individual conducting that transaction and, in any event, from the time it would have been brought to the individual's attention if the organization had exercised due diligence. An organization exercises due diligence if it maintains reasonable routines for communicating significant information to the person conducting the transaction and there is reasonable compliance with the routines. Due diligence does not require an individual acting for the organization to communicate information unless the communication is part of the individual's regular duties or the individual has reason to know of the transaction and that the transaction would be materially affected by the information.

§1-203. Lease Distinguished from Security Interest.

(a) Whether a transaction in the form of a lease creates a lease or security interest is determined by the facts of each case.

(b) A transaction in the form of a lease creates a security interest if the consideration that the lessee is to pay the lessor for the right to possession and use of the goods is an obligation for the term of the lease and is not subject to termination by the lessee, and:

(1) the original term of the lease is equal to or greater than the remaining economic life of the goods;

(2) the lessee is bound to renew the lease for the remaining economic life of the goods or is bound to become the owner of the goods;

(3) the lessee has an option to renew the lease for the remaining economic life of the goods for no additional consideration or for nominal additional consideration upon compliance with the lease agreement; or

(4) the lessee has an option to become the owner of the goods for no additional consideration or for nominal additional consideration upon compliance with the lease agreement.

(c) A transaction in the form of a lease does not create a security interest merely because:

(1) the present value of the consideration the lessee is obligated to pay the lessor for the right to possession and use of the goods is substantially equal to or is greater than the fair market value of the goods at the time the lease is entered into;

(2) the lessee assumes risk of loss of the goods;

(3) the lessee agrees to pay, with respect to the goods, taxes, insurance, filing, recording, or registration fees, or service or maintenance costs;

(4) the lessee has an option to renew the lease or to become the owner of the goods;

(5) the lessee has an option to renew the lease for a fixed rent that is equal to or greater than the reasonably predictable fair market rent for the use of the goods for the term of the renewal at the time the option is to be performed; or

(6) the lessee has an option to become the owner of the goods for a fixed price that is equal to or greater than the reasonably predictable fair market value of the goods at the time the option is to be performed.

(d) Additional consideration is nominal if it is less than the lessee's reasonably predictable cost of performing under the lease agreement if the option is not exercised. Additional consideration is not nominal if:

(1) when the option to renew the lease is granted to the lessee, the rent is stated to be the fair market rent for the use of the goods for the term of the renewal determined at the time the option is to be performed; or

(2) when the option to become the owner of the goods is granted to the lessee, the price is stated to be the fair market value of the goods determined at the time the option is to be performed.

(e) The "remaining economic life of the goods" and "reasonably predictable" fair market rent, fair market value, or cost of performing under the lease agreement must be determined with reference to the facts and circumstances at the time the transaction is entered into.

§1-204. Value.

Except as otherwise provided in Articles 3, 4, [and] 5, [and 6], a person gives value for rights if the person acquires them:

(1) in return for a binding commitment to extend credit or for the extension of immediately available credit, whether or not drawn upon and whether or not a charge-back is provided for in the event of difficulties in collection;

(2) as security for, or in total or partial satisfaction of, a preexisting claim;

(3) by accepting delivery under a preexisting contract for purchase; or

(4) in return for any consideration sufficient to support a simple contract.

§1-205. Reasonable Time; Seasonableness.

(a) Whether a time for taking an action required by [the Uniform Commercial Code] is reasonable depends on the nature, purpose, and circumstances of the action.

(b) An action is taken seasonably if it is taken at or within the time agreed or, if no time is agreed, at or within a reasonable time.

§1-206. Presumptions.

Whenever [the Uniform Commercial Code] creates a "presumption" with respect to a fact, or provides that a fact is "presumed," the trier of fact must find the existence of the fact unless and until evidence is introduced that supports a finding of its nonexistence.

Part 3—Territorial Applicability and General Rules
§1-301. Territorial Applicability; Parties' Power to Choose Applicable Law.

(a) In this section:

(1) "Domestic transaction" means a transaction other than an international transaction.

(2) "International transaction" means a transaction that bears a reasonable relation to a country other than the United States.

(b) This section applies to a transaction to the extent that it is governed by another article of the [Uniform Commercial Code].

(c) Except as otherwise provided in this section:

   (1) an agreement by parties to a domestic transaction that any or all of their rights and obligations are to be determined by the law of this State or of another State is effective, whether or not the transaction bears a relation to the State designated; and

   (2) an agreement by parties to an international transaction that any or all of their rights and obligations are to be determined by the law of this State or of another State or country is effective, whether or not the transaction bears a relation to the State or country designated.

(d) In the absence of an agreement effective under subsection (c), and except as provided in subsections (e) and (g), the rights and obligations of the parties are determined by the law that would be selected by application of this State's conflict of laws principles.

(e) If one of the parties to a transaction is a consumer, the following rules apply:

   (1) An agreement referred to in subsection (c) is not effective unless the transaction bears a reasonable relation to the State or country designated.

   (2) Application of the law of the State or country determined pursuant to subsection (c) or (d) may not deprive the consumer of the protection of any rule of law governing a matter within the scope of this section, which both is protective of consumers and may not be varied by agreement:

      (A) of the State or country in which the consumer principally resides, unless subparagraph (B) applies; or

      (B) if the transaction is a sale of goods, of the State or country in which the consumer both makes the contract and takes delivery of those goods, if such State or country is not the State or country in which the consumer principally resides.

(f) An agreement otherwise effective under subsection (c) is not effective to the extent that application of the law of the State or country designated would be contrary to a fundamental policy of the State or country whose law would govern in the absence of agreement under subsection (d).

(g) To the extent that [the Uniform Commercial Code] governs a transaction, if one of the following provisions of [the Uniform Commercial Code] specifies the applicable law, that provision governs and a contrary agreement is effective only to the extent permitted by the law so specified:

   (1) Section 2-402;

   (2) Sections 2A-105 and 2A-106;

   (3) Section 4-102;

   (4) Section 4A-507;

   (5) Section 5-116;

   (6) Section 6-103;

   (7) Section 8-110;

   (8) Sections 9-301 through 9-307.

§1-302. Variation by Agreement.

(a) Except as otherwise provided in subsection (b) or elsewhere in [the Uniform Commercial Code], the effect of provisions of [the Uniform Commercial Code] may be varied by agreement.

(b) The obligations of good faith, diligence, reasonableness, and care prescribed by [the Uniform Commercial Code] may not be disclaimed by agreement. The parties, by agreement, may determine the standards by which the performance of those obligations is to be measured if those standards are not manifestly unreasonable. Whenever [the Uniform Commercial Code] requires an action to be taken within a reasonable time, a time that is not manifestly unreasonable may be fixed by agreement.

(c) The presence in certain provisions of [the Uniform Commercial Code] of the phrase "unless otherwise agreed", or words of similar import, does not imply that the effect of other provisions may not be varied by agreement under this section.

§1-303. Course of Performance, Course of Dealing, and Usage of Trade.

(a) A "course of performance" is a sequence of conduct between the parties to a particular transaction that exists if:

   (1) the agreement of the parties with respect to the transaction involves repeated occasions for performance by a party; and

   (2) the other party, with knowledge of the nature of the performance and opportunity for objection to it, accepts the performance or acquiesces in it without objection.

(b) A "course of dealing" is a sequence of conduct concerning previous transactions between the parties to a particular transaction that is fairly to be regarded as establishing a common basis of understanding for interpreting their expressions and other conduct.

(c) A "usage of trade" is any practice or method of dealing having such regularity of observance in a place, vocation, or trade as to justify an expectation that it will be observed with respect to the transaction in question. The existence and scope of such a usage must be proved as facts. If it is established that such a usage is embodied in a trade code or similar record, the interpretation of the record is a question of law.

(d) A course of performance or course of dealing between the parties or usage of trade in the vocation or trade in which they are engaged or of which they are or should be aware is relevant in ascertaining the meaning of the parties' agreement, may give particular meaning to specific terms of the agreement, and may supplement or qualify the terms of the agreement. A usage of trade applicable in the place in which part of the performance under the agreement is to occur may be so utilized as to that part of the performance.

(e) Except as otherwise provided in subsection (f), the express terms of an agreement and any applicable course of performance, course of dealing, or usage of trade must be construed whenever reasonable as consistent with each other. If such a construction is unreasonable:

   (1) express terms prevail over course of performance, course of dealing, and usage of trade;

   (2) course of performance prevails over course of dealing and usage of trade; and

   (3) course of dealing prevails over usage of trade.

(f) Subject to Section 2-209, a course of performance is relevant to show a waiver or modification of any term inconsistent with the course of performance.

(g) Evidence of a relevant usage of trade offered by one party is not admissible unless that party has given the other party notice that the court finds sufficient to prevent unfair surprise to the other party.

§1-304. Obligation of Good Faith.

Every contract or duty within [the Uniform Commercial Code] imposes an obligation of good faith in its performance and enforcement.

§1-305. Remedies to be Liberally Administered.

(a) The remedies provided by [the Uniform Commercial Code] must be liberally administered to the end that the aggrieved party may be put in as good a position as if the other party had fully performed but neither consequential or special damages nor penal damages may be had except as specifically provided in [the Uniform Commercial Code] or by other rule of law.

(b) Any right or obligation declared by [the Uniform Commercial Code] is enforceable by action unless the provision declaring it specifies a different and limited effect.

§1-306. Waiver or Renunciation of Claim or Right After Breach.

A claim or right arising out of an alleged breach may be discharged in whole or in part without consideration by agreement of the aggrieved party in an authenticated record.

§1-307. Prima Facie Evidence by Third-party Documents.

A document in due form purporting to be a bill of lading, policy or certificate of insurance, official weigher's or inspector's certificate, consular invoice, or any other document authorized or required by the contract to be issued by a third party is prima facie evidence of its own authenticity and genuineness and of the facts stated in the document by the third party.

§1-308. Performance or Acceptance Under Reservation of Rights.

(a) A party that with explicit reservation of rights performs or promises performance or assents to performance in a manner demanded or offered by the other party does not thereby prejudice the rights reserved. Such words as "without prejudice," "under protest," or the like are sufficient.

(b) Subsection (a) does not apply to an accord and satisfaction.

§1-309. Option to Accelerate at Will.
A term providing that one party or that party's successor in interest may accelerate payment or performance or require collateral or additional collateral "at will" or when the party "deems itself insecure," or words of similar import, means that the party has power to do so only if that party in good faith believes that the prospect of payment or performance is impaired. The burden of establishing lack of good faith is on the party against which the power has been exercised.

§1-310. Subordinated Obligations.
An obligation may be issued as subordinated to performance of another obligation of the person obligated, or a creditor may subordinate its right to performance of an obligation by agreement with either the person obligated or another creditor of the person obligated. Subordination does not create a security interest as against either the common debtor or a subordinated creditor.

ARTICLE 2: SALES
Part 1—Short Title, Construction and Subject Matter
§ 2–101. Short Title.
This Article shall be known and may be cited as Uniform Commercial Code—Sales.

§ 2–102. Scope; Certain Security and Other Transactions Excluded From This Article.
Unless the context otherwise requires, this Article applies to transactions in goods; it does not apply to any transaction which although in the form of an unconditional contract to sell or present sale is intended to operate only as a security transaction nor does this Article impair or repeal any statute regulating sales to consumers, farmers or other specified classes of buyers.

§ 2–103. Definitions and Index of Definitions.
(1) In this Article unless the context otherwise requires
  (a) "Buyer" means a person who buys or contracts to buy goods.
  (b) "Good faith" in the case of a merchant means honesty in fact and the observance of reasonable commercial standards of fair dealing in the trade.
  (c) "Receipt" of goods means taking physical possession of them.
  (d) "Seller" means a person who sells or contracts to sell goods.
(2) Other definitions applying to this Article or to specified Parts thereof, and the sections in which they appear are:
"Acceptance". Section 2–606.
"Banker's credit". Section 2–325.
"Between merchants". Section 2–104.
"Cancellation". Section 2–106(4).
"Commercial unit". Section 2–105.
"Confirmed credit". Section 2–325.
"Conforming to contract". Section 2–106.
"Contract for sale". Section 2–106.
"Cover". Section 2–712.
"Entrusting". Section 2–403.
"Financing agency". Section 2–104.
"Future goods". Section 2–105.
"Goods". Section 2–105.
"Identification". Section 2–501.
"Installment contract". Section 2–612.
"Letter of Credit". Section 2–325.
"Lot". Section 2–105.
"Merchant". Section 2–104.
"Overseas". Section 2–323.
"Person in position of seller". Section 2–707.
"Present sale". Section 2–106.
"Sale". Section 2–106.

"Sale on approval". Section 2–326.
"Sale or return". Section 2–326.
"Termination". Section 2–106.
(3) The following definitions in other Articles apply to this Article:
"Check". Section 3–104.
"Consignee". Section 7–102.
"Consignor". Section 7–102.
"Consumer goods". Section 9–109.
"Dishonor". Section 3–507. "Draft". Section 3–104.
(4) In addition Article 1 contains general definitions and principles of construction and interpretation applicable throughout this Article.

§ 2–104. Definitions: "Merchant"; "Between Merchants"; "Financing Agency".
(1) "Merchant" means a person who deals in goods of the kind or otherwise by his occupation holds himself out as having knowledge or skill peculiar to the practices or goods involved in the transaction or to whom such knowledge or skill may be attributed by his employment of an agent or broker or other intermediary who by his occupation holds himself out as having such knowledge or skill.
(2) "Financing agency" means a bank, finance company or other person who in the ordinary course of business makes advances against goods or documents of title or who by arrangement with either the seller or the buyer intervenes in ordinary course to make or collect payment due or claimed under the contract for sale, as by purchasing or paying the seller's draft or making advances against it or by merely taking it for collection whether or not documents of title accompany the draft. "Financing agency" includes also a bank or other person who similarly intervenes between persons who are in the position of seller and buyer in respect to the goods (Section 2–707).
(3) "Between merchants" means in any transaction with respect to which both parties are chargeable with the knowledge or skill of merchants.

§ 2–105. Definitions: Transferability; "Goods"; "Future" Goods; "Lot"; "Commercial Unit".
(1) "Goods" means all things (including specially manufactured goods) which are movable at the time of identification to the contract for sale other than the money in which the price is to be paid, investment securities (Article 8) and things in action. "Goods" also includes the unborn young of animals and growing crops and other identified things attached to realty as described in the section on goods to be severed from realty (Section 2–107).
(2) Goods must be both existing and identified before any interest in them can pass. Goods which are not both existing and identified are "future" goods. A purported present sale of future goods or of any interest therein operates as a contract to sell.
(3) There may be a sale of a part interest in existing identified goods.
(4) An undivided share in an identified bulk of fungible goods is sufficiently identified to be sold although the quantity of the bulk is not determined. Any agreed proportion of such a bulk or any quantity thereof agreed upon by number, weight or other measure may to the extent of the seller's interest in the bulk be sold to the buyer who then becomes an owner in common.
(5) "Lot" means a parcel or a single article which is the subject matter of a separate sale or delivery, whether or not it is sufficient to perform the contract.
(6) "Commercial unit" means such a unit of goods as by commercial usage is a single whole for purposes of sale and division of which materially impairs its character or value on the market or in use. A commercial unit may be a single article (as a machine) or a set of articles (as a suite of furniture or an assortment of sizes) or a quantity (as a bale, gross, or carload) or any other unit treated in use or in the relevant market as a single whole.

§ 2–106. Definitions: "Contract"; "Agreement"; "Contract for Sale"; "Sale"; "Present Sale"; "Conforming" to Contract; "Termination"; "Cancellation".
(1) In this Article unless the context otherwise requires "contract" and "agreement" are limited to those relating to the present or future sale of goods. "Contract for sale" includes both a present sale of goods and a

contract to sell goods at a future time. A "sale" consists in the passing of title from the seller to the buyer for a price (Section 2–401). A "present sale" means a sale which is accomplished by the making of the contract.

(2) Goods or conduct including any part of a performance are "conforming" or conform to the contract when they are in accordance with the obligations under the contract.

(3) "Termination" occurs when either party pursuant to a power created by agreement or law puts an end to the contract otherwise than for its breach. On "termination" all obligations which are still executory on both sides are discharged but any right based on prior breach or performance survives.

(4) "Cancellation" occurs when either party puts an end to the contract for breach by the other and its effect is the same as that of "termination" except that the cancelling party also retains any remedy for breach of the whole contract or any unperformed balance.

§ 2–107. Goods to Be Severed From Realty: Recording.
(1) A contract for the sale of minerals or the like (including oil and gas) or a structure or its materials to be removed from realty is a contract for the sale of goods within this Article if they are to be severed by the seller but until severance a purported present sale thereof which is not effective as a transfer of an interest in land is effective only as a contract to sell.

(2) A contract for the sale apart from the land of growing crops or other things attached to realty and capable of severance without material harm thereto but not described in subsection (1) or of timber to be cut is a contract for the sale of goods within this Article whether the subject matter is to be severed by the buyer or by the seller even though it forms part of the realty at the time of contracting, and the parties can by identification effect a present sale before severance.

(3) The provisions of this section are subject to any third party rights provided by the law relating to realty records, and the contract for sale may be executed and recorded as a document transferring an interest in land and shall then constitute notice to third parties of the buyer's rights under the contract for sale.

Part 2—Form, Formation and Readjustment of Contract
§ 2–201. Formal Requirements; Statute of Frauds.
(1) Except as otherwise provided in this section a contract for the sale of goods for the price of $500 or more is not enforceable by way of action or defense unless there is some writing sufficient to indicate that a contract for sale has been made between the parties and signed by the party against whom enforcement is sought or by his authorized agent or broker. A writing is not insufficient because it omits or incorrectly states a term agreed upon but the contract is not enforceable under this paragraph beyond the quantity of goods shown in such writing.

(2) Between merchants if within a reasonable time a writing in confirmation of the contract and sufficient against the sender is received and the party receiving it has reason to know its contents, it satisfies the requirements of subsection (1) against such party unless written notice of objection to its contents is given within ten days after it is received.

(3) A contract which does not satisfy the requirements of subsection (1) but which is valid in other respects is enforceable

(a) if the goods are to be specially manufactured for the buyer and are not suitable for sale to others in the ordinary course of the seller's business and the seller, before notice of repudiation is received and under circumstances which reasonably indicate that the goods are for the buyer, has made either a substantial beginning of their manufacture or commitments for their procurement; or

(b) if the party against whom enforcement is sought admits in his pleading, testimony or otherwise in court that a contract for sale was made, but the contract is not enforceable under this provision beyond the quantity of goods admitted; or

(c) with respect to goods for which payment has been made and accepted or which have been received and accepted (Sec. 2–606).

§ 2–202. Final Written Expression: Parol or Extrinsic Evidence.
Terms with respect to which the confirmatory memoranda of the parties agree or which are otherwise set forth in a writing intended by the parties as a final expression of their agreement with respect to such terms as are

included therein may not be contradicted by evidence of any prior agreement or of a contemporaneous oral agreement but may be explained or supplemented

(a) by course of dealing or usage of trade (Section 1–205) or by course of performance (Section 2–208); and

(b) by evidence of consistent additional terms unless the court finds the writing to have been intended also as a complete and exclusive statement of the terms of the agreement.

§ 2–203. Seals Inoperative.
The affixing of a seal to a writing evidencing a contract for sale or an offer to buy or sell goods does not constitute the writing a sealed instrument and the law with respect to sealed instruments does not apply to such a contract or offer.

§ 2–204. Formation in General.
(1) A contract for sale of goods may be made in any manner sufficient to show agreement, including conduct by both parties which recognizes the existence of such a contract.

(2) An agreement sufficient to constitute a contract for sale may be found even though the moment of its making is undetermined.

(3) Even though one or more terms are left open a contract for sale does not fail for indefiniteness if the parties have intended to make a contract and there is a reasonably certain basis for giving an appropriate remedy.

§ 2–205. Firm Offers.
An offer by a merchant to buy or sell goods in a signed writing which by its terms gives assurance that it will be held open is not revocable, for lack of consideration, during the time stated or if no time is stated for reasonable time, but in no event may such period of irrevocability exceed three months; but any such term of assurance on a form supplied by the offeree must be separately signed by the offeror.

§ 2–206. Offer and Acceptance in Formation of Contract.
(1) Unless other unambiguously indicated by the language or circumstances
(a) an offer to make a contract shall be construed as inviting acceptance in any manner and by any medium reasonable in the circumstances;

(b) an order or other offer to buy goods for prompt or current shipment shall be construed as inviting acceptance either by a prompt promise to ship or by the prompt or current shipment of conforming or non-conforming goods, but such a shipment of non-conforming goods does not constitute an acceptance if the seller seasonably notifies the buyer that the shipment is offered only as an accommodation to the buyer.

(2) Where the beginning of a requested performance is a reasonable mode of acceptance an offeror who is not notified of acceptance within a reasonable time may treat the offer as having lapsed before acceptance.

§ 2–207. Additional Terms in Acceptance or Confirmation.
(1) A definite and seasonable expression of acceptance or a written confirmation which is sent within a reasonable time operates as an acceptance even though it states terms additional to or different from those offered or agreed upon, unless acceptance is expressly made conditional on assent to the additional or different terms.

(2) The additional terms are to be construed as proposals for addition to the contract. Between merchants such terms become part of the contract unless:
(a) the offer expressly limits acceptance to the terms of the offer;

(b) they materially alter it; or

(c) notification of objection to them has already been given or is given within a reasonable time after notice of them is received.

(3) Conduct by both parties which recognizes the existence of a contract is sufficient to establish a contract for sale although the writings of the parties do not otherwise establish a contract. In such case the terms of the particular contract consist of those terms on which the writings of the parties agree, together with any supplementary terms incorporated under any other provisions of this Act.

§ 2–208. Course of Performance or Practical Construction.
(1) Where the contract for sale involves repeated occasions for performance by either party with knowledge of the nature of the performance

and opportunity for objection to it by the other, any course of performance accepted or acquiesced in without objection shall be relevant to determine the meaning of the agreement.

(2) The express terms of the agreement and any such course of performance, as well as any course of dealing and usage of trade, shall be construed whenever reasonable as consistent with each other; but when such construction is unreasonable, express terms shall control course of performance and course of performance shall control both course of dealing and usage of trade (Section 1–205).

(3) Subject to the provisions of the next section on modification and waiver, such course of performance shall be relevant to show a waiver or modification of any term inconsistent with such course of performance.

§ 2–209. Modification, Rescission and Waiver.

(1) An agreement modifying a contract within this Article needs no consideration to be binding.

(2) A signed agreement which excludes modification or rescission except by a signed writing cannot be otherwise modified or rescinded, but except as between merchants such a requirement on a form supplied by the merchant must be separately signed by the other party.

(3) The requirements of the statute of frauds section of this Article (Section 2–201) must be satisfied if the contract as modified is within its provisions.

(4) Although an attempt at modification or rescission does not satisfy the requirements of subsection (2) or (3) it can operate as a waiver.

(5) A party who has made a waiver affecting an executory portion of the contract may retract the waiver by reasonable notification received by the other party that strict performance will be required of any term waived, unless the retraction would be unjust in view of a material change of position in reliance on the waiver.

§ 2–210. Delegation of Performance; Assignment of Rights.

(1) A party may perform his duty through a delegate unless otherwise agreed or unless the other party has a substantial interest in having his original promisor perform or control the acts required by the contract. No delegation of performance relieves the party delegating of any duty to perform or any liability for breach.

(2) Unless otherwise agreed all rights of either seller or buyer can be assigned except where the assignment would materially change the duty of the other party, or increase materially the burden or risk imposed on him by his contract, or impair materially his chance of obtaining return performance. A right to damages for breach of the whole contract or a right arising out of the assignor's due performance of his entire obligation can be assigned despite agreement otherwise.

(3) Unless the circumstances indicate the contrary a prohibition of assignment of "the contract" is to be construed as barring only the delegation to the assignee of the assignor's performance.

(4) An assignment of "the contract" or of "all my rights under the contract" or an assignment in similar general terms is an assignment of rights and unless the language or the circumstances (as in an assignment for security) indicate the contrary, it is a delegation of performance of the duties of the assignor and its acceptance by the assignee constitutes a promise by him to perform those duties. This promise is enforceable by either the assignor or the other party to the original contract.

(5) The other party may treat any assignment which delegates performance as creating reasonable grounds for insecurity and may without prejudice to his rights against the assignor demand assurances from the assignee (Section 2–609).

Part 3—General Obligation and Construction of Contract
§ 2–301. General Obligations of Parties.

The obligation of the seller is to transfer and deliver and that of the buyer is to accept and pay in accordance with the contract.

§ 2–302. Unconscionable Contract or Clause.

(1) If the court as a matter of law finds the contract or any clause of the contract to have been unconscionable at the time it was made the court may refuse to enforce the contract, or it may enforce the remainder of the contract without the unconscionable clause, or it may so limit the application of any unconscionable clause as to avoid any unconscionable result.

(2) When it is claimed or appears to the court that the contract or any clause thereof may be unconscionable the parties shall be afforded a reasonable opportunity to present evidence as to its commercial setting, purpose and effect to aid the court in making the determination.

§ 2–303. Allocation or Division of Risks.

Where this Article allocates a risk or a burden as between the parties "unless otherwise agreed", the agreement may not only shift the allocation, but may also divide the risk or burden.

§ 2–304. Price Payable in Money, Goods, Realty, or Otherwise.

(1) The price can be made payable in money or otherwise. If it is payable in whole or in part in goods each party is a seller of the goods which he is to transfer.

(2) Even though all or part of the price is payable in an interest in realty the transfer of the goods and the seller's obligations with reference to them are subject to this Article, but not the transfer of the interest in realty or the transferor's obligations in connection therewith.

§ 2–305. Open Price Term.

(1) The parties if they so intend can conclude a contract for sale even though the price is not settled. In such a case the price is a reasonable price at the time for delivery if

(a) nothing is said as to price; or

(b) the price is left to be agreed by the parties and they fail to agree; or

(c) the price is to be fixed in terms of some agreed market or other standard as set or recorded by a third person or agency and it is not so set or recorded.

(2) A price to be fixed by the seller or by the buyer means a price for him to fix in good faith.

(3) When a price left to be fixed otherwise than by agreement of the parties fails to be fixed through fault of one party the other may at his option treat the contract as cancelled or himself fix a reasonable price.

(4) Where, however, the parties intend not to be bound unless the price be fixed or agreed and it is not fixed or agreed there is no contract. In such a case the buyer must return any goods already received or if unable so to do must pay their reasonable value at the time of delivery and the seller must return any portion of the price paid on account.

§ 2–306. Output, Requirements and Exclusive Dealings.

(1) A term which measures the quantity by the output of the seller or the requirements of the buyer means such actual out-put or requirements as may occur in good faith, except that no quantity unreasonably disproportionate to any stated estimate or in the absence of a stated estimate to any normal or otherwise comparable prior output or requirements may be tendered or demanded.

(2) A lawful agreement by either the seller or the buyer for exclusive dealing in the kind of goods concerned imposes unless otherwise agreed an obligation by the seller to use best efforts to supply the goods and by the buyer to use best efforts to promote their sale.

§ 2–307. Delivery in Single Lot or Several Lots.

Unless otherwise agreed all goods called for by a contract for sale must be tendered in a single delivery and payment is due only on such tender but where the circumstances give either party the right to make or demand delivery in lots the price if it can be apportioned may be demanded for each lot.

§ 2–308. Absence of Specified Place for Delivery.

Unless otherwise agreed

(a) the place for delivery of goods is the seller's place of business or if he has none his residence; but

(b) in a contract for sale of identified goods which to the knowledge of the parties at the time of contracting are in some other place, that place is the place for their delivery; and

(c) documents of title may be delivered through customary banking channels.

§ 2–309. Absence of Specific Time Provisions; Notice of Termination.

(1) The time for shipment or delivery or any other action under a contract if not provided in this Article or agreed upon shall be a reasonable time.

(2) Where the contract provides for successive performances but is indefinite in duration it is valid for a reasonable time but unless otherwise agreed may be terminated at any time by either party.

(3) Termination of a contract by one party except on the happening of an agreed event requires that reasonable notification be received by the other party and an agreement dispensing with notification is invalid if its operation would be unconscionable.

§ 2–310. Open Time for Payment or Running of Credit; Authority to Ship Under Reservation.

Unless otherwise agreed

(a) payment is due at the time and place at which the buyer is to receive the goods even though the place of shipment is the place of delivery; and

(b) if the seller is authorized to send the goods he may ship them under reservation, and may tender the documents of title, but the buyer may inspect the goods after their arrival before payment is due unless such inspection is inconsistent with the terms of the contract (Section 2–513); and

(c) if delivery is authorized and made by way of documents of title otherwise than by subsection (b) then payment is due at the time and place at which the buyer is to receive the documents regardless of where the goods are to be received; and

(d) where the seller is required or authorized to ship the goods on credit the credit period runs from the time of shipment but post-dating the invoice or delaying its dispatch will correspondingly delay the starting of the credit period.

§ 2–311. Options and Cooperation Respecting Performance.

(1) An agreement for sale which is otherwise sufficiently definite (subsection (3) of Section 2–204) to be a contract is not made invalid by the fact that it leaves particulars of performance to be specified by one of the parties. Any such specification must be made in good faith and within limits set by commercial reasonableness.

(2) Unless otherwise agreed specifications relating to assortment of the goods are at the buyer's option and except as otherwise provided in subsections (1)(c) and (3) of Section 2–319 specifications or arrangements relating to shipment are at the seller's option.

(3) Where such specification would materially affect the other party's performance but is not seasonably made or where one party's cooperation is necessary to the agreed performance of the other but is not seasonably forthcoming, the other party in addition to all other remedies

(a) is excused for any resulting delay in his own performance; and

(b) may also either proceed to perform in any reasonable manner or after the time for a material part of his own performance treat the failure to specify or to cooperate as a breach by failure to deliver or accept the goods.

§ 2–312. Warranty of Title and Against Infringement; Buyer's Obligation Against Infringement.

(1) Subject to subsection (2) there is in a contract for sale a warranty by the seller that

(a) the title conveyed shall be good, and its transfer rightful; and

(b) the goods shall be delivered free from any security interest or other lien or encumbrance of which the buyer at the time of contracting has no knowledge.

(2) A warranty under subsection (1) will be excluded or modified only by specific language or by circumstances which give the buyer reason to know that the person selling does not claim title in himself or that he is purporting to sell only such right or title as he or a third person may have.

(3) Unless otherwise agreed a seller who is a merchant regularly dealing in goods of the kind warrants that the goods shall be delivered free of the rightful claim of any third person by way of infringement or the like but a buyer who furnishes specifications to the seller must hold the seller harmless against any such claim which arises out of compliance with the specifications.

§ 2–313. Express Warranties by Affirmation, Promise, Description, Sample.

(1) Express warranties by the seller are created as follows:

(a) Any affirmation of fact or promise made by the seller to the buyer which relates to the goods and becomes part of the basis of the bargain creates an express warranty that the goods shall conform to the affirmation or promise.

(b) Any description of the goods which is made part of the basis of the bargain creates an express warranty that the goods shall conform to the description.

(c) Any sample or model which is made part of the basis of the bargain creates an express warranty that the whole of the goods shall conform to the sample or model.

(2) It is not necessary to the creation of an express warranty that the seller use formal words such as "warrant" or "guarantee" or that he have a specific intention to make a warranty, but an affirmation merely of the value of the goods or a statement purporting to be merely the seller's opinion or commendation of the goods does not create a warranty.

§ 2–314. Implied Warranty: Merchantability; Usage of Trade.

(1) Unless excluded or modified (Section 2–316), a warranty that the goods shall be merchantable is implied in a contract for their sale if the seller is a merchant with respect to goods of that kind. Under this section the serving for value of food or drink to be consumed either on the premises or elsewhere is a sale.

(2) Goods to be merchantable must be at least such as

(a) pass without objection in the trade under the contract description; and

(b) in the case of fungible goods, are of fair average quality within the description; and

(c) are fit for the ordinary purpose for which such goods are used; and

(d) run, within the variations permitted by the agreement, of even kind, quality and quantity within each unit and among all units involved; and

(e) are adequately contained, packaged, and labeled as the agreement may require; and

(f) conform to the promises or affirmations of fact made on the container or label if any.

(3) Unless excluded or modified (Section 2–316) other implied warranties may arise from course of dealing or usage of trade.

§ 2–315. Implied Warranty: Fitness for Particular Purpose.

Where the seller at the time of contracting has reason to know any particular purpose for which the goods are required and that the buyer is relying on the seller's skill or judgment to select or furnish suitable goods, there is unless excluded or modified under the next section an implied warranty that the goods shall be fit for such purpose.

§ 2–316. Exclusion or Modification of Warranties.

(1) Words or conduct relevant to the creation of an express warranty and words or conduct tending to negate or limit warranty shall be construed wherever reasonable as consistent with each other, but subject to the provisions of this Article on parol or extrinsic evidence (Section 2–202) negation or limitation is inoperative to the extent that such construction is unreasonable.

(2) Subject to subsection (3), to exclude or modify the implied warranty of merchantability or any part of it the language must mention merchantability and in case of a writing must be conspicuous, and to exclude or modify any implied warranty of fitness the exclusion must be by a writing and conspicuous. Language to exclude all implied warranties of fitness is sufficient if it states, for example, that "There are no warranties which extend beyond the description on the face hereof."

(3) Notwithstanding subsection (2)

(a) unless the circumstances indicate otherwise, all implied warranties are excluded by expressions like "as is", "with all faults" or other language which in common understanding calls the buyer's attention to the exclusion of warranties and makes plain that there is no implied warranty; and

(b) when the buyer before entering into the contract has examined the goods or the sample or model as fully as he desired or has refused to examine the goods there is no implied warranty with regard to defects which an examination ought in the circumstances to have revealed to him; and

(c) an implied warranty can also be excluded or modified by course of dealing or course of performance or usage of trade.

(4) Remedies for breach of warranty can be limited in accordance with the provisions of this Article on liquidation or limitation of damages and on contractual modification of remedy (Sections 2–718 and 2–719).

§ 2–317. Cumulation and Conflict of Warranties Express or Implied.

Warranties whether express or implied shall be construed as consistent with each other and as cumulative, but if such construction is unreasonable the intention of the parties shall determine which warranty is dominant. In ascertaining that intention the following rules apply:

(a) Exact or technical specifications displace an inconsistent sample or model or general language of description.

(b) A sample from an existing bulk displaces inconsistent general language of description.

(c) Express warranties displace inconsistent implied warranties other than an implied warranty of fitness for a particular purpose.

§ 2–318. Third Party Beneficiaries of Warranties Express or Implied.

Note: *If this Act is introduced in the Congress of the United States this section should be omitted. (States to select one alternative.)*

Alternative A A seller's warranty whether express or implied extends to any natural person who is in the family or household of his buyer or who is a guest in his home if it is reasonable to expect that such person may use, consume or be affected by the goods and who is injured in person by breach of the warranty. A seller may not exclude or limit the operation of this section.

Alternative B A seller's warranty whether express or implied extends to any natural person who may reasonably be expected to use, consume or be affected by the goods and who is injured in person by breach of the warranty. A seller may not exclude or limit the operation of this section.

Alternative C A seller's warranty whether express or implied extends to any person who may reasonably be expected to use, consume or be affected by the goods and who is injured by breach of the warranty. A seller may not exclude or limit the operation of this section with respect to injury to the person of an individual to whom the warranty extends.

§ 2–319. F.O.B. and F.A.S. Terms.

(1) Unless otherwise agreed the term F.O.B. (which means "free on board") at a named place, even though used only in connection with the stated price, is a delivery term under which

(a) when the term is F.O.B. the place of shipment, the seller must at that place ship the goods in the manner provided in this Article (Section 2–504) and bear the expense and risk of putting them into the possession of the carrier; or

(b) when the term is F.O.B. the place of destination, the seller must at his own expense and risk transport the goods to that place and there tender delivery of them in the manner provided in this Article (Section 2–503);

(c) when under either (a) or (b) the term is also F.O.B. vessel, car or other vehicle, the seller must in addition at his own expense and risk load the goods on board. If the term is F.O.B. vessel the buyer must name the vessel and in an appropriate case the seller must comply with the provisions of this Article on the form of bill of lading (Section 2–323).

(2) Unless otherwise agreed the term F.A.S. vessel (which means "free alongside") at a named port, even though used only in connection with the stated price, is a delivery term under which the seller must

(a) at his own expense and risk deliver the goods alongside the vessel in the manner usual in that port or on a dock designated and provided by the buyer; and

(b) obtain and tender a receipt for the goods in exchange for which the carrier is under a duty to issue a bill of lading.

(3) Unless otherwise agreed in any case falling within subsection (1) (a) or (c) or subsection (2) the buyer must seasonably give any needed instructions for making delivery, including when the term is F.A.S. or F.O.B. the loading berth of the vessel and in an appropriate case its name and sailing date. The seller may treat the failure of needed instructions as a failure of cooperation under this Article (Section 2–311). He may also at his option move the goods in any reasonable manner preparatory to delivery or shipment.

(4) Under the term F.O.B. vessel or F.A.S. unless otherwise agreed the buyer must make payment against tender of the required documents and the seller may not tender nor the buyer demand delivery of the goods in substitution for the documents.

§ 2–320. C.I.F. and C. & F. Terms.

(1) The term C.I.F. means that the price includes in a lump sum the cost of the goods and the insurance and freight to the named destination. The term C. & F. or C.F. means that the price so includes cost and freight to the named destination.

(2) Unless otherwise agreed and even though used only in connection with the stated price and destination, the term C.I.F. destination or its equivalent requires the seller at his own expense and risk to

(a) put the goods into the possession of a carrier at the port for shipment and obtain a negotiable bill or bills of lading covering the entire transportation to the named destination; and

(b) load the goods and obtain a receipt from the carrier (which may be contained in the bill of lading) showing that the freight has been paid or provided for; and

(c) obtain a policy or certificate of insurance, including any war risk insurance, of a kind and on terms then current at the port of shipment in the usual amount, in the currency of the contract, shown to cover the same goods covered by the bill of lading and providing for payment of loss to the order of the buyer or for the account of whom it may concern; but the seller may add to the price the amount of premium for any such war risk insurance; and

(d) prepare an invoice of the goods and procure any other documents required to effect shipment or to comply with the contract; and

(e) forward and tender with commercial promptness all the documents in due form and with any indorsement necessary to perfect the buyer's rights.

(3) Unless otherwise agreed the term C. & F. or its equivalent has the same effect and imposes upon the seller the same obligations and risks as a C.I.F. term except the obligation as to insurance.

(4) Under the term C.I.F. or C. & F. unless otherwise agreed the buyer must make payment against tender of the required documents and the seller may not tender nor the buyer demand delivery of the goods in substitution for the documents.

§ 2–321. C.I.F. or C. & F.: "Net Landed Weights"; "Payment on Arrival"; Warranty of Condition on Arrival.

Under a contract containing a term C.I.F. or C. & F.

(1) Where the price is based on or is to be adjusted according to "net landed weights", "delivered weights", "out turn" quantity or quality or the like, unless otherwise agreed the seller must reasonably estimate the price. The payment due on tender of the documents called for by the contract is the amount so estimated, but after final adjustment of the price a settlement must be made with commercial promptness.

(2) An agreement described in subsection (1) or any warranty of quality or condition of the goods on arrival places upon the seller the risk of ordinary deterioration, shrinkage and the like in transportation but has no effect on the place or time of identification to the contract for sale or delivery or on the passing of the risk of loss.

(3) Unless otherwise agreed where the contract provides for payment on or after arrival of the goods the seller must before payment allow such preliminary inspection as is feasible; but if the goods are lost delivery of the documents and payment are due when the goods should have arrived.

§ 2–322. Delivery "Ex-Ship".

(1) Unless otherwise agreed a term for delivery of goods "ex-ship" (which means from the carrying vessel) or in equivalent language is not restricted to a particular ship and requires delivery from a ship which has reached a place at the named port of destination where goods of the kind are usually discharged.

(2) Under such a term unless otherwise agreed

    (a) the seller must discharge all liens arising out of the carriage and furnish the buyer with a direction which puts the carrier under a duty to deliver the goods; and

    (b) the risk of loss does not pass to the buyer until the goods leave the ship's tackle or are otherwise properly unloaded.

§ 2–323. Form of Bill of Lading Required in Overseas Shipment; "Overseas".

(1) Where the contract contemplates overseas shipment and contains a term C.I.F. or C. & F. or F.O.B. vessel, the seller unless otherwise agreed must obtain a negotiable bill of lading stating that the goods have been loaded on board or, in the case of a term C.I.F. or C. & F., received for shipment.

(2) Where in a case within subsection (1) a bill of lading has been issued in a set of parts, unless otherwise agreed if the documents are not to be sent from abroad the buyer may demand tender of the full set; otherwise only one part of the bill of lading need be tendered. Even if the agreement expressly requires a full set

    (a) due tender of a single part is acceptable within the provisions of this Article on cure of improper delivery (subsection (1) of Section 2–508); and

    (b) even though the full set is demanded, if the documents are sent from abroad the person tendering an incomplete set may nevertheless require payment upon furnishing an indemnity which the buyer in good faith deems adequate.

(3) A shipment by water or by air or a contract contemplating such shipment is "overseas" insofar as by usage of trade or agreement it is subject to the commercial, financing or shipping practices characteristic of international deep water commerce.

§ 2–324. "No Arrival, No Sale" Term.

Under a term "no arrival, no sale" or terms of like meaning, unless otherwise agreed,

(a) the seller must properly ship conforming goods and if they arrive by any means he must tender them on arrival but he assumes no obligation that the goods will arrive unless he has caused the non-arrival; and

(b) where without fault of the seller the goods are in part lost or have so deteriorated as no longer to conform to the contract or arrive after the contract time, the buyer may proceed as if there had been casualty to identified goods (Section 2–613).

§ 2–325. "Letter of Credit" Term; "Confirmed Credit".

(1) Failure of the buyer seasonably to furnish an agreed letter of credit is a breach of the contract for sale.

(2) The delivery to seller of a proper letter of credit suspends the buyer's obligation to pay. If the letter of credit is dishonored, the seller may on seasonable notification to the buyer require payment directly from him.

(3) Unless otherwise agreed the term "letter of credit" or "banker's credit" in a contract for sale means an irrevocable credit issued by a financing agency of good repute and, where the shipment is overseas, of good international repute. The term "confirmed credit" means that the credit must also carry the direct obligation of such an agency which does business in the seller's financial market.

§ 2–326. Sale on Approval and Sale or Return; Consignment Sales and Rights of Creditors.

(1) Unless otherwise agreed, if delivered goods may be returned by the buyer even though they conform to the contract, the transaction is

    (a) a "sale on approval" if the goods are delivered primarily for use, and

    (b) a "sale or return" if the goods are delivered primarily for resale.

(2) Except as provided in subsection (3), goods held on approval are not subject to the claims of the buyer's creditors until acceptance; goods held on sale or return are subject to such claims while in the buyer's possession.

(3) Where goods are delivered to a person for sale and such person maintains a place of business at which he deals in goods of the kind involved, under a name other than the name of the person making delivery, then with respect to claims of creditors of the person conducting the business the goods are deemed to be on sale or return. The provisions of this subsection are applicable even though an agreement purports to reserve title to the person making delivery until payment or resale or uses such words as "on consignment" or "on memorandum". However, this subsection is not applicable if the person making delivery

    (a) complies with an applicable law providing for a consignor's interest or the like to be evidenced by a sign, or

    (b) establishes that the person conducting the business is generally known by his creditors to be substantially engaged in selling the goods of others, or

    (c) complies with the filing provisions of the Article on Secured Transactions (Article 9).

(4) Any "or return" term of a contract for sale is to be treated as a separate contract for sale within the statute of frauds section of this Article (Section 2–201) and as contradicting the sale aspect of the contract within the provisions of this Article on parol or extrinsic evidence (Section 2–202).

§ 2–327. Special Incidents of Sale on Approval and Sale or Return.

(1) Under a sale on approval unless otherwise agreed

    (a) although the goods are identified to the contract the risk of loss and the title do not pass to the buyer until acceptance; and

    (b) use of the goods consistent with the purpose of trial is not acceptance but failure seasonably to notify the seller of election to return the goods is acceptance, and if the goods conform to the contract acceptance of any part is acceptance of the whole; and

    (c) after due notification of election to return, the return is at the seller's risk and expense but a merchant buyer must follow any reasonable instructions.

(2) Under a sale or return unless otherwise agreed

    (a) the option to return extends to the whole or any commercial unit of the goods while in substantially their original condition, but must be exercised seasonably; and

    (b) the return is at the buyer's risk and expense.

§ 2–328. Sale by Auction.

(1) In a sale by auction if goods are put up in lots each lot is the subject of a separate sale.

(2) A sale by auction is complete when the auctioneer so announces by the fall of the hammer or in other customary manner. Where a bid is made while the hammer is falling in acceptance of a prior bid the auctioneer may in his discretion reopen the bidding or declare the goods sold under the bid on which the hammer was falling.

(3) Such a sale is with reserve unless the goods are in explicit terms put up without reserve. In an auction with reserve the auctioneer may withdraw the goods at any time until he announces completion of the sale. In an auction without reserve, after the auctioneer calls for bids on an article or lot, that article or lot cannot be withdrawn unless no bid is made within a reasonable time. In either case a bidder may retract his bid until the auctioneer's announcement of completion of the sale, but a bidder's retraction does not revive any previous bid.

(4) If the auctioneer knowingly receives a bid on the seller's behalf or the seller makes or procures such a bid, and notice has not been given that liberty for such bidding is reserved, the buyer may at his option avoid the sale or take the goods at the price of the last good faith bid prior to the completion of the sale. This subsection shall not apply to any bid at a forced sale.

Part 4—Title, Creditors and Good Faith Purchasers
§ 2–401. Passing of Title; Reservation for Security; Limited Application of This Section.

Each provision of this Article with regard to the rights, obligations and remedies of the seller, the buyer, purchasers or other third parties applies irrespective of title to the goods except where the provision refers to such title. Insofar as situations are not covered by the other provisions of this Article and matters concerning title became material the following rules apply:

(1) Title to goods cannot pass under a contract for sale prior to their identification to the contract (Section 2–501), and unless otherwise explicitly agreed the buyer acquires by their identification a special property as limited by this Act. Any retention or reservation by the seller of the title (property) in goods shipped or delivered to the buyer is limited in effect to a reservation of a security interest. Subject to these provisions and to the provisions of the Article on Secured Transactions (Article 9), title to goods passes from the seller to the buyer in any manner and on any conditions explicitly agreed on by the parties.

(2) Unless otherwise explicitly agreed title passes to the buyer at the time and place at which the seller completes his performance with reference to the physical delivery of the goods, despite any reservation of a security interest and even though a document of title is to be delivered at a different time or place; and in particular and despite any reservation of a security interest by the bill of lading

  (a) if the contract requires or authorizes the seller to send the goods to the buyer but does not require him to deliver them at destination, title passes to the buyer at the time and place of shipment; but

  (b) if the contract requires delivery at destination, title passes on tender there.

(3) Unless otherwise explicitly agreed where delivery is to be made without moving the goods,

  (a) if the seller is to deliver a document of title, title passes at the time when and the place where he delivers such documents; or

  (b) if the goods are at the time of contracting already identified and no documents are to be delivered, title passes at the time and place of contracting.

(4) A rejection or other refusal by the buyer to receive or retain the goods, whether or not justified, or a justified revocation of acceptance revests title to the goods in the seller. Such revesting occurs by operation of law and is not a "sale".

§ 2–402. Rights of Seller's Creditors Against Sold Goods.

(1) Except as provided in subsections (2) and (3), rights of unsecured creditors of the seller with respect to goods which have been identified to a contract for sale are subject to the buyer's rights to recover the goods under this Article (Sections 2–502 and 2–716).

(2) A creditor of the seller may treat a sale or an identification of goods to a contract for sale as void if as against him a retention of possession by the seller is fraudulent under any rule of law of the state where the goods are situated, except that retention of possession in good faith and current course of trade by a merchant-seller for a commercially reasonable time after a sale or identification is not fraudulent.

(3) Nothing in this Article shall be deemed to impair the rights of creditors of the seller

  (a) under the provisions of the Article on Secured Transactions (Article 9); or

  (b) where identification to the contract or delivery is made not in current course of trade but in satisfaction of or as security for a pre-existing claim for money, security or the like and is made under circumstances which under any rule of law of the state where the goods are situated would apart from this Article constitute the transaction a fraudulent transfer or voidable preference.

§ 2–403. Power to Transfer; Good Faith Purchase of Goods; "Entrusting".

(1) A purchaser of goods acquires all title which his transferor had or had power to transfer except that a purchaser of a limited interest acquires rights only to the extent of the interest purchased. A person with voidable title has power to transfer a good title to a good faith purchaser for value. When goods have been delivered under a transaction of purchase the purchaser has such power even though

  (a) the transferor was deceived as to the identity of the purchaser, or

  (b) the delivery was in exchange for a check which is later dishonored, or

  (c) it was agreed that the transaction was to be a "cash sale", or

  (d) the delivery was procured through fraud punishable as larcenous under the criminal law.

(2) Any entrusting of possession of goods to a merchant who deals in goods of that kind gives him power to transfer all rights of the entruster to a buyer in ordinary course of business.

(3) "Entrusting" includes any delivery and any acquiescence in retention of possession regardless of any condition expressed between the parties to the delivery or acquiescence and regardless of whether the procurement of the entrusting or the possessor's disposition of the goods have been such as to be larcenous under the criminal law.

(4) The rights of other purchasers of goods and of lien creditors are governed by the Articles on Secured Transactions (Article 9), Bulk Transfers (Article 6) and Documents of Title (Article 7).

Part 5—Performance

§ 2–501. Insurable Interest in Goods; Manner of Identification of Goods.

(1) The buyer obtains a special property and an insurable interest in goods by identification of existing goods as goods to which the contract refers even though the goods so identified are nonconforming and he has an option to return or reject them. Such identification can be made at any time and in any manner explicitly agreed to by the parties. In the absence of explicit agreement identification occurs

  (a) when the contract is made if it is for the sale of goods already existing and identified;

  (b) if the contract is for the sale of future goods other than those described in paragraph (c), when goods are shipped, marked or otherwise designated by the seller as goods to which the contract refers;

  (c) when the crops are planted or otherwise become growing crops or the young are conceived if the contract is for the sale of unborn young to be born within twelve months after contracting or for the sale of crops to be harvested within twelve months or the next normal harvest season after contracting whichever is longer.

(2) The seller retains an insurable interest in goods so long as title to or any security interest in the goods remains in him and where the identification is by the seller alone he may until default or insolvency or notification to the buyer that the identification is final substitute other goods for those identified.

(3) Nothing in this section impairs any insurable interest recognized under any other statute or rule of law.

§ 2–502. Buyer's Right to Goods on Seller's Insolvency.

(1) Subject to subsection (2) and even though the goods have not been shipped a buyer who has paid a part or all of the price of goods in which he has a special property under the provisions of the immediately preceding section may on making and keeping good a tender of any unpaid portion of their price recover them from the seller if the seller becomes insolvent within ten days after receipt of the first installment on their price.

(2) If the identification creating his special property has been made by the buyer he acquires the right to recover the goods only if they conform to the contract for sale.

§ 2–503. Manner of Seller's Tender of Delivery.

(1) Tender of delivery requires that the seller put and hold conforming goods at the buyer's disposition and give the buyer any notification reasonably necessary to enable him to take delivery. The manner, time and place for tender are determined by the agreement and this Article, and in particular

  (a) tender must be at a reasonable hour, and if it is of goods they must be kept available for the period reasonably necessary to enable the buyer to take possession; but

  (b) unless otherwise agreed the buyer must furnish facilities reasonably suited to the receipt of the goods.

(2) Where the case is within the next section respecting shipment tender requires that the seller comply with its provisions.

(3) Where the seller is required to deliver at a particular destination tender requires that he comply with subsection (1) and also in any appropriate case tender documents as described in subsections (4) and (5) of this section.

(4) Where goods are in the possession of a bailee and are to be delivered without being moved

    (a) tender requires that the seller either tender a negotiable document of title covering such goods or procure acknowledgment by the bailee of the buyer's right to possession of the goods; but

    (b) tender to the buyer of a non-negotiable document of title or of a written direction to the bailee to deliver is sufficient tender unless the buyer seasonably objects, and receipt by the bailee of notification of the buyer's rights fixes those rights as against the bailee and all third persons; but risk of loss of the goods and of any failure by the bailee to honor the non-negotiable document of title or to obey the direction remains on the seller until the buyer has had a reasonable time to present the document or direction, and a refusal by the bailee to honor the document or to obey the direction defeats the tender.

(5) Where the contract requires the seller to deliver documents

    (a) he must tender all such documents in correct form, except as provided in this Article with respect to bills of lading in a set (subsection (2) of Section 2–323); and

    (b) tender through customary banking channels is sufficient and dishonor of a draft accompanying the documents constitutes non-acceptance or rejection.

§ 2–504. Shipment by Seller.

Where the seller is required or authorized to send the goods to the buyer and the contract does not require him to deliver them at a particular destination, then unless otherwise agreed he must

(a) put the goods in the possession of such a carrier and make such a contract for their transportation as may be reasonable having regard to the nature of the goods and other circumstances of the case; and

(b) obtain and promptly deliver or tender in due form any document necessary to enable the buyer to obtain possession of the goods or otherwise required by the agreement or by usage of trade; and

(c) promptly notify the buyer of the shipment.

Failure to notify the buyer under paragraph (c) or to make a proper contract under paragraph (a) is a ground for rejection only if material delay or loss ensues.

§ 2–505. Seller's Shipment Under Reservation.

(1) Where the seller has identified goods to the contract by or before shipment:

    (a) his procurement of a negotiable bill of lading to his own order or otherwise reserves in him a security interest in the goods. His procurement of the bill to the order of a financing agency or of the buyer indicates in addition only the seller's expectation of transferring that interest to the person named.

    (b) a non-negotiable bill of lading to himself or his nominee reserves possession of the goods as security but except in a case of conditional delivery (subsection (2) of Section 2–507) a non-negotiable bill of lading naming the buyer as consignee reserves no security interest even though the seller retains possession of the bill of lading.

(2) When shipment by the seller with reservation of a security interest is in violation of the contract for sale it constitutes an improper contract for transportation within the preceding section but impairs neither the rights given to the buyer by shipment and identification of the goods to the contract nor the seller's powers as a holder of a negotiable document.

§ 2–506. Rights of Financing Agency.

(1) A financing agency by paying or purchasing for value a draft which relates to a shipment of goods acquires to the extent of the payment or purchase and in addition to its own rights under the draft and any document of title securing it any rights of the shipper in the goods including the right to stop delivery and the shipper's right to have the draft honored by the buyer.

(2) The right to reimbursement of a financing agency which has in good faith honored or purchased the draft under commitment to or authority from the buyer is not impaired by subsequent discovery of defects with reference to any relevant document which was apparently regular on its face.

§ 2–507. Effect of Seller's Tender; Delivery on Condition.

(1) Tender of delivery is a condition to the buyer's duty to accept the goods and, unless otherwise agreed, to his duty to pay for them. Tender entitles the seller to acceptance of the goods and to payment according to the contract.

(2) Where payment is due and demanded on the delivery to the buyer of goods or documents of title, his right as against the seller to retain or dispose of them is conditional upon his making the payment due.

§ 2–508. Cure by Seller of Improper Tender or Delivery; Replacement.

(1) Where any tender or delivery by the seller is rejected because non-conforming and the time for performance has not yet expired, the seller may seasonably notify the buyer of his intention to cure and may then within the contract time make a conforming delivery.

(2) Where the buyer rejects a non-conforming tender which the seller had reasonable grounds to believe would be acceptable with or without money allowance the seller may if he seasonably notifies the buyer have a further reasonable time to substitute a conforming tender.

§ 2–509. Risk of Loss in the Absence of Breach.

(1) Where the contract requires or authorizes the seller to ship the goods by carrier

    (a) if it does not require him to deliver them at a particular destination, the risk of loss passes to the buyer when the goods are duly delivered to the carrier even though the shipment is under reservation (Section 2–505); but

    (b) if it does require him to deliver them at a particular destination and the goods are there duly tendered while in the possession of the carrier, the risk of loss passes to the buyer when the goods are there duly so tendered as to enable the buyer to take delivery.

(2) Where the goods are held by a bailee to be delivered without being moved, the risk of loss passes to the buyer

    (a) on his receipt of a negotiable document of title covering the goods; or

    (b) on acknowledgment by the bailee of the buyer's right to possession of the goods; or

    (c) after his receipt of a non-negotiable document of title or other written direction to deliver, as provided in subsection (4)(b) of Section 2–503.

(3) In any case not within subsection (1) or (2), the risk of loss passes to the buyer on his receipt of the goods if the seller is a merchant; otherwise, the risk passes to the buyer on tender of delivery.

(4) The provisions of this section are subject to contrary agreement of the parties and to the provisions of this Article on sale on approval (Section 2–327) and on effect of breach on risk of loss (Section 2–510).

§ 2–510. Effect of Breach on Risk of Loss.

(1) Where a tender or delivery of goods so fails to conform to the contract as to give a right of rejection the risk of their loss remains on the seller until cure or acceptance.

(2) Where the buyer rightfully revokes acceptance he may to the extent of any deficiency in his effective insurance coverage treat the risk of loss as having rested on the seller from the beginning.

(3) Where the buyer as to conforming goods already identified to the contract for sale repudiates or is otherwise in breach before risk of their loss has passed to him, the seller may to the extent of any deficiency in his effective insurance coverage treat the risk of loss as resting on the buyer for a commercially reasonable time.

§ 2–511. Tender of Payment by Buyer; Payment by Check.

(1) Unless otherwise agreed tender of payment is a condition to the seller's duty to tender and complete any delivery.

(2) Tender of payment is sufficient when made by any means or in any manner current in the ordinary course of business unless the seller demands payment in legal tender and gives any extension of time reasonably necessary to procure it.

(3) Subject to the provisions of this Act on the effect of an instrument on an obligation (Section 3–802), payment by check is conditional and is defeated as between the parties by dishonor of the check on due presentment.

§ 2–512. Payment by Buyer Before Inspection.
(1) Where the contract requires payment before inspection non-conformity of the goods does not excuse the buyer from so making payment unless

(a) the non-conformity appears without inspection; or

(b) despite tender of the required documents the circumstances would justify injunction against honor under the provisions of this Act (Section 5–114).

(2) Payment pursuant to subsection (1) does not constitute an acceptance of goods or impair the buyer's right to inspect or any of his remedies.

§ 2–513. Buyer's Right to Inspection of Goods.
(1) Unless otherwise agreed and subject to subsection (3), where goods are tendered or delivered or identified to the contract for sale, the buyer has a right before payment or acceptance to inspect them at any reasonable place and time and in any reasonable manner. When the seller is required or authorized to send the goods to the buyer, the inspection may be after their arrival.

(2) Expenses of inspection must be borne by the buyer but may be recovered from the seller if the goods do not conform and are rejected.

(3) Unless otherwise agreed and subject to the provisions of this Article on C.I.F. contracts (subsection (3) of Section 2–321), the buyer is not entitled to inspect the goods before payment of the price when the contract provides

(a) for delivery "C.O.D." or on other like terms; or

(b) for payment against documents of title, except where such payment is due only after the goods are to become available for inspection.

(4) A place or method of inspection fixed by the parties is presumed to be exclusive but unless otherwise expressly agreed it does not postpone identification or shift the place for delivery or for passing the risk of loss. If compliance becomes impossible, inspection shall be as provided in this section unless the place or method fixed was clearly intended as an indispensable condition failure of which avoids the contract.

§ 2–514. When Documents Deliverable on Acceptance; When on Payment.
Unless otherwise agreed documents against which a draft is drawn are to be delivered to the drawee on acceptance of the draft if it is payable more than three days after presentment; otherwise, only on payment.

§ 2–515. Preserving Evidence of Goods in Dispute.
In furtherance of the adjustment of any claim or dispute

(a) either party on reasonable notification to the other and for the purpose of ascertaining the facts and preserving evidence has the right to inspect, test and sample the goods including such of them as may be in the possession or control of the other; and

(b) the parties may agree to a third party inspection or survey to determine the conformity or condition of the goods and may agree that the findings shall be binding upon them in any subsequent litigation or adjustment.

Part 6—Breach, Repudiation and Excuse
§ 2–601. Buyer's Rights on Improper Delivery.
Subject to the provisions of this Article on breach in installment contracts (Section 2–612) and unless otherwise agreed under the sections on contractual limitations of remedy (Sections 2–718 and 2–719), if the goods or the tender of delivery fail in any respect to conform to the contract, the buyer may

(a) reject the whole; or

(b) accept the whole; or

(c) accept any commercial unit or units and reject the rest.

§ 2–602. Manner and Effect of Rightful Rejection.
(1) Rejection of goods must be within a reasonable time after their delivery or tender. It is ineffective unless the buyer seasonably notifies the seller.

(2) Subject to the provisions of the two following sections on rejected goods (Sections 2–603 and 2–604),

(a) after rejection any exercise of ownership by the buyer with respect to any commercial unit is wrongful as against the seller; and

(b) if the buyer has before rejection taken physical possession of goods in which he does not have a security interest under the provisions of this Article (subsection (3) of Section 2–711), he is under a duty after rejection to hold them with reasonable care at the seller's disposition for a time sufficient to permit the seller to remove them; but

(c) the buyer has no further obligations with regard to goods rightfully rejected.

(3) The seller's rights with respect to goods wrongfully rejected are governed by the provisions of this Article on seller's remedies in general (Section 2–703).

§ 2–603. Merchant Buyer's Duties as to Rightfully Rejected Goods.
(1) Subject to any security interest in the buyer (subsection (3) of Section 2–711), when the seller has no agent or place of business at the market of rejection a merchant buyer is under a duty after rejection of goods in his possession or control to follow any reasonable instructions received from the seller with respect to the goods and in the absence of such instructions to make reasonable efforts to sell them for the seller's account if they are perishable or threaten to decline in value speedily. Instructions are not reasonable if on demand indemnity for expenses is not forthcoming.

(2) When the buyer sells goods under subsection (1), he is entitled to reimbursement from the seller or out of the proceeds for reasonable expenses of caring for and selling them, and if the expenses include no selling commission then to such commission as is usual in the trade or if there is none to a reasonable sum not exceeding ten per cent on the gross proceeds.

(3) In complying with this section the buyer is held only to good faith and good faith conduct hereunder is neither acceptance nor conversion nor the basis of an action for damages.

§ 2–604. Buyer's Options as to Salvage of Rightfully Rejected Goods.
Subject to the provisions of the immediately preceding section on perishables if the seller gives no instructions within a reasonable time after notification of rejection the buyer may store the rejected goods for the seller's account or reship them to him or resell them for the seller's account with reimbursement as provided in the preceding section. Such action is not acceptance or conversion.

§ 2–605. Waiver of Buyer's Objections by Failure to Particularize.
(1) The buyer's failure to state in connection with rejection a particular defect which is ascertainable by reasonable inspection precludes him from relying on the unstated defect to justify rejection or to establish breach

(a) where the seller could have cured it if stated seasonably; or

(b) between merchants when the seller has after rejection made a request in writing for a full and final written statement of all defects on which the buyer proposes to rely.

(2) Payment against documents made without reservation of rights precludes recovery of the payment for defects apparent on the face of the documents.

§ 2–606. What Constitutes Acceptance of Goods.
(1) Acceptance of goods occurs when the buyer

(a) after a reasonable opportunity to inspect the goods signifies to the seller that the goods are conforming or that he will take or retain them in spite of their nonconformity; or

(b) fails to make an effective rejection (subsection (1) of Section 2–602), but such acceptance does not occur until the buyer has had a reasonable opportunity to inspect them; or

(c) does any act inconsistent with the seller's ownership; but if such act is wrongful as against the seller it is an acceptance only if ratified by him.

(2) Acceptance of a part of any commercial unit is acceptance of that entire unit.

§ 2–607. Effect of Acceptance; Notice of Breach; Burden of Establishing Breach After Acceptance; Notice of Claim or Litigation to Person Answerable Over.

(1) The buyer must pay at the contract rate for any goods accepted.

(2) Acceptance of goods by the buyer precludes rejection of the goods accepted and if made with knowledge of a non-conformity cannot be revoked because of it unless the acceptance was on the reasonable assumption that the non-conformity would be seasonably cured but acceptance does not of itself impair any other remedy provided by this Article for non-conformity.

(3) Where a tender has been accepted

    (a) the buyer must within a reasonable time after he discovers or should have discovered any breach notify the seller of breach or be barred from any remedy; and

    (b) if the claim is one for infringement or the like (subsection (3) of Section 2–312) and the buyer is sued as a result of such a breach he must so notify the seller within a reasonable time after he receives notice of the litigation or be barred from any remedy over for liability established by the litigation.

(4) The burden is on the buyer to establish any breach with respect to the goods accepted.

(5) Where the buyer is sued for breach of a warranty or other obligation for which his seller is answerable over

    (a) he may give his seller written notice of the litigation. If the notice states that the seller may come in and defend and that if the seller does not do so he will be bound in any action against him by his buyer by any determination of fact common to the two litigations, then unless the seller after seasonable receipt of the notice does come in and defend he is so bound.

    (b) if the claim is one for infringement or the like (subsection (3) of Section 2–312) the original seller may demand in writing that his buyer turn over to him control of the litigation including settlement or else be barred from any remedy over and if he also agrees to bear all expense and to satisfy any adverse judgment, then unless the buyer after seasonable receipt of the demand does turn over control the buyer is so barred.

(6) The provisions of subsections (3), (4) and (5) apply to any obligation of a buyer to hold the seller harmless against infringement or the like (subsection (3) of Section 2–312).

§ 2–608. Revocation of Acceptance in Whole or in Part.

(1) The buyer may revoke his acceptance of a lot or commercial unit whose non-conformity substantially impairs its value to him if he has accepted it

    (a) on the reasonable assumption that its non-conformity would be cured and it has not been seasonably cured; or

    (b) without discovery of such non-conformity if his acceptance was reasonably induced either by the difficulty of discovery before acceptance or by the seller's assurances.

(2) Revocation of acceptance must occur within a reasonable time after the buyer discovers or should have discovered the ground for it and before any substantial change in condition of the goods which is not caused by their own defects. It is not effective until the buyer notifies the seller of it.

(3) A buyer who so revokes has the same rights and duties with regard to the goods involved as if he had rejected them.

§ 2–609. Right to Adequate Assurance of Performance.

(1) A contract for sale imposes an obligation on each party that the other's expectation of receiving due performance will not be impaired. When reasonable grounds for insecurity arise with respect to the performance of either party the other may in writing demand adequate assurance of due performance and until he receives such assurance may if commercially reasonable suspend any performance for which he has not already received the agreed return.

(2) Between merchants the reasonableness of grounds for insecurity and the adequacy of any assurance offered shall be determined according to commercial standards.

(3) Acceptance of any improper delivery or payment does not prejudice the aggrieved party's right to demand adequate assurance of future performance.

(4) After receipt of a justified demand failure to provide within a reasonable time not exceeding thirty days such assurance of due performance as is adequate under the circumstances of the particular case is a repudiation of the contract.

§ 2–610. Anticipatory Repudiation.

When either party repudiates the contract with respect to a performance not yet due the loss of which will substantially impair the value of the contract to the other, the aggrieved party may

    (a) for a commercially reasonable time await performance by the repudiating party; or

    (b) resort to any remedy for breach (Section 2–703 or Section 2–711), even though he has notified the repudiating party that he would await the latter's performance and has urged retraction; and

    (c) in either case suspend his own performance or proceed in accordance with the provisions of this Article on the seller's right to identify goods to the contract notwithstanding breach or to salvage unfinished goods (Section 2–704).

§ 2–611. Retraction of Anticipatory Repudiation.

(1) Until the repudiating party's next performance is due he can retract his repudiation unless the aggrieved party has since the repudiation cancelled or materially changed his position or otherwise indicated that he considers the repudiation final.

(2) Retraction may be by any method which clearly indicates to the aggrieved party that the repudiating party intends to perform, but must include any assurance justifiably demanded under the provisions of this Article (Section 2–609).

(3) Retraction reinstates the repudiating party's rights under the contract with due excuse and allowance to the aggrieved party for any delay occasioned by the repudiation.

§ 2–612. "Installment Contract"; Breach.

(1) An "installment contract" is one which requires or authorizes the delivery of goods in separate lots to be separately accepted, even though the contract contains a clause "each delivery is a separate contract" or its equivalent.

(2) The buyer may reject any installment which is non-conforming if the non-conformity substantially impairs the value of that installment and cannot be cured or if the non-conformity is a defect in the required documents; but if the non-conformity does not fall within subsection (3) and the seller gives adequate assurance of its cure the buyer must accept that installment.

(3) Whenever non-conformity or default with respect to one or more installments substantially impairs the value of the whole contract there is a breach of the whole. But the aggrieved party reinstates the contract if he accepts a non-conforming installment without seasonably notifying of cancellation or if he brings an action with respect only to past installments or demands performance as to future installments.

§ 2–613. Casualty to Identified Goods.

Where the contract requires for its performance goods identified when the contract is made, and the goods suffer casualty without fault of either party before the risk of loss passes to the buyer, or in a proper case under a "no arrival, no sale" term (Section 2–324) then

    (a) if the loss is total the contract is avoided; and

    (b) if the loss is partial or the goods have so deteriorated as no longer to conform to the contract the buyer may nevertheless demand inspection and at his option either treat the contract as avoided or accept the goods with due allowance from the contract price for the deterioration or the deficiency in quantity but without further right against the seller.

§ 2–614. *Substituted Performance.*

(1) Where without fault of either party the agreed berthing, loading, or unloading facilities fail or an agreed type of carrier becomes unavailable or the agreed manner of delivery otherwise becomes commercially impracticable but a commercially reasonable substitute is available, such substitute performance must be tendered and accepted.

(2) If the agreed means or manner of payment fails because of domestic or foreign governmental regulation, the seller may withhold or stop delivery unless the buyer provides a means or manner of payment which is commercially a substantial equivalent. If delivery has already been taken, payment by the means or in the manner provided by the regulation discharges the buyer's obligation unless the regulation is discriminatory, oppressive or predatory.

§ 2–615. Excuse by Failure of Presupposed Conditions.

Except so far as a seller may have assumed a greater obligation and subject to the preceding section on substituted performance:

(a) Delay in delivery or non-delivery in whole or in part by a seller who complies with paragraphs (b) and (c) is not a breach of his duty under a contract for sale if performance as agreed has been made impracticable by the occurrence of a contingency the non-occurrence of which was a basic assumption on which the contract was made or by compliance in good faith with any applicable foreign or domestic governmental regulation or order whether or not it later proves to be invalid.

(b) Where the causes mentioned in paragraph (a) affect only a part of the seller's capacity to perform, he must allocate production and deliveries among his customers but may at his option include regular customers not then under contract as well as his own requirements for further manufacture. He may so allocate in any manner which is fair and reasonable.

(c) The seller must notify the buyer seasonably that there will be delay or non-delivery and, when allocation is required under paragraph (b), of the estimated quota thus made available for the buyer.

§ 2–616. Procedure on Notice Claiming Excuse.

(1) Where the buyer receives notification of a material or indefinite delay or an allocation justified under the preceding section he may by written notification to the seller as to any delivery concerned, and where the prospective deficiency substantially impairs the value of the whole contract under the provisions of this Article relating to breach of installment contracts (Section 2–612), then also as to the whole,

    (a) terminate and thereby discharge any unexecuted portion of the contract; or

    (b) modify the contract by agreeing to take his available quota in substitution.

(2) If after receipt of such notification from the seller the buyer fails so to modify the contract within a reasonable time not exceeding thirty days the contract lapses with respect to any deliveries affected.

(3) The provisions of this section may not be negated by agreement except in so far as the seller has assumed a greater obligation under the preceding section.

Part 7—Remedies

§ 2–701. Remedies for Breach of Collateral Contracts Not Impaired.

Remedies for breach of any obligation or promise collateral or ancillary to a contract for sale are not impaired by the provisions of this Article.

§ 2–702. Seller's Remedies on Discovery of Buyer's Insolvency.

(1) Where the seller discovers the buyer to be insolvent he may refuse delivery except for cash including payment for all goods theretofore delivered under the contract, and stop delivery under this Article (Section 2–705).

(2) Where the seller discovers that the buyer has received goods on credit while insolvent he may reclaim the goods upon demand made within ten days after the receipt, but if misrepresentation of solvency has been made to the particular seller in writing within three months before delivery the ten day limitation does not apply. Except as provided in this subsection the seller may not base a right to reclaim goods on the buyer's fraudulent or innocent misrepresentation of solvency or of intent to pay.

(3) The seller's right to reclaim under subsection (2) is subject to the rights of a buyer in ordinary course or other good faith purchaser under this Article (Section 2–403). Successful reclamation of goods excludes all other remedies with respect to them.

§ 2–703. Seller's Remedies in General.

Where the buyer wrongfully rejects or revokes acceptance of goods or fails to make a payment due on or before delivery or repudiates with respect to a part or the whole, then with respect to any goods directly affected and, if the breach is of the whole contract (Section 2–612), then also with respect to the whole undelivered balance, the aggrieved seller may

    (a) withhold delivery of such goods;

    (b) stop delivery by any bailee as hereafter provided (Section 2–705);

    (c) proceed under the next section respecting goods still unidentified to the contract;

    (d) resell and recover damages as hereafter provided (Section 2–706);

    (e) recover damages for non-acceptance (Section 2–708) or in a proper case the price (Section 2–709);

    (f) cancel.

§ 2–704. Seller's Right to Identify Goods to the Contract Notwithstanding Breach or to Salvage Unfinished Goods.

(1) An aggrieved seller under the preceding section may

    (a) identify to the contract conforming goods not already identified if at the time he learned of the breach they are in his possession or control;

    (b) treat as the subject of resale goods which have demonstrably been intended for the particular contract even though those goods are unfinished.

(2) Where the goods are unfinished an aggrieved seller may in the exercise of reasonable commercial judgment for the purposes of avoiding loss and of effective realization either complete the manufacture and wholly identify the goods to the contract or cease manufacture and resell for scrap or salvage value or proceed in any other reasonable manner.

§ 2–705. Seller's Stoppage of Delivery in Transit or Otherwise.

(1) The seller may stop delivery of goods in the possession of a carrier or other bailee when he discovers the buyer to be insolvent (Section 2–702) and may stop delivery of carload, truckload, planeload or larger shipments of express or freight when the buyer repudiates or fails to make a payment due before delivery or if for any other reason the seller has a right to withhold or reclaim the goods.

(2) As against such buyer the seller may stop delivery until

    (a) receipt of the goods by the buyer; or

    (b) acknowledgment to the buyer by any bailee of the goods except a carrier that the bailee holds the goods for the buyer; or

    (c) such acknowledgment to the buyer by a carrier by reshipment or as warehouseman; or

    (d) negotiation to the buyer of any negotiable document of title covering the goods.

(3) **(a)** To stop delivery the seller must so notify as to enable the bailee by reasonable diligence to prevent delivery of the goods.

    (b) After such notification the bailee must hold and deliver the goods according to the directions of the seller but the seller is liable to the bailee for any ensuing charges or damages.

    (c) If a negotiable document of title has been issued for goods the bailee is not obliged to obey a notification to stop until surrender of the document.

    (d) A carrier who has issued a non-negotiable bill of lading is not obliged to obey a notification to stop received from a person other than the consignor.

§ 2–706. Seller's Resale Including Contract for Resale.

(1) Under the conditions stated in Section 2–703 on seller's remedies, the seller may resell the goods concerned or the undelivered balance thereof. Where the resale is made in good faith and in a commercially reasonable manner the seller may recover the difference between the resale price and the contract price together with any incidental damages allowed under the provisions of this Article (Section 2–710), but less expenses saved in consequence of the buyer's breach.

(2) Except as otherwise provided in subsection (3) or unless otherwise agreed resale may be at public or private sale including sale by way of one or more contracts to sell or of identification to an existing contract of the seller. Sale may be as a unit or in parcels and at any time and place and on any terms but every aspect of the sale including the method, manner, time, place and terms must be commercially reasonable. The resale must be reasonably identified as referring to the broken contract, but it is not necessary that the goods be in existence or that any or all of them have been identified to the contract before the breach.

(3) Where the resale is at private sale the seller must give the buyer reasonable notification of his intention to resell.

(4) Where the resale is at public sale

    (a) only identified goods can be sold except where there is a recognized market for a public sale of futures in goods of the kind; and

    (b) it must be made at a usual place or market for public sale if one is reasonably available and except in the case of goods which are perishable or threaten to decline in value speedily the seller must give the buyer reasonable notice of the time and place of the resale; and

    (c) if the goods are not to be within the view of those attending the sale the notification of sale must state the place where the goods are located and provide for their reasonable inspection by prospective bidders; and

    (d) the seller may buy.

(5) A purchaser who buys in good faith at a resale takes the goods free of any rights of the original buyer even though the seller fails to comply with one or more of the requirements of this section.

(6) The seller is not accountable to the buyer for any profit made on any resale. A person in the position of a seller (Section 2–707) or a buyer who has rightfully rejected or justifiably revoked acceptance must account for any excess over the amount of his security interest, as hereinafter defined (subsection (3) of Section 2–711).

§ 2–707. "Person in the Position of a Seller".

(1) A "person in the position of a seller" includes as against a principal an agent who has paid or become responsible for the price of goods on behalf of his principal or anyone who otherwise holds a security interest or other right in goods similar to that of a seller.

(2) A person in the position of a seller may as provided in this Article withhold or stop delivery (Section 2–705) and resell (Section 2–706) and recover incidental damages (Section 2–710).

§ 2–708. Seller's Damages for Non-Acceptance or Repudiation.

(1) Subject to subsection (2) and to the provisions of this Article with respect to proof of market price (Section 2–723), the measure of damages for non-acceptance or repudiation by the buyer is the difference between the market price at the time and place for tender and the unpaid contract price together with any incidental damages provided in this Article (Section 2–710), but less expenses saved in consequence of the buyer's breach.

(2) If the measure of damages provided in subsection (1) is inadequate to put the seller in as good a position as performance would have done then the measure of damages is the profit (including reasonable overhead) which the seller would have made from full performance by the buyer, together with any incidental damages provided in this Article (Section 2–710), due allowance for costs reasonably incurred and due credit for payments or proceeds of resale.

§ 2–709. Action for the Price.

(1) When the buyer fails to pay the price as it becomes due the seller may recover, together with any incidental damages under the next section, the price

    (a) of goods accepted or of conforming goods lost or damaged within a commercially reasonable time after risk of their loss has passed to the buyer; and

    (b) of goods identified to the contract if the seller is unable after reasonable effort to resell them at a reasonable price or the circumstances reasonably indicate that such effort will be unavailing.

(2) Where the seller sues for the price he must hold for the buyer any goods which have been identified to the contract and are still in his control except that if resale becomes possible he may resell them at any time prior to the collection of the judgment. The net proceeds of any such resale must be credited to the buyer and payment of the judgment entitles him to any goods not resold.

(3) After the buyer has wrongfully rejected or revoked acceptance of the goods or has failed to make a payment due or has repudiated (Section 2–610), a seller who is held not entitled to the price under this section shall nevertheless be awarded damages for non-acceptance under the preceding section.

§ 2–710. Seller's Incidental Damages.

Incidental damages to an aggrieved seller include any commercially reasonable charges, expenses or commissions incurred in stopping delivery, in the transportation, care and custody of goods after the buyer's breach, in connection with return or resale of the goods or otherwise resulting from the breach.

§ 2–711. Buyer's Remedies in General; Buyer's Security Interest in Rejected Goods.

(1) Where the seller fails to make delivery or repudiates or the buyer rightfully rejects or justifiably revokes acceptance then with respect to any goods involved, and with respect to the whole if the breach goes to the whole contract (Section 2–612), the buyer may cancel and whether or not he has done so may in addition to recovering so much of the price as has been paid

    (a) "cover" and have damages under the next section as to all the goods affected whether or not they have been identified to the contract; or

    (b) recover damages for non-delivery as provided in this Article (Section 2–713).

(2) Where the seller fails to deliver or repudiates the buyer may also

    (a) if the goods have been identified recover them as provided in this Article (Section 2–502); or

    (b) in a proper case obtain specific performance or replevy the goods as provided in this Article (Section 2–716).

(3) On rightful rejection or justifiable revocation of acceptance a buyer has a security interest in goods in his possession or control for any payments made on their price and any expenses reasonably incurred in their inspection, receipt, transportation, care and custody and may hold such goods and resell them in like manner as an aggrieved seller (Section 2–706).

§ 2–712. "Cover"; Buyer's Procurement of Substitute Goods.

(1) After a breach within the preceding section the buyer may "cover" by making in good faith and without unreasonable delay any reasonable purchase of or contract to purchase goods in substitution for those due from the seller.

(2) The buyer may recover from the seller as damages the difference between the cost of cover and the contract price together with any incidental or consequential damages as hereinafter defined (Section 2–715), but less expenses saved in consequence of the seller's breach.

(3) Failure of the buyer to effect cover within this section does not bar him from any other remedy.

§ 2–713. Buyer's Damages for Non-Delivery or Repudiation.

(1) Subject to provisions of this Article with respect to the proof of market price (Section 2–723), the measure of damages for non-delivery or repudiation by the seller is the difference between the market price at the time when the buyer learned of the breach and the contract price together with any incidental and consequential damages provided in this Article (Section 2–715), but less expenses saved in consequence of the seller's breach.

(2) Market price is to be determined as of the place for tender or, in cases of rejection after arrival or revocation of acceptance, as of the place of arrival.

§ 2–714. Buyer's Damages for Breach in Regard to Accepted Goods.

(1) Where the buyer has accepted goods and given notification (subsection (3) of Section 2–607) he may recover as damages for any non-conformity of tender the loss resulting in the ordinary course of events from the seller's breach as determined in any manner which is reasonable.

(2) The measure of damages for breach of warranty is the difference at the time and place of acceptance between the value of the goods accepted and the value they would have had if they had been as warranted, unless special circumstances show proximate damages of a different amount.

(3) In a proper case any incidental and consequential damages under the next section may be recovered.

§ 2–715. Buyer's Incidental and Consequential Damages.

(1) Incidental damages resulting from the seller's breach include expenses reasonably incurred in inspection, receipt, transportation and care and custody of goods rightfully rejected, any commercially reasonable charges, expenses or commissions in connection with effecting cover and any other reasonable expense incident to the delay or other breach.

(2) Consequential damages resulting from the seller's breach include
   (a) any loss resulting from general or particular requirements and needs of which the seller at the time of contracting had reason to know and which could not reasonably be prevented by cover or otherwise; and
   (b) injury to person or property proximately resulting from any breach of warranty.

§ 2–716. Buyer's Right to Specific Performance or Replevin.

(1) Specific performance may be decreed where the goods are unique or in other proper circumstances.

(2) The decree for specific performance may include such terms and conditions as to payment of the price, damages, or other relief as the court may deem just.

(3) The buyer has a right of replevin for goods identified to the contract if after reasonable effort he is unable to effect cover for such goods or the circumstances reasonably indicate that such effort will be unavailing or if the goods have been shipped under reservation and satisfaction of the security interest in them has been made or tendered.

§ 2–717. Deduction of Damages From the Price.

The buyer on notifying the seller of his intention to do so may deduct all or any part of the damages resulting from any breach of the contract from any part of the price still due under the same contract.

§ 2–718. Liquidation or Limitation of Damages; Deposits.

(1) Damages for breach by either party may be liquidated in the agreement but only at an amount which is reasonable in the light of the anticipated or actual harm caused by the breach, the difficulties of proof of loss, and the inconvenience or nonfeasibility of otherwise obtaining an adequate remedy. A term fixing unreasonably large liquidated damages is void as a penalty.

(2) Where the seller justifiably withholds delivery of goods because of the buyer's breach, the buyer is entitled to restitution of any amount by which the sum of his payments exceeds
   (a) the amount to which the seller is entitled by virtue of terms liquidating the seller's damages in accordance with subsection (1), or
   (b) in the absence of such terms, twenty per cent of the value of the total performance for which the buyer is obligated under the contract or $500, whichever is smaller.

(3) The buyer's right to restitution under subsection (2) is subject to offset to the extent that the seller establishes
   (a) a right to recover damages under the provisions of this Article other than subsection (1), and
   (b) the amount or value of any benefits received by the buyer directly or indirectly by reason of the contract.

(4) Where a seller has received payment in goods their reasonable value or the proceeds of their resale shall be treated as payments for the purposes of subsection (2); but if the seller has notice of the buyer's breach before reselling goods received in part performance, his resale is subject to the conditions laid down in this Article on resale by an aggrieved seller (Section 2–706).

§ 2–719. Contractual Modification or Limitation of Remedy.

(1) Subject to the provisions of subsection (2) and (3) of this section and of the preceding section on liquidation and limitation of damages,
   (a) the agreement may provide for remedies in addition to or in substitution for those provided in this Article and may limit or alter the measure of damages recoverable under this Article, as by limiting the buyer's remedies to return of the goods and repayment of the price or to repair and replacement of non-conforming goods or parts; and
   (b) resort to a remedy as provided is optional unless the remedy is expressly agreed to be exclusive, in which case it is the sole remedy.

(2) Where circumstances cause an exclusive or limited remedy to fail of its essential purpose, remedy may be had as provided in this Act.

(3) Consequential damages may be limited or excluded unless the limitation or exclusion is unconscionable. Limitation of consequential damages for injury to the person in the case of consumer goods is prima facie unconscionable but limitation of damages where the loss is commercial is not.

§ 2–720. Effect of "Cancellation" or "Rescission" on Claims for Antecedent Breach.

Unless the contrary intention clearly appears, expressions of "cancellation" or "rescission" of the contract or the like shall not be construed as a renunciation or discharge of any claim in damages for an antecedent breach.

§ 2–721. Remedies for Fraud.

Remedies for material misrepresentation or fraud include all remedies available under this Article for non-fraudulent breach. Neither rescission or a claim for rescission of the contract for sale nor rejection or return of the goods shall bar or be deemed inconsistent with a claim for damages or other remedy.

§ 2–722. Who Can Sue Third Parties for Injury to Goods.

Where a third party so deals with goods which have been identified to a contract for sale as to cause actionable injury to a party to that contract
(a) a right of action against the third party is in either party to the contract for sale who has title to or a security interest or a special property or an insurable interest in the goods; and if the goods have been destroyed or converted a right of action is also in the party who either bore the risk of loss under the contract for sale or has since the injury assumed that risk as against the other;
(b) if at the time of the injury the party plaintiff did not bear the risk of loss as against the other party to the contract for sale and there is no arrangement between them for disposition of the recovery, his suit or settlement is subject to his own interest, as a fiduciary for the other party to the contract;
(c) either party may with the consent of the other sue for the benefit of whom it may concern.

§ 2–723. Proof of Market Price: Time and Place.

(1) If an action based on anticipatory repudiation comes to trial before the time for performance with respect to some or all of the goods, any damages based on market price (Section 2–708 or Section 2–713) shall be determined according to the price of such goods prevailing at the time when the aggrieved party learned of the repudiation.

(2) If evidence of a price prevailing at the times or places described in this Article is not readily available the price prevailing within any reasonable time before or after the time described or at any other place which in commercial judgment or under usage of trade would serve as a reasonable substitute for the one described may be used, making any proper allowance for the cost of transporting the goods to or from such other place.

(3) Evidence of a relevant price prevailing at a time or place other than the one described in this Article offered by one party is not admissible unless and until he has given the other party such notice as the court finds sufficient to prevent unfair surprise.

§ 2–724. Admissibility of Market Quotations.

Whenever the prevailing price or value of any goods regularly bought and sold in any established commodity market is in issue, reports in official publications or trade journals or in newspapers or periodicals of general circulation published as the reports of such market shall be admissible in evidence. The circumstances of the preparation of such a report may be shown to affect its weight but not its admissibility.

§ 2–725. Statute of Limitations in Contracts for Sale.

(1) An action for breach of any contract for sale must be commenced within four years after the cause of action has accrued. By the original agreement the parties may reduce the period of limitation to not less than one year but may not extend it.

(2) A cause of action occurs when the breach occurs, regardless of the aggrieved party's lack of knowledge of the breach. A breach of warranty occurs when tender of delivery is made, except that where a warranty explicitly extends to future performance of the goods and discovery of the breach must await the time of such performance the cause of action accrues when the breach is or should have been discovered.

(3) Where an action commenced within the time limited by subsection (1) is so terminated as to leave available a remedy by another action for the same breach such other action may be commenced after the expiration of the time limited and within six months after the termination of the first action unless the termination resulted from voluntary discontinuance or from dismissal for failure or neglect to prosecute.

(4) This section does not alter the law on tolling of the statute of limitations nor does it apply to causes of action which have accrued before this Act becomes effective.

ARTICLE 2A: LEASES
Part 1—General Provisions
§ 2A–101. Short Title.
This Article shall be known and may be cited as the Uniform Commercial Code—Leases.

§ 2A–102. Scope.
This Article applies to any transaction, regardless of form, that creates a lease.

§ 2A–103. Definitions and Index of Definitions.
(1) In this Article unless the context otherwise requires:

(a) "Buyer in ordinary course of business" means a person who in good faith and without knowledge that the sale to him [or her] is in violation of the ownership rights or security interest or leasehold interest of a third party in the goods buys in ordinary course from a person in the business of selling goods of that kind but does not include a pawnbroker. "Buying" may be for cash or by exchange of other property or on secured or unsecured credit and includes receiving goods or documents of title under a pre-existing contract for sale but does not include a transfer in bulk or as security for or in total or partial satisfaction of a money debt.

(b) "Cancellation" occurs when either party puts an end to the lease contract for default by the other party.

(c) "Commercial unit" means such a unit of goods as by commercial usage is a single whole for purposes of lease and division of which materially impairs its character or value on the market or in use. A commercial unit may be a single article, as a machine, or a set of articles, as a suite of furniture or a line of machinery, or a quantity, as a gross or carload, or any other unit treated in use or in the relevant market as a single whole.

(d) "Conforming" goods or performance under a lease contract means goods or performance that are in accordance with the obligations under the lease contract.

(e) "Consumer lease" means a lease that a lessor regularly engaged in the business of leasing or selling makes to a lessee who is an individual and who takes under the lease primarily for a personal, family, or household purpose [, if the total payments to be made under the lease contract, excluding payments for options to renew or buy, do not exceed $_____].

(f) "Fault" means wrongful act, omission, breach, or default.

(g) "Finance lease" means a lease with respect to which:
   (i) the lessor does not select, manufacture, or supply the goods;
   (ii) the lessor acquires the goods or the right to possession and use of the goods in connection with the lease; and

   (iii) one of the following occurs:
     (A) the lessee receives a copy of the contract by which the lessor acquired the goods or the right to possession and use of the goods before signing the lease contract;
     (B) the lessee's approval of the contract by which the lessor acquired the goods or the right to possession and use of the goods is a condition to effectiveness of the lease contract;
     (C) the lessee, before signing the lease contract, receives an accurate and complete statement designating the promises and warranties, and any disclaimers of warranties, limitations or modifications of remedies, or liquidated damages, including those of a third party, such as the manufacturer of the goods, provided to the lessor by the person supplying the goods in connection with or as part of the contract by which the lessor acquired the goods or the right to possession and use of the goods; or
     (D) if the lease is not a consumer lease, the lessor, before the lessee signs the lease contract, informs the lessee in writing (a) of the identity of the person supplying the goods to the lessor, unless the lessee has selected that person and directed the lessor to acquire the goods or the right to possession and use of the goods from that person, (b) that the lessee is entitled under this Article to the promises and warranties, including those of any third party, provided to the lessor by the person supplying the goods in connection with or as part of the contract by which the lessor acquired the goods or the right to possession and use of the goods, and (c) that the lessee may communicate with the person supplying the goods to the lessor and receive an accurate and complete statement of those promises and warranties, including any disclaimers and limitations of them or of remedies.

(h) "Goods" means all things that are movable at the time of identification to the lease contract, or are fixtures (Section 2A–309), but the term does not include money, documents, instruments, accounts, chattel paper, general intangibles, or minerals or the like, including oil and gas, before extraction. The term also includes the unborn young of animals.

(i) "Installment lease contract" means a lease contract that authorizes or requires the delivery of goods in separate lots to be separately accepted, even though the lease contract contains a clause "each delivery is a separate lease" or its equivalent.

(j) "Lease" means a transfer of the right to possession and use of goods for a term in return for consideration, but a sale, including a sale on approval or a sale or return, or retention or creation of a security interest is not a lease. Unless the context clearly indicates otherwise, the term includes a sublease.

(k) "Lease agreement" means the bargain, with respect to the lease, of the lessor and the lessee in fact as found in their language or by implication from other circumstances including course of dealing or usage of trade or course of performance as provided in this Article. Unless the context clearly indicates otherwise, the term includes a sublease agreement.

(l) "Lease contract" means the total legal obligation that results from the lease agreement as affected by this Article and any other applicable rules of law. Unless the context clearly indicates otherwise, the term includes a sublease contract.

(m) "Leasehold interest" means the interest of the lessor or the lessee under a lease contract.

(n) "Lessee" means a person who acquires the right to possession and use of goods under a lease. Unless the context clearly indicates otherwise, the term includes a sublessee.

(o) "Lessee in ordinary course of business" means a person who in good faith and without knowledge that the lease to him [or her] is in violation of the ownership rights or security interest or leasehold interest of a third party in the goods, leases in ordinary course from a person in the business of selling or leasing goods of that kind but does not include a pawnbroker. "Leasing" may be for cash or by exchange of other property or on secured or unsecured credit and includes receiving goods or documents of title under a pre-existing lease contract but does not include a transfer in bulk or as security for or in total or partial satisfaction of a money debt.

(p) "Lessor" means a person who transfers the right to possession and use of goods under a lease. Unless the context clearly indicates otherwise, the term includes a sublessor.

(q) "Lessor's residual interest" means the lessor's interest in the goods after expiration, termination, or cancellation of the lease contract.

(r) "Lien" means a charge against or interest in goods to secure payment of a debt or performance of an obligation, but the term does not include a security interest.

(s) "Lot" means a parcel or a single article that is the subject matter of a separate lease or delivery, whether or not it is sufficient to perform the lease contract.

(t) "Merchant lessee" means a lessee that is a merchant with respect to goods of the kind subject to the lease.

(u) "Present value" means the amount as of a date certain of one or more sums payable in the future, discounted to the date certain. The discount is determined by the interest rate specified by the parties if the rate was not manifestly unreasonable at the time the transaction was entered into; otherwise, the discount is determined by a commercially reasonable rate that takes into account the facts and circumstances of each case at the time the transaction was entered into.

(v) "Purchase" includes taking by sale, lease, mortgage, security interest, pledge, gift, or any other voluntary transaction creating an interest in goods.

(w) "Sublease" means a lease of goods the right to possession and use of which was acquired by the lessor as a lessee under an existing lease.

(x) "Supplier" means a person from whom a lessor buys or leases goods to be leased under a finance lease.

(y) "Supply contract" means a contract under which a lessor buys or leases goods to be leased.

(z) "Termination" occurs when either party pursuant to a power created by agreement or law puts an end to the lease contract otherwise than for default.

(2) Other definitions applying to this Article and the sections in which they appear are:

"Accessions". Section 2A–310(1).
"Construction mortgage". Section 2A–309(1)(d).
"Encumbrance". Section 2A–309(1)(e).
"Fixtures". Section 2A–309(1)(a).
"Fixture filing". Section 2A–309(1)(b).
"Purchase money lease". Section 2A–309(1)(c).

(3) The following definitions in other Articles apply to this Article:

"Account". Section 9–106.
"Between merchants". Section 2–104(3).
"Buyer". Section 2–103(1)(a).
"Chattel paper". Section 9–105(1)(b).
"Consumer goods". Section 9–109(1).
"Document". Section 9–105(1)(f).
"Entrusting". Section 2–403(3).
"General intangibles". Section 9–106.
"Good faith". Section 2–103(1)(b).
"Instrument". Section 9–105(1)(i).
"Merchant". Section 2–104(1).
"Mortgage". Sect 9–105(1)(j).
"Pursuant to commitment". Section 9–105(1)(k).
"Receipt". Section 2–103(1)(c).
"Sale". Section 2–106(1).
"Sale on approval". Section 2–326.
"Sale or return". Section 2–326.
"Seller". Section 2–103(1)(d).

(4) In addition Article 1 contains general definitions and principles of construction and interpretation applicable throughout this Article.

As amended in 1990.

§ 2A–104. Leases Subject to Other Law.

(1) A lease, although subject to this Article, is also subject to any applicable:

(a) certificate of title statute of this State: (list any certificate of title statutes covering automobiles, trailers, mobile homes, boats, farm tractors, and the like);

(b) certificate of title statute of another jurisdiction (Section 2A–105); or

(c) consumer protection statute of this State, or final consumer protection decision of a court of this State existing on the effective date of this Article.

(2) In case of conflict between this Article, other than Sections 2A–105, 2A–304(3), and 2A–305(3), and a statute or decision referred to in subsection (1), the statute or decision controls.

(3) Failure to comply with an applicable law has only the effect specified therein.

As amended in 1990.

§ 2A–108. Unconscionability.

(1) If the court as a matter of law finds a lease contract or any clause of a lease contract to have been unconscionable at the time it was made the court may refuse to enforce the lease contract, or it may enforce the remainder of the lease contract without the unconscionable clause, or it may so limit the application of any unconscionable clause as to avoid any unconscionable result.

(2) With respect to a consumer lease, if the court as a matter of law finds that a lease contract or any clause of a lease contract has been induced by unconscionable conduct or that unconscionable conduct has occurred in the collection of a claim arising from a lease contract, the court may grant appropriate relief.

(3) Before making a finding of unconscionability under subsection (1) or (2), the court, on its own motion or that of a party, shall afford the parties a reasonable opportunity to present evidence as to the setting, purpose, and effect of the lease contract or clause thereof, or of the conduct.

(4) In an action in which the lessee claims unconscionability with respect to a consumer lease:

(a) If the court finds unconscionability under subsection (1) or (2), the court shall award reasonable attorney's fees to the lessee.

(b) If the court does not find unconscionability and the lessee claiming unconscionability has brought or maintained an action he [or she] knew to be groundless, the court shall award reasonable attorney's fees to the party against whom the claim is made.

(c) In determining attorney's fees, the amount of the recovery on behalf of the claimant under subsections (1) and (2) is not controlling.

Part 2—Formation and Construction of Lease Contract
§ 2A–201. Statute of Frauds.

(1) A lease contract is not enforceable by way of action or defense unless:

(a) the total payments to be made under the lease contract, excluding payments for options to renew or buy, are less than $1,000; or

(b) there is a writing, signed by the party against whom enforcement is sought or by that party's authorized agent, sufficient to indicate that a lease contract has been made between the parties and to describe the goods leased and the lease term.

(2) Any description of leased goods or of the lease term is sufficient and satisfies subsection (1)(b), whether or not it is specific, if it reasonably identifies what is described.

(3) A writing is not insufficient because it omits or incorrectly states a term agreed upon, but the lease contract is not enforceable under subsection (1)(b) beyond the lease term and the quantity of goods shown in the writing.

(4) A lease contract that does not satisfy the requirements of subsection (1), but which is valid in other respects, is enforceable:

(a) if the goods are to be specially manufactured or obtained for the lessee and are not suitable for lease or sale to others in the ordinary course of the lessor's business, and the lessor, before notice of repudiation is received and under circumstances that reasonably indicate that the goods are for the lessee, has made either a substantial beginning of their manufacture or commitments for their procurement;

(b) if the party against whom enforcement is sought admits in that party's pleading, testimony or otherwise in court that a lease contract was made, but the lease contract is not enforceable under this provision beyond the quantity of goods admitted; or

(c) with respect to goods that have been received and accepted by the lessee.

(5) The lease term under a lease contract referred to in subsection (4) is:

(a) if there is a writing signed by the party against whom enforcement is sought or by that party's authorized agent specifying the lease term, the term so specified;

(b) if the party against whom enforcement is sought admits in that party's pleading, testimony, or otherwise in court a lease term, the term so admitted; or

(c) a reasonable lease term.

§ 2A–202. Final Written Expression: Parol or Extrinsic Evidence.

Terms with respect to which the confirmatory memoranda of the parties agree or which are otherwise set forth in a writing intended by the parties as a final expression of their agreement with respect to such terms as are included therein may not be contradicted by evidence of any prior agreement or of a contemporaneous oral agreement but may be explained or supplemented:

(a) by course of dealing or usage of trade or by course of performance; and

(b) by evidence of consistent additional terms unless the court finds the writing to have been intended also as a complete and exclusive statement of the terms of the agreement.

§ 2A–204. Formation in General.

(1) A lease contract may be made in any manner sufficient to show agreement, including conduct by both parties which recognizes the existence of a lease contract.

(2) An agreement sufficient to constitute a lease contract may be found although the moment of its making is undetermined.

(3) Although one or more terms are left open, a lease contract does not fail for indefiniteness if the parties have intended to make a lease contract and there is a reasonably certain basis for giving an appropriate remedy.

§ 2A–205. Firm Offers.

An offer by a merchant to lease goods to or from another person in a signed writing that by its terms gives assurance it will be held open is not revocable, for lack of consideration, during the time stated or, if no time is stated, for a reasonable time, but in no event may the period of irrevocability exceed 3 months. Any such term of assurance on a form supplied by the offeree must be separately signed by the offeror.

§ 2A–206. Offer and Acceptance in Formation of Lease Contract.

(1) Unless otherwise unambiguously indicated by the language or circumstances, an offer to make a lease contract must be construed as inviting acceptance in any manner and by any medium reasonable in the circumstances.

(2) If the beginning of a requested performance is a reasonable mode of acceptance, an offeror who is not notified of acceptance within a reasonable time may treat the offer as having lapsed before acceptance.

§ 2A–207. Course of Performance or Practical Construction.

(1) If a lease contract involves repeated occasions for performance by either party with knowledge of the nature of the performance and opportunity for objection to it by the other, any course of performance accepted or acquiesced in without objection is relevant to determine the meaning of the lease agreement.

(2) The express terms of a lease agreement and any course of performance, as well as any course of dealing and usage of trade, must be construed whenever reasonable as consistent with each other; but if that construction is unreasonable, express terms control course of performance, course of performance controls both course of dealing and usage of trade, and course of dealing controls usage of trade.

(3) Subject to the provisions of Section 2A–208 on modification and waiver, course of performance is relevant to show a waiver or modification of any term inconsistent with the course of performance.

§ 2A–208. Modification, Rescission and Waiver.

(1) An agreement modifying a lease contract needs no consideration to be binding.

(2) A signed lease agreement that excludes modification or rescission except by a signed writing may not be otherwise modified or rescinded, but, except as between merchants, such a requirement on a form supplied by a merchant must be separately signed by the other party.

(3) Although an attempt at modification or rescission does not satisfy the requirements of subsection (2), it may operate as a waiver.

(4) A party who has made a waiver affecting an executory portion of a lease contract may retract the waiver by reasonable notification received by the other party that strict performance will be required of any term waived, unless the retraction would be unjust in view of a material change of position in reliance on the waiver.

§ 2A–209. Lessee Under Finance Lease as Beneficiary of Supply Contract.

(1) The benefit of a supplier's promises to the lessor under the supply contract and of all warranties, whether express or implied, including those of any third party provided in connection with or as part of the supply contract, extends to the lessee to the extent of the lessee's leasehold interest under a finance lease related to the supply contract, but is subject to the terms of the warranty and of the supply contract and all defenses or claims arising therefrom.

(2) The extension of the benefit of a supplier's promises and of warranties to the lessee (Section 2A–209(1)) does not: (i) modify the rights and obligations of the parties to the supply contract, whether arising therefrom or otherwise, or (ii) impose any duty or liability under the supply contract on the lessee.

(3) Any modification or rescission of the supply contract by the supplier and the lessor is effective between the supplier and the lessee unless, before the modification or rescission, the supplier has received notice that the lessee has entered into a finance lease related to the supply contract. If the modification or rescission is effective between the supplier and the lessee, the lessor is deemed to have assumed, in addition to the obligations of the lessor to the lessee under the lease contract, promises of the supplier to the lessor and warranties that were so modified or rescinded as they existed and were available to the lessee before modification or rescission.

(4) In addition to the extension of the benefit of the supplier's promises and of warranties to the lessee under subsection (1), the lessee retains all rights that the lessee may have against the supplier which arise from an agreement between the lessee and the supplier or under other law.

As amended in 1990.

§ 2A–210. Express Warranties.

(1) Express warranties by the lessor are created as follows:

(a) Any affirmation of fact or promise made by the lessor to the lessee which relates to the goods and becomes part of the basis of the bargain creates an express warranty that the goods will conform to the affirmation or promise.

(b) Any description of the goods which is made part of the basis of the bargain creates an express warranty that the goods will conform to the description.

(c) Any sample or model that is made part of the basis of the bargain creates an express warranty that the whole of the goods will conform to the sample or model.

(2) It is not necessary to the creation of an express warranty that the lessor use formal words, such as "warrant" or "guarantee," or that the lessor have a specific intention to make a warranty, but an affirmation merely of the value of the goods or a statement purporting to be merely the lessor's opinion or commendation of the goods does not create a warranty.

§ 2A–211. Warranties Against Interference and Against Infringement; Lessee's Obligation Against Infringement.

(1) There is in a lease contract a warranty that for the lease term no person holds a claim to or interest in the goods that arose from an act or omission of the lessor, other than a claim by way of infringement or the like, which will interfere with the lessee's enjoyment of its leasehold interest.

(2) Except in a finance lease there is in a lease contract by a lessor who is a merchant regularly dealing in goods of the kind a warranty that the goods are delivered free of the rightful claim of any person by way of infringement or the like.

(3) A lessee who furnishes specifications to a lessor or a supplier shall hold the lessor and the supplier harmless against any claim by way of infringement or the like that arises out of compliance with the specifications.

§ 2A–212. Implied Warranty of Merchantability.

(1) Except in a finance lease, a warranty that the goods will be merchantable is implied in a lease contract if the lessor is a merchant with respect to goods of that kind.

(2) Goods to be merchantable must be at least such as

(a) pass without objection in the trade under the description in the lease agreement;

(b) in the case of fungible goods, are of fair average quality within the description;

(c) are fit for the ordinary purposes for which goods of that type are used;

(d) run, within the variation permitted by the lease agreement, of even kind, quality, and quantity within each unit and among all units involved;

(e) are adequately contained, packaged, and labeled as the lease agreement may require; and

(f) conform to any promises or affirmations of fact made on the container or label.

(3) Other implied warranties may arise from course of dealing or usage of trade.

§ 2A–213. Implied Warranty of Fitness for Particular Purpose.

Except in a finance lease, if the lessor at the time the lease contract is made has reason to know of any particular purpose for which the goods are required and that the lessee is relying on the lessor's skill or judgment to select or furnish suitable goods, there is in the lease contract an implied warranty that the goods will be fit for that purpose.

§ 2A–214. Exclusion or Modification of Warranties.

(1) Words or conduct relevant to the creation of an express warranty and words or conduct tending to negate or limit a warranty must be construed wherever reasonable as consistent with each other; but, subject to the provisions of Section 2A–202 on parol or extrinsic evidence, negation or limitation is inoperative to the extent that the construction is unreasonable.

(2) Subject to subsection (3), to exclude or modify the implied warranty of merchantability or any part of it the language must mention "merchantability", be by a writing, and be conspicuous. Subject to subsection (3), to exclude or modify any implied warranty of fitness the exclusion must be by a writing and be conspicuous. Language to exclude all implied warranties of fitness is sufficient if it is in writing, is conspicuous and states, for example, "There is no warranty that the goods will be fit for a particular purpose".

(3) Notwithstanding subsection (2), but subject to subsection (4),

(a) unless the circumstances indicate otherwise, all implied warranties are excluded by expressions like "as is," or "with all faults," or by other language that in common understanding calls the lessee's attention to the exclusion of warranties and makes plain that there is no implied warranty, if in writing and conspicuous;

(b) if the lessee before entering into the lease contract has examined the goods or the sample or model as fully as desired or has refused to examine the goods, there is no implied warranty with regard to defects that an examination ought in the circumstances to have revealed; and

(c) an implied warranty may also be excluded or modified by course of dealing, course of performance, or usage of trade.

(4) To exclude or modify a warranty against interference or against infringement (Section 2A–211) or any part of it, the language must be specific, be by a writing, and be conspicuous, unless the circumstances, including course of performance, course of dealing, or usage of trade, give the lessee reason to know that the goods are being leased subject to a claim or interest of any person.

§ 2A–215. Cumulation and Conflict of Warranties Express or Implied.

Warranties, whether express or implied, must be construed as consistent with each other and as cumulative, but if that construction is unreasonable, the intention of the parties determines which warranty is dominant. In ascertaining that intention the following rules apply:

(a) Exact or technical specifications displace an inconsistent sample or model or general language of description.

(b) A sample from an existing bulk displaces inconsistent general language of description.

(c) Express warranties displace inconsistent implied warranties other than an implied warranty of fitness for a particular purpose.

§ 2A–216. Third-Party Beneficiaries of Express and Implied Warranties.

Alternative A A warranty to or for the benefit of a lessee under this Article, whether express or implied, extends to any natural person who is in the family or household of the lessee or who is a guest in the lessee's home if it is reasonable to expect that such person may use, consume, or be affected by the goods and who is injured in person by breach of the warranty. This section does not displace principles of law and equity that extend a warranty to or for the benefit of a lessee to other persons. The operation of this section may not be excluded, modified, or limited, but an exclusion, modification, or limitation of the warranty, including any with respect to rights and remedies, effective against the lessee is also effective against any beneficiary designated under this section.

Alternative B A warranty to or for the benefit of a lessee under this Article, whether express or implied, extends to any natural person who may reasonably be expected to use, consume, or be affected by the goods and who is injured in person by breach of the warranty. This section does not displace principles of law and equity that extend a warranty to or for the benefit of a lessee to other persons. The operation of this section may not be excluded, modified, or limited, but an exclusion, modification, or limitation of the warranty, including any with respect to rights and remedies, effective against the lessee is also effective against the beneficiary designated under this section.

Alternative C A warranty to or for the benefit of a lessee under this Article, whether express or implied, extends to any person who may reasonably be expected to use, consume, or be affected by the goods and who is injured by breach of the warranty. The operation of this section may not be excluded, modified, or limited with respect to injury to the person of an individual to whom the warranty extends, but an exclusion, modification, or limitation of the warranty, including any with respect to rights and remedies, effective against the lessee is also effective against the beneficiary designated under this section.

§ 2A–219. Risk of Loss.

(1) Except in the case of a finance lease, risk of loss is retained by the lessor and does not pass to the lessee. In the case of a finance lease, risk of loss passes to the lessee.

(2) Subject to the provisions of this Article on the effect of default on risk of loss (Section 2A–220), if risk of loss is to pass to the lessee and the time of passage is not stated, the following rules apply:

(a) If the lease contract requires or authorizes the goods to be shipped by carrier

(i) and it does not require delivery at a particular destination, the risk of loss passes to the lessee when the goods are duly delivered to the carrier; but

(ii) if it does require delivery at a particular destination and the goods are there duly tendered while in the possession of the carrier, the risk of loss passes to the lessee when the goods are there duly so tendered as to enable the lessee to take delivery.

(b) If the goods are held by a bailee to be delivered without being moved, the risk of loss passes to the lessee on acknowledgment by the bailee of the lessee's right to possession of the goods.

(c) In any case not within subsection (a) or (b), the risk of loss passes to the lessee on the lessee's receipt of the goods if the lessor, or, in the case of a finance lease, the supplier, is a merchant; otherwise the risk passes to the lessee on tender of delivery.

Part 3—Effect of Lease Contract
§ 2A–302. Title to and Possession of Goods.
Except as otherwise provided in this Article, each provision of this Article applies whether the lessor or a third party has title to the goods, and whether the lessor, the lessee, or a third party has possession of the goods, notwithstanding any statute or rule of law that possession or the absence of possession is fraudulent.

§ 2A–303. Alienability of Party's Interest Under Lease Contract or of Lessor's Residual Interest in Goods; Delegation of Performance; Transfer of Rights.
(1) As used in this section, "creation of a security interest" includes the sale of a lease contract that is subject to Article 9, Secured Transactions, by reason of Section 9–102(1)(b).

(2) Except as provided in subsections (3) and (4), a provision in a lease agreement which (i) prohibits the voluntary or involuntary transfer, including a transfer by sale, sublease, creation or enforcement of a security interest, or attachment, levy, or other judicial process, of an interest of a party under the lease contract or of the lessor's residual interest in the goods, or (ii) makes such a transfer an event of default, gives rise to the rights and remedies provided in subsection (5), but a transfer that is prohibited or is an event of default under the lease agreement is otherwise effective.

(3) A provision in a lease agreement which (i) prohibits the creation or enforcement of a security interest in an interest of a party under the lease contract or in the lessor's residual interest in the goods, or (ii) makes such a transfer an event of default, is not enforceable unless, and then only to the extent that, there is an actual transfer by the lessee of the lessee's right of possession or use of the goods in violation of the provision or an actual delegation of a material performance of either party to the lease contract in violation of the provision. Neither the granting nor the enforcement of a security interest in (i) the lessor's interest under the lease contract or (ii) the lessor's residual interest in the goods is a transfer that materially impairs the prospect of obtaining return performance by, materially changes the duty of, or materially increases the burden or risk imposed on, the lessee within the purview of subsection (5) unless, and then only to the extent that, there is an actual delegation of a material performance of the lessor.

(4) A provision in a lease agreement which (i) prohibits a transfer of a right to damages for default with respect to the whole lease contract or of a right to payment arising out of the transferor's due performance of the transferor's entire obligation, or (ii) makes such a transfer an event of default, is not enforceable, and such a transfer is not a transfer that materially impairs the prospect of obtaining return performance by, materially changes the duty of, or materially increases the burden or risk imposed on, the other party to the lease contract within the purview of subsection

(5) Subject to subsections (3) and (4):
   (a) if a transfer is made which is made an event of default under a lease agreement, the party to the lease contract not making the transfer, unless that party waives the default or otherwise agrees, has the rights and remedies described in Section 2A–501(2);
   (b) if paragraph (a) is not applicable and if a transfer is made that (i) is prohibited under a lease agreement or (ii) materially impairs the prospect of obtaining return performance by, materially changes the duty of, or materially increases the burden or risk imposed on, the other party to the lease contract, unless the party not making the transfer agrees at any time to the transfer in the lease contract or otherwise, then, except as limited by contract, (i) the transferor is liable to the party not making the transfer for damages caused by the transfer to the extent that the damages could not reasonably be prevented by the party not making the transfer and (ii) a court having jurisdiction may grant other appropriate relief, including cancellation of the lease contract or an injunction against the transfer.

(6) A transfer of "the lease" or of "all my rights under the lease", or a transfer in similar general terms, is a transfer of rights and, unless the language or the circumstances, as in a transfer for security, indicate the contrary, the transfer is a delegation of duties by the transferor to the transferee. Acceptance by the transferee constitutes a promise by the transferee to perform those duties. The promise is enforceable by either the transferor or the other party to the lease contract.

(7) Unless otherwise agreed by the lessor and the lessee, a delegation of performance does not relieve the transferor as against the other party of any duty to perform or of any liability for default.

(8) In a consumer lease, to prohibit the transfer of an interest of a party under the lease contract or to make a transfer an event of default, the language must be specific, by a writing, and conspicuous.

As amended in 1990.

§ 2A–304. Subsequent Lease of Goods by Lessor.
(1) Subject to Section 2A–303, a subsequent lessee from a lessor of goods under an existing lease contract obtains, to the extent of the leasehold interest transferred, the leasehold interest in the goods that the lessor had or had power to transfer, and except as provided in subsection (2) and Section 2A–527(4), takes subject to the existing lease contract. A lessor with voidable title has power to transfer a good leasehold interest to a good faith subsequent lessee for value, but only to the extent set forth in the preceding sentence. If goods have been delivered under a transaction of purchase, the lessor has that power even though:
   (a) the lessor's transferor was deceived as to the identity of the lessor;
   (b) the delivery was in exchange for a check which is later dishonored;
   (c) it was agreed that the transaction was to be a "cash sale"; or
   (d) the delivery was procured through fraud punishable as larcenous under the criminal law.

(2) A subsequent lessee in the ordinary course of business from a lessor who is a merchant dealing in goods of that kind to whom the goods were entrusted by the existing lessee of that lessor before the interest of the subsequent lessee became enforceable against that lessor obtains, to the extent of the leasehold interest transferred, all of that lessor's and the existing lessee's rights to the goods, and takes free of the existing lease contract.

(3) A subsequent lessee from the lessor of goods that are subject to an existing lease contract and are covered by a certificate of title issued under a statute of this State or of another jurisdiction takes no greater rights than those provided both by this section and by the certificate of title statute.

As amended in 1990.

§ 2A–307. Priority of Liens Arising by Attachment or Levy on, Security Interests in, and Other Claims to Goods.
(1) Except as otherwise provided in Section 2A–306, a creditor of a lessee takes subject to the lease contract.

(2) Except as otherwise provided in subsections (3) and (4) and in Sections 2A–306 and 2A–308, a creditor of a lessor takes subject to the lease contract unless:
   (a) the creditor holds a lien that attached to the goods before the lease contract became enforceable;
   (b) the creditor holds a security interest in the goods and the lessee did not give value and receive delivery of the goods without knowledge of the security interest; or
   (c) the creditor holds a security interest in the goods which was perfected (Section 9–303) before the lease contract became enforceable.

(3) A lessee in the ordinary course of business takes the leasehold interest free of a security interest in the goods created by the lessor even though the security interest is perfected (Section 9–303) and the lessee knows of its existence.

(4) A lessee other than a lessee in the ordinary course of business takes the leasehold interest free of a security interest to the extent that it secures future advances made after the secured party acquires knowledge of the lease or more than 45 days after the lease contract becomes enforceable, whichever first occurs, unless the future advances are made pursuant to a commitment entered into without knowledge of the lease and before the expiration of the 45-day period.

As amended in 1990.

§ 2A–308. Special Rights of Creditors.
(1) A creditor of a lessor in possession of goods subject to a lease contract may treat the lease contract as void if as against the creditor retention of

possession by the lessor is fraudulent under any statute or rule of law, but retention of possession in good faith and current course of trade by the lessor for a commercially reasonable time after the lease contract becomes enforceable is not fraudulent.

(2) Nothing in this Article impairs the rights of creditors of a lessor if the lease contract (a) becomes enforceable, not in current course of trade but in satisfaction of or as security for a pre-existing claim for money, security, or the like, and (b) is made under circumstances which under any statute or rule of law apart from this Article would constitute the transaction a fraudulent transfer or voidable preference.

(3) A creditor of a seller may treat a sale or an identification of goods to a contract for sale as void if as against the creditor retention of possession by the seller is fraudulent under any statute or rule of law, but retention of possession of the goods pursuant to a lease contract entered into by the seller as lessee and the buyer as lessor in connection with the sale or identification of the goods is not fraudulent if the buyer bought for value and in good faith.

Part 4—Performance of Lease Contract: Repudiated, Substituted and Excused
§ 2A–407. Irrevocable Promises: Finance Leases.
(1) In the case of a finance lease that is not a consumer lease the lessee's promises under the lease contract become irrevocable and independent upon the lessee's acceptance of the goods.

(2) A promise that has become irrevocable and independent under subsection (1):

  (a) is effective and enforceable between the parties, and by or against third parties including assignees of the parties; and

  (b) is not subject to cancellation, termination, modification, repudiation, excuse, or substitution without the consent of the party to whom the promise runs.

(3) This section does not affect the validity under any other law of a covenant in any lease contract making the lessee's promises irrevocable and independent upon the lessee's acceptance of the goods.

As amended in 1990.

Part 5—Default
A. In General
§ 2A–503. Modification or Impairment of Rights and Remedies.
(1) Except as otherwise provided in this Article, the lease agreement may include rights and remedies for default in addition to or in substitution for those provided in this Article and may limit or alter the measure of damages recoverable under this Article.

(2) Resort to a remedy provided under this Article or in the lease agreement is optional unless the remedy is expressly agreed to be exclusive. If circumstances cause an exclusive or limited remedy to fail of its essential purpose, or provision for an exclusive remedy is unconscionable, remedy may be had as provided in this Article.

(3) Consequential damages may be liquidated under Section 2A–504, or may otherwise be limited, altered, or excluded unless the limitation, alteration, or exclusion is unconscionable. Limitation, alteration, or exclusion of consequential damages for injury to the person in the case of consumer goods is prima facie unconscionable but limitation, alteration, or exclusion of damages where the loss is commercial is not prima facie unconscionable.

(4) Rights and remedies on default by the lessor or the lessee with respect to any obligation or promise collateral or ancillary to the lease contract are not impaired by this Article.

As amended in 1990.

§ 2A–504. Liquidation of Damages.
(1) Damages payable by either party for default, or any other act or omission, including indemnity for loss or diminution of anticipated tax benefits or loss or damage to lessor's residual interest, may be liquidated in the lease agreement but only at an amount or by a formula that is reasonable in light of the then anticipated harm caused by the default or other act or omission.

(2) If the lease agreement provides for liquidation of damages, and such provision does not comply with subsection (1), or such provision is an exclusive or limited remedy that circumstances cause to fail of its essential purpose, remedy may be had as provided in this Article.

(3) If the lessor justifiably withholds or stops delivery of goods because of the lessee's default or insolvency (Section 2A–525 or 2A–526), the lessee is entitled to restitution of any amount by which the sum of his [or her] payments exceeds:

  (a) the amount to which the lessor is entitled by virtue of terms liquidating the lessor's damages in accordance with subsection (1); or

  (b) in the absence of those terms, 20 percent of the then present value of the total rent the lessee was obligated to pay for the balance of the lease term, or, in the case of a consumer lease, the lesser of such amount or $500.

(4) A lessee's right to restitution under subsection (3) is subject to offset to the extent the lessor establishes:

  (a) a right to recover damages under the provisions of this Article other than subsection (1); and

  (b) the amount or value of any benefits received by the lessee directly or indirectly by reason of the lease contract.

§ 2A–507. Proof of Market Rent: Time and Place.
(1) Damages based on market rent (Section 2A–519 or 2A–528) are determined according to the rent for the use of the goods concerned for a lease term identical to the remaining lease term of the original lease agreement and prevailing at the times specified in Sections 2A–519 and 2A–528.

(2) If evidence of rent for the use of the goods concerned for a lease term identical to the remaining lease term of the original lease agreement and prevailing at the times or places described in this Article is not readily available, the rent prevailing within any reasonable time before or after the time described or at any other place or for a different lease term which in commercial judgment or under usage of trade would serve as a reasonable substitute for the one described may be used, making any proper allowance for the difference, including the cost of transporting the goods to or from the other place.

(3) Evidence of a relevant rent prevailing at a time or place or for a lease term other than the one described in this Article offered by one party is not admissible unless and until he [or she] has given the other party notice the court finds sufficient to prevent unfair surprise.

(4) If the prevailing rent or value of any goods regularly leased in any established market is in issue, reports in official publications or trade journals or in newspapers or periodicals of general circulation published as the reports of that market are admissible in evidence. The circumstances of the preparation of the report may be shown to affect its weight but not its admissibility.
As amended in 1990.

B. Default by Lessor
§ 2A–508. Lessee's Remedies.
(1) If a lessor fails to deliver the goods in conformity to the lease contract (Section 2A–509) or repudiates the lease contract (Section 2A–402), or a lessee rightfully rejects the goods (Section 2A–509) or justifiably revokes acceptance of the goods (Section 2A–517), then with respect to any goods involved, and with respect to all of the goods if under an installment lease contract the value of the whole lease contract is substantially impaired (Section 2A–510), the lessor is in default under the lease contract and the lessee may:

  (a) cancel the lease contract (Section 2A–505(1));

  (b) recover so much of the rent and security as has been paid and is just under the circumstances;

  (c) cover and recover damages as to all goods affected whether or not they have been identified to the lease contract (Sections 2A–518 and 2A–520), or recover damages for nondelivery (Sections 2A–519 and 2A–520);

  (d) exercise any other rights or pursue any other remedies provided in the lease contract.

(2) If a lessor fails to deliver the goods in conformity to the lease contract or repudiates the lease contract, the lessee may also:

  (a) if the goods have been identified, recover them (Section 2A–522); or

  (b) in a proper case, obtain specific performance or replevy the goods (Section 2A–521).

(3) If a lessor is otherwise in default under a lease contract, the lessee may exercise the rights and pursue the remedies provided in the lease contract, which may include a right to cancel the lease, and in Section 2A–519(3).

(4) If a lessor has breached a warranty, whether express or implied, the lessee may recover damages (Section 2A–519(4)).

(5) On rightful rejection or justifiable revocation of acceptance, a lessee has a security interest in goods in the lessee's possession or control for any rent and security that has been paid and any expenses reasonably incurred in their inspection, receipt, transportation, and care and custody and may hold those goods and dispose of them in good faith and in a commercially reasonable manner, subject to Section 2A–527(5).

(6) Subject to the provisions of Section 2A–407, a lessee, on notifying the lessor of the lessee's intention to do so, may deduct all or any part of the damages resulting from any default under the lease contract from any part of the rent still due under the same lease contract.

As amended in 1990.

§ 2A–509. Lessee's Rights on Improper Delivery; Rightful Rejection.

(1) Subject to the provisions of Section 2A–510 on default in installment lease contracts, if the goods or the tender or delivery fail in any respect to conform to the lease contract, the lessee may reject or accept the goods or accept any commercial unit or units and reject the rest of the goods.

(2) Rejection of goods is ineffective unless it is within a reasonable time after tender or delivery of the goods and the lessee seasonably notifies the lessor.

§ 2A–510. Installment Lease Contracts: Rejection and Default.

(1) Under an installment lease contract a lessee may reject any delivery that is nonconforming if the nonconformity substantially impairs the value of that delivery and cannot be cured or the nonconformity is a defect in the required documents; but if the nonconformity does not fall within subsection (2) and the lessor or the supplier gives adequate assurance of its cure, the lessee must accept that delivery.

(2) Whenever nonconformity or default with respect to one or more deliveries substantially impairs the value of the installment lease contract as a whole there is a default with respect to the whole. But, the aggrieved party reinstates the installment lease contract as a whole if the aggrieved party accepts a nonconforming delivery without seasonably notifying of cancellation or brings an action with respect only to past deliveries or demands performance as to future deliveries.

§ 2A–511. Merchant Lessee's Duties as to Rightfully Rejected Goods.

(1) Subject to any security interest of a lessee (Section 2A–508(5)), if a lessor or a supplier has no agent or place of business at the market of rejection, a merchant lessee, after rejection of goods in his [or her] possession or control, shall follow any reasonable instructions received from the lessor or the supplier with respect to the goods. In the absence of those instructions, a merchant lessee shall make reasonable efforts to sell, lease, or otherwise dispose of the goods for the lessor's account if they threaten to decline in value speedily. Instructions are not reasonable if on demand indemnity for expenses is not forthcoming.

(2) If a merchant lessee (subsection (1)) or any other lessee (Section 2A–512) disposes of goods, he [or she] is entitled to reimbursement either from the lessor or the supplier or out of the proceeds for reasonable expenses of caring for and disposing of the goods and, if the expenses include no disposition commission, to such commission as is usual in the trade, or if there is none, to a reasonable sum not exceeding 10 percent of the gross proceeds.

(3) In complying with this section or Section 2A–512, the lessee is held only to good faith. Good faith conduct hereunder is neither acceptance or conversion nor the basis of an action for damages.

(4) A purchaser who purchases in good faith from a lessee pursuant to this section or Section 2A–512 takes the goods free of any rights of the lessor and the supplier even though the lessee fails to comply with one or more of the requirements of this Article.

§ 2A–512. Lessee's Duties as to Rightfully Rejected Goods.

(1) Except as otherwise provided with respect to goods that threaten to decline in value speedily (Section 2A–511) and subject to any security interest of a lessee (Section 2A–508(5)):

(a) the lessee, after rejection of goods in the lessee's possession, shall hold them with reasonable care at the lessor's or the supplier's disposition for a reasonable time after the lessee's seasonable notification of rejection;

(b) if the lessor or the supplier gives no instructions within a reasonable time after notification of rejection, the lessee may store the rejected goods for the lessor's or the supplier's account or ship them to the lessor or the supplier or dispose of them for the lessor's or the supplier's account with reimbursement in the manner provided in Section 2A–511; but

(c) the lessee has no further obligations with regard to goods rightfully rejected.

(2) Action by the lessee pursuant to subsection (1) is not acceptance or conversion.

§ 2A–513. Cure by Lessor of Improper Tender or Delivery; Replacement.

(1) If any tender or delivery by the lessor or the supplier is rejected because nonconforming and the time for performance has not yet expired, the lessor or the supplier may seasonably notify the lessee of the lessor's or the supplier's intention to cure and may then make a conforming delivery within the time provided in the lease contract.

(2) If the lessee rejects a nonconforming tender that the lessor or the supplier had reasonable grounds to believe would be acceptable with or without money allowance, the lessor or the supplier may have a further reasonable time to substitute a conforming tender if he [or she] seasonably notifies the lessee.

§ 2A–515. Acceptance of Goods.

(1) Acceptance of goods occurs after the lessee has had a reasonable opportunity to inspect the goods and

(a) the lessee signifies or acts with respect to the goods in a manner that signifies to the lessor or the supplier that the goods are conforming or that the lessee will take or retain them in spite of their nonconformity; or

(b) the lessee fails to make an effective rejection of the goods (Section 2A–509(2)).

(2) Acceptance of a part of any commercial unit is acceptance of that entire unit.

§ 2A–517. Revocation of Acceptance of Goods.

(1) A lessee may revoke acceptance of a lot or commercial unit whose nonconformity substantially impairs its value to the lessee if the lessee has accepted it:

(a) except in the case of a finance lease, on the reasonable assumption that its nonconformity would be cured and it has not been seasonably cured; or

(b) without discovery of the nonconformity if the lessee's acceptance was reasonably induced either by the lessor's assurances or, except in the case of a finance lease, by the difficulty of discovery before acceptance.

(2) Except in the case of a finance lease that is not a consumer lease, a lessee may revoke acceptance of a lot or commercial unit if the lessor defaults under the lease contract and the default substantially impairs the value of that lot or commercial unit to the lessee.

(3) If the lease agreement so provides, the lessee may revoke acceptance of a lot or commercial unit because of other defaults by the lessor.

(4) Revocation of acceptance must occur within a reasonable time after the lessee discovers or should have discovered the ground for it and before any substantial change in condition of the goods which is not caused by the nonconformity. Revocation is not effective until the lessee notifies the lessor.

(5) A lessee who so revokes has the same rights and duties with regard to the goods involved as if the lessee had rejected them.

As amended in 1990.

§ 2A–518. Cover; Substitute Goods.

(1) After a default by a lessor under the lease contract of the type described in Section 2A–508(1), or, if agreed, after other default by the lessor, the lessee may cover by making any purchase or lease of or contract to purchase or lease goods in substitution for those due from the lessor.

(2) Except as otherwise provided with respect to damages liquidated in the lease agreement (Section 2A–504) or otherwise determined pursuant to agreement of the parties (Sections 1–102(3) and 2A–503), if a lessee's cover is by a lease agreement substantially similar to the original lease agreement and the new lease agreement is made in good faith and in a commercially reasonable manner, the lessee may recover from the lessor as damages (i) the present value, as of the date of the commencement of the term of the new lease agreement, of the rent under the new lease agreement applicable to that period of the new lease term which is comparable to the then remaining term of the original lease agreement minus the present value as of the same date of the total rent for the then remaining lease term of the original lease agreement, and (ii) any incidental or consequential damages, less expenses saved in consequence of the lessor's default.

(3) If a lessee's cover is by lease agreement that for any reason does not qualify for treatment under subsection (2), or is by purchase or otherwise, the lessee may recover from the lessor as if the lessee had elected not to cover and Section 2A–519 governs.

As amended in 1990.

§ 2A–519. Lessee's Damages for Non-delivery, Repudiation, Default, and Breach of Warranty in Regard to Accepted Goods.

(1) Except as otherwise provided with respect to damages liquidated in the lease agreement (Section 2A–504) or otherwise determined pursuant to agreement of the parties (Sections 1–102(3) and 2A–503), if a lessee elects not to cover or a lessee elects to cover and the cover is by lease agreement that for any reason does not qualify for treatment under Section 2A–518(2), or is by purchase or otherwise, the measure of damages for non-delivery or repudiation by the lessor or for rejection or revocation of acceptance by the lessee is the present value, as of the date of the default, of the then market rent minus the present value as of the same date of the original rent, computed for the remaining lease term of the original lease agreement, together with incidental and consequential damages, less expenses saved in consequence of the lessor's default.

(2) Market rent is to be determined as of the place for tender or, in cases of rejection after arrival or revocation of acceptance, as of the place of arrival.

(3) Except as otherwise agreed, if the lessee has accepted goods and given notification (Section 2A–516(3)), the measure of damages for non-conforming tender or delivery or other default by a lessor is the loss resulting in the ordinary course of events from the lessor's default as determined in any manner that is reasonable together with incidental and consequential damages, less expenses saved in consequence of the lessor's default.

(4) Except as otherwise agreed, the measure of damages for breach of warranty is the present value at the time and place of acceptance of the difference between the value of the use of the goods accepted and the value if they had been as warranted for the lease term, unless special circumstances show proximate damages of a different amount, together with incidental and consequential damages, less expenses saved in consequence of the lessor's default or breach of warranty.

As amended in 1990.

§ 2A–520. Lessee's Incidental and Consequential Damages.

(1) Incidental damages resulting from a lessor's default include expenses reasonably incurred in inspection, receipt, transportation, and care and custody of goods rightfully rejected or goods the acceptance of which is justifiably revoked, any commercially reasonable charges, expenses or commissions in connection with effecting cover, and any other reasonable expense incident to the default.

(2) Consequential damages resulting from a lessor's default include:

    (a) any loss resulting from general or particular requirements and needs of which the lessor at the time of contracting had reason to know and which could not reasonably be prevented by cover or otherwise; and

    (b) injury to person or property proximately resulting from any breach of warranty.

§ 2A–521. Lessee's Right to Specific Performance or Replevin.

(1) Specific performance may be decreed if the goods are unique or in other proper circumstances.

(2) A decree for specific performance may include any terms and conditions as to payment of the rent, damages, or other relief that the court deems just.

(3) A lessee has a right of replevin, detinue, sequestration, claim and delivery, or the like for goods identified to the lease contract if after reasonable effort the lessee is unable to effect cover for those goods or the circumstances reasonably indicate that the effort will be unavailing.

§ 2A–522. Lessee's Right to Goods on Lessor's Insolvency.

(1) Subject to subsection (2) and even though the goods have not been shipped, a lessee who has paid a part or all of the rent and security for goods identified to a lease contract (Section 2A–217) on making and keeping good a tender of any unpaid portion of the rent and security due under the lease contract may recover the goods identified from the lessor if the lessor becomes insolvent within 10 days after receipt of the first installment of rent and security.

(2) A lessee acquires the right to recover goods identified to a lease contract only if they conform to the lease contract.

C. Default by Lessee

§ 2A–523. Lessor's Remedies.

(1) If a lessee wrongfully rejects or revokes acceptance of goods or fails to make a payment when due or repudiates with respect to a part or the whole, then, with respect to any goods involved, and with respect to all of the goods if under an installment lease contract the value of the whole lease contract is substantially impaired (Section 2A–510), the lessee is in default under the lease contract and the lessor may:

    (a) cancel the lease contract (Section 2A–505(1));

    (b) proceed respecting goods not identified to the lease contract (Section 2A–524);

    (c) withhold delivery of the goods and take possession of goods previously delivered (Section 2A–525);

    (d) stop delivery of the goods by any bailee (Section 2A–526);

    (e) dispose of the goods and recover damages (Section 2A–527), or retain the goods and recover damages (Section 2A–528), or in a proper case recover rent (Section 2A–529);

    (f) exercise any other rights or pursue any other remedies provided in the lease contract.

(2) If a lessor does not fully exercise a right or obtain a remedy to which the lessor is entitled under subsection (1), the lessor may recover the loss resulting in the ordinary course of events from the lessee's default as determined in any reasonable manner, together with incidental damages, less expenses saved in consequence of the lessee's default.

(3) If a lessee is otherwise in default under a lease contract, the lessor may exercise the rights and pursue the remedies provided in the lease contract, which may include a right to cancel the lease. In addition, unless otherwise provided in the lease contract:

    (a) if the default substantially impairs the value of the lease contract to the lessor, the lessor may exercise the rights and pursue the remedies provided in subsections (1) or (2); or

    (b) if the default does not substantially impair the value of the lease contract to the lessor, the lessor may recover as provided in subsection (2).

As amended in 1990.

§ 2A–524. Lessor's Right to Identify Goods to Lease Contract.

(1) After default by the lessee under the lease contract of the type described in Section 2A–523(1) or 2A–523(3)(a) or, if agreed, after other default by the lessee, the lessor may:

    (a) identify to the lease contract conforming goods not already identified if at the time the lessor learned of the default they were in the lessor's or the supplier's possession or control; and

(b) dispose of goods (Section 2A–527(1)) that demonstrably have been intended for the particular lease contract even though those goods are unfinished.

(2) If the goods are unfinished, in the exercise of reasonable commercial judgment for the purposes of avoiding loss and of effective realization, an aggrieved lessor or the supplier may either complete manufacture and wholly identify the goods to the lease contract or cease manufacture and lease, sell, or otherwise dispose of the goods for scrap or salvage value or proceed in any other reasonable manner.

As amended in 1990.

§ 2A–525. Lessor's Right to Possession of Goods.

(1) If a lessor discovers the lessee to be insolvent, the lessor may refuse to deliver the goods.

(2) After a default by the lessee under the lease contract of the type described in Section 2A–523(1) or 2A–523(3)(a) or, if agreed, after other default by the lessee, the lessor has the right to take possession of the goods. If the lease contract so provides, the lessor may require the lessee to assemble the goods and make them available to the lessor at a place to be designated by the lessor which is reasonably convenient to both parties. Without removal, the lessor may render unusable any goods employed in trade or business, and may dispose of goods on the lessee's premises (Section 2A–527).

(3) The lessor may proceed under subsection (2) without judicial process if it can be done without breach of the peace or the lessor may proceed by action.

As amended in 1990.

§ 2A–526. Lessor's Stoppage of Delivery in Transit or Otherwise.

(1) A lessor may stop delivery of goods in the possession of a carrier or other bailee if the lessor discovers the lessee to be insolvent and may stop delivery of carload, truckload, planeload, or larger shipments of express or freight if the lessee repudiates or fails to make a payment due before delivery, whether for rent, security or otherwise under the lease contract, or for any other reason the lessor has a right to withhold or take possession of the goods.

(2) In pursuing its remedies under subsection (1), the lessor may stop delivery until

  (a) receipt of the goods by the lessee;

  (b) acknowledgment to the lessee by any bailee of the goods, except a carrier, that the bailee holds the goods for the lessee; or

  (c) such an acknowledgment to the lessee by a carrier via reshipment or as warehouseman.

(3) **(a)** To stop delivery, a lessor shall so notify as to enable the bailee by reasonable diligence to prevent delivery of the goods.

  (b) After notification, the bailee shall hold and deliver the goods according to the directions of the lessor, but the lessor is liable to the bailee for any ensuing charges or damages.

  (c) A carrier who has issued a nonnegotiable bill of lading is not obliged to obey a notification to stop received from a person other than the consignor.

§ 2A–527. Lessor's Rights to Dispose of Goods.

(1) After a default by a lessee under the lease contract of the type described in Section 2A–523(1) or 2A–523(3)(a) or after the lessor refuses to deliver or takes possession of goods (Section 2A–525 or 2A–526), or, if agreed, after other default by a lessee, the lessor may dispose of the goods concerned or the undelivered balance thereof by lease, sale, or otherwise.

(2) Except as otherwise provided with respect to damages liquidated in the lease agreement (Section 2A–504) or otherwise determined pursuant to agreement of the parties (Sections 1–102(3) and 2A–503), if the disposition is by lease agreement substantially similar to the original lease agreement and the new lease agreement is made in good faith and in a commercially reasonable manner, the lessor may recover from the lessee as damages (i) accrued and unpaid rent as of the date of the commencement of the term of the new lease agreement, (ii) the present value, as of the same date, of the total rent for the then remaining lease term of the original lease agreement minus the present value, as of the same date, of the rent under the new lease agreement applicable to that period of the

new lease term which is comparable to the then remaining term of the original lease agreement, and (iii) any incidental damages allowed under Section 2A–530, less expenses saved in consequence of the lessee's default.

(3) If the lessor's disposition is by lease agreement that for any reason does not qualify for treatment under subsection (2), or is by sale or otherwise, the lessor may recover from the lessee as if the lessor had elected not to dispose of the goods and Section 2A–528 governs.

(4) A subsequent buyer or lessee who buys or leases from the lessor in good faith for value as a result of a disposition under this section takes the goods free of the original lease contract and any rights of the original lessee even though the lessor fails to comply with one or more of the requirements of this Article.

(5) The lessor is not accountable to the lessee for any profit made on any disposition. A lessee who has rightfully rejected or justifiably revoked acceptance shall account to the lessor for any excess over the amount of the lessee's security interest (Section 2A–508(5)).

As amended in 1990.

§ 2A–528. Lessor's Damages for Non-acceptance, Failure to Pay, Repudiation, or Other Default.

(1) Except as otherwise provided with respect to damages liquidated in the lease agreement (Section 2A–504) or otherwise determined pursuant to agreement of the parties (Sections 1–102(3) and 2A–503), if a lessor elects to retain the goods or a lessor elects to dispose of the goods and the disposition is by lease agreement that for any reason does not qualify for treatment under Section 2A–527(2), or is by sale or otherwise, the lessor may recover from the lessee as damages for a default of the type described in Section 2A–523(1) or 2A–523(3)(a), or, if agreed, for other default of the lessee, (i) accrued and unpaid rent as of the date of default if the lessee has never taken possession of the goods, or, if the lessee has taken possession of the goods, as of the date the lessor repossesses the goods or an earlier date on which the lessee makes a tender of the goods to the lessor, (ii) the present value as of the date determined under clause (i) of the total rent for the then remaining lease term of the original lease agreement minus the present value as of the same date of the market rent at the place where the goods are located computed for the same lease term, and (iii) any incidental damages allowed under Section 2A–530, less expenses saved in consequence of the lessee's default.

(2) If the measure of damages provided in subsection (1) is inadequate to put a lessor in as good a position as performance would have, the measure of damages is the present value of the profit, including reasonable overhead, the lessor would have made from full performance by the lessee, together with any incidental damages allowed under Section 2A–530, due allowance for costs reasonably incurred and due credit for payments or proceeds of disposition.

As amended in 1990.

§ 2A–529. Lessor's Action for the Rent.

(1) After default by the lessee under the lease contract of the type described in Section 2A–523(1) or 2A–523(3)(a) or, if agreed, after other default by the lessee, if the lessor complies with subsection (2), the lessor may recover from the lessee as damages:

  (a) for goods accepted by the lessee and not repossessed by or tendered to the lessor, and for conforming goods lost or damaged within a commercially reasonable time after risk of loss passes to the lessee (Section 2A–219), (i) accrued and unpaid rent as of the date of entry of judgment in favor of the lessor, (ii) the present value as of the same date of the rent for the then remaining lease term of the lease agreement, and (iii) any incidental damages allowed under Section 2A–530, less expenses saved in consequence of the lessee's default; and

  (b) for goods identified to the lease contract if the lessor is unable after reasonable effort to dispose of them at a reasonable price or the circumstances reasonably indicate that effort will be unavailing, (i) accrued and unpaid rent as of the date of entry of judgment in favor of the lessor, (ii) the present value as of the same date of the rent for the then remaining lease term of the lease agreement, and (iii) any incidental damages allowed under Section 2A–530, less expenses saved in consequence of the lessee's default.

(2) Except as provided in subsection (3), the lessor shall hold for the lessee for the remaining lease term of the lease agreement any goods that have been identified to the lease contract and are in the lessor's control.

(3) The lessor may dispose of the goods at any time before collection of the judgment for damages obtained pursuant to subsection (1). If the disposition is before the end of the remaining lease term of the lease agreement, the lessor's recovery against the lessee for damages is governed by Section 2A–527 or Section 2A–528, and the lessor will cause an appropriate credit to be provided against a judgment for damages to the extent that the amount of the judgment exceeds the recovery available pursuant to Section 2A–527 or 2A–528.

(4) Payment of the judgment for damages obtained pursuant to subsection (1) entitles the lessee to the use and possession of the goods not then disposed of for the remaining lease term of and in accordance with the lease agreement.

(5) After default by the lessee under the lease contract of the type described in Section 2A–523(1) or Section 2A–523(3)(a) or, if agreed, after other default by the lessee, a lessor who is held not entitled to rent under this section must nevertheless be awarded damages for non-acceptance under Section 2A–527 or Section 2A–528.

As amended in 1990.

§ 2A–530. Lessor's Incidental Damages.

Incidental damages to an aggrieved lessor include any commercially reasonable charges, expenses, or commissions incurred in stopping delivery, in the transportation, care and custody of goods after the lessee's default, in connection with return or disposition of the goods, or otherwise resulting from the default.

ARTICLE 3: NEGOTIABLE INSTRUMENTS
Part 1—General Provisions and Definitions
§ 3–101. Short Title.
This Article may be cited as Uniform Commercial Code—Negotiable Instruments.

§ 3–102. Subject Matter.
(a) This Article applies to negotiable instruments. It does not apply to money or to payment orders governed by Article 4A. A negotiable instrument that is also a certificated security under Section 8–102(1)(a) is subject to Article 8 and to this Article.

(b) In the event of conflict between the provisions of this Article and those of Article 4, Article 8, or Article 9, the provisions of Article 4, Article 8 and Article 9 prevail over those of this Article.

(c) Regulations of the Board of Governors of the Federal Reserve System and operating circulars of the Federal Reserve Banks supersede any inconsistent provision of this Article to the extent of the inconsistency.

§ 3–103. Definitions.
(a) In this Article:
  (1) "Acceptor" means a drawee that has accepted a draft.
  (2) "Drawee" means a person ordered in a draft to make payment.
  (3) "Drawer" means a person that signs a draft as a person ordering payment.
  (4) "Good faith" means honesty in fact and the observance of reasonable commercial standards of fair dealing.
  (5) "Maker" means a person that signs a note as promisor of payment.
  (6) "Order" means a written instruction to pay money signed by the person giving the instruction. The instruction may be addressed to any person, including the person giving the instruction, or to one or more persons jointly or in the alternative but not in succession. An authorization to pay is not an order unless the person authorized to pay is also instructed to pay.
  (7) "Ordinary care" in the case of a person engaged in business means observance of reasonable commercial standards, prevailing in the area in which that person is located, with respect to the business in which that person is engaged. In the case of a bank that takes an instrument for processing for collection or payment by automated

means, reasonable commercial standards do not require the bank to examine the instrument if the failure to examine does not violate the bank's prescribed procedures and the bank's procedures do not vary unreasonably from general banking usage not disapproved by this Article or Article 4.
  (8) "Party" means party to an instrument.
  (9) "Promise" means a written undertaking to pay money signed by the person undertaking to pay. An acknowledgment of an obligation by the obligor is not a promise unless the obligor also undertakes to pay the obligation.
  (10) "Prove" with respect to a fact means to meet the burden of establishing the fact (Section 1–201(8)).
  (11) "Remitter" means a person that purchases an instrument from its issuer if the instrument is payable to an identified person other than the purchaser.
(b) Other definitions applying to this Article and the sections in which they appear are:
  "Acceptance" Section 3–409.
  "Accommodated party" Section 3–419.
  "Accommodation indorsement" Section 3–205.
  "Accommodation party" Section 3–419.
  "Alteration" Section 3–407.
  "Blank indorsement" Section 3–205.
  "Cashier's check" Section 3–104.
  "Certificate of deposit" Section 3–104.
  "Certified check" Section 3–409.
  "Check" Section 3–104.
  "Consideration" Section 3–303.
  "Draft" Section 3–104.
  "Fiduciary" Section 3–307.
  "Guarantor" Section 3–417.
  "Holder in due course" Section 3–302.
  "Incomplete instrument" Section 3–115.
  "Indorsement" Section 3–204.
  "Indorser" Section 3–204.
  "Instrument" Section 3–104.
  "Issue" Section 3–105.
  "Issuer" Section 3–105.
  "Negotiable instrument" Section 3–104.
  "Negotiation" Section 3–201.
  "Note" Section 3–104.
  "Payable at a definite time" Section 3–108.
  "Payable on demand" Section 3–108.
  "Payable to bearer" Section 3–109.
  "Payable to order" Section 3–110.
  "Payment" Section 3–603.
  "Person entitled to enforce" Section 3–301.
  "Presentment" Section 3–501.
  "Reacquisition" Section 3–207.
  "Represented person" Section 3–307.
  "Special indorsement" Section 3–205.
  "Teller's check" Section 3–104.
  "Traveler's check" Section 3–104.
  "Value" Section 3–303.
(c) The following definitions in other Articles apply to this Article:
  "Bank" Section 4–105.
  "Banking day" Section 4–104.
  "Clearing house" Section 4–104.
  "Collecting bank" Section 4–105.
  "Customer" Section 4–104.
  "Depositary bank" Section 4–105.
  "Documentary draft" Section 4–104.
  "Intermediary bank" Section 4–105.
  "Item" Section 4–104.
  "Midnight deadline" Section 4–104.
  "Payor bank" Section 4–105.
  "Suspends payments" Section 4–104.
(d) In addition, Article 1 contains general definitions and principles of construction and interpretation applicable throughout this Article.

§ 3–104. Negotiable Instrument.

(a) "Negotiable instrument" means an unconditional promise or order to pay a fixed amount of money, with or without interest or other charges described in the promise or order, if it:

  (1) is payable to bearer or to order at the time it is issued or first comes into possession of a holder;

  (2) is payable on demand or at a definite time; and

  (3) does not state any other undertaking or instruction by the person promising or ordering payment to do any act in addition to the payment of money except that the promise or order may contain (i) an undertaking or power to give, maintain, or protect collateral to secure payment, (ii) an authorization or power to the holder to confess judgment or realize on or dispose of collateral, or (iii) a waiver of the benefit of any law intended for the advantage or protection of any obligor.

(b) "Instrument" means negotiable instrument.

(c) An order that meets all of the requirements of subsection (a) except subparagraph (1) and otherwise falls within the definition of "check" in subsection (f) is a negotiable instrument and a check.

(d) Notwithstanding subsection (a), a promise or order other than a check is not an instrument if, at the time it is issued or first comes into possession of a holder, it contains a conspicuous statement, however expressed, indicating that the writing is not an instrument governed by this Article.

(e) An instrument is a "note" if it is a promise, and is a "draft" if it is an order. If an instrument falls within the definition of both "note" and "draft," the person entitled to enforce the instrument may treat it as either.

(f) "Check" means (i) a draft, other than a documentary draft, payable on demand and drawn on a bank or (ii) a cashier's check or teller's check. An instrument may be a check even though it is described on its face by another term such as "money order."

(g) "Cashier's check" means a draft with respect to which the drawer and drawee are the same bank or branches of the same bank.

(h) "Teller's check" means a draft drawn by a bank (i) on another bank, or (ii) payable at or through a bank.

(i) "Traveler's check" means an instrument that (i) is payable on demand, (ii) is drawn on or payable at or through a bank, (iii) is designated by the term "traveler's check" or by a substantially similar term, and (iv) requires, as a condition to payment, a countersignature by a person whose specimen signature appears on the instrument.

(j) "Certificate of deposit" means an instrument containing an acknowledgment by a bank that a sum of money has been received by the bank, and a promise by the bank to repay the sum of money. A certificate of deposit is a note of the bank.

§ 3–105. Issue of Instrument.

(a) "Issue" means the first delivery of an instrument by the maker or drawer, whether to a holder or nonholder, for the purpose of giving rights on the instrument to any person.

(b) An unissued instrument, or an unissued incomplete instrument (Section 3–115) that is completed, is binding on the maker or drawer, but nonissuance is a defense. An instrument that is conditionally issued or is issued for a special purpose is binding on the maker or drawer, but failure of the condition or special purpose to be fulfilled is a defense.

(c) "Issuer" applies to issued and unissued instruments and means any person that signs an instrument as maker or drawer.

§ 3–106. Unconditional Promise or Order.

(a) Except as provided in subsections (b) and (c), for the purposes of Section 3–104(a), a promise or order is unconditional unless it states (i) an express condition to payment or (ii) that the promise or order is subject to or governed by another writing, or that rights or obligations with respect to the promise or order are stated in another writing; however, a mere reference to another writing does not make the promise or order conditional.

(b) A promise or order is not made conditional (i) by a reference to another writing for a statement of rights with respect to collateral, prepayment, or acceleration, or (ii) because payment is limited to resort to a particular fund or source.

(c) If a promise or order requires, as a condition to payment, a countersignature by a person whose specimen signature appears on the promise or order, the condition does not make the promise or order conditional for the purposes of Section 3–104(a). If the person whose specimen signature appears on an instrument fails to countersign the instrument, the failure to countersign is a defense to the obligation of the issuer, but the failure does not prevent a transferee of the instrument from becoming a holder of the instrument.

(d) If a promise or order at the time it is issued or first comes into possession of a holder contains a statement, required by applicable statutory or administrative law, to the effect that the rights of a holder or transferee are subject to claims or defenses that the issuer could assert against the original payee, the promise or order is not thereby made conditional for the purposes of Section 3–104(a), but there cannot be a holder in due course of the promise or order.

§ 3–107. Instrument Payable in Foreign Money.

Unless the instrument otherwise provides, an instrument that states the amount payable in foreign money may be paid in the foreign money or in an equivalent amount in dollars calculated by using the current bank-offered spot rate at the place of payment for the purchase of dollars on the day on which the instrument is paid.

§ 3–108. Payable on Demand or at a Definite Time.

(a) A promise or order is "payable on demand" if (i) it states that it is payable on demand or at sight, or otherwise indicates that it is payable at the will of the holder, or (ii) it does not state any time of payment.

(b) A promise or order is "payable at a definite time" if it is payable on elapse of a definite period of time after sight or acceptance or at a fixed date or dates or at a time or times readily ascertainable at the time the promise or order is issued, subject to rights of (i) prepayment, (ii) acceleration, or (iii) extension at the option of the holder or (iv) extension to a further definite time at the option of the maker or acceptor or automatically upon or after a specified act or event.

(c) If an instrument, payable at a fixed date, is also payable upon demand made before the fixed date, the instrument is payable on demand until the fixed date and, if demand for payment is not made before that date, becomes payable at a definite time on the fixed date.

§ 3–109. Payable to Bearer or to Order.

(a) A promise or order is payable to bearer if it:

  (1) states that it is payable to bearer or to the order of bearer or otherwise indicates that the person in possession of the promise or order is entitled to payment,

  (2) does not state a payee, or

  (3) states that it is payable to or to the order of cash or otherwise indicates that it is not payable to an identified person.

(b) A promise or order that is not payable to bearer is payable to order if it is payable (i) to the order of an identified person or (ii) to an identified person or order. A promise or order that is payable to order is payable to the identified person.

(c) An instrument payable to bearer may become payable to an identified person if it is specially indorsed as stated in Section 3–205(a). An instrument payable to an identified person may become payable to bearer if it is indorsed in blank as stated in Section 3–205(b).

§ 3–110. Identification of Person to Whom Instrument Is Payable.

(a) A person to whom an instrument is payable is determined by the intent of the person, whether or not authorized, signing as, or in the name or behalf of, the maker or drawer. The instrument is payable to the person intended by the signer even if that person is identified in the instrument by a name or other identification that is not that of the intended person. If more than one person signs in the name or behalf of the maker or drawer and all the signers do not intend the same person as payee, the instrument is payable to any person intended by one or more of the signers.

(b) If the signature of the maker or drawer of an instrument is made by automated means such as a check-writing machine, the payee of the instrument is determined by the intent of the person who supplied the name or identification of the payee, whether or not authorized to do so.

(c) A person to whom an instrument is payable may be identified in any way including by name, identifying number, office, or account number. For the purpose of determining the holder of an instrument, the following rules apply:

(1) If an instrument is payable to an account and the account is identified only by number, the instrument is payable to the person to whom the account is payable. If an instrument is payable to an account identified by number and by the name of a person, the instrument is payable to the named person, whether or not that person is the owner of the account identified by number.

(2) If an instrument is payable to:

(i) a trust, estate, or a person described as trustee or representative of a trust or estate, the instrument is payable to the trustee, the representative, or a successor of either, whether or not the beneficiary or estate is also named;

(ii) a person described as agent or similar representative of a named or identified person, the instrument is payable either to the represented person, the representative, or a successor of the representative;

(iii) a fund or organization that is not a legal entity, the instrument is payable to a representative of the members of the fund or organization; or

(iv) an office or to a person described as holding an office, the instrument is payable to the named person, the incumbent of the office, or a successor to the incumbent.

(d) If an instrument is payable to two or more persons alternatively, it is payable to any of them and may be negotiated, discharged, or enforced by any of them in possession of the instrument. If an instrument is payable to two or more persons not alternatively, it is payable to all of them and may be negotiated, discharged, or enforced only by all of them. If an instrument payable to two or more persons is ambiguous as to whether it is payable to the persons alternatively, the instrument is payable to the persons alternatively.

§ 3–111. Place of Payment.

Except as otherwise provided for items in Article 4, an instrument is payable at the place of payment stated in the instrument. If no place of payment is stated, an instrument is payable at the address of the drawee or maker stated in the instrument. If no address is stated, the place of payment is the place of business of the drawee or maker. If a drawee or maker has more than one place of business, the place of payment is any place of business of the drawee or maker chosen by the person entitled to enforce the instrument. If the drawee or maker has no place of business, the place of payment is the residence of the drawee or maker.

§ 3–112. Interest.

(a) Unless otherwise provided in the instrument, (i) an instrument is not payable with interest, and (ii) interest on an interest-bearing instrument is payable from the date of the instrument.

(b) Interest may be stated in an instrument as a fixed or variable amount of money or it may be expressed as a fixed or variable rate or rates. The amount or rate of interest may be stated or described in the instrument in any manner and may require reference to information not contained in the instrument. If an instrument provides for interest but the amount of interest payable cannot be ascertained from the description, interest is payable at the judgment rate in effect at the place of payment of the instrument and at the time interest first accrues.

§ 3–113. Date of Instrument.

(a) An instrument may be antedated or postdated. The date stated determines the time of payment if the instrument is payable at a fixed period after date. Except as provided in Section 4–401(3), an instrument payable on demand is not payable before the date of the instrument.

(b) If an instrument is undated, its date is the date of its issue or, in the case of an unissued instrument, the date it first comes into possession of a holder.

§ 3–114. Contradictory Terms of Instrument.

If an instrument contains contradictory terms, typewritten terms prevail over printed terms, handwritten terms prevail over both, and words prevail over numbers.

§ 3–115. Incomplete Instrument.

(a) "Incomplete instrument" means a signed writing, whether or not issued by the signer, the contents of which show at the time of signing that it is incomplete but that the signer intended it to be completed by the addition of words or numbers.

(b) Subject to subsection (c), if an incomplete instrument is an instrument under Section 3–104, it may be enforced (i) according to its terms if it is not completed, or (ii) according to its terms as augmented by completion. If an incomplete instrument is not an instrument under Section 3–104 but, after completion, the requirements of Section 3–104 are met, the instrument may be enforced according to its terms as augmented by completion.

(c) If words or numbers are added to an incomplete instrument without authority of the signer, there is an alteration of the incomplete instrument governed by Section 3–407.

(d) The burden of establishing that words or numbers were added to an incomplete instrument without authority of the signer is on the person asserting the lack of authority.

§ 3–116. Joint and Several Liability; Contribution.

(a) Except as otherwise provided in the instrument, two or more persons who have the same liability on an instrument as makers, drawers, acceptors, indorsers who are indorsing joint payees, or anomalous indorsers, are jointly and severally liable in the capacity in which they sign.

(b) Except as provided in Section 3–417(e) or by agreement of the affected parties, a party with joint and several liability that pays the instrument is entitled to receive from any party with the same joint and several liability contribution in accordance with applicable law.

(c) Discharge of one party with joint and several liability by a person entitled to enforce the instrument does not affect the right under subsection (b) of a party with the same joint and several liability to receive contribution from the party discharged.

§ 3–117. Other Agreements Affecting an Instrument.

Subject to applicable law regarding exclusion of proof of contemporaneous or prior agreements, the obligation of a party to an instrument to pay the instrument may be modified, supplemented, or nullified by a separate agreement of the obligor and a person entitled to enforce the instrument if the instrument is issued or the obligation is incurred in reliance on the agreement or as part of the same transaction giving rise to the agreement. To the extent an obligation is modified, supplemented, or nullified by an agreement under this section, the agreement is a defense to the obligation.

§ 3–118. Statute of Limitations.

(a) Except as provided in subsection (e), an action to enforce the obligation of a party to pay a note payable at a definite time must be commenced within six years after the payment date or dates stated in the note or, if a payment date is accelerated, within six years after the accelerated payment date.

(b) Except as provided in subsection (d) or (e), if demand for payment is made to the maker of a note payable on demand, an action to enforce the obligation of a party to pay the note must be commenced within six years after the demand. If no demand for payment is made to the maker, an action to enforce the note is barred if neither principal nor interest on the note has been paid for a continuous period of 10 years.

(c) Except as provided in subsection (d), an action to enforce the obligation of a party to an unaccepted draft to pay the draft must be commenced within six years after dishonor of the draft or 10 years after the date of the draft, whichever period expires first.

(d) An action to enforce the obligation of the acceptor of a certified check or the issuer of a teller's check, cashier's check, or traveler's check must be commenced within six years after demand for payment is made to the acceptor or issuer, as the case may be.

(e) An action to enforce the obligation of a party to a certificate of deposit to pay the instrument must be commenced within six years after demand for payment is made to the maker, but if the instrument states a maturity date and the maker is not required to pay before that date, the six-year period begins when a demand for payment is in effect and the maturity date has passed.

(f) This subsection applies to an action to enforce the obligation of a party to pay an accepted draft, other than a certified check. If the obligation of the acceptor is payable at a definite time, the action must be commenced within six years after the payment date or dates stated in the draft or acceptance. If the obligation of the acceptor is payable on demand, the action must be commenced within six years after the date of the acceptance.

(g) Unless governed by other law regarding claims for indemnity or contribution, an action (i) for conversion of an instrument, for money had and received, or like action based on conversion, (ii) for breach of warranty, or (iii) to enforce an obligation, duty, or right arising under this Article and not governed by this section must be commenced within three years after the cause of action accrues.

§ 3–119. Notice of Right to Defend Action.
In an action for breach of an obligation for which a third person is answerable over pursuant to this Article or Article 4, the defendant may give the third person written notice of the litigation, and the person notified may then give similar notice to any other person who is answerable over. If the notice states (i) that the person notified may come in and defend and (ii) that failure to do so will bind the person notified in an action later brought by the person giving the notice as to any determination of fact common to the two litigations, the person notified is so bound unless after seasonable receipt of the notice the person notified does come in and defend.

Part 2—Negotiation, Transfer and Indorsement
§ 3–201. Negotiation.
(a) "Negotiation" means a transfer of possession, whether voluntary or involuntary, of an instrument to a person who thereby becomes its holder if possession is obtained from a person other than the issuer of the instrument.

(b) Except for a negotiation by a remitter, if an instrument is payable to an identified person, negotiation requires transfer of possession of the instrument and its indorsement by the holder. If an instrument is payable to bearer, it may be negotiated by transfer of possession alone.

§ 3–202. Negotiation Subject to Rescission.
(a) Negotiation is effective even if obtained (i) from an infant, a corporation exceeding its powers, or a person without capacity, or (ii) by fraud, duress, or mistake, or in breach of duty or as part of an illegal transaction.

(b) To the extent permitted by law, negotiation may be rescinded or may be subject to other remedies, but those remedies may not be asserted against a subsequent holder in due course or a person paying the instrument in good faith and without knowledge of facts that are a basis for rescission or other remedy.

§ 3–203. Rights Acquired by Transfer.
(a) An instrument is transferred when it is delivered by a person other than its issuer for the purpose of giving to the person receiving delivery the right to enforce the instrument.

(b) Transfer of an instrument, regardless of whether the transfer is a negotiation, vests in the transferee any right of the transferor to enforce the instrument, including any right as a holder in due course, but the transferee cannot acquire rights of a holder in due course by a transfer, directly or indirectly, from a holder in due course if the purchaser engaged in fraud or illegality affecting the instrument.

(c) Unless otherwise agreed, if an instrument is transferred for value and the transferee does not become a holder because of lack of indorsement by the transferor, the transferee has a specifically enforceable right to the unqualified indorsement of the transferor, but negotiation of the instrument does not occur until the indorsement is made.

(d) If a transferor purports to transfer less than the entire instrument, negotiation of the instrument does not occur. The transferee obtains no rights under this Article and has only the rights of a partial assignee.

§ 3–204. Indorsement.
(a) "Indorsement" means a signature, other than that of a maker, drawer, or acceptor, that alone or accompanied by other words, is made on an instrument for the purpose of (i) negotiating the instrument, (ii) restricting payment of the instrument, or (iii) incurring indorser's liability on the instrument, but regardless of the intent of the signer, a signature and its accompanying words is an indorsement unless the accompanying words, the terms of the instrument, the place of the signature, or other circumstances unambiguously indicate that the signature was made for a purpose other than indorsement. For the purpose of determining whether a signature is made on an instrument, a paper affixed to the instrument is a part of the instrument.

(b) "Indorser" means a person who makes an indorsement.

(c) For the purpose of determining whether the transferee of an instrument is a holder, an indorsement that transfers a security interest in the instrument is effective as an unqualified indorsement of the instrument.

(d) If an instrument is payable to a holder under a name that is not the name of the holder, indorsement may be made by the holder in the name stated in the instrument or in the holder's name or both, but signature in both names may be required by a person paying or taking the instrument for value or collection.

§ 3–205. Special Indorsement; Blank Indorsement; Anomalous Indorsement.
(a) If an indorsement is made by the holder of an instrument, whether payable to an identified person or payable to bearer, and the indorsement identifies a person to whom it makes the instrument payable, it is a "special indorsement." When specially indorsed, an instrument becomes payable to the identified person and may be negotiated only by the indorsement of that person. The principles stated in Section 3–110 apply to special indorsements.

(b) If an indorsement is made by the holder of an instrument and it is not a special indorsement, it is a "blank indorsement." When indorsed in blank, an instrument becomes payable to bearer and may be negotiated by transfer of possession alone until specially indorsed.

(c) The holder may convert a blank indorsement that consists only of a signature into a special indorsement by writing, above the signature of the indorser, words identifying the person to whom the instrument is made payable.

(d) "Anomalous indorsement" means an indorsement made by a person that is not the holder of the instrument. An anomalous indorsement does not affect the manner in which the instrument may be negotiated.

§ 3–206. Restrictive Indorsement.
(a) An indorsement limiting payment to a particular person or otherwise prohibiting further transfer or negotiation of the instrument is not effective to prevent further transfer or negotiation of the instrument.

(b) An indorsement stating a condition to the right of the indorsee to receive payment does not affect the right of the indorsee to enforce the instrument. A person paying the instrument or taking it for value or collection may disregard the condition, and the rights and liabilities of that person are not affected by whether the condition has been fulfilled.

(c) The following rules apply to an instrument bearing an indorsement (i) described in Section 4–201(2), or (ii) in blank or to a particular bank using the words "for deposit," "for collection," or other words indicating a purpose of having the instrument collected for the indorser or for a particular account:

(1) A person, other than a bank, that purchases the instrument when so indorsed converts the instrument unless the proceeds of the instrument are received by the indorser or are applied consistently with the indorsement.

(2) A depositary bank that purchases the instrument or takes it for collection when so indorsed converts the instrument unless the proceeds of the instrument are received by the indorser or applied consistently with the indorsement.

(3) A payor bank that is also the depositary bank or that takes the instrument for immediate payment over the counter from a person other than a collecting bank converts the instrument unless the proceeds of the instrument are received by the indorser or applied consistently with the indorsement.

(4) Except as otherwise provided in paragraph (3), a payor bank or intermediary bank may disregard the indorsement and is not liable if the proceeds of the instrument are not received by the indorser or applied consistently with the indorsement.

(d) Except for an indorsement covered by subsection (c), the following rules apply to an instrument bearing an indorsement using words to the effect that payment is to be made to the indorsee as agent, trustee, or other fiduciary for the benefit of the indorser or another person.

(1) Unless there is notice of breach of fiduciary duty as provided in Section 3–307, a person that purchases the instrument from the indorsee or takes the instrument from the indorsee for collection or payment may pay the proceeds of payment or the value given for the instrument to the indorsee without regard to whether the indorsee violates a fiduciary duty to the indorser.

(2) A later transferee of the instrument or person that pays the instrument is neither given notice nor otherwise affected by the restriction in the indorsement unless the transferee or payor knows that the fiduciary dealt with the instrument or its proceeds in breach of fiduciary duty.

(e) Purchase of an instrument bearing an indorsement to which this section applies does not prevent the purchaser from becoming a holder in due course of the instrument unless the purchaser is a converter under subsection (c).

(f) In an action to enforce the obligation of a party to pay the instrument, the obligor has a defense if payment would violate an indorsement to which this section applies and the payment is not permitted by this section.

§ 3–207. Reacquisition.

Reacquisition of an instrument occurs if it is transferred, by negotiation or otherwise, to a former holder. A former holder that reacquires the instrument may cancel indorsements made after the reacquirer first became a holder of the instrument. If the cancellation causes the instrument to be payable to the reacquirer or to bearer, the reacquirer may negotiate the instrument. An indorser whose indorsement is canceled is discharged, and the discharge is effective against any later holder.

Part 3—Enforcement of Instruments
§ 3–301. Person Entitled to Enforce Instrument.

"Person entitled to enforce" an instrument means (i) the holder of the instrument, (ii) a nonholder in possession of the instrument who has the rights of a holder, or (iii) a person not in possession of the instrument who is entitled to enforce the instrument pursuant to Section 3–309. A person may be a person entitled to enforce the instrument even though the person is not the owner of the instrument or is in wrongful possession of the instrument.

§ 3–302. Holder in Due Course.

(a) Subject to subsection (c) and Section 3–106(d), "holder in due course" means the holder of an instrument if:

(1) the instrument when issued or negotiated to the holder does not bear such apparent evidence of forgery or alteration or is not otherwise so irregular or incomplete as to call into question its authenticity, and

(2) the holder took the instrument (i) for value, (ii) in good faith, (iii) without notice that the instrument is overdue or has been dishonored or that there is an uncured default with respect to payment of another instrument issued as part of the same series, (iv) without notice that the instrument contains an unauthorized signature or has been altered, (v) without notice of any claim to the instrument stated in Section 3–306, and (vi) without notice that any party to the instrument has any defense or claim in recoupment stated in Section 3–305(a).

(b) Notice of discharge of a party to the instrument, other than discharge in an insolvency proceeding, is not notice of a defense under subsection (a), but discharge is effective against a person who became a holder in due course with notice of the discharge. Public filing or recording of a document does not of itself constitute notice of a defense, claim in recoupment, or claim to the instrument.

(c) Except to the extent a transferor or predecessor in interest has rights as a holder in due course, a person does not acquire rights of a holder in due course of an instrument taken (i) by legal process or by purchase at an execution, bankruptcy, or creditor's sale or similar proceeding, (ii) by purchase as part of a bulk transaction not in ordinary course of business of the transferor, or (iii) as the successor in interest to an estate or other organization.

(d) If, under Section 3–303(a)(1), the promise of performance that is the consideration for an instrument has been partially performed, the holder may assert rights as a holder in due course of the instrument only to the fraction of the amount payable under the instrument equal to the value of the partial performance divided by the value of the promised performance.

(e) If (i) the person entitled to enforce an instrument has only a security interest in the instrument and (ii) the person obliged to pay the instrument has a defense, claim in recoupment or claim to the instrument that may be asserted against the person who granted the security interest, the person entitled to enforce the instrument may assert rights as a holder in due course only to an amount payable under the instrument which, at the time of enforcement of the instrument, does not exceed the amount of the unpaid obligation secured.

(f) To be effective, notice must be received at such time and in such manner as to give a reasonable opportunity to act on it.

(g) This section is subject to any law limiting status as a holder in due course in particular classes of transactions.

§ 3–303. Value and Consideration.

(a) An instrument is issued or transferred for value if:

(1) the instrument is issued or transferred for a promise of performance, to the extent the promise has been performed;

(2) the transferee acquires a security interest or other lien in the instrument other than a lien obtained by judicial proceedings;

(3) the instrument is issued or transferred as payment of, or as security for, an existing obligation of any person, whether or not the obligation is due;

(4) the instrument is issued or transferred in exchange for a negotiable instrument; or

(5) the instrument is issued or transferred in exchange for the incurring of an irrevocable obligation to a third party by the person taking the instrument.

(b) "Consideration" means any consideration sufficient to support a simple contract. The drawer or maker of an instrument has a defense if the instrument is issued without consideration. If an instrument is issued for a promise of performance, the drawer or maker has a defense to the extent performance of the promise is due and the promise has not been performed. If an instrument is issued for value as stated in subsection (a), the instrument is also issued for consideration.

§ 3–304. Overdue Instrument.

(a) An instrument payable on demand becomes overdue at the earliest of the following times:

(1) on the day after the day demand for payment is duly made;

(2) if the instrument is a check, 90 days after its date; or

(3) if the instrument is not a check, when the instrument has been outstanding for a period of time after its date which is unreasonably long under the circumstances of the particular case in light of the nature of the instrument and trade usage.

(b) With respect to an instrument payable at a definite time the following rules apply: (1) If the principal is payable in installments and a due date has not been accelerated, the instrument becomes overdue upon default under the instrument for nonpayment of an installment, and the instrument remains overdue until the default is cured. (2) If the principal is not payable in installments and the due date has not been accelerated, the instrument becomes overdue on the day after the due date. (3) If a due date with respect to principal has been accelerated, the instrument becomes overdue on the day after the accelerated due date.

(c) Unless the due date of principal has been accelerated, an instrument does not become overdue if there is default in payment of interest but no default in payment of principal.

§ 3–305. Defenses and Claims in Recoupment.

(a) Except as stated in subsection (b), the right to enforce the obligation of a party to pay the instrument is subject to the following:

(1) A defense of the obligor based on (i) infancy of the obligor to the extent it is a defense to a simple contract, (ii) duress, lack of legal capacity, or illegality of the transaction that nullifies the obligation of the obligor, (iii) fraud that induced the obligor to sign the instrument with neither knowledge nor reasonable opportunity to learn of its character

or its essential terms, or (iv) discharge of the obligor in insolvency proceedings.

(2) A defense of the obligor stated in another section of this Article or a defense of the obligor that would be available if the person entitled to enforce the instrument were enforcing a right to payment under a simple contract.

(3) A claim in recoupment of the obligor against the original payee of the instrument if the claim arose from the transaction that gave rise to the instrument. The claim of the obligor may be asserted against a transferee of the instrument only to reduce the amount owing on the instrument at the time the action is brought.

(b) The right of a holder in due course to enforce the obligation of a party to pay the instrument is subject to defenses of the obligor stated in subsection (a)(1), but is not subject to defenses of the obligor stated in subsection (a)(2) or claims in recoupment stated in subsection (a)(3) against a person other than the holder.

(c) Except as stated in subsection (d), in an action to enforce the obligation of a party to pay the instrument, the obligor may not assert against the person entitled to enforce the instrument a defense, claim in recoupment, or claim to the instrument (Section 3–306) of another person, but the other person's claim to the instrument may be asserted by the obligor if the other person is joined in the action and personally asserts the claim against the person entitled to enforce the instrument. An obligor is not obliged to pay the instrument if the person seeking enforcement of the instrument does not have rights of a holder in due course and the obligor proves that the instrument is a lost or stolen instrument.

(d) In an action to enforce the obligation of an accommodation party to pay an instrument, the accommodation party may assert against the person entitled to enforce the instrument any defense or claim in recoupment under subsection (a) that the accommodated party could assert against the person entitled to enforce the instrument, except the defenses of discharge in insolvency proceedings, infancy, or lack of legal capacity.

§ 3–306. Claims to an Instrument.

A person taking an instrument, other than a person having rights of a holder in due course, is subject to a claim of a property or possessory right in the instrument or its proceeds, including a claim to rescind a negotiation and to recover the instrument or its proceeds. A person having rights of a holder in due course takes free of the claim to the instrument.

§ 3–307. Notice of Breach of Fiduciary Duty.

(a) This section applies if (i) an instrument is taken from a fiduciary for payment or collection or for value, (ii) the taker has knowledge of the fiduciary status of the fiduciary, and (iii) the represented person makes a claim to the instrument or its proceeds on the basis that the transaction of the fiduciary is a breach of fiduciary duty. Notice of breach of fiduciary duty by the fiduciary is notice of the claim of the represented person. "Fiduciary" means an agent, trustee, partner, corporation officer or director, or other representative owing a fiduciary duty with respect to the instrument. "Represented person" means the principal, beneficiary, partnership, corporation, or other person to whom the duty is owed.

(b) If the instrument is payable to the fiduciary, as such, or to the represented person, the taker has notice of the breach of fiduciary duty if the instrument is (i) taken in payment of or as security for a debt known by the taker to be the personal debt of the fiduciary, (ii) taken in a transaction known by the taker to be for the personal benefit of the fiduciary, or (iii) deposited to an account other than an account of the fiduciary, as such, or an account of the represented person.

(c) If the instrument is made or drawn by the fiduciary, as such, payable to the fiduciary personally, the taker does not have notice of the breach of fiduciary duty unless the taker knows of the breach of fiduciary duty.

(d) If the instrument is made or drawn by or on behalf of the represented person to the taker as payee, the taker has notice of the breach of fiduciary duty if the instrument is (i) taken in payment of or as security for a debt known by the taker to be the personal debt of the fiduciary, (ii) taken in a transaction known by the taker to be for the personal benefit of the fiduciary, or (iii) deposited to an account other than an account of the fiduciary, as such, or an account of the represented person.

§ 3–308. Proof of Signatures and Status as Holder in Due Course.

(a) In an action with respect to an instrument, the authenticity of, and authority to make, each signature on the instrument is admitted unless specifically denied in the pleadings. If the validity of a signature is denied in the pleadings, the burden of establishing validity is on the person claiming validity, but the signature is presumed to be authentic and authorized unless the action is to enforce the liability of the purported signer and the signer is dead or incompetent at the time of trial of the issue of validity of the signature. If an action to enforce the instrument is brought against a person as the undisclosed principal of a person who signed the instrument as a party to the instrument, the plaintiff has the burden of establishing that the defendant is liable on the instrument as a represented person pursuant to Section 3–402(a).

(b) If the validity of signatures is admitted or proved and there is compliance with subsection (a), a plaintiff producing the instrument is entitled to payment if the plaintiff proves entitlement to enforce the instrument under Section 3–301, unless the defendant proves a defense or claim in recoupment. If a defense or claim in recoupment is proved, the right to payment of the plaintiff is subject to the defense or claim except to the extent the plaintiff proves that the plaintiff has rights of a holder in due course which are not subject to the defense or claim.

§ 3–309. Enforcement of Lost, Destroyed, or Stolen Instrument.

(a) A person not in possession of an instrument is entitled to enforce the instrument if (i) that person was in rightful possession of the instrument and entitled to enforce it when loss of possession occurred, (ii) the loss of possession was not the result of a voluntary transfer by that person or a lawful seizure, and (iii) that person cannot reasonably obtain possession of the instrument because the instrument was destroyed, its whereabouts cannot be determined, or it is in the wrongful possession of an unknown person or a person that cannot be found or is not amenable to service of process.

(b) A person seeking enforcement of an instrument pursuant to subsection (a) must prove the terms of the instrument and the person's right to enforce the instrument. If that proof is made, Section 3–308 applies to the case as though the person seeking enforcement had produced the instrument. The court may not enter judgment in favor of the person seeking enforcement unless it finds that the person required to pay the instrument is adequately protected against loss that might occur by reason of a claim by another person to enforce the instrument. Adequate protection may be provided by any reasonable means.

§ 3–310. Effect of Instrument on Obligation for Which Taken.

(a) Unless otherwise agreed, if a certified check, cashier's check, or teller's check is taken for an obligation, the obligation is discharged to the same extent discharge would result if an amount of money equal to the amount of the instrument were taken in payment of the obligation. Discharge of the obligation does not affect any liability that the obligor may have as an indorser of the instrument.

(b) Unless otherwise agreed and except as provided in subsection (a), if a note or an uncertified check is taken for an obligation, the obligation is suspended to the same extent the obligation would be discharged if an amount of money equal to the amount of the instrument were taken.

(1) In the case of an uncertified check, suspension of the obligation continues until dishonor of the check or until it is paid or certified. Payment or certification of the check results in discharge of the obligation to the extent of the amount of the check.

(2) In the case of a note, suspension of the obligation continues until dishonor of the note or until it is paid. Payment of the note results in discharge of the obligation to the extent of the payment.

(3) If the check or note is dishonored and the obligee of the obligation for which the instrument was taken has possession of the instrument, the obligee may enforce either the instrument or the obligation. In the case of an instrument of a third person which is negotiated to the obligee by the obligor, discharge of the obligor on the instrument also discharges the obligation.

(4) If the person entitled to enforce the instrument taken for an obligation is a person other than the obligee, the obligee may not enforce the obligation to the extent the obligation is suspended. If the obligee is the person entitled to enforce the instrument but no longer has possession of it because it was lost, stolen, or destroyed, the obligation may not be enforced to the extent of the amount payable on the instrument, and to that extent the obligee's rights against the obligor are limited to enforcement of the instrument.

(c) If an instrument other than one described in subsection (a) or (b) is taken for an obligation, the effect is (i) that stated in subsection (a) if the instrument is one on which a bank is liable as maker or acceptor, or (ii) that stated in subsection (b) in any other case.

§ 3–311. Accord and Satisfaction by Use of Instrument.

(a) This section applies if a person against whom a claim is asserted proves that (i) that person in good faith tendered an instrument to the claimant as full satisfaction of the claim, (ii) the amount of the claim was unliquidated or subject to a bona fide dispute, and (iii) the claimant obtained payment of the instrument.

(b) Unless subsection (c) applies, the claim is discharged if the person against whom the claim is asserted proves that the instrument or an accompanying written communication contained a conspicuous statement to the effect that the instrument was tendered as full satisfaction of the claim.

(c) Subject to subsection (d), a claim is not discharged under subsection (b) if the claimant is an organization and proves that within a reasonable time before the tender, the claimant sent a conspicuous statement to the person against whom the claim is asserted that communications concerning disputed debts, including an instrument tendered as full satisfaction of a debt, are to be sent to a designated person, office or place, and the instrument or accompanying communication was not received by that designated person, office, or place.

(d) Notwithstanding subsection (c), a claim is discharged under subsection (b) if the person against whom the claim is asserted proves that within a reasonable time before collection of the instrument was initiated, an agent of the claimant having direct responsibility with respect to the disputed obligation knew that the instrument was tendered in full satisfaction of the claim, or received the instrument and any accompanying written communication.

Part 4—Liability of Parties
§ 3–401. Signature.

(a) A person is not liable on an instrument unless (i) the person signed the instrument, or (ii) the person is represented by an agent or representative who signed the instrument and the signature is binding on the represented person under Section 3–402.

(b) A signature may be made (i) manually or by means of a device or machine, and (ii) by the use of any name, including any trade or assumed name, or by any word, mark, or symbol executed or adopted by a person with present intention to authenticate a writing.

§ 3–402. Signature by Representative.

(a) If a person acting, or purporting to act, as a representative signs an instrument by signing either the name of the represented person or the name of the signer, the represented person is bound by the signature to the same extent the represented person would be bound if the signature were on a simple contract. If the represented person is bound, the signature of the representative is the "authorized signature of the represented person" and the represented person is liable on the instrument, whether or not identified in the instrument.

(b) If a representative signs the name of the representative to an instrument and that signature is an authorized signature of the represented person, the following rules apply:

(1) If the form of the signature shows unambiguously that the signature is made on behalf of the represented person who is identified in the instrument, the representative is not liable on the instrument.

(2) Subject to subsection (c), if (i) the form of the signature does not show unambiguously that the signature is made in a representative capacity or (ii) the represented person is not identified in the instrument, the representative is liable on the instrument to a holder in due course that took the instrument without notice that the representative was not intended to be liable on the instrument. With respect to any other person, the representative is liable on the instrument unless the

representative proves that the original parties to the instrument did not intend the representative to be liable on the instrument.

(c) If a representative signs the name of the representative as drawer of a check without indication of the representative status and the check is payable from an account of the represented person who is identified on the check, the signer is not liable on the check if the signature is an authorized signature of the represented person.

§ 3–403. Unauthorized Signature.

(a) Except as otherwise provided in this Article, an unauthorized signature is ineffective except as the signature of the unauthorized signer in favor of a person who in good faith pays the instrument or takes it for value. An unauthorized signature may be ratified for all purposes of this Article.

(b) If the signature of more than one person is required to constitute the authorized signature of an organization, the signature of the organization is unauthorized if one of the required signatures is missing.

(c) The civil or criminal liability of a person who makes an unauthorized signature is not affected by any provision of this Article that makes the unauthorized signature effective for the purposes of this Article.

§ 3–404. Impostors; Fictitious Payees.

(a) If an impostor by use of the mails or otherwise induces the maker or drawer of an instrument to issue the instrument to the impostor, or to a person acting in concert with the impostor, by impersonating the payee of the instrument or a person authorized to act for the payee, an indorsement of the instrument by any person in the name of the payee is effective as the indorsement of the payee in favor of any person that in good faith pays the instrument or takes it for value or for collection.

(b) If (i) a person whose intent determines to whom an instrument is payable (Section 3–110(a) or (b)) does not intend the person identified as payee to have any interest in the instrument, or (ii) the person identified as payee of the instrument is a fictitious person, the following rules apply until the instrument is negotiated by special indorsement:

(1) Any person in possession of the instrument is its holder.

(2) An indorsement by any person in the name of the payee stated in the instrument is effective as the indorsement of the payee in favor of any person that in good faith pays the instrument or takes it for value or for collection.

(c) Under subsection (a) or (b) an indorsement is made in the name of a payee if (i) it is made in a name substantially similar to that of the payee or (ii) the instrument, whether or not indorsed, is deposited in a depositary bank to an account in a name substantially similar to that of the payee.

(d) With respect to an instrument to which subsection (a) or (b) applies, if a person paying the instrument or taking it for value or for collection fails to exercise ordinary care in paying or taking the instrument and that failure substantially contributes to loss resulting from payment of the instrument, the person bearing the loss may recover from the person failing to exercise ordinary care to the extent the failure to exercise ordinary care contributed to the loss.

§ 3–405. Employer Responsibility for Fraudulent Indorsement by Employee.

(a) This section applies to fraudulent indorsements of instruments with respect to which an employer has entrusted an employee with responsibility as part of the employee's duties. The following definitions apply to this section:

(1) "Employee" includes, in addition to an employee of an employer, an independent contractor and employee of an independent contractor retained by the employer.

(2) "Fraudulent indorsement" means (i) in the case of an instrument payable to the employer, a forged indorsement purporting to be that of the employer, or (ii) in the case of an instrument with respect to which the employer is drawer or maker, a forged indorsement purporting to be that of the person identified as payee.

(3) "Responsibility" with respect to instruments means authority (i) to sign or indorse instruments on behalf of the employer, (ii) to process instruments received by the employer for bookkeeping purposes, for deposit to an account, or for other disposition, (iii) to prepare or process instruments for issue in the name of the employer, (iv) to supply information determining the names or addresses of payees of instruments to be issued in the name of the employer, (v) to control the disposition of instruments to be issued in the name of the employer, or (vi) to otherwise act with respect to instruments in a responsible capacity. "Responsibility" does not include the assignment of duties that merely allow an employee to have access to instruments or blank or incomplete instrument forms that are being stored or transported or are part of incoming or outgoing mail, or similar access.

(b) For the purpose of determining the rights and liabilities of a person who, in good faith, pays an instrument or takes it for value or for collection, if an employee entrusted with responsibility with respect to the instrument or a person acting in concert with the employee makes a fraudulent indorsement to the instrument, the indorsement is effective as the indorsement of the person to whom the instrument is payable if it is made in the name of that person. If the person paying the instrument or taking it for value or for collection fails to exercise ordinary care in paying or taking the instrument and that failure substantially contributes to loss resulting from the fraud, the person bearing the loss may recover from the person failing to exercise ordinary care to the extent the failure to exercise ordinary care contributed to the loss.

(c) Under subsection (b) an indorsement is made in the name of the person to whom an instrument is payable if (i) it is made in a name substantially similar to the name of that person or (ii) the instrument, whether or not indorsed, is deposited in a depositary bank to an account in a name substantially similar to the name of that person.

§ 3–406. Negligence Contributing to Forged Signature or Alteration of Instrument.

(a) A person whose failure to exercise ordinary care substantially contributes to an alteration of an instrument or to the making of a forged signature on an instrument is precluded from asserting the alteration or the forgery against a person that, in good faith, pays the instrument or takes it for value.
(b) If the person asserting the preclusion fails to exercise ordinary care in paying or taking the instrument and that failure substantially contributes to loss, the loss is allocated between the person precluded and the person asserting the preclusion according to the extent to which the failure of each to exercise ordinary care contributed to the loss.
(c) Under subsection (a) the burden of proving failure to exercise ordinary care is on the person asserting the preclusion. Under subsection (d) the burden of proving failure to exercise ordinary care is on the person precluded.

§ 3–407. Alteration.

(a) "Alteration" means (i) an unauthorized change in an instrument that purports to modify in any respect the obligation of a party to the instrument, or (ii) an unauthorized addition of words or numbers or other change to an incomplete instrument relating to the obligation of any party to the instrument.
(b) Except as provided in subsection (c), an alteration fraudulently made by the holder discharges any party to whose obligation the alteration applies unless that party assents or is precluded from asserting the alteration. No other alteration discharges any party, and the instrument may be enforced according to its original terms.
(c) If an instrument that has been fraudulently altered is acquired by a person having rights of a holder in due course, it may be enforced by that person according to its original terms. If an incomplete instrument is completed and is then acquired by a person having rights of a holder in due course, it may be enforced by that person as completed, whether or not the completion is a fraudulent alteration.

§ 3–408. Drawee Not Liable on Unaccepted Draft.

A check or other draft does not of itself operate as an assignment of funds in the hands of the drawee available for its payment, and the drawee is not liable on the instrument until the drawee accepts it.

§ 3–409. Acceptance of Draft; Certified Check.

(a) "Acceptance" means the drawee's signed agreement to pay a draft as presented. It must be written on the draft and may consist of the drawee's

signature alone. Acceptance may be made at any time and becomes effective when notification pursuant to instructions is given or the accepted draft is delivered for the purpose of giving rights on the acceptance to any person.
(b) A draft may be accepted although it has not been signed by the drawer, is otherwise incomplete, is overdue, or has been dishonored.
(c) If a draft is payable at a fixed period after sight and the acceptor fails to date the acceptance, the holder may complete the acceptance by supplying a date in good faith.
(d) "Certified check" means a check accepted by the bank on which it is drawn. Acceptance may be made as stated in subsection (a) or by a writing on the check which indicates that the check is certified. The drawee of a check has no obligation to certify the check, and refusal to certify is not dishonor of the check.

§ 3–410. Acceptance Varying Draft.

(a) If the terms of a drawee's acceptance vary from the terms of the draft as presented, the holder may refuse the acceptance and treat the draft as dishonored. In that case, the drawee may cancel the acceptance.
(b) The terms of a draft are not varied by an acceptance to pay at a particular bank or place in the United States, unless the acceptance states that the draft is to be paid only at that bank or place.
(c) If the holder assents to an acceptance varying the terms of a draft, the obligation of each drawer and indorser that does not expressly assent to the acceptance is discharged.

§ 3–411. Refusal to Pay Cashier's Checks, Teller's Checks, and Certified Checks.

(a) In this section, "obligated bank" means the acceptor of a certified check or the issuer of a cashier's check or teller's check bought from the issuer.
(b) If the obligated bank wrongfully (i) refuses to pay a cashier's check or certified check, (ii) stops payment of a teller's check, or (iii) refuses to pay a dishonored teller's check, the person asserting the right to enforce the check is entitled to compensation for expenses and loss of interest resulting from the nonpayment and may recover consequential damages if the obligated bank refused to pay after receiving notice of particular circumstances giving rise to the damages.
(c) Expenses or consequential damages under subsection (b) are not recoverable if the refusal of the obligated bank to pay occurs because (i) the bank suspends payments, (ii) the obligated bank is asserting a claim or defense of the bank that it has reasonable grounds to believe is available against the person entitled to enforce the instrument, (iii) the obligated bank has a reasonable doubt whether the person demanding payment is the person entitled to enforce the instrument, or (iv) payment is prohibited by law.

§ 3–412. Obligation of Maker.

A maker of a note is obliged to pay the note (i) according to its terms at the time it was issued or, if not issued, at the time it first came into possession of a holder, or (ii) if the maker signed an incomplete instrument, according to its terms when completed as stated in Sections 3–115 and 3–407. The obligation is owed to a person entitled to enforce the note or to an indorser that paid the note pursuant to Section 3–415.

§ 3–413. Obligation of Acceptor.

(a) An acceptor of a draft is obliged to pay the draft (i) according to its terms at the time it was accepted, even though the acceptance states that the draft is payable "as originally drawn" or equivalent terms, (ii) if the acceptance varies the terms of the draft, according to the terms of the draft as varied, or (iii) if the acceptance is of a draft that is an incomplete instrument, according to its terms when completed as stated in Sections 3–115 and 3–407. The obligation is owed to a person entitled to enforce the draft or to the drawer or an indorser that paid the draft pursuant to Section 3–414 or 3–415.
(b) If the certification of a check or other acceptance of a draft states the amount certified or accepted, the obligation of the acceptor is that amount. If (i) the certification or acceptance does not state an amount, (ii) the instrument is subsequently altered by raising its amount, and (iii) the instrument is then negotiated to a holder in due course, the obligation of the acceptor is the amount of the instrument at the time it was negotiated to the holder in due course.

§ 3–414. Obligation of Drawer.

(a) If an unaccepted draft is dishonored, the drawer is obliged to pay the draft (i) according to its terms at the time it was issued or, if not issued, at the time it first came into possession of a holder, or (ii) if the drawer signed an incomplete instrument, according to its terms when completed as stated in Sections 3–115 and 3–407. The obligation is owed to a person entitled to enforce the draft or to an indorser that paid the draft pursuant to Section 3–415.

(b) If a draft is accepted by a bank and the acceptor dishonors the draft, the drawer has no obligation to pay the draft because of the dishonor, regardless of when or by whom acceptance was obtained.

(c) If a draft is accepted and the acceptor is not a bank, the obligation of the drawer to pay the draft if the draft is dishonored by the acceptor is the same as the obligation of an indorser stated in Section 3–415(a) and (c).

(d) Words in a draft indicating that the draft is drawn without recourse are effective to disclaim all liability of the drawer to pay the draft if the draft is not a check or a teller's check, but they are not effective to disclaim the obligation stated in subsection (a) if the draft is a check or a teller's check.

(e) If (i) a check is not presented for payment or given to a depositary bank for collection within 30 days after its date, (ii) the drawee suspends payments after expiration of the 30-day period without paying the check, and (iii) because of the suspension of payments the drawer is deprived of funds maintained with the drawee to cover payment of the check, the drawer to the extent deprived of funds may discharge its obligation to pay the check by assigning to the person entitled to enforce the check the rights of the drawer against the drawee with respect to the funds.

§ 3–415. Obligation of Indorser.

(a) Subject to subsections (b), (c) and (d) and to Section 3–419(d), if an instrument is dishonored, an indorser is obliged to pay the amount due on the instrument (i) according to the terms of the instrument at the time it was indorsed, or (ii) if the indorser indorsed an incomplete instrument, according to its terms when completed as stated in Sections 3–115 and 3–407. The obligation of the indorser is owed to a person entitled to enforce the instrument or to a subsequent indorser that paid the instrument pursuant to this section.

(b) If an indorsement states that it is made "without recourse" or otherwise disclaims liability of the indorser, the indorser is not liable under subsection (a) to pay the instrument.

(c) If notice of dishonor of an instrument is required by Section 3–503 and notice of dishonor complying with that section is not given to an indorser, the liability of the indorser under subsection (a) is discharged.

(d) If a draft is accepted by a bank after an indorsement was made and the acceptor dishonors the draft, the indorser is not liable under subsection (a) to pay the instrument.

(e) If an indorser of a check is liable under subsection (a) and the check is not presented for payment, or given to a depositary bank for collection, within 30 days after the day the indorsement was made, the liability of the indorser under subsection (a) is discharged.

§ 3–416. Transfer Warranties.

(a) A person that transfers an instrument for consideration warrants to the transferee and, if the transfer is by indorsement, to any subsequent transferee that:

> **(1)** the warrantor is a person entitled to enforce the instrument,
>
> **(2)** all signatures on the instrument are authentic and authorized,
>
> **(3)** the instrument has not been altered,
>
> **(4)** the instrument is not subject to a defense or claim in recoupment stated in Section 3–305(a) of any party that can be asserted against the warrantor, and
>
> **(5)** the warrantor has no knowledge of any insolvency proceeding commenced with respect to the maker or acceptor or, in the case of an unaccepted draft, the drawer.

(b) A person to whom the warranties under subsection (a) are made and who took the instrument in good faith may recover from the warrantor as damages for breach of warranty an amount equal to the loss suffered as a result of the breach, but not more than the amount of the instrument plus expenses and loss of interest incurred as a result of the breach.

(c) The warranties stated in subsection (a) cannot be disclaimed with respect to checks. Unless notice of a claim for breach of warranty is given to the warrantor within 30 days after the claimant has reason to know of the breach and the identity of the warrantor, the warrantor is discharged to the extent of any loss caused by the delay in giving notice of the claim.

(d) A cause of action for breach of warranty under this section accrues when the claimant has reason to know of the breach.

§ 3–417. Presentment Warranties.

(a) If an unaccepted draft is presented to the drawee for payment or acceptance and the drawee pays or accepts the draft, (i) the person obtaining payment or acceptance, at the time of presentment, and (ii) a previous transferor of the draft, at the time of transfer, warrant to the drawee making payment or accepting the draft in good faith that:

> **(1)** the warrantor is or was, at the time the warrantor transferred the draft, a person entitled to enforce the draft or authorized to obtain payment or acceptance of the draft on behalf of a person entitled to enforce the draft;
>
> **(2)** the draft has not been altered; and
>
> **(3)** the warrantor has no knowledge that the signature of the purported drawer of the draft is unauthorized.

(b) A drawee making payment may recover from any warrantor damages for breach of warranty equal to the amount paid by the drawee less the amount the drawee received or is entitled to receive from the drawer because of payment of the draft. In addition the drawee is entitled to compensation for expenses and loss of interest resulting from the breach. The right of the drawee to recover damages under this subsection is not affected by any failure of the drawee to exercise ordinary care in making payment. If the drawee accepts the draft (i) breach of warranty is a defense to the obligation of the acceptor, and (ii) if the acceptor makes payment with respect to the draft, the acceptor is entitled to recover from any warrantor for breach of warranty the amounts stated in the first two sentences of this subsection.

(c) If a drawee asserts a claim for breach of warranty under subsection (a) based on an unauthorized indorsement of the draft or an alteration of the draft, the warrantor may defend by proving that the indorsement is effective under Section 3–404 or 3–405 or the drawer is precluded under Section 3–406 or 4–406 from asserting against the drawee the unauthorized indorsement or alteration.

(d) This subsection applies if (i) a dishonored draft is presented for payment to the drawer or an indorser or (ii) any other instrument is presented for payment to a party obliged to pay the instrument, and payment is received. The person obtaining payment and a prior transferor of the instrument warrant to the person making payment in good faith that the warrantor is or was, at the time the warrantor transferred the instrument, a person entitled to enforce the instrument or authorized to obtain payment on behalf of a person entitled to enforce the instrument. The person making payment may recover from any warrantor for breach of warranty an amount equal to the amount paid plus expenses and loss of interest resulting from the breach.

(e) The warranties stated in subsections (a) and (d) cannot be disclaimed with respect to checks. Unless notice of a claim for breach of warranty is given to the warrantor within 30 days after the claimant has reason to know of the breach and the identity of the warrantor, the warrantor is discharged to the extent of any loss caused by the delay in giving notice of the claim.

(f) A cause of action for breach of warranty under this section accrues when the claimant has reason to know of the breach.

§ 3–418. Payment or Acceptance by Mistake.

(a) Except as provided in subsection (c), if the drawee of a draft pays or accepts the draft and the drawee acted on the mistaken belief that (i) payment of the draft had not been stopped under Section 4–403, (ii) the signature of the purported drawer of the draft was authorized, or (iii) the balance in the drawer's account with the drawee represented available funds, the drawee may recover the amount paid from the person to whom or for whose benefit payment was made or, in the case of acceptance, may revoke the acceptance. Rights of the drawee under this subsection are not affected by failure of the drawee to exercise ordinary care in paying or accepting the draft.

(b) Except as provided in subsection (c), if an instrument has been paid or accepted by mistake and the case is not covered by subsection (a), the person paying or accepting may recover the amount paid or revoke acceptance to the extent allowed by the law governing mistake and restitution.

(c) The remedies provided by subsection (a) or (b) may not be asserted against a person who took the instrument in good faith and for value. This subsection does not limit remedies provided by Section 3–417 for breach of warranty.

§ 3–419. Instruments Signed for Accommodation.

(a) If an instrument is issued for value given for the benefit of a party to the instrument ("accommodated party") and another party to the instrument ("accommodation party") signs the instrument for the purpose of incurring liability on the instrument without being a direct beneficiary of the value given for the instrument, the instrument is signed by the accommodation party "for accommodation."

(b) An accommodation party may sign the instrument as maker, drawer, acceptor, or indorser and, subject to subsection (d), is obliged to pay the instrument in the capacity in which the accommodation party signs. The obligation of an accommodation party may be enforced notwithstanding any statute of frauds and regardless of whether the accommodation party receives consideration for the accommodation.

(c) A person signing an instrument is presumed to be an accommodation party and there is notice that the instrument is signed for accommodation if the signature is an anomalous indorsement or is accompanied by words indicating that the signer is acting as surety or guarantor with respect to the obligation of another party to the instrument. Except as provided in Section 3–606, the obligation of an accommodation party to pay the instrument is not affected by the fact that the person enforcing the obligation had notice when the instrument was taken by that person that the accommodation party signed the instrument for accommodation.

(d) If the signature of a party to an instrument is accompanied by words indicating unambiguously that the party is guaranteeing collection rather than payment of the obligation of another party to the instrument, the signer is obliged to pay the amount due on the instrument to a person entitled to enforce the instrument only if (i) execution of judgment against the other party has been returned unsatisfied, (ii) the other party is insolvent or in an insolvency proceeding, (iii) the other party cannot be served with process, or (iv) it is otherwise apparent that payment cannot be obtained from the party whose obligation is guaranteed.

(e) An accommodation party that pays the instrument is entitled to reimbursement from the accommodated party and is entitled to enforce the instrument against the accommodated party. An accommodated party that pays the instrument has no right of recourse against, and is not entitled to contribution from, an accommodation party.

§ 3–420. Conversion of Instrument.

(a) The law applicable to conversion of personal property applies to instruments. An instrument is also converted if the instrument lacks an indorsement necessary for negotiation and it is purchased or taken for collection or the drawee takes the instrument and makes payment to a person not entitled to receive payment. An action for conversion of an instrument may not be brought by (i) the maker, drawer, or acceptor of the instrument or (ii) a payee or indorsee who did not receive delivery of the instrument either directly or through delivery to an agent or a co-payee.

(b) In an action under subsection (a), the measure of liability is presumed to be the amount payable on the instrument, but recovery may not exceed the amount of the plaintiff's interest in the instrument.

(c) A representative, other than a depositary bank, that has in good faith dealt with an instrument or its proceeds on behalf of one who was not the person entitled to enforce the instrument is not liable in conversion to that person beyond the amount of any proceeds that it has not paid out.

Part 5—Dishonor
§ 3–501. Presentment.

(a) "Presentment" means a demand (i) to pay an instrument made to the maker, drawee, or acceptor or, in the case of a note or accepted draft payable at a bank, to the bank, or (ii) to accept a draft made to the drawee, by a person entitled to enforce the instrument.

(b) Subject to Article 4, agreement of the parties, clearing house rules and the like,

(1) presentment may be made at the place of payment of the instrument and must be made at the place of payment if the instrument is payable at a bank in the United States; may be made by any commercially reasonable means, including an oral, written, or electronic communication; is effective when the demand for payment or acceptance is received by the person to whom presentment is made; is effective if made to any one of two or more makers, acceptors, drawees or other payors; and

(2) without dishonoring the instrument, the party to whom presentment is made may (i) treat presentment as occurring on the next business day after the day of presentment if the party to whom presentment is made has established a cut-off hour not earlier than 2 p.m. for the receipt and processing of instruments presented for payment or acceptance and presentment is made after the cut-off hour, (ii) require exhibition of the instrument, (iii) require reasonable identification of the person making presentment and evidence of authority to make it if made on behalf of another person, (iv) require a signed receipt on the instrument for any payment made or surrender of the instrument if full payment is made, (v) return the instrument for lack of a necessary indorsement, or (vi) refuse payment or acceptance for failure of the presentment to comply with the terms of the instrument, an agreement of the parties, or other law or applicable rule.

§ 3–502. Dishonor.

(a) Dishonor of a note is governed by the following rules:

(1) If the note is payable on demand, the note is dishonored if presentment is duly made and the note is not paid on the day of presentment.

(2) If the note is not payable on demand and is payable at or through a bank or the terms of the note require presentment, the note is dishonored if presentment is duly made and the note is not paid on the day it becomes payable or the day of presentment, whichever is later.

(3) If the note is not payable on demand and subparagraph (2) does not apply, the note is dishonored if it is not paid on the day it becomes payable.

(b) Dishonor of an unaccepted draft other than a documentary draft is governed by the following rules:

(1) If a check is presented for payment otherwise than for immediate payment over the counter, the check is dishonored if the payor bank makes timely return of the check or sends timely notice of dishonor or nonpayment under Section 4–301 or 4–302, or becomes accountable for the amount of the check under Section 4–302.

(2) If the draft is payable on demand and subparagraph (1) does not apply, the draft is dishonored if presentment for payment is duly made and the draft is not paid on the day of presentment.

(3) If the draft is payable on a date stated in the draft, the draft is dishonored if (i) presentment for payment is duly made and payment is not made on the day the draft becomes payable or the day of presentment, whichever is later, or (ii) presentment for acceptance is duly made before the day the draft becomes payable and the draft is not accepted on the day of presentment.

(4) If the draft is payable on elapse of a period of time after sight or acceptance, the draft is dishonored if presentment for acceptance is duly made and the draft is not accepted on the day of presentment.

(c) Dishonor of an unaccepted documentary draft occurs according to the rules stated in subparagraphs (2), (3), and (4) of subsection (b) except that payment or acceptance may be delayed without dishonor until no later than the close of the third business day of the drawee following the day on which payment or acceptance is required by those subparagraphs.

(d) Dishonor of an accepted draft is governed by the following rules:

(1) If the draft is payable on demand, the draft is dishonored if presentment for payment is duly made and the draft is not paid on the day of presentment.

(2) If the draft is not payable on demand, the draft is dishonored if presentment for payment is duly made and payment is not made on the day it becomes payable or the day of presentment, whichever is later.

(e) In any case in which presentment is otherwise required for dishonor under this section and presentment is excused under Section 3–504, dishonor occurs without presentment if the instrument is not duly accepted or paid.

(f) If a draft is dishonored because timely acceptance of the draft was not made and the person entitled to demand acceptance consents to a late acceptance, from the time of acceptance the draft is treated as never having been dishonored.

§ 3–503. Notice of Dishonor.

(a) The obligation of an indorser stated in Section 3–415(a) and the obligation of a drawer stated in Section 3–414(c) may not be enforced unless (i) the indorser or drawer is given notice of dishonor of the instrument complying with this section or (ii) notice of dishonor is excused under Section 3–504(c).

(b) Notice of dishonor may be given by any person; may be given by any commercially reasonable means including an oral, written, or electronic communication; is sufficient if it reasonably identifies the instrument and indicates that the instrument has been dishonored or has not been paid or accepted. Return of an instrument given to a bank for collection is a sufficient notice of dishonor.

(c) Subject to Section 3–504(d), with respect to an instrument taken for collection by a collecting bank, notice of dishonor must be given (i) by the bank before midnight of the next banking day following the banking day on which the bank receives notice of dishonor of the instrument, and (ii) by any other person within 30 days following the day on which the person receives notice of dishonor. With respect to any other instrument, notice of dishonor must be given within 30 days following the day on which dishonor occurs.

§ 3–504. Excused Presentment and Notice of Dishonor.

(a) Presentment for payment or acceptance of an instrument is excused if (i) the person entitled to present the instrument cannot with reasonable diligence make presentment, (ii) the maker or acceptor has repudiated an obligation to pay the instrument or is dead or in insolvency proceedings, (iii) by the terms of the instrument presentment is not necessary to enforce the obligation of indorsers or the drawer, or (iv) the drawer or indorser whose obligation is being enforced waived presentment or otherwise had no reason to expect or right to require that the instrument be paid or accepted.

(b) Presentment for payment or acceptance of a draft is also excused if the drawer instructed the drawee not to pay or accept the draft or the drawee was not obligated to the drawer to pay the draft.

(c) Notice of dishonor is excused if (i) by the terms of the instrument notice of dishonor is not necessary to enforce the obligation of a party to pay the instrument, or (ii) the party whose obligation is being enforced waived notice of dishonor. A waiver of presentment is also a waiver of notice of dishonor.

(d) Delay in giving notice of dishonor is excused if the delay was caused by circumstances beyond the control of the person giving the notice and the person giving the notice exercised reasonable diligence after the cause of the delay ceased to operate.

§ 3–505. Evidence of Dishonor.

(a) The following are admissible as evidence and create a presumption of dishonor and of any notice of dishonor stated:

(1) a document regular in form as provided in subsection (b) which purports to be a protest;

(2) a purported stamp or writing of the drawee, payor bank, or presenting bank on or accompanying the instrument stating that acceptance or payment has been refused unless reasons for the refusal are stated and the reasons are not consistent with dishonor;

(3) a book or record of the drawee, payor bank, or collecting bank, kept in the usual course of business which shows dishonor, even if there is no evidence of who made the entry.

(b) A protest is a certificate of dishonor made by a United States consul or vice consul, or a notary public or other person authorized to administer oaths by the law of the place where dishonor occurs. It may be made upon information satisfactory to that person. The protest must identify the instrument and certify either that presentment has been made or, if not made, the reason why it was not made, and that the instrument has been dishonored by nonacceptance or nonpayment. The protest may also certify that notice of dishonor has been given to some or all parties.

Part 6—Discharge and Payment

§ 3–601. Discharge and Effect of Discharge.

(a) The obligation of a party to pay the instrument is discharged as stated in this Article or by an act or agreement with the party which would discharge an obligation to pay money under a simple contract.

(b) Discharge of the obligation of a party is not effective against a person acquiring rights of a holder in due course of the instrument without notice of the discharge.

§ 3–602. Payment.

(a) Subject to subsection (b), an instrument is paid to the extent payment is made (i) by or on behalf of a party obliged to pay the instrument, and (ii) to a person entitled to enforce the instrument. To the extent of the payment, the obligation of the party obliged to pay the instrument is discharged even though payment is made with knowledge of a claim to the instrument under Section 3–306 by another person.

(b) The obligation of a party to pay the instrument is not discharged under subsection (a) if:

(1) a claim to the instrument under Section 3–306 is enforceable against the party receiving payment and (i) payment is made with knowledge by the payor that payment is prohibited by injunction or similar process of a court of competent jurisdiction, or (ii) in the case of an instrument other than a cashier's check, teller's check, or certified check, the party making payment accepted, from the person having a claim to the instrument, indemnity against loss resulting from refusal to pay the person entitled to enforce the instrument, or

(2) the person making payment knows that the instrument is a stolen instrument and pays a person that it knows is in wrongful possession of the instrument.

§ 3–603. Tender of Payment.

(a) If tender of payment of an obligation of a party to an instrument is made to a person entitled to enforce the obligation, the effect of tender is governed by principles of law applicable to tender of payment of an obligation under a simple contract.

(b) If tender of payment of an obligation to pay the instrument is made to a person entitled to enforce the instrument and the tender is refused, there is discharge, to the extent of the amount of the tender, of the obligation of an indorser or accommodation party having a right of recourse against the obligor making the tender.

(c) If tender of payment of an amount due on an instrument is made by or on behalf of the obligor to the person entitled to enforce the instrument, the obligation of the obligor to pay interest after the due date on the amount tendered is discharged. If presentment is required with respect to an instrument and the obligor is able and ready to pay on the due date at every place of payment stated in the instrument, the obligor is deemed to have made tender of payment on the due date to the person entitled to enforce the instrument.

§ 3–604. Discharge by Cancellation or Renunciation.

(a) A person entitled to enforce an instrument may, with or without consideration, discharge the obligation of a party to pay the instrument (i) by an intentional voluntary act such as surrender of the instrument to the party, destruction, mutilation, or cancellation of the instrument, cancellation or striking out of the party's signature, or the addition of words to the instrument indicating discharge, or (ii) by agreeing not to sue or otherwise renouncing rights against the party by a signed writing.

(b) Cancellation or striking out of an indorsement pursuant to subsection (a) does not affect the status and rights of a party derived from the indorsement.

§ 3–605. Discharge of Indorsers and Accommodation Parties.

(a) For the purposes of this section, the term "indorser" includes a drawer having the obligation stated in Section 3–414(c).

(b) Discharge of the obligation of a party to the instrument under Section 3–605 does not discharge the obligation of an indorser or accommodation party having a right of recourse against the discharged party.

(c) If a person entitled to enforce an instrument agrees, with or without consideration, to a material modification of the obligation of a party to the instrument, including an extension of the due date, there is discharge of the obligation of an indorser or accommodation party having a right of recourse against the person whose obligation is modified to the extent the modification causes loss to the indorser or accommodation party with respect to the right of recourse. The indorser or accommodation party is deemed to have suffered loss as a result of the modification equal to the amount of the right of recourse unless the person enforcing the instrument proves that no loss was caused by the modification or that the loss caused by the modification was less than the amount of the right of recourse.

(d)   If the obligation of a party to an instrument is secured by an interest in collateral and impairment of the value of the interest is caused by a person entitled to enforce the instrument, there is discharge of the obligation of an indorser or accommodation party having a right of recourse against the obligor to the extent of the impairment. The value of an interest in collateral is impaired to the extent (i) the value of the interest is reduced to an amount less than the amount of the right of recourse of the party asserting discharge, or (ii) the reduction in value of the interest causes an increase in the amount by which the amount of the right of recourse exceeds the value of the interest. The burden of proving impairment is on the party asserting discharge.

(e)   If the obligation of a party to an instrument is secured by an interest in collateral not provided by an accommodation party and the value of the interest is impaired by a person entitled to enforce the instrument, the obligation of any party who is jointly and severally liable with respect to the secured obligation is discharged to the extent the impairment causes the party asserting discharge to pay more than that party would have been obliged to pay, taking into account rights of contribution, if impairment had not occurred. If the party asserting discharge is an accommodation party not entitled to discharge under subsection (d), the party is deemed to have a right to contribution based on joint and several liability rather than a right to reimbursement. The burden of proving impairment is on the party asserting discharge.

(f)   Under subsection (d) or (e) causation of impairment includes (i) failure to obtain or maintain perfection or recordation of the interest in collateral, (ii) release of collateral without substitution of collateral of equal value, (iii) failure to perform a duty to preserve the value of collateral owed, under Article 9 or other law, to a debtor or surety or other person secondarily liable, or (iv) failure to comply with applicable law in disposing of collateral.

(g)   An accommodation party is not discharged under subsection (c) or (d) unless the person agreeing to the modification or causing the impairment knows of the accommodation or has notice under Section 3–419(c) that the instrument was signed for accommodation. There is no discharge of any party under subsection (c), (d), or (e) if (i) the party asserting discharge consents to the event or conduct that is the basis of the discharge, or (ii) the instrument or a separate agreement of the party provides for waiver of discharge under this section either specifically or by general language indicating that parties to the instrument waive defenses based on suretyship or impairment of collateral.

ARTICLE 4: BANK DEPOSITS AND COLLECTIONS
Part 1—General Provisions and Definitions
§ 4–101. Short Title.
This Article shall be known and may be cited as Uniform Commercial Code—Bank Deposits and Collections.

§ 4–102. Applicability.
(1)   To the extent that items within this Article are also within the scope of Articles 3 and 8, they are subject to the provisions of those Articles. In the event of conflict the provisions of this Article govern those of Article 3 but the provisions of Article 8 govern those of this Article.

(2)   The liability of a bank for action or non-action with respect to any item handled by it for purposes of presentment, payment or collection is governed by the law of the place where the bank is located. In the case of action or non-action by or at a branch or separate office of a bank, its liability is governed by the law of the place where the branch or separate office is located.

§ 4–103. Variation by Agreement; Measure of Damages; Certain Action Constituting Ordinary Care.
(1)   The effect of the provisions of this Article may be varied by agreement except that no agreement can disclaim a bank's responsibility for its own lack of good faith or failure to exercise ordinary care or can limit the measure of damages for such lack or failure; but the parties may by agreement determine the standards by which such responsibility is to be measured if such standards are not manifestly unreasonable.

(2)   Federal Reserve regulations and operating letters, clearing house rules, and the like, have the effect of agreements under subsection (1), whether or not specifically assented to by all parties interested in items handled.

(3)   Action or non-action approved by this Article or pursuant to Federal Reserve regulations or operating letters constitutes the exercise of ordinary care and, in the absence of special instructions, action or non-action consistent with clearing house rules and the like or with a general banking usage not disapproved by this Article, prima facie constitutes the exercise of ordinary care.

(4)   The specification or approval of certain procedures by this Article does not constitute disapproval of other procedures which may be reasonable under the circumstances.

(5)   The measure of damages for failure to exercise ordinary care in handling an item is the amount of the item reduced by an amount which could not have been realized by the use of ordinary care, and where there is bad faith it includes other damages, if any, suffered by the party as a proximate consequence.

§ 4–104. Definitions and Index of Definitions.
(1)   In this Article unless the context otherwise requires
   (a)   "Account" means any account with a bank and includes a checking, time, interest or savings account;
   (b)   "Afternoon" means the period of a day between noon and midnight;
   (c)   "Banking day" means that part of any day on which a bank is open to the public for carrying on substantially all of its banking functions;
   (d)   "Clearing house" means any association of banks or other payors regularly clearing items;
   (e)   "Customer" means any person having an account with a bank or for whom a bank has agreed to collect items and includes a bank carrying an account with another bank;
   (f)   "Documentary draft" means any negotiable or non-negotiable draft with accompanying documents, securities or other papers to be delivered against honor of the draft;
   (g)   "Item" means any instrument for the payment of money even though it is not negotiable but does not include money;
   (h)   "Midnight deadline" with respect to a bank is midnight on its next banking day following the banking day on which it receives the relevant item or notice or from which the time for taking action commences to run, whichever is later;
   (i)   "Properly payable" includes the availability of funds for payment at the time of decision to pay or dishonor;
   (j)   "Settle" means to pay in cash, by clearing house settlement, in a charge or credit or by remittance, or otherwise as instructed. A settlement may be either provisional or final;
   (k)   "Suspends payments" with respect to a bank means that it has been closed by order of the supervisory authorities, that a public officer has been appointed to take it over or that it ceases or refuses to make payments in the ordinary course of business.

(2)   Other definitions applying to this Article and the sections in which they appear are:
"Collecting bank" Section 4–105.
"Depositary bank" Section 4–105.
"Intermediary bank" Section 4–105.
"Payor bank" Section 4–105.
"Presenting bank" Section 4–105.
"Remitting bank" Section 4–105.

(3)   The following definitions in other Articles apply to this Article:
"Acceptance" Section 3–410.
"Certificate of deposit" Section 3–104.
"Certification" Section 3–411.
"Check" Section 3–104.
"Draft" Section 3–104.
"Holder in due course" Section 3–302.
"Notice of dishonor" Section 3–508.
"Presentment" Section 3–504.
"Protest" Section 3–509.
"Secondary party" Section 3–102.

(4)   In addition Article 1 contains general definitions and principles of construction and interpretation applicable throughout this Article.

§ 4–105. "Depositary Bank"; "Intermediary Bank"; "Collecting Bank"; "Payor Bank"; "Presenting Bank"; "Remitting Bank".

In this Article unless the context otherwise requires:

(a) "Depositary bank" means the first bank to which an item is transferred for collection even though it is also the payor bank;

(b) "Payor bank" means a bank by which an item is payable as drawn or accepted;

(c) "Intermediary bank" means any bank to which an item is transferred in course of collection except the depositary or payor bank;

(d) "Collecting bank" means any bank handling the item for collection except the payor bank;

(e) "Presenting bank" means any bank presenting an item except a payor bank;

(f) "Remitting bank" means any payor or intermediary bank remitting for an item.

§ 4–106. Separate Office of a Bank.

A branch or separate office of a bank [maintaining its own deposit ledgers] is a separate bank for the purpose of computing the time within which and determining the place at or to which action may be taken or notices or orders shall be given under this Article and under Article 3.

> Note: *The brackets are to make it optional with the several states whether to require a branch to maintain its own deposit ledgers in order to be considered to be a separate bank for certain purposes under Article 4. In some states "maintaining its own deposit ledgers" is a satisfactory test. In others branch banking practices are such that this test would not be suitable.*

§ 4–107. Time of Receipt of Items.

(1) For the purpose of allowing time to process items, prove balances and make the necessary entries on its books to determine its position for the day, a bank may fix an afternoon hour of two p.m. or later as a cut-off hour for the handling of money and items and the making of entries on its books.

(2) Any item or deposit of money received on any day after a cut-off hour so fixed or after the close of the banking day may be treated as being received at the opening of the next banking day.

§ 4–108. Delays.

(1) Unless otherwise instructed, a collecting bank in a good faith effort to secure payment may, in the case of specific items and with or without the approval of any person involved, waive, modify or extend time limits imposed or permitted by this Act for a period not in excess of an additional banking day without discharge of secondary parties and without liability to its transferor or any prior party.

(2) Delay by a collecting bank or payor bank beyond time limits prescribed or permitted by this Act or by instructions is excused if caused by interruption of communication facilities, suspension of payments by another bank, war, emergency conditions or other circumstances beyond the control of the bank provided it exercises such diligence as the circumstances require.

§ 4–109. Process of Posting.

The "process of posting" means the usual procedure followed by a payor bank in determining to pay an item and in recording the payment including one or more of the following or other steps as determined by the bank:

(a) verification of any signature;

(b) ascertaining that sufficient funds are available;

(c) affixing a "paid" or other stamp;

(d) entering a charge or entry to a customer's account;

(e) correcting or reversing an entry or erroneous action with respect to the item.

Part 2—Collection of Items: Depositary and Collecting Banks
§ 4–201. Presumption and Duration of Agency Status of Collecting Banks and Provisional Status of Credits; Applicability of Article; Item Indorsed "Pay Any Bank".

(1) Unless a contrary intent clearly appears and prior to the time that a settlement given by a collecting bank for an item is or becomes final (subsection (3) of Section 4–211 and Sections 4–212 and 4–213) the bank is an agent or sub-agent of the owner of the item and any settlement given for the item is provisional. This provision applies regardless of the form of indorsement or lack of indorsement and even though credit given for the item is subject to immediate withdrawal as of right or is in fact withdrawn; but the continuance of ownership of an item by its owner and any rights of the owner to proceeds of the item are subject to rights of a collecting bank such as those resulting from outstanding advances on the item and valid rights of setoff. When an item is handled by banks for purposes of presentment, payment and collection, the relevant provisions of this Article apply even though action of parties clearly establishes that a particular bank has purchased the item and is the owner of it.

(2) After an item has been indorsed with the words "pay any bank" or the like, only a bank may acquire the rights of a holder

(a) until the item has been returned to the customer initiating collection; or

(b) until the item has been specially indorsed by a bank to a person who is not a bank.

§ 4–202. Responsibility for Collection; When Action Seasonable.

(1) A collecting bank must use ordinary care in

(a) presenting an item or sending it for presentment; and

(b) sending notice of dishonor or non-payment or returning an item other than a documentary draft to the bank's transferor [or directly to the depositary bank under subsection (2) of Section 4–212] (*see note to Section 4–212*) after learning that the item has not been paid or accepted as the case may be; and

(c) settling for an item when the bank receives final settlement; and

(d) making or providing for any necessary protest; and

(e) notifying its transferor of any loss or delay in transit within a reasonable time after discovery thereof.

(2) A collecting bank taking proper action before its midnight deadline following receipt of an item, notice or payment acts seasonably; taking proper action within a reasonably longer time may be seasonable but the bank has the burden of so establishing.

(3) Subject to subsection (1)(a), a bank is not liable for the insolvency, neglect, misconduct, mistake or default of another bank or person or for loss or destruction of an item in transit or in the possession of others.

§ 4–203. Effect of Instructions.

Subject to the provisions of Article 3 concerning conversion of instruments (Section 3–419) and the provisions of both Article 3 and this Article concerning restrictive indorsements only a collecting bank's transferor can give instructions which affect the bank or constitute notice to it and a collecting bank is not liable to prior parties for any action taken pursuant to such instructions or in accordance with any agreement with its transferor.

§ 4–204. Methods of Sending and Presenting; Sending Direct to Payor Bank.

(1) A collecting bank must send items by reasonably prompt method taking into consideration any relevant instructions, the nature of the item, the number of such items on hand, and the cost of collection involved and the method generally used by it or others to present such items.

(2) A collecting bank may send

(a) any item direct to the payor bank;

(b) any item to any non-bank payor if authorized by its transferor; and

(c) any item other than documentary drafts to any non-bank payor, if authorized by Federal Reserve regulation or operating letter, clearing house rule or the like.

(3) Presentment may be made by a presenting bank at a place where the payor bank has requested that presentment be made.

§ 4–205. Supplying Missing Indorsement; No Notice from Prior Indorsement.

(1) A depositary bank which has taken an item for collection may supply any indorsement of the customer which is necessary to title unless the item contains the words "payee's indorsement required" or the like. In the absence of such a requirement a statement placed on the item by the depositary bank to the effect that the item was deposited by a customer or credited to his account is effective as the customer's indorsement.

(2) An intermediary bank, or payor bank which is not a depositary bank, is neither given notice nor otherwise affected by a restrictive indorsement of any person except the bank's immediate transferor.

§ 4-206. Transfer Between Banks.
Any agreed method which identifies the transferor bank is sufficient for the item's further transfer to another bank.

§ 4-207. Warranties of Customer and Collecting Bank on Transfer or Presentment of Items; Time for Claims.
(1) Each customer or collecting bank who obtains payment or acceptance of an item and each prior customer and collecting bank warrants to the payor bank or other payor who in good faith pays or accepts the item that

    (a) he has a good title to the item or is authorized to obtain payment or acceptance on behalf of one who has a good title; and

    (b) he has no knowledge that the signature of the maker or drawer is unauthorized, except that this warranty is not given by any customer or collecting bank that is a holder in due course and acts in good faith

        (i) to a maker with respect to the maker's own signature; or

        (ii) to a drawer with respect to the drawer's own signature, whether or not the drawer is also the drawee; or

        (iii) to an acceptor of an item if the holder in due course took the item after the acceptance or obtained the acceptance without knowledge that the drawer's signature was unauthorized; and

    (c) the item has not been materially altered, except that this warranty is not given by any customer or collecting bank that is a holder in due course and acts in good faith

        (i) to the maker of a note; or

        (ii) to the drawer of a draft whether or not the drawer is also the drawee; or

        (iii) to the acceptor of an item with respect to an alteration made prior to the acceptance if the holder in due course took the item after the acceptance, even though the acceptance provided "payable as originally drawn" or equivalent terms; or

        (iv) to the acceptor of an item with respect to an alteration made after the acceptance.

(2) Each customer and collecting bank who transfers an item and receives a settlement or other consideration for it warrants to his transferee and to any subsequent collecting bank who takes the item in good faith that

    (a) he has a good title to the item or is authorized to obtain payment or acceptance on behalf of one who has a good title and the transfer is otherwise rightful; and

    (b) all signatures are genuine or authorized; and

    (c) the item has not been materially altered; and

    (d) no defense of any party is good against him; and

    (e) he has no knowledge of any insolvency proceeding instituted with respect to the maker or acceptor or the drawer of an unaccepted item.

In addition each customer and collecting bank so transferring an item and receiving a settlement or other consideration engages that upon dishonor and any necessary notice of dishonor and protest he will take up the item.

(3) The warranties and the engagement to honor set forth in the two preceding subsections arise notwithstanding the absence of indorsement or words of guaranty or warranty in the transfer or presentment and a collecting bank remains liable for their breach despite remittance to its transferor. Damages for breach of such warranties or engagement to honor shall not exceed the consideration received by the customer or collecting bank responsible plus finance charges and expenses related to the item, if any.

(4) Unless a claim for breach of warranty under this section is made within a reasonable time after the person claiming learns of the breach, the person liable is discharged to the extent of any loss caused by the delay in making claim.

§ 4-208. Security Interest of Collecting Bank in Items, Accompanying Documents and Proceeds.
(1) A bank has a security interest in an item and any accompanying documents or the proceeds of either

    (a) in case of an item deposited in an account to the extent to which credit given for the item has been withdrawn or applied;

    (b) in case of an item for which it has given credit available for withdrawal as of right, to the extent of the credit given whether or not the credit is drawn upon and whether or not there is a right of charge-back; or

    (c) if it makes an advance on or against the item.

(2) When credit which has been given for several items received at one time or pursuant to a single agreement is withdrawn or applied in part the security interest remains upon all the items, any accompanying documents or the proceeds of either. For the purpose of this section, credits first given are first withdrawn.

(3) Receipt by a collecting bank of a final settlement for an item is a realization on its security interest in the item, accompanying documents and proceeds. To the extent and so long as the bank does not receive final settlement for the item or give up possession of the item or accompanying documents for purposes other than collection, the security interest continues and is subject to the provisions of Article 9 except that

    (a) no security agreement is necessary to make the security interest enforceable (subsection (1)(b) of Section 9-203); and

    (b) no filing is required to perfect the security interest; and

    (c) the security interest has priority over conflicting perfected security interests in the item, accompanying documents or proceeds.

§ 4-209. When Bank Gives Value for Purposes of Holder in Due Course.
For purposes of determining its status as a holder in due course, the bank has given value to the extent that it has a security interest in an item provided that the bank otherwise complies with the requirements of Section 3-302 on what constitutes a holder in due course.

§ 4-210. Presentment by Notice of Item Not Payable by, Through or at a Bank; Liability of Secondary Parties.
(1) Unless otherwise instructed, a collecting bank may present an item not payable by, through or at a bank by sending to the party to accept or pay a written notice that the bank holds the item for acceptance or payment. The notice must be sent in time to be received on or before the day when presentment is due and the bank must meet any requirement of the party to accept or pay under Section 3-505 by the close of the bank's next banking day after it knows of the requirement.

(2) Where presentment is made by notice and neither honor nor request for compliance with a requirement under Section 3-505 is received by the close of business on the day after maturity or in the case of demand items by the close of business on the third banking day after notice was sent, the presenting bank may treat the item as dishonored and charge any secondary party by sending him notice of the facts.

§ 4-211. Media of Remittance; Provisional and Final Settlement in Remittance Cases.
(1) A collecting bank may take in settlement of an item

    (a) a check of the remitting bank or of another bank on any bank except the remitting bank; or

    (b) a cashier's check or similar primary obligation of a remitting bank which is a member of or clears through a member of the same clearing house or group as the collecting bank; or

    (c) appropriate authority to charge an account of the remitting bank or of another bank with the collecting bank; or

    (d) if the item is drawn upon or payable by a person other than a bank, a cashier's check, certified check or other bank check or obligation.

(2) If before its midnight deadline the collecting bank properly dishonors a remittance check or authorization to charge on itself or presents or forwards for collection a remittance instrument of or on another bank which is of a kind approved by subsection (1) or has not been authorized by it, the collecting bank is not liable to prior parties in the event of the dishonor of such check, instrument or authorization.

(3) A settlement for an item by means of a remittance instrument or authorization to charge is or becomes a final settlement as to both the person making and the person receiving the settlement

    (a) if the remittance instrument or authorization to charge is of a kind approved by subsection (1) or has not been authorized by the person receiving the settlement and in either case the person receiving the settlement acts seasonably before its midnight deadline in presenting, forwarding for collection or paying the instrument or authorization,—at the time the remittance instrument or authorization is finally paid by the payor by which it is payable;

(b) if the person receiving the settlement has authorized remittance by a non-bank check or obligation or by a cashier's check or similar primary obligation of or a check upon the payor or other remitting bank which is not of a kind approved by subsection (1)(b),—at the time of the receipt of such remittance check or obligation; or

(c) if in a case not covered by sub-paragraphs (a) or (b) the person receiving the settlement fails to seasonably present, forward for collection, pay or return a remittance instrument or authorization to it to charge before its midnight deadline,—at such midnight deadline.

§ 4–212. Right of Charge-Back or Refund.

(1) If a collecting bank has made provisional settlement with its customer for an item and itself fails by reason of dishonor, suspension of payments by a bank or otherwise to receive a settlement for the item which is or becomes final, the bank may revoke the settlement given by it, charge-back the amount of any credit given for the item to its customer's account or obtain refund from its customer whether or not it is able to return the items if by its midnight deadline or within a longer reasonable time after it learns the facts it returns the item or sends notification of the facts. These rights to revoke, charge-back and obtain refund terminate if and when a settlement for the item received by the bank is or becomes final (subsection (3) of Section 4–211 and subsections (2) and (3) of Section 4–213).

(2) Within the time and manner prescribed by this section and Section 4–301, an intermediary or payor bank, as the case may be, may return an unpaid item directly to the depositary bank and may send for collection a draft on the depositary bank and obtain reimbursement. In such case, if the depositary bank has received provisional settlement for the item, it must reimburse the bank drawing the draft and any provisional credits for the item between banks shall become and remain final.]

Note: *Direct returns is recognized as an innovation that is not yet established bank practice, and therefore, Paragraph 2 has been bracketed. Some lawyers have doubts whether it should be included in legislation or left to development by agreement.*

(3) A depositary bank which is also the payor may charge-back the amount of an item to its customer's account or obtain refund in accordance with the section governing return of an item received by a payor bank for credit on its books (Section 4–301).

(4) The right to charge-back is not affected by

(a) prior use of the credit given for the item; or

(b) failure by any bank to exercise ordinary care with respect to the item but any bank so failing remains liable.

(5) A failure to charge-back or claim refund does not affect other rights of the bank against the customer or any other party.

(6) If credit is given in dollars as the equivalent of the value of an item payable in a foreign currency the dollar amount of any charge-back or refund shall be calculated on the basis of the buying sight rate for the foreign currency prevailing on the day when the person entitled to the charge-back or refund learns that it will not receive payment in ordinary course.

§ 4–213. Final Payment of Item by Payor Bank; When Provisional Debits and Credits Become Final; When Certain Credits Become Available for Withdrawal.

(1) An item is finally paid by a payor bank when the bank has done any of the following, whichever happens first:

(a) paid the item in cash; or

(b) settled for the item without reserving a right to revoke the settlement and without having such right under statute, clearing house rule or agreement; or

(c) completed the process of posting the item to the indicated account of the drawer, maker or other person to be charged therewith; or

(d) made a provisional settlement for the item and failed to revoke the settlement in the time and manner permitted by statute, clearing house rule or agreement.

Upon a final payment under subparagraphs (b), (c), or (d) the payor bank shall be accountable for the amount of the item.

(2) If provisional settlement for an item between the presenting and payor banks is made through a clearing house or by debits or credits in an account between them, then to the extent that provisional debits or credits for the item are entered in accounts between the presenting and payor banks or between the presenting and successive prior collecting banks seriatim, they become final upon final payment of the item by the payor bank.

(3) If a collecting bank receives a settlement for an item which is or becomes final (subsection (3) of Section 4–211, subsection (2) of Section 4–213) the bank is accountable to its customer for the amount of the item and any provisional credit given for the item in an account with its customer becomes final.

(4) Subject to any right of the bank to apply the credit to an obligation of the customer, credit given by a bank for an item in an account with its customer becomes available for withdrawal as of right

(a) in any case where the bank has received a provisional settlement for the item,—when such settlement becomes final and the bank has had a reasonable time to learn that the settlement is final;

(b) in any case where the bank is both a depositary bank and a payor bank and the item is finally paid,—at the opening of the bank's second banking day following receipt of the item.

(5) A deposit of money in a bank is final when made but, subject to any right of the bank to apply the deposit to an obligation of the customer, the deposit becomes available for withdrawal as of right at the opening of the bank's next banking day following receipt of the deposit.

§ 4–214. Insolvency and Preference.

(1) Any item in or coming into the possession of a payor or collecting bank which suspends payment and which item is not finally paid shall be returned by the receiver, trustee or agent in charge of the closed bank to the presenting bank or the closed bank's customer.

(2) If a payor bank finally pays an item and suspends payments without making a settlement for the item with its customer or the presenting bank which settlement is or becomes final, the owner of the item has a preferred claim against the payor bank.

(3) If a payor bank gives or a collecting bank gives or receives a provisional settlement for an item and thereafter suspends payments, the suspension does not prevent or interfere with the settlement becoming final if such finality occurs automatically upon the lapse of certain time or the happening of certain events (subsection (3) of Section 4–211, subsections (1)(d), (2) and (3) of Section 4–213).

(4) If a collecting bank receives from subsequent parties settlement for an item which settlement is or becomes final and suspends payments without making a settlement for the item with its customer which is or becomes final, the owner of the item has a preferred claim against such collecting bank.

Part 3—Collection of Items: Payor Banks
§ 4–301. Deferred Posting; Recovery of Payment by Return of Items; Time of Dishonor.

(1) Where an authorized settlement for a demand item (other than a documentary draft) received by a payor bank otherwise than for immediate payment over the counter has been made before midnight of the banking day of receipt the payor bank may revoke the settlement and recover any payment if before it has made final payment (subsection (1) of Section 4–213) and before its midnight deadline it

(a) returns the item; or

(b) sends written notice of dishonor or nonpayment if the item is held for protest or is otherwise unavailable for return.

(2) If a demand item is received by a payor bank for credit on its books it may return such item or send notice of dishonor and may revoke any credit given or recover the amount thereof withdrawn by its customer, if it acts within the time limit and in the manner specified in the preceding subsection.

(3) Unless previous notice of dishonor has been sent an item is dishonored at the time when for purposes of dishonor it is returned or notice sent in accordance with this section.

(4) An item is returned:

(a) as to an item received through a clearing house when it is delivered to the presenting or last collecting bank or to the clearing house or is sent or delivered in accordance with its rules; or

(b) in all other cases, when it is sent or delivered to the bank's customer or transferor or pursuant to his instructions.

§ 4–302. Payor Bank's Responsibility for Late Return of Item.

In the absence of a valid defense such as breach of a presentment warranty (subsection (1) of Section 4–207), settlement effected or the like, if an item is presented on and received by a payor bank the bank is accountable for the amount of

(a) a demand item other than a documentary draft whether properly payable or not if the bank, in any case where it is not also the depositary bank, retains the item beyond midnight of the banking day of receipt without settling for it or, regardless of whether it is also the depositary bank, does not pay or return the item or send notice of dishonor until after its midnight deadline; or

(b) any other properly payable item unless within the time allowed for acceptance or payment of that item the bank either accepts or pays the item or returns it and accompanying documents.

§ 4–303. When Items Subject to Notice, Stop-Order, Legal Process or Setoff; Order in Which Items May Be Charged or Certified.

(1) Any knowledge, notice or stop-order received by, legal process served upon or setoff exercised by a payor bank, whether or not effective under other rules of law to terminate, suspend or modify the bank's right or duty to pay an item or to charge its customer's account for the item, comes too late to so terminate, suspend or modify such right or duty if the knowledge, notice, stop-order or legal process is received or served and a reasonable time for the bank to act thereon expires or the setoff is exercised after the bank has done any of the following:

(a) accepted or certified the item;

(b) paid the item in cash;

(c) settled for the item without reserving a right to revoke the settlement and without having such right under statute, clearing house rule or agreement;

(d) completed the process of posting the item to the indicated account of the drawer, maker, or other person to be charged therewith or otherwise has evidenced by examination of such indicated account and by action its decision to pay the item; or

(e) become accountable for the amount of the item under subsection (1)(d) of Section 4–213 and Section 4–302 dealing with the payor bank's responsibility for late return of items.

(2) Subject to the provisions of subsection (1) items may be accepted, paid, certified or charged to the indicated account of its customer in any order convenient to the bank.

Part 4—Relationship Between Payor Bank and Its Customer
§ 4–401. When Bank May Charge Customer's Account.

(1) As against its customer, a bank may charge against his account any item which is otherwise properly payable from that account even though the charge creates an overdraft.

(2) A bank which in good faith makes payment to a holder may charge the indicated account of its customer according to

(a) the original tenor of his altered item; or

(b) the tenor of his completed item, even though the bank knows the item has been completed unless the bank has notice that the completion was improper.

§ 4–402. Bank's Liability to Customer for Wrongful Dishonor.

A payor bank is liable to its customer for damages proximately caused by the wrongful dishonor of an item. When the dishonor occurs through mistake liability is limited to actual damages proved. If so proximately caused and proved damages may include damages for an arrest or prosecution of the customer or other consequential damages. Whether any consequential damages are proximately caused by the wrongful dishonor is a question of fact to be determined in each case.

§ 4–403. Customer's Right to Stop Payment; Burden of Proof of Loss.

(1) A customer may by order to his bank stop payment of any item payable for his account but the order must be received at such time and in such manner as to afford the bank a reasonable opportunity to act on it prior to any action by the bank with respect to the item described in Section 4–303.

(2) An oral order is binding upon the bank only for fourteen calendar days unless confirmed in writing within that period. A written order is effective for only six months unless renewed in writing.

(3) The burden of establishing the fact and amount of loss resulting from the payment of an item contrary to a binding stop payment order is on the customer.

§ 4–404. Bank Not Obligated to Pay Check More Than Six Months Old.

A bank is under no obligation to a customer having a checking account to pay a check, other than a certified check, which is presented more than six months after its date, but it may charge its customer's account for a payment made thereafter in good faith.

§ 4–405. Death or Incompetence of Customer.

(1) A payor or collecting bank's authority to accept, pay or collect an item or to account for proceeds of its collection if otherwise effective is not rendered ineffective by incompetence of a customer of either bank existing at the time the item is issued or its collection is undertaken if the bank does not know of an adjudication of incompetence. Neither death nor incompetence of a customer revokes such authority to accept, pay, collect or account until the bank knows of the fact of death or of an adjudication of incompetence and has reasonable opportunity to act on it.

(2) Even with knowledge a bank may for ten days after the date of death pay or certify checks drawn on or prior to that date unless ordered to stop payment by a person claiming an interest in the account.

§ 4–406. Customer's Duty to Discover and Report Unauthorized Signature or Alteration.

(1) When a bank sends to its customer a statement of account accompanied by items paid in good faith in support of the debit entries or holds the statement and items pursuant to a request or instructions of its customer or otherwise in a reasonable manner makes the statement and items available to the customer, the customer must exercise reasonable care and promptness to examine the statement and items to discover his unauthorized signature or any alteration on an item and must notify the bank promptly after discovery thereof.

(2) If the bank establishes that the customer failed with respect to an item to comply with the duties imposed on the customer by subsection (1) the customer is precluded from asserting against the bank

(a) his unauthorized signature or any alteration on the item if the bank also establishes that it suffered a loss by reason of such failure; and

(b) an unauthorized signature or alteration by the same wrongdoer on any other item paid in good faith by the bank after the first item and statement was available to the customer for a reasonable period not exceeding fourteen calendar days and before the bank receives notification from the customer of any such unauthorized signature or alteration.

(3) The preclusion under subsection (2) does not apply if the customer establishes lack of ordinary care on the part of the bank in paying the item(s).

(4) Without regard to care or lack of care of either the customer or the bank a customer who does not within one year from the time the statement and items are made available to the customer (subsection (1)) discover and report his unauthorized signature or any alteration on the face or back of the item or does not within three years from that time discover and report any unauthorized indorsement is precluded from asserting against the bank such unauthorized signature or indorsement or such alteration.

(5) If under this section a payor bank has a valid defense against a claim of a customer upon or resulting from payment of an item and waives or fails upon request to assert the defense the bank may not assert against any collecting bank or other prior party presenting or transferring the item a

claim based upon the unauthorized signature or alteration giving rise to the customer's claim.

§ 4–407. Payor Bank's Right to Subrogation on Improper Payment.

If a payor bank has paid an item over the stop payment order of the drawer or maker or otherwise under circumstances giving a basis for objection by the drawer or maker, to prevent unjust enrichment and only to the extent necessary to prevent loss to the bank by reason of its payment of the item, the payor bank shall be subrogated to the rights.

> **(a)** of any holder in due course on the item against the drawer or maker; and
>
> **(b)** of the payee or any other holder of the item against the drawer or maker either on the item or under the transaction out of which the item arose; and
>
> **(c)** of the drawer or maker against the payee or any other holder of the item with respect to the transaction out of which the item arose.

Part 5—Collection of Documentary Drafts
§ 4–501. Handling of Documentary Drafts; Duty to Send for Presentment and to Notify Customer of Dishonor.

A bank which takes a documentary draft for collection must present or send the draft and accompanying documents for presentment and upon learning that the draft has not been paid or accepted in due course must seasonably notify its customer of such fact even though it may have discounted or bought the draft or extended credit available for withdrawal as of right.

§ 4–502. Presentment of "On Arrival" Drafts.

When a draft or the relevant instructions require presentment "on arrival", "when goods arrive" or the like, the collecting bank need not present until in its judgment a reasonable time for arrival of the goods has expired. Refusal to pay or accept because the goods have not arrived is not dishonor; the bank must notify its transferor of such refusal but need not present the draft again until it is instructed to do so or learns of the arrival of the goods.

§ 4–503. Responsibility of Presenting Bank for Documents and Goods; Report of Reasons for Dishonor; Referee in Case of Need.

Unless otherwise instructed and except as provided in Article 5 a bank presenting a documentary draft

> **(a)** must deliver the documents to the drawee on acceptance of the draft if it is payable more than three days after presentment; otherwise, only on payment; and
>
> **(b)** upon dishonor, either in the case of presentment for acceptance or presentment for payment, may seek and follow instructions from any referee in case of need designated in the draft or if the presenting bank does not choose to utilize his services it must use diligence and good faith to ascertain the reason for dishonor, must notify its transferor of the dishonor and of the results of its effort to ascertain the reasons therefor and must request instructions.

But the presenting bank is under no obligation with respect to goods represented by the documents except to follow any reasonable instructions seasonably received; it has a right to reimbursement for any expense incurred in following instructions and to prepayment of or indemnity for such expenses.

§ 4–504. Privilege of Presenting Bank to Deal With Goods; Security Interest for Expenses.

(1) A presenting bank which, following the dishonor of a documentary draft, has seasonably requested instructions but does not receive them within a reasonable time may store, sell, or otherwise deal with the goods in any reasonable manner.

(2) For its reasonable expenses incurred by action under subsection (1) the presenting bank has a lien upon the goods or their proceeds, which may be foreclosed in the same manner as an unpaid seller's lien.

REVISED ARTICLE 9: SECURED TRANSACTIONS
Part 1—General Provisions
§ 9–101. Short Title.

This article may be cited as Uniform Commercial Code—Secured Transactions.

§ 9–102. Definitions and Index of Definitions.

(a) [Article 9 definitions.] In this article:

(1) "Accession" means goods that are physically united with other goods in such a manner that the identity of the original goods is not lost.

(2) "Account", except as used in "account for", means a right to payment of a monetary obligation, whether or not earned by performance, (i) for property that has been or is to be sold, leased, licensed, assigned, or otherwise disposed of, (ii) for services rendered or to be rendered, (iii) for a policy of insurance issued or to be issued, (iv) for a secondary obligation incurred or to be incurred, (v) for energy provided or to be provided, (vi) for the use or hire of a vessel under a charter or other contract, (vii) arising out of the use of a credit or charge card or information contained on or for use with the card, or (viii) as winnings in a lottery or other game of chance operated or sponsored by a State, governmental unit of a State, or person licensed or authorized to operate the game by a State or governmental unit of a State. The term includes health-care-insurance receivables. The term does not include (i) rights to payment evidenced by chattel paper or an instrument, (ii) commercial tort claims, (iii) deposit accounts, (iv) investment property, (v) letter-of-credit rights or letters of credit, or (vi) rights to payment for money or funds advanced or sold, other than rights arising out of the use of a credit or charge card or information contained on or for use with the card.

(3) "Account debtor" means a person obligated on an account, chattel paper, or general intangible. The term does not include persons obligated to pay a negotiable instrument, even if the instrument constitutes part of chattel paper.

(4) "Accounting", except as used in "accounting for", means a record:

> **(A)** authenticated by a secured party;
>
> **(B)** indicating the aggregate unpaid secured obligations as of a date not more than 35 days earlier or 35 days later than the date of the record; and
>
> **(C)** identifying the components of the obligations in reasonable detail.

(5) "Agricultural lien" means an interest, other than a security interest, in farm products:

> **(A)** which secures payment or performance of an obligation for:

(i) goods or services furnished in connection with a debtor's farming operation; or

(ii) rent on real property leased by a debtor in connection with its farming operation;

> **(B)** which is created by statute in favor of a person that:

(i) in the ordinary course of its business furnished goods or services to a debtor in connection with a debtor's farming operation; or

(ii) leased real property to a debtor in connection with the debtor's farming operation; and

> **(C)** whose effectiveness does not depend on the person's possession of the personal property.

(6) "As-extracted collateral" means:

> **(A)** oil, gas, or other minerals that are subject to a security interest that:

(i) is created by a debtor having an interest in the minerals before extraction; and

(ii) attaches to the minerals as extracted; or

> **(B)** accounts arising out of the sale at the wellhead or minehead of oil, gas, or other minerals in which the debtor had an interest before extraction.

(7) "Authenticate" means:

> **(A)** to sign; or
>
> **(B)** to execute or otherwise adopt a symbol, or encrypt or similarly process a record in whole or in part, with the present intent of the authenticating person to identify the person and adopt or accept a record.

(8) "Bank" means an organization that is engaged in the business of banking. The term includes savings banks, savings and loan associations, credit unions, and trust companies.

(9) "Cash proceeds" means proceeds that are money, checks, deposit accounts, or the like.

(10) "Certificate of title" means a certificate of title with respect to which a statute provides for the security interest in question to be indicated on the certificate as a condition or result of the security interest's obtaining priority over the rights of a lien creditor with respect to the collateral.

(11) "Chattel paper" means a record or records that evidence both a monetary obligation and a security interest in specific goods, a security interest in specific goods and software used in the goods, a security interest in specific goods and license of software used in the goods, a lease of specific goods, or a lease of specific goods and license of software used in the goods. In this paragraph, "monetary obligation" means a monetary obligation secured by the goods or owed under a lease of the goods and includes a monetary obligation with respect to software used in the goods. The term does not include (i) charters or other contracts involving the use or hire of a vessel or (ii) records that evidence a right to payment arising out of the use of a credit or charge card or information contained on or for use with the card. If a transaction is evidenced by records that include an instrument or series of instruments, the group of records taken together constitutes chattel paper.

(12) "Collateral" means the property subject to a security interest or agricultural lien. The term includes:

    (A) proceeds to which a security interest attaches;

    (B) accounts, chattel paper, payment intangibles, and promissory notes that have been sold; and

    (C) goods that are the subject of a consignment.

(13) "Commercial tort claim" means a claim arising in tort with respect to which:

    (A) the claimant is an organization; or

    (B) the claimant is an individual and the claim:

(i) arose in the course of the claimant's business or profession; and

(ii) does not include damages arising out of personal injury to or the death of an individual.

(14) "Commodity account" means an account maintained by a commodity intermediary in which a commodity contract is carried for a commodity customer.

(15) "Commodity contract" means a commodity futures contract, an option on a commodity futures contract, a commodity option, or another contract if the contract or option is:

    (A) traded on or subject to the rules of a board of trade that has been designated as a contract market for such a contract pursuant to federal commodities laws; or

    (B) traded on a foreign commodity board of trade, exchange, or market, and is carried on the books of a commodity intermediary for a commodity customer.

(16) "Commodity customer" means a person for which a commodity intermediary carries a commodity contract on its books.

(17) "Commodity intermediary" means a person that:

    (A) is registered as a futures commission merchant under federal commodities law; or

    (B) in the ordinary course of its business provides clearance or settlement services for a board of trade that has been designated as a contract market pursuant to federal commodities law.

(18) "Communicate" means:

    (A) to send a written or other tangible record;

    (B) to transmit a record by any means agreed upon by the persons sending and receiving the record; or

    (C) in the case of transmission of a record to or by a filing office, to transmit a record by any means prescribed by filing-office rule.

(19) "Consignee" means a merchant to which goods are delivered in a consignment.

(20) "Consignment" means a transaction, regardless of its form, in which a person delivers goods to a merchant for the purpose of sale and:

    (A) the merchant:

(i) deals in goods of that kind under a name other than the name of the person making delivery;

(ii) is not an auctioneer; and

(iii) is not generally known by its creditors to be substantially engaged in selling the goods of others;

    (B) with respect to each delivery, the aggregate value of the goods is $1,000 or more at the time of delivery;

    (C) the goods are not consumer goods immediately before delivery; and

    (D) the transaction does not create a security interest that secures an obligation.

(21) "Consignor" means a person that delivers goods to a consignee in a consignment.

(22) "Consumer debtor" means a debtor in a consumer transaction.

(23) "Consumer goods" means goods that are used or bought for use primarily for personal, family, or household purposes.

(24) "Consumer-goods transaction" means a consumer transaction in which:

    (A) an individual incurs an obligation primarily for personal, family, or household purposes; and

    (B) a security interest in consumer goods secures the obligation.

(25) "Consumer obligor" means an obligor who is an individual and who incurred the obligation as part of a transaction entered into primarily for personal, family, or household purposes.

(26) "Consumer transaction" means a transaction in which (i) an individual incurs an obligation primarily for personal, family, or household purposes, (ii) a security interest secures the obligation, and (iii) the collateral is held or acquired primarily for personal, family, or household purposes. The term includes consumer-goods transactions.

(27) "Continuation statement" means an amendment of a financing statement which:

    (A) identifies, by its file number, the initial financing statement to which it relates; and

    (B) indicates that it is a continuation statement for, or that it is filed to continue the effectiveness of, the identified financing statement.

(28) "Debtor" means:

    (A) a person having an interest, other than a security interest or other lien, in the collateral, whether or not the person is an obligor;

    (B) a seller of accounts, chattel paper, payment intangibles, or promissory notes; or

    (C) a consignee.

(29) "Deposit account" means a demand, time, savings, passbook, or similar account maintained with a bank. The term does not include investment property or accounts evidenced by an instrument.

(30) "Document" means a document of title or a receipt of the type described in Section 7-201(2).

(31) "Electronic chattel paper" means chattel paper evidenced by a record or records consisting of information stored in an electronic medium.

(32) "Encumbrance" means a right, other than an ownership interest, in real property. The term includes mortgages and other liens on real property.

(33) "Equipment" means goods other than inventory, farm products, or consumer goods.

(34) "Farm products" means goods, other than standing timber, with respect to which the debtor is engaged in a farming operation and which are:

    (A) crops grown, growing, or to be grown, including:

(i) crops produced on trees, vines, and bushes; and

(ii) aquatic goods produced in aquacultural operations;

    (B) livestock, born or unborn, including aquatic goods produced in aquacultural operations;

    (C) supplies used or produced in a farming operation; or

    (D) products of crops or livestock in their unmanufactured states.

(35) "Farming operation" means raising, cultivating, propagating, fattening, grazing, or any other farming, livestock, or aquacultural operation.

(36) "File number" means the number assigned to an initial financing statement pursuant to Section 9-519(a).

(37) "Filing office" means an office designated in Section 9-501 as the place to file a financing statement.

(38) "Filing–office rule" means a rule adopted pursuant to Section 9–526.

(39) "Financing statement" means a record or records composed of an initial financing statement and any filed record relating to the initial financing statement.

(40) "Fixture filing" means the filing of a financing statement covering goods that are or are to become fixtures and satisfying Section 9–502(a) and (b). The term includes the filing of a financing statement covering goods of a transmitting utility which are or are to become fixtures.

(41) "Fixtures" means goods that have become so related to particular real property that an interest in them arises under real property law.

(42) "General intangible" means any personal property, including things in action, other than accounts, chattel paper, commercial tort claims, deposit accounts, documents, goods, instruments, investment property, letter-of-credit rights, letters of credit, money, and oil, gas, or other minerals before extraction. The term includes payment intangibles and software.

(43) "Good faith" means honesty in fact and the observance of reasonable commercial standards of fair dealing.

(44) "Goods" means all things that are movable when a security interest attaches. The term includes (i) fixtures, (ii) standing timber that is to be cut and removed under a conveyance or contract for sale, (iii) the unborn young of animals, (iv) crops grown, growing, or to be grown, even if the crops are produced on trees, vines, or bushes, and (v) manufactured homes. The term also includes a computer program embedded in goods and any supporting information provided in connection with a transaction relating to the program if (i) the program is associated with the goods in such a manner that it customarily is considered part of the goods, or (ii) by becoming the owner of the goods, a person acquires a right to use the program in connection with the goods. The term does not include a computer program embedded in goods that consist solely of the medium in which the program is embedded. The term also does not include accounts, chattel paper, commercial tort claims, deposit accounts, documents, general intangibles, instruments, investment property, letter-of-credit rights, letters of credit, money, or oil, gas, or other minerals before extraction.

(45) "Governmental unit" means a subdivision, agency, department, county, parish, municipality, or other unit of the government of the United States, a State, or a foreign country. The term includes an organization having a separate corporate existence if the organization is eligible to issue debt on which interest is exempt from income taxation under the laws of the United States.

(46) "Health-care-insurance receivable" means an interest in or claim under a policy of insurance which is a right to payment of a monetary obligation for health-care goods or services provided.

(47) "Instrument" means a negotiable instrument or any other writing that evidences a right to the payment of a monetary obligation, is not itself a security agreement or lease, and is of a type that in ordinary course of business is transferred by delivery with any necessary indorsement or assignment. The term does not include (i) investment property, (ii) letters of credit, or (iii) writings that evidence a right to payment arising out of the use of a credit or charge card or information contained on or for use with the card.

(48) "Inventory" means goods, other than farm products, which:

(A) are leased by a person as lessor;

(B) are held by a person for sale or lease or to be furnished under a contract of service;

(C) are furnished by a person under a contract of service; or

(D) consist of raw materials, work in process, or materials used or consumed in a business.

(49) "Investment property" means a security, whether certificated or uncertificated, security entitlement, securities account, commodity contract, or commodity account.

(50) "Jurisdiction of organization", with respect to a registered organization, means the jurisdiction under whose law the organization is organized.

(51) "Letter-of-credit right" means a right to payment or performance under a letter of credit, whether or not the beneficiary has demanded or is at the time entitled to demand payment or performance. The term does not include the right of a beneficiary to demand payment or performance under a letter of credit.

(52) "Lien creditor" means:

(A) a creditor that has acquired a lien on the property involved by attachment, levy, or the like;

(B) an assignee for benefit of creditors from the time of assignment;

(C) a trustee in bankruptcy from the date of the filing of the petition; or

(D) a receiver in equity from the time of appointment.

(53) "Manufactured home" means a structure, transportable in one or more sections, which, in the traveling mode, is eight body feet or more in width or 40 body feet or more in length, or, when erected on site, is 320 or more square feet, and which is built on a permanent chassis and designed to be used as a dwelling with or without a permanent foundation when connected to the required utilities, and includes the plumbing, heating, air-conditioning, and electrical systems contained therein. The term includes any structure that meets all of the requirements of this paragraph except the size requirements and with respect to which the manufacturer voluntarily files a certification required by the United States Secretary of Housing and Urban Development and complies with the standards established under Title 42 of the United States Code.

(54) "Manufactured-home transaction" means a secured transaction:

(A) that creates a purchase-money security interest in a manufactured home, other than a manufactured home held as inventory; or

(B) in which a manufactured home, other than a manufactured home held as inventory, is the primary collateral.

(55) "Mortgage" means a consensual interest in real property, including fixtures, which secures payment or performance of an obligation.

(56) "New debtor" means a person that becomes bound as debtor under Section 9–203(d) by a security agreement previously entered into by another person.

(57) "New value" means (i) money, (ii) money's worth in property, services, or new credit, or (iii) release by a transferee of an interest in property previously transferred to the transferee. The term does not include an obligation substituted for another obligation.

(58) "Noncash proceeds" means proceeds other than cash proceeds.

(59) "Obligor" means a person that, with respect to an obligation secured by a security interest in or an agricultural lien on the collateral, (i) owes payment or other performance of the obligation, (ii) has provided property other than the collateral to secure payment or other performance of the obligation, or (iii) is otherwise accountable in whole or in part for payment or other performance of the obligation. The term does not include issuers or nominated persons under a letter of credit.

(60) "Original debtor", except as used in Section 9–310(c), means a person that, as debtor, entered into a security agreement to which a new debtor has become bound under Section 9–203(d).

(61) "Payment intangible" means a general intangible under which the account debtor's principal obligation is a monetary obligation.

(62) "Person related to", with respect to an individual, means:

(A) the spouse of the individual;

(B) a brother, brother-in-law, sister, or sister-in-law of the individual;

(C) an ancestor or lineal descendant of the individual or the individual's spouse; or

(D) any other relative, by blood or marriage, of the individual or the individual's spouse who shares the same home with the individual.

(63) "Person related to", with respect to an organization, means:

(A) a person directly or indirectly controlling, controlled by, or under common control with the organization;

(B) an officer or director of, or a person performing similar functions with respect to, the organization;

(C) an officer or director of, or a person performing similar functions with respect to, a person described in subparagraph (A);

(D) the spouse of an individual described in subparagraph (A), (B), or (C); or

(E) an individual who is related by blood or marriage to an individual described in subparagraph (A), (B), (C), or (D) and shares the same home with the individual.

(64) "Proceeds", except as used in Section 9–609(b), means the following property:

(A) whatever is acquired upon the sale, lease, license, exchange, or other disposition of collateral;

(B) whatever is collected on, or distributed on account of, collateral;

(C) rights arising out of collateral;

(D) to the extent of the value of collateral, claims arising out of the loss, nonconformity, or interference with the use of, defects or infringement of rights in, or damage to, the collateral; or

(E) to the extent of the value of collateral and to the extent payable to the debtor or the secured party, insurance payable by reason of the loss or nonconformity of, defects or infringement of rights in, or damage to, the collateral.

(65) "Promissory note" means an instrument that evidences a promise to pay a monetary obligation, does not evidence an order to pay, and does not contain an acknowledgment by a bank that the bank has received for deposit a sum of money or funds.

(66) "Proposal" means a record authenticated by a secured party which includes the terms on which the secured party is willing to accept collateral in full or partial satisfaction of the obligation it secures pursuant to Sections 9–620, 9–621, and 9–622.

(67) "Public-finance transaction" means a secured transaction in connection with which:

(A) debt securities are issued;

(B) all or a portion of the securities issued have an initial stated maturity of at least 20 years; and

(C) the debtor, obligor, secured party, account debtor or other person obligated on collateral, assignor or assignee of a secured obligation, or assignor or assignee of a security interest is a State or a governmental unit of a State.

(68) "Pursuant to commitment", with respect to an advance made or other value given by a secured party, means pursuant to the secured party's obligation, whether or not a subsequent event of default or other event not within the secured party's control has relieved or may relieve the secured party from its obligation.

(69) "Record", except as used in "for record", "of record", "record or legal title", and "record owner", means information that is inscribed on a tangible medium or which is stored in an electronic or other medium and is retrievable in perceivable form.

(70) "Registered organization" means an organization organized solely under the law of a single State or the United States and as to which the State or the United States must maintain a public record showing the organization to have been organized.

(71) "Secondary obligor" means an obligor to the extent that:

(A) the obligor's obligation is secondary; or

(B) the obligor has a right of recourse with respect to an obligation secured by collateral against the debtor, another obligor, or property of either.

(72) "Secured party" means:

(A) a person in whose favor a security interest is created or provided for under a security agreement, whether or not any obligation to be secured is outstanding;

(B) a person that holds an agricultural lien;

(C) a consignor;

(D) a person to which accounts, chattel paper, payment intangibles, or promissory notes have been sold;

(E) a trustee, indenture trustee, agent, collateral agent, or other representative in whose favor a security interest or agricultural lien is created or provided for; or

(F) a person that holds a security interest arising under Section 2–401, 2–505, 2–711(3), 2A–508(5), 4–210, or 5–118.

(73) "Security agreement" means an agreement that creates or provides for a security interest.

(74) "Send", in connection with a record or notification, means:

(A) to deposit in the mail, deliver for transmission, or transmit by any other usual means of communication, with postage or cost of transmission provided for, addressed to any address reasonable under the circumstances; or

(B) to cause the record or notification to be received within the time that it would have been received if properly sent under subparagraph (A).

(75) "Software" means a computer program and any supporting information provided in connection with a transaction relating to the program. The term does not include a computer program that is included in the definition of goods.

(76) "State" means a State of the United States, the District of Columbia, Puerto Rico, the United States Virgin Islands, or any territory or insular possession subject to the jurisdiction of the United States.

(77) "Supporting obligation" means a letter-of-credit right or secondary obligation that supports the payment or performance of an account, chattel paper, a document, a general intangible, an instrument, or investment property.

(78) "Tangible chattel paper" means chattel paper evidenced by a record or records consisting of information that is inscribed on a tangible medium.

(79) "Termination statement" means an amendment of a financing statement which:

(A) identifies, by its file number, the initial financing statement to which it relates; and

(B) indicates either that it is a termination statement or that the identified financing statement is no longer effective.

(80) "Transmitting utility" means a person primarily engaged in the business of:

(A) operating a railroad, subway, street railway, or trolley bus;

(B) transmitting communications electrically, electromagnetically, or by light;

(C) transmitting goods by pipeline or sewer; or

(D) transmitting or producing and transmitting electricity, steam, gas, or water.

(b) [**Definitions in other articles.**] The following definitions in other articles apply to this article:

"Applicant" Section 5–102.

"Beneficiary" Section 5–102.

"Broker" Section 8–102.

"Certificated security" Section 8–102.

"Check" Section 3–104.

"Clearing corporation" Section 8–102.

"Contract for sale" Section 2–106.

"Customer" Section 4–104.

"Entitlement holder" Section 8–102.

"Financial asset" Section 8–102.

"Holder in due course" Section 3–302.

"Issuer" (with respect to a letter of credit or letter-of-credit right) Section 5–102.

"Issuer" (with respect to a security) Section 8–201.

"Lease" Section 2A–103.

"Lease agreement" Section 2A–103.

"Lease contract" Section 2A–103.

"Leasehold interest" Section 2A–103.

"Lessee" Section 2A–103.

"Lessee in ordinary course of business" Section 2A–103.

"Lessor" Section 2A–103.

"Lessor's residual interest" Section 2A–103.

"Letter of credit" Section 5–102.

"Merchant" Section 2–104.

"Negotiable instrument" Section 3–104.

"Nominated person" Section 5–102.

"Note" Section 3–104.

"Proceeds of a letter of credit" Section 5–114.

"Prove" Section 3–103.

"Sale" Section 2–106.

"Securities account" Section 8–501.

"Securities intermediary" Section 8–102.
"Security" Section 8–102.
"Security certificate" Section 8–102.
"Security entitlement" Section 8–102.
"Uncertificated security" Section 8–102.

(c) [Article 1 definitions and principles.] Article 1 contains general definitions and principles of construction and interpretation applicable throughout this article.

§ 9–103. Purchase-Money Security Interest; Application of Payments; Burden of Establishing.

(a) [Definitions.] In this section:

(1) "purchase-money collateral" means goods or software that secures a purchase-money obligation incurred with respect to that collateral; and

(2) "purchase-money obligation" means an obligation of an obligor incurred as all or part of the price of the collateral or for value given to enable the debtor to acquire rights in or the use of the collateral if the value is in fact so used.

(b) [Purchase-money security interest in goods.] A security interest in goods is a purchase-money security interest:

(1) to the extent that the goods are purchase-money collateral with respect to that security interest;

(2) if the security interest is in inventory that is or was purchase-money collateral, also to the extent that the security interest secures a purchase-money obligation incurred with respect to other inventory in which the secured party holds or held a purchase-money security interest; and

(3) also to the extent that the security interest secures a purchase-money obligation incurred with respect to software in which the secured party holds or held a purchase-money security interest.

(c) [Purchase-money security interest in software.] A security interest in software is a purchase-money security interest to the extent that the security interest also secures a purchase-money obligation incurred with respect to goods in which the secured party holds or held a purchase-money security interest if:

(1) the debtor acquired its interest in the software in an integrated transaction in which it acquired an interest in the goods; and

(2) the debtor acquired its interest in the software for the principal purpose of using the software in the goods.

(d) [Consignor's inventory purchase-money security interest.] The security interest of a consignor in goods that are the subject of a consignment is a purchase-money security interest in inventory.

(e) [Application of payment in non-consumer-goods transaction.] In a transaction other than a consumer-goods transaction, if the extent to which a security interest is a purchase-money security interest depends on the application of a payment to a particular obligation, the payment must be applied:

(1) in accordance with any reasonable method of application to which the parties agree;

(2) in the absence of the parties' agreement to a reasonable method, in accordance with any intention of the obligor manifested at or before the time of payment; or

(3) in the absence of an agreement to a reasonable method and a timely manifestation of the obligor's intention, in the following order:

(A) to obligations that are not secured; and

(B) if more than one obligation is secured, to obligations secured by purchase-money security interests in the order in which those obligations were incurred.

(f) [No loss of status of purchase-money security interest in non-consumer-goods transaction.] In a transaction other than a consumer-goods transaction, a purchase-money security interest does not lose its status as such, even if:

(1) the purchase-money collateral also secures an obligation that is not a purchase-money obligation;

(2) collateral that is not purchase-money collateral also secures the purchase-money obligation; or

(3) the purchase-money obligation has been renewed, refinanced, consolidated, or restructured.

(g) [Burden of proof in non-consumer-goods transaction.] In a transaction other than a consumer-goods transaction, a secured party claiming a purchase-money security interest has the burden of establishing the extent to which the security interest is a purchase-money security interest.

(h) [Non-consumer-goods transactions; no inference.] The limitation of the rules in subsections (e), (f), and (g) to transactions other than consumer-goods transactions is intended to leave to the court the determination of the proper rules in consumer-goods transactions. The court may not infer from that limitation the nature of the proper rule in consumer-goods transactions and may continue to apply established approaches.

§ 9–104. Control of Deposit Account.

(a) [Requirements for control.] A secured party has control of a deposit account if:

(1) the secured party is the bank with which the deposit account is maintained;

(2) the debtor, secured party, and bank have agreed in an authenticated record that the bank will comply with instructions originated by the secured party directing disposition of the funds in the deposit account without further consent by the debtor; or

(3) the secured party becomes the bank's customer with respect to the deposit account.

(b) [Debtor's right to direct disposition.] A secured party that has satisfied subsection (a) has control, even if the debtor retains the right to direct the disposition of funds from the deposit account.

§ 9–105. Control of Electronic Chattel Paper.

A secured party has control of electronic chattel paper if the record or records comprising the chattel paper are created, stored, and assigned in such a manner that:

(1) a single authoritative copy of the record or records exists which is unique, identifiable and, except as otherwise provided in paragraphs (4), (5), and (6), unalterable;

(2) the authoritative copy identifies the secured party as the assignee of the record or records;

(3) the authoritative copy is communicated to and maintained by the secured party or its designated custodian;

(4) copies or revisions that add or change an identified assignee of the authoritative copy can be made only with the participation of the secured party;

(5) each copy of the authoritative copy and any copy of a copy is readily identifiable as a copy that is not the authoritative copy; and

(6) any revision of the authoritative copy is readily identifiable as an authorized or unauthorized revision.

§ 9–106. Control of Investment Property.

(a) [Control under Section 8–106.] A person has control of a certificated security, uncertificated security, or security entitlement as provided in Section 8–106.

(b) [Control of commodity contract.] A secured party has control of a commodity contract if:

(1) the secured party is the commodity intermediary with which the commodity contract is carried; or

(2) the commodity customer, secured party, and commodity intermediary have agreed that the commodity intermediary will apply any value distributed on account of the commodity contract as directed by the secured party without further consent by the commodity customer.

(c) [Effect of control of securities account or commodity account.] A secured party having control of all security entitlements or commodity contracts carried in a securities account or commodity account has control over the securities account or commodity account.

§ 9–107. Control of Letter-of-Credit Right.

A secured party has control of a letter-of-credit right to the extent of any right to payment or performance by the issuer or any nominated person if the issuer or nominated person has consented to an assignment of proceeds of the letter of credit under Section 5–114(c) or otherwise applicable law or practice.

§ 9–108. Sufficiency of Description.

(a) [**Sufficiency of description.**] Except as otherwise provided in subsections (c), (d), and (e), a description of personal or real property is sufficient, whether or not it is specific, if it reasonably identifies what is described.

(b) [**Examples of reasonable identification.**] Except as otherwise provided in subsection (d), a description of collateral reasonably identifies the collateral if it identifies the collateral by:

  (1) specific listing;

  (2) category;

  (3) except as otherwise provided in subsection (e), a type of collateral defined in [the Uniform Commercial Code];

  (4) quantity;

  (5) computational or allocational formula or procedure; or

  (6) except as otherwise provided in subsection (c), any other method, if the identity of the collateral is objectively determinable.

(c) [**Supergeneric description not sufficient.**] A description of collateral as "all the debtor's assets" or "all the debtor's personal property" or using words of similar import does not reasonably identify the collateral.

(d) [**Investment property.**] Except as otherwise provided in subsection (e), a description of a security entitlement, securities account, or commodity account is sufficient if it describes:

  (1) the collateral by those terms or as investment property; or

  (2) the underlying financial asset or commodity contract.

(e) [**When description by type insufficient.**] A description only by type of collateral defined in [the Uniform Commercial Code] is an insufficient description of:

  (1) a commercial tort claim; or

  (2) in a consumer transaction, consumer goods, a security entitlement, a securities account, or a commodity account.

§ 9–109. Scope.

(a) [**General scope of article.**] Except as otherwise provided in subsections (c) and (d), this article applies to:

  (1) a transaction, regardless of its form, that creates a security interest in personal property or fixtures by contract;

  (2) an agricultural lien;

  (3) a sale of accounts, chattel paper, payment intangibles, or promissory notes;

  (4) a consignment;

  (5) a security interest arising under Section 2–401, 2–505, 2–711(3), or 2A–508(5), as provided in Section 9–110; and

  (6) a security interest arising under Section 4–210 or 5–118.

(b) [**Security interest in secured obligation.**] The application of this article to a security interest in a secured obligation is not affected by the fact that the obligation is itself secured by a transaction or interest to which this article does not apply.

(c) [**Extent to which article does not apply.**] This article does not apply to the extent that:

  (1) a statute, regulation, or treaty of the United States preempts this article;

  (2) another statute of this State expressly governs the creation, perfection, priority, or enforcement of a security interest created by this State or a governmental unit of this State;

  (3) a statute of another State, a foreign country, or a governmental unit of another State or a foreign country, other than a statute generally applicable to security interests, expressly governs creation, perfection, priority, or enforcement of a security interest created by the State, country, or governmental unit; or

  (4) the rights of a transferee beneficiary or nominated person under a letter of credit are independent and superior under Section 5–114.

(d) [**Inapplicability of article.**] This article does not apply to:

  (1) a landlord's lien, other than an agricultural lien;

  (2) a lien, other than an agricultural lien, given by statute or other rule of law for services or materials, but Section 9–333 applies with respect to priority of the lien;

  (3) an assignment of a claim for wages, salary, or other compensation of an employee;

  (4) a sale of accounts, chattel paper, payment intangibles, or promissory notes as part of a sale of the business out of which they arose;

  (5) an assignment of accounts, chattel paper, payment intangibles, or promissory notes which is for the purpose of collection only;

  (6) an assignment of a right to payment under a contract to an assignee that is also obligated to perform under the contract;

  (7) an assignment of a single account, payment intangible, or promissory note to an assignee in full or partial satisfaction of a preexisting indebtedness;

  (8) a transfer of an interest in or an assignment of a claim under a policy of insurance, other than an assignment by or to a health-care provider of a health-care-insurance receivable and any subsequent assignment of the right to payment, but Sections 9–315 and 9–322 apply with respect to proceeds and priorities in proceeds;

  (9) an assignment of a right represented by a judgment, other than a judgment taken on a right to payment that was collateral;

  (10) a right of recoupment or set-off, but:

    (A) Section 9–340 applies with respect to the effectiveness of rights of recoupment or set-off against deposit accounts; and

    (B) Section 9–404 applies with respect to defenses or claims of an account debtor;

  (11) the creation or transfer of an interest in or lien on real property, including a lease or rents thereunder, except to the extent that provision is made for:

    (A) liens on real property in Sections 9–203 and 9–308;

    (B) fixtures in Section 9–334;

    (C) fixture filings in Sections 9–501, 9–502, 9–512, 9–516, and 9–519; and

    (D) security agreements covering personal and real property in Section 9–604;

  (12) an assignment of a claim arising in tort, other than a commercial tort claim, but Sections 9–315 and 9–322 apply with respect to proceeds and priorities in proceeds; or

  (13) an assignment of a deposit account in a consumer transaction, but Sections 9–315 and 9–322 apply with respect to proceeds and priorities in proceeds.

§ 9–110. Security Interests Arising under Article 2 or 2A.

A security interest arising under Section 2–401, 2–505, 2–711(3), or 2A–508(5) is subject to this article. However, until the debtor obtains possession of the goods:

  (1) the security interest is enforceable, even if Section 9–203(b)(3) has not been satisfied;

  (2) filing is not required to perfect the security interest;

  (3) the rights of the secured party after default by the debtor are governed by Article 2 or 2A; and

  (4) the security interest has priority over a conflicting security interest created by the debtor.

Part 2—Effectiveness of Security Agreement; Attachment of Security Interest; Rights of Parties to Security Agreement

§ 9–201. General Effectiveness of Security Agreement.

(a) [**General effectiveness.**] Except as otherwise provided in [the Uniform Commercial Code], a security agreement is effective according to its terms between the parties, against purchasers of the collateral, and against creditors.

(b) [**Applicable consumer laws and other law.**] A transaction subject to this article is subject to any applicable rule of law which establishes a different rule for consumers and [insert reference to (i) any other statute or regulation that regulates the rates, charges, agreements, and practices for loans, credit sales, or other extensions of credit and (ii) any consumer-protection statute or regulation].

(c) [**Other applicable law controls.**] In case of conflict between this article and a rule of law, statute, or regulation described in subsection (b), the rule of law, statute, or regulation controls. Failure to comply with a statute or regulation described in subsection (b) has only the effect the statute or regulation specifies.

(d) [**Further deference to other applicable law.**] This article does not:

(1)   validate any rate, charge, agreement, or practice that violates a rule of law, statute, or regulation described in subsection (b); or

(2)   extend the application of the rule of law, statute, or regulation to a transaction not otherwise subject to it.

§ 9–203. Attachment and Enforceability of Security Interest; Proceeds; Supporting Obligations; Formal Requisites.

(a)   [**Attachment.**] A security interest attaches to collateral when it becomes enforceable against the debtor with respect to the collateral, unless an agreement expressly postpones the time of attachment.

(b)   [**Enforceability.**] Except as otherwise provided in subsections (c) through (i), a security interest is enforceable against the debtor and third parties with respect to the collateral only if:

(1)   value has been given;

(2)   the debtor has rights in the collateral or the power to transfer rights in the collateral to a secured party; and

(3)   one of the following conditions is met:

(A)   the debtor has authenticated a security agreement that provides a description of the collateral and, if the security interest covers timber to be cut, a description of the land concerned;

(B)   the collateral is not a certificated security and is in the possession of the secured party under Section 9–313 pursuant to the debtor's security agreement;

(C)   the collateral is a certificated security in registered form and the security certificate has been delivered to the secured party under Section 8–301 pursuant to the debtor's security agreement; or

(D)   the collateral is deposit accounts, electronic chattel paper, investment property, or letter-of-credit rights, and the secured party has control under Section 9–104, 9–105, 9–106, or 9–107 pursuant to the debtor's security agreement.

(c)   [**Other UCC provisions.**] Subsection (b) is subject to Section 4–210 on the security interest of a collecting bank, Section 5–118 on the security interest of a letter-of-credit issuer or nominated person, Section 9–110 on a security interest arising under Article 2 or 2A, and Section 9–206 on security interests in investment property.

(d)   [**When person becomes bound by another person's security agreement.**] A person becomes bound as debtor by a security agreement entered into by another person if, by operation of law other than this article or by contract:

(1)   the security agreement becomes effective to create a security interest in the person's property; or

(2)   the person becomes generally obligated for the obligations of the other person, including the obligation secured under the security agreement, and acquires or succeeds to all or substantially all of the assets of the other person.

(e)   [**Effect of new debtor becoming bound.**] If a new debtor becomes bound as debtor by a security agreement entered into by another person:

(1)   the agreement satisfies subsection (b)(3) with respect to existing or after-acquired property of the new debtor to the extent the property is described in the agreement; and

(2)   another agreement is not necessary to make a security interest in the property enforceable.

(f)   [**Proceeds and supporting obligations.**] The attachment of a security interest in collateral gives the secured party the rights to proceeds provided by Section 9–315 and is also attachment of a security interest in a supporting obligation for the collateral.

(g)   [**Lien securing right to payment.**] The attachment of a security interest in a right to payment or performance secured by a security interest or other lien on personal or real property is also attachment of a security interest in the security interest, mortgage, or other lien.

(h)   [**Security entitlement carried in securities account.**] The attachment of a security interest in a securities account is also attachment of a security interest in the security entitlements carried in the securities account.

(i)   [**Commodity contracts carried in commodity account.**] The attachment of a security interest in a commodity account is also attachment of a security interest in the commodity contracts carried in the commodity account.

§ 9–204. After-Acquired Property; Future Advances.

(a)   [**After-acquired collateral.**] Except as otherwise provided in subsection (b), a security agreement may create or provide for a security interest in after-acquired collateral.

(b)   [**When after-acquired property clause not effective.**] A security interest does not attach under a term constituting an after-acquired property clause to:

(1)   consumer goods, other than an accession when given as additional security, unless the debtor acquires rights in them within 10 days after the secured party gives value; or

(2)   a commercial tort claim.

(c)   [**Future advances and other value.**] A security agreement may provide that collateral secures, or that accounts, chattel paper, payment intangibles, or promissory notes are sold in connection with, future advances or other value, whether or not the advances or value are given pursuant to commitment.

§ 9–205. Use or Disposition of Collateral Permissible.

(a)   [**When security interest not invalid or fraudulent.**] A security interest is not invalid or fraudulent against creditors solely because:

(1)   the debtor has the right or ability to:

(A)   use, commingle, or dispose of all or part of the collateral, including returned or repossessed goods;

(B)   collect, compromise, enforce, or otherwise deal with collateral;

(C)   accept the return of collateral or make repossessions; or

(D)   use, commingle, or dispose of proceeds; or

(2)   the secured party fails to require the debtor to account for proceeds or replace collateral.

(b)   [**Requirements of possession not relaxed.**] This section does not relax the requirements of possession if attachment, perfection, or enforcement of a security interest depends upon possession of the collateral by the secured party.

Part 3—Perfection and Priority

§ 9–301. Law Governing Perfection and Priority of Security Interests.

Except as otherwise provided in Sections 9–303 through 9–306, the following rules determine the law governing perfection, the effect of perfection or nonperfection, and the priority of a security interest in collateral:

(1)   Except as otherwise provided in this section, while a debtor is located in a jurisdiction, the local law of that jurisdiction governs perfection, the effect of perfection or nonperfection, and the priority of a security interest in collateral.

(2)   While collateral is located in a jurisdiction, the local law of that jurisdiction governs perfection, the effect of perfection or nonperfection, and the priority of a possessory security interest in that collateral.

(3)   Except as otherwise provided in paragraph (4), while negotiable documents, goods, instruments, money, or tangible chattel paper is located in a jurisdiction, the local law of that jurisdiction governs:

(A)   perfection of a security interest in the goods by filing a fixture filing;

(B)   perfection of a security interest in timber to be cut; and

(C)   the effect of perfection or nonperfection and the priority of a nonpossessory security interest in the collateral.

(4)   The local law of the jurisdiction in which the wellhead or minehead is located governs perfection, the effect of perfection or nonperfection, and the priority of a security interest in as-extracted collateral.

§ 9–302. Law Governing Perfection and Priority of Agricultural Liens.

While farm products are located in a jurisdiction, the local law of that jurisdiction governs perfection, the effect of perfection or nonperfection, and the priority of an agricultural lien on the farm products.

§ 9–303. Law Governing Perfection and Priority of Security Interests in Goods Covered by a Certificate of Title.

(a)   [**Applicability of section.**] This section applies to goods covered by a certificate of title, even if there is no other relationship between the jurisdiction under whose certificate of title the goods are covered and the goods or the debtor.

(b) [**When goods covered by certificate of title.**] Goods become covered by a certificate of title when a valid application for the certificate of title and the applicable fee are delivered to the appropriate authority. Goods cease to be covered by a certificate of title at the earlier of the time the certificate of title ceases to be effective under the law of the issuing jurisdiction or the time the goods become covered subsequently by a certificate of title issued by another jurisdiction.

(c) [**Applicable law.**] The local law of the jurisdiction under whose certificate of title the goods are covered governs perfection, the effect of perfection or nonperfection, and the priority of a security interest in goods covered by a certificate of title from the time the goods become covered by the certificate of title until the goods cease to be covered by the certificate of title.

§ 9–307. Location of Debtor.

(a) [**"Place of business."**] In this section, "place of business" means a place where a debtor conducts its affairs.

(b) [**Debtor's location: general rules.**] Except as otherwise provided in this section, the following rules determine a debtor's location:

    (1) A debtor who is an individual is located at the individual's principal residence.

    (2) A debtor that is an organization and has only one place of business is located at its place of business.

    (3) A debtor that is an organization and has more than one place of business is located at its chief executive office.

(c) [**Limitation of applicability of subsection (b).**] Subsection (b) applies only if a debtor's residence, place of business, or chief executive office, as applicable, is located in a jurisdiction whose law generally requires information concerning the existence of a nonpossessory security interest to be made generally available in a filing, recording, or registration system as a condition or result of the security interest's obtaining priority over the rights of a lien creditor with respect to the collateral. If subsection (b) does not apply, the debtor is located in the District of Columbia.

(d) [**Continuation of location: cessation of existence, etc.**] A person that ceases to exist, have a residence, or have a place of business continues to be located in the jurisdiction specified by subsections (b) and (c).

(e) [**Location of registered organization organized under State law.**] A registered organization that is organized under the law of a State is located in that State.

(f) [**Location of registered organization organized under federal law; bank branches and agencies.**] Except as otherwise provided in subsection (i), a registered organization that is organized under the law of the United States and a branch or agency of a bank that is not organized under the law of the United States or a State are located:

    (1) in the State that the law of the United States designates, if the law designates a State of location;

    (2) in the State that the registered organization, branch, or agency designates, if the law of the United States authorizes the registered organization, branch, or agency to designate its State of location; or

    (3) in the District of Columbia, if neither paragraph (1) nor paragraph (2) applies.

(g) [**Continuation of location: change in status of registered organization.**] A registered organization continues to be located in the jurisdiction specified by subsection (e) or (f) notwithstanding:

    (1) the suspension, revocation, forfeiture, or lapse of the registered organization's status as such in its jurisdiction of organization; or

    (2) the dissolution, winding up, or cancellation of the existence of the registered organization.

(h) [**Location of United States.**] The United States is located in the District of Columbia.

(i) [**Location of foreign bank branch or agency if licensed in only one state.**] A branch or agency of a bank that is not organized under the law of the United States or a State is located in the State in which the branch or agency is licensed, if all branches and agencies of the bank are licensed in only one State.

(j) [**Location of foreign air carrier.**] A foreign air carrier under the Federal Aviation Act of 1958, as amended, is located at the designated office of the agent upon which service of process may be made on behalf of the carrier.

(k) [**Section applies only to this part.**] This section applies only for purposes of this part.

§ 9–308. When Security Interest or Agricultural Lien Is Perfected; Continuity of Perfection.

(a) [**Perfection of security interest.**] Except as otherwise provided in this section and Section 9–309, a security interest is perfected if it has attached and all of the applicable requirements for perfection in Sections 9–310 through 9–316 have been satisfied. A security interest is perfected when it attaches if the applicable requirements are satisfied before the security interest attaches.

(b) [**Perfection of agricultural lien.**] An agricultural lien is perfected if it has become effective and all of the applicable requirements for perfection in Section 9–310 have been satisfied. An agricultural lien is perfected when it becomes effective if the applicable requirements are satisfied before the agricultural lien becomes effective.

(c) [**Continuous perfection; perfection by different methods.**] A security interest or agricultural lien is perfected continuously if it is originally perfected by one method under this article and is later perfected by another method under this article, without an intermediate period when it was unperfected.

(d) [**Supporting obligation.**] Perfection of a security interest in collateral also perfects a security interest in a supporting obligation for the collateral.

(e) [**Lien securing right to payment.**] Perfection of a security interest in a right to payment or performance also perfects a security interest in a security interest, mortgage, or other lien on personal or real property securing the right.

(f) [**Security entitlement carried in securities account.**] Perfection of a security interest in a securities account also perfects a security interest in the security entitlements carried in the securities account.

(g) [**Commodity contract carried in commodity account.**] Perfection of a security interest in a commodity account also perfects a security interest in the commodity contracts carried in the commodity account.

§ 9–309. Security Interest Perfected Upon Attachment.

The following security interests are perfected when they attach:

(1) a purchase-money security interest in consumer goods, except as otherwise provided in Section 9–311(b) with respect to consumer goods that are subject to a statute or treaty described in Section 9–311(a);

(2) an assignment of accounts or payment intangibles which does not by itself or in conjunction with other assignments to the same assignee transfer a significant part of the assignor's outstanding accounts or payment intangibles;

(3) a sale of a payment intangible;

(4) a sale of a promissory note;

(5) a security interest created by the assignment of a health-care-insurance receivable to the provider of the health-care goods or services:

    (6) a security interest arising under Section 2–401, 2–505, 2–711(3), or 2A–508(5), until the debtor obtains possession of the collateral;

    (7) a security interest of a collecting bank arising under Section 4–210;

    (8) a security interest of an issuer or nominated person arising under Section 5–118;

    (9) a security interest arising in the delivery of a financial asset under Section 9–206(c);

    (10) a security interest in investment property created by a broker or securities intermediary;

    (11) a security interest in a commodity contract or a commodity account created by a commodity intermediary;

    (12) an assignment for the benefit of all creditors of the transferor and subsequent transfers by the assignee thereunder; and

    (13) a security interest created by an assignment of a beneficial interest in a decedent's estate.

§ 9–310. When Filing Required to Perfect Security Interest or Agricultural Lien; Security Interests and Agricultural Liens to Which Filing Provisions Do Not Apply.

(a) [General rule: perfection by filing.] Except as otherwise provided in subsection (b) and Section 9–312(b), a financing statement must be filed to perfect all security interests and agricultural liens.

(b) [Exceptions: filing not necessary.] The filing of a financing statement is not necessary to perfect a security interest:

　(1)　that is perfected under Section 9–308(d), (e), (f), or (g);

　(2)　that is perfected under Section 9–309 when it attaches;

　(3)　in property subject to a statute, regulation, or treaty described in Section 9–311(a);

　(4)　in goods in possession of a bailee which is perfected under Section 9–312(d)(1) or (2);

　(5)　in certificated securities, documents, goods, or instruments which is perfected without filing or possession under Section 9–312(e), (f), or (g);

　(6)　in collateral in the secured party's possession under Section 9–313;

　(7)　in a certificated security which is perfected by delivery of the security certificate to the secured party under Section 9–313;

　(8)　in deposit accounts, electronic chattel paper, investment property, or letter-of-credit rights which is perfected by control under Section 9–314;

　(9)　in proceeds which is perfected under Section 9–315; or

　(10)　that is perfected under Section 9–316.

(c) [Assignment of perfected security interest.] If a secured party assigns a perfected security interest or agricultural lien, a filing under this article is not required to continue the perfected status of the security interest against creditors of and transferees from the original debtor.

§ 9–311. Perfection of Security Interests in Property Subject to Certain Statutes, Regulations, and Treaties.

(a) [Security interest subject to other law.] Except as otherwise provided in subsection (d), the filing of a financing statement is not necessary or effective to perfect a security interest in property subject to:

　(1)　a statute, regulation, or treaty of the United States whose requirements for a security interest's obtaining priority over the rights of a lien creditor with respect to the property preempt Section 9–310(a);

　(2)　[list any certificate-of-title statute covering automobiles, trailers, mobile homes, boats, farm tractors, or the like, which provides for a security interest to be indicated on the certificate as a condition or result of perfection, and any non-Uniform Commercial Code central filing statute]; or

　(3)　a certificate-of-title statute of another jurisdiction which provides for a security interest to be indicated on the certificate as a condition or result of the security interest's obtaining priority over the rights of a lien creditor with respect to the property.

(b) [Compliance with other law.] Compliance with the requirements of a statute, regulation, or treaty described in subsection (a) for obtaining priority over the rights of a lien creditor is equivalent to the filing of a financing statement under this article. Except as otherwise provided in subsection (d) and Sections 9–313 and 9–316(d) and (e) for goods covered by a certificate of title, a security interest in property subject to a statute, regulation, or treaty described in subsection (a) may be perfected only by compliance with those requirements, and a security interest so perfected remains perfected notwithstanding a change in the use or transfer of possession of the collateral.

(c) [Duration and renewal of perfection.] Except as otherwise provided in subsection (d) and Section 9–316(d) and (e), duration and renewal of perfection of a security interest perfected by compliance with the requirements prescribed by a statute, regulation, or treaty described in subsection (a) are governed by the statute, regulation, or treaty. In other respects, the security interest is subject to this article.

(d) [Inapplicability to certain inventory.] During any period in which collateral subject to a statute specified in subsection (a)(2) is inventory held for sale or lease by a person or leased by that person as lessor and that person is in the business of selling goods of that kind, this section does not apply to a security interest in that collateral created by that person.

§ 9–312. Perfection of Security Interests in Chattel Paper, Deposit Accounts, Documents, Goods Covered by Documents, Instruments, Investment Property, Letter-of-Credit Rights, and Money; Perfection by Permissive Filing; Temporary Perfection Without Filing or Transfer of Possession.

(a) [Perfection by filing permitted.] A security interest in chattel paper, negotiable documents, instruments, or investment property may be perfected by filing.

(b) [Control or possession of certain collateral.] Except as otherwise provided in Section 9–315(c) and (d) for proceeds:

　(1)　a security interest in a deposit account may be perfected only by control under Section 9–314;

　(2)　and except as otherwise provided in Section 9–308(d), a security interest in a letter-of-credit right may be perfected only by control under Section 9–314; and

　(3)　a security interest in money may be perfected only by the secured party's taking possession under Section 9–313.

(c) [Goods covered by negotiable document.] While goods are in the possession of a bailee that has issued a negotiable document covering the goods:

　(1)　a security interest in the goods may be perfected by perfecting a security interest in the document; and

　(2)　a security interest perfected in the document has priority over any security interest that becomes perfected in the goods by another method during that time.

(d) [Goods covered by nonnegotiable document.] While goods are in the possession of a bailee that has issued a nonnegotiable document covering the goods, a security interest in the goods may be perfected by:

　(1)　issuance of a document in the name of the secured party;

　(2)　the bailee's receipt of notification of the secured party's interest; or

　(3)　filing as to the goods.

(e) [Temporary perfection: new value.] A security interest in certificated securities, negotiable documents, or instruments is perfected without filing or the taking of possession for a period of 20 days from the time it attaches to the extent that it arises for new value given under an authenticated security agreement.

(f) [Temporary perfection: goods or documents made available to debtor.] A perfected security interest in a negotiable document or goods in possession of a bailee, other than one that has issued a negotiable document for the goods, remains perfected for 20 days without filing if the secured party makes available to the debtor the goods or documents representing the goods for the purpose of:

　(1)　ultimate sale or exchange; or

　(2)　loading, unloading, storing, shipping, transshipping, manufacturing, processing, or otherwise dealing with them in a manner preliminary to their sale or exchange.

(g) [Temporary perfection: delivery of security certificate or instrument to debtor.] A perfected security interest in a certificated security or instrument remains perfected for 20 days without filing if the secured party delivers the security certificate or instrument to the debtor for the purpose of:

　(1)　ultimate sale or exchange; or

　(2)　presentation, collection, enforcement, renewal, or registration of transfer.

(h) [Expiration of temporary perfection.] After the 20-day period specified in subsection (e), (f), or (g) expires, perfection depends upon compliance with this article.

§ 9–313. When Possession by or Delivery to Secured Party Perfects Security Interest Without Filing.

(a) [Perfection by possession or delivery.] Except as otherwise provided in subsection (b), a secured party may perfect a security interest in negotiable documents, goods, instruments, money, or tangible chattel paper by taking possession of the collateral. A secured party may perfect a security interest in certificated securities by taking delivery of the certificated securities under Section 8–301.

(b) [Goods covered by certificate of title.] With respect to goods covered by a certificate of title issued by this State, a secured party may perfect a security interest in the goods by taking possession of the goods only in the circumstances described in Section 9–316(d).

(c) [**Collateral in possession of person other than debtor.**] With respect to collateral other than certificated securities and goods covered by a document, a secured party takes possession of collateral in the possession of a person other than the debtor, the secured party, or a lessee of the collateral from the debtor in the ordinary course of the debtor's business, when:

(1)   the person in possession authenticates a record acknowledging that it holds possession of the collateral for the secured party's benefit; or

(2)   the person takes possession of the collateral after having authenticated a record acknowledging that it will hold possession of collateral for the secured party's benefit.

(d) [**Time of perfection by possession; continuation of perfection.**] If perfection of a security interest depends upon possession of the collateral by a secured party, perfection occurs no earlier than the time the secured party takes possession and continues only while the secured party retains possession.

(e) [**Time of perfection by delivery; continuation of perfection.**] A security interest in a certificated security in registered form is perfected by delivery when delivery of the certificated security occurs under Section 8–301 and remains perfected by delivery until the debtor obtains possession of the security certificate.

(f) [**Acknowledgment not required.**] A person in possession of collateral is not required to acknowledge that it holds possession for a secured party's benefit.

(g) [**Effectiveness of acknowledgment; no duties or confirmation.**] If a person acknowledges that it holds possession for the secured party's benefit:

(1)   the acknowledgment is effective under subsection (c) or Section 8–301(a), even if the acknowledgment violates the rights of a debtor; and

(2)   unless the person otherwise agrees or law other than this article otherwise provides, the person does not owe any duty to the secured party and is not required to confirm the acknowledgment to another person.

(h) [**Secured party's delivery to person other than debtor.**] A secured party having possession of collateral does not relinquish possession by delivering the collateral to a person other than the debtor or a lessee of the collateral from the debtor in the ordinary course of the debtor's business if the person was instructed before the delivery or is instructed contemporaneously with the delivery:

(1)   to hold possession of the collateral for the secured party's benefit; or

(2)   to redeliver the collateral to the secured party.

(i)   [**Effect of delivery under subsection (h); no duties or confirmation.**] A secured party does not relinquish possession, even if a delivery under subsection (h) violates the rights of a debtor. A person to which collateral is delivered under subsection (h) does not owe any duty to the secured party and is not required to confirm the delivery to another person unless the person otherwise agrees or law other than this article otherwise provides.

§ 9–314. Perfection by Control.

(a) [**Perfection by control.**] A security interest in investment property, deposit accounts, letter-of-credit rights, or electronic chattel paper may be perfected by control of the collateral under Section 9–104, 9–105, 9–106, or 9–107.

(b) [**Specified collateral: time of perfection by control; continuation of perfection.**] A security interest in deposit accounts, electronic chattel paper, or letter-of-credit rights is perfected by control under Section 9–104, 9–105, or 9–107 when the secured party obtains control and remains perfected by control only while the secured party retains control.

(c) [**Investment property: time of perfection by control; continuation of perfection.**] A security interest in investment property is perfected by control under Section 9–106 from the time the secured party obtains control and remains perfected by control until:

(1)   the secured party does not have control; and

(2)   one of the following occurs:

(A) if the collateral is a certificated security, the debtor has or acquires possession of the security certificate;

(B) if the collateral is an uncertificated security, the issuer has registered or registers the debtor as the registered owner; or

(C) if the collateral is a security entitlement, the debtor is or becomes the entitlement holder.

§ 9–315. Secured Party's Rights on Disposition of Collateral and in Proceeds.

(a) [**Disposition of collateral: continuation of security interest or agricultural lien; proceeds.**] Except as otherwise provided in this article and in Section 2–403(2):

(1)   a security interest or agricultural lien continues in collateral notwithstanding sale, lease, license, exchange, or other disposition thereof unless the secured party authorized the disposition free of the security interest or agricultural lien; and

(2)   a security interest attaches to any identifiable proceeds of collateral.

(b) [**When commingled proceeds identifiable.**] Proceeds that are commingled with other property are identifiable proceeds:

(1)   if the proceeds are goods, to the extent provided by Section 9–336; and

(2)   if the proceeds are not goods, to the extent that the secured party identifies the proceeds by a method of tracing, including application of equitable principles, that is permitted under law other than this article with respect to commingled property of the type involved.

(c) [**Perfection of security interest in proceeds.**] A security interest in proceeds is a perfected security interest if the security interest in the original collateral was perfected.

(d) [**Continuation of perfection.**] A perfected security interest in proceeds becomes unperfected on the 21st day after the security interest attaches to the proceeds unless:

(1)   the following conditions are satisfied:

(A) a filed financing statement covers the original collateral;

(B) the proceeds are collateral in which a security interest may be perfected by filing in the office in which the financing statement has been filed; and

(C) the proceeds are not acquired with cash proceeds;

(2)   the proceeds are identifiable cash proceeds; or

(3)   the security interest in the proceeds is perfected other than under subsection (c) when the security interest attaches to the proceeds or within 20 days thereafter.

(e) [**When perfected security interest in proceeds becomes unperfected.**] If a filed financing statement covers the original collateral, a security interest in proceeds which remains perfected under subsection (d)(1) becomes unperfected at the later of:

(1)   when the effectiveness of the filed financing statement lapses under Section 9–515 or is terminated under Section 9–513; or

(2)   the 21st day after the security interest attaches to the proceeds.

§ 9–316. Continued Perfection of Security Interest Following Change in Governing Law.

(a) [**General rule: effect on perfection of change in governing law.**] A security interest perfected pursuant to the law of the jurisdiction designated in Section 9–301(1) or 9–305(c) remains perfected until the earliest of:

(1)   the time perfection would have ceased under the law of that jurisdiction;

(2)   the expiration of four months after a change of the debtor's location to another jurisdiction; or

(3)   the expiration of one year after a transfer of collateral to a person that thereby becomes a debtor and is located in another jurisdiction.

(b) [**Security interest perfected or unperfected under law of new jurisdiction.**] If a security interest described in subsection (a) becomes perfected under the law of the other jurisdiction before the earliest time or event described in that subsection, it remains perfected thereafter. If the security interest does not become perfected under the law of the other jurisdiction before the earliest time or event, it becomes unperfected and is deemed never to have been perfected as against a purchaser of the collateral for value.

(c) [**Possessory security interest in collateral moved to new jurisdiction.**] A possessory security interest in collateral, other than goods covered by a certificate of title and as-extracted collateral consisting of goods, remains continuously perfected if:

(1) the collateral is located in one jurisdiction and subject to a security interest perfected under the law of that jurisdiction;

(2) thereafter the collateral is brought into another jurisdiction; and

(3) upon entry into the other jurisdiction, the security interest is perfected under the law of the other jurisdiction.

(d) [**Goods covered by certificate of title from this state.**] Except as otherwise provided in subsection (e), a security interest in goods covered by a certificate of title which is perfected by any method under the law of another jurisdiction when the goods become covered by a certificate of title from this State remains perfected until the security interest would have become unperfected under the law of the other jurisdiction had the goods not become so covered.

(e) [**When subsection (d) security interest becomes unperfected against purchasers.**] A security interest described in subsection (d) becomes unperfected as against a purchaser of the goods for value and is deemed never to have been perfected as against a purchaser of the goods for value if the applicable requirements for perfection under Section 9-311(b) or 9-313 are not satisfied before the earlier of:

(1) the time the security interest would have become unperfected under the law of the other jurisdiction had the goods not become covered by a certificate of title from this State; or

(2) the expiration of four months after the goods had become so covered.

(f) [**Change in jurisdiction of bank, issuer, nominated person, securities intermediary, or commodity intermediary.**] A security interest in deposit accounts, letter-of-credit rights, or investment property which is perfected under the law of the bank's jurisdiction, the issuer's jurisdiction, a nominated person's jurisdiction, the securities intermediary's jurisdiction, or the commodity intermediary's jurisdiction, as applicable, remains perfected until the earlier of:

(1) the time the security interest would have become unperfected under the law of that jurisdiction; or

(2) the expiration of four months after a change of the applicable jurisdiction to another jurisdiction.

(g) [**Subsection (f) security interest perfected or unperfected under law of new jurisdiction.**] If a security interest described in subsection (f) becomes perfected under the law of the other jurisdiction before the earlier of the time or the end of the period described in that subsection, it remains perfected thereafter. If the security interest does not become perfected under the law of the other jurisdiction before the earlier of that time or the end of that period, it becomes unperfected and is deemed never to have been perfected as against a purchaser of the collateral for value.

§ 9-317. Interests That Take Priority over or Take Free of Security Interest or Agricultural Lien.

(a) [**Conflicting security interests and rights of lien creditors.**] A security interest or agricultural lien is subordinate to the rights of:

(1) a person entitled to priority under Section 9-322; and

(2) except as otherwise provided in subsection (e), a person that becomes a lien creditor before the earlier of the time:

(A) the security interest or agricultural lien is perfected; or

(B) one of the conditions specified in Section 9-203(b)(3) is met and a financing statement covering the collateral is filed.

(b) [**Buyers that receive delivery.**] Except as otherwise provided in subsection (e), a buyer, other than a secured party, of tangible chattel paper, documents, goods, instruments, or a security certificate takes free of a security interest or agricultural lien if the buyer gives value and receives delivery of the collateral without knowledge of the security interest or agricultural lien and before it is perfected.

(c) [**Lessees that receive delivery.**] Except as otherwise provided in subsection (e), a lessee of goods takes free of a security interest or agricultural lien if the lessee gives value and receives delivery of the collateral without knowledge of the security interest or agricultural lien and before it is perfected.

(d) [**Licensees and buyers of certain collateral.**] A licensee of a general intangible or a buyer, other than a secured party, of accounts, electronic chattel paper, general intangibles, or investment property other than a certificated security takes free of a security interest if the licensee or buyer gives value without knowledge of the security interest and before it is perfected.

(e) [**Purchase-money security interest.**] Except as otherwise provided in Sections 9-320 and 9-321, if a person files a financing statement with respect to a purchase-money security interest before or within 20 days after the debtor receives delivery of the collateral, the security interest takes priority over the rights of a buyer, lessee, or lien creditor which arise between the time the security interest attaches and the time of filing.

§ 9-320. Buyer of Goods.

(a) [**Buyer in ordinary course of business.**] Except as otherwise provided in subsection (e), a buyer in ordinary course of business, other than a person buying farm products from a person engaged in farming operations, takes free of a security interest created by the buyer's seller, even if the security interest is perfected and the buyer knows of its existence.

(b) [**Buyer of consumer goods.**] Except as otherwise provided in subsection (e), a buyer of goods from a person who used or bought the goods for use primarily for personal, family, or household purposes takes free of a security interest, even if perfected, if the buyer buys:

(1) without knowledge of the security interest;

(2) for value;

(3) primarily for the buyer's personal, family, or household purposes; and

(4) before the filing of a financing statement covering the goods.

(c) [**Effectiveness of filing for subsection (b).**] To the extent that it affects the priority of a security interest over a buyer of goods under subsection (b), the period of effectiveness of a filing made in the jurisdiction in which the seller is located is governed by Section 9-316(a) and (b).

(d) [**Buyer in ordinary course of business at wellhead or minehead.**] A buyer in ordinary course of business buying oil, gas, or other minerals at the wellhead or minehead or after extraction takes free of an interest arising out of an encumbrance.

(e) [**Possessory security interest not affected.**] Subsections (a) and (b) do not affect a security interest in goods in the possession of the secured party under Section 9-313.

§ 9-322. Priorities among Conflicting Security Interests in and Agricultural Liens on Same Collateral.

(a) [**General priority rules.**] Except as otherwise provided in this section, priority among conflicting security interests and agricultural liens in the same collateral is determined according to the following rules:

(1) Conflicting perfected security interests and agricultural liens rank according to priority in time of filing or perfection. Priority dates from the earlier of the time a filing covering the collateral is first made or the security interest or agricultural lien is first perfected, if there is no period thereafter when there is neither filing nor perfection.

(2) A perfected security interest or agricultural lien has priority over a conflicting unperfected security interest or agricultural lien.

(3) The first security interest or agricultural lien to attach or become effective has priority if conflicting security interests and agricultural liens are unperfected.

(b) [**Time of perfection: proceeds and supporting obligations.**] For the purposes of subsection (a)(1):

(1) the time of filing or perfection as to a security interest in collateral is also the time of filing or perfection as to a security interest in proceeds; and

(2) the time of filing or perfection as to a security interest in collateral supported by a supporting obligation is also the time of filing or perfection as to a security interest in the supporting obligation.

(c) [**Special priority rules: proceeds and supporting obligations.**] Except as otherwise provided in subsection (f), a security interest in collateral which qualifies for priority over a conflicting security interest under Section 9-327, 9-328, 9-329, 9-330, or 9-331 also has priority over a conflicting security interest in:

(1) any supporting obligation for the collateral; and

(2) proceeds of the collateral if:

(A) the security interest in proceeds is perfected;

(B) the proceeds are cash proceeds or of the same type as the collateral; and

(C) in the case of proceeds that are proceeds of proceeds, all intervening proceeds are cash proceeds, proceeds of the same type as the collateral, or an account relating to the collateral.

(d) **[First-to-file priority rule for certain collateral.]** Subject to subsection (e) and except as otherwise provided in subsection (f), if a security interest in chattel paper, deposit accounts, negotiable documents, instruments, investment property, or letter-of-credit rights is perfected by a method other than filing, conflicting perfected security interests in proceeds of the collateral rank according to priority in time of filing.

(e) **[Applicability of subsection (d).]** Subsection (d) applies only if the proceeds of the collateral are not cash proceeds, chattel paper, negotiable documents, instruments, investment property, or letter-of-credit rights.

(f) **[Limitations on subsections (a) through (e).]** Subsections (a) through (e) are subject to:

(1) subsection (g) and the other provisions of this part;

(2) Section 4-210 with respect to a security interest of a collecting bank;

(3) Section 5-118 with respect to a security interest of an issuer or nominated person; and

(4) Section 9-110 with respect to a security interest arising under Article 2 or 2A.

(g) **[Priority under agricultural lien statute.]** A perfected agricultural lien on collateral has priority over a conflicting security interest in or agricultural lien on the same collateral if the statute creating the agricultural lien so provides.

§ 9-323. Future Advances.

(a) **[When priority based on time of advance.]** Except as otherwise provided in subsection (c), for purposes of determining the priority of a perfected security interest under Section 9-322(a)(1), perfection of the security interest dates from the time an advance is made to the extent that the security interest secures an advance that:

(1) is made while the security interest is perfected only:

(A) under Section 9-309 when it attaches; or

(B) temporarily under Section 9-312(e), (f), or (g); and

(2) is not made pursuant to a commitment entered into before or while the security interest is perfected by a method other than under Section 9-309 or 9-312(e), (f), or (g).

(b) **[Lien creditor.]** Except as otherwise provided in subsection (c), a security interest is subordinate to the rights of a person that becomes a lien creditor to the extent that the security interest secures an advance made more than 45 days after the person becomes a lien creditor unless the advance is made:

(1) without knowledge of the lien; or

(2) pursuant to a commitment entered into without knowledge of the lien.

(c) **[Buyer of receivables.]** Subsections (a) and (b) do not apply to a security interest held by a secured party that is a buyer of accounts, chattel paper, payment intangibles, or promissory notes or a consignor.

(d) **[Buyer of goods.]** Except as otherwise provided in subsection (e), a buyer of goods other than a buyer in ordinary course of business takes free of a security interest to the extent that it secures advances made after the earlier of:

(1) the time the secured party acquires knowledge of the buyer's purchase; or

(2) 45 days after the purchase.

(e) **[Advances made pursuant to commitment: priority of buyer of goods.]** Subsection (d) does not apply if the advance is made pursuant to a commitment entered into without knowledge of the buyer's purchase and before the expiration of the 45-day period.

(f) **[Lessee of goods.]** Except as otherwise provided in subsection (g), a lessee of goods, other than a lessee in ordinary course of business, takes the leasehold interest free of a security interest to the extent that it secures advances made after the earlier of:

(1) the time the secured party acquires knowledge of the lease; or

(2) 45 days after the lease contract becomes enforceable.

(g) **[Advances made pursuant to commitment: priority of lessee of goods.]** Subsection (f) does not apply if the advance is made pursuant to a commitment entered into without knowledge of the lease and before the expiration of the 45-day period.

§ 9-324. Priority of Purchase-Money Security Interests.

(a) **[General rule: purchase-money priority.]** Except as otherwise provided in subsection (g), a perfected purchase-money security interest in goods other than inventory or livestock has priority over a conflicting security interest in the same goods, and, except as otherwise provided in Section 9-327, a perfected security interest in its identifiable proceeds also has priority, if the purchase-money security interest is perfected when the debtor receives possession of the collateral or within 20 days thereafter.

(b) **[Inventory purchase-money priority.]** Subject to subsection (c) and except as otherwise provided in subsection (g), a perfected purchase-money security interest in inventory has priority over a conflicting security interest in the same inventory, has priority over a conflicting security interest in chattel paper or an instrument constituting proceeds of the inventory and in proceeds of the chattel paper, if so provided in Section 9-330, and, except as otherwise provided in Section 9-327, also has priority in identifiable cash proceeds of the inventory to the extent the identifiable cash proceeds are received on or before the delivery of the inventory to a buyer, if:

(1) the purchase-money security interest is perfected when the debtor receives possession of the inventory;

(2) the purchase-money secured party sends an authenticated notification to the holder of the conflicting security interest;

(3) the holder of the conflicting security interest receives the notification within five years before the debtor receives possession of the inventory; and

(4) the notification states that the person sending the notification has or expects to acquire a purchase-money security interest in inventory of the debtor and describes the inventory.

(c) **[Holders of conflicting inventory security interests to be notified.]** Subsections (b)(2) through (4) apply only if the holder of the conflicting security interest had filed a financing statement covering the same types of inventory:

(1) if the purchase-money security interest is perfected by filing, before the date of the filing; or

(2) if the purchase-money security interest is temporarily perfected without filing or possession under Section 9-312(f), before the beginning of the 20-day period thereunder.

(d) **[Livestock purchase-money priority.]** Subject to subsection (e) and except as otherwise provided in subsection (g), a perfected purchase-money security interest in livestock that are farm products has priority over a conflicting security interest in the same livestock, and, except as otherwise provided in Section 9-327, a perfected security interest in their identifiable proceeds and identifiable products in their unmanufactured states also has priority, if:

(1) the purchase-money security interest is perfected when the debtor receives possession of the livestock;

(2) the purchase-money secured party sends an authenticated notification to the holder of the conflicting security interest;

(3) the holder of the conflicting security interest receives the notification within six months before the debtor receives possession of the livestock; and

(4) the notification states that the person sending the notification has or expects to acquire a purchase-money security interest in livestock of the debtor and describes the livestock.

(e) **[Holders of conflicting livestock security interests to be notified.]** Subsections (d)(2) through (4) apply only if the holder of the conflicting security interest had filed a financing statement covering the same types of livestock:

(1) if the purchase-money security interest is perfected by filing, before the date of the filing; or

(2) if the purchase-money security interest is temporarily perfected without filing or possession under Section 9-312(f), before the beginning of the 20-day period thereunder.

(f) [**Software purchase-money priority.**] Except as otherwise provided in subsection (g), a perfected purchase-money security interest in software has priority over a conflicting security interest in the same collateral, and, except as otherwise provided in Section 9–327, a perfected security interest in its identifiable proceeds also has priority, to the extent that the purchase-money security interest in the goods in which the software was acquired for use has priority in the goods and proceeds of the goods under this section.

(g) [**Conflicting purchase-money security interests.**] If more than one security interest qualifies for priority in the same collateral under subsection (a), (b), (d), or (f):

(1) a security interest securing an obligation incurred as all or part of the price of the collateral has priority over a security interest securing an obligation incurred for value given to enable the debtor to acquire rights in or the use of collateral; and

(2) in all other cases, Section 9–322(a) applies to the qualifying security interests.

§ 9–325. Priority of Security Interests in Transferred Collateral.

(a) [**Subordination of security interest in transferred collateral.**] Except as otherwise provided in subsection (b), a security interest created by a debtor is subordinate to a security interest in the same collateral created by another person if:

(1) the debtor acquired the collateral subject to the security interest created by the other person;

(2) the security interest created by the other person was perfected when the debtor acquired the collateral; and

(3) there is no period thereafter when the security interest is unperfected.

(b) [**Limitation of subsection (a) subordination.**] Subsection (a) subordinates a security interest only if the security interest:

(1) otherwise would have priority solely under Section 9–322(a) or 9–324; or

(2) arose solely under Section 2–711(3) or 2A–508(5).

§ 9–327. Priority of Security Interests in Deposit Account.

The following rules govern priority among conflicting security interests in the same deposit account:

(1) A security interest held by a secured party having control of the deposit account under Section 9–104 has priority over a conflicting security interest held by a secured party that does not have control.

(2) Except as otherwise provided in paragraphs (3) and (4), security interests perfected by control under Section 9–314 rank according to priority in time of obtaining control.

(3) Except as otherwise provided in paragraph (4), a security interest held by the bank with which the deposit account is maintained has priority over a conflicting security interest held by another secured party.

(4) A security interest perfected by control under Section 9–104(a)(3) has priority over a security interest held by the bank with which the deposit account is maintained.

§ 9–328. Priority of Security Interests in Investment Property.

The following rules govern priority among conflicting security interests in the same investment property:

(1) A security interest held by a secured party having control of investment property under Section 9–106 has priority over a security interest held by a secured party that does not have control of the investment property.

(2) Except as otherwise provided in paragraphs (3) and (4), conflicting security interests held by secured parties each of which has control under Section 9–106 rank according to priority in time of:

(A) if the collateral is a security, obtaining control;

(B) if the collateral is a security entitlement carried in a securities account and:

(i) if the secured party obtained control under Section 8–106(d)(1), the secured party's becoming the person for which the securities account is maintained;

(ii) if the secured party obtained control under Section 8–106(d)(2), the securities intermediary's agreement to comply

with the secured party's entitlement orders with respect to security entitlements carried or to be carried in the securities account; or

(iii) if the secured party obtained control through another person under Section 8–106(d)(3), the time on which priority would be based under this paragraph if the other person were the secured party; or

(C) if the collateral is a commodity contract carried with a commodity intermediary, the satisfaction of the requirement for control specified in Section 9–106(b)(2) with respect to commodity contracts carried or to be carried with the commodity intermediary.

(3) A security interest held by a securities intermediary in a security entitlement or a securities account maintained with the securities intermediary has priority over a conflicting security interest held by another secured party.

(4) A security interest held by a commodity intermediary in a commodity contract or a commodity account maintained with the commodity intermediary has priority over a conflicting security interest held by another secured party.

(5) A security interest in a certificated security in registered form which is perfected by taking delivery under Section 9–313(a) and not by control under Section 9–314 has priority over a conflicting security interest perfected by a method other than control.

(6) Conflicting security interests created by a broker, securities intermediary, or commodity intermediary which are perfected without control under Section 9–106 rank equally.

(7) In all other cases, priority among conflicting security interests in investment property is governed by Sections 9–322 and 9–323.

§ 9–329. Priority of Security Interests in Letter-of-Credit Right.

The following rules govern priority among conflicting security interests in the same letter-of-credit right:

(1) A security interest held by a secured party having control of the letter-of-credit right under Section 9–107 has priority to the extent of its control over a conflicting security interest held by a secured party that does not have control.

(2) Security interests perfected by control under Section 9–314 rank according to priority in time of obtaining control.

§ 9–330. Priority of Purchaser of Chattel Paper or Instrument.

(a) [**Purchaser's priority: security interest claimed merely as proceeds.**] A purchaser of chattel paper has priority over a security interest in the chattel paper which is claimed merely as proceeds of inventory subject to a security interest if:

(1) in good faith and in the ordinary course of the purchaser's business, the purchaser gives new value and takes possession of the chattel paper or obtains control of the chattel paper under Section 9–105; and

(2) the chattel paper does not indicate that it has been assigned to an identified assignee other than the purchaser.

(b) [**Purchaser's priority: other security interests.**] A purchaser of chattel paper has priority over a security interest in the chattel paper which is claimed other than merely as proceeds of inventory subject to a security interest if the purchaser gives new value and takes possession of the chattel paper or obtains control of the chattel paper under Section 9–105 in good faith, in the ordinary course of the purchaser's business, and without knowledge that the purchase violates the rights of the secured party.

(c) [**Chattel paper purchaser's priority in proceeds.**] Except as otherwise provided in Section 9–327, a purchaser having priority in chattel paper under subsection (a) or (b) also has priority in proceeds of the chattel paper to the extent that:

(1) Section 9–322 provides for priority in the proceeds; or

(2) the proceeds consist of the specific goods covered by the chattel paper or cash proceeds of the specific goods, even if the purchaser's security interest in the proceeds is unperfected.

(d) [**Instrument purchaser's priority.**] Except as otherwise provided in Section 9–331(a), a purchaser of an instrument has priority over a security interest in the instrument perfected by a method other than possession if the purchaser gives value and takes possession of the instrument in good faith and without knowledge that the purchase violates the rights of the secured party.

(e) [**Holder of purchase-money security interest gives new value.**] For purposes of subsections (a) and (b), the holder of a purchase-money security interest in inventory gives new value for chattel paper constituting proceeds of the inventory.

(f) [**Indication of assignment gives knowledge.**] For purposes of subsections (b) and (d), if chattel paper or an instrument indicates that it has been assigned to an identified secured party other than the purchaser, a purchaser of the chattel paper or instrument has knowledge that the purchase violates the rights of the secured party.

§ 9–331. Priority of Rights of Purchasers of Instruments, Documents, and Securities under Other Articles; Priority of Interests in Financial Assets and Security Entitlements under Article 8.

(a) [**Rights under Articles 3, 7, and 8 not limited.**] This article does not limit the rights of a holder in due course of a negotiable instrument, a holder to which a negotiable document of title has been duly negotiated, or a protected purchaser of a security. These holders or purchasers take priority over an earlier security interest, even if perfected, to the extent provided in Articles 3, 7, and 8.

(b) [**Protection under Article 8.**] This article does not limit the rights of or impose liability on a person to the extent that the person is protected against the assertion of a claim under Article 8.

(c) [**Filing not notice.**] Filing under this article does not constitute notice of a claim or defense to the holders, or purchasers, or persons described in subsections (a) and (b).

§ 9–332. Transfer of Money; Transfer of Funds from Deposit Account.

(a) [**Transferee of money.**] A transferee of money takes the money free of a security interest unless the transferee acts in collusion with the debtor in violating the rights of the secured party.

(b) [**Transferee of funds from deposit account.**] A transferee of funds from a deposit account takes the funds free of a security interest in the deposit account unless the transferee acts in collusion with the debtor in violating the rights of the secured party.

§ 9–333. Priority of Certain Liens Arising by Operation of Law.

(a) [**"Possessory lien."**] In this section, "possessory lien" means an interest, other than a security interest or an agricultural lien:

(1) which secures payment or performance of an obligation for services or materials furnished with respect to goods by a person in the ordinary course of the person's business;

(2) which is created by statute or rule of law in favor of the person; and

(3) whose effectiveness depends on the person's possession of the goods.

(b) [**Priority of possessory lien.**] A possessory lien on goods has priority over a security interest in the goods unless the lien is created by a statute that expressly provides otherwise.

§ 9–334. Priority of Security Interests in Fixtures and Crops.

(a) [**Security interest in fixtures under this article.**] A security interest under this article may be created in goods that are fixtures or may continue in goods that become fixtures. A security interest does not exist under this article in ordinary building materials incorporated into an improvement on land.

(b) [**Security interest in fixtures under real-property law.**] This article does not prevent creation of an encumbrance upon fixtures under real-property law.

(c) [**General rule: subordination of security interest in fixtures.**] In cases not governed by subsections (d) through (h), a security interest in fixtures is subordinate to a conflicting interest of an encumbrancer or owner of the related real property other than the debtor.

(d) [**Fixtures purchase-money priority.**] Except as otherwise provided in subsection (h), a perfected security interest in fixtures has priority over a conflicting interest of an encumbrancer or owner of the real property if the debtor has an interest of record in or is in possession of the real property and:

(1) the security interest is a purchase-money security interest;

(2) the interest of the encumbrancer or owner arises before the goods become fixtures; and

(3) the security interest is perfected by a fixture filing before the goods become fixtures or within 20 days thereafter.

(e) [**Priority of security interest in fixtures over interests in real property.**] A perfected security interest in fixtures has priority over a conflicting interest of an encumbrancer or owner of the real property if:

(1) the debtor has an interest of record in the real property or is in possession of the real property and the security interest:

(A) is perfected by a fixture filing before the interest of the encumbrancer or owner is of record; and

(B) has priority over any conflicting interest of a predecessor in title of the encumbrancer or owner;

(2) before the goods become fixtures, the security interest is perfected by any method permitted by this article and the fixtures are readily removable:

(A) factory or office machines;

(B) equipment that is not primarily used or leased for use in the operation of the real property; or

(C) replacements of domestic appliances that are consumer goods;

(3) the conflicting interest is a lien on the real property obtained by legal or equitable proceedings after the security interest was perfected by any method permitted by this article; or

(4) the security interest is:

(A) created in a manufactured home in a manufactured-home transaction; and

(B) perfected pursuant to a statute described in Section 9–311(a)(2).

(f) [**Priority based on consent, disclaimer, or right to remove.**] A security interest in fixtures, whether or not perfected, has priority over a conflicting interest of an encumbrancer or owner of the real property if:

(1) the encumbrancer or owner has, in an authenticated record, consented to the security interest or disclaimed an interest in the goods as fixtures; or

(2) the debtor has a right to remove the goods as against the encumbrancer or owner.

(g) [**Continuation of paragraph (f)(2) priority.**] The priority of the security interest under paragraph (f)(2) continues for a reasonable time if the debtor's right to remove the goods as against the encumbrancer or owner terminates.

(h) [**Priority of construction mortgage.**] A mortgage is a construction mortgage to the extent that it secures an obligation incurred for the construction of an improvement on land, including the acquisition cost of the land, if a recorded record of the mortgage so indicates. Except as otherwise provided in subsections (e) and (f), a security interest in fixtures is subordinate to a construction mortgage if a record of the mortgage is recorded before the goods become fixtures and the goods become fixtures before the completion of the construction. A mortgage has this priority to the same extent as a construction mortgage to the extent that it is given to refinance a construction mortgage.

(i) [**Priority of security interest in crops.**] A perfected security interest in crops growing on real property has priority over a conflicting interest of an encumbrancer or owner of the real property if the debtor has an interest of record in or is in possession of the real property.

(j) [**Subsection (i) prevails.**] Subsection (i) prevails over any inconsistent provisions of the following statutes:

§ 9–335. Accessions.

(a) [**Creation of security interest in accession.**] A security interest may be created in an accession and continues in collateral that becomes an accession.

(b) [**Perfection of security interest.**] If a security interest is perfected when the collateral becomes an accession, the security interest remains perfected in the collateral.

(c) [**Priority of security interest.**] Except as otherwise provided in subsection (d), the other provisions of this part determine the priority of a security interest in an accession.

(d) [**Compliance with certificate-of-title statute.**] A security interest in an accession is subordinate to a security interest in the whole which is perfected by compliance with the requirements of a certificate-of-title statute under Section 9–311(b).

(e) [**Removal of accession after default.**] After default, subject to Part 6, a secured party may remove an accession from other goods if the security interest in the accession has priority over the claims of every person having an interest in the whole.

(f) [**Reimbursement following removal.**] A secured party that removes an accession from other goods under subsection (e) shall promptly reimburse any holder of a security interest or other lien on, or owner of, the whole or of the other goods, other than the debtor, for the cost of repair of any physical injury to the whole or the other goods. The secured party need not reimburse the holder or owner for any diminution in value of the whole or the other goods caused by the absence of the accession removed or by any necessity for replacing it. A person entitled to reimbursement may refuse permission to remove until the secured party gives adequate assurance for the performance of the obligation to reimburse.

§ 9–336. Commingled Goods.

(a) [**"Commingled goods."**] In this section, "commingled goods" means goods that are physically united with other goods in such a manner that their identity is lost in a product or mass.

(b) [**No security interest in commingled goods as such.**] A security interest does not exist in commingled goods as such. However, a security interest may attach to a product or mass that results when goods become commingled goods.

(c) [**Attachment of security interest to product or mass.**] If collateral becomes commingled goods, a security interest attaches to the product or mass.

(d) [**Perfection of security interest.**] If a security interest in collateral is perfected before the collateral becomes commingled goods, the security interest that attaches to the product or mass under subsection (c) is perfected.

(e) [**Priority of security interest.**] Except as otherwise provided in subsection (f), the other provisions of this part determine the priority of a security interest that attaches to the product or mass under subsection (c).

(f) [**Conflicting security interests in product or mass**] If more than one security interest attaches to the product or mass under subsection (c), the following rules determine priority:

> **(1)** A security interest that is perfected under subsection (d) has priority over a security interest that is unperfected at the time the collateral becomes commingled goods.
>
> **(2)** If more than one security interest is perfected under subsection (d), the security interests rank equally in proportion to the value of the collateral at the time it became commingled goods.

§ 9–337. Priority of Security Interests in Goods Covered by Certificate of Title.

If, while a security interest in goods is perfected by any method under the law of another jurisdiction, this State issues a certificate of title that does not show that the goods are subject to the security interest or contain a statement that they may be subject to security interests not shown on the certificate:

> **(1)** a buyer of the goods, other than a person in the business of selling goods of that kind, takes free of the security interest if the buyer gives value and receives delivery of the goods after issuance of the certificate and without knowledge of the security interest; and
>
> **(2)** the security interest is subordinate to a conflicting security interest in the goods that attaches, and is perfected under Section 9–311(b), after issuance of the certificate and without the conflicting secured party's knowledge of the security interest.

Part 5—Filing
§ 9–501. Filing Office.

(a) [**Filing offices.**] Except as otherwise provided in subsection (b), if the local law of this State governs perfection of a security interest or agricultural lien, the office in which to file a financing statement to perfect the security interest or agricultural lien is:

> **(1)** the office designated for the filing or recording of a record of a mortgage on the related real property, if:
>
>> **(A)** the collateral is as-extracted collateral or timber to be cut; or
>>
>> **(B)** the financing statement is filed as a fixture filing and the collateral is goods that are or are to become fixtures; or
>
> **(2)** the office of [ ] [or any office duly authorized by [ ]], in all other cases, including a case in which the collateral is goods that are or are to become fixtures and the financing statement is not filed as a fixture filing.

(b) [**Filing office for transmitting utilities.**] The office in which to file a financing statement to perfect a security interest in collateral, including fixtures, of a transmitting utility is the office of [ ]. The financing statement also constitutes a fixture filing as to the collateral indicated in the financing statement which is or is to become fixtures.

§ 9–502. Contents of Financing Statement; Record of Mortgage as Financing Statement; Time of Filing Financing Statement.

(a) [**Sufficiency of financing statement.**] Subject to subsection (b), a financing statement is sufficient only if it:

> **(1)** provides the name of the debtor;
>
> **(2)** provides the name of the secured party or a representative of the secured party; and
>
> **(3)** indicates the collateral covered by the financing statement.

(b) [**Real-property-related financing statements.**] Except as otherwise provided in Section 9–501(b), to be sufficient, a financing statement that covers as-extracted collateral or timber to be cut, or which is filed as a fixture filing and covers goods that are or are to become fixtures, must satisfy subsection (a) and also:

> **(1)** indicate that it covers this type of collateral;
>
> **(2)** indicate that it is to be filed [for record] in the real property records;
>
> **(3)** provide a description of the real property to which the collateral is related [sufficient to give constructive notice of a mortgage under the law of this State if the description were contained in a record of the mortgage of the real property]; and
>
> **(4)** if the debtor does not have an interest of record in the real property, provide the name of a record owner.

(c) [**Record of mortgage as financing statement.**] A record of a mortgage is effective, from the date of recording, as a financing statement filed as a fixture filing or as a financing statement covering as-extracted collateral or timber to be cut only if:

> **(1)** the record indicates the goods or accounts that it covers;
>
> **(2)** the goods are or are to become fixtures related to the real property described in the record or the collateral is related to the real property described in the record and is as-extracted collateral or timber to be cut;
>
> **(3)** the record satisfies the requirements for a financing statement in this section other than an indication that it is to be filed in the real property records; and
>
> **(4)** the record is [duly] recorded.

(d) [**Filing before security agreement or attachment.**] A financing statement may be filed before a security agreement is made or a security interest otherwise attaches.

§ 9–503. Name of Debtor and Secured Party.

(a) [**Sufficiency of debtor's name.**] A financing statement sufficiently provides the name of the debtor:

> **(1)** if the debtor is a registered organization, only if the financing statement provides the name of the debtor indicated on the public record of the debtor's jurisdiction of organization which shows the debtor to have been organized;
>
> **(2)** if the debtor is a decedent's estate, only if the financing statement provides the name of the decedent and indicates that the debtor is an estate;
>
> **(3)** if the debtor is a trust or a trustee acting with respect to property held in trust, only if the financing statement:

(A) provides the name specified for the trust in its organic documents or, if no name is specified, provides the name of the settlor and additional information sufficient to distinguish the debtor from other trusts having one or more of the same settlors; and

(B) indicates, in the debtor's name or otherwise, that the debtor is a trust or is a trustee acting with respect to property held in trust; and

(4) in other cases:

(A) if the debtor has a name, only if it provides the individual or organizational name of the debtor; and

(B) if the debtor does not have a name, only if it provides the names of the partners, members, associates, or other persons comprising the debtor.

(b) [**Additional debtor-related information.**] A financing statement that provides the name of the debtor in accordance with subsection (a) is not rendered ineffective by the absence of:

(1) a trade name or other name of the debtor; or

(2) unless required under subsection (a)(4)(B), names of partners, members, associates, or other persons comprising the debtor.

(c) [**Debtor's trade name insufficient.**] A financing statement that provides only the debtor's trade name does not sufficiently provide the name of the debtor.

(d) [**Representative capacity.**] Failure to indicate the representative capacity of a secured party or representative of a secured party does not affect the sufficiency of a financing statement.

(e) [**Multiple debtors and secured parties.**] A financing statement may provide the name of more than one debtor and the name of more than one secured party.

§ 9–504. Indication of Collateral.

A financing statement sufficiently indicates the collateral that it covers if the financing statement provides:

(1) a description of the collateral pursuant to Section 9–108; or

(2) an indication that the financing statement covers all assets or all personal property.

§ 9–506. Effect of Errors or Omissions.

(a) [**Minor errors and omissions.**] A financing statement substantially satisfying the requirements of this part is effective, even if it has minor errors or omissions, unless the errors or omissions make the financing statement seriously misleading.

(b) [**Financing statement seriously misleading.**] Except as otherwise provided in subsection (c), a financing statement that fails sufficiently to provide the name of the debtor in accordance with Section 9–503(a) is seriously misleading.

(c) [**Financing statement not seriously misleading.**] If a search of the records of the filing office under the debtor's correct name, using the filing office's standard search logic, if any, would disclose a financing statement that fails sufficiently to provide the name of the debtor in accordance with Section 9–503(a), the name provided does not make the financing statement seriously misleading.

(d) [**"Debtor's correct name."**] For purposes of Section 9–508(b), the "debtor's correct name" in subsection (c) means the correct name of the new debtor.

§ 9–512. Amendment of Financing Statement.
[Alternative A]

(a) [**Amendment of information in financing statement.**] Subject to Section 9–509, a person may add or delete collateral covered by, continue or terminate the effectiveness of, or, subject to subsection (e), otherwise amend the information provided in, a financing statement by filing an amendment that:

(1) identifies, by its file number, the initial financing statement to which the amendment relates; and

(2) if the amendment relates to an initial financing statement filed [or recorded] in a filing office described in Section 9–501(a)(1), provides the information specified in Section 9–502(b).

[Alternative B]

(a) [**Amendment of information in financing statement.**] Subject to Section 9–509, a person may add or delete collateral covered by, continue or terminate the effectiveness of, or, subject to subsection (e), otherwise amend the information provided in, a financing statement by filing an amendment that:

(1) identifies, by its file number, the initial financing statement to which the amendment relates; and

(2) if the amendment relates to an initial financing statement filed [or recorded] in a filing office described in Section 9–501(a)(1), provides the date [and time] that the initial financing statement was filed [or recorded] and the information specified in Section 9–502(b).

[End of Alternatives]

(b) [**Period of effectiveness not affected.**] Except as otherwise provided in Section 9–515, the filing of an amendment does not extend the period of effectiveness of the financing statement.

(c) [**Effectiveness of amendment adding collateral.**] A financing statement that is amended by an amendment that adds collateral is effective as to the added collateral only from the date of the filing of the amendment.

(d) [**Effectiveness of amendment adding debtor.**] A financing statement that is amended by an amendment that adds a debtor is effective as to the added debtor only from the date of the filing of the amendment.

(e) [Certain amendments ineffective.] An amendment is ineffective to the extent it:

(1) purports to delete all debtors and fails to provide the name of a debtor to be covered by the financing statement; or

(2) purports to delete all secured parties of record and fails to provide the name of a new secured party of record.

§ 9–515. Duration and Effectiveness of Financing Statement; Effect of Lapsed Financing Statement.

(a) [**Five-year effectiveness.**] Except as otherwise provided in subsections (b), (e), (f), and (g), a filed financing statement is effective for a period of five years after the date of filing.

(b) [**Public-finance or manufactured-home transaction.**] Except as otherwise provided in subsections (e), (f), and (g), an initial financing statement filed in connection with a public-finance transaction or manufactured-home transaction is effective for a period of 30 years after the date of filing if it indicates that it is filed in connection with a public-finance transaction or manufactured-home transaction.

(c) [**Lapse and continuation of financing statement.**] The effectiveness of a filed financing statement lapses on the expiration of the period of its effectiveness unless before the lapse a continuation statement is filed pursuant to subsection (d). Upon lapse, a financing statement ceases to be effective and any security interest or agricultural lien that was perfected by the financing statement becomes unperfected, unless the security interest is perfected otherwise. If the security interest or agricultural lien becomes unperfected upon lapse, it is deemed never to have been perfected as against a purchaser of the collateral for value.

(d) [**When continuation statement may be filed.**] A continuation statement may be filed only within six months before the expiration of the five-year period specified in subsection (a) or the 30-year period specified in subsection (b), whichever is applicable.

(e) [**Effect of filing continuation statement.**] Except as otherwise provided in Section 9–510, upon timely filing of a continuation statement, the effectiveness of the initial financing statement continues for a period of five years commencing on the day on which the financing statement would have become ineffective in the absence of the filing. Upon the expiration of the five-year period, the financing statement lapses in the same manner as provided in subsection (c), unless, before the lapse, another continuation statement is filed pursuant to subsection (d). Succeeding continuation statements may be filed in the same manner to continue the effectiveness of the initial financing statement.

(f) [**Transmitting utility financing statement.**] If a debtor is a transmitting utility and a filed financing statement so indicates, the financing statement is effective until a termination statement is filed.

(g) [**Record of mortgage as financing statement.**] A record of a mortgage that is effective as a financing statement filed as a fixture filing under Section 9–502(c) remains effective as a financing statement filed as a fixture filing until the mortgage is released or satisfied of record or its effectiveness otherwise terminates as to the real property.

§ 9–516. What Constitutes Filing; Effectiveness of Filing.

(a) [**What constitutes filing.**] Except as otherwise provided in subsection (b), communication of a record to a filing office and tender of the filing fee or acceptance of the record by the filing office constitutes filing.

(b) [**Refusal to accept record; filing does not occur.**] Filing does not occur with respect to a record that a filing office refuses to accept because:

> **(1)** the record is not communicated by a method or medium of communication authorized by the filing office;
>
> **(2)** an amount equal to or greater than the applicable filing fee is not tendered;
>
> **(3)** the filing office is unable to index the record because:
>
> > **(A)** in the case of an initial financing statement, the record does not provide a name for the debtor;
> >
> > **(B)** in the case of an amendment or correction statement, the record:
>
> **(i)** does not identify the initial financing statement as required by Section 9–512 or 9–518, as applicable; or
>
> **(ii)** identifies an initial financing statement whose effectiveness has lapsed under Section 9–515;
>
> > **(C)** in the case of an initial financing statement that provides the name of a debtor identified as an individual or an amendment that provides a name of a debtor identified as an individual which was not previously provided in the financing statement to which the record relates, the record does not identify the debtor's last name; or
> >
> > **(D)** in the case of a record filed [or recorded] in the filing office described in Section 9–501(a)(1), the record does not provide a sufficient description of the real property to which it relates;
>
> **(4)** in the case of an initial financing statement or an amendment that adds a secured party of record, the record does not provide a name and mailing address for the secured party of record;
>
> **(5)** in the case of an initial financing statement or an amendment that provides a name of a debtor which was not previously provided in the financing statement to which the amendment relates, the record does not:
>
> > **(A)** provide a mailing address for the debtor;
> >
> > **(B)** indicate whether the debtor is an individual or an organization; or
> >
> > **(C)** if the financing statement indicates that the debtor is an organization, provide:
> >
> > > **(i)** a type of organization for the debtor;
> > >
> > > **(ii)** a jurisdiction of organization for the debtor; or
> > >
> > > **(iii)** an organizational identification number for the debtor or indicate that the debtor has none;
>
> **(6)** in the case of an assignment reflected in an initial financing statement under Section 9–514(a) or an amendment filed under Section 9–514(b), the record does not provide a name and mailing address for the assignee; or
>
> **(7)** in the case of a continuation statement, the record is not filed within the six-month period prescribed by Section 9–515(d).

(c) [**Rules applicable to subsection (b).**] For purposes of subsection (b):

> **(1)** a record does not provide information if the filing office is unable to read or decipher the information; and
>
> **(2)** a record that does not indicate that it is an amendment or identify an initial financing statement to which it relates, as required by Section 9–512, 9–514, or 9–518, is an initial financing statement.

(d) [**Refusal to accept record; record effective as filed record.**] A record that is communicated to the filing office with tender of the filing fee, but which the filing office refuses to accept for a reason other than one set forth in subsection (b), is effective as a filed record except as against a purchaser of the collateral which gives value in reasonable reliance upon the absence of the record from the files.

§ 9–520. Acceptance and Refusal to Accept Record.

(a) [**Mandatory refusal to accept record.**] A filing office shall refuse to accept a record for filing for a reason set forth in Section 9–516(b) and may refuse to accept a record for filing only for a reason set forth in Section 9–516(b).

(b) [**Communication concerning refusal.**] If a filing office refuses to accept a record for filing, it shall communicate to the person that presented the record the fact of and reason for the refusal and the date and time the record would have been filed had the filing office accepted it. The communication must be made at the time and in the manner prescribed by filing-office rule but [, in the case of a filing office described in Section 9–501(a)(2),] in no event more than two business days after the filing office receives the record.

(c) [**When filed financing statement effective.**] A filed financing statement satisfying Section 9–502(a) and (b) is effective, even if the filing office is required to refuse to accept it for filing under subsection (a). However, Section 9–338 applies to a filed financing statement providing information described in Section 9–516(b)(5) which is incorrect at the time the financing statement is filed.

(d) [**Separate application to multiple debtors.**] If a record communicated to a filing office provides information that relates to more than one debtor, this part applies as to each debtor separately.

Part 6—Default

§ 9–601. Rights after Default; Judicial Enforcement; Consignor or Buyer of Accounts, Chattel Paper, Payment Intangibles, or Promissory Notes.

(a) [**Rights of secured party after default.**] After default, a secured party has the rights provided in this part and, except as otherwise provided in Section 9–602, those provided by agreement of the parties. A secured party:

> **(1)** may reduce a claim to judgment, foreclose, or otherwise enforce the claim, security interest, or agricultural lien by any available judicial procedure; and
>
> **(2)** if the collateral is documents, may proceed either as to the documents or as to the goods they cover.

(b) [**Rights and duties of secured party in possession or control.**] A secured party in possession of collateral or control of collateral under Section 9–104, 9–105, 9–106, or 9–107 has the rights and duties provided in Section 9–207.

(c) [**Rights cumulative; simultaneous exercise.**] The rights under subsections (a) and (b) are cumulative and may be exercised simultaneously.

(d) [**Rights of debtor and obligor.**] Except as otherwise provided in subsection (g) and Section 9–605, after default, a debtor and an obligor have the rights provided in this part and by agreement of the parties.

(e) [**Lien of levy after judgment.**] If a secured party has reduced its claim to judgment, the lien of any levy that may be made upon the collateral by virtue of an execution based upon the judgment relates back to the earliest of:

> **(1)** the date of perfection of the security interest or agricultural lien in the collateral;
>
> **(2)** the date of filing a financing statement covering the collateral; or
>
> **(3)** any date specified in a statute under which the agricultural lien was created.

(f) [**Execution sale.**] A sale pursuant to an execution is a foreclosure of the security interest or agricultural lien by judicial procedure within the meaning of this section. A secured party may purchase at the sale and thereafter hold the collateral free of any other requirements of this article.

(g) [**Consignor or buyer of certain rights to payment.**] Except as otherwise provided in Section 9–607(c), this part imposes no duties upon a secured party that is a consignor or is a buyer of accounts, chattel paper, payment intangibles, or promissory notes.

§ 9–607. Collection and Enforcement by Secured Party.

(a) [**Collection and enforcement generally.**] If so agreed, and in any event after default, a secured party:

> **(1)** may notify an account debtor or other person obligated on collateral to make payment or otherwise render performance to or for the benefit of the secured party;

(2) may take any proceeds to which the secured party is entitled under Section 9-315;

(3) may enforce the obligations of an account debtor or other person obligated on collateral and exercise the rights of the debtor with respect to the obligation of the account debtor or other person obligated on collateral to make payment or otherwise render performance to the debtor, and with respect to any property that secures the obligations of the account debtor or other person obligated on the collateral;

(4) if it holds a security interest in a deposit account perfected by control under Section 9-104(a)(1), may apply the balance of the deposit account to the obligation secured by the deposit account; and

(5) if it holds a security interest in a deposit account perfected by control under Section 9-104(a)(2) or (3), may instruct the bank to pay the balance of the deposit account to or for the benefit of the secured party.

(b) [**Nonjudicial enforcement of mortgage.**] If necessary to enable a secured party to exercise under subsection (a)(3) the right of a debtor to enforce a mortgage nonjudicially, the secured party may record in the office in which a record of the mortgage is recorded:

(1) a copy of the security agreement that creates or provides for a security interest in the obligation secured by the mortgage; and

(2) the secured party's sworn affidavit in recordable form stating that:

(A) a default has occurred; and

(B) the secured party is entitled to enforce the mortgage nonjudicially.

(c) [**Commercially reasonable collection and enforcement.**] A secured party shall proceed in a commercially reasonable manner if the secured party:

(1) undertakes to collect from or enforce an obligation of an account debtor or other person obligated on collateral; and

(2) is entitled to charge back uncollected collateral or otherwise to full or limited recourse against the debtor or a secondary obligor.

(d) [**Expenses of collection and enforcement.**] A secured party may deduct from the collections made pursuant to subsection (c) reasonable expenses of collection and enforcement, including reasonable attorney's fees and legal expenses incurred by the secured party.

(e) [**Duties to secured party not affected.**] This section does not determine whether an account debtor, bank, or other person obligated on collateral owes a duty to a secured party.

§ 9-608. Application of Proceeds of Collection or Enforcement; Liability for Deficiency and Right to Surplus.

(a) [**Application of proceeds, surplus, and deficiency if obligation secured.**] If a security interest or agricultural lien secures payment or performance of an obligation, the following rules apply:

(1) A secured party shall apply or pay over for application the cash proceeds of collection or enforcement under Section 9-607 in the following order to:

(A) the reasonable expenses of collection and enforcement and, to the extent provided for by agreement and not prohibited by law, reasonable attorney's fees and legal expenses incurred by the secured party;

(B) the satisfaction of obligations secured by the security interest or agricultural lien under which the collection or enforcement is made; and

(C) the satisfaction of obligations secured by any subordinate security interest in or other lien on the collateral subject to the security interest or agricultural lien under which the collection or enforcement is made if the secured party receives an authenticated demand for proceeds before distribution of the proceeds is completed.

(2) If requested by a secured party, a holder of a subordinate security interest or other lien shall furnish reasonable proof of the interest or lien within a reasonable time. Unless the holder complies, the secured party need not comply with the holder's demand under paragraph (1)(C).

(3) A secured party need not apply or pay over for application noncash proceeds of collection and enforcement under Section 9-607 unless the failure to do so would be commercially unreasonable. A secured party that applies or pays over for application noncash proceeds shall do so in a commercially reasonable manner.

(4) A secured party shall account to and pay a debtor for any surplus, and the obligor is liable for any deficiency.

(b) [**No surplus or deficiency in sales of certain rights to payment.**] If the underlying transaction is a sale of accounts, chattel paper, payment intangibles, or promissory notes, the debtor is not entitled to any surplus, and the obligor is not liable for any deficiency.

§ 9-609. Secured Party's Right to Take Possession after Default.

(a) [**Possession; rendering equipment unusable; disposition on debtor's premises.**] After default, a secured party:

(1) may take possession of the collateral; and

(2) without removal, may render equipment unusable and dispose of collateral on a debtor's premises under Section 9-610.

(b) [**Judicial and nonjudicial process.**] A secured party may proceed under subsection (a):

(1) pursuant to judicial process; or

(2) without judicial process, if it proceeds without breach of the peace.

(c) [**Assembly of collateral.**] If so agreed, and in any event after default, a secured party may require the debtor to assemble the collateral and make it available to the secured party at a place to be designated by the secured party which is reasonably convenient to both parties.

§ 9-610. Disposition of Collateral after Default.

(a) [**Disposition after default.**] After default, a secured party may sell, lease, license, or otherwise dispose of any or all of the collateral in its present condition or following any commercially reasonable preparation or processing.

(b) [**Commercially reasonable disposition.**] Every aspect of a disposition of collateral, including the method, manner, time, place, and other terms, must be commercially reasonable. If commercially reasonable, a secured party may dispose of collateral by public or private proceedings, by one or more contracts, as a unit or in parcels, and at any time and place and on any terms.

(c) [**Purchase by secured party.**] A secured party may purchase collateral:

(1) at a public disposition; or

(2) at a private disposition only if the collateral is of a kind that is customarily sold on a recognized market or the subject of widely distributed standard price quotations.

(d) [**Warranties on disposition.**] A contract for sale, lease, license, or other disposition includes the warranties relating to title, possession, quiet enjoyment, and the like which by operation of law accompany a voluntary disposition of property of the kind subject to the contract.

(e) [**Disclaimer of warranties.**] A secured party may disclaim or modify warranties under subsection (d):

(1) in a manner that would be effective to disclaim or modify the warranties in a voluntary disposition of property of the kind subject to the contract of disposition; or

(2) by communicating to the purchaser a record evidencing the contract for disposition and including an express disclaimer or modification of the warranties.

(f) [**Record sufficient to disclaim warranties.**] A record is sufficient to disclaim warranties under subsection (e) if it indicates "There is no warranty relating to title, possession, quiet enjoyment, or the like in this disposition" or uses words of similar import.

§ 9-611. Notification Before Disposition of Collateral.

(a) [**"Notification date."**] In this section, "notification date" means the earlier of the date on which:

(1) a secured party sends to the debtor and any secondary obligor an authenticated notification of disposition; or

(2) the debtor and any secondary obligor waive the right to notification.

(b) [**Notification of disposition required.**] Except as otherwise provided in subsection (d), a secured party that disposes of collateral under Section 9-610 shall send to the persons specified in subsection (c) a reasonable authenticated notification of disposition.

(c) [**Persons to be notified.**] To comply with subsection (b), the secured party shall send an authenticated notification of disposition to:

(1) the debtor;

(2) any secondary obligor; and

(3) if the collateral is other than consumer goods:

(A) any other person from which the secured party has received, before the notification date, an authenticated notification of a claim of an interest in the collateral;

(B) any other secured party or lienholder that, 10 days before the notification date, held a security interest in or other lien on the collateral perfected by the filing of a financing statement that:

(i) identified the collateral;

(ii) was indexed under the debtor's name as of that date; and

(iii) was filed in the office in which to file a financing statement against the debtor covering the collateral as of that date; and

(C) any other secured party that, 10 days before the notification date, held a security interest in the collateral perfected by compliance with a statute, regulation, or treaty described in Section 9–311(a).

(d) [**Subsection (b) inapplicable: perishable collateral; recognized market.**] Subsection (b) does not apply if the collateral is perishable or threatens to decline speedily in value or is of a type customarily sold on a recognized market.

(e) [**Compliance with subsection (c)(3)(b).**] A secured party complies with the requirement for notification prescribed by subsection (c)(3)(B) if:

(1) not later than 20 days or earlier than 30 days before the notification date, the secured party requests, in a commercially reasonable manner, information concerning financing statements indexed under the debtor's name in the office indicated in subsection (c)(3)(B); and

(2) before the notification date, the secured party:

(A) did not receive a response to the request for information; or

(B) received a response to the request for information and sent an authenticated notification of disposition to each secured party or other lienholder named in that response whose financing statement covered the collateral.

§ 9–615. Application of Proceeds of Disposition; Liability for Deficiency and Right to Surplus.

(a) [**Application of proceeds.**] A secured party shall apply or pay over for application the cash proceeds of disposition under Section 9–610 in the following order to:

(1) the reasonable expenses of retaking, holding, preparing for disposition, processing, and disposing, and, to the extent provided for by agreement and not prohibited by law, reasonable attorney's fees and legal expenses incurred by the secured party;

(2) the satisfaction of obligations secured by the security interest or agricultural lien under which the disposition is made;

(3) the satisfaction of obligations secured by any subordinate security interest in or other subordinate lien on the collateral if:

(A) the secured party receives from the holder of the subordinate security interest or other lien an authenticated demand for proceeds before distribution of the proceeds is completed; and

(B) in a case in which a consignor has an interest in the collateral, the subordinate security interest or other lien is senior to the interest of the consignor; and

(4) a secured party that is a consignor of the collateral if the secured party receives from the consignor an authenticated demand for proceeds before distribution of the proceeds is completed.

(b) [**Proof of subordinate interest.**] If requested by a secured party, a holder of a subordinate security interest or other lien shall furnish reasonable proof of the interest or lien within a reasonable time. Unless the holder does so, the secured party need not comply with the holder's demand under subsection (a)(3).

(c) [**Application of noncash proceeds.**] A secured party need not apply or pay over for application noncash proceeds of disposition under Section 9–610 unless the failure to do so would be commercially unreasonable. A secured party that applies or pays over for application noncash proceeds shall do so in a commercially reasonable manner.

(d) [**Surplus or deficiency if obligation secured.**] If the security interest under which a disposition is made secures payment or performance of an obligation, after making the payments and applications required by subsection (a) and permitted by subsection (c):

(1) unless subsection (a)(4) requires the secured party to apply or pay over cash proceeds to a consignor, the secured party shall account to and pay a debtor for any surplus; and

(2) the obligor is liable for any deficiency.

(e) [**No surplus or deficiency in sales of certain rights to payment.**] If the underlying transaction is a sale of accounts, chattel paper, payment intangibles, or promissory notes:

(1) the debtor is not entitled to any surplus; and

(2) the obligor is not liable for any deficiency.

(f) [**Calculation of surplus or deficiency in disposition to person related to secured party.**] The surplus or deficiency following a disposition is calculated based on the amount of proceeds that would have been realized in a disposition complying with this part to a transferee other than the secured party, a person related to the secured party, or a secondary obligor if:

(1) the transferee in the disposition is the secured party, a person related to the secured party, or a secondary obligor; and

(2) the amount of proceeds of the disposition is significantly below the range of proceeds that a complying disposition to a person other than the secured party, a person related to the secured party, or a secondary obligor would have brought.

(g) [**Cash proceeds received by junior secured party.**] A secured party that receives cash proceeds of a disposition in good faith and without knowledge that the receipt violates the rights of the holder of a security interest or other lien that is not subordinate to the security interest or agricultural lien under which the disposition is made:

(1) takes the cash proceeds free of the security interest or other lien;

(2) is not obligated to apply the proceeds of the disposition to the satisfaction of obligations secured by the security interest or other lien; and

(3) is not obligated to account to or pay the holder of the security interest or other lien for any surplus.

§ 9–616. Explanation of Calculation of Surplus or Deficiency.

(a) [**Definitions.**] In this section:

(1) "Explanation" means a writing that:

(A) states the amount of the surplus or deficiency;

(B) provides an explanation in accordance with subsection (c) of how the secured party calculated the surplus or deficiency;

(C) states, if applicable, that future debits, credits, charges, including additional credit service charges or interest, rebates, and expenses may affect the amount of the surplus or deficiency; and

(D) provides a telephone number or mailing address from which additional information concerning the transaction is available.

(2) "Request" means a record:

(A) authenticated by a debtor or consumer obligor;

(B) requesting that the recipient provide an explanation; and

(C) sent after disposition of the collateral under Section 9–610.

(b) [**Explanation of calculation.**] In a consumer-goods transaction in which the debtor is entitled to a surplus or a consumer obligor is liable for a deficiency under Section 9–615, the secured party shall:

(1) send an explanation to the debtor or consumer obligor, as applicable, after the disposition and:

(A) before or when the secured party accounts to the debtor and pays any surplus or first makes written demand on the consumer obligor after the disposition for payment of the deficiency; and

(B) within 14 days after receipt of a request; or

(2) in the case of a consumer obligor who is liable for a deficiency, within 14 days after receipt of a request, send to the consumer obligor a record waiving the secured party's right to a deficiency.

(c) [**Required information.**] To comply with subsection (a)(1)(B), a writing must provide the following information in the following order:

(1) the aggregate amount of obligations secured by the security interest under which the disposition was made, and, if the amount reflects a rebate of unearned interest or credit service charge, an indication of that fact, calculated as of a specified date:

(A) if the secured party takes or receives possession of the collateral after default, not more than 35 days before the secured party takes or receives possession; or

(B) if the secured party takes or receives possession of the collateral before default or does not take possession of the collateral, not more than 35 days before the disposition;

(2) the amount of proceeds of the disposition;

(3) the aggregate amount of the obligations after deducting the amount of proceeds;

(4) the amount, in the aggregate or by type, and types of expenses, including expenses of retaking, holding, preparing for disposition, processing, and disposing of the collateral, and attorney's fees secured by the collateral which are known to the secured party and relate to the current disposition;

(5) the amount, in the aggregate or by type, and types of credits, including rebates of interest or credit service charges, to which the obligor is known to be entitled and which are not reflected in the amount in paragraph (1); and

(6) the amount of the surplus or deficiency.

(d) [**Substantial compliance.**] A particular phrasing of the explanation is not required. An explanation complying substantially with the requirements of subsection (a) is sufficient, even if it includes minor errors that are not seriously misleading.

(e) [**Charges for responses.**] A debtor or consumer obligor is entitled without charge to one response to a request under this section during any six-month period in which the secured party did not send to the debtor or consumer obligor an explanation pursuant to subsection (b)(1). The secured party may require payment of a charge not exceeding $25 for each additional response.

§ 9–617. Rights of Transferee of Collateral.

(a) [**Effects of disposition.**] A secured party's disposition of collateral after default:

(1) transfers to a transferee for value all of the debtor's rights in the collateral;

(2) discharges the security interest under which the disposition is made; and

(3) discharges any subordinate security interest or other subordinate lien [other than liens created under [cite acts or statutes providing for liens, if any, that are not to be discharged]].

(b) [**Rights of good-faith transferee.**] A transferee that acts in good faith takes free of the rights and interests described in subsection (a), even if the secured party fails to comply with this article or the requirements of any judicial proceeding.

(c) [**Rights of other transferee.**] If a transferee does not take free of the rights and interests described in subsection (a), the transferee takes the collateral subject to:

(1) the debtor's rights in the collateral;

(2) the security interest or agricultural lien under which the disposition is made; and

(3) any other security interest or other lien.

§ 9–620. Acceptance of Collateral in Full or Partial Satisfaction of Obligation; Compulsory Disposition of Collateral.

(a) [**Conditions to acceptance in satisfaction.**] Except as otherwise provided in subsection (g), a secured party may accept collateral in full or partial satisfaction of the obligation it secures only if:

(1) the debtor consents to the acceptance under subsection (c);

(2) the secured party does not receive, within the time set forth in subsection (d), a notification of objection to the proposal authenticated by:

(A) a person to which the secured party was required to send a proposal under Section 9–621; or

(B) any other person, other than the debtor, holding an interest in the collateral subordinate to the security interest that is the subject of the proposal;

(3) if the collateral is consumer goods, the collateral is not in the possession of the debtor when the debtor consents to the acceptance; and

(4) subsection (e) does not require the secured party to dispose of the collateral or the debtor waives the requirement pursuant to Section 9–624.

(b) [**Purported acceptance ineffective.**] A purported or apparent acceptance of collateral under this section is ineffective unless:

(1) the secured party consents to the acceptance in an authenticated record or sends a proposal to the debtor; and

(2) the conditions of subsection (a) are met.

(c) [**Debtor's consent.**] For purposes of this section:

(1) a debtor consents to an acceptance of collateral in partial satisfaction of the obligation it secures only if the debtor agrees to the terms of the acceptance in a record authenticated after default; and

(2) a debtor consents to an acceptance of collateral in full satisfaction of the obligation it secures only if the debtor agrees to the terms of the acceptance in a record authenticated after default or the secured party:

(A) sends to the debtor after default a proposal that is unconditional or subject only to a condition that collateral not in the possession of the secured party be preserved or maintained;

(B) in the proposal, proposes to accept collateral in full satisfaction of the obligation it secures; and

(C) does not receive a notification of objection authenticated by the debtor within 20 days after the proposal is sent.

(d) [**Effectiveness of notification.**] To be effective under subsection (a)(2), a notification of objection must be received by the secured party:

(1) in the case of a person to which the proposal was sent pursuant to Section 9–621, within 20 days after notification was sent to that person; and

(2) in other cases:

(A) within 20 days after the last notification was sent pursuant to Section 9–621; or

(B) if a notification was not sent, before the debtor consents to the acceptance under subsection (c).

(e) [**Mandatory disposition of consumer goods.**] A secured party that has taken possession of collateral shall dispose of the collateral pursuant to Section 9–610 within the time specified in subsection (f) if:

(1) 60 percent of the cash price has been paid in the case of a purchase-money security interest in consumer goods; or

(2) 60 percent of the principal amount of the obligation secured has been paid in the case of a non-purchase-money security interest in consumer goods.

(f) [**Compliance with mandatory disposition requirement.**] To comply with subsection (e), the secured party shall dispose of the collateral:

(1) within 90 days after taking possession; or

(2) within any longer period to which the debtor and all secondary obligors have agreed in an agreement to that effect entered into and authenticated after default.

(g) [**No partial satisfaction in consumer transaction.**] In a consumer transaction, a secured party may not accept collateral in partial satisfaction of the obligation it secures.

§ 9–621. Notification of Proposal to Accept Collateral.

(a) [**Persons to which proposal to be sent.**] A secured party that desires to accept collateral in full or partial satisfaction of the obligation it secures shall send its proposal to:

(1) any person from which the secured party has received, before the debtor consented to the acceptance, an authenticated notification of a claim of an interest in the collateral;

(2) any other secured party or lienholder that, 10 days before the debtor consented to the acceptance, held a security interest in or other lien on the collateral perfected by the filing of a financing statement that:

(A) identified the collateral;

(B) was indexed under the debtor's name as of that date; and

(C) was filed in the office or offices in which to file a financing statement against the debtor covering the collateral as of that date; and

(3) any other secured party that, 10 days before the debtor consented to the acceptance, held a security interest in the collateral perfected by compliance with a statute, regulation, or treaty described in Section 9–311(a).

(b) [**Proposal to be sent to secondary obligor in partial satisfaction.**] A secured party that desires to accept collateral in partial satisfaction of the obligation it secures shall send its proposal to any secondary obligor in addition to the persons described in subsection (a).

§ 9–622. Effect of Acceptance of Collateral.

(a) [**Effect of acceptance.**] A secured party's acceptance of collateral in full or partial satisfaction of the obligation it secures:

   (1) discharges the obligation to the extent consented to by the debtor;

   (2) transfers to the secured party all of a debtor's rights in the collateral;

   (3) discharges the security interest or agricultural lien that is the subject of the debtor's consent and any subordinate security interest or other subordinate lien; and

   (4) terminates any other subordinate interest.

(b) [**Discharge of subordinate interest notwithstanding noncompliance.**] A subordinate interest is discharged or terminated under subsection (a), even if the secured party fails to comply with this article.

§ 9–623. Right to Redeem Collateral.

(a) [**Persons that may redeem.**] A debtor, any secondary obligor, or any other secured party or lienholder may redeem collateral.

(b) [**Requirements for redemption.**] To redeem collateral, a person shall tender:

   (1) fulfillment of all obligations secured by the collateral; and

   (2) the reasonable expenses and attorney's fees described in Section 9–615(a)(1).

(c) [**When redemption may occur.**] A redemption may occur at any time before a secured party:

   (1) has collected collateral under Section 9–607;

   (2) has disposed of collateral or entered into a contract for its disposition under Section 9–610; or

   (3) has accepted collateral in full or partial satisfaction of the obligation it secures under Section 9–622.

§ 9–624. Waiver.

(a) [**Waiver of disposition notification.**] A debtor or secondary obligor may waive the right to notification of disposition of collateral under Section 9–611 only by an agreement to that effect entered into and authenticated after default.

(b) [**Waiver of mandatory disposition.**] A debtor may waive the right to require disposition of collateral under Section 9–620(e) only by an agreement to that effect entered into and authenticated after default.

(c) [**Waiver of redemption right.**] Except in a consumer-goods transaction, a debtor or secondary obligor may waive the right to redeem collateral under Section 9–623 only by an agreement to that effect entered into and authenticated after default.

§ 9–625. Remedies for Secured Party's Failure to Comply with Article.

(a) [**Judicial orders concerning noncompliance.**] If it is established that a secured party is not proceeding in accordance with this article, a court may order or restrain collection, enforcement, or disposition of collateral on appropriate terms and conditions.

(b) [**Damages for noncompliance.**] Subject to subsections (c), (d), and (f), a person is liable for damages in the amount of any loss caused by a failure to comply with this article. Loss caused by a failure to comply may include loss resulting from the debtor's inability to obtain, or increased costs of, alternative financing.

(c) [**Persons entitled to recover damages; statutory damages in consumer-goods transaction.**] Except as otherwise provided in Section 9–628:

   (1) a person that, at the time of the failure, was a debtor, was an obligor, or held a security interest in or other lien on the collateral may recover damages under subsection (b) for its loss; and

   (2) if the collateral is consumer goods, a person that was a debtor or a secondary obligor at the time a secured party failed to comply with this part may recover for that failure in any event an amount not less than the credit service charge plus 10 percent of the principal amount of the obligation or the time-price differential plus 10 percent of the cash price.

(d) [**Recovery when deficiency eliminated or reduced.**] A debtor whose deficiency is eliminated under Section 9–626 may recover damages for the loss of any surplus. However, a debtor or secondary obligor whose deficiency is eliminated or reduced under Section 9–626 may not otherwise recover under subsection (b) for noncompliance with the provisions of this part relating to collection, enforcement, disposition, or acceptance.

(e) [**Statutory damages: noncompliance with specified provisions.**] In addition to any damages recoverable under subsection (b), the debtor, consumer obligor, or person named as a debtor in a filed record, as applicable, may recover $500 in each case from a person that:

   (1) fails to comply with Section 9–208;

   (2) fails to comply with Section 9–209;

   (3) files a record that the person is not entitled to file under Section 9–509(a);

   (4) fails to cause the secured party of record to file or send a termination statement as required by Section 9–513(a) or (c);

   (5) fails to comply with Section 9–616(b)(1) and whose failure is part of a pattern, or consistent with a practice, of noncompliance; or

   (6) fails to comply with Section 9–616(b)(2).

(f) [**Statutory damages: noncompliance with Section 9–210.**] A debtor or consumer obligor may recover damages under subsection (b) and, in addition, $500 in each case from a person that, without reasonable cause, fails to comply with a request under Section 9–210. A recipient of a request under Section 9–210 which never claimed an interest in the collateral or obligations that are the subject of a request under that section has a reasonable excuse for failure to comply with the request within the meaning of this subsection.

(g) [**Limitation of security interest: noncompliance with Section 9–210.**] If a secured party fails to comply with a request regarding a list of collateral or a statement of account under Section 9–210, the secured party may claim a security interest only as shown in the list or statement included in the request as against a person that is reasonably misled by the failure.

§ 9–626. Action in Which Deficiency or Surplus Is in Issue.

(a) [**Applicable rules if amount of deficiency or surplus in issue.**] In an action arising from a transaction, other than a consumer transaction, in which the amount of a deficiency or surplus is in issue, the following rules apply:

   (1) A secured party need not prove compliance with the provisions of this part relating to collection, enforcement, disposition, or acceptance unless the debtor or a secondary obligor places the secured party's compliance in issue.

   (2) If the secured party's compliance is placed in issue, the secured party has the burden of establishing that the collection, enforcement, disposition, or acceptance was conducted in accordance with this part.

   (3) Except as otherwise provided in Section 9–628, if a secured party fails to prove that the collection, enforcement, disposition, or acceptance was conducted in accordance with the provisions of this part relating to collection, enforcement, disposition, or acceptance, the liability of a debtor or a secondary obligor for a deficiency is limited to an amount by which the sum of the secured obligation, expenses, and attorney's fees exceeds the greater of:

      (A) the proceeds of the collection, enforcement, disposition, or acceptance; or

      (B) the amount of proceeds that would have been realized had the noncomplying secured party proceeded in accordance with the provisions of this part relating to collection, enforcement, disposition, or acceptance.

   (4) For purposes of paragraph (3)(B), the amount of proceeds that would have been realized is equal to the sum of the secured obligation, expenses, and attorney's fees unless the secured party proves that the amount is less than that sum.

(5) If a deficiency or surplus is calculated under Section 9–615(f), the debtor or obligor has the burden of establishing that the amount of proceeds of the disposition is significantly below the range of prices that a complying disposition to a person other than the secured party, a person related to the secured party, or a secondary obligor would have brought.

(b) **[Non-consumer transactions; no inference.]** The limitation of the rules in subsection (a) to transactions other than consumer transactions is intended to leave to the court the determination of the proper rules in consumer transactions. The court may not infer from that limitation the nature of the proper rule in consumer transactions and may continue to apply established approaches.

§ 9–627. Determination of Whether Conduct Was Commercially Reasonable.

(a) **[Greater amount obtainable under other circumstances; no preclusion of commercial reasonableness.]** The fact that a greater amount could have been obtained by a collection, enforcement, disposition, or acceptance at a different time or in a different method from that selected by the secured party is not of itself sufficient to preclude the secured party from establishing that the collection, enforcement, disposition, or acceptance was made in a commercially reasonable manner.

(b) **[Dispositions that are commercially reasonable.]** A disposition of collateral is made in a commercially reasonable manner if the disposition is made:

(1) in the usual manner on any recognized market;

(2) at the price current in any recognized market at the time of the disposition; or

(3) otherwise in conformity with reasonable commercial practices among dealers in the type of property that was the subject of the disposition.

(c) **[Approval by court or on behalf of creditors.]** A collection, enforcement, disposition, or acceptance is commercially reasonable if it has been approved:

(1) in a judicial proceeding;

(2) by a bona fide creditors' committee;

(3) by a representative of creditors; or

(4) by an assignee for the benefit of creditors.

(d) **[Approval under subsection (c) not necessary; absence of approval has no effect.]** Approval under subsection (c) need not be obtained, and lack of approval does not mean that the collection, enforcement, disposition, or acceptance is not commercially reasonable.

APPENDIX C
Dictionary of Legal Terms

A

abatement Reduction or elimination of gifts by category upon the reduction in value of the estate.

absolute surety Surety liable to a creditor immediately upon the default of the principal debtor.

acceptance *Commercial paper* Acceptance is the drawee's signed engagement to honor the draft as presented. It becomes operative when completed by delivery or notification. UCC § 3–410.

    Contracts Compliance by offeree with terms and conditions of offer.

    Sale of goods UCC § 2–606 provides three ways a buyer can accept goods: (1) by signifying to the seller that the goods are conforming or that he will accept them in spite of their nonconformity, (2) by failing to make an effective rejection, and (3) by doing an act inconsistent with the seller's ownership.

acceptor Drawee who has accepted an instrument.

accession An addition to one's property by increase of the original property or by production from such property. *E.g.,* A innocently converts the wheat of B into bread. UCC § 9–315 changes the common law where a perfected security interest is involved.

accident and health insurance Provides protection from losses due to accident or sickness.

accommodation An arrangement made as a favor to another, usually involving a loan of money or commercial paper. While a party's intent may be to aid a maker of a note by lending his credit, if he seeks to accomplish thereby legitimate objects of his own and not simply to aid the maker, the act is not for accommodation.

accommodation indorser Signer not in the chain of title.

accommodation party A person who signs commercial paper in any capacity for the purpose of lending his name to another party to an instrument. UCC § 3–415.

accord and satisfaction A method of discharging a claim whereby the parties agree to accept something in settlement, the "accord" being the agreement and the "satisfaction" its execution or performance. It is a new contract that is substituted for an old contract, which is thereby discharged, or for an obligation or cause of action and that must have all of the elements of a valid contract.

account Any account with a bank, including a checking, time, interest or savings account. UCC § 4–194. Also, any right to payment, for goods or services, that is not evidenced by an instrument or chattel paper. *E.g.,* account receivable.

accounting Equitable proceeding for a complete settlement of all partnership affairs.

act of state doctrine Rule that a court should not question the validity of actions taken by a foreign government in its own country.

actual authority Power conferred upon agent by actual consent given by principal.

actual express authority Actual authority derived from written or spoken words of principal.

actual implied authority Actual authority inferred from words or conduct manifested to agent by principal.

actual notice Knowledge actually and expressly communicated.

actus reas Wrongful or overt act.

ademption The removal or extinction of a devise by act of the testator.

adequacy of consideration Not required where parties have freely agreed to the exchange.

adhesion contract Standard "form" contract, usually between a large retailer and a consumer, in which the weaker party has no realistic choice or opportunity to bargain.

adjudication The giving or pronouncing of a judgment in a case; also, the judgment given.

administrative agency Governmental entity (other than courts and legislatures) having authority to affect the rights of private parties.

administrative law Law dealing with the establishment, duties, and powers of agencies in the executive branch of government.

administrative process Entire set of activities engaged in by administrative agencies while carrying out their rulemaking, enforcement, and adjudicative functions.

administrator A person appointed by the court to manage the assets and liabilities of an intestate (a person dying without a will). A person named in the will of a testator (a person dying with a will) is called the executor. Female designations are administratrix and executrix.

adversary system System in which opposing parties initiate and present their cases.

adverse possession A method of acquiring title to real property by possession for a statutory period under certain conditions. The periods of time may differ, depending on whether the adverse possessor has color of title.

affidavit A written statement of facts, made voluntarily, confirmed by oath or affirmation of the party making it, and taken before an authorized officer.

affiliate Person who controls, is controlled by, or is under common control with the issuer.

affirm Uphold the lower court's judgment.

affirmative action Active recruitment of minority applicants.

affirmative defense A response that attacks the plaintiff's legal right to bring an action as opposed to attacking the truth of the claim. *E.g.,* accord and satisfaction; assumption of risk; contributory negligence; duress; estoppel.

affirmative disclosure Requirement that an advertiser include certain information in its advertisement so that the ad is not deceptive.

after-acquired property Property the debtor may acquire at some time after the security interest attaches.

agency Relation in which one person acts for or represents another by the latter's authority.

    Actual agency Exists where the agent is really employed by the principal.

    Agency by estoppel One created by operation of law and established by proof of such acts of the principal as reasonably lead to the conclusion of its existence.

    Implied agency One created by acts of the parties and deduced from proof of other facts.

agent Person authorized to act on another's behalf.

allegation A statement of a party setting out what he expects to prove.

allonge Piece of paper firmly affixed to the instrument.

annuity contract Agreement to pay periodic sums to insured upon reaching a designated age.

annul To annul a judgment or judicial proceeding is to deprive it of all force and operation.

answer The answer is the formal written statement made by a defendant setting forth the ground of his defense.

antecedent debt Preexisting obligation.

anticipatory breach of contract (or **anticipatory repudiation**) The unjustified assertion by a party that he will not perform an obligation that he is contractually obligated to perform at a future time. See UCC §§ 610 & 611.

apparent authority Such principal power that a reasonable person would assume an agent has in light of the principal's conduct.

appeal Resort to a superior (appellate) court to review the decision of an inferior (trial) court or administrative agency.

appeal by right Mandatory review by a higher court.

appellant A party who takes an appeal from one court to another. He may be either the plaintiff or defendant in the original court proceeding.

appellee The party in a cause against whom an appeal is taken; that is, the party who has an interest adverse to setting aside or reversing the judgment. Sometimes also called the "respondent."

appropriation Unauthorized use of another person's name or likeness for one's own benefit.

appurtenances Things appurtenant pass as incident to the principal thing. Sometimes an easement consisting of a right of way over one piece of land will pass with another piece of land as being appurtenant to it.

APR Annual percentage rate.

arbitration The reference of a dispute to an impartial (third) person chosen by the parties, who agree in advance to abide by the arbitrator's award issued after a hearing at which both parties have an opportunity to be heard.

arraignment Accused is informed of the crime against him and enters a plea.

articles of incorporation (or **certificate of incorporation**) The instrument under which a corporation is formed. The contents are prescribed in the particular state's general incorporation statute.

articles of partnership A written agreement by which parties enter into a partnership, to be governed by the terms set forth therein.

as is Disclaimer of implied warranties.

assault Unlawful attempted battery; intentional infliction of apprehension of immediate bodily harm or offensive contact.

assignee Party to whom contract rights are assigned.

assignment A transfer of the rights to real or personal property, usually intangible property such as rights in a lease, mortgage, sale agreement, or partnership.

assignment of rights Voluntary transfer to a third party of the rights arising from a contract.

assignor Party making an assignment.

assumes Delegatee agrees to perform the contractual obligation of the delegator.

assumes the mortgage Purchaser of mortgaged property becomes personally liable to pay the debt.

assumption of risk Plaintiff's express or implied consent to encounter a known danger.

attachment The process of seizing property, by virtue of a writ, summons, or other judicial order, and bringing the same into the custody of the court for the purpose of securing satisfaction of the judgment ultimately to be entered in the action. While formerly the main objective was to coerce the defendant debtor to appear in court, today the writ of attachment is used primarily to seize the debtor's property in the event a judgment is rendered.

Distinguished from execution See **execution**.

Also, the process by which a security interest becomes enforceable. Attachment may occur upon the taking of possession or upon the signing of a security agreement by the person who is pledging the property as collateral.

authority Power of an agent to change the legal status of his principal.

authorized means Any reasonable means of communication.

automatic perfection Perfection upon attachment.

award The decision of an arbitrator.

B

bad checks Issuing a check with funds insufficient to cover it.

bailee The party to whom personal property is delivered under a contract of bailment.

Extraordinary bailee Absolutely liable for the safety of the bailed property without regard to the cause of loss.

Ordinary bailee Must exercise due care.

bailment A delivery of personal property in trust for the execution of a special object in relation to such goods, beneficial either to the bailor or bailee or both, and upon a contract to either redeliver the goods to the bailor or otherwise dispose of the same in conformity with the purpose of the trust.

bailor The party who delivers goods to another in the contract of bailment.

bankrupt The state or condition of one who is unable to pay his debts as they are, or become, due.

Bankruptcy Code The Act was substantially revised in 1978 and again in 2005. Straight bankruptcy is in the nature of a liquidation proceeding and involves the collection and distribution to creditors of all the bankrupt's nonexempt property by the trustee in the manner provided by the Act. The debtor rehabilitation provisions of the Act (Chapters 11 and 13) differ from straight bankruptcy in that the debtor looks to rehabilitation and reorganization, rather than liquidation, and the creditors look to future earnings of the bankrupt, rather than to property held by the bankrupt, to satisfy their claims.

bargain Negotiated exchange.

bargained exchange Mutually agreed-upon exchange.

basis of the bargain Part of the buyer's assumption underlying the sale.

battery Unlawful touching of another; intentional infliction of harmful or offensive bodily contact.

bearer Person in possession of an instrument.

bearer paper Payable to holder of the instrument.

beneficiary One who benefits from act of another. See also **third-party beneficiary**.

Incidental A person who may derive benefit from performance on contract, though he is neither the promisee nor the one to whom performance is to be rendered. Since the incidental beneficiary is not a donee or creditor beneficiary (see **third-party beneficiary**), he has no right to enforce the contract.

Intended beneficiary Third party intended by the two contracted parties to receive a benefit from their contract.

Trust As it relates to trust beneficiaries, includes a person who has any present or future interest, vested or contingent, and also includes the owner of an interest by assignment or other transfer and, as it relates to a charitable trust, includes any person entitled to enforce the trust.

beyond a reasonable doubt Proof that is entirely convincing and satisfying to a moral certainty; criminal law standard.

bilateral contract Contract in which both parties exchange promises.

bill of lading Document evidencing receipt of goods for shipment issued by person engaged in business of transporting or forwarding goods; includes airbill. UCC § 1-201(6).

Through bill of lading A bill of lading which specifies at least one connecting carrier.

bill of sale A written agreement, formerly limited to one under seal, by which one person assigns or transfers his right to or interest in goods and personal chattels to another.

binder A written memorandum of the important terms of a contract of insurance which gives temporary protection to an insured pending investigation of risk by the insurance company or until a formal policy is issued.

blue law Prohibition of certain types of commercial activity on Sunday.

blue sky laws A popular name for state statutes providing for the regulation and supervision of securities offerings and sales, to protect citizen-investors from investing in fraudulent companies.

bona fide Latin. In good faith.

bond A certificate or evidence of a debt on which the issuing company or governmental body promises to pay the bondholders a specified amount of interest for a specified length of time and to repay the loan on the expiration date. In every case, a bond represents debt—its holder is a creditor of the corporation, not a part owner, as the shareholder is.

boycott Agreement among parties not to deal with a third party.

breach Wrongful failure to perform the terms of a contract.

Material breach Nonperformance which significantly impairs the aggrieved party's rights under the contract.

bribery Offering property to a public official to influence the official's decision.

bulk transfer Transfer not in the ordinary course of the transferor's business of a major part of his inventory.

burglary Breaking and entering the home of another at night with intent to commit a felony.

business judgment rule Protects directors from liability for honest mistakes of judgment.

business trust A trust (managed by a trustee for the benefit of a beneficiary) established to conduct a business for a profit.

but for rule Person's negligent conduct is a cause of an event if the event would not have occurred in the absence of that conduct.

buyer in ordinary course of business Person who buys in ordinary course, in good faith, and without knowledge that the sale to him is in violation of anyone's ownership rights or of a security interest.

by-laws Regulations, ordinances, rules, or laws adopted by an association or corporation for its government.

C

callable bond Bond that is subject to redemption (reacquisition) by the corporation.

cancellation One party's putting an end to a contract because of a breach by other party.

capital Accumulated goods, possessions, and assets, used for the production of profits and wealth. Owners' equity in a business. Also used to refer to the total assets of a business or to capital assets.

capital surplus Surplus other than earned surplus.

carrier Transporter of goods.

casualty insurance Covers property loss due to causes other than fire or the elements.

cause of action The ground on which an action may be sustained.

caveat emptor Latin. Let the buyer beware. This maxim is more applicable to judicial sales, auctions, and the like than to sales of consumer goods, where strict liability, warranty, and other laws protect.

certificate of deposit A written acknowledgment by a bank or banker of a deposit with promise to pay to depositor, to his order, or to some other person or to his order. UCC § 3–104(2)(c).

certificate of title Official representation of ownership.

certification Acceptance of a check by a drawee bank.

certification of incorporation See **articles of incorporation**.

certification mark Distinctive symbol, word, or design used with goods or services to certify specific characteristics.

certiorari Latin. To be informed of. A writ of common law origin issued by a superior to an inferior court requiring the latter to produce a certified record of a particular case tried therein. It is most commonly used to refer to the Supreme Court of the United States, which uses the writ of certiorari as a discretionary device to choose the cases it wishes to hear.

chancery Equity; equitable jurisdiction; a court of equity; the system of jurisprudence administered in courts of equity.

charging order Judicial lien against a partner's interest in the partnership.

charter An instrument emanating from the sovereign power, in the nature of a grant. A charter differs from a constitution in that the former is granted by the sovereign, while the latter is established by the people themselves.

Corporate law An act of a legislature creating a corporation or creating and defining the franchise of a corporation. Also a corporation's constitution or organic law; that is to say, the articles of incorporation taken in connection with the law under which the corporation was organized.

chattel mortgage A pre-Uniform Commercial Code security device whereby the mortgagee took a security interest in personal property of the mortgagor. Such security device has generally been superseded by other types of security agreements under UCC Article 9 (Secured Transactions).

chattel paper Writings that evidence both a debt and a security interest.

check A draft drawn upon a bank and payable on demand, signed by the maker or drawer, containing an unconditional promise to pay a sum certain in money to the order of the payee. UCC § 3–104(2)(b).

Cashier's check A bank's own check drawn on itself and signed by the cashier or other authorized official. It is a direct obligation of the bank.

C. & F. Cost and freight; a shipping contract.

C.I.F. Cost, insurance, and freight; a shipping contract.

civil law Laws concerned with civil or private rights and remedies, as contrasted with criminal laws.

The system of jurisprudence administered in the Roman empire, particularly as set forth in the compilation of Justinian and his successors, as distinguished from the common law of England and the canon law. The civil law (Civil Code) is followed by Louisiana.

claim A right to payment.

clearinghouse An association of banks for the purpose of settling accounts on a daily basis.

close corporation See **corporation**.

closed-ended credit Credit extended to debtor for a specific period of time.

closed shop An employer who can only hire union members.

C.O.D. Collect on delivery; generally a shipping contract.

code A compilation of all permanent laws in force consolidated and classified according to subject matter. Many states have published official codes of all laws in force, including the common law and statutes as judicially interpreted, which have been compiled by code commissions and enacted by the legislatures.

codicil A supplement or an addition to a will; it may explain, modify, add to, subtract from, qualify, alter, restrain, or revoke provisions in an existing will. It must be executed with the same formalities as a will.

cognovit judgment Written authority by debtor for entry of judgment against him in the event he defaults in payment. Such provision in a debt instrument on default confers judgment against the debtor.

collateral Secondarily liable; liable only if the party with primary liability does not perform.

collateral (security) Personal property subject to security interest.

Banking Some form of security in addition to the personal obligation of the borrower.

collateral promise Undertaking to be secondarily liable, that is, liable if the principal debtor does not perform.

collecting bank Any bank, except the payor bank, handling the item for collection. UCC § 4–105(d).

collective mark Distinctive symbol used to indicate membership in an organization.

collision insurance Protects the owner of an automobile against damage due to contact with other vehicles or objects.

commerce power Exclusive power granted by the U.S. Constitution to the federal government to regulate commerce with foreign countries and among the states.

commercial bailment Bailment in which parties derive a mutual benefit.

commercial impracticability Performance can only be accomplished with unforeseen and unjust hardship.

commercial law A phrase used to designate the whole body of substantive jurisprudence (*e.g.*, Uniform Commercial Code; Truth in Lending Act) applicable to the rights, intercourse, and relations of persons engaged in commerce, trade, or mercantile pursuits. See **Uniform Commercial Code**.

commercial paper Bills of exchange (i.e., drafts), promissory notes, bank checks, and other negotiable instruments for the payment of money, which, by their form and on their face, purport to be such instruments. UCC Article 3 is the general law governing commercial paper.

commercial reasonableness Judgment of reasonable persons familiar with the business transaction.

commercial speech Expression related to the economic interests of the speaker and its audience.

common carrier Carrier open to the general public.

common law Body of law originating in England and derived from judicial decisions. As distinguished from statutory law created by the enactment of legislatures, the common law comprises the judgments and decrees of the courts recognizing, affirming, and enforcing usages and customs of immemorial antiquity.

community property Rights of a spouse in property acquired by the other during marriage.

comparable worth Equal pay for jobs of equal value to the employer.

comparative negligence Under comparative negligence statutes or doctrines, negligence is measured in terms of percentage, and any damages allowed shall be diminished in proportion to amount of negligence attributable to the person for whose injury, damage, or death recovery is sought.

complainant One who applies to the courts for legal redress by filing a complaint (i.e., plaintiff).

complaint The pleading which sets forth a claim for relief. Such complaint (whether it be the original claim, counterclaim, cross-claim, or third-party claim) shall contain (1) a short, plain statement of the grounds upon which the court's jurisdiction depends, unless the court already has jurisdiction and the claim needs no new grounds of jurisdiction to support it, (2) a short, plain statement of the claim showing that the pleader is entitled to relief, and (3) a demand for judgment for the relief to which he deems himself entitled. Fed.R. Civil P. 8(a). The complaint, together with the summons, is required to be served on the defendant. Rule 4.

composition Agreement between debtor and two or more of her creditors that each will take a portion of his claim as full payment.

compulsory arbitration Arbitration required by statute for specific types of disputes.

computer crime Crime committed against or through the use of a computer or computer/services.

concealment Fraudulent failure to disclose a material fact.

conciliation Nonbinding process in which a third party acts as an intermediary between disputing parties.

concurrent jurisdiction Authority of more than one court to hear the same case.

condition An uncertain event which affects the duty of performance. *Concurrent conditions* The parties are to perform simultaneously. *Express condition* Performance is contingent on the happening or nonhappening of a stated event.

condition precedent An event which must occur or not occur before performance is due; event or events (presentment, dishonor, notice of dishonor) which must occur to hold a secondary party liable to commercial paper.

condition subsequent An event which terminates a duty of performance.

conditional acceptance An acceptance of an offer contingent upon the acceptance of an additional or different term.

conditional contract Obligations are contingent upon a stated event.

conditional guarantor of collection Surety liable to creditor only after creditor exhausts his legal remedies against the principal debtor.

confession of judgment Written agreement by debtor authorizing creditor to obtain a court judgment in the event debtor defaults. See also **cognovit judgment**.

confiscation Governmental taking of foreign-owned property without payment.

conflict of laws That branch of jurisprudence, arising from the diversity of the laws of different nations, states, or jurisdictions, that reconciles the inconsistencies, or decides which law is to govern in a particular case.

confusion Results when goods belonging to two or more owners become so intermixed that the property of any of them no longer can be identified except as part of a mass of like goods.

consanguinity Kinship; blood relationship; the connection or relation of persons descended from the same stock or common ancestor.

consensual arbitration Arbitration voluntarily entered into by the parties.

consent Voluntary and knowing willingness that an act should be done.

conservator Appointed by court to manage affairs of incompetent or to liquidate business.

consideration The cause, motive, price, or impelling influence which induces a contracting party to enter into a contract. Some right, interest, profit, or benefit accruing to one party or some forbearance, detriment, loss, or responsibility given, suffered, or undertaken by the other.

consignee One to whom a consignment is made. Person named in bill of lading to whom or to whose order the bill promises delivery. UCC § 7-102(b).

consignment Ordinarily implies an agency; denotes that property is committed to the consignee for care or sale.

consignor One who sends or makes a consignment; a shipper of goods. The person named in a bill of lading as the person from whom the goods have been received for shipment. UCC § 7-102(c).

consolidation In *corporate law*, the combination of two or more corporations into a newly created corporation. Thus, A Corporation and B Corporation consolidate to form C Corporation.

constitution Fundamental law of a government establishing its powers and limitations.

constructive That which is established by the mind of the law in its act of *construing* facts, conduct, circumstances, or instruments. That which has not in its essential nature the character assigned to it, but acquires such character in consequence of the way in which it is regarded by a rule or policy of law; hence, inferred, implied, or made out by legal interpretation; the word "legal" being sometimes used here in lieu of "constructive."

constructive assent An assent or consent imputed to a party from a construction or interpretation of his conduct; as distinguished from one which he actually expresses.

constructive conditions Conditions in contracts which are neither expressed nor implied but rather are imposed by law to meet the ends of justice.

constructive delivery Term comprehending all those acts which, although not truly conferring a real possession of the vendee, have been held by construction of law to be equivalent to acts of real delivery.

constructive eviction Failure by the landlord in any obligation under the lease that causes a substantial and lasting injury to the tenant's enjoyment of the premises.

constructive notice Knowledge imputed by law.

constructive trust Arising by operation of law to prevent unjust enrichment. See also **trustee**.

consumer goods Goods bought or used for personal, family, or household purposes.

consumer product Tangible personal property normally used for family, household, or personal purposes.

contingent remainder Remainder interest, conditional upon the happening of an event in addition to the termination of the preceding estate.

contract An agreement between two or more persons which creates an obligation to do or not to do a particular thing. Its essentials are competent parties, subject matter, a legal consideration, mutuality of agreement, and mutuality of obligation.

Destination contract Seller is required to tender delivery of the goods at a particular destination; seller bears the expense and risk of loss.

Executed contract Fully performed by all of the parties.

Executory contract Contract partially or entirely unperformed by one or more of the parties.

Express contract Agreement of parties that is expressed in words either in writing or orally.

Formal contract Agreement which is legally binding because of its particular form or mode or expression.

Implied-in-fact contract Contract where agreement of the parties is inferred from their conduct.

Informal contract All oral or written contracts other than formal contracts.

Installment contract Goods are delivered in separate lots.

Integrated contract Complete and total agreement.

Output contract A contract in which one party agrees to sell his entire output and the other agrees to buy it; it is not illusory, though it may be indefinite.

Quasi contract Obligation not based upon contract that is imposed to avoid injustice.

Requirements contract A contract in which one party agrees to purchase his total requirements from the other party; hence, such a contract is binding, not illusory.

Substituted contract An agreement between the parties to rescind their old contract and replace it with a new contract.

Unconscionable contract One which no sensible person not under delusion, duress, or in distress would make, and such as no honest and fair person would accept. A contract the terms of which are excessively unreasonable, overreaching, and one-sided.

Unenforceable contract Contract for the breach of which the law does not provide a remedy.

Unilateral and bilateral A unilateral contract is one in which one party makes an express engagement or undertakes a performance, without receiving in return any express engagement or promise of performance from the other. Bilateral (or reciprocal) contracts are those by which the parties expressly enter into mutual engagements.

contract clause Prohibition against the states' retroactively modifying public and private contracts.

contractual liability Obligation on a negotiable instrument, based upon signing the instrument.

contribution Payment from cosureties of their proportionate share.

contributory negligence An act or omission amounting to a want of ordinary care on the part of the complaining party, which, concurring with defendant's negligence, is proximate cause of injury.

The defense of contributory negligence is an absolute bar to any recovery in some states; because of this, it has been replaced by the doctrine of comparative negligence in many other states.

conversion Unauthorized and wrongful exercise of dominion and control over another's personal property, to exclusion of or inconsistent with rights of the owner.

convertible bond Bond that may be exchanged for other securities of the corporation.

copyright Exclusive right granted by federal government to authors of original works including literary, musical, dramatic, pictorial, graphic, sculptural, and film works.

corporation A legal entity ordinarily consisting of an association of numerous individuals. Such entity is regarded as having a personality and existence distinct from that of its several members and is vested with the capacity of continuous succession, irrespective of changes in its membership, either in perpetuity or for a limited term of years.

Closely held or close corporation Corporation that is owned by few shareholders and whose shares are not actively traded.

Corporation de facto One existing under color of law and in pursuance of an effort made in good faith to organize a corporation under the statute. Such a corporation is not subject to collateral attack.

Corporation de jure That which exists by reason of full compliance with requirements of an existing law permitting organization of such corporation.

Domestic corporation Corporation created under the laws of a given state.

Foreign corporation Corporation created under the laws of any other state, government, or country.

Publicly held corporation Corporation whose shares are owned by a large number of people and are widely traded.

Subchapter S corporation A small business corporation which, under certain conditions, may elect to have its undistributed taxable income taxed to its shareholders. I.R.C. § 1371 et seq. Of major significance is the fact that Subchapter S status usually avoids the corporate income tax, and corporate losses can be claimed by the shareholders.

Subsidiary and parent Subsidiary corporation is one in which another corporation (called parent corporation) owns at least a majority of the shares and over which it thus has control.

corrective advertising Disclosure in an advertisement that previous ads were deceptive.

costs A pecuniary allowance, made to the successful party (and recoverable from the losing party), for his expenses in prosecuting or defending an action or a distinct proceeding within an action. Generally, "costs" do not include attorneys' fees unless such fees are by a statute denominated costs or are by statute allowed to be recovered as costs in the case.

cosureties Two or more sureties bound for the same debt of a principal debtor.

co-tenants Persons who hold title concurrently.

counterclaim A claim presented by a defendant in opposition to or deduction from the claim of the plaintiff.

counteroffer A statement by the offeree which has the legal effect of rejecting the offer and of proposing a new offer to the offeror. However, the provisions of UCC § 2–207(2) modify this principle by providing that the "additional terms are to be construed as proposals for addition to the contract."

course of dealing A sequence of previous acts and conduct between the parties to a particular transaction which is fairly to be regarded as establishing a common basis of understanding for interpreting their expressions and other conduct. UCC § 1–205(1).

course of performance Conduct between the parties concerning performance of the particular contract.

court above—court below In appellate practice, the "court above" is the one to which a cause is removed for review, whether by appeal, writ of error, or certiorari, while the "court below" is the one from which the case is being removed.

covenant Used primarily with respect to promises in conveyances or other instruments dealing with real estate.

Covenants against encumbrances A stipulation against all rights to or interests in the land which may subsist in third persons to the diminution of the value of the estate granted.

Covenant appurtenant A covenant which is connected with land of the grantor, not in gross. A covenant running with the land and binding heirs, executors, and assigns of the immediate parties.

Covenant for further assurance An undertaking, in the form of a covenant, on the part of the vendor of real estate to do such further acts for the purpose of perfecting the purchaser's title as the latter may reasonably require.

Covenant for possession A covenant by which the grantee or lessee is granted possession.

Covenant for quiet enjoyment An assurance against the consequences of a defective title, and against any disturbances thereupon.

Covenants for title Covenants usually inserted in a conveyance of land, on the part of the grantor, and binding him for the completeness, security, and continuance of the title transferred to the grantee. They comprise covenants for seisin, for right to convey, against encumbrances, or quiet enjoyment, sometimes for further assurance, and almost always of warranty.

Covenant in gross Such as do not run with the land.

Covenant of right to convey An assurance by the covenantor that the grantor has sufficient capacity and title to convey the estate which he by his deed undertakes to convey.

Covenant of seisin An assurance to the purchaser that the grantor has the very estate in quantity and quality which he purports to convey.

Covenant of warranty An assurance by the grantor of an estate that the grantee shall enjoy the same without interruption by virtue of paramount title.

Covenant running with land A covenant which goes with the land, as being annexed to the estate, and which cannot be separated from the land or transferred without it. A covenant is said to run with the land when not only the original parties or their representatives, but each successive owner of the land, will be entitled to its benefit, or be liable (as the case may be) to its obligation. Such a covenant is said to be one which "touches and concerns" the land itself, so that its benefit or obligation passes with the ownership. Essentials are that the grantor and grantee must have intended that the covenant run with the land, the covenant must affect or concern the land with which it runs, and there must be privity of estate between the party claiming the benefit and the party who rests under the burden.

covenant not to compete Agreement to refrain from entering into a competing trade, profession, or business.

cover Buyer's purchase of goods in substitution for those not delivered by breaching seller.

credit beneficiary See **third-party beneficiary**.

creditor Any entity having a claim against the debtor.

crime An act or omission in violation of a public law and punishable by the government.

criminal duress Coercion by threat of serious bodily injury.

criminal intent Desired or virtually certain consequences of one's conduct.

criminal law The law that involves offenses against the entire community.

cure The right of a seller under the UCC to correct a nonconforming delivery of goods to buyer within the contract period. § 2-508.

curtesy Husband's estate in the real property of his wife.

cy-pres As near (as possible). Rule for the construction of instruments in equity, by which the intention of the party is carried out *as near as may be*, when it would be impossible or illegal to give it literal effect.

D

damage Loss, injury, or deterioration caused by the negligence, design, or accident of one person, with respect to another's person or property. The word is to be distinguished from its plural, "damages," which means a compensation in money for a loss or damage.

damages Money sought as a remedy for breach of contract or for tortious acts.

Actual damages Real, substantial, and just damages, or the amount awarded to a complainant in compensation for his actual and real loss or injury, as opposed, on the one hand, to "nominal" damages and, on the other, to "exemplary" or "punitive" damages. Synonymous with "compensatory damages" and "general damages."

Benefit-of-the-bargain damages Difference between the value received and the value of the fraudulent party's performance as represented.

Compensatory damages Compensatory damages are such as will compensate the injured party for the injury sustained, and nothing more; such as will simply make good or replace the loss caused by the wrong or injury.

Consequential damages Such damage, loss, or injury as does not flow directly and immediately from the act of the party, but only from some of the consequences or results of such act. Consequential damages resulting from a seller's breach of contract include any loss resulting from general or particular requirements and needs of which the seller at the time of contracting had reason to know and

which could not reasonably be prevented by cover or otherwise, and injury to person or property proximately resulting from any breach of warranty. UCC § 2-715(2).

Exemplary or punitive damages Damages other than compensatory damages which may be awarded against a person to punish him for outrageous conduct.

Expectancy damages Calculable by subtracting the injured party's actual dollar position as a result of the breach from that party's projected dollar position had performance occurred.

Foreseeable damages Loss of which the party in breach had reason to know when the contract was made.

Incidental damages Under UCC § 2-710, such damages include any commercially reasonable charges, expenses, or commissions incurred in stopping delivery, in the transportation, care, and custody of goods after the buyer's breach, in connection with the return or resale of the goods, or otherwise resulting from the breach. Also, such damages, resulting from a seller's breach of contract, include expenses reasonably incurred in inspection, receipt, transportation, and care and custody of goods rightfully rejected, any commercially reasonable charges, expenses, or commissions in connection with effecting cover, and any other reasonable expense incident to the delay or other breach. UCC § 2-715(1).

Irreparable damages In the law pertaining to injunctions, damages for which no certain pecuniary standard exists for measurement.

Liquidated damages and penalties Damages for breach by either party may be liquidated in the agreement but only at an amount which is reasonable in the light of the anticipated or actual harm caused by the breach, the difficulties of proof of loss, and the inconvenience or nonfeasibility of otherwise obtaining an adequate remedy. A term fixing unreasonably large liquidated damages is void as a penalty. UCC § 2-718(1).

Mitigation of damages A plaintiff may not recover damages for the effects of an injury which she reasonably could have avoided or substantially ameliorated. This limitation on recovery is generally denominated as "mitigation of damages" or "avoidance of consequences."

Nominal damages A small sum awarded where a contract has been breached but the loss is negligible or unproven.

Out-of-pocket damages Difference between the value received and the value given.

Reliance damages Contract damages placing the injured party in as good a position as he would have been in had the contract not been made.

Treble damages Three times actual loss.

de facto In fact, in deed, actually. This phrase is used to characterize an officer, a government, a past action, or a state of affairs which must be accepted for all practical purposes but which is illegal or illegitimate. See also **corporation**, *corporation de facto*.

de jure Descriptive of a condition in which there has been total compliance with all requirements of law. In this sense it is the contrary of *de facto*. See also **corporation**, *corporation de jure*.

de novo Anew; afresh; a second time.

debenture Unsecured bond.

debt security Any form of corporate security reflected as debt on the books of the corporation in contrast to equity securities such as stock; e.g., bonds, notes, and debentures are debt securities.

debtor Person who owes payment or performance of an obligation.

deceit A fraudulent and cheating misrepresentation, artifice, or device used to deceive and trick one who is ignorant of the true facts, to the prejudice and damage of the party imposed upon. See also **fraud; misrepresentation.**

decree Decision of a court of equity.

deed A conveyance of realty; a writing, signed by a grantor, whereby title to realty is transferred from one party to another.

deed of trust Interest in real property which is conveyed to a third person as trustee for the creditor.

defamation Injury of a person's reputation by publication of false statements.

default judgment Judgment against a defendant who fails to respond to a complaint.

defendant The party against whom legal action is sought.

definite term Lease that automatically expires at end of the term.

delectus personae Partner's right to choose who may become a member of the partnership.

delegatee Third party to whom the delegator's duty is delegated.

delegation of duties Transferring to another all or part of one's duties arising under a contract.

delegator Party delegating his duty to a third party.

delivery The physical or constructive transfer of an instrument or of goods from one person to another. See also **constructive delivery.**

demand Request for payment made by the holder of the instrument.

demand paper Payable on request.

demurrer An allegation of a defendant that even if the facts as stated in the pleading to which objection is taken be true, their legal consequences are not such as to require the demurring party to answer them or to proceed further with the cause.

> The Federal Rules of Civil Procedure do not provide for the use of a demurrer, but provide an equivalent to a general demurrer in the motion to dismiss for failure to state a claim on which relief may be granted. Fed.R. Civil P. 12(b).

deposition The testimony of a witness taken upon interrogatories, not in court, but intended to be used in court. See also **discovery.**

depository bank The first bank to which an item is transferred for collection even though it may also be the payor bank. UCC § 4–105(a).

descent Succession to the ownership of an estate by inheritance or by any act of law, as distinguished from "purchase."

> Descents are of two sorts, lineal and collateral. Lineal descent is descent in a direct or right line, as from father or grandfather to son or grandson. Collateral descent is descent in a collateral or oblique line, that is, up to the common ancestor and then down from him, as from brother to brother, or between cousins.

design defect Plans or specifications inadequate to ensure the product's safety.

devise A testamentary disposition of land or realty; a gift of real property by the last will and testament of the donor. When used as a noun, means a testamentary disposition of real or personal property; when used as a verb, means to dispose of real or personal property by will.

dictum Generally used as an abbreviated form of *obiter dictum*, "a remark by the way"; that is, an observation or remark made by a judge which does not embody the resolution or determination of the court and which is made without argument or full consideration of the point.

directed verdict In a case in which the party with the burden of proof has failed to present a prima facie case for jury consideration, the trial judge may order the entry of a verdict without allowing the jury to consider it because, as a matter of law, there can be only one such verdict. Fed.R. Civil P. 50(a).

disaffirmance Avoidance of a contract.

discharge Termination of certain allowed claims against a debtor.

disclaimer Negation of warranty.

discount A discount by a bank means a drawback or deduction made upon its advances or loans of money, upon negotiable paper or other evidences of debt payable at a future day, which are transferred to the bank.

discovery The pretrial devices that can be used by one party to obtain facts and information about the case from the other party in order to assist the party's preparation for trial. Under the Federal Rules of Civil Procedure, tools of discovery include depositions upon oral and written questions, written interrogatories, production of documents or things, permission to enter upon land or other property, physical and mental examinations, and requests for admission. Rules 26–37.

dishonor To refuse to accept or pay a draft or to pay a promissory note when duly presented. UCC § 3–507(1); § 4–210. See also **protest.**

disparagement Publication of false statements resulting in harm to another's monetary interests.

disputed debt Obligation whose existence or amount is contested.

dissenting shareholder One who opposes a fundamental change and has the right to receive the fair value of her shares.

dissolution The dissolution of a partnership is the change in the relation of the partners caused by any partner's ceasing to be associated with the carrying on, as distinguished from the winding up, of the business. See also **winding up.**

distribution Transfer of partnership property from the partnership to a partner; transfer of property from a corporation to any of its shareholders.

dividend The payment designated by the board of directors of a corporation to be distributed pro rata among a class or classes of the shares outstanding.

document Document of title.

document of title Instrument evidencing ownership of the document and the goods it covers.

domicile That place where a person has his true, fixed, and permanent home and principal establishment, and to which whenever he is absent he has the intention of returning.

dominant Land whose owner has rights in other land.

donee Recipient of a gift.

donee beneficiary See **third-party beneficiary**.

donor Maker of a gift.

dormant partner One who is both a silent and a secret partner.

dower A species of life-estate which a woman is, by law, entitled to claim on the death of her husband, in the lands and tenements of which he was seised in fee during the marriage, and which her issue, if any, might by possibility have inherited.

> Dower has been abolished in the majority of the states and materially altered in most of the others.

draft A written order by the first party, called the drawer, instructing a second party, called the drawee (such as a bank), to pay a third party, called the payee. An order to pay a sum certain in money, signed by a drawer, payable on demand or at a definite time, and to order or bearer. UCC § 3–104.

drawee A person to whom a bill of exchange or draft is directed, and who is requested to pay the amount of money therein mentioned. The drawee of a check is the bank on which it is drawn.

> When a drawee accepts, he engages that he will pay the instrument according to its tenor at the time of his engagement or as completed. UCC § 3–413(1).

drawer The person who draws a bill or draft. The drawer of a check is the person who signs it.

> The drawer engages that upon dishonor of the draft and any necessary notice of dishonor or protest, he will pay the amount of the draft to the holder or to any indorser who takes it up. The drawer may disclaim this liability by drawing without recourse. UCC § 3–413(2).

due negotiation Transfer of a negotiable document in the regular course of business to a holder, who takes in good faith, without notice of any defense or claim, and for value.

duress Unlawful constraint exercised upon a person, whereby he is forced to do some act against his will.
  Physical duress Coercion involving physical force or the threat of physical force.

duty Legal obligation requiring a person to perform or refrain from performing an act.

E

earned surplus Undistributed net profits, income, gains, and losses.

earnest The payment of a part of the price of goods sold, or the delivery of part of such goods, for the purpose of binding the contract.

easement A right in the owner of one parcel of land, by reason of such ownership, to use the land of another for a special purpose not inconsistent with a general property right in the owner. This right is distinguishable from a "license," which merely confers a personal privilege to do some act on the land.

Affirmative easement One where the servient estate must permit something to be done thereon, as to pass over it, or to discharge water on it.

Appurtenant easement An incorporeal right which is attached to a superior right and inheres in land to which it is attached and is in the nature of a covenant running with the land.

Easement by necessity Such arises by operation of law when land conveyed is completely shut off from access to any road by land retained by the grantor or by land of the grantor and that of a stranger.

Easement by prescription A mode of acquiring title to property by immemorial or long-continued enjoyment; refers to personal usage restricted to claimant and his ancestors or grantors.

Easement in gross An easement in gross is not appurtenant to any estate in land or does not belong to any person by virtue of ownership of an estate in other land but is a mere personal interest in or a right to use the land of another; it is purely personal and usually ends with death of grantee.

Easement of access Right of ingress and egress to and from the premises of a lot owner to a street appurtenant to the land of the lot owner.

ejectment An action to determine whether the title to certain land is in the plaintiff or is in the defendant.

electronic funds transfer A transaction with a financial institution by means of computer, telephone, or other electronic instrument.

emancipation The act by which an infant is liberated from the control of a parent or guardian and made his own master.

embezzlement The taking, in violation of a trust, of the property of one's employer.

emergency Sudden, unexpected event calling for immediate action.

eminent domain Right of the people or government to take private property for public use upon giving fair consideration.

employment discrimination Hiring, firing, compensating, promoting, or training of employees based on race, color, sex, religion, or national origin.

employment relationship One in which employer has right to control the physical conduct of employee.

endowment contract Agreement to pay insured a lump sum upon reaching a specified age or in event of death.

entirety Used to designate that which the law considers as a single whole incapable of being divided into parts.

entrapment Induced by a government official into committing a crime.

entrusting Transfer of possession of goods to a merchant who deals in goods of that kind and who may in turn transfer valid title to a buyer in the ordinary course of business.

equal pay Equivalent pay for the same work.

equal protection Requirement that similarly situated persons be treated similarly by government action.

equipment Goods used primarily in business.

equitable Just, fair, and right. Existing in equity; available or sustainable only in equity, or only upon the rules and principles of equity.

equity Justice administered according to fairness, as contrasted with the strictly formulated rules of common law. It is based on a system of rules and principles which originated in England as an alternative to the harsh rules of common law and which were based on what was fair in a particular situation.

equity of redemption The right of the mortgagor of an estate to redeem the same after it has been forfeited, at law, by a breach of the condition of the mortgage, upon paying the amount of debt, interest, and costs.

equity securities Stock or similar security, in contrast to debt securities such as bonds, notes, and debentures.

error A mistake of law, or a false or irregular application of it, such as vitiates legal proceedings and warrants reversal of the judgment.

Harmless error In appellate practice, an error committed in the progress of the trial below which was not prejudicial to the rights of the party assigning it and for which, therefore, the appellate court will not reverse the judgment.

Reversible error In appellate practice, such an error as warrants the appellate court's reversal of the judgment before it.

escrow A system of document transfer in which a deed, bond, or funds is or are delivered to a third person to hold until all conditions in a contract are fulfilled; *e.g.*, delivery of deed to escrow agent under installment land sale contract until full payment for land is made.

estate The degree, quantity, nature, and extent of interest which a person has in real and personal property. An estate in lands, tenements, and hereditaments signifies such interest as the tenant has therein.

Also, the total property of whatever kind that is owned by a decedent prior to the distribution of that property in accordance with the terms of a will or, when there is no will, by the laws of inheritance in the state of domicile of the decedent.

Future estate An estate limited to commence in possession at a future day, either without the intervention of a precedent estate or on the determination by lapse of time, or otherwise, of a precedent estate created at the same time. Examples include reversions and remainders.

estoppel A bar or impediment raised by the law which precludes a person from alleging or from denying a certain fact or state of facts, in consequence of his or her previous allegation, denial, conduct, or admission, or in consequence of a final adjudication of the matter in a court of law. See also **waiver**.

eviction Dispossession by process of law; the act of depriving a person of the possession of lands which he has held, pursuant to the judgment of a court.

evidence Any species of proof or probative matter legally presented at the trial of an issue by the act of the parties and through the medium of witnesses, records, documents, concrete objects, etc., for the purpose of inducing belief in the minds of the court or jury as to the parties' contention.

exception A formal objection to the action of the court, during the trial of a cause, in refusing a request or overruling an objection; implying that the party excepting does not acquiesce in the decision of the court but will seek to procure its reversal, and that he means to save the benefit of his request or objection in some future proceeding.

exclusionary rule Prohibition of illegally obtained evidence.

exclusive dealing Sole right to sell goods in a defined market.

exclusive jurisdiction Such jurisdiction that permits only one court (state or federal) to hear a case.

exculpatory clause Excusing oneself from fault or liability.

execution *Execution of contract* includes performance of all acts necessary to render it complete as an instrument; implies that nothing more need be done to make the contract complete and effective.

Execution upon a money judgment is the legal process of enforcing the judgment, usually by seizing and selling property of the debtor.

executive order Legislation issued by the president or a governor.

executor A person appointed by a testator to carry out the directions and requests in his will and to dispose of the property according to his testamentary provisions after his decease. The female designation is executrix. A person appointed by the court in an intestacy situation is called the administrator(rix).

executory That which is yet to be executed or performed; that which remains to be carried into operation or effect; incomplete; depending upon a future performance or event. The opposite of executed.

executory contract See **contracts**.

executory promise Unperformed obligation.

exemplary damages See **damages**.

exoneration Relieved of liability.

express Manifested by direct and appropriate language, as distinguished from that which is inferred from conduct. The word is usually contrasted with "implied."

express warranty Explicitly made contractual promise regarding property or contract rights transferred; in a sale of goods, an affirmation of fact or a promise about the goods or a description, including a sample, of goods which becomes part of the basis of the bargain.

expropriation Governmental taking of foreign-owned property for a public purpose and with payment.

ex-ship Risk of loss passes to buyer when the goods leave the ship. See UCC § 2–322. See also **F.A.S.**

extortion Making threats to obtain property.

F

fact An event that took place or a thing that exists.

false imprisonment Intentional interference with a person's freedom of movement by unlawful confinement.

false light Offensive publicity placing another in a false light.

false pretenses Intentional misrepresentation of fact in order to cheat another.

farm products Crops, livestock, or stock used or produced in farming.

F.A.S. Free alongside. Term used in sales price quotations indicating that the price includes all costs of transportation and delivery of the goods alongside the ship. See UCC § 2–319(2).

federal preemption First right of the federal government to regulate matters within its powers to the possible exclusion of state regulation.

federal question Any case arising under the Constitution, statutes, or treaties of the United States.

fee simple

Absolute A fee simple absolute is an estate that is unlimited as to duration, disposition, and descendibility. It is the largest estate and most extensive interest that can be enjoyed in land.

Conditional Type of transfer in which grantor conveys fee simple on condition that something be done or not done.

Defeasible Type of fee grant which may be defeated on the happening of an event. An estate which may last forever, but which may end upon the happening of a specified event, is a "fee simple defeasible."

Determinable Created by conveyance which contains words effective to create a fee simple and, in addition, a provision for automatic expiration of the estate on occurrence of stated event.

fee tail An estate of inheritance, descending only to a certain class or classes of heirs; *e.g.*, an estate is conveyed or devised "to A. and the heirs of his body," or "to A. and the heirs male of his body," or "to A., and the heirs female of his body."

fellow servant rule Common law defense relieving employer from liability to an employee for injuries caused by negligence of fellow employee.

felony Serious crime.

fiduciary A person or institution who manages money or property for another and who must exercise in such management activity a standard of care imposed by law or contract; *e.g.*, executor of estate; receiver in bankruptcy; trustee.

fiduciary duty Duty of utmost loyalty and good faith, such as that owed by a fiduciary such as an agent to her principal.

field warehouse Secured party takes possession of the goods but the debtor has access to the goods.

final credit Payment of the instrument by the payor bank.

financing statement Under the Uniform Commercial Code, a financing statement is used under Article 9 to reflect a public record that there is a security interest or claim to the goods in question to secure a debt. The financing statement is filed by the security holder with the secretary of state or with a similar public body; thus filed, it becomes public record. See also **secured transaction**.

fire (property) insurance Provides protection against loss due to fire or other related perils.

firm offer Irrevocable offer to sell or buy goods by a merchant in a signed writing which gives assurance that it will not be rescinded for up to three months.

fitness for a particular purpose Goods are fit for a stated purpose, provided that the seller selects the product knowing the buyer's intended use and that the buyer is relying on the seller's judgment.

fixture An article in the nature of personal property which has been so annexed to realty that it is regarded as a part of the land. Examples include a furnace affixed to a house or other building, counters permanently affixed to the floor of a store, and a sprinkler system installed in a building. UCC § 9–313(1)(a).

Trade fixtures Such chattels as merchants usually possess and annex to the premises occupied by them to enable them to store, handle,

and display their goods, which generally are removable without material injury to the premises.

F.O.B. Free on board at some location (for example, F.O.B shipping point; F.O.B destination); the invoice price includes delivery at seller's expense to that location. Title to goods usually passes from seller to buyer at the F.O.B location. UCC § 2–319(1).

foreclosure Procedure by which mortgaged property is sold on default of mortgagor in satisfaction of mortgage debt.

forgery Intentional falsification of a document with intent to defraud.

four unities Time, title, interest, and possession.

franchise A privilege granted or sold, such as to use a name or to sell products or services. The right given by a manufacturer or supplier to a retailer to use his products and name on terms and conditions mutually agreed upon.

fraud Elements include false representation; of a present or past fact; made by defendant; action in reliance thereon by plaintiff; and damage resulting to plaintiff from such misrepresentation.

fraud in the execution Misrepresentation that deceives the other party as to the nature of a document evidencing the contract.

fraud in the inducement Misrepresentation regarding the subject matter of a contract that induces the other party to enter into the contract.

fraudulent misrepresentation False statement made with knowledge of its falsity and intent to mislead.

freehold An estate for life or in fee. It must possess two qualities: (1) immobility, that is, the property must be either land or some interest issuing out of or annexed to land; and (2) indeterminate duration.

friendly fire Fire contained where it is intended to be.

frustration of purpose doctrine Excuses a promisor in certain situations when the objectives of contract have been utterly defeated by circumstances arising after formation of the agreement, and performance is excused under this rule even though there is no impediment to actual performance.

full warranty One under which warrantor will repair the product and, if unsuccessful, will replace it or refund its cost.

fungibles With respect to goods or securities, those of which any unit is, by nature or usage of trade, the equivalent of any other like unit. UCC § 1–201(17); *e.g.*, a bushel of wheat or other grain.

future estate See **estate**.

G

garnishment A statutory proceeding whereby a person's property, money, or credits in the possession or control of another are applied to payment of the former's debt to a third person.

general intangible Catchall category for collateral not otherwise covered.

general partner Member of either a general or limited partnership with unlimited liability for its debts, full management powers, and a right to share in the profits.

gift A voluntary transfer of property to another made gratuitously and without consideration. Essential requisites of "gift" are capacity of donor, intention of donor to make gift, completed delivery to or for donee, and acceptance of gift by donee.

gift causa mortis A gift in view of death is one which is made in contemplation, fear, or peril of death and with the intent that it shall take effect only in case of the death of the giver.

good faith Honesty in fact and the observance of reasonable commercial standards of fair dealing.

good faith purchaser Buyer who acts honestly, gives value, and takes the goods without notice or knowledge of any defect in the title of his transferor.

goods A term of variable content and meaning. It may include every species of personal property, or it may be given a very restricted meaning. Sometimes the meaning of "goods" is extended to include all tangible items, as in the phrase "goods and services."

All things (including specially manufactured goods) which are movable at the time of identification to a contract for sale other than the money in which the price is to be paid, investment securities, and things in action. UCC § 2–105(1).

grantee Transferee of property.

grantor A transferor of property. The creator of a trust is usually designated as the grantor of the trust.

gratuitous promise Promise made without consideration.

group insurance Covers a number of individuals.

guaranty A promise to answer for the payment of some debt, or the performance of some duty, in case of the failure of another person who, in the first instance, is liable for such payment or performance.

The terms *guaranty* and *suretyship* are sometimes used interchangeably; but they should not be confounded. The distinction between contract of suretyship and contract of guaranty is whether or not the undertaking is a joint undertaking with the principal or a separate and distinct contract; if it is the former, it is one of "suretyship," and if the latter, it is one of "guaranty." See also **surety**.

guardianship The relationship under which a person (the guardian) is appointed by a court to preserve and control the property of another (the ward).

H

heir A person who succeeds, by the rules of law, to an estate in lands, tenements, or hereditaments, upon the death of his ancestor, by descent and right of relationship.

holder Person who is in possession of a document of title or an instrument or an investment security drawn, issued, or indorsed to him or to his order, or to bearer, or in blank. UCC § 1-201(20).

holder in due course A holder who takes an instrument for value, in good faith, and without notice that it is overdue or has been dishonored or of any defense against or claim to it on the part of any person.

holograph A will or deed written entirely by the testator or grantor with his own hand and not witnessed (attested). State laws vary with respect to the validity of the holographic will.

homicide Unlawful taking of another's life.

horizontal privity Who may bring a cause of action.

horizontal restraints Agreements among competitors.

hostile fire Any fire outside its intended or usual place.

I

identified goods Designated goods as a part of a particular contract.

illegal per se Conclusively presumed unreasonable and therefore illegal.

illusory promise Promise imposing no obligation on the promisor.

implied-in-fact condition Contingencies understood but not expressed by the parties.

implied-in-law condition Contingency that arises from operation of law.

implied warranty Obligation imposed by law upon the transferor of property or contract rights; implicit in the sale arising out of certain circumstances.

implied warranty of habitability Leased premises are fit for ordinary residential purposes.

impossibility Performance that cannot be done.

in personam Against the person. Action seeking judgment against a person involving his personal rights and based on jurisdiction of his person, as distinguished from a judgment against property (i.e., in rem).

in personam jurisdiction Jurisdiction based on claims against a person, in contrast to jurisdiction over his property.

in re In the affair; in the matter of; concerning; regarding. This is the usual method of entitling a judicial proceeding in which there are no adversary parties, but merely some res concerning which judicial action is to be taken, such as a bankrupt's estate, an estate in the probate court, a proposed public highway, etc.

in rem A technical term used to designate proceedings or actions instituted *against the thing*, in contradistinction to personal actions, which are said to be *in personam*.

Quasi in rem A term applied to proceedings which are not strictly and purely *in rem*, but are brought against the defendant personally, though the real object is to deal with particular property or subject property to the discharge of claims asserted; for example, foreign attachment, or proceedings to foreclose a mortgage, remove a cloud from title, or effect a partition.

in rem jurisdiction Jurisdiction based on claims against property.

incidental beneficiary Third party whom the two parties to a contract have no intention of benefiting by their contract.

income bond Bond that conditions payment of interest on corporate earnings.

incontestability clause The prohibition of an insurer to avoid an insurance policy after a specified period of time.

indemnification Duty owed by principal to agent to pay agent for losses incurred while acting as directed by principal.

indemnify To reimburse one for a loss already incurred.

indenture A written agreement under which bonds and debentures are issued, setting forth maturity date, interest rate, and other terms.

independent contractor Person who contracts with another to do a particular job and who is not subject to the control of the other.

indicia Signs; indications. Circumstances which point to the existence of a given fact as probable, but not certain.

indictment Grand jury charge that the defendant should stand trial.

indispensable paper Chattel paper, instruments, and documents.

indorsee The person to whom a negotiable instrument, promissory note, bill of lading, etc., is assigned by indorsement.

indorsement The act of a payee, drawee, accommodation indorser, or holder of a bill, note, check, or other negotiable instrument, in writing his name upon the back of the same, with or without further or qualifying words, whereby the property in the same is assigned and transferred to another. UCC § 3-202 *et seq.*

Blank indorsement No indorsee is specified.

Qualified indorsement Without recourse, limiting one's liability on the instrument.

Restrictive indorsement Limits the rights of the indorser in some manner.

Special indorsement Designates an indorsee to be paid.

infliction of emotional distress Extreme and outrageous conduct intentionally or recklessly causing severe emotional distress.

information Formal accusation of a crime brought by a prosecutor.

infringement Unauthorized use.

injunction An equitable remedy forbidding the party defendant from doing some act which he is threatening or attempting to commit, or restraining him in the continuance thereof, such act being unjust and inequitable, injurious to the plaintiff, and not such as can be adequately redressed by an action at law.

innkeeper Hotel or motel operator.

inquisitorial system System in which the judiciary initiates, conducts, and decides cases.

insider Relative or general partner of debtor, partnership in which debtor is a partner, or corporation in which debtor is an officer, director, or controlling person.

insiders Directors, officers, employees, and agents of the issuer as well as those the issuer has entrusted with information solely for corporate purposes.

insolvency Under the UCC, a person is insolvent who either has ceased to pay his debts in the ordinary course of business or cannot pay his debts as they fall due or is insolvent within the meaning of the Federal Bankruptcy Law. UCC § 1-201(23).

Insolvency (bankruptcy) Total liabilities exceed total value of assets.

Insolvency (equity) Inability to pay debts in ordinary course of business or as they become due.

inspection Examination of goods to determine whether they conform to a contract.

instrument Negotiable instruments, stocks, bonds, and other investment securities.

insurable interest Exists where insured derives pecuniary benefit or advantage by preservation and continued existence of property or would sustain pecuniary loss from its destruction.

insurance A contract whereby, for a stipulated consideration, one party undertakes to compensate the other for loss on a specified subject by specified perils. The party agreeing to make the compensation is usually called the "insurer" or "underwriter"; the other, the "insured" or "assured"; the written contract, a "policy"; the events insured against, "risks" or "perils"; and the subject, right, or interest to be protected, the "insurable interest." Insurance is a contract whereby one undertakes to indemnify another against loss, damage, or liability arising from an unknown or contingent event.

Co-insurance A form of insurance in which a person insures property for less than its full or stated value and agrees to share the risk of loss.

Life insurance Payment of a specific sum of money to a designated beneficiary upon the death of the insured.

Ordinary life Life insurance with a savings component that runs for the life of the insured.

Term life Life insurance issued for a limited number of years that does not have a savings component.

intangible property Protected interests that are not physical.

intangibles Accounts and general intangibles.

intent Desire to cause the consequences of an act or knowledge that the consequences are substantially certain to result from the act.

inter alia Among other things.

inter se or inter sese Latin. Among or between themselves; used to distinguish rights or duties between two or more parties from their rights or duties to others.

interest in land Any right, privilege, power, or immunity in real property.

interest in partnership Partner's share in the partnership's profits and surplus.

interference with contractual relations Intentionally causing one of the parties to a contract not to perform the contract.

intermediary bank Any bank, except the depositary or payor bank, to which an item is transferred in the course of collection. UCC § 4–105(c).

intermediate test Requirement that legislation have a substantial relationship to an important governmental objective.

international law Deals with the conduct and relations of nation-states and international organizations.

interpretation Construction or meaning of a contract.

interpretative rules Statements issued by an administrative agency indicating its construction of its governing statute.

intestate A person is said to die intestate when he dies without making a will. The word is also often used to signify the person himself. *Compare* **testator**.

intrusion Unreasonable and highly offensive interference with the seclusion of another.

inventory Goods held for sale or lease or consumed in a business.

invitee A person is an "invitee" on land of another if (1) he enters by invitation, express or implied, (2) his entry is connected with the owner's business or with an activity the owner conducts or permits to be conducted on his land, and (3) there is mutual benefit or a benefit to the owner.

J

joint liability Liability where creditor must sue all of the partners as a group.

joint and several liability Liability where creditor may sue partners jointly as a group or separately as individuals.

joint stock company A general partnership with some corporate attributes.

joint tenancy See **tenancy**.

joint venture An association of two or more persons to carry on a single business transaction for profit.

judgment The official and authentic decision of a court of justice upon the respective rights and claims of the parties to an action or suit therein litigated and submitted to its determination.

judgment in personam A judgment against a particular person, as distinguished from a judgment against a thing or a right or *status*.

judgment in rem An adjudication pronounced upon the status of some particular thing or subject matter, by a tribunal having competent authority.

judgment n. o. v. Judgment non obstante veredicto in its broadest sense is a judgment rendered in favor of one party notwithstanding the finding of a verdict in favor of the other party.

judgment notwithstanding the verdict A final binding determination on the merits made by the judge after and contrary to the jury's verdict.

judgment on the pleadings Final binding determination on the merits made by the judge after the pleadings.

judicial lien Interest in property that is obtained by court action to secure payment of a debt.

judicial review Power of the courts to determine the constitutionality of legislative and executive acts.

jurisdiction The right and power of a court to adjudicate concerning the subject matter in a given case.

jurisdiction over the parties Power of a court to bind the parties to a suit.

jury A body of persons selected and summoned by law and sworn to try the facts of a case and to find according to the law and the evidence. In general, the province of the jury is to find the facts in a case, while the judge passes upon pure questions of law. As a matter of fact, however, the jury must often pass upon mixed questions of law and fact in determining the case, and in all such cases the instructions of the judge as to the law become very important.

justifiable reliance Reasonably influenced by a misrepresentation.

L

labor dispute Any controversy concerning terms or conditions of employment or union representation.

laches Based upon the maxim that equity aids the vigilant and not those who slumber on their rights. It is defined as neglect to assert a right or claim which, taken together with a lapse of time and other circumstances causing prejudice to the adverse party, operates as a bar in a court of equity.

landlord The owner of an estate in land, or a rental property, who has leased it to another person, called the "tenant." Also called "lessor."

larceny Trespassory taking and carrying away of the goods of another with the intent to permanently deprive.

last clear chance Final opportunity to avoid an injury.

lease Any agreement which gives rise to relationship of landlord and tenant (real property) or lessor and lessee (real or personal property). The person who conveys is termed the "lessor," and the person to whom conveyed, the "lessee"; and when the lessor conveys land or tenements to a lessee, he is said to lease, demise, or let them.

Sublease, or *underlease* One executed by the lessee of an estate to a third person, conveying the same estate for a shorter term than that for which the lessee holds it.

leasehold An estate in realty held under a lease. The four principal types of leasehold estates are the estate for years, periodic tenancy, tenancy at will, and tenancy at sufferance.

leasehold estate Right to possess real property.

legacy "Legacy" is a gift or bequest by will of personal property, whereas a "devise" is a testamentary disposition of real estate.

Demonstrative legacy A bequest of a certain sum of money, with a direction that it shall be paid out of a particular fund. It differs from a specific legacy in this respect: that, if the fund out of which it is payable fails for any cause, it is nevertheless entitled to come on the estate as a general legacy. And it differs from a general legacy in this: that it does not abate in that class, but in the class of specific legacies.

General legacy A pecuniary legacy, payable out of the general assets of a testator.

Residuary legacy A bequest of all the testator's personal estate not otherwise effectually disposed of by his will.

Specific legacy One which operates on property particularly designated. A legacy or gift by will of a particular specified thing, as of a horse, a piece of furniture, a term of years, and the like.

legal aggregate A group of individuals not having a legal existence separate from its members.

legal benefit Obtaining something to which one had no legal right.

legal detriment Doing an act one is not legally obligated to do or not doing an act one has a legal right to do.

legal entity An organization having a legal existence separate from that of its members.

legal sufficiency Benefit to promisor or detriment to promisee.

legislative rules Substantive rules issued by an administrative agency under the authority delegated to it by the legislature.

letter of credit An engagement by a bank or other person made at the request of a customer that the issuer will honor drafts or other demands for payment upon compliance with the conditions specified in the credit.

letters of administration Formal documents issued by probate court appointing one an administrator of an estate.

letters testamentary The formal instrument of authority and appointment given to an executor by the proper court, empowering him to enter upon the discharge of his office as executor. It corresponds to letters of administration granted to an administrator.

levy To assess; raise; execute; exact; tax; collect; gather; take up; seize. Thus, to levy (assess, exact, raise, or collect) a tax; to levy an execution, *i.e.*, to levy or collect a sum of money on an execution.

liability insurance Covers liability to others by reason of damage resulting from injuries to another's person or property.

liability without fault Crime to do a specific act or cause a certain result without regard to the care exercised.

libel Defamation communicated by writing, television, radio, or the like.

liberty Ability of individuals to engage in freedom of action and choice regarding their personal lives.

license License with respect to real property is a privilege to go on premises for a certain purpose, but does not operate to confer on or vest in the licensee any title, interest, or estate in such property.

licensee Person privileged to enter or remain on land by virtue of the consent of the lawful possessor.

lien A qualified right of property which a creditor has in or over specific property of his debtor, as security for the debt or charge or for performance of some act.

lien creditor A creditor who has acquired a lien on the property by attachment.

life estate An estate whose duration is limited to the life of the party holding it or of some other person. Upon the death of the life tenant, the property will go to the holder of the remainder interest or to the grantor by reversion.

limited liability Liability limited to amount invested in a business enterprise.

limited partner Member of a limited partnership with liability for its debts only to the extent of her capital contribution.

limited partnership See **partnership.**

limited partnership association A partnership which closely resembles a corporation.

liquidated Ascertained; determined; fixed; settled; made clear or manifest. Cleared away; paid; discharged.

liquidated damages See **damages.**

liquidated debt Obligation that is certain in amount.

liquidation The settling of financial affairs of a business or individual, usually by liquidating (turning to cash) all assets for distribution to creditors, heirs, etc. To be distinguished from dissolution.

loss of value Value of promised performance minus value of actual performance.

lost property Property with which the owner has involuntarily parted and which she does not know where to find or recover, not including property which she has intentionally concealed or deposited in a secret place for safekeeping. Distinguishable from mislaid property, which has been deliberately placed somewhere and forgotten.

M

main purpose rule Where object of promisor/surety is to provide an economic benefit for herself, the promise is considered outside of the statute of frauds.

maker One who makes or executes; as the maker of a promissory note. One who signs a check; in this context, synonymous with drawer. See **draft.**

mala in se Morally wrong.

mala prohibita Wrong by law.

mandamus Latin, we command. A legal writ compelling the defendant to do an official duty.

manslaughter Unlawful taking of another's life without malice.

Involuntary manslaughter Taking the life of another by criminal negligence or during the course of a misdemeanor.

Voluntary manslaughter Intentional killing of another under extenuating circumstances.

manufacturing defect Not produced according to specifications.

mark Trade symbol.

market allocations Division of market by customers, geographic location, or products.

marketable title Free from any defects, encumbrances, or reasonable objections to one's ownership.

marshaling of assets Segregating the assets and liabilities of a partnership from the assets and liabilities of the individual partners.

master See **principal.**

material Matters to which a reasonable investor would attach importance in deciding whether to purchase a security.

material alteration Any change that changes the contract of any party to an instrument.

maturity The date at which an obligation, such as the principal of a bond or a note, becomes due.

maxim A general legal principle.

mechanic's lien A claim created by state statutes for the purpose of securing priority of payment of the price or value of work performed and materials furnished in erecting or repairing a building or other structure; as such, attaches to the land as well as buildings and improvements erected thereon.

mediation Nonbinding process in which a third party acts as an intermediary between the disputing parties and proposes solutions for them to consider.

mens rea Criminal intent.

mentally incompetent Unable to understand the nature and effect of one's acts.

mercantile law An expression substantially equivalent to commercial law. It designates the system of rules, customs, and usages generally recognized and adopted by merchants and traders that, either in its simplicity or as modified by common law or statutes, constitutes the law for the regulation of their transactions and the solution of their controversies. The Uniform Commercial Code is the general body of law governing commercial or mercantile transactions.

merchant A person who deals in goods of the kind involved in a transaction or who otherwise by his occupation holds himself out as having knowledge or skill peculiar to the practices or goods involved in the transaction or to whom such knowledge or skill may be attributed by his employment of an agent or broker or other intermediary who by his occupation holds himself out as having such knowledge or skill. UCC § 2-104(1).

merchantability Merchant seller guarantees that the goods are fit for their ordinary purpose.

merger The fusion or absorption of one thing or right into another. In corporate law, the absorption of one company by another, the latter retaining its own name and identity and acquiring the assets, liabilities, franchises, and powers of the former, which ceases to exist as separate business entity. It differs from a consolidation, wherein all the corporations terminate their separate existences and become parties to a new one.

Conglomerate merger An acquisition, which is not horizontal or vertical, by one company of another.

Horizontal merger Merger between business competitors, such as manufacturers of the same type of products or distributors selling competing products in the same market area.

Short-form merger Merger of a 90 percent subsidiary into its parent.

Vertical merger Union with corporate customer or supplier.

midnight deadline Midnight of the next banking day after receiving an item.

mining partnership A specific type of partnership for the purpose of extracting raw minerals.

minor Under the age of legal majority (usually eighteen).

mirror image rule An acceptance cannot deviate from the terms of the offer.

misdemeanor Less serious crime.

mislaid property Property which an owner has put deliberately in a certain place that she is unable to remember, as distinguished from lost property, which the owner has left unwittingly in a location she has forgotten. See also **lost property**.

misrepresentation Any manifestation by words or other conduct by one person to another that, under the circumstances, amounts to an assertion not in accordance with the facts. A "misrepresentation" that justifies the rescission of a contract is a false statement of a substantive fact, or any conduct which leads to a belief of a substantive fact material to proper understanding of the matter in hand. See also **deceit; fraud**.

Fraudulent misrepresentation False statement made with knowledge of its falsity and intent to mislead.

Innocent misrepresentation Misrepresentation made without knowledge of its falsity but with due care.

Negligent misrepresentation Misrepresentation made without due care in ascertaining its falsity.

M'Naughten Rule Right/wrong test for criminal insanity.

modify Change the lower court's judgment.

money Medium of exchange issued by a government body.

monopoly Ability to control price or exclude others from the marketplace.

mortgage A mortgage is an interest in land created by a written instrument providing security for the performance of a duty or the payment of a debt.

mortgagor Debtor who uses real estate to secure an obligation.

multinational enterprise Business that engages in transactions involving the movement of goods, information, money, people, or services across national borders.

multiple product order Order requiring an advertiser to cease and desist from deceptive statements on all products it sells.

murder Unlawful and premeditated taking of another's life.

mutual mistake Where the common but erroneous belief of both parties forms the basis of a contract.

N

necessaries Items needed to maintain a person's station in life.

negligence The omission to do something which a reasonable person, guided by those ordinary considerations which ordinarily regulate human affairs, would do, or the doing of something which a reasonable and prudent person would not do.

Culpable negligence Greater than ordinary negligence but less than gross negligence.

negligence per se Conclusive on the issue of negligence (duty of care and breach).

negotiable Legally capable of being transferred by indorsement or delivery. Usually said of checks and notes and sometimes of stocks and bearer bonds.

negotiable instrument Signed document (such as a check or promissory note) containing an unconditional promise to pay a "sum certain" of money at a definite time to order or bearer.

negotiation Transferee becomes a holder.

net assets Total assets minus total debts.

no arrival, no sale A destination contract, but if goods do not arrive, seller is excused from liability unless such is due to the seller's fault.

no-fault insurance Compensates victims of automobile accidents regardless of fault.

nonconforming use Preexisting use not in accordance with a zoning ordinance.

nonprofit corporation One whose profits must be used exclusively for the charitable, educational, or scientific purpose for which it was formed.

nonsuit Action in form of a judgment taken against a plaintiff who has failed to appear to prosecute his action or failed to prove his case.

note See **promissory note**.

novation A novation substitutes a new party and discharges one of the original parties to a contract by agreement of all three parties. A new contract is created with the same terms as the original one; only the parties have changed.

nuisance Nuisance is that activity which arises from the unreasonable, unwarranted, or unlawful use by a person of his own property, working obstruction or injury to the right of another or to the public, and producing such material annoyance, inconvenience, and discomfort that law will presume resulting damage.

O

obiter dictum See **dictum**.

objective fault Gross deviation from reasonable conduct.

objective manifestation What a reasonable person under the circumstances would believe.

objective satisfaction Approval based upon whether a reasonable person would be satisfied.

objective standard What a reasonable person under the circumstances would reasonably believe or do.

obligee Party to whom a duty of performance is owed (by delegator and delegatee).

obligor Party owing a duty (to the assignor).

offer A manifestation of willingness to enter into a bargain, so made as to justify another person in understanding that his assent to that bargain is invited and will conclude it. Restatement, Second, Contracts, § 24.

offeree Recipient of the offer.

offeror Person making the offer.

open-ended credit Credit arrangement under which debtor has rights to enter into a series of credit transactions.

opinion Belief in the existence of a fact or a judgment as to value.

option Contract providing that an offer will stay open for a specified period of time.

order A final disposition made by an agency.

order paper Payable to a named person or to anyone designated by that person.

order to pay Direction or command to pay.

original promise Promise to become primarily liable.

output contract See **contracts**.

P

palpable unilateral mistake Erroneous belief by one party that is recognized by the other.

parent corporation Corporation which controls another corporation.

parol evidence Literally oral evidence, but now includes prior to and contemporaneous, oral, and written evidence.

parol evidence rule Under this rule, when parties put their agreement in writing, all previous oral agreements merge in the writing and the contract as written cannot be modified or changed by parol evidence, in the absence of a plea of mistake or fraud in the preparation of the writing. But the rule does not forbid a resort to parol evidence not inconsistent with the matters stated in the writing. Also, as regards sales of goods, such written agreement may be explained or supplemented by course of dealing, usage of trade, or course of conduct, and by evidence of consistent additional terms, unless the court finds the writing to have been intended also as a complete and exclusive statement of the terms of the agreement. UCC § 2–202.

part performance In order to establish part performance taking an oral contract for the sale of realty out of the statute of frauds, the acts relied upon as part performance must be of such a character that they reasonably can be naturally accounted for in no other way than that they were performed in pursuance of the contract, and they must be in conformity with its provisions. See UCC § 2–201(3).

partial assignment Transfer of a portion of contractual rights to one or more assignees.

partition The dividing of lands held by joint tenants, copartners, or tenants in common into distinct portions, so that the parties may hold those lands in severalty.

partnership An association of two or more persons to carry on, as co-owners, a business for profit.

Partnerships are treated as a conduit and are, therefore, not subject to taxation. The various items of partnership income (gains and losses, etc.) flow through to the individual partners and are reported on their personal income tax returns.

Limited partnership Type of partnership comprised of one or more general partners who manage business and who are personally liable for partnership debts, and one or more limited partners who contribute capital and share in profits but who take no part in running business and incur no liability with respect to partnership obligations beyond contribution.

Partnership at will One with no definite term or specific undertaking.

partnership capital Total money and property contributed by partners for permanent use by the partnership.

partnership property Sum of all of the partnership's assets.

past consideration An act done before the contract is made.

patent Exclusive right to an invention.

payee The person in whose favor a bill of exchange, promissory note, or check is made or drawn.

payer or payor One who pays or who is to make a payment, particularly the person who is to make payment of a check, bill, or note. Correlative to "payee."

payor bank A bank by which an item is payable as drawn or accepted. UCC § 4–105(b). Correlative to "Drawee bank."

per capita This term, derived from the civil law and much used in the law of descent and distribution, denotes that method of dividing an intestate estate by which an equal share is given to each of a number of persons, all of whom stand in equal degree to the decedent, without reference to their stocks or the right of representation. The opposite of *per stirpes*.

per stirpes This term, derived from the civil law and much used in the law of descent and distribution, denotes that method of dividing an intestate estate where a class or group of distributees takes the share to which its deceased would have been entitled, taking thus by its right of representing such ancestor and not as so many individuals. The opposite of *per capita*.

perfect tender rule Seller's tender of delivery must conform exactly to the contract.

perfection of security interest Acts required of a secured party in the way of giving at least constructive notice so as to make his security interest effective at least against lien creditors of the debtor. See UCC §§ 9–302 through 9–306. In most cases, the secured party may obtain perfection either by filing with the secretary of state or by taking possession of the collateral.

performance Fulfillment of one's contractual obligations. See also **part performance; specific performance.**

periodic tenancy Lease with a definite term that is to be continued.

personal defenses Contractual defenses which are good against holders but not holders in due course.

personal property Any property other than an interest in land.

petty crime Misdemeanor punishable by imprisonment of six months or less.

plaintiff The party who initiates a civil suit.

pleadings The formal allegations by the parties of their respective claims and defenses.

Rules or codes of civil procedure Unlike the rigid technical system of common law pleading, pleadings under federal and state rules or codes of civil procedure have a far more limited function, with determination and narrowing of facts and issues being left to discovery devices and pretrial conferences. In addition, the rules and codes permit liberal amendment and supplementation of pleadings.

Under rules of civil procedure, the pleadings consist of a complaint, an answer, a reply to a counterclaim, an answer to a cross-claim, a third-party complaint, and a third-party answer.

pledge A bailment of goods to a creditor as security for some debt or engagement.

Much of the law of pledges has been replaced by the provisions for secured transactions in Article 9 of the UCC.

possibility of reverter The interest which remains in a grantor or testator after the conveyance or devise of a fee simple determinable and which permits the grantor to be revested automatically of his estate on breach of the condition.

possibility test Under the statute of frauds, asks whether performance could possibly be completed within one year.

power of appointment A power of authority conferred by one person by deed or will upon another (called the "donee") to appoint, that is, to select and nominate, the person or persons who is or are to receive and enjoy an estate or an income therefrom or from a fund, after the testator's death, or the donee's death, or after the termination of an existing right or interest.

power of attorney An instrument authorizing a person to act as the agent or attorney of the person granting it.

power of termination The interest left in the grantor or testator after the conveyance or devise of a fee simple on condition subsequent or conditional fee.

precatory Expressing a wish.

precedent An adjudged case or decision of a court, considered as furnishing an example or authority for an identical or similar case afterwards arising or a similar question of law. See also **stare decisis**.

preemptive right The privilege of a stockholder to maintain a proportionate share of ownership by purchasing a proportionate share of any new stock issues.

preference The act of an insolvent debtor who, in distributing his property or in assigning it for the benefit of his creditors, pays or secures to one or more creditors the full amount of their claims or a larger amount than they would be entitled to receive on a *pro rata* distribution. The treatment of such preferential payments in bankruptcy is governed by the Bankruptcy Act, § 547.

preliminary hearing Determines whether there is probable cause.

premium The price for insurance protection for a specified period of exposure.

preponderance of the evidence Greater weight of the evidence; standard used in civil cases.

prescription Acquisition of a personal right to use a way, water, light, and air by reason of continuous usage. See also **easement**.

presenter's warranty Warranty given to any payor or acceptor of an instrument.

presentment The production of a negotiable instrument to the drawee for his acceptance, or to the drawer or acceptor for payment; or of a promissory note to the party liable, for payment of the same. UCC § 3–504(1).

presumption A presumption is a rule of law, statutory or judicial, by which a finding of a basic fact gives rise to the existence of presumed fact, until presumption is rebutted. A presumption imposes on the party against whom it is directed the burden of going forward with evidence to rebut or meet the presumption, but does not shift to such party the burden of proof in the sense of the risk of nonpersuasion, which remains throughout the trial upon the party on whom it was originally cast.

price discrimination Price differential.

price fixing Any agreement for the purpose and effect of raising, depressing, fixing, pegging, or stabilizing prices.

prima facie Latin. At first sight; on the first appearance; on the face of it; so far as can be judged from the first disclosure; presumably; a fact presumed to be true unless disproved by some evidence to the contrary.

primary liability Absolute obligation to pay a negotiable instrument.

principal *Law of agency* The term "principal" describes one who has permitted or directed another (*i.e.*, an agent or a servant) to act for his benefit and subject to his direction and control. Principal includes in its meaning the term "master" or employer, a species of principal who, in addition to other control, has a right to control the physical conduct of the species of agents known as servants or employees, as to whom special rules are applicable with reference to harm caused by their physical acts.

Disclosed principal One whose existence and identity are known.

Partially disclosed principal One whose existence is known but whose identity is not known.

Undisclosed principal One whose existence and identity are not known.

principal debtor Person whose debt is being supported by a surety.

priority Precedence in order of right.

private carrier Carrier which limits its service and is not open to the general public.

private corporation One organized to conduct either a privately owned business enterprise for profit or a nonprofit corporation.

private law The law involving relationships among individuals and legal entities.

privilege Immunity from tort liability.

privity Contractual relationship.

privity of contract That connection or relationship which exists between two or more contracting parties. The absence of privity as a defense in actions for damages in contract and tort actions is generally no longer viable with the enactment of warranty statutes (*e.g.*, UCC § 2–318), acceptance by states of the doctrine of strict liability, and court decisions which have extended the right to sue to third-party beneficiaries and even innocent bystanders.

probable cause Reasonable belief of the offense charged.

probate Court procedure by which a will is proved to be valid or invalid, though in current usage this term has been expanded to include generally all matters and proceedings pertaining to administration of estates, guardianships, etc.

procedural due process Requirement that governmental action depriving a person of life, liberty, or property be done through a fair procedure.

procedural law Rules for enforcing substantive law.

procedural rules Rules issued by an administrative agency establishing its organization, method of operation, and rules of conduct for practice before it.

procedural unconscionability Unfair or irregular bargaining.

proceeds Consideration for the sale, exchange, or other disposition of collateral.

process *Judicial process* In a wide sense, this term may include all the acts of a court from the beginning to the end of its proceedings in a given cause; more specifically, it means the writ, summons, mandate, or other process which is used to inform the defendant of the institution of proceedings against him and to compel his appearance, in either civil or criminal cases.

Legal process This term is sometimes used as equivalent to "lawful process." Thus, it is said that legal process means process not merely fair on its face but valid in fact. But properly it means a summons, writ, warrant, mandate, or other process issuing from a court.

profit corporation One founded for the purpose of operating a business for profit.

profit à prendre Right to make some use of the soil of another, such as a right to mine metals; carries with it the right of entry and the right to remove.

promise to pay Undertaking to pay an existing obligation.

promisee Person to whom a promise is made.

promisor Person making a promise.

promissory estoppel Arises where there is a promise which promisor should reasonably expect to induce action or forbearance on part of promisee and which does induce such action or forbearance, and where injustice can be avoided only by enforcement of the promise.

promissory note An unconditional written promise to pay a specified sum of money on demand or at a specified date. Such a note is negotiable if signed by the maker and containing an unconditional promise to pay a sum certain in money either on demand or at a definite time and payable to order or bearer. UCC § 3–104.

promoters In the law relating to corporations, those persons who first associate themselves for the purpose of organizing a company, issuing its prospectus, procuring subscriptions to the stock, securing a charter, etc.

property Interest that is legally protected.

Abandoned property Intentionally disposed of by the owner.

Lost property Unintentionally left by the owner.

Mislaid property Intentionally placed by the owner but unintentionally left.

prosecute To bring a criminal proceeding.

protest A formal declaration made by a person interested or concerned in some act about to be done, or already performed, whereby he expresses his dissent or disapproval or affirms the act against his will. The object of such a declaration usually is to preserve some right which would be lost to the protester if his assent could be implied, or to exonerate him from some responsibility which would attach to him unless he expressly negatived his assent.

Notice of protest A notice given by the holder of a bill or note to the drawer or indorser that the bill has been protested for refusal of payment or acceptance. UCC § 3–509.

provisional credit Tentative credit for the deposit of an instrument until final credit is given.

proximate cause Where the act or omission played a substantial part in bringing about or actually causing the injury or damage and where the injury or damage was either a direct result or a reasonably probable consequence of the act or omission.

proxy (Contracted from "procuracy.") Written authorization given by one person to another so that the second person can act for the first, such as that given by a shareholder to someone else to represent him and vote his shares at a shareholders' meeting.

public corporation One created to administer a unit of local civil government or one created by the United States to conduct public business.

public disclosure of private facts Offensive publicity given to private information about another person.

public law The law dealing with the relationship between government and individuals.

puffery Sales talk that is considered general bragging or overstatement.

punitive damages Damages awarded in excess of normal compensation to punish a defendant for a serious civil wrong.

purchase money security interest Security interest retained by a seller of goods in goods purchased with the loaned money.

Q

qualified fee Ownership subject to its being taken away upon the happening of an event.

quantum meruit Expression "quantum meruit" means "as much as he deserves"; describes the extent of liability on a contract implied by law. Elements essential to recovery under quantum meruit are (1) valuable services rendered or materials furnished (2) for the person sought to be charged, (3) which services and materials such person accepted, used, and enjoyed, (4) under such circumstances as reasonably notified her that plaintiff, in performing such services, was expected to be paid by the person sought to be charged.

quasi Latin. As if; almost as it were; analogous to. Negatives the idea of identity but points out that the conceptions are sufficiently similar to be classed as equals of one another.

quasi contract Legal fiction invented by common law courts to permit recovery by contractual remedy in cases where, in fact, there is no contract, but where circumstances are such that justice warrants a recovery as though a promise had been made.

quasi in rem See **in rem**.

quasi in rem jurisdiction Jurisdiction over property not based on claims against it.

quiet enjoyment Right of a tenant not to have his physical possession of premises interfered with by the landlord.

quitclaim deed A deed of conveyance operating by way of release; that is, intended to pass any title, interest, or claim which the grantor may have in the premises but neither professing that such title is valid nor containing any warranty or covenants for title.

quorum When a committee, board of directors, meeting of shareholders, legislature, or other body of persons cannot act unless at least a certain number of them are present.

R

rape Unlawful, nonconsensual sexual intercourse.

ratification In a broad sense, the confirmation of a previous act done either by the party himself or by another; as, for example, confirmation of a voidable act.

In the law of principal and agent, the adoption and confirmation by one person, with knowledge of all material facts, of an act or contract performed or entered into in his behalf by another who at the time assumed without authority to act as his agent.

rational relationship test Requirement that legislation bear a rational relationship to a legitimate governmental interest.

real defenses Defenses that are valid against all holders, including holders in due course.

real property Land, and generally whatever is erected or growing upon or affixed to land. Also, rights issuing out of, annexed to, and exercisable within or about land. See also **fixture**.

reasonable man standard Duty of care required to avoid being negligent; one who is careful, diligent, and prudent.

receiver A fiduciary of the court, whose appointment is incident to other proceedings wherein certain ultimate relief is prayed. He is a trustee or ministerial officer representing the court, all parties in interest in the litigation, and the property or funds entrusted to him.

recognizance Formal acknowledgment of indebtedness made in court.

redemption (a) The realization of a right to have the title of property restored free and clear of a mortgage, performance of the mortgage obligation being essential for such purpose. (b) Repurchase by corporation of its own shares.

reformation Equitable remedy used to reframe written contracts to reflect accurately real agreement between contracting parties when, either through mutual mistake or unilateral mistake coupled with actual or equitable fraud by the other party, the writing does not embody the contract as actually made.

regulatory license Requirement to protect the public interest.

reimbursement Duty owed by principal to pay back authorized payments agent has made on principal's behalf. Duty owed by a principal debtor to repay surety who pays principal debtor's obligation.

rejection The refusal to accept an offer; manifestation of an unwillingness to accept the goods (sales).

release The relinquishment, concession, or giving up of a right, claim, or privilege, by the person in whom it exists or to whom it accrues, to the person against whom it might have been demanded or enforced.

remainder An estate limited to take effect and be enjoyed after another estate is determined.

remand To send back. The sending by the appellate court of a cause back to the same court out of which it came, for the purpose of having some further action taken on it there.

remedy The means by which the violation of a right is prevented, redressed, or compensated. Though a remedy may be by the act of the party injured, by operation of law, or by agreement between the injurer and the injured, we are chiefly concerned with one kind of remedy, the judicial remedy, which is by action or suit.

rent Consideration paid for use or occupation of property. In a broader sense, it is the compensation or fee paid, usually periodically, for the use of any property, land, buildings, equipment, etc.

replevin An action whereby the owner or person entitled to repossession of goods or chattels may recover those goods or chattels from one who has wrongfully distrained or taken such goods or chattels or who wrongfully detains them.

reply Plaintiff's pleading in response to the defendant's answer.

repudiation Repudiation of a contract means refusal to perform duty or obligation owed to other party.

requirements contract See **contracts**.

res ipsa loquitur "The thing speaks for itself"; permits the jury to infer both negligent conduct and causation.

rescission An equitable action in which a party seeks to be relieved of his obligations under a contract on the grounds of mutual mistake, fraud, impossibility, etc.

residuary Pertaining to the residue; constituting the residue; giving or bequeathing the residue; receiving or entitled to the residue. See also **legacy, residuary legacy**.

respondeat superior Latin. Let the master answer. This maxim means that a master or employer is liable in certain cases for the wrongful acts of his servant or employee, and a principal for those of his agent.

respondent In equity practice, the party who makes an answer to a bill or other proceeding. In appellate practice, the party who contends against an appeal; *i.e.*, the appellee. The party who appeals is called the "appellant."

restitution An equitable remedy under which a person who has rendered services to another seeks to be reimbursed for the costs of his acts (but not his profits) even though there was never a contract between the parties.

restraint on alienation A provision in an instrument of conveyance which prohibits the grantee from selling or transferring the property which is the subject of the conveyance. Many such restraints are unenforceable as against public policy and the law's policy of free alienability of land.

restraint of trade Agreement that eliminates or tends to eliminate competition.

restrictive covenant Private restriction on property contained in a conveyance.

revenue license Measure to raise money.

reverse An appellate court uses the term "reversed" to indicate that it annuls or avoids the judgment, or vacates the decree, of the trial court.

reverse discrimination Employment decisions taking into account race or gender in order to remedy past discrimination.

reversion The term reversion has two meanings. First, it designates the estate left in the grantor during the continuance of a particular estate; second, it denotes the residue left in grantor or his heirs after termination of a particular estate. It differs from a remainder in that it arises by an act of law, whereas a remainder arises by an act of the parties. A reversion, moreover, is the remnant left in the grantor, while a remainder is the remnant of the whole estate disposed of after a preceding part of the same has been given away.

revocation The recall of some power, authority, or thing granted, or a destroying or making void of some deed that had existence until the act of revocation made it void.

revocation of acceptance Rescission of one's acceptance of goods based upon a nonconformity of the goods which substantially impairs their value.

right Legal capacity to require another person to perform or refrain from performing an act.

right of entry The right to take or resume possession of land by entering on it in a peaceable manner.

right of redemption The right (granted by statute only) to free property from the encumbrance of a foreclosure or other judicial sale, or to recover the title passing thereby, by paying what is due, with interest, costs, etc. Not to be confounded with the "equity of redemption," which exists independently of statute but must be exercised before sale. See also **equity of redemption**.

right to work law State statute that prohibits union shop contracts.

rights in collateral Personal property the debtor owns, possesses, or is in the process of acquiring.

risk of loss Allocation of loss between seller and buyer where the goods have been damaged, destroyed, or lost.

robbery Larceny from a person by force or threat of force.

rule Agency statement of general or particular applicability designed to implement, interpret, or process law or policy.

rule against perpetuities Principle that no interest in property is good unless it must vest, if at all, not later than twenty-one years, plus period of gestation, after some life or lives in being at time of creation of interest.

rule of reason Balancing the anticompetitive effects of a restraint against its procompetitive effects.

S

sale Transfer of title to goods from seller to buyer for a price.

sale on approval Transfer of possession without title to buyer for trial period.

sale or return Sale where buyer has option to return goods to seller.

sanction Means of enforcing legal judgments.

satisfaction The discharge of an obligation by paying a party what is due to him (as on a mortgage, lien, or contract) or what has been awarded to him by the judgment of a court or otherwise. Thus, a judgment is satisfied by the payment of the amount due to the party who has recovered such judgment, or by his levying the amount. See also **accord and satisfaction**.

scienter Latin. Knowingly.

seal Symbol that authenticates a document.

secondary liability Obligation to pay is subject to the conditions of presentment, dishonor, notice of dishonor, and sometimes protest.

secret partner Partner whose membership in the partnership is not disclosed.

Section 402A Strict liability in tort.

secured bond A bond having a lien on specific property.

secured claim Claim with a lien on property of the debtor.

secured party Creditor who possesses a security interest in collateral.

secured transaction A transaction founded on a security agreement. Such agreement creates or provides for a security interest. UCC § 9–105(h).

securities Stocks, bonds, notes, convertible debentures, warrants, or other documents that represent a share in a company or a debt owed by a company.
  Certificated security Security represented by a certificate.
  Exempt security Security not subject to registration requirements of 1933 Act.
  Exempt transaction Issuance of securities not subject to the registration requirements of 1933 Act.
  Restricted securities Securities issued under an exempt transaction.
  Uncertificated security Security not represented by a certificate.

security agreement Agreement that grants a security interest.

security interest Right in personal property securing payment or performance of an obligation.

seisin Possession with an intent on the part of him who holds it to claim a freehold interest.

self-defense Force to protect oneself against attack.

separation of powers Allocation of powers among the legislative, executive, and judicial branches of government.

service mark Distinctive symbol, word, or design that is used to identify the services of a provider.

servient Land subject to an easement.

setoff A counterclaim demand which defendant holds against plaintiff, arising out of a transaction extrinsic to plaintiff's cause of action.

settlor Creator of a trust.

severance The destruction of any one of the unities of a joint tenancy. It is so called because the estate is no longer a joint tenancy, but is severed.
  Term may also refer to the cutting of crops, such as corn, wheat, etc., or to the separation of anything from realty.

share A proportionate ownership interest in a corporation.

Shelley's case, rule in Where a person takes an estate of freehold, legally or equitably, under a deed, will, or other writing, and in the same instrument there is a limitation by way of remainder of any interest of the same legal or equitable quality to his heirs, or heirs of his body, as a class of persons to take in succession from generation to generation, the limitation to the heirs entitles the ancestor to the whole estate.
  The rule was adopted as a part of the common law of this country, though it has long since been abolished by most states.

shelter rule Transferee gets rights of transferor.

shipment contract Seller is authorized or required only to bear the expense of placing goods with the common carrier and bears the risk of loss only up to such point.

short-swing profits Profits made by insider through sale or other disposition of corporate stock within six months after purchase.

sight draft An instrument payable on presentment.

signature Any symbol executed with intent to validate a writing.

silent partner Partner who takes no part in the partnership business.

slander Oral defamation.

small claims courts Inferior civil courts with jurisdiction limited by dollar amount.

social security Measures by which the government provides economic assistance to disabled or retired employees and their dependents.

sole proprietorship A form of business in which one person owns all the assets of the business, in contrast to a partnership or a corporation.

sovereign immunity Foreign country's freedom from a host country's laws.

special warranty deed Seller promises that he has not impaired title.

specific performance The doctrine of specific performance is that where damages would compensate inadequately for the breach of an agreement, the contractor or vendor will be compelled to perform specifically what he has agreed to do; *e.g.*, ordered to execute a specific conveyance of land.
  With respect to the sale of goods, specific performance may be decreed where the goods are unique or in other proper circumstances. The decree for specific performance may include such terms and conditions as to payment of the price, damages, or other relief as the court may deem just. UCC §§ 2–711(2)(b), 2–716.

standardized business form A preprinted contract.

stare decisis Doctrine that once a court has laid down a principle of law as applicable to a certain state of facts, it will adhere to that principle and apply it to all future cases having substantially the same facts, regardless of whether the parties and property are the same or not.

state action Actions by governments, as opposed to actions taken by private individuals.

state-of-the-art Made in accordance with the level of technology at the time the product is made.

stated capital Consideration, other than that allocated to capital surplus, received for issued stock.

statute of frauds A celebrated English statute, passed in 1677, which has been adopted, in a more or less modified form, in nearly all of the United States. Its chief characteristic is the provision that no action shall be brought on certain contracts unless there be a note or memorandum thereof in writing, signed by the party to be charged or by his authorized agent.

statute of limitation A statute prescribing limitations to the right of action on certain described causes of action; that is, declaring that no suit shall be maintained on such causes of action unless brought within a specified period after the right accrued.

statutory lien Interest in property, arising solely by statute, to secure payment of a debt.

stock "Stock" is distinguished from "bonds" and, ordinarily, from "debentures" in that it gives a right of ownership in part of the assets of a corporation and a right to interest in any surplus after the payment of debt. "Stock" in a corporation is an equity, representing an ownership interest. It is to be distinguished from obligations such as notes or bonds, which are not equities and represent no ownership interest.
  Capital stock See **capital**.
  Common stock Securities which represent an ownership interest in a corporation. If the company has also issued preferred stock, both common and preferred have ownership rights. Claims of both common and preferred stockholders are junior to claims of bondholders or other creditors of the company. Common stockholders assume the greater risk, but generally exercise the greater control and may gain the greater reward in the form of dividends and capital appreciation.
  Convertible stock Stock which may be changed or converted into common stock.
  Cumulative preferred Stock having a provision that if one or more dividends are omitted, the omitted dividends must be paid before dividends may be paid on the company's common stock.

Preferred stock is a separate portion or class of the stock of a corporation that is accorded, by the charter or by-laws, a preference or priority in respect to dividends, over the remainder of the stock of the corporation, which in that case is called *common stock*.

Stock warrant A certificate entitling the owner to buy a specified amount of stock at a specified time(s) for a specified price. Differs from a stock option only in that options are granted to employees and warrants are sold to the public.

Treasury stock Shares reacquired by a corporation.

stock option Contractual right to purchase stock from a corporation.

stop payment Order for a drawee not to pay an instrument.

strict liability A concept applied by the courts in product liability cases in which a seller is liable for any and all defective or hazardous products which unduly threaten a consumer's personal safety. This concept applies to all members involved in the manufacture and sale of any facet of the product.

strict scrutiny test Requirement that legislation be necessary to promote a compelling governmental interest.

subagent Person appointed by agent to perform agent's duties.

subject matter jurisdiction Authority of a court to decide a particular kind of case.

subject to the mortgage Purchaser is not personally obligated to pay the debt, but the property remains subject to the mortgage.

subjective fault Desired or virtually certain consequences of one's conduct.

subjective satisfaction Approval based upon a party's honestly held opinion.

sublease Transfer of less than all of a tenant's interest in a leasehold.

subpoena A subpoena is a command to appear at a certain time and place to give testimony upon a certain matter. A subpoena duces tecum requires production of books, papers, and other things.

subrogation The substitution of one thing for another, or of one person into the place of another with respect to rights, claims, or securities.

Subrogation denotes the putting of a third person who has paid a debt in the place of the creditor to whom he has paid it, so that he may exercise against the debtor all the rights which the creditor, if unpaid, might have exercised.

subscribe Literally, to write underneath, as one's name. To sign at the end of a document. Also, to agree in writing to furnish money or its equivalent, or to agree to purchase some initial stock in a corporation.

subscriber Person who agrees to purchase initial stock in a corporation.

subsidiary corporation Corporation controlled by another corporation.

substantial performance Equitable doctrine protects against forfeiture for technical inadvertence, trivial variations, or omissions in performance.

substantive due process Requirement that governmental action be compatible with individual liberties.

substantive law The basic law of rights and duties (contract law, criminal law, tort law, law of wills, etc.), as opposed to procedural law (law of pleading, law of evidence, law of jurisdiction, etc.).

substantive unconscionability Oppressive or grossly unfair contractual terms.

sue To begin a lawsuit in a court.

suit "Suit" is a generic term of comprehensive signification that applies to any proceeding in a court of justice in which the plaintiff pursues, in such court, the remedy which the law affords him for the redress of an injury or the recovery of a right.

Derivative suit Suit brought by a shareholder on behalf of a corporation to enforce a right belonging to the corporation.

Direct suit Suit brought by a shareholder against a corporation based upon his ownership of shares.

summary judgment Rule of Civil Procedure 56 permits any party to a civil action to move for a summary judgment on a claim, counterclaim, or cross-claim when he believes that there is no genuine issue of material fact and that he is entitled to prevail as a matter of law.

summons Writ or process directed to the sheriff or other proper officer, requiring him to notify the person named that an action has been commenced against him in the court from which the process has

issued and that he is required to appear, on a day named, and answer the complaint in such action.

superseding cause Intervening event that occurs after the defendant's negligent conduct and relieves him of liability.

supreme law Law that takes precedence over all conflicting laws.

surety One who undertakes to pay money or to do any other act in event that his principal debtor fails therein.

suretyship A guarantee of debts of another.

surplus Excess of net assets over stated capital.

T

tangible property Physical objects.

tariff Duty or tax imposed on goods moving into or out of a country.

tenancy Possession or occupancy of land or premises under lease.

Joint tenancy Joint tenants have one and the same interest, accruing by one and the same conveyance, commencing at one and the same time, and held by one and the same undivided possession. The primary incident of joint tenancy is survivorship, by which the entire tenancy on the decease of any joint tenant remains to the survivors, and at length to the last survivor.

Tenancy at sufferance Only naked possession which continues after tenant's right of possession has terminated.

Tenancy at will Possession of premises by permission of owner or landlord, but without a fixed term.

Tenancy by the entirety A tenancy which is created between a husband and wife and by which together they hold title to the whole with right of survivorship so that, upon death of either, the other takes the whole to the exclusion of the deceased's heirs. It is essentially a "joint tenancy," modified by the common law theory that husband and wife are one person.

Tenancy for a period A tenancy for years or for some fixed period.

Tenancy in common A form of ownership whereby each tenant (i.e., owner) holds an undivided interest in property. Unlike the interest of a joint tenant or a tenant by the entirety, the interest of a tenant in common does not terminate upon his or her prior death (i.e., there is no right of survivorship).

tenancy in partnership Type of joint ownership that determines partners' rights in specific partnership property.

tenant Possessor of a leasehold interest.

tender An offer of money; the act by which one produces and offers to a person holding a claim or demand against him the amount of money which he considers and admits to be due, in satisfaction of such claim or demand, without any stipulation or condition.

Also, there may be a tender of performance of a duty other than the payment of money.

tender of delivery Seller makes available to buyer goods conforming to the contract and so notifies the buyer.

tender offer General invitation to all shareholders to purchase their shares at a specified price.

testament Will.

testator One who makes or has made a testament or will; one who dies leaving a will.

third-party beneficiary One for whose benefit a promise is made in a contract but who is not a party to the contract.

Creditor beneficiary Where performance of a promise in a contract will benefit a person other than the promisee, that person is a creditor beneficiary if no purpose to make a gift appears from the terms of the promise, in view of the accompanying circumstances, and performance of the promise will satisfy an actual, supposed, or asserted duty of the promisee to the beneficiary.

Donee beneficiary The person who takes the benefit of the contract even though there is no privity between him and the contracting parties. A third-party beneficiary who is not a creditor beneficiary. See also **beneficiary**.

time paper Payable at definite time.

time-price doctrine Permits sellers to have different prices for cash sales and credit sales.

title The means whereby the owner of lands or of personalty has the just possession of his property.

title insurance Provides protection against defect in title to real property.

tort A private or civil wrong or injury, other than breach of contract, for which a court will provide a remedy in the form of an action for damages.

Three elements of every tort action are the existence of a legal duty from defendant to plaintiff, breach of that duty, and damage as proximate result.

tortfeasor One who commits a tort.

trade acceptance A draft drawn by a seller which is presented for signature (acceptance) to the buyer at the time goods are purchased and which then becomes the equivalent of a note receivable of the seller and the note payable of the buyer.

trade name Name used in trade or business to identify a particular business or manufacturer.

trade secrets Private business information.

trademark Distinctive insignia, word, or design of a good that is used to identify the manufacturer.

transferor's warranty Warranty given by any person who transfers an instrument and receives consideration.

treaty An agreement between or among independent nations.

treble damages Three times actual loss.

trespass At common law, trespass was a form of action brought to recover damages for any injury to one's person or property or relationship with another.

Trespass to chattels or personal property An unlawful and serious interference with the possessory rights of another to personal property.

Trespass to land At common law, every unauthorized and direct breach of the boundaries of another's land was an actionable trespass. The present prevailing position of the courts finds liability for trespass only in the case of intentional intrusion, or negligence, or some "abnormally dangerous activity" on the part of the defendant.

Compare **nuisance**.

trespasser Person who enters or remains on the land of another without permission or privilege to do so.

trust Any arrangement whereby property is transferred with the intention that it be administered by a trustee for another's benefit.

A trust, as the term is used in the Restatement, when not qualified by the word "charitable," "resulting," or "constructive," is a fiduciary relationship with respect to property, subjecting the person by whom the title to the property is held to equitable duties to deal with the property for the benefit of another person, which arises through a manifestation of an intention to create such benefit. Restatement, Second, Trusts § 2.

Charitable trust To benefit humankind.

Constructive trust Wherever the circumstances of a transaction are such that the person who takes the legal estate in property cannot also enjoy the beneficial interest without necessarily violating some established principle of equity, the court will immediately raise a *constructive trust* and fasten it upon the conscience of the legal owner, so as to convert him into a trustee for the parties who in equity are entitled to the beneficial enjoyment.

Inter vivos trust Established during the settlor's lifetime.

Resulting trust One that arises by implication of law, where the legal estate in property is disposed of, conveyed, or transferred, but the intent appears or is inferred from the terms of the disposition, or from the accompanying facts and circumstances, that the beneficial interest is not to go or be enjoyed with the legal title.

Spendthrift trust Removal of the trust estate from the beneficiary's control.

Testamentary trust Established by a will.

Totten trust A tentative trust which is a joint bank account opened by the settlor.

Voting trust A trust which holds the voting rights to stock in a corporation. It is a useful device when a majority of the shareholders in a corporation cannot agree on corporate policy.

trustee In a strict sense, a "trustee" is one who holds the legal title to property for the benefit of another, while, in a broad sense, the term is sometimes applied to anyone standing in a fiduciary or confidential relation to another, such as agent, attorney, bailee, etc.

trustee in bankruptcy Representative of the estate in bankruptcy who is responsible for collecting, liquidating, and distributing the debtor's assets.

tying arrangement Conditioning a sale of a desired product (tying product) on the buyer's purchasing a second product (tied product).

U

ultra vires Acts beyond the scope of the powers of a corporation, as defined by its charter or by the laws of its state of incorporation. By the doctrine of ultra vires, a contract made by a corporation beyond the scope of its corporate powers is unlawful.

unconscionable Unfair or unduly harsh.

unconscionable contract See **contracts**.

underwriter Any person, banker, or syndicate that guarantees to furnish a definite sum of money by a definite date to a business or government in return for an issue of bonds or stock. In insurance, the one assuming a risk in return for the payment of a premium.

undisputed debt Obligation whose existence and amount are not contested.

undue influence Term refers to conduct by which a person, through his power over the mind of a testator, makes the latter's desires conform to his own, thereby overmastering the volition of the testator.

unemployment compensation Compensation awarded to workers who have lost their jobs and cannot find other employment.

unenforceable Contract under which neither party can recover.

unfair employer practice Conduct in which an employer is prohibited from engaging.

unfair labor practice Conduct in which an employer or union is prohibited from engaging.

unfair union practice Conduct in which a union is prohibited from engaging.

Uniform Commercial Code One of the Uniform Laws, drafted by the National Conference of Commissioners on Uniform State Laws, governing commercial transactions (sales of goods, commercial paper, bank deposits and collections, letters of credit, bulk transfers, warehouse receipts, bills of lading, investment securities, and secured transactions).

unilateral mistake Erroneous belief on the part of only one of the parties to a contract.

union shop Employer can hire nonunion members, but such employees must then join the union.

universal life Ordinary life divided into two components, a renewable term insurance policy and an investment portfolio.

unliquidated debt Obligation that is uncertain or contested in amount.

unqualified indorsement (see indorsement) One that imposes liability upon the indorser.

unreasonably dangerous Danger beyond that which the ordinary consumer contemplates.

unrestrictive indorsement (see indorsement) One that does not attempt to restrict the rights of the indorsee.

usage of trade Any practice or method of dealing having such regularity of observance in a place, vocation, or trade as to justify an expectation that it will be observed with respect to the transaction in question.

usury Collectively, the laws of a jurisdiction regulating the charging of interest rates. A usurious loan is one whose interest rates are determined to be in excess of those permitted by the usury laws.

V

value The performance of legal consideration, the forgiveness of an antecedent debt, the giving of a negotiable instrument, or the giving of an irrevocable commitment to a third party. UCC § 1–201(44).

variance A use differing from that provided in a zoning ordinance in order to avoid undue hardship.

vendee A purchaser or buyer; one to whom anything is sold. See also **vendor.**

vendor The person who transfers property by sale, particularly real estate; "seller" being more commonly used for one who sells personalty. See also **vendee.**

venue "Jurisdiction" of the court means the inherent power to decide a case, whereas "venue" designates the particular county or city in which a court with jurisdiction may hear and determine the case.

verdict The formal and unanimous decision or finding of a jury, impaneled and sworn for the trial of a cause, upon the matters or questions duly submitted to it upon the trial.

vertical privity Who is liable to the plaintiff.

vertical restraints Agreements among parties at different levels of the distribution chain.

vested Fixed; accrued; settled; absolute. To be "vested," a right must be more than a mere expectation based on an anticipation of the continuance of an existing law; it must have become a title, legal or equitable, to the present or future enforcement of a demand, or a legal exemption from the demand of another.

vested remainder Unconditional remainder that is a fixed present interest to be enjoyed in the future.

vicarious liability Indirect legal responsibility; for example, the liability of an employer for the acts of an employee or that of a principal for the torts and contracts of an agent.

void Null; ineffectual; nugatory; having no legal force or binding effect; unable, in law, to support the purpose for which it was intended.

This difference separates the words "void" and "voidable": *void* in the strict sense means that an instrument or transaction is nugatory and ineffectual, so that nothing can cure it; *voidable* exists when an imperfection or defect can be cured by the act or confirmation of the person who could take advantage of it.

Frequently, the word "void" is used and construed as having the more liberal meaning of "voidable."

voidable Capable of being made void. See also **void.**

voir dire Preliminary examination of potential jurors.

voluntary Resulting from free choice. The word, especially in statutes, often implies knowledge of essential facts.

voting trust Transfer of corporate shares' voting rights to a trustee.

W

wager (gambling) Agreement that one party will win or lose depending upon the outcome of an event in which the only interest is the gain or loss.

waiver Terms "estoppel" and "waiver" are not synonymous; "waiver" means the voluntary, intentional relinquishment of a known right, and "estoppel" rests upon principle that, where anyone has done an act or made a statement that would be a fraud on his part to controvert or impair, because the other party has acted upon it in belief that what was done or said was true, conscience and honest dealing require that he not be permitted to repudiate his act or gainsay his statement. See also **estoppel.**

ward An infant or insane person placed by authority of law under the care of a guardian.

warehouse receipt Receipt issued by a person storing goods.

warehouser Storer of goods for compensation.

warrant, *v.* In contracts, to engage or promise that a certain fact or state of facts, in relation to the subject matter, is, or shall be, as it is represented to be.

In conveyancing, to assure the title to property sold, by an express covenant to that effect in the deed of conveyance.

warranty A warranty is a statement or representation made by a seller of goods, contemporaneously with and as a part of a contract of sale, though collateral to express the object of the sale, having reference to the character, quality, or title of goods, and by which the seller promises or undertakes to ensure that certain facts are or shall be as he then represents them.

The general statutory law governing warranties on sales of goods is provided in UCC § 2–312 *et seq.* The three main types of warranties are (1) express warranty; (2) implied warranty of fitness; (3) implied warranty of merchantability.

warranty deed Deed in which grantor warrants good clear title. The usual covenants of title are warranties of seisin, quiet enjoyment, right to convey, freedom from encumbrances, and defense of title as to all claims.

Special warranty deed Seller warrants that he has not impaired title.

warranty liability Applies to persons who transfer an instrument or receive payment or acceptance.

warranty of title Obligation to convey the right to ownership without any lien.

waste Any act or omission that does permanent injury to the realty or unreasonably changes its value.

white-collar crime Corporate crime.

will A written instrument executed with the formalities required by statutes, whereby a person makes a disposition of his property to take effect after his death.

winding up To settle the accounts and liquidate the assets of a partnership or corporation, for the purpose of making distribution and terminating the concern.

without reserve Auctioneer may not withdraw the goods from the auction.

workers' compensation Compensation awarded to an employee who is injured, when the injury arose out of and in the course of his employment.

writ of certiorari Discretionary review by a higher court. See also **certiorari.**

writ of execution Order served by sheriff upon debtor demanding payment of a court judgment against debtor.

Z

zoning Public control over land use.

Many of the definitions are abridged and adapted from *Black's Law Dictionary,* 5th edition, West Publishing Company, 1979.

INDEX

SUGGESTIONS *for* SUMMER READING

IF YOU ENJOYED THE ECONOMICS COURSE THAT YOU
JUST FINISHED, YOU MIGHT LIKE TO READ MORE ABOUT
ECONOMIC ISSUES IN THE FOLLOWING BOOKS.

. . .

YORAM BAUMAN AND GRADY KLEIN

The Cartoon Introduction to Economics

(New York: Hill and Wang, 2010)

Basic economic principles, with humor.

. . .

NARIMAN BEHRAVESH

Spin-Free Economics

(New York: McGraw-Hill, 2008)

A straightforward guide to major economic
policy debates.

. . .

WILLIAM BREIT AND BARRY T. HIRSCH

Lives of the Laureates

(Cambridge, MA: MIT Press, 2009)

Twenty-three winners of the Nobel Prize in
Economics offer autobiographical essays about
their life and work.

. . .

. . .

BRYAN CAPLAN

*The Myth of the Rational Voter: Why
Democracies Choose Bad Policies*

(Princeton, NJ: Princeton University Press, 2008)

An economist asks why elected leaders often fail to
follow the policies that economists recommend.

. . .

PAUL COLLIER

*The Bottom Billion: Why the Poorest Countries
Are Failing and What Can Be Done About It*

(New York: Oxford University Press, 2007)

A former research director at the World Bank offers
his insights into how to help the world's poor.

. . .

AVINASH DIXIT AND BARRY NALEBUFF

*Thinking Strategically: The Competitive Edge
in Business, Politics, and Everyday Life*

(New York: Norton, 1991)

This introduction to game theory discusses how all
people—from corporate executives to criminals
under arrest—should and do make strategic decisions.

. . .